The Norton Reader

Thirteenth Edition

THE NORTON READER

An Anthology of Nonfiction

THIRTEENTH EDITION

LINDA H. PETERSON, *General Editor*
Yale University

JOHN C. BRERETON
University of Massachusetts, Boston

Joseph Bizup
Boston University

Anne E. Fernald
Fordham University

Melissa A. Goldthwaite
Saint Joseph's University

W·W·NORTON & COMPANY
NEW YORK · LONDON

W. W. Norton & Company has been independent since its founding in 1923, when William Warder Norton and Mary D. Herter Norton first published lectures delivered at the People's Institute, the adult education division of New York City's Cooper Union. The firm soon expanded its program beyond the Institute, publishing books by celebrated academics from America and abroad. By mid-century, the two major pillars of Norton's publishing program—trade books and college texts—were firmly established. In the 1950s, the Norton family transferred control of the company to its employees, and today—with a staff of four hundred and a comparable number of trade, college, and professional titles published each year—W. W. Norton & Company stands as the largest and oldest publishing house owned wholly by its employees.

Printed in the United States of America.

Acknowledgments and copyrights continue on page 1251, which serves as a continuation of the copyright page.

Editor: Marilyn Moller
Associate Editor: Betsye Mullaney
Project Editor: Melissa Atkin
Editorial Assistant: Erica Wnek
Copy Editor: Patterson Lamb
Emedia Editorial Assistant: Jennifer Barnhardt
Senior Production Manager: Eric Pier-Hocking
Art Director: Rubina Yeh
Book Designer: Martin Lubin Graphic Design
Managing Editor, College: Marian Johnson
Composition: Westchester Book Group
Manufacturing: Courier Companies

Library of Congress Cataloging-in-Publication Data

The Norton reader : an anthology of nonfiction / Linda H. Peterson . . . [et al.].—13th ed.
p. cm.
Includes bibliographical references and index.

ISBN 978-0-393-91218-0 (pbk.)

1. College readers. 2. Exposition (Rhetoric)—Problems, exercises, etc. 3. English language—Rhetoric—Problems, exercises, etc. 4. Report writing—Problems, exercises, etc.
PE1122.N68 2011
808'.0427—dc23

2011042407

W. W. Norton & Company, Inc., 500 Fifth Avenue, New York, N.Y. 10110-0017
www.wwnorton.com

W. W. Norton & Company Ltd., Castle House,
75/76 Wells Street, London W1T 3QT

5 6 7 8 9 0

Brief Contents

Preface xxvii
Acknowledgments xxix
Introduction: Reading and Writing with *The Norton Reader* xxxi

Personal Accounts 1

Journals 84

Portraits of People and Places 100
Human Nature 174
Cultural Analysis 226

Op-Eds and Public Arguments 321

Education 346
Language and Communication 401

Album of Styles 474

Nature and the Environment 496
Ethics 550
History 678
Politics and Government 784

Spoken Words 852

Science and Technology 886
Literature, the Arts, and Media 967
Philosophy and Religion 1059

Authors 1137

Permissions Acknowledgments 1171

Chronological Index 1181
Genres Index 1187
Modes Index 1193
Thematic Index 1199
Index 1205

Contents

Preface xxvii

Acknowledgments xxix

Introduction: Reading and Writing with *The Norton Reader* xxxi

Personal Accounts 1

Joan Didion *On Going Home* 1
"Sometimes I think that those of us who are now in our thirties were born into the last generation to carry the burden of 'home,' to find in family life the source of all tension and drama."

Chang-Rae Lee *Coming Home Again* 3
"Whenever I cook, I find myself working just as [my mother] would, readying the ingredients—a mash of garlic, a julienne of red peppers, fantails of shrimp—and piling them in little mounds about the cutting surface."

Zora Neale Hurston *How It Feels to Be Colored Me* 12
"I am not tragically colored. There is no great sorrow dammed up in my soul, nor lurking behind my eyes. I do not mind at all."

Maya Angelou *Graduation* 15
"Somewhere in my fatalism I had expected to die, accidentally, and never have the chance to walk up the stairs in the auditorium and gracefully receive my hard-earned diploma."

Joey Franklin *Working at Wendy's* 25
"As I hand the manager my résumé, I realize it is a mistake. He doesn't want to know my service experience, or my academic references, or my GPA. All he wants to know is if I can spell my name correctly."

Lars Eighner *On Dumpster Diving* 31
"I began Dumpster diving about a year before I became homeless."

Alberto Alvaro Ríos *Green Cards* 40
"And in Mexico, the color was green. Here, it is blue. And that Latin American green is not the green of here, in the way that this blue is not the same blue in Mexico."

J. J. Goode *Single-Handed Cooking* 43
"Disability is relative. I'd rather be incapable of prying open shellfish than allergic to them."

NANCY MAIRS *On Being a Cripple* 46
"I am a cripple. I choose this word to name me."

ALICE WALKER *Beauty: When the Other Dancer Is the Self* 55
"It was great fun being cute. But then, one day, it ended."

ANNE FADIMAN *Night Owl* 62
"Dawns are all very well (though I generally see them after staying up all night, when I may be too sleepy to appreciate them), but they can't hold a candle to a full moon, an aurora borealis, a meteor shower, or a comet."

JENNIFER SINOR *Confluences* 69
"I like to imagine that at the very moment Jerry died, my son Aidan was conceived, so that for the briefest moment, the past, present, and future stood together and recognized one another."

E. B. WHITE *Once More to the Lake* 79
"Summertime, oh summertime, pattern of life indelible, the fade-proof lake, the woods unshatterable, the pasture with the sweetfern and the juniper forever and ever, summer without end."

JOURNALS 84

JOAN DIDION *On Keeping a Notebook* 84
"Keepers of private notebooks are a different breed altogether, lonely and resistant rearrangers of things, anxious malcontents, children afflicted apparently at birth with some presentiment of loss."

RALPH WALDO EMERSON from *Journals* 90
"The things taught in colleges and schools are not an education, but the means of education."

HENRY DAVID THOREAU from *Journal* 93
"What does education often do? It makes a straight-cut ditch of a free, meandering brook."

SYLVIA PLATH from *The Journals of Sylvia Plath* 95
"I feel I have lived enough to last my life in musings, tracings of crossings and recrossings with people, mad and sane, stupid and brilliant, beautiful and grotesque, infant and antique, cold and hot, pragmatic and dream-ridden, dead and alive."

COLBY BUZZELL *Killing Time in Iraq* 97
"Car bombs are starting to become a very popular thing here in Mosul."

Portraits of People and Places 100

Scott Russell Sanders *Under the Influence* 100
"My father drank. He drank as a gut-punched boxer gasps for breath, as a starving dog gobbles food—compulsively, secretly, in pain and trembling."

Annie Dillard from *An American Childhood* 110
"Mother's energy and intelligence suited her for a greater role in a larger arena—mayor of New York, say—than the one she had."

Judith Ortiz Cofer *More Room* 116
"My grandmother's house is like a chambered nautilus; it has many rooms, yet it is not a mansion."

N. Scott Momaday *The Way to Rainy Mountain* 119
"My grandmother had a reverence for the sun, a holy regard that now is all but gone out of mankind."

Tom Wolfe *Yeager* 126
"He was master of the sky. His was a king's solitude, unique and inviolate, above the dome of the world."

Toni Morrison *Strangers* 135
"Why would we want to know a stranger when it is easier to estrange another?"

Jamaica Kincaid *Sowers and Reapers* 139
"The garden is not a place to lose your cares; the garden is not a place of rest and repose."

Jhumpa Lahiri *Rhode Island* 144
"Though I was born in London and have Indian parents, Rhode Island is the reply I give when people ask me where I am from."

Ian Frazier *Take the F* 154
"Like many Americans, I fear living in a nowhere, in a place that is no-place; in Brooklyn, that doesn't trouble me at all."

David Guterson *Enclosed, Enclopedic, Endured: The Mall of America* 161
"For a few hours we share some common ground—a fantasy of infinite commodities and comforts—and then we drift a part forever."

Human Nature 174

Anna Quindlen *Between the Sexes, a Great Divide* 174
"I've always been a feminist, and I've been one of the boys as well, and I've given both sides a pretty good shot."

PAUL THEROUX *Being a Man* 176
"I have always disliked being a man."

SCOTT RUSSELL SANDERS *Looking at Women* 179
"If there were a rule book for sex, it would be longer than the one for baseball."

AMY CUNNINGHAM *Why Women Smile* 189
"To limit a woman to one expression is like editing down an orchestra to one instrument."

ANDREW SULLIVAN *What Is a Homosexual?* 195
"I relate my experience here not to impress or to shock or to gain sympathy, but merely to convey what the homosexual experience is actually like."

HENRY PETROSKI *Falling Down Is Part of Growing Up* 199
"We are all engineers of sorts, for we all have the principles of machines and structures in our bones."

M. F. K. FISHER *Young Hunger* 206
"I unwrapped their rich brown covers and their tinfoil as silently as any prisoner slipping his way through a granite wall, and lay there breaking off the rather warm, rubbery pieces and feeling them melt down my gullet."

JANE SMILEY *Belly, Dancing, Belly, Aching, Belly, Beasts* 209
"The thing about the belly is that it is simultaneously the most real and the most abstract body part."

GLORIA STEINEM *The Good News Is: These Are Not the Best Years of Your Life* 213
"One day, an army of gray-haired women may quietly take over the earth."

ELISABETH KÜBLER-ROSS *On the Fear of Death* 219
"The more we are making advancements in science, the more we seem to fear and deny the reality of death."

CULTURAL ANALYSIS 226

NICHOLAS CARR *Is Google Making Us Stupid?* 226
"Once I was a scuba diver in the sea of words. Now I zip along the surface like a guy on a Jet Ski."

ANTHONY BURGESS *Is America Falling Apart?* 235
"During my year's stay in New Jersey I let my appetites flower into full Americanism except for one thing. I did not possess an automobile."

Adam Goodheart *9.11.01: The Skyscraper and the Airplane* 241
"Before the fire, before the ash, before the bodies tumbling solitary through space, one thin skin of metal and glass met another."

Malcolm Gladwell *Java Man* 248
"The original coffeehouse was a place where men of all types could sit all day; the tobacco they smoked made it possible to drink coffee all day; and the coffee they drank inspired them to talk all day. Out of this came the Enlightenment."

Jessica Mitford *Behind the Formaldehyde Curtain* 254
"If the funeral men are loath to discuss the subject outside the trade, the reader may, understandably, be equally loath to go on reading at this point. For those who have the stomach for it, let us part the formaldehyde curtain."

Henry Louis Gates, Jr. *In the Kitchen* 260
"Everybody I knew as a child wanted to have good hair. You could be as ugly as homemade sin dipped in misery and still be thought attractive if you had good hair."

Charles Lamb *A Dissertation upon Roast Pig* 266
"There is no flavour comparable, I will contend, to that of the crisp, tawny, well-watched, not over-roasted, crackling."

Nicholas D. Kristof *Saudis in Bikinis* 272
"I kept asking women how they felt about being repressed, and they kept answering indignantly that they aren't repressed."

Roland Barthes *Toys* 274
"French toys are usually based on imitation, they are meant to produce children who are users, not creators."

Fred Strebeigh *The Wheels of Freedom: Bicycles in China* 276
"We rode side by side through the city of Beijing, and around us streamed thousands of bicycles with red banners flying. Beijing was in revolt. And as we rode together, we broke the law."

Betty Rollin *Motherhood: Who Needs It?* 286
"For one thing, if in society's view not to be a mother is to be a freak, not to be a *blissful* mother is to be a witch."

Bill McKibben *The Case for Single-Child Families* 295
"And so I sat on the couch next to the old and dog-eared magazines and read one more time the list of questions Dr. Phil McGuire wanted his vasectomy patients to answer before he performed The Procedure."

JAMES BALDWIN *Stranger in the Village* 304
"But I remain as much a stranger today as I was the first day I arrived, and the children shout *Neger! Neger* as I walk along the streets."

BRENT STAPLES *Black Men and Public Space* 314
"After dark, on the warrenlike streets of Brooklyn where I live, I often see women who fear the worst from me."

DEBRA DICKERSON *Who Shot Johnny?* 316
"Johnny never lost consciousness. He lay in the road, trying to understand what had happened to him, why he couldn't get up."

OP-EDS AND PUBLIC ARGUMENTS 321

Anna Quindlen *Stuff Is Not Salvation* 321
"As the boom times fade, an important holiday question surfaces: why in the world did we buy all this junk in the first place?"

MOLLY IVINS *Get a Knife, Get a Dog, but Get Rid of Guns* 323
"In truth, there is no rational argument for guns in this society."

JO-ANN PILARDI *Immigration Problem Is About Us, Not Them* 325
"The immigration problem is fundamentally a demand for cheap labor—for a supply to fill our demand."

THOMAS FRIEDMAN *America's Real Dream Team* 327
"If you need any more convincing about the virtues of immigration, just come to the Intel science finals."

BRENT STAPLES *Why Colleges Shower Their Students with A's* 329
"Faced with demanding consumers and stiff competition, colleges have simply issued more and more A's, stoking grade inflation and devaluing degrees."

BARBARA EHRENREICH *Guys Just Want to Have Fun* 331
"Today, as two recent reports have revealed, it's the girls who achieve and the boys who coast along on gut courses congenial to hangovers."

DAVID BROOKS *The Gender Gap at School* 333
"Over the past two decades, there has been a steady accumulation of evidence that male and female brains work differently."

HENRY WECHSLER ET AL. *Too Many Colleges Are Still in Denial about Alcohol Abuse* 336
"Colleges have a serious problem with alcohol abuse among students, and it's not getting any better."

Jack Hitt *The Battle of the Binge* 340
"By denying the obvious pleasure of drinking and not teaching it by example, is anyone really surprised that we've loosed upon the world a generation of feral drunks?"

Kenneth A. Bruffee *Binge Drinking as a Substitute for a "Community of Learning"* 343
"It's peculiar, when you think about it, that most American colleges do not help entering students make friends through their course work."

Education 346

Frederick Douglass *Learning to Read* 346
"The more I read, the more I was led to abhor and detest my enslavers."

Eudora Welty *Clamorous to Learn* 350
"From the first I was clamorous to learn—I wanted to know and begged to be told not so much what, or how, or why, or where, as when. How soon?"

Sherman Alexie *Superman and Me* 355
"Despite all the books I read, I am still surprised I became a writer. I was going to be a pediatrician. . . . Writing was something beyond Indians."

John Holt *How Teachers Make Children Hate Reading* 358
"Why should children understand everything they read? Why should anyone? I don't, and I never did."

Jonathan Kozol *Fremont High School* 367
"'Can we talk about the bathrooms?' asked a student named Mireya."

Caroline Bird *College Is a Waste of Time and Money* 372
"I believe that college has to be judged not on what other people think is good for students, but on how good it feels to the students themselves."

William Zinsser *College Pressures* 380
"What I wish for all students is some release from the clammy grip of the future. I wish them a chance to savor each segment of their education as an experience in itself and not as a grim preparation for the next step."

Adrienne Rich *Taking Women Students Seriously* 386
"If there is any misleading concept, it is that of 'coeducation': that because women and men are sitting in the same classrooms, hearing the same lectures, reading the same books, performing the same laboratory experiments, they are receiving an equal education. They are not."

MIKE ROSE *Blue-Collar Brilliance* 393
"Although writers and scholars have often looked at the working class, they have generally focused on the values workers exhibit rather than on the thought their work requires—a subtle but pervasive omission."

LANGUAGE AND COMMUNICATION 401

MAXINE HONG KINGSTON *Tongue-Tied* 401
"It was when I found out I had to talk that school became a misery, that the silence became a misery."

RICHARD RODRIGUEZ *Aria* 405
"Because I wrongly imagined that English was intrinsically a public language and Spanish an intrinsically private one, I easily noted the difference between classroom language and the language of home."

GLORIA ANZALDÚA *How to Tame a Wild Tongue* 411
"I remember being caught speaking Spanish at recess—that was good for three licks on the knuckles with a sharp ruler."

GLORIA NAYLOR *"Mommy, What Does 'Nigger' Mean?"* 420
"Words themselves are innocuous; it is the consensus that gives them true power."

PATRICIA WILLIAMS *The Death of the Profane: The Rhetoric of Race and Rights* 423
"In the flicker of his judgmental gray eyes, that saleschild had transformed my brightly sentimental, joy-to-the-world, pre-Christmas spree to a shambles."

JOHN MCWHORTER *The Cosmopolitan Tongue: The Universality of English* 429
"Linguistic death is proceeding more rapidly even than species attrition. According to one estimate, a hundred years from now the 6,000 languages in use today will likely dwindle to 600. The question, though, is whether this is a problem."

DENNIS BARON *Who Owns Global English?* 435
"Now that English is a global language, it's taking on a life of its own in non-English-speaking countries, and the question of correctness is taking on a new spin."

BENJAMIN FRANKLIN *Learning to Write* 440
"As the chief Ends of Conversation are to *inform*, or to be *informed*, to *please* or to *persuade*, I wish well-meaning sensible Men would not lessen their Power of doing Good by a Positive assuming Manner that seldom fails to disgust, tends

to create Opposition, and to defeat every one of those Purposes for which Speech was given us, to wit, giving or receiving Information, or Pleasure."

STEPHEN KING *On Writing* 443
"Write with the door closed, rewrite with the door open. Your stuff starts out being just for you . . . but then it goes out."

GARRISON KEILLOR *How to Write a Letter* 446
Postcards 448
"We need to write, otherwise nobody will know who we are."

LEWIS THOMAS *Notes on Punctuation* 450
"Exclamation points are the most irritating of all. Look! They say, look at what I just said! How amazing is my thought!"

REBECCA SOLNIT *Locked Horns* 453
"That the natural world gives rise to metaphors by which we understand ourselves is, I have long thought, one of the most neglected reasons for protecting it and paying attention to it."

PUMLA GOBODO-MADIKIZELA *"Language Rules": Witnessing Trauma in South Africa* 455
"The language of violence is etched in the memory of many victims of violent conflict and passes on to the next generation in the way that traumatic memory so often is."

GEORGE ORWELL *Politics and the English Language* 463
"Most people who bother with the matter at all would admit that the English language is in a bad way, but it is generally assumed that we cannot by conscious action do anything about it."

ALBUM OF STYLES 474

FRANCIS BACON *Of Youth and Age* 475
"Generally, youth is like the first cogitations, not so wise as the second."

BEN JONSON *To Write Well* 477
"So did the best writers in their beginnings: they imposed upon themselves care and industry."

JOHN DONNE *No Man Is an Island* 479
"Any man's death diminishes me, because I am involved in mankind; and therefore never send to know for whom the bell tolls; it tolls for thee."

SAMUEL JOHNSON *Against Wicked Characters* 479
"If the world be promiscuously described, I cannot see what use it can be to read the account."

MARY WOLLSTONECRAFT from *A Vindication of the Rights of Woman* 480
"The education of women has, of late, been more attended to than formerly; yet they are still reckoned the frivolous sex, and ridiculed or pitied by the writers who endeavour by satire or instruction to improve them."

BENJAMIN FRANKLIN from *Poor Richard's Almanack* 481
"He that lies down with dogs, shall rise up with fleas."

WILLIAM BLAKE *Proverbs of Hell* 483
"Excess of sorrow laughs. Excess of joy weeps."

AMBROSE BIERCE from *The Devil's Dictionary* 484
"*bore*, n. A person who talks when you wish him to listen."

ABRAHAM LINCOLN *The Gettysburg Address* 486
"It is for us the living, rather, to be dedicated here to the unfinished work which they who fought here have thus far so nobly advanced."

ERNEST HEMINGWAY from *A Farewell to Arms* 486
"Abstract words such as glory, honor, courage, or hallow were obscene beside the concrete names of villages, the numbers of roads, the names of rivers, the numbers of regiments and the dates."

MARTIN LUTHER KING JR. from *I Have a Dream* 487
"We have also come to this hallowed spot to remind America of the fierce urgency of *now*. This is no time to engage in the luxury of cooling off or to take the tranquilizing drug of gradualism."

JOAN DIDION from *On Going Home* 488
"I close the drawer, and have another cup of coffee with my mother. We get along very well, veterans of a guerrilla war we never understood."

TOM WOLFE from *Yeager* 488
"How could *the captain*, the man who knows the actual situation most intimately—how could he keep on drawlin' and cucklin' and driftin' and lollygaggin' in that particular voice of his—"

JOHN MCPHEE from *Under the Snow* 490
"A mother in hibernation will readily accept a foster cub. If the need to place an orphan arises somewhat later, when mothers and their cubs are out and around, a sow will kill an alien cub as soon as she smells it."

GLORIA ANZALDÚA from *How to Tame a Wild Tongue* 490
"Being Mexican is a state of soul—not one of mind, not one of citizenship. Neither eagle nor serpent, but both."

Jamaica Kincaid from *Sowers and Reapers* 491
"It is all very beautiful, even slightly awesome; and then there is the awfulness, for those gardens and that terrace and those lakes were made by slaves."

Molly Ivins from *Get a Knife, Get a Dog, but Get Rid of Guns* 491
"Let me start this discussion by pointing out that I am not antigun. I'm proknife."

Ian Frazier from *Take the F* 492
"People in my neighborhood are mostly white, and middle class or above. People in neighborhoods nearby are mostly not white, and mostly middle class or below."

H. Bruce Franklin from *From Realism to Virtual Reality* 493
"The most profoundly deglamorizing images of that war . . . were produced not by literature but directly by technology itself."

Bill McKibben from *The Case for Single-Child Families* 494
"I have one child; she is the light of my life; she makes me care far more about the future than I used to. And I have one child; so even after my work I have some time, money and energy left to do other things."

Nature and the Environment 496

Edward Abbey *The Serpents of Paradise* 496
"I prefer not to kill animals. I'm a humanist; I'd rather kill a *man* than a snake."

Brian Doyle *Joyas Voladoras* 502
"We are utterly open with no one, in the end—not mother and father, not wife or husband, not lover, not child, not friend. We open windows to each but we live alone in the house of the heart."

John McPhee *Under the Snow* 504
"Bears in winter in the Pocono Plateau are like chocolate chips in a cookie."

Peter Matthiessen *Tigers in the Snow* 510
"On this day in the Kumalaika forest while Lena observed us from her place of hiding, I felt a kindled exaltation very close to joy."

Rachel Carson *Tides* 519
"There is no drop of water in the ocean, not even in the deepest parts of the abyss, that does not know and respond to the mysterious forces that create the tide."

JOHN MUIR *A Wind-Storm in the Forests* 525
"Winds are advertisements of all they touch, however much or little we may be able to read them; telling their wanderings even by their scents alone."

CHIEF SEATTLE *Letter to President Pierce, 1855* 532
"The whites, too, shall pass—perhaps sooner than other tribes. Continue to contaminate your bed, and you will one night suffocate in your own waste."

WILLIAM CRONON *The Trouble with Wilderness* 533
"Wilderness can hardly be the solution to our culture's problematic relationship with the nonhuman world, for wilderness is itself a part of the problem."

MARY OLIVER *Waste Land: An Elegy* 537
"I walk in the world to love it."

SANDRA STEINGRABER *Tune of the Tuna Fish* 540
"Although tuna salad sandwiches were a mainstay of my childhood diet, tuna has, during the time period between my childhood and my daughter's, become so contaminated with mercury that I choose not to buy it."

TERRY TEMPEST WILLIAMS *The Clan of One-Breasted Women* 543
"I belong to a Clan of One-Breasted Women. My mother, my grandmothers, and six aunts have all had mastectomies. Seven are dead."

ETHICS 550

MARK TWAIN *Advice to Youth* 550
"Build your character thoughtfully and painstakingly upon these precepts, and by and by, when you have got it built, you will be surprised and gratified to see how nicely and sharply it resembles everybody else's."

STEVEN PINKER *The Moral Instinct* 552
"Far from debunking morality, the science of the moral sense can advance it, by allowing us to see through the allusions that evolution and culture have saddled us with and to focus on goals we can share and defend."

JONATHAN RAUCH *In Defense of Prejudice* 569
"The realistic question is how to make the best of prejudice, not how to eradicate it."

PETER SINGER *What Should a Billionaire Give—and What Should You?* 578
"What is a human life worth? You may not want to put a price tag on it. But if we really had to, most of us would agree that the value of a human life would be in the millions."

ATUL GAWANDE *When Doctors Make Mistakes* 590
"There is a central truth in medicine. . . . *All* doctors make mistakes."

TOM REGAN *The Case for Animal Rights* 608
"The fate of animals is in our hands. God grant we are equal to the task."

MICHAEL POLLAN *An Animal's Place* 619
"The industrialization—and dehumanization—of American animal farming is a relatively new, evitable and local phenomenon: no other country raises and slaughters its food animals quite as intensively or brutally as we do."

DAVID FOSTER WALLACE *Consider the Lobster* 635
"Given the (possible) moral status and (very possible) physical suffering of the animals involved, what ethical convictions do gourmets evolve that allow them not just to eat but to savor and enjoy flesh-based viands?"

MICHAEL LEVIN *The Case for Torture* 647
"Once you have conceded that torture is justified in extreme cases, you have admitted that the decision to use torture is a matter of balancing innocent lives against the means needed to save them."

SALLIE TISDALE *We Do Abortions Here: A Nurse's Story* 650
"Women have abortions because they are too old, and too young, too poor, and too rich, too stupid, and too smart."

NORA EPHRON *The Boston Photographs* 657
"The photographs are indeed sensational. They are pictures of death in action, of the split second when luck runs out."

MICHAEL DIRDA *In Wildness Is the Preservation of the World* 663
"If you are given lined paper, write crosswise. At least occasionally."

PAUL FUSSELL *Thank God for the Atom Bomb* 664
"Experience whispers that the pity is not that we used the bomb to end the Japanese war but that it wasn't ready in time to end the German one."

HISTORY 678

LAUREL THATCHER ULRICH *The Slogan: "Well-Behaved Women Seldom Make History"* 678
"Through a strange stroke of fate I've gotten used to seeing my name on bumpers. . . . I owe this curious fame to a single line from a scholarly article I published in 1976."

BARBARA TUCHMAN *"This Is the End of the World": The Black Death* 692
"The phantom enemy had no name. Called the Black Death only in later recurrences, it was known during the first epidemic simply as the Pestilence or Great Mortality."

PHILIP ALCABES *The Bioterrorism Scare: A Historical Perspective* 705
"The lesson of history that we ignore at our peril is this: nobody can tell us how the next epidemic will happen."

WALT WHITMAN *Death of Abraham Lincoln* 716
"A moment's hush—a scream—the cry *murder*."

JAMES M. MCPHERSON *How Lincoln Won the War with Metaphors* 723
"Here lies one of the secrets of Lincoln's success as a communicator: his skill in the use of figurative language, of which metaphor is the most common example."

HANNAH ARENDT *Deportations from Western Europe* 736
"The story of the Danish Jews is *sui generis*, and the behavior of the Danish people and their government was unique among all the countries in Europe."

ALBERTO MANGUEL *The Library as Survival* 741
"From fire, water, the passage of time, neglectful readers and the hand of the censor, each of my books has escaped to tell me its story."

PHILIP GOUREVITCH *After the Genocide* 752
"Those dead Rwandans will be with me forever, I expect. That was why I had felt compelled to come to Nyarubuye: to be stuck with them—not with their experience, but with the experience of looking at them."

HENRY DAVID THOREAU *The Battle of the Ants* 758
"It was evident that their battle-cry was 'Conquer or die.'"

H. BRUCE FRANKLIN *From Realism to Virtual Reality: Images of America's Wars* 761
"The most profoundly deglamorizing images of that war . . . were produced not by literature but directly by technology itself."

FRANCES FITZGERALD *Rewriting American History* 776
"Slippery history! Not every generation but every few years the content of American-history books for children changes appreciably."

Politics and Government 784

George Orwell *Shooting an Elephant* 784
"Early one morning the sub-inspector at a police station the other end of town rang me up on the 'phone and said that an elephant was ravaging the bazaar. Would I please come and do something about it?"

Jonathan Swift *A Modest Proposal* 790
"It is a melancholy object to those who walk through this great town or travel in the country, when they see the streets, the roads, and cabin doors, crowded with beggars of the female-sex, followed by three, four, or five children, all in rags and importuning every passenger for alms."

Niccolò Machiavelli *The Morals of the Prince* 797
"Any man who tries to be good all the time is bound to come to ruin among the great number who are not good."

Thomas Jefferson and Others *The Declaration of Independence* 804
Original Draft 807
"We hold these truths to be self-evident, that all men are created equal, that they are endowed by their Creator with certain unalienable Rights, that among these are Life, Liberty, and the pursuit of Happiness.

"We hold these truths to be sacred & undeniable; that all men are created equal & independent, that from that equal creation they derive rights inherent & inalienable, among which are the preservation of life, & liberty, & the spirit of happiness."

Elizabeth Cady Stanton *Declaration of Sentiments and Resolutions* 811
"We hold these truths to be self-evident: that all men and women are created equal; that they are endowed by their Creator with certain inalienable rights; that among these are life, liberty, and the pursuit of happiness."

Abraham Lincoln *Second Inaugural Address* 813
"With malice toward none; with charity for all; with firmness in the right, as God gives us to see the right, let us strive on to finish the work we are in."

John F. Kennedy *Inaugural Address* 815
"And so, my fellow Americans, ask not what your country can do for you—ask what you can do for your country."

Martin Luther King Jr. *Letter from Birmingham Jail* 818
"Injustice anywhere is a threat to justice everywhere. . . . Whatever affects one directly, affects all indirectly."

RANDALL BALMER *Diversity and Stability: The Paradox of Religious Pluralism* 831
"Religion in America has usually served as a conservative political force—that is, its very existence as a safety valve for social discontent tends to protect the state from radical zealots and the paroxysms of revolution."

STEPHEN CARTER *The Separation of Church and State* 843
"Simply put, the metaphorical separation of church and state originated in an effort to protect religion from the state, not the state from religion."

SPOKEN WORDS 852

MARTIN LUTHER KING JR. *I Have a Dream* 852
"I have a dream that my four children will one day live in a nation where they will not be judged by the color of their skin but by the content of their character."

ELEANOR ROOSEVELT *On the Universal Declaration of Human Rights* 855
"This declaration may well become the international Magna Carta of all men everywhere."

AL GORE *The Climate Emergency* 860
"I've come to believe that global warming, the disappearance of the ocean fisheries, the destruction of the rain forests, the stratospheric ozone depletion problem, the extinction crisis, all of these are really symptoms of an underlying cause. The underlying cause is a collision between our civilization and the earth."

WILLIAM FAULKNER *Nobel Prize Award Speech* 871
"The poet's voice need not merely be the record of man, it can be one of the props, the pillars to help him endure and prevail."

BARACK OBAMA *A New Beginning* 873
"We have come here seeking a new beginning between the United States and Muslims around the world; one based upon mutual interest and mutual respect; and one based upon the truth that America and Islam are not exclusive, and need not be in competition."

SCIENCE AND TECHNOLOGY 886

JACOB BRONOWSKI *The Nature of Scientific Reasoning* 886
"What is the insight in which the scientist tries to see into nature? Can it indeed be called either imaginative or creative?"

ISAAC ASIMOV *The Eureka Phenomenon* 890
"I suspect it is the involuntary faculty of thought that gives rise to what we call "a flash of intuition," something that I imagine must be merely the result of unnoticed thinking."

THOMAS S. KUHN *The Route to Normal Science* 899
"No wonder, then, that in the early stages of the development of any science different men confronting the same range of phenomena, but not usually all the same particular phenomena, describe and interpret them in different ways."

STEPHEN HAWKING *Is Everything Determined?* 908
"It may be that everything we do is determined by some grand unified theory. If that theory has determined that we shall die by hanging, then we shall not drown. But you would have to be awfully sure that you were destined for the gallows to put to sea in a small boat during a storm."

NICHOLSON BAKER *The Charms of Wikipedia* 915
"Without the kooks and the insulters and the spray-can taggers, Wikipedia would just be the most useful encyclopedia ever made. Instead it's a fast-paced game of paintball."

HENRY WECHSLER ET AL. *Health and Behavioral Consequences of Binge Drinking in College* 925
"These findings support the view of college presidents who believe that alcohol abuse is the No. 1 problem on campus."

MELVIN KONNER *Why the Reckless Survive* 940
"People don't think clearly about risk. This is no mere insult, but a conclusion that emerges from attempts by behavioral scientists to understand how people make decisions."

EDWARD O. WILSON *Intelligent Evolution* 949
"So, will science and religion find common ground, or at least agree to divide the fundamentals into mutually exclusive domains? A great many well-meaning scholars believe that such rapprochement is both possible and desirable. A few disagree, and I am one of them."

STEPHEN JAY GOULD *Darwin's Middle Road* 959
"May we not acknowledge the personal and subjective character of creativity, but still comprehend it as a mode of thinking that emphasizes or exaggerates capacities sufficiently common to all of us that we may at least understand if not hope to imitate?"

LITERATURE, THE ARTS, AND MEDIA 967

EUDORA WELTY *One Writer's Beginnings* 967
"I learned from the age of two or three that any room in our house, at any time of day, was there to be read in, or to be read to."

VLADIMIR NABOKOV *Good Readers and Good Writers* 973
"Literature was born not the day when a boy crying wolf, wolf came running out of the Neanderthal valley with a big gray wolf at his heels: literature was born on the day when a boy came crying wolf, wolf and there was no wolf behind him."

ALLEGRA GOODMAN *Pemberley Previsited* 978
"At nine, I'd loved *Pride and Prejudice* for its humor; at fifteen, I'd read it with melancholy; but in college, I spurned it with feelings akin to those of my roommate when she broke up with her high-school sweetheart."

NORTHROP FRYE *The Motive for Metaphor* 983
"Art begins as soon as "I don't like this" turns into "this is not the way I could imagine it."

MARK DOTY *Souls on Ice* 992
"In the Stop 'n Shop in Orleans, Massachusetts, I was struck by the elegance of the mackerel in the fresh-fish display."

NGŨGĨ WA THIONG'O *Decolonizing the Mind* 997
"For colonialism, this involved two aspects of the same process: the destruction or the deliberate undervaluing of a people's culture, their art, dances, religions, history, geography, education, orature and literature, and the conscious elevation of the language of the colonizer."

VIRGINIA WOOLF *In Search of a Room of One's Own* 1005
"Let me imagine, since facts are so hard to come by, what would have happened had Shakespeare had a wonderfully gifted sister, called Judith, let us say."

MICHAEL CHABON *Kids' Stuff* 1016
"Twist endings, the unexpected usefulness of unlikely knowledge, nobility and bravery where it's least expected, and the sudden emergence of a thread of goodness in a wicked nature, those were the kind of stories told by the writers and artists of the comic books that I liked."

SCOTT MCCLOUD *Understanding Comics* 1022
"In comics at its *best* words and pictures are like *partners* in a *dance* and each one takes turns *leading*. When ***both*** partners try to lead, the competition can *subvert* the overall goals . . . YOW!"

SUSAN SONTAG *A Century of Cinema* 1028
"Cinema's hundred years appear to have the shape of a life cycle: an inevitable birth, the steady accumulation of glories, and the onset in the last decade of an ignominious, irreversible decline."

SUSAN ALLEN TOTH *Going to the Movies* 1036
"Bob takes me only to movies that he thinks have a redeeming social conscience. He doesn't call them films."

AARON COPLAND *How We Listen* 1039
"Music which always says the same thing to you will necessarily soon become dull music, but music whose meaning is slightly different with each hearing has a greater chance of remaining alive."

GENE WEINGARTEN *Pearls before Breakfast* 1043
"Do you stop and listen? Do you hurry past with a blend of guilt and irritation, aware of your cupidity but annoyed by the unbidden demand on your time and your wallet? Do you throw in a buck, just to be polite?"

PHILOSOPHY AND RELIGION 1059

LANGSTON HUGHES *Salvation* 1059
"I was saved from sin when I was going on thirteen."

RITA DOVE *The Epistle of Paul the Apostle to the Ephesians* 1061
"I was thirteen when the man who would introduce me to the apostle Paul walked into our senior Sunday-school class."

JAMES VAN THOLEN *Surprised by Death* 1070
"This is a strange day—for all of us. Most of you know that today marks my return to this pulpit after seven months of dealing with an aggressive and deadly form of cancer."

STEVEN WEINBERG *Without God* 1074
"I'm not going to say that it's easy to live without God, that science is all you need."

REG SANER *My Fall into Knowledge* 1085
"A memory lapse explains why a few years ago I accepted an invitation to debate an anti-Darwinian."

HENRY DAVID THOREAU *Where I Lived, and What I Lived For* 1098
"I went to the woods because I wished to live deliberately, to front only the essential facts of life, and see if I could not learn what it had to teach, and not, when I came to die, discover that I had not lived."

VIRGINIA WOOLF *The Death of the Moth* 1107
"Watching him, it seemed as if a fiber, very thin but pure, of the enormous energy of the world had been thrust into his frail and diminutive body."

ANNIE DILLARD *Sight into Insight* 1109
"Seeing is of course very much a matter of verbalization. Unless I call my attention to what passes before my eyes, I simply won't see it."

PLATO *The Allegory of the Cave* 1120
"But, whether true or false, my opinion is that in the world of knowledge the idea of good appears last of all, and is seen only with an effort."

JESUS *Parables of the Kingdom* 1123
"Watch therefore, for ye know neither the day nor the hour wherein the Son of man cometh."

ZEN PARABLES
Muddy Road, A Parable, Learning to Be Silent 1127
"Buddha told a parable in a sutra."

JEAN-PAUL SARTRE *Existentialism* 1128
"Man is nothing else but what he makes of himself."

AUTHORS 1137

PERMISSIONS ACKNOWLEDGMENTS 1171

CHRONOLOGICAL INDEX 1181
GENRES INDEX 1187
MODES INDEX 1193
THEMATIC INDEX 1199
INDEX 1205

Preface

The Norton Reader began as an attempt to introduce students to the essay as a genre and to create an anthology of excellent nonfiction writing. This new edition offers a wide selection of essays on a broad range of subjects—from Jhumpa Lahiri recalling the town in Rhode Island where she grew up to Peter Singer contemplating how much billionaires should give, to Rita Dove meditating on her religious heritage. At the same time, it offers many examples of the kinds of writing students are most often assigned to do, from Lahiri's profile of her home state to Singer's argument about philanthropy and Dove's personal narrative about her religious upbringing. With 180 selections in the Regular Edition and 100 in the Shorter Edition, *The Norton Reader* offers depth, breadth, and variety for teaching the essay as it's developed over time, including the seminal experiments of Francis Bacon and John Donne; the modern classics of Virginia Woolf, George Orwell, and E. B. White; and contemporary examples by such diverse writers as Anne Fadiman, Terry Tempest Williams, Malcolm Gladwell, and John McPhee.

And always, *The Norton Reader* has aimed to uphold a tradition of anthologizing excellent prose, starting with Arthur Eastman, the founding editor, who insisted that essays be selected for the quality of their writing. "Excellent prose would be their pillar of smoke by day, of fire by night," he wrote in the preface to the eighth edition. With this vision, the original editors of *The Norton Reader* chose classic essays that appealed to modern readers and that are now recognized as comprising the essay canon. We have aimed to continue this tradition, yet have also adapted the *Reader* to new pedagogies and have updated it by adding new writers whose work appeals to new generations of student readers. We believe that the essays in this volume are well-written, focus on topics that matter, and demonstrate what all of us tell our students about good writing.

The thirteenth edition welcomes three new editors, all experts in rhetoric and composition: Joseph Bizup of Boston University, Anne Fernald of Fordham University, and Melissa Goldthwaite of Saint Joseph's University. This edition blends the new and the old, the innovative and the classic.

Highlights of the Thirteenth Edition

- Both contemporary and canonical essays by authors as diverse as Toni Morrison and Mary Wollstonecraft, David Foster Wallace and Henry Thoreau, and Patricia Williams and Martin Luther King Jr.
- Unique coverage of both themes and genres. No other reader gives teachers the flexibility of focusing on both the universal themes they like to teach and the genres they assign their students to write. Thematic chapters on education, ethics, history, the environment, among others, introduce students to important academic ideas and civic conversations,

while genre chapters provide examples of cultural analysis, arguments, journals, speeches, and other kinds of writing. An Album of Styles allows students to trace the development of prose styles in English.

- Pedagogical apparatus to serve the needs of both instructors and students—but not so much as to overwhelm the essays themselves. We provide contextual notes to indicate when and where the essay was written; annotations to explain unfamiliar persons, events, and concepts; and study questions for all essays.

- Biographical information located at the end of the volume allows students either to find out about the authors before reading their essays or to encounter the authors as unknowns.

New to this Edition

- Forty-five new selections (twenty-five in the Shorter edition), including essays from American, Canadian, African, Indian, English, and Caribbean writers. Twenty-five essays have never before been anthologized. New voices include Joey Franklin describing what it's like to work at Wendy's, Sherman Alexie narrating his path to literacy via comic books, and Laurel Thatcher Ulrich explaining how she came to coin the phrase "well-behaved women seldom make history."

- A unique new Web site allows readers to sort and search for readings by genre, mode, theme, and more. Instructors can find readings according to the genres or modes they teach. For example, search for literacy narratives and find Sherman Alexie's "Superman and Me" and Frederick Douglass's "Learning to Read," among other essays. The site also features biographical notes about the authors and a short excerpt from each reading.

- Four new and expanded indexes that organize the readings according to date of publication, genre, rhetorical mode, and theme. For example, the Genres Index, including such major forms as literacy narratives, profiles of people and places, and argument, helps instructors meet crucial goals of the WPA Outcomes Statement, which urges that we teach students to write in several genres, identify conventions of format and structure, and understand how genres shape reading and writing. The Thematic Index helps instructors organize units for their courses around topics such as Law and Justice; Race, Class, and Ethnicity; Home and Family; and ten other important themes.

- More than fifty visual images—photographs, drawings, maps, graphs, and other illustrations—that accompanied the essays in their original publication form, including a visual essay on the graphic novel, "Understanding Comics," and photographs of global uses of English from Dennis Baron's blog *The Web of Language*. We hope that these images will encourage readers to think about the intersection of the visual and the verbal in modern culture, and the ways in which images enrich, highlight, and sometimes challenge the written text.

Acknowledgments

Among our many critics, advisors, and friends, the following were of special help in the preparation of the thirteenth edition, either by offering advice or by suggesting essays to be included in this edition: Amy Bennett-Zendzian (Boston University), Maria Gapotchenko (Boston University), Diane Greco Josefowicz (Boston University), Ted Fitts (Boston University), Sarah Madsen Hardy (Boston University), Mark Oppenheimer (Yale University), David Shawn (Boston University), Barbara Stuart (Yale University), and Thomas A. Underwood (Boston University). Special thanks also to our colleague and editor emeriti, Joan E. Hartman, for her advice and hands-on help with this new edition.

The editors would like to express appreciation and thanks to the many teachers who provided reviews: Alan Ainsworth (Houston Community College), Christiane Andrews (Colby-Sawyer College), Mary Angeline (University of Northern Colorado), Kim Ballerini (Nassau Community College), Barbara Bengels (Hofstra University), Margaret Benner (Towson University), Debra Berry (College of Southern Nevada), Cecilia Bonnor (Fordham University), Monica Bosson (City College of San Francisco), Rhonda Brock-Servais (Longwood University), Cheryl Brown (Towson University), Carole Clark Papper (Hofstra University), Amanda Corcoran (American River College), Sarah Cornish (Fordham University), Laurie Dawson (Sonoma State University), Marilyn Douglas-Jones (Houston Community College), Alan Fertmann (Connetquot High School), Stefan Fleischer (Houston Community College), Robert Ford (Houston Community College), George Friend (Millersville University), Wanda Fries (Somerset Community College), Kim Gainer (Radford University), Tim Giles (Georgia Southern University), C. Herbert Gilliland (U.S. Naval Academy), Linda Goldberg (Stevens Institute of Technology), Alfred Guy (Yale University), Wendy Hedrick (Community College of Philadelphia), Jacob Heller (SUNY College at Old Westbury), Faye Adele Hughes (Central Connecticut State University), Moore Jan (Frank Phillips College), Karen Keck (Texas Tech University), Carol Kushner (Dutchess Community College), Laurel Lacroix (Houston Community College Southwest), Angela Laflen (Marist College), Mary Lampman (Wilkes University), Ethna Lay (Hofstra University), Dawn (Brickey) Lee (Charleston Southern University), Robert Lunday (Houston Community College), John Magee (Ohio Northern University), Allyson McCabe (Yale University), Daisy Miller (Hofstra University), Christopher Mitchell (University of Alabama), Katie Montagna (Palomar College), Michael Moreau (Glendale Community College), Michail Mulvey (Central Connecticut State University), Kathleen Ochshorn (University of Tampa), Nancy Peterson (Eastern New Mexico University), Roger Platizky (Austin College), Doug Rice (Sacramento State University), Rich Rice (Texas Tech University), Jennifer Rich (Hofstra University), Aaron Ritzenberg

(Columbia University), Martha Robinson (Ulster County Community College), Linda Rosenkranz (Houston Community College Southwest), David Ross (Houston Community College Southwest), Douglas Rowlett (Houston Community College Southwest), Claire Schmidt (University of Missouri), Virginia Shabatay (Palomar College), Sheila Shear (Somerset Community College), Cathy Shufro (Yale University), Syble Simon (Houston Community College Central), Claude Smith (Ohio Northern University), Victor Thompson (Thomas Nelson Community College), Deborah Uman (St. John Fisher College), Clementina Verge (Central Connecticut State University), Michael Walonen (University of Alabama), John Wang (Queens College), Denise White (Kennesaw State University), Jane Wohl (Sheridan College), and Mark Wolzenburg (Champlain College).

At Boston University, special thanks goes to Amy Bennett-Zendzian and Kristin Bezio for their help with annotations and page proofs, and for their many thoughtful ideas about questions, writing assignments, and teaching suggestions. We owe thanks to Patterson Lamb for her copyediting; Greg Lauzon for his proofreading; and Michael Fleming for his work on the biographical sketches. At Norton, we thank Melissa Atkin and Eric Pier-Hocking for their help with editing and production; Megan Jackson and Margaret Gorenstein for their help with permissions; and our editors past and present: Jennifer Bartlett, Carol Hollar-Zwick, Julia Reidhead, and Marilyn Moller. A special thanks also to Betsye Mullaney, who guided this edition from conception through production with admirable patience, efficiency, and intelligence.

INTRODUCTION
Reading and Writing with The Norton Reader

Reading with a Writer's Eye

In a series of assignments for the class in which you've enrolled, your writing instructor will ask you to read a selection of essays in *The Norton Reader*. Whether you read many essays or just a few, we hope that you will enjoy them. Reading essays in a college textbook may seem different from the reading you usually do in magazines, books, or online—and reading essays for a college course *is* different, even though you will find some aspects quite familiar. When you read on your own, you choose the topics and the formats, letting your personal interests guide you. When you read in a college writing course, you will discover essays that reflect your own interests, but your instructor will also introduce you to topics you've never before encountered, to forms of writing common in college but new to you, and to levels of difficulty that will prepare you for the reading in future college classes and the writing assigned in them.

In *The Norton Reader* you will find essays that address these various interests, forms, and goals. The 180 pieces collected here originally appeared in many different venues—from a daily newspaper in Baltimore to a beautifully produced book of art photographs, from a speech given publicly by a U.S. president to a collection of private meditations by a famous author. In an anthology like *The Norton Reader*, all of these selections appear in the same format, with the same typeface and layout; all have annotations to explain references and allusions; and all have questions to urge you to think about major issues and themes. In these visible ways, the essays in this collection differ from their originals.

Even so, we hope that the original pleasure, purpose, and power of each essay will come through. To help in the reading process, we provide you with information about the context in which the essay first appeared—including the readers for whom it was intended, the magazine, book, or newspaper in which it was published, and the knowledge that its original readers brought to their reading or listening. (See "Who is the audience?" p. xxxii, and "What is the rhetorical context and purpose?" p. xxxiv.) We also suggest, in this introduction, some ways of reading essays that will help you to analyze them. (See "What is the genre and its conventions?" p. xxxvii.) Finally, we provide strategies for writing your own essays. (See "Writing in College," p. l.) Among the goals of a college reader like this one are connecting reading and writing, linking the two processes as interactive, and making your reading enrich, inspire, and improve your writing.

Most of the essays in *The Norton Reader* originally appeared in magazines or books written for general readers—educated people but not specialists in the subject. The essays were read by people like you who wanted to know—or know more—about their subjects, who knew about—or were intrigued by—their authors, or who were tempted to launch into unfamiliar subjects because they encountered them in a magazine they ordinarily read. In the world outside the classroom, readers bring their own interests and motives to the essays they read. Although putting essays in a textbook might make them seem a little artificial, we hope to make your reading process more "real" by suggesting strategies that help you understand their contexts, purposes, and ongoing relevance.

When you begin reading an essay that your instructor assigns, ask yourself some or all of the following questions. These questions—about the audience for the essay, the author and his or her purpose in writing the essay, and the genre of the essay—will help you understand the essay, re-create its original context, analyze its meaning, recognize its organization and rhetorical strategies, and imagine how you might use similar strategies for your own writing.

WHO IS THE AUDIENCE?

An *audience* consists of those to whom the essay is directed—the people who read the article, listen to the speech, or view the text. The question about audience might be posed in related ways: For whom did the author write? What readers does the author hope to reach? What readers did he or she actually reach?

Sometimes that audience is a single reader, as in an entry in a private diary; sometimes the audience is national or international, as in an editorial for a newspaper like the *Washington Post* or the *New York Times*. Often, the audience shares a common interest, as the readers of an environmental magazine might do or the buyers of books of biography or history. To help you understand the original audience for each essay, we provide *contextual notes* at the bottom of the first page of each essay. Contextual notes give information about when and where the essay first appeared and, if it began as a talk, when and where it was delivered and to what audience. If we know, we try to give a sense of what the original audience was like or, at least, what we can gauge from the publishing context.

For example, the contextual note for Scott Russell Sanders's "Looking at Women" (p. 179) tells you that it appeared in the *Georgia Review*, a small-circulation magazine that attracts readers who enjoy fiction, essays, and poetry and who like essays with a literary feel. In contrast, Nicholas Kristof's "Saudis in Bikinis" (p. 272) appeared as an editorial in the *New York Times*, a daily newspaper with a huge national readership, where Kristof has a regular column on the op-ed page. Sanders could assume that his audience would like reading personal memoirs and biographical profiles, whereas Kristof knew that he needed to speak to a large, diverse national audience of people holding very different opinions on matters of education, politics, religion, and social questions like gender. Knowing these audiences gives a window into the writers' choices, strategies, and styles. Sanders's essays begins as if it were a story, in an intriguing yet leisurely way:

> On that sizzling July afternoon, the girl who crossed at the stoplight in front of our car looked, as my mother would say, as though she had been poured into her pink shorts.

Kristof, in contrast, gets down to business quickly, since he knows he has only 750 or so words to explain the issue to his readers and convince them of his position. Kristof may begin with an intriguing observation—"On my first evening in Riyadh, I spotted a surreal scene"—but by his fourth sentence, he has reached the issue under consideration:

> Saudi women may be regarded in the West as antique doormats covered in black veils, but the women themselves vigorously reject the stereotype. "It hurts when you hear what people say about us, that we're repressed."

The expectations of the two different audiences explain, in part, the writers' different approaches and styles.

Sometimes contextual notes give information about where the selection was published and how it was received—another way to understand the audience. Maya Angelou's "Graduation" (p. 15) comes from her autobiography *I Know Why the Caged Bird Sings*, published in 1969; Angelou then continued writing her life story in five sequential volumes, most recently *A Song Flung Up to Heaven* (2002)—a sequence that testifies to her book's success and its appeal to a wide variety of readers. A different example of success with readers can be discovered from the contextual note for Dennis Baron's "Who Owns Global English?" (p. 435), originally posted on April 21, 2010, on Baron's blog, *The Web of Language*, http://illinois.edu/db/view/25. This article, written by a professor of English at the University of Illinois, had over 6,000 hits by the end of the year. In fact, a check of the top articles on Baron's blog, which is devoted to a consideration of language in the news, reveals that the stories with the greatest number of hits focus on issues in global English.

In each contextual note, we try to explain a little about the books, magazines, and newspapers that published these essays—the *New York Times Magazine*, a large-circulation weekly magazine included with the Sunday newspaper, or the *Georgia Review*, a small but well-respected literary journal published three times a year by the University of Georgia, or *I Know Why the Caged Bird Sings*, a free-standing book. As editors, we could swamp you with information about publication and authorship, but we prefer to include more essays and keep contextual information focused on the original audience and publication context—that is, on where the essay appeared, who read it, and (if we know) what reaction it received.

Who is the author?

If the audience consists of those who read the essays, the *author* is the term we use for the person who writes them. Essayists, as authors, tend to introduce themselves to their audiences, revealing personal experiences, preferences, and beliefs that bear on the subject at hand and that help explain the essayist's point of view. The essayist's self-presentation—sometimes called *persona*, sometimes *ethos*—is more important than the essayist's actual name. In "We Do Abortions Here: A Nurse's Story" (p. 650), the title gives us an important fact about the author and her perspective: she is a nurse and has seen abortions up close. Knowing this fact is more important than knowing the essayist's name (Sallie Tisdale). In "Who Shot Johnny?" (p. 316), Debra Dickerson introduces herself directly to her readers in the opening paragraph:

> I am unrepentant and vocal about having gained admittance to Harvard through affirmative action; I am a feminist, stoic about my marriage chances as a well-educated, 36-year-old black woman who won't pretend to need help taking care of herself.

Who the author is—where she comes from, what her background is, what her educational and professional experience are—becomes part of Dickerson's story, and it influences her perspective on the random shooting of her nephew about which she writes.

Not all authors are as direct as Tisdale or Dickerson. You don't really need to know who Allegra Goodman, author of "Pemberley Previsited," is—other than an avid read of Jane Austen's *Pride and Prejudice*. The fact that her parents were professors at the University of Hawaii is interesting, but not essential to her self-presentation as an Austen devotée. Nor do you need to know that David Guterson, the author of "Enclosed. Encyclopedic. Endured: The Mall of America" (p. 161), later became famous for the novel *Snow Falling on Cedars*. In his article about the largest mall in America, Guterson presents himself as a reporter, observing what he sees, shaping the information for his readers, and posing questions for himself and them about what the mall means and why it is so popular. His distance and objectivity as a reporter are important aspects of his self-presentation, of who he is as author of this essay.

Because we believe that essayists prefer to introduce themselves and reveal details of personality and experience that they consider most relevant, we do not preface each essay with a biographical note. We think they, as authors, should step forward and we, as editors, should stand back and let them speak. But if you want to learn more about the writer of an essay, you can check the *Authors* section at the end of the book. The entries there provide information about the men and women who wrote the essays. Putting this information at the end of the book gives you a choice. You may already know something about an author and not wish to consult this section. You may wish to find out something about an author before you read his or her writing. Or you may just prefer to encounter the authors on their own terms, letting them identify themselves within the essay. Sometimes knowing who authors are and where their voices come from helps readers grasp what they say—but sometimes it doesn't.

WHAT IS THE RHETORICAL CONTEXT AND PURPOSE?

The *rhetorical context*, sometimes called *rhetorical situation* or *rhetorical occasion*, refers to the context—social, political, biographical, historical—in which writing takes place and becomes public. The term *purpose*, in a writing class, refers to the author's goal—whether to inform, to persuade, to entertain, to analyze, or to do something else through the essay. We could also pose this question as follows: What goals did the writer have in composing and publishing the essay? What effect did the author wish to have on the audience?

For some selections, the rhetorical context is indicated by the *title*. Abraham Lincoln's "Second Inaugural Address" (p. 813) and John F. Kennedy's "Inaugural Address" (p. 815) were presidential speeches made on the formal occasion of their swearing in. An inauguration represents a significant moment in a leader's—and the nation's—life. The speech given on such an occasion requires a statement of the president's goals for the next four years. In addition to the title, you can discover more about the rhetorical context of a president's inaugural speech in the *opening paragraph* because he (so far it's only *he*) will often refer to the historical context early on. Lincoln, for example, refers back to his first inaugural address and the "impending civil war"; then he acknowledges that the war continues and that he prays "this mighty scourge of war may speedily pass away." In the midst of the American civil war, Lincoln knows that he must, as president, address the political conflict that faces the nation, offer hope for its resolution, and set the moral tone for the aftermath. That's his purpose.

Like the presidential speech, many essays establish the rhetorical context in their opening paragraphs. Editorials and op-eds begin with a "hook"—an opening reference to the issue at hand or the news report under consideration. You might even say that the editorial writer "creates" the rhetorical context and shows us her purpose straight away. In her op-ed "Get a Knife, Get a Dog, but Get Rid of Guns" (p. 323), Molly Ivins begins with "Guns. Everywhere guns"—letting her readers know that she's addressing the hot topic of gun control and establishing her position right up front (she's pro-control). Ivins's main purpose is to persuade others to adopt her position, but another purpose is, through humor, to amuse her readers and laugh the anti-control group out of court. Jo-Ann Pilardi's "The Immigration Problem Is About Us, Not Them" (p. 325) reveals, in its title, her rhetorical purpose: to reconsider the immigration debate. In her opening paragraphs, Pilardi reminds us of the social and political context:

> The immigration debates always focus on small brown bodies jumping fences and scooting through the brush of our Southwestern states (land that was *Mexico* about 150 years ago). Our self-righteous anger at those brown bodies is fueled by our narrow use of the word "illegal"—a term reserved only for those immigrant workers.

Even if you haven't followed newspaper reports about immigration, you can tell from this opening that the writer is engaging a highly contested American debate about what to do about immigrants who cross the U.S.-Mexico border and enter the United States. Pilardi's purpose is to disrupt the us/them thinking that hinders fruitful discussion of the issue.

Sometimes we provide information about the rhetorical context in the *contextual note* (described above) or in the *annotations* to each essay (described below). The contextual note for Martin Luther King Jr.'s "I Have a Dream" explains that the speech was

> Delivered on the steps of the Lincoln Memorial in Washington, D.C., on August 28, 1963, at one of the largest Civil Rights demonstrations in U.S. history.

The annotations (footnotes marked with small numerals) give further clues. For instance, note 3 tells us:

> George Wallace (1919–1998), Alabama's segregationist governor, used big legal terms such as "interposition" and "nullification" in his unsuccessful attempt to prevent the integration of the University of Alabama.

This annotation explains who Wallace was (a fact that King's audience would have known), but it also reveals that King is answering the arguments of his segregationist opponent, that he is debating and talking back. Use the contextual notes and annotations to help recreate the original context. But if you really want to comprehend that rhetorical occasion in 1963 when the Reverend Martin Luther King spoke in Washington, you need to use your imagination. Envision the Lincoln Memorial in the U.S. capital, fill the space with thousands of demonstrators, and wait in anticipation for one of the greatest American orators to begin his speech. Or watch a video of King at youtube.com.

Here is some additional information about *annotations* and how to use them as you read an essay: the annotations are explanatory footnotes—a common feature of a textbook. Commercial magazines and newspapers usually do not include footnotes, whereas academic writing often does. When the original authors wrote the footnotes themselves, we indicate that in square brackets, for example, [Angelou's note] or [King's note]. This tells you that the author wished to cite an expert, add information, or send the reader to another source. In most cases, however, we the editors have written the footnotes to help with difficult words, allusions, and references. We provide information about people, places, works, theories, and other unfamiliar things that the original audience may have known. For example, for Maya Angelou's "Graduation" (p. 15) we give an annotation for Gabriel Prosser and Nat Turner, but not Abraham Lincoln and Christopher Columbus. Angelou's readers, many of them African American, would have known that Prosser and Turner were executed leaders of slave rebellions in the nineteenth century. But because not all readers today know (or remember) this part of American history, we add a footnote.

Here's a final important point: Annotation, while it facilitates the making of meaning in reading, can never take its place. Reading is an active process. Experienced readers take responsibility for that action—reading critically, constructing meaning, interpreting what they read. If our annotations help you read critically, then use them; if they interfere, then just continue reading the main text and skip over them.

What is the genre and its conventions?

Genre is a term used by composition and literature teachers to refer to form—specifically, to forms that have common features and follow certain conventions of style, presentation, and subject matter. Literary genres include the short story and novel, the tragedy and comedy, the lyric and the epic poem. Essay genres include the memoir and the biographical profile, the visual analysis and op-ed, the literacy narrative and the parable. For the essay, *genre* partially determines the form's content and organization, but it should never do so in a "cookie-cutter" way.

Conventions are practices or customs commonly used in a genre—like a handshake for a social introduction or a eulogy at a funeral. Genre and convention are linked concepts, the one implying the other. Scientific articles (a genre) begin with a title and an abstract (conventions) and include sections about the methodology and the results (also conventions). Op-eds, by convention, begin with a "hook"; profiles of persons or places include a physical description of the subject; literacy narratives include a key episode in the acquisition of reading or writing skills. But in reading and writing essays, conventions should not be treated in an automatic, rigid, or insincere way. They should be seen as guidelines, strategies, or special features, not as rules.

As you read an essay, think about its form: what it includes, how the writer presents the subject, what features seem distinctive. If you read a pair or group of essays assigned by your teacher, you might ask yourself whether they represent the same genre or are noticeably different. If they are the same, you will recognize similar features; if they are different, you will notice less overlap.

Below are some common genres included in *The Norton Reader* and some features to watch for as you read.

Narrative genres

Narrative genres tell a story, using vivid details about people, events, and conflicts or crises. They also reflect on the meaning of the stories, offering the reader an interpretation or explanation of what occurred. Common narrative genres include the autobiographical essay, literacy narrative, historical narrative, and biographical narrative.

Autobiographical essay The genre of *autobiography* focuses on a significant personal experience in the writer's past and draws out the meaning as the writer tells the story and reflects on the experience. Sometimes an autobiographical essay is called *memoir, personal narrative*, or *mini-autobiography*. Its key features include a dramatic event or episode; vivid details and narration; and an interweaving of narration with reflection on and interpretation of the essayist's experience.

If you are assigned Alice Walker's "Beauty: When the Other Dancer Is the Self" (p. 55) or George Orwell's "Shooting an Elephant" (p. 784), you will immediately spot the dramatic event. For Walker, it is the day a BB pellet strikes her eye and causes "a glob of whitish scar tissue, a hideous cataract." For Orwell, it is the day when he, a young British official in Burma, must shoot an elephant that has gone "must." Walker introduces the drama in two italicized sentences: *"It was great fun being cute. But then, one day, it ended."* In the remainder of the essay she reflects on how the injury affected her sense of self, her identity. Orwell builds up to the dramatic moment more slowly, taking us through the thoughts and events that lead to his pulling the trigger. As he tells his story, Orwell reflects on the motivations of his action and reaches a point of insight:

> And it was at this moment, as I stood there with the rifle in my hands, that I first grasped the hollowness, the futility of the white man's dominion in the East.

These two essayists handle the conventions of their autobiographical essays differently, with different narrative styles and different pacing, but they both focus on a significant event and draw out its significance in the course of the essay.

Literacy narrative A subcategory of the autobiographical essay, the *literacy narrative* focuses on learning to read or write. Like other narrative genres, it uses personal experience, requires vivid details and a sharp narrative style, and gives a clear indication of the narrative's significance. Teachers frequently assign this genre in composition courses, for reading or writing or both.

If you read Frederick Douglass's "Learning to Read" (p. 346) or Ben Franklin's "Learning to Write" (p. 440), you will encounter two classic versions of the literacy narrative. For Douglass, a slave, reading was a forbidden, illegal activity, so to learn to read he was "compelled to resort to various stratagems," as he phrases it. Douglass's literacy narrative includes rich details about his life as a slave, the strategies he used to acquire literacy, and the essential value that reading held for someone who did not want to remain *"a slave for life."* For Franklin, a young man trained as a printer, writing became a means to raise himself in his social and professional world, and his narrative explains some of the tactics that allowed him to succeed. As you read Douglass or Franklin, watch for the details they choose to include and the anecdotes they recount as important to their stories. Other literacy narratives in *The Norton Reader* include Eudora Welty's "Clamorous to Learn" (p. 350), Sherman Alexis's "Superman and Me" (p. 355), and Richard Rodriguez's "Aria" (p. 405) by modern American writers who tell of their educational experiences with fascinating, sometimes painful details and with serious reflection on the meaning of reading and writing in American culture.

Historical narrative This genre also relies on narrative—on telling a story—but focuses on the larger social or political patterns that the story reveals. Like other narrative genres, *historical narrative* requires vivid details and an indication of the narrative's significance, but it may incorporate more than a single, dramatic event (though it will often begin by describing one) and offer multiple stories or episodes.

You will find several examples of historical narrative in the "History" section, including Barbara Tuchman's "'This Is the End of the World': The Black Death" (p. 692) and Philip Gourevitch's "After the Genocide" (p. 752). Both writers know that vivid descriptions and compelling anecdotes are central to good historical narratives. In her opening paragraph, Tuchman shows us—in gory detail—what the "black death" (bubonic plague) looked like:

> The diseased sailors showed strange swellings about the size of an egg or an apple in the armpits and groin. The swellings oozed blood and pus and were followed by spreading boils and black blotches on the skin from internal bleeding.

A gruesome picture, but it captures the reader's attention and fascinates us enough to read on. Gourevitch opens more quietly by setting his historical narrative in eastern Rwanda, but the vivid details of death, murder, and genocide appear very soon:

> At least fifty mostly decomposed cadavers covered the floor, wadded in clothing, their belongings strewn about and smashed. Macheted skulls had rolled here and there.

This description, which continues in almost clinical detail for a long paragraph, sets the context for the history of the Rwandan genocide that Gourevitch will tell. But it does much more: it establishes the significance of the event, justifies the label of mass murder or "genocide," and alerts the reader to the historical and international crisis in Africa. Both essayists continue with many episodes—rather than focus on a single one—because their histories require evidence of widespread events and consequences.

Biographical narrative The *biographical narrative* is a subcategory of the historical narrative discussed above, and it is related to the *biographical profile* described below. Sometimes writers choose to focus their accounts of historical events on a specific person, perhaps because that person was a "key player," the moving force in the event, or perhaps because that person allows a window into how a large historical event felt to an average citizen.

You will find both techniques—and variations on them—in essays throughout *The Norton Reader*. Walt Whitman tells the story of an American president's assassination in his "Death of Abraham Lincoln" (p. 716). Logically, Whitman focuses his narrative on the president, telling what happened on the day of the assassination but including other biographical details that he recalls from previous sightings of Lincoln and ending with his reflections on the significance of what he calls "a heroic-eminent life." In contrast, in "The Library as Survival" (p. 741), Alberto Manguel gives mini-biographies of less famous people who performed heroic deeds when the Nazis sought to destroy Jewish books and libraries during World War II. As you read historical and biographical narratives, compare their features and try to notice their conventions: people and places need to be described with accuracy and interest, stories need to be told with clarity and good pace, significance needs to emerge from the narrative, not just be tacked on at the end.

Descriptive genres

Descriptive genres let the reader know how a person, place, or thing looks, sounds, feels, or maybe even smells. But they do more: they give a dominant impression, interpret a person's actions, offer a reflection on the significance of place, or in some other way put the objective details into a larger framework. Descriptive genres in *The Norton Reader* include the profile of a person, profile of a place, and natural history.

Profile of a person Also called a *biographical sketch* or a *mini-biography*, the *profile of a person* features an individual or a group of people and uses first-hand knowledge, interviews, and/or research to present its subject. Since readers like to read about interesting subjects, it is sometimes assumed that the person must be interesting beforehand. But, really, it's the writer who makes the person interesting by discovering special characteristics or qualities through interviews or observation, by finding an interesting angle from which to present the subject, and by including engaging details, anecdotes, or dialogue to enliven the portrait. These are the special features, or conventions, of the biographical profile.

Profiles can be free-standing essays or parts of books. Tom Wolfe's "Yeager" (p. 448) is a portrait of the astronaut Chuck Yeager and part of a book about the first American astronauts in space, *The Right Stuff.* When you read this essay, you will see that Wolfe does not begin in the usual, boring way with date of birth, place of birth, parents, and education (though those details eventually make it into the profile). Instead, Wolfe lets us *hear* Yeager's voice by imitating its sound and style. Then Wolfe suggests the importance of Yeager's place in American aviation by describing how every American pilot tries to imitate this man with "the right stuff." The profile is chock-full of tales about Yeager's daring, often reckless, escapades—even as it narrates the story of how Yeager made history by breaking the sound barrier.

Profiles about family members can be difficult. Even if an essayist loves his or her parents, not every reader will find someone else's parents distinctive, memorable, or worth reading about. So it takes vivid details, humorous (or chilling) stories, and a bit of distance to succeed in the family profile. Annie Dillard *makes* her mother memorable in "An American Childhood" (p. 110) by recalling idiosyncratic stories and sayings, including the line "Terwilliger bunts one" that amuses and annoys her mother. Scott Russell Sanders, perhaps unfortunately, remembers too many characteristic episodes about his father. His profile, titled "Under the Influence" (p. 100), begins: "My father drank." Both of these writers had ordinary parents, but they make them seem extraordinary by the vividness of their memories, the special angles they take, and the overarching perspective on their parents' character that they bring to the essay.

Profile of a place Places can also become the focus of a profile, in a subcategory sometimes simply called a *place essay*. The features of this genre involve discovering the special characteristics or qualities of the place, finding an interpretive framework in which to present it, and including engaging details, anecdotes, or dialogue to enliven the essay. Since places can't speak, the essayist must speak for them and say enough about them to make them come alive.

Essayists re-create places in different ways. Ian Frazier, in "Take the F" (p. 154), uses a subway line (the F Sixth Avenue Local) to locate his Brooklyn neighborhood on the New York City grid, but he also engages the five senses—sight, sound, smell, taste, and touch—to give non-New Yorkers a feel for the place. In contrast, David Guterson begins with hard facts in "The Mall of America" (p. 161):

> 140,000 hot dogs sold each week, 10,000 permanent jobs, 44 escalators and 17 elevators, 12,750 parking spaces, 13,300 short tons of steel, $1 million in cash dispersed weekly from 8 automatic-teller machines.

Guterson's facts give us the immense scale of the mall—details that boggle the imagination but that speak to some deep-seated American desire for immensity. Both essayists bring their places to life, but in different ways and with different approaches to understanding the meaning of a place.

If a profile includes both person and place, it is what the writer Anne Fadiman calls a "Character in Context" piece. Many times, we learn about a person by seeing him or her in a characteristic space; the place defines the person, the person defines the place. N. Scott Momaday's "The Way to Rainy Mountain" (p. 119) gives us a sacred place of the Kiowas, an old landmark that they called "Rainy Mountain." Yet his profile is also about his grandmother, Abo, whom he associates with the sacred mountain:

> Her forebears came down from the high country in western Montana nearly three centuries ago. They were mountain people, a mysterious tribe of hunters whose language has never been positively classified in any major group.

To understand the significance of Momaday's return to Rainy Mountain, we must understand the mountain's associations with his grandmother. And vice versa: to understand Abo's significance to her grandson, we must understand the meaning of Rainy Mountain to the Kiowa.

Natural history The term *natural history* can refer generally to any historical writing about nature, but it also designates a genre related to the profile: the life cycle or biography of a plant or animal. (Think of it as profiling not a person but a bear or a dragonfly or a weed like goldenrod.) You will find some of these essays in the "Nature and Environment" section of this book, and you may also encounter them in biology classes. They describe a plant or animal, take it through its life cycle, and sometimes explain its significance or relationship to the human species.

In "Under the Snow" (p. 490) John McPhee focuses on a wildlife biologist, Gary Alt, who studies bears; as he describes Alt's research, McPhee includes many scientific facts about the life cycle of bears, including their breeding and feeding practices, their natural habitat, and hibernation patterns. In "Joyas Voladoras" (p. 502) Brian Doyle, too, gives a natural history—in this case of the hummingbird. But Doyle's purpose is to consider the hearts of birds and mammals and their metaphorical significance, including the human heart with its capacity to be "bruised and scarred, scored and torn, repaired by time and will, patched by force of character."

Both versions of natural history—raising scientific questions, raising questions about human actions—appear in *The Norton Reader.* Look for them in David Foster Wallace's "Consider the Lobster" (p. 635), Henry David Thoreau's "The Battle of the Ants" (p. 758), and Edward Abbey's "The Serpents of Paradise" (p. 496).

Analytic genres

Analytic genres carefully and methodically examine a text, an image, a cultural object, or a social trend by breaking it into parts, closely reading its components, and noting how the parts work in relation to the whole. In *The Norton Reader* you will find examples of textual analysis, visual analysis, and cultural analysis.

Textual analysis Also called *close reading, textual analysis* focuses on written words. It examines words and phrases for explicit and implicit meanings; it looks for similes (comparisons using *like* or *as*) and metaphors (comparisons without explicit connectors) to reveal patterns of association and hidden meanings; and it interprets the whole text on the basis of these methodical, individual observations. The *text* may be anything from the Bible or Koran, to poems and novels, to ads, billboards, or official memos.

In "The Epistle of Paul the Apostle to the Ephesians" (p. 1061), Rita Dove analyzes a book from the New Testament. Traditionally, Christians have analyzed the Bible to clarify difficult or obscure passages, to understand the book's message, and to apply it to their lives. Dove recalls her first experience with biblical analysis in a Sunday school class at her A.M.E. church.

> I was thirteen when the man who would introduce me to the apostle Paul walked into our senior Sunday-school class. He was tall, dark, and hellishly handsome, severely dressed in a matte-black narrow suit and black shirt from which rose a ring of shocking white, like a slipped halo.

In class, Dove's teacher focuses on words like "grace" and concepts like "mortal sin." But little details in this opening description—"hellishly handsome," "like a slipped halo"—clue us into the fact that Dove, the adult essayist, will do her own textual analysis, not rely on one handed down from a male clergyman. As you read her essay, notice how Dove probes the meaning of words like "human agency" and delves into the implications of textual metaphors, like Paul's "comparing the church to a marriage." For a different take on analysis, consider Mark Doty's "Souls on Ice" (p. 992), written by a poet who both explains the origin of the images he uses in his poem, "A Display of Mackerel," and the effects he tries to achieve with them. Doty compares the fish "in parallel rows / on ice" and their "scales' / radiant sections" to the "seams of lead / in a Tiffany window"—a simile that captures their unexpected beauty. Read the poem for yourself or with your class, and try a textual analysis of your own.

Visual analysis Like textual analysis, *visual analysis* looks for explicit and implicit meanings; searches for patterns of association and hidden intentions; and interprets the whole object on the basis of these methodical, individual observations. Instead of a written text, visual analysis focuses on an image, a photograph, a painting, or another visual phenomenon.

Some visual analyses have as their goal the explanation of the image itself. In "Understanding Comics" (p. 1022) Scott McCloud draws a teacher figure in the left-hand frame to explain the function of pictures and how they relate to words in a comic strip. In effect, he creates images and embeds visual analysis within the same piece. Other selections use visual analysis as part of a larger argument. An example of this appears in H. Bruce Franklin's "From Realism to Virtual Reality: Images of America's Wars" (p. 761). Franklin writes as a historian; to make his argument about how changes in technology affect our understanding of war, he analyzes a sequence of images from the Civil War through the Iraqi war of the 1990s. As you read this essay, watch how Franklin cites historical descriptions of the photographs, refers to the "dominant metaphor" or "structuring metaphor" of movies and television shows, and points to motifs repeated from image to image.

In *The Norton Reader* you will find essays that combine textual and visual analysis or that use images to trigger both kinds of analysis. (Watch for essays that include photographs, drawings, graphs, and other visual material.) In writing "Strangers" (p. 135), Toni Morrison began by thinking about a book of photographs, interpreting the images, and pondering their significance, but her essay also analyzes the ethical implications of writing narratives, of creating life stories for people she does not know. In other essays, such as N. Scott Momaday's "The Way to Rainy Mountain" (p. 119) and Fred Strebeigh's "The Wheels of Freedom: The Bicycle in China" (p. 276), the authors provide images to accompany their prose: in Momaday's case, his father's drawings; in Strebeigh's, photographs he took during his travels in China at the time of the Tiananmen uprising. These images enrich the primary analyses of the authors by underscoring key points and adding visual evidence to their arguments.

Cultural analysis This genre, called both *cultural analysis* and *cultural critique*, takes an object, trend, fad, or other phenomenon as the subject of its analysis. It uses the strategies of textual and visual analysis described above, adding personal response and library research, if desirable, to explain and interpret. Examples of this form appear in the section "Cultural Analysis."

What kinds of cultural objects and trends do essayists analyze? Almost anything and everything, it seems. The French critic Roland Barthes analyzes toys, concluding that they "*literally* prefigure the world of adult functions" (p. 274). The American writer Fred Strebeigh analyzes the Chinese bicycle (p. 276), interviewing people who rely on them for work and play, giving us a history of their manufacture, reflecting on their names ("Forever," "Flying Pigeon"), and concluding that they represent "the wheels of freedom" to many Chinese people. The African American scholar Henry Louis Gates analyzes hairstyles popular in his youth (p. 000)—how they were created, how movie stars, singers, and black icons popularized them, and why the styles remain so important for him.

Other essayists analyze trends or social practices. Jessica Mitford, for example, looks at the funeral industry, taking an outsider perspective. In "Behind the Formaldehyde Curtain" (p. 254), Mitford engages many different strategies in making her analysis—from "the arrival of the corpse at the mortuary" to the process of embalming to the presentation of the body for open-casket viewing. Her goal is to debunk the "American way of death," as she calls it, and to show how the undertaker has assumed the place formerly held by the clergyman. In "The Charms of Wikipedia" (p. 915) Nicholson Baker writes as an insider, someone who "contributed to a number of articles, some extensively, and always anonymously." As he tells the history of this now-global online resource, his larger goal involves analyzing its cultural role and defending an "inclusionist" policy for saving rather than deleting entries.

Argumentative genres

Forms of modern argument have their roots in classical Greece and Rome—that is, they go back at least 2,500 years. The Greek philosopher Aristotle held that there were really only two essential parts of an argument: (1) the statement of the case, and (2) the proof of the case. But he conceded that in practice most orators added two other parts: an introduction and a conclusion.

Roman rhetoricians like Quintillian refined and expanded this simple Aristotelian approach to include five or six parts:

(1) *exordium*: the introduction

(2) *narratio*: the statement or exposition of the case under discussion

(3) *divisio*: the outline of the points or steps in the argument

(4) *confirmatio*: the proof of the case (sometimes called *probatio*)

(5) *confutatio*: the refutation of opposing arguments

(6) *peroratio*: the conclusion

Yet Roman rhetoricians also acknowledged that, for any given argument, orators might want to omit parts. (They might, for example, omit *divisio* if the steps of the argument were simple.) And orators would often rearrange the parts of their speeches. They might, for instance, refute an opponent's arguments before advancing their own case.

Unless you participate in a debating society, you—like most modern college students—won't see this formal version of classical argument very often. Yet all Americans study it in civics class when they discuss the "Declaration of Independence" (p. 804) because Thomas Jefferson used the tactics of classical rhetoric as revived in the eighteenth century. Today, we hear its legacy in public speeches and see traces of it in newspaper editorials. The Greek and Roman philosophers weren't so much prescribing a genre as they were describing common argumentative practices. It makes sense that, if you want to argue your case effectively, you need to introduce it, outline the key points, present your evidence, and refute your opponent's position—all the steps they described. You will find these steps in the argumentative genres considered below: op-eds and editorials, public speeches and orations, and parables.

Op-eds and editorials This genre focuses on issues of public interest and encourages ordinary citizens to contribute their perspectives, opinions, and arguments to the public debate. *Op-eds* and *editorials* begin with a "hook"—a link to a recent event or news article that grabs readers' attention—as the introduction. Specific features, or conventions, include a forthright statement of position, evidence in support, often a counterargument or rebuttal of the opposition, and sometimes a formal conclusion.

Brent Staples's "Why Colleges Shower Their Students with A's" (p. 329) features most of these conventions. Staples begins by citing the principle of a famous economist, Milton Friedman, to the effect that superior products flourish and shabby ones die out. But Staples refutes this principle when applied to colleges and argues that, in fact, colleges are giving too many A's and thus "stoking grade inflation and devaluing degrees." When you read Staples's op-ed, note how he puts forward his evidence, then rebuts a common argument of his opposition:

> The argument that grades are rising because students are better prepared is simply not convincing. The evidence suggests that students and parents are demanding—and getting—what they think of as their money's worth.

Staples wraps up with some proposals to remedy grade inflation and a final stab at parents and students who are "addicted to counterfeit excellence." Although he no doubt wrote from the evidence he had gathered and the conclusion he had independently reached, you will discover that Staples uses five of the six parts of the "formal" classical argument—all but number 3.

Public speeches and orations Because *speeches* and *orations* derive directly, if also distantly, from the classical tradition of argument, they often show its formal features. Many speechwriters introduce the issue at hand, state their position, offer evidence in support and counterarguments against, and sum up—sometimes with a high rhetorical flourish. These modern tactics are based on the older classical conventions.

Elizabeth Cady Stanton, the nineteenth-century feminist, shows her knowledge of American public oratory in "Declaration of Sentiments and Resolutions" (p. 811). Stanton's declaration, presented at the first U.S. women's rights convention, is modeled on Jefferson's seminal American Declaration of Independence (p. 804). A century later, the Reverend Martin Luther King Jr., one of the great civil rights leaders and orators of modern America, continues the tradition in his "I Have a Dream" speech (p. 852) and in "A Letter from Birmingham Jail" (p. 818). In the first, King argues that America must make good on the Emancipation Proclamation and "open the doors of opportunity to all of God's children"; in the second, he makes the case for civil disobedience, taking his audience through the steps of his thinking and quietly refuting those who disagree. It is no coincidence that these important American speeches and documents use the formal conventions of argument: in so doing, the speakers demonstrate their education, ability, and right to debate the pressing issues of their day.

James van Tholen's "Surprised by Death" (p. 1070) is *not* an oration or formal argument; it is a Sunday sermon, preached upon van Tholen's return to the pulpit after months of treatment for cancer. Van Tholen uses techniques from several genres, including autobiographical narrative as he talks about his illness and fear in fighting cancer, and textual analysis as he analyzes the meaning of the Christian concept of *grace* and the Greek word *eti* in Romans 5. Yet van Tholen also makes an argument: that he is right to have hope, "unwavering hope," in God and that his listeners must have this hope, too. His personal experience and his careful study of the Bible become part of the evidence he marshals to state this conclusion.

Parables A *parable* is a story that illustrates a point, poses or answers a question, or suggests a lesson. A parable can imply an argument—though it does not make that argument directly or simply. The word *parable* means "thrown beside," and there's a sense in which any attempt to interpret a parable too specifically will always just miss the mark: the form is too complex to be reduced to a single meaning or simple moral. It is worth considering the parable as an alternative form of argument—a genre a writer might use when more formal arguments won't quite work. Feminists, for example, have sometimes turned to the parable when they find that masculine logic fails to grasp an issue. Native Americans, including Chief Seattle, have traditionally used the parable to refute the wrong-headed logic of white Americans.

Most religious traditions include parables—such as those told by Jesus or the Zen parables we include in "Philosophy and Religion." In the Zen parable "Muddy Road" (p. 1127) there's a literal-minded character, Ekido, who lives strictly by the rules, and a more knowing character, Tanzan, who has deeper wisdom. Ekido knows that a monk is supposed to avoid women, so he chastises Tanzan for picking up a "lovely girl in a silk kimono and sash" and carrying her across a muddy intersection. Tanzan responds with a question: "I left the girl there. Are you still carrying her?" Tanzan's question suggests that it's not the literal touching of a woman that matters. What matters is sexual desire. By carrying the image of the girl in his mind and brooding on it, Ekido is harboring desire within his heart, perhaps giving it space to grow. The parable is about the complexities of human desire—but it's hard to argue Tanzan's position without using many more words and perhaps being less effective. The parable—a narrative with a probing final twist—does the trick.

As you read arguments in various sections of *The Norton Reader*—whether in "Ethics" or "Politics and Government," in "Spoken Words" or "Science and Technology"—consider where and why authors use formal techniques (conventions of argument) and where and why they turn to alternative strategies—strategies identified with other genres. In the end, the goal is to make an effective argument, to convince the reader of the validity of your evidence, or urge the listener to take a prescribed course of action.

STRATEGIES FOR CRITICAL READING

The previous pages have focused on reading specific kinds of essays and on strategies for recognizing genres and their conventions. Here we offer some general tips for approaching the reading your instructor assigns this semester.

Preview the essay

Think about the essay's title, read its opening paragraph, skim the topic sentences (usually, the first sentence of each paragraph). Look at the contextual note on the first page, and try to imagine the experience, issue, or debate that motivated the essayist to write. *Previewing* is a technique widely used for college reading, but not all writing teachers encourage it. Some teachers encourage previewing for academic writing, explaining that it helps readers focus on key issues; other teachers discourage previewing, pointing out that a good essay—like a good novel or movie—can be ruined by knowing the ending.

Write in the margin

As you read, note points that seem interesting and important, forecast issues that you think the writer will address, and pose questions of your own. Talk back. Most essayists want active readers who think about what the essay says, implies, and urges as a personal response or course of action. Similarly, note points that you don't understand or that you find ambiguous. Puzzling over a sentence or a passage with your classmates can lead to crucial points of debate. Mark your queries and use them to energize class discussion.

Analyze the illustrations

Many of the essays in *The Norton Reader* include illustrations from their original publications. Think about how the essays and the images "speak" to each other. Consider whether the images enrich, highlight, or possibly challenge the essay. Does the image primarily illustrate the essay, or does it emphasize a feature unexplained by the essayist? Does the image enrich and make clearer one aspect of the writing, or does it minimize certain aspects of the subject, perhaps aspects you find important? What do you see in the images that the essayist discusses or explains? What do you see that he or she overlooks or minimizes? Thinking about images can help you clarify the author's argument or reveal points the author may have missed.

Summarize the essay

Write a summary of the essay. Begin by making a list of its key points and identifying the evidence used in support of each; then try to state briefly, in your own words, the "gist" or core of the essay. The goal is to condense the argument and evidence, while remaining faithful to the author's meaning. Your summary will be useful when you discuss the essay in class or write about it in a paper. For some genres, including the scientific report, a summary or *abstract* is included in the essay itself.

Keep a reading journal

Buy a class notebook or designate a special section of your college notebook for reflections on the essays you read. For each essay, take notes, record your responses, write questions about what puzzles you and what you want to discuss in class. Write down sentences or passages that you like and that you might want to use as models for your own essays. You may also want to list questions that the essayist raises and answers, as well as write down questions that you think the essayist has overlooked.

Use the study questions

Review the questions that follow each essay in *The Norton Reader*, and think about the issues—the subject, the structure, the language—that they pose. We include these questions to help you become an active reader, to focus attention on key issues, and to sometimes make suggestions for *doing* or *writing* something.

- Some questions ask you to locate or mark the essays' structural features, the patterns that undergird and clarify meaning. Narrative, description, exposition, persuasion, and argument follow conventional shapes—or distort them—and your ability to recognize these shapes will improve your comprehension.
- Other questions ask you to paraphrase meanings or extend them—that is, to express the meaning in your own words, to amplify points by providing your own examples, or to reframe points by connecting them with points in other essays.
- Still other questions ask you to notice special features or conventions that contribute to meaning: the author's choice of title, the author's voice

(or persona), the author's assumptions about audience (and how the author speaks to the audience), and the author's choice of style and forms of expression.

- At least one question, usually the last, asks you to write. Sometimes we ask you to demonstrate comprehension by writing about something from your experience or reading that extends an essay and enforces its argument. Sometimes, we invite you to express disagreement or dissent by writing about something from your experience or knowledge that qualifies the author's argument or calls it into question. The final question may ask you to compare or contrast two authors' positions—especially when their positions seem opposed. Or we may ask you to adapt one of the essay's rhetorical strategies to a topic of your own choice and to make the essay even more your own by basing it on personal experience.

Re-read the essay

If possible, read the essay a second time before you discuss it in class. If you're short on time, re-read the key passages and paragraphs that you marked in marginal notes. Ask yourself what you see the second time that you didn't register on first reading.

As these tactics suggest, reading need not be only a private activity; it can also become communal and cooperative. Sharing reading journals in class helps to reveal points of ambiguity and to generate debate. Discussion, with the whole class or in smaller groups, can clarify your own and others' interpretation of the essays. What interests and motives does each reader bring to particular essays? Do some interests and motives yield better readings than others? What meanings do readers agree about? What meanings do they disagree about? Can we account for our differences? What are responsive and responsible readings? Are there irresponsible readings, and how do we decide? All these questions—and others—can emerge as private reading moves into the more public arena of the classroom.

Readers write, writers read. Making meaning by writing is the flip side of making it by reading, and we hope to engage you in both processes. But in neither process are meanings passed from hand to hand like nickels, dimes, and quarters. Instead, they are constructed—as a quilt or a house or an institution. We hope that these suggestions for reading will lead you to engaged and fruitful writing.

Writing in College

Not too long ago, a college composition class usually involved a one-way conversation. Teachers gave out assignments and students wrote essays and handed them in for a grade. Teachers would generally read them once and hand them back with the errors circled and a grade. Times have changed. Now teachers still give out assignments, but students do them in stages, as drafts, and teachers often review them more than once, sometimes in a conference. Often the papers are reviewed at a tutorial session at the Writing Center. Drafts-in-process are often read by other class members, who are encouraged to give the writer frank, helpful responses about much more than the grammar, spelling, and punctuation. Today's students often get a great deal more feedback on their writing *before* it's handed in for a grade.

Additionally, the audience for student writing has changed. Papers are no longer always written to an audience of one, a "teacher as examiner." For some time now, students have been writing for peers outside of class and for larger communities as well. They have been creating discussion boards, blogs, wikis, Web sites, and other new genres with a variety of public audiences and uses. Today's students often do a great deal of writing outside of their class assignments. Finally, many writing courses today employ a portfolio approach, in which a term's worth of student papers are kept together and selectively submitted at the end, with a substantive cover letter or essay in which students reflect on their writing over the course of the semester. Obviously, different instructors will have different approaches, but every student should understand that the forms and functions of student writing have evolved and expanded in recent years.

Much of the writing you will do in a composition course will start with an assignment from your instructor. Perhaps you will be asked to respond to some of the essays in *The Norton Reader*—to expand on something a writer has said, to agree or disagree with a claim a writer has made, or to do some research to extend an author's argument and say something new about it. Or, you may be assigned a particular genre or kind of writing—a literacy narrative, a profile of a person or place, a visual or textual analysis, or an argumentative paper—and asked to use selections in this book as models of these kinds of writing. We have selected the readings because they are full of important ideas you can react to, either by agreeing or disagreeing, and also because the essays represent excellent examples of good writers at their best, models for aspiring writers to follow.

What follows is a brief guide for writing with *The Norton Reader.* We'll look at discovering your purpose, addressing your audience, finding a subject, determining what genre to employ, using rhetorical strategies, and understanding the writing process.

Knowing your purpose

Your *purpose* is, put simply, the goal for your writing. What do you want to achieve? What points do you want to make? What idea or cause motivates you to write? Anything you can do to sharpen your thinking and infuse your writing with a clear sense of purpose will be to the good: you will find it easier to stay focused and help your readers see your key point and main ideas about your subject.

What are some common purposes writers have? The authors of the essays in *The Norton Reader* had informing, persuading, entertaining, or expressing as some of their purposes. So, too, your writing will have a primary purpose, usually defined in an assignment by words such as "explain," "describe," "analyze," "argue." Each is a signal about the purpose for your writing.

For instance, if an assignment asks you to *analyze* the persuasiveness of Nicholas Kristof's op-ed "Saudis in Bikinis" (p. 272), then your purpose is to explain the claims Kristof makes, examine the evidence he uses to support them, discuss points or perspectives he misses, and develop a thesis about the reasons for the essay's persuasiveness. If an assignment asks you to *argue* for or against Kristof's claim about women in Saudi Arabia, then your purpose is to take a side, defending or refuting his claims and using evidence from your own knowledge and from reputable sources to support your argument.

Use these questions to think about your purpose for writing:

- What does the assignment ask you to do? Is the goal to inform readers, entertain them, argue a point, or express an idea or feeling? Beyond a general purpose, what does the assignment require in terms of a specific purpose?
- How does your purpose affect your choice of a subject? What do you know about the subject? How can you find out more about this subject?
- How can you connect to your readers? What will they want or need to know? How do you want them to respond to your writing?

Addressing your audience

Just as the authors in *The Norton Reader* aimed their essays at different *audiences*—readers of books, large newspapers, magazines, small journals, and scholarly publications, as well as activists, ordinary citizens, and churchgoers—so you need to imagine your audience as you write. Too wide an audience—"the general public"—and you run the risk of making your essay too diffuse, trying to reach everyone. Too narrow an audience—"my roommate Zach"—and you run the risk of being too specific.

How can you imagine an audience of your own? One way is to look around your writing classroom: that's your immediate audience, the people who are taking the course with you and your instructor. Another way is to think about your home community: your family, your neighbors, and the people of your town or city. Think of your audience as readers like yourself, with some of the same knowledge of the world and some of the same tastes. Consider your audience's range of reference: historical events they have witnessed firsthand, movies and TV shows they know about or have seen, and the books they have read or heard of. Think of them as willing to be convinced by whatever you write, but in need of good evidence.

Inevitably, some writers find that imagining an audience made only of class members seems too restrictive. That's fine; feel free to invoke another audience, say, a group of people who share a certain passion, perhaps for a team, a sport, a game, or a type of music or film. (But remember to take into account your instructor, who may need some filling in about the special knowledge you share with your audience.)

Use these questions to guide you in thinking about audience:

- What readers are you hoping to reach with your writing?
- What information can you assume your readers know? What information do you need to explain?
- In what ways will you need to adjust the style of your writing—the language, tone, sentence structure and complexity, and examples—to meet the needs of your audience?

FINDING A SUBJECT

Like the audience and purpose for your writing, the *subject* of your writing—what you write about—will often be assigned by your instructor. Some assignments are very specific, such as this study question following Stephen King's "On Writing": "Write about a time someone responded to your writing in a way that helped you learn to be a better writer. What kinds of comments and edits did that person make? Why was that response helpful to you?" Other assignments may be more general, such as the following study question on Scott Russell Sanders's profile of his father, "Under the Influence" (p. 100): "Drawing on your memories of a friend or family member, write an essay about some problem that person had and its effect on your life." This broader assignment requires you to determine the person you wish to discuss, the problem you wish to analyze, and the larger effect the person and problem had on your life.

Some assignments give you even more leeway in choosing a subject, leaving you with the inevitable question "What should I write about?" In this case, write about what you know or care about, drawing on knowledge you've already gleaned about a subject from personal experience, your reading, or research. Your knowledge does not have to be totally new, but your perspective on a subject needs to come from you—a real person writing about a subject that matters.

How do you find what you know or care about? One way is to raise questions about an essay you've read:

- What is the author's main point? Do you agree or disagree with the main point?
- Has the author said enough about the subject? What gaps or omissions do you see, if any? Are there sentences or paragraphs that you could expand into an essay of your own?
- Are the author's examples and evidence convincing? If not, why not? Can you provide a more compelling example, additional evidence, or a counter example?
- Does this reading "speak" to anything else you've read in *The Norton Reader*? Can you explain how this reading connects to the other? Do the readings agree or disagree?
- Is this reading true to your own experience? Has anything like this happened to you, or have you ever observed anything like this?

You can also choose a subject by reflecting on your own experience:

- Has someone you know affected your life in some way—by teaching you, by serving as an example (good or bad), or by changing your attitude?
- Is there a place that you can describe to others, telling them what makes it unique or special to you?
- Is there a subject you feel strongly about, something you believe others need to learn about—for example, a program on your campus or in your neighborhood, a controversial item of national significance, or a matter of global importance?
- Have you had an experience that has taught you something valuable, influenced the way you live, or made you think differently about life, school, work, family, or friends? Readers will be interested in the details of the experience, including how it affected you and what you have learned.

DETERMINING GENRE

Like the purpose, audience, and subject of your writing, the *genre* or form of your writing may be prescribed in your instructor's assignment. *The Norton Reader* contains a variety of essay genres:

- **Narrative genres**, which tell stories and include autobiographical essays, literacy narratives, historical narratives, and biographical narratives.
- **Descriptive genres**, which give details about how a person, place, or thing looks, sounds, and feels, often in a larger framework. These

include profiles of people and places and essays about nature and natural history.

- **Analytic genres**, which examine texts, images, and cultural objects and trends.
- **Argumentative genres**, which take stands and provide evidence to support them. These include op-eds, editorials, public speeches, and parables.

These genres are discussed on pp. xxxvii–xlvii and listed in the Genres Index.

If you're assigned a literacy narrative, for example, your writing will tell a vivid, detailed story about an experience you've had with reading, writing, or schooling. To write a profile of a place, you will need to give a coherent impression of it by gathering and organizing detailed descriptions of how the place looks, smells, or even feels. If you're asked to take a stand on an important issue, you will write in an argumentative genre; if you choose an op-ed or editorial, you will need to focus on a central claim, support that claim with solid evidence, consider opposing views, and be brief. Or, if your assignment is a textual analysis of one of the readings in this book, you will need to examine features of the essay—its structure, style, key metaphors and phrases—paying close attention to rhetorical details.

If you have some leeway in choosing the genre in which you will write, consider what genre best fits your purpose, audience, and subject:

- What goal do you have for your writing? What genre is most appropriate for that goal?
- Who will read your writing? What genre will best convey the point of your writing to your readers?
- What are you writing about? What genre is well-suited to your subject?

To gain more understanding of these genres, read plenty of examples, analyze the forms and strategies they use, and then try out a genre on your own. There's no better way to understand how a genre works than to try your hand at writing it.

USING RHETORICAL STRATEGIES

As you plan your essay, you will want to think about the *rhetorical strategies* by which you will present your ideas and evidence to readers. These strategies, sometimes called *rhetorical modes* or *techniques*, help a writer organize evidence, connect facts into a sequence, and provide clusters of information necessary for conveying a purpose or an argument. You might choose to *analyze* the cause of an outcome, *compare* one thing to another, *classify* your facts into categories, *define* a key term, *describe* a person, place, or phenomenon, *explain* how a process works, or *narrate* a pertinent event or experience.

Sometimes, the writing assignment that your instructor gives will determine the strategy: for example, an assignment to compare Jack Hitt's position on binge drinking with Kenneth Bruffee's (see p. 343) will require that you use a compare/contrast strategy. Similarly, the title of an essay or a study question might imply a rhetorical strategy: for example, Garrison Keillor's title, "How to Write a Letter" (p. 446), suggests a "process" essay. One of the study questions asks you to "Make a list of the suggestions that seem most helpful" and then goes on to ask, "Why might Keillor have included the other, less practical suggestions?" Here you'll need to write a list, not a paragraph, and then decide which are practical suggestions and which aren't for the process of writing a letter—an assignment you might be given.

Many essays use a mix of strategies. You might want to define a key term in an opening paragraph, narrate a story to make a point in the next paragraph, and analyze cause and effect in yet another. Except for very short pieces, most writers use several rhetorical strategies in an essay, choosing the one they think best fits their material.

Following are some rhetorical strategies that you will encounter in *The Norton Reader* and that you will want to use in your own writing.

Analyzing cause and effect

Focusing on causes helps a writer think about why something happened; focusing on effects helps a writer think about what might or could happen. Cause is oriented toward the future; effect looks back to the past. But you can use this strategy by working in either direction: from present to future, or from present to the past.

If you were writing about global warming and intending to show its harmful effects, you might lay out your evidence in this sequence:

> Cause → leads to → these effects.

If you were writing about binge drinking and trying to identify the reasons for its rise among college students, you might reverse the direction:

> Effect ← is the result of ← these causes.

Analyzing a cause (or causes) is a crucial strategy for genres such as cultural critique, op-ed, and historical narrative. But you can also use it in an autobiographical essay, where you might analyze the effects of a childhood trauma on your later life, or in a profile of a person, where you might seek the sources (the causes) of the person's adult personality or achievements.

Comparing and contrasting

Comparisons look for similarities between things; contrasts look for differences. In most uses of this rhetorical strategy, you will want to consider both similarities and differences—that is, you will want to compare *and* contrast. That's because most things worth comparing have something in common, even if they also have significant differences. You may end up finding more similarities than differences, or vice versa, but when using this strategy, think about both.

Comparison-contrast may be used for a single paragraph or for an entire essay. It tends to be set up in one of two ways: block or point-by-point. In the block technique, the writer gives all the information about one item and then follows with all the information about the other. Think of it as giving all the A's, then all the B's. Usually, the order of the information is the same for both. In the point-by-point technique, the writer focuses on specific points of comparison, alternating A, B, A, B, A, B, and so on until the main points have been covered.

Comparing and contrasting is an excellent strategy to use in writing a report, making an argument in an op-ed, or giving a speech to persuade your audience to take a specific course of action. You can set forth the pros and cons of different programs, political policies, or courses of action, leading up to the recommendation you endorse and believe is the more effective.

Classifying and dividing

Classifying and dividing involves either putting things into groups or dividing up a large block into smaller units. While this strategy might seem better suited to a biology lab than to a writing class, in fact it works well for organizing facts that seem chaotic or for handling big topics that at first glance seem overwhelming. Classifying and dividing allow the writer—and the reader—to get control of a big topic and break it into smaller units of analysis.

How does the essayist Susan Allan Toth discuss ways of "Going to the Movies" (p. 1036)? She classifies movies by the kinds of men who accompany her and who have different tastes in what they like to see. This technique gives the essayist four manageable categories: art films, movies with "a redeeming social conscience," movies that entertain, and romantic oldies that she watches on her own. In other words, Toth is classifying. How does the composer Aaron Copland discuss "How We Listen" (p. 1039)? He divides his essay—and the modes of listening to music—into three "planes" or levels of listening. This basic division helps the writer explain the different goals and experiences that listeners bring to a piece of music. Dividing goals into levels allows the writer to manage a difficult, abstract topic and to lead the reader from the simpler to the more complex level of listening.

You will find that classifying and dividing is helpful in writing all genres of analysis: textual, visual, and cultural. You will also find that it can help in argumentative genres because it enables you, as a writer or speaker, to break down a complex argument into parts or to group pieces of evidence into similar cate-gories.

Defining

Defining involves telling your reader what something means—and what it does not. It involves saying what something is—and what it is not. As a strategy, defining means making sure you—and your readers—understand what you mean by a key term. It may mean re-defining a common term to have a more precise meaning or giving nuance to a term that is commonly used too broadly. Defining and re-defining are great strategies to use in argumentative writing: they help the writer reshape the thinking of the audience and see a concept in a new light.

This rhetorical strategy is not as simple as looking up a word in a dictionary, though often that is a good place to begin. If you look up your key word in a good collegiate dictionary, you may discover that it meant something one hundred years ago that it no longer means, or that it is used in technical writing in a specific sense, or that it has a range of meanings from which you must choose to convey *your* intention. Citing one of these definitions can help in composing your essay. But defining as a rhetorical strategy may also include giving examples or providing descriptions: What does *salvation* look like to the unconverted? (See Langston Hughes's "Salvation," p. 1059.) What is a *postcard* in a literary sense? (See Garrison Keillor's "Postcards," p. 448.) In these versions of defining, the rhetorical strategy overlaps with the next one: describing.

Describing

When writers describe a person, place, or thing, they indicate what it looks like and often how it feels, smells, sounds, or tastes. As a strategy, describing involves showing rather than telling, helping readers see rather than giving them a formal definition, making the subject come alive rather than remaining abstract. When you describe, you want to choose precise verbs, specific nouns, vivid adjectives—unless your subject is dullness itself.

As a writer, you will use description in many kinds of assignments: in profiles of people and places to provide a key to their essence, in visual analysis to reveal the crucial features of a painting or photograph, in cultural critique to highlight the features of the object or phenomenon you will analyze, and in scientific lab reports to give details of an experiment. Almost no essay can be written without at least some description, and many essays rely on this strategy as a fundamental technique. In *The Norton Reader* you will find study questions in almost every section that begin with "Describe": "Describe a 'treasure' someone found and held on to," "Take a flower or tree and write a close-up description of it," "Describe some particular experience that raises a large social question"—these are just a few examples of writing assignments that ask for description.

Explaining a process

With this rhetorical strategy, the writer explains how something is done: from everyday processes like how to write a letter, how to play basketball, or how to make French fries, to unusual or extreme processes like how to embalm a corpse or how to face death. Sometimes, writers use this strategy in historical essays to show how something was done in the past. As these examples suggest, explaining a process can be useful in a range of genres: from a literacy narrative that explains learning to read, to a cultural analysis that treats the funeral industry, to a sermon or philosophical essay that explores the meaning and purpose of death and dying.

To make a process accessible to the reader, you will need to identify the main steps or stages and then explain them in order, one after the other. Sequence matters. In preparing to write a paragraph explaining a process, it might help to list the steps as a flow chart or as a cookbook recipe—and then turn your list into a paragraph (or more) of fully elaborated prose.

Narrating

This final rhetorical strategy—narrating—may be the most fundamental. We tell stories about ourselves, about our families, and about friends and neighbors. We tell stories to make a point, to illustrate an argument, to offer evidence or counter-evidence, and sometimes even to substitute for an argument. As these uses suggest, narrating appears in many genres: from memoirs and biographies, to op-eds, formal speeches, and parables. Narrating is basic to essay writing.

As you plan a paragraph or segment of narration, think about sequence: the order in which the events occurred (chronological order) or an order in which the events might be most dramatically presented (reverse chronological order or the present moment with flashback). Often, sequential order is easier for the reader to comprehend, but sometimes beginning *in medias res* (at the present moment *in the middle of things*) and then flashing back to the past creates a more compelling story. Consider incorporating time markers—not only dates, but also sequential phrases: early one evening, later that night, the next morning. And use transitions and transitional words: first, then, meanwhile, later, finally. When you've finished narrating your event or episode, re-read it and ask, What have I left out that the reader needs to know? What might I omit because the reader doesn't need to know it?

STRATEGIES FOR WRITING

If you were to watch a writer at work, you would observe that the task of writing often occurs in stages. Most writers generate ideas, write a draft, revise the draft (sometimes once, often many times), edit (make sentence- or word-level changes), and finally, proofread (check to see that the grammar, spelling, and formatting are correct). Along the way, writers develop a main point for their writing, find examples and evidence to support that point, and integrate the evidence into their work. You would be observing what teachers of writing call the *writing process*, a series of stages that writers use, though some omit a stage, some combine one or more of them, and others follow each one carefully. Your writing will benefit if you understand how the writing process works, and, even more important, how to make the process work for *you*.

Generate ideas

For many people, the hardest part of writing is looking at the blank page or empty screen. What can you say? How can you even get started? Sometimes your task is made easier when your instructor gives you a specific assignment or asks a particular question. In the next pages, we'll follow one student as she develops an essay responding to Brent Staples's "Why Colleges Shower Their Students with A's." Her instructor assigned the following study question (p. 329):

> How broad is Staples's range of examples? Would he need to adjust his position if he considered other colleges? Write an analysis of the situation at your college either to confirm or to contest Staples's argument.

The student knew she had to analyze Staples's range of examples and so began gathering ideas by rereading his essay. She noted that he cites only three colleges by name—the University of Pennsylvania, the University of Phoenix, and Duke University—and decided to do research on her own campus. Her instructor directed her to the Office of Institutional Research, which supplied her with a summary of grade distribution at her college. The summary showed that 30 percent of grades were A's, 45 percent were B's, and 25 percent were C's or below. The evidence her research produced did not seem particularly odd to her; it was about what she expected, and it refuted Staples's claim that "colleges shower their students with A's." Notice this student's process for generating ideas and getting started: she began with the question in *The Norton Reader*, reread the essay, conducted research, and discovered hard evidence that did not support Staples's claim. In fact, she developed a claim of her own, a counterclaim to Staples's.

Sometimes, the assignment your teacher gives or a study question in *The Norton Reader* is more open-ended, such as this one following Nancy Mairs's "On Being a Cripple" (p. 46):

> Mairs deliberately chooses to call herself a "cripple." Select a person or group that deliberately chooses its own name or description and explain the rationale behind the choice.

You can respond to this assignment by examining your own memory for stories you've heard, incidents you've witnessed, or people you've met, or you may need to do some research in order to have enough to say. Use one or more of the following techniques to mine your memory or generate ideas:

- Freewrite for several minutes to discover what you already know and think about a subject.

- Make a list of everything you know about the subject. Group or cluster related ideas.
- Read some articles about the subject. Take notes on what you read.
- Ask questions about the subject, starting with *who, what, when, why,* and *how.*

Different writers develop different ways of finding their material, so experiment with different techniques until you discover one or more that work for you.

Develop a main point or thesis

Most writing in college courses needs a central claim, often called a *thesis.* Most papers contain a thesis statement, often stated in the introduction, that tells readers the main point that will be supported, developed, and extended in the body of the paper.

Sometimes the thesis statement will be an arguable claim supported by evidence, such as Brent Staples's thesis, which falls at the end of the first paragraph of his op-ed: "Faced with demanding consumers and stiff competition, colleges have simply issued more and more A's, stoking grade inflation and devaluating degrees." The student who responded to Staples's essay also developed a thesis statement, narrowing a broad initial claim—"Staples is wrong about colleges showering their students with A's"—to a specific, arguable claim—"For most students at Central College, however, Staples is wrong: 70 percent of students on this campus are not being showered with A's." Her thesis statement is good because it is emerges from the research she has carried out on her own campus.

At other times, the main point of your writing won't be stated so plainly. Instead, it will be "in the air," or evident to the reader, but you won't be trying to argue a claim with evidence. If you're writing in a narrative or descriptive genre, for example, you'll have a main point, of course, particularly if you're writing a historical or biographical narrative or creating a profile of a person or place. You will make a claim about the reasons something happened or about the reasons for a person's or place's distinctive characteristics, as Scott Russell Sanders does in "Under the Influence" (p. 100):

> My father drank. He drank as a gut-punched boxer gasps for breath, as a starving dog gobbles food—

Those two sentences give the main characteristics that shape the writer's memories of his father and guide his construction of the biographical portrait.

Gather evidence

What counts as adequate evidence for your claim or thesis? The student whose response to Brent Staples's "Why Colleges Shower Students with A's" was not convinced by the evidence Staples used and found evidence that refuted his claim. Her argument would have been even stronger if she had looked for other sources, such as published survey results and reports of grade distribution at other colleges, to find out whether Staples's claim or her hunch was more accurate.

In other kinds of writing, evidence is drawn more often from personal experience than from secondary sources. In a literacy narrative, for example, the evidence will be in the examples and details of the story you tell about a formative time in your education. In a profile of a person, the evidence will also take the form of examples—the descriptive details about the person's personality, accomplishments, talents, weaknesses, looks, and behavior; anecdotes or stories about the person's life; or testimony from people who've observed the person closely. Evidence is also often drawn directly from reading. In a textual analysis, the evidence will be examples that demonstrate the text's structure, style, and language.

Organize your ideas

How you organize your ideas in a piece of writing depends to a large extent on your genre and purpose. N. Scott Momaday organizes "The Way to Rainy Mountain" (p. 119) as a journey to his grandmother's house and his native Kiowa homeland, narrating his trip in simple past tense ("I returned to Rainy Mountain in July") and interspersing family history and native American lore as he progresses (as in the legend of the Big Dipper, where Momaday comments that "the Kiowas have kinsmen in the night sky"). David Guterson organizes "Enclosed, Encyclopedic, Endured: The Mall of America" (p. 161) as an answer to a question:

> Here was a new structure that had cost more than half a billion dollars to erect—what might it tell us about ourselves?

His essay proceeds as a narrative exploration of the Mall itself, over a number of days; he links his observations to stops he makes on his trip through the complex.

For many of the essays you write in college, you will use the familiar format of an introduction, body, and conclusion, with separate paragraphs in the body for each major piece of evidence. The introduction often connects your ideas to what your readers already know and seeks to interest them in what you have to say. For instance, the student writing in response to Brent Staples's op-ed began her essay this way:

> The notion of grade inflation has been in the air for the past decade. Critics have complained that today's students are receiving far too many A's and not enough C's, D's, and F's. Things were different in the past, these critics say; grades really meant something back when the critics went to college; today's college students have it far too easy. In his recent Op-Ed piece, Brent Staples struck the familiar theme when he claimed to explain why colleges nowadays "shower" their students with A's. For most students at Central College,

> however, Staples is wrong: 70 percent of students on this campus are not being showered with A's.

In the body of an essay, you may want to place your most compelling piece of evidence first, or you may want it to come last to tie matters up for the reader. (But don't hide your best bit of evidence by placing it in the middle.) The student who wrote in response to Staples decided to use the body of her essay to present anecdotal evidence from her roommates, informal survey results from classmates about their grades, and finally the results of her research at the Office of Institutional Research. Whatever type of organization you choose, try the ideas out and write a different outline for each type of placement to see which works more successfully.

In the conclusion, you try to wrap things up, finish off your line of reasoning, and send your readers off with a final thought. Brent Staples ends "Why Colleges Shower Their Students with A's" with a predication:

> Addicted to counterfeit excellence, colleges, parents and students are unlikely to give it up. As a consequence, diplomas will become weaker and more ornamental as the years go by.

That's a fine way to conclude. Our student writer, responding to Staples, takes a different approach in her conclusion:

> Those of us who work hard and study at Central College note that we have never been "showered" with A's. We study at a place where high grades remain difficult to earn, and our situation makes me wonder whether Staples gathered only the evidence he wanted to find. Had he considered other colleges, he would not have made such a sweeping assertion.

Write multiple drafts

Even the most experienced writers know they can't do everything at once: find or invent material, assess its usefulness, arrange it in paragraphs, and write it out in well-formed sentences. If you try to produce a good essay at one sitting, in a single draft, you are likely to thin out your material, lock yourself into a structure that may not work and that you don't have time to change, and write jumbled paragraphs and clumsy sentences that won't fully convey your meaning or intention. In the end, writing a few drafts—in short periods spaced over more than a day—will produce a better essay, one that is thoughtful and deserving of a respectable grade. Here are some tips for drafting in stages:

- Get started by composing a rough draft or small sections of a draft. Don't feel obliged to start with the introduction and write straight through to the conclusion. If you don't know where to begin, write a section you know you want to include, then move to another. As you compose, you will begin to find out what you mean, what is important to your argument, what is missing, and what needs to be revised. Think of composing a rough draft as a way of discovering what you want to say.

- If you get stuck, try focused freewriting. That is, write all you can in response to a particular point or about a particular idea, not stopping for five minutes. After you're done, read what you've written looking for your thoughts on the subject. Much of what you've written won't be worthwhile, but you may have come up with key notions or put yourself in touch with useful ideas.
- Write a single paragraph for each key piece of evidence you have to support your thesis. Later on you can refine these paragraphs, combining some and breaking up others.
- At any point in this process, print out a clean version of your draft, read it through, and make changes. Add to, subtract from, rearrange, and revise the parts of your essay.

Acknowledge others' words and ideas

Your writing should reflect your own thinking, of course, but you'll often incorporate the ideas and actual words of others. Synthesizing and citing the work of others shows your readers that you have consulted reputable sources and, if you use sources honestly and skillfully, will make readers more open to your argument. It may help you to think of anything you write as part of a dialogue you are having with other writers and scholars; just be sure to credit the other writers and scholars whose words and ideas you borrow, so your readers can follow the dialogue and know who said what.

When you cite information from another source in your writing, you must credit the source. First, give the author credit by acknowledging his or her work in your text. If you cite someone's exact words, put them in quotation marks, or, if you quote more than five lines, indent them without quotation marks. Tell your readers where you got the words by including the author's name in your text and putting the page number of the book or article in parentheses right after the quote. Here is an example of a direct quotation with appropriate citation:

> Staples argues that the rise of part-time instructors is partially responsible for grade inflation: "Writing in the last issue of *Academe*, two part-timers suggest that students routinely corner adjuncts, threatening to complain if they do not turn C's into A's" (329).

If you paraphrase a source, that is, if you use another person's idea but not the exact words, you still need to cite the source of that idea, even though you have expressed it in your own words. Here is an example of a paraphrase:

> Staples dismisses the argument that grades are getting higher because of students' better preparation (329).

At the end of your paper on a separate page, list all the sources you have quoted and paraphrased. Many style guides provide directions for formatting source material. The guide used most frequently in English classes is the *MLA*

Handbook for Writers of Research Papers, Seventh Edition (2009), published by the Modern Language Association.

Sometimes writers in a hurry are tempted to absorb others' writing wholesale into their papers. This is *plagiarism*. Plagiarism is unethical because it involves the theft of another writer's words and ideas; in college courses, it is a guarantee of failure when discovered. Avoid plagiarizing at all costs. If you have fallen behind on a writing assignment, tell your instructor. You will often find that he or she will accept a late submission, and even if you are graded down for submitting the paper late, that is better than stealing others' ideas and words.

Revise alone and with peers

Although writers can and often do compose and revise alone, we all need helpful responses, whether from professional editors, classmates, or friends. You, too, will need to become a good reviser, both of your own work and of the work of your peers. It is useful first to imagine another reader for yourself and revise your work on your own, and then to give your draft to an actual reader who can read and comment on it.

All writers need to try out their arguments and ideas before they produce a final draft. Many writing classes encourage that process, teaching students to draft and revise independently but also enabling them to put less-than-final drafts forward for responses from the instructor and fellow students. Examples and arguments that seem clear to the writer may seem forced or exaggerated to another reader. In peer groups, listen to readers who disagree with you, who find your position slanted, overstated, or not fully convincing. Be responsive to their comments, and qualify interpretations or further explain points that they do not understand.

Here are some all-purpose questions that you can use to review a draft on your own or in a peer group. The questions should probably be asked in the order below, since they move from larger elements to smaller ones.

Introduction Treat the introduction as a promise by asking, "Does this essay keep the promises the introduction makes?" If it doesn't, either the introduction or the essay needs to be revised. Try to determine where the problem lies: Is the introduction off track? Does one or more of the paragraphs wander off the topic? Does the introduction promise an organization that isn't followed?

Content Next ask yourself, "Does this essay include enough material?" You may feel that some of the essays in *The Norton Reader* are dense and overspecific; your instructor, on the other hand, may find your essays skimpy and underspecific, with too few details and examples. As you read your own work and that of your classmates, look for examples and details that transmit meaning and engage your interest, understanding, and imagination. Check for adequate and persuasive evidence and multiple illustrative examples that clarify main points. If you or your readers think you need more evidence, examples, or information, revise accordingly.

Evidence and source material Then ask, "Does the essay interpret its material clearly and connect its examples to the main argument?" Your essay, and those you read as a peer reviewer, should specify the meanings of the examples you use; don't expect the examples to speak for themselves. A case in point is the use of quotations. How many are there? How necessary are they? How well are they integrated? What analysis or commentary follows each? Watch for quotations that are simply dropped in, without enough introduction or "placing" so that the reader can understand their significance. Quotations should be well integrated, clearly explaining who is speaking, where the voice is coming from, and what to attend to.

Organization and transitions Then ask, "Are the main and supporting points of this essay well-organized?" Writing puts readers in possession of material in a temporal order: that is, readers read from start to finish. Sometimes material that appears near the end of an essay might work better near the beginning; sometimes material that appears near the beginning might better be postponed. Pay attention to transitions between and within paragraphs; if they are unclear, the difficulty may lie in the organization of the material.

Tone Then ask, "Is the tone of the essay appropriate for its purpose and its audience?" Whether the tone is light-hearted, serious, reasoned, funny, enraged, thoughtful, or anything else, it needs to be appropriate to the purpose of the essay and sensitive to the expectations of the audience. Be aware of how formal your writing should be and whether contractions, abbreviations, and slang are acceptable.

Sentences Then ask, "Which sentences unfold smoothly and which sentences might cause readers to stumble?" If working in a group, ask your classmates to help you rephrase a sentence or write the thought in new words. Remember, you're trying to reach readers just like your peers, so take their questions and reactions seriously.

Learning to be a responsive reader of essays in *The Norton Reader* can teach you to respond helpfully to the essays of peer writers in your composition class—and to improve your own. Large and small elements of the composing process are reciprocal. Learn to work back and forth among wholes and parts, sections and paragraphs, introductions and conclusions. As shape and meaning come together, you can begin to refine smaller elements: sentences, phrases, specific words. You can qualify your assertions, complicate your generalizations, and tease out the implications of your examples.

Edit, proofread, and format the final draft

After you have revised the structure of your writing, you should devote time to pruning for excess, reviewing the words, and correcting errors in grammar, punctuation, and spelling—what experienced writers call editing and proofreading. This work is best done after giving the paper a rest and coming to it afresh. You may be tempted to move directly to the proofreading stage, thus shortchanging the larger, more important revision work described above. So long as the larger elements of an essay need repair, it's too soon to work on the smaller ones, so save the tinkering for last. When you're satisfied with the overall shape of your essay, turn to the work of tightening your writing by eliminating repetition and awkward phrases, correcting grammar, punctuation, and spelling, and putting your work in its final form. Be sure you know what style and format your work should take, be it that of an academic paper with set margins, double-spacing, and a title page, or some other format. Ask your instructor if you are unsure about any of these, and make the necessary changes. Then, like other writers, you will need to stop—not because there isn't more to be done but because you have other things to do.

The Norton Reader

Thirteenth Edition

Personal Accounts

Joan Didion — *On Going Home*

I am home for my daughter's first birthday. By "home" I do not mean the house in Los Angeles where my husband and I and the baby live, but the place where my family is, in the Central Valley of California. It is a vital although troublesome distinction. My husband likes my family but is uneasy in their house, because once there I fall into their ways, which are difficult, oblique, deliberately inarticulate, not my husband's ways. We live in dusty houses ("D-U-S-T," he once wrote with his finger on surfaces all over the house, but no one noticed it) filled with mementos quite without value to him (what could the Canton dessert plates mean to him? how could he have known about the assay scales, why should he care if he did know?), and we appear to talk exclusively about people we know who have been committed to mental hospitals, about people we know who have been booked on drunk-driving charges, and about property, particularly about property, land, price per acre and C-2 zoning and assessments and freeway access. My brother does not understand my husband's inability to perceive the advantage in the rather common real-estate transaction known as "sale-leaseback," and my husband in turn does not understand why so many of the people he hears about in my father's house have recently been committed to mental hospitals or booked on drunk-driving charges. Nor does he understand that when we talk about sale-leasebacks and right-of-way condemnations we are talking in code about the things we like best, the yellow fields and the cottonwoods and the rivers rising and falling and the mountain roads closing when the heavy snow comes in. We miss each other's points, have another drink and regard the fire. My brother refers to my husband, in his presence, as "Joan's husband." Marriage is the classic betrayal.

Or perhaps it is not any more. Sometimes I think that those of us who are now in our thirties were born into the last generation to carry the burden of "home," to find in family life the source of all tension and drama. I had by all objective accounts a "normal" and a "happy" family situation, and yet I was almost thirty years old before I could talk to my family on the telephone without crying after I had hung up. We did not fight. Nothing was wrong. And yet

From Slouching towards Bethlehem *(1966), Didion's first volume of nonfiction, which includes both autobiographical essays and articles analyzing American culture of the 1960s.*

some nameless anxiety colored the emotional charges between me and the place that I came from. The question of whether or not you could go home again was a very real part of the sentimental and largely literary baggage with which we left home in the fifties; I suspect that it is irrelevant to the children born of the fragmentation after World War II. A few weeks ago in a San Francisco bar I saw a pretty young girl on crystal[1] take off her clothes and dance for the cash prize in an "amateur-topless" contest. There was no particular sense of moment about this, none of the effect of romantic degradation, of "dark journey," for which my generation strived so assiduously. What sense could that girl possibly make of, say, *Long Day's Journey into Night*?[2] Who is beside the point?

That I am trapped in this particular irrelevancy is never more apparent to me than when I am home. Paralyzed by the neurotic lassitude engendered by meeting one's past at every turn, around every corner, inside every cupboard, I go aimlessly from room to room. I decide to meet it head-on and clean out a drawer, and I spread the contents on the bed. A bathing suit I wore the summer I was seventeen. A letter of rejection from *The Nation,* an aerial photograph of the site for a shopping center my father did not build in 1954. Three teacups hand-painted with cabbage roses and signed "E.M.," my grandmother's initials. There is no final solution for letters of rejection from *The Nation* and teacups hand-painted in 1900. Nor is there any answer to snapshots of one's grandfather as a young man on skis, surveying around Donner Pass in the year 1910. I smooth out the snapshot and look into his face, and do and do not see my own. I close the drawer, and have another cup of coffee with my mother. We get along very well, veterans of a guerrilla war we never understood.

Days pass. I see no one. I come to dread my husband's evening call, not only because he is full of news of what by now seems to me our remote life in Los Angeles, people he has seen, letters which require attention, but because he asks what I have been doing, suggests uneasily that I get out, drive to San Francisco or Berkeley. Instead I drive across the river to a family graveyard. It has been vandalized since my last visit and the monuments are broken, overturned in the dry grass. Because I once saw a rattlesnake in the grass I stay in the car and listen to a country-and-Western station. Later I drive with my father to a ranch he has in the foothills. The man who runs his cattle on it asks us to the roundup, a week from Sunday, and although I know that I will be in Los Angeles I say, in the oblique way my family talks, that I will come. Once home I mention the broken monuments in the graveyard. My mother shrugs.

5 I go to visit my great-aunts. A few of them think now that I am my cousin, or their daughter who died young. We recall an anecdote about a relative last seen in 1948, and they ask if I still like living in New York City. I have lived in Los Angeles for three years, but I say that I do. The baby is offered a horehound drop, and I am slipped a dollar bill "to buy a treat." Questions trail off, answers are abandoned, the baby plays with the dust motes in a shaft of afternoon sun.

1. A methamphetamine.

2. Tragedy by playwright Eugene O'Neill (1888–1952), based on the shame and deception that haunted his own family.

It is time for the baby's birthday party: a white cake, strawberry-marshmallow ice cream, a bottle of champagne saved from another party. In the evening, after she has gone to sleep, I kneel beside the crib and touch her face, where it is pressed against the slats, with mine. She is an open and trusting child, unprepared for and unaccustomed to the ambushes of family life, and perhaps it is just as well that I can offer her little of that life. I would like to give her more. I would like to promise her that she will grow up with a sense of her cousins and of rivers and of her great-grandmother's teacups, would like to pledge her a picnic on a river with fried chicken and her hair uncombed, would like to give her *home* for her birthday, but we live differently now and I can promise her nothing like that. I give her a xylophone and a sundress from Madeira, and promise to tell her a funny story.

QUESTIONS

1. Didion speaks of herself at home as "paralyzed by the neurotic lassitude engendered by meeting one's past at every turn" (paragraph 3). What about the essay helps explain these feelings?

2. What does Didion mean by "the ambushes of family life" (paragraph 6)? (Besides "ambushes," note Didion's other highly charged language: e.g., "betrayal" in paragraph 1 and "guerrilla war" in paragraph 3.)

3. In paragraph 6 Didion says she would like to give her daughter "*home* for her birthday, but we live differently now." In an essay, explain whether or not you think parents today can give their children "home." Include examples.

CHANG-RAE LEE *Coming Home Again*

WHEN MY MOTHER began using the electronic pump that fed her liquids and medication, we moved her to the family room. The bedroom she shared with my father was upstairs, and it was impossible to carry the machine up and down all day and night. The pump itself was attached to a metal stand on casters, and she pulled it along wherever she went. From anywhere in the house, you could hear the sound of the wheels clicking out a steady time over the grout lines of the slate-tiled foyer, her main thoroughfare to the bathroom and the kitchen. Sometimes you would hear her halt after only a few steps, to catch her breath or steady her balance, and whatever you were doing was instantly suspended by a pall of silence.

Published in the New Yorker *(October 16, 1995), an American magazine of literature and the arts, just after the appearance of Lee's award-winning novel,* Native Speaker *(1995).*

I was usually in the kitchen, preparing lunch or dinner, poised over the butcher block with her favorite chef's knife in my hand and her old yellow apron slung around my neck. I'd be breathless in the sudden quiet, and, having ceased my mincing and chopping, would stare blankly at the brushed sheen of the blade. Eventually, she would clear her throat or call out to say she was fine, then begin to move again, starting her rhythmic *ka-jug*; and only then could I go on with my cooking, the world of our house turning once more, wheeling through the black.

I wasn't cooking for my mother but for the rest of us. When she first moved downstairs she was still eating, though scantily, more just to taste what we were having than from any genuine desire for food. The point was simply to sit together at the kitchen table and array ourselves like a family again. My mother would gently set herself down in her customary chair near the stove. I sat across from her, my father and sister to my left and right, and crammed in the center was all the food I had made—a spicy codfish stew, say, or a casserole of gingery beef, dishes that in my youth she had prepared for us a hundred times.

It had been ten years since we'd all lived together in the house, which at fifteen I had left to attend boarding school in New Hampshire. My mother would sometimes point this out, by speaking of our present time as being "just like before Exeter," which surprised me, given how proud she always was that I was a graduate of the school.

5 My going to such a place was part of my mother's not so secret plan to change my character, which she worried was becoming too much like hers. I was clever and able enough, but without outside pressure I was readily given to sloth and vanity. The famous school—which none of us knew the first thing about—would prove my mettle. She was right, of course, and while I was there I would falter more than a few times, academically and otherwise. But I never thought that my leaving home then would ever be a problem for her, a private quarrel she would have even as her life waned.

Now her house was full again. My sister had just resigned from her job in New York City, and my father, who typically saw his psychiatric patients until eight or nine in the evening, was appearing in the driveway at four-thirty. I had been living at home for nearly a year and was in the final push of work on what would prove a dismal failure of a novel. When I wasn't struggling over my prose, I kept occupied with the things she usually did—the daily errands, the grocery shopping, the vacuuming and the cleaning, and, of course, all the cooking.

When I was six or seven years old, I used to watch my mother as she prepared our favorite meals. It was one of my daily pleasures. She shooed me away in the beginning, telling me that the kitchen wasn't my place, and adding, in her half-proud, half-deprecating way, that her kind of work would only serve to weaken me. "Go out and play with your friends," she'd snap in Korean, "or better yet, do your reading and homework." She knew that I had already done both, and that as the evening approached there was no place to go save her small and tidy kitchen, from which the clatter of her mixing bowls and pans would ring through the house.

I would enter the kitchen quietly and stand beside her, my chin lodging upon the point of her hip. Peering through the crook of her arm, I beheld the movements of her hands. For *kalbi*,[1] she would take up a butchered short rib in her narrow hand, the flinty bone shaped like a section of an airplane wing and deeply embedded in gristle and flesh, and with the point of her knife cut so that the bone fell away, though not completely, leaving it connected to the meat by the barest opaque layer of tendon. Then she methodically butterflied the flesh, cutting and unfolding, repeating the action until the meat lay out on her board, glistening and ready for seasoning. She scored it diagonally, then sifted sugar into the crevices with her pinched fingers, gently rubbing in the crystals. The sugar would tenderize as well as sweeten the meat. She did this with each rib, and then set them all aside in a large shallow bowl. She minced a half-dozen cloves of garlic, a stub of gingerroot, sliced up a few scallions, and spread it all over the meat. She wiped her hands and took out a bottle of sesame oil, and, after pausing for a moment, streamed the dark oil in two swift circles around the bowl. After adding a few splashes of soy sauce, she thrust her hands in and kneaded the flesh, careful not to dislodge the bones. I asked her why it mattered that they remain connected. "The meat needs the bone nearby," she said, "to borrow its richness." She wiped her hands clean of the marinade, except for her little finger, which she would flick with her tongue from time to time, because she knew that the flavor of a good dish developed not at once but in stages.

Whenever I cook, I find myself working just as she would, readying the ingredients—a mash of garlic, a julienne of red peppers, fantails of shrimp—and piling them in little mounds about the cutting surface. My mother never left me any recipes, but this is how I learned to make her food, each dish coming not from a list or a card but from the aromatic spread of a board.

I've always thought it was particularly cruel that the cancer was in her stomach, and that for a long time at the end she couldn't eat. The last meal I made for her was on New Year's Eve, 1990. My sister suggested that instead of a rib roast or a bird, or the usual overflow of Korean food, we make all sorts of finger dishes that our mother might fancy and pick at. 10

We set the meal out on the glass coffee table in the family room. I prepared a tray of smoked-salmon canapés,[2] fried some Korean bean cakes, and made a few other dishes I thought she might enjoy. My sister supervised me, arranging the platters, and then with some pomp carried each dish in to our parents. Finally, I brought out a bottle of champagne in a bucket of ice. My mother had moved to the sofa and was sitting up, surveying the low table. "It looks pretty nice," she said. "I think I'm feeling hungry."

This made us all feel good, especially me, for I couldn't remember the last time she had felt any hunger or had eaten something I cooked. We began to eat. My mother picked up a piece of salmon toast and took a tiny corner in her mouth. She rolled it around for a moment and then pushed it out with the tip of her tongue, letting it fall back onto her plate. She swallowed hard, as if to

1. Korean-style beef ribs.

2. Appetizers, usually toast, crackers, or bread slices with toppings.

quell a gag, then glanced up to see if we had noticed. Of course we all had. She attempted a bean cake, some cheese, and then a slice of fruit, but nothing was any use.

She nodded at me anyway, and said, "Oh, it's very good." But I was already feeling lost and I put down my plate abruptly, nearly shattering it on the thick glass. There was an ugly pause before my father asked me in a weary, gentle voice if anything was wrong, and I answered that it was nothing, it was the last night of a long year, and we were together, and I was simply relieved. At midnight, I poured out glasses of champagne, even one for my mother, who took a deep sip. Her manner grew playful and light, and I helped her shuffle to her mattress, and she lay down in the place where in a brief week she was dead.

My mother could whip up most anything, but during our first years of living in this country we ate only Korean foods. At my harangue-like behest, my mother set herself to learning how to cook exotic American dishes. Luckily, a kind neighbor, Mrs. Churchill, a tall, florid young woman with flaxen hair, taught my mother her most trusted recipes. Mrs. Churchill's two young sons, palish, weepy boys with identical crew cuts, always accompanied her, and though I liked them well enough, I would slip away from them after a few minutes, for I knew that the real action would be in the kitchen, where their mother was playing guide. Mrs. Churchill hailed from the state of Maine, where the finest Swedish meatballs and tuna casserole and angel food cake in America are made. She readily demonstrated certain techniques—how to layer wet sheets of pasta for a lasagna or whisk up a simple roux,[3] for example. She often brought gift shoeboxes containing curious ingredients like dried oregano, instant yeast, and cream of mushroom soup. The two women, though at ease and jolly with each other, had difficulty communicating, and this was made worse by the often confusing terminology of Western cuisine ("corned beef," "deviled eggs"). Although I was just learning the language myself, I'd gladly play the interlocutor, jumping back and forth between their places at the counter, dipping my fingers into whatever sauce lay about.

15 I was an insistent child, and, being my mother's firstborn, much too prized. My mother could say no to me, and did often enough, but anyone who knew us—particularly my father and sister—could tell how much the denying pained her. And if I was overconscious of her indulgence even then, and suffered the rushing pangs of guilt that she could inflict upon me with the slightest wounded turn of her lip, I was too happily obtuse and venal to let her cease. She reminded me daily that I was her sole son, her reason for living, and that if she were to lose me, in either body or spirit, she wished that God would mercifully smite her, strike her down like a weak branch.

In the traditional fashion, she was the house accountant, the maid, the launderer, the disciplinarian, the driver, the secretary, and, of course, the cook. She was also my first basketball coach. In South Korea, where girls' high school basketball is a popular spectator sport, she had been a star, the point guard for

3. Thickening agent for sauces and soups.

the national high school team that once won the all-Asia championships. I learned this one Saturday during the summer, when I asked my father if he would go down to the schoolyard and shoot some baskets with me. I had just finished the fifth grade, and wanted desperately to make the middle school team the coming fall. He called for my mother and sister to come along. When we arrived, my sister immediately ran off to the swings, and I recall being annoyed that my mother wasn't following her. I dribbled clumsily around the key, on the verge of losing control of the ball, and flung a flat shot that caromed wildly off the rim. The ball bounced to my father, who took a few not so graceful dribbles and made an easy layup. He dribbled out and then drove to the hoop for a layup on the other side. He rebounded his shot and passed the ball to my mother, who had been watching us from the foul line. She turned from the basket and began heading the other way.

"Um-mah,"[4] I cried at her, my exasperation already bubbling over, "the basket's over *here!*"

After a few steps she turned around, and from where the professional three-point line must be now, she effortlessly flipped the ball up in a two-handed set shot, its flight truer and higher than I'd witnessed from any boy or man. The ball arced cleanly into the hoop, stiffly popping the chain-link net. All afternoon, she rained in shot after shot, as my father and I scrambled after her.

When we got home from the playground, my mother showed me the photograph album of her team's championship run. For years I kept it in my room, on the same shelf that housed the scrapbooks I made of basketball stars, with magazine clippings of slick players like Bubbles Hawkins and Pistol Pete and George (the Iceman) Gervin.

It puzzled me how much she considered her own history to be immaterial, and if she never patently diminished herself, she was able to finesse a kind of self-removal by speaking of my father whenever she could. She zealously recounted his excellence as a student in medical school and reminded me, each night before I started my homework, of how hard he drove himself in his work to make a life for us. She said that because of his Asian face and imperfect English, he was "working two times the American doctors." I knew that she was building him up, buttressing him with both genuine admiration and her own brand of anxious braggadocio, and that her overarching concern was that I might fail to see him as she wished me to—in the most dawning light, his pose steadfast and solitary. 20

In the year before I left for Exeter, I became weary of her oft-repeated accounts of my father's success. I was a teenager, and so ever inclined to be dismissive and bitter toward anything that had to do with family and home. Often enough, my mother was the object of my derision. Suddenly, her life seemed so small to me. She was there, and sometimes, I thought, *always* there, as if she were confined to the four walls of our house. I would even complain about her cooking. Mostly, though, I was getting more and more impatient with the difficulty she encountered in doing everyday things. I was afraid for

4. Korean for "mommy."

her. One day, we got into a terrible argument when she asked me to call the bank, to question a discrepancy she had discovered in the monthly statement. I asked her why she couldn't call herself. I was stupid and brutal, and I knew exactly how to wound her.

"Whom do I talk to?" she said. She would mostly speak to me in Korean, and I would answer in English.

"The bank manager, who else?"

"What do I say?"

25 "Whatever you want to say."

"Don't speak to me like that!" she cried.

"It's just that you should be able to do it yourself," I said.

"You know how I feel about this!"

"Well, maybe then you should consider it *practice*," I answered lightly, using the Korean word to make sure she understood.

30 Her face blanched, and her neck suddenly became rigid, as if I were throttling her. She nearly struck me right then, but instead she bit her lip and ran upstairs. I followed her, pleading for forgiveness at her door. But it was the one time in our life that I couldn't convince her, melt her resolve with the blandishments of a spoiled son.

When my mother was feeling strong enough, or was in particularly good spirits, she would roll her machine into the kitchen and sit at the table and watch me work. She wore pajamas day and night, mostly old pairs of mine.

She said, "I can't tell, what are you making?"

"*Mahn-doo*[5] filling."

"You didn't salt the cabbage and squash."

35 "Was I supposed to?"

"Of course. Look, it's too wet. Now the skins will get soggy before you can fry them."

"What should I do?"

"It's too late. Maybe it'll be OK if you work quickly. Why didn't you ask me?"

"You were finally sleeping."

40 "You should have woken me."

"No way."

She sighed, as deeply as her weary lungs would allow.

"I don't know how you were going to make it without me."

"I don't know, either. I'll remember the salt next time."

45 "You better. And not too much."

We often talked like this, our tone decidedly matter-of-fact, chin up, just this side of being able to bear it. Once, while inspecting a potato fritter batter I was making, she asked me if she had ever done anything that I wished she hadn't done. I thought for a moment, and told her no. In the next breath, she wondered aloud if it was right of her to have let me go to Exeter, to live away

5. Korean dumplings, usually filled with cabbage and meat.

from the house while I was so young. She tested the batter's thickness with her finger and called for more flour. Then she asked if, given a choice, I would go to Exeter again.

I wasn't sure what she was getting at, and I told her that I couldn't be certain, but probably yes, I would. She snorted at this and said it was my leaving home that had once so troubled our relationship. "Remember how I had so much difficulty talking to you? Remember?"

She believed back then that I had found her more and more ignorant each time I came home. She said she never blamed me, for this was the way she knew it would be with my wonderful new education. Nothing I could say seemed to quell the notion. But I knew that the problem wasn't simply the *education*; the first time I saw her again after starting school, barely six weeks later, when she and my father visited me on Parents Day, she had already grown nervous and distant. After the usual campus events, we had gone to the motel where they were staying in a nearby town and sat on the beds in our room. She seemed to sneak looks at me, as though I might discover a horrible new truth if our eyes should meet.

My own secret feeling was that I had missed my parents greatly, my mother especially, and much more than I had anticipated. I couldn't tell them that these first weeks were a mere blur to me, that I felt completely overwhelmed by all the studies and my much brighter friends and the thousand irritating details of living alone, and that I had really learned nothing, save perhaps how to put on a necktie while sprinting to class. I felt as if I had plunged too deep into the world, which, to my great horror, was much larger than I had ever imagined.

I welcomed the lull of the motel room. My father and I had nearly dozed off when my mother jumped up excitedly, murmured how stupid she was, and hurried to the closet by the door. She pulled out our old metal cooler and dragged it between the beds. She lifted the top and began unpacking plastic containers, and I thought she would never stop. One after the other they came out, each with a dish that traveled well—a salted stewed meat, rolls of Korean-style sushi. I opened a container of radish kimchi[6] and suddenly the room bloomed with its odor, and I reveled in the very peculiar sensation (which perhaps only true kimchi lovers know) of simultaneously drooling and gagging as I breathed it all in. For the next few minutes, they watched me eat. I'm not certain that I was even hungry. But after weeks of pork parmigiana and chicken patties and wax beans, I suddenly realized that I had lost all the savor in my life. And it seemed I couldn't get enough of it back. I ate and I ate, so much and so fast that I actually went to the bathroom and vomited. I came out dizzy and sated with the phantom warmth of my binge.

50

And beneath the face of her worry, I thought, my mother was smiling.

From that day, my mother prepared a certain meal to welcome me home. It was always the same. Even as I rode the school's shuttle bus from Exeter to Logan airport, I could already see the exact arrangement of my mother's table.

6. Spicy Korean relish.

I knew that we would eat in the kitchen, the table brimming with plates. There was the *kalbi*, of course, broiled or grilled depending on the season. Leaf lettuce, to wrap the meat with. Bowls of garlicky clam broth with miso and tofu and fresh spinach. Shavings of cod dusted in flour and then dipped in egg wash and fried. Glass noodles with onions and shiitake. Scallion-and-hot-pepper pancakes. Chilled steamed shrimp. Seasoned salads of bean sprouts, spinach, and white radish. Crispy squares of seaweed. Steamed rice with barley and red beans. Homemade kimchi. It was all there—the old flavors I knew, the beautiful salt, the sweet, the excellent taste.

After the meal, my father and I talked about school, but I could never say enough for it to make any sense. My father would often recall his high school principal, who had gone to England to study the methods and traditions of the public schools, and regaled students with stories of the great Eton man. My mother sat with us, paring fruit, not saying a word but taking everything in. When it was time to go to bed, my father said good night first. I usually watched television until the early morning. My mother would sit with me for an hour or two, perhaps until she was accustomed to me again, and only then would she kiss me and head upstairs to sleep.

55 During the following days, it was always the cooking that started our conversations. She'd hold an inquest over the cold leftovers we ate at lunch, discussing each dish in terms of its balance of flavors or what might have been prepared differently. But mostly I begged her to leave the dishes alone. I wish I had paid more attention. After her death, when my father and I were the only ones left in the house, drifting through the rooms like ghosts, I sometimes tried to make that meal for him. Though it was too much for two, I made each dish anyway, taking as much care as I could. But nothing turned out quite right—not the color, not the smell. At the table, neither of us said much of anything. And we had to eat the food for days.

I remember washing rice in the kitchen one day and my mother's saying in English, from her usual seat, "I made a big mistake."

"About Exeter?"

"Yes. I made a big mistake. You should be with us for that time. I should never let you go there."

"So why did you?" I said.

60 "Because I didn't know I was going to die."

I let her words pass. For the first time in her life, she was letting herself speak her full mind, so what else could I do?

"But you know what?" she spoke up. "It was better for you. If you stayed home, you would not like me so much now."

I suggested that maybe I would like her even more.

She shook her head. "Impossible."

65 Sometimes I still think about what she said, about having made a mistake. I would have left home for college, that was never in doubt, but those years I was away at boarding school grew more precious to her as her illness progressed. After many months of exhaustion and pain and the haze of the drugs, I thought that her mind was beginning to fade, for more and more it seemed that she

was seeing me again as her fifteen-year-old boy, the one she had dropped off in New Hampshire on a cloudy September afternoon.

I remember the first person I met, another new student, named Zack, who walked to the welcome picnic with me. I had planned to eat with my parents—my mother had brought a coolerful of food even that first day—but I learned of the cookout and told her that I should probably go. I wanted to go, of course. I was excited, and no doubt fearful and nervous, and I must have thought I was only thinking ahead. She agreed wholeheartedly, saying I certainly should. I walked them to the car, and perhaps I hugged them, before saying goodbye. One day, after she died, my father told me what happened on the long drive home to Syracuse.

He was driving the car, looking straight ahead. Traffic was light on the Massachusetts Turnpike, and the sky was nearly dark. They had driven for more than two hours and had not yet spoken a word. He then heard a strange sound from her, a kind of muffled chewing noise, as if something inside her were grinding its way out.

"So, what's the matter?" he said, trying to keep an edge to his voice.

She looked at him with her ashen face and she burst into tears. He began to cry himself, and pulled the car over onto the narrow shoulder of the turnpike, where they stayed for the next half hour or so, the blank-faced cars droning by them in the cold, onrushing night.

Every once in a while, when I think of her, I'm driving alone somewhere on the highway. In the twilight, I see their car off to the side, a blue Olds coupe with a landau top, and as I pass them by I look back in the mirror and I see them again, the two figures huddling together in the front seat. Are they sleeping? Or kissing? Are they all right? 70

Questions

1. Chang-Rae Lee begins his essay *in medias res*—in the middle of things. How does his choice create drama, sympathy, and significance for the personal experience that he narrates?

2. Because Lee begins his account at a late stage of his mother's illness, he often flashes back to earlier points in their relationship. Mark the flashbacks in the text and explain the purpose of each.

3. Details of food and cooking appear throughout the essay—for example, in paragraphs 8–9, 11–13, and 32–34. Besides giving us a flavor of Korean food, what function do these details serve?

4. Lee titles his essay "Coming Home Again," whereas Joan Didion titles hers "On Going Home" (see the previous essay in "Personal Accounts"). What different connotations do "coming home" and "going home" suggest? How do these differences emerge in the personal accounts of each writer?

5. Write a personal essay about "coming home" or "going home."

Zora Neale Hurston *How It Feels to Be Colored Me*

I am colored but I offer nothing in the way of extenuating circumstances except the fact that I am the only Negro in the United States whose grandfather on the mother's side was not an Indian chief.

I remember the very day that I became colored. Up to my thirteenth year I lived in the little Negro town of Eatonville, Florida. It is exclusively a colored town. The only white people I knew passed through the town going to or coming from Orlando. The native whites rode dusty horses, the Northern tourists chugged down the sandy village road in automobiles. The town knew the Southerners and never stopped cane chewing[1] when they passed. But the Northerners were something else again. They were peered at cautiously from behind curtains by the timid. The more venturesome would come out on the porch to watch them go past and got just as much pleasure out of the tourists as the tourists got out of the village.

The front porch might seem a daring place for the rest of the town, but it was a gallery seat for me. My favorite place was atop the gate-post. Proscenium box for a born first-nighter. Not only did I enjoy the show, but I didn't mind the actors knowing that I liked it. I usually spoke to them in passing. I'd wave at them and when they returned my salute, I would say something like this: "Howdy-do-well-I-thank-you-where-you-goin'?" Usually automobile or the horse paused at this, and after a queer exchange of compliments, I would probably "go a piece of the way" with them, as we say in farthest Florida. If one of my family happened to come to the front in time to see me, of course negotiations would be rudely broken off. But even so, it is clear that I was the first "welcome-to-our-state" Floridian, and I hope the Miami Chamber of Commerce will please take notice.

During this period, white people differed from colored to me only in that they rode through town and never lived there. They liked to hear me "speak pieces" and sing and wanted to see me dance the parse-me-la, and gave me generously of their small silver for doing these things, which seemed strange to me for I wanted to do them so much that I needed bribing to stop. Only they didn't know it. The colored people gave no dimes. They deplored any joyful tendencies in me, but I was their Zora nevertheless. I belonged to them, to the nearby hotels, to the county—everybody's Zora.

5 But changes came in the family when I was thirteen, and I was sent to school in Jacksonville. I left Eatonville, the town of the oleanders,[2] as Zora.

Originally published in the World Tomorrow *in May 1928, just as Hurston was graduating from Barnard College; collected and reprinted in* I Love Myself When I Am Laughing . . . and Then Again When I Am Looking Mean and Impressive *(1973), a volume of Hurston's writings edited by the African American writer Alice Walker.*

1. Chewing sugar cane.
2. Fragrant tropical flowers, common in the South.

When I disembarked from the river-boat at Jacksonville, she was no more. It seemed that I had suffered a sea change. I was not Zora of Orange County any more, I was now a little colored girl. I found it out in certain ways. In my heart as well as in the mirror, I became a fast brown—warranted not to rub nor run.

But I am not tragically colored. There is no great sorrow dammed up in my soul, nor lurking behind my eyes. I do not mind at all. I do not belong to the sobbing school of Negrohood who hold that nature somehow has given them a lowdown dirty deal and whose feelings are all hurt about it. Even in the helter-skelter skirmish that is my life, I have seen that the world is to the strong regardless of a little pigmentation more or less. No, I do not weep at the world—I am too busy sharpening my oyster knife.[3]

Someone is always at my elbow reminding me that I am the granddaughter of slaves. It fails to register depression with me. Slavery is sixty years in the past. The operation was successful and the patient is doing well, thank you. The terrible struggle[4] that made me an American out of a potential slave said "On the line!" The Reconstruction said "Get set!"; and the generation before said "Go!" I am off to a flying start and I must not halt in the stretch to look behind and weep. Slavery is the price I paid for civilization, and the choice was not with me. It is a bully adventure and worth all that I have paid through my ancestors for it. No one on earth ever had a greater chance for glory. The world to be won and nothing to be lost. It is thrilling to think—to know that for any act of mine, I shall get twice as much praise or twice as much blame. It is quite exciting to hold the center of the national stage, with the spectators not knowing whether to laugh or to weep.

The position of my white neighbor is much more difficult. No brown specter pulls up a chair beside me when I sit down to eat. No dark ghost thrusts its leg against mine in bed. The game of keeping what one has is never so exciting as the game of getting.

I do not always feel colored. Even now I often achieve the unconscious Zora of Eatonville before the Hegira.[5] I feel most colored when I am thrown against a sharp white background.

For instance at Barnard. "Beside the waters of the Hudson"[6] I feel my race. Among the thousand white persons, I am a dark rock surged upon, and overswept, but through it all, I remain myself. When covered by the waters, I am; and the ebb but reveals me again. 10

3. Cf. the popular expression "The world is my oyster."

4. The Civil War. The Reconstruction was the period immediately following the war; one of its better effects was that northern educators came South to teach newly freed slaves.

5. A journey undertaken away from a dangerous situation into a more highly desirable one (literally, the flight of Muhammad from Mecca in 622 C.E.).

6. Barnard is an American women's college in New York City, near the Hudson River; cf. the psalmist's "by the waters of Babylon."

Sometimes it is the other way around. A white person is set down in our midst, but the contrast is just as sharp for me. For instance, when I sit in the drafty basement that is The New World Cabaret with a white person, my color comes. We enter chatting about any little nothing that we have in common and are seated by the jazz waiters. In the abrupt way that jazz orchestras have, this one plunges into a number. It loses no time in circumlocutions, but gets right down to business. It constricts the thorax and splits the heart with its tempo and narcotic harmonies. This orchestra grows rambunctious, rears on its hind legs and attacks the tonal veil with primitive fury, rending it, clawing it until it breaks through to the jungle beyond. I follow those heathen—follow them exultingly. I dance wildly inside myself; I yell within, I whoop; I shake my assegai[7] above my head, I hurl it true to the mark *yeeeeooww*! I am in the jungle and living in the jungle way. My face is painted red and yellow and my body is painted blue. My pulse is throbbing like a war drum. I want to slaughter something—give pain, give death to what, I do not know. But the piece ends. The men of the orchestra wipe their lips and rest their fingers. I creep back slowly to the veneer we call civilization with the last tone and find the white friend sitting motionless in his seat, smoking calmly.

"Good music they have here," he remarks, drumming the table with his fingertips.

Music. The great blobs of purple and red emotion have not touched him. He has only heard what I felt. He is far away and I see him but dimly across the ocean and the continent that have fallen between us. He is so pale with his whiteness then and I am *so* colored.

At certain times I have no race, I am *me*. When I set my hat at a certain angle and saunter down Seventh Avenue, Harlem City, feeling as snooty as the lions in front of the Forty-Second Street Library, for instance. So far as my feelings are concerned, Peggy Hopkins Joyce on the Boule Mich[8] with her gorgeous raiment, stately carriage, knees knocking together in a most aristocratic manner, has nothing on me. The cosmic Zora emerges. I belong to no race nor time. I am the eternal feminine with its string of beads.

15 I have no separate feeling about being an American citizen and colored. I am merely a fragment of the Great Soul that surges within the boundaries. My country, right or wrong.

Sometimes, I feel discriminated against, but it does not make me angry. It merely astonishes me. How *can* any deny themselves the pleasure of my company? It's beyond me.

But in the main, I feel like a brown bag of miscellany propped against a wall. Against a wall in company with other bags, white, red and yellow. Pour out the contents, and there is discovered a jumble of small things priceless and

7. South African hunting spear.

8. Peggy Hopkins Joyce, American beauty and fashion-setter of the twenties; the Boule Mich, the Boulevard Saint-Michel, a fashionable Parisian street.

worthless. A first-water diamond, an empty spool, bits of broken glass, lengths of string, a key to a door long since crumbled away, a rusty knife-blade, old shoes saved for a road that never was and never will be, a nail bent under the weight of things too heavy for any nail, a dried flower or two still a little fragrant. In your hand is the brown bag. On the ground before you is the jumble it held—so much like the jumble in the bags, could they be emptied, that all might be dumped in a single heap and the bags refilled without altering the content of any greatly. A bit of colored glass more or less would not matter. Perhaps that is how the Great Stuffer of Bags filled them in the first place—who knows?

QUESTIONS

1. From the beginning Hurston startles us: "I remember the very day that I became colored." Why does Hurston insist that one *becomes* colored? What happened on that day to make her so?

2. Each section of Hurston's essay explores a different possible identity, some based on skin color, others emphasizing history, culture, or gender. What does Hurston accomplish by such an approach?

3. The final paragraph introduces a key metaphor: "like a brown bag of miscellany propped against a wall." How does Hurston develop this metaphor? What does she mean by it?

4. Like another writer in "Personal Accounts," Nancy Mairs in "On Being a Cripple," Hurston chooses a label, "colored me," to explore questions of personal identity. Compare Hurston's use of "colored" with Mairs's use of "cripple."

MAYA ANGELOU *Graduation*

THE CHILDREN IN STAMPS[1] trembled visibly with anticipation. Some adults were excited too, but to be certain the whole young population had come down with graduation epidemic. Large classes were graduating from both the grammar school and the high school. Even those who were years removed from their own day of glorious release were anxious to help with preparations as a kind of dry run. The junior students who were moving into the vacating classes' chairs were tradition-bound to show their talents for leadership and management.

From I Know Why the Caged Bird Sings *(1970), the first volume of Angelou's autobiography of growing up in a segregated southern town. After its popular success, Angelou continued her life story in five sequential volumes, ending with* A Song Flung Up to Heaven *(2002), an account of the turbulent years of the civil rights movement and the assassinations of Malcolm X and Martin Luther King Jr.*

1. A town in Arkansas.

They strutted through the school and around the campus exerting pressure on the lower grades. Their authority was so new that occasionally if they pressed a little too hard it had to be overlooked. After all, next term was coming, and it never hurt a sixth grader to have a play sister in the eighth grade, or a tenth-year student to be able to call a twelfth grader Bubba. So all was endured in a spirit of shared understanding. But the graduating classes themselves were the nobility. Like travelers with exotic destinations on their minds, the graduates were remarkably forgetful. They came to school without their books or tablets or even pencils. Volunteers fell over themselves to secure replacements for the missing equipment. When accepted, the willing workers might or might not be thanked, and it was of no importance to the pregraduation rites. Even teachers were respectful of the now quiet and aging seniors, and tended to speak to them, if not as equals, as beings only slightly lower than themselves. After tests were returned and grades given, the student body, which acted like an extended family, knew who did well, who excelled, and what piteous ones had failed.

Unlike the white high school, Lafayette County Training School distinguished itself by having neither lawn, nor hedges, nor tennis court, nor climbing ivy. Its two buildings (main classrooms, the grade school and home economics) were set on a dirt hill with no fence to limit either its boundaries or those of bordering farms. There was a large expanse to the left of the school which was used alternately as a baseball diamond or basketball court. Rusty hoops on swaying poles represented the permanent recreational equipment, although bats and balls could be borrowed from the P.E. teacher if the borrower was qualified and if the diamond wasn't occupied.

Over this rocky area relieved by a few shady tall persimmon trees the graduating class walked. The girls often held hands and no longer bothered to speak to the lower students. There was a sadness about them, as if this old world was not their home and they were bound for higher ground. The boys, on the other hand, had become more friendly, more outgoing. A decided change from the closed attitude they projected while studying for finals. Now they seemed not ready to give up the old school, the familiar paths and classrooms. Only a small percentage would be continuing on to college—one of the South's A & M (agricultural and mechanical) schools, which trained Negro youths to be carpenters, farmers, handymen, masons, maids, cooks and baby nurses. Their future rode heavily on their shoulders, and blinded them to the collective joy that had pervaded the lives of the boys and girls in the grammar school graduating class.

Parents who could afford it had ordered new shoes and readymade clothes for themselves from Sears and Roebuck or Montgomery Ward. They also engaged the best seamstresses to make the floating graduating dresses and to cut down secondhand pants which would be pressed to a military slickness for the important event.

5 Oh, it was important, all right. Whitefolks would attend the ceremony, and two or three would speak of God and home, and the Southern way of life, and Mrs. Parsons, the principal's wife, would play the graduation march while the lower-grade graduates paraded down the aisles and took their seats below

the platform. The high school seniors would wait in empty classrooms to make their dramatic entrance.

In the Store I was the person of the moment. The birthday girl. The center. Bailey[2] had graduated the year before, although to do so he had had to forfeit all pleasures to make up for his time lost in Baton Rouge.

My class was wearing butter-yellow piqué dresses, and Momma launched out on mine. She smocked the yoke into tiny crisscrossing puckers, then shirred the rest of the bodice. Her dark fingers ducked in and out of the lemony cloth as she embroidered raised daisies around the hem. Before she considered herself finished she had added a crocheted cuff on the puff sleeves, and a pointy crocheted collar.

I was going to be lovely. A walking model of all the various styles of fine hand sewing and it didn't worry me that I was only twelve years old and merely graduating from the eighth grade. Besides, many teachers in Arkansas Negro schools had only that diploma and were licensed to impart wisdom.

The days had become longer and more noticeable. The faded beige of former times had been replaced with strong and sure colors. I began to see my classmates' clothes, their skin tones, and the dust that waved off pussy willows. Clouds that lazed across the sky were objects of great concern to me. Their shiftier shapes might have held a message that in my new happiness and with a little bit of time I'd soon decipher. During that period I looked at the arch of heaven so religiously my neck kept a steady ache. I had taken to smiling more often, and my jaws hurt from the unaccustomed activity. Between the two physical sore spots, I suppose I could have been uncomfortable, but that was not the case. As a member of the winning team (the graduating class of 1940) I had outdistanced unpleasant sensations by miles. I was headed for the freedom of open fields.

10 Youth and social approval allied themselves with me and we trammeled memories of slights and insults. The wind of our swift passage remodeled my features. Lost tears were pounded to mud and then to dust. Years of withdrawal were brushed aside and left behind, as hanging ropes of parasitic moss.

My work alone had awarded me a top place and I was going to be one of the first called in the graduating ceremonies. On the classroom blackboard, as well as on the bulletin board in the auditorium, there were blue stars and white stars and red stars. No absences, no tardinesses, and my academic work was among the best of the year. I could say the preamble to the Constitution even faster than Bailey. We timed ourselves often: "We the people of the United States in order to form a more perfect union . . ." I had memorized the Presidents of the United States from Washington to Roosevelt in chronological as well as alphabetical order.

My hair pleased me too. Gradually the black mass had lengthened and thickened, so that it kept at last to its braided pattern, and I didn't have to yank my scalp off when I tried to comb it.

2. The author's brother.

Louise and I had rehearsed the exercises until we tired out ourselves. Henry Reed was class valedictorian. He was a small, very black boy with hooded eyes, a long, broad nose and an oddly shaped head. I had admired him for years because each term he and I vied for the best grades in our class. Most often he bested me, but instead of being disappointed I was pleased that we shared top places between us. Like many Southern Black children, he lived with his grandmother, who was as strict as Momma and as kind as she knew how to be. He was courteous, respectful and soft-spoken to elders, but on the playground he chose to play the roughest games. I admired him. Anyone, I reckoned, sufficiently afraid or sufficiently dull could be polite. But to be able to operate at a top level with both adults and children was admirable.

His valedictory speech was entitled "To Be or Not to Be." The rigid tenth-grade teacher had helped him write it. He'd been working on the dramatic stresses for months.

15 The weeks until graduation were filled with heady activities. A group of small children were to be presented in a play about buttercups and daisies and bunny rabbits. They could be heard throughout the building practicing their hops and their little songs that sounded like silver bells. The older girls (nongraduates, of course) were assigned the task of making refreshments for the night's festivities. A tangy scent of ginger, cinnamon, nutmeg and chocolate wafted around the home economics building as the budding cooks made samples for themselves and their teachers.

In every corner of the workshop, axes and saws split fresh timber as the woodshop boys made sets and stage scenery. Only the graduates were left out of the general bustle. We were free to sit in the library at the back of the building or look in quite detachedly, naturally, on the measures being taken for our event.

Even the minister preached on graduation the Sunday before. His subject was, "Let your light so shine that men will see your good works and praise your Father, Who is in Heaven." Although the sermon was purported to be addressed to us, he used the occasion to speak to backsliders, gamblers and general ne'er-do-wells. But since he had called our names at the beginning of the service we were mollified.

Among Negroes the tradition was to give presents to children going only from one grade to another. How much more important this was when the person was graduating at the top of the class. Uncle Willie and Momma had sent away for a Mickey Mouse watch like Bailey's. Louise gave me four embroidered handkerchiefs. (I gave her crocheted doilies.) Mrs. Sneed, the minister's wife, made me an undershirt to wear for graduation, and nearly every customer gave me a nickel or maybe even a dime with the instruction "Keep on moving to higher ground," or some such encouragement.

Amazingly the great day finally dawned and I was out of bed before I knew it. I threw open the back door to see it more clearly, but Momma said, "Sister, come away from that door and put your robe on."

20 I hoped the memory of that morning would never leave me. Sunlight was itself young, and the day had none of the insistence maturity would bring it in a few hours. In my robe and barefoot in the backyard, under cover of going to see

about my new beans, I gave myself up to the gentle warmth and thanked God that no matter what evil I had done in my life He had allowed me to live to see this day. Somewhere in my fatalism I had expected to die, accidentally, and never have the chance to walk up the stairs in the auditorium and gracefully receive my hard-earned diploma. Out of God's merciful bosom I had won reprieve.

Bailey came out in his robe and gave me a box wrapped in Christmas paper. He said he had saved his money for months to pay for it. It felt like a box of chocolates, but I knew Bailey wouldn't save money to buy candy when we had all we could want under our noses.

He was as proud of the gift as I. It was a soft-leather-bound copy of a collection of poems by Edgar Allan Poe, or, as Bailey and I called him, "Eap." I turned to "Annabel Lee" and we walked up and down the garden rows, the cool dirt between our toes, reciting the beautifully sad lines.

Momma made a Sunday breakfast although it was only Friday. After we finished the blessing, I opened my eyes to find the watch on my plate. It was a dream of a day. Everything went smoothly and to my credit, I didn't have to be reminded or scolded for anything. Near evening I was too jittery to attend to chores, so Bailey volunteered to do all before his bath.

Days before, we had made a sign for the Store, and as we turned out the lights Momma hung the cardboard over the doorknob. It read clearly: CLOSED. GRADUATION.

My dress fitted perfectly and everyone said that I looked like a sunbeam in it. On the hill, going toward the school, Bailey walked behind with Uncle Willie, who muttered, "Go on, Ju." He wanted him to walk ahead with us because it embarrassed him to have to walk so slowly. Bailey said he'd let the ladies walk together, and the men would bring up the rear. We all laughed, nicely. 25

Little children dashed by out of the dark like fireflies. Their crepe-paper dresses and butterfly wings were not made for running and we heard more than one rip, dryly, and the regretful "uh uh" that followed.

The school blazed without gaiety. The windows seemed cold and unfriendly from the lower hill. A sense of ill-fated timing crept over me, and if Momma hadn't reached for my hand I would have drifted back to Bailey and Uncle Willie, and possibly beyond. She made a few slow jokes about my feet getting cold, and tugged me along to the now-strange building.

Around the front steps, assurance came back. There were my fellow "greats," the graduating class. Hair brushed back, legs oiled, new dresses and pressed pleats, fresh pocket handkerchiefs and little handbags, all homesewn. Oh, we were up to snuff, all right. I joined my comrades and didn't even see my family go in to find seats in the crowded auditorium.

The school band struck up a march and all classes filed in as had been rehearsed. We stood in front of our seats, as assigned, and on a signal from the choir director, we sat. No sooner had this been accomplished than the band started to play the national anthem. We rose again and sang the song, after which we recited the pledge of allegiance. We remained standing for a brief minute before the choir director and the principal signaled to us, rather desperately I thought, to take our seats. The command was so unusual that our carefully rehearsed and smooth-running machine was thrown off. For a full minute we fumbled for our chairs and bumped into each other awkwardly. Habits change or solidify under pressure, so in our state of nervous tension we had been ready to follow our usual assembly pattern: the American national anthem, then the pledge of allegiance, then the song every Black person I knew called the Negro National Anthem. All done in the same key, with the same passion and most often standing on the same foot.

30 Finding my seat at last, I was overcome with a presentiment of worse things to come. Something unrehearsed, unplanned, was going to happen, and we were going to be made to look bad. I distinctly remember being explicit in the choice of pronoun. It was "we," the graduating class, the unit, that concerned me then.

The principal welcomed "parents and friends" and asked the Baptist minister to lead us in prayer. His invocation was brief and punchy, and for a second I thought we were getting on the high road to right action. When the principal came back to the dais, however, his voice had changed. Sounds always affected me profoundly and the principal's voice was one of my favorites. During assembly it melted and lowed weakly into the audience. It had not been in my plan to listen to him, but my curiosity was piqued and I straightened up to give him my attention.

He was talking about Booker T. Washington, our "late great leader," who said we can be as close as the fingers on the hand, etc. . . . Then he said a few vague things about friendship and the friendship of kindly people to those less fortunate than themselves. With that his voice nearly faded, thin, away. Like a river diminishing to a stream and then to a trickle. But he cleared his throat and said, "Our speaker tonight, who is also our friend, came from Texarkana to deliver the commencement address, but due to the irregularity of the train schedule, he's going to, as they say, 'speak and run.'" He said that we understood and wanted the man to know that we were most grateful for the time he was able to give us and then something about how we were willing always to adjust to another's program, and without more ado—"I give you Mr. Edward Donleavy."

Not one but two white men came through the door off-stage. The shorter one walked to the speaker's platform, and the tall one moved to the center seat and sat down. But that was our principal's seat, and already occupied. The dislodged gentleman bounced around for a long breath or two before the Baptist minister gave him his chair, then with more dignity than the situation deserved, the minister walked off the stage.

Donleavy looked at the audience once (on reflection, I'm sure that he wanted only to reassure himself that we were really there), adjusted his glasses and began to read from a sheaf of papers.

35 He was glad "to be here and to see the work going on just as it was in the other schools."

At the first "Amen" from the audience I willed the offender to immediate death by choking on the word. But Amens and Yes, sirs began to fall around the room like rain through a ragged umbrella.

He told us of the wonderful changes we children in Stamps had in store. The Central School (naturally, the white school was Central) had already been granted improvements that would be in use in the fall. A well-known artist was coming from Little Rock to teach art to them. They were going to have the newest microscopes and chemistry equipment for their laboratory. Mr. Donleavy didn't leave us long in the dark over who made these improvements available to Central High. Nor were we to be ignored in the general betterment scheme he had in mind.

He said that he had pointed out to people at a very high level that one of the first-line football tacklers at Arkansas Agricultural and Mechanical College had graduated from good old Lafayette County Training School. Here fewer Amens were heard. Those few that did break through lay dully in the air with the heaviness of habit.

He went on to praise us. He went on to say how he had bragged that "one of the best basketball players at Fisk sank his first ball right here at Lafayette County Training School."

40 The white kids were going to have a chance to become Galileos and Madame Curies and Edisons and Gauguins, and our boys (the girls weren't even in on it) would try to be Jesse Owenses and Joe Louises.

Owens and the Brown Bomber were great heroes in our world, but what school official in the white-goddom of Little Rock had the right to decide that those two men must be our only heroes? Who decided that for Henry Reed to become a scientist he had to work like George Washington Carver, as a bootblack, to buy a lousy microscope? Bailey was obviously always going to be too small to be an athlete, so which concrete angel glued to what country seat had decided that if my brother wanted to become a lawyer he had to first pay penance for his skin by picking cotton and hoeing corn and studying correspondence books at night for twenty years?

The man's dead words fell like bricks around the auditorium and too many settled in my belly. Constrained by hard-learned manners I couldn't look behind me, but to my left and right the proud graduating class of 1940 had dropped their heads. Every girl in my row had found something new to do with her handkerchief. Some folded the tiny squares into love knots, some into triangles, but most were wadding them, then pressing them flat on their yellow laps.

On the dais, the ancient tragedy was being replayed. Professor Parsons sat, a sculptor's reject, rigid. His large, heavy body seemed devoid of will or willingness, and his eyes said he was no longer with us. The other teachers examined the flag (which was draped stage right) or their notes, or the windows which opened on our now-famous playing diamond.

Graduation, the hush-hush magic time of frills and gifts and congratulations and diplomas, was finished for me before my name was called. The accomplishment was nothing. The meticulous maps, drawn in three colors of ink, learning and spelling decasyllabic words, memorizing the whole of *The Rape of Lucrece*[3]—it was for nothing. Donleavy had exposed us.

3. A 1,855-line narrative poem by Shakespeare, which recounts the story of the daughter of a Roman prefect. When she was defiled, she stabbed herself in the presence of her father and her husband.

45 We were maids and farmers, handymen and washerwomen, and anything higher that we aspired to was farcical and presumptuous.

Then I wished that Gabriel Prosser and Nat Turner[4] had killed all whitefolks in their beds and that Abraham Lincoln had been assassinated before the signing of the Emancipation Proclamation, and that Harriet Tubman[5] had been killed by that blow on her head and Christopher Columbus had drowned in the *Santa Maria*.

It was awful to be a Negro and have no control over my life. It was brutal to be young and already trained to sit quietly and listen to charges brought against my color with no chance of defense. We should all be dead. I thought I should like to see us all dead, one on top of the other. A pyramid of flesh with the whitefolks on the bottom, as the broad base, then the Indians with their silly tomahawks and teepees and wigwams and treaties, the Negroes with their mops and recipes and cotton sacks and spirituals sticking out of their mouths. The Dutch children should all stumble in their wooden shoes and break their necks. The French should choke to death on the Louisiana Purchase (1803) while silkworms ate all the Chinese with their stupid pigtails. As a species, we were an abomination. All of us.

Donleavy was running for election, and assured our parents that if he won we could count on having the only colored paved playing field in that part of Arkansas. Also—he never looked up to acknowledge the grunts of acceptance—also, we were bound to get some new equipment for the home economics building and the workshop.

He finished, and since there was no need to give any more than the most perfunctory thank-you's, he nodded to the men on the stage, and the tall white man who was never introduced joined him at the door. They left with the attitude that now they were off to something really important. (The graduation ceremonies at Lafayette County Training School had been a mere preliminary.)

50 The ugliness they left was palpable. An uninvited guest who wouldn't leave. The choir was summoned and sang a modern arrangement of "Onward, Christian Soldiers," with new words pertaining to graduates seeking their place in the world. But it didn't work. Elouise, the daughter of the Baptist minister, recited "Invictus,"[6] and I could have cried at the impertinence of "I am the master of my fate, I am the captain of my soul."

My name had lost its ring of familiarity and I had to be nudged to go and receive my diploma. All my preparations had fled. I neither marched up to the stage like a conquering Amazon, nor did I look in the audience for Bailey's nod

4. Gabriel Prosser (c. 1776–1800) and Nat Turner (1800–1831), executed leaders of slave rebellions in Virginia.

5. Black abolitionist (c. 1820–1913), known for her work as a "conductor" on the Underground Railroad.

6. An inspirational poem by William Ernest Henley (1849–1903), once very popular for occasions such as this one.

of approval. Marguerite Johnson, I heard the name again, my honors were read, there were noises in the audience of appreciation, and I took my place on the stage as rehearsed.

I thought about colors I hated: ecru, puce, lavender, beige and black.

There was shuffling and rustling around me, then Henry Reed was giving his valedictory address, "To Be or Not to Be." Hadn't he heard the white-folks? We couldn't *be,* so the question was a waste of time. Henry's voice came out clear and strong. I feared to look at him. Hadn't he got the message? There was no "nobler in the mind" for Negroes because the world didn't think we had minds, and they let us know it. "Outrageous fortune"? Now, that was a joke. When the ceremony was over I had to tell Henry Reed some things. That is, if I still cared. Not "rub," Henry, "erase." "Ah, there's the erase." Us.

Henry had been a good student in elocution. His voice rose on tides of promise and fell on waves of warnings. The English teacher had helped him to create a sermon winging through Hamlet's soliloquy. To be a man, a doer, a builder, a leader, or to be a tool, an unfunny joke, a crusher of funky toadstools. I marveled that Henry could go through with the speech as if we had a choice.

I had been listening and silently rebutting each sentence with my eyes closed; then there was a hush, which in an audience warns that something unplanned is happening. I looked up and saw Henry Reed, the conservative, the proper, the A student, turn his back to the audience and turn to us (the proud graduating class of 1940) and sing, nearly speaking, 55

> "Lift ev'ry voice and sing
> Till earth and heaven ring
> Ring with the harmonies of Liberty . . ."

It was the poem written by James Weldon Johnson. It was the music composed by J. Rosamond Johnson. It was the Negro national anthem. Out of habit we were singing it.

Our mothers and fathers stood in the dark hall and joined the hymn of encouragement. A kindergarten teacher led the small children onto the stage and the buttercups and daisies and bunny rabbits marked time and tried to follow:

> "Stony the road we trod
> Bitter the chastening rod
> Felt in the days when hope, unborn, had died.
> Yet with a steady beat
> Have not our weary feet
> Come to the place for which our fathers sighed?"

Each child I knew had learned that song with his ABC's and along with "Jesus Loves Me This I Know." But I personally had never heard it before. Never heard the words, despite the thousands of times I had sung them. Never thought they had anything to do with me.

On the other hand, the words of Patrick Henry had made such an impression on me that I had been able to stretch myself tall and trembling and say, "I know not what course others may take, but as for me, give me liberty or give me death."

And now I heard, really for the first time:

> "We have come over a way that with tears
> has been watered,
> We have come, treading our path through
> the blood of the slaughtered."

60 While echoes of the song shivered in the air, Henry Reed bowed his head, said "Thank you," and returned to his place in the line. The tears that slipped down many faces were not wiped away in shame.

We were on top again. As always, again. We survived. The depths had been icy and dark, but now a bright sun spoke to our souls. I was no longer simply a member of the proud graduating class of 1940; I was a proud member of the wonderful, beautiful Negro race.

Oh, Black known and unknown poets, how often have your auctioned pains sustained us? Who will compute the lonely nights made less lonely by your songs, or the empty pots made less tragic by your tales?

If we were a people much given to revealing secrets, we might raise monuments and sacrifice to the memories of our poets, but slavery cured us of that weakness. It may be enough, however, to have it said that we survive in exact relationship to the dedication of our poets (include preachers, musicians and blues singers).

QUESTIONS

1. Presumably, all of Angelou's readers would have witnessed a graduation ceremony and brought their memories to her essay. How does she fulfill the reader's expectations for what graduation includes? How does she surprise us with details we don't expect?

2. In paragraph 43 Angelou writes that "the ancient tragedy was being replayed." What does she mean? How does her essay help to resist the tragic script?

3. Write a personal essay about an event you anticipated hopefully but that did not fulfill your expectations, incorporating an explanation of your disappointment into your account, as Angelou does.

Joey Franklin *Working at Wendy's*

It's 8:45 P.M., and I am standing in front of the counter at Wendy's. It smells of French fries and mop water. In my right hand I hold my résumé. I don't know if I need a résumé to apply for the Wendy's night shift, but I bring it anyway. It anchors me as I drift toward the sixteen-year-old kid behind the counter and ask to speak to his manager.

"One mandarin orange salad?" the boy asks.

"Uh, no. Actually, I'd like to speak to the *manager*." As the cashier retreats to the back of the store, I recognize a large kid with curly hair working the fryer—he used to play football with some of the members of my Boy Scout troop. He looks up at me, and I avert my eyes. Part of me wants to turn around and leave before the manager comes out. A couple in their twenties walks into the restaurant behind me. I step away from the counter and pretend to read the menu, holding my résumé close to my chest. The urge to leave increases. Just then the manager comes out and asks, "You here about the night shift?"

As I hand the manager my résumé, I realize it is a mistake. He doesn't want to know my service experience, or my academic references, or my GPA. All he wants to know is if I can spell my name correctly.

5 "Er, the application is over there," the manager says, handing me back my résumé and pointing to a file folder mounted on the wall next to the counter. I take the application to an empty table in the corner of the restaurant and hunch over it, wishing I had a drink, or a hamburger, or something to put on the table beside me.

The next day I go for an interview with the hiring manager. I sit down at a table in the lobby and answer two questions: "What hours do you want to work?" and "When can you start?"

When he was sixteen, my brother, Josh, got his first job at McDonald's. He lasted two weeks before deciding the greasy uniform and salty mop water weren't worth $5.25 an hour. His manager used to show off rejected applications to the other employees in the back of the store. Most were high school dropouts looking for spending money, but a few had college degrees. One application was from a doctor who had recently left his practice because he "couldn't handle the mortality rate."

I think about that doctor now as I sit in a small back room at Wendy's. I have just watched thirty minutes of training videos about customer service, floor mopping, heavy lifting, and armed robbery. Chelsea, the training manager, hands me two neatly folded uniforms and a brand-new hat. Holding the hat in my hand, I look out into the kitchen at my new coworkers. At the fryer is the large high school kid I remember from the night before. A skinny brown-haired

Written when Franklin was an English major at Brigham Young University in Provo, Utah; published in Twentysomething Essays by Twentysomething Writers *(2006).*

Asian-looking boy who must be about nineteen years old is washing dishes. Two girls are at the front of the store taking orders, and the manager is on the phone with an angry customer. "Can I do this?" I ask myself, and put on my hat.

Chelsea is pregnant. During our training session, I guess she is about six months along. It turns out she is due in three days. "This is my last week on the day shift," she says. "After the baby is born, I'll be back on nights." This is her first child, she explains, and says she is looking forward to being a mom. She smiles as she pats her stomach and asks about my son.

10 "Eighteen months," I tell her, "a real handful." I explain that I want to work nights so I can take care of my son during the day while my wife finishes her last semester of college. I ask about the pay, but I already know her answer. "We start at five-seventy-five," she says, "but the night guys get six." I ask her what she thinks about $7. She says she'll see what she can do.

Chelsea trains me on Tuesday and goes into labor on Wednesday. I don't see her again for three weeks.

Kris Livingston's mom ran the register at the Taco Bell on the corner of Lombard Street and Allen Boulevard in a poorer section of Beaverton, Oregon. Her name was Dawn. She was divorced and had three boys. She shared a three-bedroom apartment with another single mom and her own five children. They listened to Snoop Dogg and Ice-T, drank forty-ounce malt liquors, and walked over two miles round-trip every Saturday to watch the neighborhood boys play basketball at Schiffler Park.

On welfare-check days, Dawn went grocery shopping and brought home twelve-packs of Pepsi, stacks of frozen steaks, crinkly bags of potato chips, several gallons of 2-percent milk, and bag after bag of Malt-O-Meal cereal. The week before welfare checks came, they ate eggs and instant ramen—lots of ramen.

Her son Kris was my best friend in sixth grade. We often walked to Taco Bell together to visit his mother. She usually bought us a taco while we sat in a booth in the corner of the store and talked about bicycles, girls, and football. Once, on the way home from visiting his mom, Kris said, "She used to sell drugs, you know. We had plenty of money, and nobody thought she was a bad mom then."

15 My first night on the job, I work with Dave. He is seventeen years old, five-ten, and keeps his hair short, like a soldier. He goes to an alternative high school if he wakes up in time and is looking forward to enlisting in the military when he turns eighteen. His dad, who recently remarried and moved, told Dave he would have to find his own place to live. When Dave isn't sleeping on his friends' couches, he lives in his car, a 1982 Volkswagen Rabbit with a hole in the floor just beneath the gas pedal.

Dave works with me a few nights a week and knows the business well. He's quick with a mop, can make all the sandwiches blindfolded, and has the entire computer memorized. When he's not working, he hangs out in the restaurant lobby trying to steal Frosties and old fries when no one is looking. The manager says she will give him food if he needs it and asks that he not steal anymore. "Asking gets you nowhere," he says, and keeps stealing.

Because I live just two blocks from the store, I recognize a disproportionate number of the late-night drive-through customers. Mostly, I see parents of the scouts I work with, or other scout leaders, and occasionally a friend from school. When they pull up to the window and see me in the Wendy's hat and headphones, the following conversation ensues:

"Joey, I didn't know you worked here! How's it going?"

"Good, good. Just flipping burgers."

"Hey, you've got to do what you've got to do." 20

Then I explain the job is temporary, and it's the only job in town that allows me to work at night so I can watch my son during the day while my wife finishes school. I tell them in another month I'll be back in school and working at a better-paying, less humiliating campus job.

One evening a fellow scout leader comes through, and after an exchange similar to the one described above, he says, "Hey, more power to ya. I know a lot of people who think they're above that." He thanks me as I hand him his triple cheeseburger, and he drives around the corner and out of sight.

At 250 pounds, Danny really fills out his uniform. He played varsity football for the local high school, has earned his Eagle Scout award, and knows his way around a car engine. On several occasions he has changed spark plugs, jumped batteries, and even replaced brakes on the cars of fellow employees, usually right in the store parking lot.

Wendy's is the first job Danny has ever had. With six months' experience, he is the senior employee and is being considered for a management position. He brings in about $1,000 a month, much of which he gives to his grandmother. At closing, he always saves the good salads for me and talks the manager into letting me go home early. He likes listening to Metallica, working on his Trans Am, and talking with Tonya, a high school junior who also works at the store.

While I'm washing my hands in the bathroom at work, a well-groomed twenty-something man standing at the sink next to me starts a conversation. "Do you like working the night shift?" he asks. 25

"It's not bad," I say, shaking my wet hands over the sink.

"How long have you worked here?"

"Two weeks."

"Have you ever thought about college?" he asks. I want to tell him I'm in the top 5 percent of students at my college, that I am two semesters away from graduating, and that I'm on my way to grad school to get a Ph.D. in English literature. Instead, I shrug and tell him the same line I tell everyone: "Oh yeah, I'm just working here until my wife finishes." He doesn't believe me. To him, I look like another wasted life, another victim. He thinks I got my girlfriend pregnant, that I never graduated from high school, that I can't do any better than flip burgers at two in the morning. He feels sorry for my kids.

30 "I only applied here because I knew I would get hired," says Sara the first night I work with her. She is a nineteen-year-old single mother with a sixteen-month-old boy. She is very tall and wears her long brown hair in a ponytail pulled through the hole in the back of her Wendy's hat. I ask her why she needed a job so bad.

"I had to get one," she tells me. "My parole officer said it was the only way to stay out of jail." I start at this and then ask, "Why were you in jail?"

"Drugs," she says, and pauses, testing me. "I was wearing my boyfriend's jacket, and the cops found a heroin pipe in the pocket." I ask how long she was in jail. "One year," she tells me. "I just got out a month ago."

When I was in fifth grade, my dad got a job delivering pizza. As an eleven-year-old, pivoting on that blurry edge between boyhood and adolescence, I found myself bragging to my friends about the prospect of free pizza and then wishing I hadn't told them anything about my father's job. He worked a few nights a week, and when he came home, his uniform smelled like steaming cardboard and burnt cheese, but he always brought home pizza.

Oren is nineteen years old and works at Wendy's to pay for a cell-phone bill and to get out of the house. His parents are devout Mormons and think he is a disgrace to their entire family. He wants to sell marijuana because he believes he can do nothing else. "I don't do anything well," he tells me one night while washing dishes. "I don't know what I want to do with my life." He asks Sara to find some pot for him to sell.

35 Oren's mother is Japanese, born and raised, and speaks to her children in her native tongue. That means Oren speaks Japanese and has family connections in Japan.

Oren also owns an AK-47 and likes to go up into the canyons and shoot jackrabbits. He showed me a picture once of a rabbit carcass out in the desert, its innards all blown out and dangling for the camera.

Tonight, while working the grill, Danny tells me he has never been on a date. "Girls don't like me," he says as he flips a row of sizzling, square quarter-pound patties. I can tell he believes it. Danny, by his own admission, is the kind of guy whom girls like for support. He is a gentleman, he asks thoughtful questions, and he's always willing to talk. He thinks his weight and his scruff turn girls off. He tells me he is going to ask Tonya to a movie this weekend but isn't sure she'll say yes. Later, Tonya comes into the store, and Danny disappears with her for a few minutes out in the lobby. He comes back with a large smile on his face and says, "I've got a date this weekend, can you work for me?"

I don't like when Dave works the front line with me. I can't make sandwiches very fast yet, and he gets tired of waiting. More than once he pushes me aside to finish an order. If he sees me hesitate on a step, he barks at me, "Red, green, red, green! Ketchup, pickle, tomato, lettuce! Come on, Joe, it's not that hard."

Later, while I'm mopping the floor at closing, Dave comes by and takes the mop from my hand. "Like this," he says, scrubbing the tile vigorously. He thrusts the mop back in my hands and walks away, rolling his eyes.

Chelsea is back at work tonight for the first time since having her baby. She appears fairly happy, and I am surprised at how well adjusted she seems to being a working mom. The phone rings several times, and Chelsea takes the calls in her office. She tells me her husband has lots of questions about putting the baby to bed. After the lobby closes, Chelsea disappears into the bathroom for nearly half an hour. This happens every time I work with her. I wonder if she is sick. Then I notice the breast pump in a case on her desk. Another employee tells me Chelsea has been expressing milk in one of the bathroom stalls on her breaks. 40

Danny and Tonya have been dating for two weeks. He shows up for his shift an hour early to see her before she gets off. They sit in the lobby holding hands and talking for almost the entire hour. When they're not in the store together, she sends text messages to his phone, which I catch him reading while he stands at the grill.

Tonight Danny approaches me while I'm opening boxes of French fries. He wants advice on how to ask Tonya to her junior prom. "I want to do something romantic," he says. I suggest Shakespeare's eighteenth sonnet. He has never heard of it. "'Shall I compare thee to a summer's day . . .'" I recite. "She'll love it." I print off the sonnet at home and bring it to work for him the next day. He writes it in a card and delivers it with flowers. Two weeks later, in a rented tux at Tonya's junior prom, Danny gets his first kiss.

I call my dad tonight. He asks about school, about my son, and about work. I tell him about Wendy's.

"What? Who?" he says.

"Me. I got a job at Wendy's." Long pause. "I needed a job I could do at night." More silence. "It's not so bad." Still silence. "I work from nine P.M. to one A.M. a few nights a week." 45

Just when I think the line must be disconnected, Dad clears his throat and asks, "What happened to your computer job?"

"The guy ran out of work for me."

"Oh." More silence. I imagine he looks around the room to make sure no one is listening before he says, "Wendy's? When did that happen?" I want to tell him that it didn't *happen,* that it wasn't an accident, but I am stuck wondering how to make him understand, and at the same time wondering why I should have to explain anything at all. I wonder what his reaction would be if I had chosen to get more student loans instead of the part-time job. I choose to say nothing. Then I offer him my employee discount on fries next time he is in town. He says he'll take me up on it.

When I come into the store tonight, Dave is talking loudly to some employees gathered in the lobby. I ask what all the laughing is about. They tell me that last night Dave and Oren siphoned all the gas out of Dave's stepmother's four-wheeler, and then they urinated on her car handles.

50 Everyone dreads working with Chelsea. When she is not in her office counting the till or on the phone with her husband, she sits on the front counter and complains about her mother-in-law. She does very little to help prep the store for closing, and we rarely get out before two A.M.

Tonight she tells me about her mother-in-law's most recent visit. "I cleaned the house for hours before she came," Chelsea says, nursing a Diet Coke. "And the first thing she says when she gets there is how disgusting the place looks. She won't even eat my cooking." According to Chelsea, her mother-in-law has hated her ever since she got engaged. She wouldn't even visit except that Chelsea has a baby now, and the mother-in-law feels obligated. Chelsea's mother-in-law is disappointed that she is still working. "A mother's place is in the home," she says to Chelsea. "Your kids will be ruined."

Tonight Waymon Hamilton comes through the drive-up window with his family. Waymon lives around the corner from me, and his two sons are in my scout troop, but they spend most of their free time traveling around the state playing premier Little League baseball. They order a few value meals, some drinks, and they ask how I'm doing. There is no hint of concern or condolence in their voices, and I appreciate it.

I hand them their food and watch them drive away. Most people know Waymon the way I know him, as a dedicated father who works hard at a thankless job to provide for his family. His unassuming nature and warm smile are what I see when I think about him. Few people know him as the fleet-footed running back who helped Brigham Young University win Holiday Bowls in 1981 and 1983. Few people know he holds several BYU scoring records, including second place for touchdowns in a season, third in career touchdowns, and fifth for both season and career points scored. I didn't even know he played college football until someone mentioned it at a scout meeting. I once worked all day with Waymon, putting in a new driveway for a neighbor, and he never mentioned his football days once. He told me about his boys, about teaching public school in California, and about pouring lots of concrete.

After the store closes, I come home, take off my uniform, and climb into bed with my wife. She rolls over, tells me she loves me, and murmurs something about the smell of French fries. I kiss her on the cheek and close my eyes. It is winter, but the house is warm. My son is asleep in the next room. There is food in the fridge, and I have a job that pays an honest wage. In the morning I will make breakfast and send my wife off to school. And then, after the dishes are done, if the weather permits, my son and I will take a walk to the park.

Questions

1. What is Joey Franklin's attitude toward working at Wendy's? How does he demonstrate it? In answering these questions, look especially at the conclusion of the essay and at the details he chooses about how others respond to him.

2. Franklin uses considerable detail to develop his coworkers as characters (see paragraph 13 for an example). Which details do you find especially effective? Why?

3. Most of this essay is written in the present tense (with past-tense reflections about former jobs held by family members). What is the effect of Franklin's use of this verb tense? How would the essay differ if he wrote the entire essay in past tense?

4. Write an essay about a job you've held. Use dialogue and details to develop characters.

Lars Eighner — *On Dumpster Diving*

Long before I began Dumpster diving I was impressed with Dumpsters, enough so that I wrote the Merriam-Webster[1] research service to discover what I could about the word *Dumpster*. I learned from them that it is a proprietary word belonging to the Dempster Dumpster company. Since then I have dutifully capitalized the word, although it was lowercased in almost all the citations Merriam-Webster photocopied for me. Dempster's word is too apt. I have never heard these things called anything but Dumpsters. I do not know anyone who knows the generic name for these objects. From time to time I have heard a wino or hobo give some corrupted credit to the original and call them Dipsy Dumpsters.

I began Dumpster diving about a year before I became homeless.

I prefer the word *scavenging* and use the word *scrounging* when I mean to be obscure. I have heard people, evidently meaning to be polite, use the word *foraging*, but I prefer to reserve that word for gathering nuts and berries and such, which I do also according to the season and the opportunity. *Dumpster diving* seems to me to be a little too cute and, in my case, inaccurate because I lack the athletic ability to lower myself into the Dumpsters as the true divers do, much to their increased profit.

I like the frankness of the word *scavenging*, which I can hardly think of without picturing a big black snail on an aquarium wall. I live from the refuse of others. I am a scavenger. I think it a sound and honorable niche, although if I could I would naturally prefer to live the comfortable consumer life, perhaps—and only perhaps—as a slightly less wasteful consumer, owing to what I have learned as a scavenger.

From Travels with Lizbeth *(1993), an account of Eighner's life as a homeless person.*

1. A large publisher of dictionaries.

5 While Lizbeth[2] and I were still living in the shack on Avenue B as my savings ran out, I put almost all my sporadic income into rent. The necessities of daily life I began to extract from Dumpsters. Yes, we ate from them. Except for jeans, all my clothes came from Dumpsters. Boom boxes, candles, bedding, toilet paper, a virgin male love doll, medicine, books, a typewriter, dishes, furnishings, and change, sometimes amounting to many dollars—I acquired many things from the Dumpsters.

I have learned much as a scavenger. I mean to put some of what I have learned down here, beginning with the practical art of Dumpster diving and proceeding to the abstract.

What is safe to eat?

After all, the finding of objects is becoming something of an urban art. Even respectable employed people will sometimes find something tempting sticking out of a Dumpster or standing beside one. Quite a number of people, not all of them of the bohemian type, are willing to brag that they found this or that piece in the trash. But eating from Dumpsters is what separates the dilettanti from the professionals. Eating safely from the Dumpsters involves three principles: using the senses and common sense to evaluate the condition of the found materials, knowing the Dumpsters of a given area and checking them regularly, and seeking always to answer the question, "Why was this discarded?"

Perhaps everyone who has a kitchen and a regular supply of groceries has, at one time or another, made a sandwich and eaten half of it before discovering mold on the bread or got a mouthful of milk before realizing the milk had turned. Nothing of the sort is likely to happen to a Dumpster diver because he is constantly reminded that most food is discarded for a reason. Yet a lot of perfectly good food can be found in Dumpsters.

10 Canned goods, for example, turn up fairly often in the Dumpsters I frequent. All except the most phobic people would be willing to eat from a can, even if it came from a Dumpster. Canned goods are among the safest of foods to be found in Dumpsters but are not utterly foolproof.

Although very rare with modern canning methods, botulism is a possibility. Most other forms of food poisoning seldom do lasting harm to a healthy person, but botulism is almost certainly fatal and often the first symptom is death. Except for carbonated beverages, all canned goods should contain a slight vacuum and suck air when first punctured. Bulging, rusty, and dented cans and cans that spew when punctured should be avoided, especially when the contents are not very acidic or syrupy.

Heat can break down the botulin, but this requires much more cooking than most people do to canned goods. To the extent that botulism occurs at all, of course, it can occur in cans on pantry shelves as well as in cans from Dumpsters. Need I say that home-canned goods are simply too risky to be recommended.

2. The author's dog.

From time to time one of my companions, aware of the source of my provisions, will ask, "Do you think these crackers are really safe to eat?" For some reason it is most often the crackers they ask about.

This question has always made me angry. Of course I would not offer my companion anything I had doubts about. But more than that, I wonder why he cannot evaluate the condition of the crackers for himself. I have no special knowledge and I have been wrong before. Since he knows where the food comes from, it seems to me he ought to assume some of the responsibility for deciding what he will put in his mouth. For myself I have few qualms about dry foods such as crackers, cookies, cereal, chips, and pasta if they are free of visible contaminates and still dry and crisp. Most often such things are found in the original packaging, which is not so much a positive sign as it is the absence of a negative one.

Raw fruits and vegetables with intact skins seem perfectly safe to me, excluding of course the obviously rotten. Many are discarded for minor imperfections that can be pared away. Leafy vegetables, grapes, cauliflower, broccoli, and similar things may be contaminated by liquids and may be impractical to wash. 15

Candy, especially hard candy, is usually safe if it has not drawn ants. Chocolate is often discarded only because it has become discolored as the cocoa butter de-emulsified. Candying, after all, is one method of food preservation because pathogens do not like very sugary substances.

All of these foods might be found in any Dumpster and can be evaluated with some confidence largely on the basis of appearance. Beyond these are foods that cannot be correctly evaluated without additional information.

I began scavenging by pulling pizzas out of the Dumpster behind a pizza delivery shop. In general, prepared food requires caution, but in this case I knew when the shop closed and went to the Dumpster as soon as the last of the help left.

Such shops often get prank orders; both the orders and the products made to fill them are called *bogus.* Because help seldom stays long at these places, pizzas are often made with the wrong topping, refused on delivery for being cold, or baked incorrectly. The products to be discarded are boxed up because inventory is kept by counting boxes: A boxed pizza can be written off; an unboxed pizza does not exist.

I never placed a bogus order to increase the supply of pizzas and I believe no one else was scavenging in this Dumpster. But the people in the shop became suspicious and began to retain their garbage in the shop overnight. While it lasted I had a steady supply of fresh, sometimes warm pizza. Because I knew the Dumpster I knew the source of the pizza, and because I visited the Dumpster regularly I knew what was fresh and what was yesterday's. 20

The area I frequent is inhabited by many affluent college students. I am not here by chance; the Dumpsters in this area are very rich. Students throw out many good things, including food. In particular they tend to throw everything out when they move at the end of a semester, before and after breaks, and around midterm, when many of them despair of college. So I find it advantageous to keep an eye on the academic calendar.

Students throw food away around breaks because they do not know whether it has spoiled or will spoil before they return. A typical discard is a half jar of peanut butter. In fact, nonorganic peanut butter does not require refrigeration and is unlikely to spoil in any reasonable time. The student does not know that, and since it is Daddy's money, the student decides not to take a chance. Opened containers require caution and some attention to the question, "Why was this discarded?" But in the case of discards from student apartments, the answer may be that the item was thrown out through carelessness, ignorance, or wastefulness. This can sometimes be deduced when the item is found with many others, including some that are obviously perfectly good.

Some students, and others, approach defrosting a freezer by chucking out the whole lot. Not only do the circumstances of such a find tell the story, but also the mass of frozen goods stays cold for a long time and items may be found still frozen or freshly thawed.

Yogurt, cheese, and sour cream are items that are often thrown out while they are still good. Occasionally I find a cheese with a spot of mold, which of course I just pare off, and because it is obvious why such a cheese was discarded, I treat it with less suspicion than an apparently perfect cheese found in similar circumstances. Yogurt is often discarded, still sealed, only because the expiration date on the carton had passed. This is one of my favorite finds because yogurt will keep for several days, even in warm weather.

Students throw out canned goods and staples at the end of semesters and when they give up college at midterm. Drugs, pornography, spirits, and the like are often discarded when parents are expected—Dad's Day, for example. And spirits also turn up after big party weekends, presumably discarded by the newly reformed. Wine and spirits, of course, keep perfectly well even once opened, but the same cannot be said of beer.

My test for carbonated soft drinks is whether they still fizz vigorously. Many juices or other beverages are too acidic or too syrupy to cause much concern, provided they are not visibly contaminated. I have discovered nasty molds in vegetable juices, even when the product was found under its original seal; I recommend that such products be decanted slowly into a clear glass. Liquids always require some care. One hot day I found a large jug of Pat O'Brien's Hurricane mix. The jug had been opened but was still ice cold. I drank three large glasses before it became apparent to me that someone had added the rum to the mix, and not a little rum. I never tasted the rum, and by the time I began to feel the effects I had already ingested a very large quantity of the beverage. Some divers would have considered this a boon, but being suddenly intoxicated in a public place in the early afternoon is not my idea of a good time.

I have heard of people maliciously contaminating discarded food and even handouts, but mostly I have heard of this from people with vivid imaginations who have had no experience with the Dumpsters themselves. Just before the pizza shop stopped discarding its garbage at night, jalapeños began showing up on most of the thrown-out pizzas. If indeed this was meant to discourage me, it was a wasted effort because I am a native Texan.

For myself, I avoid game, poultry, pork, and egg-based foods, whether I find them raw or cooked. I seldom have the means to cook what I find, but when I do I avail myself of plentiful supplies of beef, which is often in very good condition. I suppose fish becomes disagreeable before it becomes dangerous. Lizbeth is happy to have any such thing that is past its prime and, in fact, does not recognize fish as food until it is quite strong.

Home leftovers, as opposed to surpluses from restaurants, are very often bad. Evidently, especially among students, there is a common type of personality that carefully wraps up even the smallest leftover and shoves it into the back of the refrigerator for six months or so before discarding it. Characteristic of this type are the reused jars and margarine tubs to which the remains are committed. I avoid ethnic foods I am unfamiliar with. If I do not know what it is supposed to look like when it is good, I cannot be certain I will be able to tell if it is bad.

30 No matter how careful I am I still get dysentery at least once a month, oftener in warm weather. I do not want to paint too romantic a picture. Dumpster diving has serious drawbacks as a way of life.

I learned to scavenge gradually, on my own. Since then I have initiated several companions into the trade. I have learned that there is a predictable series of stages a person goes through in learning to scavenge.

At first the new scavenger is filled with disgust and self-loathing. He is ashamed of being seen and may lurk around, trying to duck behind things, or he may try to dive at night. (In fact, most people instinctively look away from a scavenger. By skulking around, the novice calls attention to himself and arouses suspicion. Diving at night is ineffective and needlessly messy.)

Every grain of rice seems to be a maggot. Everything seems to stink. He can wipe the egg yolk off the found can, but he cannot erase from his mind the stigma of eating garbage.

That stage passes with experience. The scavenger finds a pair of running shoes that fit and look and smell brand-new. He finds a pocket calculator in perfect working order. He finds pristine ice cream, still frozen, more than he can eat or keep. He begins to understand: People throw away perfectly good stuff, a lot of perfectly good stuff.

35 At this stage, Dumpster shyness begins to dissipate. The diver, after all, has the last laugh. He is finding all manner of good things that are his for the taking. Those who disparage his profession are the fools, not he.

He may begin to hang on to some perfectly good things for which he has neither a use nor a market. Then he begins to take note of the things that are not perfectly good but are nearly so. He mates a Walkman with broken earphones and one that is missing a battery cover. He picks up things that he can repair.

At this stage he may become lost and never recover. Dumpsters are full of things of some potential value to someone and also of things that never have much intrinsic value but are interesting. All the Dumpster divers I have known come to the point of trying to acquire everything they touch. Why not take it, they reason, since it is all free? This is, of course, hopeless. Most divers come to realize that they must restrict themselves to items of relatively immediate utility. But in some cases the diver simply cannot control himself. I have met several of these pack-rat types. Their ideas of the values of various pieces of junk verge on the psychotic. Every bit of glass may be a diamond, they think, and all that glisters, gold.

I tend to gain weight when I am scavenging. Partly this is because I always find far more pizza and doughnuts than water-packed tuna, nonfat yogurt, and fresh vegetables. Also I have not developed much faith in the reliability of Dumpsters as a food source, although it has been proven to me many times. I tend to eat as if I have no idea where my next meal is coming from. But mostly I just hate to see food go to waste and so I eat much more than I should. Something like this drives the obsession to collect junk.

As for collecting objects, I usually restrict myself to collecting one kind of small object at a time, such as pocket calculators, sunglasses, or campaign buttons. To live on the street I must anticipate my needs to a certain extent: I must pick up and save warm bedding I find in August because it will not be found in Dumpsters in November. As I have no access to health care, I often hoard essential drugs, such as antibiotics and antihistamines. (This course can be recommended only to those with some grounding in pharmacology. Antibiotics, for example, even when indicated are worse than useless if taken in insufficient amounts.) But even if I had a home with extensive storage space, I could not save everything that might be valuable in some contingency.

40 I have proprietary feelings about my Dumpsters. As I have mentioned, it is no accident that I scavenge from ones where good finds are common. But my limited experience with Dumpsters in other areas suggests to me that even in poorer areas, Dumpsters, if attended with sufficient diligence, can be made to yield a livelihood. The rich students discard perfectly good kiwifruit; poorer people discard perfectly good apples. Slacks and Polo shirts are found in the one place; jeans and T-shirts in the other. The population of competitors rather than the affluence of the dumpers most affects the feasibility of survival by scavenging. The large number of competitors is what puts me off the idea of trying to scavenge in places like Los Angeles.

Curiously, I do not mind my direct competition, other scavengers, so much as I hate the can scroungers.

People scrounge cans because they have to have a little cash. I have tried scrounging cans with an able-bodied companion. Afoot a can scrounger simply cannot make more than a few dollars a day. One can extract the necessities of life from the Dumpsters directly with far less effort than would be required to accumulate the equivalent value in cans. (These observations may not hold in places with container redemption laws.)

Can scroungers, then, are people who must have small amounts of cash. These are drug addicts and winos, mostly the latter because the amounts of cash are so small. Spirits and drugs do, like all other commodities, turn up in Dumpsters and the scavenger will from time to time have a half bottle of a rather good wine with his dinner. But the wino cannot survive on these occasional finds; he must have his daily dose to stave off the DTs. All the cans he can carry will buy about three bottles of Wild Irish Rose.

I do not begrudge them the cans, but can scroungers tend to tear up the Dumpsters, mixing the contents and littering the area. They become so specialized that they can see only cans. They earn my contempt by passing up change, canned goods, and readily hockable items.

There are precious few courtesies among scavengers. But it is common practice to set aside surplus items: pairs of shoes, clothing, canned goods, and such. A true scavenger hates to see good stuff go to waste, and what he cannot use he leaves in good condition in plain sight. 45

Can scroungers lay waste to everything in their path and will stir one of a pair of good shoes to the bottom of a Dumpster, to be lost or ruined in the muck. Can scroungers will even go through individual garbage cans, something I have never seen a scavenger do.

Individual garbage cans are set out on the public easement only on garbage days. On other days going through them requires trespassing close to a dwelling. Going through individual garbage cans without scattering litter is almost impossible. Litter is likely to reduce the public's tolerance of scavenging. Individual cans are simply not as productive as Dumpsters; people in houses and duplexes do not move so often and for some reason do not tend to discard as much useful material. Moreover, the time required to go through one garbage can that serves one household is not much less than the time required to go through a Dumpster that contains the refuse of twenty apartments.

But my strongest reservation about going through individual garbage cans is that this seems to me a very personal kind of invasion to which I would object if I were a householder. Although many things in Dumpsters are obviously meant never to come to light, a Dumpster is somehow less personal.

I avoid trying to draw conclusions about the people who dump in the Dumpsters I frequent. I think it would be unethical to do so, although I know many people will find the idea of scavenger ethics too funny for words.

Dumpsters contain bank statements, correspondence, and other documents, just as anyone might expect. But there are also less obvious sources of information. Pill bottles, for example. The labels bear the name of the patient, the name of the doctor, and the name of the drug. AIDS drugs and antipsychotic medicines, to name but two groups, are specific and are seldom prescribed for any other disorders. The plastic compacts for birth-control pills usually have complete label information. 50

Despite all of this sensitive information, I have had only one apartment resident object to my going through the Dumpster. In that case it turned out the resident was a university athlete who was taking bets and who was afraid I would turn up his wager slips.

Occasionally a find tells a story. I once found a small paper bag containing some unused condoms, several partial tubes of flavored sexual lubricants, a partially used compact of birth-control pills, and the torn pieces of a picture of a young man. Clearly she was through with him and planning to give up sex altogether.

Dumpster things are often sad—abandoned teddy bears, shredded wedding books, despaired-of sales kits. I find many pets lying in state in Dumpsters. Although I hope to get off the streets so that Lizbeth can have a long and comfortable old age, I know this hope is not very realistic. So I suppose when her time comes she too will go into a Dumpster. I will have no better place for her. And after all, it is fitting, since for most of her life her livelihood has come from the Dumpster. When she finds something I think is safe that has been spilled from a Dumpster, I let her have it. She already knows the route around the best ones. I like to think that if she survives me she will have a chance of evading the dog catcher and of finding her sustenance on the route.

Silly vanities also come to rest in the Dumpsters. I am a rather accomplished needleworker. I get a lot of material from the Dumpsters. Evidently sorority girls, hoping to impress someone, perhaps themselves, with their mastery of a womanly art, buy a lot of embroider-by-number kits, work a few stitches horribly, and eventually discard the whole mess. I pull out their stitches, turn the canvas over, and work an original design. Do not think I refrain from chuckling as I make gifts from these kits.

55 I find diaries and journals. I have often thought of compiling a book of literary found objects. And perhaps I will one day. But what I find is hopelessly commonplace and bad without being, even unconsciously, camp. College students also discard their papers. I am horrified to discover the kind of paper that now merits an A in an undergraduate course. I am grateful, however, for the number of good books and magazines the students throw out.

In the area I know best I have never discovered vermin in the Dumpsters, but there are two kinds of kitty surprise. One is alley cats whom I meet as they leap, claws first, out of Dumpsters. This is especially thrilling when I have Lizbeth in tow. The other kind of kitty surprise is a plastic garbage bag filled with some ponderous, amorphous mass. This always proves to be used cat litter.

City bees harvest doughnut glaze and this makes the Dumpster at the doughnut shop more interesting. My faith in the instinctive wisdom of animals is always shaken whenever I see Lizbeth attempt to catch a bee in her mouth, which she does whenever bees are present. Evidently some birds find Dumpsters profitable, for birdie surprise is almost as common as kitty surprise of the first kind. In hunting season all kinds of small game turn up in Dumpsters, some of it, sadly, not entirely dead. Curiously, summer and winter, maggots are uncommon.

The worst of the living and near-living hazards of the Dumpsters are the fire ants. The food they claim is not much of a loss, but they are vicious and aggressive. It is very easy to brush against some surface of the Dumpster and pick up half a dozen or more fire ants, usually in some sensitive area such as the underarm. One advantage of bringing Lizbeth along as I make Dumpster rounds is that, for obvious reasons, she is very alert to ground-based fire ants. When Lizbeth recognizes a fire-ant infestation around our feet, she does the Dance of the Zillion Fire Ants. I have learned not to ignore this warning from Lizbeth, whether I perceive the tiny ants or not, but to remove ourselves at

Lizbeth's first pas de bourée. All the more so because the ants are the worst in the summer months when I wear flip-flops if I have them. (Perhaps someone will misunderstand this. Lizbeth does the Dance of the Zillion Fire Ants when she recognizes more fire ants than she cares to eat, not when she is being bitten. Since I have learned to react promptly, she does not get bitten at all. It is the isolated patrol of fire ants that falls in Lizbeth's range that deserves pity. She finds them quite tasty.)

By far the best way to go through a Dumpster is to lower yourself into it. Most of the good stuff tends to settle at the bottom because it is usually weightier than the rubbish. My more athletic companions have often demonstrated to me that they can extract much good material from a Dumpster I have already been over.

60 To those psychologically or physically unprepared to enter a Dumpster, I recommend a stout stick, preferably with some barb or hook at one end. The hook can be used to grab plastic garbage bags. When I find canned goods or other objects loose at the bottom of a Dumpster, I lower a bag into it, roll the desired object into the bag, and then hoist the bag out—a procedure more easily described than executed. Much Dumpster diving is a matter of experience for which nothing will do except practice.

Dumpster diving is outdoor work, often surprisingly pleasant. It is not entirely predictable; things of interest turn up every day and some days there are finds of great value. I am always very pleased when I can turn up exactly the thing I most wanted to find. Yet in spite of the element of chance, scavenging more than most other pursuits tends to yield returns in some proportion to the effort and intelligence brought to bear. It is very sweet to turn up a few dollars in change from a Dumpster that has just been gone over by a wino.

The land is now covered with cities. The cities are full of Dumpsters. If a member of the canine race is ever able to know what it is doing, then Lizbeth knows that when we go around to the Dumpsters, we are hunting. I think of scavenging as a modern form of self-reliance. In any event, after having survived nearly ten years of government service, where everything is geared to the lowest common denominator, I find it refreshing to have work that rewards initiative and effort. Certainly I would be happy to have a sinecure again, but I am no longer heartbroken that I left one.

I find from the experience of scavenging two rather deep lessons. The first is to take what you can use and let the rest go by. I have come to think that there is no value in the abstract. A thing I cannot use or make useful, perhaps by trading, has no value however rare or fine it may be. I mean useful in a broad sense—some art I would find useful and some otherwise.

I was shocked to realize that some things are not worth acquiring, but now I think it is so. Some material things are white elephants that eat up the possessor's substance. The second lesson is the transience of material being. This has not quite converted me to a dualist, but it has made some headway in that direction. I do not suppose that ideas are immortal, but certainly mental things are longer lived than other material things.

65 Once I was the sort of person who invests objects with sentimental value. Now I no longer have those objects, but I have the sentiments yet.

Many times in our travels I have lost everything but the clothes I was wearing and Lizbeth. The things I find in Dumpsters, the love letters and rag dolls of so many lives, remind me of this lesson. Now I hardly pick up a thing without envisioning the time I will cast it aside. This I think is a healthy state of mind. Almost everything I have now has already been cast out at least once, proving that what I own is valueless to someone.

Anyway, I find my desire to grab for the gaudy bauble has been largely sated. I think this is an attitude I share with the very wealthy—we both know there is plenty more where what we have came from. Between us are the rat-race millions who nightly scavenge the cable channels looking for they know not what.

I am sorry for them.

QUESTIONS

1. How does Eighner organize his essay? What does such an organization imply?

2. Eighner's simple, understated tone suggests that anyone can adapt to Dumpster diving with a little practice. Why do you think he uses such a tone?

3. Write about someone who does what Eighner deplores in his closing paragraphs, "invests objects with sentimental value." Let your description reveal whether or not you agree with Eighner.

ALBERTO ALVARO RÍOS *Green Cards*

ALL COLORS EXIST to satisfy the longing for blue.

There's a folk saying in Spanish, *el que quiera azul qu ele cueste.* One must pay for what one wants; it's a variation of the older Spanish proverb, "Take what you want and pay for it, says God." But the phrase means, more literally, *he who wants blue, let it cost him.*

A green card is what you get if you are a citizen of another country but you find yourself in, or cross over to, the United States. The card is a first step toward applying for citizenship. My wife, who was born in Mexico, had one. My mother, who was born in England, had one. My father, who was born in Mexico, didn't have one. But that's another story, involving some curious papers and shady explanations. My mother-in-law, after more than forty years here, still has one. She's never been quite sure what to do next. But she's learned well that you don't raise your hand to ask the Immigration Service anything. They notice you then. Everybody knows that.

They notice you, and then they do something. And they're everywhere, maybe. So you don't speak loudly, you don't ask questions, you don't make trou-

First appeared in the Spring 1995 issue of Indiana Review, *a small-circulation quarterly magazine; included in Ríos's memoir,* Capirotada: A Nogales Memoir *(1999).*

ble. Run away when you have to. Don't sign anything. Get a job only where everybody else is getting one, where it's safe.

There were all kinds of stories. The one my mother-in-law lived with the longest was how, her sister in Guaymas told her, they had heard that when you become a citizen of the United States, you have to spit on the flag of Mexico. And they would all shake their heads in a *no*.

My mother, when she became a citizen, recalls a curious moment. After the ceremony, the high-school band came in to the courtroom and, because she was special—which is to say, in this border town with Mexico, she was not Mexican—they played the British national anthem. Someone thought it was a good idea. At that moment, though, she says she felt a little funny. She never forgot.

None of this is easy, and nobody knows what will happen when you come, and everybody is not treated the same. And things do happen. I think, finally, they were right.

Crossing over from Mexico, for example, was more than just being there and then being here. It was a change in how one walked, and a change in color. Over there, the ground moved one way, coiled and trailed and offered itself. Here was not there, and the coiling and trailing and offering were to the left and to the right, but never the same. To this, the legs and the body had to adjust. It was not the same ground.

And in Mexico, the color was green. Here, it is blue. And that Latin-American green is not the green of here, in the way that this blue is not the same blue in Mexico. The eyes, like the legs, have to learn over.

It is more than the music and the food and the clothing. It is the walk, and the color. And smell—not of food, but of things. And if one walked this other walk, and smells were new so the nose had to accommodate itself, one then began to look different. The body and the mirror made their changes.

I remember something from the middle of all this, from the middle of color and the middle of the century. During the '50s, I remember driving through town and seeing pickup trucks full of men dressed in white. They were *braceros*, the workers imported specifically from Mexico for a brief time, sometimes only a day, just to work. After work, either at the end of the day or the end of the growing season, they had to go back to Mexico. What that meant was taking the pickup truck to the border and dropping them all off.

Arizona was the last state to hold out against minimum wage, championing the *laissez-faire* system of government oversight; in this case, let the growers pay what the workers will accept and don't get in the way. And these workers worked for almost nothing. It seemed, for a while, like a good idea to the growers and to the government, whose program this was.

As a kid, I remember only all these men dressed in white. It was a color that meant they didn't belong anywhere.

Crossing over from Mexico to the United States is not a small thing, but not large either. This is an incorrect vocabulary. To cross over was big, but that part was easy. The big is like that. It was the small that was difficult.

To cross the border was made up of these smaller things, then. It was lived as these more difficult-to-explain changes in color, more like that, more something of the body than one might suspect. It was the different way of walking because the ground was new, in all things. A different way of walking or a different way of hiding. More surprise, or more dullness, dullness or quiet. Something.

It is a movement from green, but who would know it? How to explain it? This is what I've heard all my life. It is a movement like the planet's, a movement that is there absolute, but who can feel it? A movement from green, from green to what is next.

For my family, crossing over was crossing over from green, not from Mexico. Green from before, but sorted out, from all the moments of green in a life, sorted and lifted out and then assembled together, into a big green, into green only. Fresh from the inhuman jungles of Chiapas and farther still, somewhere middle on the Western-hemisphere map, into the green day, into the green night, into the in-between—the light and the dark greens, the green that is brown and the green that is white—but green, and inside green, green incarnate, from the back and from the front, from the shoulders and the feet, green from yesterday and green from before yesterday, all of it ocean-like, all of it water, all of it moving as claws and tendrils and tongues, as eyes, as webs, and as base and rough flight, so that to navigate upon it one needed to ride above it to move through it, and even then to be careful and to look around. One needed to paddle and to chart, the paddle as a half-weapon and a half-tool, remembering never to dangle foolishly—for the one moment green takes—an arm into it.

From green utterly and in whispers, green eyes and green tongue, green taste and green sound; green from tea; but then from coffee; from bitter, but then from sweet; green from garden, and a little then from bean and root and tuber, but then from sky and from air and from light.

But at light, and in dream, sound and strong, four-square and, yet, in that moment of pellucid strength, in that moment also inexplicably tinged with rue, there it is that green wavers and is for a moment inconstant, is for a moment green that is hollowed, or absent; is, for a moment, blue. There is the pivotal point, the narrows in this repeating hourglass of colors, in this life. There for a second, but there absolutely: green shifts to blue, and it is done.

20 It is Blue. Only and just blue. It is the log sawed and in its moment of breaking. It is the yawn pushed fully and then fully engaged. It is a blue. Blue and not green. Only blue. Only blue and the memory of green. Not a desire yet—green is too close—but a memory.

So much was the green.

On the far other side of green was a yellow, somewhere out there, somewhere only in imagination perhaps, yellow and red and some other colors on the other side of memory. Yellow, then the green, but now blue. It was the end at last, or the beginning. It was not the middle. But it was the discovery of the middle.

In this way, the green stayed, the way the Virgin Mary was painted, and in the shades of the hillside houses. It stayed in the Chinese teas, in the *yerba buena*,[1] how that green was a cure for things, and in the afternoons, in talk.

1. A species of mint used for medicinal purposes.

Green stayed, and had a place in my family, but always as a memory. It stayed as a sadness for something.

It stayed as what used to be.

Questions

1. What do you think Ríos means when he says that Mexico is green and the United States is blue (paragraph 9)?

2. What is Ríos's attitude toward immigration, both legal and illegal?

3. Even though Ríos lives in the United States, he has elements of green left, as he says in the next-to-last paragraph. Do those elements serve as an argument against his blue–green dichotomy?

4. Characterize some thing or some person you know well in terms of colors, as Ríos does, especially in paragraph 17.

J. J. Goode

Single-Handed Cooking

My back aches. My eyes burn. I've been peeling and chopping for an hour, but I'm still being taunted by a pile of untouched vegetables. My problem is not the quantity. It's that the task of steadying each item falls to an almost useless appendage: the short, goofy arm, inexplicably bent into an L-shape and graced by just three fingers, that dangles from my right shoulder.

No one knows why I was born like this. My mom wasn't exposed to any radiation while she was pregnant, nor did she, say, have one too many sips of wine. Yet I do occasionally wonder whether my dad's Ph.D. dissertation subject—a pre-PETA endeavor for which he plucked the legs from frogs and studied their regeneration—sparked some sort of cosmic payback.

Whatever the reason, I occupy a sort of upper middle class of the handicapped. Sure, there's plenty to complain about, but all in all, things aren't so bad. While the wheelchair-bound struggle to reach their stoves, it feels a bit "Princess and the Pea" of me to grumble that peeling potatoes is as grueling as making *mole*.[1] ("Vegetables are distressingly round," said a commiserating friend.) Or to lament that day last winter when my girlfriend took a trip to Philadelphia, leaving me at home in Brooklyn with a dozen oysters and not enough hands to shuck them with. Disability is relative: I'd rather be incapable of prying open shellfish than allergic to them. Still, I see jimmying an oyster,

Published in Gourmet *(July 2009), a monthly magazine devoted to food and wine, which began publication in January 1941 and ceased print publication in November 1999.*

1. Mole: Spanish word for a variety of sauces used in Mexican cuisine, the most common being *mole poblano*, which includes chili peppers and chocolate.

which otters manage without much difficulty, as an ability that's not too much to ask for.

I happily live without most of the things I can't do. The kitchen, however, is where what I love butts up against what can be so discouragingly difficult. Forget shucking an oyster; even a mundane task such as draining a pot of pasta can be death-defying. After swathing my right arm in towels to prevent it from searing (the last thing I need is for it to be less useful), I lodge it beneath the pot's handle with the same care that I imagine a window washer uses to secure his harness to a skyscraper. Then I inch toward the sink, the whole time bracing for scalding disaster and indulging in an equally scalding torrent of self-pity. Some people say the kitchen is where they clear their heads; for me, it's where I face my demons.

Every meal is a proving ground, and I suffer mistakes as though they were failures, even when they have nothing to do with my arm. "It's really good," friends insist, as I sulk over hanger steak that doesn't have a perfectly rosy center or a gratin whose top has barely browned, forever fighting the feeling that somehow it all would have gone right had I been born a little more symmetrical. I can even find fault with the faultless because what I'm truly after is unreachable: two normal arms.

When I first started to cook, I developed a crush on any ingredient that leveled the playing field. I adored canned anchovies, since the fillets simply melted in hot oil. I loved beets because after I roasted them in foil, their skins would slip right off. But soon my attraction to convenience gave way to a relishing of the arduous.

Having previously avoided anything that required peeling, I now dove into recipes that called for celery root and butternut squash. I embraced Thai stir-fries, which had me meticulously slicing raw pork into matching strips so they'd all finish cooking at the same time. I can't count the times friends have watched me tackle an overly complicated prep job—always girding themselves for a bloodbath—and anxiously urged me to try using a food processor. I refuse for the same reason I insist on balancing a pan on my raised right knee when I sauce tableside instead of asking anyone for help. (It's the same reason I refused to sit out in baseball when it came time for me to bat.) I appreciate the thought, I sniff, but I can handle it.

This masochistic streak is why I'm still chopping. I'm having some friends over for dinner and I'm making braised chicken, a dish that's a breeze for most cooks but presents, for me, just the right level of hardship for a dinner party. The only way to get what I casually call my right arm to act like one is to hunch awkwardly over my cutting board, so it can reach the food that needs to be stabilized. For an hour, that was celery, onions, and carrots. A rough chop would surely suffice, but I'm attempting to dice, chasing the satisfaction of seeing perfect cubes conjured by a blur of hand and knife.

My back is bent again. This time, I'm close enough to a chicken to kiss it—unfortunate no matter how comfortable you are with raw poultry. As I try to detach a leg, it slips from my right hand's feeble grasp, spattering my cheek with cold chicken liquid. I seethe but rinse off and continue. I could, of course, have bought chicken parts. But a whole chicken is always cheaper by the pound, and why shouldn't I have access? I like to think of the price discrepancy as a one-arm tax.

10 Half an hour later, I've successfully dismantled the thing and begun the rewarding task of browning it, savoring the knowledge that any cook would, at this point in the process, be upright at the stove and wielding tongs in exactly the same manner as I am. After setting the chicken aside and spooning some of the golden fat from the pot, I take a seat, sweep the vegetables from my cutting board into a big bowl supported by my knees, and ferry the bowl to the stove. The vegetables sizzle when I dump them in. Now, to add the wine.

The wine! I forgot I'd have to open a bottle, a potential catastrophe. I should turn off the burner, just in case I take as long to open this bottle as I did the last one. Instead, I bet my hard-won diced vegetables that I won't scorch them. Springing into action, I wedge the bottle between my thighs, wrap my right arm around the neck (its effect is almost purely symbolic), and struggle to work the screw through the cork. I already detect a faint acridity wafting from the pot, a whiff of defeat. I quickly adjust my technique, somehow wrenching the cork out in one piece, and rush back to the stove. The vegetables have more color than I wanted, but they're fine. In goes some wine, a few sprigs of thyme, and the chicken. I cover the pot and shove it into the oven.

I know there are more compelling examples of fortitude than me braising chicken. Like a paraplegic racing uphill in a tricked-out wheelchair on marathon day, or my late grandfather, who at 90 walked down and up 20-odd flights in the pitch darkness of New York City's 2003 blackout to get groceries for his wife. But turn a spotlight on any accomplishment, however minor, and it seems like a triumph. Away from that glare, though, there's only the struggle.

My right arm swathed again, my back contorted, I stoop down and heave the pot out of the oven without incident (once I dipped so low to retrieve a casserole dish perched on the bottom rack that I singed my forehead on the top one). I call in my friends, and we sit down to a dinner that, I have to admit, is pretty good. Someone even admires my fastidious touch, the precise little cubes of carrots and celery scattered beneath the burnished chicken. "Thanks," I say. "It was nothing."

Questions

1. How would you characterize J. J. Goode's attitude toward his disability? What parts of the essay reveal his attitude?

2. Goode presents cooking as an adventure, writing, for example, that when he adds wine to a dish he springs into action and wedges the wine bottle between his thighs (paragraph 11). Two strategies he uses to heighten this sense of adventure are present tense and strong verbs. Which verb choices do you find especially effective? Why?

3. Goode writes, "turn a spotlight on any accomplishment, however minor, and it seems like a triumph" (paragraph 12). Write an essay about a minor accomplishment you've had. Use present tense, strong verbs, and detail to make that accomplishment seem like a triumph.

NANCY MAIRS *On Being a Cripple*

To escape is nothing. Not to escape is nothing.
—LOUISE BOGAN

THE OTHER DAY I was thinking of writing an essay on being a cripple. I was thinking hard in one of the stalls of the women's room in my office building, as I was shoving my shirt into my jeans and tugging up my zipper. Preoccupied, I flushed, picked up my book bag, took my cane down from the hook, and unlatched the door. So many movements unbalanced me, and as I pulled the door open I fell over backward, landing fully clothed on the toilet seat with my legs splayed in front of me: the old beetle-on-its-back routine. Saturday afternoon, the building deserted, I was free to laugh aloud as I wriggled back to my feet, my voice bouncing off the yellowish tiles from all directions. Had anyone been there with me, I'd have been still and faint and hot with chagrin. I decided that it was high time to write the essay.

First, the matter of semantics. I am a cripple. I choose this word to name me. I choose from among several possibilities, the most common of which are "handicapped" and "disabled." I made the choice a number of years ago, without thinking, unaware of my motives for doing so. Even now, I'm not sure what those motives are, but I recognize that they are complex and not entirely flattering. People—crippled or not—wince at the word "cripple," as they do not at "handicapped" or "disabled." Perhaps I want them to wince. I want them to see me as a tough customer, one to whom the fates/gods/viruses have not been kind, but who can face the brutal truth of her existence squarely. As a cripple, I swagger.

But, to be fair to myself, a certain amount of honesty underlies my choice. "Cripple" seems to me a clean word, straightforward and precise. It has an honorable history, having made its first appearance in the Lindisfarne Gospel[1] in the tenth century. As a lover of words, I like the accuracy with which it describes my condition: I have lost the full use of my limbs. "Disabled," by contrast, suggests any incapacity, physical or mental. And I certainly don't like "handicapped," which implies that I have deliberately been put at a disadvantage, by whom I can't imagine (my God is not a Handicapper General), in order to equalize chances in the great race of life. These words seem to me to be moving away from my condition, to be widening the gap between word and reality. Most remote is the recently coined euphemism "differently abled," which partakes of the same semantic hopefulness that transformed countries from "undeveloped"

From Plaintext *(1986), a collection of personal essays, many about Mairs's life with multiple sclerosis.*

1. Illustrated manuscript of the four gospels of the New Testament done by Irish monks; English commentaries were added in the tenth century.

to "underdeveloped," then to "less developed," and finally to "developing" nations. People have continued to starve in those countries during the shift. Some realities do not obey the dictates of language.

Mine is one of them. Whatever you call me, I remain crippled. But I don't care what you call me, so long as it isn't "differently abled," which strikes me as pure verbal garbage designed, by its ability to describe anyone, to describe no one. I subscribe to George Orwell's thesis that "the slovenliness of our language makes it easier for us to have foolish thoughts."[2] And I refuse to participate in the degeneration of the language to the extent that I deny that I have lost anything in the course of this calamitous disease; I refuse to pretend that the only differences between you and me are the various ordinary ones that distinguish any one person from another. But call me "disabled" or "handicapped" if you like. I have long since grown accustomed to them; and if they are vague, at least they hint at the truth. Moreover, I use them myself. Society is no readier to accept crippledness than to accept death, war, sex, sweat, or wrinkles. I would never refer to another person as a cripple. It is the word I use to name only myself.

5 I haven't always been crippled, a fact for which I am soundly grateful. To be whole of limb is, I know from experience, infinitely more pleasant and useful than to be crippled; and if that knowledge leaves one open to bitterness at my loss, the physical soundness I once enjoyed (though I did not enjoy it half enough) is well worth the occasional stab of regret. Though never any good at sports, I was a normally active child and young adult. I climbed trees, played hopscotch, jumped rope, skated, swam, rode my bicycle, sailed. I despised team sports, spending some of the wretchedest afternoons of my life, sweaty and humiliated, behind a field-hockey stick and under a basketball hoop. I tramped alone for miles along the bridle paths that webbed the woods behind the house I grew up in. I swayed through countless dim hours in the arms of one man or another under the scattered shot of light from mirrored balls, and gyrated through countless more as Tab Hunter and Johnny Mathis[3] gave way to the Rolling Stones, Creedence Clearwater Revival, Cream. I walked down the aisle. I pushed baby carriages, changed tires in the rain, marched for peace.

When I was twenty-eight I started to trip and drop things. What at first seemed my natural clumsiness soon became too pronounced to shrug off. I consulted a neurologist, who told me that I had a brain tumor. A battery of tests, increasingly disagreeable, revealed no tumor. About a year and a half later I developed a blurred spot in one eye. I had, at last, the episodes "disseminated in space and time" requisite for a diagnosis: multiple sclerosis. I have never been sorry for the doctor's initial misdiagnosis, however. For almost a week, until

2. A quotation from "Politics and the English Language" (included in the section "Language and Communication") by Orwell (1903–1950), British essayist and novelist, famous for his political commentaries.

3. Tab Hunter (b. 1931), American actor and singer popular in the 1960s; Johnny Mathis (b. 1935), American singer popular in the 1950s and 1960s and well known for his love ballads.

the negative results of the tests were in, I thought that I was going to die right away. Every day for the past nearly ten years, then, has been a kind of gift. I accept all gifts.

Multiple sclerosis is a chronic degenerative disease of the central nervous system, in which the myelin that sheathes the nerves is somehow eaten away and scar tissue forms in its place, interrupting the nerves' signals. During its course, which is unpredictable and uncontrollable, one may lose vision, hearing, speech, the ability to walk, control of bladder and/or bowels, strength in any or all extremities, sensitivity to touch, vibration, and/or pain, potency, coordination of movements—the list of possibilities is lengthy and, yes, horrifying. One may also lose one's sense of humor. That's the easiest to lose and the hardest to survive without.

In the past ten years, I have sustained some of these losses. Characteristic of MS are sudden attacks, called exacerbations, followed by remissions, and these I have not had. Instead, my disease has been slowly progressive. My left leg is now so weak that I walk with the aid of a brace and a cane; and for distances I use an Amigo, a variation on the electric wheelchair that looks rather like an electrified kiddie car. I no longer have much use of my left hand. Now my right side is weakening as well. I still have the blurred spot in my right eye. Overall, though, I've been lucky so far. My world has, of necessity, been circumscribed by my losses, but the terrain left me has been ample enough for me to continue many of the activities that absorb me: writing, teaching, raising children and cats and plants and snakes, reading, speaking publicly about MS and depression, even playing bridge with people patient and honorable enough to let me scatter cards every which way without sneaking a peek.

Lest I begin to sound like Pollyanna, however, let me say that I don't like having MS. I hate it. My life holds realities—harsh ones, some of them—that no right-minded human being ought to accept without grumbling. One of them is fatigue. I know of no one with MS who does not complain of bone-weariness; in a disease that presents an astonishing variety of symptoms, fatigue seems to be a common factor. I wake up in the morning feeling the way most people do at the end of a bad day, and I take it from there. As a result, I spend a lot of time *in extremis*[4] and, impatient with limitation, I tend to ignore my fatigue until my body breaks down in some way and forces rest. Then I miss picnics, dinner parties, poetry readings, the brief visits of old friends from out of town. The offspring of a puritanical tradition of exceptional venerability, I cannot view these lapses without shame. My life often seems a series of small failures to do as I ought.

10 I lead, on the whole, an ordinary life, probably rather like the one I would have led had I not had MS. I am lucky that my predilections were already solitary, sedentary, and bookish—unlike the world-famous French cellist I have read about, or the young woman I talked with one long afternoon who wanted only to be a jockey. I had just begun graduate school when I found out something was wrong with me, and I have remained, interminably, a graduate stu-

4. Latin for "in the last straits"—here it means "at the limits of endurance."

dent. Perhaps I would not have if I'd thought I had the stamina to return to a full-time job as a technical editor; but I've enjoyed my studies.

In addition to studying, I teach writing courses. I also teach medical students how to give neurological examinations. I pick up freelance editing jobs here and there. I have raised a foster son and sent him into the world, where he has made me two grandbabies, and I am still escorting my daughter and son through adolescence. I go to Mass every Saturday. I am a superb, if messy, cook. I am also an enthusiastic laundress, capable of sorting a hamper full of clothes into five subtly differentiated piles, but a terrible housekeeper. I can do italic writing and, in an emergency, bathe an oil-soaked cat. I play a fiendish game of Scrabble. When I have the time and the money, I like to sit on my front steps with my husband, drinking Amaretto and smoking a cigar, as we imagine our counterparts in Leningrad and make sure that the sun gets down once more behind the sharp childish scrawl of the Tucson Mountains.

This lively plenty has its bleak complement, of course, in all the things I can no longer do. I will never run again, except in dreams, and one day I may have to write that I will never walk again. I like to go camping, but I can't follow George and the children along the trails that wander out of a campsite through the desert or into the mountains. In fact, even on the level I've learned never to check the weather or try to hold a coherent conversation: I need all my attention for my wayward feet. Of late, I have begun to catch myself wondering how people can propel themselves without canes. With only one usable hand, I have to select my clothing with care not so much for style as for ease of ingress and egress, and even so, dressing can be laborious. I can no longer do fine stitchery, pick up babies, play the piano, braid my hair. I am immobilized by acute attacks of depression, which may or may not be physiologically related to MS but are certainly its logical concomitant.

These two elements, the plenty and the privation, are never pure, nor are the delight and wretchedness that accompany them. Almost every pickle that I get into as a result of my weakness and clumsiness—and I get into plenty—is funny as well as maddening and sometimes painful. I recall one May afternoon when a friend and I were going out for a drink after finishing up at school. As we were climbing into opposite sides of my car, chatting, I tripped and fell, flat and hard, onto the asphalt parking lot, my abrupt departure interrupting him in mid-sentence. "Where'd you go?" he called as he came around the back of the car to find me hauling myself up by the door frame. "Are you all right?" Yes, I told him, I was fine, just a bit rattly, and we drove off to find a shady patio and some beer. When I got home an hour or so later, my daughter greeted me with "What have you done to yourself?" I looked down. One elbow of my white turtleneck with the green froggies, one knee of my white trousers, one white kneesock were blood-soaked. We peeled off the clothes and inspected the damage, which was nasty enough but not alarming. That part wasn't funny: The abrasions took a long time to heal, and one got a little infected. Even so, when I think of my friend talking earnestly, suddenly, to the hot thin air while I dropped from his view as though through a trap door, I find the image as silly as something from a Marx Brothers movie.

I may find it easier than other cripples to amuse myself because I live propped by the acceptance and the assistance and, sometimes, the amusement of those around me. Grocery clerks tear my checks out of my checkbook for me, and sales clerks find chairs to put into dressing rooms when I want to try on clothes. The people I work with make sure I teach at times when I am least likely to be fatigued, in places I can get to, with the materials I need. My students, with one anonymous exception (in an end-of-the-semester evaluation), have been unperturbed by my disability. Some even like it. One was immensely cheered by the information that I paint my own fingernails; she decided, she told me, that if I could go to such trouble over fine details, she could keep on writing essays. I suppose I became some sort of bright-fingered muse. She wrote good essays, too.

15 The most important struts in the framework of my existence, of course, are my husband and children. Dismayingly few marriages survive the MS test, and why should they? Most twenty-two- and nineteen-year-olds, like George and me, can vow in clear conscience, after a childhood of chicken pox and summer colds, to keep one another in sickness and in health so long as they both shall live. Not many are equipped for catastrophe: the dismay, the depression, the extra work, the boredom that a degenerative disease can insinuate into a relationship. And our society, with its emphasis on fun and its association of fun with physical performance, offers little encouragement for a whole spouse to stay with a crippled partner. Children experience similar stresses when faced with a crippled parent, and they are more helpless, since parents and children can't usually get divorced. They hate, of course, to be different from their peers, and the child whose mother is tacking down the aisle of a school auditorium packed with proud parents like a Cape Cod dinghy in a stiff breeze jolly well stands out in a crowd. Deprived of legal divorce, the child can at least deny the mother's disability, even her existence, forgetting to tell her about recitals and PTA meetings, refusing to accompany her to stores or church or the movies, never inviting friends to the house. Many do.

But I've been limping along for ten years now, and so far George and the children are still at my left elbow, holding tight. Anne and Matthew vacuum floors and dust furniture and haul trash and rake up dog droppings and button my cuffs and bake lasagna and Toll House cookies with just enough grumbling so I know that they don't have brain fever. And far from hiding me, they're forever dragging me by racks of fancy clothes or through teeming school corridors, or welcoming gaggles of friends while I'm wandering through the house in Anne's filmy pink babydoll pajamas. George generally calls before he brings someone home, but he does just as many dumb thankless chores as the children. And they all yell at me, laugh at some of my jokes, write me funny letters when we're apart—in short, treat me as an ordinary human being for whom they have some use. I think they like me. Unless they're faking. . . .

Faking. There's the rub. Tugging at the fringes of my consciousness always is the terror that people are kind to me only because I'm a cripple. My mother almost shattered me once, with that instinct mothers have—blind, I think, in this case, but unerring nonetheless—for striking blows along the fault-lines of their children's hearts, by telling me, in an attack on my selfishness, "We all have to make allowances for you, of course, because of the way you are." From the distance of a couple of years, I have to admit that I haven't any idea just what she meant, and I'm not sure that she knew either. She was awfully angry. But at the time, as the words thudded home, I felt my worst fear, suddenly realized. I could bear being called selfish: I am. But I couldn't bear the corroboration that those around me were doing in fact what I'd always suspected them of doing, professing fondness while silently putting up with me because of the way I am. A cripple. I've been a little cracked ever since.

Along with this fear that people are secretly accepting shoddy goods comes a relentless pressure to please—to prove myself worth the burdens I impose, I guess, or to build a substantial account of goodwill against which I may write drafts in times of need. Part of the pressure arises from social expectations. In our society, anyone who deviates from the norm had better find some way to compensate. Like fat people, who are expected to be jolly, cripples must bear their lot meekly and cheerfully. A grumpy cripple isn't playing by the rules. And much of the pressure is self-generated. Early on I vowed that, if I had to have MS, by God I was going to do it well. This is a class act, ladies and gentlemen. No tears, no recriminations, no faintheartedness.

One way and another, then, I wind up feeling like Tiny Tim,[5] peering over the edge of the table at the Christmas goose, waving my crutch, piping down God's blessing on us all. Only sometimes I don't want to play Tiny Tim. I'd rather be Caliban,[6] a most scurvy monster. Fortunately, at home no one much cares whether I'm a good cripple or a bad cripple as long as I make vichyssoise with fair regularity. One evening several years ago, Anne was reading at the dining-room table while I cooked dinner. As I opened a can of tomatoes, the can slipped in my left hand and juice spattered me and the counter with bloody spots. Fatigued and infuriated, I bellowed, "I'm so sick of being crippled!" Anne glanced at me over the top of her book. "There now," she said, "do you feel better?" "Yes," I said, "yes, I do." She went back to her reading. I felt better. That's about all the attention my scurviness ever gets.

20 Because I hate being crippled, I sometimes hate myself for being a cripple. Over the years I have come to expect—even accept—attacks of violent self-loathing. Luckily, in general our society no longer connects deformity and disease directly with evil (though a charismatic once told me that I have MS because a devil is in me) and so I'm allowed to move largely at will, even among small children. But I'm not sure that this revision of attitude has been particularly helpful. Physical imperfection, even freed of moral disapprobation, still defies and violates the ideal, especially for women, whose confinement in their bodies as objects of desire is far from over. Each age, of course, has its ideal, and I doubt that ours is any better or worse than any other. Today's ideal woman, who lives on the glossy pages of dozens of magazines, seems to be

5. A crippled, frail young boy saved by Scrooge's eventual generosity in Charles Dickens's novel *A Christmas Carol.*

6. The monstrous son of the witch Sycorax in Shakespeare's play *The Tempest.*

between the ages of eighteen and twenty-five; her hair has body, her teeth flash white, her breath smells minty, her underarms are dry; she has a career but is still a fabulous cook, especially of meals that take less than twenty minutes to prepare; she does not ordinarily appear to have a husband or children; she is trim and deeply tanned; she jogs, swims, plays tennis, rides a bicycle, sails, but does not bowl; she travels widely, even to out-of-the-way places like Finland and Samoa, always in the company of the ideal man, who possesses a nearly identical set of characteristics. There are a few exceptions. Though usually white and often blonde, she may be black, Hispanic, Asian, or Native American, so long as she is unusually sleek. She may be old, provided she is selling a laxative or is Lauren Bacall. If she is selling a detergent, she may be married and have a flock of strikingly messy children. But she is never a cripple.

Like many women I know, I have always had an uneasy relationship with my body. I was not a popular child, largely, I think now, because I was peculiar: intelligent, intense, moody, shy, given to unexpected actions and inexplicable notions and emotions. But as I entered adolescence, I believed myself unpopular because I was homely: my breasts too flat, my mouth too wide, my hips too narrow, my clothing never quite right in fit or style. I was not, in fact, particularly ugly, old photographs inform me, though I was well off the ideal; but I carried this sense of self-alienation with me into adulthood, where it regenerated in response to the depredations of MS. Even with my brace I walk with a limp so pronounced that, seeing myself on the videotape of a television program on the disabled, I couldn't believe that anything but an inchworm could make progress humping along like that. My shoulders droop and my pelvis thrusts forward as I try to balance myself upright, throwing my frame into a bony S. As a result of contractures, one shoulder is higher than the other and I carry one arm bent in front of me, the fingers curled into a claw. My left arm and leg have wasted into pipe-stems, and I try always to keep them covered. When I think about how my body must look to others, especially to men, to whom I have been trained to display myself, I feel ludicrous, even loathsome.

At my age, however, I don't spend much time thinking about my appearance. The burning egocentricity of adolescence, which assures one that all the world is looking all the time, has passed, thank God, and I'm generally too caught up in what I'm doing to step back, as I used to, and watch myself as though upon a stage. I'm also too old to believe in the accuracy of self-image. I know that I'm not a hideous crone, that in fact, when I'm rested, well dressed, and well made up, I look fine. The self-loathing I feel is neither physically nor intellectually substantial. What I hate is not me but a disease.

I am not a disease.

And a disease is not—at least not singlehandedly—going to determine who I am, though at first it seemed to be going to. Adjusting to a chronic incurable illness, I have moved through a process similar to that outlined by Elisabeth Kübler-Ross in *On Death and Dying*. The major difference—and it is far more significant than most people recognize—is that I can't be sure of the outcome, as the terminally ill cancer patient can. Research studies indicate that, with proper medical care, I may achieve a "normal" life span. And in our society, with its vision of death as the ultimate evil, worse even than decrepitude, the response to such news is, "Oh well, at least you're not going to *die*." Are there worse things than dying? I think that there may be.

25 I think of two women I know, both with MS, both enough older than I to have served me as models. One took to her bed several years ago and has been there ever since. Although she can sit in a high-backed wheelchair, because she is incontinent she refuses to go out at all, even though incontinence pants, which are readily available at any pharmacy, could protect her from embarrassment. Instead, she stays at home and insists that her husband, a small quiet man, a retired civil servant, stay there with her except for a quick weekly foray to the supermarket. The other woman, whose illness was diagnosed when she was eighteen, a nursing student engaged to a young doctor, finished her training, married her doctor, accompanied him to Germany when he was in the service, bore three sons and a daughter, now grown and gone. When she can, she travels with her husband; she plays bridge, embroiders, swims regularly; she works, like me, as a symptomatic-patient instructor of medical students in neurology. Guess which woman I hope to be.

At the beginning, I thought about having MS almost incessantly. And because of the unpredictable course of the disease, my thoughts were always terrified. Each night I'd get into bed wondering whether I'd get out again the next morning, whether I'd be able to see, to speak, to hold a pen between my fingers. Knowing that the day might come when I'd be physically incapable of killing myself, I thought perhaps I ought to do so right away, while I still had the strength. Gradually I came to understand that the Nancy who might one day lie inert under a bedsheet, arms and legs paralyzed, unable to feed or bathe herself, unable to reach out for a gun, a bottle of pills, was not the Nancy I was at present, and that I could not presume to make decisions for that future Nancy, who might well not want in the least to die. Now the only provision I've made for the future Nancy is that when the time comes—and it is likely to come in the form of pneumonia, friend to the weak and the old—I am not to be treated with machines and medications. If she is unable to communicate by then, I hope she will be satisfied with these terms.

Thinking all the time about having MS grew tiresome and intrusive, especially in the large and tragic mode in which I was accustomed to considering my plight. Months and even years went by without catastrophe (at least without one related to MS), and really I was awfully busy, what with George and children and snakes and students and poems, and I hadn't the time, let alone the inclination, to devote myself to being a disease. Too, the richer my life became, the funnier it seemed, as though there were some connection between largesse and laughter, and so my tragic stance began to waver until, even with the aid of a brace and a cane, I couldn't hold it for very long at a time.

After several years I was satisfied with my adjustment. I had suffered my grief and fury and terror, I thought, but now I was at ease with my lot. Then one summer day I set out with George and the children across the desert for a vacation in California. Part way to Yuma I became aware that my right leg felt funny. "I think I've had an exacerbation," I told George. "What shall we do?"

he asked. "I think we'd better get the hell to California," I said, "because I don't know whether I'll ever make it again." So we went on to San Diego and then to Orange, up the Pacific Coast Highway to Santa Cruz, across to Yosemite, down to Sequoia and Joshua Tree, and so back over the desert to home. It was a fine two-week trip, filled with friends and fair weather, and I wouldn't have missed it for the world, though I did in fact make it back to California two years later. Nor would there have been any point in missing it, since in MS, once the symptoms have appeared, the neurological damage has been done, and there's no way to predict or prevent that damage.

The incident spoiled my self-satisfaction, however. It renewed my grief and fury and terror, and I learned that one never finishes adjusting to MS. I don't know now why I thought one would. One does not, after all, finish adjusting to life, and MS is simply a fact of my life—not my favorite fact, of course—but as ordinary as my nose and my tropical fish and my yellow Mazda station wagon. It may at any time get worse, but no amount of worry or anticipation can prepare me for a new loss. My life is a lesson in losses. I learn one at a time.

30 And I had best be patient in the learning, since I'll have to do it like it or not. As any rock fan knows, you can't always get what you want. Particularly when you have MS. You can't, for example, get cured. In recent years researchers and the organizations that fund research have started to pay MS some attention even though it isn't fatal; perhaps they have begun to see that life is something other than a quantitative phenomenon, that one may be very much alive for a very long time in a life that isn't worth living. The researchers have made some progress toward understanding the mechanism of the disease: It may well be an autoimmune reaction triggered by a slowacting virus. But they are nowhere near its prevention, control, or cure. And most of us want to be cured. Some, unable to accept incurability, grasp at one treatment after another, no matter how bizarre: megavitamin therapy, gluten-free diet, injections of cobra venom, hypothermal suits, lymphocytopharesis, hyperbaric chambers. Many treatments are probably harmless enough, but none are curative.

The absence of a cure often makes MS patients bitter toward their doctors. Doctors are, after all, the priests of modern society, the new shamans, whose business is to heal, and many an MS patient roves from one to another, searching for the "good" doctor who will make him well. Doctors too think of themselves as healers, and for this reason many have trouble dealing with MS patients, whose disease in its intransigence defeats their aims and mocks their skills. Too few doctors, it is true, treat their patients as whole human beings, but the reverse is also true. I have always tried to be gentle with my doctors, who often have more at stake in terms of ego than I do. I may be frustrated, maddened, depressed by the incurability of my disease, but I am not diminished by it, and they are. When I push myself up from my seat in the waiting room and stumble toward them, I incarnate the limitation of their powers. The least I can do is refuse to press on their tenderest spots.

This gentleness is part of the reason that I'm not sorry to be a cripple. I didn't have it before. Perhaps I'd have developed it anyway—how could I know such a thing?—and I wish I had more of it, but I'm glad of what I have. It has opened and enriched my life enormously, this sense that my frailty and need must be mirrored in others, that in searching for and shaping a stable core in a life wrenched by change and loss, change and loss, I must recognize the same process, under individual conditions, in the lives around me. I do not deprecate such knowledge, however I've come by it.

All the same, if a cure were found, would I take it? In a minute. I may be a cripple, but I'm only occasionally a loony and never a saint. Anyway, in my brand of theology God doesn't give bonus points for a limp. I'd take a cure; I just don't need one. A friend who also has MS startled me once by asking, "Do you ever say to yourself, 'Why me, Lord?'" "No, Michael, I don't," I told him, "because whenever I try, the only response I can think of is 'Why not?'" If I could make a cosmic deal, who would I put in my place? What in my life would I give up in exchange for sound limbs and a thrilling rush of energy? No one. Nothing. I might as well do the job myself. Now that I'm getting the hang of it.

Questions

1. How does Mairs organize her essay? What connects the different parts to each other?

2. What stereotypes of "disabled" people does Mairs expect us to believe in? How does she set out to counter them?

3. Mairs deliberately chooses to call herself a "cripple." Select a person or group that deliberately chooses its own name or description and explain the rationale behind the choice.

Alice Walker

Beauty: When the Other Dancer Is the Self

It is a bright summer day in 1947. My father, a fat, funny man with beautiful eyes and a subversive wit, is trying to decide which of his eight children he will take with him to the county fair. My mother, of course, will not go. She is knocked out from getting most of us ready: I hold my neck stiff against the pressure of her knuckles as she hastily completes the braiding and then beribboning of my hair.

My father is the driver for the rich old white lady up the road. Her name is Miss Mey. She owns all the land for miles around, as well as the house in which we live. All I remember about her is that she once offered to pay my mother

From In Search of Our Mother's Gardens: Womanist Prose *(1983), a collection of essays meditating on African American and feminist sources of inspiration, published the year after Walker's highly successful novel* The Color Purple.

thirty-five cents for cleaning her house, raking up piles of her magnolia leaves, and washing her family's clothes, and that my mother—she of no money, eight children, and a chronic earache—refused it. But I do not think of this in 1947. I am two and a half years old. I want to go everywhere my daddy goes. I am excited at the prospect of riding in a car. Someone has told me fairs are fun. That there is room in the car for only three of us doesn't faze me at all. Whirling happily in my starchy frock, showing off my biscuit-polished patent-leather shoes and lavender socks, tossing my head in a way that makes my ribbons bounce, I stand, hands on hips, before my father. "Take me, Daddy," I say with assurance; "I'm the prettiest!"

Later, it does not surprise me to find myself in Miss Mey's shiny black car, sharing the back seat with the other lucky ones. Does not surprise me that I thoroughly enjoy the fair. At home that night I tell the unlucky ones all I can remember about the merry-go-round, the man who eats live chickens, and the teddy bears, until they say: that's enough, baby Alice. Shut up now, and go to sleep.

It is Easter Sunday, 1950. I am dressed in a green, flocked, scalloped-hem dress (handmade by my adoring sister, Ruth) that has its own smooth satin petticoat and tiny hot-pink roses tucked into each scallop. My shoes, new T-strap patent leather, again highly biscuit-polished. I am six years old and have learned one of the longest Easter speeches to be heard that day, totally unlike the speech I said when I was two: "Easter lilies/pure and white/blossom in/the morning light." When I rise to give my speech I do so on a great wave of love and pride and expectation. People in the church stop rustling their new crinolines. They seem to hold their breath. I can tell they admire my dress, but it is my spirit, bordering on sassiness (womanishness), they secretly applaud.

5 "That girl's a little *mess*," they whisper to each other, pleased.

Naturally I say my speech without stammer or pause, unlike those who stutter, stammer, or, worst of all, forget. This is before the word "beautiful" exists in people's vocabulary, but "Oh, isn't she the *cutest* thing!" frequently floats my way. "And got so much sense!" they gratefully add . . . for which thoughtful addition I thank them to this day.

It was great fun being cute. But then, one day, it ended.

I am eight years old and a tomboy. I have a cowboy hat, cowboy boots, checkered shirt and pants, all red. My playmates are my brothers, two and four years older than I. Their colors are black and green, the only difference in the way we are dressed. On Saturday nights we all go to the picture show, even my mother; Westerns are her favorite kind of movie. Back home, "on the ranch," we pretend we are Tom Mix, Hopalong Cassidy, Lash LaRue (we've even named one of our dogs Lash LaRue); we chase each other for hours rustling cattle, being outlaws, delivering damsels from distress. Then my parents decide to buy my brothers guns. These are not "real" guns. They shoot "BBs," copper pellets my brothers say will kill birds. Because I am a girl, I do not get a gun. Instantly I am relegated to the position of Indian. Now there appears a great distance between us. They shoot and shoot at everything with their new guns. I try to keep up with my bow and arrows.

One day while I am standing on top of our makeshift "garage"—pieces of tin nailed across some poles—holding my bow and arrow and looking out toward the fields, I feel an incredible blow in my right eye. I look down just in time to see my brother lower his gun.

Both brothers rush to my side. My eye stings, and I cover it with my hand. "If you tell," they say, "we will get a whipping. You don't want that to happen, do you?" I do not. "Here is a piece of wire," says the older brother, picking it up from the roof; "say you stepped on one end of it and the other flew up and hit you." The pain is beginning to start. "Yes," I say, "Yes, I will say that is what happened." If I do not say this is what happened, I know my brothers will find ways to make me wish I had. But now I will say anything that gets me to my mother.

Confronted by our parents we stick to the lie agreed upon. They place me on a bench on the porch and I close my left eye while they examine the right. There is a tree growing from underneath the porch that climbs past the railing to the roof. It is the last thing my right eye sees. I watch as its trunk, its branches, and then its leaves are blotted out by the rising blood.

I am in shock. First there is intense fever, which my father tries to break using lily leaves bound around my head. Then there are chills: my mother tries to get me to eat soup. Eventually, I do not know how, my parents learn what has happened. A week after the "accident" they take me to see a doctor. "Why did you wait so long to come?" he asks, looking into my eye and shaking his head. "Eyes are sympathetic," he says. "If one is blind, the other will likely become blind too."

This comment of the doctor's terrifies me. But it is really how I look that bothers me most. Where the BB pellet struck there is a glob of whitish scar tissue, a hideous cataract, on my eye. Now when I stare at people—a favorite pastime, up to now—they will stare back. Not at the "cute" little girl, but at her scar. For six years I do not stare at anyone, because I do not raise my head.

Years later, in the throes of a mid-life crisis, I ask my mother and sister whether I changed after the "accident." "No," they say, puzzled. "What do you mean?"

What do I mean?

I am eight, and, for the first time, doing poorly in school, where I have been something of a whiz since I was four. We have just moved to the place where the "accident" occurred. We do not know any of the people around us because this is a different county. The only time I see the friends I knew is when we go back to our old church. The new school is the former state penitentiary. It is a large stone building, cold and drafty, crammed to overflowing with boisterous, ill-disciplined children. On the third floor there is a huge circular imprint of some partition that has been torn out.

"What used to be here?" I ask a sullen girl next to me on our way past it to lunch.

"The electric chair," says she.

At night I have nightmares about the electric chair, and about all the people reputedly "fried" in it. I am afraid of the school, where all the students seem to be budding criminals.

20 "What's the matter with your eye?" they ask, critically.

When I don't answer (I cannot decide whether it was an "accident" or not), they shove me, insist on a fight.

My brother, the one who created the story about the wire, comes to my rescue. But then brags so much about "protecting" me, I become sick.

After months of torture at the school, my parents decide to send me back to our old community, to my old school. I live with my grandparents and the teacher they board. But there is no room for Phoebe, my cat. By the time my grandparents decide there *is* room, and I ask for my cat, she cannot be found. Miss Yarborough, the boarding teacher, takes me under her wing, and begins to teach me to play the piano. But soon she marries an African—a "prince," she says—and is whisked away to his continent.

At my old school there is at least one teacher who loves me. She is the teacher who "knew me before I was born" and bought my first baby clothes. It is she who makes life bearable. It is her presence that finally helps me turn on the one child at the school who continually calls me "one-eyed bitch." One day I simply grab him by his coat and beat him until I am satisfied. It is my teacher who tells me my mother is ill.

25 My mother is lying in bed in the middle of the day, something I have never seen. She is in too much pain to speak. She has an abscess in her ear. I stand looking down on her, knowing that if she dies, I cannot live. She is being treated with warm oils and hot bricks held against her cheek. Finally a doctor comes. But I must go back to my grandparents' house. The weeks pass but I am hardly aware of it. All I know is that my mother might die, my father is not so jolly, my brothers still have their guns, and I am the one sent away from home.

"You did not change," they say.

Did I imagine the anguish of never looking up?

I am twelve. When relatives come to visit I hide in my room. My cousin Brenda, just my age, whose father works in the post office and whose mother is a nurse, comes to find me. "Hello," she says. And then she asks, looking at my recent school picture, which I did not want taken, and on which the "glob," as I think of it, is clearly visible, "You still can't see out of that eye?"

"No," I say, and flop back on the bed over my book.

30 That night, as I do almost every night, I abuse my eye. I rant and rave at it, in front of the mirror. I plead with it to clear up before morning. I tell it I hate and despise it. I do not pray for sight. I pray for beauty.

"You did not change," they say.

I am fourteen and baby-sitting for my brother Bill, who lives in Boston. He is my favorite brother and there is a strong bond between us. Understanding my feelings of shame and ugliness he and his wife take me to a local hospital, where the "glob" is removed by a doctor named O. Henry. There is still a small bluish crater where the scar tissue was, but the ugly white stuff is gone. Almost immediately I become a different person from the girl who does not raise her head. Or so I think. Now that I've raised my head I win the boyfriend of my dreams. Now that I've raised my head I have plenty of friends. Now that I've raised my head classwork comes from my lips as faultlessly as Easter speeches did, and I leave high school as valedictorian, most popular student, and *queen,* hardly believing my luck. Ironically, the girl who was voted most beautiful in our class (and was) was later shot twice through the chest by a male companion, using a "real" gun, while she was pregnant. But that's another story in itself. Or is it?

"You did not change," they say.

It is now thirty years since the "accident." A beautiful journalist comes to visit and to interview me. She is going to write a cover story for her magazine that focuses on my latest book. "Decide how you want to look on the cover," she says. "Glamorous, or whatever."

Never mind "glamorous," it is the "whatever" that I hear. Suddenly all I can think of is whether I will get enough sleep the night before the photography session: if I don't, my eye will be tired and wander, as blind eyes will. 35

At night in bed with my lover I think up reasons why I should not appear on the cover of a magazine. "My meanest critics will say I've sold out," I say. "My family will now realize I write scandalous books."

"But what's the real reason you don't want to do this?" he asks.

"Because in all probability," I say in a rush, "my eye won't be straight."

"It will be straight enough," he says. Then, "Besides, I thought you'd made your peace with that."

And I suddenly remember that I have. 40

I remember:

I am talking to my brother Jimmy, asking if he remembers anything unusual about the day I was shot. He does not know I consider that day the last time my father, with his sweet home remedy of cool lily leaves, chose me, and that I suffered and raged inside because of this. "Well," he says, "all I remember is standing by the side of the highway with Daddy, trying to flag down a car. A white man stopped, but when Daddy said he needed somebody to take his little girl to the doctor, he drove off."

I remember:

I am in the desert for the first time. I fall totally in love with it. I am so overwhelmed by its beauty, I confront for the first time, consciously, the meaning of the doctor's words years ago: "Eyes are sympathetic. If one is blind, the other will likely become blind too." I realize I have dashed about the world madly, looking at this, looking at that, storing up images against the fading of the light. *But I might have missed seeing the desert!* The shock of that possibility—and gratitude for over twenty-five years of sight—sends me literally to my knees. Poem after poem comes—which is perhaps how poets pray.

On Sight

I am so thankful I have seen
The Desert
And the creatures in the desert
And the desert Itself.

The desert has its own moon
Which I have seen
With my own eye.
There is no flag on it.

Trees of the desert have arms
All of which are always up
That is because the moon is up
The sun is up

Also the sky
The stars
Clouds
None with flags.

If there were flags, I doubt
the trees would point.
Would you?

45 *But mostly, I remember this:*

I am twenty-seven, and my baby daughter is almost three. Since her birth I have worried about her discovery that her mother's eyes are different from other people's. Will she be embarrassed? I think. What will she say? Every day she watches a television program called "Big Blue Marble." It begins with a picture of the earth as it appears from the moon. It is bluish, a little battered-looking, but full of light, with whitish clouds swirling around it. Every time I see it I weep with love, as if it is a picture of Grandma's house. One day when I am putting Rebecca down for her nap, she suddenly focuses on my eye. Something inside me cringes, gets ready to try to protect myself. All children are cruel about physical differences, I know from experience, and that they don't always mean to be is another matter. I assume Rebecca will be the same.

But no-o-o-o. She studies my face intently as we stand, her inside and me outside her crib. She even holds my face maternally between her dimpled little hands. Then, looking every bit as serious and lawyerlike as her father, she says, as if it may just possibly have slipped my attention: "Mommy, there's a *world* in your eye." (As in, "Don't be alarmed, or do anything crazy.") And then, gently, but with great interest: "Mommy, where did you *get* that world in your eye?"

For the most part, the pain left then. (So what, if my brothers grew up to buy even more powerful pellet guns for their sons and to carry real guns themselves. So what, if a young "Morehouse man"[1] once nearly fell off the steps of Trevor Arnett Library because he thought my eyes were blue.) Crying and laughing I ran to the bathroom, while Rebecca mumbled and sang herself off to sleep. Yes indeed, I realized, looking into the mirror. There *was* a world in my eye. And I saw that it was possible to love it: that in fact, for all it had taught me of shame and anger and inner vision, I *did* love it. Even to see it drifting out of orbit in boredom, or rolling up out of fatigue, not to mention floating back at attention in excitement (bearing witness, a friend has called it), deeply suitable to my personality, and even characteristic of me.

That night I dream I am dancing to Stevie Wonder's[2] song "Always" (the name of the song is really "As," but I hear it as "Always"). As I dance, whirling and joyous, happier than I've ever been in my life, another bright-faced dancer joins me. We dance and kiss each other and hold each other through the night. The other dancer has obviously come through all right, as I have done. She is beautiful, whole and free. And she is also me.

1. A student at Morehouse College in Atlanta, Georgia.
2. African American singer, songwriter, and music producer (b. 1950).

Questions

1. Throughout her essay Walker refers to the "accident." Why does she put the word in quotation marks? Has Walker made her peace with the "accident" and its consequences?

2. Walker writes her essay by selecting particular moments in her life. What does each moment show? How do these moments relate to Walker's theme?

3. What is the effect of ending the essay by recounting a dream? How does the dream relate to the essay's title?

4. Write an essay comparing and contrasting Walker's essay and Mairs's "On Being a Cripple." Consider especially the two authors' responses to injury or illness and their attitudes toward those subjects.

Anne Fadiman

Night Owl

My husband and I sleep in a white wooden bed whose head posts are surmounted by two birds, carved and painted by an artist friend. On George's side there is a meadowlark, brown of back, yellow of breast, with a black pectoral V as trig and sporty as the neck of a tennis sweater. On my side there is a snowy owl, more muted in coloration, its feathers a frowzy tessellation of white and black. *Sturnella magna* and *Nyctea scandiaca*[1] have one thing in common: they are both fast asleep, their eyes shut tight, their beaks resting peacefully on their breasts.

Alas, the lark and the owl who rest beneath their wooden familiars have a far harder time synchronizing their circadian rhythms. George is an early riser, a firm believer in seizing the day while it is still fresh. I am not fully alive until the sun sets. In the morning, George is quick and energetic, while I blink in the sunlight, move as if through honey, and pour salt in the coffee. When we turn off the light at 11:30—too late for him, too early for me—George falls instantly asleep, while I, mocked by the bird that slumbers above my head, arrange and rearrange the pillows, searching for the elusive cool sides.

In the fourth century B.C., Androsthenes, a scribe who accompanied Alexander the Great to India, observed that the tamarind tree opened its leaves during the day and folded them at night. He assumed that it was worshiping the sun. Twenty-two centuries later, the great Swedish taxonomist Carolus Linnaeus designed a flower clock—a circular garden whose twelve wedge-shaped flower beds, each planted with species whose petals opened at a different hour, told the time from 6:00 A.M. (white water lily) to 6:00 P.M. (evening primrose). In humans, the circadian clock is centered in the suprachiasmatic nucleus, a freckle-sized, sickle-shaped cluster of nerve cells in the hypothalamus, but it can be activated by proteins produced by genes all over the body. Scientists at Cornell have successfully reset human biological clocks (though only temporarily) by shining bright lights on the backs of people's knees, suggesting that the mechanisms for controlling sleeping and waking are embedded in nearly every human cell—as well as in every flower petal, every insect antenna, every bird wing.

Chronobiologists have also established that out of every ten people, eight follow a normal circadian cycle (that is, rising naturally at around 7:30 A.M.); one is a lark; and one is an owl. These settings are genetically encoded and cannot

This essay appeared in an earlier version under the pseudonym "Philonoe" in the American Scholar *(Winter 1999) and was later included in* At Large and at Small: Familiar Essays *(2007), a collection of essays reminiscent of the writing of Charles Lamb (1775–1834) in its attention to personal experience shared in the context of literary and historical comparisons.*

1. *Sturnella magna*, Eastern Meadowlark; *Nyctea scandiaca*, Snowy Owl.

be erased. Once an owl, always an owl. (The same goes for other species. Wilse Webb, a psychologist at the University of Florida, spent five years trying to teach rats not to sleep between noon and 6:00 P.M. "They, by their contrary nature," he told Lynne Lamberg, an expert on sleep patterns, "spent five years teaching me otherwise.") I would wager my softest down pillow that the Cornell scientist who thought up the light-on-the-backs-of-the-knees experiment was an owl. At 8:00 A.M., could any biologist dream up something so lunatic (from *luna*, moon), so surreal, so redolent of the punchy wee hours and so incompatible with the rational light of morning?

"When I write after dark," observed Cyril Connolly, "the shades of evening [5] scatter their purple through my prose. Then why not write in the morning? Unfortunately in my case there is never very much of the morning, and it is curious that although I do not despise people who go to bed earlier than I, almost everyone is impatient with me for not getting up." Connolly put his finger on the human owl's perennial problem. The natural world discovered the benefits of shift work long ago: it is easier to share a given territory when not everyone is out and about at once. No one faults the bandicoot for prowling after dusk; no one chides the night-flying cecropia moth for its decadence; no one calls the whippoorwill a lazy slugabed for sleeping by day and singing by night—but people who were born to follow similar rhythms are viewed by the other nine tenths of the population as a tad threadbare in the moral fiber department.

"Those who would bring great things to pass," cautioned the eighteenth-century theologian Matthew Henry, "must rise early." In the medieval Benedictine horarium, the first of the monk's seven daily offices was observed at 3:15 A.M., the better to get a corner on virtue before anyone else could put in a competing bid. And at 4:30 A.M., is it any surprise that in 1660 one would have found John Milton, lustrous with matutinal rectitude, listening to a servant read aloud from the Hebrew Bible, while in 1890 one would have found the Irish journalist and pornographer Frank Harris (on the rare nights when he was sleeping alone) finally nodding off after a night of unspeakable debauch?

The owl's reputation may be beyond salvation. Who gets up early? Farmers, bakers, doctors. Who stays up late? Muggers, streetwalkers, cat burglars. It's assumed that if you're sneaking around after midnight, you must have something to hide. Night is the time of goblins, ghouls, vampires, zombies, witches, warlocks, demons, wraiths, fiends, banshees, poltergeists, werefolk, bogeymen, and things that go bump. (It is also the time of fairies and angels, but, like many comforting things, these are all too easily crowded out of the imagination. The nightmare trumps the pleasant dream.) Night, like winter, is a metaphor for death: one does not say "the dead of morning" or "the dead of spring." In a strange and tenebrous book called *Night* (which every lark should be forced to read, preferably by moonlight), the British critic A. Alvarez (an owl) points out, glumly, that Christ is known as the Light of the World and Satan as the Prince of Darkness. With such a powerful pro-lark tradition arrayed against us, must we owls be forever condemned to the infernal regions—which, despite their inextinguishable flames, are always described as *dark?*

I have tried hard to understand the lark's perspective. Campbell Geeslin, the artist who carved our bedpost finials, retires at nine and rises at five. "I've gotten up early ever since I was a boy in West Texas," he told me. "You'd look out of the window at dawn, and the sky would stretch on forever. It was a special creamy color at that hour, before the clouds came. It was the only time when it was cool. The morning was clean and blank and full of promise, like a piece of paper no one had written on yet. I couldn't wait to jump out of bed and invent something: a car, an airplane, a vacuum cleaner made from a spice can. By sunset, the day was used up, exhausted. Night was a time of disappointment, when you thought about all the things you'd hoped to do and hadn't done. There's nothing as sad and lonely as the bark of a coyote somewhere off in the West Texas night, and the moon hanging outside your window as bone-white as an old cow skull."

That's persuasive testimony, but it's not going to make me jump out of bed at five any more than a panegyric by a white water lily on the splendors of the morning is going to make the evening primrose transplant itself in Linnaeus's 6:00 A.M. flower bed. My suprachiasmatic nucleus is stuck in the owl position, and there's nothing I can do about it. Dawns are all very well (though I generally see them after staying up all night, when I may be too sleepy to appreciate them), but they can't hold a candle to a full moon, an aurora borealis, a meteor shower, or a comet.

10 In March of 1986, I was climbing with a friend on the Tasman Glacier in New Zealand. It occurred to us that if we got up at 1:00 A.M. and walked northeast across the glacier, we might be able to see Halley's Comet, which was making its every-seventy-sixth-year swing that month and could be best viewed (or so we had read) from the Southern Hemisphere. For my larkish companion, 1:00 A.M. was an early start; for me, it was simply an excuse to postpone my bedtime. We left the Tasman Saddle promptly at one, roped up, and put on our crampons in what seemed at first like pitch darkness but soon, once our eyes grew accustomed to the light of thousands of stars reflected on the shimmering glacier, seemed more like dusk. After crunching a mile or so across the clean hard snow, which had been unpleasantly slushy in the afternoon sun, we stopped on a narrow col[2] with a thousand-foot drop-off on either side. And there it was: a small white cornucopia above the northern horizon, not solid, but delicately stippled, as if produced by a heavenly dot-matrix printer. We spread our sleeping bags on the snow and crawled inside. The vantage point was dizzying. It was impossible to tell whether the comet was above us or we were above the comet; we were all falling through space, missing the stars by inches.

Surely the best thing about camping is the night. Night is what differentiates a camping trip from a series of day hikes. There are few greater pleasures than stretching out in your tent, inside which a glowing candle lantern makes your muddy boots and damp wool socks look as if they were painted by Georges de La Tour, and glimpsing, through the open flap, the corner of a constellation that is invisible from your hometown. (Since I live in New York City, that

2. A gap in a ridge.

includes just about everything, even the Big Dipper.) There are sounds you wouldn't hear at home, either: crickets, cicadas, tree frogs, loons, owls—even, on a memorable Catskills backpacking trip in my husband's youth, the urgent rustles of copulating porcupines. The contrast between the infinite space outside the tent and the cozily delimited interior, whose little zippers and pouches (for glasses, handkerchiefs, pocketknives) form a miniature simulacrum of a well-ordered pantry, nudges my memory back to the houses I used to make in my childhood by suspending a blanket over a table, dragging in a tray of cocoa and cookies, and creating a private domestic zone in which the temperature was always warm and the light was always crepuscular. Hell may be a dark place, but so is the womb.

My husband inherited his larkishness, along with his Roman nose and his shaggy eyebrows, from his father, who would feel he had committed an act of irreparable sloth if he slept past 4:30 A.M. I inherited my owlishness from a father who shares Jimmy Walker's conviction that it is a sin to go to bed on the same day you get up. Even if he retires at 2:00 A.M., my father cannot fall asleep without at least an hour of rigorous mental games. (He is the sort of person who could never get drowsy counting sheep; he once told me that he just got wider and wider awake as the numbers mounted, since he had to make sure he was counting correctly.) He composes puns, limericks, clerihews, palindromes, anagrams, and alphabetical lists of various kinds. An example of the last of these genres: Excluding the refractory *x*, which was long ago thrown out of the game, proceed through the alphabet from *a* to *z*, finding words that end with the letters *el*. Proper names are allowed. Solution: Abel, babel, channel, diesel, Edel, Fidel, Gödel . . . and so on. The sailing was reasonably clear until my father got to *z*, a perennial troublemaker. It took an hour, from 4:00 A.M. to 5:00 A.M., to come up with the name of a fellow reviewer at *The Nation* whom he had last seen sixty years earlier: Morton Dauwen Zabel. My father says that at the moment Mr. Zabel sidled into his consciousness, he was suffused with a sense of transcendent completion greater than he had ever felt on signing a book contract or closing a deal.

Insomnia need not be disagreeable. When Annie Proulx can't sleep, she puts on Quebec reels and dances around for half an hour in her bunny slippers. Until the fantasy wore thin with repetition, F. Scott Fitzgerald quarterbacked the Princeton team to hundreds of nocturnal victories over Yale. Lewis Carroll, like my father, posed himself problems:

> Q: If 70 per cent [of a group of pensioners] have lost an eye, 75 per cent an ear, 80 per cent an arm, 85 per cent a leg; what percentage, *at least*, must have lost all four?
>
> A: Ten. Adding the wounds together, we get 70 + 75 + 80 + 85 = 310, among 100 men; which gives 3 to each, and 4 to 10 men. Therefore the least percentage is 10.

Not everyone's cup of somnifacient tea—but, as Carroll put it, "I believe that an hour of calculation is much better for me than half-an-hour of worry."

I feel certain that Morton Dauwen Zabel would never have paid my father an extrasensory visit during the day, nor would Lewis Carroll have performed his amputations with such accuracy had he been operating when the rest of the world was awake. Owls think better at night. It is true, however, that many people make mistakes when they stay up late. The *Exxon Valdez* ran aground at 12:04 A.M.; the pesticide tank at Bhopal ruptured at 12:40 A.M.; the Chernobyl reactor exploded at 1:23 A.M.; the reactor at Three Mile Island spewed radiation at 3:53 A.M. These accidents were all attributable to human error. But surely the errant humans were among the non-owl 90 percent: day folk, maybe even dyed-in-the-wool larks, who had been forced by the exigencies of shift work to disobey the ticking of their circadian clocks. At Three Mile Island, the workers had just rotated to the night shift *that very day* and must have been as groggy as a planeful of New Yorkers disembarking in Kuala Lumpur.

15 It was therefore with a distinct sense of unease that I read *Night as Frontier*, a book by a Boston University sociologist named Murray Melbin. Melbin believes that night, like the American West in the nineteenth century, is a territory to be colonized. We have run out of space, so if we wish to increase our productivity and uncrowd our cities, the only dimension we have left to occupy is time: the hours after the normal workday. Many factories have already discovered that it is cheaper to operate around the clock, even if wages are higher on the nonstandard shifts. If Melbin is right, those factory nightworkers—along with locksmiths, bartenders, bail bondsmen, twenty-four-hour gas-station attendants, police officers, paramedics, security guards, taxi drivers, talk-show hosts, and suicide hotline volunteers—are the advance wave of a vast nocturnal migration. There are many parallels between night work and the settlement of the Western frontier: the pioneers tend to be young and nonconformist (the middle-aged are home watching Jay Leno); the population is sparse (owls tend to be mavericks); authority is decentralized (supervisors are asleep); life is informal (no coats and ties are required); there is hardship (fatigue, isolation, disruption of family routines) and lawlessness (parking-lot muggings).

Melbin may be right. But in my view, if the night is like the Wild West, *let's leave it that way*. If too many settlers start putting down stakes in the territory beyond midnight, California is going to happen. The wide open spaces will become the Los Angeles freeway system, and with too few owls behind the wheel, there will be accidents.

Because I savor the illusion of having the small hours to myself, when I am in the city I prefer to spend them at home. The noirish melancholy of the after-hours club and the all-night diner suits many owls, but I'd rather be in our bedroom, looking out the window every once in a while at the flocks of chic, black-garbed young couples, their laughter floating upward through the night, who cross the patch of lamplight at Houston and West Broadway. Even if the city were safer, I doubt I would go for late walks. Dickens once had a period of insomnia during which he spent several nights walking the London streets between half past twelve and half past five: Haymarket, Newgate Prison, Bethlehem Hospital, Westminster Bridge, Covent Garden. He was searching for comfort but found only drunkards, thieves, rain, shadows, silence, and scudding clouds "as restless as an evil conscience in a tumbled bed." The night he described in *The Uncommercial Traveller* is not the sable goddess of Edward Young or the bare-bosomed nurturer that Walt Whitman beseeched to press him close; it is more like the horrid place of "distempered gloom of thought/And deadly weariness of heart" that James Thomson visited in "The City of Dreadful Night," the most depressing of all nocturnal poems. For Dickens, as for me, the urban night was best enjoyed indoors, preferably with a book in hand.

"There is absolutely no such thing as reading but by a candle," wrote Charles Lamb.

> We have tried the affectation of a book at noon-day in gardens, and in sultry arbours; but it was labour thrown away. Those gay motes in the beam come about you, hovering and teasing, like so many coquets, that will have you all to their self, and are jealous of your abstractions. By the midnight taper, the writer digests his meditations. By the same light we must approach to their perusal, if we would catch the flame, the odour.

I prefer a 150-watt halogen bulb, but I know just what he meant. Reading by day seems prosaic and businesslike, the stuff of duty rather than of pleasure. When I was ten or twelve, I would close my schoolbooks without protest at bedtime, but after my mother left the room, I'd flip the switch of my bedside lamp and snatch a stolen hour (or two or three) of novel-reading, my heart beating wildly if I heard footsteps in the hall. Had my mother glimpsed the light under the door? She always had the grace to pretend she hadn't. Her steps would grow fainter, the book would grow shorter, and I would fall asleep at an ungodly hour, suffused with the goody-goody's secret pride at having sinned.

The child who reads at night is likely to become the adult who writes at night. During the day, I pop out of my chair a dozen times an hour. The phone rings, the fax beeps, the mailbox needs to be checked, the coffee needs to be brewed, the letter needs to be filed, the Post-its need to be rearranged—and possibly color-coded—*right this instant*. How can the writer's distractive sirens be resisted? During a phase when his muse was particularly obdurate, John McPhee used to tie himself to his chair with his bathrobe sash. Schiller heightened his powers of concentration by inhaling the fumes from a cache of rotten apples he kept in a drawer. All I need to do is stay up past midnight.

Something amazing happens when the rest of the world is sleeping. I am glued to my chair. I forget that I ever wanted to do anything but write. The crowded city, the crowded apartment, and the crowded calendar suddenly seem spacious. Three or four hours pass in a moment; I have no idea what time it is, because I never check the clock. If I chose to listen, I could hear the swish of taxis bound for downtown bars or the soft saxophone riffs that drift from a neighbor's window, but nothing gets through. I am suspended in a sensory deprivation tank, and the very lack of sensation is delicious.

A few years ago, I was inching along with excruciating slowness on a book I was trying to write. It was clear that the only way I would finish it was by surrendering unconditionally to my owl self. For several months, I worked all night, ate breakfast with my family, and slept from 9:00 A.M. to 4:00 P.M. The pages piled up as speedily as the Tailor of Gloucester's piecework. The only problem was that even though my husband and I inhabited the same zip code, he was living on New York time and I had apparently moved to Auckland. The jet lag on weekends was terrible.

I finished the book and promised I'd never do it again, except for occasional binges of three or four nights: just long enough to write an essay. I have kept my word. I am even more attached to George than I am to my circadian rhythm, so the trade-off has been worth it. And unlike most recovering alcoholics, I seem to be able to indulge in a bender now and then without permanently falling off the wagon.

It is now 3:42 A.M. Everyone here has been asleep for hours except my daughter's hamster, the other nocturnal mammal in the family, who is busy carrying sunflower seeds from one end of his terrarium to the other. After Silkie completes this task, he will change his mind and bring the seeds back again. I will do more or less the same thing with several paragraphs. Then, when the light breaks over Houston Street and the pigeons begin to coo on the window ledge, Silkie and I will retire. "And so by faster and faster degrees," wrote Dickens at the end of his long night walk, "until the last degrees were very fast, the day came, and I was tired and could sleep." Good night.

QUESTIONS

1. Anne Fadiman develops her essay through comparing and contrasting "morning" people and "night" people. What are the benefits she sees in being a night person? What literary devices (such as similes) does she use to highlight similarities and differences between the two groups of people she describes?

2. Fadiman's tone is somewhat elevated in this essay. Her tone is in part determined by word choice. Which words did you have to look up in a dictionary to understand? Bring a list of those words and definitions to class with you for discussion.

3. Write an essay in which you use comparisons and contrasts to make an argument about the value of something others might undervalue.

Jennifer Sinor

Confluences

(for my father)

For the first 12 hours after my father returned—wearing clothes that were three days old, his body still wrinkled from time spent immersed in water—he faced investigation for the murder of his brother. I imagine it was only protocol for the rangers and the Fairbanks police; death in a national park requires the federal government to file a report, whether that death results from a grizzly, an avalanche, or a body that has just given out. Still, I wonder if there was a moment in the police station, days away from the last time he had slept, his brother's body on its way to a temporary morgue, when my father's thoughts turned to questions of intention—his own or his brother's—and the ease with which a body can leave this earth.

The headwaters of the Alatna River, along with those of the Killik and Nigu Rivers, gather in the Gates of the Arctic National Park in northern Alaska, high up in the Brooks Range. One of six rivers in the park dedicated "wild and scenic" and therefore federally protected, the Alatna begins as a trickle and eventually builds to class III rapids on its 83-mile journey to confluence with the Koyukuk. The park itself, over eight million acres of protected wildlife, roadless and therefore one of the most remote regions in the United States, is home to the Arrigetch Mountains whose granitic spires reach 6,000 feet in the air. On the river one might see caribou, moose, Dall sheep, eagles, grizzlies, and even the occasional seagull far from the shores of the Pacific.

Though the river snakes lazily across a valley floor, through an idyllic landscape of open tundra and boreal forests, the Alatna has earned its wild and scenic designation. At the headwaters, the river is no more than a large drainage basin pooling in barren Summit Lake. With little water in the river, adventurers beginning at Summit must drag their Avon rafts for miles over gravel bars and sand barriers. But the lack of water is deceiving. An atypically hot day or a little rain can cause a dramatic rise in the water level, as much as six feet at once, due to glacial melting or the refusal of the thick layer of permafrost to absorb the rainfall. Within minutes, the river becomes a series of chutes, some as narrow as a canoe, where water rages down the mountain. Every guidebook, map, and Web site surveying the region reminds potential visitors that these rivers are ultimately unmappable.

My son was conceived the night my uncle died. Curling his body and holding fast to the slender strands of willow growing nearby, my uncle left this world on a day with no night while the collection of cells that would become my son clung to the walls of my body, defying the odds and remaining viable. The following day, my uncle still dead and the cells still holding on and dividing, I whined in my journal about how quickly pens seem to lose their ink.

Published in the American Scholar *(Winter 2008), the magazine of the Phi Beta Kappa Society.*

5 My father and his brother Jerry had gone to the northern reaches of Alaska to run the Alatna River for many reasons, some articulated and others not: my dad had never seen the headwaters; my uncle Jerry had run the river before and knew no wilder place; returning was on his life list; Jerry was sick and his time spent on trails and in tents was becoming limited; and Alaska is enormous and unknown, a place worthy of reckoning. I imagine they went because Alaska hovered like a dream from their childhood when they spent long afternoons in the hayloft considering what lay beyond the landlocked plains.

Written first on a legal pad in thin blue lines of ink that run like waves across the page, then later transferred to the computer, the journal my dad made of the trip, composed on the flight back, begins: "Jerry and I met in St. Louis to begin our incredible journey."

He then moves quickly to describe those few hours, not even 24, when everything was still okay—arriving in Fairbanks, flying to the hinterlands, renting gear from the outfitter. He names the few people they met, the meals they ate, the conversations they had with the taxi driver. I imagine his pen pausing for lengths of time as he begins the story. I imagine him nursing a drink, staring into the clouds, and willing himself to recall more of what would typically pass unnoticed, not wanting to set out on what he knows will lead to pain. I imagine he clings to these moments the way he clung to their raft; I imagine he is frightened when he must leave them behind. Yet he begins.

By the time my dad is on the second page of his journal, the ordinary fades like fog at the rising sun. He writes that well into the morning of their first day in the Alaskan wilderness, long after the bush pilot has left them at Summit Lake, Jerry fell while trying to fish. It is the first glimmer. After recording the number of fish Jerry catches, their length and type, my dad writes that Jerry told him he had fallen while walking back to the camp and was worried he had cracked a rib. In amongst the arctic char comes a hint, like frost, of fragility.

And then on the morning of the second day, they realize that fuel is running low. My dad does not write why, but I know it is because my uncle overhauled the fuel canisters before they left and did a poor job of it. The irony is bitter, for my uncle was a chemical engineer, a specialist, in fact, in fuels. The founder and editor of what became *The Sinor Synthetic Fuels Report*, a man who helped design the first space shuttle in the '80s and worked on alternative fuel sources in the '90s, Jerry is faced, on July 12, 2003, with the knowledge that he and my father are two days into a 14-day trip and have already used half their fuel.

10 *Aidan has not yet been conceived on July 12. His being waits in the universe for a body, and in my journal I remain transfixed by the ordinary in my life: a new puppy that won't behave, a deadline for an essay, heat that has clamped the intermountain west and refused to let go. I mow the lawn, riding the tractor up and down the hill beside our house, and consider calling my mom to make sure my dad has gotten off okay. The day before my father left for Alaska, I chose not to call him to wish him a safe journey. Our last interaction, an argument over a card game, had left me angry and resentful, feelings as familiar and worn as my favorite shoes. I will not learn for several days of his ordeal. When I do, I will, at the age of 34, believe that I am somehow to blame because I failed to call.*

My dad and Jerry spend that afternoon falling as they struggle in inch-deep water, using ropes to line, or drag, the raft down the shallow headwaters of the Alatna. It is hard work, lining a boat. I say this not from experience but from the way my father's hands looked when he returned from Alaska. Swollen and scabbed, they were so bloated that my mother had to type the initial draft of his journal. His hands betrayed the difficulty of the trip in a way his words never would; their stretched skin remained with me later when he suggested that he had done nothing at all.

Others had been asked to come along on the trip, including my husband, Michael, and me. Being in the backcountry was something my extended family did together, like others might see a movie or eat out. Every summer we backpacked in the Rockies, choosing wilderness areas over national parks or forests in hopes that the additional work of getting there would mean having part of the planet to ourselves. A dozen people from three generations around a campfire in the Mt. Zirkel Wilderness was not unusual; only two people in the central Brooks Range was.

That evening Jerry admits to my father that he had to lie to his doctor about coming to Alaska. His prostate cancer and Parkinson's were becoming more complicated and he had, just days before, been placed on new medication that is giving him trouble. My dad writes:

> After dinner, we sat around the fire talking about successes and failures, investment strategies, future trips, hopes for our children and life in general. It was a very good evening, but it was also the first time he mentioned the third member of our group (Cynde) and why she wasn't with us. When I said, "Cynde did not come on this trip." He responded, "I know, I just forgot."

Crystal clear in thought only 48 hours before, Jerry now confuses white rocks for sand dollars and imagines people who aren't there. Reeling my mother, Cynde, into the story, my uncle's mind was taking refuge in the familiar—she usually accompanied them on their trips. In fact, she'd been on their last trip to Alaska when the same river, the Alatna, had pulled her under with its giant river arms, leaving her bruised and sore but not broken. Reading this as a warning, she chose not go on this trip—the cold, the mosquitoes, the lack of dry land. We all found excuses; mine had something to do with a porch that needed painting and a new dog that couldn't be left alone. When we learned that Jerry was dead, when we learned that my dad had, by himself, paddled the body of his dead brother for 60 miles in search of help, we wondered, as Jerry had, why we weren't there.

Jerry, though, refuses to allow us to remain outside the warmth of the campfire and brings us into the story—first my mother, then, the following day, his daughter, his wife, his son, and others—weaving us into the landscape. Perhaps he imagines my mother gone for a minute to the tent to put on a layer of fleece, or his daughter down by the river watching for eagles, or his son on a night hike, waiting for stars that will never appear. For Jerry, it seems, we are all there in Alaska, poking a stick at the coals in the campfire as the night declines to come to an end and the sun lingers forever on the horizon.

15 Because I am the oldest in my family, I cannot say what it is like to have an older sibling, one whom, perhaps, you have revered your entire life, whose path you have followed, whose choices you have been taught to see as good and right, and whose decline you must witness. Instead, I am familiar with the responsibility of being the eldest, of making a path, of always being watched. "I know, I just forgot," says Jerry, the one who never failed his siblings or his children. My first thoughts are of how hard that moment must have been for two men born in the Corn Belt just after the Depression, when weakness and error simply were not options. I imagine the shifting of feet, the stoking of fire, the busying of hands with mess kits and fishing line, anything to ignore the monster that has crept into camp threatening to disrupt a pattern, a practiced way of being, that these two men lived for over 60 years.

But later, I reconsider this moment in my dad's story. My dad reads the early signs of mental deterioration in Jerry's inability to distinguish between reality and figment, but I wonder if the dementia is not working to refigure a truer truth, not bound by actual truth, that seeps into the emotional truth of things. What if Jerry's failing mind is only failing to erect the boundaries and borders we typically build? What if, in those moments, the possibility exists that those who are not "there" actually are there warming themselves by the fire? What if, rather than being alone in the Alaskan wilds without fuel, with physical and mental loss pressing in, my dad and his brother are surrounded by family? What if the felt truth is the actual truth?

Or maybe I am just wishing it had been so. Maybe Jerry doesn't feel grace in the dissolving line between fact and fiction but rather experiences the swirling hysteria that must accompany the declining grip on reality. Maybe when he says "I know, I just forgot," he is really wishing with all his heart to stand firmly on the banks of reality.

I will not know that I am pregnant for several weeks. Only Aidan will know of his existence and then only in a cellular way. That I could be inhabited by another without my knowledge unnerves me. Hormones busily make preparations for my body to do what it has never been taught but must somehow now do, and I open another carton of milk for my breakfast cereal. In my journal I worry that friends no longer like me, that I am getting nothing done this summer, that I want to back out of a conference in September, that I should call my mom but don't. All the while an egg is waiting and a favorite uncle dying.

When I look back at these journal entries years later, days when I know my dad was fighting to stay alive, I am at first embarrassed by what fills the page. Though I could not know of the miracles happening around me, I wish I had been less concerned about the mundane and more outwardly focused. I find it hard to imagine that I could write several lines about the inadequacy of my pen and the failures of an eight-week-old puppy. But recently I have begun to see these pages as a kind of tether, a line connecting me to these ordinary moments in my past, allowing me to recover what would typically have been left to fade. On July 14, 2003, hormones releasing, my father fighting, and my uncle failing, I worried about taking our new puppy running. To have left this moment unwritten would have severed the only connection I have to a day in my life where the world split open without my notice.

Day three is, my dad writes with typical understatement, a difficult day. By late morning, Jerry can no longer stand upright. As long as he keeps walking, he can remain erect, but as soon as he stops moving, he falls into the river, into the raft, onto the rocks on the shore. The Alatna is painfully dry. My dad and uncle continue to line the 15-foot Avon down the shallows and over the sand and gravel bars, heaving their belongings, wishing for more water. Rain falls. Granitic rock formations appear in the far distance, holding court above the U-shaped valley where nothing grows above a foot. There are only tussocks, sedge, and the occasional willow, beaten low by a wind that hammers the landscape. Every now and then, an eagle flies overhead, a herd of caribou flees their approach, the rains desist for a minute, then the sky opens. 20

Every now and then, my uncle asks where they are and where everyone else is. When this happens, my dad responds, "Jerry, we are in the middle of Alaska going down the Alatna and there are only two of us."

Only two.

Only two days ago, all was right in the world. Two years ago, the signs of Parkinson's were less apparent. Two decades ago, Jerry and my dad were in the prime of life, building shuttles that could return to earth and writing treaties dictating how the world should act in time of war. Two score ago, they were getting married, finishing school, taking road trips to Florida to see the alligators. Only two.

More falling. One moment my dad looks up and Jerry isn't there. Beaching the raft, he goes in search of his brother only to find him near the shoreline, soaking wet; gloves, glasses, hat missing. He has been looking for my mother in the cotton grass. She has been gone so long. Time bends like the river. Now and then, here and there, near and far move closer together. I am at home writing in my journal an entry that will forever root me to this day long after the day has passed, the egg that will become my son knits into my body either to grow or to perish, and over a campfire the night before, my dad and his brother bring us onto the river in the stories they tell.

Though he only admits "real concern" at this point, there must be terror for my father. He is 200 miles from a city of any size with a brother who is gradually leaving him. He searches for the missing gloves and hat and then abandons the search. Who knows what the river might have taken? Is it at this point, I wonder, surrounded by acres of tundra, with so much missing, that he remembers a conversation he had had with Jerry shortly after the Parkinson's diagnosis? Knowing that the disease would leave him bedridden and imprisoned in a body that had once been able to bushwhack through the Rockies for miles without rest, Jerry asked his younger brother to make sure he died in the natural world. When the time came, help him find a cliff, a valley, a bottomless river, a final ceiling out of sky. Using the raft to steady Jerry's failing body and guiding both down a river that has grown steadily in the rain and the lower elevation, perhaps my father turns to the now clear sky and considers what he is being asked to do. 25

They set up camp, my dad erecting Jerry's tent, and eat a cold dinner. The lighters and the waterproof matches had been soaked during the day's struggles and would not light. Somehow the plastic bag had been left open. My dad does not have to write that Jerry was in charge of these things. More than 10 years of backpacking with my family tells me that Jerry held the matches. He was the one who made the fire, cooked the food, called us from our tents when the sun was just beginning to chase away the morning chill. He was the one who chose the routes, found the campsite, told us how close to the river we could pitch our tents. He was the one who held the map, named the stars, and warned us repeatedly about the three greatest threats in wilderness backpacking: lightning, sunstroke, and falling.

Day Four. Jerry can no longer speak. His voice is a whisper, words slurring together. They decide over breakfast that they are in real trouble and need to head to Lake Takahula for help, a journey of 60 miles. Two retired school teachers live in a remote cabin in the woods near the lake with their dog and a satellite phone, information handed to my father and Jerry with their fishing licenses and now more precious than fuel.

This, then, is the way things are. My dad writes, "Jerry was gone part of the time." In these moments, he is utterly alone.

The last time I had seen my uncle was only a week or so before the Alaska trip. We had had a Sinor Family Reunion in Grand Island, Nebraska. My dad's younger brother, Keith, lives on a lake and the family gathered for a weekend of swimming and boating and beach picnics. The entire family was there, uncles and aunts, nieces and nephews, brothers and sisters, sweating under the Midwestern sun while the black flies bit our ankles.

On the first morning of the reunion, I took a picture of my uncle and his family, the camera holding what would soon be lost. They were dressed in blue and stood in the shade. It is the intimacy of that moment, their bodies touching at the elbows, our eyes meeting through the lens, that I remember. All of us, for a fraction of time, holding the pose and each other.

Jerry was very thin. While his no-fat diet gave his prostate cancer little to invade, it left his body with little to live on. Each time I saw him, his belt was cinched tighter and his clothes hung more loosely from his limbs. Yet, he seemed strong. We all said so, watching him play badminton. Yes, we assured ourselves, he was well despite the drugs, the treatments, the long slide to immobility that is Parkinson's.

When the thunderstorm came, we all ran for the garage, carrying beach chairs and leftover food—all of us except Jerry. He headed in the opposite direction, to the lake, where waves were competing with each other to touch the sky. We saw him push off from the boat dock on the Jet Ski and ride to the center of the lake, where he whirled in tight circles as the lightning and the thunder began. We only pointed. Rain hit the tin roof like hail, making it impossible to hear one another. In my mind's eye, he raises his fist to the storm and transgresses, for a moment, his own mortality. He demands participation in life. He will not remain offstage for the drama. The lightning does not strike him down, and he grows in my eyes.

Remembering how this once thick man rode a Jet Ski like a weapon a week before he died, I recall also a moment of vulnerability in a small hotel near Lake Titicacca, our final day in Peru. We were all there: my brother, his wife, my mom and dad, Michael, my aunt, Jerry, his daughter and her husband, a group that typically fished together every summer, now staying in a motel that bordered the world's highest navigable lake. Because Jerry wanted to see Machu Picchu before he died, we spent our frequent flyer miles, hired a guide to take us on the Inca Trail, and found ourselves a year before his death exploring the city of Cuzco,[1] the bellybutton of the world.

It was an amazing trip, but tiring, tiring for all of us—the altitude, the constant travel, the food, the water. We were weathered. On the last day, we were gathering our suitcases and backpacks one last time. Ivan, our guide, was trying to hustle us out of the hotel and into the van to Lima and our flight home. There was a chance we would miss the plane. The commotion—11 adults trying to get organized and into a van, some leaving that night, others the next day—filled the tiny lobby of the hotel and bounced against the low ceiling and narrow door. Amidst the chaos, Jerry came into the lobby, unsteady like a child, eyes wide in alarm. "Ivan, Ivan," he said, his voice matching the shakiness of his limbs, "I have lost my tickets."

We stopped, all of us, bags half-zipped, water bottles dangling at our sides, and looked to Jerry—the man whose knowledge and experience had seemed as boundless as space itself—willing him with our eyes not to reveal himself. Please, I thought, please do not show me this tender part of your belly. I do not want to know that you are anything except what you have ever been. I do not want you to be anything but whole. 35

Day four still. Afternoon. 67°44' north latitude. The GPS places them, roots them to a locatable spot on the spinning globe, but they are far from motionless. They start the raft down a narrow chute. Rainfall, permafrost, and the many small creeks that run into the Alatna have conspired to create a torrent. Water rushes them headlong down the river, sweepers leaning like animals of prey, ready to pull them from the raft and send them into the roiling water. When they turn the corner and see the giant shale outcrop, a wall of rock that cuts across the chute, they can do nothing but slam into it. The raft buckles and climbs the wall; my dad, in front, is thrown out of the raft and pulled under the outcrop. Somehow the raft, too, goes under or around or over. No one knows. When my dad comes up for air, Jerry and the raft are also on the other side.

The bottom of the raft has been shredded, but miraculously neither my dad nor Jerry is seriously injured. They decide to camp for the night while they try to repair the raft with duct tape. Jerry repeatedly suggests that they just walk to the car and go home. Unable to stand at all, Jerry gathers wood on his hands and knees in hopes of building a fire to warm my father.

That night Jerry insists that they find their location on the GPS. My dad argues, seeing no point in knowing their longitude when their only choice is to

1. Machu Picchu, Inca site built in the fifteenth century; Cuzco, a city in southeastern Peru.

head south on the river, but Jerry will not surrender the point. Finally, my dad agrees and they find the coordinates of the camp.

I wonder at Jerry's insistence. Is it, in a sense, the final act of caretaking in a life dedicated to securing the safety of others, of making sure there is order in the world before leaving it? Or is it because he feels at some deep level that a final resting place should be a known place, a place that holds itself, in its specificity, its repeatability, against the vastness that is the Alaskan wilds, the vastness of the universe? Or is it because his mind, cast to sea, unable to latch onto anyone or anything long enough to recover rationality, holds the GPS like a flotation device, willing the linear to return? For whatever reason, Jerry insists, and because of his insistence, we, as a family, will be able to return someday to that shore, to those willows, to those rocks, and stand in the thicket where he lay down to die.

40 My dad gets Jerry ready for bed, dressing him in his long johns and tucking him into his sleeping bag, as he had done for me as a child, perhaps as Jerry had once done for him. Hours later, from his own tent, my dad hears Jerry struggling with the zipper on his tent. "What are you doing?" he asks. And Jerry responds that he wants to try his new fly line. The first coherent words in more than a day. My dad takes them as a sign that the new Parkinson's drugs are kicking in. "Go to bed," he says. And this time, when my dad lies down to sleep, it is the sleep of release. Things will be okay, he tells himself. The drugs are working.

In the early morning hours of July 15, my dad hears Jerry struggle again with the zipper on his tent. When he goes over and asks Jerry what he is doing, Jerry responds, "What are you doing here?" My dad repeats the question; Jerry repeats the answer. Unlike all the other times in which my dad has explained that they are in the middle of Alaska trying to get home and Jerry has responded that he knows but has just forgotten, this time Jerry never returns to the here. He remains there, wherever there is, and wonders what my dad is doing at his side.

When the sun comes up the next day, Jerry has disappeared.

My dad spends two hours looking for him, following his footprints, worrying that he tried to go fishing and has been pulled into the Alatna. But fishing was not what Jerry had in mind. Jerry's boot tracks lead north and west of their tents, meandering for close to 50 yards, until they stop near the river. By following his trail, my father finds his brother curled up like a baby in a thicket of willows some yards from the river. Jerry has been careful to lie down next to the willows rather than on them, sharing the ground, choosing a place. Sometime in the night he had reached into his dry bag, to the very bottom, and put on his "going home" clothes, the clean shirt and pants meant for the plane ride back. Earlier in the evening, he could not zip his tent. Now he had laced his own boots. Clothes clean, no sign of a fall or struggle, he is holding a small branch in his hand, holding it like you might a walking stick.

My dad, who must serve simultaneously as brother, oarsman, and priest, blesses the land and loads the boat. In this story, the heroes do not live to see another day. I know my father well enough to know that such an ending is unacceptable.

45 Jerry was diagnosed with Parkinson's in 1995. The following August my extended family backpacked in the Mt. Zirkel Wilderness of Colorado. It was the first backpacking trip since Jerry's diagnosis and the first since my divorce. Loss, it seems, is democratic.

That we would both carry on with our lives was never a question. His illness and my failed marriage did not even warrant conversation. No one said anything to either of us. We hiked, fished, and ate as we always had. Around the campfire we talked about books, or legal questions, or politics, or what the fish seemed to be biting this year. At times I wanted to scream, hold out my emptiness like an amputated limb and demand it be acknowledged, but instead I stirred the soup in my cup and waited for it to cool.

On the last day, we were breaking camp for the final climb out to the cars. Everyone was busy stuffing backpacks, filtering water, or laying ground cloths in the sun to dry. My aunt and I were folding the tent that I had shared in the past with my husband. We were absorbed in one of the greatest pleasures of backpacking—the economy with which you travel, the fact that each thing has its own place—and all seemed fine.

I looked over at Jerry who was busy attending to his own possessions and those of the community. He looked as he had always looked. But then so did I. To anyone else, we were the same as ever. I walked over to him.

What I said was, "I am sorry that you have Parkinson's." What I meant was thank you for taking me into the natural world and showing me how mountains rest their tired bodies against one another and rivers scrape out plains the size of entire states, how meteors return like swallows every year in August to flash across the sky and wildflowers fill valleys so that you can no longer see the trail. What I meant was that I hoped he would find peace, that he would always be able to recognize himself, that he would not be in pain. What I meant was that I felt like I was a failure because John had left me, that sometimes when I sat very still on my couch at home, loneliness suffocated me, that I could not understand how things would ever feel okay again. What I meant was that I was scared. What I meant was that I would bear witness to his loss in hopes that he would bear witness to mine.

50 After getting my uncle's body into the raft, my dad pushes off. For 60 miles, he would be thrown from the raft some 30 or 40 times, each time fearing he would lose the raft, his brother's body, his only way home. Sandbars would catch him and roll his body across their stretches, wearing holes in his neoprene waders and gloves and plunging him repeatedly into ice-cold water. A night and a day would pass. Finally, after wandering for miles in the woods, he would find the cabin with the satellite phone.

About pushing off from the site where Jerry died, my dad writes, "By luck, not by plan, Jerry was facing me for the rest of the trip." With no one else to talk to and a river that seemed to wish them gone, my father turns one last time to his brother for support and begins to talk. For close to two days, he paddles, swims, climbs, falls, and tells stories. Perhaps, he recalls moments from their childhood: throwing rocks over the barn, swimming in the irrigation ditch, the taste of tomatoes fresh from the vine. Perhaps, he thanks Jerry for going to college and showing him and his siblings another way of being in the world, a life different from anything my father had imagined while inoculating pigs and driving the tractor through the corn. Perhaps, he describes the scenery as they move from tundra into boreal forests, into the winking greens of the white and black spruce. I know he sang songs, and I know my father well enough to know that when he forgot the words to "Tom Dooley" or "John Henry,"[2] he made them up, fanciful songs about heroes and lovers and trains that go all night. I know my father told Jerry he loved him.

In his journal he writes, "We talked," blurring once again the boundary between here and there. And for this I am grateful. Because when I think of what my father went through, what it would have been like to make the trip to Takahulu, the only comfort I can take is in knowing my father had company. As he had several nights before over the campfire, my dad brings all of us onto the raft, a raft on which Jerry is not dead and they are not alone. Weaving together stories of the past, he creates a net that holds all of us, a net that carries him to safety, to home.

The morning my father arrives at Lake Takahulu, I write in my journal that I am going rafting in two days down the Snake River. Worried that the time away from my desk is time poorly spent, I imagine writing an essay about the experience, what it is like to float down a river that begins in the mountains and runs to the sea. Mostly I complain about the dog and how easily I am distracted by household projects. Still, this is the last entry I make before I learn of Jerry's death, the last recorded narrative of what my life was like when Jerry was alive, my father whole, and my son the size of a period.

I like to imagine that at the very moment Jerry died, my son Aidan was conceived, so that for the briefest moment, the past, present, and future stood together and recognized one another. I like to imagine that the suffering my dad experienced, pain that has haunted him every day since his return, is measured out among us, so that we all carry part of the burden. I like to imagine that the stories I tell here, like the stories my dad told me as a child and the ones he recited as a way to remain sane on the river, have the power to reach across distance and time and death to connect me to him, and him to Jerry, and Jerry to Aidan. Jerry can no longer tell his story and I must carry Aidan's for him until he is older. Someday he will carry mine and I will tell my father's and loss will be found in language.

2. "Tom Dooley," folk song based on the execution of Tom Dula, who was convicted of Laura Foster's 1866 murder in Wilkes County, North Carolina; "John Henry," folk song based on the legend of John Henry, believed to have competed against a steam-powered hammer in erecting a railroad, winning the competition but dying of exhaustion with his hammer still in his hand.

QUESTIONS

1. Jennifer Sinor's essay brings together seeming opposites, such as life and death, memory and loss of memory, past and present. What other opposites does Sinor write about? Locate specific places in the essay where you identify these opposites.

2. Sinor uses both her own journals and her father's journals to reconstruct the events about which she writes. How does her use of journals help her accomplish her purpose in this essay?

3. In this essay, Sinor uses rhetorical questions (see, for example, paragraphs 16 and 25). What is the effect of her use of questions? Why do you think she uses them?

4. Sinor uses different typefaces to separate descriptive sections about others and reflective sections about herself. Write an essay in which you use a similar format to do the same.

E. B. White

Once More to the Lake

One summer, along about 1904, my father rented a camp on a lake in Maine and took us all there for the month of August. We all got ringworm from some kittens and had to rub Pond's Extract on our arms and legs night and morning, and my father rolled over in a canoe with all his clothes on; but outside of that the vacation was a success and from then on none of us ever thought there was any place in the world like that lake in Maine. We returned summer after summer—always on August 1st for one month. I have since become a salt-water man, but sometimes in summer there are days when the restlessness of the tides and the fearful cold of the sea water and the incessant wind which blows across the afternoon and into the evening make me wish for the placidity of a lake in the woods. A few weeks ago this feeling got so strong I bought myself a couple of bass hooks and a spinner and returned to the lake where we used to go, for a week's fishing and to revisit old haunts.

I took along my son, who had never had any fresh water up his nose and who had seen lily pads only from train windows. On the journey over to the lake I began to wonder what it would be like. I wondered how time would have marred this unique, this holy spot—the coves and streams, the hills that the sun set behind, the camps and the paths behind the camps. I was sure the tarred road would have found it out and I wondered in what other ways it would be desolated. It is strange how much you can remember about places like that once you allow your mind to return into the grooves which lead back. You remember one thing, and that suddenly reminds you of another thing. I guess I remembered clearest of all the early mornings, when the lake was cool and motionless, remembered how the bedroom smelled of the lumber it was made of and of the wet woods whose scent entered through the screen. The partitions in the camp were thin and did not extend clear to the top of the rooms, and as I was always the first up I would dress softly so as not to wake the others, and sneak out into

Originally appeared in "One Man's Meat," White's column for Harper's Magazine *(October 1941); later included in* One Man's Meat *(1942), a collection of his columns about life on a Maine saltwater farm, and then in* Essays of E. B. White *(1977).*

the sweet outdoors and start out in the canoe, keeping close along the shore in the long shadows of the pines. I remembered being very careful never to rub my paddle against the gunwale for fear of disturbing the stillness of the cathedral.

The lake had never been what you would call a wild lake. There were cottages sprinkled around the shores, and it was in farming country although the shores of the lake were quite heavily wooded. Some of the cottages were owned by nearby farmers, and you would live at the shore and eat your meals at the farmhouse. That's what our family did. But although it wasn't wild, it was a fairly large and undisturbed lake and there were places in it which, to a child at least, seemed infinitely remote and primeval.

I was right about the tar: it led to within half a mile of the shore. But when I got back there, with my boy, and we settled into a camp near a farmhouse and into the kind of summertime I had known, I could tell that it was going to be pretty much the same as it had been before—I knew it, lying in bed the first morning, smelling the bedroom, and hearing the boy sneak quietly out and go off along the shore in a boat. I began to sustain the illusion that he was I, and therefore, by simple transposition, that I was my father. This sensation persisted, kept cropping up all the time we were there. It was not an entirely new feeling, but in this setting it grew much stronger. I seemed to be living a dual existence. I would be in the middle of some simple act, I would be picking up a bait box or laying down a table fork, or I would be saying something, and suddenly it would be not I but my father who was saying the words or making the gesture. It gave me a creepy sensation.

5 We went fishing the first morning. I felt the same damp moss covering the worms in the bait can, and saw the dragonfly alight on the tip of my rod as it hovered a few inches from the surface of the water. It was the arrival of this fly that convinced me beyond any doubt that everything was as it always had been, that the years were a mirage and there had been no years. The small waves were the same, chucking the rowboat under the chin as we fished at anchor, and the boat was the same boat, the same color green and the ribs broken in the same places, and under the floor-boards the same fresh-water leavings and débris—the dead helgrammite,[1] the wisps of moss, the rusty discarded fishhook, the dried blood from yesterday's catch. We stared silently at the tips of our rods, at the dragonflies that came and went. I lowered the tip of mine into the water, tentatively, pensively dislodging the fly, which darted two feet away, poised, darted two feet back, and came to rest again a little farther up the rod. There had been no years between the ducking of this dragonfly and the other one—the one that was part of memory. I looked at the boy, who was silently watching his fly, and it was my hands that held his rod, my eyes watching. I felt dizzy and didn't know which rod I was at the end of.

We caught two bass, hauling them in briskly as though they were mackerel, pulling them over the side of the boat in a businesslike manner without any landing net, and stunning them with a blow on the back of the head. When we got back for a swim before lunch, the lake was exactly where we had left it, the same number of inches from the dock, and there was only the merest sugges-

1. The larvae of the dobsonfly (usually spelled "hellgrammite").

tion of a breeze. This seemed an utterly enchanted sea, this lake you could leave to its own devices for a few hours and come back to, and find that it had not stirred, this constant and trustworthy body of water. In the shallows, the dark, water-soaked sticks and twigs, smooth and old, were undulating in clusters on the bottom against the clean ribbed sand, and the track of the mussel was plain. A school of minnows swam by, each minnow with its small individual shadow, doubling the attendance, so clear and sharp in the sunlight. Some of the other campers were in swimming, along the shore, one of them with a cake of soap, and the water felt thin and clear and unsubstantial. Over the years there had been this person with the cake of soap, this cultist, and here he was. There had been no years.

Up to the farmhouse to dinner through the teeming, dusty field, the road under our sneakers was only a two-track road. The middle track was missing, the one with the marks of the hooves and the splotches of dried, flaky manure. There had always been three tracks to choose from in choosing which track to walk in; now the choice was narrowed down to two. For a moment I missed terribly the middle alternative. But the way led past the tennis court, and something about the way it lay there in the sun reassured me; the tape had loosened along the backline, the alleys were green with plantains and other weeds, and the net (installed in June and removed in September) sagged in the dry noon, and the whole place steamed with midday heat and hunger and emptiness. There was a choice of pie for dessert, and one was blueberry and one was apple, and the waitresses were the same country girls, there having been no passage of time, only the illusion of it as in a dropped curtain—the waitresses were still fifteen; their hair had been washed, that was the only difference—they had been to the movies and seen the pretty girls with the clean hair.

Summertime, oh summertime, pattern of life indelible, the fade-proof lake, the woods unshatterable, the pasture with the sweetfern and the juniper forever and ever, summer without end; this was the background, and the life along the shore was the design, the cottagers with their innocent and tranquil design, their tiny docks with the flagpole and the American flag floating against the white clouds in the blue sky, the little paths over the roots of the trees leading from camp to camp and the paths leading back to the outhouses and the can of lime for sprinkling, and at the souvenir counters at the store the miniature birch-bark canoes and the post cards that showed things looking a little better than they looked. This was the American family at play, escaping the city heat, wondering whether the newcomers in the camp at the head of the cove were "common" or "nice," wondering whether it was true that the people who drove up for Sunday dinner at the farmhouse were turned away because there wasn't enough chicken.

It seemed to me, as I kept remembering all this, that those times and those summers had been infinitely precious and worth saving. There had been jollity and peace and goodness. The arriving (at the beginning of August) had been so big a business in itself, at the railway station the farm wagon drawn up, the first smell of the pine-laden air, the first glimpse of the smiling farmer, and the great importance of the trunks and your father's enormous authority in such matters, and the feel of the wagon under you for the long ten-mile haul, and at the top of the last long hill catching the first view of the lake after eleven months of not seeing this cherished body of water. The shouts and cries of the other campers when they saw you, and the trunks to be unpacked, to give up their rich burden. (Arriving was less exciting nowadays, when you sneaked up in your car and parked it under a tree near the camp and took out the bags and in five minutes it was all over, no fuss, no loud wonderful fuss about trunks.)

10 Peace and goodness and jollity. The only thing that was wrong now, really, was the sound of the place, an unfamiliar nervous sound of the outboard motors. This was the note that jarred, the one thing that would sometimes break the illusion and set the years moving. In those other summertimes all motors were inboard; and when they were at a little distance, the noise they made was a sedative, an ingredient of summer sleep. They were one-cylinder and two-cylinder engines, and some were make-and-break and some were jump-spark,[2] but they all made a sleepy sound across the lake. The one-lungers throbbed and fluttered, and the twin-cylinder ones purred and purred, and that was a quiet sound too. But now the campers all had outboards. In the daytime, in the hot mornings, these motors made a petulant, irritable sound; at night, in the still evening when the afterglow lit the water, they whined about one's ears like mosquitoes. My boy loved our rented outboard, and his great desire was to achieve singlehanded mastery over it, and authority, and he soon learned the trick of choking it a little (but not too much), and the adjustment of the needle valve. Watching him I would remember the things you could do with the old one-cylinder engine with the heavy flywheel, how you could have it eating out of your hand if you got really close to it spiritually. Motor boats in those days didn't have clutches, and you would make a landing by shutting off the motor at the proper time and coasting in with a dead rudder. But there was a way of reversing them, if you learned the trick, by cutting the switch and putting it on again exactly on the final dying revolution of the flywheel, so that it would kick back against compression and begin reversing. Approaching a dock in a strong following breeze, it was difficult to slow up sufficiently by the ordinary coasting method, and if a boy felt he had complete mastery over his motor, he was tempted to keep it running beyond its time and then reverse it a few feet from the dock. It took a cool nerve, because if you threw the switch a twentieth of a second too soon you would catch the flywheel when it still had speed enough to go up past center, and the boat would leap ahead, charging bull-fashion at the dock.

We had a good week at the camp. The bass were biting well and the sun shone endlessly, day after day. We would be tired at night and lie down in the accumulated heat of the little bedrooms after the long hot day and the breeze would stir almost imperceptibly outside and the smell of the swamp drift in through the rusty screens. Sleep would come easily and in the morning the red squirrel would be on the roof, tapping out his gay routine. I kept remembering everything, lying in bed in the mornings—the small steamboat that had a long rounded stern like the lip of a Ubangi, and how quietly she ran on the moonlight sails, when the older boys played their mandolins and the girls sang and we ate doughnuts dipped in sugar, and how sweet the music was on the water in the shining night, and what it had felt like to think about girls then. After

2. Methods of ignition timing.

breakfast we would go up to the store and the things were in the same place—the minnows in a bottle, the plugs and spinners disarranged and pawed over by the youngsters from the boys' camp, the fig newtons and the Beeman's gum. Outside, the road was tarred and cars stood in front of the store. Inside, all was just as it had always been, except there was more Coca-Cola and not so much Moxie and root beer and birch beer and sarsaparilla. We would walk out with a bottle of pop apiece and sometimes the pop would backfire up our noses and hurt. We explored the streams, quietly, where the turtles slid off the sunny logs and dug their way into the soft bottom; and we lay on the town wharf and fed worms to the tame bass. Everywhere we went I had trouble making out which was I, the one walking at my side, the one walking in my pants.

One afternoon while we were there at that lake a thunderstorm came up. It was like the revival of an old melodrama that I had seen long ago with childish awe. The second-act climax of the drama of the electrical disturbance over a lake in America had not changed in any important respect. This was the big scene, still the big scene. The whole thing was so familiar, the first feeling of oppression and heat and a general air around camp of not wanting to go very far away. In midafternoon (it was all the same) a curious darkening of the sky, and a lull in everything that had made life tick; and then the way the boats suddenly swung the other way at their moorings with the coming of a breeze out of the new quarter, and the premonitory rumble. Then the kettle drum, then the snare, then the bass drum and cymbals, then crackling light against the dark, and the gods grinning and licking their chops in the hills. Afterward the calm, the rain steadily rustling in the calm lake, the return of light and hope and spirits, and the campers running out in joy and relief to go swimming in the rain, their bright cries perpetuating the deathless joke about how they were getting simply drenched, and the children screaming with delight at the new sensation of bathing in the rain, and the joke about getting drenched linking the generations in a strong indestructible chain. And the comedian who waded in carrying an umbrella.

When the others went swimming my son said he was going in too. He pulled his dripping trunks from the line where they had hung all through the shower, and wrung them out. Languidly, and with no thought of going in, I watched him, his hard little body, skinny and bare, saw him wince slightly as he pulled up around his vitals the small, soggy, icy garment. As he buckled the swollen belt suddenly my groin felt the chill of death.

Questions

1. What has guided White in his selection of the details he gives about the trip? Why, for example, does he talk about the road, the dragonfly, and the boat's motor?

2. White speaks of the lake as a "holy spot." What about it was holy?

3. White's last sentence often surprises first-time readers. Go back through the essay and pick out sections, words, or phrases that seem to prepare for the ending.

4. Write about revisiting a place that has a special meaning for you.

JOURNALS

JOAN DIDION

On Keeping a Notebook

"'THAT WOMAN ESTELLE,'" the note reads, "'is partly the reason why George Sharp and I are separated today.' *Dirty crepe-de-Chine wrapper, hotel bar, Wilmington RR, 9:45 a.m. August Monday morning.*"

Since the note is in my notebook, it presumably has some meaning to me. I study it for a long while. At first I have only the most general notion of what I was doing on an August Monday morning in the bar of the hotel across from the Pennsylvania Railroad station in Wilmington, Delaware (waiting for a train? missing one? 1960? 1961? why Wilmington?), but I do remember being there. The woman in the dirty crepe-de-Chine wrapper had come down from her room for a beer, and the bartender had heard before the reason why George Sharp and she were separated today. "Sure," he said, and went on mopping the floor. "You told me." At the other end of the bar is a girl. She is talking, pointedly, not to the man beside her but to a cat lying in the triangle of sunlight cast through the open door. She is wearing a plaid silk dress from Peck & Peck, and the hem is coming down.

Here is what it is: the girl has been on the Eastern Shore, and now she is going back to the city, leaving the man beside her, and all she can see ahead are the viscous summer sidewalks and the 3 a.m. long-distance calls that will make her lie awake and then sleep drugged through all the steaming mornings left in August (1960? 1961?). Because she must go directly from the train to lunch in New York, she wishes that she had a safety pin for the hem of the plaid silk dress, and she also wishes that she could forget about the hem and the lunch and stay in the cool bar that smells of disinfectant and malt and make friends with the woman in the crepe-de-Chine wrapper. She is afflicted by a little self-pity, and she wants to compare Estelles. That is what that was all about.

Why did I write it down? In order to remember, of course, but exactly what was it I wanted to remember? How much of it actually happened? Did any of it? Why do I keep a notebook at all? It is easy to deceive oneself on all those scores. The impulse to write things down is a peculiarly compulsive one, inexplicable to those who do not share it, useful only accidentally, only secondarily, in the way that any compulsion tries to justify itself. I suppose that it begins or does not begin in the cradle. Although I have felt compelled to write things down since I was five years old, I doubt that my daughter ever will, for she is a singu-

From Slouching towards Bethlehem *(1966), Didion's first volume of nonfiction, which includes both autobiographical essays and articles analyzing American culture of the 1960s.*

larly blessed and accepting child, delighted with life exactly as life presents itself to her, unafraid to go to sleep and unafraid to wake up. Keepers of private notebooks are a different breed altogether, lonely and resistant rearrangers of things, anxious malcontents, children afflicted apparently at birth with some presentiment of loss.

5 My first notebook was a Big Five tablet, given to me by my mother with the sensible suggestion that I stop whining and learn to amuse myself by writing down my thoughts. She returned the tablet to me a few years ago; the first entry is an account of a woman who believed herself to be freezing to death in the Arctic night, only to find, when day broke, that she had stumbled onto the Sahara Desert, where she would die of the heat before lunch. I have no idea what turn of a five-year-old's mind could have prompted so insistently "ironic" and exotic a story, but it does reveal a certain predilection for the extreme which has dogged me into adult life; perhaps if I were analytically inclined I would find it a truer story than any I might have told about Donald Johnson's birthday party or the day my cousin Brenda put Kitty Litter in the aquarium.

So the point of my keeping a notebook has never been, nor is it now, to have an accurate factual record of what I have been doing or thinking. That would be a different impulse entirely, an instinct for reality which I sometimes envy but do not possess. At no point have I ever been able successfully to keep a diary; my approach to daily life ranges from the grossly negligent to the merely absent, and on those few occasions when I have tried dutifully to record a day's events, boredom has so overcome me that the results are mysterious at best. What is this business about "shopping, typing piece, dinner with E, depressed"? Shopping for what? Typing what piece? Who is E? Was this "E" depressed, or was I depressed? Who cares?

In fact I have abandoned altogether that kind of pointless entry; instead I tell what some would call lies. "That's simply not true," the members of my family frequently tell me when they come up against my memory of a shared event. "The party was *not* for you, the spider was *not* a black widow, *it wasn't that way at all.*" Very likely they are right, for not only have I always had trouble distinguishing between what happened and what merely might have happened, but I remain unconvinced that the distinction, for my purposes, matters. The cracked crab that I recall having for lunch the day my father came home from Detroit in 1945 must certainly be embroidery, worked into the day's pattern to lend verisimilitude; I was ten years old and would not now remember the cracked crab. The day's events did not turn on cracked crab. And yet it is precisely that fictitious crab that makes me see the afternoon all over again, a home movie run all too often, the father bearing gifts, the child weeping, an exercise in family love and guilt. Or that is what it was to me. Similarly, perhaps it never did snow that August in Vermont; perhaps there never were flurries in the night wind, and maybe no one else felt the ground hardening and summer already dead even as we pretended to bask in it, but that was how it felt to me, and it might as well have snowed, could have snowed, did snow.

How it felt to me: that is getting closer to the truth about a notebook. I sometimes delude myself about why I keep a notebook, imagine that some thrifty virtue derives from preserving everything observed. See enough and write it down, I tell myself, and then some morning when the world seems drained of wonder, some day when I am only going through the motions of doing what I am supposed to do, which is write—on that bankrupt morning I will simply open my notebook and there it will all be, a forgotten account with accumulated interest, paid passage back to the world out there: dialogue overheard in hotels and elevators and at the hat-check counter in Pavillon (one middle-aged man shows his hat check to another and says, "That's my old football number"); impressions of Bettina Aptheker and Benjamin Sonnenberg and Teddy ("Mr. Acapulco") Stauffer; careful *aperçus*[1] about tennis bums and failed fashion models and Greek shipping heiresses, one of whom taught me a significant lesson (a lesson I could have learned from F. Scott Fitzgerald, but perhaps we all must meet the very rich for ourselves) by asking, when I arrived to interview her in her orchid-filled sitting room on the second day of a paralyzing New York blizzard, whether it was snowing outside.

I imagine, in other words, that the notebook is about other people. But of course it is not. I have no real business with what one stranger said to another at the hat-check counter in Pavillon; in fact I suspect that the line "That's my old football number" touched not my own imagination at all, but merely some memory of something once read, probably "The Eighty-Yard Run."[2] Nor is my concern with a woman in a dirty crepe-de-Chine wrapper in a Wilmington bar. My stake is always, of course, in the unmentioned girl in the plaid silk dress. *Remember what it was to be me:* that is always the point.

10 It is a difficult point to admit. We are brought up in the ethic that others, any others, all others, are by definition more interesting than ourselves; taught to be diffident, just this side of self-effacing. ("You're the least important person in the room and don't forget it," Jessica Mitford's[3] governess would hiss in her ear on the advent of any social occasion; I copied that into my notebook because it is only recently that I have been able to enter a room without hearing some such phrase in my inner ear.) Only the very young and the very old may recount their dreams at breakfast, dwell upon self, interrupt with memories of beach picnics and favorite Liberty lawn dresses and the rainbow trout in a creek near Colorado Springs. The rest of us are expected, rightly, to affect absorption in other people's favorite dresses, other people's trout.

And so we do. But our notebooks give us away, for however dutifully we record what we see around us, the common denominator of all we see is always, transparently, shamelessly, the implacable "I." We are not talking here about the kind of notebook that is patently for public consumption, a structural conceit for binding together a series of graceful *pensées;*[4] we are talking about

1. Perceptions, insights (French).
2. Short story by Irwin Shaw (1914–1984).
3. British essayist and social critic (1917–1996).
4. Thoughts, meditations (French).

something private, about bits of the mind's string too short to use, an indiscriminate and erratic assemblage with meaning only for its maker.

And sometimes even the maker has difficulty with the meaning. There does not seem to be, for example, any point in my knowing for the rest of my life that, during 1964, 720 tons of soot fell on every square mile of New York City, yet there it is in my notebook, labeled "FACT." Nor do I really need to remember that Ambrose Bierce liked to spell Leland Stanford's[5] name "£eland $tanford" or that "smart women almost always wear black in Cuba," a fashion hint without much potential for practical application. And does not the relevance of these notes seem marginal at best?:

> In the basement museum of the Inyo County Courthouse in Independence, California, sign pinned to a mandarin coat: "This MANDARIN COAT was often worn by Mrs. Minnie S. Brooks when giving lectures on her TEAPOT COLLECTION."
>
> Redhead getting out of car in front of Beverly Wilshire Hotel, chinchilla stole, Vuitton bags with tags reading:
>
> MRS LOU FOX
> HOTEL SAHARA
> VEGAS

Well, perhaps not entirely marginal. As a matter of fact, Mrs. Minnie S. Brooks and her MANDARIN COAT pull me back into my own childhood, for although I never knew Mrs. Brooks and did not visit Inyo County until I was thirty, I grew up in just such a world, in houses cluttered with Indian relics and bits of gold ore and ambergris and the souvenirs my Aunt Mercy Farnsworth brought back from the Orient. It is a long way from that world to Mrs. Lou Fox's world, where we all live now, and is it not just as well to remember that? Might not Mrs. Minnie S. Brooks help me to remember what I am? Might not Mrs. Lou Fox help me to remember what I am not?

But sometimes the point is harder to discern. What exactly did I have in mind when I noted down that it cost the father of someone I know $650 a month to light the place on the Hudson in which he lived before the Crash?[6] What use was I planning to make of this line by Jimmy Hoffa:[7] "I may have my faults, but being wrong ain't one of them"? And although I think it interesting to know where the girls who travel with the Syndicate have their hair done when they find themselves on the West Coast, will I ever make suitable use of it? Might I not be better off just passing it on to John O'Hara?[8] What is a recipe for sauerkraut doing in my notebook? What kind of magpie keeps this notebook? *"He was born the night the Titanic went down."* That seems a nice enough line, and I even

5. Bierce (1842–1914), American journalist and fiction writer, known for such ironic writing as *The Devil's Dictionary* (see p. 483); Stanford (1824–1893), railroad magnate, governor of California, and founder of Stanford University.

6. The stock market crash of 1929.

7. Head of the Teamsters' Union who disappeared in 1975 and is presumed dead (1932–1982).

8. American novelist (1905–1970).

recall who said it, but is it not really a better line in life than it could ever be in fiction?

15 But of course that is exactly it: not that I should ever use the line, but that I should remember the woman who said it and the afternoon I heard it. We were on her terrace by the sea, and we were finishing the wine left from lunch, trying to get what sun there was, a California winter sun. The woman whose husband was born the night the *Titanic* went down wanted to rent her house, wanted to go back to her children in Paris. I remember wishing that I could afford the house, which cost $1,000 a month. "Someday you will," she said lazily. "Someday it all comes." There in the sun on her terrace it seemed easy to believe in someday, but later I had a low-grade afternoon hangover and ran over a black snake on the way to the supermarket and was flooded with inexplicable fear when I heard the checkout clerk explaining to the man ahead of me why she was finally divorcing her husband. "He left me no choice," she said over and over as she punched the register. "He has a little seven-month-old baby by her, he left me no choice." I would like to believe that my dread then was for the human condition, but of course it was for me, because I wanted a baby and did not then have one and because I wanted to own the house that cost $1,000 a month to rent and because I had a hangover.

It all comes back. Perhaps it is difficult to see the value in having one's self back in that kind of mood, but I do see it; I think we are well advised to keep on nodding terms with the people we used to be whether we find them attractive company or not. Otherwise they turn up unannounced and surprise us, come hammering on the mind's door at 4 a.m. of a bad night and demand to know who deserted them, who betrayed them, who is going to make amends. We forget all too soon the things we thought we could never forget. We forget the loves and the betrayals alike, forget what we whispered and what we screamed, forget who we were. I have already lost touch with a couple of people I used to be; one of them, a seventeen-year-old, presents little threat, although it would be of some interest to me to know again what it feels like to sit on a river levee drinking vodka-and-orange-juice and listening to Les Paul and Mary Ford[9] and their echoes sing "How High the Moon" on the car radio. (You see I still have the scenes, but I no longer perceive myself among those present, no longer could even improvise the dialogue.) The other one, a twenty-three-year-old, bothers me more. She was always a good deal of trouble, and I suspect she will reappear when I least want to see her, skirts too long, shy to the point of aggravation, always the injured party, full of recriminations and little hurts and stories I do not want to hear again, at once saddening me and angering me with her vulnerability and ignorance, an apparition all the more insistent for being so long banished.

It is a good idea, then, to keep in touch, and I suppose that keeping in touch is what notebooks are all about. And we are all on our own when it comes to keeping those lines open to ourselves: your notebook will never help me, nor mine you. *"So what's new in the whiskey business?"* What could that

9. Husband-and-wife musical team of the 1940s and 1950s.

possibly mean to you? To me it means a blonde in a Pucci bathing suit sitting with a couple of fat men by the pool at the Beverly Hills Hotel. Another man approaches, and they all regard one another in silence for a while. "So what's new in the whiskey business?" one of the fat men finally says by way of welcome, and the blonde stands up, arches one foot and dips it in the pool, looking all the while at the cabaña where Baby Pignatari[10] is talking on the telephone. That is all there is to that, except that several years later I saw the blonde coming out of Saks Fifth Avenue in New York with her California complexion and a voluminous mink coat. In the harsh wind that day she looked old and irrevocably tired to me, and even the skins in the mink coat were not worked the way they were doing them that year, not the way she would have wanted them done, and there is the point of the story. For a while after that I did not like to look in the mirror, and my eyes would skim the newspapers and pick out only the deaths, the cancer victims, the premature coronaries, the suicides, and I stopped riding the Lexington Avenue IRT[11] because I noticed for the first time that all the strangers I had seen for years—the man with the seeing-eye dog, the spinster who read the classified pages every day, the fat girl who always got off with me at Grand Central—looked older than they once had.

It all comes back. Even that recipe for sauerkraut: even that brings it back. I was on Fire Island when I first made that sauerkraut, and it was raining, and we drank a lot of bourbon and ate the sauerkraut and went to bed at ten, and I listened to the rain and the Atlantic and felt safe. I made the sauerkraut again last night and it did not make me feel any safer, but that is, as they say, another story.

10. Brazilian playboy (1916–1977).

11. A New York City subway line; one of its stops is the Grand Central railway terminal.

Questions

1. What distinction does Didion make between a diary and a notebook? What uses does a notebook have for Didion?

2. Didion says she uses her notebook to "tell what some would call lies" (paragraph 7). Why does she do this? Would some people call these things truths? Why?

3. Didion says, "*How it felt to me:* that is getting closer to the truth about a notebook." What writing strategies does she use to convey "how it felt"?

4. Try keeping a notebook for a week, jotting down the sorts of things that Didion does. At the end of the week, take one or two of your entries and expand on them, as Didion does with the entries on Mrs. Minnie S. Brooks and Mrs. Lou Fox.

Ralph Waldo Emerson from *Journals*

I like to have a man's knowledge comprehend more than one class of topics, one row of shelves. I like a man who likes to see a fine barn as well as a good tragedy. [1828]

The Religion that is afraid of science dishonors God and commits suicide. [1831]

The things taught in colleges and schools are not an education, but the means of education. [1831]

Don't tell me to get ready to die. I know not what shall be. The only preparation I can make is by fulfilling my present duties. This is the everlasting life. [1832]

5 My aunt [Mary Moody Emerson] had an eye that went through and through you like a needle. "She was endowed," she said, "with the fatal gift of penetration." She disgusted everybody because she knew them too well. [1832]

I am sure of this, that by going much alone a man will get more of a noble courage in thought and word than from all the wisdom that is in books. [1833]

I fretted the other night at the hotel at the stranger who broke into my chamber after midnight, claiming to share it. But after his lamp had smoked the chamber full and I had turned round to the wall in despair, the man blew out his lamp, knelt down at his bedside, and made in low whisper a long earnest prayer. Then was the relation entirely changed between us. I fretted no more, but respected and liked him. [1835]

I believe I shall some time cease to be an individual, that the eternal tendency of the soul is to become Universal, to animate the last extremities of organization. [1837]

It is very hard to be simple enough to be good. [1837]

10 A man must have aunts and cousins, must buy carrots and turnips, must have barn and woodshed, must go to market and to the blacksmith's shop, must saunter and sleep and be inferior and silly. [1838]

From The Journals of Ralph Waldo Emerson, *begun in 1819, when he was a college sophomore, and continued throughout his life. The journals, which reached one hundred volumes by 1839, were mined for public essays during Emerson's lifetime, but only after his death were his journals and notebooks published in ten book-length volumes between 1909 and 1914.*

How sad a spectacle, so frequent nowadays, to see a young man after ten years of college education come out, ready for his voyage of life—and to see that the entire ship is made of rotten timber, of rotten, honeycombed, traditional timber without so much as an inch of new plank in the hull. [1839]

A sleeping child gives me the impression of a traveler in a very far country. [1840]

In reading these letters of M.M.E.[1] I acknowledge (with surprise that I could ever forget it) the debt of myself and my brothers to that old religion which, in those years, still dwelt like a Sabbath peace in the country population of New England, which taught privation, self-denial, and sorrow. A man was born, not for prosperity, but to suffer for the benefit of others, like the noble rock-maple tree which all around the villages bleeds for the service of man.[2] Not praise, not men's acceptance of our doing, but the Spirit's holy errand through us, absorbed the thought. How dignified is this! how all that is called talents and worth in Paris and in Washington dwindles before it! [1841]

All writing is by the grace of God. People do not deserve to have good writing, they are so pleased with bad. In these sentences that you show me, I can find no beauty, for I see death in every clause and every word. There is a fossil or a mummy character which pervades this book. The best sepulchers, the vastest catacombs, Thebes and Cairo, Pyramids, are sepulchers to me. I like gardens and nurseries. Give me initiative, spermatic, prophesying, man-making words. [1841]

When summer opens, I see how fast it matures, and fear it will be short; but after the heats of July and August, I am reconciled, like one who has had his swing, to the cool of autumn. So will it be with the coming of death. [1846]

In England every man you meet is some man's son; in America, he may be some man's father. [1848]

Every poem must be made up of lines that are poems. [1848]

Love is necessary to righting the estate of woman in this world. Otherwise nature itself seems to be in conspiracy against her dignity and welfare; for the cultivated, high-thoughted, beauty-loving, saintly woman finds herself unconsciously desired for her sex, and even enhancing the appetite of her savage pursuers by these fine ornaments she has piously laid on herself. She finds with indignation that she is herself a snare, and was made such. I do not wonder at her occasional protest, violent protest against nature, in fleeing to nunneries, and taking black veils. Love rights all this deep wrong. [1848]

Natural Aristocracy. It is a vulgar error to suppose that a gentleman must be ready to fight. The utmost that can be demanded of the gentleman is that he be incapable of a lie. There is a man who has good sense, is well informed,

1. Mary Moody Emerson (1774–1863), Emerson's aunt, his father's sister.
2. The sap of the rock or sugar maple is collected and made into maple syrup.

well-read, obliging, cultivated, capable, and has an absolute devotion to truth. He always means what he says, and says what he means, however courteously. You may spit upon him—nothing could induce him to spit upon you—no praises, and no possessions, no compulsion of public opinion. You may kick him—he will think it the kick of a brute—but he is not a brute, and will not kick you in return. But neither your knife and pistol, nor your gifts and courting will ever make the smallest impression on his vote or word; for he is the truth's man, and will speak and act the truth until he dies. [1849]

20 Love is temporary and ends with marriage. Marriage is the perfection which love aimed at, ignorant of what it sought. Marriage is a good known only to the parties—a relation of perfect understanding, aid, contentment, possession of themselves and of the world—which dwarfs love to green fruit. [1850]

I found when I had finished my new lecture that it was a very good house, only the architect had unfortunately omitted the stairs. [1851]

This filthy enactment [The Fugitive Slave Law][3] was made in the nineteenth century, by people who could read and write. I will not obey it, by God. [1851]

Henry [Thoreau] is military. He seemed stubborn and implacable; always manly and wise, but rarely sweet. One would say that, as Webster[4] could never speak without an antagonist, so Henry does not feel himself except in opposition. He wants a fallacy to expose, a blunder to pillory, requires a little sense of victory, a roll of the drums, to call his powers into full exercise. [1853]

Shall we judge the country by the majority or by the minority? Certainly, by the minority. The mass are animal, in state of pupilage, and nearer the chimpanzee. [1854]

25 All the thoughts of a turtle are turtle. [1854]

Resources or feats. I like people who can do things. When Edward and I struggled in vain to drag our big calf into the barn, the Irish girl put her finger into the calf's mouth, and led her in directly. [1862]

George Francis Train said in a public speech in New York, "Slavery is a divine institution." "So is hell," exclaimed an old man in the crowd. [1862]

You complain that the Negroes are a base class. Who makes and keeps the Jew or the Negro base, who but you, who exclude them from the rights which others enjoy? [1867]

3. A law enacted in 1850 to compel the arrest of runaway slaves and their return to their owners.

4. Daniel Webster (1782–1852), American statesman and orator, known for his advocacy of nationalism, as opposed to state sovereignty.

Henry David Thoreau from *Journal*

As the least drop of wine tinges the whole goblet, so the least particle of truth colors our whole life. It is never isolated, or simply added as treasure to our stock. When any real progress is made, we unlearn and learn anew what we thought we knew before. [1837]

Not by constraint or severity shall you have access to true wisdom, but by abandonment, and childlike mirthfulness. If you would know aught, be gay before it. [1840]

It is the man determines what is said, not the words. If a mean person uses a wise maxim, I bethink me how it can be interpreted so as to commend itself to his meanness; but if a wise man makes a commonplace remark, I consider what wider construction it will admit. [1840]

Nothing goes by luck in composition. It allows of no tricks. The best you can write will be the best you are. Every sentence is the result of a long probation. The author's character is read from title-page to end. Of this he never corrects the proofs. We read it as the essential character of a handwriting without regard to the flourishes. And so of the rest of our actions; it runs as straight as a ruled line through them all, no matter how many curvets about it. Our whole life is taxed for the least thing well done: it is its net result. How we eat, drink, sleep, and use our desultory hours, now in these indifferent days, with no eye to observe and no occasion [to] excite us, determines our authority and capacity for the time to come. [1841]

What does education often do? It makes a straight-cut ditch of a free, meandering brook. [1850] 5

All perception of truth is the detection of an analogy; we reason from our hands to our head. [1851]

To set down such choice experiences that my own writings may inspire me and at last I may make wholes of parts. Certainly it is a distinct profession to rescue from oblivion and to fix the sentiments and thoughts which visit all men more or less generally, that the contemplation of the unfinished picture may suggest its harmonious completion. Associate reverently and as much as you can with your loftiest thoughts. Each thought that is welcomed and recorded is a nest egg, by the side of which more will be laid. Thoughts accidentally thrown together become a frame in which more may be developed and exhibited.

From The Journal of Henry David Thoreau, *kept from 1837, when Thoreau was twenty years old, until his death in 1861; first published in 1906 and reissued with additional volumes in 1984.*

Perhaps this is the main value of a habit of writing, of keeping a journal—that so we remember our best hours and stimulate ourselves. My thoughts are my company. They have a certain individuality and separate existence, aye, personality. Having by chance recorded a few disconnected thoughts and then brought them into juxtaposition, they suggest a whole new field in which it was possible to labor and to think. Thought begat thought. [1852]

There is no such thing as pure *objective* observation. Your observation, to be interesting, *i.e.* to be significant, must be *subjective*. The sum of what the writer of whatever class has to report is simply some human experience, whether he be poet or philosopher or man of science. The man of most science is the man most alive, whose life is the greatest event. Senses that take cognizance of outward things merely are of no avail. It matters not where or how far you travel—the farther commonly the worse—but how much alive you are. If it is possible to conceive of an event outside to humanity, it is not of the slightest significance, though it were the explosion of a planet. Every important worker will report what life there is in him. It makes no odds into what seeming deserts the poet is born. Though all his neighbors pronounce it a Sahara, it will be a paradise to him; for the desert which we see is the result of the barrenness of our experience. No mere willful activity whatever, whether in writing verses or collecting statistics, will produce true poetry or science. If you are really a sick man, it is indeed to be regretted, for you cannot accomplish so much as if you were well. All that a man has to say or do that can possibly concern mankind, is in some shape or other to tell the story of his love—to sing, and, if he is fortunate and keeps alive, he will be forever in love. This alone is to be alive to the extremities. It is a pity that this divine creature should ever suffer from cold feet; a still greater pity that the coldness so often reaches to his heart. I look over the report of the doings of a scientific association and am surprised that there is so little life to be reported; I am put off with a parcel of dry technical terms. Anything living is easily and naturally expressed in popular language. I cannot help suspecting that the life of these learned professors has been almost as inhuman and wooden as a rain-gauge or self-registering magnetic machine. They communicate no fact which rises to the temperature of bloodheat. It doesn't all amount to one rhyme. [1854]

It is pardonable when we spurn the proprieties, even the sanctities, making them stepping-stones to something higher. [1858]

10 There is always some accident in the best things, whether thoughts or expressions or deeds. The memorable thought, the happy expression, the admirable deed are only partly ours. The thought came to us because we were in a fit mood; also we were unconscious and did not know that we had said or done a good thing. We must walk consciously only part way toward our goal, and then leap in the dark to our success. What we do best or most perfectly is what we have most thoroughly learned by the longest practice, and at length it falls from us without our notice, as a leaf from a tree. It is the *last* time we shall do it—our unconscious leavings. [1859]

The expression "a *liberal* education" originally meant one worthy of freemen. Such is education simply in a true and broad sense. But education ordinarily so called—the learning of trades and professions which is designed to enable men to earn their living, or to fit them for a particular station in life—is *servile*. [1859]

Questions for Emerson and Thoreau

1. Emerson frequently uses similes and metaphors in his journal—for example, "My aunt had an eye that went through and through you like a needle" (1832) or "A sleeping child gives me the impression of a traveler in a very far country" (1840). Unpack these and other metaphors you find in his journals, and discuss what they add to his thoughts.

2. Thoreau writes that "Nothing goes by luck in composition. . . . The best you can write will be the best you are." In what sense are his journal entries examples of this belief?

3. Both Thoreau and Emerson write journal entries on the subject of education, both using metaphorical language. Compare their beliefs on education, in part by comparing the metaphors they use.

4. Choose one journal entry from either Emerson or Thoreau and write an essay by expanding, amplifying, or showing exceptions to it.

Sylvia Plath

from *The Journals of Sylvia Plath*

Sunday night, *February* 23. This must be the 26th February 23rd I have lived through: over a quarter century of Februaries, and would I could cut a slice of recollection back through them all and trace the spiraling stair of my ascent adultward—or is it a descent? I feel I have lived enough to last my life in musings, tracings of crossings and recrossings with people, mad and sane, stupid and brilliant, beautiful and grotesque, infant and antique, cold and hot, pragmatic and dream-ridden, dead and alive. My house of days and masks is rich enough so that I might and must spend years fishing, hauling up the pearl-eyed, horny, scaled and sea-bearded monsters sunk long, long in the Sargasso of my imagination. I feel myself grip on my past as if it were my life: I shall make it my future business: every casual wooden monkey-carving, every pane of orange-and-purple nubbled glass on my grandmother's stair-landing window, every white hexagonal bathroom tile found by Warren[1] and me on

From The Journals of Sylvia Plath *(1982) edited by Ted Hughes (1930–1998), who was Plath's husband from 1956 until her suicide in 1963, though they separated in 1962;* The Unabridged Journals of Sylvia Plath (2000) *was edited by Karen V. Kukil and restored passages and entries not included by Hughes.*

1. Warren Joseph Plath (b. 1935), Sylvia Plath's brother.

our way digging to China, becomes radiant, magnetic, sucking meaning to it and shining with strange significance: unriddle the riddle: why is every doll's shoelace a revelation? Every wishing-box dream an annunciation? Because these are the sunk relics of my lost selves that I must weave, wordwise, into future fabrics. Today, from coffee till teatime at six, I read in *Lady Chatterley's Lover*, drawn back again with the joy of a woman living with her own game-keeper, and *Women in Love* and *Sons and Lovers*. Love, love: Why do I feel I would have known and loved Lawrence.[2] How many women must feel this and be wrong! I opened *The Rainbow*, which I have never read, and was sucked into the concluding Ursula and Skrebensky episode and sank back, breath knocked out of me, as I read of their London hotel, their Paris trip, their riverside loving while Ursula studied at college. This is the stuff of my life—my life, different, but no less brilliant and splendid—and the flow of my story will take me beyond this in my way—arrogant? I felt mystically that if I read Woolf,[3] read Lawrence (these two, why? their vision, so different, is so like mine) I can be itched and kindled to a great work: burgeoning, fat with the texture and substance of life: This my call, my work. This gives my being a name, a meaning—"to make of the moment something permanent": I, in my sphere, taking my place beside Dr. Beuscher and Doris Krook[4] in theirs—neither psychologist, priestess nor philosopher—teacher but a blending of both rich vocations in my own worded world. A book dedicated to each of them. Fool. Dreamer. When my first novel is written and accepted (a year hence? longer?) I shall permit myself the luxury of writing above: "I am no liar." I worked on two pages of carefully worded criticism of the Lawrence thesis: feel I am right, but wonder as always: will they see? will they scornfully smile me into the wrong? No: I stated clearly my case and I feel there is a good case made. Cups of scalding tea: how it rests me. We walked out about seven into the pleasant mild-cold still night to the library: the campus snow-blue, lit from myriad windows, deserted. Cleared, cleansed, stung fresh-cheeked chill, we walked the creaking-cricking plank paths through the botanical gardens and while Ted[5] delivered thesis and book I walked four times round the triangle flanked by Lawrence House, the Student's Building and the street running from Paradise Pond to College Hall, meeting no one, secretly gleeful and in control, summoning all my past green, gilded gray, sad, sodden and loveless, ecstatic, and in-love selves to be with me and rejoice. . . .

2. D. H. Lawrence (1885–1930), an English novelist who wrote *Lady Chatterley's Lover* (1928), *Women in Love* (1920), *Sons and Lovers* (1913), and *The Rainbow* (1915), all of which Plath references in this journal entry.

3. Virginia Woolf (1882–1941), modernist English writer, known for her fiction and nonfiction.

4. Dr. Ruth Tiffany Barnhouse Beuscher (1923–1999) was Plath's psychiatrist starting in 1953; after her divorce, she dropped Beuscher from her last name; Dorothea (Doris) Krook (1920–1989), a literary scholar and professor of English literature, was Plath's tutor at Cambridge University; she later married and took the name Dorothea Krook-Gilead.

5. Ted Hughes (1930–1998) was a British poet and Sylvia Plath's husband from 1956 until Plath's suicide in 1963.

QUESTIONS

1. Sylvia Plath writes, "I feel myself grip on my past as if it were my life: I shall make it my future business" (paragraph 1). Identify places where she links past, present, and future in this journal entry.

2. Plath uses many lists in this journal entry. Why do you think she does so? Which list do you find most effective and why?

3. Plath reflects on her reading of D. H. Lawrence. Write a journal entry in which you reflect on the influence of someone whose writing, music, or visual art you admire.

COLBY BUZZELL *Killing Time in Iraq*

BRUTAL ATTACK ON A COUNTERMORTAR MISSION

IT WAS AT NIGHT, the moon was gone, and the visibility was almost zero. Had my night vision goggles on. We set our gun position down on this hill, me and Pfc. Pointz. I laid down in the prone position and scanned my sector. I was only on the ground for like thirty seconds when I started feeling a tingling sensation all down my back and up my arms. I was like, What the f*** is that?? I had my NODs on and I looked down on the ground, and at first it looked like the TV screen when the cable goes out, you know like millions of bees in a snowstorm, but once I took a closer look I realized that I was lying down on a huge pile of literally thousands and thousands of ants. I looked at my arms and there were hundreds of ants crawling all over me, in fact I could hear them crawling on me. The ants here are not like the itty-bitty house ants back home, the ones in Iraq are f***ing huge, like as big as the ones at Fort Benning. I freaked out, they were all over me, crawling all up and down my back, up my arms, on my face, everywhere. I jumped up, threw my helmet off, tore my vest off as fast as I could, swearing and cussing every profanity in the f***ing book, slapping and hitting myself all over trying to get them off of me as fast as I could. Every now and then I could feel one of them biting into me and I'd grit my teeth in pain. I yelled at my assistant gunner to help me out and start slapping them off me as well.

Pfc. Pointz and Spc. Cummings both found all of this very comical. I tore my top off, my T-shirt, they were down my pants as well now. That wasn't too pleasant a feeling.

Lesson: Don't be a f***ing idiot like me, and always look before you lie down anywhere, especially in this country.

On the way back to the FOB, our shocks and hydraulics completely went tits up and the vehicle was bouncing up and down like an East L.A. low-rider Impala the whole way. It was sort of fun for like the first couple minutes, but then after a while I started feeling seasick, and I almost barfed up my beef

Taken from Buzzell's blog, composed while he was serving in Iraq and collected in his book My War: Killing Time in Iraq *(2005).*

enchilada MRE. (That wasn't a racist joke, I seriously ate a beef enchilada MRE prior to this.)

Posted by CBFTW[1] at 8:11 a.m., July 26, 2004

CAR BOMB

5 Last night a car bomb was discovered along a busy freeway here in Mosul. My platoon was placed on QRF while 3rd Platoon rolled out to secure the area and blow the thing up.

Car bombs are starting to become a very popular thing here in Mosul. The car bombs in Iraq are not like the car bombs you see in the movies, where they just blow up and the car just catches on fire. The psychopaths who are making these things have got the art of car bomb making down to a f***ing science, where they can produce the highest amount of casualties and damage humanly possible. It's mind blowing the amount of damage one single car bomb can do.

When they go off there will literally be nothing left of the VBIED, there'll be a huge hole in the street where the car once was. The explosions create these huge mushroom clouds of dust that can be seen miles away and the cars that were around it will all be thrown on their backs, and windows in buildings blocks away will be shattered from the concussion of the blast.

> We like the cars, the cars that go boom.
> —Some rap song in the eighties

Posted by CBFTW on July 18, 2004

ANOTHER DAMN CAR BOMB

At 0330 last night I woke up to a very loud explosion. At first I thought it was another bad dream, but my roommate also heard it and woke up and said, "Hey, did you hear that?!" Yeah, I told him. We stayed up for a couple minutes silently after that, wondering what the hell was that, and then we both went back to sleep. We later found out that it was an IED.

This morning we all went to breakfast and when we returned I took my weekly dose of anti-malaria medication and went to my room. Shortly after that, Sgt. L banged on my door and said that our platoon just got placed on QRF (Quick Reaction Force) and to stand by and be ready to go at any minute, today might be another 24th of June (that was the day of the Mohammed Al Noory Mosque/Sheikh Fatih police attack). The main gate to the airfield to our FOB just got hit by a vehicle-borne IED (car bomb) and there's mass casualties.

10 The vehicle-borne IED was a Toyota pickup with a female driver.

The airfield here also got mortared several times today.

Posted by CBFTW at 8:11 p.m., July 26, 2004

AND ANOTHER DAMN CAR BOMB

I'm getting pretty good at guessing just from the noise an explosion makes if it was a mortar impact, vehicle-borne IED, or a controlled detonation. This

1. This is the name of Buzzell's blog.

morning I went to breakfast at the chow hall. Had the usual—eggs, sausage, side of bacon. And as I was leaving the chow hall with my morning dose of coffee in my hand, I heard a loud explosion off in the distance and observed a huge cloud of dust. I thought to myself, damn, that was probably a car bomb.

Guess what? It was.

Posted by CBFTW at 9:53 a.m., August 2, 2004

"MASSEM?"

Today my squad had gate guard duty.

My platoon had a countermortar observation post up on OP Abrams to attend during the afternoon. My squad on the other hand lucked out and had gate guard duty. When the guys exited our gate they all cursed at us and flipped us off as they drove by. We all just waved and smiled at them. Suckers. They were just jealous that they didn't have gate guard, instead of an OP. I don't blame them, anything is better than an OP. We have a lot of Iraqis working on our FOB, building shit and doing stuff. We had an Iraqi come up to us in the heat of the afternoon with two large bags of ice. With a smile he said that he wanted to help us, because we were helping them. That was very cool of him. 15

Pfc. Evans and I ripped open one of the bags of ice and started cooling ourselves off with it, rubbing our foreheads with it and stuff. Pfc. Evans then looked over at me and said, "Damn, that was the nicest thing I've heard from an Iraqi the whole time I've been here."

Later on in the afternoon, another Iraqi contractor came up to our gate and kept on saying, "Massem? Massem?"

What the hell is "Massem"?

After a couple minutes of trying to figure out what the hell "Massem" was, we finally realized that he was asking us if we had a *Maxim* magazine.

Every Stryker pretty much has a *Maxim* inside of it, it's like required reading or something here in the Stryker Brigade. The ceilings of some of the Strykers are actually covered in pinup girls from *Maxim*. So we lent him the latest issue, and he just sat there turning the pages with an ear-to-ear smile, wide-eyed and saying, "Good! Good!" every time there was a photo of some girl in skimpy underwear looking all sexy. After flipping through the *Maxim*, he handed it back to us, thanked us, and walked off. 20

Happy.

Posted by CBFTW at 4:01 p.m., July 20, 2004

QUESTIONS

1. Does Buzzell write the way you'd expect a soldier to write? What signs of his profession appear in his writing? What elements surprise you?

2. What seems to be Buzzell's attitude toward warfare? Toward Iraqis? Toward his fellow soldiers?

3. Begin and maintain a journal or blog about your own daily actions, and then compare what you write with Buzzell's blog. What is different? What is the same?

Portraits of People and Places

Scott Russell Sanders *Under the Influence*

My father drank. He drank as a gut-punched boxer gasps for breath, as a starving dog gobbles food—compulsively, secretly, in pain and trembling. I use the past tense not because he ever quit drinking but because he quit living. That is how the story ends for my father, age sixty-four, heart bursting, body cooling and forsaken on the linoleum of my brother's trailer. The story continues for my brother, my sister, my mother, and me, and will continue so long as memory holds.

In the perennial present of memory, I slip into the garage or barn to see my father tipping back the flat green bottles of wine, the brown cylinders of whiskey, the cans of beer disguised in paper bags. His Adam's apple bobs, the liquid gurgles, he wipes the sandy-haired back of a hand over his lips, and then, his bloodshot gaze bumping into me, he stashes the bottle or can inside his jacket, under the workbench, between two bales of hay, and we both pretend the moment has not occurred.

"What's up, buddy?" he says, thick-tongued and edgy.

"Sky's up," I answer, playing along.

5 "And don't forget prices," he grumbles. "Prices are always up. And taxes."

In memory, his white 1951 Pontiac with the stripes down the hood and the Indian head on the snout jounces to a stop in the driveway; or it is the 1956 Ford station wagon, or the 1963 Rambler shaped like a toad, or the sleek 1969 Bonneville that will do 120 miles per hour on straightaways; or it is the robin's-egg blue pickup, new in 1980, battered in 1981, the year of his death. He climbs out, grinning dangerously, unsteady on his legs, and we children interrupt our game of catch, our building of snow forts, our picking of plums, to watch in silence as he weaves past into the house, where he slumps into his overstuffed chair and falls asleep. Shaking her head, our mother stubs out the cigarette he has left smoldering in the ashtray. All evening, until our bedtimes, we tiptoe past him, as past a snoring dragon. Then we curl in our fearful sheets, listening. Eventually he wakes with a grunt, Mother slings accusations at him, he snarls back, she yells, he growls, their voices clashing. Before long, she retreats to their bedroom,

Originally published in Harper's Magazine *(November 1989), a monthly dedicated to discussing American politics, literature, and culture.*

sobbing—not from the blows of fists, for he never strikes her, but from the force of words.

Left alone, our father prowls the house, thumping into furniture, rummaging in the kitchen, slamming doors, turning the pages of the newspaper with a savage crackle, muttering back at the late-night drivel from television. The roof might fly off, the walls might buckle from the pressure of his rage. Whatever my brother and sister and mother may be thinking on their own rumpled pillows, I lie there hating him, loving him, fearing him, knowing I have failed him. I tell myself he drinks to ease an ache that gnaws at his belly, an ache I must have caused by disappointing him somehow, a murderous ache I should be able to relieve by doing all my chores, earning A's in school, winning baseball games, fixing the broken washer and the burst pipes, bringing in money to fill his empty wallet. He would not hide the green bottles in his tool box, would not sneak off to the barn with a lump under his coat, would not fall asleep in the daylight, would not roar and fume, would not drink himself to death, if only I were perfect.

I am forty-two as I write these words, and I know full well now that my father was an alcoholic, a man consumed by disease rather than by disappointment. What had seemed to me a private grief is in fact a public scourge. In the United States alone some ten or fifteen million people share his ailment, and behind the doors they slam in fury or disgrace, countless other children tremble. I comfort myself with such knowledge, holding it against the throb of memory like an ice pack against a bruise. There are keener sources of grief: poverty, racism, rape, war. I do not wish to compete for a trophy in suffering. I am only trying to understand the corrosive mixture of helplessness, responsibility, and shame that I learned to feel as the son of an alcoholic. I realize now that I did not cause my father's illness, nor could I have cured it. Yet for all this grown-up knowledge, I am still ten years old, my own son's age, and as that boy I struggle in guilt and confusion to save my father from pain.

Consider a few of our synonyms for *drunk*: tipsy, tight, pickled, soused, and plowed; stoned and stewed, lubricated and inebriated, juiced and sluiced; three sheets to the wind, in your cups, out of your mind, under the table; lit up, tanked up, wiped out; besotted, blotto, bombed, and buzzed; plastered, polluted, putrified; loaded or looped, boozy, woozy, fuddled, or smashed; crocked and shit-faced, corked and pissed, snockered and sloshed.

10 It is a mostly humorous lexicon, as the lore that deals with drunks—in jokes and cartoons, in plays, films, and television skits—is largely comic. Aunt Matilda nips elderberry wine from the sideboard and burps politely during supper. Uncle Fred slouches to the table glassy-eyed, wearing a lamp shade for a hat and murmuring, "Candy is dandy but liquor is quicker." Inspired by cocktails, Mrs. Somebody recounts the events of her day in a fuzzy dialect, while Mr. Somebody nibbles her ear and croons a bawdy song. On the sofa with Boyfriend, Daughter giggles, licking gin from her lips, and loosens the bows in her hair. Junior knocks back some brews with his chums at the Leopard Lounge and stumbles home to the wrong house, wonders foggily why he cannot locate

his pajamas, and crawls naked into bed with the ugliest girl in school. The family dog slurps from a neglected martini and wobbles to the nursery, where he vomits in Baby's shoe.

It is all great fun. But if in the audience you notice a few laughing faces turn grim when the drunk lurches on stage, don't be surprised, for these are the children of alcoholics. Over the grinning mask of Dionysus,[1] the leering mask of Bacchus,[2] these children cannot help seeing the bloated features of their own parents. Instead of laughing, they wince, they mourn. Instead of celebrating the drunk as one freed from constraints, they pity him as one enslaved. They refuse to believe *in vino veritas,*[3] having seen their befuddled parents skid away from truth toward folly and oblivion. And so these children bite their lips until the lush staggers into the wings.

My father, when drunk, was neither funny nor honest; he was pathetic, frightening, deceitful. There seemed to be a leak in him somewhere, and he poured in booze to keep from draining dry. Like a torture victim who refuses to squeal, he would never admit that he had touched a drop, not even in his last year, when he seemed to be dissolving in alcohol before our very eyes. I never knew him to lie about anything, ever, except about this one ruinous fact. Drowsy, clumsy, unable to fix a bicycle tire, throw a baseball, balance a grocery sack, or walk across the room, he was stripped of his true self by drink. In a matter of minutes, the contents of a bottle could transform a brave man into a coward, a buddy into a bully, a gifted athlete and skilled carpenter and shrewd businessman into a bumbler. No dictionary of synonyms for *drunk* would soften the anguish of watching our prince turn into a frog.

Father's drinking became the family secret. While growing up, we children never breathed a word of it beyond the four walls of our house. To this day, my brother and sister rarely mention it, and then only when I press them. I did not confess the ugly, bewildering fact to my wife until his wavering walk and slurred speech forced me to. Recently, on the seventh anniversary of my father's death, I asked my mother if she ever spoke of his drinking to friends. "No, no, never," she replied hastily. "I couldn't bear for anyone to know."

The secret bores under the skin, gets in the blood, into the bone, and stays there. Long after you have supposedly been cured of malaria, the fever can flare up, the tremors can shake you. So it is with the fevers of shame. You swallow the bitter quinine[4] of knowledge, and you learn to feel pity and compassion toward the drinker. Yet the shame lingers in your marrow, and, because of the shame, anger.

15 For a long stretch of my childhood we lived on a military reservation in Ohio, an arsenal where bombs were stored underground in bunkers, vintage airplanes

1. Greek god of wine and intoxication.
2. Roman god of wine and intoxication.
3. "In wine is truth."
4. Drug from the bark of the South American cinchona tree, used to treat malaria.

burst into flames, and unstable artillery shells boomed nightly at the dump. We had the feeling, as children, that we played in a mine field, where a heedless footfall could trigger an explosion. When Father was drinking, the house, too, became a mine field. The least bump could set off either parent.

The more he drank, the more obsessed Mother became with stopping him. She hunted for bottles, counted the cash in his wallet, sniffed at his breath. Without meaning to snoop, we children blundered left and right into damning evidence. On afternoons when he came home from work sober, we flung ourselves at him for hugs, and felt against our ribs the telltale lump in his coat. In the barn we tumbled on the hay and heard beneath our sneakers the crunch of buried glass. We tugged open a drawer in his workbench, looking for screwdrivers or crescent wrenches, and spied a gleaming six-pack among the tools. Playing tag, we darted around the house just in time to see him sway on the rear stoop and heave a finished bottle into the woods. In his good night kiss we smelled the cloying sweetness of Clorets, the mints he chewed to camouflage his dragon's breath.

I can summon up that kiss right now by recalling Theodore Roethke's[5] lines about his own father in "My Papa's Waltz":

> The whiskey on your breath
> Could make a small boy dizzy;
> But I hung on like death:
> Such waltzing was not easy.

Such waltzing was hard, terribly hard, for with a boy's scrawny arms I was trying to hold my tipsy father upright.

For years, the chief source of those incriminating bottles and cans was a grimy store a mile from us, a cinder block place called Sly's, with two gas pumps outside and a moth-eaten dog asleep in the window. A strip of flypaper, speckled the year round with black bodies, coiled in the doorway. Inside, on rusty metal shelves or in wheezing coolers, you could find pop and Popsicles, cigarettes, potato chips, canned soup, raunchy postcards, fishing gear, Twinkies, wine, and beer. When Father drove anywhere on errands, Mother would send us kids along as guards, warning us not to let him out of our sight. And so with one or more of us on board, Father would cruise up to Sly's, pump a dollar's worth of gas or plump the tires with air, and then, telling us to wait in the car, he would head for that fly-spangled doorway.

Dutiful and panicky, we cried, "Let us go in with you!"

"No," he answered. "I'll be back in two shakes." 20

"Please!"

"No!" he roared. "Don't you budge, or I'll jerk a knot in your tails!"

So we stayed put, kicking the seats, while he ducked inside. Often, when he had parked the car at a careless angle, we gazed in through the window and saw Mr. Sly fetching down from a shelf behind the cash register two green

5. American poet (1908–1963) whose father also drank too much.

pints of Gallo wine. Father swigged one of them right there at the counter, stuffed the other in his pocket, and then out he came, a bulge in his coat, a flustered look on his red face.

Because the Mom and Pop who ran the dump were neighbors of ours, living just down the tar-blistered road, I hated them all the more for poisoning my father. I wanted to sneak in their store and smash the bottles and set fire to the place. I also hated the Gallo brothers, Ernest and Julio, whose jovial faces shone from the labels of their wine, labels I would find, torn and curled, when I burned the trash. I noted the Gallo brothers' address, in California, and I studied the road atlas to see how far that was from Ohio, because I meant to go out there and tell Ernest and Julio what they were doing to my father, and then, if they showed no mercy, I would kill them.

25 While growing up on the back roads and in the country schools and cramped Methodist churches of Ohio and Tennessee, I never heard the word *alcoholism,* never happened across it in books or magazines. In the nearby towns, there were no addiction treatment programs, no community mental health centers, no Alcoholics Anonymous chapters, no therapists. Left alone with our grievous secret, we had no way of understanding Father's drinking except as an act of will, a deliberate folly or cruelty, a moral weakness, a sin. He drank because he chose to, pure and simple. Why our father, so playful and competent and kind when sober, would choose to ruin himself and punish his family, we could not fathom.

Our neighborhood was high on the Bible, and the Bible was hard on drunkards. "Woe to those who are heroes at drinking wine, and valiant men in mixing strong drink," wrote Isaiah. "The priest and the prophet reel with strong drink, they are confused with wine, they err in vision, they stumble in giving judgment. For all tables are full of vomit, no place is without filthiness." We children had seen those fouled tables at the local truck stop where the notorious boozers hung out, our father occasionally among them. "Wine and new wine take away the understanding," declared the prophet Hosea. We had also seen evidence of that in our father, who could multiply seven-digit numbers in his head when sober, but when drunk could not help us with fourth-grade math. Proverbs warned: "Do not look at wine when it is red, when it sparkles in the cup and goes down smoothly. At the last it bites like a serpent, and stings like an adder. Your eyes will see strange things, and your mind utter perverse things." Woe, woe.

Dismayingly often, these biblical drunkards stirred up trouble for their own kids. Noah made fresh wine after the flood, drank too much of it, fell asleep without any clothes on, and was glimpsed in the buff by his son Ham, whom Noah promptly cursed. In one passage—it was so shocking we had to read it under our blankets with flashlights—the patriarch Lot fell down drunk and slept with his daughters. The sins of the fathers set their children's teeth on edge.

Our ministers were fond of quoting St. Paul's pronouncement that drunkards would not inherit the kingdom of God. These grave preachers assured us that the wine referred to during the Last Supper was in fact grape juice. Bible and sermons and hymns combined to give us the impression that Moses should have brought down from the mountain another stone tablet, bearing the Eleventh Commandment: Thou shalt not drink.

The scariest and most illuminating Bible story apropos of drunkards was the one about the lunatic and the swine. Matthew, Mark, and Luke each told a version of the tale. We knew it by heart: When Jesus climbed out of his boat one day, this lunatic came charging up from the graveyard, stark naked and filthy, frothing at the mouth, so violent that he broke the strongest chains. Nobody would go near him. Night and day for years this madman had been wailing among the tombs and bruising himself with stones. Jesus took one look at him and said, "Come out of the man, you unclean spirits!" for he could see that the lunatic was possessed by demons. Meanwhile, some hogs were conveniently rooting nearby. "If we have to come out," begged the demons, "at least let us go into those swine." Jesus agreed. The unclean spirits entered the hogs, and the hogs rushed straight off a cliff and plunged into a lake. Hearing the story in Sunday school, my friends thought mainly of the pigs. (How big a splash did they make? Who paid for the lost pork?) But I thought of the redeemed lunatic, who bathed himself and put on clothes and calmly sat at the feet of Jesus, restored—so the Bible said—to "his right mind."

When drunk, our father was clearly in his wrong mind. He became a stranger, as fearful to us as any graveyard lunatic, not quite frothing at the mouth but fierce enough, quick-tempered, explosive; or else he grew maudlin and weepy, which frightened us nearly as much. In my boyhood despair, I reasoned that maybe he wasn't to blame for turning into an ogre. Maybe, like the lunatic, he was possessed by demons. I found support for my theory when I heard liquor referred to as "spirits," when the newspapers reported that somebody had been arrested for "driving under the influence," and when church ladies railed against that "demon drink." 30

If my father was indeed possessed, who would exorcise him? If he was a sinner, who would save him? If he was ill, who would cure him? If he suffered, who would ease his pain? Not ministers or doctors, for we could not bring ourselves to confide in them; not the neighbors, for we pretended they had never seen him drunk; not Mother, who fussed and pleaded but could not budge him; not my brother and sister, who were only kids. That left me. It did not matter that I, too, was only a child, and a bewildered one at that. I could not excuse myself.

On first reading a description of delirium tremens—in a book on alcoholism I smuggled from the library—I thought immediately of the frothing lunatic and the frenzied swine. When I read stories or watched films about grisly metamorphoses—Dr. Jekyll becoming Mr. Hyde,[6] the mild husband changing into a werewolf, the kindly neighbor taken over by a brutal alien—I could not help seeing my own father's mutation from sober to drunk. Even today, knowing better, I am attracted by the demonic theory of drink, for when I recall my

6. London physician and his evil alter ego, in Robert Louis Stevenson's novel.

father's transformation, the emergence of his ugly second self, I find it easy to believe in possession by unclean spirits. We never knew which version of Father would come home from work, the true or the tainted, nor could we guess how far down the slope toward cruelty he would slide.

How far a man *could* slide we gauged by observing our back-road neighbors—the out-of-work miners who had dragged their families to our corner of Ohio from the desolate hollows of Appalachia, the tight-fisted farmers, the surly mechanics, the balked and broken men. There was, for example, whiskey-soaked Mr. Jenkins, who beat his wife and kids so hard we could hear their screams from the road. There was Mr. Lavo the wino, who fell asleep smoking time and again, until one night his disgusted wife bundled up the children and went outside and left him in his easy chair to burn; he awoke on his own, staggered out coughing into the yard, and pounded her flat while the children looked on and the shack turned to ash. There was the truck driver, Mr. Sampson, who tripped over his son's tricycle one night while drunk and got so mad that he jumped into his semi and drove away, shifting through the dozen gears, and never came back. We saw the bruised children of these fathers clump onto our school bus, we saw the abandoned children huddle in the pews at church, we saw the stunned and battered mothers begging for help at our doors.

Our own father never beat us, and I don't think he ever beat Mother, but he threatened often. The Old Testament Yahweh was not more terrible in his wrath. Eyes blazing, voice booming, Father would pull out his belt and swear to give us a whipping, but he never followed through, never needed to, because we could imagine it so vividly. He shoved us, pawed us with the back of his hand, as an irked bear might smack a cub, not to injure, just to clear a space. I can see him grabbing Mother by the hair as she cowers on a chair during a nightly quarrel. He twists her neck back until she gapes up at him, and then he lifts over her skull a glass quart bottle of milk, the milk running down his forearm; and he yells at her, "Say just one more word, one goddamn word, and I'll shut you up!" I fear she will prick him with her sharp tongue, but she is terrified into silence, and so am I, and the leaking bottle quivers in the air, and milk slithers through the red hair of my father's uplifted arm, and the entire scene is there to this moment, the head jerked back, the club raised.

35 When the drink made him weepy, Father would pack a bag and kiss each of us children on the head, and announce from the front door that he was moving out. "Where to?" we demanded, fearful each time that he would leave for good, as Mr. Sampson had roared away for good in his diesel truck. "Someplace where I won't get hounded every minute," Father would answer, his jaw quivering. He stabbed a look at Mother, who might say, "Don't run into the ditch before you get there," or, "Good riddance," and then he would slink away. Mother watched him go with arms crossed over her chest, her face closed like the lid on a box of snakes. We children bawled. Where could he go? To the truck stop, that den of iniquity? To one of those dark, ratty flophouses in town? Would he wind up sleeping under a railroad bridge or on a park bench or in a cardboard box, mummied in rags, like the bums we had seen on our trips to Cleveland and Chicago? We bawled and bawled, wondering if he would ever come back.

He always did come back, a day or a week later, but each time there was a sliver less of him.

In Kafka's[7] *The Metamorphosis,* which opens famously with Gregor Samsa waking up from uneasy dreams to find himself transformed into an insect, Gregor's family keep reassuring themselves that things will be just fine again, "When he comes back to us." Each time alcohol transformed our father, we held out the same hope, that he would really and truly come back to us, our authentic father, the tender and playful and competent man, and then all things would be fine. We had grounds for such hope. After his weepy departures and chapfallen returns, he would sometimes go weeks, even months without drinking. Those were glad times. Joy banged inside my ribs. Every day without the furtive glint of bottles, every meal without a fight, every bedtime without sobs encouraged us to believe that such bliss might go on forever.

Mother was fooled by just such a hope all during the forty-odd years she knew this Greeley Ray Sanders. Soon after she met him in a Chicago delicatessen on the eve of World War II and fell for his butter-melting Mississippi drawl and his wavy red hair, she learned that he drank heavily. But then so did a lot of men. She would soon coax or scold him into breaking the nasty habit. She would point out to him how ugly and foolish it was, this bleary drinking, and then he would quit. He refused to quit during their engagement, however, still refused during the first years of marriage, refused until my sister came along. The shock of fatherhood sobered him, and he remained sober through my birth at the end of the war and right on through until we moved in 1951 to the Ohio arsenal, that paradise of bombs. Like all places that make a business of death, the arsenal had more than its share of alcoholics and drug addicts and other varieties of escape artists. There I turned six and started school and woke into a child's flickering awareness, just in time to see my father begin sneaking swigs in the garage.

He sobered up again for most of a year at the height of the Korean War, to celebrate the birth of my brother. But aside from that dry spell, his only breaks from drinking before I graduated from high school were just long enough to raise and then dash our hopes. Then during the fall of my senior year—the time of the Cuban missile crisis, when it seemed that the nightly explosions at the munitions dump and the nightly rages in our household might spread to engulf the globe—Father collapsed. His liver, kidneys, and heart all conked out. The doctors saved him, but only by a hair. He stayed in the hospital for weeks, going through a withdrawal so terrible that Mother would not let us visit him. If he wanted to kill himself, the doctors solemnly warned him, all he had to do was hit the bottle again. One binge would finish him.

Father must have believed them, for he stayed dry the next fifteen years. It was an answer to prayer, Mother said, it was a miracle. I believe it was a reflex of fear, which he sustained over the years through courage and pride. He knew a man could die from drink, for his brother Roscoe had. We children never laid

40

7. Franz Kafka (1883–1924), Prague-born novelist and short-story writer whose works raise puzzling moral, spiritual, and political dilemmas.

eyes on doomed Uncle Roscoe, but in the stories Mother told us he became a fairy-tale figure, like a boy who took the wrong turning in the woods and was gobbled up by the wolf.

The fifteen-year dry spell came to an end with Father's retirement in the spring of 1978. Like many men, he gave up his identity along with his job. One day he was a boss at the factory, with a brass plate on his door and a reputation to uphold; the next day he was a nobody at home. He and Mother were leaving Ontario, the last of the many places to which his job had carried them, and they were moving to a new house in Mississippi, his childhood stomping grounds. As a boy in Mississippi, Father sold Coca-Cola during dances while the moonshiners peddled their brew in the parking lot; as a young blade, he fought in bars and in the ring, seeking a state Golden Gloves championship; he gambled at poker, hunted pheasants, raced motorcycles and cars, played semiprofessional baseball, and, along with all his buddies—in the Black Cat Saloon, behind the cotton gin, in the woods—he drank. It was a perilous youth to dream of recovering.

After his final day of work, Mother drove on ahead with a car full of begonias and violets, while Father stayed behind to oversee the packing. When the van was loaded, the sweaty movers broke open a six-pack and offered him a beer.

"Let's drink to retirement!" they crowed. "Let's drink to freedom! to fishing! hunting! loafing! Let's drink to a guy who's going home!"

At least I imagine some such words, for that is all I can do, imagine, and I see Father's hand trembling in midair as he thinks about the fifteen sober years and about the doctors' warning, and he tells himself *God damnit, I am a free man,* and *Why can't a free man drink one beer after a lifetime of hard work?* and I see his arm reaching, his fingers closing, the can tilting to his lips. I even supply a label for the beer, a swaggering brand that promises on television to deliver the essence of life. I watch the amber liquid pour down his throat, the alcohol steal into his blood, the key turn in his brain.

45 Soon after my parents moved back to Father's treacherous stomping ground, my wife and I visited them in Mississippi with our five-year-old daughter. Mother had been too distraught to warn me about the return of the demons. So when I climbed out of the car that bright July morning and saw my father napping in the hammock, I felt uneasy, for in all his sober years I had never known him to sleep in daylight. Then he lurched upright, blinked his bloodshot eyes, and greeted us in a syrupy voice. I was hurled back helpless into childhood.

"What's the matter with Papaw?" our daughter asked.

"Nothing," I said. "Nothing!"

Like a child again, I pretended not to see him in his stupor, and behind my phony smile I grieved. On that visit and on the few that remained before his death, once again I found bottles in the workbench, bottles in the woods. Again his hands shook too much for him to run a saw, to make his precious miniature furniture, to drive straight down back roads. Again he wound up in the ditch, in the hospital, in jail, in treatment centers. Again he shouted and wept. Again he lied. "I never touched a drop," he swore. "Your mother's making it up."

I no longer fancied I could reason with the men whose names I found on the bottles—Jim Beam, Jack Daniels—nor did I hope to save my father by burning down a store. I was able now to press the cold statistics about alcoholism against the ache of memory: ten million victims, fifteen million, twenty. And yet, in spite of my age, I reacted in the same blind way as I had in childhood, ignoring biology, forgetting numbers, vainly seeking to erase through my efforts whatever drove him to drink. I worked on their place twelve and sixteen hours a day, in the swelter of Mississippi summers, digging ditches, running electrical wires, planting trees, mowing grass, building sheds, as though what nagged at him was some list of chores, as though by taking his worries on my shoulders I could redeem him. I was flung back into boyhood, acting as though my father would not drink himself to death if only I were perfect.

I failed of perfection; he succeeded in dying. To the end, he considered himself not sick but sinful. "Do you want to kill yourself?" I asked him. "Why not?" he answered. "Why the hell not? What's there to save?" To the end, he would not speak about his feelings, would not or could not give a name to the beast that was devouring him. 50

In silence, he went rushing off the cliff. Unlike the biblical swine, however, he left behind a few of the demons to haunt his children. Life with him and the loss of him twisted us into shapes that will be familiar to other sons and daughters of alcoholics. My brother became a rebel, my sister retreated into shyness, I played the stalwart and dutiful son who would hold the family together. If my father was unstable, I would be a rock. If he squandered money on drink, I would pinch every penny. If he wept when drunk—and only when drunk—I would not let myself weep at all. If he roared at the Little League umpire for calling my pitches balls, I would throw nothing but strikes. Watching him flounder and rage, I came to dread the loss of control. I would go through life without making anyone mad. I vowed never to put in my mouth or veins any chemical that would banish my everyday self. I would never make a scene, never lash out at the ones I loved, never hurt a soul. Through hard work, relentless work, I would achieve something dazzling—in the classroom, on the basketball floor, in the science lab, in the pages of books—and my achievement would distract the world's eyes from his humiliation. I would become a worthy sacrifice, and the smoke of my burning would please God.

It is far easier to recognize these twists in my character than to undo them. Work has become an addiction for me, as drink was an addiction for my father. Knowing this, my daughter gave me a placard for the wall: WORKAHOLIC. The labor is endless and futile, for I can no more redeem myself through work than I could redeem my father. I still panic in the face of other people's anger, because his drunken temper was so terrible. I shrink from causing sadness or disappointment even to strangers, as though I were still concealing the family shame. I still notice every twitch of emotion in the faces around me, having learned as a child to read the weather in faces, and I blame myself for their least pang of unhappiness or anger. In certain moods I blame myself for everything. Guilt burns like acid in my veins.

I am moved to write these pages now because my own son, at the age of ten, is taking on himself the griefs of the world, and in particular the griefs of his father. He tells me that when I am gripped by sadness he feels responsible; he feels there must be something he can do to spring me from depression, to fix my life. And that crushing sense of responsibility is exactly what I felt at the age of ten in the face of my father's drinking. My son wonders if I, too, am possessed. I write, therefore, to drag into the light what eats at me—the fear, the guilt, the shame—so that my own children may be spared.

I still shy away from nightclubs, from bars, from parties where the solvent is alcohol. My friends puzzle over this, but it is no more peculiar than for a man to shy away from the lions' den after seeing his father torn apart. I took my own first drink at the age of twenty-one, half a glass of burgundy. I knew the odds of my becoming an alcoholic were four times higher than for the sons of nonalcoholic fathers. So I sipped warily.

55 I still do—once a week, perhaps, a glass of wine, a can of beer, nothing stronger, nothing more. I listen for the turning of a key in my brain.

QUESTIONS

1. Sanders frequently punctuates his memories of his father with information from other sources—dictionaries, medical encyclopedias, poems and short stories, the Bible. What function do these sources perform? How do they enlarge and enrich Sanders's essay?

2. Why does Sanders include the final three paragraphs (53–55)? What effect do they create that would be lost without them?

3. Drawing on your memories of a friend or family member, write an essay about some problem that person had and its effect on your life.

ANNIE DILLARD from *An American Childhood*

ONE SUNDAY AFTERNOON Mother wandered through our kitchen, where Father was making a sandwich and listening to the ball game. The Pirates were playing the New York Giants at Forbes Field. In those days, the Giants had a utility infielder named Wayne Terwilliger. Just as Mother passed through, the radio announcer cried—with undue drama—"Terwilliger bunts one!"

"Terwilliger bunts one?" Mother cried back, stopped short. She turned. "Is that English?"

"The player's name is Terwilliger," Father said. "He bunted."

From An American Childhood, *Dillard's 1987 memoir of growing up in Pittsburgh.*

"That's marvelous," Mother said. "'Terwilliger bunts one.' No wonder you listen to baseball. 'Terwilliger bunts one.'"

For the next seven or eight years, Mother made this surprising string of syllables her own. Testing a microphone, she repeated, "Terwilliger bunts one"; testing a pen or a typewriter, she wrote it. If, as happened surprisingly often in the course of various improvised gags, she pretended to whisper something else in my ear, she actually whispered, "Terwilliger bunts one." Whenever someone used a French phrase, or a Latin one, she answered solemnly, "Terwilliger bunts one." If Mother had had, like Andrew Carnegie, the opportunity to cook up a motto for a coat of arms, hers would have read simply and tellingly, "Terwilliger bunts one." (Carnegie's was "Death to Privilege.")

She served us with other words and phrases. On a Florida trip, she repeated tremulously, "That . . . is a royal poinciana." I don't remember the tree; I remember the thrill in her voice. She pronounced it carefully, and spelled it. She also liked to say "portulaca."

The drama of the words "Tamiami Trail" stirred her, we learned on the same Florida trip. People built Tampa on one coast, and they built Miami on another. Then—the height of visionary ambition and folly—they piled a slow, tremendous road through the terrible Everglades to connect them. To build the road, men stood sunk in muck to their armpits. They fought off cottonmouth moccasins and six-foot alligators. They slept in boats, wet. They blasted muck with dynamite, cut jungle with machetes; they laid logs, dragged drilling machines, hauled dredges, heaped limestone. The road took fourteen years to build up by the shovelful, a Panama Canal in reverse, and cost hundreds of lives from tropical, mosquito-carried diseases. Then, capping it all, some genius thought of the word Tamiami: they called the road from Tampa to Miami, this very road under our spinning wheels, the Tamiami Trail. Some called it Alligator Alley. Anyone could drive over this road without a thought.

Hearing this, moved, I thought all the suffering of road building was worth it (it wasn't my suffering), now that we had this new thing to hang these new words on—Alligator Alley for those who liked things cute, and, for connoisseurs like Mother, for lovers of the human drama in all its boldness and terror, the Tamiami Trail.

Back home, Mother cut clips from reels of talk, as it were, and played them back at leisure. She noticed that many Pittsburghers confuse "leave" and "let." One kind relative brightened our morning by mentioning why she'd brought her son to visit: "He wanted to come with me, so I left him." Mother filled in Amy and me on locutions we missed. "I can't do it on Friday," her pretty sister told a crowded dinner party, "because Friday's the day I lay in the stores."

(All unconsciously, though, we ourselves used some pure Pittsburghisms. We said "tele pole," pronounced "telly pole," for that splintery sidewalk post I loved to climb. We said "slippy"—the sidewalks are "slippy." We said, "That's all the farther I could go." And we said, as Pittsburghers do say, "This glass needs washed," or "The dog needs walked"—a usage our father eschewed; he knew it was not standard English, nor even comprehensible English, but he never let on.)

"Spell 'poinsettia,'" Mother would throw out at me, smiling with pleasure. "Spell 'sherbet.'" The idea was not to make us whizzes, but, quite the contrary, to remind us—and I, especially, needed reminding—that we didn't know it all just yet.

"There's a deer standing in the front hall," she told me one quiet evening in the country.

"Really?"

"No. I just wanted to tell you something once without your saying, 'I know.'"

15 Supermarkets in the middle 1950s began luring, or bothering, customers by giving out Top Value Stamps or Green Stamps. When, shopping with Mother, we got to the head of the checkout line, the checker, always a young man, asked, "Save stamps?"

"No," Mother replied genially, week after week, "I build model airplanes." I believe she originated this line. It took me years to determine where the joke lay.

Anyone who met her verbal challenges she adored. She had surgery on one of her eyes. On the operating table, just before she conked out, she appealed feelingly to the surgeon, saying, as she had been planning to say for weeks, "Will I be able to play the piano?" "Not on me," the surgeon said. "You won't pull that old one on me."

It was, indeed, an old one. The surgeon was supposed to answer, "Yes, my dear, brave woman, you will be able to play the piano after this operation," to which Mother intended to reply, "Oh, good, I've always wanted to play the piano." This pat scenario bored her; she loved having it interrupted. It must have galled her that usually her acquaintances were so predictably unalert; it must have galled her that, for the length of her life, she could surprise everyone so continually, so easily, when she had been the same all along. At any rate, she loved anyone who, as she put it, saw it coming, and called her on it.

She regarded the instructions on bureaucratic forms as straight lines. "Do you advocate the overthrow of the United States government by force or violence?" After some thought she wrote, "Force." She regarded children, even babies, as straight men. When Molly learned to crawl, Mother delighted in buying her gowns with drawstrings at the bottom, like Swee'pea's,[1] because, as she explained energetically, you could easily step on the drawstring without the baby's noticing, so that she crawled and crawled and crawled and never got anywhere except into a small ball at the gown's top.

20 When we children were young, she mothered us tenderly and dependably; as we got older, she resumed her career of anarchism. She collared us into her gags. If she answered the phone on a wrong number, she told the caller, "Just a minute," and dragged the receiver to Amy or me, saying, "Here, take this, your name is Cecile," or, worse, just, "It's for you." You had to think on your feet. But did you want to perform well as Cecile, or did you want to take pity on the wretched caller?

1. The infant in the comic strip *Popeye* by Elzie Crisler Segar.

During a family trip to the Highland Park Zoo, Mother and I were alone for a minute. She approached a young couple holding hands on a bench by the seals, and addressed the young man in dripping tones: "Where have you been? Still got those baby-blue eyes; always did slay me. And this"—a swift nod at the dumbstruck young woman, who had removed her hand from the man's—"must be the one you were telling me about. She's not so bad, really, as you used to make out. But listen, you know how I miss you, you know where to reach me, same old place. And there's Ann over there—see how she's grown? See the blue eyes?"

And off she sashayed, taking me firmly by the hand, and leading us around briskly past the monkey house and away. She cocked an ear back, and both of us heard the desperate man begin, in a high-pitched wail, "I swear, I never saw her before in my life. . . ."

On a long, sloping beach by the ocean, she lay stretched out sunning with Father and friends, until the conversation gradually grew tedious, when without forethought she gave a little push with her heel and rolled away. People were stunned. She rolled deadpan and apparently effortlessly, arms and legs extended and tidy, down the beach to the distant water's edge, where she lay at ease just as she had been, but half in the surf, and well out of earshot.

She dearly loved to fluster people by throwing out a game's rules at whim—when she was getting bored, losing in a dull sort of way, and when everybody else was taking it too seriously. If you turned your back, she moved the checkers around on the board. When you got them all straightened out, she denied she'd touched them; the next time you turned your back, she lined them up on the rug or hid them under your chair. In a betting rummy game called Michigan, she routinely played out of turn, or called out a card she didn't hold, or counted backward, simply to amuse herself by causing an uproar and watching the rest of us do double takes and have fits. (Much later, when serious suitors came to call, Mother subjected them to this fast card game as a trial by ordeal; she used it as an intelligence test and a measure of spirit. If the poor man could stay a round without breaking down or running out, he got to marry one of us, if he still wanted to.)

25

She excelled at bridge, playing fast and boldly, but when the stakes were low and the hands dull, she bid slams for the devilment of it, or raised her opponents' suit to bug them, or showed her hand, or tossed her cards in a handful behind her back in a characteristic swift motion accompanied by a vibrantly innocent look. It drove our stolid father crazy. The hand was over before it began, and the guests were appalled. How do you score it, who deals now, what do you do with a crazy person who is having so much fun? Or they were down seven, and the guests were appalled. "Pam!" "Dammit, Pam!" He groaned. What ails such people? What on earth possesses them? He rubbed his face.

She was an unstoppable force; she never let go. When we moved across town, she persuaded the U.S. Post Office to let her keep her old address—forever—because she'd had stationery printed. I don't know how she did it. Every new post office worker, over decades, needed to learn that although the Doaks' mail is addressed to here, it is delivered to there.

Mother's energy and intelligence suited her for a greater role in a larger arena—mayor of New York, say—than the one she had. She followed American politics closely; she had been known to vote for Democrats. She saw how things should be run, but she had nothing to run but our household. Even there, small minds bugged her; she was smarter than the people who designed the things she had to use all day for the length of her life.

"Look," she said. "Whoever designed this corkscrew never used one. Why would anyone sell it without trying it out?" So she invented a better one. She showed me a drawing of it. The spirit of American enterprise never faded in Mother. If capitalizing and tooling up had been as interesting as theorizing and thinking up, she would have fired up a new factory every week, and chaired several hundred corporations.

"It grieves me," she would say, "it grieves my heart," that the company that made one superior product packaged it poorly, or took the wrong tack in its advertising. She knew, as she held the thing mournfully in her two hands, that she'd never find another. She was right. We children wholly sympathized, and so did Father; what could she do, what could anyone do, about it? She was Samson in chains.[2] She paced.

30 She didn't like the taste of stamps so she didn't lick stamps; she licked the corner of the envelope instead. She glued sandpaper to the sides of kitchen drawers, and under kitchen cabinets, so she always had a handy place to strike a match. She designed, and hounded workmen to build against all norms, doubly wide kitchen counters and elevated bathroom sinks. To splint a finger, she stuck it in a lightweight cigar tube. Conversely, to protect a pack of cigarettes, she carried it in a Band-Aid box. She drew plans for an over-the-finger toothbrush for babies, an oven rack that slid up and down, and—the family favorite—Lendalarm. Lendalarm was a beeper you attached to books (or tools) you loaned friends. After ten days, the beeper sounded. Only the rightful owner could silence it.

She repeatedly reminded us of P. T. Barnum's dictum: You could sell anything to anybody if you marketed it right. The adman who thought of making Americans believe they needed underarm deodorant was a visionary. So, too, was the hero who made a success of a new product, Ivory soap. The executives were horrified, Mother told me, that a cake of this stuff floated. Soap wasn't supposed to float. Anyone would be able to tell it was mostly whipped-up air. Then some inspired adman made a leap: Advertise that it floats. Flaunt it. The rest is history.

She respected the rare few who broke through to new ways. "Look," she'd say, "here's an intelligent apron." She called upon us to admire intelligent control knobs and intelligent pan handles, intelligent andirons and picture frames and knife sharpeners. She questioned everything, every pair of scissors, every knitting needle, gardening glove, tape dispenser. Hers was a restless mental vigor that just about ignited the dumb household objects with its force.

2. The Israelite champion against the Philistines, to whom he was betrayed by Delilah (see Judges 14–16).

Torpid conformity was a kind of sin; it was stupidity itself, the mighty stream against which Mother would never cease to struggle. If you held no minority opinions, or if you failed to risk total ostracism for them daily, the world would be a better place without you.

Always I heard Mother's emotional voice asking Amy and me the same few questions: Is that your own idea? Or somebody else's? "*Giant* is a good movie," I pronounced to the family at dinner. "Oh, really?" Mother warmed to these occasions. She all but rolled up her sleeves. She knew I hadn't seen it. "Is that your considered opinion?"

35 She herself held many unpopular, even fantastic, positions. She was scathingly sarcastic about the McCarthy hearings[3] while they took place, right on our living-room television; she frantically opposed Father's wait-and-see calm. "We don't know enough about it," he said. "I do," she said. "I know all I need to know."

She asserted, against all opposition, that people who lived in trailer parks were not bad but simply poor, and had as much right to settle on beautiful land, such as rural Ligonier, Pennsylvania, as did the oldest of families in the finest of hidden houses. Therefore, the people who owned trailer parks, and sought zoning changes to permit trailer parks, needed our help. Her profound belief that the country-club pool sweeper was a person, and that the department-store saleslady, the bus driver, telephone operator, and housepainter were people, and even in groups the steelworkers who carried pickets and the Christmas shoppers who clogged intersections were people—this was a conviction common enough in democratic Pittsburgh, but not altogether common among our friends' parents, or even, perhaps, among our parents' friends.

Opposition emboldened Mother, and she would take on anybody on any issue—the chairman of the board, at a cocktail party, on the current strike; she would fly at him in a flurry of passion, as a songbird selflessly attacks a big hawk.

"Eisenhower's going to win," I announced after school. She lowered her magazine and looked me in the eyes: "How do you know?" I was doomed. It was fatal to say, "Everyone says so." We all knew well what happened. "Do you consult this Everyone before you make your decisions? What if Everyone decided to round up all the Jews?" Mother knew there was no danger of cowing me. She simply tried to keep us all awake. And in fact it was always clear to Amy and me, and to Molly when she grew old enough to listen, that if our classmates came to cruelty, just as much as if the neighborhood or the nation came to madness, we were expected to take, and would be each separately capable of taking, a stand.

3. In televised hearings in 1954, the Army accused Wisconsin senator Joseph R. McCarthy (1908–1957) of improperly seeking preferential treatment for a former colleague then in the service. Senator McCarthy, widely known as a Communist hunter, accused the Army of covering up certain espionage action, which led to the senator's loss of public favor and contributed to his "condemnation" by the Senate in December 1954.

QUESTIONS

1. Dillard piles up examples in this excerpt, barely creating transitions between them. What do the many examples add up to? Is there an overall point she wishes to make about her mother? Try to state it in your own words.

2. When this piece was originally published in Dillard's *An American Childhood*, the chapter had no title. If you could title this piece, what would that title be? Why?

3. Do some free-writing about one of your own parents (or someone important in your life when you were a child). Like Dillard, use as many specific examples as possible to communicate that person's character and personality.

JUDITH ORTIZ COFER *More Room*

MY GRANDMOTHER'S HOUSE is like a chambered nautilus; it has many rooms, yet it is not a mansion. Its proportions are small and its design simple. It is a house that has grown organically, according to the needs of its inhabitants. To all of us in the family it is known as *la casa de Mamá*.[1] It is the place of our origin; the stage for our memories and dreams of Island life.

I remember how in my childhood it sat on stilts; this was before it had a downstairs. It rested on its perch like a great blue bird, not a flying sort of bird, more like a nesting hen, but with spread wings. Grandfather had built it soon after their marriage. He was a painter and housebuilder by trade, a poet and meditative man by nature. As each of their eight children were born, new rooms were added. After a few years, the paint did not exactly match, nor the materials, so that there was a chronology to it, like the rings of a tree, and Mamá could tell you the history of each room in her *casa*, and thus the genealogy of the family along with it.

Her room is the heart of the house. Though I have seen it recently, and both woman and room have diminished in size, changed by the new perspective of my eyes, now capable of looking over countertops and tall beds, it is not this picture I carry in my memory of Mamá's *casa*. Instead, I see her room as a queen's chamber where a small woman loomed large, a throne-room with a massive four-poster bed in its center which stood taller than a child's head. It was on this bed where her own children had been born that the smallest grandchildren were allowed to take naps in the afternoons; here too was where Mamá secluded herself to dispense private advice to her daughters, sitting on the edge of the bed, looking down at whoever sat on the rocker where genera-

From Cofer's 1990 book, Silent Dancing: A Partial Reminiscence of a Puerto Rican Childhood, *which won the 1991 PEN/Martha Albrand Special Citation for Nonfiction.*

1. Mama's house.

tions of babies had been sung to sleep. To me she looked like a wise empress right out of the fairy tales I was addicted to reading.

Though the room was dominated by the mahogany four-posters, it also contained all of Mamá's symbols of power. On her dresser instead of cosmetics there were jars filled with herbs: *yerba buena, yerba mala,*[2] the making of purgatives and teas to which we were all subjected during childhood crises. She had a steaming cup for anyone who could not, or would not, get up to face life on any given day. If the acrid aftertaste of her cures for malingering did not get you out of bed, then it was time to call *el doctor.*

And there was the monstrous chifforobe she kept locked with a little golden key she did not hide. This was a test of her dominion over us; though my cousins and I wanted a look inside that massive wardrobe more than anything, we never reached for that little key lying on top of her Bible on the dresser. This was also where she placed her earrings and rosary at night. God's word was her security system. This chifforobe was the place where I imagined she kept jewels, satin slippers, and elegant sequined, silk gowns of heart-breaking fineness. I lusted after those imaginary costumes. I had heard that Mamá had been a great beauty in her youth, and the belle of many balls. My cousins had other ideas as to what she kept in that wooden vault: its secret could be money (Mamá did not hand cash to strangers, banks were out of the question, so there were stories that her mattress was stuffed with dollar bills, and that she buried coins in jars in her garden under rosebushes, or kept them in her inviolate chifforobe); there might be that legendary gun salvaged from the Spanish-American conflict over the Island. We went wild over suspected treasures that we made up simply because children have to fill locked trunks with something wonderful. 5

On the wall above the bed hung a heavy silver crucifix. Christ's agonized head hung directly over Mamá's pillow. I avoided looking at this weapon suspended over where her head would lay; and on the rare occasions when I was allowed to sleep on that bed, I scooted down to the safe middle of the mattress, where her body's impression took me in like a mother's lap. Having taken care of the obligatory religious decoration with a crucifix, Mamá covered the other walls with objects sent to her over the years by her children in the States. *Los Nueva Yores*[3] were represented by, among other things, a postcard of Niagara Falls from her son Hernán, postmarked, Buffalo, N.Y. In a conspicuous gold frame hung a large color photograph of her daughter Nena, her husband and their five children at the entrance to Disneyland in California. From us she had gotten a black lace fan. Father had brought it to her from a tour of duty with the Navy in Europe (on Sundays she would remove it from its hook on the wall to fan herself at Sunday mass). Each year more items were added as the family grew and dispersed, and every object in the room had a story attached to it, a *cuento*[4] which Mamá would bestow on anyone who received the privilege of a day alone with her. It was almost worth pretending to be sick, though the

2. Good herbs, bad herbs.
3. The New Yorkers.
4. Tale.

bitter herb purgatives of the body were a big price to pay for the spirit revivals of her story-telling.

Mamá slept alone on her large bed, except for the times when a sick grandchild warranted the privilege, or when a heartbroken daughter came home in need of more than herbal teas. In the family there is a story about how this came to be.

When one of the daughters, my mother or one of her sisters, tells the *cuento* of how Mamá came to own her nights, it is usually preceded by the qualifications that Papá's exile from his wife's room was not a result of animosity between the couple, but that the act had been Mamá's famous bloodless coup for her personal freedom. Papá was the benevolent dictator of her body and her life who had had to be banished from her bed so that Mamá could better serve her family. Before the telling, we had to agree that the old man was not to blame. We all recognized that in the family Papá was as an *alma de Dios*,[5] a saintly, soft-spoken presence whose main pleasures in life, such as writing poetry and reading the Spanish large-type editions of *Reader's Digest*, always took place outside the vortex of Mamá's crowded realm. It was not his fault, after all, that every year or so he planted a babyseed in Mamá's fertile body, keeping her from leading the active life she needed and desired. He loved her and the babies. Papá composed odes and lyrics to celebrate births and anniversaries and hired musicians to accompany him in singing them to his family and friends at extravagant pig-roasts he threw yearly. Mamá and the oldest girls worked for days preparing the food. Papá sat for hours in his painter's shed, also his study and library, composing the songs. At these celebrations he was also known to give long speeches in praise of God, his fecund wife, and his beloved island. As a middle child, my mother remembers these occasions as a time when the women sat in the kitchen and lamented their burdens, while the men feasted out in the patio, their rum-thickened voice rising in song and praise for each other, *compañeros* all.[6]

It was after the birth of her eighth child, after she had lost three at birth or in infancy, that Mamá made her decision. They say that Mamá had had a special way of letting her husband know that they were expecting, one that had begun when, at the beginning of their marriage, he had built her a house too confining for her taste. So, when she discovered her first pregnancy, she supposedly drew plans for another room, which he dutifully executed. Every time a child was due, she would demand, *more space, more space.* Papá acceded to her wishes, child after child, since he had learned early that Mamá's renowned temper was a thing that grew like a monster along with a new belly. In this way Mamá got the house that she wanted, but with each child she lost in heart and energy. She had knowledge of her body and perceived that if she had any more children, her dreams and her plans would have to be permanently forgotten, because she would be a chronically ill woman, like Flora with her twelve children: asthma, no teeth, in bed more than on her feet.

10 And so, after my youngest uncle was born, she asked Papá to build a large room at the back of the house. He did so in joyful anticipation. Mamá had

5. Literally, "soul of God." A thoroughly good person.

6. Companions.

asked him special things this time: shelves on the walls, a private entrance. He thought that she meant this room to be a nursery where several children could sleep. He thought it was a wonderful idea. He painted it his favorite color, sky blue, and made large windows looking out over a green hill and the church spires beyond. But nothing happened. Mamá's belly did not grow, yet she seemed in a frenzy of activity over the house. Finally, an anxious Papá approached his wife to tell her that the new room was finished and ready to be occupied. And Mamá, they say, replied: "Good, it's for *you*."

And so it was that Mamá discovered the only means of birth control available to a Catholic woman of her time: sacrifice. She gave up the comfort of Papá's sexual love for something she deemed greater: the right to own and control her body, so that she might live to meet her grandchildren—me among them—so that she could give more of herself to the ones already there, so that she could be more than a channel for other lives, so that even now that time has robbed her of the elasticity of her body and of her amazing reservoir of energy, she still emanates the kind of joy that can only be achieved by living according to the dictates of one's own heart.

Questions

1. At the end of the essay, Cofer explains in fairly direct terms why her grandmother wanted "more room." Why do you think she uses narration as the primary mode in the rest of the essay? What does she gain by first narrating, then explaining?

2. Cofer uses many similes and metaphors—for example, in paragraph 1 she says that her grandmother's house was "like a chambered nautilus" and in paragraph 5 that her grandmother's Bible was "her security system." Discuss the use of one or two such comparisons that you find particularly effective.

3. What are the possible meanings of the title?

4. Write about a favorite or mysterious place you remember from childhood.

N. Scott Momaday *The Way to Rainy Mountain*

A single knoll rises out of the plain in Oklahoma, north and west of the Wichita Range. For my people, the Kiowas, it is an old landmark, and they gave it the name Rainy Mountain. The hardest weather in the world is there. Winter brings blizzards, hot tornadic winds arise in the spring, and in summer the prairie is an anvil's edge. The grass turns brittle and brown, and it cracks beneath your feet. There are green belts along the rivers and creeks, linear groves of hickory

First published in 1967 in the Reporter, *a now defunct small-circulation American magazine; reprinted in* The Way to Rainy Mountain, *Momaday's 1969 book about the west. The illustrations were drawn by the author's father, Al Momaday.*

and pecan, willow and witch hazel. At a distance in July or August the steaming foliage seems almost to writhe in fire. Great green and yellow grasshoppers are everywhere in the tall grass, popping up like corn to sting the flesh, and tortoises crawl about on the red earth, going nowhere in the plenty of time. Loneliness is an aspect of the land. All things in the plain are isolate; there is no confusion of objects in the eye, but *one* hill or *one* tree or *one* man. To look upon that landscape in the early morning, with the sun at your back, is to lose the sense of proportion. Your imagination comes to life, and this, you think, is where Creation was begun.

I returned to Rainy Mountain in July. My grandmother had died in the spring, and I wanted to be at her grave. She had lived to be very old and at last infirm. Her only living daughter was with her when she died, and I was told that in death her face was that of a child.

I like to think of her as a child. When she was born, the Kiowas were living the last great moment of their history. For more than a hundred years they had controlled the open range from the Smoky Hill River to the Red, from the headwaters of the Canadian to the fork of the Arkansas and Cimarron. In alliance with the Comanches, they had ruled the whole of the southern Plains. War was their sacred business, and they were among the finest horsemen the world has ever known. But warfare for the Kiowas was preeminently a matter of disposition rather than of survival, and they never understood the grim, unrelenting advance of the U.S. Cavalry. When at last, divided and ill-provisioned, they were driven onto the Staked Plains in the cold rains of autumn, they fell into panic. In Palo Duro Canyon they abandoned their crucial stores to pillage and had nothing then but their lives. In order to save themselves, they surrendered to the soldiers at Fort Sill and were imprisoned in the old stone corral that now stands as a military museum. My grandmother was spared the humiliation of those high gray walls by eight or ten years, but she must have known from birth the affliction of defeat, the dark brooding of old warriors.

Her name was Aho, and she belonged to the last culture to evolve in North America. Her forebears came down from the high country in western Montana nearly three centuries ago. They were a mountain people, a mysterious tribe of hunters whose language has never been positively classified in any major group. In the late seventeenth century they began a long migration to the south and east. It was a journey toward the dawn, and it led to a golden age. Along the way the Kiowas were befriended by the Crows, who gave them the culture and religion of the Plains. They acquired horses, and their ancient nomadic spirit was

suddenly free of the ground. They acquired Tai-me, the sacred Sun Dance doll, from that moment the object and symbol of their worship, and so shared in the divinity of the sun. Not least, they acquired the sense of destiny, therefore courage and pride. When they entered upon the southern Plains they had been transformed. No longer were they slaves to the simple necessity of survival; they were a lordly and dangerous society of fighters and thieves, hunters and priests of the sun. According to their origin myth, they entered the world through a hollow log. From one point of view, their migration was the fruit of an old prophecy, for indeed they emerged from a sunless world.

Although my grandmother lived out her long life in the shadow of Rainy Mountain, the immense landscape of the continental interior lay like memory in her blood. She could tell of the Crows, whom she had never seen, and of the Black Hills, where she had never been. I wanted to see in reality what she had seen more perfectly in the mind's eye, and traveled fifteen hundred miles to begin my pilgrimage. 5

Yellowstone, it seemed to me, was the top of the world, a region of deep lakes and dark timber, canyons and waterfalls. But, beautiful as it is, one might have the sense of confinement there. The skyline in all directions is

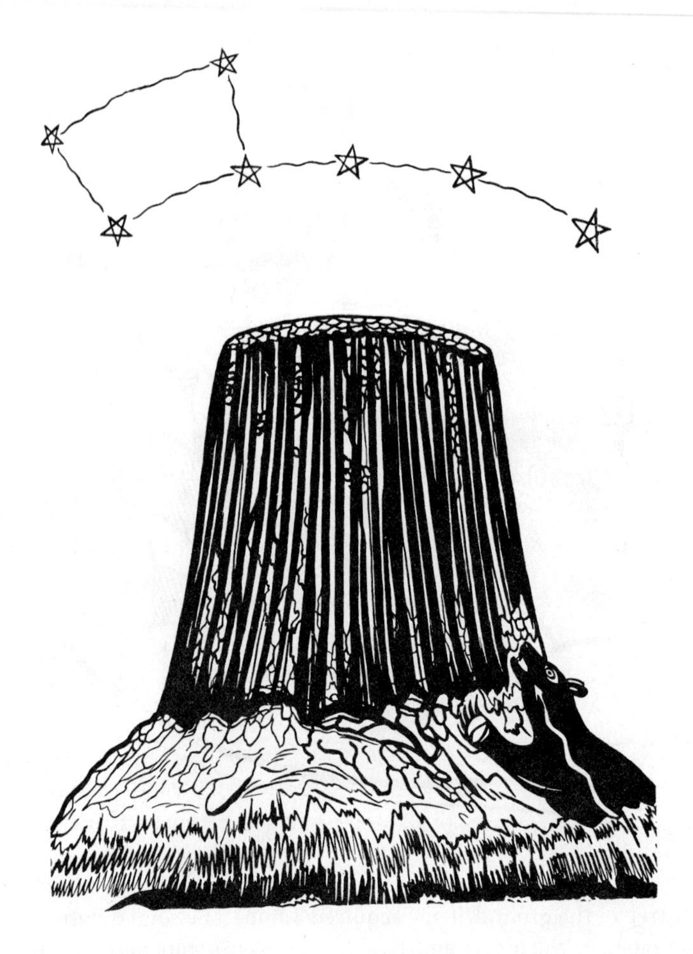

close at hand, the high wall of the woods and deep cleavages of shade. There is a perfect freedom in the mountains, but it belongs to the eagle and the elk, the badger and the bear. The Kiowas reckoned their stature by the distance they could see, and they were bent and blind in the wilderness.

Descending eastward, the highland meadows are a stairway to the plain. In July the inland slope of the Rockies is luxuriant with flax and buckwheat, stonecrop and larkspur. The earth unfolds and the limit of the land recedes. Clusters of trees, and animals grazing far in the distance, cause the vision to reach away and wonder to build upon the mind. The sun follows a longer course in the day, and the sky is immense beyond all comparison. The great billowing clouds that sail upon it are the shadows that move upon the grain like water, dividing light. Farther down, in the land of the Crows and Blackfeet, the plain is yellow. Sweet clover takes hold of the hills and bends upon itself to cover and seal the soil. There the Kiowas paused on their way; they had come to the place where they must change their lives. The sun is at home on the plains. Precisely there does it have the certain character of a god. When the Kiowas came to the land of the Crows, they could see the dark lees of the hills at dawn across the Bighorn River, the profusion of light on the grain shelves, the oldest deity ranging after the solstices. Not yet would they veer southward to the caldron of the land that lay below; they must wean their blood from the northern winter and hold the mountains a while longer in their view. They bore Tai-me in procession to the east.

A dark mist lay over the Black Hills, and the land was like iron. At the top of a ridge I caught sight of Devil's Tower upthrust against the gray sky as if in the birth of time the core of the earth had broken through its crust and the motion of the world was begun. There are things in nature that engender an awful quiet in the heart of man; Devil's Tower is one of them. Two centuries ago, because they could not do otherwise, the Kiowas made a legend at the base of the rock. My grandmother said:

> Eight children were there at play, seven sisters and their brother. Suddenly the boy was struck dumb; he trembled and began to run upon his hands and feet. His fingers became claws, and his body was covered with fur. Directly there was a bear where the boy had been. The sisters were terrified; they ran, and the bear after them. They came to the stump of a great tree, and the tree spoke to them. It bade them climb upon it, and as they did so it began to rise into the air. The bear came to kill them, but they were just beyond its reach. It reared against the tree and scored the bark all around with its claws. The seven sisters were borne into the sky, and they became the stars of the Big Dipper.

From that moment, and so long as the legend lives, the Kiowas have kinsmen in the night sky. Whatever they were in the mountains, they could be no more. However tenuous their well-being, however much they had suffered and would suffer again, they had found a way out of the wilderness.

My grandmother had a reverence for the sun, a holy regard that now is all but gone out of mankind. There was a wariness in her, and an ancient awe. She was a Christian in her later years, but she had come a long way about, and she never forgot her birthright. As a child she had been to the Sun Dances; she had taken part in those annual rites, and by them she had learned the restoration of her people in the presence of Tai-me. She was about seven when the last Kiowa Sun Dance was held in 1887 on the Washita River above Rainy Mountain Creek. The buffalo were gone. In order to consummate the ancient sacrifice—to impale the head of a buffalo bull upon the medicine tree—a delegation of old men journeyed into Texas, there to beg and barter for an animal from the Goodnight herd. She was ten when the Kiowas came together for the last time as a living Sun Dance culture. They could find no buffalo; they had to hang an old hide from the sacred tree. Before the dance could begin, a company of soldiers rode out from Fort Sill under orders to disperse the tribe. Forbidden without cause the essential act of their faith, having seen the wild herds slaughtered and left to rot upon the ground, the Kiowas backed away forever from the medicine tree. That was July 20, 1890, at the great bend of the Washita. My grandmother was there. Without bitterness, and for as long as she lived, she bore a vision of deicide.

10 Now that I can have her only in memory, I see my grandmother in the several postures that were peculiar to her: standing at the wood stove on a winter morning and turning meat in a great iron skillet; sitting at the south window, bent above her beadwork, and afterwards, when her vision failed, looking down for a long time into the fold of her hands; going out upon a cane, very slowly as she did when the weight of age came upon her; praying. I remember her most often at prayer. She made long, rambling prayers out of suffering and hope, having seen many things. I was never sure that I had the right to hear, so exclusive were they of all mere custom and company. The last time I saw her she prayed standing by the side of her bed at night, naked to the waist, the light of a kerosene lamp moving upon her dark skin. Her long, black hair, always drawn and braided in the day, lay upon her shoulders and against her breasts like a shawl. I do not speak Kiowa, and I never understood her prayers, but there was something inherently sad in the sound, some merest hesitation upon the syllables of sorrow. She began in a high and descending pitch, exhausting her breath to silence; then again and again—and always the same intensity of effort, of something that is, and is not, like urgency in the human voice. Transported so in the dancing light among the shadows of her room, she seemed beyond the reach of time. But that was illusion; I think I knew then that I should not see her again.

Houses are like sentinels in the plain, old keepers of the weather watch. There, in a very little while, wood takes on the appearance of great age. All colors wear soon away in the wind and rain, and then the wood is burned gray and the grain appears and the nails turn red with rust. The windowpanes are black and opaque; you imagine there is nothing within, and indeed there are many ghosts, bones given up to the land. They stand here and there against the sky, and you approach them for a longer time than you expect. They belong in the distance; it is their domain.

Once there was a lot of sound in my grandmother's house, a lot of coming and going, feasting and talk. The summers there were full of excitement and reunion. The Kiowas are a summer people; they abide the cold and keep to themselves, but when the season turns and the land becomes warm and vital they cannot hold still; an old love of going returns upon them. The aged visitors who came to my grandmother's house when I was a child were made of lean and leather, and they bore themselves upright. They wore great black hats and bright ample shirts that shook in the wind. They rubbed fat upon their hair and wound their braids with strips of colored cloth. Some of them painted their faces and carried the scars of old and cherished enmities. They were an old council of warlords, come to remind and be reminded of who they were. Their wives and daughters served them well. The women might indulge themselves; gossip was at once the mark and compensation of their servitude. They made loud and elaborate talk among themselves, full of jest and gesture, fright and false alarm. They went abroad in fringed and flowered shawls, bright beadwork and German silver. They were at home in the kitchen, and they prepared meals that were banquets.

There were frequent prayer meetings, and great nocturnal feasts. When I was a child I played with my cousins outside, where the lamplight fell upon the ground and the singing of the old people rose up around us and carried away into the darkness. There were a lot of good things to eat, a lot of laughter and surprise. And afterwards, when the quiet returned, I lay down with my grandmother and could hear the frogs away by the river and feel the motion of the air.

Now there is a funeral silence in the rooms, the endless wake of some final word. The walls have closed in upon my grandmother's house. When I returned to it in mourning, I saw for the first time in my life how small it was. It was late at night, and there was a white moon, nearly full. I sat for a long time on the stone steps by the kitchen door. From there I could see out across the land; I could see the long row of trees by the creek, the low light upon the rolling plains, and the stars of the Big Dipper. Once I looked at the moon and caught sight of a strange thing. A cricket had perched upon the handrail, only a few inches away from me. My line of vision was such that the creature filled the moon like a fossil. It had gone there, I thought, to live and die, for there, of all places, was its small definition made whole and eternal. A warm wind rose up and purled like the longing within me.

15 The next morning I awoke at dawn and went out on the dirt road to Rainy Mountain. It was already hot, and the grasshoppers began to fill the air. Still, it was early in the morning, and the birds sang out of the shadows. The long yellow grass on the mountain shone in the bright light, and a scissortail hied above the land. There, where it ought to be, at the end of a long and legendary way, was my grandmother's grave. Here and there on the dark stones were ancestral names. Looking back once, I saw the mountain and came away.

Questions

1. Throughout this essay, Momaday uses similes (comparisons with "like" or "as") and metaphors (comparisons without specific connectors). Which comparisons were most helpful in aiding your understanding? Which comparison was most surprising?

2. Momaday connects personal and cultural history to a particular place. Find another essay, either in "Portraits of People and Places" or "Nature and the Environment," that makes similar connections. Write a comparison of the two essays.

3. In paragraph 10, Momaday describes the roles that women played in his grandmother's Kiowa culture. Consider the roles women played in your grandmother's generation and culture; perhaps ask your mother or grandmother about their experiences. To what extent have those roles remained the same or changed in your generation? Write an account based on your conversations with older family members and your own personal knowledge.

Tom Wolfe *Yeager*

ANYONE WHO TRAVELS very much on airlines in the United States soon gets to know the voice of *the airline pilot* . . . coming over the intercom . . . with a particular drawl, a particular folksiness, a particular down-home calmness that is so exaggerated it begins to parody itself (nevertheless!—it's reassuring) . . . the voice that tells you, as the airliner is caught in thunderheads and goes bolting up and down a thousand feet at a single gulp, to check your seat belts because "it might get a little choppy" . . . the voice that tells you (on a flight from Phoenix preparing for its final approach into Kennedy Airport, New York, just after dawn): "Now, folks, uh . . . this is the captain . . . ummmm . . . We've got a little ol' red light up here on the control panel that's tryin' to tell us that the *lan*din' gears're not . . . uh . . . *lock*in' into position when we lower 'em . . . Now . . . *I* don't believe that little ol' red light knows what it's *talk*in' about—I believe it's that little ol' red light that iddn' workin' right" . . . faint chuckle, long pause, as if to say, *I'm not even sure all this is really worth going into—still, it may amuse you* . . . "*But* . . . I guess to play it by the rules, we oughta *humor* that little ol' light . . . so we're gonna take her down to about, oh, two or three hundred feet over the runway at Kennedy, and the folks down there on the ground are gonna see if they caint give us a *vis*ual inspection of those ol' landin' gears"—with which he is obviously on intimate ol'-buddy terms, as with every other working part of this mighty ship—"and if I'm right . . . they're gonna tell us everything is copa*cet*ic all the way aroun' an' we'll jes take her on in" . . . and, after a couple of low passes over the field, the voice returns: "Well, folks, those folks down there on the ground—it must be too early for 'em or somethin'—I 'spect they still got the *sleep*ers in their eyes . . . 'cause they say they caint tell if those ol' landin' gears are all the way down or not . . . But, you know, up here in the cockpit we're convinced they're all the way down, so we're jes gonna take her on in . . . And oh" . . . *(I almost forgot)* . . . "while we take a little swing out over the ocean an' empty some of that surplus fuel we're not gonna be needin' anymore—that's what you might be seein' comin' out of the wings—our lovely little ladies . . . if they'll be so kind . . . they're gonna go up and down the aisles and show you how we do what we call 'assumin' the position'" . . . another faint chuckle *(We do this so often, and it's so much fun, we even have a funny little name for it)* . . . and the stewardesses, a bit grimmer, by the looks of them, than *that voice,* start telling the passengers to take their glasses off and take the ballpoint pens and other sharp objects out of their pockets, and they show them *the position,* with the head lowered . . . while down on the field at Kennedy the little yellow emergency trucks start roaring across the field—and even though in your pounding heart and your sweating palms and your broiling brainpan you *know* this is a critical moment in your life, you still can't quite bring yourself to be*lieve* it,

From The Right Stuff, *Wolfe's 1979 account of the first astronauts, which was made into a 1983 movie.*

because if it were . . . how could *the captain,* the man who knows the actual situation most intimately . . . how could he keep on drawlin' and chucklin' and driftin' and lollygaggin' in that particular voice of his—

Well!—who doesn't know that voice! And who can forget it!—even after he is proved right and the emergency is over.

That particular voice may sound vaguely Southern or Southwestern, but it is specifically Appalachian in origin. It originated in the mountains of West Virginia, in the coal country, in Lincoln County, so far up in the hollows that, as the saying went, "they had to pipe in daylight." In the late 1940's and early 1950's this up-hollow voice drifted down from on high, from over the high desert of California, down, down, down, from the upper reaches of the Brotherhood into all phases of American aviation. It was amazing. It was *Pygmalion*[1] in reverse. Military pilots and then, soon, airline pilots, pilots from Maine and Massachusetts and the Dakotas and Oregon and everywhere else, began to talk in that poker-hollow West Virginia drawl, or as close to it as they could bend their native accents. It was the drawl of the most righteous of all the possessors of the right stuff: Chuck Yeager.

Yeager had started out as the equivalent, in the Second World War, of the legendary Frank Luke of the 27th Aero Squadron in the First. Which is to say, he was the boondocker, the boy from the back country, with only a high-school education, no credentials, no cachet or polish of any sort, who took off the feed-store overalls and put on a uniform and climbed into an airplane and lit up the skies over Europe.

Yeager grew up in Hamlin, West Virginia, a town on the Mud River not far from Nitro, Hurricane Whirlwind, Salt Rock, Mud, Sod, Crum, Leet, Dollie, Ruth, and Alum Creek. His father was a gas driller (drilling for natural gas in the coalfields), his older brother was a gas driller, and he would have been a gas driller had he not enlisted in the Army Air Force in 1941 at the age of eighteen. In 1943, at twenty, he became a flight officer, i.e., a non-com who was allowed to fly, and went to England to fly fighter planes over France and Germany. Even in the tumult of the war Yeager was somewhat puzzling to a lot of other pilots. He was a short, wiry, but muscular little guy with dark curly hair and a tough-looking face that seemed (to strangers) to be saying: "You best not be lookin' me in the eye, you peckerwood, or I'll put four more holes in your nose." But that wasn't what was puzzling. What was puzzling was the way Yeager talked. He seemed to talk with some older forms of English elocution, syntax, and conjugation that had been preserved up-hollow in the Appalachians. There were people up there who never said they disapproved of anything, they said: "I don't hold with it." In the present tense they were willing to *help* out, like anyone else; but in the past tense they only *holped.* "H'it weren't nothin' I hold with, but I holped him out with it, anyways."

1. An allusion to the play by Bernard Shaw (1856–1950), in which a teacher of phonetics attempts to transform a Cockney flower girl into an elegant lady by means of transforming her speech.

In his first eight missions, at the age of twenty, Yeager shot down two German fighters. On his ninth he was shot down over German-occupied French territory, suffering flak wounds; he bailed out, was picked up by the French underground, which smuggled him across the Pyrenees into Spain disguised as a peasant. In Spain he was jailed briefly, then released, whereupon he made it back to England and returned to combat during the Allied invasion of France. On October 12, 1944, Yeager took on and shot down five German fighter planes in succession. On November 6, flying a propeller-driven P-51 Mustang, he shot down one of the new jet fighters the Germans had developed, the Messerschmitt-262, and damaged two more, and on November 20 he shot down four FW-190s. It was a true Frank Luke–style display of warrior fury and personal prowess. By the end of the war he had thirteen and a half kills. He was twenty-two years old.

In 1946 and 1947 Yeager was trained as a test pilot at Wright Field in Dayton. He amazed his instructors with his ability at stunt-team flying, not to mention the unofficial business of hassling. That plus his up-hollow drawl had everybody saying, "He's a natural-born stick 'n' rudder man." Nevertheless, there was something extraordinary about it when a man so young, with so little experience in flight test, was selected to go to Muroc Field in California for the XS-1 project.

Muroc was up in the high elevations of the Mojave Desert. It looked like some fossil landscape that had long since been left behind by the rest of terrestrial evolution. It was full of huge dry lake beds, the biggest being Rogers Lake. Other than sagebrush the only vegetation was Joshua trees, twisted freaks of the plant world that looked like a cross between cactus and Japanese bonsai. They had a dark petrified green color and horribly crippled branches. At dusk the Joshua trees stood out in silhouette on the fossil wasteland like some arthritic nightmare. In the summer the temperature went up to 110 degrees as a matter of course, and the dry lake beds were covered in sand, and there would be windstorms and sandstorms right out of a Foreign Legion movie. At night it would drop to near freezing, and in December it would start raining, and the dry lakes would fill up with a few inches of water, and some sort of putrid prehistoric shrimps would work their way up from out of the ooze, and sea gulls would come flying in a hundred miles or more from the ocean, over the mountains, to gobble up these squirming little throwbacks. A person had to see it to believe it: flocks of sea gulls wheeling around in the air out in the middle of the high desert in the dead of winter and grazing on antediluvian crustaceans in the primordial ooze.

When the wind blew the few inches of water back and forth across the lake beds, they became absolutely smooth and level. And when the water evaporated in the spring, and the sun baked the ground hard, the lake beds became the greatest natural landing fields ever discovered, and also the biggest, with miles of room for error. That was highly desirable, given the nature of the enterprise at Muroc.

10 Besides the wind, sand, tumbleweed, and Joshua trees, there was nothing at Muroc except for two quonset-style hangars, side by side, a couple of gasoline pumps, a single concrete runway, a few tarpaper shacks, and some tents. The officers stayed in the shacks marked "barracks," and lesser souls stayed

in the tents and froze all night and fried all day. Every road into the property had a guardhouse on it manned by soldiers. The enterprise the Army had undertaken in this godforsaken place was the development of supersonic jet and rocket planes.

At the end of the war the Army had discovered that the Germans not only had the world's first jet fighter but also a rocket plane that had gone 596 miles an hour in tests. Just after the war a British jet, the Gloster Meteor, jumped the official world speed record from 469 to 606 in a single day. The next great plateau would be Mach 1, the speed of sound, and the Army Air Force considered it crucial to achieve it first.

The speed of sound, Mach 1, was known (thanks to the work of the physicist Ernst Mach) to vary at different altitudes, temperatures, and wind speeds. On a calm 60-degree day at sea level it was about 760 miles an hour, while at 40,000 feet, where the temperature would be at least sixty below, it was about 660 miles an hour. Evil and baffling things happened in the transonic zone, which began at about .7 Mach. Wind tunnels choked out at such velocities. Pilots who approached the speed of sound in dives reported that the controls would lock or "freeze" or even alter their normal functions. Pilots had crashed and died because they couldn't budge the stick. Just last year Geoffrey de Havilland, son of the famous British aircraft designer and builder, had tried to take one of his father's DH 108s to Mach 1. The ship started buffeting and then disintegrated, and he was killed. This led engineers to speculate that the shock waves became so severe and unpredictable at Mach 1, no aircraft could survive them. They started talking about "the sonic wall" and "the sound barrier."

So this was the task that a handful of pilots, engineers, and mechanics had at Muroc. The place was utterly primitive, nothing but bare bones, bleached tarpaulins, and corrugated tin rippling in the heat with caloric waves; and for an ambitious young pilot it was perfect. Muroc seemed like an outpost on the dome of the world, open only to a righteous few, closed off to the rest of humanity, including even the Army Air Force brass of command control, which was at Wright Field. The commanding officer at Muroc was only a colonel, and his superiors at Wright did not relish junkets to the Muroc rat shacks in the first place. But to pilots this prehistoric throwback of an airfield became . . . shrimp heaven! the rat-shack plains of Olympus!

Low Rent Septic Tank Perfection . . . yes; and not excluding those traditional essentials for the blissful hot young pilot: Flying & Drinking and Drinking & Driving.

Just beyond the base, to the southwest, there was a rickety windblown 1930's-style establishment called Pancho's Fly Inn, owned, run, and bartended by a woman named Pancho Barnes. Pancho Barnes wore tight white sweaters and tight pants, after the mode of Barbara Stanwyck in *Double Indemnity*.[2] She   15

2. A 1944 film featuring a femme fatale housewife (played by Stanwyck) and a likable insurance salesman (played by Fred MacMurray) who concoct a cold-blooded scheme to murder her husband for purposes of lustful desire and financial gain; because the murder doesn't pass for an accident, their scheme ultimately fails.

was only forty-one when Yeager arrived at Muroc, but her face was so weather-beaten, had so many hard miles on it, that she looked older, especially to the young pilots at the base. She also shocked the pants off them with her vulcanized tongue. Everybody she didn't like was an old bastard or a sonofabitch. People she liked were old bastards and sonsabitches, too. "I tol' 'at ol' bastard to get 'is ass on over here and I'd g'im a drink." But Pancho Barnes was anything but Low Rent. She was the granddaughter of the man who designed the old Mount Lowe cable-car system, Thaddeus S. C. Lowe. Her maiden name was Florence Leontine Lowe. She was brought up in San Marino, which adjoined Pasadena and was one of Los Angeles' wealthiest suburbs, and her first husband—she was married four times—was the pastor of the Pasadena Episcopal Church, the Rev. C. Rankin Barnes. Mrs. Barnes seemed to have few of the conventional community interests of a Pasadena matron. In the late 1920's, by boat and plane, she ran guns for Mexican revolutionaries and picked up the nickname Pancho. In 1930 she broke Amelia Earhart's[3] air-speed record for women. Then she barnstormed around the country as the featured performer of "Pancho Barnes's Mystery Circus of the Air." She always greeted her public in jodhpurs and riding boots, a flight jacket, a white scarf, and a white sweater that showed off her terrific Barbara Stanwyck chest. Pancho's desert Fly Inn had an airstrip, a swimming pool, a dude ranch corral, plenty of acreage for horseback riding, a big old guest house for the lodgers, and a connecting building that was the bar and restaurant. In the barroom the floors, the tables, the chairs, the walls, the beams, the bar were of the sort known as extremely weatherbeaten, and the screen doors kept banging. Nobody putting together such a place for a movie about flying in the old days would ever dare make it as dilapidated and generally go-to-hell as it actually was. Behind the bar were many pictures of airplanes and pilots, lavishly autographed and inscribed, badly framed and crookedly hung. There was an old piano that had been dried out and cracked to the point of hopeless desiccation. On a good night a huddle of drunken aviators could be heard trying to bang, slosh, and navigate their way through old Cole Porter[4] tunes. On average nights the tunes were not that good to start with. When the screen door banged and a man walked through the door into the saloon, every eye in the place checked him out. If he wasn't known as somebody who had something to do with flying at Muroc, he would be eyed like some lame goddamned mouseshit sheepherder from *Shane*.[5]

The plane the Air Force wanted to break the sound barrier with was called the X-1 at the outset and later on simply the X-1. The Bell Aircraft Corporation had built it under an Army contract. The core of the ship was a rocket of the type first developed by a young Navy inventor, Robert Truax, during the war. The fuselage was shaped like a 50-caliber bullet—an object that was known to

3. Pioneering aviator (1897–1937) who disappeared while attempting a world flight in 1937.

4. American composer of popular music (1891–1964), including Broadway show tunes.

5. A 1953 classic Western set in Jackson Hole, Wyoming, about an impressionable young boy, Joey Starrett, who idolizes a mysterious golden-haired gunslinger (Shane).

go supersonic smoothly. Military pilots seldom drew major test assignments; they went to highly paid civilians working for the aircraft corporations. The prime pilot for the X-1 was a man whom Bell regarded as the best of the breed. This man looked like a movie star. He looked like a pilot from out of *Hell's Angels.*[6] And on top of everything else there was his name: Slick Goodlin.

The idea in testing the X-1 was to nurse it carefully into the transonic zone, up to seven-tenths, eight-tenths, nine-tenths the speed of sound (.7 Mach, .8 Mach, .9 Mach) before attempting the speed of sound itself, Mach 1, even though Bell and the Army already knew the X-1 had the rocket power to go to Mach 1 and beyond, if there *was* any *beyond.* The consensus of aviators and engineers, after Geoffrey de Havilland's death, was that the speed of sound was an absolute, like the firmness of the earth. The sound barrier was a farm you could buy in the sky. So Slick Goodlin began to probe the transonic zone in the X-1, going up to .8 Mach. Every time he came down he'd have a riveting tale to tell. The buffeting, it was so fierce—and the listeners, their imaginations aflame, could practically see poor Geoffrey de Havilland disintegrating in midair. And the goddamned aerodynamics—and the listeners got a picture of a man in ballroom pumps skidding across a sheet of ice, pursued by bears. A controversy arose over just how much bonus Slick Goodlin should receive for assaulting the dread Mach 1 itself. Bonuses for contract test pilots were not unusual; but the figure of $150,000 was now bruited about. The Army balked, and Yeager got the job. He took it for $283 a month, or $3,396 a year; which is to say, his regular Army captain's pay.

The only trouble they had with Yeager was in holding him back. On his first powered flight in the X-1 he immediately executed an unauthorized zero-g roll with a full load of rocket fuel, then stood the ship on its tail and went up to .85 Mach in a vertical climb, also unauthorized. On subsequent flights, at speeds between .85 Mach and .9 Mach, Yeager ran into most known airfoil problems—loss of elevator, aileron, and rudder control, heavy trim pressures, Dutch rolls, pitching and buffeting, the lot—yet was convinced, after edging over .9 Mach, that this would all get better, not worse, as you reached Mach 1. The attempt to push beyond Mach 1—"breaking the sound barrier"—was set for October 14, 1947. Not being an engineer, Yeager didn't believe the "barrier" existed.

October 14 was a Tuesday. On Sunday evening, October 12, Chuck Yeager dropped in at Pancho's, along with his wife. She was a brunette named Glennis, whom he had met in California while he was in training, and she was such a number, so striking, he had the inscription "Glamorous Glennis" written on the nose of his P-51 in Europe and, just a few weeks back, on the X-1 itself. Yeager didn't go to Pancho's and knock back a few because two days later the big test was coming up. Nor did he knock back a few because it was the weekend. No, he knocked back a few because night had come and he was a pilot at Muroc. In keeping with the military tradition of Flying & Drinking, that was what you did, for no other reason than that the sun had gone down. You went to Pancho's and knocked back a few and listened to the screen doors banging

6. A 1930 movie about World War I aviation.

and to other aviators torturing the piano and the nation's repertoire of Familiar Favorites and to lonesome mouseturd strangers wandering in through the banging doors and to Pancho classifying the whole bunch of them as old bastards and miserable peckerwoods. That was what you did if you were a pilot at Muroc and the sun went down.

20 So about eleven Yeager got the idea that it would be a hell of a kick if he and Glennis saddled up a couple of Pancho's dude-ranch horses and went for a romp, a little rat race, in the moonlight. This was in keeping with the military tradition of Flying & Drinking and Drinking & Driving, except that this was prehistoric Muroc and you rode horses. So Yeager and his wife set off on a little proficiency run at full gallop through the desert in the moonlight amid the arthritic silhouettes of the Joshua trees. Then they start racing back to the corral, with Yeager in the lead and heading for the gateway. Given the prevailing conditions, it being nighttime, at Pancho's, and his head being filled with a black sandstorm of many badly bawled songs and vulcanized oaths, he sees too late that the gate has been closed. Like many a hard-driving midnight pilot before him, he does not realize that he is not equally gifted in the control of all forms of locomotion. He and the horse hit the gate, and he goes flying off and lands on his right side. His side hurts like hell.

The next day, Monday, his side still hurts like hell. It hurts every time he moves. It hurts every time he breathes deep. It hurts every time he moves his right arm. He knows that if he goes to a doctor at Muroc or says anything to anybody even remotely connected with his superiors, he will be scrubbed from the flight on Tuesday. They might even go so far as to put some other miserable peckerwood in his place. So he gets on his motorcycle, an old junker that Pancho had given him, and rides over to see a doctor in the town of Rosamond, near where he lives. Every time the goddamned motorcycle hits a pebble in the road, his side hurts like a sonofabitch. The doctor in Rosamond informs him he has two broken ribs and he tapes them up and tells him that if he'll just keep his right arm immobilized for a couple of weeks and avoid any physical exertion or sudden movements, he should be all right.

Yeager gets up before daybreak on Tuesday morning—which is supposed to be the day he tries to break the sound barrier—and his ribs still hurt like a sonofabitch. He gets his wife to drive him over to the field, and he has to keep his right arm pinned down to his side to keep his ribs from hurting so much. At dawn, on the day of a flight, you could hear the X-1 screaming long before you got there. The fuel for the X-1 was alcohol and liquid oxygen, oxygen converted from a gas to a liquid by lowering its temperature to 297 degrees below zero. And when the lox, as it was called, rolled out of the hoses and into the belly of the X-1, it started boiling off and the X-1 started steaming and screaming like a teakettle. There's quite a crowd on hand, by Muroc standards . . . perhaps nine or ten souls. They're still fueling the X-1 with the lox, and the beast is wailing.

The X-1 looked like a fat orange swallow with white markings. But it was really just a length of pipe with four rocket chambers in it. It had a tiny cockpit and a needle nose, two little straight blades (only three and a half inches thick at the thickest part) for wings, and a tail assembly set up high to avoid the "sonic wash" from the wings. Even though his side was throbbing and his right arm felt practically useless, Yeager figured he could grit his teeth and get through the flight—except for one specific move he had to make. In the rocket launches, the X-1, which held only two and a half minutes' worth of fuel, was carried up to twenty-six thousand feet underneath a B-29. At seven thousand feet, Yeager was to climb down a ladder from the bomb bay of the B-29 to the open doorway of the X-1, hook up to the oxygen system and the radio microphone and earphones, and put his crash helmet on and prepare for the launch, which would come at twenty-five thousand feet. This helmet was a homemade number. There had never been any such thing as a crash helmet before, except in stunt flying. Throughout the war pilots had used the old skin-tight leather helmet-and-goggles. But the X-1 had a way of throwing the pilot around so violently that there was danger of getting knocked out against the walls of the cockpit. So Yeager had bought a big leather football helmet—there were no plastic ones at the time—and he butchered it with a hunting knife until he carved the right kind of holes in it, so that it would fit down over his regular flying helmet and the earphones and the oxygen rig. Anyway, then his flight engineer, Jack Ridley, would climb down the ladder, out in the breeze, and shove into place the cockpit door, which had to be lowered out of the belly of the B-29 on a chain. Then Yeager had to push a handle to lock the door airtight. Since the X-1's cockpit was minute, you had to push the handle with your right hand. It took quite a shove. There was no way you could move into position to get enough leverage with your left hand.

Out in the hangar Yeager makes a few test shoves on the sly, and the pain is so incredible he realizes that there is no way a man with two broken ribs is going to get the door closed. It is time to confide in somebody, and the logical man is Jack Ridley. Ridley is not only the flight engineer but a pilot himself and a good old boy from Oklahoma to boot. He will understand about Flying & Drinking and Drinking & Driving through the goddamned Joshua trees. So Yeager takes Ridley off to the side in the tin hangar and says: Jack, I got me a little ol' problem here. Over at Pancho's the other night I sorta . . . dinged my goddamned ribs. Ridley says, Whattya mean . . . *dinged?* Yeager says, Well, I guess you might say I damned near like to . . . *broke* a coupla the sonsabitches. Whereupon Yeager sketches out the problem he foresees.

Not for nothing is Ridley the engineer on this project. He has an inspiration. He tells a janitor named Sam to cut him about nine inches off a broom handle. When nobody's looking, he slips the broomstick into the cockpit of the X-1 and gives Yeager a little advice and counsel. 25

So with that added bit of supersonic flight gear Yeager went aloft.

At seven thousand feet he climbed down the ladder into the X-1's cockpit, clipped on his hoses and lines, and managed to pull the pumpkin football helmet over his head. Then Ridley came down the ladder and lowered the door into place. As Ridley had instructed, Yeager now took the nine inches of broomstick and slipped it between the handle and the door. This gave him just enough mechanical advantage to reach over with his left hand and whang the thing shut. So he whanged the door shut with Ridley's broomstick and was ready to fly.

At 26,000 feet the B-29 went into a shallow dive, then pulled up and released Yeager and the X-1 as if it were a bomb. Like a bomb it dropped and shot forward (at the speed of the mother ship) at the same time. Yeager had been launched straight into the sun. It seemed to be no more than six feet in front of him, filling up the sky and blinding him. But he managed to get his bearings and set off the four rocket chambers one after the other. He then experienced something that became known as the ultimate sensation in flying: "booming and zooming." The surge of the rockets was so tremendous, forced him back into his seat so violently, he could hardly move his hands forward the few inches necessary to reach the controls. The X-1 seemed to shoot straight up in an absolutely perpendicular trajectory, as if determined to snap the hold of gravity via the most direct route possible. In fact, he was only climbing at the 45-degree angle called for in the flight plan. At about .87 Mach the buffeting started.

On the ground the engineers could no longer see Yeager. They could only hear . . . that poker-hollow West Virginia drawl.

30 "Had a mild buffet there . . . jes the usual instability . . ."

Jes the usual instability?

Then the X-1 reached the speed of .96 Mach, and that incredible caint-hardlyin' aw-shuckin' drawl said:

"Say, Ridley . . . make a note here, will ya?" *(if you ain't got nothin' better to do)* ". . . elevator effectiveness *re*gained."

Just as Yeager had predicted, as the X-1 approached Mach 1, the stability improved. Yeager had his eyes pinned on the machometer. The needle reached .96, fluctuated, and went off the scale.

35 And on the ground they heard . . . that voice:

"Say, Ridley . . . make another note, will ya?" *(if you ain't too bored yet)* ". . . there's somethin' wrong with this ol' machometer . . ." (faint chuckle) ". . . it's gone kinda screwy on me . . ."

And in that moment, on the ground, they heard a boom rock over the desert floor—just as the physicist Theodore von Kármán had predicted many years before.

Then they heard Ridley back in the B-29: "If it is, Chuck, we'll fix it. Personally I think you're seeing things."

Then they heard Yeager's poker-hollow drawl again:

40 "Well, I guess I am, Jack . . . And I'm still goin' upstairs like a bat."

The X-1 had gone through "the sonic wall" without so much as a bump. As the speed topped out at Mach 1.05, Yeager had the sensation of shooting straight through the top of the sky. The sky turned a deep purple and all at once the stars and the moon came out—and the sun shone at the same time. He had reached a layer of the upper atmosphere where the air was too thin to contain reflecting dust particles. He was simply looking out into space. As the X-1 nosed over at the top of the climb, Yeager now had seven minutes of . . . Pilot Heaven . . . ahead of him. He was going faster than any man in history, and it was almost silent up here, since he had exhausted his rocket fuel, and he was so high in such a vast space that there was no sensation of motion. He was master of the sky. His was a king's solitude, unique and inviolate, above the dome of the world. It would take him seven minutes to glide back down and land at Muroc. He spent the time doing victory rolls and wing-over-wing aerobatics while Rogers Lake and the High Sierras spun around below.

QUESTIONS

1. Before recounting Yeager's personal history or the story of breaking the sound barrier, Wolfe begins with the voice of an airline pilot. Why does he begin this way? What connection does the first paragraph have with the rest of the essay?

2. Wolfe interweaves Yeager's personal history with a more public, official history of the space program. Make a flowchart or diagram to show how this interweaving works.

3. Write an essay that interweaves some part of your personal history with some larger, public story.

TONI MORRISON *Strangers*

I AM IN THIS RIVER PLACE—newly mine—walking in the yard when I see a woman sitting on the seawall at the edge of a neighbor's garden. A homemade fishing pole arcs into the water some twenty feet from her hand. A feeling of welcome washes over me. I walk toward her, right up to the fence that separates my place from the neighbor's, and notice with pleasure the clothes she wears: men's shoes, a man's hat, a well-worn colorless sweater over a long black dress. The woman turns her head and greets me with an easy smile and a "How you doing?" She tells me her name (Mother Something) and we talk for some time—fifteen minutes or so—about fish recipes and weather and children. When I ask her if she lives there, she answers no. She lives in a nearby village, but the owner of the house lets her come to this spot any time she wants to fish, and she comes every week, sometimes several days in a row when the perch or catfish are running and even if they aren't because she likes eel, too, and they are always there. She is witty and full of the wisdom that older women always seem to have a lock on. When we part, it is with an understanding that she will be there the next day or very soon after and we will visit again. I imagine more conversations with her. I will invite her into my house for coffee, for tales, for laughter. She reminds me of someone, something. I imagine a friendship, casual, effortless, delightful.

She is not there the next day. She is not there the following days, either. And I look for her every morning. The summer passes, and I have not seen her at all. Finally, I approach the neighbor to ask about her and am bewildered to learn that the neighbor does not know who or what I am talking about. No

Morrison wrote this essay to introduce a book of photographs by Robert Bergman, A Kind of Rapture *(1998).*

old woman fished from her wall—ever—and none had permission to do so. I decide that the fisherwoman fibbed about the permission and took advantage of the neighbor's frequent absences to poach. The fact of the neighbor's presence is proof that the fisherwoman would not be there. During the months following, I ask lots of people if they know Mother Something. No one, not even people who have lived in nearby villages for seventy years, has ever heard of her.

I feel cheated, puzzled, but also amused, and wonder off and on if I have dreamed her. In any case, I tell myself, it was an encounter of no value other than anecdotal. Still. Little by little, annoyance then bitterness takes the place of my original bewilderment. A certain view from my windows is now devoid of her, reminding me every morning of her deceit and my disappointment. What was she doing in that neighborhood, anyway? She didn't drive, had to walk four miles if indeed she lived where she said she did. How could she be missed on the road in that hat, those awful shoes? I try to understand the intensity of my chagrin, and why I am missing a woman I spoke to for fifteen minutes. I get nowhere except for the stingy explanation that she had come into my space (next to it, anyway—at the property line, at the edge, just at the fence, where the most interesting things always happen), and had implied promises of female camaraderie, of opportunities for me to be generous, of protection and protecting. Now she is gone, taking with her my good opinion of myself, which, of course, is unforgivable.

Isn't that the kind of thing that we fear strangers will do? Disturb. Betray. Prove they are not like us. That is why it is so hard to know what to do with them. The love that prophets have urged us to offer the stranger is the same love

that Jean-Paul Sartre[1] could reveal as the very mendacity of Hell. The signal line of *No Exit*, "*L'enfer, c'est les autres*," raises the possibility that "other people" are responsible for turning a personal world into a public hell. In the admonition of a prophet and the sly warning of an artist, strangers as well as the beloved are understood to tempt our gaze, to slide away or to stake claims. Religious prophets caution against the slide, the looking away; Sartre warns against love as possession.

The resources available to us for benign access to each other, for vaulting the mere blue air that separates us, are few but powerful: language, image, and experience, which may involve both, one, or neither of the first two. Language (saying, listening, reading) can encourage, even mandate, surrender, the breach of distances among us, whether they are continental or on the same pillow, whether they are distances of culture or the distinctions and indistinctions of age or gender, whether they are the consequences of social invention or biology. Image increasingly rules the realm of shaping, sometimes becoming, often contaminating, knowledge. Provoking language or eclipsing it, an image can determine not only what we know and feel but also what we believe is worth knowing about what we feel. 5

These two godlings, language and image, feed and form experience. My instant embrace of an outrageously dressed fisherwoman was due in part to an image on which my representation of her was based. I immediately sentimentalized and appropriated her. I owned her or wanted to (and I suspect she glimpsed

1. French existentialist philosopher (1905–1980). The line in Sartre's 1944 play *No Exit* is usually translated as "Hell is other people."

it). I had forgotten the power of embedded images and stylish language to seduce, reveal, control. Forgot, too, their capacity to help us pursue the human project—which is to remain human and to block the dehumanization of others.

But something unforeseen has entered into this admittedly oversimplified menu of our resources. Far from our original expectations of increased intimacy and broader knowledge, routine media presentations deploy images and language that narrow our view of what humans look like (or ought to look like) and what in fact we are like. Succumbing to the perversions of media can blur vision, resisting them can do the same. I was clearly and aggressively resisting such influences in my encounter with the fisherwoman. Art as well as the market can be complicit in the sequestering of form from formula, of nature from artifice, of humanity from commodity. Art gesturing toward representation has, in some exalted quarters, become literally beneath contempt. The concept of what it is to be human has altered, and the word *truth* needs quotation marks around it so that its absence (its elusiveness) is stronger than its presence.

Why would we want to know a stranger when it is easier to estrange another? Why would we want to close the distance when we can close the gate? Appeals in arts and religion for comity in the Common Wealth are faint.

It took some time for me to understand my unreasonable claims on that fisherwoman. To understand that I was longing for and missing some aspect of myself, and that there are no strangers. There are only versions of ourselves, many of which we have not embraced, most of which we wish to protect ourselves from. For the stranger is not foreign, she is random, not alien but remembered; and it is the randomness of the encounter with our already known—although unacknowledged—selves that summons a ripple of alarm. That makes us reject the figure and the emotions it provokes—especially when these emotions are profound. It is also what makes us want to own, govern, administrate the Other. To romance her, if we can, back into our own mirrors. In either instance (of alarm or false reverence), we deny her personhood, the specific individuality we insist upon for ourselves.

10 Robert Bergman's radiant portraits of strangers provoked this meditation. Occasionally, there arises an event or a moment that one knows immediately will forever mark a place in the history of artistic endeavor. Bergman's portraits represent such a moment, such an event. In all its burnished majesty his gallery refuses us unearned solace, and one by one by one the photographs unveil *us*, asserting a beauty, a kind of rapture, that is as close as can be to a master template of the singularity, the community, the unextinguishable sacredness of the human race.

QUESTIONS

1. In his book, *A Kind of Rapture*, Robert Bergman included people he encountered on the streets of America. Why does Morrison not dwell on that fact?

2. In the opening paragraphs (1–3) Morrison relates a story about a woman she sees fishing near her property; later in the essay she expresses regret, even guilt, that her

story "sentimentalized and appropriated" the woman (paragraphs 6–7). What does Morrison mean by this self-criticism? Do you agree that it may be ethically wrong to create stories about the strangers we see?

3. What do you see in these photographs? More than Morrison does? Different things? Write an interpretation of one of the portraits that intrigues you.

Jamaica Kincaid *Sowers and Reapers*

Why must people insist that the garden is a place of rest and repose, a place to forget the cares of the world, a place in which to distance yourself from the painful responsibility that comes with being a human being?

The day after I spoke to a group of people at the Garden Conservancy's tenth-anniversary celebration, in Charleston, South Carolina, an American man named Frank Cabot, the chairman and founder of the organization and a very rich man, who has spent some of his money creating a spectacular garden in the surprisingly hospitable climate of eastern Canada, told me that he was sorry I had been invited, that he was utterly offended by what I had said and the occasion I had used to say it, for I had done something unforgivable—I had introduced race and politics into the garden.

There were three of us on a panel, and our topic was "My Favorite Garden." One of the speakers said that his favorite was Hidcote Manor, in England, created by an American Anglophile named Lawrence Johnston. (A very nice climbing yellow rose, which is sometimes available through the Wayside Gardens catalogue, is named after him.) There are at least a thousand gardens in every corner of the world, but especially in England, that should come before Hidcote as a choice for favorite garden. The garden of the filmmaker Derek Jarman, who succumbed to AIDS in 1994, is a particularly good example. Dramatically set in the shadow of a nuclear-power station in Dungeness, Kent, surrounding a one-story house that has been painted black, this garden, when I saw it, was abloom with poppies in brilliant shades and with *Crambe maritima* (sea kale) and pathways lined with pebbles, the kind found at the seashore, and all sorts of worn-down objects that looked as if they were the remains of a long-ago shipwreck just found. When you see it for the first time, it so defies what you expect that this thought really will occur to you: Now, what is a garden? And, at the same time, you will be filled with pleasure and inspiration.

Another man spoke of a garden he was designing in Chicago which would include a re-creation of a quadripartite garden made by prisoners in Auschwitz. (This way of organizing a garden is quite common, and it has a history that

First published in the New Yorker *(January 22, 2001), a magazine of literature and the arts. Kincaid is perhaps best known as a novelist, but as a staff writer for the* New Yorker *she has produced many essays like this one examining her own experiences.*

begins with Genesis 2:10—"A river issues from Eden to water the garden, and it then divides and becomes four branches.") The garden in Auschwitz was created over many years and by many people, all of whom were facing death, and it gave me a sharp pang to realize that, while waiting to be brutally murdered, some people had made a garden.

5 I had prepared a talk in which I was going to say that my favorite garden is the Garden of Eden, because every time I see a garden that I love it becomes my favorite garden until I see another garden that I love and completely forget the garden that so dominated my affections a short time before; and also because this garden, Eden, is described in the fewest words I have ever seen used to describe a garden, and yet how unforgettable and vivid the description remains: "And from the ground the Lord God caused to grow every tree that was pleasing to the sight and good for food, with the tree of life in the middle of the garden, and the tree of knowledge of good and bad."

But after that man spoke of the Holocaust garden, a nice speech on Eden was no longer possible.

I heard myself telling my audience that I had been surprised to see, on the way into my hotel, in the little park across the way, a statue of John Caldwell Calhoun,[1] that inventor of the rhetoric of states' rights and the evil encoded in it, who was elected Vice-President of the United States twice. I remarked on how hard it must be for the black citizens of Charleston to pass each day by the statue of a man who hated them, cast in a heroic pose. And then I wondered if anyone in the audience had seen the Holocaust memorial right next to the statue of John Caldwell Calhoun: a strange cryptlike, criblike structure, another commemoration of some of the people who were murdered by the Germans. Then I said that John Caldwell Calhoun was not altogether so far removed from Adolf Hitler; that these two men seem to be more in the same universe than not.

It was all this and more that I said that made Frank Cabot angry at me, but not long after his outburst I joined a group of attendees to the conference who were going off to tour and have dinner at Middleton Place, the famous plantation. Middleton is a popular destination for Americans who are interested in gardens, garden history, or a whiff of the sweet stench that makes up so much of American history. It is, on the one hand, a series of beautiful rooms in the garden sense: there is a part for roses only, there is a part for azaleas, there is a part for camellias, and so on and so on. The most spectacular part of the garden is a grassy terrace made by human hands, and on the slope of the terrace are small and perfectly regular risings, so that when seen from below they look like stiff pleats in a skirt that has just been disturbed by a faint breeze. At the foot of the terrace are two small lakes that have been fashioned to look like a butterfly stilled by chloroform. It is all very beautiful, even slightly awesome; and then there is the awfulness, for those gardens and that terrace and those lakes were

1. Calhoun (1782–1850), senator from South Carolina, U.S. vice president 1825–32, and ardent segregationist and theoretician of States' Rights, the doctrine of limited federal power, and individual states' choice in such matters as slavery.

made by slaves. The water from the river adjacent to the plantation was channelled to flood the rice fields, and this was done by slaves, who had brought their rice-cultivation skills with them from Africa. For, as far as I know, there are no rice fields in England, Scotland, Ireland, or Wales. I was feeling quite sad about all this when I came upon a big rubble of bricks. It was all that remained of the main house on the plantation in the wake of the strategy, conceived by that ingenious pyromaniac and great general from the North, William Tecumseh Sherman,[2] which had helped to bring the traitorous South to its knees. As I walked toward a tent to have a dinner of black-eyed peas and rice, ribs and chicken and sweet potatoes, a dinner that I think of as the cuisine of black people from the American South, and where I would hear the Lester Lanin[3] orchestra accompany a white man imitating the voice of Louis Armstrong as he sang songs made famous by Louis Armstrong, I ran into Mr. Frank Cabot, and I kept from him a fact that I happen to know: Arthur Middleton, of Middleton plantation, was one of the signers of the Declaration of Independence.

Nowhere is the relationship between the world and the garden better documented than in Thomas Jefferson's "Garden and Farm Books," an obsessively detailed account of his domestic life. People like to say that Jefferson is an enigma, that he was a man of contradictions, as if those things could not be said of just about anybody. But you have only to read anything he wrote, and you will find the true man, Thomas Jefferson, who is always so unwittingly transparent, always most revealing when confident that he has covered his tracks. He tried to write an autobiography, but he stopped before he had written a hundred pages. In it he states that he was born, that his father's name was Peter, that he wrote the Declaration of Independence, that he went to France and witnessed the French Revolution. The whole thing reads as if it were composed by one of the many marble busts of him which decorate the vestibules of government buildings. The Jefferson to be found in the autobiography is the unwittingly transparent Jefferson. The Jefferson who is confident that he has covered his tracks is to be found in the "Garden and Farm Books." The first entry in the "Garden" book is so beautiful, and so simple a statement: "1766. Shadwell. Mar. 30. Purple hyacinth begins to bloom." It goes on: "Apr. 6. Narcissus and Puckoon open. [Apr.] 13. Puckoon flowers fallen. [Apr.] 16. a bluish colored, funnel-formed flower in low-grounds in bloom." (This must have been *Mertensia virginica*.) The entries continue in this way for years, until 1824: the peas are sown, the asparagus planted, the fruit trees planted, the vegetables reaped. Each entry reads as if it were a single line removed from a poem: something should come before, and something should come after. And what should come before and after is to be found in the "Farm" book, and it comes in the form of a list of names: Ursula, George, Jupiter, Davy, Minerva, Caesar, and Jamy; and the Hemings, Beverly, Betty, Peter, John, and Sally. (Why is it that people who

2. Union Civil War general (1820–1891) famous for his scorched-earth policy designed to destroy the South's means of production.

3. Orchestra leader (1911–2004) associated with upper-class social events.

readily agree that Jefferson owned Sally Hemings cannot believe that he slept with her?)[4] It is they who sowed the peas, dug the trenches, and filled them with manure. It is they who planted and harvested the corn. And when Jefferson makes this entry in his "Garden" book, on April 8, 1794—"our first dish of Asparagus"—it is they who have made it possible for him to enjoy asparagus. None of these names appear in the "Garden" book; the garden is free of their presence, but they turn up in the "Farm" book, and in painful, but valuable-to-know, detail. Little Beverly Hemings, Jefferson's son by Sally, must have been a very small boy the year that he was allotted one and a half yards of wool. One year, John Hemings, Sally's uncle, received, along with Sally's mother, seven yards of linen, five yards of blue wool, and a pair of shoes. On and on it goes: the garden emerging from the farm, the garden unable to exist without the farm, the garden kept apart from the farm, race and politics kept out of the garden.

10 But, you know, the garden Jefferson made at Monticello is not really very good. You don't see it and think, Now, there is something I would like to do. It is not beautiful in the way that the garden George Washington's slaves made at Mount Vernon is beautiful. (I owe this new appreciation of Mount Vernon to Mac Griswold and her excellent book "Washington's Gardens at Mount Vernon: Landscape of the Inner Man.") There is hardly anything featured in the garden at Monticello that makes you want to rush home, subdue a few people, and re-create it. And the reason might be that Jefferson was less interested in the garden than in the marvellous things grown there. Each year, I order packets of something he grew, *Dolichos lablab*, purple hyacinth beans, something no garden should be without. What is beautiful about Monticello is the views, whether you are looking out from the house or looking at it from far away. Jefferson did not so much make a garden as a landscape. The explanation for this may be very simple: his father was a surveyor. This might also explain why he is responsible for some of the great vistas we know—the American West.

Not long after I returned from Charleston, a small amount of money that I had not expected came my way. In my ongoing conversation with my garden, I had for a very long time wanted to build a wall to add to its shape and character. So I immediately called Ron Pembroke, the maker of the most excellent landscapes in the area where I live. My house is situated on a little rise, a knoll, and I find the way it looks from many angles in the general landscape to be very pleasing, and so I had firmly in mind just the kind of wall I wanted. But Ron Pembroke, after walking me up and down and back and forth with a measuring tape in his hand, and taking me in his truck to see the other walls he had built, convinced me that my design was really quite ugly and that his was beautiful and superior.

And so began the building of two hundred-foot-long walls, one above the other, separated by a terrace eight feet wide. One day, four men arrived in the yard, and they were accompanied by big pieces of machinery, including, of course, an earthmover. The men began to rearrange the slope that fell away

4. Sally Hemings (1773–1835) was Jefferson's slave who had a long-term relationship with him and several children.

from the house, and by the end of the day my nice house looked as if it were the only thing left standing after a particularly disastrous natural event. The construction of the walls went on. Day after day, four men, whose names were Jared Clawson, Dan, Tony, and John, came and dug trenches and pounded stakes into the ground after they had looked through a surveyor's instrument many times. One day, truckloads of coarsely pummelled gray stone were deposited in the driveway and carefully laid at the bottom of the trenches. Another day, truckloads of a beautiful gray, blue, yellowish, and glistening stone were delivered and left on the lawn. This stone came from a quarry in Goshen, Massachusetts, Ron Pembroke told me. It is the stone he prefers to use when he builds walls, and it is more expensive than other kinds of stone, but it does display his work to best advantage. My two walls, he said, would most likely require a hundred tons of stone.

The walls started to take shape, at first almost mysteriously. The four men began by placing stones atop one another, in a staggered arrangement, so that always one stone was resting on top of two. In the beginning, each stone they picked up seemed to be just the perfect one needed. But then things began to get more difficult. Sometimes a stone would be carried to the wall with great effort and, after being pounded into place, it would not look quite right to Tony and Dan and John and Jared Clawson.

And did I say that all this was being done in the autumn? I do not know if that is the ideal time to build a wall, but I was so happy to see my walls being made that I became very possessive of the time spent on them and wanted the four men to be building only my walls. I didn't begrudge them lunchtime or time taken to smoke a cigarette, but why did they have to stop working when the day was at an end, and why did the day have to come to an end, for that matter? How I loved to watch those men work, especially the man named Jared Clawson. It was he who built the stairs that made it possible to walk from the lower wall to the eight-foot-wide terrace, and then up to the level ground of a patio, which was made flush with the top of the upper wall. And the stairs were difficult to make, or so it seemed to me, for it took Jared Clawson ten days to make them.

15 One day, it was finished. The walls were built, and they looked fantastic. My friend Paige had given me twelve bottles of champagne, a present for my twentieth wedding anniversary. I loved the taste of this champagne so much that I gave a bottle to each of the men who had helped build my walls. How glad was my spirit when, at the end of all this, Ron Pembroke presented me with a bill, and I in turn gave him a check for the complete amount, and there was nothing between us but complete respect and admiration and no feeling of the injustice of it all, no disgust directed toward me and my nice house, beautifully set off by those dramatic walls, for he had his own house and his own wall and his own spouse and his own anniversary.

At the foot of the lower wall, I have planted five hundred daffodils, ranging in shade from bright yellow to creamy white. In the terrace separating the lower and the upper walls, I have planted two hundred *Tulipa* 'Mrs. J.T. Scheepers,' which is perhaps my favorite tulip in the world. In the four beds on either side of the patio, I have planted two hundred *Tulipa* 'Blue Diamond,' a hundred *Tulipa* 'Angélique,' and only fifty of *Tulipa* 'Black Hero' because they were so expensive. Towering above these hundreds of bulbs, I planted the magnolias 'Woodsman' and 'Elizabeth' and 'Miss Honeybee'; and then *Magnolia zenii* and *Magnolia denudata*. At the beginning of the woodland, which I can see from a certain angle if I am standing on the upper wall, I planted a hundred *Fritillaria meleagris* and fifty each of *Galanthus elwesii* and *Galanthus nivalis*.

Ron Pembroke refilled the trenches with a rich topsoil, a mixture of composted organic material and riverbank soil, but I did not see one earthworm wriggling around in it, and this made me worry, for I have such a reverence for earthworms, whose presence signifies that the soil is good. Their anxious, iridescent, wriggly form, when confronted with broad daylight, is very reassuring. We may be made from dust (the dust of the garden, I presume), but it is not to dust that we immediately return; first, we join the worms.

The garden is not a place to lose your cares; the garden is not a place of rest and repose. Even God did not find it so.

QUESTIONS

1. According to Kincaid, Frank Cabot, chairman of the Garden Conservancy, said she did the "unforgivable—I had introduced race and politics into the garden" (paragraph 2). Can you imagine how race and politics could ever have been left out? What might have led some garden people to ignore or suppress them?

2. The essay has two parts: the Charleston speech and the garden building project. What is the relationship between the two? Why does Kincaid spend so much time on her admiration for the workers?

3. Write an essay describing how you took on a task and completed it successfully. Or write about how someone you know did a good job on a difficult assignment. Go into the kind of detail Kincaid does about her wall.

JHUMPA LAHIRI

Rhode Island

RHODE ISLAND IS NOT an island. Most of it is attached to the continental United States, tucked into a perfect-looking corner formed by the boundaries of Connecticut to the west and Massachusetts above. The rest is a jagged confusion of shoreline: delicate slivers of barrier beach, numerous inlets and peninsulas, and a cluster of stray puzzle pieces, created by the movement of glaciers, nestled in the Narragansett Bay. The tip of Watch Hill, in the extreme southwest, extends like a curving rib bone into the Atlantic Ocean. The salt

Published in State by State: A Panoramic Portrait of America (2008), *a collection edited by Matt Weiland and Sean Wiley to show the regional diversity of the United States. All fifty contributors wrote about their home states, exploring the intersections of personal, regional, and national history.*

ponds lining the edge of South Kingstown,[1] where I grew up, resemble the stealthy work of insects who have come into contact with nutritious, antiquated paper.

In 1524, Giovanni Verrazzano[2] thought that the pear-shaped contours of Block Island, nine miles off the southern coast, resembled the Greek island of Rhodes. In 1644, subsequent explorers, mistaking one of Rhode Island's many attendant islands—there are over thirty of them—for another, gave the same name to Aquidneck Island, famous for Newport, and it has now come to represent the state as a whole. Though the name is misleading it is also apt, for despite Rhode Island's physical connection to the mainland, a sense of insularity prevails. Typical to many island communities, there is a combination of those who come only in the warm months, for the swimming and the clamcakes, and those full-time residents who seem never to go anywhere else. Jacqueline Kennedy Onassis and Cornelius Vanderbilt[3] were among Rhode Island's summer people. Given its diminutive proportions there is a third category: those who pass through without stopping. Forty-eight miles long and thirty-seven wide, it is a brief, unavoidable part of the journey by train between Boston and New York and also, if one chooses to take I–95, by car.

Historically it has harbored the radical and the seditious, misfits and minorities. Roger Williams, the liberal theologian who is credited with founding Rhode Island in 1636, was banished from the Massachusetts Bay Colony by, among others, Nathaniel Hawthorne's great grandfather.[4] Williams's unorthodox views on matters religious and otherwise made him an enemy of the Puritans. He eventually became and remained until his death a Seeker, rejecting any single body of doctrine and respecting the good in all branches of faith. Rhode Island, the thirteenth of the original thirteen colonies, had the greatest degree of self-rule, and was the first to renounce allegiance to King George in 1776. The Rhode Island Charter of 1663 guaranteed "full liberty in religious concernments," and, to its credit, the state accommodated the nation's first Baptists, its first Quakers, and is the site of its oldest synagogue, dedicated in 1763. A different attitude greeted the indigenous population, effectively decimated by 1676 in the course of King Philip's War.[5] Rhode Island is the only state that continues to celebrate, the second Monday of every August, VJ Day,

1. South Kingstown, a small town in the southern part of the state, is home to the University of Rhode Island.

2. Giovanni Verrazzano (1485–1528), an Italian explorer working for King Francis I of France, sailed the North American coast between South Carolina and Newfoundland.

3. Jacqueline Kennedy Onassis (1929–1994), wife of U.S. president John Fitzgerald Kennedy and later of Greek shipping magnate Aristotle Onassis; Cornelius Vanderbilt (1794–1877), American multimillionaire who made his wealth from steamships and railroads, built "The Breakers," a summer house in Newport, Rhode Island.

4. Roger Williams (c. 1603–1683) was banished by Colonel John Hawthorne (1641–1717), the judge most famous for presiding over the Salem witch trials in 1692. His descendent was the novelist Nathaniel Hawthorne (1804–1864).

5. King Philip's War (1675–1676) is sometimes called Metacom's Rebellion, after the Native American leader whom the English called "King Philip."

which commemorates the surrender of Japan after the bombings of Hiroshima and Nagasaki. On a lesser but also disturbing note, it has not managed to pass the bottle bill, which means that all those plastic containers of Autocrat Coffee Syrup, used to make coffee milk (Rhode Island's official beverage), are destined for the purgatory of landfills.

Though I was born in London and have Indian parents, Rhode Island is the reply I give when people ask me where I am from. My family came in the summer of 1970, from Cambridge, Massachusetts, so that my father could begin work as a librarian at the University of Rhode Island. I had just turned three years old. URI is located in the village of Kingston, a place originally called Little Rest. The name possibly stems from accounts of Colonial troops pausing on their way to fight the Narragansett tribe on the western banks of Worden Pond, an event known as the Great Swamp Massacre.[6] We lived on Kingston's main historic tree-lined drag, in a white house with a portico and black shutters. It had been built in 1829 (a fact stated by a plaque next to the front door) to contain the law office of Asa Potter, who was at one point Rhode Island's secretary of state, and whose main residence was the larger, more spectacular house next door. After Asa Potter left Rhode Island to work in a bank in New York, the house became the site of a general store, with a tailor's shop at the front. By 1970 it was an apartment house owned by a fellow Indian, a professor of mathematics named Dr. Suryanarayan.

5 My family was a hybrid; year-rounders who, like the summer people, didn't fundamentally belong. We rented the first floor of the house; an elderly American woman named Miss Tay lived above us, alone, and her vulnerable, solitary presence was a constant reminder, to my parents, of America's harsh ways. A thick iron chain threaded through wooden posts separated us from our neighbors, the Fishers. A narrow path at the back led to a brown shingled shed I never entered. Hanging from one of the outbuildings on the Fisher's property was an oxen yoke, an icon of old New England agriculture, at once elegant and menacing, that both intrigued and scared me as a child. Its bowed shape caused me to think it was a weapon, not merely a restraint. Until I was an adult, I never knew exactly what it was for.

Kingston in those days was a mixture of hippies and Yankees and professors and students. The students arrived every autumn, taking up all the parking spaces, crowding the tables in the Memorial Union with their trays of Cokes and French fries, one year famously streaking on the lawn outside a fraternity building. After commencement in May, things were quiet again, to the point of feeling deserted. I imagine this perpetual ebb and flow, segments of the population ritually coming and going, made it easier for my foreign-born parents to feel that they, too, were rooted to the community in some way. Apart from the Suryanarayans, there were a few other Indian families, women other than my mother in saris walking now and then across the quad. My parents sought them

6. Great Swamp Massacre, a pivotal battle in King Philip's War, fought in November 1675 between the colonial militia and the Narragansett tribe.

out, invited them over for Bengali[7] dinners, and consider a few of these people among their closest friends today.

The gravitational center of Kingston was, and remains, the Kingston Congregational Church ("King Kong" to locals), where my family did not worship but where I went for Girl Scout meetings once a week, and where my younger sister eventually had her high-school graduation party. Across the street from the church, just six houses down from ours, was the Kingston Free Library. It was constructed as a courthouse, and also served as the state house between 1776 and 1791. The building's staid Colonial bones later incorporated Victorian flourishes, including a belfry and a mansard roof. If you stand outside and look up at a window to the right on the third floor, three stern white life-sized busts will stare down at you through the glass. They are thought to be likenesses of Abraham Lincoln, Oliver Wendell Holmes, and John Greenleaf Whittier.[8] For many years now, the bust of Lincoln has worn a long red-and-white striped hat, *Cat in the Hat*–style, on its head.[9]

From my earliest memories I was obsessed with the library, with its creaky, cramped atmosphere and all the things it contained. The books used to live on varnished wooden shelves, the modest card catalog contained in two bureau-sized units, sometimes arranged back to back. Phyllis Goodwin, then and for decades afterward the children's librarian, conducted the story hours I faithfully attended when I was little, held upstairs in a vaulted space called Potter Hall. Light poured in through enormous windows on three sides, and Asa Potter's portrait, predominantly black apart from the pale shade of his face, presided over the fireplace. Along with Phyllis there were two other women in charge of the library—Charlotte Schoonover, the director, and Pam Stoddard. Charlotte and Pam, roughly my mother's generation, were friends, and they both had sons about my age. For many years, Charlotte, Pam, and Phyllis represented the three graces to me, guardians of a sacred place that seemed both to represent the heart of Kingston and also the means of escaping it. They liked to play Corelli or Chopin[10] on the little tape recorder behind the desk, but ordered Patti Smith's *Horses* for the circulating album collection.

When I was sixteen I was hired to work as a page at the library, which meant shelving books, working at the circulation desk, and putting plastic wrappers on the jackets of new arrivals. A lot of older people visited daily, to sit at a table with an arrangement of forsythia or cattails at the center, and read the newspaper. I remember a tall, slightly harried mother with wire-rimmed glasses who would come every two weeks with many children behind her and

7. From the historic region now in northern India and southern Bangladesh.

8. Abraham Lincoln (1809–1865), president of the United States during the Civil War; Oliver Wendell Holmes (1841–1935), legal theorist and associate justice of the U.S. Supreme Court from 1902 until 1932; John Greenleaf Whittier (1807–1892), American Quaker poet now most famous for "Snow-Bound."

9. The children's book that launched the career of Dr. Seuss, published in 1957.

10. Arcangelo Corelli (1653–1713), Italian composer; Frédéric François Chopin (1811–1849), Polish composer and virtuoso pianist.

a large canvas tote bag over her shoulder, which she would dump out and then fill up again with more volumes of *The Borrowers* and Laura Ingalls Wilder[11] for the next round of collective reading. Jane Austen was popular with the patrons, enough for me to remember that the books had red cloth covers. I was an unhappy adolescent, lacking confidence, boyfriends, a proper sense of myself. When I was in the library it didn't matter. I took my cue from the readers who came and went and understood that books were what mattered, that they were above high school, above an adolescent's petty trials, above life itself.

10 By this time we no longer lived in Kingston. We had moved, when I was eight and my sister was one, to a house of our own. I would have preferred to stay in Kingston and live in an enclave called Biscuit City, not only because of the name but because it was full of professors and their families and had a laid-back, intellectual feel. Instead we moved to a town called Peace Dale, exactly one mile away. Peace Dale was a former mill town, an area where the university didn't hold sway. Our housing development, called Rolling Acres, was a leafy loop of roads without sidewalks. The turn into the neighborhood, off the main road, is between a John Deere showroom[12] and a bingo hall. Our house, a style called Colonial Garrison according to the developer's brochure, was historical in name only. In 1975 it was built before our eyes—the foundation dug, concrete poured, pale yellow vinyl siding stapled to the exterior.

After we moved into that house, something changed; whether it was my growing older or the place itself, I was aware that the world immediately outside our door, with its red-flagged mailboxes and children's bicycles left overnight on well-seeded grass, was alien to my parents. Some of our neighbors were friendly. Others pretended we were not there. I remember hot days when the mothers of my American friends in the neighborhood would lie in their bikinis on reclining chairs, chatting over wine coolers as my friends and I ran through a sprinkler, while my fully dressed mother was alone in our house, deep-frying a carp or listening to Bengali folk songs. In Rolling Acres we became car-bound. We couldn't walk, as we had been able to do in Kingston, to see a movie on campus, or buy milk and bread at Evan's Market, or get stamps at the post office. While one could walk (or run or bike) endlessly around the looping roads of Rolling Acres, without a car we were cut off from the rest of the world. When my parents first moved to Rhode Island, I think they both assumed that it was an experiment, just another port of call on their unfolding immigrant journey. The fact that they now owned a house, along with my father getting tenure, brought the journey to a halt. Thirty-seven years later, my parents still live there. The Little Rest they took in 1970 has effectively become the rest of their lives.

The sense of the environment radically shifting from mile to mile holds true throughout Rhode Island, almost the way life can vary block by block in certain

11. *The Borrowers* (1952), the first in a series of children's books by Mary Norton about little people who live in the houses of big people and "borrow" things; Laura Ingalls Wilder (1867–1957), author of the popular "Little House" series for children.

12. For the sale of John Deere tractors and other agricultural equipment.

cities. In South Kingstown alone there is a startling mixture of the lovely and the ugly—of resort, rural, and run-of-the-mill. There are strip malls, most of them radiating from a frenetic intersection called Dale Carlia corner, and no one who lives in my town can avoid negotiating its many traffic lights and lanes on a regular basis. There are countless housing developments, filled with energy-efficient split-levels when I was growing up, these days with McMansions. There are several Dunkin' Donut shops (Rhode Island has more per capita than any other state). There are also quiet farms where horses graze, and remote, winding roads through woods, flanked by low stone walls. There are places to buy antiques and handmade pottery. Along South Road is a sloping, empty field that resembles the one where Wyeth painted *Christina's World*.[13] There is a house on Route 108, just after the traffic light on 138, with the most extraordinary show of azaleas I have ever seen. And then, of course, there are the beaches.

We did not live on the ocean proper, but it was close enough, about five miles away. The ocean was where we took all our visitors from Massachusetts (which was where the majority of my parents' Bengali friends lived), either to Scarborough, which is the state beach, or to Point Judith Light. They used to sit on the grassy hill speaking a foreign tongue, sometimes bringing a picnic of packaged white bread and a pot of *aloo dum*.[14] On the way back they liked to stop in the fishing village of Galilee, where the parking lots of the shops and restaurants were covered with broken seashells. They did not go to eat stuffies, a local delicacy made from quahogs and bread crumbs, but to see if the daily catch included any butterfish or mackerel, to turn into a mustard curry at home. Occasionally my mother's best friend from Massachusetts, Koely Das, wanted to get lobsters or crabs, but these, too, received the curry treatment, a far, fiery cry from a side of melted butter.

The Atlantic I grew up with lacks the color and warmth of the Caribbean, the grandeur of the Pacific, the romance of the Mediterranean. It is generally cold, and full of rust-colored seaweed. Still, I prefer it. The waters of Rhode Island, as much a part of the state's character, if not more, as the land, never asked us questions, never raised a brow. Thanks to its very lack of welcome, its unwavering indifference, the ocean always made me feel accepted, and to my dying day, the seaside is the only place where I can feel truly and recklessly happy.

My father, a global traveler, considers Rhode Island paradise. For nearly four decades he has dedicated himself there to a job he loves, rising through the ranks in the library's cataloging department to become its head. But in addition to the job, he loves the place. He loves that it is quiet, and moderate, and is, in the great scheme of things, uneventful. He loves that he lives close to his work, and that he does not have to spend a significant portion of his life sitting in a car on the highway, or on a crowded subway, commuting. (Lately, because my parents have downsized to one car, he has begun to take a bus, on which he is

13. Andrew Wyeth (1917–2009), a Maine artist whose most famous work, *Christina's World* (1948), shows a woman in a field of golden grass struggling to reach a farmhouse at the top of the hill.

14. Potato curry.

frequently the sole passenger.) Though Rhode Island is a place of four proper seasons, he loves that both winters and summers, tempered by the ocean breezes, are relatively mild. He loves working in his small garden, and going once a week to buy groceries, coupons in hand, at Super Stop&Shop. In many ways he is a spiritual descendant of America's earliest Puritan settlers: thrifty, hard-working, plain in his habits. Like Roger Williams, he is something of a Seeker, aloof from organized religions but appreciating their philosophical worth. He also embodies the values of two of New England's greatest thinkers, demonstrating a profound lack of materialism and self-reliance that would have made Thoreau and Emerson proud. "The great man is he who in the midst of the crowd keeps with perfect sweetness the independence of solitude," Emerson wrote.[15] This is the man who raised me.

My mother, a gregarious and hard-wired urbanite, has struggled; to hear her recall the first time she was driven down from Massachusetts, along I–95 and then a remote, lightless stretch of Route 138, is to understand that Rhode Island was and in many ways remains the heart of darkness for her. She stayed at home to raise me and my sister, frequently taking in other children as well, but apart from a stint as an Avon Lady she had no job. In 1987, when my sister was a teenager, my mother finally ventured out, directing a day care and also working as a classroom assistant at South Road Elementary School, which both my sister and I had attended. One day, after she'd been working at the school for a decade, she started to receive anonymous hate mail. It came in the form of notes placed in her mailbox at school, and eventually in her coat pocket. There were nine notes in total. The handwriting was meant to look like a child's awkward scrawl. The content was humiliating, painful to recount. "Go back to India," one of them said. "Many people here do not like to see your face," read another. By then my mother had been a resident of Rhode Island for twenty-seven years. In Rhode Island she had raised two daughters, given birth to one. She had set up a home and potted geraniums year after year and thrown hundreds of dinner parties for her ever-expanding circle of Bengali friends. In Rhode Island she had renounced her Indian passport for an American one, pledged allegiance to the flag. My mother was ashamed of the notes, and for a while, hoping they would stop, she kept them to herself.

The incident might make a good start to a mystery novel, the type that always flew out of the Kingston Free Library: poison-pen letters appearing in a quaint, sleepy town. But there was nothing cozily intriguing about the cold-blooded correspondence my mother received. After finding the note in her coat pocket (it was February, recess time, and she had been expecting to pull out a glove), she told the school principal, and she also told my family what was going on. In the wake of this incident, many kind people reached out to my mother to express their outrage on her behalf, and for each of those nine notes, she received many sympathetic ones, including words of support from the former president of the university, Francis Horn. The majority of these people were Americans; one of the things that continues to upset my mother was that very

15. A quotation from Ralph Waldo Emerson's essay "Self-Reliance" (1841).

few members of Rhode Island's Indian community, not insignificant by then, were willing to stand by her side. Some resented my mother for creating controversy, for drawing attention to their being foreign, a fact they worked to neutralize. Others told her that she might not have been targeted if she had worn skirts and trousers instead of saris and bindis. Meetings were held at the elementary school, calling for increased tolerance and sensitivity. The story was covered by the *Providence Journal-Bulletin* and the local television news. Montel Williams[16] called our house, wanting my mother to appear on his show (she declined). A detective was put on the case, but the writer of the notes never came forward, was never found. Over ten years have passed. South Road School has shut down, for reasons having nothing to do with what happened to my mother. She worked for another school, part of the same system, in West Kingston, and has recently retired.

I left Rhode Island at eighteen to attend college in New York City, which is where, following a detour up to Boston, I continue to live.[17] Because my parents still live in Rhode Island I still visit, though the logistics of having two small children mean they come to me these days more often than I go to them. I was there in August 2007. My parents, children, sister, and I had just been to Vermont, renting a cabin on a lake. There was a screened-in porch, a Modern Library first edition of *To the Lighthouse*[18] in the bookcase, and a severe mouse problem in the kitchen. In the end the mice drove us away, and during the long drive back to my parents' house, I was aware how little Vermont and Rhode Island, both New England states, have in common. Vermont is dramatically northern, rural, mountainous, landlocked. Rhode Island is flat, briny, more densely populated. Vermont is liberal enough to sanction gay marriage but feels homogenous, lacking Rhode Island's deep pockets of immigration from Ireland, Portugal, and Italy. Rhode Island's capital, Providence, was run for years by a Republican Italian, Buddy Cianci. In 1984 he was convicted of kidnapping his then-estranged wife's boyfriend, beating him with a fire log, and burning him with a lighted cigarette. In 1991 he ran again for mayor, and the citizens of Rhode Island handed him 97 percent of the vote.

It was hotter in Rhode Island than it had been in Vermont. The Ghiorse Beach Factor, courtesy of John Ghiorse, the meteorologist on Channel 10, was a perfect 10 for the weekend we were there. On my way to buy sunscreen at the CVS pharmacy in Kingston, I stopped by the library, excited to see the sign outside indicating that the summer book sale was still going on. The library has been expanded and renovated since I worked there, the circulation desk much larger now and facing the entering visitor, with a computer system instead of the clunky machine that stamped due date cards. The only familiar thing, apart from the books, was Pam. "Just the dregs," she warned me about the book sale.

16. Montel Williams (b. 1956), host of *The Montel Williams Show*.

17. Lahiri went to Barnard College in New York City as an undergraduate, and then pursued graduate degrees at Boston University.

18. Novel (1927) by Virginia Woolf set in a summer house by the sea.

As we were catching up, an elderly couple with British accents approached. "Excuse me," the woman interrupted. "Can you recommend something decent? I'm tired of murder mysteries and people being killed. I just want to hear a decent family story." Pam led her away to the books on tape section, and I went upstairs to Potter Hall to look at the sale. It was just the dregs, as Pam had said, but I managed to find a few things I'd always meant to read—a paperback copy of Donna Tartt's *The Secret History*, and *Monkeys* by Susan Minot.[19] The curtained stage that used to be at one end of the room, on which I had performed, among other things, the role of the Queen of Hearts in *Alice in Wonderland*, was gone, so that the space seemed even bigger. The grand piano was still there, but Asa Potter's portrait was at the Museum of Fine Arts in Boston, Pam later explained, for repairs. She told me she was thinking of retiring soon, and that Phyllis, who had retired long before, had discovered a late-blooming talent for portrait painting. "It's a quirky place," Pam reflected when I asked her about Rhode Island, complaining, "There's no zoning. No united front." And practically in the same breath, proudly: "Kingston is the melting pot of the state."

20 In the afternoon I took my children, along with my mother and sister, to Scarborough. The beach was packed, the tide high and rough. As soon as we set down our things, a wave hit us, forcing us to pick up a drenched blanket and move. Scarborough is a large beach with a paved parking lot that feels even larger. The parking lot itself is also useful in the off-season, for learning how to drive. Scarborough lacks the steep, dramatic dunes and isolated aura of lower Cape Cod, a stretch of New England coastline I have come, in my adult life, to love more than the beach of my childhood. The sand at Scarborough is extremely fine and gray and, when moist, resembles wet ash. A large tide pool had formed that day, and it was thick with young muddied children lying on their bellies, pretending to swim. My son darted off to chase seagulls. The breeze blew impressively in spite of the sultry weather, justifying Ghiorse's ten out of ten. In the distance I could see Point Judith Light. The giant billboard for Coppertone, the Dr. T. J. Eckleburg of my youth,[20] has vanished, but I imagined it was still there—the model's toasted bikini-clad seventies body sprawled regally, indifferently, above the masses.

An announcement on the loudspeaker informed us that a little girl was lost, asking her to meet her mother under the flag on the boardwalk. Another announcement followed: The men's hot water showers were temporarily out of service. The population was democratic, unpretentious, inclusive: ordinary bodies of various sizes and shades, the shades both genetic and cultivated, reading paperback bestsellers and reaching into big bags of chips. I saw no *New Yorker* magazines being read, no heirloom tomato sandwiches or organic peaches being

19. Donna Tartt's *The Secret History* (1992) follows the lives of six college students and their classics professor; Susan Minot's *Monkeys* (1987) focuses on the siblings of a Boston suburban family as they cope with their mother's death and father's alcoholism.

20. Lahiri alludes to a billboard in F. Scott Fitzgerald's novel *The Great Gatsby* (1925), which shows the eyes of Dr. T. J. Eckleburg, "blue and gigantic—their irises are one yard high."

consumed. A trio of deeply tanned adolescent boys tripped past, collectively courting, one could imagine, the same elusive girl. The sun began to set, and within an hour the crowd had thinned to the point where a man started to drag his metal detector through the sand, and the only kids in the tide pool were my own. As we were getting up to go, our bodies sticky with salt, it occurred to me that Scarborough Beach on a summer day is one of the few places that is not a city but still manages, reassuringly, to feel like one. Two days later, I headed home with my sister and my children to Brooklyn. On our way through West Kingston to catch the highway, a lone green truck selling Dell's, Rhode Island's beloved frozen lemonade, beckoned at an otherwise desolate intersection, but my sister and I drove on, accepting the fact that we would not taste Dell's for another year.

As long as my mother and father live, I will continue to visit Rhode Island. They are, respectively, in their late sixties and seventies now, and each time I drive by the local funeral home in Wakefield, I try to prepare myself. Just after I'd finished a draft of this essay, early one November morning, my mother had a heart attack at home. An Indian doctor at Rhode Island Hospital, Arun Singh, performed the bypass operation that has saved her life. When I was a child, I remember my mother often wondering who, in the event of an emergency or other crisis, would come running to help us. During the weeks when I feared she might slip away, everyone did. Our mailbox was stuffed with get-well cards from my mother's students, the refrigerator stuffed with food from her friends. My father's colleagues at the library took up a collection to buy my family Thanksgiving dinner. Our next door neighbor, Mrs. Hyde, who had seen the ambulance pulling up to our house, crossed over to our yard as I was heading to the hospital one day, and told me she'd said a special prayer for my mother at her church.

Due to my parents' beliefs, whenever and wherever they do die, they will not be buried in Rhode Island soil. The house in Rolling Acres will belong to other people; there will be no place there to pay my respects. At the risk of predicting the future, I can see myself, many years from now, driving up I–95, on my way to another vacation on the Cape. We will cross the border after Connecticut, turn off at exit 3A for Kingston, and then continue along an alternative, prettier route that will take us across Jamestown and over the Newport Bridge, where the sapphire bay spreads out on either side, a breathtaking sight that will never grow old. There will no longer be a reason to break the journey in Little Rest. Like many others, we will pass through without stopping.

Questions

1. One purpose of the collection in which Lahiri's essay appeared is to show the diversity of the fifty American states. How does Lahiri achieve this purpose? What details does she provide that are unique to Rhode Island or New England?

2. Lahiri is a novelist who obviously loves books. Choose one allusion to a novel or short story, and explain how this reference enriches the narrative Lahiri tells.

3. Lahiri gives both her personal history and a brief history of the state in which she grew up. What connections might be drawn between the personal and the regional? Consider both the explicit and implicit connections.

4. Write an account of the region or state in which you grew up, integrating some of its history with your personal experience.

IAN FRAZIER

Take the F

BROOKLYN, NEW YORK, has the undefined, hard-to-remember shape of a stain. I never know what to tell people when they ask me where in it I live. It sits at the western tip of Long Island at a diagonal that does not conform neatly to the points of the compass. People in Brooklyn do not describe where they live in terms of north or west or south. They refer instead to their neighborhoods and to the nearest subway lines. I live on the edge of Park Slope, a neighborhood by the crest of a low ridge that runs through the borough. Prospect Park is across the street. Airplanes in the landing pattern for LaGuardia Airport sometimes fly right over my building; every few minutes, on certain sunny days, perfectly detailed airplane shadows slide down my building and up the building opposite in a blink. You can see my building from the plane—it's on the left-hand side of Prospect Park, the longer patch of green you cross after the expanse of Green-Wood Cemetery.

We moved to a co-op apartment in a four-story building a week before our daughter was born. She is now six. I grew up in the country and would not have expected ever to live in Brooklyn. My daughter is a city kid, with less sympathy for certain other parts of the country. When we visited Montana, she was disappointed by the scarcity of pizza places. I overheard her explaining—she was three or four then—to a Montana kid about Brooklyn. She said, "In Brooklyn, there is a lot of broken glass, so you have to wear shoes. And, there is good pizza." She is stern in her judgment of pizza. At the very low end of the pizza-ranking scale is some pizza she once had in New Hampshire, a category now called New Hampshire pizza. In the middle is some okay pizza she once had at the Bronx Zoo, which she calls zoo pizza. At the very top is the pizza at the pizza place where the big kids go, about two blocks from our house.

Our subway is the F train. It runs under our building and shakes the floor. The F is generally a reliable train, but one spring as I walked in the park I saw emergency vehicles gathered by a concrete-sheathed hole in the lawn. Firemen lifted a metal lid from the hole and descended into it. After a while, they reappeared, followed by a few people, then dozens of people, then a whole lot of

First published as a "Letter from Brooklyn" in the New Yorker *(February 25, 1995), a magazine of American literature and the arts, to which Frazier is a regular contributor; later included in his book,* Gone to New York: Adventures in the City *(2005).*

people—passengers from a disabled F train, climbing one at a time out an exit shaft. On the F, I sometimes see large women in straw hats reading a newspaper called the *Caribbean Sunrise*, and Orthodox Jews bent over Talmudic texts[1] in which the footnotes have footnotes, and groups of teenagers wearing identical red bandannas with identical red plastic baby pacifiers in the corners of their mouths, and female couples in porkpie hats, and young men with the silhouettes of the Manhattan skyline razored into their short side hair from one temple around to the other, and Russian-speaking men with thick wrists and big wristwatches, and a hefty, tall woman with long, straight blond hair who hums and closes her eyes and absently practices cello fingerings on the metal subway pole. As I watched the F train passengers emerge among the grass and trees of Prospect Park, the faces were as varied as usual, but the expressions of indignant surprise were all about the same.

Just past my stop, Seventh Avenue, Manhattan-bound F trains rise from underground to cross the Gowanus Canal. The train sounds different—lighter, quieter—in the open air. From the elevated tracks, you can see the roofs of many houses stretching back up the hill to Park Slope, and a bumper crop of rooftop graffiti, and neon signs for Eagle Clothes and Kentile Floors, and flat expanses of factory roofs where seagulls stand on one leg around puddles in the sagging spots. There are fuel-storage tanks surrounded by earthen barriers, and slag piles, and conveyor belts leading down to the oil-slicked waters of the canal. On certain days, the sludge at the bottom of the canal causes it to bubble. Two men fleeing the police jumped in the canal a while ago; one made it across, the other quickly died. When the subway doors open at the Smith–Ninth Street stop, you can see the bay and sometimes smell the ocean breeze. This stretch of elevated is the highest point of the New York subway system. To the south you can see the Verrazano-Narrows Bridge, to the north the World Trade towers.[2] For just a few moments, the Statue of Liberty appears between passing buildings. Pieces of a neighborhood—laundry on clotheslines, a standup swimming pool, a plaster saint, a satellite dish, a rectangle of lawn—slide by like quickly dealt cards. Then the train descends again; growing over the wall just before the tunnel is a wisteria bush, which blooms pale blue every May.

I have spent days, weeks on the F train. The trip from Seventh Avenue to midtown Manhattan is long enough so that every ride can produce its own minisociety of riders, its own forty-minute Ship of Fools.[3] Once a woman an arm's length from me on a crowded train pulled a knife on a man who threatened her. I remember the argument and the principals, but mostly I remember the knife—its flat, curved wood-grain handle inlaid with brass fittings at each end, its long, tapered blade. Once a man sang the words of the Lord's Prayer to a mournful, syncopated tune, and he fitted the mood of the morning so exactly 5

1. The Talmud, a collection of rabbinic discussions of law, ethics, philosophy, and history, is a key text of Judaism.

2. Destroyed by terrorist attacks on September 11, 2001 (9/11).

3. An ancient Western allegory depicting a ship with human passengers who are mad, frivolous, or witlessly ignorant of their fate.

that when he asked for money at the end the riders reached for their wallets and purses as if he'd pulled a gun. Once a big white kid with some friends was teasing a small old Hispanic lady, and when he got off the train I looked at him through the window and he slugged it hard next to my face. Once a thin woman and a fat woman sitting side by side had a long and loud conversation about someone they intended to slap silly: "Her butt be in the *hospital*!" "Bring out the ar-*tillery*!" The terminus of the F in Brooklyn is at Coney Island, not far from the beach. At an off hour, I boarded the train and found two or three passengers and, walking around on the floor, a crab. The passengers were looking at the crab. Its legs clicked on the floor like varnished fingernails. It moved in this direction, then that, trying to get comfortable. It backed itself under a seat, against the wall. Then it scooted out just after some new passengers had sat down there, and they really screamed. Passengers at the next stop saw it and laughed. When a boy lifted his foot as if to stomp it, everybody cried, "Noooh!" By the time we reached Jay Street–Borough Hall,[4] there were maybe a dozen of us in the car, all absorbed in watching the crab. The car doors opened and a heavyset woman with good posture entered. She looked at the crab; then, sternly, at all of us. She let a moment pass. Then she demanded, "*Whose* is *that*?" A few stops later, a short man with a mustache took a manila envelope, bent down, scooped the crab into it, closed it, and put it in his coat pocket.

The smells in Brooklyn: coffee, fingernail polish, eucalyptus, the breath from laundry rooms, pot roast, Tater Tots. A woman I know who grew up here says she moved away because she could not stand the smell of cooking food in the hallway of her parents' building. I feel just the opposite. I used to live in a converted factory above an army-navy store, and I like being in a place that smells like people live there. In the mornings, I sometimes wake to the smell of toast, and I still don't know exactly whose toast it is. And I prefer living in a borough of two and a half million inhabitants, the most of any borough in the city. I think of all the rural places, the pine-timbered canyons and within-commuting-distance farmland, that we are preserving by not living there. I like the immensities of the borough, the unrolling miles of Eastern Parkway and Ocean Parkway and Linden Boulevard, and the disheveled outlying parks strewn with tree limbs and with shards of glass held together by liquor bottle labels, and the tough bridges—the Williamsburg and the Manhattan—and the gentle Brooklyn Bridge. And I like the way the people talk; some really do have Brooklyn accents, really do say "dese" and "dose." A week or two ago, a group of neighbors stood on a street corner watching a peregrine falcon on a building cornice contentedly eating a pigeon it had caught, and the sunlight came through its tail feathers, and a woman said to a man, "Look at the tail, it's so ah-range," and the man replied, "Yeah, I soar it." Like many Americans, I fear living in a nowhere, in a place that is no-place; in Brooklyn, that doesn't trouble me at all.

4. A station on the IND Fulton Street Line and IND Culver Line of the New York City subway system.

Everybody, it seems, is here. At Grand Army Plaza, I have seen traffic tie-ups caused by Haitians and others rallying in support of President Aristide,[5] and by St. Patrick's Day parades, and by Jews of the Lubavitcher sect celebrating the birthday of their Grand Rebbe with a slow procession of ninety-three motor homes—one for each year of his life. Local taxis have bumper stickers that say "Allah Is Great"; one of the men who made the bomb that blew up the World Trade Center used an apartment just a few blocks from me. When an election is held in Russia, crowds line up to cast ballots at a Russian polling place in Brighton Beach. A while ago, I volunteer-taught reading at a public elementary school across the park. One of my students, a girl, was part Puerto Rican, part Greek, and part Welsh. Her looks were a lively combination, set off by sea-green eyes. I went to a map store in Manhattan and bought maps of Puerto Rico, Greece, and Wales to read with her, but they didn't interest her. A teacher at the school was directing a group of students to set up chairs for a program in the auditorium, and she said to me, "We have a problem here—each of these kids speaks a different language." She asked the kids to tell me where they were from. One was from Korea, one from Brazil, one from Poland, one from Guyana, one from Taiwan. In the program that followed, a chorus of fourth and fifth graders sang "God Bless America," "You're a Grand Old Flag," and "I'm a Yankee-Doodle Dandy."

People in my neighborhood are mostly white, and middle class or above. People in neighborhoods nearby are mostly not white, and mostly middle class or below. Everybody uses Prospect Park. On summer days, the park teems with sound—the high note is kids screaming in the water sprinklers at the playground, the midrange is radios and tape players, and the bass is idling or speeding cars. People bring lawn furniture and badminton nets and coolers, and then they barbecue. Charcoal smoke drifts into the neighborhood. Last year, local residents upset about the noise and litter and smoke began a campaign to outlaw barbecuing in the park. There was much unfavorable comment about "the barbecuers." Since most of the barbecuers, as it happens, are black or Hispanic, the phrase "Barbecuers Go Home," which someone spray-painted on the asphalt at the Ninth Street entrance to the park, took on a pointed, unkind meaning. But then park officials set up special areas for barbecuing, and the barbecuers complied, and the controversy died down.

Right nearby is a shelter for homeless people. Sometimes people sleep on the benches along the park, sometimes they sleep in the foyer of our building. Once I went downstairs, my heart pounding, to evict a homeless person who I had been told was there. The immediate, unquestioning way she left made me feel bad; later I always said "Hi" to her and gave her a dollar when I ran into her. One night, late, I saw her on the street, and I asked her her last name (by then I already knew her first name) and for a moment she couldn't recall it. At this, she shook her head in mild disbelief.

10 There's a guy I see on a bench along Prospect Park West all the time. Once I walked by carrying my year-old son, and the man said, "Someday he be

5. Jean-Bertrand Aristide (b. 1953), president of Haiti briefly in 1991, and again in 1994–1996 and 2001–2004.

carrying you." At the local copy shop one afternoon, a crowd was waiting for copies and faxes when a man in a houndstooth fedora came in seeking signatures for a petition to have the homeless shelter shut down. To my surprise, and his, the people in the copy shop instantly turned on him. "I suppose because they're poor they shouldn't even have a place to sleep at night," a woman said as he backed out the door. On the park wall across the street from my building, someone has written in black marker:

COPS PROTECT CITIZENS
WHO PROTECT US FROM COPS.

Sometimes I walk from my building downhill and north, along the Brooklyn waterfront, where cargo ships with scuffed sides and prognathous bows lean overhead. Sometimes I walk by the Brooklyn Navy Yard, its docks now too dormant to attract saboteurs, its long expanses of chain-link fence tangled here and there with the branches of ailanthus trees growing through. Sometimes I head southwest, keeping more or less to the high ground—Bay Ridge—along Fifth Avenue, through Hispanic neighborhoods that stretch in either direction as far as you can see, and then through block after block of Irish. I follow the ridge to its steep descent to the water at the Verrazano Narrows; Fort Hamilton, an army post dating from 1814, is there, and a small Episcopal church called the Church of the Generals. Robert E. Lee once served as a vestryman of this church, and Stonewall Jackson was baptized here. Today the church is in the shade of a forest of high concrete columns supporting an access ramp to the Verrazano-Narrows Bridge.

Sometimes I walk due south, all the way out Coney Island Avenue. In that direction, as you approach the ocean, the sky gets bigger and brighter, and the buildings seem to flatten beneath it. Dry cleaners advertise "Tallis[6] Cleaned Free with Every Purchase Over Fifteen Dollars." Then you start to see occasional lines of graffiti written in Cyrillic.[7] Just past a Cropsey Avenue billboard welcoming visitors to Coney Island is a bridge over a creek filled nearly to the surface with metal shopping carts that people have tossed there over the years. A little farther on, the streets open onto the beach. On a winter afternoon, bundled-up women sit on the boardwalk on folding chairs around a portable record player outside a restaurant called Gastronom Moscow. The acres of trash-dotted sand are almost empty. A bottle of Peter the Great vodka lies on its side, drops of water from its mouth making a small depression in the sand. A man with trousers rolled up to his shins moves along the beach, chopping at driftwood with an axe. Another passerby says, "He's vorking hard, that guy!" The sunset unrolls light along the storefronts like tape. From the far distance, little holes in the sand at the water's edge mark the approach of a short man wearing hip boots and earphones and carrying a long-handled metal detector. Treasure hunters dream of the jewelry that people must have lost here over the years.

6. Jewish prayer shawl.
7. The alphabet used for Russian and other Slavic languages.

Some say that this is the richest treasure beach in the Northeast. The man stops, runs the metal detector again over a spot, digs with a clamming shovel, lifts some sand, brushes through it with a gloved thumb, discards it. He goes on, leaving a trail of holes behind him.

I like to find things myself, and I always try to keep one eye on the ground as I walk. So far I have found seven dollars (a five and two ones), an earring in the shape of a strawberry, several personal notes, a matchbook with a 900 number to call to hear "prison sex fantasies," and two spent .25-caliber shells. Once on Carroll Street, I saw a page of text on the sidewalk, and I bent over to read it. It was page 191 from a copy of *Anna Karenina*.[8] I read the whole page. It described Vronsky leaving a gathering and riding off in a carriage. In a great book, the least fragment is great. I looked up and saw a woman regarding me closely from a few feet away. "You're reading," she said wonderingly. "From a distance, I t'ought you were watchin' ants."

My favorite place to walk is the Brooklyn Botanic Garden, not more than fifteen minutes away. It's the first place I take out-of-towners, who may not associate Brooklyn with flowers. In the winter, the garden is drab as pocket lint, and you can practically see all the way through from Flatbush Avenue to Washington Avenue. But then in February or March a few flowerings begin, the snowdrops and the crocuses, and then the yellow of the daffodils climbs Daffodil Hill, and then the magnolias—star magnolias, umbrella magnolias, saucer magnolias—go off all at once, and walking among them is like flying through cumulus clouds. Then the cherry trees blossom, some a soft and glossy red like makeup, others pink as a dessert, and crowds fill the paths on weekends and stand in front of the blossoms in their best clothes and have their pictures taken. Security guards tell people, "No eating, no sitting on the grass—this is a garden, not a park." There are traffic jams of strollers and kids running loose. One security guard jokes into his radio, "There's a pterodactyl on the overlook!" In the pond in the Japanese Garden, ducks lobby for pieces of bread. A duck quacks, in Brooklynese, "Yeah, yeah, yeah," having heard it all before.

Then the cherry blossoms fall, they turn some paths completely pink next to the grass's green, and the petals dry, and people tread them into a fine pink powder. Kids visit on end-of-school-year field trips, and teachers yell, "Shawon, get back on line!" and boys with long T-shirts printed from neck to knee with an image of Martin Luther King's face run by laughing and swatting at one another. The yellow boxes that photographic film comes in fall on the ground, and here and there an empty bag of Crazy Calypso potato chips. The lilacs bloom, each bush with a scent slightly different from the next, and yellow tulips fill big round planters with color so bright it ascends in a column, like a searchlight beam. The roses open on the trellises in the Rose Garden and attract a lively air traffic of bees, and June wedding parties, brides and grooms and their

8. *Anna Karenina*, novel by the Russian writer Leo Tolstoy, published in serial installments between 1873 to 1877.

subsidiaries, adjust themselves minutely for photographers there. A rose called the Royal Gold smells like a new bathing suit and is as yellow.

15 In our building of nine apartments, two people have died and six have been born since we moved in. I like our neighbors—a guy who works for Off-Track Betting, a guy who works for the Department of Correction, a woman who works for Dean Witter,[9] an in-flight steward, a salesperson of subsidiary rights at a publishing house, a restaurant manager, two lawyers, a retired machinist, a Lebanese-born woman of ninety-five—as well as any I've ever had. We keep track of the bigger events in the building with the help of Chris, our downstairs neighbor. Chris lives on the ground floor and often has conversations in the hall while her foot props her door open. When our kids are sick, she brings them her kids' videos to watch, and when it rains she gives us rides to school. One year, Chris became pregnant and had to take a blood-thinning medicine and was in and out of the hospital. Finally, she had a healthy baby and came home, but then began to bleed and didn't stop. Her husband brought the baby to us about midnight and took Chris to the nearest emergency room. Early the next morning, the grandmother came and took the baby. Then for two days nobody heard anything. When we knocked on Chris's door we got no answer and when we called we got an answering machine. The whole building was expectant, spooky, quiet. The next morning I left the house and there in the foyer was Chris. She held her husband's arm, and she looked pale, but she was returning from the hospital under her own steam. I hugged her at the door, and it was the whole building hugging her. I walked to the garden seeing glory everywhere. I went to the Rose Garden and took a big Betsy McCall rose to my face and breathed into it as if it were an oxygen mask.

(1995)

9. Dean Witter, an American stock brokerage and securities firm, which merged with the investment banking house Morgan Stanley in 1997.

QUESTIONS

1. According to Frazier, Brooklynites identify themselves by neighborhood and subway line (see paragraph 1). In addition to his subway line, how does Frazier describe where he lives? What techniques help him present his Brooklyn neighborhood to readers who are nonresidents?

2. Frazier engages all of the senses: sight, sound, smell, taste, and touch. Choose one example of each that you find effective, and explain why.

3. Like Jhumpa Lahiri in "Rhode Island" (pp. 144–153), Frazier wishes to establish the uniqueness of his home. What features seem to be unique? What features seem universal? What relation do you see between the unique and the universal?

4. Write an essay about your neighborhood, using techniques you identified in questions 1 and 2.

David Guterson

Enclosed. Encyclopedic. Endured: The Mall of America

Last April, on a visit to the new Mall of America near Minneapolis, I carried with me the public-relations press kit provided for the benefit of reporters. It included an assortment of "fun facts" about the mall: 140,000 hot dogs sold each week, 10,000 permanent jobs, 44 escalators and 17 elevators, 12,750 parking places, 13,300 short tons of steel, $1 million in cash disbursed weekly from 8 automatic-teller machines. Opened in the summer of 1992, the mall was built on the 78-acre site of the former Metropolitan Stadium, a five-minute drive from the Minneapolis–St. Paul International Airport. With 4.2 million square feet of floor space—including twenty-two times the retail footage of the average American shopping center—the Mall of America was "the largest fully enclosed combination retail and family entertainment complex in the United States."

Eleven thousand articles, the press kit warned me, had already been written on the mall. Four hundred trees had been planted in its gardens, $625 million had been spent to build it, 350 stores had been leased. Three thousand bus tours were anticipated each year along with a half-million Canadian visitors and 200,000 Japanese tourists. Sales were projected at $650 million for 1993 and at $1 billion for 1996. Donny and Marie Osmond had visited the mall, as had Janet Jackson and Sally Jesse Raphael, Arnold Schwarzenegger, and the 1994 Winter Olympic Committee. The mall was five times larger than Red Square and twenty times larger than St. Peter's Basilica; it incorporated 2.3 miles of hallways and almost twice as much steel as the Eiffel Tower. It was also home to the nation's largest indoor theme park, a place called Knott's Camp Snoopy.

On the night I arrived, a Saturday, the mall was spotlit dramatically in the manner of a Las Vegas casino. It resembled, from the outside, a castle or fort, the Emerald City or Never-Never Land, impossibly large and vaguely unreal, an unbroken, windowless multi-storied edifice the size of an airport terminal.

Published in Harper's Magazine *(August 1993), a monthly magazine that often prints critical accounts of American cultural phenomena.*

Surrounded by parking lots and new freeway ramps, monolithic and imposing in the manner of a walled city, it loomed brightly against the Minnesota night sky with the disturbing magnetism of a mirage.

I knew already that the Mall of America had been imagined by its creators not merely as a marketplace but as a national tourist attraction, an immense zone of entertainments. Such a conceit raised provocative questions, for our architecture testifies to our view of ourselves and to the condition of our souls. Large buildings stand as markers in the lives of nations and in the stream of a people's history. Thus I could only ask myself: Here was a new structure that had cost more than half a billion dollars to erect—what might it tell us about ourselves? If the Mall of America was part of America, what was that going to mean?

5 I passed through one of the mall's enormous entranceways and took myself inside. Although from a distance the Mall of America had appeared menacing—exuding the ambience of a monstrous hallucination—within it turned out to be simply a shopping mall, certainly more vast than other malls but in tone and aspect, design and feel, not readily distinguishable from them. Its nuances were instantly familiar as the generic features of the American shopping mall at the tail end of the twentieth century: polished stone, polished tile, shiny chrome and brass, terrazzo floors, gazebos. From third-floor vistas, across vaulted spaces, the Mall of America felt endlessly textured—glass-enclosed elevators, neon-tube lighting, bridges, balconies, gas lamps, vaulted skylights—and densely crowded with hordes of people circumambulating in an endless promenade. Yet despite the mall's expansiveness, it elicited claustrophobia, sensory deprivation, and an unnerving disorientation. Everywhere I went I spied other pilgrims who had found, like me, that the straight way was lost and that the YOU ARE HERE landmarks on the map kiosks referred to nothing in particular.

Getting lost, feeling lost, being lost—these states of mind are intentional features of the mall's psychological terrain. There are, one notices, no clocks or windows, nothing to distract the shopper's psyche from the alternate reality the mall conjures. Here we are free to wander endlessly and to furtively watch our fellow wanderers, thousands upon thousands of milling strangers who have come with the intent of losing themselves in the mall's grand, stimulating design. For a few hours we share some common ground—a fantasy of infinite commodities and comforts—and then we drift apart forever. The mall exploits our acquisitive instincts without honoring our communal requirements, our eternal desire for discourse and intimacy, needs that until the twentieth century were traditionally met in our marketplaces but that are not met at all in giant shopping malls.

On this evening a few thousand young people had descended on the mall in pursuit of alcohol and entertainment. They had come to Gators, Hooters, and Knuckleheads, Puzzles, Fat Tuesday, and Ltl Ditty's. At Players, a sports bar, the woman beside me introduced herself as "the pregnant wife of an Iowa pig

farmer" and explained that she had driven five hours with friends to "do the mall party scene together." She left and was replaced by Kathleen from Minnetonka, who claimed to have "a real shopping thing—I can't go a week without buying new clothes. I'm not fulfilled until I buy something."

Later a woman named Laura arrived, with whom Kathleen was acquainted. "I *am* the mall," she announced ecstatically upon discovering I was a reporter. "I'd move in here if I could bring my dog," she added. "This place is heaven, it's a *mecca*."

"We egg each other on," explained Kathleen, calmly puffing on a cigarette. "It's like, sort of, an addiction."

"You want the truth?" Laura asked. "I'm constantly suffering from megamall withdrawal. I come here all the time." 10

Kathleen: "It's a sickness. It's like cocaine or something; it's a drug."

Laura: "Kathleen's got this thing about buying, but I just need to *be* here. If I buy something it's an added bonus."

Kathleen: "She buys stuff all the time; don't listen."

Laura: "Seriously, I feel sorry for other malls. They're so small and *boring*."

Kathleen seemed to think about this: "Richdale Mall," she blurted finally. 15 She rolled her eyes and gestured with her cigarette. "Oh, my God, Laura. Why did we even *go* there?"

There is, of course, nothing naturally abhorrent in the human impulse to dwell in marketplaces or the urge to buy, sell, and trade. Rural Americans traditionally looked forward to the excitement and sensuality of market day; Native Americans traveled long distances to barter and trade at sprawling, festive encampments. In Persian bazaars and in the ancient Greek agoras the very soul of the community was preserved and could be seen, felt, heard, and smelled as it might be nowhere else. All over the planet the humblest of people have always gone to market with hope in their hearts and in expectation of something beyond mere goods—seeking a place where humanity is temporarily in ascendance, a palette for the senses, one another.

But the illicit possibilities of the marketplace also have long been acknowledged. The Persian bazaar was closed at sundown; the Greek agora was off-limits to those who had been charged with certain crimes. One myth of the Old West we still carry with us is that market day presupposes danger; the faithful were advised to make purchases quickly and repair without delay to the farm, lest their attraction to the pleasures of the marketplace erode their purity of spirit.

In our collective discourse the shopping mall appears with the tract house, the freeway, and the backyard barbecue as a product of the American postwar years, a testament to contemporary necessities and desires and an invention not only peculiarly American but peculiarly of our own era too. Yet the mall's varied and far-flung predecessors—the covered bazaars of the Middle East, the stately arcades of Victorian England, Italy's vaulted and skylit gallerias, Asia's monsoon-protected urban markets—all suggest that the rituals of indoor shopping, although in their nuances not often like our own, are nevertheless broadly known. The late twentieth-century American contribution has been to transform the enclosed bazaar into an economic institution that is vastly profitable yet socially enervated, one that redefines in fundamental ways the human relationship to the marketplace. At the Mall of America—an extreme example—we discover ourselves thoroughly lost among strangers in a marketplace intentionally designed to serve no community needs.

In the strict sense the Mall of America is not a marketplace at all—the soul of a community expressed as a *place*—but rather a tourist attraction. Its promoters have peddled it to the world at large as something more profound than a local marketplace and as a destination with deep implications. "I believe we can make Mall of America stand for all of America," asserted the mall's general manager, John Wheeler, in a promotional video entitled *There's a Place for Fun in Your Life*. "I believe there's a shopper in all of us," added the director of marketing, Maureen Hooley. The mall has memorialized its opening-day proceedings by producing a celebratory videotape: Ray Charles singing "America the Beautiful," a laser show followed by fireworks, "The Star-Spangled Banner" and "The Stars and Stripes Forever," the Gatlin Brothers, and Peter Graves. "Mall of America . . . ," its narrator intoned. "The name alone conjures up images of greatness, of a retail complex so magnificent it could only happen in America."

20 Indeed, on the day the mall opened, Miss America visited. The mall's logo—a red, white, and blue star bisected by a red, white, and blue ribbon—decorated everything from the mall itself to coffee mugs and the flanks of buses. The idea, director of tourism Colleen Hayes told me, was to position America's largest mall as an institution on the scale of Disneyland or the Grand Canyon, a place simultaneously iconic and totemic, a revered symbol of the United States and a mecca to which the faithful would flock in pursuit of all things purchasable.

On Sunday I wandered the hallways of the pleasure dome with the sensation that I had entered an M. C. Escher drawing—there was no such thing as up or down, and the escalators all ran backward. A 1993 Ford Probe GT was displayed as if popping out of a giant packing box; a full-size home, complete with artificial lawn, had been built in the mall's rotunda. At the Michael Ricker Pewter Gallery I came across a miniature tableau of a pewter dog peeing on a pewter man's leg; at Hologram Land I pondered 3-D hallucinations of the Medusa and Marilyn Monroe. I passed a kiosk called The Sportsman's Wife; I stood beside a life-size statue of the Hamm's Bear, carved out of pine and available for $1,395 at a store called Minnesot-ah! At Pueblo Spirit I examined a "dream catcher"—a small hoop made from deer sinew and willow twigs and designed to be hung over its owner's bed as a tactic for filtering bad dreams. For a while I sat in front of Glamour Shots and watched while women were groomed and brushed for photo sessions yielding high-fashion self-portraits at $34.95 each. There was no stopping, no slowing down. I passed Mug Me, Queen for a Day, and Barnyard Buddies, and stood in the Brookstone store examining a catalogue: a gopher "eliminator" for $40 (it's a vibrating, anodized-aluminum stake), a "no-stoop" shoehorn for $10, a nose-hair trimmer for $18. At the arcade inside Knott's Camp Snoopy I watched while teenagers played Guardians of the 'Hood, Total Carnage, Final Fight, and Varth Operation Thunderstorm; a small crowd of them had gathered around a lean, cool character who stood calmly shooting video cowpokes in a game called Mad Dog McCree. Left thumb on his silver belt buckle, biceps pulsing, he banged away without remorse while dozens of his enemies crumpled and died in alleyways and dusty streets.

At Amazing Pictures a teenage boy had his photograph taken as a bodybuilder—his face smoothly grafted onto a rippling body—then proceeded to purchase this pleasing image on a poster, a sweatshirt, and a coffee mug. At Painted Tipi there was wild rice for sale, hand-harvested from Leech Lake, Minnesota. At Animalia I came across a polyresin figurine of a turtle retailing for $3,200. At Bloomingdale's I pondered a denim shirt with its sleeves ripped away, the sort of thing available at used-clothing stores (the "grunge look," a

Bloomingdale's employee explained), on sale for $125. Finally, at a gift shop in Knott's Camp Snoopy, I came across a game called Electronic Mall Madness, put out by Milton Bradley. On the box, three twelve-year-old girls with good features happily vied to beat one another to the game-board mall's best sales.

At last I achieved an enforced self-arrest, anchoring myself against a bench while the mall tilted on its axis. Two pubescent girls in retainers and braces sat beside me sipping coffees topped with whipped cream and chocolate sprinkles, their shopping bags gathered tightly around their legs, their eyes fixed on the passing crowds. They came, they said, from Shakopee—"It's nowhere," one of them explained. The megamall, she added, was "a buzz at first, but now it seems pretty normal. 'Cept my parents are like Twenty Questions every time I want to come here. 'Specially since the shooting."

On a Sunday night, she elaborated, three people had been wounded when shots were fired in a dispute over a San Jose Sharks jacket. "In the *mall*," her friend reminded me. "Right here at megamall. A shooting."

"It's like nowhere's safe," the first added.

They sipped their coffees and explicated for me the plot of a film they saw as relevant, a horror movie called *Dawn of the Dead*, which they had each viewed a half-dozen times. In the film, they explained, apocalypse had come, and the survivors had repaired to a shopping mall as the most likely place to make their last stand in a poisoned, impossible world. And this would have been perfectly all right, they insisted, except that the place had also attracted hordes of the infamous living dead—sentient corpses who had not relinquished their attraction to indoor shopping.

I moved on and contemplated a computerized cash register in the infant's section of the Nordstrom store: "The Answer Is Yes!!!" its monitor reminded clerks. "Customer Service Is Our Number One Priority!" Then back at Bloomingdale's I contemplated a bank of televisions playing incessantly an advertisement for Egoïste, a men's cologne from Chanel. In the ad a woman on a wrought-iron balcony tossed her black hair about and screamed long and passionately; then there were many women screaming passionately, too, and throwing balcony shutters open and closed, and this was all followed by a bottle of the cologne displayed where I could get a good look at it. The brief, strange drama repeated itself until I could no longer stand it.

America's first fully enclosed shopping center—Southdale Center, in Edina, Minnesota—is a ten-minute drive from the Mall of America and thirty-six years its senior. (It is no coincidence that the Twin Cities area is such a prominent player in mall history: Minnesota is subject to the sort of severe weather that makes climate-controlled shopping seductive.) Opened in 1956, Southdale spawned an era of fervid mall construction and generated a vast new industry. Shopping centers proliferated so rapidly that by the end of 1992, says the National Research Bureau, there were nearly 39,000 of them operating everywhere across the country. But while malls recorded a much-ballyhooed success in the America of the 1970s and early 1980s, they gradually became less profitable to run as the exhausted and overwhelmed American worker inevitably lost interest in leisure shopping. Pressed for time and short on money, shoppers turned to factory outlet centers, catalogue purchasing, and "category killers" (specialty stores such as Home Depot and Price Club) at the expense of shopping malls. The industry, unnerved, reinvented itself, relying on smaller and more convenient local centers—especially the familiar neighborhood strip mall—and building far fewer large regional malls in an effort to stay afloat through troubled times. With the advent of cable television's Home Shopping Network and the proliferation of specialty catalogue retailers (whose access to computerized market research has made them, in the Nineties, powerful competitors), the mall industry reeled yet further. According to the International Council of Shopping Centers, new mall construction in 1992 was a third of what it had been in 1989, and the value of mall-construction contracts dropped 60 percent in the same three-year period.

Anticipating a future in which millions of Americans will prefer to shop in the security of their living rooms—conveniently accessing online retail companies as a form of quiet evening entertainment—the mall industry, after less than forty years, experienced a full-blown mid-life crisis. It was necessary for the industry to re-invent itself once more, this time with greater attentiveness to the qualities that would allow it to endure relentless change. Anxiety-ridden and sapped of vitality, mall builders fell back on an ancient truth, one capable of sustaining them through troubled seasons: they discovered what humanity had always understood, that shopping and frivolity go hand in hand and are inherently symbiotic. *If you build it fun, they will come.*

The new bread-and-circuses approach to mall building was first ventured in 1985 by the four Ghermezian brothers—Raphael, Nader, Bahman, and Eskandar—builders of Canada's $750 million West Edmonton Mall, which included a water slide, an artificial lake, a miniature-golf course, a hockey rink, and forty-seven rides in an amusement park known as Fantasyland. The complex quickly generated sales revenues at twice the rate per square foot of retail space that could be squeezed from a conventional outlet mall, mostly by developing its own shopping synergy: people came for a variety of reasons and to do a variety of things. West Edmonton's carnival atmosphere, it gradually emerged, lubricated pocketbooks and inspired the sort of impulse buying on which malls everywhere thrive. To put the matter another way, it was time for a shopping-and-pleasure palace to be attempted in the United States.

After selling the Mall of America concept to Minnesotans in 1985, the Ghermezians joined forces with their American counterparts—Mel and Herb Simon of Indianapolis, owners of the NBA's Indiana Pacers and the nation's second-largest developers of shopping malls. The idea, in the beginning, was to outdo West Edmonton by building a mall far larger and more expensive—something visionary, a wonder of the world—and to include such attractions as fashionable hotels, an elaborate tour de force aquarium, and a monorail to the Minneapolis–St. Paul airport. Eventually the project was downscaled substantially: a million square feet of floor space was eliminated, the construction budget was cut, and the aquarium and hotels were never built (reserved, said marketing director Maureen Hooley, for "phase two" of the mall's development). Japan's Mitsubishi Bank, Mitsui Trust, and Chuo Trust together put up a reported $400 million to finance the cost of construction, and Teachers Insurance and Annuity Association (the majority owner of the Mall of America) came through with another $225 million. At a total bill of $625 million, the mall was ultimately a less ambitious project than its forebear up north on the Canadian plains, and neither as large nor as gaudy. Reflecting the economy's downturn, the parent companies of three of the mall's anchor tenants—Sears, Macy's, and Bloomingdale's—were battling serious financial trouble and needed substantial transfusions from mall developers to have their stores ready by opening day.

The mall expects to spend millions on marketing itself during its initial year of operation and has lined up the usual corporate sponsors—Ford, Pepsi, US West—in an effort to build powerful alliances. Its public-relations representatives travel to towns such as Rapid City, South Dakota, and Sioux City, Iowa, in order to drum up interest within the Farm Belt. Northwest Airlines, another corporate sponsor, offers package deals from London and Tokyo and fare adjustments for those willing to come from Bismarck, North Dakota; Cedar Rapids, Iowa; and Kalamazoo or Grand Rapids, Michigan. Calling itself a "premier tourism destination," the mall draws from a primary tourist market that incorporates the eleven Midwest states (and two Canadian provinces) lying within a day's drive of its parking lots. It also estimates that in its first six months of operation, 5.3 million out of 16 million visitors came from beyond the Twin Cities metropolitan area.

The mall has forecast a much-doubted figure of 46 million annual visits by 1996—four times the number of annual visits to Disneyland, for example, and twelve times the visits to the Grand Canyon. The number, Maureen Hooley explained, seems far less absurd when one takes into account that mall pilgrims make far more repeat visits—as many as eighty in a single year—than visitors to theme parks such as Disneyland. Relentless advertising and shrewd promotion, abetted by the work of journalists like myself, assure the mall that visitors will come in droves—at least for the time being. The national media have comported themselves as if the new mall were a place of light and promise, full of hope and possibility. Meanwhile the Twin Cities' media have been shameless: on opening night Minneapolis's WCCO-TV aired a one-hour mall special, hosted by local news anchors Don Shelby and Colleen Needles, and the *St. Paul Pioneer Press* (which was named an "official" sponsor of the opening) dedicated both a phone line and a weekly column to answering esoteric mall questions. Not to be outdone, the *Minneapolis Star Tribune* developed a special graphic to draw readers to mall stories and printed a vast Sunday supplement before opening day under the heading A WHOLE NEW MALLGAME. By the following Wednesday all perspective was in eclipse: the local press reported that at 9:05 A.M., the mall's Victoria's Secret outlet had recorded its first sale, a pair of blue/green silk men's boxer shorts; that mall developers Mel and Herb Simon ate black-bean soup for lunch at 12:30 P.M.; that Kimberly Levis, four years old, constructed a rectangular column nineteen bricks high at the mall's Lego Imagination Center; and that mall officials had retained a plumber on standby in case difficulties arose with the mall's toilets.

From all of this coverage—and from the words you now read—the mall gains status as a phenomenon worthy of our time and consideration: place as celebrity. The media encourage us to visit our megamall in the obligatory fashion we flock to *Jurassic Park*—because it is there, all glitter and glow, a piece of the terrain, a season's diversion, an assumption on the cultural landscape. All of us will want to be in on the conversation and, despite ourselves, we will go.

Lost in the fun house I shopped till I dropped, but the scale of the mall eventually overwhelmed me and I was unable to make a purchase. Finally I met Chuck Brand on a bench in Knott's Camp Snoopy; he was seventy-two and, in his personal assessment of it, had lost at least 25 percent of his mind. "It's fun being a doozy," he confessed to me. "The security cops got me figured and keep their distance. I don't get hassled for hanging out, not shopping. Because the deal is, when you're seventy-two, man, you're just about all done shopping." 35

After forty-seven years of selling houses in Minneapolis, Chuck comes to the mall every day. He carries a business card with his picture on it, his company name and phone number deleted and replaced by his pager code. His wife drops him at the mall at 10:00 A.M. each morning and picks him up again at six; in between he sits and watches. "I can't sit home and do nothing," he insisted. When I stood to go he assured me he understood: I was young and had things I had to do. "Listen," he added, "thanks for talking to me, man. I've been sitting in this mall for four months now and nobody ever said nothing."

The next day I descended into the mall's enormous basement, where its business offices are located. "I'm sorry to have to bring this up," my prearranged mall guide, Michelle Biesiada, greeted me. "But you were seen talking to one of our housekeepers—one of the people who empty the garbage?—and really, you aren't supposed to do that."

Later we sat in the mall's security center, a subterranean computerized command post where two uniformed officers manned a bank of television screens. The Mall of America, it emerged, employed 109 surveillance cameras to monitor the various activities of its guests, and had plans to add yet more. There were cameras in the food courts and parking lots, in the hallways and in Knott's Camp Snoopy. From where we sat, it was possible to monitor thirty-six locations simultaneously; it was also possible, with the use of a zoom feature, to narrow in on an object as small as a hand, a license plate, or a wallet.

While we sat in the darkness of the security room, enjoying the voyeuristic pleasures it allowed (I, for one, felt a giddy sense of power), a security guard noted something of interest occurring in one of the parking lots. The guard engaged a camera's zoom feature, and soon we were given to understand that a couple of bored shoppers were enjoying themselves by fornicating in the front seat of a parked car. An officer was dispatched to knock on their door and discreetly suggest that they move themselves along; the Mall of America was no place for this. "If they want to have sex they'll have to go elsewhere," a security officer told me. "We don't have anything against sex, per se, but we don't want it happening in our parking lots."

40 I left soon afterward for a tour of the mall's basement, a place of perpetual concrete corridors and home to a much-touted recyclery. Declaring itself "the most environmentally conscious shopping center in the industry," the Mall of America claims to recycle up to 80 percent of its considerable refuse and points to its "state-of-the-art" recycling system as a symbol of its dedication to Mother Earth. Yet Rick Doering of Browning-Ferris Industries—the company contracted to manage the mall's 700 tons of monthly garbage—described the on-site facility as primarily a public-relations gambit that actually recycles only a third of the mall's tenant waste and little of what is discarded by its thousands of visitors; furthermore, he admitted, the venture is unprofitable to Browning-Ferris, which would find it far cheaper to recycle the mall's refuse somewhere other than in its basement.

A third-floor "RecycleNOW Center," located next to Macy's and featuring educational exhibits, is designed to enhance the mall's self-styled image as a national recycling leader. Yet while the mall's developers gave Macy's $35 million to cover most of its "build-out" expenses (the cost of transforming the mall's basic structure into finished, customer-ready floor space), Browning-Ferris got nothing in build-out costs and operates the center at a total loss, paying rent equivalent to that paid by the mall's retailers. As a result, the company has had to look for ways to keep its costs to a minimum, and the mall's garbage is now sorted by developmentally disabled adults working a conveyor belt in the basement. Doering and I stood watching them as they picked at a stream of paper and plastic bottles; when I asked about their pay, he flinched and grimaced, then deflected me toward another supervisor, who said that wages were based on daily productivity. Did this mean that they made less than minimum wage? I inquired. The answer was yes.

Upstairs once again, I hoped for relief from the basement's oppressive, concrete gloom, but the mall felt densely crowded and with panicked urgency I made an effort to leave. I ended up instead at Knott's Camp Snoopy—the seven-acre theme park at the center of the complex—a place intended to alleviate claustrophobia by "bringing the outdoors indoors." Its interior landscape, the press kit claims, "was inspired by Minnesota's natural habitat—forests, meadows, river banks, and marshes . . ." And "everything you see, feel, smell and hear adds to the illusion that it's summertime, seventy degrees and you're outside enjoying the awesome splendor of the Minnesota woods."

Creators of this illusion had much to contend with, including sixteen carnival-style midway rides, such as the Pepsi Ripsaw, the Screaming Yellow Eagle, Paul Bunyan's Log Chute by Brawny, Tumbler, Truckin', and Huff 'n' Puff; fifteen places for visitors to eat, such as Funnel Cakes, Stick Dogs and Campfire Burgers, Taters, Pizza Oven, and Wilderness Barbecue; seven shops with names like Snoopy's Boutique, Joe Cool's Hot Shop, and Camp Snoopy Toys; and such assorted attractions as Pan for Gold, Hunter's Paradise Shooting Gallery, the Snoopy Fountain, and the video arcade that includes the game Mad Dog McCree.

As if all this were not enough to cast a serious pall over the Minnesota woods illusion, the theme park's designers had to contend with the fact that they could use few plants native to Minnesota. At a constant temperature of seventy degrees, the mall lends itself almost exclusively to tropical varieties—orange jasmine, black olive, oleander, hibiscus—and not at all to the conifers of Minnesota, which require a cold dormancy period. Deferring ineluctably to this troubling reality, Knott's Camp Snoopy brought in 526 tons of plants—tropical rhododendrons, willow figs, buddhist pines, azaleas—from such places as Florida, Georgia, and Mississippi.

45

Anne Pryor, a Camp Snoopy marketing representative, explained to me that these plants were cared for via something called "integrated pest management," which meant the use of predators such as ladybugs instead of pesticides. Yet every member of the landscape staff I spoke to described a campaign of late-night pesticide spraying as a means of controlling the theme park's enemies—mealybugs, aphids, and spider mites. Two said they had argued for integrated pest management as a more environmentally sound method of controlling insects but that to date it had not been tried.

Even granting that Camp Snoopy is what it claims to be—an authentic version of Minnesota's north woods tended by environmentally correct means—the question remains whether it makes sense to place a forest in the middle of the country's largest shopping complex. Isn't it true that if people want woods, they are better off not going to a mall?

On Valentine's Day last February—cashing in on the promotional scheme of a local radio station—ninety-two couples were married en masse in a ceremony at the Mall of America. They rode the roller coaster and the Screaming Yellow Eagle and were photographed beside a frolicking Snoopy, who wore an immaculate tuxedo. "As we stand here together at the Mall of America," presiding district judge Richard Spicer declared, "we are reminded that there is a place for fun in your life and you have found it in each other." Six months earlier, the Reverend Leith Anderson of the Wooddale Church in Eden Prairie conducted services in the mall's rotunda. Six thousand people had congregated by 10:00 A.M., and Reverend Anderson delivered a sermon entitled "The Unknown God of the Mall." Characterizing the mall as a "direct descendant" of the ancient Greek agoras, the reverend pointed out that, like the Greeks before us, we Americans have many gods. Afterward, of course, the flock went shopping, much to the chagrin of Reverend Delton Krueger, president of the Mall Area Religious Council, who told the *Minneapolis Star Tribune* that as a site for church services, the mall may trivialize religion. "A good many people in the churches," said Krueger, "feel a lot of the trouble in the world is because of materialism."

But a good many people in the mall business today apparently think the trouble lies elsewhere. They are moving forward aggressively on the premise that the dawning era of electronic shopping does not preclude the building of shopping-and-pleasure palaces all around the globe. Japanese developers, in a joint venture with the Ghermezians known as International Malls Incorporated, are planning a $400 million Mall of Japan, with an ice rink, a water park, a fantasy-theme hotel, three breweries, waterfalls, and a sports center. We might shortly predict, too, a Mall of Europe, a Mall of New England, a Mall of California, and perhaps even a Mall of the World. The concept of shopping in a frivolous atmosphere, concocted to loosen consumers' wallets, is poised to proliferate globally. We will soon see monster malls everywhere, rooted in the soil of every nation and offering a preposterous, impossible variety of commodities and entertainments.

The new malls will be planets unto themselves, closed off from this world in the manner of space stations or of science fiction's underground cities. Like the Mall of America and West Edmonton Mall—prototypes for a new generation of shopping centers—they will project a separate and distinct reality in which an "outdoor café" is not outdoors, a "bubbling brook" is a concrete watercourse, and a "serpentine street" is a hallway. Safe, surreal, and outside of time and space, they will offer the mind a potent dreamscape from which there is no present waking. This carefully controlled fantasy—now operable in Minnesota—is so powerful as to inspire psychological addiction or to elicit in visitors a catatonic obsession with the mall's various hallucinations. The new malls will be theatrical, high-tech illusions capable of attracting enormous crowds from distant points and foreign ports. Their psychology has not yet been tried pervasively on the scale of the Mall of America, nor has it been perfected. But in time our marketplaces, all over the world, will be in essential ways interchangeable, so thoroughly divorced from the communities in which they sit that they will appear to rest like permanently docked spaceships against the landscape, windowless and turned in upon their own affairs. The affluent will travel as tourists to each, visiting the holy sites and taking photographs in the catacombs of far-flung temples.

50 Just as Victorian England is acutely revealed beneath the grandiose domes of its overwrought train stations, so is contemporary America well understood from the upper vistas of its shopping malls, places without either windows or clocks where the temperature is forever seventy degrees. It is facile to believe, from this vantage point, that the endless circumambulations of tens of thousands of strangers—all loaded down with the detritus of commerce—resemble anything akin to community. The shopping mall is not, as the architecture critic Witold Rybczynski has concluded, "poised to become a real urban place" with "a variety of commercial and noncommercial functions." On the contrary, it is poised to multiply around the world as an institution offering only a desolate substitute for the rich, communal lifeblood of the traditional marketplace, which will not survive its onslaught.

Standing on the Mall of America's roof, where I had ventured to inspect its massive ventilation units, I finally achieved a full sense of its vastness, of how it overwhelmed the surrounding terrain—the last sheep farm in sight, the Mississippi River incidental in the distance. Then I peered through the skylights down into Camp Snoopy, where throngs of my fellow citizens caroused happily in the vast entrails of the beast.

Questions

1. In this article, Guterson often uses lists. Why do you think he does so? What effect do the long lists have on readers?

2. At various points in the article, the Mall of America is compared to Mecca, heaven, or a church, and those who shop and seek entertainment there are referred to as "pilgrims." In other places, the mall is referred to as "an addiction" or a drug. Which metaphor do you find more persuasive? Why?

3. Guterson claims that "our architecture testifies to our view of ourselves and to the condition of our souls" (paragraph 4). Write an article about a building you frequently go to (for example, the building in which your classroom is housed; a church, mosque, or synagogue; your dorm; or your parents' home). What does the architecture of that building say about those who frequent it? How does the architecture influence behavior or beliefs?

Human Nature

Anna Quindlen *Between the Sexes, a Great Divide*

Perhaps we all have the same memory of the first boy-girl party we attended. The floors were waxed, the music loud, the air thick with the smell of cologne. The boys stood on one side of the room and the girls on the other, each affecting a nonchalance belied by the shuffling male loafers and the occasional high birdlike sound of a female giggle.

Eventually, one of the taller, better-looking boys, perhaps dogged by two slightly shorter, squeakier acolytes, would make the big move across the chasm to ask the cutest girl to dance. Eventually, one of the girls would brave the divide to start a conversation on the other side. We would immediately develop a certain opinion of that girl, so that for the rest of our school years together, pajama parties would fairly crackle when she was not there.

None of us would consciously know it then, but what we were seeing, that great empty space in the center of the floor as fearful as a trapdoor, was the great division between the sexes. It was wonderful to think of the time when it would no longer be there, when the school gym would be a great meeting ground in which we would mingle freely, girl and boy, boy and girl, person to person, all alike. And maybe that's going to happen sometime in my lifetime, but I can't say I know when.

I've thought about this for some time, because I've written some loving things about men, and some nasty things too, and I meant them all. And I've always been a feminist, and I've been one of the boys as well, and I've given both sides a pretty good shot. I've spent a lot of time telling myself that men and women are fundamentally alike, mainly in the service of arguing that women should not only be permitted but be welcomed into a variety of positions and roles that only men occupied.

5 And then something happens, a little thing usually, and all I can see is that great shiny space in the middle of the dance floor where no one ever meets. "I swear to God we are a different species," one of my friends said on the telephone recently. I can't remember whether the occasion was a fight with her husband, a scene at work or a contretemps with a mutual male friend of ours. No matter. She's said it before and she'll say it again, just like all my other friends have said it to me, and I to them. Men are the other.

Quindlen wrote a twice-weekly op-ed column for the New York Times *from 1981 to 1994. This essay appeared in the "Hers" column of the* Times *on March 24, 1988.*

We are the other, too, of course. That's why we want to believe so badly that there are no others at all, because over the course of human history being other has meant being symbols of divinity, evil, carnal degeneration, perfect love, fertility and death, to name a few. And anybody who has ever been a symbol knows that it's about as relaxing as sitting on a piece of Louis XV furniture. It is also true that over the course of history, we have been subordinate to others, symbols of weakness, dependency and emotions run amok.

Yet isn't it odd that I feel that the prejudice is somehow easier to deal with than the simple difference? Prejudice is evil and can be fought, while difference simply is. I live with three males, one husband and two sons, and occasionally I realize with great clarity that they are gazing across a divide at me, not because of big differences among us, but because of small ones.

The amaryllis bulb haunts me. "Why did you put an onion in a pot in the bathroom?" my elder son asked several months ago. I explained that it was not an onion but an amaryllis bulb and that soon it would grow into fabulous flowers. "What is that thing in the bathroom?" his father said later the same day. Impatiently I explained again. A look flashed between them, and then the littlest boy, too. Mom. Weird. Women.

Once I would have felt anger flame inside me at that. But I've done the same so many times now. On the telephone a friend and I will be commiserating about the failure of our husbands to listen when we talk, or their inexorable linear thinking, or their total blindness to the use and necessity of things like amaryllis bulbs. One of us will sigh, and the other will know what the sigh means. Husband. Strange. Men. Is it any wonder that our relationships are so often riddled with misunderstandings and disappointments?

In the children you can see the beginnings, even though we raise them in households in which mothers do things fathers once did, and vice versa. Children try to nail down the world, and themselves, early on and in a very primitive and real way. I remember a stage with my elder son in which, going through the supermarket or walking down the street, he would pin me down on each person walking by, and on such disparate cultural influences as Vanna White and Captain Kangaroo, by demanding that I tell him which genitalia category they fell in. Very soon, he got the idea: us and them, him and her. It was all very well to say that all people are the same inside (even if I had believed it) but he thought the outside was very important, too, and it helped him classify the world. 10

I must never forget, I suppose, that even in the gym, with all that space between us, we still managed to pick partners and dance. It's the dance that's important, not the difference. (I shouldn't leave out who leads and who follows. But I speak to that from a strange perspective, since any man who has ever danced with me can attest to the fact that I have never learned to follow.)

I have just met the dance downstairs. My elder son has one of his best friends over, and he does not care that she is a girl, and she does not care that he is a boy. But she is complaining that he is chasing her with the plastic spider and making her scream, and he is grinning maniacally because that is just exactly the response he is looking for, and they are both having a great time.

Two children, raised in egalitarian households in the 1980s. Between them the floor already stretches, an ocean to cross before they can dance uneasily in one another's arms.

QUESTIONS

1. Mark the places in this essay where Quindlen, after describing "the first boy-girl party we attended" (paragraph 1), returns to it. How does she turn an event into a symbol of male–female differences?

2. Consider Quindlen's statement, "I've spent a lot of time telling myself that men and women are fundamentally alike, mainly in the service of arguing that women should not only be permitted but be welcomed into a variety of positions and roles that only men occupied" (paragraph 4). Does her admission that they are not fundamentally alike mean that women should not be welcomed into male positions and roles? Why?

3. As Quindlen in this essay casts men as the Other, so Scott Russell Sanders in "Looking at Women" (p. 179) casts women as the Other. How do they present and try to decipher what they do not fully know or understand?

4. Write an essay in which you turn an event into a symbol.

PAUL THEROUX *Being a Man*

THERE IS A PATHETIC sentence in the chapter "Fetishism" in Dr. Norman Cameron's book *Personality Development and Psychopathology.* It goes, "Fetishists are nearly always men; and their commonest fetish is a woman's shoe." I cannot read that sentence without thinking that it is just one more awful thing about being a man—and perhaps it is an important thing to know about us.

I have always disliked being a man. The whole idea of manhood in America is pitiful, in my opinion. This version of masculinity is a little like having to wear an ill-fitting coat for one's entire life (by contrast, I imagine femininity to be an oppressive sense of nakedness). Even the expression "Be a man!" strikes me as insulting and abusive. It means: Be stupid, be unfeeling, obedient, soldierly and stop thinking. Man means "manly"—how can one think about men without considering the terrible ambition of manliness? And yet it is part of every man's life. It is a hideous and crippling lie; it not only insists on difference and connives at superiority, it is also by its very nature destructive—emotionally damaging and socially harmful.

The youth who is subverted, as most are, into believing in the masculine ideal is effectively separated from women and he spends the rest of his life finding women a riddle and a nuisance. Of course, there is a female version of this

From Theroux's collection of essays Sunrise with Seamonsters *(1985).*

male affliction. It begins with mothers encouraging little girls to say (to other adults) "Do you like my new dress?" In a sense, little girls are traditionally urged to please adults with a kind of coquettishness, while boys are enjoined to behave like monkeys toward each other. The nine-year-old coquette proceeds to become womanish in a subtle power game in which she learns to be sexually indispensable, socially decorative and always alert to a man's sense of inadequacy.

Femininity—being lady-like—implies needing a man as witness and seducer; but masculinity celebrates the exclusive company of men. That is why it is so grotesque; and that is also why there is no manliness without inadequacy—because it denies men the natural friendship of women.

5 It is very hard to imagine any concept of manliness that does not belittle women, and it begins very early. At an age when I wanted to meet girls—let's say the treacherous years of thirteen to sixteen—I was told to take up a sport, get more fresh air, join the Boy Scouts, and I was urged not to read so much. It was the 1950s and if you asked too many questions about sex you were sent to camp—boy's camp, of course: the nightmare. Nothing is more unnatural or prison-like than a boy's camp, but if it were not for them we would have no Elks' Lodges, no pool rooms, no boxing matches, no Marines.

And perhaps no sports as we know them. Everyone is aware of how few in number are the athletes who behave like gentlemen. Just as high school basketball teaches you how to be a poor loser, the manly attitude toward sports seems to be little more than a recipe for creating bad marriages, social misfits, moral degenerates, sadists, latent rapists and just plain louts. I regard high school sports as a drug far worse than marijuana, and it is the reason that the average tennis champion, say, is a pathetic oaf.

Any objective study would find the quest for manliness essentially right-wing, puritanical, cowardly, neurotic and fueled largely by a fear of women. It is also certainly philistine. There is no book-hater like a Little League coach. But indeed all the creative arts are obnoxious to the manly ideal, because at their best the arts are pursued by uncompetitive and essentially solitary people. It makes it very hard for a creative youngster, for any boy who expresses the desire to be alone seems to be saying that there is something wrong with him.

It ought to be clear by now that I have something of an objection to the way we turn boys into men. It does not surprise me that when the President of the United States has his customary weekend off he dresses like a cowboy—it is both a measure of his insecurity and his willingness to please. In many ways, American culture does little more for a man than prepare him for modeling clothes in the L. L. Bean catalog. I take this as a personal insult because for many years I found it impossible to admit to myself that I wanted to be a writer. It was my guilty secret, because being a writer was incompatible with being a man.

There are people who might deny this, but that is because the American writer, typically, has been so at pains to prove his manliness that we have come to see literariness and manliness as mingled qualities. But first there was a fear that writing was not a manly profession—indeed, not a profession at all. (The paradox in American letters is that it has always been easier for a woman to write and for a man to be published.) Growing up, I had thought of sports as wasteful and humiliating, and the idea of manliness was a bore. My wanting to become a writer was not a flight from that oppressive roleplaying, but I quickly saw that it was at odds with it. Everything in stereotyped manliness goes against the life of the mind. The Hemingway personality is too tedious to go into here, and in any case his exertions are well known, but certainly it was not until this aberrant behavior was examined by feminists in the 1960s that any male writer dared question the pugnacity in Hemingway's fiction. All the bullfighting and arm wrestling and elephant shooting diminished Hemingway as a writer, but it is consistent with a prevailing attitude in American writing: one cannot be a male writer without first proving that one is a man.

10 It is normal in America for a man to be dismissive or even somewhat apologetic about being a writer. Various factors make it easier. There is a heartiness about journalism that makes it acceptable—journalism is the manliest form of American writing and, therefore, the profession the most independent-minded women seek (yes, it is an illusion, but that is my point). Fiction-writing is equated with a kind of dispirited failure and is only manly when it produces wealth—money is masculinity. So is drinking. Being a drunkard is another assertion, if misplaced, of manliness. The American male writer is traditionally proud of his heavy drinking. But we are also a very literal-minded people. A man proves his manhood in America in old-fashioned ways. He kills lions, like Hemingway; or he hunts ducks, like Nathanael West; or he makes pronouncements like, "A man should carry enough knife to defend himself with," as James Jones once said to a *Life* interviewer. Or he says he can drink you under the table. But even tiny drunken William Faulkner loved to mount a horse and go fox hunting, and Jack Kerouac roistered up and down Manhattan in a lumberjack shirt (and spent every night of *The Subterraneans* with his mother in Queens). And we are familiar with the lengths to which Norman Mailer is prepared, in his endearing way, to prove that he is just as much a monster as the next man.[1]

When the novelist John Irving was revealed as a wrestler, people took him to be a very serious writer; and even a bubble reputation like Erich (*Love Story*) Segal's was enhanced by the news that he ran the marathon in a respectable time. How surprised we would be if Joyce Carol Oates were revealed as a sumo wrestler or Joan Didion active in pumping iron. "Lives in New York City with her three children" is the typical woman writer's biographical note, for just as the male writer must prove he has achieved a sort of muscular manhood, the woman writer—or rather her publicists—must prove her motherhood.

There would be no point in saying any of this if it were not generally accepted that to be a man is somehow—even now in feminist-influenced America—a privilege. It is on the contrary an unmerciful and punishing burden. Being a man is bad enough; being manly is appalling (in this sense, women's lib has done much more for men than for women). It is the sinister silliness of men's fashions, and a clubby attitude in the arts. It is the subversion of good students. It is the

1. The writers named in this paragraph and the next are twentieth-century Americans whose personal lives may be seen as conforming (or not conforming, in the cases of Oates and Didion) to stereotypical ideas of masculinity.

so-called Dress Code of the Ritz-Carlton Hotel in Boston, and it is the institutionalized cheating in college sports. It is the most primitive insecurity.

And this is also why men often object to feminism but are afraid to explain why: of course women have a justified grievance, but most men believe—and with reason—that their lives are just as bad.

Questions

1. In this essay, Theroux makes many negative statements about being a man—or worse, being manly. Do you agree with his assessment of what it means to be a man or to be "manly"? Why or why not?

2. In paragraph 2, Theroux uses similes to describe his feelings about masculinity and femininity, claiming that "masculinity is . . . like having to wear an ill-fitting coat for one's entire life" and imagining "femininity to be an oppressive sense of nakedness." Write two similes, one describing your sense of what it is to be masculine, the other describing your sense of what it is to be feminine. How do your similes supplement, or differ from, Theroux's?

3. In paragraph 6, Theroux says he regards "high school sports as a drug far worse than marijuana." Consider his attitude toward sports throughout the essay. How does his sense of sports compare to yours? Explain the differences and similarities in a brief essay.

Scott Russell Sanders *Looking at Women*

On that sizzling July afternoon, the girl who crossed at the stoplight in front of our car looked, as my mother would say, as though she had been poured into her pink shorts. The girl's matching pink halter bared her stomach and clung to her nubbin breasts, leaving little to the imagination, as my mother would also say. Until that moment, it had never made any difference to me how much or little a girl's clothing revealed, for my imagination had been entirely devoted to other mysteries. I was eleven. The girl was about fourteen, the age of my buddy Norman who lounged in the back seat with me. Staring after her, Norman elbowed me in the ribs and murmured, "Check out that chassis."

His mother glared around from the driver's seat. "Hush your mouth."

"I was talking about that sweet Chevy," said Norman, pointing out a souped-up jalopy at the curb.

"I know what you were talking about," his mother snapped.

5 No doubt she did know, since mothers could read minds, but at first I did not have a clue. Chassis? I knew what it meant for a car, an airplane, a radio,

First published in the Georgia Review *(Spring 1989); later reprinted in Sanders's essay collection* Secrets of the Universe *(1991).*

or even a cannon to have a chassis. But could a girl have one as well? I glanced after the retreating figure, and suddenly noticed with a sympathetic twitching in my belly the way her long raven ponytail swayed in rhythm to her walk and the way her fanny jostled in those pink shorts. In July's dazzle of sun, her swinging legs and arms beamed at me a semaphore I could almost read.

As the light turned green and our car pulled away, Norman's mother cast one more scowl at her son in the rearview mirror, saying, "Just think how it makes her feel to have you two boys gawking at her."

How? I wondered.

"Makes her feel like hot stuff," said Norman, owner of a bold mouth.

"If you don't get your mind out of the gutter, you're going to wind up in the state reformatory," said his mother.

10 Norman gave a snort. I sank into the seat, and tried to figure out what power had sprung from that sashaying girl to zap me in the belly.

Only after much puzzling did it dawn on me that I must finally have drifted into the force-field of sex, as a space traveler who has lived all his years in free fall might rocket for the first time within gravitational reach of a star. Even as a bashful eleven-year-old I knew the word *sex*, of course, and I could paste that name across my image of the tantalizing girl. But a label for a mystery no more explains a mystery than the word *gravity* explains gravity. As I grew a beard and my taste shifted from girls to women, I acquired a more cagey language for speaking of desire, I picked up disarming theories. First by hearsay and then by experiment, I learned the delicious details of making babies. I came to appreciate the urgency for propagation that litters the road with maple seeds and drives salmon up waterfalls and yokes the newest crop of boys to the newest crop of girls. Books in their killjoy wisdom taught me that all the valentines and violins, the waltzes and glances, the long fever and ache of romance, were merely embellishments on biology's instructions that we multiply our kind. And yet, the fraction of desire that actually leads to procreation is so vanishingly small as to seem irrelevant. In his lifetime a man sways to a million longings, only a few of which, or perhaps none at all, ever lead to the fathering of children. Now, thirty years away from that July afternoon, firmly married, twice a father, I am still humming from the power unleashed by the girl in pink shorts, still wondering how it made her feel to have two boys gawk at her, still puzzling over how to dwell in the force-field of desire.

How should a man look at women? It is a peculiarly and perhaps neurotically human question. Billy goats do not fret over how they should look at nanny goats. They look or don't look, as seasons and hormones dictate, and feel what they feel without benefit of theory. There is more billy goat in most men than we care to admit. None of us, however, is pure goat. To live utterly as an animal would make the business of sex far tidier but also drearier. If we tried, like Rousseau,[1]

1. Jean-Jacques Rousseau (1712–1778), Swiss-born French philosopher, author, political theorist, and composer. His closeness to nature, individualism, rebellion against the established social and political order, and glorification of the emotions made him the father of French romanticism.

to peel off the layers of civilization and imagine our way back to some pristine man and woman who have not yet been corrupted by hand-me-down notions of sexuality, my hunch is that we would find, in our speculative state of nature, that men regarded women with appalling simplicity. In any case, unlike goats, we dwell in history. What attracts our eyes and rouses our blood is only partly instinctual. Other forces contend in us as well: the voices of books and religions, the images of art and film and advertising, the entire chorus of culture. Norman's telling me to relish the sight of females and his mother's telling me to keep my eyes to myself are only two of the many voices quarreling in my head.

If there were a rule book for sex, it would be longer than the one for baseball (that byzantine sport), more intricate and obscure than tax instructions from the Internal Revenue Service. What I present here are a few images and reflections that cling, for me, to this one item in such a compendium of rules: How should a man look at women?

Well before I was to see any women naked in the flesh, I saw a bevy of them naked in photographs, hung in a gallery around the bed of my freshman roommate at college. A *Playboy* subscriber, he would pluck the centerfold from its staples each month and tape another airbrushed lovely to the wall. The gallery was in place when I moved in, and for an instant before I realized what I was looking at, all that expanse of skin reminded me of a meat locker back in Newton Falls, Ohio. I never quite shook that first impression, even after I had inspected the pinups at my leisure on subsequent days. Every curve of buttock and breast was news to me, an innocent kid from the Puritan back roads. Today you would be hard pressed to find a college freshman as ignorant as I was of female anatomy, if only because teenagers now routinely watch movies at home that would have been shown, during my teen years, exclusively on the fly-speckled screens of honky-tonk cinemas or in the basement of the Kinsey Institute.[2] I studied those alien shapes on the wall with a curiosity that was not wholly sexual, a curiosity tinged with the wonder that astronomers must have felt when they pored over the early photographs of the far side of the moon.

15 The paper women seemed to gaze back at me, enticing or mocking, yet even in my adolescent dither I was troubled by the phony stare, for I knew this was no true exchange of looks. Those mascaraed eyes were not fixed on me but on a camera. What the models felt as they posed I could only guess—perhaps the boredom of any numbskull job, perhaps the weight of dollar bills, perhaps the sweltering lights of fame, perhaps a tingle of the power that launched a thousand ships.

Whatever their motives, these women had chosen to put themselves on display. For the instant of the photograph, they had become their bodies, as a prizefighter does in the moment of landing a punch, as a weightlifter does in the moment of hoisting a barbell, as a ballerina does in the whirl of a pirouette, as we all do in the crisis of making love or dying. Men, ogling such photographs,

2. Indiana University's Institute for Sex Research, directed, beginning in 1942, by American biologist Alfred Charles Kinsey (1894–1956).

are supposed to feel that where so much surface is revealed there can be no depths. Yet I never doubted that behind the makeup and the plump curves and the two dimensions of the image there was an inwardness, a feeling self as mysterious as my own. In fact, during moments when I should have been studying French or thermodynamics, I would glance at my roommate's wall and invent mythical lives for those goddesses. The lives I made up were adolescent ones, to be sure; but so was mine. Without that saving aura of inwardness, these women in the glossy photographs would have become merely another category of objects for sale, alongside the sports cars and stereo systems and liquors advertised in the same pages. If not extinguished, however, their humanity was severely reduced. And if by simplifying themselves they had lost some human essence, then by gaping at them I had shared in the theft.

What did that gaping take from me? How did it affect my way of seeing other women, those who would never dream of lying nude on a fake tiger rug before the million-faceted eye of a camera? The bodies in the photographs were implausibly smooth and slick and inflated, like balloon caricatures that might be floated overhead in a parade. Free of sweat and scars and imperfections, sensual without being fertile, tempting yet impregnable, they were Platonic ideals of the female form, divorced from time and the fluster of living, excused from the perplexities of mind. No actual woman could rival their insipid perfection.

The swains who gathered to admire my roommate's gallery discussed the pinups in the same tones and in much the same language as the farmers back home in Ohio used for assessing cows. The relevant parts of male or female bodies are quickly named—and, the *Kamasutra* and Marquis de Sade[3] notwithstanding, the number of ways in which those parts can be stimulated or conjoined is touchingly small—so these studly conversations were more tedious than chitchat about the weather. I would lie on my bunk pondering calculus or Aeschylus and unwillingly hear the same few nouns and fewer verbs issuing from one mouth after another, and I would feel smugly superior. Here I was, improving my mind, while theirs wallowed in the notorious gutter. Eventually the swains would depart, leaving me in peace, and from the intellectual heights of my bunk I would glance across at those photographs—and yield to the gravity of lust. Idiot flesh! How stupid that a counterfeit stare and artful curves, printed in millions of copies on glossy paper, could arouse me. But there it was, not the first proof of my body's automatism and not the last.

Nothing in men is more machinelike than the flipping of sexual switches. I have never been able to read with a straight face the claims made by D. H. Lawrence[4] and lesser pundits that the penis is a god, a lurking dragon. It more

3. The *Kamasutra*, detailed account (fourth-to-seventh centuries C.E.) of the art and technique of Indian erotics by the sage Vātsyāyana; Marquis de Sade (1740–1814), French author whose works, because of their pornographic and blasphemous subject matter, led to his repeated imprisonment and have been suppressed by the French courts as recently as 1957.

4. David Herbert Lawrence (1885–1930), English novelist and author of *Lady Chatterley's Lover* (1928).

nearly resembles a railroad crossing signal, which stirs into life at intervals to announce, "Here comes a train." Or, if the penis must be likened to an animal, let it be an ill-trained circus dog, sitting up and playing dead and heeling whenever it takes a notion, oblivious of the trainer's commands. Meanwhile, heart, lungs, blood vessels, pupils, and eyelids all assert their independence like the members of a rebellious troupe. Reason stands helpless at the center of the ring, cracking its whip.

20 While he was president, Jimmy Carter raised a brouhaha by confessing in a *Playboy* interview, of all shady places, that he occasionally felt lust in his heart for women. What man hasn't, aside from those who feel lust in their hearts for other men? The commentators flung their stones anyway. Naughty, naughty, they chirped. Wicked Jimmy. Perhaps Mr. Carter could derive some consolation from psychologist Allen Wheelis, who blames male appetite on biology: "We have been selected for desiring. Nothing could have convinced us by argument that it would be worthwhile to chase endlessly and insatiably after women, but something has transformed us from within, a plasmid has invaded our DNA, has twisted our nature so that now this is exactly what we *want* to do." Certainly, by Darwinian logic, those males who were most avid in their pursuit of females were also the most likely to pass on their genes. Consoling it may be, yet it is finally no solution to blame biology. "I am extremely sexual in my desires: I carry them everywhere and at all times," William Carlos Williams[5] tells us on the opening page of his autobiography. "I think that from that arises the drive which empowers us all. Given that drive, a man does with it what his mind directs. In the manner in which he directs that power lies his secret." Whatever the contents of my DNA, however potent the influence of my ancestors, I still must direct that rebellious power. I still must live with the consequences of my looking and my longing.

Aloof on their blankets like goddesses on clouds, the pinups did not belong to my funky world. I was invisible to them, and they were immune to my gaze. Not so the women who passed me on the street, sat near me in classes, shared a table with me in the cafeteria: it was risky to stare at them. They could gaze back, and sometimes did, with looks both puzzling and exciting. It only complicated matters for me to realize that so many of these strangers had taken precautions that men should notice them. The girl in matching pink halter and shorts who set me humming in my eleventh year might only have wanted to keep cool in the sizzle of July. But these alluring college femmes had deeper designs. Perfume, eye shadow, uplift bras (about which I learned in the Sears catalog), curled hair, stockings, jewelry, lipstick, lace—what were these if not hooks thrown out into male waters?

I recall being mystified in particular by spike heels. They looked painful to me, and dangerous. Danger may have been the point, since the spikes would have made good weapons—they were affectionately known, after all, as stilettos. Or danger may have been the point in another sense, because a woman

5. American poet and physician (1883–1963).

teetering along on such heels is tipsy, vulnerable, broadcasting her need for support. And who better than a man to prop her up, some guy who clomps around in brogans wide enough for the cornerstones of flying buttresses? (For years after college, I felt certain that spike heels had been forever banned, like bustles and foot-binding, but lately they have come back in fashion, and once more one encounters women teetering along on knife points.)

Back in those days of my awakening to women, I was also baffled by lingerie. I do not mean underwear, the proletariat of clothing, and I do not mean foundation garments, pale and sensible. I mean what the woman who lives in the house behind ours—owner of a shop called "Bare Essentials"—refers to as "intimate apparel." Those two words announce that her merchandise is both sexy and expensive. These flimsy items cost more per ounce than truffles, more than frankincense and myrrh. They are put-ons whose only purpose is in being taken off. I have a friend who used to attend the men's-only nights at Bare Essentials, during which he would invariably buy a slinky outfit or two, by way of proving his serious purpose, outfits that wound up in the attic because his wife would not be caught dead in them. Most of the customers at the shop are women, however, as the models are women, and the owner is a woman. What should one make of that? During my college days I knew about intimate apparel only by rumor, not being that intimate with anyone who would have tricked herself out in such finery, but I could see the spike heels and other female trappings everywhere I turned. Why, I wondered then and wonder still, do so many women decorate themselves like dolls? And does that mean they wish to be viewed as dolls?

On this question as on many others, Simone de Beauvoir has clarified matters for me, writing in *The Second Sex*:[6] "The 'feminine' woman in making herself prey tries to reduce man, also, to her carnal passivity; she occupies herself in catching him in her trap, in enchaining him by means of the desires she arouses in him in submissively making herself a thing." Those women who transform themselves into dolls, in other words, do so because that is the most potent identity available to them. "It must be admitted," Beauvoir concedes, "that the males find in woman more complicity than the oppressor usually finds in the oppressed. And in bad faith they take authorization from this to declare that she has *desired* the destiny they have imposed on her."

25 *Complicity, oppressor, bad faith:* such terms yank us into a moral realm unknown to goats. While I am saddled with enough male guilt to believe three-quarters of Beauvoir's claim, I still doubt that men are so entirely to blame for the turning of women into sexual dolls. I believe human history is more collaborative than her argument would suggest. It seems unlikely to me that one-half the species could have "imposed" a destiny on the other half, unless that other half were far more craven than the females I have known. Some women have

6. de Beauvoir, French novelist and essayist (1908–1986) who served as one of the most articulate exponents of existentialism; *Le Deuxième Sexe* (1949; translated as *The Second Sex*, 1953), a thorough analysis of women's status in society, became a classic of feminist literature.

expressed their own skepticism on this point. Thus Joan Didion: "That many women are victims of condescension and exploitation and sex-role stereotyping was scarcely news, but neither was it news that other women are not: nobody forces women to buy the package." Beauvoir herself recognized that many members of her sex refuse to buy the "feminine" package: "The emancipated woman, on the contrary, wants to be active, a taker, and refuses the passivity man means to impose on her."

Since my college years, back in the murky 1960s, emancipated women have been discouraging their unemancipated sisters from making spectacles of themselves. Don't paint your face like a clown's or drape your body like a mannequin's, they say. Don't bounce on the sidelines in skimpy outfits, screaming your fool head off, while men compete in the limelight for victories. Don't present yourself to the world as a fluff pastry, delicate and edible. Don't waddle across the stage in a bathing suit in hopes of being named Miss This or That.

A great many women still ignore the exhortations. Wherever a crown for beauty is to be handed out, many still line up to stake their claims. Recently, Miss Indiana Persimmon Festival was quoted in our newspaper about the burdens of possessing the sort of looks that snag men's eyes. "Most of the time I enjoy having guys stare at me," she said, "but every once in a while it makes me feel like a piece of meat." The news photograph showed a cheerleader's perky face, heavily made-up, with starched hair teased into a blond cumulus. She put me in mind not of meat but of a plastic figurine, something you might buy from a booth outside a shrine. Nobody should ever be seen as meat, mere juicy stuff to satisfy an appetite. Better to appear as a plastic figurine, which is not meant for eating, and which is a gesture, however crude, toward art. Joyce[7] described the aesthetic response as a contemplation of form without the impulse to action. Perhaps that is what Miss Indiana Persimmon Festival wishes to inspire in those who look at her, perhaps that is what many women who paint and primp themselves desire: to withdraw from the touch of hands and dwell in the eye alone, to achieve the status of art.

By turning herself (or allowing herself to be turned into) a work of art, does a woman truly escape men's proprietary stare? Not often, says the British critic John Berger. Summarizing the treatment of women in Western painting, he concludes that—with a few notable exceptions, such as works by Rubens and Rembrandt—the woman on canvas is a passive object displayed for the pleasure of the male viewer, especially for the owner of the painting, who is, by extension, owner of the woman herself. Berger concludes: "Men look at women. Women watch themselves being looked at. This determines not only most relations between men and women but also the relation of women to themselves. The surveyor of woman in herself is male: the surveyed female. Thus she turns herself into an object—and most particularly an object of vision: a sight."

That sweeping claim, like the one quoted earlier from Beauvoir, also seems to me about three-quarters truth and one-quarter exaggeration. I know men who outdo the peacock for show, and I know women who are so fully possessed

7. James Joyce (1882–1941), Irish novelist.

of themselves that they do not give a hang whether anybody notices them or not. The flamboyant gentlemen portrayed by Van Dyck are no less aware of being *seen* than are the languid ladies portrayed by Ingres.[8] With or without clothes, both gentlemen and ladies may conceive of themselves as objects of vision, targets of envy or admiration or desire. Where they differ is in their potential for action: the men are caught in the midst of a decisive gesture or on the verge of making one; the women wait like fuel for someone else to strike a match.

30 I am not sure the abstract nudes favored in modern art are much of an advance over the inert and voluptuous ones of the old school. Think of two famous examples: Duchamp's *Nude Descending a Staircase* (1912), where the faceless woman has blurred into a waterfall of jagged shards, or Picasso's *Les Demoiselles d'Avignon* (1907), where the five angular damsels have been hammered as flat as cookie sheets and fitted with African masks. Neither painting invites us to behold a woman, but instead to behold what Picasso or Duchamp can make of one.

The naked women in Rubens, far from being passive, are gleefully active, exuberant, their sumptuous pink bodies like rainclouds or plump nebulae. "His nudes are the first ones that ever made me feel happy about my own body," a woman friend told me in one of the Rubens galleries of the Prado Museum. I do not imagine any pinup or store-window mannequin or bathing-suited Miss Whatsit could have made her feel that way. The naked women in Rembrandt, emerging from the bath or rising from bed, are so private, so cherished in the painter's gaze, that we as viewers see them not as sexual playthings but as loved persons. A man would do well to emulate that gaze.

I have never thought of myself as a sight. How much that has to do with being male and how much with having grown up on the back roads where money was scarce and eyes were few, I cannot say. As a boy, apart from combing my hair when I was compelled to and regretting the patches on my jeans (only the poor wore patches), I took no trouble over my appearance. It never occurred to me that anybody outside my family, least of all a girl, would look at me twice. As a young man, when young women did occasionally glance my way, without any prospect of appearing handsome I tried at least to avoid appearing odd. A standard haircut and the cheapest versions of the standard clothes were camouflage enough. Now as a middle-aged man I have achieved once more that boyhood condition of invisibility, with less hair to comb and fewer patches to humble me.

Many women clearly pass through the world aspiring to invisibility. Many others just as clearly aspire to be conspicuous. Women need not make spectacles of themselves in order to draw the attention of men. Indeed, for my taste, the less paint and fewer bangles the better. I am as helpless in the presence of subtle lures as a male moth catching a whiff of pheromones. I am a sucker for hair ribbons, a scarf at the throat, toes leaking from sandals, teeth bared in a smile. By contrast, I have always been more amused than attracted by the

8. Anthony Van Dyck (1599–1641), Flemish painter who settled in England in 1632; Jean-Auguste-Dominique Ingres (1780–1867), French painter.

enameled exhibitionists whom our biblical mothers would identify as brazen hussies or painted Jezebels or, in the extreme cases, as whores of Babylon.

To encounter female exhibitionists in their full glory and variety, you need to go to a city. I never encountered ogling as a full-blown sport until I visited Rome, where bands of Italian men joined with gusto in appraising the charms of every passing female, and the passing females vied with one another in demonstrating their charms. In our own cities the most notorious bands of oglers tend to be construction gangs or street crews, men who spend much of their day leaning on the handles of shovels or pausing between bursts of riveting guns, their eyes tracing the curves of passersby. The first time my wife and kids and I drove into Boston we followed the signs to Chinatown, only to discover that Chinatown's miserably congested main street was undergoing repairs. That street also proved to be the city's home for X-rated cinemas and girlie shows and skin shops. LIVE SEX ACTS ON STAGE. PEEP SHOWS. PRIVATE BOOTHS. Caught in a traffic jam, we spent an hour listening to jackhammers and wolf whistles as we crept through the few blocks of pleasure palaces, my son and daughter with their noses hanging out the windows, my wife and I steaming. Lighted marquees peppered by burnt-out bulbs announced the titles of sleazy flicks; life-size posters of naked women flanked the doorways of clubs: leggy strippers in miniskirts, the originals for some of the posters, smoked on the curb between numbers.

After we had finally emerged from the zone of eros, eight-year-old Jesse 35
inquired, "What was *that* place all about?"

"Sex for sale," my wife Ruth explained.

That might carry us some way toward a definition of pornography: making flesh into a commodity, flaunting it like any other merchandise, divorcing bodies from selves. By this reckoning, there is a pornographic dimension to much advertising, where a charge of sex is added to products ranging from cars to shaving cream. In fact, the calculated imagery of advertising may be more harmful than the blatant imagery of the pleasure palaces, that frank raunchiness which Kate Millett refers to as the "truthful explicitness of pornography." One can leave the X-rated zone of the city, but one cannot escape the sticky reach of commerce, which summons girls to the high calling of cosmetic glamor, fashion, and sexual display, while it summons boys to the panting chase.

You can recognize pornography, according to D. H. Lawrence, "by the insult it offers, invariably, to sex, and to the human spirit." He should know, Millett argues in *Sexual Politics,* for in her view Lawrence himself was a purveyor of patriarchal and often sadistic pornography. I think she is correct about the worst of Lawrence, and that she identifies a misogynist streak in his work; but she ignores his career-long struggle to achieve a more public, tolerant vision of sexuality as an exchange between equals. Besides, his novels and stories all bear within themselves their own critiques. George Steiner reminds us that "the list of writers who have had the genius to enlarge our actual compass of sexual awareness, who have given the erotic play of the mind a novel focus, an area of recognition previously unknown or fallow, is very small." Lawrence belongs on that brief list. The chief insult to the human spirit is to deny it, to claim that we are merely conglomerations of molecules, to pretend that we exist purely as bundles of appetites or as food for the appetites of others.

Men commit that insult toward women out of ignorance, but also out of dread. Allen Wheelis again: "Men gather in pornographic shows, not to stimulate desire, as they may think, but to diminish fear. It is the nature of the show to reduce the woman, discard her individuality, her soul, make her into an object, thereby enabling the man to handle her with greater safety, to use her as a toy. . . . As women move increasingly toward equality, the felt danger to men increases, leading to an increase in pornography and, since there are some men whose fears cannot even so be stilled, to an increase also in violence against women."

40 *Make her into an object:* all the hurtful ways for men to look at women are variations on this betrayal. "Thus she turns herself into an object," writes Berger. A woman's ultimate degradation is in "submissively making herself a thing," writes Beauvoir. To be turned into an object—whether by the brush of a painter or the lens of a photographer or the eye of a voyeur, whether by hunger or poverty or enslavement, by mugging or rape, bullets or bombs, by hatred, racism, car crashes, fires, or falls—is for each of us the deepest dread; and to reduce another person to an object is the primal wrong.

Caught in the vortex of desire, we have to struggle to recall the wholeness of persons, including ourselves. Beauvoir speaks of the temptation we all occasionally feel to give up the struggle for a self and lapse into the inertia of an object: "Along with the ethical urge of each individual to affirm his subjective existence, there is also the temptation to forgo liberty and become a thing." A woman in particular, given so much encouragement to lapse into thinghood, "is often very well pleased with her role as the *Other.*"

Yet one need not forgo liberty and become a thing, without a center or a self, in order to become the Other. In our mutual strangeness, men and women can be doorways one for another, openings into the creative mystery that we share by virtue of our existence in the flesh. "To be sensual," James Baldwin writes, "is to respect and rejoice in the force of life, of life itself, and to be *present* in all that one does, from the effort of loving to the breaking of bread." The effort of loving is reciprocal, not only in act but in desire, an *I* addressing a *Thou,* a meeting in that vivid presence. The distance a man stares across at a woman, or a woman at a man, is a gulf in the soul, out of which a voice cries, *Leap, leap.* One day all men may cease to look on themselves as prototypically human and on women as lesser miracles; women may cease to feel themselves the targets for desire; men and women both may come to realize that we are all mere flickerings in the universal fire; and then none of us, male or female, need give up humanity in order to become the *Other.*

Ever since I gawked at the girl in pink shorts, I have dwelt knowingly in the force-field of sex. Knowingly or not, it is where we all dwell. Like the masses of planets and stars, our bodies curve the space around us. We radiate signals constantly, radio sources that never go off the air. We cannot help being centers of attraction and repulsion for one another. That is not all we are by a long shot, nor all we are capable of feeling, and yet, even after our much-needed revolution in sexual consciousness, the power of eros will still turn our heads and hearts. In a world without beauty pageants, there will still be beauty, however its definition may have changed. As long as men have eyes, they will gaze with yearning and confusion at women.

When I return to the street with the ancient legacy of longing coiled in my DNA, and the residues from a thousand generations of patriarchs silting my brain, I encounter women whose presence strikes me like a slap of wind in the face. I must prepare a gaze that is worthy of their splendor.

Questions

1. Several sections of this essay are grounded in specific episodes from Sanders's life. Identify the episodes and explain how he uses them.

2. The five sections of this essay are separated by typographical space rather than connected by prose transitions. Determine the content of each section and explain its relation to the content of the section that precedes it. Describe Sanders's strategies of organization and development.

3. In paragraph 12 Sanders asks, "How should a man look at women?" What is his answer? Where does he provide it?

4. Write an essay in which you answer, in your own terms, Sanders's question, "How should a man look at women?"

Amy Cunningham *Why Women Smile*

After smiling brilliantly for nearly four decades, I now find myself trying to quit. Or, at the very least, seeking to lower the wattage a bit.

Not everyone I know is keen on this. My smile has gleamed like a cheap plastic night-light so long and so reliably that certain friends and relatives worry that my mood will darken the moment my smile dims. "Gee," one says, "I associate you with your smile. It's the essence of you. I should think you'd want to smile more!" But the people who love me best agree that my smile—which springs forth no matter where I am or how I feel—hasn't been serving me well. Said my husband recently, "Your smiling face and unthreatening demeanor make people like you in a fuzzy way, but that doesn't seem to be what you're after these days."

Smiles are not the small and innocuous things they appear to be: Too many of us smile in lieu of showing what's really on our minds. Indeed, the success of the women's movement might be measured by the sincerity—and lack of it—in

Many of Cunningham's writings have appeared in wide-circulation magazines aimed at women, like this 1993 essay from Lear's Magazine, *a periodical no longer published.*

our smiles. Despite all the work we American women have done to get and maintain full legal control of our bodies, not to mention our destinies, we still don't seem to be fully in charge of a couple of small muscle groups in our faces.

We smile so often and so promiscuously—when we're angry, when we're tense, when we're with children, when we're being photographed, when we're interviewing for a job, when we're meeting candidates to employ—that the Smiling Woman has become a peculiarly American archetype. This isn't entirely a bad thing, of course. A smile lightens the load, diffuses unpleasantness, redistributes nervous tension. Women doctors smile more than their male counterparts, studies show, and are better liked by their patients.

5 Oscar Wilde's[1] old saw that "a woman's face is her work of fiction" is often quoted to remind us that what's on the surface may have little connection to what we're feeling. What is it in our culture that keeps our smiles on automatic pilot? The behavior seems to be an equal blend of nature and nurture. Research has demonstrated that since females often mature earlier than males and are less irritable, girls smile more than boys from the very beginning. But by adolescence, the differences in the smiling rates of boys and girls are so robust that it's clear the culture has done more than its share of the dirty work. Just think of the mothers who painstakingly embroidered the words ENTER SMILING on little samplers, and then hung their handiwork on doors by golden chains. Translation: "Your real emotions aren't welcome here."

Clearly, our instincts are another factor. Our smiles have their roots in the greetings of monkeys, who pull their lips up and back to show their fear of attack, as well as their reluctance to vie for a position of dominance. And like the opossum caught in the light by the clattering garbage cans, we, too, flash toothy grimaces when we make major mistakes. By declaring ourselves nonthreatening, our smiles provide an extremely versatile means of protection.

Our earliest baby smiles are involuntary reflexes having only the vaguest connection to contentment or comfort. In short, we're genetically wired to pull on our parents' heartstrings. As Desmond Morris explains in *Babywatching*, this is our way of attaching ourselves to our caretakers, as truly as baby chimps clench their mothers' fur. Even as babies we're capable of projecting onto others (in this case, our parents) the feelings we know we need to get back in return.

Bona fide social smiles occur at two-and-a-half to three months of age, usually a few weeks after we first start gazing with intense interest into the faces of our parents. By the time we are six months old, we are smiling and laughing regularly in reaction to tickling, feedings, blown raspberries, hugs, and peekaboo games. Even babies who are born blind intuitively know how to react to pleasurable changes with a smile, though their first smiles start later than those of sighted children.

Psychologists and psychiatrists have noted that babies also smile and laugh with relief when they realize that something they thought might be dangerous is not dangerous after all. Kids begin to invite their parents to indulge

1. Irish-born Victorian dramatist (1854–1900).

them with "scary" approach-avoidance games; they love to be chased or tossed up into the air. (It's interesting to note that as adults, we go through the same gosh-that's-shocking-and-dangerous-but-it's-okay-to-laugh-and-smile cycles when we listen to raunchy stand-up comics.)

10 From the wilds of New Guinea to the sidewalks of New York, smiles are associated with joy, relief, and amusement. But smiles are by no means limited to the expression of positive emotions: People of many different cultures smile when they are frightened, embarrassed, angry, or miserable. In Japan, for instance, a smile is often used to hide pain or sorrow.

Psychologist Paul Ekman, the head of the University of California's Human Interaction Lab in San Francisco, has identified 18 distinct types of smiles, including those that show misery, compliance, fear, and contempt. The smile of true merriment, which Dr. Ekman calls the Duchenne Smile, after the 19th century French doctor who first studied it, is characterized by heightened circulation, a feeling of exhilaration, and the employment of two major facial muscles: the zygomaticus major of the lower face, and the orbicularis oculi, which crinkles the skin around the eyes. But since the average American woman's smile often has less to do with her actual state of happiness than it does with the social pressure to smile no matter what, her baseline social smile isn't apt to be a felt expression that engages the eyes like this. Ekman insists that if people learned to read smiles, they could see the sadness, misery, or pain lurking there, plain as day.

Evidently, a woman's happy, willing deference is something the world wants visibly demonstrated. Woe to the waitress, the personal assistant or receptionist, the flight attendant, or any other woman in the line of public service whose smile is not offered up to the boss or client as proof that there are no storm clouds—no kids to support, no sleep that's been missed—rolling into the sunny workplace landscape. Women are expected to smile no matter where they line up on the social, cultural, or economic ladder: College professors are criticized for not smiling, political spouses are pilloried for being too serious, and women's roles in films have historically been smiling ones. It's little wonder that men on the street still call out, "Hey, baby, smile! Life's not *that* bad, is it?" to women passing by, lost in thought.

A friend remembers being pulled aside by a teacher after class and asked, "What is wrong, dear? You sat there for the whole hour looking so sad!" "All I could figure," my friend says now, "is that I wasn't smiling. And the fact that *she* felt sorry for me for looking normal made me feel horrible."

Ironically, the social laws that govern our smiles have completely reversed themselves over the last 2,000 years. Women weren't always expected to seem animated and responsive; in fact, immoderate laughter was once considered one of the more conspicuous vices a woman could have, and mirth was downright sinful. Women were kept apart, in some cultures even veiled, so that they couldn't perpetuate Eve's seductive, evil work. The only smile deemed appropriate on a privileged woman's face was the serene, inward smile of the Virgin Mary at Christ's birth, and even that expression was best directed exclusively at young children. Cackling laughter and wicked glee were the kinds of sounds heard only in hell.

15 What we know of women's facial expressions in other centuries comes mostly from religious writings, codes of etiquette, and portrait paintings. In 15th century Italy, it was customary for artists to paint lovely, blank-faced women in profile. A viewer could stare endlessly at such a woman, but she could not gaze back. By the Renaissance, male artists were taking some pleasure in depicting women with a semblance of complexity, Leonardo da Vinci's *Mona Lisa*, with her veiled enigmatic smile, being the most famous example.

The Golden Age of the Dutch Republic marks a fascinating period for studying women's facial expressions. While we might expect the drunken young whores of Amsterdam to smile devilishly (unbridled sexuality and lasciviousness were *supposed* to addle the brain), it's the faces of the Dutch women from fine families that surprise us. Considered socially more free, these women demonstrate a fuller range of facial expressions than their European sisters. Frans Hals's 1622 portrait of Stephanus Geraerdt and Isabella Coymans, a married couple, is remarkable not just for the full, friendly smiles on each face, but for the frank and mutual pleasure the couple take in each other.

In the 1800s, sprightly, pretty women began appearing in advertisements for everything from beverages to those newfangled Kodak Land cameras. Women's faces were no longer impassive, and their willingness to bestow status, to offer, proffer, and yield, was most definitely promoted by their smiling images. The culture appeared to have turned the smile, originally a bond shared between intimates, into a socially required display that sold capitalist ideology as well as kitchen appliances. And female viewers soon began to emulate these highly idealized pictures. Many longed to be more like her, that perpetually smiling female. She seemed so beautiful. So content. So whole.

By the middle of the 19th century, the bulk of America's smile burden was falling primarily to women and African-American slaves, providing a very portable means of protection, a way of saying, "I'm harmless. I won't assert myself here." It reassured those in power to see signs of gratitude and contentment in the faces of subordinates. As long ago as 1963, adman David Ogilvy declared the image of a woman smiling approvingly at a product clichéd, but we've yet to get the message. Cheerful Americans still appear in ads today, smiling somewhat less disingenuously than they smiled during the middle of the century, but smiling broadly nonetheless.

Other countries have been somewhat reluctant to import our "Don't worry, be happy" American smiles. When McDonald's opened in Moscow not long ago and when EuroDisney debuted in France last year, the Americans involved in both business ventures complained that they couldn't get the natives they'd employed to smile worth a damn.

20 Europeans visiting the United States for the first time are often surprised at just how often Americans smile. But when you look at our history, the relentless good humor (or, at any rate, the pretense of it) falls into perspective. The American wilderness was developed on the assumption that this country had a short-

age of people in relation to its possibilities. In countries with a more rigid class structure or caste system, fewer people are as captivated by the idea of quickly winning friends and influencing people. Here in the States, however, every stranger is a potential associate. Our smiles bring new people on board. The American smile is a democratic version of a curtsy or doffed hat, since, in this land of free equals, we're not especially formal about the ways we greet social superiors.

The civil rights movement never addressed the smile burden by name, but activists worked on their own to set new facial norms. African-American males stopped smiling on the streets in the 1960s, happily aware of the unsettling effect this action had on the white population. The image of the simple-minded, smiling, white-toothed black was rejected as blatantly racist, and it gradually retreated into the distance. However, like the women of Sparta and the wives of samurai, who were expected to look happy upon learning their sons or husbands had died in battle, contemporary American women have yet to unilaterally declare their faces their own property.

For instance, imagine a woman at a morning business meeting being asked if she could make a spontaneous and concise summation of a complicated project she's been struggling to get under control for months. She might draw the end of her mouth back and clench her teeth—*Eek!*—in a protective response, a polite, restrained expression of her surprise, not unlike the expression of a conscientious young schoolgirl being told to get out paper and pencil for a pop quiz. At the same time, the woman might be feeling resentful of the supervisor who sprang the request, but she fears taking that person on. So she holds back a comment. The whole performance resolves in a weird grin collapsing into a nervous smile that conveys discomfort and unpreparedness. A pointed remark by way of explanation or self-defense might've worked better for her—but her mouth was otherwise engaged.

We'd do well to realize just how much our smiles misrepresent us, and swear off for good the self-deprecating grins and ritual displays of deference. Real smiles have beneficial physiological effects, according to Paul Ekman. False ones do nothing for us at all.

"Smiles are as important as sound bites on television," insists producer and media coach Heidi Berenson, who has worked with many of Washington's most famous faces. "And women have always been better at understanding this than men. But the smile I'm talking about is not a cutesy smile. It's an authoritative smile. A genuine smile. Properly timed, it's tremendously powerful."

To limit a woman to one expression is like editing down an orchestra to one instrument. And the search for more authentic means of expression isn't easy in a culture in which women are still expected to be magnanimous smilers, helpmates in crisis, and curators of everybody else's morale. But change is already floating in the high winds. We see a boon in assertive female comedians who are proving that women can *dish out* smiles, not just wear them. Actress Demi Moore has stated that she doesn't like to take smiling roles. Nike is running ads that show unsmiling women athletes sweating, reaching, pushing themselves.

25

These women aren't overly concerned with issues of rapport; they're not being "nice" girls—they're working out.

If a woman's smile were truly her own, to be smiled or not, according to how the *woman* felt, rather than according to what someone else needed, she would smile more spontaneously, without ulterior, hidden motives. As Rainer Maria Rilke wrote in *The Journal of My Other Self*, "Her smile was not meant to be seen by anyone and served its whole purpose in being smiled."

That smile is my long-term aim. In the meantime, I hope to stabilize on the smile continuum somewhere between the eliciting grin of Farrah Fawcett and the haughty smirk of Jeane Kirkpatrick.[2]

2. Fawcett (1947–2009), television star and pinup girl of the 1970s, famous for her feathered hair; Kirkpatrick (1926–2006), American educator, diplomat, and U.S. ambassador to the United Nations under Ronald Reagan, 1981–85.

QUESTIONS

1. Were you or some people you know urged to smile or to smile more? How was the advice given? What do you think was the motive?

2. Collect some observational data on the way men and women interact with strangers and see if you can confirm any part of Cunningham's essay.

3. Several years after Cunningham wrote "Why Women Smile," she discovered new research on smiling (see "All Smiles Now," below). This research has made her change her view on women's smiles. Write a brief account of what these changes are and what new evidence they reflect.

4. Do you think that Paul Ekman's research on Buddhist monks fully applies to American women and their smiles? What issues remain? Write about the issues in an essay that draws on your own experience and observation.

FRIDAY, DECEMBER 29, 2006[3]
ALL SMILES NOW

I once wrote an essay called "Why Women Smile" for the women's magazine *Lear's*. More than fifteen years later, I'm still receiving checks from academic presses planning to re-run the article because, apparently, it "teaches well" in first-year college writing classes. . . .

But here's the quandary: I now know that a whole chunk of my article is incorrect. . . . For my research at the time, I interviewed a noted psychologist and facial expression expert Paul Ekman. I remember that when the piece was published, Ekman didn't seem so thrilled with it. He didn't write me back. I now know that's because he had been trying to tell me that he was conceiving of the human smile in a new way and that the feminists who thought women should smile less weren't approaching smiles from the right perspective. But I couldn't

3. Posted on Cunningham's blog (on Beliefnet.com) on this date.

hear him. Ekman then was just a short time from researching Tibetan monks and the Dalai Lama's smiling meditations. He was on his way to substantiating that smiles—even fake plastered-on smiles—can indeed lift our moods and keep us happier. So actually, smiling women have had the right idea all along.

But I was so attached to the notion that feminine niceness was some kind of pathology that I couldn't hear what Ekman was telling me. Indeed, I couldn't imagine that if you smiled while seated quietly in meditation, you would spread the energy of cheer throughout the world and rise up feeling better. I couldn't conceive of the topic spiritually.

Since then, Ekman has published his findings. And my melancholy little prose piece (which my mother always hated anyway) is out there like the Energizer Bunny banging its drum. So until I can make this wrong a right, do me a favor: Smile freely and broadly. Get happy.

Andrew Sullivan *What Is a Homosexual?*

Gay adolescents are offered what every heterosexual teenager longs for: to be invisible in the girls' locker room. But you are invisible in the boys' locker room, your desire as unavoidable as its object. In that moment, you learn the first homosexual lesson: that your survival depends upon self-concealment. I remember specifically coming back to high school after a long summer when I was fifteen and getting changed in the locker room for the first time again with a guy I had long had a crush on. But since the vacation, he had developed enormously: suddenly he had hair on his chest, his body had grown and strengthened, he was—clearly—no longer a boy. In front of me, he took off his shirt, and unknowingly, slowly, erotically stripped. I became literally breathless, overcome by the proximity of my desire. The gay teenager learns in that kind of event a form of control and sublimation, of deception and self-contempt, that never leaves his consciousness. He learns that that which would most give him meaning is most likely to destroy him in the eyes of others; that the condition of his friendships is the subjugation of himself.

In the development of any human being, these are powerful emotions. They form a person. The homosexual learns to make distinctions between his sexual desire and his emotional longings—not because he is particularly prone to objectification of the flesh, but because he needs to survive as a social and sexual being. The society separates these two entities, and for a long time the homosexual has no option but to keep them separate. He learns certain rules; and, as with a child learning grammar, they are hard, later on in life, to unlearn.

It's possible, I think, that whatever society teaches or doesn't teach about homosexuality, this fact will always be the case. No homosexual child,

From Sullivan's 1995 book, Virtually Normal: An Argument about Homosexuality.

surrounded overwhelmingly by heterosexuals, will feel at home in his sexual and emotional world, even in the most tolerant of cultures. And every homosexual child will learn the rituals of deceit, impersonation, and appearance. Anyone who believes political, social, or even cultural revolution will change this fundamentally is denying reality. This isolation will always hold. It is definitional of homosexual development. And children are particularly cruel. At the age of eleven, no one wants to be the odd one out; and in the arena of dating and hormones, the exclusion is inevitably a traumatic one.

It's also likely to be forlorn. Most people are liable to meet emotional rejection by sheer force of circumstance; but for a homosexual, the odds are simply far, far higher. My own experience suggests that somewhere between two and five percent of the population have involuntarily strong emotional and sexual attractions to the same sex. Which means that the pool of possible partners *starts* at one in twenty to one in fifty. It's no wonder, perhaps, that male homosexual culture has developed an ethic more of anonymous or promiscuous sex than of committed relationships. It's as if the hard lessons of adolescence lower permanently—by the sheer dint of the odds—the aspiration for anything more.

5 Did I know what I was? Somewhere, maybe. But it was much easier to know what I wasn't. I wasn't going to be able to enter into the world of dating girls; I wasn't going to be able to feel fully comfortable among the heterosexual climate of the male teenager. So I decided, consciously or subconsciously, to construct a trajectory of my life that would remove me from their company; give me an excuse, provide a dignified way out. In Anglo-Saxon culture, the wonk has such an option: he's too nerdy or intellectual to be absorbed by girls. And there is something masculine and respected in the discipline of the arts and especially the sciences. You can gain respect and still be different.

So I threw myself into my schoolwork, into (more dubiously) plays, into creative writing, into science fiction. Other homosexuals I have subsequently met pursued other strategies: some paradoxically threw themselves into sports, outjocking the jocks, gaining ever greater proximity, seeking respect, while knowing all the time that they were doomed to rejection. Others withdrew into isolation and despair. Others still, sensing their difference, flaunted it. At my high school, an older boy insisted on wearing full makeup to class; and he was accepted in a patronizing kind of way, his brazen otherness putting others at ease. They knew where they were with him; and he felt at least comfortable with their stable contempt. The rest of us who lived in a netherworld of sexual insecurity were not so lucky.

Most by then had a far more acute sense of appearances than those who did not need to hide anything; and our sense of irony, and of aesthetics, assumed a precociously arch form, and drew us subtly together. Looking back, I realize that many of my best friends in my teen years were probably homosexual; and that somewhere in our coded, embarrassed dialogue we admitted it. Many of us also embraced those ideologies that seemed most alien to what we feared we might be: of the sports jock, of the altar boy, of the young conservative. They were the ultimate disguises. And our recognition of ourselves in the other only confirmed our desire to keep it quiet.

I should add that many young lesbians and homosexuals seem to have had a much easier time of it. For many, the question of sexual identity was not a critical factor in their life choices or vocation, or even a factor at all. Perhaps because of a less repressive upbringing or because of some natural ease in the world, they affected a simple comfort with their fate, and a desire to embrace it. These people alarmed me: their very ease was the sternest rebuke to my own anxiety, because it rendered it irrelevant. But later in life, I came to marvel at the naturalness of their self-confidence, in the face of such concerted communal pressure, and to envy it. I had the more common self-dramatizing urge of the tortured homosexual, trapped between feeling wicked and feeling ridiculous. It's shameful to admit it, but I was more traumatized by the latter than by the former: my pride was more formidable a force than my guilt.

When people ask the simple question, *What is a homosexual?* I can only answer with stories like these. I could go on, but too many stories have already been told. Ask any lesbian or homosexual, and they will often provide a similar account. I was once asked at a conservative think tank what evidence I had that homosexuality was far more of an orientation than a choice, and I was forced to reply quite simply: my life. It's true that I have met a handful of lesbians and gay men over the years who have honestly told me that they genuinely had a choice in the matter (and a few heterosexuals who claim they too chose their orientation). I believe them; but they are the exception and not the rule. As homosexual lives go, my own was somewhat banal and typical.

10 This is not, of course, the end of the matter. Human experience begins with such facts, it doesn't end with them. There's a lamentable tendency to try to find some definitive solution to permanent human predicaments—in a string of DNA, in a conclusive psychological survey, in an analysis of hypothalami, in a verse of the Bible—in order to cut the argument short. Or to insist on the emotional veracity of a certain experience and expect it to trump any other argument on the table. But none of these things can replace the political and moral argument about how a society should deal with the presence of homosexuals in its midst. I relate my experience here not to impress or to shock or to gain sympathy, but merely to convey what the homosexual experience is actually like. You cannot discuss something until you know roughly what it is. * * *

In a society more and more aware of its manifold cultures and subcultures, we have been educated to be familiar and comfortable with what has been called "diversity": the diversity of perspective, culture, meaning. And this diversity is usually associated with what are described as cultural constructs: race, gender, sexuality, and so on. But as the obsession with diversity intensifies, the possibility of real difference alarms and terrifies all the more. The notion of collective characteristics—of attributes more associated with blacks than with whites, with Asians than with Latinos, with gay men than with straight men, with men than with women—has become anathema. They are marginalized as "stereotypes." The acceptance of diversity has come to mean the acceptance of the essential sameness of all types of people, and the danger of generalizing among them at all. In fact, it has become virtually a definition of "racist" to make any substantive generalizations about a particular ethnicity, and a definition of "homophobic" to make any generalizations about homosexuals.

What follows, then, is likely to be understood as "homophobic." But I think it's true that certain necessary features of homosexual life lead to certain unavoidable features of homosexual character. This is not to say that they define any random homosexual: they do not. As with any group or way of life, there are many, many exceptions. Nor is it to say that they define the homosexual life: it should be clear by now that I believe that the needs and feelings of homosexual children and adolescents are largely interchangeable with those of their heterosexual peers. But there are certain generalizations that can be made about adult homosexuals and lesbians that have the ring of truth.

Of course, in a culture where homosexuals remain hidden and wrapped in self-contempt, in which their emotional development is often stunted and late, in which the closet protects all sorts of self-destructive behavior that a more open society would not, it is still very hard to tell what is inherent in a homosexual life that makes it different, and what is simply imposed upon it. Nevertheless, it seems to me that even in the most tolerant societies, some of the differences that I have just described would inhere.

The experience of growing up profoundly different in emotional and psychological makeup inevitably alters a person's self-perception, tends to make him or her more wary and distant, more attuned to appearance and its foibles, more self-conscious and perhaps more reflective. The presence of homosexuals in the arts, in literature, in architecture, in design, in fashion could be understood, as some have, as a simple response to oppression. Homosexuals have created safe professions within which to hide and protect each other. But why these professions? Maybe it's also that these are professions of appearance. Many homosexual children, feeling distant from their peers, become experts at trying to figure out how to disguise their inner feelings, to "pass." They notice the signs and signals of social interaction, because they do not come instinctively. They develop skills early on that help them notice the inflections of a voice, the quirks of a particular movement, and the ways in which meaning can be conveyed in code. They have an ear for irony and for double meanings. Sometimes, by virtue of having to suppress their natural emotions, they find formal outlets to express themselves: music, theater, art. And so their lives become set on a trajectory which reinforces these trends.

15 As a child, I remember, as I suppressed the natural emotions of an adolescent, how I naturally turned in on myself—writing, painting, and participating in amateur drama. Or I devised fantasies of future exploits—war leader, parliamentarian, famous actor—that could absorb those emotions that were being diverted from meeting other boys and developing natural emotional relationships with them. And I developed mannerisms, small ways in which I could express myself, tiny revolts of personal space—a speech affectation, a ridiculous piece of clothing—that were, in retrospect, attempts to communicate something in code which could not be communicated in language. In this homosexual archness there was, of course, much pain. And it came as no surprise that once I had become more open about my homosexuality, these mannerisms declined. Once I found the strength to be myself, I had no need to act myself. So my

clothes became progressively more regular and slovenly; I lost interest in drama; my writing moved from fiction to journalism; my speech actually became less affected.

This, of course, is not a universal homosexual experience. Many homosexuals never become more open, and the skills required to survive the closet remain skills by which to earn a living. And many homosexuals, even once they no longer need those skills, retain them. My point is simply that the universal experience of self-conscious difference in childhood and adolescence—common, but not exclusive, to homosexuals—develops identifiable skills. They are the skills of mimesis; and one of the goods that homosexuals bring to society is undoubtedly a more highly developed sense of form, of style. Even in the most open of societies, I think, this will continue to be the case. It is not something genetically homosexual; it is something environmentally homosexual. And it begins young.

Questions

1. Throughout this essay Sullivan distinguishes between the "human experience" of all adolescents and experiences particular to or common among "homosexuals." Make a list of each. Were there features that you would have listed in the opposite column? What features did you expect Sullivan to mention that he did not?

2. Sullivan notes that it is currently unfashionable to think in terms of "stereotypes" of any group, whether based on race, gender, sexuality, or some other classification (paragraph 11). Even so, he has set himself the task of answering the question "What is a homosexual?" How does he define this key term without resorting to stereotypes?

3. Although Sullivan does not advance a political agenda or a set of social reforms, his essay implies actions that would be beneficial to homosexuals and, more generally, to American society. What are these?

4. Write an essay that attempts to define the characteristics of a particular group, using a variation of Sullivan's title, "What Is a ——?"

Henry Petroski

Falling Down Is Part of Growing Up

We are all engineers of sorts, for we all have the principles of machines and structures in our bones. We have learned to hold our bodies against the forces of nature as surely as we have learned to walk. We calculate the paths of our arms and legs with the computer of our brain, and we catch baseballs and footballs with

Included in To Engineer Is Human: The Role of Failure in Successful Design *(1985), the first of many books Petroski has written on industrial design, including everyday objects such as pencils, paper clips, toothpicks, and Post-it notes.*

more dependability than the most advanced weapons systems intercept missiles. We may wonder if human evolution may not have been the greatest engineering feat of all time. And though many of us forget how much we once knew about the principles and practice of engineering, the nursery rhymes and fairy tales of our youth preserve the evidence that we did know quite a bit.

We are born into a world swathed in trust and risk. And we become accustomed from the instant of birth to living with the simultaneous possibilities that there *will* be and that there will *not* be catastrophic structural failure. The doctor who delivers us and the nurses who carry us about the delivery room are cavalier human cranes and forklifts who have moved myriad babies from delivery to holding upside down to showing to mother to cleansing to footprinting to wristbanding to holding right-side up to showing to father to taking to the nursery. I watched with my heart in my mouth as my own children were so moved and rearranged, and the experience exhausted me. Surely sometime, somewhere, a baby has been dropped, surely a doctor has had butterfingers or a nurse a lapse of attention. But we as infants and we as parents cannot and do not and should not dwell on those remotely possible, hideous scenarios, or we might immobilize the human race in the delivery room. Instead, our nursery rhymes help us think about the unthinkable in terms of serenity.

Rock-a-bye baby
In the tree top.
When the wind blows,
The cradle will rock.
When the bough breaks,
The cradle will fall.
And down will come baby,
Cradle and all.

Home from the hospital, we are in the hands of our parents and friends and relatives—and structurally weak siblings. We are held up helpless over deep pile carpets and hard terrazzo floors alike, and we ride before we walk, risking the sudden collapse of an uncle's trick knee. We are transported across impromptu bridges of arms thrown up without plans or blueprints between mother and aunt, between neighbor and father, between brother and sister—none of whom is a registered structural engineer. We come to Mama and to Papa eventually to forget our scare reflex and we learn to trust the beams and girders and columns of their arms and our cribs. We become one with the world and nap in the lap of gravity. Our minds dream weightlessly, but our ears come to hear the sounds of waking up. We listen to the warm whispers giving structure to the world of silence, and we learn from the bridges of lullabyes and play that not only we but also the infrastructure needs attention.

London Bridge is falling down,
Falling down, falling down.

London Bridge is falling down,
My fair lady.

Build it up with wood and stone,
Wood and stone, wood and stone.
Build it up with wood and stone,
My fair lady.

The parts of our bodies learn to function as levers, beams, columns, and even structures like derricks and bridges as we learn to turn over in our cribs, to sit up, to crawl, to walk, and generally to support the weight of our own bodies as well as what we lift and carry. At first we do these things clumsily, but we learn from our mistakes. Each time the bridge of our body falls down, we build it up again. We pile back on hands and knees to crawl over the river meandering beneath us. We come to master crawling, and we come to elaborate upon it, moving faster and freer and with less and less concern for collapsing all loose in the beams and columns of our back and limbs. We extend our infant theory of structures and hypothesize that we can walk erect, cantilevering our semicircular canals in the stratosphere. We think these words in the Esperanto[1] of babble, and with the arrogance of youth we reach for the stars. With each tottering attempt to walk, our bodies learn from the falls what not to do next time. In time we walk without thinking and think without falling, but it is not so much that we have learned how to walk as we have learned not to fall. Sometimes we have accidents and we break our arms and legs. We have them fixed and we go on as before. Barring disease, we walk erect and correctly throughout our lives until our structure deteriorates with old age and we need to be propped up with canes or the like. For the majority of our lives walking generally becomes as dependable as one can imagine it to be, but if we choose to load the structure of our bodies beyond the familiar limits of walking, say by jogging or marathoning, then we run the risk of structural failure in the form of muscle pulls and bone fractures. But our sense of pain stops most of us from overexerting ourselves and from coming loose at our connections as we go round and round, hand in hand, day in and day out.

Ring around the rosie,
A pocket full of posies,
Ashes, ashes,
We all fall down.

If ontogeny recapitulates phylogeny,[2] if all that has come to be human races before the fetus floating in its own prehistory, then the child playing relives the 5

1. An artificial international language first constructed in the 1870s.

2. A late-nineteenth-century theory about evolution claimed that ontogeny, the growth of an individual organism, is a repetition of phylogeny, the evolutionary history of a species.

evolution of structural engineering in its blocks. And the blocks will be as stone and will endure as monuments to childhood, as Erector Sets and Tinker Toys and Legos will not. Those modern optimizations will long have folded and snapped in the frames and bridges of experiment, though not before the child will have learned from them the limitations of metal and wood and plastic. These lessons will be carried in the tool box of the mind to serve the carpenter in all of us in time.

Step on a crack
And break your mother's back.

The child will play with mud and clay, making cakes and bricks in the wonderful oven of the sun. The child will learn that concrete cracks a mother's back but that children's backs are as resilient as springs and pliant as saplings. The child will watch the erection of flowers on columns of green but break them for the smiles of its parents. Summer will roof houses in the bushes, vault cathedrals in the trees. The child will learn the meaning of time, and watch the structures fall into winter and become skeletons of shelters that will be built again out of the dark in the ground and the light in the sky. The child angry and victimized by other children angry will learn the meanings of vandalism and sabotage, of demolition and destruction, of collapse and decline, of the lifetime of structures—and the structure of life.

The Sphinx asked, "What walks on four legs in the morning,
two legs in the afternoon, and three legs in the evening?"

The child learns that the arms and legs of dolls and soldiers break, the wheels of wagons and tricycles turn against their purpose, and the bats and balls of games do not last forever. No child articulates it, but everyone learns that toys are mean. They teach us not the vocabulary but the reality of structural failure and product liability. They teach us that as we grow, the toys that we could not carry soon cannot carry us. They are as bridges built for the traffic of a lighter age, and their makers are as blameless as the builders of a lighter bridge. We learn that not everything can be fixed.

Humpty Dumpty sat on a wall;
Humpty Dumpty had a great fall.
All the King's horses and all the King's men
Couldn't put Humpty together again.

The adolescent learns that bones can break. The arms counterbalancing the legs locomoting are as fragile as the steel and iron railroad bridges under the reciprocating blows of the behemoths rushing through the nineteenth century. The cast of thousands of childhoods reminds the arms and legs, while they have grown stronger but brittle, that they have also grown taller and wiser. They fall less and less. They grow into the arms and legs of young adults making babies fly between them, wheeeee, up in the air unafraid of the gravity parents can throw away. But the weight of responsibility and bills and growing babies brings the parents down to earth and they begin to think of things besides their bridges of muscles and columns of bones. They think of jobs and joys of a different kind, perhaps even if they are engineers.

Jack and Jill went up the hill
To fetch a pail of water,
Jack fell down and broke his crown
And Jill came tumbling after.

The natural fragileness of things comes to be forgotten, for we have learned to take it easy on the man-made world. We do not pile too high or reach too far. We make our pencil points sharper, but we do not press as hard. We learn to write without snap, and the story of our life goes smoothly, but quickly becomes dull. (Everyone wishes secretly to be the writer pushing the pencil to its breaking point.) We feel it in our bones as we grow old and then we remember how brittle but exhilarating life can be. And we extend ourselves beyond our years and break our bones again, thinking what the hell. We have wisdom and we understand the odds and probabilities. We know that nothing is forever.

Three wise men of Gotham
Went to sea in a bowl:
If the vessel had been stronger,
My song would be longer.

10

As if it were not enough that the behavior of our very bodies accustoms us to the limitations of engineering structures, our language itself is ambiguous about the daily trials to which life and limb are subjected. Both human beings and inhuman beams are said to be under stress and strain that may lead to fatigue if not downright collapse. Breakdowns of man and machine can occur if they are called upon to carry more than they can bear. The anthropomorphic language of engineering is perhaps no accident since man is not only the archetypal machine but also the Ur-structure.

Furniture is among the oldest of inanimate engineering structures designed to carry a rather well-defined load under rather well-defined circumstances. We are not surprised that furniture used beyond its intended purpose is broken, and we readily blame the child who abuses the furniture rather than the designer of the furniture or the furniture itself when it is abused. Thus a chair must support a person in a sitting position, but it might not be expected to survive a brawl in a saloon. A bed might be expected to support a recumbent child, a small rocking chair only a toddler. But the child's bed would not necessarily be considered badly designed if it collapsed under the child's wild use of it as a trampoline, and a child's chair cannot be faulted for breaking under the weight of a heavier child using it as a springboard. The arms and legs of chairs, the heads and feet of beds, just like those of the people whom they serve, cannot be expected to be strong without limit.

Mother Goose is as full of structural failures as human history. The nursery rhymes acknowledge the limitations of the strength of the objects man builds as readily as fairy tales recognize the frailties of human nature. The story of Goldilocks and the Three Bears teaches us how we can unwittingly proceed from engineering success to failure. Papa Bear's chair is so large and so hard and so unyielding under the weight of Goldilocks that apparently without thinking she gains a confidence in the strength of all rocking chairs. Goldilocks next tries Mama Bear's chair, which is not so large but is softer, perhaps because it is built with a lighter wood. Goldilocks finds this chair too soft, however, too yielding in the cushion. Yet it is strong enough to support her. Thus the criterion of strength becomes less a matter of concern than the criteria of "give" and comfort, and Goldilocks is distracted by her quest for a comfortable chair at the expense of one sufficiently strong. Finally Goldilocks approaches Baby Bear's chair, which is apparently stiffer but weaker than Mama Bear's, with little if any apprehension about its safety, for Goldilocks' experience is that all chairs are overdesigned. At first the smallest chair appears to be "just right," but, as with all marginal engineering designs, whether chairs or elevated walkways, the chair suddenly gives way under Goldilocks and sends her crashing to the floor.

The failure of the chair does not keep Goldilocks from next trying beds without any apparent concern for their structural integrity. When Papa Bear's bed is too hard and Mama's is too soft, Goldilocks does not seem to draw a parallel with the chairs. She finds Baby Bear's bed "just right" and falls asleep in it without worrying about its collapsing under her. One thing the fairy tale implicitly teaches us as children is to live in a world of seemingly capricious structural failure and success without anxiety. While Goldilocks may worry about having broken Baby Bear's chair, she does not worry about all chairs and beds breaking. According to Bruno Bettelheim, the tale of Goldilocks and the Three Bears lacks some of the important features of a true fairy tale, for in it there is neither recovery nor consolation, there is no resolution of conflict, and Goldilocks' running away from the bears is not exactly a happy ending. Yet there is structural recovery and consolation in that the bed does not break, and there is thereby a structural happy ending.

If the story of Goldilocks demonstrates how the user of engineering products can be distracted into overestimating their strength, the story of the Three Little Pigs shows how the designer can underestimate the strength his structure may need in an emergency or, as modern euphemisms would put it, under extreme load or hypothetical accident conditions. We recall that each of the three pigs has the same objective: to build a house. It is implicit in the mother pig's admonishment as they set out that their houses not only will have to shelter the little pigs from ordinary weather, but must also stand up against any extremes to which the Big Bad Wolf may subject them.

15 The three little pigs are all aware of the structural requirements necessary to keep the wolf out, but they differ in their beliefs of how severe a wolf's onslaught can be, and some of the pigs would like to get by with the least work and the most play. Thus the individual pigs make different estimates of how strong their houses must be, and each reaches a different conclusion about how

much strength he can sacrifice to availability of materials and time of construction. That each pig thinks he is building his house strong enough is demonstrated by the first two pigs dancing and singing, "Who's afraid of the Big Bad Wolf." They think their houses are safe enough and that their brother laboring over his brick house has overestimated the strength of the wolf and overdesigned his structure. Finally, when the third pig's house is completed, they all dance and sing their assurances. It is only the test of the wolf's full fury that ultimately proves the third pig correct. Had the wolf been a bugaboo,[3] all three houses might have stood for many a year and the first two pigs never been proven wrong.

Thus the nursery rhymes, riddles, and fairy tales of childhood introduce us to engineering. From lullabyes that comfort us even as they sing of structural failure to fairy tales that teach us that we can build our structures so strong that they can withstand even the huffing and puffing of a Big Bad Wolf, we learn the rudiments and the humanness of engineering.

Our own bodies, the oral tradition of our language and our nursery rhymes, our experiences with blocks and sand, all serve to accustom us to the idea that structural failure is part of the human condition. Thus we seem to be preconditioned, or at least emotionally prepared, to expect bridges and dams, buildings and boats, to break now and then. But we seem not at all resigned to the idea of major engineering structures having the same mortality as we. Somehow, as adults who forget their childhood, we expect our constructions to have evolved into monuments, not into mistakes. It is as if engineers and non-engineers alike, being human, want their creations to be superhuman. And that may not seem to be an unrealistic aspiration, for the flesh and bone of steel and stone can seem immortal when compared with the likes of man.

3. Source of fear, real or imagined.

Questions

1. How well does Petroski's opening metaphor—"we are all engineers of sorts"—work? By the end of the essay does he convince you of this point? How are we not like engineers?

2. Have you ever used fairy tales to "prove" a point? What is gained by such a use—in Petroski's essay or in your own experience?

3. Describe a time when you or someone you know overstressed his or her body or a piece of furniture. What happened?

M. F. K. Fisher *Young Hunger*

It is very hard for people who have passed the age of, say, fifty to remember with any charity the hunger of their own puberty and adolescence when they are dealing with the young human animals who may be frolicking about them. Too often I have seen good people helpless with exasperation and real anger upon finding in the morning that cupboards and iceboxes have been stripped of their supplies by two or three youths—or even *one*—who apparently could have eaten four times their planned share at the dinner table the night before.

Such avidity is revolting, once past. But I can recall its intensity still; I am not yet too far from it to understand its ferocious demands when I see a fifteen-year-old boy wince and whiten at the prospect of waiting politely a few more hours for food, when his guts are howling for meat-bread-candy-fruit-cheese-milkmilkmilk-ANYTHING IN THE WORLD TO EAT.

I can still remember my almost insane desperation when I was about eighteen and was staying overnight with my comparatively aged godparents. I had come home alone from France in a bad continuous storm and was literally concave with solitude and hunger. The one night on the train seemed even rougher than those on board ship, and by the time I reached my godparents' home I was almost lightheaded.

I got there just in time for lunch. It is clear as ice in my mind: a little cup of very weak chicken broth, one salted cracker, one-half piece of thinly sliced toast, and then, ah then, a whole waffle, crisp and brown and with a piece of beautiful butter melting in its middle—which the maid deftly cut into four sections! One section she put on my godmother's plate. The next *two,* after a nod of approval from her mistress, she put on mine. My godfather ate the fourth.

5 There was a tiny pot of honey, and I dutifully put a dab of it on my piggish portion, and we all nibbled away and drank one cup apiece of tea with lemon. Both my godparents left part of their waffles.

It was simply that they were old and sedentary and quite out of the habit of eating amply with younger people: a good thing for them, but pure hell for me. I did not have the sense to explain to them how starved I was—which I would not hesitate to do now. Instead I prowled around my bedroom while the house slumbered through its afternoon siesta, wondering if I dared sneak to the strange kitchen for something, anything, to eat, and knowing I would rather die than meet the silent, stern maid or my nice, gentle little hostess.

Later we walked slowly down to the village, and I was thinking sensuously of double malted ice-cream sodas at the corner drugstore, but there was no possibility of such heaven. When we got back to the quiet house, the maid brought

From The Gastronomical Me *(1943), a memoir about Fisher's gastronomical coming of age and one of several books in which she draws on her experience of food in its social settings. The original chapter title was "To Feed Such Hunger" (1930).*

my godfather a tall glass of exquisitely rich milk, with a handful of dried fruit on the saucer under it, because he had been ill; but as we sat and watched him unwillingly down it, his wife said softly that it was such a short time until dinner that she was sure I did not want to spoil my appetite, and I agreed with her because I was young and shy.

When I dressed, I noticed that the front of my pelvic basin jutted out like two bricks under my skirt: I looked like a scarecrow.

Dinner was very long, but all I can remember is that it had, as *pièce de résistance,* half of the tiny chicken previously boiled for broth at luncheon, which my godmother carved carefully so that we should each have a bit of the breast and I, as guest, should have the leg, after a snippet had been sliced from it for her husband, who liked dark meat too.

There were hot biscuits, yes, the smallest I have ever seen, two apiece under a napkin on a silver dish. Because of them we had no dessert: it would be too rich, my godmother said. 10

We drank little cups of decaffeinized coffee on the screened porch in the hot Midwestern night, and when I went up to my room I saw that the maid had left a large glass of rich malted milk beside my poor godfather's bed.

My train would leave before five in the morning, and I slept little and unhappily, dreaming of the breakfast I would order on it. Of course when I finally saw it all before me, twinkling on the Pullman[1] silver dishes, I could eat very little, from too much hunger and a sense of outrage.

I felt that my hosts had been indescribably rude to me, and selfish and conceited and stupid. Now I know that they were none of these things. They had simply forgotten about any but their own dwindling and cautious needs for nourishment. They had forgotten about being hungry, being young, being . . .

In an essay by Max Beerbohm[2] about hosts and guests, the tyrants and the tyrannized, there is a story of what happened to him once when he was a schoolboy and someone sent him a hamper that held, not the usual collection of marmalade, sardines, and potted tongue, but twelve whole sausage-rolls.

"Of sausage-rolls I was particularly fond," he says. He could have dominated all his friends with them, of course, but "I carried the box up to my cubicle, and, having eaten two of the sausage-rolls, said nothing that day about the other ten, nor anything about them when, three days later, I had eaten them all—all, up there, alone." 15

What strange secret memories such a tale evokes! Is there a grown-up person anywhere who cannot remember some such shameful, almost insane act of greediness of his childhood? In recollection his scalp will prickle, and his palms will sweat, at the thought of the murderous risk he may have run from his outraged companions.

1. Pullman, the company that built and ran sleeping cars on American railroads from the 1890s to the 1960s.

2. English comic writer and caricaturist (1872–1956).

When I was about sixteen, and in boarding-school, we were allowed one bar of chocolate a day, which we were supposed to eat sometime between the sale of them at the little school bookstore at four-thirty and the seven o'clock dinner gong. I felt an almost unbearable hunger for them—not for one, but for three or four or five at a time, so that I should have *enough,* for once, in my yawning stomach.

I hid my own purchases for several days, no mean trick in a school where every drawer and cupboard was inspected, openly and snoopingly too, at least twice a week. I cannot remember now how I managed it, with such lack of privacy and my own almost insurmountable hunger every afternoon, but by Saturday I had probably ten chocolate bars—my own and a few I had bribed my friends who were trying to lose weight to buy for me.

I did not sign up for any of the usual weekend debauchery such as a walk to the village drugstore for a well-chaperoned double butterscotch and pecan sundae. Instead I lay languidly on my bed, trying to look as if I had a headache and pretending to read a very fancy book called, I think, *Martin Pippin in the Apple Orchard,*[3] until the halls quieted.

20 Then I arranged all my own and my roommate's pillows in a voluptuous pile, placed so that I could see whether a silent housemotherly foot stood outside the swaying monk's-cloth curtain that served as a door (to cut down our libidinous chitchat, the school board believed), and I put my hoard of Hersheys discreetly under a fold of the bedspread.

I unwrapped their rich brown covers and their tinfoil as silently as any prisoner chipping his way through a granite wall, and lay there breaking off the rather warm, rubbery, delicious pieces and feeling them melt down my gullet, and reading the lush symbolism of the book; and all the time I was hot and almost panting with the fear that people would suddenly walk in and see me there. And the strange thing is that nothing would have happened if they had!

It is true that I had more than my allotted share of candy, but that was not a crime. And my friends, full of their Saturday delights, would not have wanted ordinary chocolate. And anyway I had much more than I could eat, and was basically what Beerbohm calls, somewhat scornfully, "a host" and not "a guest": I loved to entertain people and dominate them with my generosity.

Then why was I breathless and nervous all during that solitary and not particularly enjoyable orgy? I suppose there is a Freudian explanation for it, or some other kind. Certainly the experience does not make me sound very attractive to myself. Even the certainty of being in good company is no real solace.

3. An illustrated children's book written by Eleanor Farjeon (1881–1965) and published in 1921.

Questions

1. Fisher's world is highly class-stratified. What markers of the upper class did you notice in her essay? Did they interfere with your enjoyment of it, or add to your pleasure as a reader?

2. Describe a time when you have been truly hungry. Was your experience like Fisher's—or different?

3. Narrate an episode when you or someone you know went on an eating binge. Was it truly enjoyable? Use Fisher as a model to describe your experience.

Jane Smiley

Belly, Dancing, Belly, Aching, Belly, Beasts

1. Vanity

A week or so ago, I told my fifteen-year-old daughter that I thought I would get my navel pierced. This sort of thing is not unusual for women whose husbands have left them. A friend of mine saw his ex-wife for the first time in two years not long ago, and she (aged fifty-five) revealed that she had been doing a lot of surfing and snowboarding lately. When he exclaimed that in their thirty-five years of marriage, he had maybe seen her in a bathing suit twice, she shrugged heartlessly and went back to her book. A navel-piercing, I thought, would be just the sort of secret, sexy act to put me in the right mood for the last third of my life, which I plan to model on that of either Pamela Harriman[1] or Victoria Woodhull[2]—two independent women who seem to have crossed back and forth over the border between men and women with ease and without being taken captive by either side. A nice diamond stud in my navel, or the more classic gold loop, would be something I could reveal on selected occasions as a code for other soon to be revealed things about me that no one would suspect. My daughter was not at all charmed by the idea, either of revelations of my inner nature or of the piercing itself. In fact, she declared that me piercing my navel was both disgusting to think about and outdated, and she couldn't say which was worse.

The thing about the belly is that it is simultaneously the most real and the most abstract body part. It is a region rather than a spot on the map, rather like the Sargasso Sea is a region of the Atlantic Ocean that is defined but unbounded. The navel is the single little rocky island in the region. It would be nice to put a lighthouse on it, not to warn travelers away, but to give the region something to be or do. My particular belly region is about as small as it could be, which is the way I like it. I know that the real problem with the navel-piercing would be that I would do it only to show off, a bad motive if ever there was one. But even though the belly is only a region, it is one we are often obsessed with. Over the

From Body: Writers Reflect on Parts of the Body *(1999), a collection edited by Sharon Sloan Fiffer and Steve Fiffer that includes essays on the brain, eyes, nose, teeth, skin, breasts, knees, and other body parts.*

1. English-born socialite (1920–1997) known for her affairs with and marriages to important, wealthy men. After taking U.S. citizenship, she became U.S. ambassador to France, 1993–1997.

2. American suffragist (1838–1927) who advocated sexual freedom.

years, I have spent more time contemplating my belly than contemplating my face. After all, you need a mirror to contemplate your face, but you can look down any time and wonder what your belly is saying about you. My belly is my vanity—I never wear makeup and never do anything more to my hair than wash it and comb it, I think because as long as my belly is flat, everything is generally okay and I can forget the other stuff.

2. HUNGER

Right around the time I was pondering navel-piercing, a woman said to me, "Why are you so thin? You eat like a field hand!" It's true. I know how to shovel it in. When I was married to my first husband, who was six foot ten, I used to make recipes designed for six. He would eat enough for four. I would eat enough for two. Our ongoing conversation, which was the best thing about our marriage, always stopped completely when we sat down to eat, and we never dined for longer than ten minutes. We shoveled fast but we shoveled with pure pleasure. I also drink with gusto, big gulps of lemonade, Diet Coke, cranberry juice, water, whatever. Thus my life comes back, over and over, every day, to the belly, which harbors the stomach and the intestines. I know that appetite is in the mind, that taste is in the tongue, that hunger, perhaps, is in the gullet, but I am never quite satisfied until I feel that little stretch of the belly. James Fallows[3] once wrote that Americans couldn't get enough to eat in Japan, because the food was fat-free; Americans, he felt, couldn't be satisfied without sensing that little smear of grease that lingers on the lips at the end of a good meal. I honor his opinion, but I don't share it. Volume is what I pay attention to, volume inside my belt. When there is no place left to put it, you have to take a rest.

Here are my favorite belly-fillers: French bread and French butter; eggplant parmesan; chicken cooked with saffron, garlic, and cream; chicken in a sweet red pepper sauce with Indian spices; jalapeno/artichoke dip with tortilla chips; sourdough toast; grilled ham and cheese; pork tamales; blue potatoes mashed with cream and butter. I like to cook and sing along to country music. If I find myself in a region of the country where it is difficult to find a good meal, I get impatient. Fortunately, I now live in California, where it is difficult not to find a good meal.

3. LOVE

5 Right around the time of the belly-piercing idea and the field-hand remark, I was sitting and talking to a friend of mine. I was recalling my first pregnancy, twenty years back, with a man now long ago and far away. I smiled, because that is what mothers do when they recall their first pregnancies. My friend laid his hand upon my flat belly with sudden and unconscious tenderness, the most loving gesture I have ever experienced.

3. American journalist (b. 1949) most noted for his affiliation with the *Atlantic Monthly*, but who has also written for *Slate*, the *New Yorker*, and the *New York Times*.

Love, of course, shares the belly with hunger, and it is, from first to last, an uneasy association. Until pregnancy, the stomach and the womb are easily distinguishable. A gas pain is a gas pain is a gas pain, a cramp is a cramp is a cramp. No woman ever mixes up the two. But one little conception, and pretty soon the stomach has a lot of complaints to make. Particular foods are in demand—my last pregnancy featured a hankering, at all hours, for guacamole. Others called out for steak or buttered toast. Morning sickness was noon sickness and evening sickness, too. And then, as soon as that subsided, there was movement. At first it felt like bubbles popping, then it felt like fluttering from side to side, then it organized itself into kicks and punches and rollings-over. The bulbous shape of a little foot could be seen pushing against the now vast hump of the belly. The stomach and the womb talked back and forth to one another—whenever the stomach hurt, the womb responded with Braxton Hicks contractions.[4] Once I ate lobster and I thought the result would be premature birth. I gained forty pounds with one, forty-five with the other two. The stomach in its endless hunger expressed the needs of the womb, and the babies weighed in at eight, nine and ten pounds.

Even though I knew what pregnancy was, even though I knew the baby was not "coming" but was indeed here, active within, the vastness of the belly and the counterweight I developed behind dismayed me. No mirror or photograph could capture how large I was, no reassurance that I wasn't very big could convince me. My spreading pelvis and aching uterine ligaments told me that I wasn't well-designed for mammalian reproduction; no woman is. It's a miracle humans have survived as well as they have. I knew for a fact that pregnancy, and, say, hunting and gathering could not possibly go together. The only things that go together comfortably with the last month of pregnancy are floating in the bathtub and complaining. And that was before I brought my mind to bear upon the child's eventual mode of exit, which was one of those things that has to be experienced to be imagined, and even then seems impossible.

Oh the little horned womb, that fills up with love and then pings back into shape, leaving the belly once again looking bland and complacent.

4. Animals

How fortunate we are to carry our bellies upright, the organs packed neatly, tightly, into the pelvis like items in a suitcase. Consider the Great Dane or the German shepherd, whose bellies have room, whose stomachs zig and zag, who, when leaping for a Frisbee, may feel a sudden twinge of pain that they don't understand and then die within hours of a torsion. My old Great Dane bloated twice, once after eating grass, which fermented in his stomach and locked the pyloric valve[5] shut, so he couldn't throw up. Within twenty minutes of our noticing the first symptoms, he was going into shock, but he was immediately relieved,

4. A sporadic tightening of the uterine wall in the second or third trimester of pregnancy.

5. The pylorus canal is part of the stomach. The pyloric valve is the muscle at the end of the pyloric canal that allows food to pass to the small intestine.

with a burp, when the vet put a tube down his throat. The second time was neither so easy nor so cheap. This time the stomach did turn halfway over, and required surgery. They tacked the stomach to the wall of the belly and cut away part of the valve into the small intestine so that nothing could get stuck in there ever again. And then there is the horse, ever and always in thrall to his digestive system. The horse evolved to eat vast quantities of poor forage fifteen to eighteen hours a day. The horse's belly is only really happy with a steady progress of greenery that never stops, never gets stuck, and never tries to back up. As they say in Pony Club, if your horse manages to regurgitate, he is about to die. The finest, best cared-for horse in the world can colic and pass on in an hour or two, the victim of a cascade of toxic effects that may grow out of a little belly pain. As with big dogs, the belly's position in the horse hinders rather than helps him. Once things get to sloshing around in that flexible space, they can turn over, get hung up, lose themselves. No matter how pregnant women ever get, they never, like mares, suffer from uterine torsion; gravity doesn't permit it.

10 Comparative anatomy is a trade-off—no mammal is quite right or quite wrong. Biomechanics giveth and it taketh away. Uprightness has given us back pain, on the one hand, but it has taken the pressure of gravity off our abdominal muscles.

5. Strength

The last time I was in this post-marriage state, I studied modern dance with the eighteen-year-olds. Every day, we put on our leotards and our tights and began our instruction by turning out our feet, stacking our vertebrae, neck to tailbone, and then slowly and deliberately rolling our heads forward and down. We simultaneously dropped our pelvises and bent our knees. After suspending ourselves for a moment in the final downward position, we slowly and deliberately rolled ourselves upward again. The strength for this was all in the belly. It is the belly that protects and cares for the delicate spine. It is the belly out of which, in dance, all movement grows, until every dancer is the Indian god Shiva,[6] balanced on one leg, arms spread in every direction, the other leg lifted high, energy flowing like light out of the mighty belly and spreading through the universe.

This time, I study horseback riding, which is quite like modern dance in its way. Once again, the belly is all, the center of the connection between the horse and the rider. Horses and riders are all backs—the horse's back muscles pass his strength and energy from his springing haunches to his supple shoulders and neck; the rider's back muscles flex and absorb the shock of the horse's movement as it moves upward from the rider's pelvic triangle to her shoulders, neck, and head. The rider's belly sustains and centers all this energy and prevents it from passing to her hands on the reins and locking there, against the horse's delicate mouth. Every day, the rider, like the dancer, puts her mind into her belly, and finds power there.

6. A Hindu deity, one of whose manifestations is the dancer Smiley describes.

6. Pain

My daughter reported to me that a girl she knew still has not recovered from her navel-piercing. Things seemed to be going well enough, with loose clothing and hip-hugging sweatpants, until the infection set in. Now it's been several months of agony, and she still can't wear a belt. I began at once to backpedal on my own navel-piercing fantasy. Perhaps a discreet tattoo would serve just as well, also on the belly, but at a distance from the navel and its nerve endings. The problem with a tattoo is that it has to be representational. A flower? How dull. A face? Whose? A name? Not erotic in the least. A butterfly or a dog? How like a bumper sticker. Actually, the only thing I can imagine that would be really fun to have tattooed onto your belly would be another navel, maybe with a picture of a diamond stud in it, and a line from Magritte[7] underneath, *This is not a navel.*

7. Belgian surrealist painter (1898–1967), one of whose famous paintings is *The Treachery of Images*, a realistic picture of a pipe with the caption, "This is not a pipe."

Questions

1. Have you had part of your body pierced or tattooed? Give your reasons for having it done or, if you didn't, for resisting having it done.

2. What is the organizing principle of Smiley's essay? Consider, among other things, her subtitles.

3. Compare and contrast Smiley's attitudes toward food with those described by M. F. K. Fisher in "Young Hunger" (pp. 206–208). Write a brief essay comparing and contrasting their attitudes.

Gloria Steinem

The Good News Is: These Are Not the Best Years of Your Life

If you had asked me a decade or more ago, I certainly would have said the campus was the first place to look for the feminist or any other revolution. I also would have assumed that student-age women, like student-age men, were much more likely to be activist and open to change than their parents. After all, campus revolts have a long and well-publicized tradition, from the students of medieval France, whose "heresy" was suggesting that the university be separate from the church, through the anticolonial student riots of

First published in Ms. *(September 1979), a feminist magazine started in 1971 at the beginning of the modern women's movement and aimed at "exploring the truths and complexities of women's lives and patriarchal oppression." Steinem was a founding editor.*

British India; from students who led the cultural revolution of the People's Republic of China, to campus demonstrations against the Shah of Iran. Even in this country, with far less tradition of student activism, the populist movement to end the war in Vietnam was symbolized by campus protests and mistrust of anyone over thirty.

It has taken me many years of traveling as a feminist speaker and organizer to understand that I was wrong about women; at least, about women acting on their own behalf. In activism, as in so many other things, I had been educated to assume that men's cultural pattern was the natural or the only one. If student years were the peak time of rebellion and openness to change for men, then the same must be true for women. In fact, a decade of listening to every kind of women's group—from brown-bag lunchtime lectures organized by office workers to all-night rap sessions at campus women's centers; from housewives' self-help groups to campus rallies—has convinced me that the reverse is more often true. Women may be the one group that grows more radical with age. Though some students are big exceptions to this rule, women in general don't begin to challenge the politics of our own lives until later.

Looking back, I realize that this pattern has been true for my life, too. My college years were full of uncertainties and the personal conservatism that comes from trying to win approval and fit into the proper grown-up and womanly role whether that means finding a well-to-do man to be supported by or a male radical to support. Nonetheless, I went right on assuming that brave exploring youth and cowardly conservative old age were the norms for everybody, and that I must be just an isolated and guilty accident. Though every generalization based on female culture has many exceptions, and should never be used as a crutch or excuse, I think we might be less hard on ourselves and each other as students, feel better about our potential for change as we grow older—and educate reporters who announce feminism's demise because its red-hot center is not on campus—if we figured out that for most of us as women, the traditional college period is an unrealistic and cautious time. Consider a few of the reasons.

As students, women are probably treated with more equality than we ever will be again. For one thing, we're consumers. The school is only too glad to get the tuitions we pay, or that our families or government grants pay on our behalf. With population rates declining because of women's increased power over childbearing, that money is even more vital to a school's existence. Yet more than most consumers, we're too transient to have much power as a group. If our families are paying our tuition, we may have even less power.

5 As young women, whether students or not, we're still in the stage most valued by male-dominant cultures: We have our full potential as workers, wives, sex partners, and childbearers.

That means we haven't yet experienced the life events that are most radicalizing for women: entering the paid-labor force and discovering how women are treated there; marrying and finding out that it is not yet an equal partnership; having children and discovering who is responsible for them and who is not; and aging, still a greater penalty for women than for men.

Furthermore, new ambitions nourished by the rebirth of feminism may make young women feel and behave a little like a classical immigrant group. We are determined to prove ourselves, to achieve academic excellence, and to prepare for interesting and successful careers. More noses are kept to more grindstones in an effort to demonstrate newfound abilities, and perhaps to allay suspicions that women still have to have more and better credentials than men. This doesn't leave much time for activism. Indeed, we may not yet know that it is necessary.

In addition, the very progress into previously all-male careers that may be revolutionary for women is seen as conservative and conformist by outside critics. Assuming male radicalism to be the measure of change, they interpret any concern with careers as evidence of "campus conservatism." In fact, "dropping out" may be a departure for men, but "dropping in" is a new thing for women. Progress lies in the direction we have not been.

Like most groups of the newly arrived or awakened, our faith in education and paper degrees also has yet to be shaken. For instance, the percentage of women enrolled in colleges and universities has been increasing at the same time that the percentage of men has been decreasing. Among students entering college in 1978, women *outnumbered* men for the first time. This hope of excelling at the existing game is probably reinforced by the greater cultural pressure on females to be "good girls" and observe somebody else's rules.

10 Though we may know intellectually that we need to have new games with new rules, we probably haven't quite absorbed such facts as the high unemployment rate among female Ph.D.s; the lower average salary among women college graduates of all races than among counterpart males who graduated from high school or less; the middle-management ceiling against which even those eagerly hired new business-school graduates seem to bump their heads after five or ten years; and the barrier-breaking women in nontraditional fields who become the first fired when recession hits. Sadly enough, we may have to personally experience some of these reality checks before we accept the idea that lawsuits, activism, and group pressure will have to accompany our individual excellence and crisp new degrees.

Then there is the female guilt trip, student edition. If we're not sailing along as planned, it must be *our* fault. If our mothers didn't "do anything" with their educations, it must have been *their* fault. If we can't study as hard as we think we must (because women still have to be better prepared than men), and have a substantial personal and sexual life at the same time (because women are supposed to care more about relationships than men do), then we feel inadequate, as if each of us were individually at fault for a problem that is actually culture-wide.

I've yet to be on a campus where most women weren't worrying about some aspect of combining marriage, children, and a career. I've yet to find one where many men were worrying about the same thing. Yet women will go right on suffering from the double-role problem and terminal guilt until men are encouraged, pressured, or otherwise forced, individually and collectively, to integrate themselves into the "women's work" of raising children and home-making. Until then, and until there are changed job patterns to allow equal parenthood, children will go right on growing up with the belief that only women can be loving and nurturing, and only men can be intellectual or active outside the home. Each half of the world will go on limiting the full range of its human talent.

Finally, there is the intimate political training that hits women in the teens and early twenties: the countless ways we are still brainwashed into assuming that women are dependent on men for our basic identities, both in our work and our personal lives, much more than vice versa. After all, if we're going to enter a marriage system that's still legally designed for a person and a half, submit to an economy in which women still average about fifty-nine cents on the dollar earned by men, and work mainly as support staff and assistants, or *co*-directors and *vice*-presidents at best, then we have to be convinced that we are not whole people on our own.

In order to make sure that we will see ourselves as half-people, and thus be addicted to getting our identity from serving others, society tries hard to convert us as young women into "man junkies"; that is, into people who are addicted to regular shots of male-approval and presence, both professionally and personally. We need a man standing next to us, actually and figuratively, whether it's at work, on Saturday night, or throughout life. (If only men realized how little it matters *which* man is standing there, they would understand that this addiction depersonalizes them, too.) Given the danger to a male-dominant system if young women stop internalizing this political message of derived identity, it's no wonder that those who try to kick the addiction—and, worse yet, to help other women do the same—are likely to be regarded as odd or dangerous by everyone from parents to peers.

15 With all that pressure combined with little experience, it's no wonder that younger women are often less able to support each other. Even young women who espouse feminist goals as individuals may refrain from identifying themselves as "feminist": it's okay to want equal pay for yourself (just one small reform) but it's not okay to want equal pay for women as a group (an economic revolution). Some retreat into individualized career obsessions as a way of avoiding this dangerous discovery of shared experience with women as a group. Others retreat into the safe middle ground of "I'm not a feminist but . . ." Still others become politically active, but only on issues that are taken seriously by their male counterparts.

The same lesson about the personal conservatism of younger women is taught by the history of feminism. If I hadn't been conned into believing the masculine stereotype of youth as the "natural" time for freedom and rebellion, a time of "sowing wild oats" that actually is made possible by the assurance of power and security later on, I could have figured out the female pattern of activism by looking at women's movements of the past.

In this country, for instance, the nineteenth-century wave of feminism was started by older women who had been through the radicalizing experience of getting married and becoming the legal chattel of their husbands (or the equally radicalizing experience of *not* getting married and being treated as spinsters). Most of them had also worked in the antislavery movement and learned from the political parallels between race and sex. In other countries, that wave was also led by women who were past the point of maximum pressure toward marriageability and conservatism.

Looking at the first decade of this second wave, it's clear that the early feminist activist and consciousness-raising groups of the 1960s were organized by women who had experienced the civil rights movement, or homemakers who had discovered that raising kids and cooking didn't occupy all their talents. While most campuses of the late sixties were still circulating the names of illegal abortionists privately (after all, abortion could damage our marriage value), slightly older women were holding press conferences and speak-outs about the reality of abortions (including their own, even though that often meant confessing to an illegal act) and demanding reform or repeal of anti-choice laws. Though rape had been a quiet epidemic on campus for generations, younger women victims were still understandably fearful of speaking up, and campuses encouraged silence in order to retain their reputation for safety with tuition-paying parents. It took many off-campus speak-outs, demonstrations against laws of evidence and police procedures, and testimonies in state legislatures before most student groups began to make demands on campus and local cops for greater rape protection. In fact, "date rape"—the common campus phenomenon of a young woman being raped by someone she knows, perhaps even by several students in a fraternity house—is just now being exposed. Marital rape, a more difficult legal issue, was taken up several years ago. As for battered women and the attendant exposé of husbands and lovers as more statistically dangerous than unknown muggers in the street, that issue still seems to be thought of as a largely noncampus concern, yet at many of the colleges and universities where I've spoken, there has been at least one case within current student memory of a young woman beaten or murdered by a jealous lover.

This cultural pattern of youthful conservatism makes the growing number of older women going back to school very important. They are life examples and pragmatic activists who radicalize women young enough to be their daughters. Now that the median female undergraduate age in this country is twenty-seven because so many older women have returned, the campus is becoming a major place for cross-generational connections.

None of this should denigrate the courageous efforts of young women, especially women on campus, and the many changes they've pioneered. On the contrary, they should be seen as even more remarkable for surviving the conservative pressures, recognizing societal problems they haven't yet fully experienced, and organizing successfully in the midst of a transient student population. Every women's history course, rape hot line, or campus newspaper that is finally covering *all* the news; every feminist professor whose job has been created or tenure saved by student pressure, or male administrator whose consciousness has been permanently changed; every counselor who's stopped guiding women one way and men another; every lawsuit that's been fueled by student energies against unequal athletic funds or graduate school requirements: all those accomplishments are even more impressive when seen against the backdrop of the female pattern of activism. 20

Finally, it would help to remember that a feminist revolution rarely resembles a masculine-style one—just as a young woman's most radical act toward her mother (that is, connecting as women in order to help each other get some power) doesn't look much like a young man's most radical act toward his father (that is, breaking the father-son connection in order to separate identities or take over existing power).

It's those father-son conflicts at a generational, national level that have often provided the conventional definition of revolution; yet they've gone on for centuries without basically changing the role of the female half of the world. They have also failed to reduce the level of violence in society, since both fathers and sons have included some degree of aggressiveness and superiority to women in their definition of masculinity, thus preserving the anthropological model of dominance.

Furthermore, what current leaders and theoreticians define as revolution is usually little more than taking over the army and the radio stations. Women have much more in mind than that. We have to uproot the sexual caste system that is the most pervasive power structure in society, and that means transforming the patriarchal values of those who run the institutions, whether they are politically the "right" or the "left," the fathers or the sons. This cultural part of the change goes very deep, and is often seen as too intimate, and perhaps too threatening, to be considered as either serious or possible. Only conflicts among men are "serious." Only a takeover of existing institutions is "possible."

That's why the definition of "political," on campus as elsewhere, tends to be limited to who's running for president, who's demonstrating against corporate investments in South Africa, or which is the "moral" side of some conventional revolution, preferably one that is thousands of miles away.

25 As important as such activities are, they are also the most comfortable ones when we're young. They provide a sense of virtue without much disruption in the power structure of our daily lives. Even when the most consistent energies on campus are actually concentrated around feminist issues, they may be treated as apolitical and invisible. Asked "What's happening on campus?" a student may reply, "The antinuke movement," even though that resulted in one demonstration of two hours, while student antirape squads have been patrolling the campus every night for two years and women's studies have begun to transform the very textbooks we read.

No wonder reporters and sociologists looking for revolution on campus often miss the depth of feminist change and activity that is really there. Women students themselves may dismiss it as not political and not serious. Certainly, it rarely comes in the masculine sixties style of bombing buildings or burning draft cards. In fact, it goes much deeper than protesting a temporary sympton—say, the draft—and challenges the right of one group to dominate another, which is the disease itself.

Young women have a big task of resisting pressures and challenging definitions. Their increasing success is a miracle of foresight and courage that should make us all proud. But they should know that they, too, may grow more radical with age.

One day, an army of gray-haired women may quietly take over the earth.

Questions

1. Trace Steinem's use of pronouns (I, we, they) throughout this piece. Why does she use "we" to refer to college-age women in some places and "they" in other places? What is the effect of her choice of pronouns?

2. In "Being a Man," Paul Theroux bristles against what seems to be expected of men, rejecting current definitions of masculinity. Steinem, in paragraph 22 of her essay, seems to imply that men have control over definitions of masculinity, arguing that "both fathers and sons have included some degree of aggressiveness and superiority to women in their definition of masculinity." Where do you think definitions of masculinity and femininity come from? Who can change them?

3. Steinem's article was originally published in 1979. Are her observations of college-age women applicable to women on your campus today? Write a brief essay discussing the differences and similarities between the young women she describes and the young women on your campus.

Elisabeth Kübler-Ross

On the Fear of Death

Let me not pray to be sheltered from dangers but to be fearless in facing them.
Let me not beg for the stilling of my pain but for the heart to conquer it.
Let me not look for allies in life's battlefield but to my own strength.
Let me not crave in anxious fear to be saved but hope for the patience to win my freedom.
Grant me that I may not be a coward, feeling your mercy in my success alone; but let me find the grasp of your hand in my failure.

—Rabindranath Tagore, *Fruit-Gathering*

Epidemics have taken a great toll of lives in past generations. Death in infancy and early childhood was frequent and there were few families who didn't lose a member of the family at an early age. Medicine has changed greatly in the last decades. Widespread vaccinations have practically eradicated many illnesses, at least in western Europe and the United States. The use of chemotherapy, especially the antibiotics, has contributed to an ever decreasing

A chapter from Kübler-Ross's celebrated 1969 book, On Death and Dying, *which traces the "stages of grief"—denial, anger, bargaining, depression, and acceptance—through which a dying person passes when faced with a terminal illness.*

number of fatalities in infectious diseases. Better child care and education has effected a low morbidity and mortality among children. The many diseases that have taken an impressive toll among the young and middle-aged have been conquered. The number of old people is on the rise, and with this fact come the number of people with malignancies and chronic diseases associated more with old age.

Pediatricians have less work with acute and life-threatening situations as they have an ever increasing number of patients with psychosomatic disturbances and adjustment and behavior problems. Physicians have more people in their waiting rooms with emotional problems than they have ever had before, but they also have more elderly patients who not only try to live with their decreased physical abilities and limitations but who also face loneliness and isolation with all its pains and anguish. The majority of these people are not seen by a psychiatrist. Their needs have to be elicited and gratified by other professional people, for instance, chaplains and social workers. It is for them that I am trying to outline the changes that have taken place in the last few decades, changes that are ultimately responsible for the increased fear of death, the rising number of emotional problems, and the greater need for understanding of and coping with the problems of death and dying.

When we look back in time and study old cultures and people, we are impressed that death has always been distasteful to man and will probably always be. From a psychiatrist's point of view this is very understandable and can perhaps best be explained by our basic knowledge that, in our unconscious, death is never possible in regard to ourselves. It is inconceivable for our unconscious to imagine an actual ending of our own life here on earth, and if this life of ours has to end, the ending is always attributed to a malicious intervention from the outside by someone else. In simple terms, in our unconscious mind we can only be killed; it is inconceivable to die of a natural cause or of old age. Therefore death in itself is associated with a bad act, a frightening happening, something that in itself calls for retribution and punishment.

One is wise to remember these fundamental facts as they are essential in understanding some of the most important, otherwise unintelligible communications of our patients.

5 The second fact that we have to comprehend is that in our unconscious mind we cannot distinguish between a wish and a deed. We are all aware of some of our illogical dreams in which two completely opposite statements can exist side by side—very acceptable in our dreams but unthinkable and illogical in our wakening state. Just as our unconscious mind cannot differentiate between the wish to kill somebody in anger and the act of having done so, the young child is unable to make this distinction. The child who angrily wishes his mother to drop dead for not having gratified his needs will be traumatized greatly by the actual death of his mother—even if this event is not linked closely in time with his destructive wishes. He will always take part or the whole blame for the loss of his mother. He will always say to himself—rarely to others—"I did it, I am responsible, I was bad, therefore Mommy left me." It is well to remember that the child will react in the same manner if he loses a

parent by divorce, separation, or desertion. Death is often seen by a child as an impermanent thing and has therefore little distinction from a divorce in which he may have an opportunity to see a parent again.

Many a parent will remember remarks of their children such as, "I will bury my doggy now and next spring when the flowers come up again, he will get up." Maybe it was the same wish that motivated the ancient Egyptians to supply their dead with food and goods to keep them happy and the old American Indians to bury their relatives with their belongings.

When we grow older and begin to realize that our omnipotence is really not so omnipotent, that our strongest wishes are not powerful enough to make the impossible possible, the fear that we have contributed to the death of a loved one diminishes—and with it the guilt. The fear remains diminished, however, only so long as it is not challenged too strongly. Its vestiges can be seen daily in hospital corridors and in people associated with the bereaved.

A husband and wife may have been fighting for years, but when the partner dies, the survivor will pull his hair, whine and cry louder and beat his chest in regret, fear and anguish, and will hence fear his own death more than before, still believing in the law of talion—an eye for an eye, a tooth for a tooth—"I am responsible for her death, I will have to die a pitiful death in retribution."

Maybe this knowledge will help us understand many of the old customs and rituals which have lasted over the centuries and whose purpose is to diminish the anger of the gods or the people as the case may be, thus decreasing the anticipated punishment. I am thinking of the ashes, the torn clothes, the veil, the *Klage Weiber*[1] of the old days—they are all means to ask you to take pity on them, the mourners, and are expressions of sorrow, grief, and shame. If someone grieves, beats his chest, tears his hair, or refuses to eat, it is an attempt at self-punishment to avoid or reduce the anticipated punishment for the blame that he takes on the death of a loved one.

This grief, shame, and guilt are not very far removed from feelings of anger and rage. The process of grief always includes some qualities of anger. Since none of us likes to admit anger at a deceased person, these emotions are often disguised or repressed and prolong the period of grief or show up in other ways. It is well to remember that it is not up to us to judge such feelings as bad or shameful but to understand their true meaning and origin as something very human. In order to illustrate this I will again use the example of the child—and the child in us. The five-year-old who loses his mother is both blaming himself for her disappearance and being angry at her for having deserted him and for no longer gratifying his needs. The dead person then turns into something the child loves and wants very much but also hates with equal intensity for this severe deprivation.

10

The ancient Hebrews regarded the body of a dead person as something unclean and not to be touched. The early American Indians talked about the evil spirits and shot arrows in the air to drive the spirits away. Many other cultures have rituals to take care of the "bad" dead person, and they all originate

1. Wailing wives.

in this feeling of anger which still exists in all of us, though we dislike admitting it. The tradition of the tombstone may originate in this wish to keep the bad spirits deep down in the ground, and the pebbles that many mourners put on the grave are left-over symbols of the same wish. Though we call the firing of guns at military funerals a last salute, it is the same symbolic ritual as the Indian used when he shot his spears and arrows into the skies.

I give these examples to emphasize that man has not basically changed. Death is still a fearful, frightening happening, and the fear of death is a universal fear even if we think we have mastered it on many levels.

What has changed is our way of coping and dealing with death and dying and our dying patients.

Having been raised in a country in Europe where science is not so advanced, where modern techniques have just started to find their way into medicine, and where people still live as they did in this country half a century ago, I may have had an opportunity to study a part of the evolution of mankind in a shorter period.

15 I remember as a child the death of a farmer. He fell from a tree and was not expected to live. He asked simply to die at home, a wish that was granted without questioning. He called his daughters into the bedroom and spoke with each one of them alone for a few moments. He arranged his affairs quietly, though he was in great pain, and distributed his belongings and his land, none of which was to be split until his wife should follow him in death. He also asked each of his children to share in the work, duties, and tasks that he had carried on until the time of the accident. He asked his friends to visit him once more, to bid good-bye to them. Although I was a small child at the time, he did not exclude me or my siblings. We were allowed to share in the preparations of the family just as we were permitted to grieve with them until he died. When he did die, he was left at home, in his own beloved home which he had built, and among his friends and neighbors who went to take a last look at him where he lay in the midst of flowers in the place he had lived in and loved so much. In that country today there is still no make-believe slumber room, no embalming, no false makeup to pretend sleep. Only the signs of very disfiguring illnesses are covered up with bandages and only infectious cases are removed from the home prior to the burial.

Why do I describe such "old-fashioned" customs? I think they are an indication of our acceptance of a fatal outcome, and they help the dying patient as well as his family to accept the loss of a loved one. If a patient is allowed to terminate his life in the familiar and beloved environment, it requires less adjustment for him. His own family knows him well enough to replace a sedative with a glass of his favorite wine; or the smell of a home-cooked soup may give him the appetite to sip a few spoons of fluid which, I think, is still more enjoyable than an infusion. I will not minimize the need for sedatives and infusions and realize full well from my own experience as a country doctor that they are sometimes life-saving and often unavoidable. But I also know that patience and familiar people and foods could replace many a bottle of intravenous fluids given for the simple reason that it fulfills the physiological need without involving too many people and/or individual nursing care.

The fact that children are allowed to stay at home where a fatality has stricken and are included in the talk, discussions, and fears gives them the feeling that they are not alone in the grief and gives them the comfort of shared responsibility and shared mourning. It prepares them gradually and helps them view death as part of life, an experience which may help them grow and mature.

This is in great contrast to a society in which death is viewed as taboo, discussion of it is regarded as morbid, and children are excluded with the presumption and pretext that it would be "too much" for them. They are then sent off to relatives, often accompanied with some unconvincing lies of "Mother has gone on a long trip" or other unbelievable stories. The child senses that something is wrong, and his distrust in adults will only multiply if other relatives add new variations of the story, avoid his questions or suspicions, shower him with gifts as a meager substitute for a loss he is not permitted to deal with. Sooner or later the child will become aware of the changed family situation and, depending on the age and personality of the child, will have an unresolved grief and regard this incident as a frightening, mysterious, in any case very traumatic experience with untrustworthy grownups, which he has no way to cope with.

It is equally unwise to tell a little child who lost her brother that God loved little boys so much that he took little Johnny to heaven. When this little girl grew up to be a woman she never solved her anger at God, which resulted in a psychotic depression when she lost her own little son three decades later.

20 We would think that our great emancipation, our knowledge of science and of man, has given us better ways and means to prepare ourselves and our families for this inevitable happening. Instead the days are gone when a man was allowed to die in peace and dignity in his own home.

The more we are making advancements in science, the more we seem to fear and deny the reality of death. How is this possible?

We use euphemisms, we make the dead look as if they were asleep, we ship the children off to protect them from the anxiety and turmoil around the house if the patient is fortunate enough to die at home, we don't allow children to visit their dying parents in the hospitals, we have long and controversial discussions about whether patients should be told the truth—a question that rarely arises when the dying person is tended by the family physician who has known him from delivery to death and who knows the weaknesses and strengths of each member of the family.

I think there are many reasons for this flight away from facing death calmly. One of the most important facts is that dying nowadays is more gruesome in many ways, namely, more lonely, mechanical, and dehumanized; at times it is even difficult to determine technically when the time of death has occurred.

Dying becomes lonely and impersonal because the patient is often taken out of his familiar environment and rushed to an emergency room. Whoever has been very sick and has required rest and comfort especially may recall his experience of being put on a stretcher and enduring the noise of the ambulance siren and hectic rush until the hospital gates open. Only those who have lived through this may appreciate the discomfort and cold necessity of such transportation which is only the beginning of a long order—hard to endure when you are well, difficult to express in words when noise, light, pumps, and voices are all too much to put up with. It may well be that we might consider more the patient under the sheets and blankets and perhaps stop our well-meant efficiency and rush in order to hold the patient's hand, to smile, or to listen to a question. I include the trip to the hospital as the first episode in dying, as it is for many. I am putting it exaggeratedly in contrast to the sick man who is left at home—not to say that lives should not be saved if they can be saved by a hospitalization but to keep the focus on the patient's experience, his needs and his reactions.

When a patient is severely ill, he is often treated like a person with no right to an opinion. It is often someone else who makes the decision if and when and where a patient should be hospitalized. It would take so little to remember that the sick person too has feelings, has wishes and opinions, and has—most important of all—the right to be heard.

Well, our presumed patient has now reached the emergency room. He will be surrounded by busy nurses, orderlies, interns, residents, a lab technician perhaps who will take some blood, an electrocardiogram technician who takes the cardiogram. He may be moved to X-ray and he will overhear opinions of his condition and discussions and questions to members of the family. He slowly but surely is beginning to be treated like a thing. He is no longer a person. Decisions are made often without his opinion. If he tries to rebel he will be sedated and after hours of waiting and wondering whether he has the strength, he will be wheeled into the operating room or intensive treatment unit and become an object of great concern and great financial investment.

He may cry for rest, peace, and dignity, but he will get infusions, transfusions, a heart machine, or tracheotomy if necessary. He may want one single person to stop for one single minute so that he can ask one single question—but he will get a dozen people around the clock, all busily preoccupied with his heart rate, pulse, electrocardiogram or pulmonary functions, his secretions or excretions but not with him as a human being. He may wish to fight it all but it is going to be a useless fight since all this is done in the fight for his life, and if they can save his life they can consider the person afterwards. Those who consider the person first may lose precious time to save his life! At least this seems to be the rationale or justification behind all this—or is it? Is the reason for this increasingly mechanical, depersonalized approach our own defensiveness? Is this approach our own way to cope with and repress the anxieties that a terminally or critically ill patient evokes in us? Is our concentration on equipment, on blood pressure our desperate attempt to deny the impending death which is so frightening and discomforting to us that we displace all our knowledge onto machines, since they are less close to us than the suffering face of another human being which would remind us once more of our lack of omnipotence, our own limits and failures, and last but not least perhaps our own mortality?

Maybe the question has to be raised: Are we becoming less human or more human?

[I]t is clear that whatever the answer may be, the patient is suffering more—not physically, perhaps, but emotionally. And his needs have not changed over the centuries, only our ability to gratify them.

Questions

1. In this essay Kübler-Ross incorporates various kinds of evidence: experience, observation, and reading. Mark the various kinds and describe how she integrates them into her text.

2. Kübler-Ross attends to the needs of the living and the rights of the dying. Describe where and how she attends to each and how she presents the conflicts, actual and potential, between them.

3. In paragraphs 24–27 Kübler-Ross describes the experience of the trip by ambulance, the emergency room, and the hospital from a patient's point of view. What does this shift in point of view contribute to the essay?

4. Imagine a situation in which a child or children are not isolated from death. What might be the consequences? Using this situation and its possible consequences, write an essay in which you agree or disagree with Kübler-Ross's views.

Cultural Analysis

Nicholas Carr — *Is Google Making Us Stupid?*

"Dave, stop. stop, will you? Stop, Dave. Will you stop, Dave?" So the supercomputer HAL pleads with the implacable astronaut Dave Bowman in a famous and weirdly poignant scene toward the end of Stanley Kubrick's *2001: A Space Odyssey*.[1] Bowman, having nearly been sent to a deep-space death by the malfunctioning machine, is calmly, coldly disconnecting the memory circuits that control its artificial "brain." "Dave, my mind is going," HAL says, forlornly. "I can feel it. I can feel it."

I can feel it, too. Over the past few years I've had an uncomfortable sense that someone, or something, has been tinkering with my brain, remapping the neural circuitry, reprogramming the memory. My mind isn't going—so far as I can tell—but it's changing. I'm not thinking the way I used to think. I can feel it most strongly when I'm reading. Immersing myself in a book or a lengthy article used to be easy. My mind would get caught up in the narrative or the turns of the argument, and I'd spend hours strolling through long stretches of prose. That's rarely the case anymore. Now my concentration often starts to drift after two or three pages. I get fidgety, lose the thread, begin looking for something else to do. I feel as if I'm always dragging my wayward brain back to the text. The deep reading that used to come naturally has become a struggle.

I think I know what's going on. For more than a decade now, I've been spending a lot of time online, searching and surfing and sometimes adding to the great databases of the Internet. The Web has been a godsend to me as a writer. Research that once required days in the stacks or periodical rooms of libraries can now be done in minutes. A few Google searches, some quick clicks on hyperlinks, and I've got the telltale fact or pithy quote I was after. Even when I'm not working, I'm as likely as not to be foraging in the Web's info-thickets—reading and writing e-mails, scanning headlines and blog posts, watching videos and listening to podcasts, or just tripping from link to link to link. (Unlike footnotes, to which they're sometimes likened, hyperlinks don't merely point to related works; they propel you toward them.)

First published in the Atlantic Monthly, *July/August 2008, and expanded into a book,* The Shallows: What the Internet Is Doing to Our Brains *(2010). Carr has written widely on the impact of technology; he blogs at roughtype.com.*

1. A 1968 science fiction film about artificial intelligence in which HAL, a computer, threatens to take control of a human space mission.

For me, as for others, the Net is becoming a universal medium, the conduit for most of the information that flows through my eyes and ears and into my mind. The advantages of having immediate access to such an incredibly rich store of information are many, and they've been widely described and duly applauded. "The perfect recall of silicon memory," *Wired*'s Clive Thompson has written, "can be an enormous boon to thinking." But that boon comes at a price. As the media theorist Marshall McLuhan[2] pointed out in the 1960s, media are not just passive channels of information. They supply the stuff of thought, but they also shape the process of thought. And what the Net seems to be doing is chipping away my capacity for concentration and contemplation. My mind now expects to take in information the way the Net distributes it: in a swiftly moving stream of particles. Once I was a scuba diver in the sea of words. Now I zip along the surface like a guy on a Jet Ski.

5 I'm not the only one. When I mention my troubles with reading to friends and acquaintances—literary types, most of them—many say they're having similar experiences. The more they use the Web, the more they have to fight to stay focused on long pieces of writing. Some of the bloggers I follow have also begun mentioning the phenomenon. Scott Karp, who writes a blog about online media, recently confessed that he has stopped reading books altogether. "I was a lit major in college, and used to be [a] voracious book reader," he wrote.

2. Marshall McLuhan (1911–1980), pioneering Canadian media critic and author of the 1964 book *Understanding Media*. His phrase "the medium is the message" encapsulates his argument that the form (medium) by which we receive information affects how we understand it.

"What happened?" He speculates on the answer: "What if I do all my reading on the web not so much because the way I read has changed, i.e. I'm just seeking convenience, but because the way I THINK has changed?"

Bruce Friedman, who blogs regularly about the use of computers in medicine, also has described how the Internet has altered his mental habits. "I now have almost totally lost the ability to read and absorb a longish article on the web or in print," he wrote earlier this year. A pathologist who has long been on the faculty of the University of Michigan Medical School, Friedman elaborated on his comment in a telephone conversation with me. His thinking, he said, has taken on a "staccato" quality, reflecting the way he quickly scans short passages of text from many sources online. "I can't read *War and Peace*[3] anymore," he admitted. "I've lost the ability to do that. Even a blog post of more than three or four paragraphs is too much to absorb. I skim it."

Anecdotes alone don't prove much. And we still await the long-term neurological and psychological experiments that will provide a definitive picture of how Internet use affects cognition. But a recently published study of online research habits, conducted by scholars from University College London, suggests that we may well be in the midst of a sea change in the way we read and think. As part of the five-year research program, the scholars examined computer logs documenting the behavior of visitors to two popular research sites, one operated by the British Library and one by a U.K. educational consortium, that provide access to journal articles, e-books, and other sources of written information. They found that people using the sites exhibited "a form of skimming activity," hopping from one source to another and rarely returning to any source they'd already visited. They typically read no more than one or two pages of an article or book before they would "bounce" out to another site. Sometimes they'd save a long article, but there's no evidence that they ever went back and actually read it. The authors of the study report:

> It is clear that users are not reading online in the traditional sense; indeed there are signs that new forms of "reading" are emerging as users "power browse" horizontally through titles, contents pages and abstracts going for quick wins. It almost seems that they go online to avoid reading in the traditional sense.

Thanks to the ubiquity of text on the Internet, not to mention the popularity of text-messaging on cell phones, we may well be reading more today than we did in the 1970s or 1980s, when television was our medium of choice. But it's a different kind of reading, and behind it lies a different kind of thinking—perhaps even a new sense of the self. "We are not only *what* we read," says Maryanne Wolf, a developmental psychologist at Tufts University and the author of *Proust and the Squid: The Story and Science of the Reading Brain*. "We are *how* we read." Wolf worries that the style of reading promoted by the Net, a style that

3. *War and Peace* (1869), Leo Tolstoy's epic five-volume novel depicting five Russian families' experiences during the Napoleonic Wars (1803–1814), during which Napoleon's armies invaded Russia.

puts "efficiency" and "immediacy" above all else, may be weakening our capacity for the kind of deep reading that emerged when an earlier technology, the printing press, made long and complex works of prose commonplace. When we read online, she says, we tend to become "mere decoders of information." Our ability to interpret text, to make the rich mental connections that form when we read deeply and without distraction, remains largely disengaged.

Reading, explains Wolf, is not an instinctive skill for human beings. It's not etched into our genes the way speech is. We have to teach our minds how to translate the symbolic characters we see into the language we understand. And the media or other technologies we use in learning and practicing the craft of reading play an important part in shaping the neural circuits inside our brains. Experiments demonstrate that readers of ideograms, such as the Chinese, develop a mental circuitry for reading that is very different from the circuitry found in those of us whose written language employs an alphabet. The variations extend across many regions of the brain, including those that govern such essential cognitive functions as memory and the interpretation of visual and auditory stimuli. We can expect as well that the circuits woven by our use of the Net will be different from those woven by our reading of books and other printed works.

10 Sometime in 1882, Friedrich Nietzsche[4] bought a typewriter—a Malling-Hansen Writing Ball, to be precise. His vision was failing, and keeping his eyes focused on a page had become exhausting and painful, often bringing on crushing headaches. He had been forced to curtail his writing, and he feared that he would soon have to give it up. The typewriter rescued him, at least for a time. Once he had mastered touch-typing, he was able to write with his eyes closed, using only the tips of his fingers. Words could once again flow from his mind to the page.

But the machine had a subtler effect on his work. One of Nietzsche's friends, a composer, noticed a change in the style of his writing. His already terse prose had become even tighter, more telegraphic. "Perhaps you will through this instrument even take to a new idiom," the friend wrote in a letter, noting that, in his own work, his "thoughts in music and language often depend on the quality of pen and paper."

"You are right," Nietzsche replied, "our writing equipment takes part in the forming of our thoughts." Under the sway of the machine, writes the German media scholar Friedrich A. Kittler, Nietzsche's prose "changed from arguments to aphorisms, from thoughts to puns, from rhetoric to telegram style."

The human brain is almost infinitely malleable. People used to think that our mental meshwork, the dense connections formed among the 100 billion or so neurons inside our skulls, was largely fixed by the time we reached adulthood. But brain researchers have discovered that that's not the case. James Olds, a professor of neuroscience who directs the Krasnow Institute for Advanced Study at George Mason University, says that even the adult mind "is very plastic." Nerve cells routinely break old connections and form new ones. "The brain,"

4. Friedrich Nietzsche (1844–1900), German philosopher whose books challenged conventional assumptions about Christianity and morality.

according to Olds, "has the ability to reprogram itself on the fly, altering the way it functions."

As we use what the sociologist Daniel Bell has called our "intellectual technologies"—the tools that extend our mental rather than our physical capacities—we inevitably begin to take on the qualities of those technologies. The mechanical clock, which came into common use in the 14th century, provides a compelling example. In *Technics and Civilization*, the historian and cultural critic Lewis Mumford described how the clock "disassociated time from human events and helped create the belief in an independent world of mathematically measurable sequences." The "abstract framework of divided time" became "the point of reference for both action and thought."

15 The clock's methodical ticking helped bring into being the scientific mind and the scientific man. But it also took something away. As the late MIT computer scientist Joseph Weizenbaum observed in his 1976 book, *Computer Power and Human Reason: From Judgment to Calculation*, the conception of the world that emerged from the widespread use of timekeeping instruments "remains an impoverished version of the older one, for it rests on a rejection of those direct experiences that formed the basis for, and indeed constituted, the old reality." In deciding when to eat, to work, to sleep, to rise, we stopped listening to our senses and started obeying the clock.

The process of adapting to new intellectual technologies is reflected in the changing metaphors we use to explain ourselves to ourselves. When the mechanical clock arrived, people began thinking of their brains as operating "like clockwork." Today, in the age of software, we have come to think of them as operating "like computers." But the changes, neuroscience tells us, go much deeper than metaphor. Thanks to our brain's plasticity, the adaptation occurs also at a biological level.

The Internet promises to have particularly far-reaching effects on cognition. In a paper published in 1936, the British mathematician Alan Turing proved that a digital computer, which at the time existed only as a theoretical machine, could be programmed to perform the function of any other information-processing device. And that's what we're seeing today. The Internet, an immeasurably powerful computing system, is subsuming most of our other intellectual technologies. It's becoming our map and our clock, our printing press and our typewriter, our calculator and our telephone, and our radio and TV.

When the Net absorbs a medium, that medium is re-created in the Net's image. It injects the medium's content with hyperlinks, blinking ads, and other digital gewgaws, and it surrounds the content with the content of all the other media it has absorbed. A new e-mail message, for instance, may announce its arrival as we're glancing over the latest headlines at a newspaper's site. The result is to scatter our attention and diffuse our concentration.

The Net's influence doesn't end at the edges of a computer screen, either. As people's minds become attuned to the crazy quilt of Internet media, traditional media have to adapt to the audience's new expectations. Television programs add text crawls and pop-up ads, and magazines and newspapers shorten their articles, introduce capsule summaries, and crowd their pages with easy-to-browse info-snippets. When, in March of this year, *The New York Times* decided to devote the second and third pages of every edition to article abstracts, its design director, Tom Bodkin, explained that the "shortcuts" would give harried readers a quick "taste" of the day's news, sparing them the "less efficient" method of actually turning the pages and reading the articles. Old media have little choice but to play by the new-media rules.

20 Never has a communications system played so many roles in our lives—or exerted such broad influence over our thoughts—as the Internet does today. Yet, for all that's been written about the Net, there's been little consideration of how, exactly, it's reprogramming us. The Net's intellectual ethic remains obscure.

About the same time that Nietzsche started using his typewriter, an earnest young man named Frederick Winslow Taylor carried a stopwatch into the Midvale Steel plant in Philadelphia and began a historic series of experiments aimed at improving the efficiency of the plant's machinists. With the approval of Midvale's owners, he recruited a group of factory hands, set them to work on various metalworking machines, and recorded and timed their every movement as well as the operations of the machines. By breaking down every job into a sequence of small, discrete steps and then testing different ways of performing each one, Taylor created a set of precise instructions—an "algorithm," we might say today—for how each worker should work. Midvale's employees grumbled about the strict new regime, claiming that it turned them into little more than automatons, but the factory's productivity soared.

More than a hundred years after the invention of the steam engine, the Industrial Revolution had at last found its philosophy and its philosopher. Taylor's tight industrial choreography—his "system," as he liked to call it—was embraced by manufacturers throughout the country and, in time, around the world. Seeking maximum speed, maximum efficiency, and maximum output, factory owners used time-and-motion studies to organize their work and configure the jobs of their workers. The goal, as Taylor defined it in his celebrated 1911 treatise, *The Principles of Scientific Management*, was to identify and adopt, for every job, the "one best method" of work and thereby to effect "the gradual substitution of science for rule of thumb throughout the mechanic arts." Once his system was applied to all acts of manual labor, Taylor assured his followers, it would bring about a restructuring not only of industry but of society, creating a utopia of perfect efficiency. "In the past the man has been first," he declared; "in the future the system must be first."

Taylor's system is still very much with us; it remains the ethic of industrial manufacturing. And now, thanks to the growing power that computer engineers and software coders wield over our intellectual lives, Taylor's ethic is beginning to govern the realm of the mind as well. The Internet is a machine designed for the efficient and automated collection, transmission, and manipulation of information, and its legions of programmers are intent on finding the "one best method"—the perfect algorithm—to carry out every mental movement of what we've come to describe as "knowledge work."

Google's headquarters, in Mountain View, California—the Googleplex—is the Internet's high church, and the religion practiced inside its walls is Taylorism. Google, says its chief executive, Eric Schmidt, is "a company that's founded around the science of measurement," and it is striving to "systematize everything" it does. Drawing on the terabytes of behavioral data it collects through its search engine and other sites, it carries out thousands of experiments a day, according to the *Harvard Business Review*, and it uses the results to refine the algorithms that increasingly control how people find information and extract meaning from it. What Taylor did for the work of the hand, Google is doing for the work of the mind.

25 The company has declared that its mission is "to organize the world's information and make it universally accessible and useful." It seeks to develop "the perfect search engine," which it defines as something that "understands exactly what you mean and gives you back exactly what you want." In Google's view, information is a kind of commodity, a utilitarian resource that can be mined and processed with industrial efficiency. The more pieces of information we can "access" and the faster we can extract their gist, the more productive we become as thinkers.

Where does it end? Sergey Brin and Larry Page, the gifted young men who founded Google while pursuing doctoral degrees in computer science at Stanford, speak frequently of their desire to turn their search engine into an artificial intelligence, a HAL-like machine that might be connected directly to our brains. "The ultimate search engine is something as smart as people—or smarter," Page said in a speech a few years back. "For us, working on search is a way to work on artificial intelligence." In a 2004 interview with *Newsweek*, Brin said, "Certainly if you had all the world's information directly attached to your brain, or an artificial brain that was smarter than your brain, you'd be better off." Last year, Page told a convention of scientists that Google is "really trying to build artificial intelligence and to do it on a large scale."

Such an ambition is a natural one, even an admirable one, for a pair of math whizzes with vast quantities of cash at their disposal and a small army of computer scientists in their employ. A fundamentally scientific enterprise, Google is motivated by a desire to use technology, in Eric Schmidt's words, "to solve problems that have never been solved before," and artificial intelligence is the hardest problem out there. Why wouldn't Brin and Page want to be the ones to crack it?

Still, their easy assumption that we'd all "be better off" if our brains were supplemented, or even replaced, by an artificial intelligence is unsettling. It suggests a belief that intelligence is the output of a mechanical process, a series of discrete steps that can be isolated, measured, and optimized. In Google's world, the world we enter when we go online, there's little place for the fuzziness of contemplation. Ambiguity is not an opening for insight but a bug to be fixed. The human brain is just an outdated computer that needs a faster processor and a bigger hard drive.

The idea that our minds should operate as high-speed data-processing machines is not only built into the workings of the Internet, it is the network's reigning business model as well. The faster we surf across the Web—the more links we click and pages we view—the more opportunities Google and other companies gain to collect information about us and to feed us advertisements. Most of the proprietors of the commercial Internet have a financial stake in collecting the crumbs of data we leave behind as we flit from link to link—the more crumbs, the better. The last thing these companies want is to encourage leisurely reading or slow, concentrated thought. It's in their economic interest to drive us to distraction.

Maybe I'm just a worrywart. Just as there's a tendency to glorify technological progress, there's a countertendency to expect the worst of every new tool or machine. In Plato's *Phaedrus*,[5] Socrates bemoaned the development of writing. He feared that, as people came to rely on the written word as a substitute for the knowledge they used to carry inside their heads, they would, in the words of one of the dialogue's characters, "cease to exercise their memory and become forgetful." And because they would be able to "receive a quantity of information without proper instruction," they would "be thought very knowledgeable when they are for the most part quite ignorant." They would be "filled with the conceit of wisdom instead of real wisdom." Socrates wasn't wrong—the new technology did often have the effects he feared—but he was shortsighted. He couldn't foresee the many ways that writing and reading would serve to spread information, spur fresh ideas, and expand human knowledge (if not wisdom). 30

The arrival of Gutenberg's printing press, in the 15th century, set off another round of teeth gnashing. The Italian humanist Hieronimo Squarciafico worried that the easy availability of books would lead to intellectual laziness, making men "less studious" and weakening their minds. Others argued that cheaply printed books and broadsheets would undermine religious authority, demean the work of scholars and scribes, and spread sedition and debauchery. As New York University professor Clay Shirky notes, "Most of the arguments made against the printing press were correct, even prescient." But, again, the doomsayers were unable to imagine the myriad blessings that the printed word would deliver.

So, yes, you should be skeptical of my skepticism. Perhaps those who dismiss critics of the Internet as Luddites[6] or nostalgists will be proved correct, and from our hyperactive, data-stoked minds will spring a golden age of intellectual discovery and universal wisdom. Then again, the Net isn't the alphabet, and although it may replace the printing press, it produces something altogether different. The kind of deep reading that a sequence of printed pages promotes is valuable not just for the knowledge we acquire from the author's words but for the intellectual vibrations those words set off within our own minds. In the

5. Plato (c. 428–348 BCE), Greek philosopher. The dialogue *Phaedrus* contains an extended discussion of the relative merits of speech versus writing.

6. Luddites originally referred to nineteenth-century textile workers who opposed new technology; the term now refers to anyone who opposes new technologies or automation.

quiet spaces opened up by the sustained, undistracted reading of a book, or by any other act of contemplation, for that matter, we make our own associations, draw our own inferences and analogies, foster our own ideas. Deep reading, as Maryanne Wolf argues, is indistinguishable from deep thinking.

If we lose those quiet spaces, or fill them up with "content," we will sacrifice something important not only in our selves but in our culture. In a recent essay, the playwright Richard Foreman eloquently described what's at stake:

> I come from a tradition of Western culture, in which the ideal (my ideal) was the complex, dense and "cathedral-like" structure of the highly educated and articulate personality—a man or woman who carried inside themselves a personally constructed and unique version of the entire heritage of the West. [But now] I see within us all (myself included) the replacement of complex inner density with a new kind of self—evolving under the pressure of information overload and the technology of the "instantly available."

As we are drained of our "inner repertory of dense cultural inheritance," Foreman concluded, we risk turning into "pancake people—spread wide and thin as we connect with that vast network of information accessed by the mere touch of a button."

I'm haunted by that scene in *2001*. What makes it so poignant, and so weird, is the computer's emotional response to the disassembly of its mind: its despair as one circuit after another goes dark, its childlike pleading with the astronaut—"I can feel it. I can feel it. I'm afraid"—and its final reversion to what can only be called a state of innocence. HAL's outpouring of feeling contrasts with the emotionlessness that characterizes the human figures in the film, who go about their business with an almost robotic efficiency. Their thoughts and actions feel scripted, as if they're following the steps of an algorithm. In the world of *2001*, people have become so machinelike that the most human character turns out to be a machine. That's the essence of Kubrick's dark prophecy: as we come to rely on computers to mediate our understanding of the world, it is our own intelligence that flattens into artificial intelligence.

QUESTIONS

1. Carr's title is a question. How would you answer it? What are his main examples of how Google is making us stupid? What counterexamples does he offer? What examples, on either side, would you add?

2. What are the most important advantages of "Taylorism," or the application of scientific methods to human behavior? Are there aspects of human behavior that cannot be improved by such methods?

3. As Carr notes, we tend to explain our minds as working like the most advanced technology around—be that papyrus, a typewriter, or a computer. Choose one or two such metaphors and discuss how the mind is—and is not—like the thing to which it is compared.

4. Interview a few people, including some who grew up using the Internet and some who remember doing research mainly using books. Write your own analysis of the impact of the Internet on our ability to think, reason, and research, building on Carr's essay and the anecdotes you collect.

Anthony Burgess *Is America Falling Apart?*

I am back in Bracciano, a castellated town about 13 miles north of Rome, after a year in New Jersey. I find the Italian Government still unstable, gasoline more expensive than anywhere in the world, butchers and bank clerks and tobacconists (which also means saltsellers) ready to go on strike at the drop of a *cappello*,[1] neo-Fascists at their dirty work, the hammer and sickle painted on the rumps of public statues, a thousand-lire note (officially worth about $1.63) shrunk to the slightness of a dollar bill.

Nevertheless, it's delightful to be back. People are underpaid but they go through an act of liking their work, the open markets are luscious with esculent color, the community is more important than the state, the human condition is humorously accepted. The *tramontana*[2] blows viciously today, and there's no central heating to turn on, but it will be pleasant when the wind drops. The two television channels are inadequate, but next Wednesday's rerun of an old Western, with Gary Cooper coming into a saloon saying "*Ciao, ragazzi*,"[3] is something to look forward to. Manifold consumption isn't important here. The quality of life has nothing to do with the quantity of brand names. What matters is talk, family, cheap wine in the open air, the wresting of minimal sweetness out of the long-known bitterness of living. I was spoiled in New Jersey. The Italian for *spoiled* is *viziato,* cognate with *vitiated,* which has to do with vice.

Spoiled? Well, yes. I never had to shiver by a fire that wouldn't draw, or go without canned kraut juice or wild rice. America made me develop new appetites in order to make proper use of the supermarket. A character in Evelyn Waugh's *Put Out More Flags* said that the difference between prewar and postwar life[4] was that, prewar, if one thing went wrong the day was ruined; postwar, if one thing went right the day would be made. America is a prewar country, psychologically unprepared for one thing to go wrong. Now everything seems to

Written during 1970–71, when Burgess, an English novelist then famous for A Clockwork Orange, *was a visiting professor at Princeton University; published in the* New York Times *(November 7, 1971).*

1. Hat.
2. North wind.
3. "Hi, boys."
4. Waugh published *Put Out More Flags* in 1942. "Prewar" refers to conditions before World War II.

be going wrong. Hence the neurosis, despair, the Kafka feeling that the whole marvelous fabric of American life is coming apart at the seams. Italy is used to everything going wrong. This is what the human condition is about.

Let me stay for a while on this subject of consumption. American individualism, on the face of it an admirable philosophy, wishes to manifest itself in independence of the community. You don't share things in common; you have your own things. A family's strength is signalized by its possessions. Herein lies a paradox. For the desire for possessions must eventually mean dependence on possessions. Freedom is slavery. Once let the acquisitive instinct burgeon (enough flour for the winter, not just for the week), and there are ruggedly individual forces only too ready to make it come to full and monstrous blossom. New appetites are invented; what to the European are bizarre luxuries become, to the American, plain necessities.

5 During my year's stay in New Jersey I let my appetites flower into full Americanism except for one thing. I did not possess an automobile. This self-elected deprivation was a way into the nastier side of the consumer society. Where private ownership prevails, public amenities decay or are prevented from coming into being. The wretched run-down rail services of America are something I try, vainly, to forget. The nightmare of filth, outside and in, that enfolds the trip from Springfield, Mass., to Grand Central Station would not be accepted in backward Europe. But far worse is the nightmare of travel in and around Los Angeles, where public transport does not exist and people are literally choking to death in their exhaust fumes. This is part of the price of the metaphysic of individual ownership.

But if the car owner can ignore the lack of public transport, he can hardly ignore the decay of services in general. His car needs mechanics, and mechanics grow more expensive and less efficient. The gadgets in the home are cheaper to replace than repair. The more efficiently self-contained the home, primary fortress of independence, seems to be, the more dependent it is on the great impersonal corporations, as well as a diminishing army of servitors. Skills at the lowest level have to be wooed slavishly and exorbitantly rewarded. Plumbers will not come. Nor, at the higher level, will doctors. And doctors and dentists, in a nation committed to maiming itself with sugar and cholesterol, know their scarcity value and behave accordingly.

Americans are at last realizing that the acquisition of goods is not the whole of life. Consumption, on one level, is turning insipid, especially as the quality of the artifacts themselves seems to be deteriorating. Planned obsolescence is not conducive to pride in workmanship. On another level, consumption is turning sour. There is a growing guilt about the masses of discarded junk—rusting automobiles and refrigerators and washing machines and dehumidifiers—that it is uneconomical to recycle. Indestructible plastic hasn't even the grace to undergo chemical change. America, the world's biggest consumer, is the world's biggest polluter. Awareness of this is a kind of redemptive grace, but it doesn't appreciably lead to repentance and a revolution in consumer habits. Citizens of Los Angeles are horrified by that daily pall of golden smog, but they don't noticeably clamor for a decrease in the number of owner-vehicles. There is no worse neurosis than that which derives from a consciousness of guilt and an inability to reform.

America is anachronistic in so many ways, and not least in its clinging to a belief—now known to be unviable—in the capacity of the individual citizen to do everything for himself. Americans are admirable in their distrust of the corporate state—they have fought both Fascism and Communism—but they forget that there is a use for everything, even the loathesome bureaucratic machine. America needs a measure of socialization, as Britain needed it. Things—especially those we need most—don't always pay their way, and it is here that the state must enter, dismissing the profit element. Part of the present American neurosis, again, springs from awareness of this but inability to do anything about practical implementation. Perhaps only a country full of bombed cities feels capable of this kind of social revolution.

It would be supererogatory for me to list those areas in which thoughtful Americans feel that collapse is coming. It is enough for me to concentrate on what, during my New Jersey stay, impinged on my own life. Education, for instance, since I have a 6-year-old son to be brought up. America has always despised its teachers and, as a consequence, it has been granted the teachers it deserves. The quality of first-grade education that my son received, in a New Jersey town noted for the excellence of its public schools, could not, I suppose, be faulted on the level of dogged conscientiousness. The principal had read all the right pedagogic books, and was ready to quote these in the footnotes to his circular exhortations to parents. The teachers worked rigidly from the approved rigidly programed primers, ensuring that school textbook publication remains the big business it is.

But there seemed to be no spark; no daring, no madness, no readiness to engage the individual child's mind as anything other than raw material for statistical reductions. The fear of being unorthodox is rooted in the American teacher's soul: you can be fired for treading the path of experimental enterprise. In England, teachers cannot be fired, except for raping girl students and getting boy students drunk. In consequence, there is the kind of security that breeds eccentric genius, the capacity for firing mad enthusiasms. 10

I know that American technical genius, and most of all the moon landings, seems to give the lie to too summary a condemnation of the educational system, but there is more to education than the segmental equipping of the mind. There is that transmission of the value of the past as a force still miraculously fertile and moving—mostly absent from American education at all levels.

Of course, America was built on a rejection of the past. Even the basic Christianity which was brought to the continent in 1620 was of a novel and bizarre kind that would have nothing to do with the great rank river of belief that produced Dante and Michelangelo. America as a nation has never been able to settle to a common belief more sophisticated than the dangerous naiveté of the Declaration of Independence. "Life, liberty and the pursuit of happiness," indeed. And now America, filling in the vacuum left by the liquefied

British Empire, has the task of telling the rest of the world that there's something better than Communism. The something better can only be moneymaking and consumption for its own sake. In the name of this ghastly creed the jungles must be defoliated.[5]

No wonder the guilt of the thoughtful Americans I met in Princeton and New York and, indeed, all over the Union tended to express itself as an extravagant masochism, a desire for flagellation. Americans want to take on all the blame they can find, gluttons for punishment. "What do Europeans really think of us?" is a common question at parties. The expected answer is: "They think you're a load of decadent, gross-lipped, potbellied, callous, overbearing neoimperialists." Then the head can be bowed and the chest smitten: "*Nostra culpa, nostra maxima culpa. . . .*"[6] But the fact is that such an answer, however much desired, would not be an honest one. Europeans think more highly of Americans now than they ever did. Let me try to explain why.

When Europe, after millennia of war, rapine, slavery, famine, intolerance, had sunk to the level of a sewer, America became the golden dream, the Eden where innocence could be recovered. Original sin was the monopoly of that dirty continent over there; in America man could glow in an aura of natural goodness, driven along his shining path by divine reason. The Declaration of Independence itself is a monument to reason. Progress was possible, and the wrongs committed against the Indians, the wildlife, the land itself, could be explained away in terms of the rational control of environment necessary for the building of a New Jerusalem.[7] Right and wrong made up the moral dichotomy; evil—that great eternal inextirpable entity—had no place in America.

15 At last, with the Vietnam war and especially the Mylai horror,[8] Americans are beginning to realize that they are subject to original sin as much as Europeans are. Some things—the massive crime figures, for instance—can now be explained only in terms of absolute evil. Europe, which has long known about evil and learned to live with it (*live* is *evil* spelled backwards), is now grimly pleased to find that America is becoming like Europe. America is no longer Europe's daughter nor her rich stepmother: she is Europe's sister. The agony that America is undergoing is not to be associated with breakdown so much as with the parturition of self-knowledge.

It has been assumed by many that the youth of America has been in the vanguard of the discovery of both the disease and the cure. The various

5. That is, in order to deny the enemy protective cover—a part of American strategy during the Vietnam War.

6. "Through our fault, through our most grievous fault," a modification of *Mea culpa, mea maxima culpa* ("Through my fault . . ."), part of the act of confession in the Roman Catholic Church.

7. The holy city described by John in Revelation 21, here a figurative expression for a perfected society.

8. A massacre by American troops of more than three hundred Vietnamese civilians in the village of My Lai.

copping-out movements, however, from the Beats on, have committed the gross error of assuming that original sin rested with their elders, their rulers, and that they themselves could manifest their essential innocence by building little neo-Edens. The drug culture could confirm that the paradisal vision was available to all who sought it. But instant ecstasy has to be purchased, like any other commodity, and, in economic terms, that passive life of pure being involves parasitism. Practically all of the crime I encountered in New York—directly or through report—was a preying of the opium-eaters on the working community. There has to be a snake in paradise. You can't escape the heritage of human evil by building communes, usually on an agronomic ignorance that, intended to be a rejection of inherited knowledge, that suspect property of the elders, does violence to life. The American young are well-meaning but misguided, and must not themselves be taken as guides.

The guides, as always, lie among the writers and artists. And Americans ought to note that, however things may seem to be falling apart, arts and the humane scholarship are flourishing here, as they are not, for instance, in England. I'm not suggesting that Bellow, Mailer, Roth[9] and the rest have the task of finding a solution to the American mess, but they can at least clarify its nature and show how it relates to the human condition in general. Literature, that most directly human of the arts, often reacts magnificently to an ambience of unease or apparent breakdown. The Elizabethans,[10] to whose era we look back as to an irrecoverable Golden Age, were far more conscious than modern Americans of the chaos and corruption and incompetence of the state. Shakespeare's period was one of poverty, unemployment, ghastly inflation, violence in the streets. Twenty-six years after his death there was a bloody civil war, followed by a dictatorship of religious fanatics, followed by a calm respite in which the seeds of a revolution were sown. England survived. America will survive.

I'm not suggesting that Americans sit back and wait for a transient period of mistrust and despair to resolve itself, like a disease, through the unconscious healing forces which lie deep in organic nature. Man, as Thornton Wilder showed in *The Skin of Our Teeth,*[11] always comes through—though sometimes only just. Americans living here and now have a right to an improvement in the quality of their lives, and they themselves, not the remote governors, must do something about it. It is not right that men and women should fear to go on the streets at night, and that they should sometimes fear the police as much as the criminals, both of whom sometimes look like mirror images of each other. I have had too much evidence, in my year in New Jersey, of the police behaving like the "Fascist pigs" of the revolutionary press. There are too many guns about, and the disarming of the police should be a natural aspect of the disarming of the entire citizenry.

9. Saul Bellow (1915–2005), Norman Mailer (1923–2007), and Philip Roth (b. 1933)—all American writers.

10. The British during the reign of Elizabeth I, 1558–1603.

11. Pulitzer Prize–winning comedy, written in 1942 by Thornton Wilder (1897–1975).

American politics, at both the state and the Federal levels, is too much concerned with the protection of large fortunes, America being the only example in history of a genuine timocracy.[12] The wealth qualification for the aspiring politician is taken for granted; a governmental system dedicated to the promotion of personal wealth in a few selected areas will never act for the public good. The time has come, nevertheless, for citizens to demand, from their government, a measure of socialization—the provision of amenities for the many, of which adequate state pensions and sickness benefits, as well as nationalized transport, should be priorities.

20 As for those remoter solutions to the American nightmare—only an aspect, after all, of the human nightmare—an Englishman must be diffident about suggesting that America made her biggest mistake in becoming America—meaning a revolutionary republic based on a romantic view of human nature. To reject a limited monarchy in favor of an absolute one (which is, after all, what the American Presidency is) argues a trust in the disinterestedness of an elected ruler which is, of course, no more than a reflection of belief in the innate goodness of man—so long as he happens to be American man. The American Constitution is out of date. Republics tend to corruption. Canada and Australia have their own problems, but they are happier countries than America.

This *Angst*[13] about America coming apart at the seams, which apparently is shared by nearly 50 per cent of the entire American population, is something to rejoice about. A sense of sin is always admirable, though it must not be allowed to become neurotic. If electric systems break down and gadgets disintegrate, it doesn't matter much. There is always wine to be drunk by candlelight, uniced. If America's position as a world power collapses, and the Union dissolves into independent states, there is still the life of the family or the individual to be lived. England has survived her own dissolution as an imperial power, and Englishmen seem to be happy enough. But I ask the reader to note that I, an Englishman, no longer live in England, and I can't spend more than six months at a stretch in Italy—or any other European country, for that matter. I come to America as to a country more stimulating than depressing. The future of mankind is being worked out there on a scale typically American—vast, dramatic, almost apocalyptical. I brave the brutality and the guilt in order to be in on the scene. I shall be back.

12. A state in which power depends on wealth.
13. Anxiety.

Questions

1. This essay appeared in 1971. What might Burgess leave out, add, or modify if he were to write it today?

2. Burgess says that in his son's school there was "no readiness to engage the individual child's mind as anything other than raw material for statistical reductions" (paragraph 10).

Precisely what is he referring to? Does your own experience support or counter Burgess's claim?

3. Visitors like Burgess can sometimes see things natives miss; they can also overlook the obvious. Write a response to Burgess, pointing out where he is on target and what he has missed.

Adam Goodheart — *9.11.01: The Skyscraper and the Airplane*

And as the smart ship grew
In stature, grace, and hue,
In shadowy silent distance grew the Iceberg too.
—Thomas Hardy,[1]
"The Convergence of the Twain"

Before the fire, before the ash, before the bodies tumbling solitary through space, one thin skin of metal and glass met another. Miles apart only moments before, then feet, and then, in an almost inconceivable instant, only a fraction of an inch. Try to imagine them there, suspended: two man-made behemoths joined in a fatal kiss.

Fatal, fated: perhaps even long foreseen. The skyscraper and the airplane were born side by side, and ever since then have occupied adjacent rooms in our collective unconscious. To call September 11th a nightmare is to be clinically precise about it, for like all true nightmares, it was grafted together out of preexisting elements, fragments of our waking lives and our imaginations.

Nearly a century ago, just five years after the first scrawny aircraft left the ground at Kitty Hawk, a widely circulated illustration by a Manhattan publisher named Moses King—"King's Dream of New York," he titled it—showed a fantasy cityscape in which biplanes buzzed among the downtown office towers and a vast dirigible brushed the uppermost cupola. In that same year, 1908, E. M. Forster[2] wrote a short story envisioning a world of the future where humans lived in huge structures composed of tiny, airless chambers, each one "like the cell of a bee," leaving them to travel in airships that crisscrossed the globe (though the earth had become so drably uniform, he observed, that "what was the good of going to Pekin when it was just like Shrewsbury?"). In the last

Originally published in the American Scholar *(Winter 2002), a journal of the Phi Beta Kappa Society that "strives to preserve the essay."*

1. Hardy (1840–1928), English novelist and poet, whose poem "The Convergence of the Twain" meditates on the sinking of the *Titanic*, the largest and most luxurious ocean liner of the day.

2. English novelist (1879–1970).

paragraph of the story, "The Machine Stops," Forster imagined this world coming to an end: "The whole city was broken like a honeycomb. An air-ship . . . crashed downwards, exploding as it went, rending gallery after gallery with its wings of steel."

Skyscraper and airplane: fragile containers for even-more-fragile flesh and blood. Each an artificial shell of our own manufacture—or not quite of our own manufacture, since, strictly speaking, very few of us, as individuals, have any direct involvement in their creation. Each a capsule of recycled air, with windows sealed shut against the blue. Each an innovation that, in Forsterian terms, has made Pekin more and more like Shrewsbury. Each a honeycomb that traps us side by side with strangers. Each a rig that suspends us far above the ground, half-willing aerialists, and then whispers: *Trust me*. Each a machine that teaches us, in similar ways, how to be modern.

5 What keeps it up? What, that is to say, keeps *us* up? Perhaps one person in a thousand really knows, understanding coolly why it is that the contraption doesn't plummet back to earth under our weight. For the rest of us, the precise functioning of wing and girder, the mathematical intricacies of gravitational thrust and counterthrust, remain lifelong mysteries. Our animal selves, quite sensibly, would rather stick close to solid ground. But this is where we must steel ourselves to be something more than animals. We must summon up the will to trust—not so much in the metal armature beneath us as in the faceless experts who designed and built it, in the corporations that own and maintain it, in the armature of civilization and science. No wonder we sometimes get dizzy.

The cultural critic Marshall Berman,[3] in selecting a title for his 1982 treatise on the experience of modernity, borrowed a newly resonant phrase from Karl Marx:[4] *All That Is Solid Melts Into Air.* "To be modern," he wrote, "is to find ourselves in an environment that promises us adventure, power, joy, growth, transformation of ourselves and the world—and, at the same time, that threatens to destroy everything we have, everything we know, everything we are." It is to ride atop a skyscraper, to soar in an airplane. And both threatened us with such destruction, not just on that machine-bright morning in September, but long before.

Both sprang from the late nineteenth century, and from the American Middle West (Louis Sullivan's Chicago, the Wright Brothers' Ohio)[5]—a place where earth and sky were blank canvases waiting to be filled with movement and form. Yet both had deeper roots as well. In England in the 1780s, the decade in which the Montgolfiers took to the air in their balloons, and the young Wordsworth and Coleridge sharpened their pens at grammar school, the Duke of Bedford owned an exceptionally large racehorse that one of his grooms named Skyscraper—the first recorded appearance of the word. (The mare finished first at the Epson Derby in 1789.) In the years that followed, *skyscraper* was used to

3. Writer and political theorist (b. 1940).
4. Author of *Das Kapital* and famous originator of communist theory (1818–1883).
5. Sullivan (1856–1924), American architect; Wright brothers, inventors of the airplane.

describe the uppermost sail on a ship's rigging (1794), a high hat or bonnet (1800), or simply a very tall person (1857). After crossing the Atlantic, it was used by American sportswriters as early as the 1860s to describe a towering fly ball. Like so many of the next century's most important words (*computer, rocket, network*), *skyscraper* jostled around indecisively for a while, hesitating between one meaning and another before settling into its ultimate niche. However they used the word, people were clearly grasping toward the sky, toward something up there that they could almost brush with their fingertips—and that they were determined to reach by one contrivance or another.

When the earliest buildings to be called skyscrapers appeared, in the 1870s and 1880s, they sprang into shape so suddenly as to seem born in a single piece. The pioneering architects of Chicago, one recent historian has written, "learned almost everything of importance that would be known a century later about how to build skyscrapers." Yet the skyscraper was not, as it seems to us now, a single unified invention, but rather many inventions knit into one.

First and foremost, of course, was the ability to produce cheap, high-quality structural steel—the first truly revolutionary architectural innovation since the Romans invented the arch and the dome two millennia before. One nineteenth-century engineer couched this development in almost Darwinian terms: For the first time, he explained, tall buildings were designed as vertebrates instead of crustaceans. For the first time, their loads and stresses could be carried not by massive carapaces of masonry but by a web of slender struts and braces whose strength lay in its interconnectedness: a prototypical modern form, destined to be replicated in everything from computer chips to international airline routes. Louis Sullivan might have boasted of his buildings' pure functionalism, but in fact the skyscraper's exterior was merely its skin, its only function (besides shelter from the elements) to provide a kind of movie screen onto which the architect could project any embellishment he chose: rich Gothic traceries, Art Deco's silvery sheen, or, eventually, the stern theatrics of high modernism.

Still, if architects had had only steel to work with, the interiors of their skyscrapers would have just been little more than dark and dreary warrens. Office towers of ten and twenty stories required, for their basic functioning, a whole list of innovations that are now taken for granted, but that were still brand new in the second half of the nineteenth century: electric lights and central heating, passenger elevators and fire escapes, telephones and flush toilets. As fate had it, all of these appeared on the American scene at approximately the same time. And all of them, moreover, required a wholly new type of city to support them: one with reliable, centrally managed electric and gas companies, sewer systems, water mains, fire departments, elevator inspectors, telephone operators, trash collectors. Did the modern city give birth to the skyscraper, or vice versa? The answer, probably, is a bit of both.

Of all these varied accoutrements, none was more critical to the skyscraper's development than the passenger elevator. At New York's Crystal Palace exposition in 1854, a Yonkers mechanic named Elisha Graves Otis would periodically ascend high above the crowds on an open platform of wrought iron. As the machine creaked up to its zenith, the inventor gestured to an assistant, who cut through the hoisting rope with a hatchet. The spectators gasped in horror—but instead of plummeting to the ground, the elevator merely settled back into its ratcheted safety lock. "All safe, gentlemen, all safe," Otis announced.

Otis's words would become the constant refrain of the dawning era. In the nineteenth century, for the first time in human history, millions of ordinary people would be required to entrust their lives, on a daily basis, to technologies whose inner workings remained a mystery. They were a generation of pioneers, the men and women of New York and Chicago, no less than the settlers of the Great Plains. The odd thing, in retrospect, is how easily they seem to have taken the changes in stride. When the architect Bradford Gilbert,[6] in 1888, topped off his Tower Building at eleven stories, many New York pedestrians avoided that block of Broadway, certain that the structure would topple in the first stiff breeze. But Gilbert, in an Otis-like show of confidence, moved his own office onto the uppermost floor; the building withstood a hurricane soon after, and before long was taken for granted. Barely two decades later, when the Metropolitan Life Building reached a record fifty stories, the only question was who would try for sixty. (It would be the retailing magnate Frank Woolworth, who began planning his skyscraper a few weeks after the Metropolitan tower opened.)

Even more remarkable, the mythology of the skyscraper was born full-fledged with the building itself. Here is the earliest recorded appearance of the word in its contemporary sense, from an 1883 issue of *American Architect and Building News*: "This form of sky-scraper gives that peculiar refined, independent, self-contained, daring, bold, heaven-reaching, erratic, piratic, Quixotic, American thought." (Those were the days when even trade journals waxed Whitmanesque.)[7]

A century earlier, Thomas Jefferson, proclaiming American exceptionalism in his *Notes on Virginia*, cited the extraordinary size of native bears and elk, caverns and waterfalls. (He even vigorously defended American Indians against a French naturalist's insinuation that their "organs of generation" were smaller than average.) But the skyscraper rendered all of Jefferson's examples irrelevant. Here was the final proof of America's towering stature, in a tower raised not by God but by its citizens.

15 Before long, the race to scrape the sky lifted off the ground. And like the skyscraper's, the airplane's infancy was shortlived, its full maturity quick to arrive: Orville Wright would live to see the era of inflight movies. Strut and brace, spar and rib formed the bones of the plane as they did of the skyscraper, stiffening an outer shell designed to cut through hostile wind. And the airplane, too, would become a sort of capsule of human amenities, but to an even greater degree: a mobile life-support system, no less than a spaceship would be.

6. American architect (1853–1911) who built some of the first skyscrapers, including the Tower Building (1889) in New York City, now demolished.

7. Referring to Walt Whitman (1819–1892), American poet known for his romantic, democratic, all-embracing *Leaves of Grass*.

And yet, after nearly a century aloft, we have never learned to occupy planes as comfortably as we do skyscrapers. Antoine de Saint-Exupéry,[8] in the 1930s, predicted that within a generation or two, the airplane would come to seem a perfectly commonplace thing, "an object as natural as a pebble polished by the waves." Instead, it still seems the very epitome of what is artificial and mechanical. Stepping aboard one, even the most habitual of flyers must exercise a small act of conscious will. The passenger never forgets that he is wagering his life on the journey, even if he knows that the odds in this type of roulette are relatively good.

Air travel is a unique experience in modern life, the sociologist Mark Gottdiener[9] recently wrote, "because, deep down inside us, it is a 'near death' experience. It is the most common way individuals surrender control and voluntarily place themselves in harm's way in contemporary society. If they drive, they are also at risk, but they remain in control behind the wheel." Strapped into our seats, waiting on the runway, staring out the window at the stained frailty of the wing, we toy with fantasies of annihilation. We look at our fellow travelers and wonder what it would be like to face death alongside these strangers. A terribly intimate, terribly modern way to go: so close to one another in these well-lit rows, so far from family and home.

In a seminar for phobic flyers offered by American Airlines, participants spend ten consecutive hours being lectured by pilots, flight attendants, mechanics, and psychologists, who repeat this phrase like a mantra: "Airplanes do not drop, dive, plummet, or fall." In doing so, they merely voice the silent chant of every airborne congregation. For flying requires an act of almost religious faith, the surrender of oneself, in absolute trust, to the wisdom and benevolent expertise of corporations, pilots, governments, engineers—the whole apparatus of modernity. In this setting, the smallest acts take on ritual significance: the pantomimed instructions of flight attendants, the dimming of lights, the serving of food. Airline meals, tiny and perfectly formed, are like the Japanese tea ceremony, in which gesture is more important than nourishment. In giving us food, the airline offers us a promise of sustenance; in eating, we accept. All of us know one or two stiff-necked dissenters who refuse to fly at all, and they irritate us more than their mild neurosis would warrant, as if they had renounced their citizenship in the commonwealth of flight.

If the skyscraper, with its crudely phallic thrust, is male, the airplane is female. Entering, we pass into a place that promises—if rarely quite delivering—all the amenities of the womb: shelter, nourishment, warmth, dimness, sleep. The earliest flight attendants, in the 1920s, were men, but airlines quickly discovered that passengers preferred to be cared for by women, and before long they were openly competing with one another to provide the most beautiful and provocatively clad stewardesses. Erotic currents move among the passengers as

8. French poet and aviator (1900–1944), best known for *The Little Prince* (1943).

9. Professor of sociology at the State University of New York–Buffalo, author of *The Social Production of Urban Space* (1985), and editor of *The City and the Sign: Introduction to Urban Semiotics* (1986).

well. Skyscrapers place us alongside strangers and demand that we work; airplanes seat us side by side and whisper idle fantasies of sex. This is the double face of modern alienation: the limitless pain of loneliness, the limitless promise of random encounters. Proximity, anonymity: the world of skyscrapers and airplanes is one in which terrorists stalk freely among their prey.

20 The architect of the World Trade Center, Minoru Yamasaki,[10] was afraid of heights. He once wrote that in a world of perfect freedom, he'd have created nothing but one-story buildings overlooking fields of flowers. He designed the Trade Center with narrow windows framed by vertical columns like prison bars, close enough together that he could steady himself against them when looking out. Instead of one-story buildings overlooking fields of flowers, he built gargantuan monoliths overlooking a windswept plaza. Their scale was brutal, unsoftened by the slightest hint of stylishness. Only at a great distance did they impress, jutting like a double bowsprit from the prow of Manhattan, from the prow of America itself. Or, if you preferred, like a pair of middle fingers, raised against the hostile vastness of the Atlantic Ocean.

But to take in this view you had to stand far away: in Hoboken, or Hamburg, or Kabul. (Or to observe the towers through a lens. Like so many twentieth-century creations, they seemed designed to be seen not in person but on film, as though the cinematic eye were the only one that mattered.) Standing at the base of the towers and looking up, the human observer had the sense mostly not of their height, but of their immense weight. They were two mountains of trapped kinetic energy, perpetually poised at the brink of release. The irony of architecture, all architecture, is that we create structures to shelter ourselves, yet in building them, we set ourselves at risk. The surest way to stay safe from fires, earthquakes, and bombs is never to go indoors. The surest way not to fall is to stay on the ground.

In *Anna Karenina*,[11] Levin is terrified by the birth of his first child, for he realizes that he has brought into the world a new means for him to be hurt beyond all previous imagining. Tolstoy recognized that every act of creation has its shadow double, a coequal act of destruction. When Yamasaki created buildings on an unprecedented scale, he also created the potential for disaster on an unprecedented scale, a nightmare knit into every cubic inch of glass and steel. (The man who would eventually engineer their destruction understood this: he came from a family of builders.) They fascinated us, as airplanes do, because part of us always imagined them falling. It is the same part of us that loves our children because we can imagine them dying.

And when the towers did fall, we watched with the horror of witnesses to a death half foreseen, in dreams and shadowy portents. They buckled, released their long-held burden, and wearily sank to earth.

10. Founder of the Michigan-based architectural firm that built the World Trade Center in 1973.
11. Novel (1875–77) by Russian author Leo Tolstoy (1828–1910).

The authors of the catastrophe—who can doubt it?—created something terrible and permanent: an image that will stand for as long as any tower. In a thousand years, anyone who knows anything at all about us, the ancient Modern Americans, will probably know about the skyscraper and the airplane, and about the bright September morning that welded them together.

Eight days after the collapse, I stood on lower Broadway near where the skycrapers had been. The destruction was all strangely contained behind chain-link fences and squads of stolid cops: all the familiar markers of a Situation Under Control. The mounded ruins poured out a thick column of white smoke, its innards glowing sickly yellow under the slanting rays of late-afternoon sun. It looked exactly as if the crater of a volcano had somehow opened up among the downtown office buildings, and now was being probed and monitored by businesslike teams of geologists and seismologists, lest it erupt again without warning, I was reminded of being atop Mount Etna,[12] and peering alongside other tourists into the gassy abyss of the caldera, looking fruitlessly for some deep-buried source of smoke and heat. Above everything, above the place where the towers had stood, a helicopter whirred, miraculously suspended, riding on a column of newly liberated air. 25

12. Still-active volcano in Sicily.

Questions

1. After the destruction of the World Trade Center towers on September 11, 2001, many writers attempted to analyze and comprehend the event. What is Goodheart's approach? As you (re)read the essay, mark sentences that articulate or summarize his key points.

2. Goodheart chooses an epigraph from Thomas Hardy's poem "The Convergence of the Twain," originally subtitled "Lines on the Loss of the Titanic," to introduce his analysis. To what extent is the tragedy of the *Titanic* like or unlike the tragedy of September 11?

3. Throughout his analysis Goodheart quotes other writers, thinkers, and inventors. Choose one quotation that you think is particularly effective and explain why.

4. Goodheart's essay is, in a sense, an analysis of a visual image from September 11; he calls it "an image that will stand for as long as any tower" (paragraph 24). Choose another image from that day or the aftermath and, like Goodheart, write an essay in which you analyze its meaning and significance.

MALCOLM GLADWELL *Java Man*

THE ORIGINAL COCA-COLA was a late-nineteenth-century concoction known as Pemberton's French Wine Coca, a mixture of alcohol, the caffeine-rich kola nut, and coca, the raw ingredient of cocaine. In the face of social pressure, first the wine and then the coca were removed, leaving the more banal modern beverage in its place: carbonated, caffeinated sugar water with less kick to it than a cup of coffee. But is that the way we think of Coke? Not at all. In the nineteen-thirties, a commercial artist named Haddon Sundblom had the bright idea of posing a portly retired friend of his in a red Santa Claus suit with a Coke in his hand, and plastering the image on billboards and advertisements across the country. Coke, magically, was reborn as caffeine for children, caffeine without any of the weighty adult connotations of coffee and tea. It was—as the ads with Sundblom's Santa put it—"the pause that refreshes." It added life. It could teach the world to sing.

One of the things that have always made drugs so powerful is their cultural adaptability, their way of acquiring meanings beyond their pharmacology. We think of marijuana, for example, as a drug of lethargy, of disaffection. But in Colombia, the historian David T. Courtwright points out in "Forces of Habit," "peasants boast that cannabis helps them to *quita el cansancio* or reduce fatigue; increase their *fuerza* and *ánimo*, force and spirit; and become *incansable*, tireless." In Germany right after the Second World War, cigarettes briefly and suddenly became the equivalent of crack cocaine. "Up to a point, the majority of the habitual smokers preferred to do without food even under extreme conditions of nutrition rather than to forgo tobacco," according to one account of the period. "Many housewives . . . bartered fat and sugar for cigarettes." Even a drug as demonized as opium has been seen in a more favorable light. In the eighteen-thirties, Franklin Delano Roosevelt's grandfather Warren Delano II made the family fortune exporting the drug to China, and Delano was able to sugar-coat his activities so plausibly that no one ever accused his grandson of being the scion of a drug lord. And yet, as Bennett Alan Weinberg and Bonnie K. Bealer remind us in their marvellous book "The World of Caffeine," there is no drug quite as effortlessly adaptable as caffeine, the Zelig of chemical stimulants.

At one moment, in one form, it is the drug of choice of café intellectuals and artists; in another, of housewives; in another, of Zen monks; and, in yet another, of children enthralled by a fat man who slides down chimneys. King Gustav III, who ruled Sweden in the latter half of the eighteenth century, was so convinced of the particular perils of coffee over all other forms of caffeine that he devised an elaborate experiment. A convicted murderer was sentenced to drink cup after cup of coffee until he died, with another murderer sentenced to a lifetime of tea drinking, as a control. (Unfortunately, the two doctors in charge

First published in the New Yorker *(July 30, 2001), an American magazine of literature, culture, and the arts, to which Gladwell has been a regular contributor since 1996.*

of the study died before anyone else did; then Gustav was murdered; and finally the tea drinker died, at eighty-three, of old age—leaving the original murderer alone with his espresso, and leaving coffee's supposed toxicity in some doubt.) Later, the various forms of caffeine began to be divided up along sociological lines. Wolfgang Schivelbusch, in his book "Tastes of Paradise," argues that, in the eighteenth century, coffee symbolized the rising middle classes, whereas its great caffeinated rival in those years—cocoa, or, as it was known at the time, chocolate—was the drink of the aristocracy. "Goethe, who used art as a means to lift himself out of his middle class background into the aristocracy, and who as a member of a courtly society maintained a sense of aristocratic calm even in the midst of immense productivity, made a cult of chocolate, and avoided coffee," Schivelbusch writes. "Balzac, who despite his sentimental allegiance to the monarchy, lived and labored for the literary marketplace and for it alone, became one of the most excessive coffee-drinkers in history. Here we see two fundamentally different working styles and means of stimulation—fundamentally different psychologies and physiologies." Today, of course, the chief cultural distinction is between coffee and tea, which, according to a list drawn up by Weinberg and Bealer, have come to represent almost entirely opposite sensibilities:

Coffee Aspect	*Tea Aspect*
Male	Female
Boisterous	Decorous
Indulgence	Temperance
Hardheaded	Romantic
Topology	Geometry
Heidegger	Carnap
Beethoven	Mozart
Libertarian	Statist
Promiscuous	Pure

That the American Revolution began with the symbolic rejection of tea in Boston Harbor, in other words, makes perfect sense. Real revolutionaries would naturally prefer coffee. By contrast, the freedom fighters of Canada, a hundred years later, were most definitely tea drinkers. And where was Canada's autonomy won? Not on the blood-soaked fields of Lexington and Concord but in the genteel drawing rooms of Westminster, over a nice cup of Darjeeling and small, triangular cucumber sandwiches.

All this is a bit puzzling. We don't fetishize the difference between salmon eaters and tuna eaters, or people who like their eggs sunny-side up and those who like them scrambled. So why invest so much importance in the way people prefer their caffeine? A cup of coffee has somewhere between a hundred and two hundred and fifty milligrams; black tea brewed for four minutes has between forty and a hundred milligrams. But the disparity disappears if you consider that many tea drinkers drink from a pot, and have more than one cup. Caffeine is caffeine. "The more it is pondered," Weinberg and Bealer write, "the more paradoxical this duality within the culture of caffeine appears. After all, both coffee and tea are aromatic infusions of vegetable matter, 5 served hot or cold in similar quantities; both are often mixed with cream or sugar; both are universally available in virtually any grocery or restaurant in civilized society; and both contain the identical psychoactive alkaloid stimulant, caffeine."

It would seem to make more sense to draw distinctions based on the way caffeine is metabolized rather than on the way it is served. Caffeine, whether it is in coffee or tea or a soft drink, moves easily from the stomach and intestines into the bloodstream, and from there to the organs, and before long has penetrated almost every cell of the body. This is the reason that caffeine is such a wonderful stimulant. Most substances can't cross the blood-brain barrier, which is the body's defensive mechanism, preventing viruses or toxins from entering the central nervous system. Caffeine does so easily. Within an hour or so, it reaches its peak concentration in the brain, and there it does a number of things—principally, blocking the action of adenosine, the neuromodulator that makes you sleepy, lowers your blood pressure, and slows down your heartbeat. Then, as quickly as it builds up in your brain and tissues, caffeine is gone—which is why it's so safe. (Caffeine in ordinary quantities has never been conclusively linked to serious illness.)

But how quickly it washes away differs dramatically from person to person. A two-hundred-pound man who drinks a cup of coffee with a hundred milligrams of caffeine will have a maximum caffeine concentration of one milligram per kilogram of body weight. A hundred-pound woman having the same cup of coffee will reach a caffeine concentration of two milligrams per kilogram of body weight, or twice as high. In addition, when women are on the Pill, the rate at which they clear caffeine from their bodies slows considerably. (Some of the side effects experienced by women on the Pill may in fact be caffeine jitters caused by their sudden inability to tolerate as much coffee as they could before.) Pregnancy reduces a woman's ability to process caffeine still further. The half-life of caffeine in an adult is roughly three and a half hours. In a pregnant woman, it's eighteen hours. (Even a four-month-old child processes caffeine more efficiently.) An average man and woman sitting down for a cup of coffee are thus not pharmaceutical equals: in effect, the woman is under the influence of a vastly more powerful drug. Given these differences, you'd think that, instead of contrasting the caffeine cultures of tea and coffee, we'd contrast the caffeine cultures of men and women.

But we don't, and with good reason. To parse caffeine along gender lines does not do justice to its capacity to insinuate itself into every aspect of our lives, not merely to influence culture but even to create it. Take coffee's reputation as the "thinker's" drink. This dates from eighteenth-century Europe, where coffeehouses played a major role in the egalitarian, inclusionary spirit that was then sweeping the continent. They sprang up first in London, so alarming Charles II that in 1676 he tried to ban them. It didn't work. By 1700, there were hundreds of coffeehouses in London, their subversive spirit best captured by a couplet from a comedy of the period: "In a coffeehouse just now among the rabble I bluntly asked, which is the treason table." The movement then spread to Paris, and by the end of the eighteenth century coffeehouses numbered in the hundreds—most famously; the Café de la Régence, near the Palais Royal, which counted among its customers Robespierre, Napoleon, Voltaire, Victor Hugo, Théophile Gautier, Rousseau, and the Duke of Richelieu. Previously, when men had gathered together to talk in public places, they had done so in bars, which drew from specific socioeconomic niches and, because of the alcohol they served, created a specific kind of talk. The new coffeehouses, by contrast, drew from many different classes and trades, and they served a stimulant, not a depressant. "It is not extravagant to claim that it was in these gathering spots that the art of conversation became the basis of a new literary style and that a new ideal of general education in letters was born," Weinberg and Bealer write.

It is worth nothing, as well, that in the original coffeehouses nearly everyone smoked, and nicotine also has a distinctive physiological effect. It moderates mood and extends attention, and, more important, it doubles the rate of caffeine metabolism: it allows you to drink twice as much coffee as you could otherwise. In other words, the original coffeehouse was a place where men of all types could sit all day; the tobacco they smoked made it possible to drink coffee all day; and the coffee they drank inspired them to talk all day. Out of this came the Enlightenment. (The next time we so perfectly married pharmacology and place, we got Joan Baez.)[1]

In time, caffeine moved from the café to the home. In America, coffee triumphed because of the country's proximity to the new Caribbean and Latin American coffee plantations, and the fact that throughout the nineteenth century duties were negligible. Beginning in the eighteen-twenties, Courtwright tells us, Brazil "unleashed a flood of slave-produced coffee. American per capita consumption, three pounds per year in 1830, rose to eight pounds by 1859." 10

What this flood of caffeine did, according to Weinberg and Bealer, was to abet the process of industrialization—to help "large numbers of people to coordinate their work schedules by giving them the energy to start work at a given time and continue it as long as necessary." Until the eighteenth century, it must be remembered, many Westerners drank beer almost continuously, even beginning their day with something called "beer soup." (Bealer and Weinberg helpfully provide the following eighteenth-century German recipe: "Heat the beer in a saucepan; in a separate small pot beat a couple of eggs. Add a chunk of butter to the hot beer. Stir in some cool beer to cool it, then pour over the eggs. Add a bit of salt, and finally mix all the ingredients together, whisking it well to keep it from curdling.") Now they began each day with a strong cup of coffee. One way to explain the industrial revolution is as the inevitable consequence of a world where people suddenly preferred being jittery to being drunk. In the modern world, there was no other way to keep up. That's what Edison meant when he said that genius was ninety-nine per cent perspiration and one per cent inspiration. In the old paradigm, working with your mind had been associated with leisure. It was only the poor who worked hard. (The quintessential

1. Joan Baez (b. 1941), American folksinger and political activist.

preindustrial narrative of inspiration belonged to Archimedes, who made his discovery, let's not forget, while taking a bath.) But Edison was saying that the old class distinctions no longer held true—that in the industrialized world there was as much toil associated with the life of the mind as there had once been with the travails of the body.

In the twentieth century, the professions transformed themselves accordingly: medicine turned the residency process into an ordeal of sleeplessness, the legal profession borrowed a page from the manufacturing floor and made its practitioners fill out time cards like union men. Intellectual heroics became a matter of endurance. "The pace of computation was hectic," James Gleick writes of the Manhattan Project in "Genius," his biography of the physicist Richard Feynman. "Feynman's day began at 8:30 and ended fifteen hours later. Sometimes he could not leave the computing center at all. He worked through for thirty-one hours once and the next day found that an error minutes after he went to bed had stalled the whole team. The routine allowed just a few breaks." Did Feynman's achievements reflect a greater natural talent than his less productive forebears had? Or did he just drink a lot more coffee? Paul Hoffman, in "The Man Who Loved Only Numbers," writes of the legendary twentieth-century mathematician Paul Erdös that "he put in nineteen-hour days, keeping himself fortified with 10 to 20 milligrams of Benzedrine or Ritalin, strong espresso and caffeine tablets. 'A mathematician,' Erdös was fond of saying, 'is a machine for turning coffee into theorems.'" Once, a friend bet Erdös five hundred dollars that he could not quit amphetamines for a month. Erdös took the bet and won, but, during his time of abstinence, he found himself incapable of doing any serious work. "You've set mathematics back a month," he told his friend when he collected, and immediately returned to his pills.

Erdös's unadulterated self was less real and less familiar to him than his adulterated self, and that is a condition that holds, more or less, for the rest of society as well. Part of what it means to be human in the modern age is that we have come to construct our emotional and cognitive states not merely from the inside out—with thought and intention—but from the outside in, with chemical additives. The modern personality is, in this sense, a synthetic creation: skillfully regulated and medicated and dosed with caffeine so that we can always be awake and alert and focussed when we need to be. On a bet, no doubt, we could walk away from caffeine if we had to. But what would be the point? The lawyers wouldn't make their billable hours. The young doctors would fall behind in their training. The physicists might still be stuck out in the New Mexico desert. We'd set the world back a month.

That the modern personality is synthetic is, of course, a disquieting notion. When we talk of synthetic personality—or of constructing new selves through chemical means—we think of hard drugs, not caffeine. Timothy Leary used to make such claims about LSD, and the reason his revolution never took flight was that most of us found the concept of tuning in, turning on, and dropping out to be a bit creepy. Here was this shaman, this visionary—and yet, if his consciousness was so great, why was he so intent on altering it? More important, what exactly were we supposed to be tuning in to? We were given hints, with psychedelic colors and deep readings of "Lucy in the Sky with Diamonds," but that was never enough. If we are to re-create ourselves, we would like to know what we will become.

15 Caffeine is the best and most useful of our drugs because in every one of its forms it can answer that question precisely. It is a stimulant that blocks the action of adenosine, and comes in a multitude of guises, each with a ready-made story attached, a mixture of history and superstition and whimsy which infuses the daily ritual of adenosine blocking with meaning and purpose. Put caffeine in a red can and it becomes refreshing fun. Brew it in a teapot and it becomes romantic and decorous. Extract it from little brown beans and, magically, it is hardheaded and potent. "There was a little known Russian émigré, Trotsky by name, who during World War I was in the habit of playing chess in Vienna's Café Central every evening," Bealer and Weinberg write, in one of the book's many fascinating café yarns:

> A typical Russian refugee, who talked too much but seemed utterly harmless, indeed, a pathetic figure in the eyes of the Viennese. One day in 1917 an official of the Austrian Foreign Ministry rushed into the minister's room, panting and excited, and told his chief, "Your excellency . . . Your excellency . . . Revolution has broken out in Russia." The minister, less excitable and less credulous than his official, rejected such a wild claim and retorted calmly, "Go away . . . Russia is not a land where revolutions break out. Besides, who on earth would make a revolution in Russia? Perhaps Herr Trotsky from the Café Central?"

The minister should have known better. Give a man enough coffee and he's capable of anything.

QUESTIONS

1. How serious do you think Gladwell is when he says that we're all drugged on caffeine? How can you tell?

2. Gladwell creates a binary between coffee and tea. Describe another binary between two closely similar forms—such as seashore vs. mountains; Coke vs. Pepsi; skis vs. snowboards. How do binaries work? What limitations do you see in the binary you created or in Gladwell's?

3. Gladwell offers several hypotheses for caffeine's success as the drug of choice for the modern world. Discuss which one you find most persuasive.

4. Write a description of some of the rituals that you or someone you know indulges in with coffee or tea.

Jessica Mitford *Behind the Formaldehyde Curtain*

The drama begins to unfold with the arrival of the corpse at the mortuary.

Alas, poor Yorick![1] How surprised he would be to see how his counterpart of today is whisked off to a funeral parlor and is in short order sprayed, sliced, pierced, pickled, trussed, trimmed, creamed, waxed, painted, rouged and neatly dressed—transformed from a common corpse into a Beautiful Memory Picture. This process is known in the trade as embalming and restorative art, and is so universally employed in the United States and Canada that the funeral director does it routinely, without consulting corpse or kin. He regards as eccentric those few who are hardy enough to suggest that it might be dispensed with. Yet no law requires embalming, no religious doctrine commends it, nor is it dictated by considerations of health, sanitation, or even of personal daintiness. In no part of the world but in Northern America is it widely used. The purpose of embalming is to make the corpse presentable for viewing in a suitably costly container; and here too the funeral director routinely, without first consulting the family, prepares the body for public display.

Is all this legal? The processes to which a dead body may be subjected are after all to some extent circumscribed by law. In most states, for instance, the signature of next of kin must be obtained before an autopsy may be performed, before the deceased may be cremated, before the body may be turned over to a medical school for research purposes; or such provision must be made in the decedent's will. In the case of embalming, no such permission is required nor is it ever sought. A textbook, *The Principles and Practices of Embalming,* comments on this: "There is some question regarding the legality of much that is done within the preparation room." The author points out that it would be most unusual for a responsible member of a bereaved family to instruct the mortician, in so many words, to "embalm" the body of a deceased relative. The very term "embalming" is so seldom used that the mortician must rely upon custom in the matter. The author concludes that unless the family specifies otherwise, the act of entrusting the body to the care of a funeral establishment carries with it an implied permission to go ahead and embalm.

Embalming is indeed a most extraordinary procedure, and one must wonder at the docility of Americans who each year pay hundreds of millions of dollars for its perpetuation, blissfully ignorant of what it is all about, what is done, how it is done. Not one in ten thousand has any idea of what actually

From The American Way of Death *(1963), an exposé of the funeral industry, which was revised and updated by Mitford just before her death in 1996 as* The American Way of Death Revisited *(1998).*

1. Hamlet says this (V.i.184) upon seeing the skull of the court clown he had known as a child.

takes place. Books on the subject are extremely hard to come by. They are not to be found in most libraries or bookshops.

In an era when huge television audiences watch surgical operations in the comfort of their living rooms, when, thanks to the animated cartoon, the geography of the digestive system has become familiar territory even to the nursery school set, in a land where the satisfaction of curiosity about almost all matters is a national pastime, the secrecy surrounding embalming can, surely, hardly be attributed to the inherent gruesomeness of the subject. Custom in this regard has within this century suffered a complete reversal. In the early days of American embalming, when it was performed in the home of the deceased, it was almost mandatory for some relative to stay by the embalmer's side and witness the procedure. Today, family members who might wish to be in attendance would certainly be dissuaded by the funeral director. All others, except apprentices, are excluded by law from the preparation room. 5

A close look at what does actually take place may explain in large measure the undertaker's intractable reticence concerning a procedure that has become his major *raison d'être*.[2] Is it possible he fears that public information about embalming might lead patrons to wonder if they really want this service? If the funeral men are loath to discuss the subject outside the trade, the reader may, understandably, be equally loath to go on reading at this point. For those who have the stomach for it, let us part the formaldehyde curtain. . . .

The body is first laid out in the undertaker's morgue—or rather, Mr. Jones is reposing in the preparation room—to be readied to bid the world farewell.

The preparation room in any of the better funeral establishments has the tiled and sterile look of a surgery, and indeed the embalmer-restorative artist who does his chores there is beginning to adopt the term "dermasurgeon" (appropriately corrupted by some mortician-writers as "demi-surgeon") to describe his calling. His equipment, consisting of scalpels, scissors, augers, forceps, clamps, needles, pumps, tubes, bowls and basins, is crudely imitative of the surgeon's, as is his technique, acquired in a nine- or twelve-month post-high-school course in an embalming school. He is supplied by an advanced chemical industry with a bewildering array of fluids, sprays, pastes, oils, powders, creams, to fix or soften tissue, shrink or distend it as needed, dry it here, restore the moisture there. There are cosmetics, waxes and paints to fill and cover features, even plaster of Paris to replace entire limbs. There are ingenious aids to prop and stabilize the cadaver: a Vari-Pose Head Rest, the Edwards Arm and Hand Positioner, the Repose Block (to support the shoulders during the embalming), and the Throop Foot Positioner, which resembles an old-fashioned stocks.

Mr. John H. Eckels, president of the Eckels College of Mortuary Science, thus describes the first part of the embalming procedure: "In the hands of a skilled practitioner, this work may be done in a comparatively short time and without mutilating the body other than by slight incision—so slight that it scarcely would cause serious inconvenience if made upon a living person. It is

2. Reason for being.

necessary to remove the blood, and doing this not only helps in the disinfecting, but removes the principal cause of disfigurements due to discoloration."

10 Another textbook discusses the all-important time element: "The earlier this is done, the better, for every hour that elapses between death and embalming will add to the problems and complications encountered. . . ." Just how soon should one get going on the embalming? The author tells us, "On the basis of such scanty information made available to this profession through its rudimentary and haphazard system of technical research, we must conclude that the best results are to be obtained if the subject is embalmed before life is completely extinct—that is, before cellular death has occurred. In the average case, this would mean within an hour after somatic death." For those who feel that there is something a little rudimentary, not to say haphazard, about this advice, a comforting thought is offered by another writer. Speaking of fears entertained in early days of premature burial, he points out, "One of the effects of embalming by chemical injection, however, has been to dispel fears of live burial." How true; once the blood is removed, chances of live burial are indeed remote.

To return to Mr. Jones, the blood is drained out through the veins and replaced by embalming fluid pumped in through the arteries. As noted in *The Principles and Practices of Embalming,* "every operator has a favorite injection and drainage point—a fact which becomes a handicap only if he fails or refuses to forsake his favorites when conditions demand it." Typical favorites are the carotid artery, femoral artery, jugular vein, subclavian vein. There are various choices of embalming fluid. If Flextone is used, it will produce a "mild, flexible rigidity. The skin retains a velvety softness, the tissues are rubbery and pliable. Ideal for women and children." It may be blended with B. and G. Products Company's Lyf-Lyk tint, which is guaranteed to reproduce "nature's own skin texture . . . the velvety appearance of living tissue." Suntone comes in three separate tints: Suntan; Special Cosmetic Tint, a pink shade "especially indicated for young female subjects"; and Regular Cosmetic Tint, moderately pink.

About three to six gallons of a dyed and perfumed solution of formaldehyde, glycerin, borax, phenol, alcohol and water is soon circulating through Mr. Jones, whose mouth has been sewn together with a "needle directed upward between the upper lip and gum and brought out through the left nostril," with the corners raised slightly "for a more pleasant expression." If he should be bucktoothed, his teeth are cleaned with Bon Ami and coated with colorless nail polish. His eyes, meanwhile, are closed with flesh-tinted eye caps and eye cement.

The next step is to have at Mr. Jones with a thing called a trocar. This is a long, hollow needle attached to a tube. It is jabbed into the abdomen, poked around the entrails and chest cavity, the contents of which are pumped out and replaced with "cavity fluid." This done, and the hole in the abdomen sewn up, Mr. Jones's face is heavily creamed (to protect the skin from burns which may be caused by leakage of the chemicals), and he is covered with a sheet and left unmolested for a while. But not for long—there is more, much more, in store for him. He has been embalmed, but not yet restored, and the best time to start the restorative work is eight to ten hours after embalming, when the tissues have become firm and dry.

The object of all this attention to the corpse, it must be remembered, is to make it presentable for viewing in an attitude of healthy repose. "Our customs require the presentation of our dead in the semblance of normality . . . unmarred by the ravages of illness, disease or mutilation," says Mr. J. Sheridan Mayer in his *Restorative Art.* This is rather a large order since few people die in the full bloom of health, unravaged by illness and unmarked by some disfigurement. The funeral industry is equal to the challenge: "In some cases the gruesome appearance of a mutilated or disease-ridden subject may be quite discouraging. The task of restoration may seem impossible and shake the confidence of the embalmer. This is the time for intestinal fortitude and determination. Once the formative work is begun and affected tissues are cleaned or removed, all doubts of success vanish. It is surprising and gratifying to discover the results which may be obtained."

15 The embalmer, having allowed an appropriate interval to elapse, returns to the attack, but now he brings into play the skill and equipment of sculptor and cosmetician. Is a hand missing? Casting one in plaster of Paris is a simple matter. "For replacement purposes, only a cast of the back of the hand is necessary; this is within the ability of the average operator and is quite adequate." If a lip or two, a nose or an ear should be missing, the embalmer has at hand a variety of restorative waxes with which to model replacements. Pores and skin texture are simulated by stippling with a little brush, and over this cosmetics are laid on. Head off? Decapitation cases are rather routinely handled. Ragged edges are trimmed, and head joined to torso with a series of splints, wires and sutures. It is a good idea to have a little something at the neck—a scarf or a high collar—when time for viewing comes. Swollen mouth? Cut out tissue as needed from inside the lips. If too much is removed, the surface contour can easily be restored by padding with cotton. Swollen necks and cheeks are reduced by removing tissue through vertical incisions made down each side of the neck. "When the deceased is casketed, the pillow will hide the suture incisions . . . as an extra precaution against leakage, the suture may be painted with liquid sealer."

The opposite condition is more likely to present itself—that of emaciation. His hypodermic syringe now loaded with massage cream, the embalmer seeks out and fills the hollowed and sunken areas by injection. In this procedure the backs of the hands and fingers and the under-chin area should not be neglected.

Positioning the lips is a problem that recurrently challenges the ingenuity of the embalmer. Closed too tightly, they tend to give a stern, even disapproving expression. Ideally, embalmers feel, the lips should give the impression of being ever so slightly parted, the upper lip protruding slightly for a more youthful appearance. This takes some engineering, however, as the lips tend to drift apart. Lip drift can sometimes be remedied by pushing one or two straight pins through the inner margin of the lower lip and then inserting them between the two front upper teeth. If Mr. Jones happens to have no teeth, the pins can just as easily be anchored in his Armstrong Face Former and Denture Replacer. Another method to maintain lip closure is to dislocate the lower jaw, which is then held in its new position by a wire run through holes which have been drilled through the upper and lower jaws at the midline. As the French are fond of saying, *il faut souffrir pour être belle.*[3]

If Mr. Jones has died of jaundice, the embalming fluid will very likely turn him green. Does this deter the embalmer? Not if he has intestinal fortitude. Masking pastes and cosmetics are heavily laid on, burial garments and casket interiors are color-correlated with particular care, and Jones is displayed beneath rose-colored lights. Friends will say "How *well* he looks." Death by carbon monoxide, on the other hand, can be rather a good thing from the embalmer's viewpoint: "One advantage is the fact that this type of discoloration is an exaggerated form of a natural pink coloration." This is nice because the healthy glow is already present and needs but little attention.

The patching and filling completed, Mr. Jones is now shaved, washed and dressed. Cream-based cosmetic, available in pink, flesh, suntan, brunette and blond, is applied to his hands and face, his hair is shampooed and combed (and, in the case of Mrs. Jones, set), his hands manicured. For the horny-handed son of toil special care must be taken; cream should be applied to remove ingrained grime, and the nails cleaned. "If he were not in the habit of having them manicured in life, trimming and shaping is advised for better appearance—never questioned by kin."

20 Jones is now ready for casketing (this is the present participle of the verb "to casket"). In this operation his right shoulder should be depressed slightly "to turn the body a bit to the right and soften the appearance of lying flat on the back." Positioning the hands is a matter of importance, and special rubber positioning blocks may be used. The hands should be cupped slightly for a more lifelike, relaxed appearance. Proper placement of the body requires a delicate sense of balance. It should lie as high as possible in the casket, yet not so high that the lid, when lowered, will hit the nose. On the other hand, we are cautioned, placing the body too low "creates the impression that the body is in a box."

Jones is next wheeled into the appointed slumber room where a few last touches may be added—his favorite pipe placed in his hand or, if he was a great reader, a book propped into position. (In the case of little Master Jones a Teddy bear may be clutched.) Here he will hold open house for a few days, visiting hours 10 A.M. to 9 P.M.

All now being in readiness, the funeral director calls a staff conference to make sure that each assistant knows his precise duties. Mr. Wilber Kriege writes: "This makes your staff feel that they are a part of the team, with a definite assignment that must be properly carried out if the whole plan is to succeed. You never heard of a football coach who failed to talk to his entire team before they go on the field. They have drilled on the plays they are to execute for hours and days, and yet the successful coach knows the importance of making even the bench-warming third-string substitute feel that he is important if the game is to be won." The winning of *this* game is predicated upon glass-smooth handling of the logistics. The funeral director has notified the

3. It is necessary to suffer to be beautiful.

pallbearers whose names were furnished by the family, has arranged for the presence of clergyman, organist, and soloist, has provided transportation for everybody, has organized and listed the flowers sent by friends. In *Psychology of Funeral Service* Mr. Edward A. Martin points out: "He may not always do as much as the family thinks he is doing, but it is his helpful guidance that they appreciate in knowing they are proceeding as they should. . . . The important thing is how well his services can be used to make the family believe they are giving unlimited expression to their own sentiment."

The religious service may be held in a church or in the chapel of the funeral home; the funeral director vastly prefers the latter arrangement, for not only is it more convenient for him but it affords him the opportunity to show off his beautiful facilities to the gathered mourners. After the clergyman has had his say, the mourners queue up to file past the casket for a last look at the deceased. The family is *never* asked whether they want an open-casket ceremony; in the absence of their instruction to the contrary, this is taken for granted. Consequently well over 90 per cent of all American funerals feature the open casket—a custom unknown in other parts of the world. Foreigners are astonished by it. An English woman living in San Francisco described her reaction in a letter to the writer:

> I myself have attended only one funeral here—that of an elderly fellow worker of mine. After the service I could not understand why everyone was walking towards the coffin (sorry, I mean casket), but thought I had better follow the crowd. It shook me rigid to get there and find the casket open and poor old Oscar lying there in his brown tweed suit, wearing a suntan makeup and just the wrong shade of lipstick. If I had not been extremely fond of the old boy, I have a horrible feeling that I might have giggled. Then and there I decided that I could never face another American funeral—even dead.

The casket (which has been resting throughout the service on a Classic Beauty Ultra Metal Casket Bier) is now transferred by a hydraulically operated device called Porto-Lift to a balloon-tired, Glide Easy casket carriage which will wheel it to yet another conveyance, the Cadillac Funeral Coach. This may be lavender, cream, light green—anything but black. Interiors, of course, are color-correlated, "for the man who cannot stop short of perfection."

At graveside, the casket is lowered into the earth. This office, once the prerogative of friends of the deceased, is now performed by a patented mechanical lowering device. A "Lifetime Green" artificial grass mat is at the ready to conceal the sere earth, and overhead, to conceal the sky, is a portable Steril Chapel Tent ("resists the intense heat and humidity of summer and the terrific storms of winter . . . available in Silver Grey, Rose or Evergreen"). Now is the time for the ritual scattering of earth over the coffin, as the solemn words "earth to earth, ashes to ashes, dust to dust" are pronounced by the officiating cleric. This can today be accomplished "with a mere flick of the wrist with the Gordon Leak-Proof Earth Dispenser. No grasping of a handful of dirt, no soiled fingers. Simple, dignified, beautiful, reverent! The modern way!" The

Gordon Earth Dispenser (at $5) is of nickel-plated brass construction. It is not only "attractive to the eye and long wearing"; it is also "one of the 'tools' for building better public relations" if presented as "an appropriate non-commercial gift" to the clergyman. It is shaped something like a saltshaker.

Untouched by human hand, the coffin and the earth are now united.

It is in the function of directing the participants through this maze of gadgetry that the funeral director has assigned to himself his relatively new role of "grief therapist." He has relieved the family of every detail, he has revamped the corpse to look like a living doll, he has arranged for it to nap for a few days in a slumber room, he has put on a well-oiled performance in which the concept of *death* has played no part whatsoever—unless it was inconsiderately mentioned by the clergyman who conducted the religious service. He has done everything in his power to make the funeral a real pleasure for everybody concerned. He and his team have given their all to score an upset victory over death.

QUESTIONS

1. Mitford's description might be called a "process analysis"—that is, it describes the process by which a corpse becomes a "Beautiful Memory Picture." What are the stages of the process? Mark them in the margins of the essay, and think about how Mitford treats each one.

2. Mitford objects to the American funeral industry and its manipulation of death, yet she never directly says so. How do we as readers know her attitude? Cite words, phrases, or sentences that reveal her position.

3. Describe a process that you object to, letting your choice of words reveal your attitude.

HENRY LOUIS GATES, JR. *In the Kitchen*

WE ALWAYS HAD a gas stove in the kitchen, in our house in Piedmont, West Virginia, where I grew up. Never electric, though using electric became fashionable in Piedmont in the sixties, like using Crest toothpaste rather than Colgate, or watching Huntley and Brinkley rather than Walter Cronkite.[1] But not us: gas, Colgate, and good ole Walter Cronkite, come what may. We used gas partly out of loyalty to Big Mom, Mama's Mama, because she was mostly blind and still loved to cook, and could feel her way more easily with gas than with electric. But

Originally published in the New Yorker *(April 18, 1994), a magazine distinguished for its fiction, essays, and reviews, in advance of the publication of Gates's memoir,* Colored People *(1994).*

1. Newscasters of the 1960s: Chet Huntley and David Brinkley were on NBC; Walter Cronkite was on CBS.

the most important thing about our gas-equipped kitchen was that Mama used to do hair there. The "hot comb" was a fine-toothed iron instrument with a long wooden handle and a pair of iron curlers that opened and closed like scissors. Mama would put it in the gas fire until it glowed. You could smell those prongs heating up.

I liked that smell. Not the smell so much, I guess, as what the smell meant for the shape of my day. There was an intimate warmth in the women's tones as they talked with my Mama, doing their hair. I knew what the women had been through to get their hair ready to be "done," because I would watch Mama do it to herself. How that kink could be transformed through grease and fire into that magnificent head of wavy hair was a miracle to me, and still is.

Mama would wash her hair over the sink, a towel wrapped around her shoulders, wearing just her slip and her white bra. (We had no shower—just a galvanized tub that we stored in the kitchen—until we moved down Rat Tail Road into Doc Wolverton's house, in 1954.) After she dried it, she would grease her scalp thoroughly with blue Bergamot hair grease, which came in a short, fat jar with a picture of a beautiful colored lady on it. It's important to grease your scalp real good, my Mama would explain, to keep from burning yourself. Of course, her hair would return to its natural kink almost as soon as the hot water and shampoo hit it. To me, it was another miracle how hair so "straight" would so quickly become kinky again the second it even approached some water.

My Mama had only a few "clients" whose heads she "did"—did, I think, because she enjoyed it, rather than for the few pennies it brought in. They would sit on one of our red plastic kitchen chairs, the kind with the shiny metal legs, and brace themselves for the process. Mama would stroke that red-hot iron—which by this time had been in the gas fire for half an hour or more—slowly but firmly through their hair, from scalp to strand's end. It made a scorching, crinkly sound, the hot iron did, as it burned its way through kink, leaving in its wake straight strands of hair, standing long and tall but drooping over at the ends, their shape like the top of a heavy willow tree. Slowly, steadily, Mama's hands would transform a round mound of Odetta[2] kink into a darkened swamp of everglades. The Bergamot made the hair shiny; the heat of the hot iron gave it a brownish-red cast. Once all the hair was as straight as God allows kink to get, Mama would take the wellheated curling iron and twirl the straightened strands into more or less loosely wrapped curls. She claimed that she owed her skill as a hairdresser to the strength in her wrists, and as she worked her little finger would poke out, the way it did when she sipped tea. Mama was a southpaw, and wrote upside down and backward to produce the cleanest, roundest letters you've ever seen.

5 The "kitchen" she would all but remove from sight with a handheld pair of shears, bought just for this purpose. Now, the kitchen was the room in which we were sitting—the room where Mama did hair and washed clothes, and where we all took a bath in that galvanized tub. But the word has another meaning, and the kitchen that I'm speaking of is the very kinky bit of hair at the back of

2. Singer Odetta Holmes (1930–2008) of blues and spirituals in the 1950s and a leading figure in the American folk revival of the 1960s; she wore her hair in an Afro.

your head, where your neck meets your shirt collar. If there was ever a part of our African past that resisted assimilation, it was the kitchen. No matter how hot the iron, no matter how powerful the chemical, no matter how stringent the mashed-potatoes-and-lye formula of a man's "process," neither God nor woman nor Sammy Davis, Jr.,[3] could straighten the kitchen. The kitchen was permanent, irredeemable, irresistible kink. Unassimilably African. No matter what you did, no matter how hard you tried, you couldn't de-kink a person's kitchen. So you trimmed it off as best you could.

When hair had begun to "turn," as they'd say—to return to its natural kinky glory—it was the kitchen that turned first (the kitchen around the back, and nappy edges at the temples). When the kitchen started creeping up the back of the neck, it was time to get your hair done again.

Sometimes, after dark, a man would come to have his hair done. It was Mr. Charlie Carroll. He was very light-complected and had a ruddy nose—it made me think of Edmund Gwenn, who played Kris Kringle in "Miracle on 34th Street." At first, Mama did him after my brother, Rocky, and I had gone to sleep. It was only later that we found out that he had come to our house so Mama could iron his hair—not with a hot comb or a curling iron but with our very own Proctor-Silex steam iron. For some reason I never understood, Mr. Charlie would conceal his Frederick Douglass–like mane[4] under a big white Stetson hat. I never saw him take it off except when he came to our house, at night, to have his hair pressed. (Later, Daddy would tell us about Mr. Charlie's most prized piece of knowledge, something that the man would only confide after his hair had been pressed, as a token of intimacy. "Not many people know this," he'd say, in a tone of circumspection, "but George Washington was Abraham Lincoln's daddy." Nodding solemnly, he'd add the clincher: "A white man told me." Though he was in dead earnest, this became a humorous refrain around our house—"a white man told me"—which we used to punctuate especially preposterous assertions.)

My mother examined my daughters' kitchens whenever we went home to visit, in the early eighties. It became a game between us. I had told her not to do it, because I didn't like the politics it suggested—the notion of "good" and "bad" hair. "Good" hair was "straight," "bad" hair kinky. Even in the late sixties, at the height of Black Power, almost nobody could bring themselves to say "bad" for good and "good" for bad. People still said that hair like white people's hair was "good," even if they encapsulated it in a disclaimer, like "what we used to call 'good.'"

Maggie would be seated in her high chair, throwing food this way and that, and Mama would be cooing about how cute it all was, how I used to do just like Maggie was doing, and wondering whether her flinging her food with her left hand meant that she was going to be left-handed like Mama. When my daughter

3. African American singer, dancer, and entertainer (1925–1990) with notably "processed" hair.

4. Douglass (1817–1895) was an escaped slave turned abolitionist; photographs show him with a lionlike mane of hair.

was just about covered with Chef Boyardee Spaghetti-O's, Mama would seize the opportunity: wiping her clean, she would tilt Maggie's head to one side and reach down the back of her neck. Sometimes Mama would even rub a curl between her fingers, just to make sure that her bifocals had not deceived her. Then she'd sigh with satisfaction and relief: No kink . . . yet. Mama! I'd shout, pretending to be angry. Every once in a while, if no one was looking, I'd peek, too.

I say "yet" because most black babies are born with soft, silken hair. But after a few months it begins to turn, as inevitably as do the seasons or the leaves on a tree. People once thought baby oil would stop it. They were wrong. 10

Everybody I knew as a child wanted to have good hair. You could be as ugly as homemade sin dipped in misery and still be thought attractive if you had good hair. "Jesus moss," the girls at Camp Lee, Virginia, had called Daddy's naturally "good" hair during the war. I know that he played that thick head of hair for all it was worth, too.

My own hair was "not a bad grade," as barbers would tell me when they cut it for the first time. It was like a doctor reporting the results of the first full physical he has given you. Like "You're in good shape" or "Blood pressure's kind of high—better cut down on salt."

I spent most of my childhood and adolescence messing with my hair. I definitely wanted straight hair. Like Pop's. When I was about three, I tried to stick a wad of Bazooka bubble gum to that straight hair of his. I suppose what fixed that memory for me is the spanking I got for doing so: he turned me upside down, holding me by my feet, the better to paddle my behind. Little *nigger,* he had shouted, walloping away. I started to laugh about it two days later, when my behind stopped hurting.

When black people say "straight," of course, they don't usually mean literally straight—they're not describing hair like, say, Peggy Lipton's (she was the white girl on "The Mod Squad"), or like Mary's of Peter, Paul & Mary[5] fame; black people call that "stringy" hair. No, "straight" just means not kinky, no matter what contours the curl may take. I would have done *anything* to have straight hair—and I used to try everything, short of getting a process.[6]

Of the wide variety of techniques and methods I came to master in the challenging prestidigitation of the follicle, almost all had two things in common: a heavy grease and the application of pressure. It's not an accident that some of the biggest black-owned companies in the fifties and sixties made hair products. And I tried them all, in search of that certain silken touch, the one that would leave neither the hand nor the pillow sullied by grease. 15

I always wondered what Frederick Douglass put on *his* hair, or what Phillis Wheatley[7] put on hers. Or why Wheatley has that rag on her head in the little engraving in the frontispiece of her book. One thing is for sure: you can bet that when Phillis Wheatley went to England and saw the Countess of Huntingdon

5. Folksinging group famous in the 1960s for "Puff the Magic Dragon" and a version of Bob Dylan's "Blowing in the Wind."

6. Hair-straightening treatment that used chemicals for smoothing out kinks.

7. African American poet and slave (1753–1784) and America's first published black writer. She was taken to England to meet royalty.

she did not stop by the Queen's coiffeur on her way there. So many black people still get their hair straightened that it's a wonder we don't have a national holiday for Madame C. J. Walker, the woman who invented the process of straightening kinky hair. Call it Jheri-Kurled or call it "relaxed," it's still fried hair.

I used all the greases, from sea-blue Bergamot and creamy vanilla Duke (in its clear jar with the orange-white-and-green label) to the godfather of grease, the formidable Murray's. Now, Murray's was some *serious* grease. Whereas Bergamot was like oily jello, and Duke was viscous and sickly sweet, Murray's was light brown and *hard*. Hard as lard and twice as greasy, Daddy used to say. Murray's came in an orange can with a press-on top. It was so hard that some people would put a match to the can, just to soften the stuff and make it more manageable. Then, in the late sixties, when Afros came into style, I used Afro Sheen. From Murray's to Duke to Afro Sheen: that was my progression in black consciousness.

We used to put hot towels or washrags over our Murray-coated heads, in order to melt the wax into the scalp and the follicles. Unfortunately, the wax also had the habit of running down your neck, ears, and forehead. Not to mention your pillowcase. Another problem was that if you put two palmfuls of Murray's on your head your hair turned white. (Duke did the same thing.) The challenge was to get rid of that white color. Because if you got rid of the white stuff you had a magnificent head of wavy hair. That was the beauty of it: Murray's was so hard that it froze your hair into the wavy style you brushed it into. It looked really good if you wore a part. A lot of guys had parts *cut* into their hair by a barber, either with the clippers or with a straight-edge razor. Especially if you had kinky hair—then you'd generally wear a short razor cut, or what we called a Quo Vadis.

We tried to be as innovative as possible. Everyone knew about using a stocking cap, because your father or your uncle wore one whenever something really big was about to happen, whether sacred or secular: a funeral or a dance, a wedding or a trip in which you confronted official white people. Any time you were trying to look really sharp, you wore a stocking cap in preparation. And if the event was really a big one, you made a new cap. You asked your mother for a pair of her hose, and cut it with scissors about six inches or so from the open end—the end with the elastic that goes up to the top of the thigh. Then you knotted the cut end, and it became a beehive-shaped hat, with an elastic band that you pulled down low on your forehead and down around your neck in the back. To work well, the cap had to fit tightly and snugly, like a press. And it had to fit that tightly because it *was* a press: it pressed your hair with the force of the hose's elastic. If you greased your hair down real good, and left the stocking cap on long enough, voilà: you got a head of pressed-against-the-scalp waves. (You also got a ring around your forehead when you woke up, but it went away.) And then you could enjoy your concrete do. Swore we were bad, too, with all that grease and those flat heads. My brother and I would brush it out a bit in the mornings, so that it looked—well, "natural." Grown men still wear stocking caps—especially older men, who generally keep their stocking caps in their top drawers, along with their cufflinks and their see-through silk socks, their "Maverick" ties, their silk handkerchiefs, and whatever else they prize the most.

A Murrayed-down stocking cap was the respectable version of the process, which, by contrast, was most definitely not a cool thing to have unless you were an entertainer by trade. Zeke and Keith and Poochie and a few other stars of the high-school basketball team all used to get a process once or twice a year. It was expensive, and you had to go somewhere like Pittsburgh or D.C. or Uniontown—somewhere where there were enough colored people to support a trade. The guys would disappear, then reappear a day or two later, strutting like peacocks, their hair burned slightly red from the lye base. They'd also wear "rags"—cloths or handkerchiefs—around their heads when they slept or played basketball. Do-rags, they were called. But the result was straight hair, with just a hint of wave. No curl. Do-it-yourselfers took their chances at home with a concoction of mashed potatoes and lye. 20

The most famous process of all, however, outside of the process Malcolm X describes in his "Autobiography," and maybe the process of Sammy Davis, Jr., was Nat King Cole's[8] process. Nat King Cole had patent-leather hair. That man's got the finest process money can buy, or so Daddy said the night we saw Cole's TV show on NBC. It was November 5, 1956. I remember the date because everyone came to our house to watch it and to celebrate one of Daddy's buddies' birthdays. Yeah, Uncle Joe chimed in, they can do shit to his hair that the average Negro can't even *think* about—secret shit.

Nat King Cole was *clean*. I've had an ongoing argument with a Nigerian friend about Nat King Cole for twenty years now. Not about whether he could sing—any fool knows that he could—but about whether or not he was a handkerchief head for wearing that patent-leather process.

Sammy Davis, Jr.'s process was the one I detested. It didn't look good on him. Worse still, he liked to have a fried strand dangling down the middle of his forehead, so he could shake it out from the crown when he sang. But Nat King Cole's hair was a thing unto itself, a beautifully sculpted work of art that he and he alone had the right to wear. The only difference between a process and a stocking cap, really, was taste; but Nat King Cole, unlike, say, Michael Jackson, looked *good* in his. His head looked like Valentino's[9] head in the twenties, and some say it was Valentino the process was imitating. But Nat King Cole wore a process because it suited his face, his demeanor, his name, his style. He was as clean as he wanted to be.

I had forgotten all about that patent-leather look until one day in 1971, when I was sitting in an Arab restaurant on the island of Zanzibar surrounded by men in fezzes and white caftans, trying to learn how to eat curried goat and rice with the fingers of my right hand and feeling two million miles from home. All of a sudden, an old transistor radio sitting on top of a china cupboard stopped blaring out its Swahili music and started playing "Fly Me to the Moon," by Nat King Cole. The restaurant's din was not affected at all, but in

8. Singer and jazz pianist (1919–1965).

9. Film star (1895–1926) known, among other things, for his slicked-back hair.

my mind's eye I saw it: the King's magnificent sleek black tiara. I managed, barely, to blink back the tears.

QUESTIONS

1. "Kitchen" has two meanings in Gates's essay; write a brief summary of the essay explaining the significance of both uses of "kitchen."

2. Why do you think Gates uses so many allusions to celebrities (mostly from the 1950s and 1960s) and brand-name products? Note his preferences and progression. What is the significance of the allusions and brand names?

3. Write an essay in which you use memories from childhood—including sensory details, popular allusions, and brand-name products—to describe some element of your culture or identity.

CHARLES LAMB

A Dissertation upon Roast Pig

MANKIND, SAYS A Chinese manuscript, which my friend M. was obliging enough to read and explain to me, for the first seventy thousand ages ate their meat raw, clawing or biting it from the living animal, just as they do in Abyssinia to this day. This period is not obscurely hinted at by their great Confucius[1] in the second chapter of his *Mundane Mutations*, where he designates a kind of golden age by the term Cho-fang, literally the Cooks' Holiday. The manuscript goes on to say, that the art of roasting, or rather broiling (which I take to be the elder brother) was accidentally discovered in the manner following. The swineherd, Ho-ti, having gone out into the woods one morning, as his manner was, to collect mast for his hogs, left his cottage in the care of his eldest son Bo-bo, a great lubberly boy, who being fond of playing with fire, as younkers of his age commonly are, let some sparks escape into a bundle of straw, which kindling quickly, spread the conflagration over every part of their poor mansion till it was reduced to ashes. Together with the cottage (a sorry antediluvian make-shift of a building, you may think it), what was of much more importance, a fine litter of new-farrowed pigs, no less than nine in number, perished. China pigs have been esteemed a luxury all over the East from the remotest periods that we read of.

Originally published under his pseudonym, Elia, in London Magazine *(1822) and collected in* Essays of Elia *(1823), a celebrated collection of essays on ordinary subjects such as being a bachelor or visiting a college town.*

1. Confucius (Kong zi c. 571–479 BCE), preeminent Chinese philosopher whose *Analects* argued for self-discipline, obedience to family, and good government. The descriptions of the manuscript that follow are a fiction of Lamb's.

Bo-bo was in the utmost consternation, as you may think, not so much for the sake of the tenement, which his father and he could easily build up again with a few dry branches, and the labor of an hour or two, at any time, as for the loss of the pigs. While he was thinking what he should say to his father, and wringing his hands over the smoking remnants of one of those untimely sufferers, an odor assailed his nostrils, unlike any scent which he had before experienced. What could it proceed from?—not from the burnt cottage—he had smelt that smell before—indeed this was by no means the first accident of the kind which had occurred through the negligence of this unlucky young fire-brand. Much less did it resemble that of any known herb, weed, or flower. A premonitory moistening at the same time overflowed his nether lip. He knew not what to think. He next stooped down to feel the pig, if there were any signs of life in it. He burnt his fingers, and to cool them he applied them in his booby fashion to his mouth. Some of the crumbs of the scorched skin had come away with his fingers, and for the first time in his life (in the world's life indeed, for before him no man had known it) he tasted—*crackling!* Again he felt and fumbled at the pig. It did not burn him so much now, still he licked his fingers from a sort of habit. The truth at length broke into his slow understanding, that it was the pig that smelt so, and the pig that tasted so delicious; and, surrendering himself up to the new-born pleasure, he fell to tearing up whole handfuls of the scorched skin with the flesh next it, and was cramming it down his throat in his beastly fashion, when his sire entered amid the smoking rafters, armed with retributory cudgel, and finding how affairs stood, began to rain blows upon the young rogue's shoulders, as thick as hail-stones, which Bo-bo heeded not any more than if they had been flies. The tickling pleasure, which he experienced in his lower regions, had rendered him quite callous to any inconveniences he might feel in those remote quarters. His father might lay on, but he could not beat him from his pig, till he had fairly made an end of it, when, becoming a little more sensible of his situation, something like the following dialogue ensued.

"You graceless whelp, what have you got there devouring? Is it not enough that you have burnt me down three houses with your dog's tricks, and be hanged to you, but you must be eating fire, and I know not what—what have you got there, I say?"

"O father, the pig, the pig, do come and taste how nice the burnt pig eats."

The ears of Ho-ti tingled with terror. He cursed his son, and he cursed himself that ever he should beget a son that should eat burnt pig.

Bo-bo, whose scent was wonderfully sharpened since morning, soon raked out another pig, and fairly rending it asunder, thrust the lesser half by main force into the fists of Ho-ti, still shouting out "Eat, eat, eat the burning pig, father, only taste—O Lord,"—with such-like barbarous ejaculations, cramming all the while as if he would choke. 5

Ho-ti trembled in every joint while he grasped the abominable thing, wavering whether he should not put his son to death for an unnatural young monster, when the crackling scorching his fingers, as it had done his son's, and applying the same remedy to them, he in his turn tasted some of its flavor, which, make what sour mouths he would for a pretence, proved not altogether displeasing to him. In conclusion (for the manuscript here is a little tedious) both father and son fairly sat down to the mess, and never left off till they had despatched all that remained of the litter.

Bo-bo was strictly enjoined not to let the secret escape, for the neighbors would certainly have stoned them for a couple of abominable wretches, who could think of improving upon the good meat which God had sent them. Nevertheless, strange stories got about. It was observed that Ho-ti's cottage was burnt down now more frequently than ever. Nothing but fires from this time forward. Some would break out in broad day, others in the night-time. As often as the sow farrowed, so sure was the house of Ho-ti to be in a blaze; and Ho-ti himself, which was the more remarkable, instead of chastising his son, seemed to grow more indulgent to him than ever. At length they were watched, the terrible mystery discovered, and father and son summoned to take their trial at Pekin, then an inconsiderable assize town. Evidence was given, the obnoxious food itself produced in court, and verdict about to be pronounced, when the foreman of the jury begged that some of the burnt pig, of which the culprits stood accused, might be handed into the box. He handled it, and they all handled it, and burning their fingers, as Bo-bo and his father had done before them, and nature prompting to each of them the same remedy, against the face of all the facts, and the clearest charge which judge had ever given—to the surprise of the whole court, townsfolk, strangers, reporters, and all present—without leaving the box, or any manner of consultation whatever, they brought in a simultaneous verdict of Not Guilty.

The judge, who was a shrewd fellow, winked at the manifest iniquity of the decision: and, when the court was dismissed, went privily, and bought up all the pigs that could be had for love or money. In a few days his Lordship's town house was observed to be on fire. The thing took wing, and now there was nothing to be seen but fires in every direction. Fuel and pigs grew enormously dear all over the district. The insurance offices one and all shut up shop. People built slighter and slighter every day, until it was feared that the very science of architecture would in no long time be lost to the world. Thus this custom of firing houses continued, till in process of time, says my manuscript, a sage arose, like our Locke,[2] who made a discovery, that the flesh of swine, or indeed of any other animal, might be cooked (*burnt*, as they called it) without the necessity of consuming a whole house to dress it. Then first began the rude form of a gridiron. Roasting by the string, or spit, came in a century or two later; I forget in whose dynasty. By such slow degrees, concludes the manuscript, do the most useful and seemingly the most obvious arts, make their way among mankind.

Without placing too implicit faith in the account above given, it must be agreed, that if a worthy pretext for so dangerous an experiment as setting houses on fire (especially in these days) could be assigned in favor of any culinary object, that pretext and excuse might be found in ROAST PIG.

2. John Locke (1632–1704), Enlightenment philosopher whose work continues to influence theories of democracy and the self.

Of all the delicacies in the whole *mundus edibilis*,[3] I will maintain it to be the most delicate—*princeps obsoniorum*.[4] 10

I speak not of your grown porkers—things between pig and pork—those hobbydehoys[5]—but a young and tender suckling—under a moon old—guiltless as yet of the sty—with no original speck of the *amor immunditiæ*,[6] the hereditary failing of the first parent, yet manifest—his voice as yet not broken, but something between a childish treble, and a grumble—the mild forerunner, or *prœludium*,[7] of a grunt.

He must be roasted. I am not ignorant that our ancestors ate them seethed, or boiled—but what a sacrifice of the exterior tegument!

There is no flavor comparable, I will contend, to that of the crisp, tawny, well-watched, not over-roasted, *crackling*, as it is well called—the very teeth are invited to their share of the pleasure at this banquet in overcoming the coy, brittle resistance—with the adhesive oleaginous—O call it not fat—but an indefinable sweetness growing up to it—the tender blossoming of fat—fat cropped in the bud—taken in the shoot—in the first innocence—the cream and quintessence of the child-pig's yet pure food——the lean, no lean, but a kind of animal manna—or, rather, fat and lean (if it must be so) blended and running into each other, that both together make but one ambrosian result, or common substance.

Behold him, while he is doing—it seemeth rather a refreshing warmth, than a scorching heat, that he is so passive to. How equably he twirleth round the string!—Now he is just done. To see the extreme sensibility of that tender age, he hath wept out his pretty eyes—radiant jellies—shooting stars—

See him in the dish, his second cradle, how meek he lieth!—wouldst thou have had this innocent grow up to the grossness and indocility which too often accompany maturer swinehood? Ten to one he would have proved a glutton, a sloven, an obstinate, disagreeable animal—wallowing in all manner of filthy conversation—from these sins he is happily snatched away— 15

> Ere sin could blight, or sorrow fade,
> Death came with timely care——[8]

his memory is odoriferous—no clown curseth, while his stomach half rejecteth, the rank bacon—no coal-heaver bolteth him in reeking sausages—he hath a fair sepulchre in the grateful stomach of the judicious epicure—and for such a tomb might be content to die.

He is the best of sapors. Pine-apple is great. She is indeed almost too transcendent—a delight, if not sinful, yet so like to sinning, that really a

3. Edible world (Latin).
4. Chief of delicacies (Latin).
5. Usually hobbledehoy: an awkward or clumsy youth.
6. Love of filth (Latin).
7. Prelude (Latin).
8. From "Epitaph on an Infant," by Samuel Taylor Coleridge (1772–1834).

tender-conscienced person would do well to pause—too ravishing for mortal taste, she woundeth and excoriateth the lips that approach her—like lovers' kisses, she biteth—she is a pleasure bordering on pain from the fierceness and insanity of her relish—but she stoppeth at the palate—she meddleth not with the appetite—and the coarsest hunger might barter her consistently for a mutton chop.

Pig—let me speak his praise—is no less provocative of the appetite, than he is satisfactory to the criticalness of the censorious palate. The strong man may batten on him, and the weakling refuseth not his mild juices.

Unlike to mankind's mixed characters, a bundle of virtues and vices, inexplicably intertwisted, and not to be unravelled without hazard, he is—good throughout. No part of him is better or worse than another. He helpeth, as far as his little means extend, all around. He is the least envious of banquets. He is all neighbors' fare.

I am one of those who freely and ungrudgingly impart a share of the good things of this life which fall to their lot (few as mine are in this kind), to a friend, I protest I take as great an interest in my friend's pleasures, his relishes, and proper satisfactions, as in mine own. "Presents," I often say, "endear Absents." Hares, pheasants, partridges, snipes, barn-door chicken (those "tame villatic fowl"[9]), capons, plovers, brawn, barrels of oysters, I dispense as freely as I receive them. I love to taste them, as it were, upon the tongue of my friend. But a stop must be put somewhere. One would not, like Lear, "give everything." I make my stand upon pig. Methinks it is an ingratitude to the Giver of all good flavors, to extra-domiciliate, or send out of the house, slightingly, (under pretext of friendship, or I know not what) a blessing so particularly adapted, predestined, I may say, to my individual taste.—It argues an insensibility.

20 I remember a touch of conscience in this kind at school. My good old aunt, who never parted from me at the end of a holiday without stuffing a sweet-meat, or some nice thing, into my pocket, had dismissed me one evening with a smoking plum-cake, fresh from the oven. In my way to school (it was over London bridge) a gray-headed old beggar saluted me (I have no doubt at this time of day that he was a counterfeit). I had no pence to console him with, and in the vanity of self-denial, and the very coxcombry of charity, school-boy-like, I made him a present of—the whole cake! I walked on a little, buoyed up, as one is on such occasions, with a sweet soothing of self-satisfaction; but before I had got to the end of the bridge, my better feelings returned, and I burst into tears, thinking how ungrateful I had been to my good aunt, to go and give her good gift away to a stranger, that I had never seen before, and who might be a bad man for aught I knew; and then I thought of the pleasure my aunt would be taking in thinking that I—I myself, and not another—would eat her nice cake—and what should I say to her the next time I saw her—how naughty I was to part with her pretty present—and the odor of that spicy cake came back upon my recollection, and the pleasure and the curiosity I had taken in seeing her make it, and her joy when she sent it to the oven, and how disappointed she would feel that I had never had a bit of it in my mouth at

9. From *Samson Agonistes*, by John Milton (1608–1674).

last—and I blamed my impertinent spirit of alms-giving, and out-of-place hypocrisy of goodness, and above all I wished never to see the face again of that insidious, good-for-nothing, old gray impostor.

Our ancestors were nice[10] in their methods of sacrificing these tender victims. We read of pigs whipt to death with something of a shock, as we hear of any other obsolete custom. The age of discipline is gone by, or it would be curious to inquire (in a philosophical light merely) what effect this process might have towards intenerating and dulcifying a substance, naturally so mild and dulcet as the flesh of young pigs. It looks like refining a violet. Yet we should be cautious, while we condemn the inhumanity, how we censure the wisdom of the practice. It might impart a gusto—

I remember an hypothesis, argued upon by the young students, when I was at St. Omer's,[11] and maintained with much learning and pleasantry on both sides, "Whether, supposing that the flavor of a pig who obtained his death by whipping (*per flagellationem extremam*[12]) superadded a pleasure upon the palate of a man more intense than any possible suffering we can conceive in the animal, is man justified in using that method of putting the animal to death?" I forget the decision.

His sauce should be considered. Decidedly, a few bread crumbs, done up with his liver and brains, and a dash of mild sage. But, banish, dear Mrs. Cook, I beseech you, the whole onion tribe. Barbecue your whole hogs to your palate, steep them in shalots, stuff them out with plantations of the rank and guilty garlic; you cannot poison them, or make them stronger than they are—but consider, he is a weakling—a flower.

10. Archaic: fastidious (used ironically here).
11. St. Omer, France, where there was a Catholic college for English students.
12. By fatal whipping (Latin).

Questions

1. What is the relation between the story of the discovery of roast pig and the second half of the essay?

2. To explain his reluctance to share roast pig with any of his friends, Lamb offers an anecdote about giving a cake to a beggar. What lesson did he learn from giving the cake away? How does that apply to his behavior with pig?

3. Usually "dissertation" refers to a long scholarly work. How does Lamb use the word? What other examples of irony and humor do you find here? Which of them remain funny and which have gone stale since 1822?

4. Lamb refers to a school debate about the connection between the pain of an animal's death and the flavor of the meat. How has our thinking about the treatment and eating of animals changed since Lamb's day?

5. Write your own imaginary account of the discovery of an improbably delicious food: artichokes, lobster, the French fry. Then, in the manner of Lamb, turn the story into an essay by framing it within a larger story of the food and what it means to you.

Nicholas D. Kristof *Saudis in Bikinis*

Riyadh, Saudi Arabia—On my first evening in Riyadh, I spotted a surreal scene: three giggly black ghosts, possibly young women enveloped in black cloaks called abayas, clustered around a display in a shopping mall, enthusiastically fingering a blouse so sheer and low-cut that my wife would never be caught dead in it. Afterward, I delicately asked a Saudi woman to explicate the scene.

"What do you think the 'black ghosts' wear underneath their abayas?" she replied archly.

Saudi women may be regarded in the West as antique doormats covered in black veils, but the women themselves vigorously reject that stereotype. "It hurts when you hear what people say about us, that we're repressed," Monira Abdulaziz, an assistant professor, said reproachfully.

"I cover up my body and my face, and I'm happy that I'm a religious girl obeying God's rules," a dietician named Lana scolded me after I wrote a typically snide reference to repressed Saudi women. "I can swim and do sports and go to restaurants and wear what I want, but not in front of men. Why should I show my legs and breasts to men? Is that really freedom?"

5 In Riyadh, several Saudi women offered the same scathing critique, effectively arguing that Saudi women are the free ones—free from sexual harassment, free from pornography, free from seeing their bodies used to market cars and colas. It is Western women, they say, who have been manipulated into becoming the toys of men.

Saudi Arabia is a bizarre place. It has McDonald's restaurants that look just like those at home except that there is one line for men and one for women. *Al Riyadh* newspaper has women journalists, but they're kept in their own room; when a male editor must edit a woman's copy, he does it by phone. Saudi women wear bikinis—but only in home swimming pools or in all-women pools. They claim all this reflects not repression but a culture they cherish.

"You can't go to an Indian woman and say, 'Why are you wearing a sari?'" fumed Hend al-Khuthaila, a university professor who was the first female university dean in Saudi Arabia. "You can't go up to a Western woman and say, 'Why are you wearing a short dress?' Well, this is our abaya. This is part of my culture. It's part of my tradition. It never bothered me."

Maha Muneef, a female pediatrician, emphasized that Saudi Arabia is progressing, albeit more slowly than many women would like. "My mother didn't go to any school at all, because then there were no girls' schools at all," she said. "My older sister, who is 20 years older than me, she went up to the sixth grade and then quit, because the feeling was that a girl only needs to

Published on October 25, 2002, in the New York Times, *where Kristof has written a twice-weekly op-ed column since 2001.*

learn to read and write. Then I went to college and medical school on scholarship to the States. My daughter, maybe she'll be president, or an astronaut."

Another doctor, Hanan Balkhy, seemed ambivalent. "I don't think women here have equal opportunities," she acknowledged. "There are meetings I can't go to. There are buildings I can't go into. But you have to look at the context of development. Discrimination will take time to overcome."

Dr. Balkhy emphasized that Saudi women want to solve their problems themselves. These days in particular, she said, even liberal Saudis feel on the defensive and are reluctant to discuss their concerns for fear that foreigners will seize upon the problems to discredit their country. 10

All this created an awkward series of interviews. I kept asking women how they felt about being repressed, and they kept answering indignantly that they aren't repressed.

So what should we make of this? Is it paternalistic of us in the West to try to liberate women who insist that they're happy as they are?

No, I think we're on firm ground.

If most Saudi women want to wear a tent, if they don't want to drive, then that's fine. But why not give them the choice? Why ban women drivers and why empower the religious police, the mutawwa, to scold those loose hussies who choose to show a patch of hair?

If Saudi Arabians choose to kill their economic development and sacrifice international respect by clinging to the 15th century, if the women prefer to remain second-class citizens, then I suppose that's their choice. But if anyone chooses to behave so foolishly, is it any surprise that outsiders point and jeer? 15

Questions

1. Kristof believes that Saudi Arabia's strict rules for women—no driving, no public mixing of the sexes, no revealing clothing—are "foolish." What do you think? And what do you think of the Saudi Arabian women who defend such practices?

2. How should one country behave toward another that has starkly different standards of morality (e.g., capital punishment, polygamy, repression of women)? Think about the evidence you might give in support of your view.

3. Describe a time when you got into an argument or dispute over standards of behavior with someone you disagreed with. What triggered it? How did it get resolved? What happened?

Roland Barthes *Toys*

French toys: One could not find a better illustration of the fact that the adult Frenchman sees the child as another self. All the toys one commonly sees are essentially a microcosm of the adult world; they are all reduced copies of human objects, as if in the eyes of the public the child was, all told, nothing but a smaller man, a homunculus to whom must be supplied objects of his own size.

Invented forms are very rare: a few sets of blocks, which appeal to the spirit of do-it-yourself, are the only ones which offer dynamic forms. As for the others, French toys *always mean something*, and this something is always entirely socialized, constituted by the myths or the techniques of modern adult life: the army, broadcasting, the post office, medicine (miniature instrument-cases, operating theaters for dolls), school, hair styling (driers for permanent-waving), the air force (parachutists), transport (trains, Citroëns, Vedettes, Vespas,[1] petrol stations), science (Martian toys).

The fact that French toys *literally* prefigure the world of adult functions obviously cannot but prepare the child to accept them all, by constituting for him, even before he can think about it, the alibi of a Nature which has at all times created soldiers, postmen and Vespas. Toys here reveal the list of all the things the adult does not find unusual: war, bureaucracy, ugliness, Martians, etc. It is not so much, in fact, the imitation which is a sign of an abdication, as its literalness. French toys are like a Jivaro[2] head, in which one recognizes, shrunken to the size of an apple, the wrinkles and hair of an adult. There exist, for instance, dolls which urinate; they have an esophagus, one gives them a bottle, they wet their nappies; soon, no doubt, milk will turn to water in their stomachs. This is meant to prepare the little girl for the causality of housekeeping, to "condition" her to her future role as mother. However, faced with this world of faithful and complicated objects, the child can only identify himself as owner, as user, never as creator; he does not invent the world, he uses it: There are, prepared for him, actions without adventure, without wonder, without joy. He is turned into a little stay-at-home householder who does not even have to invent the mainsprings of adult causality; they are supplied to him ready-made: He has only to help himself, he is never allowed to discover anything from start to finish. The merest set of blocks, provided it is not too refined, implies a very different learning of the world: Then, the child does not in any way create meaningful objects, it matters little to him whether they have an adult name; the actions he performs are not those of a user but those of a demiurge. He creates forms

From Mythologies *(1957), a collection of brief essays on French culture that originally appeared as general-circulation newspaper pieces; selected and translated for American readers by Annette Lavers in* Mythologies *(1972).*

1. French automobiles, French motorboats, Italian motor scooters.
2. South American Indian head-hunting tribe.

which walk, which roll, he creates life, not property: Objects now act by themselves, they are no longer an inert and complicated material in the palm of his hand. But such toys are rather rare: French toys are usually based on imitation, they are meant to produce children who are users, not creators.

The bourgeois status of toys can be recognized not only in their forms, which are all functional, but also in their substances. Current toys are made of a graceless material, the product of chemistry, not of nature. Many are now molded from complicated mixtures; the plastic material of which they are made has an appearance at once gross and hygienic, it destroys all the pleasure, the sweetness, the humanity of touch. A sign which fills one with consternation is the gradual disappearance of wood, in spite of its being an ideal material because of its firmness and its softness, and the natural warmth of its touch. Wood removes, from all the forms which it supports, the wounding quality of angles which are too sharp, the chemical coldness of metal. When the child handles it and knocks it, it neither vibrates nor grates, it has a sound at once muffled and sharp. It is a familiar and poetic substance, which does not sever the child from close contact with the tree, the table, the floor. Wood does not wound or break down; it does not shatter, it wears out, it can last a long time, live with the child, alter little by little the relations between the object and the hand. If it dies, it is in dwindling, not in swelling out like those mechanical toys which disappear behind the hernia of a broken spring. Wood makes essential objects, objects for all time. Yet there hardly remain any of these wooden toys from the Vosges, these fretwork farms with their animals, which were only possible, it is true, in the days of the craftsman. Henceforth, toys are chemical in substance and color; their very material introduces one to a coenaesthesis[3] of use, not pleasure. These toys die in fact very quickly, and once dead, they have no posthumous life for the child.

3. General awareness of the body and its condition.

Questions

1. What parts of Barthes's critique of French toys could also be applied to American toys? Think of specific toys that you might use as evidence in class discussion.

2. Consider the use of punctuation in this essay. What is the effect of the frequent use of colons and the frequent use of commas to separate independent clauses? (Barthes originally wrote this piece in French, and Annette Lavers translated it into English.) To what extent might translation affect punctuation choices?

3. Write a two-page essay that begins with your own version of the following sentence: "American toys: One could not find a better illustration of the fact that the adult American sees the child as . . ."

4. Write an analysis of a toy you remember from childhood. What meaning can you find in that toy? As Barthes does, note its shape, function, purpose, materials, and so forth.

Fred Strebeigh

The Wheels of Freedom: Bicycles in China

"Hello." She appeared at my right shoulder, her face inches from mine. We were cycling together, though I had never seen her before. We rode side by side through the city of Beijing, and around us streamed thousands of bicycles with red banners flying. Beijing was in revolt. And as we rode together we broke the law.

I had gone to China with an odd goal: to learn a bit about what the bicycle means to people who live in a country with only a few thousand privately owned cars but some 220 million cycles—vastly more than any other nation. And I had arrived at an odd time.

My first day in China was also the first day of what became known as the Beijing Spring of 1989. As I awoke, students and citizens by the hundreds of thousands were flowing from all over Beijing to Tiananmen Square, the vast plaza at the city's heart, creating the largest spontaneous demonstration in the history of China and perhaps the world. They came on foot and by bus and subway, of course, but mostly they came by bicycle, calling for freedom. (I could see why bicycles are forbidden in the capital of North Korea, China's more repressive neighbor. Its government reportedly fears that bikes give people too much independence.)

Within hours of my arrival in Beijing, bicycles became more crucial than ever. Buses stopped. Subways shut. Taxis struck. But on flowed the bikes of Beijing. Bicyclists carried messages from university to university. Tricyclists rushed round delivering food to demonstrators. Families and schoolmates and couples and commuters smiled and waved as they rode, in twos and threes and throngs.

5 On my own bicycle, hesitant at first and then lost in the cycling masses, I roamed freely. Daily I rode to Tiananmen Square, with its mood of carnival, its students from all regions, and its uncountable cycles. Bicycles and tricycles became flag holders and tent supporters. They became tea dispensers and cold-drink stands. They became photographers' perches, families' viewing platforms, old men's reading chairs, and children's racing toys.

On my bicycle I also strayed far from Tiananmen, to the quiet corners of the city. Everywhere the bicycle set the rhythm of life. Martial artists rode to practice with swords strapped to their bikes. Women in jet-black business suits pedalled their daughters to school. Boys fished beside parked bicycles at placid lakes. Bakers in white toques headed for work on transport tricycles. Pedalling beside them at their slow pace, I felt at ease and oddly at home. I felt as I had

Sent to China on a magazine assignment to analyze the cultural role of the bicycle, Strebeigh found himself immersed in a political uprising in Beijing, its capital. The essay was first published in Bicycling Magazine *(April 1991) and then adapted for* China Update *(Winter 1991), a magazine published by the Yale–China Association. The latter version is reprinted here.*

years ago in my small hometown, where automobiles never clogged the streets and where the bicycle offered a mix of peace and freedom.

Riding among the bicycles of Beijing, I began to recognize dozens of China's famous brands: Golden Lion and Mountain River, Plum Flower and Chrysanthemum, Red Flag and Red Cotton, Flying Arrival and Flying Pigeon, Pheasant and Phoenix and Forever. Long and stately bicycles, recalling decades past, they possessed the rake and sheer and grace that today I associate less with cycling than with yachting. I felt as if I were cruising, on the wake of clippers like *Red Jacket* or *Flying Cloud*, in a regatta of tall ships.

Afternoon rush hour in Chengdu.

Then the Chinese government declared martial law. It forbade citizens to attend the student demonstrations and forbade foreigners, like me, to visit Tiananmen or talk to students. It sent its army in a first push into the city, but citizens peacefully blocked its way. My Chinese hosts (I had been invited to lecture at a couple of universities) warned me to obey the government, and I said I would try.

In the second day under martial law, as I was riding down one of Beijing's leafy boulevards, suddenly a young woman appeared at my shoulder. She said "hello," and we were cycling together.

10 I had been rolling at Beijing speed, eight miles an hour—in synch with commuters, demonstrators, and vegetable haulers. To catch me she had accelerated, maybe to eight-and-a-half miles an hour.

"What," she wanted to know, did I "think about the students?" She wore tinted glasses, a shy smile in a radiant face, a lab coat—she was a science student, and by law we were forbidden to talk.

"I think what they are doing is very brave," I said, "and very scary." And so we became two petty criminals, riding handlebar-to-handlebar.

We floated together and others floated past. But they travelled fractions of a pedal-turn faster or fractions slower, and we were left alone in talk, our handle-bars occasionally nudging each other, in the bizarre intimacy of Beijing cycling. I worried aloud about the Chinese army—now half a mile to our west, still blocked but still pressing towards us. She praised George Washington. We would not have talked so freely in a restaurant or hotel, I realized; police could have demanded our names. But here we were just two bicycles lost in the mass—the most private place in Beijing.

Ahead of us appeared Tiananmen Square, where some of her classmates had been starving themselves in protest and others had been singing "We Shall Overcome." Within moments, she drifted south and I north. Soon I was at the American embassy. They warned me against talking to students.

15 To stay in Beijing, I decided, was to endanger anyone I met. And so I resolved to travel out from the capital and return later, in order to talk about bicycles in a time of greater calm and, I hoped, greater freedom.

One of the people I most wanted to meet outside Beijing was a student in Sichuan Province named Fang Hui. The year before, she had become the first woman to ride a bicycle from Chengdu, the capital of Sichuan in central China, to Lhasa, the capital of Tibet—bumping for thirteen hundred miles over one of China's worst roads, a sawtooth of rock tracks and mountain passes which reach altitudes above 15,000 feet. In recognition, China honored her as one of the nation's "Ten Brave Young People."

I didn't care much about Fang Hui's honors. I cared more about her motivations, her goals. I guess I expected her to be a hot but somewhat dull athlete, the sort who wins Chinese honors by excelling in volleyball. When we met at her university in Chengdu, where she is a graduate student in English, she surprised me.

As we pedalled through the streets of Chengdu, I asked Fang Hui if she had always been a cyclist. Not really, she said. Before her trip she had not owned a bicycle. The day before departing for Tibet she bought an old, single-speed Arched Eyebrow for 75 yuan ($15). She then taught herself to ride, over a thousand miles of mountains.

I asked how she chose Tibet. She said she had answered a poster advertisement. I was shocked. So, apparently, were the five men, mostly teachers from a local school, who had planned the trip and posted invitations for fellow travellers. Only Fang Hui accepted.

20 The men doubted she could reach Tibet, perhaps because she looked like a pudgy schoolgirl. Uphill she always rode more slowly than they, falling miles behind. Downhill, because her old bike had wretched brakes, she squeezed its levers with all her strength as the Arched Eyebrow hurtled down pitted roads. "I went very fast," she said. "I felt as if I would become light." At the end of each day of clinging to her brake levers, her hands were so cramped she could not open them.

Eventually, the men admitted that her strength egged them on. "If even a girl can do this," they said, "how shameful for a man to give up."

Fang Hui had not really worried about giving up on the journey, she told me. But, earlier, she had worried about giving up on life. "Before," she said, "yesterday, today, tomorrow were all alike—so dull. What I most wanted was to meet something unexpected."

Not just the road's pain but also its loneliness changed Fang Hui. At remote outposts she would meet soldiers, mere isolated boys, who would write love letters that followed her up the Lhasa road, carried by lone truck drivers. In yet remoter terrain she would ride half a day, she recalled, and "not see a single man. So when I heard a dog bark, it would arouse a tender feeling—a reminder of the human world. When I came back, people all said I had changed. Now I can find something new in every day." And now at night, she added with glee, "sometimes I dream I am riding very fast downhill."

As I rode through Chengdu, sometimes talking with Fang Hui or with other university students and teachers, I began to see that the bicycle offered an escape not just *from* everyday life. It also offered escape within everyday life.

25 One day as Fang Hui and I rode through a crush of cyclists, a young couple passed us riding two bicycles side-by-side. They rode pedal-to-pedal and almost arm-in-arm. At first the girl rode with her left hand on the boy's right, controlling his hand and handlebar, steering them both. Then he moved his hand to round the small of her back. They reminded me of partners in a waltz.

The boy lowered his hand to the girl's bicycle seat and leaned to her, and as they rode they whispered. In the often-dehumanizing crush of urban China, two bicycles had made space for romance. Fang Hui said that young "lovers" often ride so utterly together, so alone in their world.

Providing such measures of human dignity, one professor told me, was one of the bicycle's gifts to China—and particularly to people like his parents, who were "peasants" (the term in China for all people who work the land). Here in the center of China's richest farmlands, he said, I could watch the bicycle making life less hard. Flower farmers with hollyhocks and asters tied to their bicycles arrived in Chengdu at dawn, flicked down their kickstands on side streets, and

began to sell. Farmers' sons strapped saws and other carpenters' tools to their bicycles, rode into the city, and waited at curbside for customers to hire them to build beds or bureaus. In Sichuan's booming "free markets" (free, that is, of government control), geese came to town on the backs of farmers' tricycles, were sold to families for domestic egg laying, and then departed with their wings still flapping, strapped to the buyers' handlebars. Everywhere, cycles kept life rolling.

The professor told me that peasants in his parents' remote village always refer to the bicycle, appreciatively, as the "foreign horse." The government opposes the name, he said, but it helps explain the history of the bicycle in China. The first bicycle arrived in 1886, carrying Thomas Stevens, a young San Franciscan who was completing the first cycling journey around the world. With its huge front wheel and small rear one, his penny-farthing[1] cycle must have looked very foreign but, unlike a good horse, not very practical.

The first practical bicycle to reach China came in 1891, again transporting a round-the-world cyclist. By the early twentieth century, the foreign horse had won the fascination of China's last emperor, the young Puyi, who rode one around his palace, Beijing's "Forbidden City."

30 Slowly cycling trickled down from the throne toward the masses. By the 1940s China's bicycle factories were producing a vehicle like today's most common model, a virtual twin of England's stately Raleigh Tourist.

In the years before the Chinese revolution of 1949, the professor told me, almost everyone called the bicycle "foreign horse," because "foreign" suggested both "modern" and "admirable." Since peasants carried most goods on their backs, they particularly admired the bicycle. Every peasant longed to shift his burden to the back of a foreign horse—a longing frustrated by high price and short supply.

Then came the revolution of 1949. Hoping to "raise the people's dignity," the professor continued, the young government made two decisions. Happily, in an effort to give wheels to an impoverished population, it encouraged bicycle production, which began doubling and redoubling. But sadly, because the old name suggested blind worship of foreign things, the government banned the lyrical phrase "foreign horse" (which, pronounced *yang ma* in Chinese,

1. Referring to wheels of unequal size: pennies were big, farthings small.

resounds like a ringing gong). The government imposed, instead, the unpoetic "self-running cart" (*zi xing che* in Chinese, which sounds like a dental problem).

Not surprisingly, the cycle's foreign resonance remains. Peasants in remote villages still pedal "foreign horses." And many Chinese factories, seeking a touch of class, still adorn their bicycles with prominent English names: "Forever" or "Light Roadster" or, on the most celebrated of foreign horses, "Flying Pigeon—The All-Steel Bicycle." (When George Bush[2] made his first presidential visit to China, his welcoming gift from the nation was a pair of Flying Pigeons.)

A regional branch of the Flying Pigeon Bicycle Factory lies an hour's ride from the center of Chengdu, and one day I was given a tour of its old-style assembly line by Jiang Guoji, the factory's present director—the first ever elected by its workers. He spoke with the ease of a manager whose workers trust his judgment and whose society trusts his product.

Since Jiang Guoji's factory sits in the middle of China's best farmland, he and his co-workers decided to specialize in what Jiang called the "ZA-62" or "Reinforced Flying Pigeon." This bike, which I came to think of as the "Peasant Pigeon," comes with massive tubing, a formidable rack, a second set of forks to hold the front wheels, and—probably unique among Chinese bicycles—a three-year warranty. It contains 68 pounds of steel which, together with

2. George H. W. Bush (b. 1924), president of the United States from 1989 to 1993.

some leather and rubber, brings its total weight above 72 pounds—three times that of my average American bike.

Jiang Guoji's factory has raised production steadily, along with all Chinese cycle factories, creating an unprecedented problem. The year before my visit, Chinese bicycle production reached 42 million cycles—dwarfing any other nation's output and, more significantly, overtaking Chinese demand for the first time in history. For years, bicycles had been rationed, and families had longed to own a good one. Now "if a person has money, he can buy," Jiang told me, with a mix of pride and regret—because prices have begun dropping and "bicycle factories have real competition."

In response, Jiang said, he was trying to spur international demand for Peasant Pigeons. Looking for good "propaganda," two years earlier he donated "Peasant Pigeons" to five local riders who wanted to go around the world. Alas, one had been run down by a truck in Pakistan. But the other four were riding on, circling the globe back towards his factory. He expected his 72-pound Pigeons home within a year, still under warranty. (He added that, despite transport costs and import duties, he would gladly sell Peasant Pigeons wholesale in America for less than a dollar a pound.)

All Chinese bicycles—whether sturdy Flying Pigeons or sad Arched Eyebrows—must survive long after their warranties have expired. To help them along, repairmen have set up roadside stands in every city. Entering the business proves simple. A would-be repairman chooses a site, asks the city to license it to him, and lays down his tools. He then puts up his advertisement—a circle of overlapping innertubes, colored black and deep pink, perhaps hung on a tree limb.

Some Chinese portray repairmen in a style that outdoes American caricatures of car mechanics. Most of my Chinese acquaintances knew one repairman they relied on and dozens they distrusted. One university professor insisted that underemployed repairmen scatter tacks to puncture passing tires and inflate profits.

40

Another professor invited me to meet her revered neighborhood repairman. Since he worked incessantly and had little time for chatter, she devised a ruse to buy time for asking questions: we would take him her Flying Arrival, which had a useless rear brake.

We found him at the back gate of her university beneath a circle of innertubes. When my friend arrived, the repairman put aside a Phoenix he was polishing and greeted her as a long-term client. She presented the brake problem. He took a quick look, produced two sets of pliers, loosened a nut, tightened a cable, tensioned a spring and, after 30 seconds of work, handed the bike back to her—fixed. He refused payment. The job was too small. He resumed polishing the Phoenix.

Though her ruse had failed, the professor pressed forward: How did he become a repairman? Three years ago when he was twenty-seven, he told us, he stopped working his family's farm because the land was small and the family had more than enough laborers—including his wife, their three children, his two sisters and two brothers, and their aging parents. He still lives on the

A bike repairman's job may be the freest in China. All that's needed is a street corner and a few tools.

farm but commutes three miles to the city on his Forever. He works seven days a week, from 9 A.M. to 8 P.M., except when it rains.

He likes bike repair because it "makes *money*," he said, emphasizing the word as if it were a novelty. Back on the farm, where he hopes never to work again, he "just produced *crops*," which sold for "not-so-much money."

When we asked him how much he made in a month, he told us 800 yuan ($216). The professor gasped. To me she said, quietly, "That's five university professors!" Still, she seemed to believe him. She pointed out to me that he had paid the government's penalty for having three children. The penalty in recent years has run as high as 2,000 yuan ($540), she said, too much for most professors—but not for an industrious bike fixer.

As I talked to more repairmen, I saw that their job may be the freest in China. A hard worker needed only a street corner and a few tools. Before his eyes bikes would inevitably break down and, if he was skilled, clients would multiply. Bicycle repair seemed to offer an extension of what the bike itself offered and what so many Chinese sought: modest dignity, new choices, ample freedom. 45

The farm country outside Chengdu, contrary to the complaints of one peasant-turned-repairman, generates much of the new agricultural wealth enjoyed by the Chinese people. In early June, by train and by bicycle, I travelled to the southern mountains that rim this rich agricultural bowl within Sichuan province. There I was the guest at another university, tucked in verdant hills.

During my stay, one teacher lent me an old "Peasant Pigeon"—one well past its warranty. I rode it daily over farm tracks of rut and rock that would have jolted the nuts off my light American bike. The big Pigeon just bobbed along, high and easy.

One midday while I was exploring narrow paths through emerald-colored rice paddies, two girls whizzed past me, riding double on a black Forever. Both wore red uniforms and one carried an abacus—students dashing home for lunch.

With me was a professor who was fluent not only in English but also the quite-obscure local dialect. She suggested we follow the students so I could meet a "peasant family."

50 We travelled through flooded paddies, past water buffaloes, up to a newly built home that stretched around a cement courtyard, and found the older of the two girls talking with her mother next to their vegetable garden. The professor introduced us. Their mother, Mrs. Fang, invited us for tea and introduced her daughters: Liya, third-grader and bicycle passenger, and Jianmei, sixth-grader and bicyclist. Because Jianmei's Forever still had protective wrapping paper on its top bar, as if it had just come from the store, I asked if it was new.

Jianmei, who was gulping down rice in preparation for her afternoon at school, said proudly that she won it just last year. Her mother explained that the family offers their daughters prizes for each year that they sustain grades of 90% or better. In autumn each daughter names a prize she wants, and then for the rest of the school year she tries to win it. In third grade Jianmei won a set of nice clothes; in fourth grade, a golden wristwatch; in fifth grade, the Forever. (I said to the professor, in English, "Are you sure we're talking to *peasants*?")

Mrs. Fang then led us through her tiled kitchen to a room that held, along with awards won by Jianmei for track and basketball, another full-sized bicycle—a cherry-red "Cuckoo," also still wrapped to protect its paint. It was Jianmei's earlier bike. I was astonished; ten years ago here, the professor had told me, only one family in ten could afford even a single bicycle.

Jianmei explained that she wanted the Forever because it was strong and smooth enough to carry her little sister. With it, she rides not just to school but up to the university, off to a nearby temple, even to a town 22 miles away to see the world's largest carved Buddha.

As we walked away from the Fang household—so imbued with work and reward and independence—I said to the professor: "Don't you wish you grew up in a place like that?" A bit later I thought to myself: "I *did* grow up in a place like that." Riding off to school, studying hard, cycling ten and twenty miles on a whim—this was like being back in sixth grade in my small hometown.

55 On the same day I talked with the Fang family, stories of the Beijing massacre—of hundreds or perhaps thousands of citizens killed by army troops and tanks—were reaching our remote region. Soon travellers arrived with tales of killing in other provincial cities. Students began to flee our rural campus, fearing the army would next descend on them. I returned to Chengdu.

There, I tried to continue the work I had planned—looking for the city's used bicycle market, avoiding the army troops who had arrived to quell outbursts, gathering statistics on bicycle ownership. But I could not concentrate. My mind was on Beijing. Finally I decided to return, to what just days before had been the world's most exuberant city.

These bicycles were more than crushed machines. They represented crushed dignity, humanity, and freedom.

Again I rode its leafy boulevards, but no excited voice at my shoulder asked what I thought of the students. No banners waved. No people smiled. All faces seemed as if carved, years ago, in soft stone—at once fixed and badly weathered.

Each evening, Beijing television proudly showed the now-barren Tiananmen Square, cleared of all students and, for that matter, all life. Understandably, the TV cameras did not show what people in Beijing had seen: citizens trying to stop tanks by shoving bicycles at them, flatbed tricycles turned into ambulances for slaughtered children. Less understandably, the cameras often began their pan across the square with an image of a pile of crumpled bicycles.

That odd image haunted me for months, long after I had left China. Only slowly did I realize that the government had chosen that scene precisely. The government cameras wanted to show more than a few crushed machines. They wanted to show crushed dignity, crushed humanity, crushed freedom—so much that the bicycle means in China.

And finally I realized that of course the old men who cling to power in China would want to show off the crumpled bicycles of the young men and women who had called for freedom. How terrifying it must have been, to those old men, to see millions of young people cycling towards them—so independent, so alive, so free—all those wheels turning and turning beyond the control of fear or fiat. Of course those old men would want to crush the cycles of the young. For they would know too well that history itself runs in cycles—sometimes foreign horses, sometimes self-running carts, always wheels of change. How sad: Four decades earlier these same old men, seeking to "raise the people's dignity," had set rolling the cycles of modern China. And then, in a few days of a Beijing spring, they sought to crush, all at once, cycles and dignity and change together. They might as easily have sought to stop the circling, round the sun, of earth's revolution. For as each spring comes round, the old fade and the young quicken. And every day throughout China, the wheels of freedom roll.

QUESTIONS

1. Strebeigh's magazine assignment was to depict and analyze the role of bicycles in modern-day China. What important roles does the bicycle play? Which do you think are most important—to Strebeigh? to the Chinese people he interviewed?

2. The article is titled "The Wheels of Freedom." Why? What relationship between bicycles and freedom does the essay suggest?

3. Write about an important product or artifact in American culture, analyzing its significance to its users and, if relevant, to yourself.

BETTY ROLLIN

Motherhood: Who Needs It?

MOTHERHOOD IS in trouble, and it ought to be. A rude question is long overdue: Who needs it? The answer used to be (1) society and (2) women. But now, with the impending horrors of overpopulation, society desperately *doesn't* need it. And women don't need it either. Thanks to the Motherhood Myth—the idea that having babies is something that all normal women instinctively want and need and will enjoy doing—they just *think* they do.

The notion that the maternal wish and the activity of mothering are instinctive or biologically predestined is baloney. Try asking most sociologists, psychologists, psychoanalysts, biologists—many of whom are mothers—about motherhood being instinctive: it's like asking department store presidents if their Santa Clauses are real. "Motherhood—instinctive?" shouts distinguished sociologist/author Dr. Jessie Bernard. "Biological destiny? Forget biology! If it were biology, people would die from not doing it."

"Women don't need to be mothers any more than they need spaghetti," says Dr. Richard Rabkin, a New York psychiatrist. "But if you're in a world where everyone is eating spaghetti, thinking they need it and want it, you will think so too. Romance has really contaminated science. So-called instincts have to do with stimulation. They are not things that well up inside of you."

"When a woman says with feeling that she craved her baby from within, she is putting into biological language what is psychological," says University of Michigan psychoanalyst and motherhood-researcher Dr. Frederick Wyatt.

Originally published in Look *(September 22, 1970), a popular general-interest magazine that ceased publication in 1971.*

"There are no instincts," says Dr. William Goode, president-elect of the American Sociological Association. "There are reflexes, like eye-blinking, and drives, like sex. There is no innate drive for children. Otherwise, the enormous cultural pressures that there are to reproduce wouldn't exist. There are no cultural pressures to sell you on getting your hand out of the fire."

There are, to be sure, biologists and others who go on about biological destiny, that is, the innate or instinctive goal of motherhood. (At the turn of the century, even good old capitalism was explained by a theorist as "the *instinct* of acquisitiveness.") And many psychoanalysts will hold the Freudian view that women feel so rotten about not having a penis that they are necessarily propelled into the child-wish to replace the missing organ. Psychoanalysts also make much of the psychological need to repeat what one's parent of the same sex has done. Since every woman has a mother, it is considered normal to wish to imitate one's mother by being a mother. 5

There is, surely, a wish to pass on love if one has received it, but to insist women must pass it on in the same way is like insisting that every man whose father is a gardener has to be a gardener. One dissenting psychoanalyst says, simply, "There is a wish to comply with one's biology, yes, but we needn't and sometimes we shouldn't." (Interestingly, the woman who has been the greatest contributor to child therapy and who has probably given more to children than anyone alive is Dr. Anna Freud, Freud's magnificent daughter, who is not a mother.)

Anyway, what an expert cast of hundreds is telling us is, simply, that biological *possibility* and desire are not the same as biological *need*. Women have childbearing equipment. To choose not to use the equipment is no more blocking what is instinctive than it is for a man who, muscles or no, chooses not to be a weight lifter.

So much for the wish. What about the "instinctive" *activity* of mothering? One animal study shows that when a young member of a species is put in a cage, say, with an older member of the same species, the latter will act in a protective, "maternal" way. But that goes for both males and females who have been "mothered" themselves. And studies indicate that a human baby will also respond to whoever is around playing mother—even if it's father. Margaret Mead and many others frequently point out that mothering can be a fine occupation, if you want it, for either sex. Another experiment with monkeys who were brought up without mothers found them lacking in maternal behavior toward their own offspring. A similar study showed that monkeys brought up without other monkeys of the opposite sex had no interest in mating—all of which suggests that both mothering and mating behavior are learned, not instinctual. And, to turn the cart (or the baby carriage) around, baby ducks who lovingly follow their mothers seemed, in the mother's absence, to just as lovingly follow wooden ducks or even vacuum cleaners.

If motherhood isn't instinctive, when and why, then, was the Motherhood Myth born? Until recently, the entire question of maternal motivation was academic. Sex, like it or not, meant babies. Not that there haven't always been a lot of interesting contraceptive tries. But until the creation of the diaphragm in the 1880's, the birth of babies was largely unavoidable. And, generally speaking, nobody really seemed to mind. For one thing, people tend to be sort of good sports about what seems to be inevitable. For another, in the past, the population needed beefing up. Mortality rates were high, and agricultural cultures, particularly, have always needed children to help out. So because it "just happened" and because it was needed, motherhood was assumed to be innate.

10 Originally, it was the word of God that got the ball rolling with "Be fruitful and multiply," a practical suggestion, since the only people around then were Adam and Eve. But in no time, supermoralists like St. Augustine changed the tone of the message: "Intercourse, even with one's legitimate wife, is unlawful and wicked where the conception of the offspring is prevented," he, we assume, thundered. And the Roman Catholic position was thus cemented. So then and now, procreation took on a curious value among people who viewed (and view) the pleasures of sex as sinful. One could partake in the sinful pleasure, but feel vindicated by the ensuing birth. Motherhood cleaned up sex. Also, it cleaned up women, who have always been considered somewhat evil, because of Eve's transgression (". . . but the woman was deceived and became a transgressor. Yet woman will be saved through bearing children . . . ," I Timothy, 2:14–15), and somewhat dirty because of menstruation.

And so, based on need, inevitability, and pragmatic fantasy—the Myth *worked,* from society's point of view—the Myth grew like corn in Kansas. And society reinforced it with both laws and propaganda—laws that made woman a chattel, denied her education and personal mobility, and madonna propaganda that she was beautiful and wonderful doing it and it was all beautiful and wonderful to do. (One rarely sees a madonna washing dishes.)

In fact, the Myth persisted—breaking some kind of record for long-lasting fallacies—until something like yesterday. For as the truth about the Myth trickled in—as women's rights increased, as women gradually got the message that it was certainly possible for them to do most things that men did, that they live longer, that their brains were not tinier—then, finally, when the really big news rolled in, that they could *choose* whether or not to be mothers—what happened? The Motherhood Myth soared higher than ever. As Betty Friedan made oh-so-clear in *The Feminine Mystique,*[1] the '40's and '50's produced a group of ladies who not only had babies as if they were going out of style (maybe they were) but, as never before, they turned motherhood into a cult. First, they wallowed in the aesthetics of it all—natural childbirth and nursing became maternal musts. Like heavy-bellied ostriches, they grounded their heads in the sands of motherhood, only coming up for air to say how utterly happy and fulfilled they were. But, as Mrs. Friedan says only too plainly, they weren't. The Myth galloped

1. Friedan began writing *The Feminine Mystique* (1963) after she sent a questionnaire to women in her 1942 Smith College class and discovered that many of them felt a general dissatisfaction with their lives. Friedan defined this "mystique"—"the problem that has no name"—as the worthlessness women feel in roles that make them dependent financially, intellectually, and emotionally on their husbands.

on, moreover, long after making babies had turned from practical asset to liability for both individual parents *and* society. With the average cost of a middle-class child figured conservatively at $30,000 (not including college), any parent knows that the only people who benefit economically from children are manufacturers of consumer goods. Hence all those gooey motherhood commercials. And the Myth gathered momentum long after sheer numbers, while not yet extinguishing us, have made us intensely uncomfortable. Almost all of our societal problems, from minor discomforts like traffic to major ones like hunger, the population people keep reminding us, have to do with there being too many people. And who suffers most? The kids who have been so mindlessly brought into the world, that's who. They are the ones who have to cope with all of the difficult and dehumanizing conditions brought on by overpopulation. They are the ones who have to cope with the psychological nausea of feeling unneeded by society. That's not the only reason for drugs, but, surely, it's a leading contender.

Unfortunately, the population curbers are tripped up by a romantic, stubborn, ideological hurdle. How can birth-control programs really be effective as long as the concept of glorious motherhood remains unchanged? (Even poor old Planned Parenthood has to euphemize—why not Planned Unparenthood?) Particularly among the poor, motherhood is one of the few inherently positive institutions that are accessible. As Berkeley demographer Judith Blake points out, "Poverty-oriented birth control programs do not make sense as a welfare measure . . . as long as existing pronatalist policies . . . encourage mating, pregnancy, and the care, support, and rearing of children." Or, she might have added, as long as the less-than-idyllic childrearing part of motherhood remains "in small print."

Sure, motherhood gets dumped on sometimes: Philip Wylie's Momism[2] got going in the '40's and Philip Roth's *Portnoy's Complaint* did its best to turn rancid the chicken-soup concept of Jewish motherhood. But these are viewed as the sour cries of a black humorist here, a malcontent there. Everyone shudders, laughs, but it's like the mouse and the elephant joke. Still, the Myth persists. Last April, a Brooklyn woman was indicted on charges of manslaughter and negligent homicide—eleven children died in a fire in a building she owned and criminally neglected—"But," sputtered her lawyer, "my client, Mrs. Breslow, is a mother, a grandmother, and a great-grandmother!"

15 Most remarkably, the Motherhood Myth persists in the face of the most overwhelming maternal unhappiness and incompetence. If reproduction were merely superfluous and expensive, if the experience were as rich and rewarding as the cliché would have us believe, if it were a predominantly joyous trip for everyone riding—mother, father, child—then the going everybody-should-have-two-children plan would suffice. Certainly, there are a lot of joyous mothers, and their children and (sometimes, not necessarily) their husbands reflect their joy. But a lot of evidence suggests that for more women than anyone wants to

2. Wylie's *A Generation of Vipers* (1942) blamed many of the ills of American society on dominating mothers.

admit, motherhood can be miserable. ("If it weren't," says one psychiatrist wryly, "the world wouldn't be in the mess it's in.")

There is a remarkable statistical finding from a recent study of Dr. Bernard's, comparing the mental illness and unhappiness of married mothers and single women. The latter group, it turned out, was both markedly less sick and overtly more happy. Of course, it's not easy to measure slippery attitudes like happiness. "Many women have achieved a kind of reconciliation—a conformity," says Dr. Bernard,

> that they interpret as happiness. Since feminine happiness is supposed to lie in devoting one's life to one's husband and children, they do that; so *ipso facto,* they assume they are happy. And for many women, untrained for independence and "processed" for motherhood, they find their state far preferable to the alternatives, which don't really exist.

Also, unhappy mothers are often loath to admit it. For one thing, if in society's view not to be a mother is to be a freak, not to be a *blissful* mother is to be a witch. Besides, unlike a disappointing marriage, disappointing motherhood cannot be terminated by divorce. Of course, none of that stops such a woman from expressing her dissatisfaction in a variety of ways. Again, it is not only she who suffers but her husband and children as well. Enter the harridan housewife, the carping shrew. The realities of motherhood can turn women into terrible people. And, judging from the 50,000 cases of child abuse in the U.S. each year, some are worse than terrible.

In some cases, the unpleasing realities of motherhood begin even before the beginning. In *Her Infinite Variety,* Morton Hunt describes young married women pregnant for the first time as "very likely to be frightened and depressed, masking these feelings in order not to be considered contemptible. The arrival of pregnancy interrupts a pleasant dream of motherhood and awakens them to the realization that they have too little money, or not enough space, or unresolved marital problems. . . ."

The following are random quotes from interviews with some mothers in Ann Arbor, Mich., who described themselves as reasonably happy. They all had positive things to say about their children, although when asked about the best moment of their day, they *all* confessed it was when the children were in bed. Here is the rest:

> Suddenly I had to devote myself to the child totally. I was under the illusion that the baby was going to fit into my life, and I found that I had to switch my life and my schedule to fit *him.* You think, "I'm in love, I'll get married, and we'll have a baby." First there's two, then three, it's simple and romantic. You don't even think about the work. . . .
>
> You never get away from the responsibility. Even when you leave the children with a sitter, you are not out from under the pressure of the responsibility. . . .
>
> I hate ironing their pants and doing their underwear, and they never put their clothes in the laundry basket. . . . As they get older, they make less demands on our time because they're in school, but the demands are

> greater in forming their values. . . . Best moment of the day is when all the children are in bed. . . . The worst time of the day is 4 P.M., when you have to get dinner started, the kids are tired, hungry and crabby—everybody wants to talk to you about *their* day . . . your day is only half over.
>
> Once a mother, the responsibility and concern for my children became so encompassing. . . . It took a great deal of will to keep up other parts of my personality. . . . To me, motherhood gets harder as they get older because you have less control. . . . In an abstract sense, I'd have several. . . . In the non-abstract, I would not have any. . . .
>
> I had anticipated that the baby would sleep and eat, sleep and eat. Instead, the experience was overwhelming. I really had not thought particularly about what motherhood would mean in a realistic sense. I want to do *other* things, like to become involved in things that are worthwhile—I don't mean women's clubs—but I don't have the physical energy to go out in the evenings. I feel like I'm missing something . . . the experience of being somewhere with people and having them talking about something—something that's going on in the world.

Every grownup person expects to pay a price for his pleasures, but seldom is the price as vast as the one endured "however happily" by most mothers. We have mentioned the literal cost factor. But what does that mean? For middle-class American women, it means a life style with severe and usually unimagined limitations; i.e., life in the suburbs, because who can afford three bedrooms in the city? And what do suburbs mean? For women, suburbs mean other women and children and leftover peanut-butter sandwiches and car pools and seldom-seen husbands. Even the Feminine Mystiqueniks—the housewives who finally admitted that their lives behind brooms (OK, electric brooms) were driving them crazy—were loath to trace their predicament to their children. But it is simply a fact that a childless married woman has no child-work and little housework. She can live in a city, or, if she still chooses the suburbs or the country, she can leave on the commuter train with her husband if she wants to. Even the most ardent job-seeking mother will find little in the way of great opportunities in Scarsdale.[3] Besides, by the time she wakes up, she usually lacks both the preparation for the outside world and the self-confidence to get it. You will say there are plenty of city-dwelling working mothers. But most of those women do additional-funds-for-the-family kind of work, not the interesting career kind that takes plugging during child-bearing years. 20

Nor is it a bed of petunias for the mother who does make it professionally. Says writer critic Marya Mannes:

> If the creative woman has children, she must pay for this indulgence with a long burden of guilt, for her life will be split three ways between them and her husband and her work. . . . No woman with any heart can compose a paragraph when her child is in trouble. . . . The creative woman has no wife to protect her from intrusion. A man at his desk in a room with closed door is a man at work. A woman at a desk in any room is available.

3. A wealthy suburb of New York City.

Speaking of jobs, do remember that mothering, salary or not, is a job. Even those who can afford nurses to handle the nitty-gritty still need to put out emotionally. "Well-cared-for" neurotic rich kids are not exactly unknown in our society. One of the more absurd aspects of the Myth is the underlying assumption that, since most women are biologically equipped to bear children, they are psychologically, mentally, emotionally, and technically equipped (or interested) to rear them. Never mind happiness. To assume that such an exacting, consuming, and important task is something almost all women are equipped to do is far more dangerous and ridiculous than assuming that everyone with vocal cords should seek a career in the opera.

A major expectation of the Myth is that children make a not-so-hot marriage hotter, or a hot marriage, hotter still. Yet almost every available study indicates that childless marriages are far happier. One of the biggest, of 850 couples, was conducted by Dr. Harold Feldman of Cornell University, who states his finding in no uncertain terms: "Those couples with children had a significantly lower level of marital satisfaction than did those without children." Some of the reasons are obvious. Even the most adorable children make for additional demands, complications, and hardships in the lives of even the most loving parents. If a woman feels disappointed and trapped in her mother role, it is bound to affect her marriage in any number of ways: she may take out her frustrations directly on her husband, or she may count on him too heavily for what she feels she is missing in her daily life.

". . . You begin to grow away from your husband," says one of the Michigan ladies. "He's working on his career and you're working on your family. But you both must gear your lives to the children. You do things the children enjoy, more than things you might enjoy." More subtle and possibly more serious is what motherhood may do to a woman's sexuality. Often when the stork flies in, sexuality flies out. Both in the emotional minds of some women *and* in the minds of their husbands, when a woman becomes a mother, she stops being a woman. It's not only that motherhood may destroy her physical attractiveness, but its madonna concept may destroy her *feelings* of sexuality.

25 And what of the payoff? Usually, even the most self-sacrificing of maternal self-sacrificers expects a little something back. Gratified parents are not unknown to the Western world, but there are probably at least just as many who feel, to put it crudely, shortchanged. The experiment mentioned earlier—where the baby ducks followed vacuum cleaners instead of their mothers—indicates that what passes for love from baby to mother is merely a rudimentary kind of object attachment. Without necessarily feeling like a Hoover, a lot of women become disheartened because babies and children are not only not interesting to talk to (not everyone thrills at the wonders of da-da-ma-ma talk) but they are generally not empathetic, considerate people. Even the nicest children are not capable of empathy, surely a major ingredient of love, until they are much older. Sometimes they're never capable of it. Dr. Wyatt says that often, in later years particularly, when most of the "returns" are in, it is the "good mother" who suffers most of all. It is then she must face a reality: The child—the appendage with her genes—is not an appendage, but a separate person. What's more, he

or she may be a separate person who doesn't even like her—or whom she doesn't really like.

So if the music is lousy, how come everyone's dancing? Because the motherhood minuet is taught freely from birth, and whether or not she has rhythm or likes the music, every woman is expected to do it. Indeed, she *wants* to do it. Little girls start learning what to want—and what to be—when they are still in their cribs. Dr. Miriam Keiffer, a young social psychologist at Bensalem, the Experimental College of Fordham University, points to studies showing that

> at six months of age, mothers are already treating their baby girls and boys quite differently. For instance, mothers have been found to touch, comfort, and talk to their females more. If these differences can be found at such an early stage, it's not surprising that the end product is as different as it is. What is surprising is that men and women are, in so many ways, similar.

Some people point to the way little girls play with dolls as proof of their innate motherliness. But remember, little girls are *given* dolls. When Margaret Mead[4] presented some dolls to New Guinea children, it was the boys, not the girls, who wanted to play with them, which they did by crooning lullabies and rocking them in the most maternal fashion.

By the time they reach adolescence, most girls, unconsciously or not, have learned enough about role definition to qualify for a master's degree. In general, the lesson has been that no matter what kind of career thoughts one may entertain, one must, first and foremost, be a wife and mother. A girl's mother is usually her first teacher. As Dr. Goode says, "A woman is not only taught by society to have a child; she is taught to have a child who will have a child." A woman who has hung her life on the Motherhood Myth will almost always reinforce her young married daughter's early training by pushing for grandchildren. Prospective grandmothers are not the only ones. Husbands, too, can be effective sellers. After all, they have the Fatherhood Myth to cope with. A married man is *supposed* to have children. Often, particularly among Latins, children are a sign of potency. They help him assure the world—and himself—that he is the big man he is supposed to be. Plus, children give him both immortality (whatever that means) and possibly the chance to become more in his lifetime through the accomplishments of his children, particularly his son. (Sometimes it's important, however, for the son to do better, but not *too* much better.)

Friends, too, can be counted on as myth-pushers. Naturally one wants to do what one's friends do. One study, by the way, found a correlation between a woman's fertility and that of her three closest friends. The negative sell comes into play here, too. We have seen what the concept of non-mother means (cold, selfish, unwomanly, abnormal). In practice, particularly in the suburbs, it can mean, simply, exclusion—both from child-centered activities (that is, most

4. American anthropologist (1901–1978) whose groundbreaking research in *Coming of Age in Samoa* (1928) demonstrated that individual development is shaped by cultural demands and expectations and that the stage of adolescence, especially sexual development, will be more or less problematic depending on the culture.

activities) and child-centered conversations (that is, most conversations). It can also mean being the butt of a lot of unfunny jokes. ("Whaddya waiting for? An immaculate conception? Ha ha.") Worst of all, it can mean being an object of pity.

In case she's escaped all those pressures (that is, if she was brought up in a cave), a young married woman often wants a baby just so that she'll (1) have something to do (motherhood is better than clerk/typist, which is often the only kind of job she can get, since little more has been expected of her and, besides, her boss also expects her to leave and be a mother); (2) have something to hug and possess, to be needed by and have power over; and (3) have something to *be*—e.g., a baby's mother. Motherhood affords an instant identity. First, through wifehood, you are somebody's wife; then you are somebody's mother. Both give not only identity and activity, but status and stardom of a kind. During pregnancy, a woman can look forward to the kind of attention and pampering she may not ever have gotten or may never otherwise get. Some women consider birth the biggest accomplishment of their lives, which may be interpreted as saying not much for the rest of their lives. As Dr. Goode says, "It's like the gambler who may know the roulette wheel is crooked, but it's the only game in town." Also, with motherhood, the feeling of accomplishment is immediate. It is really much faster and easier to make a baby than paint a painting, or write a book, or get to the point of accomplishment in a job. It is also easier in a way to shift focus from self-development to child development—particularly since, for women, self-development is considered selfish. Even unwed mothers may achieve a feeling of this kind. (As we have seen, little thought is given to the aftermath.) And, again, since so many women are underdeveloped as people, they feel that, besides children, they have little else to give—to themselves, their husbands, to their world.

30 You may ask why then, when the realities do start pouring in, does a woman want to have a second, third, even fourth child? OK, (1) just because reality is pouring in doesn't mean she wants to *face* it. A new baby can help bring back some of the old illusions. Says psychoanalyst Dr. Natalie Shainess, "She may view each successive child as a knight in armor that will rescue her from being a 'bad unhappy mother.'" (2) Next on the horror list of having no children, is having one. It suffices to say that only children are not only OK, they even have a high rate of exceptionality. (3) Both parents usually want at least one child of each sex. The husband, for reasons discussed earlier, probably wants a son. (4) The more children one has, the more of an excuse one has not to develop in any other way.

What's the point? A world without children? Of course not. Nothing could be worse or more unlikely. No matter what anyone says in *Look* or anywhere else, motherhood isn't about to go out like a blown bulb, and who says it should? Only the Myth must go out, and now it seems to be dimming.

The younger-generation females who have been reared on the Myth have not rejected it totally, but at least they recognize it can be more loving to children not to have them. And at least they speak of adopting children instead of bearing them. Moreover, since the new nonbreeders are "less hung-up" on ownership, they seem to recognize that if you dig loving children, you don't necessarily have to own one. The end of the Motherhood Myth might make available more loving women (and men!) for those children who already exist.

When motherhood is no longer culturally compulsory, there will, certainly, be less of it. Women are now beginning to think and do more about development of self, of their individual resources. Far from being selfish, such development is probably our only hope. That means more alternatives for women. And more alternatives mean more selective, better, happier, motherhood—and childhood and husbandhood (or manhood) and peoplehood. It is not a question of whether or not children are sweet and marvelous to have and rear; the question is, even if that's so, whether or not one wants to pay the price for it. It doesn't make sense any more to pretend that women need babies, when what they really need is themselves. If God were still speaking to us in a voice we could hear, even He would probably say, "Be fruitful. Don't multiply."

QUESTIONS

1. Why does Rollin use the term "myth" to describe what she believes is the common attitude toward motherhood?

2. Arguing against motherhood is likely to cause problems in persuading an audience. How does Rollin go about dealing with those problems?

3. Rollin allows that "nothing could be worse or more unlikely" than "a world without children" (paragraph 31). Does this contradict her previous argument?

4. Choose a common "myth" in contemporary society and argue against it.

BILL MCKIBBEN

The Case for Single-Child Families

THE BUILDING was nondescript; four stories of modern concrete just down the street from Ottawa's Civic Hospital. The receptionist greeted me politely, told me the doctor was running a little late. And so I sat on the couch next to the old and dog-eared magazines and read one more time the list of questions Dr. Phil McGuire wanted his vasectomy patients to answer before he performed The Procedure:

"What would you and your partner feel if you were told tomorrow that she was pregnant? Joy? Despair? Resignation? What about in five years?

Published on May 13, 1998, in The Christian Century, *a Protestant magazine with a stated mission to nurture faith and examine issues of politics, culture, and theology. This essay was included in* Maybe One: A Personal and Environmental Argument for Single-Child Families *(1998), a book that extends McKibben's work as a well-known environmental writer, most famous for* The End of the Earth *(1989).*

"Would you want the chance to have children with another partner if your current relationship ended through separation or death?

"Would you want to have the chance to have more children if one or more of your children died?

5 "Would more children be in your picture now if your financial circumstances improved significantly?"

These are tougher questions than you usually get asked in a doctor's office. If you have heart disease, you have to choose *what* to do; it's rare to have to choose, until the very end, whether you want to do *anything at all.* But I could have gotten up and left, no harm done. I have one child. I'd decided to have no more. But this seemed so final.

Then Dr. McGuire came in, wearing khakis, old Nikes, an earring, a plaid shirt. So far that day, he said, he'd done nine vasectomies, pruned branches of nine family trees. He was calm, gentle—sweet. "I had a couple this morning who'd had one child when they were in their 30s, spent the next ten years trying to have another, and failed. Now they were in their early 40s and just couldn't conceive of conceiving again, so they wanted some insurance." He'd had a police officer, and a guy who builds Web pages, and several couples in their early 30s, each with two kids.

And he'd talked with all of them. "I try to protect people if I don't think they're ready," he said. "I'm a general practitioner and I've seen so many women come in who are unexpectedly pregnant, and completely delighted about it." But when people have made up their minds, he's ready to help—he's done 1,100 vasectomies, more and more each year. "Someday I hope to have a clinic just devoted to vasectomies—a fish tank and all the hunting and fishing and outdoors magazines," he said.

I'd come to him because Ottawa is not far from my home, because I could afford him (he charged just over $200, less than most American operations), and because I could tell from his Web site (www.ottawa-vas.com) that he thought pretty deeply about the whole issue. He had a sense of humor (his toll-free number is 1-800-LASTKID), but he also had a sense of purpose. "Sometimes I turn people down," he said. "But it's so much safer than having a woman get a tubal ligation, which is a big operation inside a major body cavity with general anaesthesia."

10 So I sat on the table and pulled my pants down around my ankles. He swabbed my scrotum with iodine ("The iodine needs to be a little warm—the last thing we want is any shrinkage before we start") and then injected a slug of anaesthetic into each side of my testicles. Yes, it was a needle down there, but no, it didn't hurt much—by chance I'd spent the previous afternoon in the dentist's chair, and this was much less painful. (And no flossing!) He cut a small hole in my scrotum, and with a forceps pulled out the vas deferens, the tube that carried sperm to my penis. Then he cauterized it and put it back inside, repeating the procedure on the other side. I could feel a little tugging, nothing more. The wound was so small it didn't require stitches, or even a Band-Aid. For a few days, he said, my groin would be a little sore. After that it would take 20 ejacula-

tions or so to drain the last of the sperm already in my system. And that would be that. In evolutionary terms, I'd be out of business.

It's easy for me to explain why I was lying on the table at the Ottawa Vasectomy Clinic: all I need is a string of statistics. In one recent study, condoms broke 4.8 percent of the time that they were used. Sixty percent of all pregnancies in the U.S. are unintended—60 percent. That doesn't mean all those children are unwanted; half just come when their parents weren't planning on it. But half end in abortion. In fact, six in ten women having abortions did so because their contraceptives failed; among typical couples, 18 percent using diaphragms and 12 percent using condoms managed to get pregnant. And no one's doing much to improve the situation—a nation that spends $600 million developing new cosmetics and fragrances each year has exactly one pharmaceutical company still conducting research on improved methods of birth control. So if I was serious about stopping at one child, this was where I belonged. For my wife, Sue, getting sterilized would have meant a real operation, real risk; for me it meant a bag of ice on my lap as I drove home. It all added up.

Not that we'd come to our decision to have one child easily. Although my work on environmental issues keeps bringing population questions front and center, I have avoided the issue of population for years. I know that by 2050 there will be almost 50 percent more Americans (and nearly 100 percent more human beings) than there are now. I know that in the last ten or 20 or 30 years, our impact has grown so much that we're changing even those places we don't inhabit—changing the way the weather works, changing the plants and animals that live at the poles and deep in the jungle.

I am convinced, too, that simplifying lifestyles alone, although crucial, will not do enough to reduce our impact in the next 50 years. Americans' lifestyles are just so "big." During the next decade India and China will each add to the planet about ten times as many people as the U.S., but the stress on the natural world by those new Americans may exceed that from the new Indians and Chinese combined. My five-year-old daughter has already used more stuff and added more waste to the environment than many of the world's residents do in a lifetime.

When Sue and I faced the issue of how many children to have, these abstract issues of population became personal and practical. What about Sophie? Would being an only child damage her spirit and mind? I explored the myths surrounding "the only child," and the clichés about one child being spoiled and overly dependent. Although these questions are emotionally charged and complex, every bit of research in recent decades shows that only kids do just fine—that they achieve as much and are as well adjusted as children with siblings. So that wasn't the hitch.

15 Along with doing all the research, however, I had to confront the deeply ingrained sense in many of us that there's something inherently *selfish* about not being willing to have children. It's not as strong as the sense of selfishness that can attach itself to abortion, but it's there nonetheless, and particularly strong, I think, in people of faith. It's the relic of our long theological wrestle

with the issue of birth control. And it is not easily dismissed. Condoms may not be sinful, but selfishness must be, if anything is. The children of small families are no more selfish than any other kids—but are the parents?

In a consumer society, where we've been drilled relentlessly in selfishness, it's a peril to take seriously. In her book *Beyond Motherhood,* Jeanne Safer interviews dozens of men and women who have decided against children. I have no wish to judge them, for it's often an honorable decision, and people should not bear children if they feel they can't cope with them. On the other hand, I have no wish to *become* them. They are selfish, and proudly; one New York literary agent describes herself as "an advocate of selfishness." Safer says she herself felt her biological clock ticking, but heard other clocks as well:

> My practice is just starting to take off—I'll lose all the momentum if I cut back to part-time. That summer I thought, it'll have to wait until after we get back from Bali and I'm no longer taking medication to prevent malaria. And what about the trip to Turkey we want to take next summer.

She was, she said, "particularly aware that children would change my marriage drastically. . . . Parenthood, I believed, would certainly spell the end of our nightly candlelit sandalwood-scented bubble baths complete with silly bath toys, where we played like children in a deliciously adult incarnation." Not only that, "I realized that having a child of my own would force me to spend a great deal of time doing things I'd disliked; I'd never been crazy about children's birthday parties when I'd attended them years earlier, and a trip to the circus is my idea of purgatory."

Safer found many like-minded folk. Sandra Singer, for instance, a photographer who moonlights as a belly dancer to "guarantee her allure" and who insists that "I've seen too many women who have children lose their sexuality as well as their identity. They let their bodies go, and they complain about their husband's sexual advances. I complain about the lack."

Safer reconciles herself to her decision not to have kids, and celebrates by giving her own belly-dancing performance. "Working through feelings about motherhood had unleashed hidden reserves of creativity and femininity, and I emerged liberated, energized and strong," she reports. In fact one night she dreams of a cantaloupe growing on a vine in her parents' garden in the middle of winter: "The cantaloupe was myself, the fruit of my parents' loins, which, though barren in the biological sense, was ripening out of season."

20 It's wrong to ridicule such attitudes, at least in a culture that still assigns the work of raising kids mostly to women and allows men to continue their careers at full tilt. Sometimes people have to rescue themselves; in Toni Morrison's novel *Sula*, the heroine won't marry or bear children in order to preserve her "Me-ness." When her grandmother wants her to have babies to "settle" her, Sula says, "I don't want to make somebody else. I want to make myself." Often it's women from very poor backgrounds who decide to remain childless, realizing that it's their best hope for upward mobility against strong odds; in a 1985 study of poor Southern high school students, the 16 percent who wanted no

children were the ones with the loftiest ambitions, the ambitions that in other contexts we want such children to have.

But it's also possible to understand the concern of popes and rabbis and just ordinary folk that, for some people, the decision to have no children or a small family represents a decision to indulge yourself without a thought for anyone else, a decision to take sandalwood-scented candlelit baths without the danger that there might be stray Legos left in the tub to poke you in the backside.

Theologian Gilbert Meilaender quotes one young man who says, "When you have children, the focus changes from the couple to the kids. Suddenly everything is done for them. Well, I'm 27, I've used up a good portion of my life already. Why should I want to sacrifice for someone who's still got his whole life ahead of him?" Such an attitude is, among other things, environmentally problematic; even if this fellow has no kids, thereby sparing the planet some burden, he seems unlikely to do much else to ensure its future—he's the same guy who's going to be voting against gas taxes and demanding the right to drive his Suburban into the overheated sunset.

John Ryan, an American Catholic theologian of the first half of the 20th century, made this argument most powerfully. A man of impeccable progressive credentials, Ryan was known as "the Right Reverend New Dealer" for his unwavering support of the Roosevelt administration. But this same John Ryan also wanted everyone who married to have many children, not simply as proof that they weren't using birth control but because he thought that raising large families makes people better human beings.

Ryan argued that supporting large families demands "forms of discipline necessary for the successful life," a life "accomplished only at the cost of continuous and considerable sacrifice, of compelling ourselves to do without the immediate and pleasant goods for the sake of remote and permanent goods." One of eleven children himself, Ryan thought that most people practicing birth control would be doing it from a "decadent" frame of mind; that bachelors were not building the kind of character necessary to contribute to the common good of society. Not only that, those with few children might become too wealthy, which was as dangerous as being too poor. In the words of ethicist John Berkman, "He was appealing to hard work, and building character, and he thought that was best achieved for most people in the context of having a large family."

25

This pragmatic argument comes straight from the American sense of purpose. And it is by no means a negligible or stupid argument: successfully raising a large brood of well-adjusted children is a great accomplishment, one that cannot help but change and deepen the parents. You emerge different people when you spend your life focusing, as good parents must, on *someone else's* well-being. If maturity is the realization that you are not at the center of the world, then the most time-honored way to become mature is to be a parent many times over, and a good one. Not just because parenting is tough, but also because it's so *joyful*, because it shows you that real transcendent pleasure comes from putting someone else first. It teaches you how dull self-absorption can be.

Such lessons don't always take, of course. As essayist Katha Pollitt points out, the tendency to ascribe "particular virtues—compassion, patience, common sense, nonviolence—to mothers" is an overdone, and in some ways oppressive, cliché; telling yourself that toilet training a string of two-year-olds is good for your soul may keep you away from other worlds. And in a country where incredible numbers of fathers walk away from their kids, you could argue that fatherhood seems to barely dent the culture's pervasive selfishness. And yet when I think of my circle of friends and acquaintances, the single most common route to maturity has been through raising children, often lots of them.

The problem, of course, is that now we live in an era—maybe only a brief one, maybe only for a few generations—when parenting a bunch of kids clashes with the good of the planet. So is there a different way to achieve some of that maturity, with no children or only a single child to change your life? It's not that one kid won't alter most things in your life; he or she will. But Ryan was right—it's not the total commitment that comes with a large brood. Your career or a calling continues, however hobbled you may sometimes be. Alice Walker, in a pithy essay titled "*One* Child of One's Own," called her single daughter a "meaningful digression," and that's right in many ways; if she had borne five children, she probably wouldn't have been writing many books. But those books represent a serious attempt at maturity in another way, and perhaps that's a clue. We need to find ways to be adults, grownups, *people who focus on others,* without being parents of large families.

In the weeks leading up to the 1994 Cairo Conference on population, the pope led the fight against many of the provisions in the draft documents for that conclave. Though I disagreed with some of his stands, I found much of his language powerful and intriguing. The Catholic Church, he said, does not support "an ideology of fertility at all costs," but instead an ethic in which the decision "whether or not to have a child" is not "motivated by selfish or carelessness, but by a prudent, conscious generosity that weighs the possibilities and circumstances." True, he added that such an ethic "gives priority to the welfare of the unborn child," but several weeks later, arguing that radical individualism and "a sexuality apart from ethical references" was inhuman, he called for a "culture of responsible procreation."

In those words, and the words of many others, I think we can see the outline of an ethic that avoids self-indulgence yet does not deny the physical facts of a planet with 6 billion people who may soon nearly double their numbers—a planet that grows hotter, stormier and less stable by the day, a planet where huge swaths of God's creation are being wiped out by the one species told to tend this particular garden. I don't pretend it is an ethic that can be embraced by the Vatican, or the Hasidim; but I do think it is an ethic that might undergird a more sustainable world.

30 The beginning of Genesis contains the fateful command, repeated elsewhere in the Hebrew Bible, to "be fruitful and multiply, and fill the earth." That this was the first commandment gave it special priority. And it was biological, too, a command that echoed what our genes already shouted.

But there is something else unique about it—it is the first commandment we have fulfilled. There's barely a habitable spot on the planet without a human being; in our lifetimes we've filled every inch of the planet with our presence. Everywhere the temperature climbs, the ultraviolet penetrates more deeply. In furthest Alaska, always our national metaphor for emptiness, the permafrost now melts at a rapid pace, trees move on to the tundra, insects infest forests in record numbers, and salmon turn back down streams because the water's gotten too warm to spawn. "There's been a permanent and significant climate regime shift," says an Alaskan scientist. "There has been nothing like this in the record." There's not a creature anywhere on earth whose blood doesn't show the presence of our chemicals, not an ocean that isn't higher because of us. For better and for worse, we are everywhere. We can check this commandment off the list.

And we can check it off for happier reasons as well. There's no denying that we've done great environmental damage, but it's also true that we've spread wondrous and diverse cultures, full of love and song, across the wide earth. We should add a holiday to the calendar of every church to celebrate this achievement.

But when you check something off a list, you don't just throw the list away. You look further down the list, see what comes next. And the list, of course, is long. The Gospels, the Torah, the Koran and a thousand other texts sacred and profane give us plenty of other goals toward which to divert some of the energy we've traditionally used in raising large families, goals on which we've barely begun. Feed the hungry, clothe the naked, comfort the oppressed; love your neighbor as yourself; heal the earth. We live on a planet where 3 billion people don't have clean water, where species die by the score each day, where kids grow up without fathers, where violence overwhelms us, where people judge each other by the color of their skin, where a hypersexualized culture poisons the adolescence of girls, where old people and young people need each other's support. And the energy freed by having smaller families may be some of the energy needed to take on these next challenges. To really take them on, not just to announce that they're important, or to send a check, or to read an article, but to make them central to our lives.

I have one child; she is the light of my life; she makes me care far more about the future than I used to. And I have one child; so even after my work I have some time, money and energy left to do other things. I get to work on Adirondack conservation issues and assist those who are fighting global warming; I've helped my wife start a new school in our town; I can teach Sunday school and help run a nationwide effort to decommercialize Christmas and sit on the board of the local college. (And I belly dance too, though in my case it's hiking, cross-country skiing, mountain biking.) If I had three kids, I would still do those things, but less of them; either that, or my work would come at their expense. As it is, once in a while I'm stretched too thin and don't see Sophie for a day, and that reminds me to slow down, to find the real center of my life. But I want to get further down that list.

35 So the pope strikes me as largely right in his reasoning if not his conclusions. Radical individualism is inhuman. Living as if you were the most important thing on earth is, literally, blasphemy; recreational sex may not bother me, but recreational life does. Our decisions should be motivated "not by selfishness or carelessness, but by a prudent conscious generosity." It's just that at the end of the twentieth century, on this planet, the signs of the times point me in the direction of the kinds of caring, the ways of maturing, that come with small, not large, families.

The church should not find that argument so foreign. Priests are celibate at least in part because it allows them to make Christ their bride, to devote all their energies to the other tasks set before us on this earth. And the wisdom of that argument is proved daily in a million places around the globe where committed priests and nuns take on the hardest and dirtiest challenges the earth has to offer. If we now have plenty of people to guarantee our survival as a race, and if lots more people may make that survival harder, then it's time to follow the lead of those clerics a little—not to embrace celibacy necessarily, but to love your child to pieces, and with whatever you have left to start working your way down the list.

And the same logic should make it clear, of course, that all sorts of other kinds of people—childless gay people, infertile people, people who do not feel called to parenthood—can become every bit as mature (or immature) as a parent of six, as long as they can find some substitute discipline for repeatedly placing someone or something else at the center of their lives.

Sometimes those disciplines are quiet and private, sometimes public. In Allan Gurganus's novel *Plays Well with Others*, his main character describes taking care of one friend after another as they succumbed to AIDS—describes the almost hydraulic outpouring of love it took to tend them. "My own loved ones were not brought into the world by me, but only, in my company, let out of it," he writes. His own obituary, he knows, will show that he left "no immediate survivors." "And yet I feel I've earned a family too." More so, of course, than many parents.

When she began studying the differences between pro-choice and pro-life advocates in the abortion dispute, Kristin Luker noticed something interesting. It was true that they differed over the morality of terminating pregnancy, but those differences were the product of other, more fundamental splits in their view of the world. They felt differently about God, about the role of women and, most interestingly, they felt very differently about the nature of planning.

40 Pro-choice activists, she observed, were almost obsessed with planning for their children, trying to give them "maximum parental guidance and every possible advantage," while parents active in the antiabortion movement "tend to be *laissez-faire* individualists in their attitude" toward child-rearing. "Pro-life people," she wrote, "believe that one becomes a parent by *being* a parent; parenthood is for them a 'natural' rather than a social role. The values implied by the in-vogue term 'parenting' (as in parenting classes) are alien to them." One woman she interviewed said, "I think people are foolish to worry about

things in the future. The future takes care of itself." Too much planning, including too much family planning, means "playing God."

One of my favorite magazines comes from a small Ohio town. Called *Plain*, it is edited (and its type hand-set) by "conservative" Quakers, which is to say a group of men and women who live more or less in the fashion of Old Order Amish. The magazine recently reprinted a dinner conversation about the subject of family planning. The participants, each of them the parent of four children, were discussing their unease with contraception, and in terms very reminiscent of Luker's study:

> Miriam: It breeds the mentality that "I want what I want, when I want."
>
> Scott: It leads back to self-seeking, which eventually knows no bounds.
>
> Marvin: Actually, it leads to a bottom-line refusal to accept God's will for our lives.
>
> Scott: I think that one of the things Mary Ann and I have learned along the way, and which has further separated us from the mainstream culture, is the realization that we can always make room for one more. Because the room to be made is in our hearts.

That way of seeing the world attracts me—there is in its spontaneity and confidence something of real beauty. It offers a kind of freedom. Not the freedom of unlimited options that we've come to idolize, but a freedom from constant worrying and fretting. Sometimes I hate the calculator instinct in me, the part of me that constantly weighs benefits and risks, the part that keeps me safe and solvent at the expense of experience. There is something incredibly attractive about the mystery of the next child, and the next; I'd love to meet them. I'd love to leave it to God, or to chance, or to biology, or to destiny, or to the wind. Part of me thinks that those conservative Quakers, those pro-lifers, are unequivocally right.

The trouble is, there are now other ways to play God in this world, and *not* planning is one of them.

This was not always the case. In the Book of Job, God appears as a taunting voice from the whirlwind: "Where were you when I laid the foundations of the earth?" God asks Job. "Who shut up the sea with doors . . . and said here shall thy proud waves be stayed? . . . Who has cleft a channel for the torrents of rain, and a way for the thunderbolt?" Job has no way to reply, and no need; the earth is infinitely bigger than he; how absurd he would look standing at the edge of the sea and trying to whistle up the waves. God—the world—was huge, and we were tiny. Creation dwarfed us.

But now there are so many of us, and we have done such a poor job of planning for our numbers, that for the first time we can answer God back. We can say: we set the boundaries of the ocean. If we keep heating the planet at our current pace, the seas will rise two feet in the next century. Every one foot will bring the water 90 feet further inland across the typical American beach, drowning wetland and marsh. It's our lack of planning that changes the rainfall, that means more severe storms and worse flooding. It's not an "act of God." It's an act of us.

45 We no longer have the luxury of not planning; we're simply too big. We dominate the earth. When people first headed west across the plains, they didn't need a zoning board; now Californians try to channel and control growth lest they choke on it. In a crowded world, not planning has as many consequences as planning. This is a special time, and that turns everything on its head.

QUESTIONS

1. McKibben ends his essay by stating, "This is a special time, and that turns everything on its head." How does he demonstrate that this is "a special time"? Do you agree with him? In what sense does his argument depend on this being "a special time"?

2. McKibben tells of how his five-year-old daughter Sophie "has already used more stuff and added more waste to the environment than many of the world's residents do in a lifetime." Make an inventory of how much "stuff" you use in an average week, and then discuss whether your inventory proves McKibben's point.

3. Write an essay arguing that people who decide not to have children are or are not selfish.

JAMES BALDWIN *Stranger in the Village*

FROM ALL AVAILABLE evidence no black man had ever set foot in this tiny Swiss village before I came. I was told before arriving that I would probably be a "sight" for the village; I took this to mean that people of my complexion were rarely seen in Switzerland, and also that city people are always something of a "sight" outside of the city. It did not occur to me—possibly because I am an American—that there could be people anywhere who had never seen a Negro.

It is a fact that cannot be explained on the basis of the inaccessibility of the village. The village is very high, but it is only four hours from Milan and three hours from Lausanne. It is true that it is virtually unknown. Few people making plans for a holiday would elect to come here. On the other hand, the villagers are able, presumably, to come and go as they please—which they do: to another town at the foot of the mountain, with a population of approximately five thousand, the nearest place to see a movie or go to the bank. In the village there is no movie house, no bank, no library, no theater; very few radios, one jeep, one station wagon; and at the moment, one typewriter, mine, an invention which the woman next door to me here had never seen. There are about six hundred people living here, all Catholic—I conclude this from the fact that the Catholic church

Written in 1953 and included in Notes of a Native Son *(1955), an autobiographical collection that describes and analyzes the experience of being black in America and Europe.*

is open all year round, whereas the Protestant chapel, set off on a hill a little removed from the village, is open only in the summertime when the tourists arrive. There are four or five hotels, all closed now, and four or five *bistros,* of which, however, only two do any business during the winter. These two do not do a great deal, for life in the village seems to end around nine or ten o'clock. There are a few stores, butcher, baker, *épicerie,*[1] a hardware store, and a money-changer—who cannot change travelers' checks, but must send them down to the bank, an operation which takes two or three days. There is something called the *Ballet Haus,* closed in the winter and used for God knows what, certainly not ballet, during the summer. There seems to be only one schoolhouse in the village, and this for the quite young children; I suppose this to mean that their older brothers and sisters at some point descend from these mountains in order to complete their education—possibly, again, to the town just below. The landscape is absolutely forbidding, mountains towering on all four sides, ice and snow as far as the eye can reach. In this white wilderness, men and women and children move all day, carrying washing, wood, buckets of milk or water, sometimes skiing on Sunday afternoons. All week long boys and young men are to be seen shoveling snow off the rooftops, or dragging wood down from the forest in sleds.

The village's only real attraction, which explains the tourist season, is the hot spring water. A disquietingly high proportion of these tourists are cripples, or semi-cripples, who come year after year—from other parts of Switzerland, usually—to take the waters. This lends the village, at the height of the season, a rather terrifying air of sanctity, as though it were a lesser Lourdes. There is often something beautiful, there is always something awful, in the spectacle of a person who has lost one of his faculties, a faculty he never questioned until it was gone, and who struggles to recover it. Yet people remain people, on crutches or indeed on deathbeds; and wherever I passed, the first summer I was here, among the native villagers or among the lame, a wind passed with me—of astonishment, curiosity, amusement, and outrage. That first summer I stayed two weeks and never intended to return. But I did return in the winter, to work; the village offers, obviously, no distractions whatever and has the further advantage of being extremely cheap. Now it is winter again, a year later, and I am here again. Everyone in the village knows my name, though they scarcely ever use it, knows that I come from America—though, this, apparently, they will never really believe: black men come from Africa—and everyone knows that I am the friend of the son of a woman who was born here, and that I am staying in their chalet. But I remain as much a stranger today as I was the first day I arrived, and the children shout *Neger! Neger!* as I walk along the streets.

It must be admitted that in the beginning I was far too shocked to have any real reaction. In so far as I reacted at all, I reacted by trying to be pleasant—it being a great part of the American Negro's education (long before he goes to school) that he must make people "like" him. This smile-and-the-world-smiles-with-you routine worked about as well in this situation as it had in the situation for which it was designed, which is to say that it did not work at all.

1. A grocery shop.

No one, after all, can be liked whose human weight and complexity cannot be, or has not been, admitted. My smile was simply another unheard-of phenomenon which allowed them to see my teeth—they did not, really, see my smile and I began to think that, should I take to snarling, no one would notice any difference. All of the physical characteristics of the Negro which had caused me, in America, a very different and almost forgotten pain were nothing less than miraculous—or infernal—in the eyes of the village people. Some thought my hair was the color of tar, that it had the texture of wire, or the texture of cotton. It was jocularly suggested that I might let it all grow long and make myself a winter coat. If I sat in the sun for more than five minutes some daring creature was certain to come along and gingerly put his fingers on my hair, as though he were afraid of an electric shock, or put his hand on my hand, astonished that the color did not rub off. In all of this, in which it must be conceded there was the charm of genuine wonder and in which there were certainly no element of intentional unkindness, there was yet no suggestion that I was human: I was simply a living wonder.

5 I knew that they did not mean to be unkind, and I know it now; it is necessary, nevertheless, for me to repeat this to myself each time that I walk out of the chalet. The children who shout *Neger!* have no way of knowing the echoes this sound raises in me. They are brimming with good humor and the more daring swell with pride when I stop to speak with them. Just the same, there are days when I cannot pause and smile, when I have no heart to play with them; when, indeed, I mutter sourly to myself, exactly as I muttered on the streets of a city these children have never seen, when I was no bigger than these children are now: *Your* mother *was a nigger.* Joyce is right about history being a nightmare[2]—but it may be the nightmare from which no one *can* awaken. People are trapped in history and history is trapped in them.

There is a custom in the village—I am told it is repeated in many villages—of "buying" African natives for the purpose of converting them to Christianity. There stands in the church all year round a small box with a slot for money, decorated with a black figurine, and into this box the villagers drop their francs. During the *carnaval* which precedes Lent, two village children have their faces blackened—out of which bloodless darkness their blue eyes shine like ice—and fantastic horsehair wigs are placed on their blond heads; thus disguised, they solicit among the villagers for money for the missionaries in Africa. Between the box in the church and the blackened children, the village "bought" last year six or eight African natives. This was reported to me with pride by the wife of one of the *bistro* owners and I was careful to express astonishment and pleasure at the solicitude shown by the village for the souls of black folks. The *bistro* owner's wife beamed with a pleasure far more genuine than my own and seemed to feel that I might now breathe more easily concerning the souls of at least six of my kinsmen.

2. James Joyce (1882–1941), Irish novelist; Stephen Daedalus, in Joyce's novel *Ulysses*, says, "History is a nightmare from which I am trying to escape."

I tried not to think of these so lately baptized kinsmen, of the price paid for them, or the peculiar price they themselves would pay, and said nothing about my father, who having taken his own conversion too literally never, at bottom, forgave the white world (which he described as heathen) for having saddled him with a Christ in whom, to judge at least from their treatment of him, they themselves no longer believed. I thought of white men arriving for the first time in an African village, strangers there, as I am a stranger here, and tried to imagine the astounded populace touching their hair and marveling at the color of their skin. But there is a great difference between being the first white man to be seen by Africans and being the first black man to be seen by whites. The white man takes the astonishment as tribute, for he arrives to conquer and to convert the natives, whose inferiority in relation to himself is not even to be questioned; whereas I, without a thought of conquest, find myself among a people whose culture controls me, has even, in a sense, created me, people who have cost me more in anguish and rage than they will ever know, who yet do not even know of my existence. The astonishment with which I might have greeted them, should they have stumbled into my African village a few hundred years ago, might have rejoiced their hearts. But the astonishment with which they greet me today can only poison mine.

And this is so despite everything I may do to feel differently, despite my friendly conversations with the *bistro* owner's wife, despite their three-year-old son who has at last become my friend, despite the *saluts* and *bonsoirs*[3] which I exchange with people as I walk, despite the fact that I know that no individual can be taken to task for what history is doing, or has done. I say that the culture of these people controls me—but they can scarcely be held responsible for European culture. America comes out of Europe, but these people have never seen America, nor have most of them seen more of Europe than the hamlet at the foot of their mountain. Yet they move with an authority which I shall never have; and they regard me, quite rightly, not only as a stranger in their village but as a suspect latecomer, bearing no credentials, to everything they have—however unconsciously—inherited.

For this village, even were it incomparably more remote and incredibly more primitive, is the West, the West onto which I have been so strangely grafted. These people cannot be, from the point of view of power, strangers anywhere in the world; they have made the modern world, in effect, even if they do not know it. The most illiterate among them is related, in a way that I am not, to Dante, Shakespeare, Michelangelo, Aeschylus, Da Vinci, Rembrandt, and Racine; the cathedral at Chartres says something to them which it cannot say to me, as indeed would New York's Empire State Building, should anyone here ever see it. Out of their hymns and dances come Beethoven and Bach. Go back a few centuries and they are in their full glory—but I am in Africa, watching the conquerors arrive.

10 The rage of the disesteemed is personally fruitless, but it is also absolutely inevitable; this rage, so generally discounted, so little understood even among

3. "Hellos" and "good evenings."

the people whose daily bread it is, is one of the things that makes history. Rage can only with difficulty, and never entirely, be brought under the domination of the intelligence and is therefore not susceptible to any arguments whatever. This is a fact which ordinary representatives of the *Herren volk,*[4] having never felt this rage and being unable to imagine, quite fail to understand. Also, rage cannot be hidden, it can only be dissembled. This dissembling deludes the thoughtless, and strengthens rage and adds, to rage, contempt. There are, no doubt, as many ways of coping with the resulting complex of tensions as there are black men in the world, but no black man can hope ever to be entirely liberated from this internal warfare—rage, dissembling, and contempt having inevitably accompanied his first realization of the power of white men. What is crucial here is that, since white men represent in the black man's world so heavy a weight, white men have for black men a reality which is far from being reciprocal; and hence all black men have toward all white men an attitude which is designed, really, either to rob the white man of the jewel of his naïveté, or else to make it cost him dear.

The black man insists, by whatever means he finds at his disposal, that the white man cease to regard him as an exotic rarity and recognize him as a human being. This is a very charged and difficult moment, for there is a great deal of will power involved in the white man's naïveté. Most people are not naturally reflective any more than they are naturally malicious, and the white man prefers to keep the black man at a certain human remove because it is easier for him thus to preserve his simplicity and avoid being called to account for crimes committed by his forefathers, or his neighbors. He is inescapably aware, nevertheless, that he is in a better position in the world than black men are, nor can he quite put to death the suspicion that he is hated by black men therefore. He does not wish to be hated, neither does he wish to change places, and at this point in his uneasiness he can scarcely avoid having recourse to those legends which white men have created about black men, the most usual effect of which is that the white man finds himself enmeshed, so to speak, in his own language which describes hell, as well as the attributes which lead one to hell, as being as black as night.

Every legend, moreover, contains its residuum of truth, and the root function of language is to control the universe by describing it. It is of quite considerable significance that black men remain, in the imagination, and in overwhelming numbers in fact, beyond the disciplines of salvation; and this despite the fact that the West has been "buying" African natives for centuries. There is, I should hazard, an instantaneous necessity to be divorced from this so visibly unsaved stranger, in whose heart, moreover, one cannot guess what dreams of vengeance are being nourished; and, at the same time, there are few things on earth more attractive than the idea of the unspeakable liberty which is allowed the unredeemed. When, beneath the black mask, a human being begins to make himself felt one cannot escape a certain awful wonder as to what kind of human being it is. What one's imagination makes of other people

4. Master race.

is dictated, of course, by the laws of one's own personality and it is one of the ironies of black-white relations that, by means of what the white man imagines the black man to be, the black man is enabled to know who the white man is.

I have said, for example, that I am as much a stranger in this village today as I was the first summer I arrived, but this is not quite true. The villagers wonder less about the texture of my hair than they did then, and wonder rather more about me. And the fact that their wonder now exists on another level is reflected in their attitudes and in their eyes. There are the children who make those delightful, hilarious, sometimes astonishingly grave overtures of friendship in the unpredictable fashion of children; other children, having been taught that the devil is a black man, scream in genuine anguish as I approach. Some of the older women never pass without a friendly greeting, never pass, indeed, if it seems that they will be able to engage me in conversation; other women look down or look away or rather contemptuously smirk. Some of the men drink with me and suggest that I learn how to ski—partly, I gather, because they cannot imagine what I would look like on skis—and want to know if I am married, and ask questions about my *métier.* But some of the men have accused *le sale nègre*[5]—behind my back—of stealing wood and there is already in the eyes of some of them that peculiar, intent, paranoiac malevolence which one sometimes surprises in the eyes of American white men when, out walking with their Sunday girl, they see a Negro male approach.

There is a dreadful abyss between the streets of this village and the streets of the city in which I was born, between the children who shout *Neger!* today and those who shouted *Nigger!* yesterday—the abyss is experience, the American experience. The syllable hurled behind me today expresses, above all, wonder: I am a stranger here. But I am not a stranger in America and the same syllable riding on the American air expresses the war my presence has occasioned in the American soul.

For this village brings home to me this fact: that there was a day, and not really a very distant day, when Americans were scarcely Americans at all but discontented Europeans, facing a great unconquered continent and strolling, say, into a marketplace and seeing black men for the first time. The shock this spectacle afforded is suggested, surely, by the promptness with which they decided that these black men were not really men but cattle. It is true that the necessity on the part of the settlers of the New World of reconciling their moral assumptions with the fact—and the necessity—of slavery enhanced immensely the charm of this idea, and it is also true that this idea expresses, with a truly American bluntness, the attitude which to varying extents all masters have had toward all slaves. 15

But between all former slaves and slave-owners and the drama which begins for Americans over three hundred years ago at Jamestown, there are at least two differences to be observed. The American Negro slave could not suppose, for one thing, as slaves in past epochs had supposed and often done, that he would ever be able to wrest the power from his master's hands. This

5. The dirty Negro.

was a supposition which the modern era, which was to bring about such vast changes in the aims and dimensions of power, put to death; it only begins, in unprecedented fashion, and with dreadful implications, to be resurrected today. But even had this supposition persisted with undiminished force, the American Negro slave could not have used it to lend his condition dignity, for the reason that this supposition rests on another: that the slave in exile yet remains related to his past, has some means—if only in memory—of revering and sustaining the forms of his former life, is able, in short, to maintain his identity.

This was not the case with the American Negro slave. He is unique among the black men of the world in that his past was taken from him, almost literally, at one blow. One wonders what on earth the first slave found to say to the first dark child he bore. I am told that there are Haitians able to trace their ancestry back to African kings, but any American Negro wishing to go back so far will find his journey through time abruptly arrested by the signature on the bill of sale which served as the entrance paper for his ancestor. At the time—to say nothing of the circumstances—of the enslavement of the captive black man who was to become the American Negro, there was not the remotest possibility that he would ever take power from his master's hands. There was no reason to suppose that his situation would ever change, nor was there, shortly, anything to indicate that his situation had ever been different. It was his necessity, in the words of E. Franklin Frazier,[6] to find a "motive for living under American culture or die." The identity of the American Negro comes out of this extreme situation, and the evolution of this identity was a source of the most intolerable anxiety in the minds and the lives of his masters.

For the history of the American Negro is unique also in this: that the question of his humanity, and of his rights therefore as a human being, became a burning one for several generations of Americans, so burning a question that it ultimately became one of those used to divide the nation. It is out of this argument that the venom of the epithet *Nigger!* is derived. It is an argument which Europe has never had, and hence Europe quite sincerely fails to understand how or why the argument arose in the first place, why its effects are frequently disastrous and always so unpredictable, why it refuses until today to be entirely settled. Europe's black possessions remained—and do remain—in Europe's colonies, at which remove they represented no threat whatever to European identity. If they posed any problem at all for the European conscience it was a problem which remained comfortingly abstract: in effect, the black man, as a *man* did not exist for Europe. But in America, even as a slave, he was an inescapable part of the general social fabric and no American could escape having an attitude toward him. Americans attempt until today to make an abstraction of the Negro, but the very nature of these abstractions reveals the tremendous effects the presence of the Negro has had on the American character.

When one considers the history of the Negro in America it is of the greatest importance to recognize that the moral beliefs of a person, or a people, are never really as tenuous as life—which is not moral—very often causes them to

6. African American sociologist (1894–1962).

appear; these create for them a frame of reference and a necessary hope, the hope being that when life has done its worst they will be enabled to rise above themselves and to triumph over life. Life would scarcely be bearable if this hope did not exist. Again, even when the worst has been said, to betray a belief is not by any means to have put oneself beyond its power; the betrayal of a belief is not the same thing as ceasing to believe. If this were not so there would be no moral standards in the world at all. Yet one must also recognize that morality is based on ideas and that all ideas are dangerous—dangerous because ideas can only lead to action and where the action leads no man can say. And dangerous in this respect: that confronted with the impossibility of remaining faithful to one's beliefs, and the equal impossibility of becoming free of them, one can be driven to the most inhuman excesses. The ideas on which American beliefs are based are not, though Americans often seem to think so, ideas which originated in America. They came out of Europe. And the establishment of democracy on the American continent was scarcely as radical a break with the past as was the necessity, which Americans faced, of broadening this concept to include black men.

This was, literally, a hard necessity. It was impossible, for one thing, for Americans to abandon their beliefs, not only because these beliefs alone seemed able to justify the sacrifices they had endured and the blood that they had spilled, but also because these beliefs afforded them their only bulwark against a moral chaos as absolute as the physical chaos of the continent it was their destiny to conquer. But in the situation in which Americans found themselves, these beliefs threatened an idea which, whether or not one likes to think so, is the very warp and woof of the heritage of the West, the idea of white supremacy. 20

Americans have made themselves notorious by the shrillness and the brutality with which they have insisted on this idea, but they did not invent it; and it has escaped the world's notice that those very excesses of which Americans have been guilty imply a certain, unprecedented uneasiness over the idea's life and power, if not, indeed, the idea's validity. The idea of white supremacy rests simply on the fact that white men are the creators of civilization (the present civilization, which is the only one that matters; all previous civilizations are simply "contributions" to our own) and are therefore civilization's guardians and defenders. Thus it was impossible for Americans to accept the black man as one of themselves, for to do so was to jeopardize their status as white men. But not so to accept him was to deny his human reality, his human weight and complexity, and the strain of denying the overwhelmingly undeniable forced Americans into rationalizations so fantastic that they approached the pathological.

At the root of the American Negro problem is the necessity of the American white man to find a way of living with the Negro in order to be able to live with himself. And the history of this problem can be reduced to the means used by Americans—lynch law and law, segregation and legal acceptance, terrorization and concession—either to come to terms with this necessity, or to find a way around it, or (most usually) to find a way of doing both these things at once. The resulting spectacle, at once foolish and dreadful, led someone to make the quite accurate observation that "the Negro-in-America is a form of insanity which overtakes white men."

In this long battle, a battle by no means finished, the unforeseeable effects of which will be felt by many future generations, the white man's motive was the protection of his identity; the black man was motivated by the need to establish an identity. And despite the terrorization which the Negro in America endured and endures sporadically until today, despite the cruel and totally inescapable ambivalence of his status in his country, the battle for his identity has long ago been won. He is not a visitor to the West, but a citizen there, an American; as American as the Americans who despise him, the Americans who fear him, the Americans who love him—the Americans who became less than themselves, or rose to be greater than themselves by virtue of the fact that the challenge he represented was inescapable. He is perhaps the only black man in the world whose relationship to white men is more terrible, more subtle, and more meaningful than the relationship of bitter possessed to uncertain possessors. His survival depended, and his development depends, on his ability to turn his peculiar status in the Western world to his own advantage and, it may be, to the very great advantage of that world. It remains for him to fashion out of his experience that which will give him sustenance, and a voice.

The cathedral at Chartres, I have said, says something to the people of this village which it cannot say to me; but it is important to understand that this cathedral says something to me which it cannot say to them. Perhaps they are struck by the power of the spires, the glory of the windows; but they have known God, after all, longer than I have known him, and in a different way, and I am terrified by the slippery bottomless well to be found in the crypt, down which heretics were hurled to death, and by the obscene, inescapable gargoyles jutting out of the stone and seeming to say that God and the devil can never be divorced. I doubt that the villagers think of the devil when they face a cathedral because they have never been identified with the devil. But I must accept the status which myth, if nothing else, gives me in the West before I can hope to change the myth.

25 Yet, if the American Negro has arrived at his identity by virtue of the absoluteness of his estrangement from his past, American white men still nourish the illusion that there is some means of recovering the European innocence, of returning to a state in which black men do not exist. This is one of the greatest errors Americans can make. The identity they fought so hard to protect has, by virtue of that battle, undergone a change: Americans are as unlike any other white people in the world as it is possible to be. I do not think, for example, that it is too much to suggest that the American vision of the world—which allows so little reality, generally speaking, for any of the darker forces in human life, which tends until today to paint moral issues in glaring black and white—owes a great deal to the battle waged by Americans to maintain between themselves and black men a human separation which could not be bridged. It is only now beginning to be borne in on us—very faintly, it must be admitted, very slowly, and very much against our will—that this vision of the world is dangerously inaccurate, and perfectly useless. For it protects our moral high-mindedness at

the terrible expense of weakening our grasp of reality. People who shut their eyes to reality simply invite their own destruction, and anyone who insists on remaining in a state of innocence long after that innocence is dead turns himself into a monster.

The time has come to realize that the interracial drama acted out on the American continent has not only created a new black man, it has created a new white man, too. No road whatever will lead Americans back to the simplicity of this European village where white men still have the luxury of looking on me as a stranger. I am not, really, a stranger any longer for any American alive. One of the things that distinguishes Americans from other people is that no other people has ever been so deeply involved in the lives of black men, and vice versa. This fact faced, with all its implications, it can be seen that the history of the American Negro problem is not merely shameful, it is also something of an achievement. For even when the worst has been said, it must also be added that the perpetual challenge posed by this problem was always, somehow, perpetually met. It is precisely this black-white experience which may prove of indispensable value to us in the world we face today. This world is white no longer, and it will never be white again.

Questions

1. Baldwin begins with the narration of his experience in a Swiss village. At what point do you become aware that he has a larger point? What purpose does he make his experience serve?

2. Trace the use of the word "stranger" over the course of the essay. How does Baldwin's use of the word evolve as the essay develops?

3. Baldwin relates the white man's language and legends about black men to the "laws" of the white man's personality. What conviction about the source and the nature of language does this reveal?

4. Describe some particular experience that raises a large social question or shows the workings of large social forces. Does Baldwin offer any help in the problem of connecting the particular and the general?

Brent Staples *Black Men and Public Space*

My first victim was a woman—white, well dressed, probably in her early twenties. I came upon her late one evening on a deserted street in Hyde Park, a relatively affluent neighborhood in an otherwise mean, impoverished section of Chicago. As I swung onto the avenue behind her, there seemed to be a discreet, uninflammatory distance between us. Not so. She cast back a worried glance. To her, the youngish black man—a broad six feet two inches with a beard and billowing hair, both hands shoved into the pockets of a bulky military jacket—seemed menacingly close. After a few more quick glimpses, she picked up her pace and was soon running in earnest. Within seconds she disappeared into a cross street.

That was more than a decade ago, I was twenty-two years old, a graduate student newly arrived at the University of Chicago. It was in the echo of that terrified woman's footfalls that I first began to know the unwieldy inheritance I'd come into—the ability to alter public space in ugly ways. It was clear that she thought herself the quarry of a mugger, a rapist, or worse. Suffering a bout of insomnia, however, I was stalking sleep, not defenseless wayfarers. As a softy who is scarcely able to take a knife to a raw chicken—let alone hold one to a person's throat—I was surprised, embarrassed, and dismayed all at once. Her flight made me feel like an accomplice in tyranny. It also made it clear that I was indistinguishable from the muggers who occasionally seeped into the area from the surrounding ghetto. That first encounter, and those that followed, signified that a vast, unnerving gulf lay between nighttime pedestrians—particularly women—and me. And I soon gathered that being perceived as dangerous is a hazard in itself. I only needed to turn a corner into a dicey situation, or crowd some frightened, armed person in a foyer somewhere, or make an errant move after being pulled over by a policeman. Where fear and weapons meet—and they often do in urban America—there is always the possibility of death.

In that first year, my first away from my hometown, I was to become thoroughly familiar with the language of fear. At dark, shadowy intersections, I could cross in front of a car stopped at a traffic light and elicit the *thunk, thunk, thunk, thunk* of the driver—black, white, male, or female—hammering down the door locks. On less traveled streets after dark, I grew accustomed to but never comfortable with people crossing to the other side of the street rather than pass me. Then there were the standard unpleasantries with policemen, doormen, bouncers, cabdrivers, and others whose business it is to screen out troublesome individuals *before* there is any nastiness.

Originally appeared in Harper's Magazine *(December 1986), an American monthly that continues its mission to "explore the issues and ideas in politics, science, and the arts that drive our national conversation." The essay was later incorporated into* Parallel Time: Growing Up in Black and White *(1994), an award-winning memoir of Staples's formative years in Chester, Pennsylvania, that chronicles his escape from poverty and crime and his brother's violent destruction.*

I moved to New York nearly two years ago and I have remained an avid night walker. In central Manhattan, the near-constant crowd cover minimizes tense one-on-one street encounters. Elsewhere—in SoHo, for example, where sidewalks are narrow and tightly spaced buildings shut out the sky—things can get very taut indeed.

5 After dark, on the warrenlike streets of Brooklyn where I live, I often see women who fear the worst from me. They seem to have set their faces on neutral, and with their purse straps strung across their chests bandolier-style, they forge ahead as though bracing themselves against being tackled. I understand, of course, that the danger they perceive is not a hallucination. Women are particularly vulnerable to street violence, and young black males are drastically overrepresented among the perpetrators of that violence. Yet these truths are no solace against the kind of alienation that comes of being ever the suspect, a fearsome entity with whom pedestrians avoid making eye contact.

It is not altogether clear to me how I reached the ripe old age of twenty-two without being conscious of the lethality nighttime pedestrians attributed to me. Perhaps it was because in Chester, Pennsylvania, the small, angry industrial town where I came of age in the 1960s, I was scarcely noticeable against a backdrop of gang warfare, street knifings, and murders. I grew up one of the good boys, had perhaps a half-dozen fistfights. In retrospect, my shyness of combat has clear sources.

As a boy, I saw countless tough guys locked away; I have since buried several, too. They were babies, really—a teenage cousin, a brother of twenty-two, a childhood friend in his mid-twenties—all gone down in episodes of bravado played out in the streets. I came to doubt the virtues of intimidation early on. I chose, perhaps unconsciously, to remain a shadow—timid, but a survivor.

The fearsomeness mistakenly attributed to me in public places often has a perilous flavor. The most frightening of these confusions occurred in the late 1970s and early 1980s, when I worked as a journalist in Chicago. One day, rushing into the office of a magazine I was writing for with a deadline story in hand, I was mistaken for a burglar. The office manager called security and, with an ad hoc[1] posse, pursued me through the labyrinthine halls, nearly to my editor's door. I had no way of proving who I was. I could only move briskly toward the company of someone who knew me.

Another time I was on assignment for a local paper and killing time before an interview. I entered a jewelry store on the city's affluent Near North Side. The proprietor excused herself and returned with an enormous red Doberman pinscher straining at the end of a leash. She stood, the dog extended toward me, silent to my questions, her eyes bulging nearly out of her head. I took a cursory look around, nodded, and bade her good night.

10 Relatively speaking, however, I never fared as badly as another black male journalist. He went to nearby Waukegan, Illinois, a couple of summers ago to work on a story about a murderer who was born there. Mistaking the reporter for the killer, police officers hauled him from his car at gunpoint and but for

1. For a particular purpose; improvised.

his press credentials would probably have tried to book him. Such episodes are not uncommon. Black men trade tales like this all the time.

Over the years, I learned to smother the rage I felt at so often being taken for a criminal. Not to do so would surely have led to madness. I now take precautions to make myself less threatening. I move about with care, particularly late in the evening. I give a wide berth to nervous people on subway platforms during the wee hours, particularly when I have exchanged business clothes for jeans. If I happen to be entering a building behind some people who appear skittish, I may walk by, letting them clear the lobby before I return, so as not to seem to be following them. I have been calm and extremely congenial on those rare occasions when I've been pulled over by the police.

And on late-evening constitutionals I employ what has proved to be an excellent tension-reducing measure: I whistle melodies from Beethoven and Vivaldi and the more popular classical composers. Even steely New Yorkers hunching toward nighttime destinations seem to relax, and occasionally they even join in the tune. Virtually everybody seems to sense that a mugger wouldn't be warbling bright, sunny selections from Vivaldi's *Four Seasons*.[2] It is my equivalent of the cowbell that hikers wear when they know they are in bear country.

2. Work by composer Antonio Vivaldi (1678–1741), celebrating the seasons.

QUESTIONS

1. Staples writes of situations rightly perceived as threatening and of situations misperceived as threatening. Give specific instances of each and tell how they are related.

2. Staples's essay contains a mixture of rage and humor. Does this mix distract from or contribute to the seriousness of the matter?

3. Write of a situation in which someone was wrongly perceived as threatening.

DEBRA DICKERSON *Who Shot Johnny?*

GIVEN MY LEVEL of political awareness, it was inevitable that I would come to view the everyday events of my life through the prism of politics and the national discourse. I read *The Washington Post, The New Republic, The New Yorker, Harper's, The Atlantic Monthly, The Nation, National Review, Black Enterprise* and *Essence* and wrote a weekly column for the *Harvard Law School Record* during my three years just ended there. I do this because I know

Published in the New Republic *(January 1, 1996), an American journal of politics and the arts. The essay was selected for* Best American Essays *(1997), a yearly series that reprints distinguished nonfiction pieces from national and regional American magazines.*

that those of us who are not well-fed white guys in suits must not yield the debate to them, however well-intentioned or well-informed they may be. Accordingly, I am unrepentant and vocal about having gained admittance to Harvard through affirmative action; I am a feminist, stoic about my marriage chances as a well-educated, 36-year-old black woman who won't pretend to need help taking care of herself. My strength flags, though, in the face of the latest role assigned to my family in the national drama. On July 27, 1995, my 16-year-old nephew was shot and paralyzed.

Talking with friends in front of his home, Johnny saw a car he thought he recognized. He waved boisterously—his trademark—throwing both arms in the air in a full-bodied, hip-hop Y. When he got no response, he and his friends sauntered down the walk to join a group loitering in front of an apartment building. The car followed. The driver got out, brandished a revolver and fired into the air. Everyone scattered. Then he took aim and shot my running nephew in the back.

Johnny never lost consciousness. He lay in the road, trying to understand what had happened to him, why he couldn't get up. Emotionlessly, he told the story again and again on demand, remaining apologetically firm against all demands to divulge the missing details that would make sense of the shooting but obviously cast him in a bad light. Being black, male and shot, he must, apparently, be gang- or drug-involved. Probably both. Witnesses corroborate his version of events.

Nearly six months have passed since that phone call in the night and my nightmarish, headlong drive from Boston to Charlotte. After twenty hours behind the wheel, I arrived haggard enough to reduce my mother to fresh tears and to find my nephew reassuring well-wishers with an eerie sangfroid.[1]

5

I take the day shift in his hospital room; his mother and grandmother, a clerk and cafeteria worker, respectively, alternate nights there on a cot. They don their uniforms the next day, gaunt after hours spent listening to Johnny moan in his sleep. How often must his subconscious replay those events and curse its host for saying hello without permission, for being carefree and young while a would-be murderer hefted the weight of his uselessness and failure like Jacob Marley's chains?[2] How often must he watch himself lying stubbornly immobile on the pavement of his nightmares while the sound of running feet syncopate his attacker's taunts?

I spend these days beating him at gin rummy and Scrabble, holding a basin while he coughs up phlegm and crying in the corridor while he catheterizes himself. There are children here much worse off than he. I should be grateful. The doctors can't, or won't, say whether he'll walk again.

I am at once repulsed and fascinated by the bullet, which remains lodged in his spine (having done all the damage it can do, the doctors say). The wound is undramatic—small, neat and perfectly centered—an impossibly pink pit

1. Cold blood (French). Composure; self-assurance in the face of difficulty.

2. The ghost of Marley, in chains, visits Ebenezer Scrooge in Dickens's *A Christmas Carol.*

surrounded by an otherwise undisturbed expanse of mahogany. Johnny has asked me several times to describe it but politely declines to look in the mirror I hold for him.

Here on the pediatric rehab ward, Johnny speaks little, never cries, never complains, works diligently to become independent. He does whatever he is told; if two hours remain until the next pain pill, he waits quietly. Eyes bloodshot, hands gripping the bed rails. During the week of his intravenous feeding when he was tormented by the primal need to masticate, he never asked for food. He just listened while we counted down the days for him and planned his favorite meals. Now required to dress himself unassisted, he does so without demur, rolling himself back and forth valiantly on the bed and shivering afterwards, exhausted. He "ma'am"s and "sir"s everyone politely. Before his "accident," a simple request to take out the trash could provoke a firestorm of teenage attitude. We, the women who have raised him, have changed as well; we've finally come to appreciate those boxer-baring, oversized pants we used to hate—it would be much more difficult to fit properly sized pants over his diaper.

He spends a lot of time tethered to rap music still loud enough to break my concentration as I read my many magazines. I hear him try to soundlessly mouth the obligatory "mothafuckers" overlaying the funereal dirge of the music tracks. I do not normally tolerate disrespectful music in my or my mother's presence, but if it distracts him now . . .

10 "Johnny," I ask later, "do you still like gangster rap?" During the long pause I hear him think loudly, *I'm paralyzed Auntie, not stupid.* "I mostly just listen to hip hop," he says evasively into his *Sports Illustrated.*

Miserable though it is, time passes quickly here. We always seem to be jerking awake in our chairs just in time for the next pill, his every-other-night bowel program, the doctor's rounds. Harvard feels a galaxy away—the world revolves around Family Members Living With Spinal Cord Injury class, Johnny's urine output and strategizing with my sister to find affordable, accessible housing. There is always another long-distance uncle in need of an update, another church member wanting to pray with us or Johnny's little brother in need of some attention.

We Dickerson women are so constant a presence the ward nurses and cleaning staff call us by name and join us for cafeteria meals and cigarette breaks. At Johnny's birthday pizza party, they crack jokes and make fun of each other's husbands (there are no men here). I pass slices around and try not to think, "17 with a bullet."

Oddly, we feel little curiosity or specific anger toward the man who shot him. We have to remind ourselves to check in with the police. Even so, it feels pro forma, like sending in those $2 rebate forms that come with new pantyhose: you know your request will fall into a deep, dark hole somewhere but, still, it's your duty to try. We push for an arrest because we owe it to Johnny and to ourselves as citizens. We don't think about it otherwise—our low expectations are too ingrained. A Harvard aunt notwithstanding, for people like Johnny, Marvin Gaye[3] was right that only three things are sure: taxes, death and trouble. At least it wasn't the second.

We rarely wonder about or discuss the brother who shot him because we already know everything about him. When the call came, my first thought was the same one I'd had when I'd heard about Rosa Parks's beating:[4] a brother did it. A non-job-having, middle-of-the-day malt-liquor-drinking, crotch-clutching, loud-talking brother with many neglected children born of many forgotten women. He lives in his mother's basement with furniture rented at an astronomical interest rate, the exact amount of which he does not know. He has a car phone, an $80 monthly cable bill and every possible phone feature but no savings. He steals Social Security numbers from unsuspecting relatives and assumes their identities to acquire large TV sets for which he will never pay. On the slim chance that he is brought to justice, he will have a colorful criminal history and no coherent explanation to offer for this act. His family will raucously defend him and cry cover-up. Some liberal lawyer just like me will help him plea bargain his way to yet another short stay in a prison pesthouse that will serve only to add another layer to the brother's sociopathology and formless, mindless nihilism. We know him. We've known and feared him all our lives.

15 As a teenager, he called, "Hey, baby, gimme somma that boodie!" at us from car windows. Indignant at our lack of response, he followed up with, "Fuck you, then, 'ho!" He called me a "white-boy lovin' nigger bitch oreo" for being in the gifted program and loving it. At 27, he got my 17-year-old sister pregnant with Johnny and lost interest without ever informing her that he was married. He snatched my widowed mother's purse as she waited in pre-dawn darkness for the bus to work and then broke into our house while she soldered on an assembly line. He chased all the small entrepreneurs from our neighborhood with his violent thievery, and put bars on our windows. He kept us from sitting on our own front porch after dark and laid the foundation for our periodic bouts of self-hating anger and racial embarrassment. He made our neighborhood a ghetto. He is the poster fool behind the maddening community knowledge that there are still some black mothers who raise their daughters but merely love their sons. He and his cancerous carbon copies eclipse the vast majority of us who are not sociopaths and render us invisible. He is the Siamese twin who has died but cannot be separated from his living, vibrant sibling; which of us must attract more notice? We despise and disown this anomalous loser but, for many, he *is* black America. We know him, we know that he is outside the fold, and we know that he will only get worse. What we didn't know is that, because of him, my little sister would one day be the latest hysterical black mother wailing over a fallen child on TV.

3. African American soul singer (1939–1984) who was shot to death in an altercation with his father.

4. The elderly Rosa Parks, the 1950s civil rights pioneer, was the victim of a beating in the 1990s.

Alone, lying in the road bleeding and paralyzed but hideously conscious, Johnny had lain helpless as he watched his would-be murderer come to stand over him and offer this prophecy: "Betch'ou won't be doin' nomo' wavin', motha'fucker."

Fuck you, asshole. He's fine from the waist up. You just can't do anything right, can you?

QUESTIONS

1. Why did the *New Republic* include the first paragraph? Do you think the essay would be more or less effective if it began simply with the sentence "On July 27, 1995, my 16-year-old nephew was shot and paralyzed"?

2. Dickerson feels—and expresses—anger throughout this essay. How? Against what or whom?

3. Why does Dickerson use the term "brother" in the final paragraphs? How does this composite characterization work? How does it answer the question "Who shot Johnny?"

Op-Eds and Public Arguments

Anna Quindlen *Stuff Is Not Salvation*

As the boom times fade, an important holiday question surfaces: why in the world did we buy all this junk in the first place?

What passes for the holiday season began before dawn the day after Thanksgiving, when a worker at a Wal-Mart in Valley Stream, N.Y., was trampled to death by a mob of bargain hunters. Afterward, there were reports that some people, mesmerized by cheap consumer electronics and discounted toys, kept shopping even after announcements to clear the store.

These are dark days in the United States: the cataclysmic stock-market declines, the industries edging up on bankruptcy, the home foreclosures and the waves of layoffs. But the prospect of an end to plenty has uncovered what may ultimately be a more pernicious problem, an addiction to consumption so out of control that it qualifies as a sickness. The suffocation of a store employee by a stampede of shoppers was horrifying, but it wasn't entirely surprising.

Americans have been on an acquisition binge for decades. I suspect television advertising, which made me want a Chatty Cathy doll[1] so much as a kid that when I saw her under the tree my head almost exploded. By contrast, my father will be happy to tell you about the excitement of getting an orange in his stocking during the Depression. The depression before this one.

A critical difference between then and now is credit. The orange had to be paid for. The rite of passage for a child when I was young was a solemn visit to the local bank, there to exchange birthday money for a savings passbook. Every once in a while, like magic, a bit of extra money would appear. Interest. Yippee. 5

The passbook was replaced by plastic, so that today Americans are overwhelmed by debt and the national savings rate is calculated, like an algebra equation, in negatives. By 2010 Americans will be a trillion dollars in the hole on credit-card debt alone.

But let's look, not at the numbers, but the atmospherics. Appliances, toys, clothes, gadgets. Junk. There's the sad truth. Wall Street executives may have

First appeared in Quindlen's Newsweek *magazine column on December 22, 2008, at the height of the Christmas shopping season.*

1. Chatty Cathy dolls, which speak when a ring in their neck is pulled, have been manufactured by Mattel since 1959.

made investments that lost their value, but, in a much smaller way, so did the rest of us. "I looked into my closet the other day and thought, why did I buy all this stuff?" one friend said recently. A person in the United States replaces a cell phone every 16 months, not because the cell phone is old, but because it is oldish. My mother used to complain that the Christmas toys were grubby and forgotten by Easter. (I didn't even really like dolls, especially dolls who introduced themselves to you over and over again when you pulled the ring in their necks.) Now much of the country is made up of people with the acquisition habits of a 7-year-old, desire untethered from need, or the ability to pay. The result is a booming business in those free-standing storage facilities, where junk goes to linger in a persistent vegetative state, somewhere between eBay and the dump.

Oh, there is still plenty of need. But it is for real things, things that matter: college tuition, prescription drugs, rent. Food pantries and soup kitchens all over the country have seen demand for their services soar. Homelessness, which had fallen in recent years, may rebound as people lose their jobs and their houses. For the first time this month, the number of people on food stamps will exceed the 30 million mark.

Hard times offer the opportunity to ask hard questions, and one of them is the one my friend asked, staring at sweaters and shoes: why did we buy all this stuff? Did anyone really need a flat-screen in the bedroom, or a designer handbag, or three cars? If the mall is our temple, then Marc Jacobs[2] is God. There's a scary thought.

10 The drumbeat that accompanied Black Friday[3] this year was that the numbers had to redeem us, that if enough money was spent by shoppers it would indicate that things were not so bad after all. But what the economy required was at odds with a necessary epiphany. Because things are dire, many people have become hesitant to spend money on trifles. And in the process they began to realize that it's all trifles.

Here I go, stating the obvious: stuff does not bring salvation. But if it's so obvious, how come for so long people have not realized it? The happiest families I know aren't the ones with the most square footage, living in one of those cavernous houses with enough garage space to start a homeless shelter. (There's a holiday suggestion right there.) And of course they are not people who are in real want. Just because consumption is bankrupt doesn't mean that poverty is ennobling.

But somewhere in between there is a family like one I know in rural Pennsylvania, raising bees for honey (and for the science, and the fun, of it), digging a pond out of the downhill flow of the stream, with three kids who somehow, incredibly, don't spend six months of the year whining for the toy du jour. (The youngest once demurred when someone offered him another box on his birthday; "I already have a present," he said.) The mother of the household says hav-

2. Marc Jacobs (b. 1963) sells a widely distributed line of clothing and accessories.

3. Black Friday is the day after Thanksgiving, the beginning of the Christmas shopping season.

ing less means her family appreciates possessions more. "I can give you a story about every item, really," she says of what they own. In other words, what they have has meaning. And meaning, real meaning, is what we are always trying to possess. Ask people what they'd grab if their house were on fire, the way our national house is on fire right now. No one ever says it's the tricked-up microwave they got at Wal-Mart.

Questions

1. What does Quindlen gain from tying her essay so closely to the recession that began in 2008, the year her column appeared? What in it might soon appear dated and what will be enduring?

2. Does Quindlen talk enough about the stuff in her own life? How is she like the "us" she analyzes, and how might she be different?

3. Write an essay about the stuff in your life. You may take Quindlen's approach, condemning Americans as a nation of shallow "collectors," or try a completely different approach.

Molly Ivins

Get a Knife, Get a Dog, but Get Rid of Guns

GUNS. EVERYWHERE GUNS.

Let me start this discussion by pointing out that I am not antigun. I'm proknife. Consider the merits of the knife.

In the first place, you have to catch up with someone in order to stab him. A general substitution of knives for guns would promote physical fitness. We'd turn into a whole nation of great runners. Plus, knives don't ricochet. And people are seldom killed while cleaning their knives.

As a civil libertarian, I, of course, support the Second Amendment. And I believe it means exactly what it says:

A well-regulated militia being necessary to the security of a free state, the right of the people to keep and bear arms shall not be infringed. Fourteen-year-old boys are not part of a well-regulated militia. Members of wacky religious cults are not part of a well-regulated militia. Permitting unregulated citizens to have guns is destroying the security of this free state. 5

Written for Ivins's regular column in the Fort Worth Star-Telegraph *and collected in* Nothin' but Good Times Ahead *(1993). Ivins (1944–2007) was famous for her outspoken style, as suggested in the title of her book* Molly Ivins Can't Say That, Can She? *(1991).*

I am intrigued by the arguments of those who claim to follow the judicial doctrine of original intent. How do they know it was the dearest wish of Thomas Jefferson's heart that teenage drug dealers should cruise the cities of this nation perforating their fellow citizens with assault rifles? Channeling?

There is more hooey spread about the Second Amendment. It says quite clearly that guns are for those who form part of a well-regulated militia, that is, the armed forces, including the National Guard. The reasons for keeping them away from everyone else get clearer by the day.

The comparison most often used is that of the automobile, another lethal object that is regularly used to wreak great carnage. Obviously, this society is full of people who haven't enough common sense to use an automobile properly. But we haven't outlawed cars yet.

We do, however, license them and their owners, restrict their use to presumably sane and sober adults, and keep track of who sells them to whom. At a minimum, we should do the same with guns.

10 In truth, there is no rational argument for guns in this society. This is no longer a frontier nation in which people hunt their own food. It is a crowded, overwhelmingly urban country in which letting people have access to guns is a continuing disaster. Those who want guns—whether for target shooting, hunting, or potting rattlesnakes (get a hoe)—should be subject to the same restrictions placed on gun owners in England, a nation in which liberty has survived nicely without an armed populace.

The argument that "guns don't kill people" is patent nonsense. Anyone who has ever worked in a cop shop knows how many family arguments end in murder because there was a gun in the house. Did the gun kill someone? No. But if there had been no gun, no one would have died. At least not without a good foot race first. Guns do kill. Unlike cars, that is all they do.

Michael Crichton makes an interesting argument about technology in his thriller *Jurassic Park*.[1] He points out that power without discipline is making this society into a wreckage. By the time someone who studies the martial arts becomes a master—literally able to kill with bare hands—that person has also undergone years of training and discipline. But any fool can pick up a gun and kill with it.

"A well-regulated militia" surely implies both long training and long discipline. That is the least, the very least, that should be required of those who are permitted to have guns, because a gun is literally the power to kill. For years I used to enjoy taunting my gun-nut friends about their psychosexual hang-ups—always in a spirit of good cheer, you understand. But letting the noisy minority in the NRA[2] force us to allow this carnage to continue is just plain insane.

I do think gun nuts have a power hang-up. I don't know what is missing in their psyches that they need to feel they have the power to kill. But no sane society would allow this to continue.

1. The 1990 novel *Jurassic Park*, made into a movie in 1994.
2. National Rifle Association.

Ban the damn things. Ban them all. 15
You want protection? Get a dog.

Questions

1. What do you think of Ivins's examination of the Constitution? What kind of evidence would convince you even more? Why doesn't Ivins provide more evidence?

2. Characterize Ivins's language. What words, phrases, or structures seem typical of her style?

3. Examine the analogy between guns and cars. How does it hold up? Where does it break down?

Jo-Ann Pilardi

Immigration Problem Is About Us, Not Them

The immigration debates always focus on small brown bodies jumping fences and scooting through the brush of our Southwestern states (land that was Mexico about 150 years ago).

Our self-righteous anger at those brown bodies is fueled by our narrow use of the word "illegal"—a term reserved only for those immigrant workers. Yet aren't there other "illegals" hiding in the American underbrush, and isn't it time to add to the American immigration lexicon a new term?

But where are those other "illegals"—the illegal employers of the illegal workers? Let's call them "illegal native employers." These INEs run the gamut from executives of hotel chains to presidents of agribusiness corporations in California, from nanny-employing parents to restaurant owners, from contractors to employment agencies. And let's not forget the INEs who own huge chicken-processing plants.

Where are the TV news videotapes of those illegals? Let's film them as they leave their homes and arrive at their corporate headquarters, their law offices, their retail establishments, their hotels, their construction sites. Do we dare humiliate them with our cameras—and call them felons?

I'd like to see the Minutemen set up a chapter far from the Arizona border and patrol Wall Street, binoculars in hand, to set their sights on those "illegals"—brokers selling stocks for INE companies. 5

Published as an op-ed in the Baltimore Sun *on June 7, 2006. Like many op-eds, this piece was not written by a professional journalist on the staff of the newspaper, but contributed by one of its readers, a professor of philosophy and women's studies at a nearby university.*

Let's build fences outside the INE businesses, to separate and stigmatize them. Maybe the National Guard should patrol those fences. Not to worry, though, because President Bush assures us the troops will not be "militarized." (The word is still out, though, on whether there will be bullets in their guns.)

No doubt, these suggestions make us squirm. Maybe that's because many of these "illegals" are us, or our friends or relatives. If 12 million undocumented workers are employed here, thousands of employers must be signing their paychecks.

If 12 million undocumented workers toil in this country as construction workers, gardeners, housekeepers, nannies, agricultural workers, food processers, then thousands of business owners, homeowners, politicians and government officials condone or welcome their work—and look the other way at their illegal status.

Many of our political leaders talk a hard line about "immigration reform" even though they know our country is mired in its demand for the immigrant work force. We use and exploit the labor of these millions every day. In doing so, we also weaken the wages, benefits and organizing power of all our workers.

10 The Senate voted 62-36 to approve its version of an immigration bill, with most GOP senators opposing it. A battle with the more conservative House over its more vicious bill begins shortly. Evidently, the Senate version includes most of the so-called Ag Jobs bill, which has languished for years under the Bush administration and which has been supported in the past by the United Farm Workers.

Immigrants in the United States for two to five years would be put into a "temporary-worker" program; those here longer would be eligible for citizenship after an 11-year probationary period, with other criteria also to be met.

Conservatives describe the bill as "amnesty" for undocumented workers. So, once again, virtually all of the media attention centers on the workers, not the employers.

This is not the first time, nor will it be the last, that workers have come across the southern border in great numbers to make a living and to contribute to the U.S. economy. We need to create a fair immigration program for those who want to stay, not one that separates them by creating a national caste system of "guest workers." Europeans have learned the hard way that guest-worker programs lead to further national divisions and to virulent racism.

But whatever we do, we should stop thinking the problem is just about "securing our borders"—from them. The immigration problem is fundamentally a demand for cheap labor—for a supply to fill our demand.

15 Noting the problems that arose from Germany's guest-worker program, which imported masses of Turkish and southern European workers, the writer Max Frisch[1] observed, "Labor was called, but it was people who came." This—the moral, economic and political problem—is not the immigrants' problem; it's ours. I hope we have the courage to solve it humanely.

1. Swiss novelist (1911–1991) who often wrote about questions of personal identity.

Questions

1. What do you think the reaction would be if people did as Pilardi says and started hounding employers, the ones she terms INEs?

2. Who benefits from illegal immigration? Who loses?

3. What does Pilardi have against the idea of "guest workers"? Why doesn't she think that solution would work? What do you think?

Thomas Friedman *America's Real Dream Team*[1]

Went to a big Washington dinner last week. You know the kind: Large hall; black ties; long dresses. But this was no ordinary dinner. There were 40 guests of honor. So here's my Sunday news quiz: I'll give you the names of most of the honorees, and you tell me what dinner I was at. Ready?

Linda Zhou, Alice Wei Zhao, Lori Ying, Angela Yu-Yun Yeung, Lynnelle Lin Ye, Kevin Young Xu, Benjamin Chang Sun, Jane Yoonhae Suh, Katheryn Cheng Shi, Sunanda Sharma, Sarine Gayaneh Shahmirian, Arjun Ranganath Puranik, Raman Venkat Nelakant, Akhil Mathew, Paul Masih Das, David Chienyun Liu, Elisa Bisi Lin, Yifan Li, Lanair Amaad Lett, Ruoyi Jiang, Otana Agape Jakpor, Peter Danming Hu, Yale Wang Fan, Yuval Yaacov Calev, Levent Alpoge, John Vincenzo Capodilupo and Namrata Anand.

No, sorry, it was not a dinner of the China-India Friendship League. Give up?

O.K. All these kids are American high school students. They were the majority of the 40 finalists in the 2010 Intel Science Talent Search, which, through a national contest, identifies and honors the top math and science high school students in America, based on their solutions to scientific problems. The awards dinner was Tuesday, and, as you can see from the above list, most finalists hailed from immigrant families, largely from Asia.

Indeed, if you need any more convincing about the virtues of immigration, just come to the Intel science finals. I am a pro-immigration fanatic. I think keeping a constant flow of legal immigrants into our country—whether they wear blue collars or lab coats—is the key to keeping us ahead of China. Because when you mix all of these energetic, high-aspiring people with a democratic system and free markets, magic happens. If we hope to keep that magic, we need immigration reform that guarantees that we will always attract and 5

First appeared on March 21, 2010, in the New York Times, *where Friedman is a regular columnist specializing in international affairs, particularly in the Middle East.*

1. "Dream Team" is a reference to the U.S. basketball team assembled for the 1992 Olympics that contained Magic Johnson, Larry Bird, and Michael Jordan. Now it can mean any assemblage of superb players, in or out of a sport.

retain, in an orderly fashion, the world's first-round aspirational and intellectual draft choices.

This isn't complicated. In today's wired world, the most important economic competition is no longer between countries or companies. The most important economic competition is actually between you and your own imagination. Because what your kids imagine, they can now act on farther, faster, cheaper than ever before—as individuals. Today, just about everything is becoming a commodity, except imagination, except the ability to spark new ideas.

If I just have the spark of an idea now, I can get a designer in Taiwan to design it. I can get a factory in China to produce a prototype. I can get a factory in Vietnam to mass manufacture it. I can use Amazon.com to handle fulfillment. I can use freelancer.com to find someone to do my logo and manage my backroom. And I can do all this at incredibly low prices. The one thing that is not a commodity and never will be is that spark of an idea. And this Intel dinner was all about our best sparklers.

Before the dinner started, each contestant stood by a storyboard explaining their specific project. Namrata Anand, a 17-year-old from the Harker School in California, patiently explained to me her research, which used spectral analysis and other data to expose information about the chemical enrichment history of "Andromeda Galaxy." I did not understand a word she said, but I sure caught the gleam in her eye.

My favorite chat, though, was with Amanda Alonzo, a 30-year-old biology teacher at Lynbrook High School in San Jose, Calif. She had taught two of the finalists. When I asked her the secret, she said it was the resources provided by her school, extremely "supportive parents" and a grant from Intel that let her spend part of each day inspiring and preparing students to enter this contest. Then she told me this: Local San Jose realtors are running ads in newspapers in China and India telling potential immigrants to "buy a home" in her Lynbrook school district because it produced "two Intel science winners."

10

Seriously, ESPN or MTV should broadcast the Intel finals live. All of the 40 finalists are introduced, with little stories about their lives and aspirations. Then the winners of the nine best projects are announced. And finally, with great drama, the overall winner of the $100,000 award for the best project of the 40 is identified. This year it was Erika Alden DeBenedictis of New Mexico for developing a software navigation system that would enable spacecraft to more efficiently "travel through the solar system." After her name was called, she was swarmed by her fellow competitor-geeks.

Gotta say, it was the most inspiring evening I've had in D.C. in 20 years. It left me thinking, "If we can just get a few things right—immigration, education standards, bandwidth, fiscal policy—maybe we'll be O.K." It left me feeling that maybe Alice Wei Zhao of North High School in Sheboygan, Wis., chosen by her fellow finalists to be their spokeswoman, was right when she told the audience: "Don't sweat about the problems our generation will have to deal with. Believe me, our future is in good hands."

As long as we don't shut our doors.

Questions

1. Does Friedman's sports metaphor in the title have resonance throughout the essay? Where else do you see signs of it? What is his version of a "real" Dream Team?

2. Friedman assumes there is a worldwide competition. What are some signs of this competition that you have noticed, besides those in Friedman's essay?

3. How would you characterize Friedman's tone? What are some of its markers? Why do you think he chose to write his op-ed in such a manner?

4. Precisely what kind of immigration is Friedman writing about? Does the presence of bright children of immigrants speak to the larger issues of immigration? Why or why not?

Brent Staples

Why Colleges Shower Their Students with A's

The economist Milton Friedman taught that superior products flourished and shabby ones died out when consumers voted emphatically with their dollars. But the truth of the marketplace is that shabby products can do just fine if they sustain the veneer of quality while slipping downhill, as has much of higher education. Faced with demanding consumers and stiff competition, colleges have simply issued more and more A's, stoking grade inflation and devaluing degrees.

Grade inflation is in full gallop at every level, from struggling community institutions to the elites of the Ivy League. In some cases, campuswide averages have crept up from a C just 10 years ago to B-plus today.

Some departments shower students with A's to fill poorly attended courses that might otherwise be canceled. Individual professors inflate grades after consumer-conscious administrators hound them into it. Professors at every level inflate to escape negative evaluations by students, whose opinions now figure in tenure and promotion decisions.

The most vulnerable teachers are the part-timers who have no job security and who now teach more than half of all college courses. Writing in the last issue of the journal *Academe*, two part-timers suggest that students routinely corner adjuncts, threatening to complain if they do not turn C's into A's. An Ivy League professor said recently that if tenure disappeared, universities would be "free to sell diplomas outright."

5 The consumer appetite for less rigorous education is nowhere more evident than in the University of Phoenix, a profit-making school that shuns traditional scholarship and offers a curriculum so superficial that critics compare

Published on the op-ed page of the New York Times *(March 8, 1998).*

it to a drive-through restaurant. Two hundred colleges have closed since a businessman dreamed up Phoenix 20 years ago. Meanwhile, the university has expanded to 60 sites spread around the country, and more than 40,000 students, making it the country's largest private university.

Phoenix competes directly with the big state universities and lesser-known small colleges, all of which fear a student drain. But the elite schools fear each other and their customers, the students, who are becoming increasingly restive about the cost of a first-tier diploma, which now exceeds $120,000. Faced with the prospect of crushing debt, students are treating grades as a matter of life and death—occasionally even suing to have grades revised upward.

Twenty years ago students grumbled, then lived with the grades they were given. Today, colleges of every stature permit them to appeal low grades through deans or permanent boards of inquiry. In *The Chronicle of Higher Education*, Prof. Paul Korshin of the University of Pennsylvania recently described his grievance panel as the "rhinoplasty committee," because it does "cosmetic surgery" on up to 500 transcripts a year.

The argument that grades are rising because students are better prepared is simply not convincing. The evidence suggests that students and parents are demanding—and getting—what they think of as their money's worth.

One way to stanch inflation is to change the way the grade point average is calculated. Under most formulas, all courses are given equal weight, so math, science and less-challenging courses have equal impact on the averages. This arrangement rewards students who gravitate to courses where high marks are generously given and punishes those who seek out math and science courses, where far fewer students get the top grade.

10 Valen Johnson, a Duke University statistics professor, came under heavy fire from both students and faculty when he proposed recalculating the grade point average to give rigorously graded courses greater weight. The student government beat back the plan with the help of teachers in the humanities, who worried that students might abandon them for other courses that they currently avoided. Other universities have expressed interest in adopting the Johnson plan, but want their names kept secret to avoid a backlash.

Addicted to counterfeit excellence, colleges, parents and students are unlikely to give it up. As a consequence, diplomas will become weaker and more ornamental as the years go by.

QUESTIONS

1. What is the grade situation on your campus? Have you been showered with A's recently? Have you noticed professors inflating grades?

2. Staples writes, "An Ivy League professor said recently that if tenure disappeared, universities would be 'free to sell diplomas outright'" (paragraph 4). Analyze this statement. What are its implications? Why does the professor think tenured faculty serve as protection against the "selling" of diplomas? What level of confidence does this professor have in the administration?

3. A Duke University statistics professor proposed "recalculating the grade point average to give rigorously graded courses greater weight" (paragraph 10). He was opposed by humanities professors. What might have been the source of their opposition? What do you think is meant by "rigorously graded"? What is the situation on your campus: do math profs grade more "rigorously" than English profs? Who are the hardest graders?

4. How broad is Staples's range of examples? Would he need to adjust his position if he considered other colleges? Write an analysis of the situation at your college either to confirm or to contest Staples's argument.

Barbara Ehrenreich *Guys Just Want to Have Fun*

When I was in college, I followed a simple strategy: Go where the boys are. Sure, that led me into many settings where inebriants flowed, but my reasoning was strictly practical. Men ruled the world, as anyone could see, so the trick was to do as they did. No girlie major like art history or French lit for me. I started in chemistry and then proceeded up the gender gradient to physics, finally achieving in Classical Mechanics the exalted status of only girl in the class.

But that was an era when the cool kids smoked Gauloises[1] and argued about Kierkegaard and Trotsky.[2] Today, as two recent reports have revealed, it's the girls who achieve and the boys who coast along on gut courses congenial to hangovers. Boys are less likely to go to college in the first place (only 45% of college students under 25 are male) and are less likely to graduate as well. If I tried to follow my original strategy now, I would probably end up with an M.A. in Madden, the football video game, and a postgraduate stay in rehab.

The trend has occasioned some predictions of a coming matriarchy in which high-achieving women will rule over a nation of slacker guys. We've all seen the movie, an endless loop culminating most recently in *You, Me and Dupree.*[3] That little girls' T shirt slogan—GIRLS RULE, BOYS DROOL—is beginning to look less like a slur and more like an empirical observation.

But it may be that the boys still know what they're doing. Among other things that have changed since the '60s is the corporate culture, which once valued literacy, numeracy, high GPAs and the ability to construct a simple

Published in Time *magazine (July 23, 2006) and later on Ehrenreich's blog, ehrenreich .blogs.com. Like many of her writings, including the books* Bait and Switch *and* Nickeled and Dimed, *it has a light tone but a serious purpose.*

1. Strong French cigarettes.

2. Kierkegaard: Danish philosopher (1813–1855), a precursor of existentialism; Trotsky: Russian revolutionary (1879–1940), Lenin's top assistant, assassinated at Stalin's command.

3. A 2006 film comedy starring Kate Hudson, Matt Dillon, Seth Rogen, Owen Wilson, and Michael Douglas.

sentence. No doubt there are still workplaces where such achievements are valued, but when I set out as an undercover journalist seeking a white-collar corporate job for my book *Bait and Switch*, I was shocked to find the emphasis entirely on such elusive qualities as "personality," "attitude" and "likability." Play down the smarts, the career coaches and self-help books advised, cull the experience and exude a "positive attitude."

5 In a June article on corporate personality testing, the *Washington Post* reported on a woman who passed the skills test for a customer-care job but wasn't hired because she failed the personality test. Those tests, including the ubiquitous Myers-Briggs test,[4] have no scientific credibility or predictive value, as Annie Murphy Paul showed in her 2004 book, *Cult of Personality*. You can have one Myers-Briggs personality on Tuesday and another when you retake the test on Thursday. Their chief function, as far as I could tell when I took them, was to weed out the introverts. When asked whether you'd rather be the life of the party or curl up with a book, the correct answer is always "Party!"

So the best preparation for that all-important personality test may well be a college career spent playing poker and doing tequila shots. An Atlanta woman I interviewed, a skilled website writer, was fired without explanation after a few weeks at a job. "I tried to fit in," she told me. "I went to lunch with the guys, but all they talked about was sports, which I know nothing about, and they all seemed to know each other from college." Poor thing, she had probably wasted her college years in the library.

The business world isn't totally hostile to higher education—an M.B.A. still counts for something. But as G.J. Meyer wrote in his classic 1995 book, *Executive Blues: Down and Out in Corporate America*, a higher degree in something other than business or law—or, worse, a stint of college teaching—can impart a deadly "academic stench" to one's résumé. And what are we to make of the growing corporate defiance of elementary grammar? At a job fair I attended, AT&T Wireless solicited sales reps with the question, if it was a question, "Are you ready to put your skills to work. Like the way you're a quick study. How you're good at finding solutions." Take that, you irritating, irrelevant English 101 professors!

Maybe we need a return to gender-segregated higher education, with the academic equivalent of Pinocchio's Pleasure Island for boys, where they can hone their "people skills" at keg parties. But we will need those high-achieving girls more than ever. Someone, after all, is going to have to figure out how to make an economy run by superannuated slacker boys competitive again in a world filled with Chinese and Indian brainiacs. I'd still major in physics if I were doing it again, just because there ought to be at least a few Americans, of whatever gender, who know something beyond the technology of beer bongs.

4. A widely used test of personality types.

QUESTIONS

1. Ehrenreich claims that the guys may be onto something: corporate culture now tends to value "personality," "attitude," and "likability." But aren't these traits commonly associated with women? What do you think has happened?

2. Precisely what's wrong with the AT&T quotation in paragraph 7? Do you think AT&T's error was intentional, an oversight, or just ignorance?

3. Do Ehrenreich's observations about sex roles among college students agree with your own observations? Write about your observations in an essay that might be humorous, as Ehrenreich's piece is, or serious.

DAVID BROOKS

The Gender Gap at School

THERE ARE THREE gender-segregated sections in any airport: the restrooms, the security pat-down area and the bookstore. In the men's sections of the bookstore, there are books describing masterly men conquering evil. In the women's sections there are novels about, well, I guess feelings and stuff.

The same separation occurs in the home. Researchers in Britain asked 400 accomplished women and 500 accomplished men to name their favorite novels. The men preferred novels written by men, often revolving around loneliness and alienation. Camus's *The Stranger*, Salinger's *Catcher in the Rye* and Vonnegut's *Slaughterhouse-Five* topped the male list.

The women leaned toward books written by women. The women's books described relationships and are a lot better than the books the men chose. The top six women's books were *Jane Eyre*, *Wuthering Heights*, *The Handmaid's Tale*, *Middlemarch*, *Pride and Prejudice* and *Beloved*.

There are a couple of reasons why the two lists might diverge so starkly. It could be men are insensitive dolts who don't appreciate subtle human connections and good literature. Or, it could be that the part of the brain where men experience negative emotion, the amygdala,[1] is not well connected to the part of the brain where verbal processing happens, whereas the part of the brain where women experience negative emotion, the cerebral cortex,[2] is well connected. It could be that women are better at processing emotion through words.

5 Over the past two decades, there has been a steady accumulation of evidence that male and female brains work differently. Women use both sides of their brain more symmetrically than men. Men and women hear and smell differently (women are much more sensitive). Boys and girls process colors

Published on June 11, 2006, in the New York Times, *where Brooks writes a regular op-ed column.*

1. The portion of the brain that controls emotions and memory.
2. The part of the brain that controls awareness, language, and consciousness.

differently (young girls enjoy an array of red, green and orange crayons whereas young boys generally stick to black, gray and blue). Men and women experience risk differently (men enjoy it more).

It could be, in short, that biological factors influence reading tastes, even after accounting for culture. Women who have congenital adrenal hyperplasia,[3] which leads to high male hormone secretions, are more likely to choose violent stories than other women.

This wouldn't be a problem if we all understood these biological factors and if teachers devised different curriculums to instill an equal love of reading in both boys and girls.

The problem is that even after the recent flurry of attention about why boys are falling behind, there is still intense social pressure not to talk about biological differences between boys and girls (ask Larry Summers).[4] There is still resistance, especially in the educational world, to the findings of brain researchers. Despite some innovations here and there, in most classrooms boys and girls are taught the same books in the same ways.

Young boys are compelled to sit still in schools that have sacrificed recess for test prep. Many are told in a thousand subtle ways they are not really good students. They are sent home with these new-wave young adult problem novels, which all seem to be about introspectively morose young women whose parents are either suicidal drug addicts or fatally ill manic depressives.

10 It shouldn't be any surprise that according to a National Endowment for the Arts study, the percentage of young men who read has plummeted over the past 14 years. Reading rates are falling three times as fast among young men as among young women. Nor should it be a surprise that men are drifting away from occupations that involve reading and school. Men now make up a smaller share of teachers than at any time in the past 40 years.

Dr. Leonard Sax,[5] whose book *Why Gender Matters* is a lucid guide to male and female brain differences, emphasizes that men and women can excel at any subject. They just have to be taught in different ways. Sax is a big believer in single-sex schools, which he says allow kids to open up and break free from gender stereotypes. But for most kids it would be a start if they were assigned books they might actually care about. For boys, that probably means more Hemingway, Tolstoy, Homer and Twain.

During the 1970's, it was believed that gender is a social construct and that gender differences could be eliminated via consciousness-raising. But it turns out gender is not a social construct. Consciousness-raising doesn't turn boys into sensitively poetic pacifists. It just turns many of them into high school and college dropouts who hate reading.

3. A genetic defect of the adrenal glands. A person with adrenal hyperplasia cannot produce several vital hormones known as corticosteroids, which are significant in sex identification.

4. President of Harvard, 2001–06, who resigned after making controversial remarks about women's biological fitness to pursue careers in science.

5. A Maryland family physician and psychologist who wrote *Why Gender Matters* and *Boys Adrift: What's Really behind the Growing Epidemic of Unmotivated Boys?*

QUESTIONS

1. Does your experience bear out Brooks's claim that boys and girls read differently? Use some examples from people you know.

2. Examine the evidence that Brooks marshals for his claim that girls' and boys' brains are different. Do you think Brooks produces enough evidence to support his claim? Do you know of evidence that he omits?

3. Do a brief survey of favorite books of males and females, and see if it bears out Brooks's claim. Write up your findings in a brief report or counterargument.

BINGE DRINKING

The three op-ed pieces that follow all deal with binge drinking by contemporary college students. Drinking too much is not, of course, a recent phenomenon. We know from diaries, letters, and memoirs that many young people in the eighteenth and nineteenth centuries drank too much, whether after work in a pub or tavern, during their school days in a university room, or when out for an occasional night on the town. We also know that overdrinking in those centuries was railed against (in moral treatises), lamented (in sermons and lectures), and satirized (as in William Hogarth's famous print depicting a drunken "Idle Apprentice" or in George Cruikshank's "Gin Lane").

Why, then, has binge drinking—a recently defined term—become a matter of such serious concern in the public press and in educational journals and newsletters? You may want to propose answers in class discussion, but surely one cause lies in the research of medical scientists at the Harvard School of Public Health who, in the early 1990s, identified and studied the problem, then published their findings in scholarly journals, including the prestigious Journal of the American Medical Association (JAMA).

We have included one example of this medical research in the section "Science and Technology": the article "Health and Behavioral Consequences of Binge Drinking in College: A National Survey of Students at 140 Campuses" (p. 924). For this op-ed section, however, we have chosen the scientists' expression of personal concern, written for the educational journal the Chronicle of Higher Education, *which devotes its final page to opinion pieces submitted by members of the academic community. Also included in this section are two very different responses to the research, one from the* New York Times Magazine, *another from the* Chronicle of Higher Education, *both drawing on personal experience but reaching quite different conclusions.*

The debate over binge drinking is ongoing today. Consult the Harvard School of Public Health Web site (www.hsph.harvard.edu/cas) for the latest research—or look in your own local newspaper or alumni magazine for the latest exchange.

HENRY WECHSLER, CHARLES DEUTSCH, AND GEORGE DOWDALL

Too Many Colleges Are Still in Denial about Alcohol Abuse

Colleges have a serious problem with alcohol abuse among students, and it's not getting any better. In 1989, a survey by the Carnegie Foundation for the Advancement of Teaching found that college presidents viewed alcohol abuse as their top campus-life problem. The recent national surveys of college students' drinking that we conducted for Harvard University's School of Public Health documented that alcohol abuse is still rife. Perhaps the second-largest problem in campus life is that many colleges are still in denial, just as many family members who live with alcohol abusers are.

To be sure, on some campuses officials are making great efforts to reduce alcohol abuse. At others, however, they seem oblivious to the magnitude and effects of the abuse. Those in denial act as if they believe that this deep-seated American problem can be changed by someone, able and dedicated, working part time in a basement office at the student-health service.

Alcohol abuse is a common, not a marginal, activity at most colleges, and we only fool ourselves if we expect marginal efforts to reduce it. If we really want to deal with the problem, administrators, faculty members, students, and parents must first gain a better understanding of how excessive drinking is affecting the academic and social climate of their institutions. Second, they must believe there are promising, practical strategies they can adopt that will improve the situation. Finally, they must be prepared to contend with the skepticism and resistance bound to be aroused by actions designed to curb the abuse.

We should stress that our concern is with students' alcohol *abuse*—the drinking of amounts large enough to create problems for the drinker or for others around him or her. The crux of the problem is the *behavior* of the drinker, not the quantity of alcohol consumed. When people do dangerous or obnoxious things when they drink, that's alcohol abuse. Unfortunately, behavior that anywhere else would be classified as alcohol abuse now is not only acceptable but actually the norm on many campuses, in spite of excessive drinking's documented role in automobile crashes, violence, suicide, and high-risk sexual behavior.

5 Certainly, excessive drinking is not a new problem, on campus or in the society the campus reflects. A local sheriff still leads Harvard University's graduation procession, a tradition that began in Colonial days, not for a ceremonial purpose but to control drunk and rowdy celebrants. Generations of college alumni have wistfully recalled the boozy high jinks of their student days, filtering out memories of illness, insane risk, unwanted consequences, and friends who never made it out of the hole they had dug for themselves.

Written for the Chronicle of Higher Education *(April 14, 1995) and based on the research of the authors in the Harvard School of Public Health. For an overview of the extensive findings of these scientists and the implications of their research for college campuses, see the book, coauthored by Wechsler and Bernice Wuethrich,* Dying to Drink: Confronting Binge Drinking on College Campuses *(2002); for a scientific version of the research, see Wechsler et al., "Health and Behavioral Consequences of Binge Drinking," included in "Science and Technology," p. 924.*

Some alumni no doubt think their children and grandchildren deserve the same "good times." The problem is that, because of lethal sexually transmitted diseases, the easy availability of weapons, and roads filled with high-speed automobiles, the consequences of alcohol abuse are much more deadly today.

Binge drinking—defined as the heavy, episodic use of alcohol—has persisted on campuses despite both a general decrease in alcohol consumption among Americans and an increase in the number of abstainers. Some people (including the author of a recent front-page article in *The New York Times*) have assumed that the latter two trends have translated into more-moderate drinking on the campuses. Nothing could be further from the truth.

Our recent research, which received support from the Robert Wood Johnson Foundation, was the only large-scale study to date of the extent and consequences of binge drinking at a representative sample of American colleges and universities. Our detailed findings from surveys of 17,592 students at 140 randomly selected four-year colleges were published in the December 7, 1994, issue of the *Journal of the American Medical Association*.

For men, our study used the generally accepted criterion for binge drinking: the consumption of five or more drinks in a row at least once in the previous two weeks. We reduced the number of drinks to four in a row for women, to take into account our findings that for the average college woman four drinks produce the same level of alcohol-related problems as do five drinks for the average college man.

10 Our study found that 44 per cent of all students in the sample were binge drinkers—50 per cent of the men and 39 per cent of the women. Although our 1993 study was the only one to survey a representative sample of colleges, the findings were very similar to those of two other national surveys conducted at about the same time. A study done in 1993 by the Institute for Social Research of the University of Michigan found that 40 per cent of the college students surveyed were binge drinkers. And a similar study, conducted from 1990 to 1992 by the Core Institute at Southern Illinois University, also put the figure at 40 per cent. Had our study used a five-drink standard for women, as the other two studies did, 41 per cent of the students surveyed would have been classified as binge drinkers. The agreement among these three independent national studies is remarkable.

Certainly, not all students who have ever binged have an alcohol problem, but colleges with large numbers of binge drinkers *do*. The proportion of binge drinkers among students varied considerably among the 140 colleges in our study—from as low as 1 per cent to as high as 70 per cent. At 44 colleges, more than half of the students responding to the survey were binge drinkers. This variation contradicts the belief that among college students we will find a fairly constant and intractable proportion who will drink to excess. It suggests, instead, that colleges create or perpetuate their own drinking cultures through their selection of students, traditions, policies, and other practices.

Not surprisingly, our study shows a strong relationship between the frequency of binge drinking and alcohol-related problems. Nineteen per cent of all students qualify as frequent binge drinkers—those who binge more than once a week. They were found to be from seven to ten times as likely as non-binge drinkers to fail to use protection when having sex, to engage in unplanned sexual activity, to get into trouble with campus police, to damage property, or to suffer an injury. Half of the frequent binge drinkers reported experiencing five or more *different* alcohol-related problems. Yet very few of those students considered themselves to have an alcohol problem or even to be heavy drinkers.

Our findings break new ground in exploring the extent to which alcohol-related behavior obstructs the possibility of "building communities of civility and respect on campuses," to borrow the title of this year's annual convention of the American Council on Education. On campuses where more than half of the students were binge drinkers, the vast majority of the non-binge drinkers who lived on campus—fully 87 per cent—reported experiencing one or more problems as a result of others' binge drinking. They were the victims of what we call "second-hand binge effects." Such students were up to three times as likely as students on campuses where 35 per cent or fewer of students binge to report being pushed, hit, or assaulted, experiencing an unwanted sexual advance, or otherwise being bothered by the alcohol-related behavior of other students.

Colleges cannot claim to create a supportive learning environment when they tolerate such behavior. To fulfill their missions, colleges will have to reduce alcohol abuse markedly. How can this be done? Each college has its own level of binge drinking, traditions, and circumstances and thus must craft its own response to the problem. Still, our findings suggest strategies that could be effective.

15 Administrators must first decide where to focus their energies. They should realize that about 85 per cent of all college students drink (although they do not all binge) and that alcohol is easily available to students regardless of age. Thus programs at many colleges that seek to reduce drinking among all students are doomed to failure. Other programs try to inform binge drinkers about ways to avoid harmful consequences—for example, by designating a nondrinking friend to drive. But in a social system rife with alcohol abuse, whether a family or a campus, the least effective intervention point is the abuser.

Prevention cannot depend solely on the individual alcohol abuser's recognition of the problem and his or her willingness to accept help, nor can it depend on the cooperation of student organizations that are heavily involved in alcohol abuse. In fact, our study found that more than 80 per cent of the students residing in fraternities or sororities were binge drinkers. If a college or university really aspires to be a community of civility and respect, the principal goal of its prevention efforts must be to help students who are adversely affected by the binge drinking of others to assert their rights. These students deserve to learn that college life need not include cleaning up after a vomiting roommate; being awakened at 3 A.M. several nights a week by revelers; or being physically, verbally, or sexually assaulted.

Students, faculty and staff members, administrators, and trustees should establish and enforce explicit rules about what kinds of behavior will not be tolerated. And since binge drinking is a highly social activity, colleges must offer better ways to help students make friends, find romance, and keep busy. We found that the students who spent the most time studying, performing community service, or working were the least likely to be binge drinkers.

Furthermore, because half of the students who binge in college were binge drinkers in high school, colleges should use the admission process to influence the drinking culture on campus. They can do this by making clear in their promotional material and through the information that recruiters provide to high-school teachers and counselors that they will protect the right of all students to an educational environment free from alcohol abuse and abusive behavior.

College officials also need to work more closely with city officials and with local businesses that sell alcohol to eliminate the sales to minors and to discourage "half-price beer nights" and other practices that encourage drunkenness. For their part, athletics directors can have enormous influence on the drinking culture of a campus if they can be pressed to use it constructively with their athletes. Finally, residence-hall advisers and academic counselors can play a key role in preventing alcohol abuse by intervening quickly in incidents of public drunkenness that violate codes of conduct. But they need much better training and support from the administration than most of them now receive.

20 Before these or other constructive steps can be taken, campus authorities must stop denying the extent of the problem. Denial includes failing to recognize the impact and extensiveness of campus alcohol abuse and acting as if easy stratagems will produce change.

We recommend a weekend tour, beginning on Thursday night. As the night progresses, observe the campus and the clubs on its outskirts. Drop in on the health services, the fraternity houses, and the dorms in the early morning hours. Take a late-night ride with a security guard. Check out class attendance on Friday.

On Saturday, repeat the process. And later station yourself outside sorority houses and residence halls on Sunday morning and witness "the walk of shame"—a phrase students use to describe women's returning from a night's unplanned, and often unprotected, sex. Ask students to describe drinking behavior. Above all, fight the temptation to think of the alcohol abuse you see as merely the problem of "troubled" individuals. When the faces change but the numbers don't, something much more powerful and institutional is happening.

Don't expect change to be easy. Opponents of significant change will cite longstanding traditions, the need not to scare students away in a highly competitive marketplace, the damage to the institution's image of publicly acknowledging an alcohol problem, the real or imagined vulnerability of the institution to legal action, the displeasure of local merchants who depend on student drinking, and opposition from campus newspapers that depend on advertisements from those businesses.

But if you want change, acknowledge the existence of alcohol abuse and the challenge it poses to the college's mission. Commit resources from all parts of the institution, with visible support from the president, to coordinated, long-term actions. Make your intentions clear, not just in speeches but also in the budget. And expect change to be gradual. Remember, not so long ago we resigned ourselves to smoke-filled offices and thought little could be done to stop drunk driving.

QUESTIONS

1. This article, written for college administrators, is a heavily revised version of a scientific study (see the authors' research article in "Science and Technology," p. 925). Note the changes you see between the original study and this version. Are there changes in style? In audience? In format? In details? Which changes matter most to the overall impact of the essays?

2. What does the term "in denial" mean? Where does it come from? Do authorities on your campus act as if they are "in denial" about alcohol abuse?

3. Take the "weekend tour" the authors recommend on your own campus or a campus you know. Write up your results as a newspaper article.

JACK HITT *The Battle of the Binge*

Back in the 70's—my college time—an English professor I barely knew named Ted Stirling spotted me on the quad and invited me to a small, informal reading after supper. Maybe he felt sorry for me. I had marooned myself in the French ghetto of *la littérature comparative*, and had further exiled myself in the cul-de-sac between Latin and Spanish. So I went that night to sit on stuffed sofas beneath scowling bishops in gilt frames and to discuss Wallace Stevens's poem "Thirteen Ways of Looking at a Blackbird." Afterward, Stirling bought the students a pitcher of beer at the pub, and we strained to act intelligently and comfortably while drinking with an elder. ("Stevens an insurance agent! Surely you jest, Professor. Why, that would make poets the unacknowledged underwriters of the world, wouldn't you agree?")

I started thinking about how I learned to drink at college—I went to Sewanee, in Tennessee—when I read about a recent Harvard study that found that 43 percent, nearly half, of all college students today "binge drink," defined as regularly pounding down four or five stiff ones in a row in order to get blasted. The pandemic is so severe that 113 college presidents united a few weeks ago to publicly admit that a generation is in peril. They have also rolled out a public-service ad, which employs that brand of sarcasm Madison Avenue thinks young people find amusing. "Binge Beer," it says. "Who says falling off a balcony is such a bad thing?" See, you're supposed to realize that falling off a balcony is, in fact, a bad thing.

Published in the New York Times Magazine *(October 24, 1999) in the section titled "The Way We Live Now."*

Other educational tactics include dry rock concerts, abstinent fraternities, "mock 'tail" parties, a Web site of course (www.nasulgc.org/bingedrink) and a new CD-ROM called "Alcohol 101" and featuring a "virtual party" that segues into an anatomical lecture about how quickly the bloodstream absorbs alcohol. Look out, Myst.

What no one seems to have noticed is that the rise in binging has occurred at the very same time that the legal drinking age has been raised everywhere to 21. If you're 18 to 21, it's the 1920's again and a mini-Prohibition is in full swing. As a result, moderate drinking has almost vanished among students and, more tellingly, from school-sponsored events. How anachronistic it feels to describe what used to be routine college functions, like a Dizzy Gillespie concert or a Robert Penn Warren reading, followed by a reception, with drinks and hors d'oeuvres, at which students were expected to at least pretend to be cool about it, i.e., practice drinking. I frequently received dinner invitations from faculty members like Tom Spaccarelli, a Spanish professor who served up tapas while uncorking a Rioja for a few students. We handled the long stems of our wineglasses as confidently as a colt its legs.

5 And there was always another occasion. Sewanee had dozens of those inane college societies like Green Ribbon, a group whose invitation to membership I haughtily trashed after Professor Paschall, my sponsor, explained that the point was nothing more than "getting dressed up and having cocktails with some alumni."

But I began to see the point about 10 years after graduation when I returned to Sewanee to give a little talk. Afterward, I took some students to the pub where they sheepishly ordered cider. At first, I thought this new college life—clean and sober—was a good idea. Then my nephew, a junior there at that time, explained the typical partygoer's schedule: drive off campus or hide in the woods (often alone), guzzle a pint of bourbon, eat a box of breath mints and then stumble into the dry sorority party serenely blotto. My nephew knew two students who had died—falling off a cliff, blood poisoning—and five others who had been paralyzed or seriously injured in car accidents because of binging. For a college with roughly 1,300 students, this constitutes a statistical massacre.

We drank wildly in the 70's, too. The Phi's had their seasonal Screaming Bull blowout. Kegs were easy to find on weekends. I have drunk tequila only once in my life, and this being a family newspaper, my account of that evening can proceed no further. I was a member of the Sewanee Temperance League, whose annual outdoor party pledged to "rid the world of alcohol by consuming it all ourselves." But all those events were crowded social occasions, almost always with professors and their spouses in attendance—not prowling alone in the woods with a pint. After college, when you got a job, Screaming Bull opportunities quickly tapered off; the working world was different yet, in time, quite familiar, like an evening with Ted Stirling or a dinner at Tom Spaccarelli's.

This year, Ohio University's zero-tolerance program has proudly outlawed *empty* beer cans in the dorm. Nearly 7 percent of the entire 16,000-student enrollment last year was disciplined for alcohol abuse, often handed over as criminals to the Athens Municipal Court. Despite all the tough bluster, the binge rate among students there hasn't budged from an astounding 60 percent.

For college students, booze has been subsumed into the Manichaean battle of our drug war. It's either Prohibition or cave into the hippies' legalization schemes. And it seems fairly unreversible. Legislatures raised the drinking minimum in reaction to the raw emotion deployed by Mothers Against Drunk Driving. Then colleges were bullied by insurance companies that threatened to jack up liability rates if administrators didn't take aggressive action. The old days of looking the other way, when the police used to pick up toasted students and quietly drive them to their dorms, seems like collaboration in today's harsh light.

10 There probably is a way out of this, but it is going to require some larger cultural changes that will make us see the irony, even cruelty, of infantilizing certain young adults. The very people who have urged this situation into existence are too often the people who vent about the increasing lack of "responsibility" in our society (demanding, for example, that juvenile offenders be treated in court as adults). But for middle-class kids in college, they make responsibility an ever-receding ideal, never quite grasped in the pampered ease of an extended adolescence.

In the early 70's, the big political fight among college students was for the right to vote. The argument held that kids who were considered old enough to die for their country and order a drink in a bar should be able to choose their political leaders. It is back to two out of three again. But booze is not like the vote, which can be ignored to no one's immediate peril. Rather, alcohol consumption, like table manners or sexual behavior, is a socialized phenomenon, which if not taught, yields up a kind of wild child. By denying the obvious pleasure of drinking and not teaching it by example, is anyone really surprised that we've loosed upon the world a generation of feral drunks?

QUESTIONS

1. The research by Wechsler and his colleagues at the Harvard School of Public Health has provoked a national debate about the drinking habits of college students. To what extent does Jack Hitt engage the scientific research? To what extent does he agree with the public opinions expressed by Wechsler and his colleagues about actions that should be taken to stop binge drinking?

2. Is Hitt's op-ed focused more on the problem of binge drinking or on its solution? Does Hitt propose a solution?

3. Enter the public debate by writing your own op-ed on this topic, perhaps for your college or hometown newspaper. Consider your personal experience or other evidence you can add to public knowledge, and use it, as well as existing research, to make your argument.

Kenneth A. Bruffee *Binge Drinking as a Substitute for a "Community of Learning"*

The Harvard School of Public Health found in 1993 that binge drinking is widespread on American college campuses, particularly among members of fraternities and sororities. The school's most recent report documents the disturbing fact that binge drinking has not declined in the five years since that first study. Even though the proportion of students who declare themselves teetotalers is slightly larger, the effects of binge drinking continue to be widespread and severe. They range from poor grades to destruction of property, assault, drunk driving, and death (*The Chronicle*, September 18, 1998).

To stem the tide of binge drinking, colleges have tried closing fraternities and sororities, punishing heavy drinkers, enlisting the help of liquor-store owners, and banning alcohol on their campuses. So far, those efforts have largely failed. One reason may be that missing from most of them, and from most research on the subject, is an understanding of why first-year students join fraternities and sororities in the first place.

I know why I joined one, many more years ago than I care to mention. I arrived on that gracious, learned, sophisticated campus to find myself among people—professors, administrators, upperclassmen (yes, all were men in those days)—who were committed (it seemed to me) to making me feel just how green, scared, lonely, and small-town I was. They all seemed vexed that I wasn't already what they hoped I would become. Administrators told me how much I had to learn and how hard I had to work to learn it. Professors told me how little they valued what I already knew, and how trivial and misleading would be anything that I learned from anyone but themselves. I was an intrusive rube. I didn't belong.

Most of my fellow freshmen seemed committed to making me feel like a rube, too. Today I think I know why, though I certainly did not know it then. They were trying as hard as I was to conceal from everyone, including themselves, that they, too, were green, scared, lonely, and small-town.

I joined a fraternity because I wanted, desperately, to belong. 5

Fraternity members were the only people on the campus who seemed to know what it meant to feel like a rube, who knew the depth and overwhelming intensity of an 18-year-old's need to belong. They knew how to marshal and exploit that need, because they'd been there themselves not long before. Fraternities seemed to be the only place on the campus with a ready supply of friends for freshmen.

There were certainly no friends to be had where I thought I would achieve my most consequential goals as a college student—in my classes. I made no friends there until my last year in college, and then only by chance. Even

From the back page of the Chronicle of Higher Education *(February 9, 1999), which publishes opinion pieces by faculty members, students, and academic administrators.*

today, most college students make few friends through their classes until late in their college careers, if at all.

That's one reason college students become binge drinkers.

Such a claim may sound like some kind of bad joke, so I hasten to explain.

10 Most of the talk about binge drinking, the research into it, and the administrative attempts to curb it assume a sharp distinction between the "academic" and the "social" connections of college students with their peers. Students also make that distinction. If you ask a cross section of college students about their friends, some may say they occasionally talk with a few of them about their course work and (if they admit at all to such eccentricities) their intellectual and aesthetic interests. With the rest of their friends, they'll say, such topics seldom come up.

It's peculiar, when you think about it, that most American colleges do not help entering students make friends through their course work. Presumably, one goal of liberal education is to enrich life with the kind of conversation that comes with substantive friendship. And when colleges actively provide students with the opportunity to make friends through their classes, they eagerly grasp the chance.

A study of 183 students who entered Brooklyn College in the fall of 1987 and took courses that were organized into "learning communities"—in which the same group of students was registered for three courses together—showed that 73 per cent agreed with the statement that the experience "helps students make new friends more easily." The retention rate of the students studied was 73 per cent, compared with the college's normal average of 59 per cent.

Many students who do make it to their junior and senior years are likely to concede (if only in private) that most of their friendships then tend to merge social interests with academic and aesthetic interests—from pursuing genetic research to listening to Mozart concertos. By then, their sense of belonging is rooted in the academic major they have chosen and in the new interests they have developed in elective courses.

Of course, some freshmen arrive on the campus in the company of old high-school friends. But those students, too—most of them similarly green, scared, lonely 18-year-olds—feel the pressing need to belong to the new world they have entered. And they, too, are willing to belong on any terms, even terms that require them to continue to keep their curiosity and thought deeply buried.

15 Those are the terms of membership that fraternities and sororities offer. In return, these social clubs provide companionship that is predictable, reliable, aesthetically unimaginative, and intellectually unchallenging. So-called "wild parties" and the binge drinking that fuels them are misguided attempts to breathe life into stultifying conventionality.

In contrast, many traditional college classrooms—organized around lectures and class discussions—offer surprise, change, and intellectual stimulation. But their structure emphasizes individual mastery, self-sufficiency, and exclusion of outside distractions. While encouraging individual achievement, such courses often foster little substantive social interaction among students.

Colleges can do a great deal more than they generally do to make classrooms a source of social engagement around substantive issues. One approach is collaborative learning and related ways of organizing course work into learning communities, team projects, and peer tutoring.

Research can guide colleges in such efforts. We need to know whether collaborative learning actually does help students bring to the surface suppressed curiosity and thought, and, if so, how. Most of all, we need to know whether collaborative learning—especially, but not exclusively, during the first year of college—can give students opportunities to make friends in settings that are not merely social, vapid encounters, and, as a result, reduce the social desperation that drives students to binge drinking.

Granted, research is unlikely to show that collaborative learning is a universal solution to social problems at colleges. Research certainly will not demonstrate that collaborative learning alone can empty out fraternity and sorority houses.

But I am confident that research will show that collaborative learning can give entering college students a chance to experience a refreshingly new kind of social intimacy with their peers. It could help American colleges chip away at the problem of binge drinking, by helping to generate social cohesion, civil discourse, and, yes, even friendship among young people who arrive on campuses green, scared, lonely, and small-town. 20

Questions

1. To what extent does Kenneth Bruffee engage the scientific research about the drinking habits of college students? To what extent does he agree with the public opinions expressed by Wechsler and his colleagues about actions that should be taken to stop binge drinking?

2. Is Bruffee's op-ed focused more on the causes of binge drinking or on its solution? Does Bruffee propose a solution? How is a "community of learning" a solution?

3. Enter the public debate by writing your own op-ed on this topic, perhaps for your college or hometown newspaper. Consider your personal experience or other evidence you can add to public knowledge, and use it, as well as existing research, to make your argument.

Questions on Op-Eds and Public Arguments

1. What characteristics do the op-ed pieces in this section have in common? Consider technique, argument, and attitude.

2. Examine the five column-length op-ed pieces: those by Ivins, Staples, Quindlen, Friedman, and Ehrenreich. What features do they have in common? What kinds of arguments do they tend to make? How would you characterize their language? From your reading of these five, discuss the range available to the writer of a newspaper op-ed column.

3. Look for three essays in other sections of *The Norton Reader* that also fit into the category "op-ed." Do they have features similar to or different from those you identified in question 2?

EDUCATION

FREDERICK DOUGLASS *Learning to Read*

I LIVED IN Master Hugh's family about seven years.[1] During this time, I succeeded in learning to read and write. In accomplishing this, I was compelled to resort to various stratagems. I had no regular teacher. My mistress, who had kindly commenced to instruct me, had, in compliance with the advice and direction of her husband, not only ceased to instruct, but had set her face against my being instructed by any one else. It is due, however, to my mistress to say of her, that she did not adopt this course of treatment immediately. She at first lacked the depravity indispensable to shutting me up in mental darkness. It was at least necessary for her to have some training in the exercise of irresponsible power, to make her equal to the task of treating me as though I were a brute.

My mistress was, as I have said, a kind and tender-hearted woman; and in the simplicity of her soul she commenced, when I first went to live with her, to treat me as she supposed one human being ought to treat another. In entering upon the duties of a slaveholder, she did not seem to perceive that I sustained to her the relation of a mere chattel, and that for her to treat me as a human being was not only wrong, but dangerously so. Slavery proved as injurious to her as it did to me. When I went there, she was a pious, warm, and tender-hearted woman. There was no sorrow or suffering for which she had not a tear. She had bread for the hungry, clothes for the naked, and comfort for every mourner that came within her reach. Slavery soon proved its ability to divest her of these heavenly qualities. Under its influence, the tender heart became stone, and the lamblike disposition gave way to one of tigerlike fierceness. The first step in her downward course was in her ceasing to instruct me. She now commenced to practise her husband's precepts. She finally became even more violent in her opposition than her husband himself. She was not satisfied with simply doing as well as he had commanded; she seemed anxious to do better. Nothing seemed to make her more angry than to see me with a newspaper. She seemed to think that here lay the danger. I have had her rush at me with a face made all up of fury, and snatch from me a newspaper, in a manner that fully revealed her apprehension. She was an apt woman; and a little experience soon

From Douglass's autobiography, Narrative of the Life of Frederick Douglass, an American Slave, Written by Himself *(1845), a landmark of African American literature.*

1. In Baltimore, Maryland.

demonstrated, to her satisfaction, that education and slavery were incompatible with each other.

From this time I was most narrowly watched. If I was in a separate room any considerable length of time, I was sure to be suspected of having a book, and was at once called to give an account of myself. All this, however, was too late. The first step had been taken. Mistress, in teaching me the alphabet, had given me the *inch*, and no precaution could prevent me from taking the *ell*.[2]

The plan which I adopted, and the one by which I was most successful, was that of making friends of all the little white boys whom I met in the street. As many of these as I could, I converted into teachers. With their kindly aid, obtained at different times and in different places, I finally succeeded in learning to read. When I was sent of errands, I always took my book with me, and by going one part of my errand quickly, I found time to get a lesson before my return. I used also to carry bread with me, enough of which was always in the house, and to which I was always welcome; for I was much better off in this regard than many of the poor white children in our neighborhood. This bread I used to bestow upon the hungry little urchins, who, in return, would give me that more valuable bread of knowledge. I am strongly tempted to give the names of two or three of those little boys, as a testimonial of the gratitude and affection I bear them; but prudence forbids;—not that it would injure me, but it might embarrass them; for it is almost an unpardonable offence to teach slaves to read in this Christian country. It is enough to say of the dear little fellows, that they lived on Philpot Street, very near Durgin and Bailey's ship-yard. I used to talk this matter of slavery over with them. I would sometimes say to them, I wished I could be as free as they would be when they got to be men. "You will be free as soon as you are twenty-one, *but I am a slave for life!* Have not I as good a right to be free as you have?" These words used to trouble them; they would express for me the liveliest sympathy, and console me with the hope that something would occur by which I might be free.

5

I was now about twelve years old, and the thought of being *a slave for life* began to bear heavily upon my heart. Just about this time, I got hold of a book entitled "The Columbian Orator."[3] Every opportunity I got, I used to read this book. Among much of other interesting matter, I found in it a dialogue between a master and his slave. The slave was represented as having run away from his master three times. The dialogue represented the conversation which took place between them, when the slave was retaken the third time. In this dialogue, the whole argument in behalf of slavery was brought forward by the master, all of which was disposed of by the slave. The slave was made to say some very smart as well as impressive things in reply to his master—things which had the desired though unexpected effect; for the conversation resulted in the voluntary emancipation of the slave on the part of the master.

2. Once a unit of measurement equal to forty-five inches; the saying is proverbial.

3. A popular collection of poems, dialogues, plays, and speeches.

In the same book, I met with one of Sheridan's mighty speeches on and in behalf of Catholic emancipation.[4] These were choice documents to me. I read them over and over again with unabated interest. They gave tongue to interesting thoughts of my own soul, which had frequently flashed through my mind, and died away for want of utterance. The moral which I gained from the dialogue was the power of truth over the conscience of even a slaveholder. What I got from Sheridan was a bold denunciation of slavery, and a powerful vindication of human rights. The reading of these documents enabled me to utter my thoughts, and to meet the arguments brought forward to sustain slavery; but while they relieved me of one difficulty, they brought on another even more painful than the one of which I was relieved. The more I read, the more I was led to abhor and detest my enslavers. I could regard them in no other light than a band of successful robbers, who had left their homes, and gone to Africa, and stolen us from our homes, and in a strange land reduced us to slavery. I loathed them as being the meanest as well as the most wicked of men. As I read and contemplated the subject, behold! that very discontentment which Master Hugh had predicted would follow my learning to read had already come, to torment and sting my soul to unutterable anguish. As I writhed under it, I would at times feel that learning to read had been a curse rather than a blessing. It had given me a view of my wretched condition, without the remedy. It opened my eyes to the horrible pit, but to no ladder upon which to get out. In moments of agony, I envied my fellow-slaves for their stupidity. I have often wished myself a beast. I preferred the condition of the meanest reptile to my own. Any thing, no matter what, to get rid of thinking! It was this everlasting thinking of my condition that tormented me. There was no getting rid of it. It was pressed upon me by every object within sight or hearing, animate or inanimate. The silver trump of freedom had roused my soul to eternal wakefulness. Freedom now appeared, to disappear no more forever. It was heard in every sound, and seen in every thing. It was ever present to torment me with a sense of my wretched condition. I saw nothing without seeing it, I heard nothing without hearing it, and felt nothing without feeling it. It looked from every star, it smiled in every calm, breathed in every wind, and moved in every storm.

I often found myself regretting my own existence, and wishing myself dead; and but for the hope of being free, I have no doubt but that I should have killed myself, or done something for which I should have been killed. While in this state of mind, I was eager to hear any one speak of slavery. I was a ready listener. Every little while, I could hear something about the abolitionists. It was some time before I found what the word meant. It was always used in such connections as to make it an interesting word to me. If a slave ran away and succeeded in getting clear, or if a slave killed his master, set fire to a barn, or did any thing very wrong in the mind of a slaveholder, it was spoken of as the

4. Richard Brinsley Sheridan (1751–1815), Irish dramatist and political leader. The speech, arguing for the abolition of laws denying Roman Catholics in Great Britain and Ireland civil and political liberties, was actually made by the Irish patriot Arthur O'Connor.

fruit of *abolition*. Hearing the word in this connection very often, I set about learning what it meant. The dictionary afforded me little or no help. I found it was "the act of abolishing"; but then I did not know what was to be abolished. Here I was perplexed. I did not dare to ask any one about its meaning, for I was satisfied that it was something they wanted me to know very little about. After a patient waiting, I got one of our city papers, containing an account of the number of petitions from the north, praying for the abolition of slavery in the District of Columbia, and of the slave trade between the States. From this time I understood the words *abolition* and *abolitionist,* and always drew near when that word was spoken, expecting to hear something of importance to myself and fellow-slaves. The light broke in upon me by degrees. I went one day down on the wharf of Mr. Waters; and seeing two Irishmen unloading a scow of stone, I went, unasked, and helped them. When we had finished, one of them came to me and asked me if I were a slave. I told him I was. He asked, "Are ye a slave for life?" I told him that I was. The good Irishman seemed to be deeply affected by the statement. He said to the other that it was a pity so fine a little fellow as myself should be a slave for life. He said it was a shame to hold me. They both advised me to run away to the north; that I should find friends there, and that I should be free. I pretended not to be interested in what they said, and treated them as if I did not understand them; for I feared they might be treacherous. White men have been known to encourage slaves to escape, and then, to get the reward, catch them and return them to their masters. I was afraid that these seemingly good men might use me so; but I nevertheless remembered their advice, and from that time I resolved to run away. I looked forward to a time at which it would be safe for me to escape. I was too young to think of doing so immediately; besides, I wished to learn how to write, as I might have occasion to write my own pass. I consoled myself with the hope that I should one day find a good chance. Meanwhile, I would learn to write.

The idea as to how I might learn to write was suggested to me by being in Durgin and Bailey's ship-yard, and frequently seeing the ship carpenters, after hewing, and getting a piece of timber ready for use, write on the timber the name of that part of the ship for which it was intended. When a piece of timber was intended for the larboard side, it would be marked thus—"L." When a piece was for the starboard side, it would be marked thus—"S." A piece for the larboard side forward, would be marked thus—"L. F." When a piece was for starboard side forward, it would be marked thus—"S. F." For larboard aft, it would be marked thus— "L. A." For starboard aft, it would be marked thus—"S. A." I soon learned the names of these letters, and for what they were intended when placed upon a piece of timber in the shipyard. I immediately commenced copying them, and in a short time was able to make the four letters named. After that, when I met with any boy who I knew could write, I would tell him I could write as well as he. The next word would be, "I don't believe you. Let me see you try it." I would then make the letters which I had been so fortunate as to learn, and ask him to beat that. In this way I got a good many lessons in writing, which it is quite possible I should never have gotten in any other way. During this time, my copy-book was the board fence, brick wall, and pavement; my pen and ink was a lump of chalk. With these, I learned mainly how to write. I then commenced and continued copying the Italics in Webster's Spelling Book,[5] until I could make them all without looking on the book. By this time, my little Master Thomas had gone to school, and learned how to write, and had written over a number of copy-books. These had been brought home, and shown to some of our near neighbors, and then laid aside. My mistress used to go to class meeting at the Wilk Street meetinghouse every Monday afternoon, and leave me to take care of the house. When left thus, I used to spend the time in writing in the spaces left in Master Thomas's copy-book, copying what he had written. I continued to do this until I could write a hand very similar to that of Master Thomas. Thus, after a long, tedious effort for years, I finally succeeded in learning how to write.

5. *The American Spelling Book* (1783) by Noah Webster (1758–1843), American lexicographer.

QUESTIONS

1. Douglass's story might today be called a "literacy narrative"—an account of how someone gains the skills of reading and writing. What are the key features of this narrative? What obstacles did Douglass face? How did he overcome them?

2. Many literacy narratives include an enabling figure, someone who helps the young learner along his or her way. Is there such a figure in Douglass's narrative? Why or why not?

3. At the end of this narrative, Douglass mentions that he wrote "in the spaces left in Master Thomas's copy-book, copying what he had written" (paragraph 8). To what extent is imitation (copying) part of learning? To what extent does this narrative show originality?

4. Write your own literacy narrative—an account of how you learned to read and write.

EUDORA WELTY *Clamorous to Learn*

FROM THE FIRST I was clamorous to learn—I wanted to know and begged to be told not so much what, or how, or why, or where, as when. How soon?

> Pear tree by the garden gate,
> How much longer must I wait?

This rhyme from one of my nursery books was the one that spoke for me. But I lived not at all unhappily in this craving, for my wild curiosity was in large

Originally delivered as part of a lecture series at Harvard University in 1983, then published in Welty's memoir, One Writer's Beginnings *(1985).*

part suspense, which carries its own secret pleasure. And so one of the godmothers of fiction was already bending over me.

When I was five years old, I knew the alphabet, I'd been vaccinated (for smallpox), and I could read. So my mother walked across the street to Jefferson Davis Grammar School[1] and asked the principal if she would allow me to enter the first grade after Christmas.

"Oh, all right," said Miss Duling. "Probably the best thing you could do with her."

Miss Duling, a lifelong subscriber to perfection, was a figure of authority, the most whole-souled I have ever come to know. She was a dedicated schoolteacher who denied herself all she might have done or whatever other way she might have lived (this possibility was the last that could have occurred to us, her subjects in school). I believe she came of well-off people, well-educated, in Kentucky, and certainly old photographs show she was a beautiful, high-spirited-looking young lady—and came down to Jackson to its new grammar school that was going begging for a principal. She must have earned next to nothing; Mississippi then as now was the nation's lowest-ranking state economically, and our legislature has always shown a painfully loud reluctance to give money to public education. That challenge *brought* her.

In the long run she came into touch, as teacher or principal, with three generations of Jacksonians. My parents had not, but everybody else's parents had gone to school to her. She'd taught most of our leaders somewhere along the line. When she wanted something done—some civic oversight corrected, some injustice made right overnight, or even a tree spared that the fool telephone people were about to cut down—she telephoned the mayor, or the chief of police, or the president of the power company, or the head doctor at the hospital, or the judge in charge of a case, or whoever, and calling them by their first names, *told* them. It is impossible to imagine her meeting with anything less than compliance. The ringing of her brass bell from their days at Davis School would still be in their ears. She also proposed a spelling match between the fourth grade at Davis School and the Mississippi Legislature, who went through with it; and that told the Legislature.

5

Her standards were very high and of course inflexible, her authority was total; why *wouldn't* this carry with it a brass bell that could be heard ringing for a block in all directions? That bell belonged to the figure of Miss Duling as though it grew directly out of her right arm, as wings grew out of an angel or a tail out of the devil. When we entered, marching, into her school, by strictest teaching, surveillance, and order we learned grammar, arithmetic, spelling, reading, writing, and geography; and she, not the teachers, I believe, wrote out the examinations: need I tell you, they were "hard."

She's not the only teacher who has influenced me, but Miss Duling, in some fictional shape or form, has stridden into a larger part of my work than I'd realized until now. She emerges in my perhaps inordinate number of

1. Named after the president of the Confederate States of America (1861–65) and located in Jackson, Mississippi.

schoolteacher characters. I loved those characters in the writing. But I did not, in life, love Miss Duling. I was afraid of her high-arched bony nose, her eyebrows lifted in half-circles above her hooded, brilliant eyes, and of the Kentucky R's in her speech, and the long steps she took in her hightop shoes. I did nothing but fear her bearing-down authority, and did not connect this (as of course we were meant to) with our own need or desire to learn, perhaps because I already had this wish, and did not need to be driven.

She was impervious to lies or foolish excuses or the insufferable plea of not knowing any better. She wasn't going to have any frills, either, at Davis School. When a new governor moved into the mansion, he sent his daughter to Davis School; her name was Lady Rachel Conner. Miss Duling at once called the governor to the telephone and told him, "She'll be plain Rachel here."

Miss Duling dressed as plainly as a Pilgrim on a Thanksgiving poster we made in the schoolroom, in a longish black-and-white checked gingham dress, a bright thick wool sweater the red of a railroad lantern—she'd knitted it herself—black stockings and her narrow elegant feet in black hightop shoes with heels you could hear coming, rhythmical as a parade drum down the hall. Her silky black curly hair was drawn back out of curl, fastened by high combs, and knotted behind. She carried her spectacles on a gold chain hung around her neck. Her gaze was in general sweeping, then suddenly at the point of concentration upon you. With a swing of her bell that took her whole right arm and shoulder, she rang it, militant and impartial, from the head of the front steps of Davis School when it was time for us all to line up, girls on one side, boys on the other. We were to march past her into the school building, while the fourth-grader she nabbed played time on the piano, mostly to a tune we could have skipped to, but we didn't skip into Davis School.

10 Little recess (open-air exercises) and big recess (lunch-boxes from home opened and eaten on the grass, on the girls' side and the boys' side of the yard) and dismissal were also regulated by Miss Duling's bell. The bell was also used to catch us off guard with fire drill.

It was examinations that drove my wits away, as all emergencies do. Being expected to measure up was paralyzing. I failed to make 100 on my spelling exam because I missed one word and that word was "uncle." Mother, as I knew she would, took it personally. "You couldn't spell *uncle*? When you've got those five perfectly splendid uncles in West Virginia? What would *they* say to that?"

It was never that Mother wanted me to beat my classmates in grades; what she wanted was for me to have my answers right. It was unclouded perfection I was up against.

My father was much more tolerant of possible error. He only said, as he steeply and impeccably sharpened my pencils on examination morning, "Now just keep remembering: the examinations were made out for the *average* student to pass. That's the majority. And if the majority can pass, think how much better *you* can do."

I looked to my mother, who had her own opinions about the majority. My father wished to treat it with respect, she didn't. I'd been born left-handed, but the habit was broken when I entered the first grade in Davis School. My father had insisted. He pointed out that everything in life had been made for the convenience of right-handed people, because they were the majority, and he often used "what the majority wants" as a criterion for what was for the best. My mother said she could not promise him, could not promise him at all, that I wouldn't stutter as a consequence. Mother had been born left-handed too; her family consisted of five left-handed brothers, a left-handed mother, and a father who could write with both hands at the same time, also backwards and forwards and upside down, different words with each hand. She had been broken of it when she was young, and she said she used to stutter.

"But you still stutter," I'd remind her, only to hear her say loftily, "You should have heard me when I was your age." 15

In my childhood days, a great deal of stock was put, in general, in the value of doing well in school. Both daily newspapers in Jackson saw the honor roll as news and published the lists, and the grades, of all the honor students. The city fathers gave the children who made the honor roll free season tickets to the baseball games down at the grandstand. We all attended and all worshiped some player on the Jackson Senators: I offered up my 100's in arithmetic and spelling, reading and writing, attendance and, yes, deportment—I must have been a prig!—to Red McDermott, the third baseman. And our happiness matched that of knowing Miss Duling was on her summer vacation, far, far away in Kentucky.

Every school week, visiting teachers came on their days for special lessons. On Mondays, the singing teacher blew into the room fresh from the early outdoors, singing in her high soprano "How do you do?" to do-mi-sol-do,[2] and we responded in chorus from our desks, "I'm ve-ry well" to do-sol-mi-do. Miss Johnson taught us rounds—"Row row row your boat gently down the stream"—and "Little Sir Echo," with half the room singing the words and the other half being the echo, a competition. She was from the North, and she was the one who wanted us all to stop the Christmas carols and see snow. The snow falling that morning outside the window was the first most of us had ever seen, and Miss Johnson threw up the window and held out wide her own black cape and caught flakes on it and ran, as fast as she could go, up and down the aisles to show us the real thing before it melted.

Thursday was Miss Eyrich and Miss Eyrich was Thursday. She came to give us physical training. She wasted no time on nonsense. Without greeting, we were marched straight outside and summarily divided into teams (no choosing sides), put on the mark, and ordered to get set for a relay race. Miss Eyrich cracked out "Go!" Dread rose in my throat. My head swam. Here was my turn, nearly upon me. (Wait, have I been touched—was that slap the touch? Go on! Do I go on without our passing a word? What word? Now am I racing too fast to turn around? Now I'm nearly home, but where is the hand waiting for mine to touch? Am I too late? Have I lost the whole race for our side?) I lost the relay race for our side before I started, through living ahead of myself, dreading to make my start, feeling too late prematurely, and standing transfixed by

2. Syllables indicating the first, third, fifth, and eighth tones of the scale.

emergency, trying to think of a password. Thursdays still can make me hear Miss Eyrich's voice. "On your mark—get set—GO!"

Very composedly and very slowly, the art teacher, who visited each room on Fridays, paced the aisle and looked down over your shoulder at what you were drawing for her. This was Miss Ascher. Coming from behind you, her deep, resonant voice reached you without being a word at all, but a sort of purr. It was much the sound given out by our family doctor when he read the thermometer and found you were running a slight fever: "Um-hm. Um-hm." Both alike, they let you go right ahead with it.

20 The school toilets were in the boys' and girls' respective basements. After Miss Duling had rung to dismiss school, a friend and I were making our plans for Saturday from adjoining cubicles. "Can you come spend the day with me?" I called out, and she called back, "I might could."

"Who—said—MIGHT—COULD?" It sounded like "Fe Fi Fo Fum!"

We both were petrified, for we knew whose deep measured words those were that came from just outside our doors. That was the voice of Mrs. McWillie, who taught the other fourth grade across the hall from ours. She was not even our teacher, but a very heavy, stern lady who dressed entirely in widow's weeds with a pleated black shirtwaist with a high net collar and velvet ribbon, and a black skirt to her ankles, with black circles under her eyes and a mournful, Presbyterian expression. We children took her to be a hundred years old. We held still.

"You might as well tell me," continued Mrs. McWillie. "I'm going to plant myself right here and wait till you come out. Then I'll see who it was I heard saying 'MIGHT-COULD.'"

If Elizabeth wouldn't go out, of course I wouldn't either. We knew her to be a teacher who would not flinch from standing there in the basement all afternoon, perhaps even all day Saturday. So we surrendered and came out. I priggishly hoped Elizabeth would clear it up which child it was—it wasn't me.

25 "So it's you." She regarded us as a brace, made no distinction: whoever didn't say it was guilty by association. "If I ever catch you down here one more time saying 'MIGHT-COULD,' I'm going to carry it to Miss Duling. You'll be kept in every day for a week! I hope you're both sufficiently ashamed of yourselves?" Saying "might-could" was bad, but saying it in the basement made bad grammar a sin. I knew Presbyterians believed that you could go to Hell.

Mrs. McWillie never scared us into grammar, of course. It was my first-year Latin teacher in high school who made me discover I'd fallen in love with it. It took Latin to thrust me into bona fide alliance with words in their true meaning. Learning Latin (once I was free of Caesar) fed my love for words upon words, words in continuation and modification, and the beautiful, sober, accretion of a sentence. I could see the achieved sentence finally standing there, as real, intact, and built to stay as the Mississippi State Capitol at the top of my street, where I could walk through it on my way to school and hear underfoot the echo of its marble floor, and over me the bell of its rotunda.

On winter's rainy days, the schoolrooms would grow so dark that sometimes you couldn't see the figures on the blackboard. At that point, Mrs. McWillie, that stern fourth-grade teacher, would let her children close their books, and she would move, broad in widow's weeds like darkness itself, to the window and by what light there was she would stand and read aloud "The King of the Golden River."[3] But I was excluded—in the other fourth grade, across the hall. Miss Louella Varnado, my teacher, didn't copy Mrs. McWillie; we had a spelling match: you could spell in the dark. I did not then suspect that there was any other way I could learn the story of "The King of the Golden River" than to have been assigned in the beginning to Mrs. McWillie's cowering fourth grade, then wait for her to treat you to it on the rainy day of her choice. I only now realize how much the treat depended, too, on there not having been money enough to put electric lights in Davis School. John Ruskin had to come in through courtesy of darkness. When in time I found the story in a book and read it to myself, it didn't seem to live up to my longings for a story with that name; as indeed, how could it?

3. A fantasy for children by the English author John Ruskin (1819–1900).

Questions

1. Like Frederick Douglass's narrative (see previous essay), Welty's essay might be called a "literacy narrative"—an account of how someone gains the skills of reading and writing. What are the key features of this narrative?

2. If you have read Douglass's narrative, compare the similarities and differences. Might both learners be described as "clamorous to learn"?

3. Write your own literacy narrative—an account of how you learned to read and write.

Sherman Alexie — *Superman and Me*

I learned to read with a Superman[1] comic book. Simple enough, I suppose. I cannot recall which particular Superman comic book I read, nor can I remember which villain he fought in that issue. I cannot remember the plot, nor the means by which I obtained the comic book. What I can remember is this: I was 3 years old, a Spokane Indian boy living with his family on the

Originally appearing in the book The Most Wonderful Books: Writers on Discovering the Pleasures of Reading *(1997), this essay was also published in the* Los Angeles Times *series "The Joy of Reading and Writing" (April 19, 1998). Like other essays Alexie has published, this one concerns contemporary Native American life and his experience as a Spokane/Coeur d'Alene Indian.*

1. Iconic superhero created in the 1930s.

Spokane Indian Reservation in eastern Washington state. We were poor by most standards, but one of my parents usually managed to find some minimum-wage job or another, which made us middle-class by reservation standards. I had a brother and three sisters. We lived on a combination of irregular pay-checks, hope, fear and government surplus food.

My father, who is one of the few Indians who went to Catholic school on purpose, was an avid reader of westerns, spy thrillers, murder mysteries, gangster epics, basketball player biographies and anything else he could find. He bought his books by the pound at Dutch's Pawn Shop, Goodwill, Salvation Army and Value Village. When he had extra money, he bought new novels at supermarkets, convenience stores and hospital gift shops. Our house was filled with books. They were stacked in crazy piles in the bathroom, bedrooms and living room. In a fit of unemployment-inspired creative energy, my father built a set of bookshelves and soon filled them with a random assortment of books about the Kennedy assassination,[2] Watergate,[3] the Vietnam War[4] and the entire 23-book series of the Apache westerns.[5] My father loved books, and since I loved my father with an aching devotion, I decided to love books as well.

I can remember picking up my father's books before I could read. The words themselves were mostly foreign, but I still remember the exact moment when I first understood, with a sudden clarity, the purpose of a paragraph. I didn't have the vocabulary to say "paragraph," but I realized that a paragraph was a fence that held words. The words inside a paragraph worked together for a common purpose. They had some specific reason for being inside the same fence. This knowledge delighted me. I began to think of everything in terms of paragraphs. Our reservation was a small paragraph within the United States. My family's house was a paragraph, distinct from the other paragraphs of the LeBrets to the north, the Fords to our south and the Tribal School to the west. Inside our house, each family member existed as a separate paragraph but still had genetics and common experiences to link us. Now, using this logic, I can see my changed family as an essay of seven paragraphs: mother, father, older brother, the deceased sister, my younger twin sisters and our adopted little brother.

At the same time I was seeing the world in paragraphs, I also picked up that Superman comic book. Each panel, complete with picture, dialogue and narrative was a three-dimensional paragraph. In one panel, Superman breaks through a door. His suit is red, blue and yellow. The brown door shatters into many pieces. I look at the narrative above the picture. I cannot read the words,

2. John F. Kennedy (1917–1963), thirty-fifth president of the United States (1961–1963), was assassinated in Dallas, Texas, on November 22, 1963, by Lee Harvey Oswald.

3. Hotel in Washington, D.C.; here refers to a political scandal that surrounded Richard M. Nixon (1913–1994), thirty-seventh president of the United States (1969–1974), and led to his resignation.

4. A twenty-year conflict (1954–1975) between South Vietnam, which was allied with the United States, and communist North Vietnam.

5. A series of pulp novels published between 1975 and 1984, written by several authors under the pseudonym "William M. James."

but I assume it tells me that "Superman is breaking down the door." Aloud, I pretend to read the words and say, "Superman is breaking down the door." Words, dialogue, also float out of Superman's mouth. Because he is breaking down the door, I assume he says, "I am breaking down the door." Once again, I pretend to read the words and say aloud, "I am breaking down the door." In this way, I learned to read.

5 This might be an interesting story all by itself. A little Indian boy teaches himself to read at an early age and advances quickly. He reads "Grapes of Wrath"[6] in kindergarten when other children are struggling through "Dick and Jane."[7] If he'd been anything but an Indian boy living on the reservation, he might have been called a prodigy. But he is an Indian boy living on the reservation and is simply an oddity. He grows into a man who often speaks of his childhood in the third-person, as if it will somehow dull the pain and make him sound more modest about his talents.

A smart Indian is a dangerous person, widely feared and ridiculed by Indians and non-Indians alike. I fought with my classmates on a daily basis. They wanted me to stay quiet when the non-Indian teacher asked for answers, for volunteers, for help. We were Indian children who were expected to be stupid. Most lived up to those expectations inside the classroom but subverted them on the outside. They struggled with basic reading in school but could remember how to sing a few dozen powwow songs. They were monosyllabic in front of their non-Indian teachers but could tell complicated stories and jokes at the dinner table. They submissively ducked their heads when confronted by a non-Indian adult but would slug it out with the Indian bully who was 10 years older. As Indian children, we were expected to fail in the non-Indian world. Those who failed were ceremonially accepted by other Indians and appropriately pitied by non-Indians.

I refused to fail. I was smart. I was arrogant. I was lucky. I read books late into the night, until I could barely keep my eyes open. I read books at recess, then during lunch, and in the few minutes left after I had finished my classroom assignments. I read books in the car when my family traveled to powwows or basketball games. In shopping malls, I ran to the bookstores and read bits and pieces of as many books as I could. I read the books my father brought home from the pawnshops and secondhand. I read the books I borrowed from the library. I read the backs of cereal boxes. I read the newspaper. I read the bulletins posted on the walls of the school, the clinic, the tribal offices, the post office. I read junk mail. I read auto-repair manuals. I read magazines. I read anything that had words and paragraphs. I read with equal parts joy and desperation. I loved those books, but I also knew that love had only one purpose. I was trying to save my life.

Despite all the books I read, I am still surprised I became a writer. I was going to be a pediatrician. These days, I write novels, short stories, and poems. I visit schools and teach creative writing to Indian kids. In all my years in the

6. A 1939 novel about the Great Depression by American novelist John Steinbeck (1902–1968).

7. Textbook series used to teach reading from the 1930s through the 1970s.

reservation school system, I was never taught how to write poetry, short stories or novels. I was certainly never taught that Indians wrote poetry, short stories and novels. Writing was something beyond Indians. I cannot recall a single time that a guest teacher visited the reservation. There must have been visiting teachers. Who were they? Where are they now? Do they exist? I visit the schools as often as possible. The Indian kids crowd the classroom. Many are writing their own poems, short stories and novels. They have read my books. They have read many other books. They look at me with bright eyes and arrogant wonder. They are trying to save their lives. Then there are the sullen and already defeated Indian kids who sit in the back rows and ignore me with theatrical precision. The pages of their notebooks are empty. They carry neither pencil nor pen. They stare out the window. They refuse and resist. "Books," I say to them. "Books," I say. I throw my weight against their locked doors. The door holds. I am smart. I am arrogant. I am lucky. I am trying to save our lives.

QUESTIONS

1. Twice Alexie asserts that he is (or was) "smart," "arrogant," and "lucky." Why does he place so much emphasis on these qualities?

2. "Despite all the books I read," Alexie observes in his final paragraph, "I am still surprised I became a writer." Why is he surprised?

3. Alexie writes that from the moment he realized the reason for paragraphs, he "began to think of everything in terms of paragraphs." How does the structure and arrangement of Alexie's own paragraphs contribute to the development of the essay's themes?

4. Alexie's essay is a literacy narrative, an account of how he learned to read and write. Write your own literacy narrative.

JOHN HOLT

How Teachers Make Children Hate Reading

WHEN I WAS TEACHING English at the Colorado Rocky Mountain School, I used to ask my students the kinds of questions that English teachers usually ask about reading assignments—questions designed to bring out the points that *I* had decided *they* should know. They, on their part, would try to get me to give them hints and clues as to what I wanted. It was a game of wits. I never gave my students an opportunity to say what they really thought about a book.

From The Under-Achieving School *(1969), Holt's third book-length critique of American education. Its predecessors were* How Children Fail *(1964) and* How Children Learn *(1967). In 1977 Holt founded* Growing without Schooling, *the nation's first home education newsletter.*

I gave vocabulary drills and quizzes too. I told my students that every time they came upon a word in their book they did not understand, they were to look it up in the dictionary. I even devised special kinds of vocabulary tests, allowing them to use their books to see how the words were used. But looking back, I realize that these tests, along with many of my methods, were foolish.

My sister was the first person who made me question my conventional ideas about teaching English. She had a son in the seventh grade in a fairly good public school. His teacher had asked the class to read Cooper's *The Deerslayer.*[1] The choice was bad enough in itself; whether looking at man or nature, Cooper was superficial, inaccurate and sentimental, and his writing is ponderous and ornate. But to make matters worse, this teacher had decided to give the book the microscope and x-ray treatment. He made the students look up and memorize not only the definitions but the derivations of every big word that came along—and there were plenty. Every chapter was followed by close questioning and testing to make sure the students "understood" everything.

Being then, as I said, conventional, I began to defend the teacher, who was a good friend of mine, against my sister's criticisms. The argument soon grew hot. What was wrong with making sure that children understood everything they read? My sister answered that until this year her boy had always loved reading, and had read a lot on his own; now he had stopped. (He was not really to start again for many years.)

5 Still I persisted. If children didn't look up the words they didn't know, how would they ever learn them? My sister said, "Don't be silly! When you were little you had a huge vocabulary, and were always reading very grown-up books. When did you ever look up a word in a dictionary?"

She had me. I don't know that we had a dictionary at home; if we did, I didn't use it. I don't use one today. In my life I doubt that I have looked up as many as fifty words, perhaps not even half that.

Since then I have talked about this with a number of teachers. More than once I have said, "According to tests, educated and literate people like you have a vocabulary of about twenty-five thousand words. How many of these did you learn by looking them up in a dictionary?" They usually are startled. Few claim to have looked up even as many as a thousand. How did they learn the rest?

They learned them just as they learned to talk—by meeting words over and over again, in different contexts, until they saw how they fitted.

Unfortunately, we English teachers are easily hung up on this matter of understanding. Why should children understand everything they read? Why should anyone? Does anyone? I don't, and I never did. I was always reading books that teachers would have said were "too hard" for me, books full of words I didn't know. That's how I got to be a good reader. When about ten, I read all

1. James Fenimore Cooper (1789–1851), American novelist; *The Deerslayer* was published in 1841.

the D'Artagnan stories[2] and loved them. It didn't trouble me in the least that I didn't know why France was at war with England or who was quarreling with whom in the French court or why the Musketeers should always be at odds with Cardinal Richelieu's men. I didn't even know who the Cardinal was, except that he was a dangerous and powerful man that my friends had to watch out for. This was all I needed to know.

10 Having said this, I will now say that I think a big, unabridged dictionary is a fine thing to have in any home or classroom. No book is more fun to browse around in—*if* you're not made to. Children, depending on their age, will find many pleasant and interesting things to do with a big dictionary. They can look up funny-sounding words, which they like, or words that nobody else in the class has ever heard of, which they like, or long words, which they like, or forbidden words, which they like best of all. At a certain age, and particularly with a little encouragement from parents or teachers, they may become very interested in where words came from and when they came into the language and how their meanings have changed over the years. But exploring for the fun of it is very different from looking up words out of your reading because you're going to get into trouble with your teacher if you don't.

While teaching fifth grade two years or so after the argument with my sister, I began to think again about reading. The children in my class were supposed to fill out a card—just the title and author and a one-sentence summary—for every book they read. I was not running a competition to see which child could read the most books, a competition that almost always leads to cheating. I just wanted to know what the children were reading. After a while it became clear that many of these very bright kids, from highly literate and even literary backgrounds, read very few books and deeply disliked reading. Why should this be?

At this time I was coming to realize, as I described in my book *How Children Fail,* that for most children school was a place of danger, and their main business in school was staying out of danger as much as possible. I now began to see also that books were among the most dangerous things in school.

From the very beginning of school we make books and reading a constant source of possible failure and public humiliation. When children are little we make them read aloud, before the teacher and other children, so that we can be sure they "know" all the words they are reading. This means that when they don't know a word, they are going to make a mistake, right in front of everyone. Instantly they are made to realize that they have done something wrong. Perhaps some of the other children will begin to wave their hands and say, "Ooooh! O-o-o-oh!" Perhaps they will just giggle, or nudge each other, or make a face. Perhaps the teacher will say, "Are you sure?" or ask someone else what

2. Alexandre Dumas (1802–1870), called Dumas *père* to distinguish him from his son Alexandre, called Dumas *fils,* wrote *The Three Musketeers* (1844), a historical novel set in seventeenth-century France. D'Artagnan, the hero of the novel, meets three friends, already musketeers (soldiers who carry muskets), and joins them in fighting cardinals, dodging assassins, and seeking romance.

he thinks. Or perhaps, if the teacher is kindly, she will just smile a sweet, sad smile—often one of the most painful punishments a child can suffer in school. In any case, the child who has made the mistake knows he has made it, and feels foolish, stupid, and ashamed, just as any of us would in his shoes.

Before long many children associate books and reading with mistakes, real or feared, and penalties and humiliation. This may not seem sensible, but it is natural. Mark Twain once said that a cat that sat on a hot stove lid would never sit on one again—but it would never sit on a cold one either. As true of children as of cats. If they, so to speak, sit on a hot book a few times, if books cause them humiliation and pain, they are likely to decide that the safest thing to do is to leave all books alone.

15 After having taught fifth-grade classes for four years I felt quite sure of this theory. In my next class were many children who had had great trouble with schoolwork, particularly reading. I decided to try at all costs to rid them of their fear and dislike of books, and to get them to read oftener and more adventurously.

One day soon after school had started, I said to them, "Now I'm going to say something about reading that you have probably never heard a teacher say before. I would like you to read a lot of books this year, but I want you to read them only for pleasure. I am not going to ask you questions to find out whether you understand the books or not. If you understand enough of a book to enjoy it and want to go on reading it, that's enough for me. Also I'm not going to ask you what words mean.

"Finally," I said, "I don't want you to feel that just because you start a book, you have to finish it. Give an author thirty or forty pages or so to get his story going. Then if you don't like the characters and don't care what happens to them, close the book, put it away, and get another. I don't care whether the books are easy or hard, short or long, as long as you enjoy them. Furthermore I'm putting all this in a letter to your parents, so they won't feel they have to quiz and heckle you about books at home."

The children sat stunned and silent. Was this a teacher talking? One girl, who had just come to us from a school where she had had a very hard time, and who proved to be one of the most interesting, lively, and intelligent children I have ever known, looked at me steadily for a long time after I had finished. Then, still looking at me, she said slowly and solemnly, "Mr. Holt, do you really mean that?" I said just as solemnly, "I mean every word of it."

Apparently she decided to believe me. The first book she read was Dr. Seuss's *How the Grinch Stole Christmas,* not a hard book even for most third graders. For a while she read a number of books on this level. Perhaps she was clearing up some confusion about reading that her teachers, in their hurry to get her up to "grade level," had never given her enough time to clear up. After she had been in the class six weeks or so and we had become good friends, I very tentatively suggested that, since she was a skillful rider and loved horses, she might like to read *National Velvet.*[3] I made my sell as soft as possible, saying

3. Enid Bagnold (1889–1981), British author, published *National Velvet* in 1935.

only that it was about a girl who loved and rode horses, and that if she didn't like it, she could put it back. She tried it, and though she must have found it quite a bit harder than what she had been reading, finished it and liked it very much.

20 During the spring she really astonished me, however. One day, in one of our many free periods, she was reading at her desk. From a glimpse of the illustrations I thought I knew what the book was. I said to myself, "It can't be," and went to take a closer look. Sure enough, she was reading *Moby-Dick,* in the edition with woodcuts by Rockwell Kent. When I came close to her desk she looked up. I said, "Are you really reading that?" She said she was. I said, "Do you like it?" She said, "Oh, yes, it's neat!" I said, "Don't you find parts of it rather heavy going?" She answered, "Oh, sure, but I just skip over those parts and go on to the next good part."

This is exactly what reading should be and in school so seldom is—an exciting, joyous adventure. Find something, dive into it, take the good parts, skip the bad parts, get what you can out of it, go on to something else. How different is our mean-spirited, picky insistence that every child get every last little scrap of "understanding" that can be dug out of a book.

For teachers who really enjoy doing it, and will do it with gusto, reading aloud is a very good idea. I have found that not just fifth graders but even ninth and eleventh graders enjoy it. Jack London's "To Build a Fire" is a good read-aloud story. So are ghost stories, and "August Heat," by W. F. Harvey, and "The Monkey's Paw," by W. W. Jacobs, are among the best. Shirley Jackson's "The Lottery" is sure-fire, and will raise all kinds of questions for discussion and argument.[4] Because of a TV program they had seen and that excited them, I once started reading my fifth graders William Golding's *Lord of the Flies,*[5] thinking to read only a few chapters, but they made me read it to the end.

In my early fifth-grade classes the children usually were of high IQ, came from literate backgrounds and were generally felt to be succeeding in school. Yet it was astonishingly hard for most of those children to express themselves in speech or in writing. I have known a number of five-year-olds who were considerably more articulate than most of the fifth graders I have known in school. Asked to speak, my fifth graders were covered with embarrassment; many refused altogether. Asked to write, they would sit for minutes on end, staring at the paper. It was hard for most of them to get down a half page of writing, even on what seemed to be interesting topics or topics they chose themselves.

In desperation I hit on a device that I named the Composition Derby. I divided the class into teams, and told them that when I said, "Go," they were to start writing something. It could be about anything they wanted, but it had to be about something—they couldn't just write "dog dog dog dog" on the paper. It could be true stories, descriptions of people or places or events, wishes, made-up stories, dreams—anything they liked. Spelling didn't count, so they didn't

4. London (1876–1916) and Jackson (1919–1965) are American novelists; Harvey (1885–1937) and Jacobs (1863–1943) are British novelists.

5. British novelist (1911–1993), published *Lord of the Flies* in 1954.

have to worry about it. When I said, "Stop," they were to stop and count up the words they had written. The team that wrote the most words would win the derby.

It was a success in many ways and for many reasons. The first surprise was that the two children who consistently wrote the most words were two of the least successful students in the class. They were bright, but they had always had a very hard time in school. Both were very bad spellers, and worrying about this had slowed down their writing without improving their spelling. When they were free of this worry and could let themselves go, they found hidden and unsuspected talents.

One of the two, a very driven and anxious little boy, used to write long adventures, or misadventures, in which I was the central character—"The Day Mr. Holt Went to Jail," "The Day Mr. Holt Fell Into the Hole," "The Day Mr. Holt Got Run Over," and so on. These were very funny, and the class enjoyed hearing me read them aloud. One day I asked the class to write a derby on a topic I would give them. They groaned; they liked picking their own. "Wait till you hear it," I said. "It's 'The Day the School Burned Down.'"

With a shout of approval and joy they went to work, and wrote furiously for 20 minutes or more, laughing and chuckling as they wrote. The papers were all much alike; in them the children danced around the burning building, throwing in books and driving me and the other teachers back in when we tried to escape.

In our first derby the class wrote an average of about ten words a minute; after a few months their average was over 20. Some of the slower writers tripled their output. Even the slowest, one of whom was the best student in the class, were writing 15 words a minute. More important, almost all the children enjoyed the derbies and wrote interesting things.

Some time later I learned that Professor S. I. Hayakawa, teaching freshman English, had invented a better technique. Every day in class he asked his students to write without stopping for about half an hour. They could write on whatever topic or topics they chose, but the important thing was not to stop. If they ran dry, they were to copy their last sentence over and over again until new ideas came. Usually they came before the sentence had been copied once. I use this idea in my own classes, and call this kind of paper a Non-Stop. Sometimes I ask students to write a Non-Stop on an assigned topic, more often on anything they choose. Once in a while I ask them to count up how many words they have written, though I rarely ask them to tell me; it is for their own information. Sometimes these papers are to be handed in; often they are what I call private papers, for the students' eyes alone.

The private paper has proved very useful. In the first place, in any English class—certainly any large English class—if the amount the students write is limited by what the teacher can find time to correct, or even to read, the students will not write nearly enough. The only remedy is to have them write a great deal that the teacher does not read. In the second place, students writing for themselves will write about many things that they would never write on a paper to be handed in, once they have learned (sometimes it takes a while) that the teacher means what he says about the papers' being private. This is important, not just because it enables them to get things off their chest, but also because they are most likely to write well, and to pay attention to how they write, when they are writing about something important to them.

Some English teachers, when they first hear about private papers, object that students do not benefit from writing papers unless the papers are corrected. I disagree for several reasons. First, most students, particularly poor students, do not read the corrections on their papers; it is boring, even painful. Second, even when they do read these corrections, they do not get much help from them, do not build the teacher's suggestions into their writing. This is true even when they really believe the teacher knows what he is talking about.

Third, and most important, we learn to write by writing, not by reading other people's ideas about writing. What most students need above all else is practice in writing, and particularly in writing about things that matter to them, so that they will begin to feel the satisfaction that comes from getting important thoughts down in words and will care about stating these thoughts forcefully and clearly.

Teachers of English—or, as some schools say (ugh!), Language Arts—spend a lot of time and effort on spelling. Most of it is wasted; it does little good, and often more harm than good. We should ask ourselves, "How do good spellers spell? What do they do when they are not sure which spelling of a word is right?" I have asked this of a number of good spellers. Their answer never varies. They do not rush for a dictionary or rack their brains trying to remember some rules. They write down the word both ways, or several ways, look at them and pick the one that looks best. Usually they are right.

Good spellers know what words look like and even, in their writing muscles, feel like. They have a good set of word images in their minds, and are willing to trust these images. The things we do to "teach" spelling to children do little to develop these skills or talents, and much to destroy them or prevent them from developing.

35 The first and worst thing we do is to make children anxious about spelling. We treat a misspelled word like a crime and penalize the misspeller severely; many teachers talk of making children develop a "spelling conscience," and fail otherwise excellent papers because of a few spelling mistakes. This is self-defeating. When we are anxious, we don't perceive clearly or remember what we once perceived. Everyone knows how hard it is to recall even simple things when under emotional pressure; the harder we rack our brains, the less easy it is to find what we are looking for. If we are anxious enough, we will not trust the messages that memory sends us. Many children spell badly because although their first hunches about how to spell a word may be correct, they are afraid to trust them. I have often seen on children's papers a word correctly spelled, then crossed out and misspelled.

There are some tricks that might help children get sharper word images. Some teachers may be using them. One is the trick of air writing; that is, of "writing" a word in the air with a finger and "seeing" the image so formed. I did this quite a bit with fifth graders, using either the air or the top of a desk, on which their fingers left no mark. Many of them were tremendously excited by this. I can still hear them saying, "There's nothing there, but I can see it!" It seemed like black magic. I remember that when I was little I loved to write in the air. It was effortless, voluptuous, satisfying, and it was fun to see the word appear in the air. I used to write "Money Money Money," not so much because I didn't have any as because I liked the way it felt, particularly that *y* at the end, with its swooping tail.

Another thing to help sharpen children's image-making machinery is taking very quick looks at words—or other things. The conventional machine for doing this is the tachistoscope. But these are expensive, so expensive that most children can have few chances to use them, if any at all. With some three-by-five and four-by-eight file cards you can get the same effect. On the little cards you put the words or the pictures that the child is going to look at. You hold the larger card over the card to be read, uncover it for a split second with a quick wrist motion, then cover it up again. Thus you have a tachistoscope that costs one cent and that any child can work by himself.

Once when substituting in a first-grade class, I thought that the children, who were just beginning to read and write, might enjoy some of the kind of free, nonstop writing that my fifth graders had. One day about 40 minutes before lunch, I asked them all to take pencil and paper and start writing about anything they wanted to. They seemed to like the idea, but right away one child said anxiously, "Suppose we can't spell a word."

"Don't worry about it," I said. "Just spell it the best way you can."

A heavy silence settled on the room. All I could see were still pencils and anxious faces. This was clearly not the right approach. So I said, "All right, I'll tell you what we'll do. Any time you want to know how to spell a word, tell me and I'll write it on the board." 40

They breathed a sigh of relief and went to work. Soon requests for words were coming fast; as soon as I wrote one, someone asked me another. By lunchtime, when most of the children were still busily writing, the board was full. What was interesting was that most of the words they had asked for were much longer and more complicated than anything in their reading books or workbooks. Freed from worry about spelling, they were willing to use the most difficult and interesting words that they knew.

The words were still on the board when we began school next day. Before I began to erase them, I said to the children, "Listen, everyone. I have to erase these words, but before I do, just out of curiosity I'd like to see if you remember some of them."

The result was surprising. I had expected that the child who had asked for and used a word might remember it, but I did not think many others would. But many of the children still knew many of the words. How had they learned them? I suppose each time I wrote a word on the board a number of children had looked up, relaxed yet curious, just to see what the word looked like, and these images and the sound of my voice saying the word had stuck in their minds until the next day. This, it seems to me, is how children may best learn to write and spell.

What can a parent do if a school, or a teacher, is spoiling the language for a child by teaching it in some tired way? First, try to get them to change, or at least let them know that you are eager for change. Talk to other parents; push some of these ideas in the PTA; talk to the English department at the school; talk to the child's own teacher. Many teachers and schools want to know what the parents want.

45 If the school or teacher cannot be persuaded, then what? Perhaps all you can do is try not to let your child become too bored or discouraged or worried by what is happening in school. Help him meet the school's demands, foolish though they may seem, and try to provide more interesting alternatives at home—plenty of books and conversation, and a serious and respectful audience when a child wants to talk. Nothing that ever happened to me in English classes at school was as helpful to me as the long conversations I used to have every summer with my uncle, who made me feel that the difference in our ages was not important and that he was really interested in what I had to say.

At the end of her freshman year in college a girl I know wrote home to her mother, "Hooray! Hooray! Just think—I never have to take English any more!" But this girl had always been an excellent English student, had always loved books, writing, ideas. It seems unnecessary and foolish and wrong that English teachers should so often take what should be the most flexible, exciting, and creative of all school courses and make it into something that most children can hardly wait to see the last of. Let's hope that we can and soon will begin to do much better.

QUESTIONS

1. Mark the anecdotes that Holt uses and describe how he orders them in time and by theme. Consider the advantages and disadvantages of his organizing this essay to reflect his own learning.

2. "[F]or most children," Holt observes, "school was a place of danger, and their main business in school was staying out of danger as much as possible" (paragraph 12). Locate instances in which he makes this point explicit and instances in which he implies it.

3. Holt's "Composition Derby" and Hayakawa's "Non-Stop" are now usually called free writing. Have your teachers used free writing? In what grades? From your own experience, how much has the teaching of writing changed since 1967, when Holt wrote this essay?

4. Holt begins this essay by describing the "game of wits" played by teachers and students alike: teachers ask students what teachers want students to know and students ask teachers for clues about what teachers want (paragraph 1). Do you recognize this game? Do you remember learning to play it? Do you think you play it well? Do you like playing it? Write an essay that answers these questions. Be sure to include anecdotes from your own experience.

Jonathan Kozol *Fremont High School*

Fremont High School in Los Angeles enrolls almost 5,000 students on a three-track schedule, with about 3,300 in attendance at a given time. The campus "sprawls across a city block, between San Pedro Street and Avalon Boulevard in South Central Los Angeles,"[1] the Los Angeles Times observes. A "neighborhood fortress, its perimeter protected by an eight-foot steel fence topped by spikes," the windows of the school are "shielded from gunfire by thick screens." According to teachers at the school, the average ninth grade student reads at fourth or fifth grade level. Nearly a third read at third grade level or below. About two thirds of the ninth grade students drop out prior to twelfth grade.

There were 27 homerooms for the first-year students, nine homerooms for seniors at the time I visited in spring of 2003. Thirty-five to 40 classrooms, nearly a third of all the classrooms in the school, were located in portables.[2] Some classes also took place in converted storage closets—"windowless and nasty," said one of the counselors—or in converted shop rooms without blackboards. Class size was high, according to a teacher who had been here for six years and who invited me into her tenth grade social studies class. Nearly 220 classes had enrollments ranging between 33 and over 40 students. The class I visited had 40 students, almost all of whom were present on the day that I was there.

Unlike the staggered luncheon sessions I observed at Walton High, lunch was served in a single sitting to the students in this school. "It's physically impossible to feed 3,300 kids at once," the teacher said. "The line for kids to get their food is very long and the entire period lasts only 30 minutes. It takes them 15 minutes just to walk there from their classes and get through the line. They get 10 minutes probably to eat their meals. A lot of them don't try. You've been a teacher, so you can imagine what it does to students when they have no food to eat for an entire day. The schoolday here at Fremont is eight hours long."

For teachers, too, the schedule sounded punishing. "I have six classes every day, including my homeroom," she said. "I've had *more* than 40 students in a class some years. My average class this year is 36. I see more than 200 students every day. Classes start at seven-thirty. I don't usually leave until four or four-thirty. . . ."

High school students, when I meet them first, are often more reluctant than the younger children are to open up their feelings and express their personal 5

From The Shame of the Nation: The Restoration of Apartheid Schooling in America *(2005), a book documenting the recent resurgence of social and racial inequities in America's public schools.*

1. Former designation of an area of Los Angeles associated with poverty and crime; in 2003 the area's name was changed to "South Los Angeles."

2. Portable classrooms; temporary buildings or trailers used for classroom space.

concerns; but hesitation on the part of students did not prove to be a problem in this class at Fremont High. The students knew I was a writer (they were told this by their teacher) and they took no time in getting down to matters that were on their minds.

"Can we talk about the bathrooms?" asked a student named Mireya.

In almost any classroom there are certain students who, by force of the directness or unusual sophistication of their way of speaking, tend to capture your attention from the start. Mireya later spoke insightfully of academic problems at the school, but her observations on the physical and personal embarrassments she and her schoolmates had to undergo cuts to the heart of questions of essential dignity or the denial of such dignity that kids in squalid schools like this one have to deal with.

Fremont High School, as court papers document, has "15 fewer bathrooms than the law requires." Of the limited number of bathrooms that are working in the school, "only one or two . . . are open and unlocked for girls to use." Long lines of girls are "waiting to use the bathrooms," which are generally "unclean" and "lack basic supplies," including toilet paper. Some of the classrooms "do not have air-conditioning," so that students "become red-faced and unable to concentrate" during "the extreme heat of summer." The rats observed by children in their elementary schools proliferate at Fremont High as well. "Rats in eleven . . . classrooms," maintenance records of the school report. "Rat droppings" are recorded "in the bins and drawers" of the high school's kitchen. "Hamburger buns" are being "eaten off [the] bread-delivery rack," school records note.

No matter how many times I read these tawdry details in court filings and depositions, I'm always surprised again to learn how often these unsanitary physical conditions are permitted to continue in a public school even after media accounts describe them vividly. But hearing of these conditions in Mireya's words was even more unsettling, in part because this student was so fragile-seeming and because the need even to speak of these indignities in front of me and all the other students seemed like an additional indignity.

10 "The problem is this," she carefully explained. "You're not allowed to use the bathroom during lunch, which is a 30-minute period. The only time that you're allowed to use it is between your classes." But "this is a huge building," she went on. "It has long corridors. If you have one class at one end of the building and your next class happens to be way down at the other end, you don't have time to use the bathroom and still get to class before it starts. So you go to your class and then you ask permission from your teacher to go to the bathroom and the teacher tells you, 'No. You had your chance between the periods. . . .'

"I feel embarrassed when I have to stand there and explain it to a teacher."

"This is the question," said a wiry-looking boy named Edward, leaning forward in his chair close to the door, a little to the right of where I stood. "Students are not animals, but even animals need to relieve themselves sometimes. We're in this building for eight hours. What do they think we're supposed to do?"

"It humiliates you," said Mireya, who went on to make the interesting statement that "the school provides solutions that don't actually work," and this idea was taken up by other students in describing course requirements within the school. A tall black student, for example, told me that she hoped to be a social worker or a doctor but was programmed into "Sewing Class" this year. She also had to take another course, called "Life Skills," which she told me was a very basic course—"a retarded class," to use her words—that "teaches things like the six continents," which she said she'd learned in elementary school.

When I asked her why she had to take these courses, she replied that she'd been told they were required, which reminded me of the response the sewing teacher I had met at Roosevelt Junior High School gave to the same question. As at Roosevelt, it turned out that this was not exactly so. What *was* required was that high school students take two courses in an area of study that was called "the Technical Arts," according to the teacher. At schools that served the middle class or upper middle class, this requirement was likely to be met by courses that had academic substance and, perhaps, some relevance to college preparation. At Beverly Hills High School,[3] for example, the technical arts requirement could be fulfilled by taking subjects such as residential architecture, the designing of commercial structures, broadcast journalism, advanced computer graphics, a sophisticated course in furniture design, carving and sculpture, or an honors course in engineering research and design. At Fremont High, in contrast, this requirement was far more likely to be met by courses that were basically vocational.

Mireya, for example, who had plans to go to college, told me that she had to take a sewing class last year and now was told she'd been assigned to take a class in hair-dressing as well. When I asked the teacher why Mireya could not skip these subjects and enroll in classes that would help her to pursue her college aspirations, she replied, "It isn't a question of what students want. It's what the school may have available. If all the other elective classes that a student wants to take are full, she has to take one of these classes if she wants to graduate." 15

A very small girl named Obie who had big blue-tinted glasses tilted up across her hair interrupted then to tell me with a kind of wild gusto that she took hair-dressing *twice*! When I expressed surprise that this was possible, she said there were two levels of hair-dressing offered here at Fremont High. "One is in hair-styling," she said. "The other is in braiding."

Mireya stared hard at this student for a moment and then suddenly began to cry. "I don't *want* to take hair-dressing. I did not need sewing either. I knew how to sew. My mother is a seamstress in a factory. I'm trying to go to college. I don't need to sew to go to college. My mother sews. I hoped for something else."

"What would you rather take?" I asked.

"I wanted to take an AP class,"[4] she answered.

Mireya's sudden tears elicited a strong reaction from one of the boys who had been silent up to now. A thin and dark-eyed student, named Fortino, with 20

3. Main public high school for Beverly Hills, an affluent city in the Los Angeles area.

4. A class that prepares students to take one of the College Board's "Advanced Placement" examinations, for which students may receive college credit or placement in advanced classes.

long hair down to his shoulders who was sitting on the left side of the classroom, he turned directly to Mireya.

"Listen to me," he said. "The owners of the sewing factories need laborers. Correct?"

"I guess they do," Mireya said.

"It's not going to be their own kids. Right?"

"Why not?" another student said.

25 "So they can grow beyond themselves," Mireya answered quietly. "But we remain the same."

"You're ghetto," said Fortino, "so we send you to the factory." He sat low in his desk chair, leaning on one elbow, his voice and dark eyes loaded with a cynical intelligence. "You're ghetto—so you sew!"

"There are higher positions than these," said a student named Samantha.

"You're ghetto," said Fortino unrelentingly to her. "So sew!"

Mireya was still crying.

30 Several students spoke then of a problem about frequent substitute teachers, which was documented also in court papers. One strategy for staffing classes in these three- and four-track schools when substitutes could not be found was to assign a teacher who was not "on track"—that is, a teacher who was on vacation—to come back to school and fill in for the missing teacher. "Just yesterday I was subbing [for] a substitute who was subbing for a teacher who never shows up," a teacher told the ACLU[5] lawyers. "That's one scenario. . . ."

Obie told me that she stopped coming to class during the previous semester because, out of her six teachers, three were substitutes. "Come on now! Like—hello? We live in a rich country? Like the richest country in the world? Hello?"

The teacher later told me that three substitutes in one semester, if the student's words were accurate, would be unusual. But "on average, every student has a substitute teacher in at least one class. Out of 180 teacher-slots, typically 25 or so cannot be filled and have to be assigned to substitutes."

Hair-dressing and sewing, it turned out, were not the only classes students at the school were taking that appeared to have no relevance to academic education. A number of the students, for example, said that they were taking what were known as "service classes" in which they would sit in on an academic class but didn't read the texts or do the lessons or participate in class activities but passed out books and did small errands for the teachers. They were given half-credits for these courses. Students received credits, too, for jobs they took outside of school, in fast-food restaurants for instance, I was told. How, I wondered, was a credit earned or grade determined for a job like this outside of school? "Best behavior and great customer service," said a student who was working in a restaurant, as she explained the logic of it all to ACLU lawyers in her deposition.

The teacher gave some other examples of the ways in which the students were shortchanged in academic terms. The year-round calendar, she said, gave

5. The American Civil Liberties Union, a nonprofit organization founded in 1920 to protect rights guaranteed to individuals by the U.S. Constitution.

these students 20 fewer schooldays than the students who attended school on normal calendars receive. In compensation, they attended classes for an extra hour, up until three-thirty, and students in the higher grades who had failed a course and had to take a make-up class remained here even later, until six, or sometimes up to nine.

"They come out of it just totally glassed-over," said the teacher, and, as one result, most teachers could not realistically give extra homework to make up for fewer days of school attendance and, in fact, because the kids have been in school so long each day, she said, "are likely to give less." 35

Students who needed to use the library to do a research paper for a class ran into problems here as well, because, as a result of the tight scheduling of classes, they were given no free time to use the library except at lunch, or for 30 minutes after school, unless a teacher chose to bring a class into the library to do a research project during a class period. But this was frequently impossible because the library was often closed when it was being used for other purposes such as administration of examinations, typically for "make-up tests," as I was told. "It's been closed now for a week because they're using it for testing," said Samantha.

"They were using it for testing last week also," said Fortino, who reported that he had a research paper due for which he had to locate 20 sources but had made no progress on it yet because he could not get into the library.

"You have to remember," said the teacher, "that the school's in session all year long, so if repairs need to be made in wiring or something like that in the library, they have to do it while the kids are here. So at those times the library is closed. Then, if there's testing taking place in there, the library is closed. And if an AP teacher needs a place to do an AP prep, the library is closed. And sometimes when the teachers need a place to meet, the library is closed." In all, according to the school librarian, the library was closed more than a quarter of the year.

During a meeting with a group of teachers later in the afternoon, it was explained to me in greater detail how the overcrowding of the building limited course offerings for students. "Even when students *ask* to take a course that interests them and teachers want to teach it," said one member of the faculty—she gave the example of a class in women's studies she said she would like to teach—"the physical shortages of space repeatedly prevent this." Putting students into service classes, on the other hand, did not require extra space. So, instead of the enrichment students might have gained from taking an elective course that had some academic substance, they were obliged to sit through classes in which they were not enrolled and from which they said that they learned virtually nothing.

Mireya had asked her teacher for permission to stay in the room with us during my meeting with the other teachers and remained right to the end. At five p.m., as I was about to leave the school, she stood beside the doorway of the classroom as the teacher, who was giving me a ride, assembled all the work she would be taking home. 40

"Why is it," she asked, "that students who do not need what we need get so much more? And we who need it so much more get so much less?"

I told her I'd been asking the same question now for nearly 40 years and still had no good answer. She answered, maturely, that she did not think there was an answer.

QUESTIONS

1. Kozol draws on a range of evidence in his portrait of Fremont High School: numerical data, court documents, comparisons to other schools, and testimony from teachers and students. How does he combine these various sorts of evidence? Which sort of evidence does he emphasize? Why?

2. Kozol writes about a number of students, but he gives particular attention to Mireya. Why?

3. Kozol adopts a journalistic style, but he also puts himself into the story. How does Kozol use the first person ("I")?

4. Using Kozol's essay as a model, write a portrait of another school that you know well.

CAROLINE BIRD *College Is a Waste of Time and Money*

A GREAT MAJORITY of our nine million college students are not in school because they want to be or because they want to learn. They are there because it has become the thing to do or because college is a pleasant place to be; because it's the only way they can get parents or taxpayers to support them without working at a job they don't like; because Mother wanted them to go, or some other reason entirely irrelevant to the course of studies for which college is supposedly organized.

As I crisscross the United States lecturing on college campuses, I am dismayed to find that professors and administrators, when pressed for a candid opinion, estimate that no more than 25 percent of their students are turned on by classwork. For the rest, college is at best a social center or aging vat, and at worst a young folks' home or even a prison that keeps them out of the mainstream of economic life for a few more years.

The premise—which I no longer accept—that college is the best place for all high-school graduates grew out of a noble American ideal. Just as the United States was the first nation to aspire to teach every small child to read and write, so, during the 1950s, we became the first and only great nation to aspire to higher education for all. During the '60s we damned the expense and built great state university systems as fast as we could. And adults—parents,

From Bird's book The Case Against College *(1975).*

employers, high-school counselors—began to push, shove and cajole youngsters to "get an education."

It became a mammoth industry, with taxpayers footing more than half the bill. By 1970, colleges and universities were spending more than 30 billion dollars annually. But still only half our high-school graduates were going on. According to estimates made by the economist Fritz Machlup, if we had been educating every young person until age 22 in that year of 1970, the bill for higher education would have reached 47.5 billion dollars, 12.5 billion more than the total corporate profits for the year.

5 Figures such as these have begun to make higher education for all look financially prohibitive, particularly now when colleges are squeezed by the pressures of inflation and a drop-off in the growth of their traditional market.

Predictable demography has caught up with the university empire builders. Now that the record crop of postwar babies has graduated from college, the rate of growth of the student population has begun to decline. To keep their mammoth plants financially solvent, many institutions have begun to use hard-sell, Madison-Avenue techniques to attract students. They sell college like soap, promoting features they think students want: innovative programs, an environment conducive to meaningful personal relationships, and a curriculum so free that it doesn't sound like college at all.

Pleasing the customers is something new for college administrators. Colleges have always known that most students don't like to study, and that at least part of the time they are ambivalent about college, but before the student riots of the 1960s educators never thought it either right or necessary to pay any attention to student feelings. But when students rebelling against the Vietnam war and the draft discovered they could disrupt a campus completely, administrators had to act on some student complaints. Few understood that the protests had tapped the basic discontent with college itself, a discontent that did not go away when the riots subsided.

Today students protest individually rather than in concert. They turn inward and withdraw from active participation. They drop out to travel to India or to feed themselves on subsistence farms. Some refuse to go to college at all. Most, of course, have neither the funds nor the self-confidence for constructive articulation of their discontent. They simply hang around college unhappily and reluctantly.

All across the country, I have been overwhelmed by the prevailing sadness on American campuses. Too many young people speak little, and then only in drowned voices. Sometimes the mood surfaces as diffidence, wariness, or coolness, but whatever its form, it looks like a defense mechanism, and that rings a bell. This is the way it used to be with women, and just as society had systematically damaged women by insisting that their proper place was in the home, so we may be systematically damaging 18-year-olds by insisting that their proper place is in college.

10 Campus watchers everywhere know what I mean when I say students are sad, but they don't agree on the reason for it. During the Vietnam war some

ascribed the sadness to the draft; now others blame affluence, or say it has something to do with permissive upbringing.

Not satisfied with any of these explanations, I looked for some answers with the journalistic tools of my trade—scholarly studies, economic analyses, the historical record, the opinions of the especially knowledgeable, conversations with parents, professors, college administrators, and employers, all of whom spoke as alumni too. Mostly I learned from my interviews with hundreds of young people on and off campuses all over the country.

My unnerving conclusion is that students are sad because they are not needed. Somewhere between the nursery and the employment office, they become unwanted adults. No one has anything in particular against them. But no one knows what to do with them either. We already have too many people in the world of the 1970s, and there is no room for so many newly minted 18-year-olds. So we temporarily get them out of the way by sending them to college where in fact only a few belong.

To make it more palatable, we fool ourselves into believing that we are sending them there for their own best interests, and that it's good for them, like spinach. Some, of course, learn to like it, but most wind up preferring green peas.

Educators admit as much. Nevitt Sanford, distinguished student of higher education, says students feel they are "capitulating to a kind of voluntary servitude." Some of them talk about their time in college as if it were a sentence to be served. I listened to a 1970 Mount Holyoke graduate: "For two years I was really interested in science, but in my junior and senior years I just kept saying, 'I've done two years; I'm going to finish.' When I got out I made up my mind that I wasn't going to school anymore because so many of my courses had been bullshit."

15 But bad as it is, college is often preferable to a far worse fate. It is better than the drudgery of an uninspiring nine-to-five job, and better than doing nothing when no jobs are available. For some young people, it is a graceful way to get away from home and become independent without losing the financial support of their parents. And sometimes it is the only alternative to an intolerable home situation.

It is difficult to assess how many students are in college reluctantly. The conservative Carnegie Commission estimates from 5 to 30 percent. Sol Linowitz, who was once chairman of a special committee on campus tension of the American Council on Education, found that "a significant number were not happy with their college experience because they felt they were there only in order to get the 'ticket to the big show' rather than to spend the years as productively as they otherwise could."

Older alumni will identify with Richard Baloga, a policeman's son, who stayed in school even though he "hated it" because he thought it would do him some good. But fewer students each year feel this way. Daniel Yankelovich has surveyed undergraduate attitudes for a number of years, and reported in 1971 that 74 percent thought education was "very important." But just two years earlier, 80 percent thought so.

The doubters don't mind speaking up. Leon Lefkowitz, chairman of the department of social studies at Central High School in Valley Stream, New

York, interviewed 300 college students at random, and reports that 200 of them didn't think that the education they were getting was worth the effort. "In two years I'll pick up a diploma," said one student, "and I can honestly say it was a waste of my father's bread."

Nowadays, says one sociologist, you don't have to have a reason for going to college; it's an institution. His definition of an institution is an arrangement everyone accepts without question; the burden of proof is not on why you go, but why anyone thinks there might be a reason for not going. The implication is that an 18-year-old is too young and confused to know what he wants to do, and that he should listen to those who know best and go to college.

I don't agree. I believe that college has to be judged not on what other people think is good for students, but on how good it feels to the students themselves. 20

I believe that people have an inside view of what's good for them. If a child doesn't want to go to school some morning, better let him stay at home, at least until you find out why. Maybe he knows something you don't. It's the same with college. If high-school graduates don't want to go, or if they don't want to go right away, they may perceive more clearly than their elders that college is not for them. It is no longer obvious that adolescents are best off studying a core curriculum that was constructed when all educated men could agree on what made them educated, or that professors, advisors, or parents can be of any particular help to young people in choosing a major or a career. High-school graduates see college graduates driving cabs, and decide it's not worth going. College students find no intellectual stimulation in their studies and drop out.

If students believe that college isn't necessarily good for them, you can't expect them to stay on for the general good of mankind. They don't go to school to beat the Russians to Jupiter, improve the national defense, increase the GNP, or create a new market for the arts—to mention some of the benefits taxpayers are supposed to get for supporting higher education.

Nor should we expect to bring about social equality by putting all young people through four years of academic rigor. At best, it's a roundabout and expensive way to narrow the gap between the highest and lowest in our society anyway. At worst, it is unconsciously elitist. Equalizing opportunity through universal higher education subjects the whole population to the intellectual mode natural only to a few. It violates the fundamental egalitarian principle of respect for the differences between people.

Of course, most parents aren't thinking of the "higher" good at all. They send their children to college because they are convinced young people benefit financially from those four years of higher education. But if money is the only goal, college is the dumbest investment you can make. I say this because a young banker in Poughkeepsie, New York, Stephen G. Necel, used a computer to compare college as an investment with other investments available in 1974 and college did not come out on top.

For the sake of argument, the two of us invented a young man whose rich uncle gave him, in cold cash, the cost of a four-year education at any college he chose, but the young man didn't have to spend the money on college. After bales of computer paper, we had our mythical student write to his uncle: 25

"Since you said I could spend the money foolishly if I wished, I am going to blow it all on Princeton."

The much respected financial columnist Sylvia Porter echoed the common assumption when she said last year, "A college education is among the very best investments you can make in your entire life." But the truth is not quite so rosy, even if we assume that the Census Bureau is correct when it says that as of 1972, a man who completed four years of college would expect to earn $199,000 more between the ages of 22 and 64 than a man who had only a high-school diploma.

If a 1972 Princeton-bound high-school graduate had put the $34,181 that his four years of college would have cost him into a savings bank at 7.5 per cent interest compounded daily, he would have had at age 64 a total of $1,129,200, or $528,200 more than the earnings of a male college graduate, and more than five times as much as the $199,000 extra the more educated man could expect to earn between 22 and 64.

The big advantage of getting your college money in cash now is that you can invest it in something that has a higher return than a diploma. For instance, a Princeton-bound high-school graduate of 1972 who liked fooling around with cars could have banked his $34,181, and gone to work at the local garage at close to $1,000 more per year than the average high-school graduate. Meanwhile, as he was learning to be an expert auto mechanic, his money would be ticking away in the bank. When he became 28, he would have earned $7,199 less on his job from age 22 to 28 than his college-educated friend, but he would have had $73,113 in his passbook—enough to buy out his boss, go into the used-car business, or acquire his own new-car dealership. If successful in business, he could expect to make more than the average college graduate. And if he had the brains to get into Princeton, he would be just as likely to make money without the four years spent on campus. Unfortunately, few college-bound high-school graduates get the opportunity to bank such a large sum of money, and then wait for it to make them rich. And few parents are sophisticated enough to understand that in financial returns alone, their children would be better off with the money than with the education.

Rates of return and dollar signs on education are fascinating brain teasers, but obviously there is a certain unreality to the game. Quite aside from the noneconomic benefits of college, and these should loom larger once the dollars are cleared away, there are grave difficulties in assigning a dollar value to college at all.

30 In fact there is no real evidence that the higher income of college graduates is due to college. College may simply attract people who are slated to earn more money anyway; those with higher IQs, better family backgrounds, a more enterprising temperament. No one who has wrestled with the problem is prepared to attribute all of the higher income to the impact of college itself.

Christopher Jencks, author of *Inequality,* a book that assesses the effect of family and schooling in America, believes that education in general accounts for less than half of the difference in income in the American population. "The biggest single source of income differences," writes Jencks, "seems to be the fact that men from high-status families have higher incomes than men from low-status families even when they enter the same occupations, have the same amount of education, and have the same test scores."

Jacob Mincer of the National Bureau of Economic Research and Columbia University states flatly that of "20 to 30 percent of students at any level, the additional schooling has been a waste, at least in terms of earnings." College fails to work its income-raising magic for almost a third of those who go. More than half of those people in 1972 who earned $15,000 or more reached that comfortable bracket without the benefit of a college diploma. Jencks says that financial success in the U.S. depends a good deal on luck, and the most sophisticated regression analyses have yet to demonstrate otherwise.

But most of today's students don't go to college to earn more money anyway. In 1968, when jobs were easy to get, Daniel Yankelovich made his first nationwide survey of students. Sixty-five percent of them said they "would welcome less emphasis on money." By 1973, when jobs were scarce, that figure jumped to 80 percent.

The young are not alone. Americans today are all looking less to the pay of a job than to the work itself. They want "interesting" work that permits them "to make a contribution," "express themselves" and "use their special abilities," and they think college will help them find it.

35 Jerry Darring of Indianapolis knows what it is to make a dollar. He worked with his father in the family plumbing business, on the line at Chevrolet, and in the Chrysler foundry. He quit these jobs to enter Wright State University in Dayton, Ohio, because "in a job like that a person only has time to work, and after that he's so tired that he can't do anything else but come home and go to sleep."

Jerry came to college to find work "helping people." And he is perfectly willing to spend the dollars he earns at dull, well-paid work to prepare for lower-paid work that offers the reward of service to others.

Jerry's case is not unusual. No one works for money alone. In order to deal with the nonmonetary rewards of work, economists have coined the concept of "psychic income," which according to one economic dictionary means "income that is reckoned in terms of pleasure, satisfaction, or general feelings of euphoria."

Psychic income is primarily what college students mean when they talk about getting a good job. During the most affluent years of the late 1960s and early 1970s college students told their placement officers that they wanted to be researchers, college professors, artists, city planners, social workers, poets, book publishers, archeologists, ballet dancers, or authors.

The psychic income of these and other occupations popular with students is so high that these jobs can be filled without offering high salaries. According to one study, 93 percent of urban university professors would choose the same vocation again if they had the chance, compared with only 16 per cent of unskilled auto workers. Even though the monetary gap between college professor and auto worker is now surprisingly small, the difference in psychic income is enormous.

40 But colleges fail to warn students that jobs of these kinds are hard to come by, even for qualified applicants, and they rarely accept the responsibility of helping students choose a career that will lead to a job. When a young person says he is interested in helping people, his counselor tells him to become a psychologist. But jobs in psychology are scarce. The Department of Labor, for instance, estimates there will be 4,300 new jobs for psychologists in 1975 while colleges are expected to turn out 58,430 B.A.s in psychology that year.

Of 30 psych majors who reported back to Vassar what they were doing a year after graduation in 1972, only five had jobs in which they could possibly use their courses in psychology, and two of these were working for Vassar.

The outlook isn't much better for students majoring in other psychic-pay disciplines: sociology, English, journalism, anthropology, forestry, education. Whatever college graduates want to do, most of them are going to wind up doing what there is to do.

John Shingleton, director of placement at Michigan State University, accuses the academic community of outright hypocrisy. "Educators have never said, 'Go to college and get a good job,' but this has been implied, and now students expect it. . . . If we care what happens to students after college, then let's get involved with what should be one of the basic purposes of education: career preparation."

In the 1970s, some of the more practical professors began to see that jobs for graduates meant jobs for professors too. Meanwhile, students themselves reacted to the shrinking job market, and a "new vocationalism" exploded on campus. The press welcomed the change as a return to the ethic of achievement and service. Students were still idealistic, the reporters wrote, but they now saw that they could best make the world better by healing the sick as physicians or righting individual wrongs as lawyers.

45 But there are no guarantees in these professions either. The American Enterprise Institute estimated in 1971 that there would be more than the target ratio of 100 doctors for every 100,000 people in the population by 1980. And the odds are little better for would-be lawyers. Law schools are already graduating twice as many new lawyers every year as the Department of Labor thinks will be needed, and the oversupply is growing every year.

And it's not at all apparent that what is actually learned in a "professional" education is necessary for success. Teachers, engineers and others I talked to said they find that on the job they rarely use what they learned in school. In order to see how well college prepared engineers and scientists for actual paid work in their fields, The Carnegie Commission queried all the employees with degrees in these fields in two large firms. Only one in five said the work they were doing bore a "very close relationship" to their college studies, while almost a third saw "very little relationship at all." An overwhelming majority could think of many people who were doing their same work, but had majored in different fields.

Majors in nontechnical fields report even less relationship between their studies and their jobs. Charles Lawrence, a communications major in college and now the producer of "Kennedy & Co.," the Chicago morning television show, says, "You have to learn all that stuff and you never use it again. I learned my job doing it." Others employed as architects, nurses, teachers and other members of the so-called learned professions report the same thing.

Most college administrators admit that they don't prepare their graduates for the job market. "I just wish I had the guts to tell parents that when you get out of this place you aren't prepared to do anything," the academic head of a famous liberal-arts college told us. Fortunately, for him, most people believe that you don't have to defend a liberal-arts education on those grounds. A liberal-arts education is supposed to provide you with a value system, a standard, a set of ideas, not a job. "Like Christianity, the liberal arts are seldom practiced and would probably be hated by the majority of the populace if they were," said one defender.

The analogy is apt. The fact is, of course, that the liberal arts are a religion in every sense of that term. When people talk about them, their language becomes elevated, metaphorical, extravagant, theoretical and reverent. And faith in personal salvation by the liberal arts is professed in a creed intoned on ceremonial occasions such as commencements.

If the liberal arts are a religious faith, the professors are its priests. But disseminating ideas in a four-year college curriculum is slow and most expensive. If you want to learn about Milton, Camus, or even Margaret Mead you can find them in paperback books, the public library, and even on television. 50

And when most people talk about the value of a college education, they are not talking about great books. When at Harvard commencement, the president welcomes the new graduates into "the fellowship of educated men and women," what he could be saying is, "Here is a piece of paper that is a passport to jobs, power and instant prestige." As Glenn Bassett, a personnel specialist at G.E. says, "In some parts of G.E., a college degree appears completely irrelevant to selection to, say, a manager's job. In most, however, it is a ticket of admission."

But now that we have doubled the number of young people attending college, a diploma cannot guarantee even that. The most charitable conclusion we can reach is that college probably has very little, if any, effect on people and things at all. Today, the false premises are easy to see:

First, college doesn't make people intelligent, ambitious, happy, or liberal. It's the other way around. Intelligent, ambitious, happy, liberal people are attracted to higher education in the first place.

Second, college can't claim much credit for the learning experiences that really change students while they are there. Jobs, friends, history, and most of all the sheer passage of time have as big an impact as anything even indirectly related to the campus.

Third, colleges have changed so radically that a freshman entering in the fall of 1974 can't be sure to gain even the limited value research studies assigned to colleges in the '60s. The sheer size of undergraduate campuses of the 1970s makes college even less stimulating now than it was 10 years ago. Today even motivated students are disappointed with their college courses and professors. 55

Finally, a college diploma no longer opens as many vocational doors. Employers are beginning to realize that when they pay extra for someone with a diploma, they are paying only for an empty credential. The fact is that most of the work for which employers now expect college training is now or has been capably done in the past by people without higher educations.

College, then, may be a good place for those few young people who are really drawn to academic work, who would rather read than eat, but it has become too expensive, in money, time, and intellectual effort to serve as a holding pen for large numbers of our young. We ought to make it possible for those reluctant, unhappy students to find alternative ways of growing up, and more realistic preparation for the years ahead.

QUESTIONS

1. Much of Bird's article focuses on the economic value (or lack thereof) of a college education. Are there other reasons, beyond (or in addition to) economics, why you or your classmates are attending college? To what extent does Bird consider or ignore these other reasons for attending college?

2. In paragraphs 48–50, Bird compares liberal arts education to religion. Why does she make this comparison? What do you think her attitude is toward the liberal arts? Is it similar to or different from yours?

3. In paragraphs 5–6, Bird discusses the hard-sell advertising techniques of many academic institutions. Look into your own school's "advertising techniques" (view books, pamphlets, information sent to homes and high schools, Web sites, etc.). How do these sources present the school to parents and potential students? Write an analysis of one of these sources.

WILLIAM ZINSSER *College Pressures*

Dear Carlos: I desperately need a dean's excuse for my chem midterm which will begin in about 1 hour. All I can say is that I totally blew it this week. I've fallen incredibly, inconceivably behind.

Carlos: Help! I'm anxious to hear from you. I'll be in my room and won't leave it until I hear from you. Tomorrow is the last day for . . .

Carlos: I left town because I started bugging out again. I stayed up all night to finish a take-home make-up exam & am typing it to hand in on the 10th. It was due on the 5th. P.S. I'm going to the dentist. Pain is pretty bad.

Carlos: Probably by Friday I'll be able to get back to my studies. Right now I'm going to take a long walk. This whole thing has taken a lot out of me.

Carlos: I'm really up the proverbial creek. The problem is I really *bombed* the history final. Since I need that course for my major I . . .

Written when Zinsser was Master (head) of a Yale residential college and published in a small circulation bimonthly magazine about rural life, Blair and Ketchum's Country Journal *(April 1979), which has since ceased publication.*

Carlos: Here follows a tale of woe. I went home this weekend, had to help my Mom, & caught a fever so didn't have much time to study. My professor . . .

Carlos: Aargh! Trouble. Nothing original but everything's piling up at once. To be brief, my job interview . . .

Hey Carlos, good news! I've got mononucleosis.

Who are these wretched supplicants, scribbling notes so laden with anxiety, seeking such miracles of postponement and balm? They are men and women who belong to Branford College, one of the twelve residential colleges at Yale University, and the messages are just a few of the hundreds that they left for their dean, Carlos Hortas—often slipped under his door at 4 A.M.—last year.

But students like the ones who wrote those notes can also be found on campuses from coast to coast—especially in New England and at many other private colleges across the country that have high academic standards and highly motivated students. Nobody could doubt that the notes are real. In their urgency and their gallows humor they are authentic voices of a generation that is panicky to succeed.

My own connection with the message writers is that I am master of Branford College. I live in its Gothic quadrangle and know the students well. (We have 485 of them.) I am privy to their hopes and fears—and also to their stereo music and their piercing cries in the dead of night ("Does anybody *ca-a-are*?"). If they went to Carlos to ask how to get through tomorrow, they come to me to ask how to get through the rest of their lives.

Mainly I try to remind them that the road ahead is a long one and that it will have more unexpected turns than they think. There will be plenty of time to change jobs, change careers, change whole attitudes and approaches. They don't want to hear such liberating news. They want a map—right now—that they can follow unswervingly to career security, financial security, Social Security and, presumably, a prepaid grave.

5 What I wish for all students is some release from the clammy grip of the future. I wish them a chance to savor each segment of their education as an experience in itself and not as a grim preparation for the next step. I wish them the right to experiment, to trip and fall, to learn that defeat is as instructive as victory and is not the end of the world.

My wish, of course, is naive. One of the few rights that America does not proclaim is the right to fail. Achievement is the national god, venerated in our media—the million-dollar athlete, the wealthy executive—and glorified in our praise of possessions. In the presence of such a potent state religion, the young are growing up old.

I see four kinds of pressure working on college students today: economic pressure, parental pressure, peer pressure, and self-induced pressure. It is easy to look around for villains—to blame the colleges for charging too much money, the professors for assigning too much work, the parents for pushing their children too far, the students for driving themselves too hard. But there are no villains; only victims.

"In the late 1960s," one dean told me, "the typical question that I got from students was 'Why is there so much suffering in the world?' or 'How can I make a contribution?' Today it's 'Do you think it would look better for getting into law school if I did a double major in history and political science, or just majored in one of them?'" Many other deans confirmed this pattern. One said: "They're trying to find an edge—the intangible something that will look better on paper if two students are about equal."

Note the emphasis on looking better. The transcript has become a sacred document, the passport to security. How one appears on paper is more important than how one appears in person. *A* is for Admirable and *B* is for Borderline, even though, in Yale's official system of grading, *A* means "excellent" and *B* means "very good." Today, looking very good is no longer good enough, especially for students who hope to go on to law school or medical school. They know that entrance into the better schools will be an entrance into the better law firms and better medical practices where they will make a lot of money. They also know that the odds are harsh. Yale Law School, for instance, matriculates 170 students from an applicant pool of 3,700; Harvard enrolls 550 from a pool of 7,000.

10 It's all very well for those of us who write letters of recommendation for our students to stress the qualities of humanity that will make them good lawyers or doctors. And it's nice to think that admission officers are really reading our letters and looking for the extra dimension of commitment or concern. Still, it would be hard for a student not to visualize these officers shuffling so many transcripts studded with *A*s that they regard a *B* as positively shameful.

The pressure is almost as heavy on students who just want to graduate and get a job. Long gone are the days of the "gentleman's C," when students journeyed through college with a certain relaxation, sampling a wide variety of courses—music, art, philosophy, classics, anthropology, poetry, religion—that would send them out as liberally educated men and women. If I were an employer I would rather employ graduates who have this range and curiosity than those who narrowly pursued safe subjects and high grades. I know countless students whose inquiring minds exhilarate me. I like to hear the play of their ideas. I don't know if they are getting *A*s or *C*s, and I don't care. I also like them as people. The country needs them, and they will find satisfying jobs. I tell them to relax. They can't.

Nor can I blame them. They live in a brutal economy. Tuition, room, and board at most private colleges now comes to at least $7,000, not counting books and fees. This might seem to suggest that the colleges are getting rich. But they are equally battered by inflation. Tuition covers only 60 percent of what it costs to educate a student, and ordinarily the remainder comes from what colleges receive in endowments, grants, and gifts. Now the remainder keeps being swallowed by the cruel costs—higher every year—of just opening the doors. Heating oil is up. Insurance is up. Postage is up. Health-premium costs are up. Everything is up. Deficits are up. We are witnessing in America the creation of a brotherhood of paupers—colleges, parents, and students, joined by the common bond of debt.

Today it is not unusual for a student, even if he works part time at college and full time during the summer, to accrue $5,000 in loans after four years—loans that he must start to repay within one year after graduation. Exhorted at commencement to go forth into the world, he is already behind as he goes forth. How could he not feel under pressure throughout college to prepare for this day of reckoning? I have used "he," incidentally, only for brevity. Women at Yale are under no less pressure to justify their expensive education to themselves, their parents, and society. In fact, they are probably under more pressure. For although they leave college superbly equipped to bring fresh leadership to traditionally male jobs, society hasn't yet caught up with this fact.

Along with economic pressure goes parental pressure. Inevitably, the two are deeply intertwined.

I see many students taking pre-medical courses with joyless tenacity. They go off to their labs as if they were going to the dentist. It saddens me because I know them in other corners of their life as cheerful people. 15

"Do you want to go to medical school?" I ask them.

"I guess so," they say, without conviction, or "Not really."

"Then why are you going?"

"Well, my parents want me to be a doctor. They're paying all this money and . . ."

Poor students, poor parents. They are caught in one of the oldest webs of love and duty and guilt. The parents mean well; they are trying to steer their sons and daughters toward a secure future. But the sons and daughters want to major in history or classics or philosophy—subjects with no "practical" value. Where's the payoff on the humanities? It's not easy to persuade such loving parents that the humanities do indeed pay off. The intellectual faculties developed by studying subjects like history and classics—an ability to synthesize and relate, to weigh cause and effect, to see events in perspective—are just the faculties that make creative leaders in business or almost any general field. Still, many fathers would rather put their money on courses that point toward a specific profession—courses that are pre-law, pre-medical, pre-business, or, as I sometimes heard it put, "pre-rich." 20

But the pressure on students is severe. They are truly torn. One part of them feels obligated to fulfill their parents' expectations; after all, their parents are older and presumably wiser. Another part tells them that the expectations that are right for their parents are not right for them.

I know a student who wants to be an artist. She is very obviously an artist and will be a good one—she has already had several modest local exhibits. Meanwhile she is growing as a well-rounded person and taking humanistic subjects that will enrich the inner resources out of which her art will grow. But her father is strongly opposed. He thinks that an artist is a "dumb" thing to be. The student vacillates and tries to please everybody. She keeps up with her art somewhat furtively and takes some of the "dumb" courses her father wants her to take—at least they are dumb courses for her. She is a free spirit on a campus of tense students—no small achievement in itself—and she deserves to follow her muse.

Peer pressure and self-induced pressure are also intertwined, and they begin almost at the beginning of freshman year.

"I had a freshman student I'll call Linda," one dean told me, "who came in and said she was under terrible pressure because her roommate, Barbara, was much brighter and studied all the time. I couldn't tell her that Barbara had come in two hours earlier to say the same thing about Linda."

25 The story is almost funny—except that it's not. It's symptomatic of all the pressures put together. When every student thinks every other student is working harder and doing better, the only solution is to study harder still. I see students going off to the library every night after dinner and coming back when it closes at midnight. I wish they would sometimes forget about their peers and go to a movie. I hear the clacking of typewriters in the hours before dawn. I see the tension in their eyes when exams are approaching and papers are due: *"Will I get everything done?"*

Probably they won't. They will get sick. They will get "blocked." They will sleep. They will oversleep. They will bug out. *Hey Carlos, help!*

Part of the problem is that they do more than they are expected to do. A professor will assign five-page papers. Several students will start writing ten-page papers to impress him. Then more students will write ten-page papers, and a few will raise the ante to fifteen. Pity the poor student who is still just doing the assignment.

"Once you have twenty or thirty percent of the student population deliberately overexerting," one dean points out, "it's bad for everybody. When a teacher gets more and more effort from his class, the student who is doing normal work can be perceived as not doing well. The tactic works, psychologically."

Why can't the professor just cut back and not accept longer papers? He can, and he probably will. But by then the term will be half over and the damage done. Grade fever is highly contagious and not easily reversed. Besides, the professor's main concern is with his course. He knows his students only in relation to the course and doesn't know that they are also overexerting in their other courses. Nor is it really his business. He didn't sign up for dealing with the student as a whole person and with all the emotional baggage the student brought along from home. That's what deans, masters, chaplains, and psychiatrists are for.

30 To some extent this is nothing new: a certain number of professors have always been self-contained islands of scholarship and shyness, more comfortable with books than with people. But the new pauperism has widened the gap still further, for professors who actually like to spend time with students don't have as much time to spend. They also are overexerting. If they are young, they are busy trying to publish in order not to perish, hanging by their finger nails onto a shrinking profession. If they are old and tenured, they are buried under the duties of administering departments—as departmental chairmen or members of committees—that have been thinned out by the budgetary axe.

Ultimately it will be the students' own business to break the circles in which they are trapped. They are too young to be prisoners of their parents' dreams and their classmates' fears. They must be jolted into believing in themselves as unique men and women who have the power to shape their own future.

"Violence is being done to the undergraduate experience," says Carlos Hortas. "College should be open-ended: at the end it should open many, many roads. Instead, students are choosing their goal in advance, and their choices narrow as they go along. It's almost as if they think that the country has been codified in the type of jobs that exist—that they've got to fit into certain slots. Therefore, fit into the best-paying slot.

"They ought to take chances. Not taking chances will lead to a life of colorless mediocrity. They'll be comfortable. But something in the spirit will be missing."

I have painted too drab a portrait of today's students, making them seem a solemn lot. That is only half of their story; if they were so dreary I wouldn't so thoroughly enjoy their company. The other half is that they are easy to like. They are quick to laugh and to offer friendship. They are not introverts. They are unusually kind and are more considerate of one another than any student generation I have known.

35 Nor are they so obsessed with their studies that they avoid sports and extracurricular activities. On the contrary, they juggle their crowded hours to play on a variety of teams, perform with musical and dramatic groups, and write for campus publications. But this in turn is one more cause of anxiety. There are too many choices. Academically, they have 1,300 courses to select from; outside class they have to decide how much spare time they can spare and how to spend it.

This means that they engage in fewer extracurricular pursuits than their predecessors did. If they want to row on the crew and play in the symphony they will eliminate one; in the '60s they would have done both. They also tend to choose activities that are self-limiting. Drama, for instance, is flourishing in all twelve of Yale's residential colleges as it never has before. Students hurl themselves into these productions—as actors, directors, carpenters, and technicians—with a dedication to create the best possible play, knowing that the day will come when the run will end and they can get back to their studies.

They also can't afford to be the willing slave of organizations like the *Yale Daily News*. Last spring at the one-hundredth anniversary banquet of that paper—whose past chairmen include such once and future kings as Potter Stewart, Kingman Brewster, and William F. Buckley, Jr.—much was made of the fact that the editorial staff used to be small and totally committed and that "newsies" routinely worked fifty hours a week. In effect they belonged to a club; Newsies is how they defined themselves at Yale. Today's student will write one or two articles a week, when he can, and he defines himself as a student. I've never heard the word Newsie except at the banquet.

If I have described the modern undergraduate primarily as a driven creature who is largely ignoring the blithe spirit inside who keeps trying to come out and play, it's because that's where the crunch is, not only at Yale but throughout American education. It's why I think we should all be worried about the values that are nurturing a generation so fearful of risk and so goal-obsessed at such an early age.

I tell students that there is no one "right" way to get ahead—that each of them is a different person, starting from a different point and bound for a different destination. I tell them that change is a tonic and that all the slots are not codified nor the frontiers closed. One of my ways of telling them is to invite men and women who have achieved success outside the academic world to come and talk informally with my students during the year. They are heads of companies or ad agencies, editors of magazines, politicians, public officials, television magnates, labor leaders, business executives, Broadway producers, artists, writers, economists, photographers, scientists, historians—a mixed bag of achievers.

40 I ask them to say a few words about how they got started. The students assume that they started in their present profession and knew all along that it was what they wanted to do. Luckily for me, most of them got into their field by a circuitous route, to their surprise, after many detours. The students are startled. They can hardly conceive of a career that was not pre-planned. They can hardly imagine allowing the hand of God or chance to nudge them down some unforeseen trail.

QUESTIONS

1. What are the four kinds of pressure Zinsser describes for the 1970s? Are they the same kinds of pressure that trouble students today? Or have new ones taken their place?

2. Some people believe that students perform best when subjected to pressure, others that they perform best when relatively free of pressure. How do you respond to pressure? How much pressure is enough? How much is too much?

3. Write an essay in which you compare your expectations of college pressures with the reality as you have experienced it to date.

ADRIENNE RICH

Taking Women Students Seriously

I SEE MY FUNCTION here today as one of trying to create a context, delineate a background, against which we might talk about women as students and students as women. I would like to speak for a while about this background, and then I hope that we can have, not so much a question period, as a raising of concerns, a sharing of questions for which we as yet may have no answers, an opening of conversations which will go on and on.

The talk that follows was addressed to teachers of women. . . . It was given for the New Jersey College and University Coalition on Women's Education, May 9, 1978 [Rich's note]. Reprinted in On Lies, Secrets, and Silence: Selected Prose, 1966–1978 *(1979).*

When I went to teach at Douglass, a women's college,[1] it was with a particular background which I would like briefly to describe to you. I had graduated from an all-girls' school in the 1940s, where the head and the majority of the faculty were independent, unmarried women. One or two held doctorates, but had been forced by the Depression (and by the fact that they were women) to take secondary school teaching jobs. These women cared a great deal about the life of the mind, and they gave a great deal of time and energy—beyond any limit of teaching hours—to those of us who showed special intellectual interest or ability. We were taken to libraries, art museums, lectures at neighboring colleges, set to work on extra research projects, given extra French or Latin reading. Although we sometimes felt "pushed" by them, we held those women in a kind of respect which even then we dimly perceived was not generally accorded to women in the world at large. They were vital individuals, defined not by their relationships but by their personalities; and although under the pressure of the culture we were all certain we wanted to get married, their lives did not appear empty or dreary to us. In a kind of cognitive dissonance, we knew they were "old maids" and therefore supposed to be bitter and lonely; yet we saw them vigorously involved with life. But despite their existence as alternate models of women, the *content* of the education they gave us in no way prepared us to survive as women in a world organized by and for men.

From that school, I went on to Radcliffe, congratulating myself that now I would have great men as my teachers. From 1947 to 1951, when I graduated, I never saw a single woman on a lecture platform, or in front of a class, except when a woman graduate student gave a paper on a special topic. The "great men" talked of other "great men," of the nature of Man, the history of Mankind, the future of Man; and never again was I to experience, from a teacher, the kind of prodding, the insistence that my best could be even better, that I had known in high school. Women students were simply not taken very seriously. Harvard's message to women was an elite mystification: we were, of course, part of Mankind; we were special, achieving women, or we would not have been there; but of course our real goal was to marry—if possible, a Harvard graduate.

In the late sixties, I began teaching at the City College of New York—a crowded, public, urban, multiracial institution as far removed from Harvard as possible. I went there to teach writing in the SEEK Program,[2] which predated Open Admissions and which was then a kind of model for programs designed to open up higher education to poor, black, and Third World students. Although during the next few years we were to see the original concept of SEEK diluted, then violently attacked and betrayed, it was for a short time an extraordinary and intense teaching and learning environment. The characteristics of this

1. Part of Rutgers University in New Jersey.

2. SEEK is an acronym for "Search for Education, Elevation, and Knowledge"; the instructors in the program included not only college teachers but also creative artists and writers.

environment were a deep commitment on the part of teachers to the minds of their students; a constant, active effort to create or discover the conditions for learning, and to educate ourselves to meet the needs of the new college population; a philosophical attitude based on open discussion of racism, oppression, and the politics of literature and language; and a belief that learning in the classroom could not be isolated from the student's experience as a member of an urban minority group in white America. Here are some of the kinds of questions we, as teachers of writing, found ourselves asking:

> (1) What has been the student's experience of education in the inadequate, often abusively racist public school system, which rewards passivity and treats a questioning attitude or independent mind as a behavior problem? What has been her or his experience in a society that consistently undermines the selfhood of the poor and the nonwhite? How can such a student gain that sense of self which is necessary for active participation in education? What does all this mean for us as teachers?
>
> (2) How do we go about teaching a canon of literature which has consistently excluded or depreciated nonwhite experience?
>
> (3) How can we connect the process of learning to write well with the student's own reality, and not simply teach her/him how to write acceptable lies in standard English?

5 When I went to teach at Douglass College in 1976, and in teaching women's writing workshops elsewhere, I came to perceive stunning parallels to the questions I had first encountered in teaching the so-called disadvantaged students at City. But in this instance, and against the specific background of the women's movement, the questions framed themselves like this:

> (1) What has been the student's experience of education in schools which reward female passivity, indoctrinate girls and boys in stereotypic sex roles, and do not take the female mind seriously? How does a woman gain a sense of her *self* in a system—in this case, patriarchal capitalism—which devalues work done by women, denies the importance and uniqueness of female experience, and is physically violent toward women? What does this mean for a woman teacher?
>
> (2) How do we, as women, teach women students a canon of literature which has consistently excluded or depreciated female experience, and which often expresses hostility to women and validates violence against us?
>
> (3) How can we teach women to move beyond the desire for male approval and getting "good grades" and seek and write their own truths that the culture has distorted or made taboo? (For women, of course, language itself is exclusive: I want to say more about this further on.)

In teaching women, we have two choices: to lend our weight to the forces that indoctrinate women to passivity, self-depreciation, and a sense of powerlessness, in which case the issue of "taking women students seriously" is a moot one; or to consider what we have to work against, as well as with, in ourselves, in our students, in the content of the curriculum, in the structure of the institution, in the society at large. And this means, first of all, taking ourselves seriously: Recognizing that central responsibility of a woman to herself, without which we remain always the Other, the defined, the object, the victim; believing that there is a unique quality of validation, affirmation, challenge, support, that one woman can offer another. Believing in the value and significance of women's experience, traditions, perceptions. Thinking of ourselves seriously, not as one of the boys, not as neuters, or androgynes, but *as women*.

Suppose we were to ask ourselves, simply: What does a woman need to know? Does she not, as a self-conscious, self-defining human being, need a knowledge of her own history, her much-politicized biology, an awareness of the creative work of women of the past, the skills and crafts and techniques and powers exercised by women in different times and cultures, a knowledge of women's rebellions and organized movements against our oppression and how they have been routed or diminished? Without such knowledge women live and have lived without context, vulnerable to the projections of male fantasy, male prescriptions for us, estranged from our own experience because our education has not reflected or echoed it. I would suggest that not biology, but ignorance of our selves, has been the key to our powerlessness.

But the university curriculum, the high-school curriculum, do not provide this kind of knowledge for women, the knowledge of Womankind, whose experience has been so profoundly different from that of Mankind. Only in the precariously budgeted, much-condescended-to area of women's studies is such knowledge available to women students. Only there can they learn about the lives and work of women other than the few select women who are included in the "mainstream" texts, usually misrepresented even when they do appear. Some students, at some institutions, manage to take a majority of courses in women's studies, but the message from on high is that this is self-indulgence, soft-core education: the "real" learning is the study of Mankind.

If there is any misleading concept, it is that of "coeducation": that because women and men are sitting in the same classrooms, hearing the same lectures, reading the same books, performing the same laboratory experiments, they are receiving an equal education. They are not, first because the content of education itself validates men even as it invalidates women. Its very message is that men have been the shapers and thinkers of the world, and that this is only natural. The bias of higher education, including the so-called sciences, is white and male, racist and sexist; and this bias is expressed in both subtle and blatant ways. I have mentioned already the exclusiveness of grammar itself: "The student should test himself on the above questions"; "The poet is representative. He stands among partial men for the complete man." Despite a few half-hearted departures from custom, what the linguist Wendy Martyna has named "He-Man" grammar prevails throughout the culture. The efforts of feminists to reveal the profound ontological implications of sexist grammar are routinely ridiculed by academicians and journalists, including the professedly liberal *Times* columnist, Tom Wicker, and the professed humanist, Jacques Barzun. Sexist grammar burns into the brains of little girls and young women a message that the male is the norm, the standard, the central figure beside which we are the deviants, the marginal, the dependent variables. It lays the foundation for androcentric thinking, and leaves men safe in their solipsistic tunnel-vision.

10 Women and men do not receive an equal education because outside the classroom women are perceived not as sovereign beings but as prey. The growing incidence of rape on and off the campus may or may not be fed by the proliferations of pornographic magazines and X-rated films available to young males in fraternities and student unions; but it is certainly occurring in a context of widespread images of sexual violence against women, on billboards and in so-called high art. More subtle, more daily than rape is the verbal abuse experienced by the woman student on many campuses—Rutgers for example—where, traversing a street lined with fraternity houses, she must run a gauntlet of male commentary and verbal assault. The undermining of self, of a woman's sense of her right to occupy space and walk freely in the world, is deeply relevant to education. The capacity to think independently, to take intellectual risks, to assert ourselves mentally, is inseparable from our physical way of being in the world, our feelings of personal integrity. If it is dangerous for me to walk home late of an evening from the library, *because I am a woman and can be raped,* how self-possessed, how exuberant can I feel as I sit working in that library? how much of my working energy is drained by the subliminal knowledge that, as a woman, I test my physical right to exist each time I go out alone? Of this knowledge, Susan Griffin has written:

> . . . more than rape itself, the fear of rape permeates our lives. And what does one do from day to day, with *this* experience, which says, without words and directly to the heart, *your existence, your experience, may end at any moment.* Your experience may end, and the best defense against this is not to be, to deny being in the body, as a self, to . . . avert your gaze, make yourself, as a presence in the world, less felt.[3]

Finally, rape of the mind. Women students are more and more often now reporting sexual overtures by male professors—one part of our overall growing consciousness of sexual harassment in the workplace. At Yale a legal suit has been brought against the university by a group of women demanding an explicit policy against sexual advances toward female students by male professors. Most young women experience a profound mixture of humiliation and intellectual self-doubt over seductive gestures by men who have the power to award grades, open doors to grants and graduate school, or extend special knowledge and training. Even if turned aside, such gestures constitute mental rape, destructive to a woman's ego. They are acts of domination, as despicable as the molestation of the daughter by the father.

But long before entering college the woman student has experienced her alien identity in a world which misnames her, turns her to its own uses, denying her the resources she needs to become self-affirming, self-defined. The nuclear family teaches her that relationships are more important than selfhood or work;

3. Rich is quoting from the manuscript of Griffin's *Rape: The Power of Consciousness* (New York, 1979).

that "whether the phone rings for you, and how often," having the right clothes, doing the dishes, take precedence over study or solitude; that too much intelligence or intensity may make her unmarriageable; that marriage and children—service to others—are, finally, the points on which her life will be judged a success or a failure. In high school, the polarization between feminine attractiveness and independent intelligence comes to an absolute. Meanwhile, the culture resounds with messages. During Solar Energy Week in New York I saw young women wearing "ecology" T-shirts with the legend: CLEAN, CHEAP AND AVAILABLE; a reminder of the 1960s antiwar button which read: CHICKS SAY YES TO MEN WHO SAY NO. Department store windows feature female mannequins in chains, pinned to the wall with legs spread, smiling in positions of torture. Feminists are depicted in the media as "shrill," "strident," "puritanical," or "humorless," and the lesbian choice—the choice of the woman-identified woman—as pathological or sinister. The young woman sitting in the philosophy classroom, the political science lecture, is already gripped by tensions between her nascent sense of self-worth, and the battering force of messages like these.

Look at a classroom: look at the many kinds of women's faces, postures, expressions. Listen to the women's voices. Listen to the silences, the unasked questions, the blanks. Listen to the small, soft voices, often courageously trying to speak up, voices of women taught early that tones of confidence, challenge, anger, or assertiveness, are strident and unfeminine. Listen to the voices of the women and the voices of the men; observe the space men allow themselves, physically and verbally, the male assumption that people will listen, even when the majority of the group is female. Look at the faces of the silent, and of those who speak. Listen to a woman groping for language in which to express what is on her mind, sensing that the terms of academic discourse are not her language, trying to cut down her thought to the dimensions of a discourse not intended for her (*for it is not fitting that a woman speak in public*); or reading her paper aloud at breakneck speed, throwing her words away, deprecating her own work by a reflex prejudgment: *I do not deserve to take up time and space.*

As women teachers, we can either deny the importance of this context in which women students think, write, read, study, project their own futures; or try to work with it. We can either teach passively, accepting these conditions, or actively, helping our students identify and resist them.

15 One important thing we can do is *discuss* the context. And this need not happen only in a women's studies course; it can happen anywhere. We can refuse to accept passive, obedient learning and insist upon critical thinking. We can become harder on our women students, giving them the kinds of "cultural prodding" that men receive, but on different terms and in a different style. Most young women need to have their intellectual lives, their work, legitimized against the claims of family, relationships, the old message that a woman is always available for service to others. We need to keep our standards very high, not to accept a woman's preconceived sense of her limitations; we need to be hard to please, while supportive of risk-taking, because self-respect often comes only when exacting standards have been met. At a time when adult literacy is generally low, we need to demand more, not less, of women, both for the sake

of their futures as thinking beings, and because historically women have always had to be better than men to do half as well. A romantic sloppiness, an inspired lack of rigor, a self-indulgent incoherence, are symptoms of female self-depreciation. We should help our women students to look very critically at such symptoms, and to understand where they are rooted.

Nor does this mean we should be training women students to "think like men." Men in general think badly: in disjuncture from their personal lives, claiming objectivity where the most irrational passions seethe, losing, as Virginia Woolf[4] observed, their senses in the pursuit of professionalism. It is not easy to think like a woman in a man's world, in the world of the professions; yet the capacity to do that is a strength which we can try to help our students develop. To think like a woman in a man's world means thinking critically, refusing to accept the givens, making connections between facts and ideas which men have left unconnected. It means remembering that every mind resides in a body; remaining accountable to the female bodies in which we live; constantly retesting given hypotheses against lived experience. It means a constant critique of language, for as Wittgenstein[5] (no feminist) observed, "The limits of my language are the limits of my world." And it means that most difficult thing of all: listening and watching in art and literature, in the social sciences, in all the descriptions we are given of the world, for the silences, the absences, the nameless, the unspoken, the encoded—for there we will find the true knowledge of women. And in breaking those silences, naming our selves, uncovering the hidden, making ourselves present, we begin to define a reality which resonates to *us*, which affirms *our* being, which allows the woman teacher and the woman student alike to take ourselves, and each other, seriously: meaning, to begin taking charge of our lives.

4. British novelist, essayist, and feminist (1882–1941).
5. Ludwig Wittgenstein (1889–1951), Austrian-born British philosopher.

QUESTIONS

1. Rich discusses the importance of listening to silences and of paying attention to absences. In one of your classes, listen and observe; take note of who speaks and who doesn't; and watch for responses from the instructor. What sense can you make of these silences and absences? Do your conclusions correspond to Rich's, or do they differ?

2. Rich and David Brooks (in "The Gender Gap at School" in the op-eds section) come to very different conclusions. What do you think accounts for their differences?

3. In paragraph 10, Rich discusses the relationship between intellectual independence and physical safety. Do some research on the public safety policies on your own campus (escorts, lighting, etc.) and also consider your own experiences. Do you feel safe walking alone on campus? To what extent does your sense of physical safety affect your intellectual work? Write a journal entry or article for your school's newspaper on these issues.

MIKE ROSE

Blue-Collar Brilliance

My mother, Rose Meraglio rose (Rosie), shaped her adult identity as a waitress in coffee shops and family restaurants. When I was growing up in Los Angeles during the 1950s, my father and I would occasionally hang out at the restaurant until her shift ended, and then we'd ride the bus home with her. Sometimes she worked the register and the counter, and we sat there; when she waited booths and tables, we found a booth in the back where the waitresses took their breaks.

There wasn't much for a child to do at the restaurants, and so as the hours stretched out, I watched the cooks and waitresses and listened to what they said. At mealtimes, the pace of the kitchen staff and the din from customers picked up. Weaving in and out around the room, waitresses warned *behind you* in impassive but urgent voices. Standing at the service window facing the kitchen, they called out abbreviated orders. *Fry four on two*, my mother would say as she clipped a check onto the metal wheel. Her tables were *deuces*, *four-tops*, or *six-tops* according to their size; seating areas also were nicknamed. The *racetrack*, for instance, was the fast-turnover front section. Lingo conferred authority and signaled know-how.

Rosie took customers' orders, pencil poised over pad, while fielding questions about the food. She walked full tilt through the room with plates stretching up her left arm and two cups of coffee somehow cradled in her right hand. She stood at a table or booth and removed a plate for this person, another for that person, then another, remembering who had the hamburger, who had the fried shrimp, almost always getting it right. She would haggle with the cook about a returned order and rush by us, saying. *He gave me lip, but I got him.* She'd take a minute to flop down in the booth next to my father. *I'm all in*, she'd say, and whisper something about a customer. Gripping the outer edge of the table with one hand, she'd watch the room and note, in the flow of our conversation, who needed a refill, whose order was taking longer to prepare than it should, who was finishing up.

I couldn't have put it in words when I was growing up, but what I observed in my mother's restaurant defined the world of adults, a place where competence was synonymous with physical work. I've since studied the working habits of blue-collar workers and have come to understand how much my mother's kind of work demands of both body and brain. A waitress acquires knowledge and intuition about the ways and the rhythms of the restaurant business. Waiting on seven to nine tables, each with two to six customers, Rosie devised memory strategies so that she could remember who ordered what. And because

Published in the summer 2009 issue of the American Scholar, *the magazine of the Phi Beta Kappa society. In this essay, as in much of his other work, Rose approaches his arguments about class, education, and literacy through his personal experience and family history.*

Rosie solved technical and human problems on the fly.

she knew the average time it took to prepare different dishes, she could monitor an order that was taking too long at the service station.

5 Like anyone who is effective at physical work, my mother learned *to work smart*, as she put it, *to make every move count.* She'd sequence and group tasks: What could she do first, then second, then third as she circled through her station? What tasks could be clustered? She did everything on the fly, and when problems arose—technical or human—she solved them within the flow of work, while taking into account the emotional state of her co-workers. Was the manager in a good mood? Did the cook wake up on the wrong side of the bed? If so, how could she make an extra request or effectively return an order?

And then, of course, there were the customers who entered the restaurant with all sorts of needs, from physiological ones, including the emotions that accompany hunger, to a sometimes complicated desire for human contact. Her tip depended on how well she responded to these needs, and so she became adept at reading social cues and managing feelings, both the customers' and her own. No wonder, then, that Rosie was intrigued by psychology. The restaurant became the place where she studied human behavior, puzzling over the problems of her regular customers and refining her ability to deal with people in a difficult world. She took pride in *being among the public*, she'd say. *There isn't a day that goes by in the restaurant that you don't learn something.*

My mother quit school in the seventh grade to help raise her brothers and sisters. Some of those siblings made it through high school, and some dropped out to find work in railroad yards, factories, or restaurants. My father finished a grade or two in primary school in Italy and never darkened the schoolhouse door again. I didn't do well in school either. By high school I had accumulated a spotty academic record and many hours of hazy disaffection. I spent a few years on the vocational track, but in my senior year I was inspired by my English teacher and managed to squeak into a small college on probation.

My freshman year was academically bumpy, but gradually I began to see formal education as a means of fulfillment and as a road toward making a living. I studied the humanities and later the social and psychological sciences and taught for 10 years in a range of situations—elementary school, adult education courses, tutoring centers, a program for Vietnam veterans[1] who wanted to go to college. Those students had socioeconomic and educational backgrounds similar to mine. Then I went back to graduate school to study education and cognitive psychology[2] and eventually became a faculty member in a school of education.

Intelligence is closely associated with formal education—the type of schooling a person has, how much and how long—and most people seem to move comfortably from that notion to a belief that work requiring less schooling requires less intelligence. These assumptions run through our cultural history, from the post–Revolutionary War period, when mechanics were characterized by political rivals as illiterate and therefore incapable of participating in government, until today. More than once I've heard a manager label his workers as "a bunch of dummies." Generalizations about intelligence, work, and social class deeply affect our assumptions about ourselves and each other, guiding the ways we use our minds to learn, build knowledge, solve problems, and make our way through the world.

10 Although writers and scholars have often looked at the working class, they have generally focused on the values such workers exhibit rather than on the thought their work requires—a subtle but pervasive omission. Our cultural iconography promotes the muscled arm, sleeve rolled tight against biceps, but no brightness behind the eye, no image that links hand and brain.

One of my mother's brothers, Joe Meraglio, left school in the ninth grade to work for the Pennsylvania Railroad.[3] From there he joined the Navy,

1. American veterans of a twenty-year (1954–1975) conflict between South Vietnam, which was allied with the United States, and communist North Vietnam.

2. The branch of psychology concerned with such subjects as perception, memory, thinking, and learning.

3. A railroad (1846–1968) that extended from the mid-Atlantic region of the United States to the Midwest.

returned to the railroad, which was already in decline, and eventually joined his older brother at General Motors[4] where, over a 33-year career, he moved from working on the assembly line to supervising the paint-and-body department. When I was a young man, Joe took me on a tour of the factory. The floor was loud—in some places deafening—and when I turned a corner or opened a door, the smell of chemicals knocked my head back. The work was repetitive and taxing, and the pace was inhumane.

Still, for Joe the shop floor provided what school did not; it was *like schooling*, he said, a place where *you're constantly learning*. Joe learned the most efficient way to use his body by acquiring a set of routines that were quick and preserved energy. Otherwise he would never have survived on the line.

As a foreman, Joe constantly faced new problems and became a consummate multi-tasker, evaluating a flurry of demands quickly, parceling out physical and mental resources, keeping a number of ongoing events in his mind, returning to whatever task had been interrupted, and maintaining a cool head under the pressure of grueling production schedules. In the midst of all this, Joe learned more and more about the auto industry, the technological and social dynamics of the shop floor, the machinery and production processes, and the basics of paint chemistry and of plating and baking. With further promotions, he not only solved problems but also began to find problems to solve: Joe initiated the redesign of the nozzle on a paint sprayer, thereby eliminating costly and unhealthy overspray. And he found a way to reduce energy costs on the baking ovens without affecting the quality of the paint. He lacked formal knowledge of how the machines under his supervision worked, but he had direct experience with them, hands-on knowledge, and was savvy about their quirks and operational capabilities. He could experiment with them.

In addition, Joe learned about budgets and management. Coming off the line as he did, he had a perspective of workers' needs and management's demands, and this led him to think of ways to improve efficiency on the line while relieving some of the stress on the assemblers. He had each worker in a unit learn his or her co-workers' jobs so they could rotate across stations to relieve some of the monotony. He believed that rotation would allow assemblers to get longer and more frequent breaks. It was an easy sell to the people on the line. The union, however, had to approve any modification in job duties, and the managers were wary of the change. Joe had to argue his case on a number of fronts, providing him a kind of rhetorical education.

15 Eight years ago I began a study of the thought processes involved in work like that of my mother and uncle. I catalogued the cognitive demands of a range of blue-collar and service jobs, from waitressing and hair styling to plumbing and welding. To gain a sense of how knowledge and skill develop, I observed experts as well as novices. From the details of this close examination, I tried to fashion what I called "cognitive biographies" of blue-collar workers. Biographi-

4. American company that for much of the twentieth century was the world's largest automaker.

With an eighth-grade education, Joe (hands together) advanced to supervisor of a G.M. paint-and-body department.

cal accounts of the lives of scientists, lawyers, entrepreneurs, and other professionals are rich with detail about the intellectual dimension of their work. But the life stories of working-class people are few and are typically accounts of hardship and courage or the achievements wrought by hard work.

Our culture—in Cartesian[5] fashion—separates the body from the mind, so that, for example, we assume that the use of a tool does not involve abstraction. We reinforce this notion by defining intelligence solely on grades in school and numbers on IQ tests.[6] And we employ social biases pertaining to a person's place on the occupational ladder. The distinctions among blue, pink, and white collars carry with them attributions of character, motivation, and intelligence. Although we rightly acknowledge and amply compensate the play of mind in white-collar and professional work, we diminish or erase it in considerations about other endeavors—physical and service work particularly. We also often ignore the experience of everyday work in administrative deliberations and policymaking.

But here's what we find when we get in close. The plumber seeking leverage in order to work in tight quarters and the hair stylist adroitly handling scissors and comb manage their bodies strategically. Though work-related actions become routine with experience, they were learned at some point through

5. Recalling the dualist philosophy of René Descartes (1596–1650), a French scientist, mathematician, and philosopher.

6. Tests that give a numerical measure of intelligence, the "Intelligence Quotient."

observation, trial and error, and, often, physical or verbal assistance from a co-worker or trainer. I've frequently observed novices talking to themselves as they take on a task, or shaking their head or hand as if to erase an attempt before trying again. In fact, our traditional notions of routine performance could keep us from appreciating the many instances within routine where quick decisions and adjustments are made. I'm struck by the thinking-in-motion that some work requires, by all the mental activity that can be involved in simply getting from one place to another: the waitress rushing back through her station to the kitchen or the foreman walking the line.

The use of tools requires the studied refinement of stance, grip, balance, and fine-motor skills. But manipulating tools is intimately tied to knowledge of what a particular instrument can do in a particular situation and do better than other similar tools. A worker must also know the characteristics of the material one is engaging—how it reacts to various cutting or compressing devices, to degrees of heat, or to lines of force. Some of these things demand judgment, the weighing of options, the consideration of multiple variables, and, occasionally, the creative use of a tool in an unexpected way.

In manipulating material, the worker becomes attuned to aspects of the environment, a training or disciplining of perception that both enhances knowledge and informs perception. Carpenters have an eye for length, line, and angle; mechanics troubleshoot by listening; hair stylists are attuned to shape, texture, and motion. Sensory data merge with concept, as when an auto mechanic relies on sound, vibration, and even smell to understand what cannot be observed.

20 Planning and problem solving have been studied since the earliest days of modern cognitive psychology and are considered core elements in Western definitions of intelligence. To work is to solve problems. The big difference between the psychologist's laboratory and the workplace is that in the former the problems are isolated and in the latter they are embedded in the real-time flow of work with all its messiness and social complexity.

Much of physical work is social and interactive. Movers determining how to get an electric range down a flight of stairs require coordination, negotiation, planning, and the establishing of incremental goals. Words, gestures, and sometimes a quick pencil sketch are involved, if only to get the rhythm right. How important it is, then, to consider the social and communicative dimension of physical work, for it provides the medium for so much of work's intelligence.

Given the ridicule heaped on blue-collar speech, it might seem odd to value its cognitive content. Yet, the flow of talk at work provides the channel for organizing and distributing tasks, for troubleshooting and problem solving, for learning new information and revising old. A significant amount of teaching, often informal and indirect, takes place at work. Joe Meraglio saw that much of his job as a supervisor involved instruction. In some service occupations, language and communication are central: observing and interpreting behavior and expression, inferring mood and motive, taking on the perspective of others, responding appropriately to social cues, and knowing when you're understood. A good hair stylist, for instance, has the ability to convert vague requests *(I want something light and summery)* into an appropriate cut through questions, pictures, and hand gestures.

Verbal and mathematical skills drive measures of intelligence in the Western Hemisphere, and many of the kinds of work I studied are thought to require relatively little proficiency in either. Compared to certain kinds of white-collar occupations, that's true. But written symbols flow through physical work.

Numbers are rife in most workplaces: on tools and gauges, as measurements, as indicators of pressure or concentration or temperature, as guides to sequence, on ingredient labels, on lists and spreadsheets, as markers of quantity and price. Certain jobs require workers to make, check, and verify calculations, and to collect and interpret data. Basic math can be involved, and some workers develop a good sense of numbers and patterns. Consider, as well, what might be called material mathematics: mathematical functions embodied in materials and actions, as when a carpenter builds a cabinet or a flight of stairs. A simple mathematical act can extend quickly beyond itself. Measuring, for example, can involve more than recording the dimensions of an object. As I watched a cabinetmaker measure a long strip of wood, he read a number off the tape out loud, looked back over his shoulder to the kitchen wall, turned back to his task, took another measurement, and paused for a moment in thought. He was solving a problem involving the molding, and the measurement was important to his deliberation about structure and appearance.

25 In the blue-collar workplace, directions, plans, and reference books rely on illustrations, some representational and others, like blueprints, that require training to interpret. Esoteric symbols—visual jargon—depict switches and receptacles, pipe fittings, or types of welds. Workers themselves often make sketches on the job. I frequently observed them grab a pencil to sketch something on a scrap of paper or on a piece of the material they were installing.

Though many kinds of physical work don't require a high literacy level, more reading occurs in the blue-collar workplace than is generally thought, from manuals and catalogues to work orders and invoices, to lists, labels, and forms. With routine tasks, for example, reading is integral to understanding production quotas, learning how to use an instrument, or applying a product. Written notes can initiate action, as in restaurant orders or reports of machine malfunction, or they can serve as memory aids.

True, many uses of writing are abbreviated, routine, and repetitive, and they infrequently require interpretation or analysis. But analytic moments can be part of routine activities, and seemingly basic reading and writing can be cognitively rich. Because workplace language is used in the flow of other activities, we can overlook the remarkable coordination of words, numbers, and drawings required to initiate and direct action.

If we believe everyday work to be mindless, then that will affect the work we create in the future. When we devalue the full range of everyday cognition, we offer limited educational opportunities and fail to make fresh and meaningful instructional connections among disparate kinds of skill and knowledge. If we think that whole categories of people—identified by class or occupation—are not that bright, then we reinforce social separations and cripple our ability to talk across cultural divides.

Affirmation of diverse intelligence is not a retreat to a softhearted definition of the mind. To acknowledge a broader range of intellectual capacity is to take seriously the concept of cognitive variability, to appreciate in all the Rosies and Joes the thought that drives their accomplishments and defines who they are. This is a model of the mind that is worthy of a democratic society.

QUESTIONS

1. In his closing paragraph, Rose asserts that the expanded understanding of intelligence for which he is arguing suggests "a model of the mind that is worthy of a democratic society." What are the social or political implications of this connection between mind and democracy?

2. Rose's essay was originally subtitled "Questioning assumptions about intelligence, work, and social class." What assumptions is Rose questioning, either directly or indirectly?

3. Rose introduces his general argument with detailed accounts of the work-lives of two family members: his mother and his uncle. Why do you think he makes this choice?

4. Rose describes himself as writing "'cognitive biographies' of blue-collar workers" (paragraph 15). Drawing as Rose does on interviews and careful observation, write a cognitive biography of your own.

Language and Communication

Maxine Hong Kingston *Tongue-Tied*

Long ago in China, knot-makers tied string into buttons and frogs, and rope into bell pulls. There was one knot so complicated that it blinded the knot-maker. Finally an emperor outlawed this cruel knot, and the nobles could not order it anymore. If I had lived in China, I would have been an outlaw knot-maker.

Maybe that's why my mother cut my tongue. She pushed my tongue up and sliced the frenum.[1] Or maybe she snipped it with a pair of nail scissors. I don't remember her doing it, only her telling me about it, but all during childhood I felt sorry for the baby whose mother waited with scissors or knife in hand for it to cry—and then, when its mouth was wide open like a baby bird's, cut. The Chinese say "a ready tongue is an evil."

I used to curl up my tongue in front of the mirror and tauten my frenum into a white line, itself as thin as a razor blade. I saw no scars in my mouth. I thought perhaps I had had two frena, and she had cut one. I made other children open their mouths so I could compare theirs to mine. I saw perfect pink membranes stretching into precise edges that looked easy enough to cut. Sometimes I felt very proud that my mother committed such a powerful act upon me. At other times I was terrified—the first thing my mother did when she saw me was to cut my tongue.

"Why did you do that to me, Mother?"

"I told you." 5

"Tell me again."

"I cut it so that you would not be tongue-tied. Your tongue would be able to move in any language. You'll be able to speak languages that are completely different from one another. You'll be able to pronounce anything. Your frenum looked too tight to do those things, so I cut it."

"But isn't 'a ready tongue an evil'?"

Published as the first chapter of The Woman Warrior: Memoirs of a Girlhood among Ghosts *(1976), Kingston's highly acclaimed account of her Asian American girlhood and her family history.*

1. The connecting fold of membrane on the underside of the tongue.

"Things are different in this ghost country."[2]

10 "Did it hurt me? Did I cry and bleed?"

"I don't remember. Probably."

She didn't cut the other children's. When I asked cousins and other Chinese children whether their mothers had cut their tongues loose, they said, "What?"

"Why didn't you cut my brothers' and sisters' tongues?"

"They didn't need it."

15 "Why not? Were theirs longer than mine?"

"Why don't you quit blabbering and get to work?"

If my mother was not lying she should have cut more, scraped away the rest of the frenum skin, because I have a terrible time talking. Or she should not have cut at all, tampering with my speech. When I went to kindergarten and had to speak English for the first time, I became silent. A dumbness—a shame—still cracks my voice in two, even when I want to say "hello" casually, or ask an easy question in front of the check-out counter, or ask directions of a bus driver. I stand frozen, or I hold up the line with the complete, grammatical sentence that comes squeaking out at impossible length. "What did you say?" says the cab driver, or "Speak up," so I have to perform again, only weaker the second time. A telephone call makes my throat bleed and takes up that day's courage. It spoils my day with self-disgust when I hear my broken voice come skittering out into the open. It makes people wince to hear it. I'm getting better, though. Recently I asked the postman for special-issue stamps; I've waited since childhood for postmen to give me some of their own accord. I am making progress, a little every day.

My silence was thickest—total—during the three years that I covered my school paintings with black paint. I painted layers of black over houses and flowers and suns, and when I drew on the blackboard, I put a layer of chalk on top. I was making a stage curtain, and it was the moment before the curtain parted or rose. The teachers called my parents to school, and I saw they had been saving my pictures, curling and cracking, all alike and black. The teachers pointed to the pictures and looked serious, talked seriously too, but my parents did not understand English. ("The parents and teachers of criminals were executed," said my father.) My parents took the pictures home. I spread them out (so black and full of possibilities) and pretended the curtains were swinging open, flying up, one after another, sunlight underneath, mighty operas.

During the first silent year I spoke to no one at school, did not ask before going to the lavatory, and flunked kindergarten. My sister also said nothing for three years, silent in the playground and silent at lunch. There were other quiet Chinese girls not of our family, but most of them got over it sooner than we did. I enjoyed the silence. At first it did not occur to me I was supposed to talk or to pass kindergarten. I talked at home and to one or two of the Chinese kids in class. I made motions and even made some jokes. I drank out of a toy saucer

2. In Kingston's story, the Chinese immigrants see white Americans as "ghosts," whose language and values they must adopt to become American.

when the water spilled out of the cup, and everybody laughed, pointing at me, so I did it some more. I didn't know that Americans don't drink out of saucers.

I liked the Negro students (Black Ghosts) best because they laughed the loudest and talked to me as if I were a daring talker too. One of the Negro girls had her mother coil braids over her ears Shanghai-style like mine; we were Shanghai twins except that she was covered with black like my paintings. Two Negro kids enrolled in Chinese school, and the teachers gave them Chinese names. Some Negro kids walked me to school and home, protecting me from the Japanese kids, who hit me and chased me and stuck gum in my ears. The Japanese kids were noisy and tough. They appeared one day in kindergarten, released from concentration camp,[3] which was a tic-tac-toe mark, like barbed wire, on the map. 20

It was when I found out I had to talk that school became a misery, that the silence became a misery. I did not speak and felt bad each time that I did not speak. I read aloud in first grade, though, and heard the barest whisper with little squeaks come out of my throat. "Louder," said the teacher, who scared the voice away again. The other Chinese girls did not talk either, so I knew the silence had to do with being a Chinese girl.

Reading out loud was easier than speaking because we did not have to make up what to say, but I stopped often, and the teacher would think I'd gone quiet again. I could not understand "I." The Chinese "I" had seven strokes, intricacies. How could the American "I," assuredly wearing a hat like the Chinese, have only three strokes, the middle so straight? Was it out of politeness that this writer left off strokes the way a Chinese has to write her own name small and crooked? No, it was not politeness; "I" is a capital and "you" is a lower-case. I stared at that middle line and waited so long for its black center to resolve into tight strokes and dots that I forgot to pronounce it. The other troublesome word was "here," no strong consonant to hang on to, and so flat, when "here" is two mountainous ideographs. The teacher, who had already told me every day how to read "I" and "here," put me in the low corner under the stairs again, where the noisy boys usually sat.

When my second grade class did a play, the whole class went to the auditorium except the Chinese girls. The teacher, lovely and Hawaiian, should have understood about us, but instead left us behind in the classroom. Our voices were too soft or nonexistent, and our parents never signed the permission slips anyway. They never signed anything unnecessary. We opened the door a crack and peeked out, but closed it again quickly. One of us (not me) won every spelling bee, though.

I remember telling the Hawaiian teacher, "We Chinese can't sing 'land where our fathers died.'" She argued with me about politics, while I meant because of curses. But how can I have that memory when I couldn't talk? My mother says that we, like the ghosts, have no memories.

3. During World War II, more than 100,000 Japanese Americans were imprisoned in "War Relocation Camps" in the United States.

25 After American school, we picked up our cigar boxes, in which we had arranged books, brushes, and an inkbox neatly, and went to Chinese school, from 5:00 to 7:30 P.M. There we chanted together, voices rising and falling, loud and soft, some boys shouting, everybody reading together, reciting together and not alone with one voice. When we had a memorization test, the teacher let each of us come to his desk and say the lesson to him privately, while the rest of the class practiced copying or tracing. Most of the teachers were men. The boys who were so well behaved in the American school played tricks on them and talked back to them. The girls were not mute. They screamed and yelled during recess, when there were no rules; they had fistfights. Nobody was afraid of children hurting themselves or of children hurting school property. The glass doors to the red and green balconies with the gold joy symbols were left wide open so that we could run out and climb the fire escapes. We played capture-the-flag in the auditorium, where Sun Yat-sen and Chiang Kai-shek's[4] pictures hung at the back of the stage, the Chinese flag on their left and the American flag on their right. We climbed the teak ceremonial chairs and made flying leaps off the stage. One flag headquarters was behind the glass door and the other on stage right. Our feet drummed on the hollow stage. During recess the teachers locked themselves up in their office with the shelves of books, copybooks, inks from China. They drank tea and warmed their hands at a stove. There was no play supervision. At recess we had the school to ourselves, and also we could roam as far as we could go—downtown, Chinatown stores, home—as long as we returned before the bell rang.

At exactly 7:30 the teacher again picked up the brass bell that sat on his desk and swung it over our heads, while we charged down the stairs, our cheering magnified in the stairwell. Nobody had to line up.

Not all of the children who were silent at American school found voice at Chinese school. One new teacher said each of us had to get up and recite in front of the class, who was to listen. My sister and I had memorized the lesson perfectly. We said it to each other at home, one chanting, one listening. The teacher called on my sister to recite first. It was the first time a teacher had called on the second-born to go first. My sister was scared. She glanced at me and looked away; I looked down at my desk. I hoped that she could do it because if she could, then I wouldn't have to. She opened her mouth and a voice came out that wasn't a whisper, but it wasn't a proper voice either. I hoped that she would not cry, fear breaking up her voice like twigs underfoot. She sounded as if she were trying to sing through weeping and strangling. She did not pause or stop to end the embarrassment. She kept going until she said the last word, and then she sat down. When it was my turn, the same voice came out, a crippled animal running on broken legs. You could hear splinters in my voice, bones rubbing jagged against one another. I was loud, though. I was glad I didn't whisper. There was one little girl who whispered.

4. Sun Yat-sen (1866–1925) and his successor, Chiang Kai-shek (1888–1975), led the Guomindang (or Nationalist party) campaign to unify China in the 1920s and 1930s.

Questions

1. Like Gloria Anzaldúa in "How to Tame a Wild Tongue" (p. 411), Kingston uses the tongue as both a physical body part and a metaphor for speech. Locate examples of these uses of "tongue" and explain them.

2. Why does Kingston call non-Asians "ghosts"? Are these the only ghosts Kingston confronts? Discuss her usage of this term in the essay and in the subtitle of her autobiography, *Memoirs of a Girlhood among Ghosts.*

3. If you have had difficulty speaking up or if you have faced a language problem in your past, write about it in an essay that explains your experience in terms of a family or social context.

Richard Rodriguez *Aria*

Supporters of bilingual education today imply that students like me miss a great deal by not being taught in their family's language. What they seem not to recognize is that, as a socially disadvantaged child, I considered Spanish to be a private language. What I needed to learn in school was that I had the right—and the obligation—to speak the public language of *los gringos*. The odd truth is that my first-grade classmates could have become bilingual, in the conventional sense of that word, more easily than I. Had they been taught (as upper-middle-class children are often taught early) a second language like Spanish or French, they could have regarded it simply as that: another public language. In my case such bilingualism could not have been so quickly achieved. What I did not believe was that I could speak a single public language.

Without question, it would have pleased me to hear my teachers address me in Spanish when I entered the classroom. I would have felt much less afraid. I would have trusted them and responded with ease. But I would have delayed—for how long postponed?—having to learn the language of public society. I would have evaded—and for how long could I have afforded to delay?—learning the great lesson of school, that I had a public identity.

Fortunately, my teachers were unsentimental about their responsibility. What they understood was that I needed to speak a public language. So their voices would search me out, asking me questions. Each time I'd hear them, I'd look up in surprise to see a nun's face frowning at me. I'd mumble, not really meaning to answer. The nun would persist, "Richard, stand up. Don't look at the floor. Speak up. Speak to the entire class, not just to me!" But I couldn't believe that the English language was mine to use. (In part, I did not want to

From Hunger of Memory: The Education of Richard Rodriguez *(1982), an autobiography of Rodriguez's experiences as a student, including his controversial argument against bilingual education.*

believe it.) I continued to mumble. I resisted the teacher's demands. (Did I somehow suspect that once I learned public language my pleasing family life would be changed?) Silent, waiting for the bell to sound, I remained dazed, diffident, afraid.

Because I wrongly imagined that English was intrinsically a public language and Spanish an intrinsically private one, I easily noted the difference between classroom language and the language of home. At school, words were directed to a general audience of listeners. ("Boys and girls.") Words were meaningfully ordered. And the point was not self-expression alone but to make oneself understood by many others. The teacher quizzed: "Boys and girls, why do we use that word in this sentence? Could we think of a better word to use there? Would the sentence change its meaning if the words were differently arranged? And wasn't there a better way of saying much the same thing?" (I couldn't say. I wouldn't try to say.)

5 Three months. Five. Half a year passed. Unsmiling, ever watchful, my teachers noted my silence. They began to connect my behavior with the difficult progress my older sister and brother were making. Until one Saturday morning three nuns arrived at the house to talk to our parents. Stiffly, they sat on the blue living room sofa. From the doorway of another room, spying the visitors, I noted the incongruity—the clash of two worlds, the faces and voices of school intruding upon the familiar setting of home. I overheard one voice gently wondering, "Do your children speak only Spanish at home, Mrs. Rodriguez?" While another voice added, "That Richard especially seems so timid and shy."

That Rich-heard!

With great tact the visitors continued, "Is it possible for you and your husband to encourage your children to practice their English when they are home?" Of course, my parents complied. What would they not do for their children's well-being? And how could they have questioned the Church's authority which those women represented? In an instant, they agreed to give up the language (the sounds) that had revealed and accentuated our family's closeness. The moment after the visitors left, the change was observed. "*Ahora,* speak to us *en inglés,*"[1] my father and mother united to tell us.

At first, it seemed a kind of game. After dinner each night, the family gathered to practice "our" English. (It was still then *inglés,* a language foreign to us, so we felt drawn as strangers to it.) Laughing, we would try to define words we could not pronounce. We played with strange English sounds, often overanglicizing our pronunciations. And we filled the smiling gaps of our sentences with familiar Spanish sounds. But that was cheating, somebody shouted. Everyone laughed. In school, meanwhile, like my brother and sister, I was required to attend a daily tutoring session. I needed a full year of special attention. I also needed my teachers to keep my attention from straying in class by calling out, *Rich-heard*—their English voices slowly prying loose my ties to my other name, its three notes, *Ri-car-do.* Most of all I needed to hear my mother and father speak to me in a moment of seriousness in broken—suddenly heartbreaking—

1. "*Now,* speak to us *in English.*"

English. The scene was inevitable: One Saturday morning I entered the kitchen where my parents were talking in Spanish. I did not realize that they were talking in Spanish however until, at the moment they saw me, I heard their voices change to speak English. Those *gringo* sounds they uttered startled me. Pushed me away. In that moment of trivial misunderstanding and profound insight, I felt my throat twisted by unsounded grief. I turned quickly and left the room. But I had no place to escape to with Spanish. (The spell was broken.) My brother and sisters were speaking English in another part of the house.

Again and again in the days following, increasingly angry, I was obliged to hear my mother and father: "Speak to us *en inglés*." (*Speak*.) Only then did I determine to learn classroom English. Weeks after, it happened: One day in school I raised my hand to volunteer an answer. I spoke out in a loud voice. And I did not think it remarkable when the entire class understood. That day, I moved very far from the disadvantaged child I had been only days earlier. The belief, that calming assurance that I belonged in public, had at last taken hold.

10 Shortly after, I stopped hearing the high and loud sounds of *los gringos*. A more and more confident speaker of English, I didn't trouble to listen to *how* strangers sounded, speaking to me. And there simply were too many English-speaking people in my day for me to hear American accents anymore. Conversations quickened. Listening to persons who sounded eccentrically pitched voices, I usually noted their sounds for an initial few seconds before I concentrated on *what* they were saying. Conversations became content-full. Transparent. Hearing someone's *tone* of voice—angry or questioning or sarcastic or happy or sad—I didn't distinguish it from the words it expressed. Sound and word were thus tightly wedded. At the end of a day, I was often bemused, always relieved, to realize how "silent," though crowded with words, my day in public had been. (This public silence measured and quickened the change in my life.)

At last, seven years old, I came to believe what had been technically true since my birth: I was an American citizen.

But the special feeling of closeness at home was diminished by then. Gone was the desperate, urgent, intense feeling of being at home; rare was the experience of feeling myself individualized by family intimates. We remained a loving family, but one greatly changed. No longer so close; no longer bound tight by the pleasing and troubling knowledge of our public separateness. Neither my older brother nor sister rushed home after school anymore. Nor did I. When I arrived home there would often be neighborhood kids in the house. Or the house would be empty of sounds.

Following the dramatic Americanization of their children, even my parents grew more publicly confident. Especially my mother. She learned the names of all the people on our block. And she decided we needed to have a telephone installed in the house. My father continued to use the word *gringo*. But it was no longer charged with the old bitterness or distrust. (Stripped of any emotional content, the word simply became a name for those Americans not of Hispanic descent.) Hearing him, sometimes, I wasn't sure if he was pronouncing the Spanish word *gringo* or saying gringo in English.

Matching the silence I started hearing in public was a new quiet at home. The family's quiet was partly due to the fact that, as we children learned more and more English, we shared fewer and fewer words with our parents. Sentences needed to be spoken slowly when a child addressed his mother or father. (Often the parent wouldn't understand.) The child would need to repeat himself. (Still the parent misunderstood.) The young voice, frustrated, would end up saying, "Never mind"—the subject was closed. Dinners would be noisy with the clinking of knives and forks against dishes. My mother would smile softly between her remarks; my father at the other end of the table would chew and chew at his food, while he stared over the heads of his children.

15 My *mother*! My *father*! After English became my primary language, I no longer knew what words to use in addressing my parents. The old Spanish words (those tender accents of sound) I had used earlier—*mamá* and *papá*—I couldn't use anymore. They would have been too painful reminders of how much had changed in my life. On the other hand, the words I heard neighborhood kids call *their* parents seemed equally unsatisfactory. *Mother* and *Father; Ma, Papa, Pa, Dad, Pop* (how I hated the all American sound of that last word especially)—all these terms I felt were unsuitable, not really terms of address for *my* parents. As a result, I never used them at home. Whenever I'd speak to my parents, I would try to get their attention with eye contact alone. In public conversations, I'd refer to "my parents" or "my mother and father."

My mother and father, for their part, responded differently, as their children spoke to them less. She grew restless, seemed troubled and anxious at the scarcity of words exchanged in the house. It was she who would question me about my day when I came home from school. She smiled at small talk. She pried at the edges of my sentences to get me to say something more. (What?) She'd join conversations she overheard, but her intrusions often stopped her children's talking. By contrast, my father seemed reconciled to the new quiet. Though his English improved somewhat, he retired into silence. At dinner he spoke very little. One night his children and even his wife helplessly giggled at his garbled English pronunciation of the Catholic Grace before Meals. Thereafter he made his wife recite the prayer at the start of each meal, even on formal occasions, when there were guests in the house. Hers became the public voice of the family. On official business, it was she, not my father, one would usually hear on the phone or in stores, talking to strangers. His children grew so accustomed to his silence that, years later, they would speak routinely of his shyness. (My mother would often try to explain: Both his parents died when he was eight. He was raised by an uncle who treated him like little more than a menial servant. He was never encouraged to speak. He grew up alone. A man of few words.) But my father was not shy, I realized, when I'd watch him speaking Spanish with relatives. Using Spanish, he was quickly effusive. Especially when talking with other men, his voice would spark, flicker, flare alive with sounds. In Spanish, he expressed ideas and feelings he rarely revealed in English. With firm Spanish sounds, he conveyed confidence and authority English would never allow him.

The silence at home, however, was finally more than a literal silence. Fewer words passed between parent and child, but more profound was the silence that resulted from my inattention to sounds. At about the time I no longer bothered to listen with care to the sounds of English in public, I grew careless about listening to the sounds family members made when they spoke. Most of the time I heard someone speaking at home and didn't distinguish his sounds from the words people uttered in public. I didn't even pay much attention to my parents' accented and ungrammatical speech. At least not at home. Only when I was with them in public would I grow alert to their accents. Though, even then, their sounds caused me less and less concern. For I was increasingly confident of my own public identity.

I would have been happier about my public success had I not sometimes recalled what it had been like earlier, when my family had conveyed its intimacy through a set of conveniently private sounds. Sometimes in public, hearing a stranger, I'd hark back to my past. A Mexican farmworker approached me downtown to ask directions to somewhere, "*¿Hijito . . . ?*"[2] he said. And his voice summoned deep longing. Another time, standing beside my mother in the visiting room of a Carmelite convent,[3] before the dense screen which rendered the nuns shadowy figures, I heard several Spanish-speaking nuns—their busy, singsong overlapping voices—assure us that yes, yes, we were remembered, all our family was remembered in their prayers. (Their voices echoed faraway family sounds.) Another day, a dark-faced old woman—her hand light on my shoulder—steadied herself against me as she boarded a bus. She murmured something I couldn't quite comprehend. Her Spanish voice came near, like the face of a never-before-seen relative in the instant before I was kissed. Her voice, like so many of the Spanish voices I'd hear in public, recalled the golden age of my youth. Hearing Spanish then, I continued to be a careful, if sad, listener to sounds. Hearing a Spanish-speaking family walking behind me, I turned to look. I smiled for an instant, before my glance found the Hispanic-looking faces of strangers in the crowd going by.

Today I hear bilingual educators say that children lose a degree of "individuality" by becoming assimilated into public society. (Bilingual schooling was popularized in the seventies, that decade when middle-class ethnics began to resist the process of assimilation—the American melting pot.) But the bilingualists simplistically scorn the value and necessity of assimilation. They do not seem to realize that there are *two* ways a person is individualized. So they do not realize that while one suffers a diminished sense of *private* individuality by becoming assimilated into public society, such assimilation makes possible the achievement of *public* individuality.

20 The bilingualists insist that a student should be reminded of his difference from others in mass society, his heritage. But they equate mere separateness with individuality. The fact is that only in private—with intimates—is separateness from the crowd a prerequisite for individuality. (An intimate draws me apart, tells me that I am unique, unlike all others.) In public, by

2. "Little boy . . . ?"
3. Of the Catholic Order of Our Lady of Mount Carmel.

contrast, full individuality is achieved, paradoxically, by those who are able to consider themselves members of the crowd. Thus it happened for me: Only when I was able to think of myself as an American, no longer an alien in *gringo* society, could I seek the rights and opportunities necessary for full public individuality. The social and political advantages I enjoy as a man result from the day that I came to believe that my name, indeed, is *Rich-heard Road-ree-guess*. It is true that my public society today is often impersonal. (My public society is usually mass society.) Yet despite the anonymity of the crowd and despite the fact that the individuality I achieve in public is often tenuous—because it depends on my being one in a crowd—I celebrate the day I acquired my new name. Those middle-class ethnics who scorn assimilation seem to me filled with decadent self-pity, obsessed by the burden of public life. Dangerously, they romanticize public separateness and they trivialize the dilemma of the socially disadvantaged.

My awkward childhood does not prove the necessity of bilingual education. My story discloses instead an essential myth of childhood—inevitable pain. If I rehearse here the changes in my private life after my Americanization, it is finally to emphasize the public gain. The loss implies the gain: The house I returned to each afternoon was quiet. Intimate sounds no longer rushed to the door to greet me. There were other noises inside. The telephone rang. Neighborhood kids ran past the door of the bedroom where I was reading my schoolbooks—covered with shopping-bag paper. Once I learned public language, it would never again be easy for me to hear intimate family voices. More and more of my day was spent hearing words. But that may only be a way of saying that the day I raised my hand in class and spoke loudly to an entire roomful of faces, my childhood started to end.

QUESTIONS

1. What, according to Rodriguez, did he lose because he attended an English-speaking (Catholic) school without a bilingual program? What did he gain?

2. Rodriguez frames this section of his autobiography with an argument against bilingual education. How convincing is his evidence? Does he claim that all nonnative speakers of English educated in English would have the same losses and gains as he did?

3. According to Rodriguez, what are the differences between private and public languages, private and public individuality? Can both exist when the family language and the school language are English? How might a native speaker of English describe the differences?

4. Make a case, in writing, for or against bilingual education using material from Gloria Naylor's "Mommy, What Does 'Nigger' Mean?" (p. 420), Maxine Hong Kingston's "Tongue-Tied" (p. 401), and Gloria Anzaldúa's "How to Tame a Wild Tongue" (p. 411), as well as your own experience, observation, and reading.

Gloria Anzaldúa *How to Tame a Wild Tongue*

"We're going to have to control your tongue," the dentist says, pulling out all the metal from my mouth. Silver bits plop and tinkle into the basin. My mouth is a motherlode.

The dentist is cleaning out my roots. I get a whiff of the stench when I gasp. "I can't cap that tooth yet, you're still draining," he says.

"We're going to have to do something about your tongue," I hear the anger rising in his voice. My tongue keeps pushing out the wads of cotton, pushing back the drills, the long thin needles. "I've never seen anything as strong or as stubborn," he says. And I think, how do you tame a wild tongue, train it to be quiet, how do you bridle and saddle it? How do you make it lie down?

> "Who is to say that robbing a people of
> its language is less violent than war?"
>
> —Ray Gwyn Smith[1]

I remember being caught speaking Spanish at recess—that was good for three licks on the knuckles with a sharp ruler. I remember being sent to the corner of the classroom for "talking back" to the Anglo teacher when all I was trying to do was tell her how to pronounce my name. "If you want to be American, speak 'American.' If you don't like it, go back to Mexico where you belong."

5 "I want you to speak English. *Pa'hallar buen trabajo tienes que saber hablar el inglés bien. Qué vale toda tu educación si todavía hablas inglés con un* 'accent,'" my mother would say, mortified that I spoke English like a Mexican. At Pan American University, I, and all Chicano students were required to take two speech classes. Their purpose: to get rid of our accents.

Attacks on one's form of expression with the intent to censor are a violation of the First Amendment. *El Anglo con cara de inocente nos arrancó la lengua.* Wild tongues can't be tamed, they can only be cut out.

Overcoming the Tradition of Silence

> *Ahogadas, escupimos el oscuro.*
> *Peleando con nuestra propia sombra*
> *el silencio nos sepulta.*

En boca cerrada no entran moscas. "Flies don't enter a closed mouth" is a saying I kept hearing when I was a child. *Ser habladora* was to be a gossip and a liar, to talk too much. *Muchachitas bien criadas,* well-bred girls don't answer

From Borderlands/La Frontera *(1987), a collection of experimental essays and memoirs that combine English, Spanish, and Chicano Spanish. All notes are the author's. The author has asked that no translations of Spanish or Chicano Spanish be included.*

1. Ray Gwyn Smith, *Moorland Is Cold Country*, unpublished book.

back. *Es una falta de respeto* to talk back to one's mother or father. I remember one of the sins I'd recite to the priest in the confession box the few times I went to confession: talking back to my mother, *hablar pa' 'trás, repelar. Hocicona, repelona, chismosa,* having a big mouth, questioning, carrying tales are all signs of being *mal criada.* In my culture they are all words that are derogatory if applied to women—I've never heard them applied to men.

The first time I heard two women, a Puerto Rican and a Cuban, say the word "*nosotras*," I was shocked. I had not known the word existed. Chicanas use *nosotros* whether we're male or female. We are robbed of our female being by the masculine plural. Language is a male discourse.

> And our tongues have become
> dry the wilderness has
> dried out our tongues and
> we have forgotten speech.
>
> —IRENA KLEPFISZ[2]

Even our own people, other Spanish speakers *nos quieren poner candados en la boca.* They would hold us back with their bag of *reglas de académia.*

Oyé como ladra: el lenguaje de la frontera

> *Quien tiene boca se equivoca.*
>
> —MEXICAN SAYING

10 "*Pocho,* cultural traitor, you're speaking the oppressor's language by speaking English, you're ruining the Spanish language," I have been accused by various Latinos and Latinas. Chicano Spanish is considered by the purist and by most Latinos deficient, a mutilation of Spanish.

But Chicano Spanish is a border tongue which developed naturally. Change, *evolución, enriquecimiento de palabras nuevas por invención o adopción* have created variants of Chicano Spanish, *un nuevo lenguaje. Un lenguaje que corresponde a un modo de vivir.* Chicano Spanish is not incorrect, it is a living language.

For a people who are neither Spanish nor live in a country in which Spanish is the first language; for a people who live in a country in which English is the reigning tongue but who are not Anglo; for a people who cannot entirely identify with either standard (formal, Castilian) Spanish nor standard English, what recourse is left to them but to create their own language? A language which they can connect their identity to, one capable of communicating the realities and values true to themselves—a language with terms that are neither *español ni inglés,* but both. We speak a patois, a forked tongue, a variation of two languages.

2. Irena Klepfisz, "*Di rayze aheym*/The Journey Home," in *The Tribe of Dina: A Jewish Women's Anthology,* Melanie Kaye/Kantrowitz and Irena Klepfisz, eds. (Montpelier, VT: Sinister Wisdom Books, 1986), 49.

Chicano Spanish sprang out of the Chicanos' need to identify ourselves as a distinct people. We needed a language with which we could communicate with ourselves, a secret language. For some of us, language is a homeland closer than the Southwest—for many Chicanos today live in the Midwest and the East. And because we are a complex, heterogeneous people, we speak many languages. Some of the languages we speak are:

1. Standard English
2. Working class and slang English
3. Standard Spanish
4. Standard Mexican Spanish
5. North Mexican Spanish dialect
6. Chicano Spanish (Texas, New Mexico, Arizona and California have regional variations)
7. Tex-Mex
8. *Pachuco* (called *caló*)

My "home" tongues are the languages I speak with my sister and brothers, with my friends. They are the last five listed, with 6 and 7 being closest to my heart. From school, the media and job situations, I've picked up standard and working class English. From Mamagrande Locha and from reading Spanish and Mexican literature, I've picked up Standard Spanish and Standard Mexican Spanish. From *los recién llegados,* Mexican immigrants, and *braceros*, I learned the North Mexican dialect. With Mexicans I'll try to speak either Standard Mexican Spanish or the North Mexican dialect. From my parents and Chicanos living in the Valley, I picked up Chicano Texas Spanish, and I speak it with my mom, younger brother (who married a Mexican and who rarely mixes Spanish with English), aunts and older relatives.

15 With Chicanas from *Nuevo México* or *Arizona* I will speak Chicano Spanish a little, but often they don't understand what I'm saying. With most California Chicanas I speak entirely in English (unless I forget). When I first moved to San Francisco, I'd rattle off something in Spanish, unintentionally embarrassing them. Often it is only with another Chicana *tejana* that I can talk freely.

Words distorted by English are known as anglicisms or *pochismos*. The *pocho* is an anglicized Mexican or American of Mexican origin who speaks Spanish with an accent characteristic of North Americans and who distorts and reconstructs the language according to the influence of English.[3] Tex-Mex, or Spanglish, comes most naturally to me. I may switch back and forth from English to Spanish in the same sentence or in the same word. With my sister and my brother Nune and with Chicano *tejano* contemporaries I speak in Tex-Mex.

3. R. C. Ortega, *Dialectología Del Barrio*, trans. Hortencia S. Alwan (Los Angeles, CA: R. C. Ortega Publisher & Bookseller, 1977), 132.

From kids and people my own age I picked up *Pachuco. Pachuco* (the language of the zoot suiters) is a language of rebellion, both against Standard Spanish and Standard English. It is a secret language. Adults of the culture and outsiders cannot understand it. It is made up of slang words from both English and Spanish. *Ruca* means girl or woman, *vato* means guy or dude, *chale* means no, *simón* means yes, *churo* is sure, talk is *periquiar, pigionear* means petting, *que gacho* means how nerdy, *ponte águila* means watch out, death is called *la pelona*. Through lack of practice and not having others who can speak it, I've lost most of the *Pachuco* tongue.

CHICANO SPANISH

Chicanos, after 250 years of Spanish/Anglo colonization, have developed significant differences in the Spanish we speak. We collapse two adjacent vowels into a single syllable and sometimes shift the stress in certain words such as *maíz/maiz, cohete/cuete*. We leave out certain consonants when they appear between vowels: *lado/lao, mojado/mojao*. Chicanos from South Texas pronounced *f* as *j* as in *jue (fue)*. Chicanos use "archaisms," words that are no longer in the Spanish language, words that have been evolved out. We say *semos, truje, haiga, ansina,* and *naiden*. We retain the "archaic" *j*, as in *jalar*, that derives from an earlier *h* (the French *halar* or the Germanic *halon* which was lost to standard Spanish in the 16th century), but which is still found in several regional dialects such as the one spoken in South Texas. (Due to geography, Chicanos from the Valley of South Texas were cut off linguistically from other Spanish speakers. We tend to use words that the Spaniards brought over from Medieval Spain. The majority of the Spanish colonizers in Mexico and the Southwest came from Extremadura—Hernán Cortés was one of them—and Andalucía. Andalucians pronounce *ll* like a *y*, and their *d*'s tend to be absorbed by adjacent vowels: *tirado* becomes *tirao*. They brought *el lenguaje popular, dialectos y regionalismos.*[4])

Chicanos and other Spanish speakers also shift *ll* to *y* and *z* to *s*.[5] We leave out initial syllables, saying *tar* for *estar, toy* for *estoy, hora* for *ahora* (*cubanos* and *puertorriqueños* also leave out initial letters of some words). We also leave out the final syllable such as *pa* for *para*. The intervocalic *y*, the *ll* as in *tortilla, ella, botella,* gets replaced by *tortia* or *tortiya, ea, botea*. We add an additional syllable at the beginning of certain words: *atocar* for *tocar, agastar* for *gastar*. Sometimes we'll say *lavaste las vacijas,* other times *lavates* (substituting the *ates* verb endings for the *aste*).

20 We use anglicisms, words borrowed from English: *bola* from ball, *carpeta* from carpet, *máchina de lavar* (instead of *lavadora*) from washing machine. Tex-Mex argot, created by adding a Spanish sound at the beginning or end of an English word such as *cookiar* for cook, *watchar* for watch, *parkiar* for park,

4. Eduardo Hernandéz-Chávez, Andrew D. Cohen, and Anthony F. Beltramo, *El Lenguaje de los Chicanos: Regional and Social Characteristics of Language Used by Mexican Americans* (Arlington, VA: Center for Applied Linguistics, 1975), 39.

5. Hernandéz-Chávez, xvii.

and *rapiar* for rape, is the result of the pressures on Spanish speakers to adapt to English.

We don't use the word *vosotros/as* or its accompanying verb form. We don't say *claro* (to mean yes), *imagínate*, or *me emociona,* unless we picked up Spanish from Latinas, out of a book, or in a classroom. Other Spanish-speaking groups are going through the same, or similar, development in their Spanish.

Linguistic Terrorism

> *Deslenguadas. Somos los del español deficiente.* We are your linguistic nightmare, your linguistic aberration, your linguistic *mestizaje*, the subject of your *burla*. Because we speak with tongues of fire we are culturally crucified. Racially, culturally and linguistically *somos huérfanos*—we speak an orphan tongue.

Chicanas who grew up speaking Chicano Spanish have internalized the belief that we speak poor Spanish. It is illegitimate, a bastard language. And because we internalize how our language has been used against us by the dominant culture, we use our language differences against each other.

Chicana feminists often skirt around each other with suspicion and hesitation. For the longest time I couldn't figure it out. Then it dawned on me. To be close to another Chicana is like looking into the mirror. We are afraid of what we'll see there. *Pena.* Shame. Low estimation of self. In childhood we are told that our language is wrong. Repeated attacks on our native tongue diminish our sense of self. The attacks continue throughout our lives.

Chicanas feel uncomfortable talking in Spanish to Latinas, afraid of their censure. Their language was not outlawed in their countries. They had a whole lifetime of being immersed in their native tongue; generations, centuries in which Spanish was a first language, taught in school, heard on radio and TV, and read in the newspaper.

25 If a person, Chicana or Latina, has a low estimation of my native tongue, she also has a low estimation of me. Often with *mexicanas y latinas* we'll speak English as a neutral language. Even among Chicanas we tend to speak English at parties or conferences. Yet, at the same time, we're afraid the other will think we're *agringadas* because we don't speak Chicano Spanish. We oppress each other trying to out-Chicano each other, vying to be the "real" Chicanas, to speak like Chicanos. There is no one Chicano language just as there is no one Chicano experience. A monolingual Chicana whose first language is English or Spanish is just as much a Chicana as one who speaks several variants of Spanish. A Chicana from Michigan or Chicago or Detroit is just as much a Chicana as one from the Southwest. Chicano Spanish is as diverse linguistically as it is regionally.

By the end of this century, Spanish speakers will comprise the biggest minority group in the U.S., a country where students in high schools and colleges are encouraged to take French classes because French is considered more "cultured." But for a language to remain alive it must be used.[6] By the

6. Irena Klepfisz, "Secular Jewish Identity: Yidishkayt in America," in *The Tribe of Dina*, Kaye/Kantrowitz and Klepfisz, eds., 43.

end of this century English, and not Spanish, will be the mother tongue of most Chicanos and Latinos.

So, if you want to really hurt me, talk badly about my language. Ethnic identity is twin skin to linguistic identity—I am my language. Until I can take pride in my language, I cannot take pride in myself. Until I can accept as legitimate Chicano Texas Spanish, Tex-Mex and all the other languages I speak, I cannot accept the legitimacy of myself. Until I am free to write bilingually and to switch codes without having always to translate, while I still have to speak English or Spanish when I would rather speak Spanglish, and as long as I have to accommodate the English speakers rather than having them accommodate me, my tongue will be illegitimate.

I will no longer be made to feel ashamed of existing. I will have my voice: Indian, Spanish, white. I will have my serpent's tongue—my woman's voice, my sexual voice, my poet's voice. I will overcome the tradition of silence.

> My fingers
> move sly against your palm
> Like women everywhere, we speak in code. . . .
>
> —MELANIE KAYE/KANTROWITZ[7]

"Vistas," corridos, y comida: My Native Tongue

In the 1960s, I read my first Chicano novel. It was *City of Night* by John Rechy, a gay Texan, son of a Scottish father and a Mexican mother. For days I walked around in stunned amazement that a Chicano could write and could get published. When I read *I Am Joaquín*[8] I was surprised to see a bilingual book by a Chicano in print. When I saw poetry written in Tex-Mex for the first time, a feeling of pure joy flashed through me. I felt like we really existed as a people. In 1971, when I started teaching High School English to Chicano students, I tried to supplement the required texts with works by Chicanos, only to be reprimanded and forbidden to do so by the principal. He claimed that I was supposed to teach "American" and English literature. At the risk of being fired, I swore my students to secrecy and slipped in Chicano short stories, poems, a play. In graduate school, while working toward a Ph.D., I had to "argue" with one advisor after the other, semester after semester, before I was allowed to make Chicano literature an area of focus.

30 Even before I read books by Chicanos or Mexicans, it was the Mexican movies I saw at the drive-in—the Thursday night special of $1.00 a carload—that gave me a sense of belonging. *"Vámonos a las vistas,"* my mother would call out and we'd all—grandmother, brothers, sister and cousins—squeeze into the

7. Melanie Kaye/Kantrowitz, "Sign," in *We Speak in Code: Poems and Other Writings* (Pittsburgh, PA: Motheroot Publications, Inc., 1980), 85.

8. Rodolfo Gonzales, *I Am Joaquín/Yo Soy Joaquín* (New York, NY: Bantam Books, 1972). It was first published in 1967.

car. We'd wolf down cheese and bologna white bread sandwiches while watching Pedro Infante in melodramatic tear-jerkers like *Nosotros los pobres,* the first "real" Mexican movie (that was not an imitation of European movies). I remember seeing *Cuando los hijos se van* and surmising that all Mexican movies played up the love a mother has for her children and what ungrateful sons and daughters suffer when they are not devoted to their mothers. I remember the singing-type "westerns" of Jorge Negrete and Miguel Aceves Mejía. When watching Mexican movies, I felt a sense of homecoming as well as alienation. People who were to amount to something didn't go to Mexican movies, or *bailes* or tune their radios to *bolero, rancherita,* and *corrido* music.

The whole time I was growing up, there was *norteño* music sometimes called North Mexican border music, or Tex-Mex music, or Chicano music, or *cantina* (bar) music. I grew up listening to *conjuntos,* three- or four-piece bands made up of folk musicians playing guitar, *bajo sexto,* drums and button accordion, which Chicanos had borrowed from the German immigrants who had come to Central Texas and Mexico to farm and build breweries. In the Rio Grande Valley, Steve Jordan and Little Joe Hernández were popular, and Flaco Jiménez was the accordion king. The rhythms of Tex-Mex music are those of the polka, also adapted from the Germans, who in turn had borrowed the polka from the Czechs and Bohemians.

I remember the hot, sultry evenings when *corridos*—songs of love and death on the Texas-Mexican borderlands—reverberated out of cheap amplifiers from the local *cantinas* and wafted in through my bedroom window.

Corridos first became widely used along the South Texas/Mexican border during the early conflict between Chicanos and Anglos. The *corridos* are usually about Mexican heroes who do valiant deeds against the Anglo oppressors. Pancho Villa's song, "*La cucaracha,*" is the most famous one. *Corridos* of John F. Kennedy and his death are still very popular in the Valley. Older Chicanos remember Lydia Mendoza, one of the great border *corrido* singers who was called *la Gloria de Tejas*. Her "*El tango negro,*" sung during the Great Depression, made her a singer of the people. The everpresent *corridos* narrated one hundred years of border history, bringing news of events as well as entertaining. These folk musicians and folk songs are our chief cultural mythmakers, and they made our hard lives seem bearable.

I grew up feeling ambivalent about our music. Country-western and rock-and-roll had more status. In the 50s and 60s, for the slightly educated and *agringado* Chicanos, there existed a sense of shame at being caught listening to our music. Yet I couldn't stop my feet from thumping to the music, could not stop humming the words, nor hide from myself the exhilaration I felt when I heard it.

35 There are more subtle ways that we internalize identification, especially in the forms of images and emotions. For me food and certain smells are tied to my identity, to my homeland. Woodsmoke curling up to an immense blue sky; woodsmoke perfuming my grandmother's clothes, her skin. The stench of cow manure and the yellow patches on the ground; the crack of a .22 rifle and the

reek of cordite. Homemade white cheese sizzling in a pan, melting inside a folded *tortilla*. My sister Hilda's hot, spicy *menudo, chile colorado* making it deep red, pieces of *panza* and hominy floating on top. My brother Carito barbecuing *fajitas* in the backyard. Even now and 3,000 miles away, I can see my mother spicing the ground beef, pork and venison with *chile*. My mouth salivates at the thought of the hot steaming *tamales* I would be eating if I were home.

Si le preguntas a mi mamá, "¿Qué eres?"

> "Identity is the essential core of who we are as individuals, the conscious experience of the self inside."
>
> —KAUFMAN[9]

Nosotros los Chicanos straddle the borderlands. On one side of us, we are constantly exposed to the Spanish of the Mexicans, on the other side we hear the Anglos' incessant clamoring so that we forget our language. Among ourselves we don't say *nosotros los americanos, o nosotros los españoles, o nosotros los hispanos.* We say *nosotros los mexicanos* (by *mexicanos* we do not mean citizens of Mexico; we do not mean a national identity, but a racial one). We distinguish between *mexicanos del otro lado* and *mexicanos de este lado.* Deep in our hearts we believe that being Mexican has nothing to do with which country one lives in. Being Mexican is a state of soul—not one of mind, not one of citizenship. Neither eagle nor serpent, but both. And like the ocean, neither animal respects borders.

> *Dime con quien andas y te diré quien eres.*
> (Tell me who your friends are and I'll tell you who you are.)
>
> —MEXICAN SAYING

Si le preguntas a mi mamá, "¿Qué eres?" te dirá, "Soy mexicana." My brothers and sister say the same. I sometimes will answer "*soy mexicana*" and at others will say "*soy Chicana*" *o* "*soy tejana.*" But I identified as "*Raza*" before I ever identified as "*mexicana*" or "Chicana."

As a culture, we call ourselves Spanish when referring to ourselves as a linguistic group and when copping out. It is then that we forget our predominant Indian genes. We are 70 to 80% Indian.[10] We call ourselves Hispanic[11] or Spanish-American or Latin American or Latin when linking ourselves to other Spanish-speaking peoples of the Western hemisphere and when copping out. We call ourselves Mexican-American[12] to signify we are neither Mexican nor

9. Kaufman, 68.

10. Chávez, 88–90.

11. "Hispanic" is derived from *Hispanis* (*España*, a name given to the Iberian Peninsula in ancient times when it was a part of the Roman Empire) and is a term designated by the U.S. government to make it easier to handle us on paper.

12. The Treaty of Guadalupe Hidalgo created the Mexican-American in 1848.

American, but more the noun "American" than the adjective "Mexican" (and when copping out).

Chicanos and other people of color suffer economically for not acculturating. This voluntary (yet forced) alienation makes for psychological conflict, a kind of dual identity—we don't identify with the Anglo-American cultural values and we don't totally identify with the Mexican cultural values. We are a synergy of two cultures with various degrees of Mexicanness or Angloness. I have so internalized the borderland conflict that sometimes I feel like one cancels out the other and we are zero, nothing, no one. *A veces no soy nada ni nadie. Pero hasta cuando no lo soy, lo soy.*

40 When not copping out, when we know we are more than nothing, we call ourselves Mexican, referring to race and ancestry; *mestizo* when affirming both our Indian and Spanish (but we hardly ever own our Black ancestry); Chicano when referring to a politically aware people born and/or raised in the U.S.; *Raza* when referring to Chicanos; *tejanos* when we are Chicanos from Texas.

Chicanos did not know we were a people until 1965 when Cesar Chavez and the farmworkers united and *I Am Joaquín* was published and *la Raza Unida* party was formed in Texas. With that recognition, we became a distinct people. Something momentous happened to the Chicano soul—we became aware of our reality and acquired a name and a language (Chicano Spanish) that reflected that reality. Now that we had a name, some of the fragmented pieces began to fall together—who we were, what we were, how we had evolved. We began to get glimpses of what we might eventually become.

Yet the struggle of identities continues, the struggle of borders is our reality still. One day the inner struggle will cease and a true integration take place. In the meantime, *tenemos que hacerla lucha. ¿Quién está protegiendo los ranchos de mi gente? ¿Quién está tratando de cerrar la fisura entre la india y el blanco en nuestra sangre? El Chicano, sí, el Chicano que anda como un ladrón en su propia casa.*

Los Chicanos, how patient we seem, how very patient. There is the quiet of the Indian about us.[13] We know how to survive. When other races have given up their tongue, we've kept ours. We know what it is to live under the hammer blow of the dominant *norteamericano* culture. But more than we count the blows, we count the days the weeks the years the centuries the eons until the white laws and commerce and customs will rot in the deserts they've created, lie bleached. *Humildes* yet proud, *quietos* yet wild, *nosotros los mexicanos*-Chicanos will walk by the crumbling ashes as we go about our business. Stubborn, persevering, impenetrable as stone, yet possessing a malleability that renders us unbreakable, we, the *mestizas* and *mestizos*, will remain.

13. Anglos, in order to alleviate their guilt for dispossessing the Chicano, stressed the Spanish part of us and perpetrated the myth of the Spanish Southwest. We have accepted the fiction that we are Hispanic, that is Spanish, in order to accommodate ourselves to the dominant culture and its abhorrence of Indians. Chávez, 88–91.

QUESTIONS

1. Anzaldúa includes many Spanish words and phrases, some of which she explains, others which she leaves untranslated. Why? What different responses might bilingual versus English-only readers have to her writing?

2. The essay begins with an example of Anzaldúa's "untamed tongue." What meanings, many metaphoric, does Anzaldúa give for "tongue" or "wild tongue"? How does the essay develop these meanings?

3. Anzaldúa speaks of Chicano Spanish as a "living language" (paragraph 11). What does she mean? What is her evidence for this point? What other languages do you know that are living, and how do you know they are living?

4. If you speak or write more than one language, or if you come from a linguistic community that has expressions specific to itself, write an essay in which you incorporate that language and/or alternate it with English. Think about the ways that Anzaldúa uses both English and Spanish.

GLORIA NAYLOR *"Mommy, What Does 'Nigger' Mean?"*

LANGUAGE IS THE SUBJECT. It is the written form with which I've managed to keep the wolf away from the door and, in diaries, to keep my sanity. In spite of this, I consider the written word inferior to the spoken, and much of the frustration experienced by novelists is the awareness that whatever we manage to capture in even the most transcendent passages falls far short of the richness of life. Dialogue achieves its power in the dynamics of a fleeting moment of sight, sound, smell and touch.

I'm not going to enter the debate here about whether it is language that shapes reality or vice versa. That battle is doomed to be waged whenever we seek intermittent reprieve from the chicken and egg dispute. I will simply take the position that the spoken word, like the written word, amounts to a nonsensical arrangement of sounds or letters without a consensus that assigns "meaning." And building from the meanings of what we hear, we order reality. Words themselves are innocuous; it is the consensus that gives them true power.

Originally published in the "Hers" column of the New York Times *(February 20, 1986), which featured essays and commentary by women writers. The author wants it understood that the use of the word "nigger" is reprehensible in today's society. This essay speaks to a specific time and place when that word was utilized to empower African Americans; today it is used to degrade them even if spoken from their own mouths.*

I remember the first time I heard the word nigger. In my third-grade class, our math tests were being passed down the rows, and as I handed the papers to a little boy in back of me, I remarked that once again he had received a much lower mark than I did. He snatched his test from me and spit out that word. Had he called me a nymphomaniac or a necrophiliac, I couldn't have been more puzzled. I didn't know what a nigger was, but I knew that whatever it meant, it was something he shouldn't have called me. This was verified when I raised my hand, and in a loud voice repeated what he had said and watched the teacher scold him for using a "bad" word. I was later to go home and ask the inevitable question that every black parent must face—"Mommy, what does 'nigger' mean?"

And what exactly did it mean? Thinking back, I realize that this could not have been the first time the word was used in my presence. I was part of a large extended family that had migrated from the rural South after World War II and formed a close-knit network that gravitated around my maternal grandparents. Their ground-floor apartment in one of the buildings they owned in Harlem was a weekend mecca for my immediate family, along with countless aunts, uncles and cousins who brought along assorted friends. It was a bustling and open house with assorted neighbors and tenants popping in and out to exchange bits of gossip, pick up an old quarrel or referee the ongoing checkers game in which my grandmother cheated shamelessly. They were all there to let down their hair and put up their feet after a week of labor in the factories, laundries and shipyards of New York.

5 Amid the clamor, which could reach deafening proportions—two or three conversations going on simultaneously, punctuated by the sound of a baby's crying somewhere in the back rooms or out on the street—there was still a rigid set of rules about what was said and how. Older children were sent out of the living room when it was time to get into the juicy details about "you-know-who" up on the third floor who had gone and gotten herself "p-r-e-g-n-a-n-t!" But my parents, knowing that I could spell well beyond my years, always demanded that I follow the others out to play. Beyond sexual misconduct and death, everything else was considered harmless for our young ears. And so among the anecdotes of the triumphs and disappointments in the various workings of their lives, the word nigger was used in my presence, but it was set within contexts and inflections that caused it to register in my mind as something else.

In the singular, the word was always applied to a man who had distinguished himself in some situation that brought their approval for his strength, intelligence or drive:

"Did Johnny really do that?"

"I'm telling you, that nigger pulled in $6,000 of overtime last year. Said he got enough for a down payment on a house."

When used with a possessive adjective by a woman—"my nigger"—it became a term of endearment for husband or boyfriend. But it could be more than just a term applied to a man. In their mouths it became the pure essence of manhood—a disembodied force that channeled their past history of struggle and present survival against the odds into a victorious statement of being: "Yeah, that old foreman found out quick enough—you don't mess with a nigger."

10 In the plural, it became a description of some group within the community that had overstepped the bounds of decency as my family defined it: Parents who neglected their children, a drunken couple who fought in public, people who simply refused to look for work, those with excessively dirty mouths or unkempt households were all "trifling niggers." This particular circle could forgive hard times, unemployment, the occasional bout of depression—they had gone through all of that themselves—but the unforgivable sin was lack of self-respect.

A woman could never be a "nigger" in the singular, with its connotation of confirming worth. The noun girl was its closest equivalent in that sense, but only when used in direct address and regardless of the gender doing the addressing. "Girl" was a token of respect for a woman. The one-syllable word was drawn out to sound like three in recognition of the extra ounce of wit, nerve or daring that the woman had shown in the situation under discussion.

"G-i-r-l, stop. You mean you said that to his face?"

But if the word was used in a third-person reference or shortened so that it almost snapped out of the mouth, it always involved some element of communal disapproval. And age became an important factor in these exchanges. It was only between individuals of the same generation, or from an older person to a younger (but never the other way around), that "girl" would be considered a compliment.

I don't agree with the argument that use of the word nigger at this social stratum of the black community was an internalization of racism. The dynamics were the exact opposite: the people in my grandmother's living room took a word that whites used to signify worthlessness or degradation and rendered it impotent. Gathering there together, they transformed "nigger" to signify the varied and complex human beings they knew themselves to be. If the word was to disappear totally from the mouths of even the most liberal of white society, no one in that room was naïve enough to believe it would disappear from white minds. Meeting the word head-on, they proved it had absolutely nothing to do with the way they were determined to live their lives.

15 So there must have been dozens of times that the word "nigger" was spoken in front of me before I reached the third grade. But I didn't "hear" it until it was said by a small pair of lips that had already learned it could be a way to humiliate me. That was the word I went home and asked my mother about. And since she knew that I had to grow up in America, she took me in her lap and explained.

QUESTIONS

1. In her opening paragraph, Naylor writes that she considers "the written word inferior to the spoken." In what ways does she demonstrate the superiority of the spoken word in this essay?

2. Naylor claims that "[w]ords themselves are innocuous; it is the consensus that gives them true power" (paragraph 2). As a class, brainstorm a list of words that can have different meanings and connotations, depending on who uses the words.

3. Think of a word that has several different meanings in your own family or community. Write a personal essay in which you detail those meanings. Like Naylor, use grammatical terms (as well as age- and gender-specifics, if applicable) to categorize the different meanings.

PATRICIA WILLIAMS *The Death of the Profane: The Rhetoric of Race and Rights*

BUZZERS ARE BIG IN NEW YORK CITY. Favored particularly by smaller stores and boutiques, merchants throughout the city have installed them as screening devices to reduce the incidence of robbery: if the face at the door looks desirable, the buzzer is pressed and the door is unlocked. If the face is that of an undesirable, the door stays locked. Predictably, the issue of undesirability has revealed itself to be a racial determination. While controversial enough at first, even civil-rights organizations backed down eventually in the face of arguments that the buzzer system is a "necessary evil," that it is a "mere inconvenience" in comparison to the risks of being murdered, that suffering discrimination is not as bad as being assaulted, and that in any event it is not all blacks who are barred, just "17-year-old black males wearing running shoes and hooded sweatshirts."[1]

The installation of these buzzers happened swiftly in New York; stores that had always had their doors wide open suddenly became exclusive or received people by appointment only. I discovered them and their meaning one Saturday in 1986. I was shopping in Soho and saw in a store window a sweater that I wanted to buy for my mother. I pressed my round brown face to the window and my finger to the buzzer, seeking admittance. A narrow-eyed, white teenager wearing running shoes and feasting on bubble gum glared out, evaluating me for signs that would pit me against the limits of his social understanding. After about five seconds, he mouthed "We're closed," and blew pink rubber at me. It was two Saturdays before Christmas, at one o'clock in the afternoon; there were several white people in the store who appeared to be shopping for things for *their* mothers.

I was enraged. At that moment I literally wanted to break all the windows of the store and *take* lots of sweaters for my mother. In the flicker of his judgmental gray eyes, that saleschild had transformed my brightly sentimental,

A chapter in Williams's book The Alchemy of Race and Rights *(1991), which probes the roots of racism through anecdote and personal witness, as well as scholarly analysis of the law's inadequacies. All notes in the essay are the author's.*

1. "When 'By Appointment' Means Keep Out," *New York Times*, December 17, 1986, p. B1. Letter to the Editor from Michael Levin and Marguerita Levin, *New York Times*, January 11, 1987, p. E32.

joy-to-the-world, pre-Christmas spree to a shambles. He snuffed my sense of humanitarian catholicity, and there was nothing I could do to snuff his, without making a spectacle of myself.

I am still struck by the structure of power that drove me into such a blizzard of rage. There was almost nothing I could do, short of physically intruding upon him, that would humiliate him the way he humiliated me. No words, no gestures, no prejudices of my own would make a bit of difference to him; his refusal to let me into the store—it was Benetton's, whose colorfully punnish ad campaign is premised on wrapping every one of the world's peoples in its cottons and woolens—was an outward manifestation of his never having let someone like me into the realm of his reality. He had no compassion, no remorse, no reference to me; and no desire to acknowledge me even at the estranged level of arm's-length transactor. He saw me only as one who would take his money and therefore could not conceive that I was there to give him money.

5 In this weird ontological imbalance, I realized that buying something in that store was like bestowing a gift, the gift of my commerce, the lucre of my patronage. In the wake of my outrage, I wanted to take back the gift of appreciation that my peering in the window must have appeared to be. I wanted to take it back in the form of unappreciation, disrespect, defilement. I wanted to work so hard at wishing he could feel what I felt that he would never again mistake my hatred for some sort of plaintive wish to be included. I was quite willing to disenfranchise myself, in the heat of my need to revoke the flattery of my purchasing power. I was willing to boycott Benetton's, random white-owned businesses, and anyone who ever blew bubble gum in my face again.

My rage was admittedly diffuse, even self-destructive, but it was symmetrical. The perhaps loose-ended but utter propriety of that rage is no doubt lost not just to the young man who actually barred me, but to those who would appreciate my being barred only as an abstract precaution, who approve of those who would bar even as they deny that they would bar *me*.

The violence of my desire to burst into Benetton's is probably quite apparent. I often wonder if the violence, the exclusionary hatred, is equally apparent in the repeated public urgings that blacks understand the buzzer system by putting themselves in the shoes of white storeowners—that, in effect, blacks look into the mirror of frightened white faces for the reality of their undesirability; and that then blacks would "just as surely conclude that [they] would not let [themselves] in under similar circumstances."[2] (That some blacks might agree merely shows that some of us have learned too well the lessons of privatized intimacies of self-hatred and rationalized away the fullness of our public, participatory selves.)

On the same day I was barred from Benetton's, I went home and wrote the above impassioned account in my journal. On the day after that, I found I was still brooding, so I turned to a form of catharsis I have always found healing. I typed up as much of the story as I have just told, made a big poster of it, put a nice colorful border around it, and, after Benetton's was truly closed, stuck it

2. *New York Times*, January 11, 1987, p. E32.

to their big sweater-filled window. I exercised my first-amendment right to place my business with them right out in the street.

So that was the first telling of this story. The second telling came a few months later, for a symposium on Excluded Voices sponsored by a law review. I wrote an essay summing up my feelings about being excluded from Benetton's and analyzing "how the rhetoric of increased privatization, in response to racial issues, functions as the rationalizing agent of public unaccountability and, ultimately, irresponsibility." Weeks later, I received the first edit. From the first page to the last, my fury had been carefully cut out. My rushing, run-on rage had been reduced to simple declarative sentences. The active personal had been inverted in favor of the passive impersonal. My words were different; they spoke to me upside down. I was afraid to read too much of it at a time—meanings rose up at me oddly, stolen and strange.

A week and a half later, I received the second edit. All reference to Benetton's had been deleted because, according to the editors and the faculty adviser, it was defamatory; they feared harassment and liability; they said printing it would be irresponsible. I called them and offered to supply a footnote attesting to this as my personal experience at one particular location and of a buzzer system not limited to Benetton's; the editors told me that they were not in the habit of publishing things that were unverifiable. I could not but wonder, in this refusal even to let me file an affadavit, what it would take to make my experience verifiable. The testimony of an independent white bystander? (a requirement in fact imposed in U.S. Supreme Court holdings through the first part of the century[3]). 10

Two days *after* the piece was sent to press, I received copies of the final page proofs. All reference to my race had been eliminated because it was against "editorial policy" to permit descriptions of physiognomy. "I realize," wrote one editor, "that this was a very personal experience, but any reader will know what you must have looked like when standing at that window." In a telephone conversation to them, I ranted wildly about the significance of such an omission. "It's irrelevant," another editor explained in a voice gummy with soothing and patience; "It's nice and poetic," but it doesn't "advance the discussion of any principle . . . This is a law review, after all." Frustrated, I accused him of censorship; calmly he assured me it was not. "This is just a matter of style," he said with firmness and finality.

Ultimately I did convince the editors that mention of my race was central to the whole sense of the subsequent text; that my story became one of extreme paranoia without the information that I am black; or that it became one in which the reader had to fill in the gap by assumption, presumption, prejudgment, or prejudice. What was most interesting to me in this experience was how the blind application of principles of neutrality, through the device of omission, acted either to make me look crazy or to make the reader participate in old habits of cultural bias.

3. See generally *Blyew v. U.S.*, 80 U.S. 581 (1871), upholding a state's right to forbid blacks to testify against whites.

That was the second telling of my story. The third telling came last April, when I was invited to participate in a law-school conference on Equality and Difference. I retold my sad tale of exclusion from Soho's most glitzy boutique, focusing in this version on the law-review editing process as a consequence of an ideology of style rooted in a social text of neutrality. I opined:

> Law and legal writing aspire to formalized, color-blind, liberal ideals. Neutrality is the standard for assuring these ideals; yet the adherence to it is often determined by reference to an aesthetic of uniformity, in which difference is simply omitted. For example, when segregation was eradicated from the American lexicon, its omission led many to actually believe that racism therefore no longer existed. Race-neutrality in law has become the presumed antidote for race bias in real life. With the entrenchment of the notion of race-neutrality came attacks on the concept of affirmative action and the rise of reverse discrimination suits. Blacks, for so many generations deprived of jobs based on the color of our skin, are now told that we ought to find it demeaning to be hired, based on the color of our skin. Such is the silliness of simplistic either-or inversions as remedies to complex problems.
>
> What is truly demeaning in this era of double-speak-no-evil is going on interviews and not getting hired because someone doesn't think we'll be comfortable. It is demeaning not to get promoted because we're judged "too weak," then putting in a lot of energy the next time and getting fired because we're "too strong." It is demeaning to be told what we find demeaning. It is very demeaning to stand on street corners unemployed and begging. It is downright demeaning to have to explain why we haven't been employed for months and then watch the job go to someone who is "more experienced." It is outrageously demeaning that none of this can be called racism, even if it happens only to, or to large numbers of, black people; as long as it's done with a smile, a handshake and a shrug; as long as the phantom-word "race" is never used.
>
> The image of race as a phantom-word came to me after I moved into my late godmother's home. In an attempt to make it my own, I cleared the bedroom for painting. The following morning the room asserted itself, came rushing and raging at me through the emptiness, exactly as it had been for twenty-five years. One day filled with profuse and overwhelming complexity, the next day filled with persistently recurring memories. The shape of the past came to haunt me, the shape of the emptiness confronted me each time I was about to enter the room. The force of its spirit still drifts like an odor throughout the house.
>
> The power of that room, I have thought since, is very like the power of racism as status quo: it is deep, angry, eradicated from view, but strong enough to make everyone who enters the room walk around the bed that isn't there, avoiding the phantom as they did the substance, for fear of bodily harm. They do not even know they are avoiding; they defer to the unseen shapes of things with subtle responsiveness, guided by an impulsive awareness of nothingness, and the deep knowledge and denial of witchcraft at work.
>
> The phantom room is to me symbolic of the emptiness of formal equal opportunity, particularly as propounded by President Reagan, the Reagan Civil Rights Commission and the Reagan Supreme Court. Blindly formalized constructions of equal opportunity are the creation of a space that is

> filled in by a meandering stream of unguided hopes, dreams, fantasies, fears, recollections. They are the presence of the past in imaginary, imagistic form—the phantom-roomed exile of our longing.
>
> It is thus that I strongly believe in the efficacy of programs and paradigms like affirmative action. Blacks are the objects of a constitutional omission which has been incorporated into a theory of neutrality. It is thus that omission is really a form of expression, as oxymoronic as that sounds: racial omission is a literal part of original intent; it is the fixed, reiterated prophecy of the Founding Fathers. It is thus that affirmative action is an affirmation; the affirmative act of hiring—or hearing—blacks is a recognition of individuality that re-places blacks as a social statistic, that is profoundly interconnective to the fate of blacks and whites either as sub-groups or as one group. In this sense, affirmative action is as mystical and beyond-the-self as an initiation ceremony. It is an act of verification and of vision. It is an act of social as well as professional responsibility.

The following morning I opened the local newspaper, to find that the event of my speech had commanded two columns on the front page of the Metro section. I quote only the opening lines: "Affirmative action promotes prejudice by denying the status of women and blacks, instead of affirming them as its name suggests. So said New York City attorney Patricia Williams to an audience Wednesday."[4]

I clipped out the article and put it in my journal. In the margin there is a note to myself: eventually, it says, I should try to pull all these threads together into yet another law-review article. The problem, of course, will be that in the hierarchy of law-review citation, the article in the newspaper will have more authoritative weight about me, as a so-called "primary resource," than I will have; it will take precedence over my own citation of the unverifiable testimony of my speech. 15

I have used the Benetton's story a lot, in speaking engagements at various schools. I tell it whenever I am too tired to whip up an original speech from scratch. Here are some of the questions I have been asked in the wake of its telling:

Am I not privileging a racial perspective, by considering only the black point of view? Don't I have an obligation to include the "salesman's side" of the story?

Am I not putting the salesman on trial and finding him guilty of racism without giving him a chance to respond to or cross-examine me?

Am I not using the store window as a "metaphorical fence" against the potential of his explanation in order to represent my side as "authentic"?

How can I be sure I'm right? 20

What makes my experience the real black one anyway?

4. "Attorney Says Affirmative Action Denies Racism, Sexism," *Dominion Post* (Morgantown, West Virginia), April 8, 1988, p. B1.

Isn't it possible that another black person would disagree with my experience? If so, doesn't that render my story too unempirical and subjective to pay any attention to?

Always a major objection is to my having put the poster on Benetton's window. As one law professor put it: "It's one thing to publish this in a law review, where no one can take it personally, but it's another thing altogether to put your own interpretation right out there, just like that, uncontested, I mean, with nothing to counter it."*

*At the end of her essay, Williams added these observations. "These questions put me on trial—an imaginary trial where it is I who have the burden of proof—and proof being nothing less than the testimony of the salesman actually confessing yes yes I am a racist. These questions question my own ability to know, to assess, to be objective. And of course, since anything that happens to me is inherently subjective, they take away my power to know what happens to me in the world. Others, by this standard, will always know better than I. And my insistence on recounting stories from my own perspective will be treated as presumption, slander, paranoid hallucination, or just plain lies.

"Recently I got an urgent call from Thomas Grey of Stanford Law School. He had used this piece in his jurisprudence class, and a rumor got started that the Benetton's story wasn't true, that I had made it up, that it was a fantasy, a lie that was probably the product of a diseased mind trying to make all white people feel guilty. At this point I realized it almost didn't make any difference whether I was telling the truth or not—that the greater issue I had to face was the overwhelming weight of a disbelief that goes beyond mere disinclination to believe and becomes active suppression of anything I might have to say. The greater problem is a powerfully oppressive mechanism for denial of black self-knowledge and expression. And this denial cannot be separated from the simultaneously pathological willingness to believe certain things about blacks—not to believe them, but things about them.

"When students in Grey's class believed and then claimed that I had made it all up, they put me in a position like that of Tawana Brawley [a black woman who falsely claimed she was abducted and raped by white men (eds.)]. I mean that specifically: the social consequence of concluding that we are liars operates as a kind of public absolution of racism—the conclusion is not merely that we are troubled or that I am eccentric, but that we, as liars, are the norm. Therefore, the nonbelievers can believe, things of this sort really don't happen (even in the face of statistics to the contrary). Racism or rape is all a big fantasy concocted by troublesome minorities and women. It is interesting to recall the outcry in every national medium, from the *New York Post* to the *Times* to the major networks, in the wake of the Brawley case: who will ever again believe a black woman who cries rape by a white man? Now shift the frame a bit, and imagine a white male facing a consensus that he lied. Would there be a difference? Consider Charles Stuart, for example, the white Bostonian who accused a black man of murdering his pregnant wife and whose brother later alleged that in fact the brothers had conspired to murder her. Most people and the media not only did not claim but actively resisted believing that Stuart represented any kind of 'white male' norm. Instead he was written off as a troubled weirdo, a deviant—again even in the face of spousal-abuse statistics to the contrary. There was not a story I could find that carried on about 'who will ever believe' the next white man who cries murder."

QUESTIONS

1. Williams's essay is about how the "objective," "neutral" forms writing often takes can drain away the significance of a particular person's story. Can you find examples of this phenomenon in other writing you read? Or can you find examples of it on TV or radio talk shows, for instance?

2. How does Williams move from the Benetton story to her larger point?

3. How would you characterize the tone of Williams's essay? Does any of her original rage remain?

4. What do you think of Williams's posting her reaction on the Benetton window? Write your opinion of the function and effectiveness of this action.

JOHN MCWHORTER

The Cosmopolitan Tongue: The Universality of English

IN DEPICTING THE EMERGENCE of the world's languages as a curse of gibberish, the biblical tale of the Tower of Babel makes us moderns smile. Yet, considering the headache that 6,000 languages can induce in real life, the story makes a certain sense.

Not long ago, 33 of the FBI's 12,000 employees spoke Arabic, as did 6 of the 1,000 employees at the American Embassy in Iraq. How can we significantly improve that situation is a good question. It's hard to learn Arabic, and not only because it's hard to pick up any new language. Iraqi Arabic is actually one of several "dialects" of Arabic that is as different from the others as one Romance language is from another. Using Iraqi Arabic even in a country as close as Egypt would be like sitting down at a trattoria in Milan and ordering lunch in Portuguese.

Bookstore shelves groan under the weight of countless foreign-language self-teaching sets that are about as useful as the tonics and elixirs that passed as medicine a century ago and leave their students with anemic vocabularies and paltry grammar that are of little use in real conversation.

Even with good instruction, it is fiendishly difficult to learn any new language well, at least after about the age of 15. While vilified in certain quarters as threatening the future of the English language in America, most immigrants who actually try to improve their English skills here in the United States find that they have trouble communicating effectively even with doctors or their children's schoolteachers.

Yet the going idea among linguists and anthropologists is that we must keep as many languages alive as possible, and that the death of each one is 5

Published in World Affairs *(Fall 2009), a bimonthly journal devoted to conversations and debate about issues related to U.S. foreign policy.*

another step on a treadmill toward humankind's cultural oblivion. This accounted for the melancholy tone, for example, of the obituaries for the Eyak language of southern Alaska last year when its last speaker died.

That death did mean, to be sure, that no one will again use the word *demexch*, which refers to a soft spot in the ice where it is good to fish. Never again will we hear the word *'ał* for an evergreen branch, a word whose final sound is a whistling past the sides of the tongue that sounds like wind passing through just such a branch. And behind this small death is a larger context. Linguistic death is proceeding more rapidly even than species attrition. According to one estimate, a hundred years from now the 6,000 languages in use today will likely dwindle to 600. The question, though, is whether this is a problem.

As someone who has taught himself languages as a hobby since childhood and is an academic linguist, I hardly rejoice when a language dies. Other languages can put concepts together in ways that make them more fascinatingly different from English than most of us are aware they can be. In the Berik language in New Guinea, for example, verbs have to mark the sex of the person you are affecting, the size of the object you are wielding, and whether it is light outside. (*Kitobana* means "gives three large objects to a male in the sunlight.") Berik is doing fine for now, but is probably one of the languages we won't see around in 2109.

Assuming that we can keep 6,000 languages alive is the rough equivalent of supposing that we can stop, say, ice from developing soft spots. Here's why. As people speaking indigenous languages migrate to cities, inevitably they learn globally dominant languages like English and use them in their interactions with one another. The immigrants' children may use their parents' indigenous languages at home. But they never know those languages as part of their public life, and will therefore be more comfortable with the official language of the world they grow up in. For the most part, they will speak this language to their own children. These children will not know the indigenous languages of their grandparents, and thus pretty soon they will not be spoken. This is language death.

Many scholars hope that we can turn back the tide with programs to revive indigenous languages, but the sad fact is that this will almost never be very effective. Learning small indigenous languages tends to be a tough business for people raised in European languages: they tend to be more like Berik than like French.

10 I saw what this meant when I was assigned to teach some Native Americans their ancestral language. Filled with sounds it's hard to make unless you were born to them, it seemed almost *designed* to frustrate someone who grew up with English.

In the Central Pomo language of California, if one person sits, the word is—get ready—*'c*^{ˇh}*áw*. The mark at the beginning signifies a catch in the throat, and what the raised little *h* requires shall not detain us here, but rest assured that it's a distinct challenge to render if you grew up speaking English. But if more than one person sits, it's a different word, *naphów*. If it's liquid that is sitting, as in a container, then the word is *cˇóm*. The whole language is like this.

Yes, there is the success story of Hebrew, but that unlikely revival came about because of a happenstantial confluence of religion, the birth of a nation, and the obsession of Eliezer Ben-Yehuda, who settled in Palestine and insisted on speaking only Hebrew to all Jews. This extended to reducing his wife to tears when he caught her singing a lullaby to their child in her native Russian.

Few people not involved with nation building would be inclined to such a violent dedication to learning a new language, as is proven by the merely genuflective level of Hebrew that American Jews today typically master in Hebrew school. It also helped Hebrew's successful comeback that it had a long tradition of written materials. Only about 200 languages are truly written: most are only spoken.

What makes the potential death of a language all the more emotionally charged is the belief that if a language dies, a cultural worldview will die with it. But this idea is fragile. Certainly language is a key aspect of what distinguishes one group from another. However, a language itself does not correspond to the particulars of a culture but to a faceless process that creates new languages as the result of geographical separation. For example, most Americans pronounce disgusting as "diss-kussting" with a *k* sound. (Try it—you probably do too.) However, some people say "dizz-gusting"—it's easier to pronounce the *g* after a softer sound like *z*. Imagine a language with the word pronounced as it is spelled (and as it was in Latin): "diss-gusting." The group speaking the language splits into two groups that go their separate ways. Come back five hundred years later, and one group is pronouncing the word "diss-kussting," while the other is pronouncing it "dizz-gusting." After even more time, the word would start shortening, just as we pronounce "let us" as "let's." After a thousand years, in one place it would be something like "skussting," while in the other it might be "zgustin." After another thousand, perhaps "skusty" and "zguss." By this time, these are no longer even the same language.

This is exactly why there are different languages—what began in Latin as *augustus* became *agosto* in Spanish and, in French, *août*, pronounced as just the single vowel sound. Estonian is what happened when speakers of an earlier language migrated away from other ones; in one place, Estonian happened, in the other, Finnish did. And so while Finnish for *horse* is *hevonen*, in Estonian it's *hobune*. 15

Notice that this is not about culture, any more than saying "diss-kusting" rather than "diz-gusting" reflects anything about one's soul. In fact, all human groups could, somehow, exhibit the exact same culture—and yet their languages would be as different as they are now, because the differences are the result of geographical separation, leading to chance linguistic drifting of the kind that turn *augustus* into *agosto* and *août*. In this we would be like whales, whose species behave similarly everywhere, but have distinct "songs" as the result of happenstance. Who argues that we must preserve each pod of whales because of the particular songs they happen to have developed? The diversity of human languages is subject to the same evaluation: each one is the result of a roll of the dice.

One school of thought proposes that there is more than mere chance in how a language's words emerge, and that if we look closely we see culture peeping through. For example, in its obituary for Eyak, the *Economist* proposed that the fact that *kultahl* meant both leaf and feather signified a cultural appreciation of the unique spiritual relationship of trees and birds. But in English we use *hover* to refer both to the act of waiting, suspended, in the air and the act of staying close to a mate at a cocktail party to ward off potential rivals. Notice how much less interesting that is to us than the bit about the Eyak and leaves and feathers.

For the better part of a century, all attempts to conjure any meaningful indication of thought patterns or cultural outlook from the vocabularies and grammars of languages have fallen apart in that sort of way, with researchers picking up only a few isolated shards of evidence. For example, because "table" has feminine gender in Spanish (*la mesa*), a Spanish speaker is more likely—if pressed—to imagine a cartoon table having a high voice. But this isn't exactly what most of us would think of as meaningfully "cultural," nor as having to do with "thought." And in fact, Spanish speakers do not go about routinely imagining tables as cooing in feminine tones.

Thus the oft-heard claim that the death of a language means the death of a culture puts the cart before the horse. When the culture dies, naturally the language dies along with it. The reverse, however, is not necessarily true. Groups do not find themselves in the bizarre circumstance of having all of their traditional cultural accoutrements in hand only to find themselves incapable of indigenous expression because they no longer speak the corresponding language. Native American groups would bristle at the idea that they are no longer meaningfully "Indian" simply because they no longer speak their ancestral tongue. Note also the obvious and vibrant black American culture in the United States, among people who speak not Yoruba but English.

20 The main loss when a language dies is not cultural but aesthetic. The click sounds in certain African languages are magnificent to hear. In many Amazonian languages, when you say something you have to specify, with a suffix, where you got the information. The Ket language of Siberia is so awesomely irregular as to seem a work of art.

But let's remember that this aesthetic delight is mainly savored by the outside observer, often a professional savorer like myself. Professional linguists or anthropologists are part of a distinct human minority. Most people, in the West or anywhere else, find the fact that there are so many languages in the world no more interesting than I would find a list of all the makes of Toyota. So our case for preserving the world's languages cannot be based on how fascinating their variegation appears to a few people in the world. The question is whether there is some urgent benefit to humanity from the fact that some people speak click languages, while others speak Ket or thousands of others, instead of everyone speaking in a universal tongue.

As 5,500 languages slowly disappear, the aesthetic loss is not to be dismissed. And in fact dying languages become museum pieces. For this reason it is fortunate and crucial that modern technology is recording and analyzing them more thoroughly than ever before. Perhaps a future lies before us in which English will be a sort of global tongue while people continue to speak about 600 other languages among themselves. English already is a de facto universal language—yet those who would consider it a blessing if everyone over 15 spoke an artificial language like Esperanto are often somewhat *diss-kussted* that this is the status English is moving closer toward decade by decade.

Obviously, the discomfort with English "taking over" is due to associations with imperialism, first on the part of the English and then, of course, the American behemoth. We cannot erase from our minds the unsavory aspects of history. Nor should we erase from our minds the fact that countless languages—such as most of the indigenous languages of North America and Australia—have become extinct not because of something as abstract and gradual as globalization, but because of violence, annexation, and cultural extermination. But we cannot change that history, nor is it currently conceivable how we could arrange for some other language to replace the growing universality of English. Like the QWERTY keyboard,[1] this particular horse is out of the barn.

Even if the world's currencies are someday tied to the *renmimbi*,[2] English's head start as the lingua franca[3] of popular culture, scholarship, and international discourse would ensure its linguistic dominance. To change this situation would require a great many centuries, certainly too long a span to figure meaningfully in our assessment of the place of English in world communications in our present moment.

25

And notice how daunting the prospect of Chinese as a world language is, with a writing system that demands mastery of 2,000 characters in order to be able to read even a tabloid newspaper. For all of its association with Pepsi and the CIA, English is very user-friendly as the world's 6,000 languages go. English verb conjugation is spare compared to, say, that of Italian—just the third-person singular s in the present, for example. There are no pesky genders to memorize (and no feminine-gendered tables that talk like Penelope Cruz). There are no sounds under whose dispensation you almost have to be born as a prerequisite for rendering them anywhere near properly, like the notorious trilly *r*ˇ sound in Czech.

Each language is hard in its own way. Try explaining to a foreigner why, if you get a busy signal, you might say, "I'll try her tomorrow," but you can also say, "Tomorrow I turn 25," without using the *will* to indicate the future. But as a language all people are required to learn, would it really be better to have one like Russian, with three genders, fiercely subtle and irregular verb marking,

1. The QWERTY keyboard is based on a layout designed by Christopher Latham Sholes (1819–1890) in 1874 and patented in 1878.

2. *Renmimbi* is the official currency of the People's Republic of China.

3. Lingua franca, a common language.

and numbers so hard to express properly that Russians themselves have trouble with them?

There are those who worry not only that English will become *primus inter pares*,[4] but that it will finally eat up even the last remaining 600 languages as well. But this stretches the imagination, to be sure. As long as there are Japanese people meeting and raising children in Japan, amidst a culture in which Japanese is enshrined as the language of not only speech but education, literature, and journalism, it is hard to conceive even of the first step toward the day when a child raised in Osaka would speak English and think of Japanese as a language his parents spoke when they "didn't want me to understand." Eyak is one thing, but the languages spoken by substantial populations and well entrenched in writing are another.

However, as is increasingly clear today, under the terms of the present order we must prepare for unforeseen circumstances and treat the surprising as normal. Suppose global warming patterns forced population relocations of unprecedented volume and speed: perhaps this could lead to the use of English as a lingua franca among displaced hordes of assorted extractions, such that children raised in these new settings would speak English instead of Finnish or Japanese or Croatian.

Or just maybe the process could happen as the result of some less dramatic and more gradual process. We might conceive of humanity continuing to benefit from the extinct 600 languages as taught ones. People could savor Tolstoy in the original Russian as we today read Virgil in Latin.

30 Viscerally, as a great fan of Russian for many years, I am as uncomfortable as anyone else with the prospect of Russian no longer being passed on to children. However, I am also aware that mine is not necessarily a logical discomfort. Coming back to the Tower of Babel, can we say that the benefits of linguistic diversity are more important, in a way that a representative number of humans could agree upon, than the impediment to communication that they entail? Especially when their differentiation from one another is, ultimately, a product of the same kind of accretionary accidents that distinguish a woodchuck from a groundhog?

At the end of the day, language death is, ironically, a symptom of people coming together. Globalization means hitherto isolated peoples migrating and sharing space. For them to do so and still maintain distinct languages across generations happens only amidst unusually tenacious self-isolation—such as that of the Amish—or brutal segregation. (Jews did not speak Yiddish in order to revel in their diversity but because they lived in an apartheid society.) Crucially, it is black Americans, the Americans whose English is most distinct from that of the mainstream, who are the ones most likely to live separately from whites geographically and spiritually.

The alternative, it would seem, is indigenous groups left to live in isolation—complete with the maltreatment of women and lack of access to modern medicine and technology typical of such societies. Few could counte-

4. *Primus inter pares*, Latin for "the first among equals."

nance this as morally justified, and attempts to find some happy medium in such cases are frustrated by the simple fact that such peoples, upon exposure to the West, tend to seek membership in it.

As we assess our linguistic future as a species, a basic question remains. Would it be inherently evil if there were not 6,000 spoken languages but one? We must consider the question in its pure, logical essence, apart from particular associations with English and its history. Notice, for example, how the discomfort with the prospect in itself eases when you imagine the world's language being, say, Eyak.

QUESTIONS

1. John McWhorter argues against the belief that the death of a language means the death of a cultural worldview. What support does he provide for his argument? Do you find it convincing? Why or why not?

2. McWhorter incorporates stylistic elements that give this article a conversational tone; for example, he addresses readers when he writes "get ready" (paragraph 11) and "Try it—you probably do too" (paragraph 14). How does this use of direct address affect you as a reader?

3. McWhorter asks whether we can "say that the benefits of linguistic diversity are more important . . . than the impediment to communication that they entail" (paragraph 30). Write a response paper in which you take a position on this question.

DENNIS BARON

Who Owns Global English?

A 1.8 MILLION EURO advertising campaign for Madrid's new Spanish-English public schools is being ridiculed for its slogan "Yes, we want," which critics are calling bad English.

English is what the chanters of "Yes, we want," want to learn, because English is the new global language. The ads, which evoke Barack Obama's "Yes, we can," have appeared on Spanish television, radio, billboards, and buses, prompting complaints that the Education Ministry should be promoting its bilingual public elementary and high schools in correct English if it wants pupils to pick them.

After all, one professional translator sniffed, "any of the students in these schools would be suspended if they repeated this slogan on a test." But a representative of the Ministry of Education insisted that "Yes, we want," is not a test item, it's a "creative publicity slogan, one of the best in recent years."

Posted April 21, 2010, on Baron's blog, The Web of Language, *which is devoted to a consideration of language in the news.*

Is the slogan really bad English, or is it simply new English? Now that English is a global language, it's taking on a life of its own in non-English-speaking countries, and the question of correctness is taking on a new spin. There are plenty of websites chronicling the depredations of "Engrish," Asian signs and product labels translated into inadvertently funny English.

The proliferation of non-idiomatic English in international settings is hardly new, and it's not confined to East Asia or to former British colonies. Thirty years ago, in a small French city, my daughter's sixth-grade English teacher marked *phone number* wrong on a test. The correct idiom, Mme la prof told me when I complained, was "number phone," a translation of the French idiom *numéro de téléphone. Phone number* might be "O.K." in American English, she conceded, but only British English was acceptable in her class. She had been to England, and she had it on good authority that the Queen said "number phone." She didn't change the grade.

While much of the world has joined Spain in chanting, "What do we want? English! When do we want it? Now!" or words to that effect, some governments are trying to stop global English before it undermines their own national language.

Recently a Slovak television station came under fire for three untranslated English sentences uttered on a talk show. A guest, British musician Andy Hillard, a Bratislava resident fairly fluent in Slovak, had trouble understanding a question in Slovak, so the host translated it into English. Hillard automatically answered in English, violating the new official language law requiring that

One of many examples from engrish.com.

only Slovak be used in public. Someone complained, and the government quickly launched an investigation which could result in a $7,300 fine for "misusing the language." While English is taught in almost every Slovak school, the government doesn't want English on the air.

In another move to combat the spread of English, the Chinese government has ordered its television stations to stop using English abbreviations, including GDP (gross domestic product), CPI (consumer price index), and NBA (National Basketball Association). Supporters of the English ban see it protecting the purity of Chinese, while opponents of the restriction point out that Chinese was never a pure language: up to 30,000 ancient Chinese words, like *shijie*, 'word,' and *zhendi*, 'truth,' come from Sanskrit and Pali, while more recent borrowings include *gongchandang*, 'communist,' which comes from Japanese. Not to mention that, as in Spain, Slovakia, and France, English is the most widely studied foreign language in China.

What's also curious, considering the global status of English, is that some English speakers actually fear that their language is threatened by other languages. Just as Slovakia and France declared their languages official in order to protect them from English, and from the languages of indigenous minorities and immigrants, anglophones think that making English official will protect it, though it's not clear what protection the global language needs.

10

In some cases the protectionists go even further, campaigning to get rid of borrowed words in English. So Oliver Kamm complained when the London *Times* TV critic, reviewing the new actor playing Dr. Who, wrote, "Plus ça change, plus c'est la même Doctor Who."[1] Kamm, a *Times* leader writer, believes that to be correct, the reviewer should have written "le même Dr. Who," since Dr. Who is a male character. But Kamm would prefer no French at all, or any other foreign language, for that matter, since in his view, readers of the *Times*, who don't attend bilingual schools and aren't very good at languages, won't understand foreignisms unless they're translated (*The Times*, Mar. 27, 2010, p. 107; *leader writer* is British for op-ed columnist).

No matter how much we object to "mistakes" in other people's language, there doesn't seem to be much we can do about it. Plus English speakers, who can't effectively control the English of fellow anglophones, are actually in a much weaker position when trying to control the English of foreigners. And objecting to the English of advertising seems hopeless. To anglophones, "Yes, we want" may seem funny, and Spanish authorities may even find it embarrassing, but whatever happens to the slogan, its very existence is one more sign that English, now that it's global, is no longer the exclusive property of English-speaking nations.

The ancient Romans may have felt a similar loss of linguistic control as their empire slipped away and Latin started its long segue into Italian, Spanish, French, Portuguese, Romanian, Catalan, and the other romance tongues. For now it doesn't look like English is breaking up the way Latin did. But it could. As the Queen might put it, it's early days yet. And that's British for "it's too soon to tell."

UPDATE: FWIW,[2] additional campaign placards like the Madrid subway poster reproduced here show more clearly that "Yes, we want" is actually part of a bilingual sentence: "Yes, we want estudiar el próximo curso . . ."[3] That new information hasn't calmed the anglophones objecting to what they still regard as irregular English, or the Spanish-speakers who think it's Spanglish, and it has prompted further complaints from purists who object to language mixing. What the campaign does demonstrate is the popularity of English in schools, and the well-known tendency of advertisers to stretch language in order to attract attention to their message.

1. *Plus ça change, plus c'est la même*, French for "The more it changes, the more it remains."
2. FWIW; for what it's worth.
3. *Estudiar el proximo curso*, Spanish for "Study the next course."

Madrid subway placard showing the text of the beleaguered ad in more detail.

Questions

1. Dennis Baron titles this blog entry "Who Owns Global English?" Does he answer that question? If you answer "yes," point to the place in the text you find that answer. If you answer "no," what potential answers can you locate?

2. How does Baron's use of visual images support or illustrate the points he makes in this blog post?

3. Write an essay or blog post in which you consider some aspect of language and communication. Use three visual images to support or illustrate your points.

BENJAMIN FRANKLIN *Learning to Write*

ABOUT THIS TIME I met with an odd Volume of the *Spectator*.[1] I had never before seen any of them. I bought it, read it over and over, and was much delighted with it. I thought the Writing excellent, and wish'd if possible to imitate it. With that View, I took some of the Papers, and making short Hints of the Sentiment in each Sentence, laid them by a few Days, and then without looking at the Book, tried to complete the Papers again, by expressing each hinted Sentiment at length and as fully as it had been express'd before in any suitable Words that should come to hand.

Then I compar'd my *Spectator* with the Original, discover'd some of my Faults and corrected them. But I found I wanted a Stock of Words or a Readiness in recollecting and using them which I thought I should have acquir'd before that time, if I had gone on making Verses, since the continual Occasion for Words of the same Import but of different Length, to suit the Measure,[2] or of different Sound for the Rhyme, would have laid me under a constant Necessity of searching for Variety, and also have tended to fix that Variety in my Mind, and make me Master of it. Therefore I took some of the Tales and turn'd them into Verse: And after a time, when I had pretty well forgotten the Prose, turn'd them back again. I also sometimes jumbled my Collections of Hints into Confusion, and after some Weeks, endeavor'd to reduce them into the best Order, before I began to form the full Sentences, and complete the Paper. This was to teach me Method in the Arrangement of Thoughts. By comparing my Work afterwards with the original, I discover'd many faults and amended them; but I sometimes had the Pleasure of Fancying that in certain Particulars of small Import, I had been lucky enough to improve the Method or the Language and this encourag'd me to think I might possibly in time come to be a tolerable English Writer, of which I was extremely ambitious.

My Time for these Exercises and for Reading, was at Night after Work, or before Work began in the Morning; or on Sundays, when I contrived to be in the Printing-House alone, evading as much as I could the common Attendance on public Worship, which my Father used to exact of me when I was under his Care: And which indeed I still thought a Duty; tho' I could not, as it seemed to me, afford the Time to practice it.

When about 16 Years of Age, I happen'd to meet with a Book written by one Tryon,[3] recommending a Vegetable Diet. I determined to go into it. My Brother being yet unmarried, did not keep House, but boarded himself and his Apprentices in another Family. My refusing to eat Flesh occasioned an Inconveniency, and I was frequently chid for my singularity. I made myself acquainted

Drawn from Franklin's Autobiography, *his classic account of his life, first published in 1791.*

1. Daily English periodical noted for its excellence in prose.
2. Meter.
3. Thomas Tryon (1634–1703), author of *Way to Health and Happiness* (1682).

with Tryon's Manner of preparing some of his Dishes, such as Boiling Potatoes or Rice, making Hasty Pudding,[4] and a few others, and then propos'd to my Brother, that if he would give me Weekly half the Money he paid for my Board, I would board myself. He instantly agreed to it, and I presently found that I could save half what he paid me. This was an additional Fund for buying Books: But I had another Advantage in it. My Brother and the rest going from the Printing-House to their Meals, I remain'd there alone, and dispatching presently my light Repast, (which often was no more than a Biscuit or a Slice of Bread, a Handful of Raisins or a Tart from the Pastry Cook's, and a Glass of Water) had the rest of the Time till their Return, for Study, in which I made the greater Progress from that greater Clearness of Head and quicker Apprehension which usually attend Temperance in Eating and Drinking. And now it was that being on some Occasion made asham'd of my Ignorance in Figures; which I had twice fail'd in learning when at School, I took Cocker's Book of Arithmetic,[5] and went thro' the whole by myself with great Ease. I also read Seller's[6] and Sturmy's[7] Books of Navigation, and became acquainted with the little Geometry they contain, but never proceeded far in that Science. And I read about this Time Locke on Human Understanding and the Art of Thinking by Messrs. du Port Royal.[8]

5

While I was intent on improving my Language, I met with an English Grammar (I think it was Greenwood's[9]) at the End of which there were two little Sketches of the Arts of Rhetoric and Logic, the latter finishing with a Specimen of a Dispute in the Socratic Method. And soon after I procur'd Xenophon's Memorable Things of Socrates,[10] wherein there are many Instances of the same Method. I was charm'd with it, adopted it, dropped my abrupt Contradiction and positive Argumentation, and put on the humble Enquirer and Doubter. And being then, from reading Shaftesbury[11] and Collins,[12] became a real Doubter in many Points of our Religious Doctrine. I found this Method safest for myself and very embarrassing to those against whom I used it, therefore I took a Delight in it, practic'd it continually and grew very artful and expert in drawing People even of superior Knowledge into Concessions the Consequences of which they did not foresee, entangling them in Difficulties out of which they

4. Cornmeal mush.

5. Well-known textbook, first published in 1677.

6. John Seller (c. 1658–1698), author of *Practical Navigation* (1694).

7. Samuel Sturmy (1633–1669), author of *The Mariner's Magazine* (1699).

8. John Locke (1632–1704), British philosopher and author of *An Essay Concerning Human Understanding* (1690); Pierre Nicole (1625–1695) of Port Royal published his book in 1662; it was translated into English as *Logic: Or the Art of Thinking* in 1687.

9. James Greenwood (d. 1737), author of *An Essay towards a Practical English Grammar* (1711).

10. Xenophon's (c. 430–355 B.C.E.) *The Memorable Things of Socrates* was published in English translation by Edward Bysshe in 1712.

11. Anthony Ashley Cooper, earl of Shaftesbury (1671–1713), famous for his *Characteristics of Men, Manners, Opinions, Times* (1711).

12. Anthony Collins (1676–1729), a friend of Locke; author of *A Discourse of Free Thinking* (1713).

could not extricate themselves, and so obtaining Victories that neither myself nor my Cause always deserved. I continu'd this Method some few Years, but gradually left it, retaining only the Habit of expressing myself in Terms of modest Diffidence, never using when I advance any thing that may possibly be disputed, the Words, *Certainly, undoubtedly*, or any others that give the Air of Positiveness to an Opinion; but rather say, *I conceive*, or I *apprehend* a Thing to be so or so. *It appears to me*, or I *should think it so or so for such and such Reasons*, or *I imagine* it to be so, or *it is so if I am not mistaken*. This Habit I believe has been of great Advantage to me, when I have had occasion to inculcate my Opinions and persuade Men into Measures that I have been from time to time engag'd in promoting. And as the chief Ends of Conversation are to *inform*, or to be *informed*, to *please* or to *persuade*, I wish well-meaning sensible Men would not lessen their Power of doing Good by a Positive assuming Manner that seldom fails to disgust, tends to create Opposition, and to defeat every one of those Purposes for which Speech was given us, to wit, giving or receiving Information, or Pleasure: For if you would *inform*, a positive dogmatical Manner in advancing your Sentiments, may provoke Contradiction and prevent a candid Attention. If you wish Information and Improvement from the Knowledge of others and yet at the same time express yourself as firmly fix'd in your present Opinions, modest sensible Men, who do not love Disputation, will probably leave you undisturb'd in the Possession of your Error; and by such a Manner you can seldom hope to recommend yourself in *pleasing* your Hearers, or to persuade those whose Concurrence you desire. Pope says, judiciously,

> Men should be taught as if you taught them not,
> And things unknown propos'd as things forgot,

farther recommending it to us,

> To speak tho' sure, with seeming Diffidence.[13]

And he might have coupled with this Line that which he has coupled with another, I think less properly,

> For want of Modesty is want of Sense.

If you ask why *less properly*, I must repeat the Lines;

> "Immodest Words admit of *no* Defence;
> For Want of Modesty is Want of Sense."[14]

Now is not *Want of Sense*, (where a Man is so unfortunate as to want it) some Apology for his *Want of Modesty*? and would not the Lines stand more justly thus?

13. Adapted from Alexander Pope's (1688–1744) *An Essay on Criticism* (1711).

14. Franklin wrongly attributes these two lines to Pope. They are by Wentworth Dillon (1633?–1685), from his *Essay on Translated Verse* (1684). The second line should read "For want of Decency is want of Sense."

Immodest Words admit *but this* Defence.
That Want of Modesty is Want of Sense.

This however I should submit to better Judgments.

Questions

1. Franklin describes his youthful practice of imitating successful writers' sentences. Have you ever done this? What do you think of the practice? What are writers likely to learn from such a practice?

2. Franklin is a classic auto-didact, a self-teacher. Recount what Franklin learned in this manner, and note what he failed to teach himself. What kinds of knowledge did Franklin seek to acquire? Was his learning broad or narrow? What kinds of endeavors was this knowledge most suited for?

3. When he was sixteen, Franklin read a book about vegetarian diets and immediately was converted. Write about how you or someone you know was converted to following a distinct path, either religious, ethical, or physical (examples you might choose: a religious sect, a strict diet, exercise). Did the conversion happen suddenly, as it did with Franklin, or did it take place slowly, over time? How long did the conversion last?

Stephen King

On Writing

Hardly a week after being sprung from detention hall, I was once more invited to step down to the principal's office. I went with a sinking heart, wondering what new shit I'd stepped in.

It wasn't Mr. Higgins who wanted to see me, at least; this time the school guidance counselor had issued the summons. There had been discussions about me, he said, and how to turn my "restless pen" into more constructive channels. He had enquired of John Gould, editor of Lisbon's weekly newspaper,[1] and had discovered Gould had an opening for a sports reporter. While the school couldn't *insist* that I take this job, everyone in the front office felt it would be a good idea. *Do it or die,* the G.C.'s eyes suggested. Maybe that was just paranoia, but even now, almost forty years later, I don't think so.

I groaned inside. I was shut of *Dave's Rag*, almost shut of *The Drum*, and now here was the Lisbon *Weekly Enterprise*. Instead of being haunted by

Although he is primarily known for his horror and suspense writing, King also wrote On Writing: A Memoir of the Craft *(2000), from which this piece was excerpted.*

1. John Gould (1908–2003) was a columnist, editor, and essayist who lived most of his life in Lisbon Falls, Maine.

waters, like Norman Maclean in *A River Runs Through It*,[2] I was as a teenager haunted by newspapers. Still, what could I do? I rechecked the look in the guidance counselors eyes and said I would be delighted to interview for the job.

Gould—not the well-known New England humorist or the novelist who wrote *The Greenleaf Fires*[3] but a relation of both, I think—greeted me warily but with some interest. We would try each other out, he said, if that suited me.

5 Now that I was away from the administrative offices of Lisbon High, I felt able to muster a little honesty. I told Mr. Gould that I didn't know much about sports. Gould said, "These are games people understand when they're watching them drunk in bars. You'll learn if you try."

He gave me a huge roll of yellow paper on which to type my copy—I think I still have it somewhere—and promised me a wage of half a cent a word. It was the first time someone had promised me wages for writing.

The first two pieces I turned in had to do with a basketball game in which an LHS player broke the school scoring record. One was a straight piece of reporting. The other was a sidebar about Robert Ransom's record-breaking performance. I brought both to Gould the day after the game so he'd have them for Friday, which was when the paper came out. He read the game piece, made two minor corrections, and spiked it. Then he started in on the feature piece with a large black pen.

I took my fair share of English Lit classes in my two remaining years at Lisbon, and my fair share of composition, fiction, and poetry classes in college, but John Gould taught me more than any of them, and in no more than ten minutes. I wish I still had the piece—it deserves to be framed, editorial corrections and all—but I can remember pretty well how it went and how it looked after Gould had combed through it with that black pen of his. Here's an example:

> Last night, in the ~~well-loved~~ gymnasium of Lisbon High School, partisans and Jay Hills fans alike were stunned by an athletic performance unequalled in school history. Bob Ransom~~, known as "Bullet" Bob for both his size and accuracy,~~ scored thirty-seven points. Yes, you heard me right. ~~Plus~~ he did it with grace, speed . . . and with an odd courtesy as well, committing only two personal fouls in his ~~knight-like~~ quest for a record which has eluded Lisbon ~~thinclads~~ players since ~~the years of Korea~~ 1953. . . .

2. Norman Maclean (1902–1990) wrote *A River Runs Through It and Other Stories* (1976), which includes the often-quoted words, "I am haunted by waters."
3. *The Greenleaf Fires* (1978) was written by John A. Gould.

Gould stopped at "the years of Korea" and looked up at me. "What year was the last record made?" he asked.

Luckily, I had my notes. "1953," I said. Gould grunted and went back to work. When he finished marking my copy in the manner indicated above, he looked up and saw something on my face. I think he must have mistaken it for horror. It wasn't; it was pure revelation. Why, I wondered, didn't English teachers ever do this? It was like the Visible Man Old Raw Diehl had on his desk in the biology room. 10

"I only took out the bad parts, you know," Gould said. "Most of it's pretty good."

"I know," I said, meaning both things: yes, most of it was good—okay anyway, serviceable—and yes, he had only taken out the bad parts. "I won't do it again."

He laughed. "If that's true, you'll never have to work for a living. You can do *this* instead. Do I have to explain any of these marks?"

"No," I said.

"When you write a story, you're telling yourself the story," he said. "When you rewrite, your main job is taking out all the things that are *not* the story." 15

Gould said something else that was interesting on the day I turned in my first two pieces: write with the door closed, rewrite with the door open. Your stuff starts out being just for you, in other words, but then it goes out. Once you know what the story is and get it right—as right as you can, anyway—it belongs to anyone who wants to read it. Or criticize it. If you're very lucky (this is my idea, not John Gould's, but I believe he would have subscribed to the notion), more will want to do the former than the latter.

Questions

1. Stephen King provides an example of the way his editor marked up his work. What rationale can you provide for the edits? Would you have made different choices if you were the editor? Why?

2. King uses dialogue and description to help characterize his editor. In which parts of the text do you get the best sense of who Gould is? Why are those parts effective?

3. Write about a time someone responded to your writing in a way that helped you learn to be a better writer. What kinds of comments and edits did that person make? Why was that response helpful to you?

GARRISON KEILLOR *How to Write a Letter*

WE SHY PERSONS need to write a letter now and then, or else we'll dry up and blow away. It's true. And I speak as one who loves to reach for the phone, dial the number, and talk. I say, "Big Bopper[1] here—what's shakin', babes?" The telephone is to shyness what Hawaii is to February, it's a way out of the woods, *and yet*: a letter is better.

Such a sweet gift—a piece of handmade writing, in an envelope that is not a bill, sitting in our friend's path when she trudges home from a long day spent among wahoos and savages, a day our words will help repair. They don't need to be immortal, just sincere. She can read them twice and again tomorrow: *You're someone I care about, Corinne, and think of often and every time I do you make me smile.*

We need to write, otherwise nobody will know who we are. They will have only a vague impression of us as A Nice Person, because, frankly, we don't shine at conversation, we lack the confidence to thrust our faces forward and say, "Hi, I'm Heather Hooten; let me tell you about my week." Mostly we say "Uh-huh" and "Oh, really." People smile and look over our shoulder, looking for someone else to meet.

So a shy person sits down and writes a letter. To be known by another person—to meet and talk freely on the page—to be close despite distance. To escape from anonymity and be our own sweet selves and express the music of our souls.

5 Same thing that moves a giant rock star to sing his heart out in front of 123,000 people moves us to take ballpoint in hand and write a few lines to our dear Aunt Eleanor. *We want to be known.* We want her to know that we have fallen in love, that we quit our job, that we're moving to New York, and we want to say a few things that might not get said in casual conversation: *Thank you for what you've meant to me, I am very happy right now.*

The first step in writing letters is to get over the guilt of *not* writing. You don't "owe" anybody a letter. Letters are a gift. The burning shame you feel when you see unanswered mail makes it harder to pick up a pen and makes for a cheerless letter when you finally do. *I feel bad about not writing, but I've been so busy,* etc. Skip this. Few letters are obligatory, and they are *Thanks for the wonderful gift* and *I am terribly sorry to hear about George's death* and *Yes, you're welcome to stay with us next month*, and not many more than that. Write those promptly if you want to keep your friends. Don't worry about the others, except love letters, of course. When your true love writes, *Dear Light of My Life, Joy of My Heart, O Lovely Pulsating Core of My Sensate Life*, some response is called for.

From We Are Still Married *(1989), a collection of Keillor's stories, letters, and skits. Many of Keillor's humorous pieces are aired on his popular radio program,* A Prairie Home Companion.

1. American disc-jockey turned rock star (1930–1959), popular in the late 1950s.

Some of the best letters are tossed off in a burst of inspiration, so keep your writing stuff in one place where you can sit down for a few minutes and (*Dear Roy, I am in the middle of a book entitled* We Are Still Married *but thought I'd drop you a line. Hi to your sweetie, too*) dash off a note to a pal. Envelopes, stamps, address book, everything in a drawer so you can write fast when the pen is hot.

A blank white eight-by-eleven sheet can look as big as Montana if the pen's not so hot—try a smaller page and write boldly. Or use a note card with a piece of fine art on the front; if your letter ain't good, at least they get the Matisse.[2] Get a pen that makes a sensuous line, get a comfortable typewriter, a friendly word processor—which feels easy to the hand.

Sit for a few minutes with the blank sheet in front of you, and meditate on the person you will write to, let your friend come to mind until you can almost see her or him in the room with you. Remember the last time you saw each other and how your friend looked and what you said and what perhaps was unsaid between you, and when your friend becomes real to you, start to write.

Write the salutation—*Dear* You—and take a deep breath and plunge in. A simple declarative sentence will do, followed by another and another and another. Tell us what you're doing and tell it like you were talking to us. Don't think about grammar, don't think about lit'ry style, don't try to write dramatically, just give us your news. Where did you go, who did you see, what did they say, what do you think? 10

If you don't know where to begin, start with the present moment: *I'm sitting at the kitchen table on a rainy Saturday morning. Everyone is gone and the house is quiet.* Let your simple description of the present moment lead to something else, let the letter drift gently along.

The toughest letter to crank out is one that is meant to impress, as we all know from writing job applications; if it's hard work to slip off a letter to a friend, maybe you're trying too hard to be terrific. A letter is only a report to someone who already likes you for reasons other than your brilliance. Take it easy.

Don't worry about form. It's not a term paper. When you come to the end of one episode, just start a new paragraph. You can go from a few lines about the sad state of pro football to the fight with your mother to your fond memories of Mexico to your cat's urinary-tract infection to a few thoughts on personal indebtedness and on to the kitchen sink and what's in it. The more you write, the easier it gets, and when you have a True True Friend to write to, a *compadre*, a soul sibling, then it's like driving a car down a country road, you just get behind the keyboard and press on the gas.

Don't tear up the page and start over when you write a bad line—try to write your way out of it. Make mistakes and plunge on. Let the letter cook along and let yourself be bold. Outrage, confusion, love—whatever is in your mind, let it find a way to the page. Writing is a means of discovery, always, and when you come to the end and write *Yours ever* or *Hugs and kisses*, you'll know something you didn't when you wrote *Dear Pal*.

Probably your friend will put your letter away, and it'll be read again a few years from now—and it will improve with age. And forty years from now, your 15

2. French painter (1869–1954).

friend's grandkids will dig it out of the attic and read it, a sweet and precious relic of the ancient eighties that gives them a sudden clear glimpse of you and her and the world we old-timers knew. You will then have created an object of art. Your simple lines about where you went, who you saw, what they said, will speak to those children and they will feel in their hearts the humanity of our times.

You can't pick up a phone and call the future and tell them about our times. You have to pick up a piece of paper.

GARRISON KEILLOR *Postcards*

A POSTCARD TAKES ABOUT FIFTY WORDS gracefully, which is how to write one. A few sweet strokes in a flowing hand—pink roses, black-face sheep in a wet meadow, the sea, the Swedish coast—your friend in Washington gets the idea. She doesn't need your itinerary to know that you remember her.

Fifty words is a strict form but if you write tiny and sneak over into the address side to squeeze in a hundred, the grace is gone and the result is not a poem but notes for a letter you don't have time to write, which will make her feel cheated.

So many persons traveling to a strange land are inclined to see its life so clearly, its essential national character, they could write a book about it as other foreign correspondents have done ("highly humorous . . . definitely a must"), but fifty words is a better length for what you really know.

Fifty words and a picture. Say you are in Scotland, the picture is of your hotel, a stone pile looking across the woods of Druimindarroch to Loch Nan Uamh near the village of Arisaig. You've never seen this country. For the past year you've worked like a prisoner in the mines. Write.

---

5 Scotland is the most beautiful country in the world and I am drinking coffee in the library of what once was the manor of people who inherited everything and eventually lost it. Thus it became a hotel. I'm with English people whose correctness is overpowering. What wild good luck to be here. And to be an American! I'm so happy, bubba.

In the Highlands, many one-lane roads which widen at curves and hills—a driving thrill, especially when following a native who drives like hell—you stick close to him, like the second car of the roller-coaster, but lose your nerve. Sixty mph down a one-lane winding road. I prefer a career.

The arrogance of Americans who, without so much as a *"mi scusi"* or *"bitte"* or *"s'il vous plaît,"* words that a child could learn easily, walk up to a stranger and say, "Say, where's the museum?" as if English and rudeness rule the world, never ceases to amaze. You hear the accent and sink under the table.

Woke up at six, dark. Switzerland. Alps. Raining. Lights of villages high in the sky. Too dark to see much so snoozed awhile. Woke up in sunny Italy. Field after field of corn, like Iowa in August. Mamas, papas, grammas, grampas, little babies. Skinny trees above the whitewashed houses.

Arrived in Venice. A pipe had burst at the hotel and we were sent to another not as good. Should you spend time arguing for a refund? Went to San Marco,[3] on which the doges overspent. A cash register in the sanctuary: five hundred lire to see the gold altar. Now we understand the Reformation.

On the train to Vienna, she, having composed the sentences carefully from old memory of intermediate German, asked the old couple if the train went to Vienna. *"Ja, ja!"* Did we need to change trains? *"Nein."* Later she successfully ordered dinner and registered at the hotel. *Mein wundercompanion.*

People take me for an American tourist and stare at me, maybe because I walk slow and stare at them, so today I walked like a bat out of hell along the Ringstrasse, past the Hofburg Palace to Stephans Platz and back, and if anyone stared, I didn't notice. Didn't see much of Vienna but felt much better.

One week in a steady drizzle of German and now I am starting to lose my grip on English, I think. Don't know what to write. How are you? Are the Twins going to be in the World Series?

You get to Mozart's apartment[4] through the back door of a restaurant. Kitchen smells, yelling, like at Burger King. The room where he wrote *Figaro* is bare, as if he moved out this morning. It's a nice apartment. His grave at the cemetery is now marked, its whereabouts being unknown. Mozart our brother.

Copenhagen is raining and all the Danes seem unperturbed. A calm humorous people. Kids are the same as anywhere, wild, and nobody hits them. Men wear pastels, especially turquoise. Narrow streets, no cars, little shops, and in the old square a fruit stand and an old woman with flowers yelling, "WŌSA FOR TEW-VA!"

Sunbathing yesterday. A fine woman took off her shirt, jeans, pants, nearby, and lay on her belly, then turned over. Often she sat up to apply oil. Today my back is burned bright red (as St. Paul warns) from my lying and looking at her so long but who could ignore such beauty and *so generous.*

3. The Basilica di San Marco of Venice, a magnificent hodgepodge of Byzantine domes, mosaics, and plundered treasure from the Near East and Asia, is one of the largest and most famous cathedrals in the world.

4. Mozart's "Figarohaus," where he lived from October 1784 to April 1787, is behind St. Stephen's Cathedral in Vienna.

QUESTIONS

1. In "How to Write a Letter," Keillor offers several suggestions. Make a list of the suggestions that seem most helpful. Why might Keillor have included the other, less practical suggestions?

2. Keillor addresses "How to Write a Letter" to shy people (a group in which he includes himself—"We shy persons . . ."). Does his advice also apply to those who are not shy? Why or why not?

3. Analyze the progression of "Postcards." How is the piece organized? Why do you think Keillor chose this organization?

4. Keillor wrote these pieces in the 1980s before people communicated by e-mail. Does any of his advice fit e-mail correspondence? Write a how-to piece entitled "How to Write an E-mail." E-mail it to the class.

5. Pick up several postcards from your college bookstore. Write fifty-word messages on each and send them to family and friends, or, if assigned, to your classmates and teacher.

LEWIS THOMAS

Notes on Punctuation

THERE ARE NO precise rules about punctuation (Fowler[1] lays out some general advice (as best he can under the complex circumstances of English prose (he points out, for example, that we possess only four stops (the comma, the semicolon, the colon and the period (the question mark and exclamation point are not, strictly speaking, stops; they are indicators of tone (oddly enough, the Greeks employed the semicolon for their question mark (it produces a strange sensation to read a Greek sentence which is a straightforward question: Why weepest thou; (instead of Why weepest thou? (and, of course, there are parentheses (which are surely a kind of punctuation making this whole much more complicated by having to count up the left-handed parentheses in order to be sure of closing with the right number (but if the parentheses were left out, with nothing to work with but the stops, we would have considerably more flexibility in the deploying of layers of meaning than if we tried to separate all the clauses by physical barriers (and in the latter case, while we might have more precision and exactitude for our meaning, we would lose the essential flavor of language, which is its wonderful ambiguity))))))))))))).

The commas are the most useful and usable of all the stops. It is highly important to put them in place as you go along. If you try to come back after

From The Medusa and the Snail: More Notes of a Biology Watcher *(1979), a collection of science writing.*

1. H. W. Fowler, author of *Modern English Usage* (1926).

doing a paragraph and stick them in the various spots that tempt you you will discover that they tend to swarm like minnows into all sorts of crevices whose existence you hadn't realized and before you know it the whole long sentence becomes immobilized and lashed up squirming in commas. Better to use them sparingly, and with affection, precisely when the need for each one arises, nicely, by itself.

I have grown fond of semicolons in recent years. The semicolon tells you that there is still some question about the preceding full sentence; something needs to be added; it reminds you sometimes of the Greek usage. It is almost always a greater pleasure to come across a semicolon than a period. The period tells you that that is that; if you didn't get all the meaning you wanted or expected, anyway you got all the writer intended to parcel out and now you have to move along. But with a semicolon there you get a pleasant little feeling of expectancy; there is more to come; read on; it will get clearer.

Colons are a lot less attractive, for several reasons: firstly, they give you the feeling of being rather ordered around, or at least having your nose pointed in a direction you might not be inclined to take if left to yourself, and, secondly, you suspect you're in for one of those sentences that will be labeling the points to be made: firstly, secondly and so forth, with the implication that you haven't sense enough to keep track of a sequence of notions without having them numbered. Also, many writers use this system loosely and incompletely, starting out with number one and number two as though counting off on their fingers but then going on and on without the succession of labels you've been led to expect, leaving you floundering about searching for the ninthly or seventeenthly that ought to be there but isn't.

Exclamation points are the most irritating of all. Look! they say, look at what I just said! How amazing is my thought! It is like being forced to watch someone else's small child jumping up and down crazily in the center of the living room shouting to attract attention. If a sentence really has something of importance to say, something quite remarkable, it doesn't need a mark to point it out. And if it is really, after all, a banal sentence needing more zing, the exclamation point simply emphasizes its banality!   5

Quotation marks should be used honestly and sparingly, when there is a genuine quotation at hand, and it is necessary to be very rigorous about the words enclosed by the marks. If something is to be quoted, the *exact* words must be used. If part of it must be left out because of space limitations, it is good manners to insert three dots to indicate the omission, but it is unethical to do this if it means connecting two thoughts which the original author did not intend to have tied together. Above all, quotation marks should not be used for ideas that you'd like to disown, things in the air so to speak. Nor should they be put in place around clichés; if you want to use a cliché you must take full responsibility for it yourself and not try to job it off on anon., or on society. The most objectionable misuse of quotation marks, but one which illustrates the dangers of misuse in ordinary prose, is seen in advertising, especially in advertisements for small restaurants, for example "just around the corner," or "a good place to eat." No single, identifiable, citable person ever really said, for the record, "just around the corner," much less "a good place to eat," least likely of all for restaurants of the type that use this type of prose.

The dash is a handy device, informal and essentially playful, telling you that you're about to take off on a different tack but still in some way connected with the present course—only you have to remember that the dash is there, and either put a second dash at the end of the notion to let the reader know that he's back on course, or else end the sentence, as here, with a period.

The greatest danger in punctuation is for poetry. Here it is necessary to be as economical and parsimonious with commas and periods as with the words themselves, and any marks that seem to carry their own subtle meanings, like dashes and little rows of periods, even semicolons and question marks, should be left out altogether rather than inserted to clog up the thing with ambiguity. A single exclamation point in a poem, no matter what else the poem has to say, is enough to destroy the whole work.

The things I like best in T. S. Eliot's poetry, especially in the *Four Quartets*, are the semicolons. You cannot hear them, but they are there, laying out the connections between the images and the ideas. Sometimes you get a glimpse of a semicolon coming, a few lines farther on, and it is like climbing a steep path through woods and seeing a wooden bench just at a bend in the road ahead, a place where you can expect to sit for a moment, catching your breath.

10 Commas can't do this sort of thing; they can only tell you how the different parts of a complicated thought are to be fitted together, but you can't sit, not even take a breath, just because of a comma,

QUESTIONS

1. The title of this piece begins with the word "notes." Is that the right word? Is this a series of notes or something else?

2. How long did it take you to realize that Thomas is playing a kind of game with his readers? (For instance, paragraph 1 is a single sentence.) Is punctuation the kind of thing people usually play games with?

3. Choose one or two writers from the next section, "Album of Styles," and describe how they employ commas, colons, and semicolons. Do any of the semicolons serve as "a wooden bench just at a bend in the road ahead" (paragraph 9)?

4. Compare Thomas's technique of illustrating his points as he explains them with Garrison Keillor's similar technique in "Postcards" (p. 448). What other forms of writing might be treated this way? Find other examples that, like Thomas's "Notes" or Keillor's "Postcards," merge form and content.

Rebecca Solnit *Locked Horns*

ONE DAY NOT long ago, I went to see a show of animal skulls at the local science museum. I like skulls. What's ordinarily hidden under the upholstery of flesh, skin, hair, and other tissue is revealed in bones, the foundations of bodies and, in the size of craniums, perhaps the seat of consciousness, a sort of naked essence of what makes each animal so distinctly itself. The barn-size room was full of them, from the gray throne of an elephant's head to the yellowish hacksaws of crocodile smiles, all the same raw ingredients of teeth and craniums and eye sockets in spectacularly different proportions corresponding to vision and diet and defense and thought. A wall was covered with a grid of hundreds of sea lion skulls to show their subtle variation, and antlered and horned creatures were lined up on other walls, all the splendor of what in that room seemed apt to call the animal kingdom.

Something I'd missed on a previous visit stopped me cold and made me think for days afterward: a glass case containing four stag skulls, or, rather, two pairs of stag skulls. Each pair of opponents had locked antlers and, unable to disentangle themselves, had died face to face, probably of hunger. The antlers were intricately intertwined like branches of trees that had grown together, and it must have taken only an instant of coincidence when the antlers were angled to fit together like two pieces of a puzzle rather than to clash, a moment when the stags sealed their fates. Such a tangle is fairly common among antlered creatures and some horned ones, such as bighorn sheep, and it's given rise to the phrase "lock horns," which I'd never thought about, any more than I had ever thought why a penknife is called a penknife until I came across Wordsworth[1] mentioning that he used one to trim his quill pen.

Language is full of such fossils of the actual and the natural, but what struck me on this visit was the grimness of the stags' fate and the ease with which it turned to metaphor and to warning. I quickly reviewed my own life to see if any conflicts were so intractable and vowed not to let any so consume me. A lot of people have died of being right, and some of them have taken their opponents with them. Everyone's encountered bad divorces, noise-obsessed neighbors, monomaniacs who let a grievance take over their lives to the exclusion of everything else, a sort of psychological starvation. It's not hard to expand this notion to politics, to the locked horns of the cold war between the Soviet Union and the United States. Nor is it hard to extend the idea to the way the United States seems lost without an opponent abroad—an evil empire, an axis of evil—with which to lock horns, so that rather than reap a peace dividend

Originally published under the title "Writing the Metaphor Home" in Orion Magazine *(2003) and included with this title in Solnit's essay collection* Storming the Gates of Paradise: Landscapes for Politics *(2007), which deals with the connections between place and politics, nature and culture.*

1. William Wordsworth (1770–1850), English Romantic poet.

since 1989, we've watched political leaders look for the familiar embrace of an enemy's antlers.

But it's important to remember that it's a metaphor, that stags are no more prone to divorces than to first-strike missile deployment. Theodor Adorno[2] objected to astrology (or, more specifically, to the astrology column in an American newspaper) because people thought that the stars were about them; better to say that we are about the stars. That is, it's not that stags are like us but that we are like stags. One of the uses of the natural world is the generation of striking images and actions that let us define and redefine ourselves and connect ourselves to everything else. That the natural world gives rise to metaphors by which we understand ourselves is, I have long thought, one of the most neglected reasons for protecting it and paying attention to it. It's important to remember too that biological determinism is just bad analogy: all that stuff claiming we are like our primordial selves, therefore we must eat raw food or copulate with those who look this way or act out that way, is just saying that the stars are about us.

5 The definition is always partial; the door at the far end is always open for something else to happen, for redefinition. "My love is like a red, red rose," wrote the poet Robert Burns;[3] we assume that there is something about roses—sweetness, redness, delicacy, beauty, ephemerality—that he has in mind and do not picture his sweetheart with thorns, roots, and maybe aphids. Partial resemblance, because metaphor takes us only so far; then we must travel by other means.

The same week I saw the skulls of the stags who'd starved of intractable combat, I went downtown to meet my friend Claire and see the last day of a big show of Yoko Ono's art.[4] It was a magnificent show, and Ono's work managed to do all the things the conceptualists of that era most prized, but with a kind of tender hopefulness that wasn't theirs but hers. At the entrance to the exhibition were two tables, each with two chairs, and the tabletop was a chessboard set with chess pieces, ready to play. But all the chessmen—and the tables, and the chairs, and the board—were white, whiter than the stags' antlers, than their skulls, than their teeth, pure white. In Ono's game, your opponent was no longer different from yourself and maybe no longer your opponent. Can you fight yourself? How do you know when you're winning?

Claire, who has gone around the world doing antinuclear and peace work and now heads Oakland's Martin Luther King Jr. Freedom Center, has many surprising talents, and it turned out that she is an avid chess player. I am not, and I was tired, but that was all to the good, because she was delighted that it took only three moves for me to mistake her rook for mine and move it against her—at which point the game was over, we had unhooked antlers, and Ono

2. Theodor Adorno (1903–1969), a German-born philosopher and sociologist.

3. Robert Burns (1759–1796), a Scottish poet who adapted and preserved Scottish folk songs, including "My Love Is Like a Red, Red Rose" (1794).

4. Yoko Ono (b. 1933), Japanese American artist and musician known for her marriage to John Lennon and her peace activism.

had firmly suggested that difference is negligible and conflict avoidable, in this artwork that was about remaking the games and metaphors for war into a playful merging. Further in the exhibition was documentation of Ono's billboards and placards from the Vietnam War era, which said things like "The War Is Over If You Want It." Ono makes it clear not only that we could disengage from conflict but also that with open imagination we could transform it into something else—perhaps into love, a word that crops up all over her work. Stags are stags, but chess doesn't have to be war. Neither does war.

Questions

1. Rebecca Solnit both values and considers the limits of metaphor. What, according to Solnit, can metaphor accomplish? What are its limits?

2. In this essay about the functions of metaphor, Solnit uses many metaphors, such as "the gray throne of an elephant's head" and "the yellowish hacksaws of crocodile smiles" (paragraph 1). Trace Solnit's use of metaphor throughout the essay. Which metaphors are most effective for you? Why?

3. Solnit considers "locked horns" both literally and figuratively in this essay. Write about a phrase or cliché that you came to understand in a new or deeper way either because of personal experience or through learning the origins of that phrase or cliché.

Pumla Gobodo-Madikizela

"Language Rules": Witnessing about Trauma in South Africa

"Let's play a game."

It was strange, almost surreal, to see a group of young girls seven to ten years old laughing and cavorting in the streets of an Eastern Cape township in South Africa—the Mlungisi Township, the same township that in the mid-1980s had become the scene of so much misery, a tinderbox of inflamed emotion against the inhumanities of apartheid. But that was before these children were even born. I was doing some work in Mlungisi Township and happened to be walking through their neighborhood when I saw them. Their squeals and cries were the very embodiment of joy. My heart leapt. They looked like little tender shoots of foliage—little blades of life—poking out from under the cooled lava of the township once utterly devastated by apartheid's volcano.

Published in River Teeth: A Journal of Nonfiction Narrative *(Spring 2007), this essay recounts some of Gobodo-Madikizela's experiences serving on the Truth and Reconciliation Commission, which was created to promote national unity and reconciliation after apartheid ended in South Africa.*

"What game?" the others shouted back, skipping back and forth.

"Let me show you," the first one said. She was about eight and looked as if she might be the informal leader of the group. She began to demonstrate. The other girls didn't seem too enthusiastic about this new game. What was wrong with just playing skip? But slowly, they became intrigued.

5 "It is called the necklace game," the leader said. "This is just going to be pretend necklace, not the real thing," she said. She pushed the other girls aside as if to open up the stage. Rotating through the role of victim, then killers, then onlookers, she seemed to my amazement to recall virtually everything that actually happened in a real "necklace" murder, even though she hadn't been born when the last necklace killing occurred in her township.

She flailed her arms, screaming in mock anguish as if being beaten, swaying back and forth, turning her head from left to right, and begging for mercy with eyes wide open to show fright. Then she switched roles and play-acted someone going off to find petrol, then another person offering matches, then someone running to demand a car tire from an imaginary passing motorist.

"Give me your tire," she ordered with mock hostility. She narrated the part of the motorist dutifully obeying, then the petrol man, then the matches man. Finally, she returned to her victim role, struggling against the make-believe tire placed around her neck. Nervously, she made a gesture simulating the striking of a match, as if her friends—now a crowd of executioners—had forced her to set herself alight.

As imaginary flames engulfed her, she threw her arms wildly into the air. "Now sing and clap your hands and dance. I'm dying," she said. Her friends started clapping and singing in a discordant rhythm. They formed a circle and went round and round her "body." Gradually, the high-pitched screams of the girl with the imaginary tire around her neck faded into a whimper as her life ebbed away. Consumed by the flames, she slowly lowered herself to the ground and "died." It was all make-believe.

None of the girls I saw reenacting the necklace game that morning had actually witnessed a necklace murder. But the unspoken events of the past—the silence of Mlungisi's lambs—had become imprinted on their minds. It was not just the outward form of the game, but its inner meaning, the sense of trauma to communal life that it carried with it. They carried the collective horror somewhere deep within them. Reenacting the death dance of the necklace victim may well have been a way of transforming its memory into something more accessible and less fearful for the girls.

10 This incident provides an illuminating metaphor for the way in which trauma is passed on intergenerationally "in ways subtle and not so subtle" through silences, fear, and through the psychological scars and pain that are often left unacknowledged. The questions that remain for us when we witness a scene such as this one are: Did they witness it? If they only heard about it without witnessing it, how could they so accurately reenact it?

The language of violence is etched in the memory of many victims of violent conflict and passed on to the next generation in the way that traumatic memory so often is. The notion of intergenerational transmission of trauma has been well established, particularly in the surviving families of the Holocaust, where it has been observed that second- and third-generation descendants of survivors *know* their parents' trauma without their parents ever discussing their experiences in any detail. The traumatic stories are communicated in behaviorally subtle and unconscious ways. The externalized skit of a necklace murder by the young girls in the story above could be seen as an expression of that which cannot be spoken but expressed only through symbolic language.

This repetition of real events from the past seems like a transformation of traumatic experience into ritual, perhaps a cathartic way of putting into action the struggle to find language that expresses the frustrations, helplessness, disempowerment, and dire poverty of people whose lives never counted in the past and continue to count for little in the greater scheme of things.

The notion of "language rules"—which I have borrowed from Hannah Arendt's reflections in her book on Eichmann[1]—is an interesting one.[2] Arendt uses the phrase in reference to the use of euphemistic language, where nothing is called by its proper name. The phrase "language rules" implies, on the one hand, that one has to obey rules of communication and, on the other hand, that these rules of communication often fail us, and that words may fall short of adequately conveying the meaning of experience, especially experiences that are imbued with painful memories.

The stories of trauma told by victims who testified before South Africa's Truth and Reconciliation Commission (TRC) illustrate this struggle with language. Traumatic experience overwhelms the senses so that even in the retelling of the trauma, language is inadequate. Language does not sufficiently capture what happened. As victims navigate the world of language to try to communicate these painful memories to witnesses of their traumatic testimony, the essence of their experience may be lost in the words they choose in order to convey what they went through. I would like to illustrate this "loss" of meaning with two stories from the TRC.

The first story is drawn from our work in the early stages of the TRC process. We were conducting outreach meetings throughout the country to invite communities to submit testimonies in preparation for the TRC's public hearings. I was part of a team leading the TRC's outreach program in the black township of Mlungisi in the Eastern Cape region. In the 1980s Mlungisi had suffered unspeakable violence both at the hands of apartheid government police and also as a result of the atrocities of the necklace murders committed by young people affiliated with the anti-apartheid struggle. The history of Mlungisi was a bloody one that left the community ravaged, where memories of an unspeakable past were performed through children's reenactment games. 15

1. Hannah Arendt (1906–1975), German-Jewish political theorist and philosopher; Adolf Eichmann (1906–1962), a German Nazi who facilitated the deportation of Jews to ghettos and extermination camps during World War II.

2. Hannah Arendt, *Eichmann in Jerusalem: A Report on the Banality of Evil* (New York: Penguin, 1994) [Author's note].

Ten years after the raging fires of the necklace murders in the streets of Mlungisi were extinguished, one could still see the brokenness in the faces of the people sitting in the community hall waiting to hear our message.

We gathered on the stage of the community hall to give speeches about the different TRC committees, inviting the audience to remember the past and bear witness to their pain and suffering. In the midst of my presentation, I noticed that a woman in the audience was shifting and turning in her seat. By the time I completed my presentation, she had defiantly turned her back to us. I wondered if her body language was a reaction to something I had said. I walked down from the stage to talk to her. As I touched her on her shoulder she got up angrily and walked away. I followed her outside to a spot under a tree. With a look of pain and anger in her eyes, she asked why we were asking them to bring up "buried pain." She wondered why the commission wanted to open up old wounds.

"We have laid these stories to rest," she said. "Now you are asking us to talk about things that we have forgotten!"

Like an unwelcome messenger I sat there next to her, not looking at her and not knowing what to say. It started to rain—a sign from above to rescue me from my guilt for having caused her pain—and I offered to drive her home. Driving in silence, I knew what unbearable horrors our presence in the township of Mlungisi was forcing its residents to remember. Our quick arrival at her home brought simultaneously some relief—I would soon be alone with my guilt and not have to face her—and a sense of anxious anticipation—I did not trust myself to say the right parting words that would express my regret for having caused her pain. As I opened the door to let her out of the car, I expected to say my good-byes and return back to the hall. But instead, Mrs. Plaatjie invited me into her home. She asked me to sit on one of only two chairs in her kitchen while she sat in the other. She then told me her story:

> My son was eleven years old. He had come home during school break at ten o'clock. I was sitting right there, where you are sitting, just sitting exactly where you are sitting in that chair. He walked in, dressed in his school uniform, went to the cupboard over there, and opened the drawer to get a knife. He cut himself a slice of bread. He was in a rush; he is like that when he comes home during break. He got some peanut butter and spread it on his bread. He put the bread back, but there were crumbs left on the cupboard. And the knife was still smudged with peanut butter. He ran out, still chewing his bread and holding it in his hand.
>
> It wasn't long. I heard shots outside—some commotion and shots. I went flying out of the house. Now I am dazed. I run. My eyes are on the crowd that has gathered. Here is my son, my only child. My anguish was beyond anything I thought I could experience. They have killed him. I threw myself over him. I can feel the wetness of his blood. I felt his last breath leave him. He was my only child.

This is a compelling example of how witnesses of trauma continue to live in the grip of the images of their traumatic memories and of what Ruth Glynn calls the "ceaseless repetitions" of traumatic experience.[3] The images, emotions,

3. Ruth Glynn, "Trauma on the Line: Terrorism and Testimony in the *anni di piombo*," in *The Value of Literature in and after the Seventies: The Case of Italy and Portugal*, ed.

and voices from the past are etched in her memory—the crumbs left on the cupboard, the knife her son leaves behind still smudged with peanut butter, and her anguish reappear as if the *event* is happening in the present. Each memory—the chair on which I was sitting, the jar of peanut butter always on the cupboard—seems to take on new significance, to become a symbol of her little boy's final act in his home. Even the crumbs are treasured as a kind of sacred memory.

As she told the story, the event was so vivid in my mind that it was as if it were happening at that very moment. Her use of tense defies the rules of grammar as she crosses and recrosses the boundaries of past and present. *He ran out. He is still chewing his bread. Now I am dazed. I can feel his blood. I ran.* The final moment comes when she recalls seeing her son's lifeless body. "Here is my son." My eyes follow her hand as if I would see her son lying on the floor. I feel like a witness standing both outside of her memory and participating *in* the act of remembering: Are we in the past, or the present? Is the past even "past"? The answer to these questions lies in Lawrence Langer's notion of the "timelessness" of traumatic memory. Trauma, according to Langer, is "immune to the vicissitudes of time."[4]

20

Another example that illustrates the timelessness of traumatic memory is from the testimony of a mother whose son was killed on army duty in the South African Defense Force (SADF) during the apartheid government's war against the liberation struggle in Namibia. Wallace McGregor was second in command in a unit responsible for minesweeping operations in an area occupied by the SADF across the Namibian–South African border. He died after suffering injuries from a mortar bomb explosion. According to army policy, all his mother, Anne-Marie McGregor, was told was that her son died "in operation." Not only was she prevented by official SADF policy from knowing the details of how her son was killed, but Wallace's body was brought home in a sealed body bag, which deprived her of any last moments she might have wanted to have with him before he was buried.

Mrs. McGregor was invited to the TRC to talk about the loss of her son and her experience with the SADF. She told the TRC about the years of agony, of knowing that she would never see Wallace again, yet *not knowing* whether the body brought back by the SADF officials was actually her son's body. Over the years that followed Wallace's death, Mrs. McGregor was plagued by this sense of uncertainty, and she "saw" her son in many young men she encountered in the streets who bore some resemblance to him.

Mrs. McGregor's apparent inability fully to grasp the inevitable reality of her loss is articulated in her encounter with the man who was the commander of Wallace's unit in Namibia. The man approached us at the TRC after watching a television screening of Mrs. McGregor's TRC testimony. In the television program Mrs. McGregor made a plea to anyone who was present when her son died

---

Monica Jansen and Paula Jordão (Utrecht: University of Utrecht Igitur Publishing, 2006) [Author's note].

4. Lawrence Langer, *Holocaust Testimonies: The Ruins of Memory* (New Haven CT: Yale University Press, 1991), 112 [Author's note].

to come forward. Arrangements were made for the former commander, who was accompanied by his wife, and Mrs. McGregor and her two sons to meet at the offices of the TRC.[5] Sitting in the room as a witness to the conversation about Wallace, I was struck again by the fusion of past and present in the retelling of traumatic events. For almost two hours the conversation between Mrs. McGregor and the former commander focused on Wallace, his habits and mannerisms, his words and his values. They compared "notes" on what they knew about Wallace, speaking in present tense as if Wallace had just gone out for awhile and would return to join us in the room. "Oh yes," Mrs. McGregor would respond to a statement about a particular characteristic of Wallace's, "he is very finicky. Wallace is a perfectionist. He will always do that . . ." She beamed with warmth and fondness when the former commander confirmed what she knew about her son: "That's exactly the way he is," she concurred. "He loves to be clean."

It seemed that for Mrs. McGregor the clock had stopped and that the story of her son's death had never occurred. So dramatic was the denial of time and reality that it seemed that we as witnesses were forced to suspend our judgment and our ability to "know better"—that is, to understand that Mrs. McGregor was only temporarily propelled to a past that she seemed to be experiencing as present, a state that Jennifer Willging calls the "disintegration of linear time."[6] What brought Mrs. McGregor to the reality of her loss was the commander's shift of focus in his narrative to a description of the critical event that led to Wallace's death. For the former commander, too, it seemed as if the images of that moment from the past flooded his memory, for as he began to describe the tragic scene, his voice started to crack and tears ran down his cheeks. He described the anxious moment when the paramedics' helicopter touched down in the operational area, how they rushed Wallace to the nearest hospital, and how he held Wallace's hand, "because I wanted my hand to be his heart." As he uttered these words, the former commander collapsed with the sheer intensity of the memory of that moment. He broke down in tears as he described the moment when he realized that his hand-heart was not enough to save Wallace's life. His wife sat motionless next to him, the quiet tears rolling down her face the only sign of emotion. In response, Mrs. McGregor, letting go of her younger son's hand, let out a deep mournful cry and buried her head against my chest. Her deep pain, expressed in her heart-wrenching sobs, symbolized both the pain of what was revealed by the former commander and the uncertainty she had endured over the years since her son's death. It had been ten years since Wallace died, but this was the first time anyone had spoken to her about how her son was killed. She was sobbing uncontrollably like a child, repeating the words "*Hy is rerig dood. Wallace is dood*" (He really *is* dead. Wallace is dead) over and

5. The man requested that his identity not be disclosed since he still felt bound by the SADF secrecy code [Author's note].

6. Jennifer Willging, "Annie Ernaux's Shameful Narration," *French Forum* 26.1 (2001), 83–103, 90 [Author's note].

over again. There was stillness in the room when, with apparent calm, she lifted her head, reaching out with her eyes to the former commander.

The radical shift in Mrs. McGregor's response from cheerfulness in the first part of her conversation as she recounted her son's special characteristics to the utter anguish expressed through her tears exemplifies several characteristics of trauma. One is the dissociation that helps victims and survivors of traumatic experience cope with the distressing elements of their trauma.[7] By engaging in an apparently "normal" conversation about her son, Mrs. McGregor was delaying confrontation with the reality of her loss. A second illustrative moment in her encounter with the former commander is her extremely emotional reaction to the "confirmation" of what she already "knew": that her son had died on army duty. Her breaking down, as if confronted for the first time with the news of her son's death, is suggestive of the fragmentation and compartmentalization that allows victims and survivors to escape, even if only briefly, from the ravages of traumatic memory.[8]

25

Mrs. McGregor's heart-wrenching sobs could be seen as the "second blow" of her traumatic loss. The first was ten years earlier when the news of her son's death came with a sealed body bag that deprived her of the deeper level of knowing that she needed to have some closure without any official acknowledgment by a witness who was present when her son was killed. Her tears seem to symbolize "the wound that cries out," a wound that "addresses us in the attempt to tell us of a reality or a truth" that cannot be articulated.[9]

As Eija Harjula and Timo Heiskanen remind us, when people are traumatized, a "silent language" begins to occupy the space between words, rupturing speech and changing its rhythm.[10] This "silent language" in essence conveys the "*lived* memory" of her trauma and her struggle with its disruptive impact.[11] When language failed, her anguished silence and speechlessness "spoke" through her tears. Paradoxically, this language of silence may also be a path toward the possibility, no matter how small, of closure. Complete closure after massive trauma is, of course, not possible. This is partially because of what has been termed the "indelible" imprint of traumatic memory.[12]

7. In its broadest sense, *dissociation* means the "splitting off" of memories of a traumatic event from consciousness. Traumatic memories that become dissociated may be too painful and evoke too much anxiety to be consciously experienced [Author's note].

8. Judith Herman, *Trauma and Recovery: The Aftermath of Violence—From Domestic Abuse to Political Terror* (London: Pandora, 1992) [Author's note].

9. Cathy Caruth, *Unclaimed Experience: Trauma, Narrative, and History* (Baltimore MD: Johns Hopkins University Press, 1996), 4, 6 [Author's note].

10. Eija Harjula and Timo Heiskanen, "Trauma Lives in Speech: The Rhythm of Speech Breaks, Words Disappear, A Hole Is Torn in Speech," *International Forum of Psychoanalysis* 11.3 (2002), 198–201, 198 [Author's note].

11. Pumla Gobodo-Madikizela, *A Human Being Died that Night: A South African Story of Forgiveness* (Boston: Houghton Mifflin, 2003) [Author's note].

12. Herman, *Trauma and Recovery*; Langer, *Holocaust Testimonies* [Author's note].

Mrs. McGregor and her sons, who sat in painful silence on both sides of their mother, may have been taking the first small steps toward some form of healing—a first layer of closure. As we left the room, there was a certain calm about the young men and their mother. There appeared to be a lightness about Mrs. McGregor as she got up to leave. As the former commander and his wife were escorted by one of my colleagues in the opposite direction, Mrs. McGregor turned with a warm smile and followed them with her eyes until they disappeared into the busy corridors of the TRC. "You know," she said, turning back to us, "Wallace would have been growing bits of gray hair just like him." She then wondered if her son would have allowed his gray hair to grow, and thought that the perfectionist in him would have led him to pluck out the gray hair. It is precisely this level of engaging with the memory of her son that opens the possibility of the transformation of pain from her loss into a narrative that becomes part of her life.

QUESTIONS

1. Pumla Gobodo-Madikizela tells stories of times when "Traumatic experience overwhelms the senses so that even in the retelling of the trauma, language is inadequate" (paragraph 14). Which story in this essay is most memorable to you? Why? Is there something about the way the story is told—Gobodo-Madikizela's use of language—that makes it memorable?

2. Gobodo-Madikizela begins with a narrative about children playing a game and ends with a narrative about a mother seeking closure in dealing with the death of her son. Why do you think she begins and ends where she does? Do these stories illustrate something different or something similar about trauma and how individuals and groups deal with it?

3. Gobodo-Madikizela describes, provides history, analyzes, and reports on her own experience and the experiences of others. The essay is a complex mix of reportage, personal narrative, research, and analysis. Note the places in the essay where you recognize these different approaches to the material. In what places do you think the author is most successful? Least successful?

4. Gobodo-Madikizela writes about times when words themselves are inadequate; she also describes different uses of body language. Write an autobiographical narrative about a time when body language communicated more than words.

George Orwell — *Politics and the English Language*

MOST PEOPLE who bother with the matter at all would admit that the English language is in a bad way, but it is generally assumed that we cannot by conscious action do anything about it. Our civilization is decadent and our language—so the argument runs—must inevitably share in the general collapse. It follows that any struggle against the abuse of language is a sentimental archaism, like preferring candles to electric light or hansom cabs to aeroplanes. Underneath this lies the half-conscious belief that language is a natural growth and not an instrument which we shape for our own purposes.

Now, it is clear that the decline of a language must ultimately have political and economic causes: it is not due simply to the bad influence of this or that individual writer. But an effect can become a cause, reinforcing the original cause and producing the same effect in an intensified form, and so on indefinitely. A man may take to drink because he feels himself to be a failure, and then fail all the more completely because he drinks. It is rather the same thing that is happening to the English language. It becomes ugly and inaccurate because our thoughts are foolish, but the slovenliness of our language makes it easier for us to have foolish thoughts. The point is that the process is reversible. Modern English, especially written English, is full of bad habits which spread by imitation and which can be avoided if one is willing to take the necessary trouble. If one gets rid of these habits one can think more clearly, and to think clearly is a necessary first step towards political regeneration: so that the fight against bad English is not frivolous and is not the exclusive concern of professional writers. I will come back to this presently, and I hope that by that time the meaning of what I have said here will have become clearer. Meanwhile, here are five specimens of the English language as it is now habitually written.

These five passages have not been picked out because they are especially bad—I could have quoted far worse if I had chosen—but because they illustrate various of the mental vices from which we now suffer. They are a little below the average, but are fairly representative samples. I number them so that I can refer back to them when necessary:

> "(1) I am not, indeed, sure whether it is not true to say that the Milton who once seemed not unlike a seventeenth-century Shelley had not become, out of an experience ever more bitter in each year, more alien [*sic*] to the founder of that Jesuit sect which nothing could induce him to tolerate."
>
> PROFESSOR HAROLD LASKI (ESSAY IN FREEDOM OF EXPRESSION).

From Shooting an Elephant, and Other Essays *(1950), a collection of Orwell's best-known essays. "Politics and the English Language" is the most famous modern argument for a clear, unadorned writing style—not only as a matter of good sense, but as a political virtue.*

"(2) Above all, we cannot play ducks and drakes with a native battery of idioms which prescribes such egregious collocations of vocables as the Basic *put up with* for *tolerate* or *put at a loss* for *bewilder.*"

PROFESSOR LANCELOT HOGBEN (*INTERGLOSSA*).

"(3) On the one side we have the free personality: by definition it is not neurotic, for it has neither conflict nor dream. Its desires, such as they are, are transparent, for they are just what institutional approval keeps in the forefront of consciousness; another institutional pattern would alter their number and intensity; there is little in them that is natural, irreducible, or culturally dangerous. But *on the other side,* the social bond itself is nothing but the mutual reflection of these self-secure integrities. Recall the definition of love. Is not this the very picture of a small academic? Where is there a place in this hall of mirrors for either personality or fraternity?"

ESSAY ON PSYCHOLOGY IN POLITICS (NEW YORK).

"(4) All the 'best people' from the gentlemen's clubs, and all the frantic fascist captains, united in common hatred of Socialism and bestial horror of the rising tide of the mass revolutionary movement, have turned to acts of provocation, to foul incendiarism, to medieval legends of poisoned wells, to legalize their own destruction of proletarian organizations, and rouse the agitated petty-bourgeoisie to chauvinistic fervour on behalf of the fight against the revolutionary way out of the crisis."

COMMUNIST PAMPHLET.

"(5) If a new spirit *is* to be infused into this old country, there is one thorny and contentious reform which must be tackled, and that is the humanization and galvanization of the B.B.C. Timidity here will bespeak cancer and atrophy of the soul. The heart of Britain may be sound and of strong beat, for instance, but the British lion's roar at present is like that of Bottom in Shakespeare's *Midsummer Night's Dream*—as gentle as any sucking dove. A virile new Britain cannot continue indefinitely to be traduced in the eyes or rather ears, of the world by the effete languors of Langham Place, brazenly masquerading as 'standard English'. When the Voice of Britain is heard at nine o'clock, better far and infinitely less ludicrous to hear aitches honestly dropped than the present priggish, inflated, inhibited, school-ma'amish arch braying of blameless bashful mewing maidens!"

LETTER IN *TRIBUNE.*

Each of these passages has faults of its own, but, quite apart from avoidable ugliness, two qualities are common to all of them. The first is staleness of imagery; the other is lack of precision. The writer either has a meaning and cannot express it, or he inadvertently says something else, or he is almost indifferent as to whether his words mean anything or not. This mixture of vagueness and sheer incompetence is the most marked characteristic of modern English prose, and especially of any kind of political writing. As soon as certain topics are raised, the concrete melts into the abstract and no one seems able to think of turns of speech that are not hackneyed: prose consists less and less of *words* chosen for the sake of their meaning, and more and more of *phrases* tacked together like the sections of a prefabricated henhouse. I list below, with notes and examples, various of the tricks by means of which the work of prose-construction is habitually dodged:

Dying Metaphors

A newly invented metaphor assists thought by evoking a visual image, while on the other hand a metaphor which is technically "dead" (e.g. *iron resolution*) has in effect reverted to being an ordinary word and can generally be used without loss of vividness. But in between these two classes there is a huge dump of worn-out metaphors which have lost all evocative power and are merely used because they save people the trouble of inventing phrases for themselves. Examples are: *Ring the changes on, take up the cudgels for, toe the line, ride roughshod over, stand shoulder to shoulder with, play into the hands of, no axe to grind, grist to the mill, fishing in troubled waters, on the order of the day, Achilles' heel, swan song, hotbed.* Many of these are used without knowledge of their meaning (what is a "rift," for instance?), and incompatible metaphors are frequently mixed, a sure sign that the writer is not interested in what he is saying. Some metaphors now current have been twisted out of their original meaning without those who use them even being aware of the fact. For example, *toe the line* is sometimes written *tow the line*. Another example is *the hammer and the anvil,* now always used with the implication that the anvil gets the worst of it. In real life it is always the anvil that breaks the hammer, never the other way about: a writer who stopped to think what he was saying would be aware of this, and would avoid perverting the original phrase. 5

Operators or Verbal False Limbs

These save the trouble of picking out appropriate verbs and nouns, and at the same time pad each sentence with extra syllables which give it an appearance of symmetry. Characteristic phrases are: *render inoperative, militate against, make contact with, be subjected to, give rise to, give grounds for, have the effect of, play a leading part (role) in, make itself felt, take effect, exhibit a tendency to, serve the purpose of, etc., etc.* The keynote is the elimination of simple verbs. Instead of being a single word, such as *break, stop, spoil, mend, kill,* a verb becomes a *phrase,* made up of a noun or adjective tacked on to some general-purposes verb such as *prove, serve, form, play, render.* In addition, the passive voice is wherever possible used in preference to the active, and noun constructions are used instead of gerunds (*by examination of* instead of *by examining*). The range of verbs is further cut down by means of the *-ize* and *de-* formation, and the banal statements are given an appearance of profundity by means of the *not un-* formation. Simple conjunctions and prepositions are replaced by such phrases as *with respect to, having regard to, the fact that, by dint of, in view of, in the interests of, on the hypothesis that;* and the ends of sentences are saved from anticlimax by such resounding commonplaces as *greatly to be desired, cannot be left out of account, a development to be expected in the near future, deserving of serious consideration, brought to a satisfactory conclusion,* and so on and so forth.

PRETENTIOUS DICTION

Words like *phenomenon, element, individual* (as noun), *objective, categorical, effective, virtual, basic, primary, promote, constitute, exhibit, exploit, utilize, eliminate, liquidate,* are used to dress up simple statements and give an air of scientific impartiality to biased judgments. Adjectives like *epoch-making, epic, historic, unforgettable, triumphant, age-old, inevitable, inexorable, veritable,* are used to dignify the sordid processes of international politics, while writing that aims at glorifying war usually takes on an archaic colour, its characteristic words being: *realm, throne, chariot, mailed fist, trident, sword, shield, buckler, banner, jackboot, clarion.* Foreign words and expressions such as *cul de sac, ancien régime, deus ex machina, mutatis mutandis, status quo, gleichschaltung, weltanschauung,* are used to give an air of culture and elegance. Except for the useful abbreviations *i.e., e.g.,* and *etc.*, there is no real need for any of the hundreds of foreign phrases now current in English. Bad writers, and especially scientific, political and sociological writers, are nearly always haunted by the notion that Latin or Greek words are grander than Saxon ones, and unnecessary words like *expedite, ameliorate, predict, extraneous, deracinated, clandestine, subaqueous* and hundreds of others constantly gain ground from their Anglo-Saxon opposite numbers.[1] The jargon peculiar to Marxist writing (*hyena, hangman, cannibal, petty bourgeois, these gentry, lackey, flunkey, mad dog, White Guard,* etc.) consists largely of words and phrases translated from Russian, German or French; but the normal way of coining a new word is to use a Latin or Greek root with the appropriate affix and, where necessary, the *-ize* formation. It is often easier to make up words of this kind (*deregionalize, impermissible, extramarital, nonfragmentatory* and so forth) than to think up the English words that will cover one's meaning. The result, in general, is an increase in slovenliness and vagueness.

MEANINGLESS WORDS

In certain kinds of writing, particularly in art criticism and literary criticism, it is normal to come across long passages which are almost completely lacking in meaning.[2] Words like *romantic, plastic, values, human, dead, sentimental, natural, vitality,* as used in art criticism, are strictly meaningless in the sense that

1. An interesting illustration of this is the way in which the English flower names which were in use till very recently are being ousted by Greek ones, *snapdragon* becoming *antirrhinum, forget-me-not* becoming *myosotis,* etc. It is hard to see any practical reason for this change of fashion: it is probably due to an instinctive turning-away from the more homely word and a vague feeling that the Greek word is scientific [Orwell's note].

2. Example: "Comfort's catholicity of perception and image, strangely Whitmanesque in range, almost the exact opposite in aesthetic compulsion, continues to evoke that trembling atmospheric accumulative hinting at a cruel, an inexorably serene timelessness. . . . Wrey Gardiner scores by aiming at simple bull's-eyes with precision. Only they are not so simple, and through this contented sadness runs more than the surface bittersweet of resignation" (*Poetry Quarterly*) [Orwell's note].

they not only do not point to any discoverable object, but are hardly ever expected to do so by the reader. When one critic writes, "The outstanding feature of Mr. X's work is its living quality," while another writes, "The immediately striking thing about Mr. X's work is its peculiar deadness," the reader accepts this as a simple difference of opinion. If words like *black* and *white* were involved, instead of the jargon words *dead* and *living,* he would see at once that language was being used in an improper way. Many political words are similarly abused. The word *Fascism* has now no meaning except in so far as it signifies "something not desirable." The words *democracy, socialism, freedom, patriotic, realistic, justice,* have each of them several different meanings which cannot be reconciled with one another. In the case of a word like *democracy,* not only is there no agreed definition, but the attempt to make one is resisted from all sides. It is almost universally felt that when we call a country democratic we are praising it: consequently the defenders of every kind of régime claim that it is a democracy, and fear that they might have to stop using the word if it were tied down to any one meaning. Words of this kind are often used in a consciously dishonest way. That is, the person who uses them has his own private definition, but allows his hearer to think he means something quite different. Statements like *Marshal Pétain was a true patriot, The Soviet Press is the freest in the world, The Catholic Church is opposed to persecution,* are almost always made with intent to deceive. Other words used in variable meanings, in most cases more or less dishonestly, are: *class, totalitarian, science, progressive, reactionary, bourgeois, equality.*

Now that I have made this catalogue of swindles and perversions, let me give another example of the kind of writing that they lead to. This time it must of its nature be an imaginary one. I am going to translate a passage of good English into modern English of the worst sort. Here is a well-known verse from *Ecclesiastes:*

> "I returned and saw under the sun, that the race is not to the swift, nor the battle to the strong, neither yet bread to the wise, nor yet riches to men of understanding, nor yet favour to men of skill; but time and chance happeneth to them all."

Here it is in modern English: 10

> "Objective consideration of contemporary phenomena compels the conclusion that success or failure in competitive activities exhibits no tendency to be commensurate with innate capacity, but that a considerable element of the unpredictable must invariably be taken into account."

This is a parody, but not a very gross one. Exhibit (3), above, for instance, contains several patches of the same kind of English. It will be seen that I have not made a full translation. The beginning and ending of the sentence follow the original meaning fairly closely, but in the middle the concrete illustrations—race, battle, bread—dissolve into the vague phrase "success or failure in competitive activities." This had to be so, because no modern writer of the kind I am discussing—no one capable of using phrases like "objective consideration of contemporary phenomena"—would ever tabulate his thoughts in that precise and detailed way. The whole tendency of modern prose is away from concreteness. Now analyse these two sentences a little more closely. The first contains forty-nine words but only sixty syllables, and all its words are those of everyday life. The second contains thirty-eight words of ninety syllables: eighteen of its words are from Latin roots, and one from Greek. The first sentence contains six vivid images, and only one phrase ("time and chance") that could be called vague. The second contains not a single fresh, arresting phrase, and in spite of its ninety syllables it gives only a shortened version of the meaning contained in the first. Yet without a doubt it is the second kind of sentence that is gaining ground in modern English. I do not want to exaggerate. This kind of writing is not yet universal, and outcrops of simplicity will occur here and there in the worst-written page. Still, if you or I were told to write a few lines on the uncertainty of human fortunes, we should probably come much nearer to my imaginary sentence than to the one from *Ecclesiastes*.

As I have tried to show, modern writing at its worst does not consist in picking out words for the sake of their meaning and inventing images in order to make the meaning clearer. It consists in gumming together long strips of words which have already been set in order by someone else, and making the results presentable by sheer humbug. The attraction of this way of writing is that it is easy. It is easier—even quicker, once you have the habit—to say *In my opinion it is a not unjustifiable assumption that* than to say *I think*. If you use ready-made phrases, you not only don't have to hunt about for words; you also don't have to bother with the rhythms of your sentences, since these phrases are generally so arranged as to be more or less euphonious. When you are composing in a hurry—when you are dictating to a stenographer, for instance, or making a public speech—it is natural to fall into a pretentious, Latinized style. Tags like *a consideration which we should do well to bear in mind* or *a conclusion to which all of us would readily assent* will save many a sentence from coming down with a bump. By using stale metaphors, similes and idioms, you save much mental effort, at the cost of leaving your meaning vague, not only for your reader but for yourself. This is the significance of mixed metaphors. The sole aim of a metaphor is to call up a visual image. When these images clash—as in *The Fascist octopus has sung its swan song, the jackboot is thrown into the melting pot*—it can be taken as certain that the writer is not seeing a mental image of the objects he is naming; in other words he is not really thinking. Look again at the examples I gave at the beginning of this essay. Professor Laski (1) uses five negatives in fifty-three words. One of these is superfluous, making nonsense of the whole passage, and in addition there is the slip *alien* for akin, making further nonsense, and several avoidable pieces of clumsiness which increase the general vagueness. Professor Hogben (2) plays ducks and drakes with a battery which is able to write prescriptions, and, while disapproving of the everyday phrase *put up with*, is unwilling to look *egregious* up in the dictionary and see what it means. (3), if one takes an uncharitable attitude towards it, is simply meaningless: probably one could work out its intended meaning by reading the whole of the article in which it occurs. In (4), the writer knows more or less what he wants to say, but an accumulation of stale phrases chokes him like tea leaves blocking a sink. In (5), words and meaning have almost parted company. People who write in this manner usually have a general emotional meaning—they dislike one thing and want to express solidarity with another—but they are not interested in the detail of what they are saying. A scrupulous writer, in every sentence that he writes, will ask himself at least four questions, thus: What am I trying to say? What words will express it? What image or idiom will make it clearer? Is this image fresh enough to have an effect? And he will probably ask himself two more: Could I put it more shortly? Have I said anything that is avoidably ugly? But you are not obliged to go to all this trouble. You can shirk it by simply throwing your mind open and letting the ready-made phrases come crowding in. They will construct your sentences for you—even think your thoughts for you, to a certain extent—and at need they will perform the important service of partially concealing your meaning even from yourself. It is at this point that the special connection between politics and the debasement of language becomes clear.

In our time it is broadly true that political writing is bad writing. Where it is not true, it will generally be found that the writer is some kind of rebel, expressing his private opinions and not a "party line." Orthodoxy, of whatever colour, seems to demand a lifeless, imitative style. The political dialects to be found in pamphlets, leading articles, manifestos, White Papers and the speeches of under-secretaries do, of course, vary from party to party, but they are all alike in that one almost never finds in them a fresh, vivid, homemade turn of speech. When one watches some tired hack on the platform mechanically repeating the familiar phrases—*bestial atrocities, iron heel, blood-stained tyranny, free peoples of the world, stand shoulder to shoulder*—one often has a curious feeling that one is not watching a live human being but some kind of dummy: a feeling which suddenly becomes stronger at moments when the light catches the speaker's spectacles and turns them into blank discs which seem to have no eyes behind them. And this is not altogether fanciful. A speaker who uses that kind of phraseology has gone some distance towards turning himself into a machine. The appropriate noises are coming out of his larynx, but his brain is not involved as it would be if he were choosing his words for himself. If the speech he is making is one that he is accustomed to make over and over again, he may be almost unconscious of what he is saying, as one is when one utters the responses in church. And this reduced state of consciousness, if not indispensable, is at any rate favourable to political conformity.

In our time, political speech and writing are largely the defence of the indefensible. Things like the continuance of British rule in India, the Russian purges and deportations, the dropping of the atom bombs on Japan, can indeed be defended, but only by arguments which are too brutal for most people to face, and which do not square with the professed aims of political parties. Thus political language has to consist largely of euphemism, question-begging and sheer cloudy vagueness. Defenceless villages are bombarded from the air, the inhabitants driven out into the countryside, the cattle machine-gunned, the huts set on fire with incendiary bullets: this is called *pacification*. Millions of peasants are robbed of their farms and sent trudging along the roads with no more than they can carry: this is called *transfer of population* or *rectification of frontiers*. People are imprisoned for years without trial, or shot in the back of the neck or sent to die of scurvy in Arctic lumber camps: this is called *elimination of unreliable elements*. Such phraseology is needed if one wants to name things without calling up mental pictures of them. Consider for instance some comfortable English professor defending Russian totalitarianism. He cannot say outright, "I believe in killing off your opponents when you can get good results by doing so." Probably, therefore, he will say something like this:

15 "While freely conceding that the Soviet régime exhibits certain features which the humanitarian may be inclined to deplore, we must, I think, agree that a certain curtailment of the right to political opposition is an unavoidable concomitant of transitional periods, and that the rigors which the Russian people have been called upon to undergo have been amply justified in the sphere of concrete achievement."

The inflated style is itself a kind of euphemism. A mass of Latin words falls upon the facts like soft snow, blurring the outlines and covering up all the details. The great enemy of clear language is insincerity. When there is a gap between one's real and one's declared aims, one turns as it were instinctively to long words and exhausted idioms, like a cuttlefish squirting out ink. In our age there is no such thing as "keeping out of politics." All issues are political issues, and politics itself is a mass of lies, evasions, folly, hatred and schizophrenia. When the general atmosphere is bad, language must suffer. I should expect to find—this is a guess which I have not sufficient knowledge to verify—that the German, Russian and Italian languages have all deteriorated in the last ten or fifteen years, as a result of dictatorship.

But if thought corrupts language, language can also corrupt thought. A bad usage can spread by tradition and imitation, even among people who should and do know better. The debased language that I have been discussing is in some ways very convenient. Phrases like *a not unjustifiable assumption, leaves much to be desired, would serve no good purpose, a consideration which we should do well to bear in mind,* are a continuous temptation, a packet of aspirins always at one's elbow. Look back through this essay, and for certain you will find that I have again and again committed the very faults I am protesting against. By this morning's post I have received a pamphlet dealing with conditions in Germany. The author tells me that he "felt impelled" to write it. I open it at random, and here is almost the first sentence that I see: "(The Allies) have an opportunity not only of achieving a radical transformation of Germany's social and political structure in such a way as to avoid a nationalistic reaction in Germany itself, but at the same time of laying the foundations of a co-operative and unified Europe." You see, he "feels impelled" to write—feels, presumably, that he has something new to say—and yet his words, like cavalry horses answering the bugle, group themselves automatically into the familiar dreary pattern. This invasion of one's mind by ready-made phrases (*lay the foundations, achieve a radical transformation*) can only be prevented if one is constantly on guard against them, and every such phrase anaesthetizes a portion of one's brain.

I said earlier that the decadence of our language is probably curable. Those who deny this would argue, if they produced an argument at all, that language merely reflects existing social conditions, and that we cannot influence its development by any direct tinkering with words and constructions. So far as the general tone or spirit of a language goes, this may be true, but it is not true in detail. Silly words and expressions have often disappeared, not through any evolutionary process but owing to the conscious action of a minority. Two recent examples were *explore every avenue* and *leave no stone unturned,* which were killed by the jeers of a few journalists. There is a long list of fly-blown metaphors which could similarly be got rid of if enough people would interest themselves in the job; and it should also be possible to laugh the *not un-* formation out of existence,[3] to reduce the amount of Latin and Greek in the average sentence, to drive out foreign phrases and strayed scientific words, and, in general, to make pretentiousness unfashionable. But all these are minor points. The defence of the English language implies more than this, and perhaps it is best to start by saying what it does *not* imply.

To begin with it has nothing to do with archaism, with the salvaging of obsolete words and turns of speech, or with the setting up of a "standard English" which must never be departed from. On the contrary, it is especially concerned with the scrapping of every word or idiom which has outworn its usefulness. It has nothing to do with correct grammar and syntax, which are of no importance so long as one makes one's meaning clear, or with the avoidance of Americanisms, or with having what is called a "good prose style." On the other hand it is not concerned with fake simplicity and the attempt to make written English colloquial. Nor does it even imply in every case preferring the Saxon word to the Latin one, though it does imply using the fewest and shortest words that will cover one's meaning. What is above all needed is to let the meaning choose the word, and not the other way about. In prose, the worst thing one can do with words is to surrender to them. When you think of a concrete object, you think wordlessly, and then, if you want to describe the thing you have been visualizing you probably hunt about till you find the exact words that seem to fit. When you think of something abstract you are more inclined to use words from the start, and unless you make a conscious effort to prevent it, the existing dialect will come rushing in and do the job for you, at the expense of blurring or even changing your meaning. Probably it is better to put off using words as long as possible and get one's meaning as clear as one can through pictures or sensations. Afterwards one can choose—not simply *accept*—the phrases that will best cover the meaning, and then switch round and decide what impression one's words are likely to make on another person. This last effort of the mind cuts out all stale or mixed images, all prefabricated phrases, needless repetitions, and humbug and vagueness generally. But one can often

3. One can cure oneself of the *not un-* formation by memorizing this sentence: *A not unblack dog was chasing a not unsmall rabbit across a not ungreen field* [Orwell's note].

be in doubt about the effect of a word or a phrase, and one needs rules that one can rely on when instinct fails. I think the following rules will cover most cases:

(i) Never use a metaphor, simile or other figure of speech which you are used to seeing in print.

(ii) Never use a long word where a short one will do.

(iii) If it is possible to cut a word out, always cut it out.

(iv) Never use the passive where you can use the active.

(v) Never use a foreign phrase, a scientific word or a jargon word if you can think of an everyday English equivalent.

(vi) Break any of these rules sooner than say anything outright barbarous.

These rules sound elementary, and so they are, but they demand a deep change of attitude in anyone who has grown used to writing in the style now fashionable. One could keep all of them and still write bad English, but one could not write the kind of stuff that I quoted in those five specimens at the beginning of this article.

20 I have not here been considering the literary use of language, but merely language as an instrument for expressing and not for concealing or preventing thought. Stuart Chase[4] and others have come near to claiming that all abstract words are meaningless, and have used this as a pretext for advocating a kind of political quietism. Since you don't know what Fascism is, how can you struggle against Fascism? One need not swallow such absurdities as this, but one ought to recognize that the present political chaos is connected with the decay of language, and that one can probably bring about some improvement by starting at the verbal end. If you simplify your English, you are freed from the worst follies of orthodoxy. You cannot speak any of the necessary dialects, and when you make a stupid remark its stupidity will be obvious, even to yourself. Political language—and with variations this is true of all political parties, from Conservatives to Anarchists—is designed to make lies sound truthful and murder respectable, and to give an appearance of solidity to pure wind. One cannot change this all in a moment, but one can at least change one's own habits, and from time to time one can even, if one jeers loudly enough, send some worn-out and useless phrase—some *jackboot, Achilles' heel, hotbed, melting pot, acid test, veritable inferno* or other lump of verbal refuse—into the dustbin where it belongs.

4. Chase (in *The Tyranny of Words* [1938] and *The Power of Words* [1954]) and S. I. Hayakawa (in *Language in Action* [1939]) popularized the semantic theories of Alfred Korzybski.

Questions

1. State Orwell's main point as precisely as possible.

2. What kinds of prose does Orwell analyze in this essay? Look, in particular, at the passages he quotes in paragraph 3. Where would you find their contemporary equivalents?

3. Apply Orwell's rule iv, "Never use the passive where you can use the active" (paragraph 19), to paragraph 14 of his essay. What happens when you change his passive constructions to active? Has Orwell forgotten rule iv or is he covered by rule vi, "Break any of these rules sooner than say anything outright barbarous"?

4. Orwell wrote this essay in 1946. Choose at least two examples of political discourse from current media and discuss, in an essay, whether Orwell's analysis of the language of politics is still valid. If it is, which features that he singles out for criticism appear most frequently in your examples?

Album of Styles: Introduction

What is style? The question eludes easy answers. "Le style est l'homme meme," the Count de Buffon observed in 1753, in an address on his admission to the French Academy. His words, translated into English, have become proverbial: "The style is the person."

Buffon's words suggest that we can gain insight into a person's character by considering the mode of self-presentation, whether in actions or in words. A writer's style is a recognizable expression of self that permeates a text: the clear, distinct, and individual voice that readers "hear" when they read an essay. We can work toward an understanding of a writer's style by examining the elements that create it—words, metaphors, syntax, and rhetorical techniques and maneuvers.

Although a writer's style reflects an individual personality and a personal set of preferences, it is also influenced by the historical context in which the writer lives. Different historical periods have privileged different prose styles. For example, the "metaphysical" writers of the early seventeenth century used elaborate metaphors called "conceits." This stylistic preference appears in the selection from John Donne's meditation, "No Man Is an Island," where Donne reflects on the interconnectedness of all humankind by positing that each of us is part of a continent or mainland, and no one an "island, entire of itself."

The "Augustan" writers of the eighteenth century preferred periodic sentences—sentences that used frequent parallel construction; introductory, dependent clauses before the main, independent clause; and balanced correlatives such as neither and nor, not only with but also, or both and and. Examples of the periodic style appear in the excerpts from Samuel Johnson and Mary Wollstonecraft—as in, for example, Johnson's second sentence, which begins with a dependent clause and balances two parallel clauses in the predicate (of what use it can be and why it may not be as safe). When Wollstonecraft uses the periodic sentence in A Vindication of the Rights of Woman (1792), she is not only expressing her feminist sentiments but also demonstrating her mastery of the dominant literary style of the day.

If the periodic style requires careful attention to the logic of a long, balanced sentence, the aphoristic style emphasizes the swiftness and wit of a quick insight. A single perfect sentence can become a proverb expressing conventional wisdom or an aphorism exposing hypocrisy. The selections here from Blake, Franklin, and Bierce show how brevity can communicate wisdom, profundity, or humor. Remembering that an American wrote "haste makes waste" before the Revolution reinvigorates the proverb and reawakens us to the power of the sharp, well expressed insight.

Throughout this album, you will see that American writers, shaped by a spirit of innovation and revolution, have created styles distinct from their British ancestors. If *we hear echoes of the periodic style in Abraham Lincoln and Martin Luther King Jr., we also hear both asserting the power of distinctly American ideals of union and integration with concision and repetition. Lincoln was a master of simple sentences, often arranged to build to a climax, as in the third paragraph of the "Gettysburg Address." King was a master of biblical cadences, drawing on the rhetorical style of American preachers.*

Modern writers may at first appear more simple, direct, and concise than their literary predecessors. No doubt Ernest Hemingway's crisp, precise style—dominated by strong nouns and verbs, virtually free of adjectives and Latinate diction—has influenced recent generations of American writers. We can find its impact in William Zinsser's preference for strong verbs and minimal adjectives in "College Pressures" *(pp. 380–86) or Molly Ivins's direct, no-nonsense sentences in* "Get a Knife, Get a Dog, but Get Rid of Guns" *(pp. 323–25). But as literacy and education have spread to more and more people, from more and more cultural and linguistic backgrounds, styles of English have blossomed in new and abundant directions. When Gloria Anzaldúa writes* "Nosotros los Chicanos straddle the borderlands," *she introduces a new English, and reminds us of the many new Englishes being born every day as new immigrants arrive, settle, and make the language their own.*

Even within the field of journalism, in which an absence of style might seem to be preferred, writers have distinct styles, such as Joan Didion, the detached observer at the eye of the storm, and Tom Wolfe, whose sensory details thrill us with their immediacy. Didion, who testified in an interview to the influence of Hemingway's style on her own prose, often adopts his short, crisp sentences, but she also incorporates elaborately complex sentences as she analyzes complex cultural phenomena.

Reading the prose and studying the styles of authors, both old and new, can help aspiring writers develop their own styles. Ben Franklin tells us in his Autobiography *that, as a young man, he would read the essays of Joseph Addison and Richard Steele, then close his book and try to write out the essays in his (and their) best style. Ben Jonson advises us, in the selection "To Write Well" from his commonplace book,* Timber, or Discoveries, *"For a man to write well, there are required three necessaries: to read the best authors, observe the best speakers, and much exercise of his own style." As usual, Samuel Johnson's reflections on writing speak volumes: "What is written without effort is in general read without pleasure."*

Francis Bacon: *Of Youth and Age*

A man that is young in years may be old in hours, if he have lost no time. But that happeneth rarely. Generally, youth is like the first cogitations, not so wise as the second. For there is a youth in thoughts as well as in ages. And yet the invention of young men is more lively than that of old, and imaginations stream into their minds better, and as it were more divinely. Natures that have much heat, and great and violent desires and perturbations, are not ripe for

From Bacon's Essays, *the first edition of which appeared in 1597, with augmented and revised editions in 1612 and 1625. Bacon's essays are known for their objective, judicial style.*

action till they have passed the meridian of their years: as it was with Julius Caesar,[1] and Septimius Severus. Of the latter of whom it is said, *Juventutem egit erroribus, imo furoribus, plenam:*[2] and yet he was the ablest emperor, almost, of all the list. But reposed natures may do well in youth. As it is seen in Augustus Caesar, Cosmus, Duke of Florence, Gaston de Foix,[3] and others. On the other side, heat and vivacity in age is an excellent composition for business. Young men are fitter to invent than to judge, fitter for execution than for counsel, and fitter for new projects than for settled business. For the experience of age, in things that fall within the compass of it, directeth them, but in new things abuseth them. The errors of young men are the ruin of business; but the errors of aged men amount but to this, that more might have been done, or sooner. Young men, in the conduct and manage of actions, embrace more than they can hold; stir more than they can quiet; fly to the end, without consideration of the means and degrees; pursue some few principles which they have chanced upon absurdly; care not to innovate,[4] which draws unknown inconveniences; use extreme remedies at first; and, that which doubleth all errors, will not acknowledge or retract them; like an unready horse that will neither stop nor turn. Men of age object too much, consult too long, adventure too little, repent too soon, and seldom drive business home to the full period, but content themselves with a mediocrity of success. Certainly it is good to compound employments of both; for that will be good for the present, because the virtues of either age may correct the defects of both; and good for succession, that young men may be learners while men in age are actors; and, lastly, good for extern accidents, because authority followeth old men, and favour and popularity youth. But for the moral part, perhaps youth will have the pre-eminence, as age hath for the politic. A certain rabbin, upon the text, *Your young men shall see visions, and your old men shall dream dreams,*[5] inferreth that young men are admitted nearer to God than old, because vision is a clearer revelation than a dream. And certainly, the more a man drinketh of the world, the more it intoxicateth; and age doth profit rather in the powers of understanding than in the virtues of the will and affections. There be some have an over-early ripeness in their years, which fadeth betimes. These are, first, such as have brittle wits, the edge whereof is soon turned; such as was Hermogenes the rhetorician, whose books are exceeding subtle, who afterwards waxed stupid.[6] A second sort is of those that have some natural dispositions which have better grace in youth than in age, such as is a fluent and

1. Julius Caesar (100–44 B.C.E.) became dictator of Rome in 49 B.C.E.

2. Severus (145/6–211 C.E.) became emperor of Rome in 193 C.E. "He passed a youth full of folly, or rather of madness," according to Spartianus (*Life of Severus*).

3. Augustus Caesar (63 B.C.E.–14 C.E.) became ruler of Rome in 27 B.C.E.; Cosimo de' Medici (1519–1574) became ruler of Florence in 1537; Gaston de Foix, duke of Nemours and nephew of Louis XII of France, died in battle in 1512, at twenty-two.

4. Are not careful about innovating.

5. Joel 2.28. "Rabbin" means "rabbi."

6. Hermogenes, Greek rhetorician of the 2nd century C.E., is said to have lost his memory when young.

luxuriant speech, which becomes youth well, but not age: so Tully saith of Hortensius, *Idem manebat, neque idem docebat.*[7] The third is of such as take too high a strain at the first, and are magnanimous more than tract of years can uphold. As was Scipio Africanus, of whom Livy saith in effect, *Ultima primis cedebant.*[8]

7. "He remained the same when the same style no longer became him" (Cicero, *Brutus*); said by Cicero (or Tully) of a rival orator.

8. "His last actions were not the equal of his first" (*Heroides* 9); Bacon quotes from the poet Ovid (43 B.C.E.–17 C.E.) to express the gist of what the historian Livy (59 B.C.E.–17 C.E.) said of Africanus (236–183/4 B.C.E.), Roman conqueror of Africa.

Questions

1. List the positive attributes Bacon assigns to both youth and age. Does he prefer one stage over another? How can you tell?

2. Bacon's title suggests that his essay will compare and contrast *youth* with *age*. Locate two or three sentences that contain a comparison, and describe the words or phrases Bacon uses to emphasize his point of similarity or contrast.

3. Bacon uses the rhetorical mode of classifying and dividing to analyze his two main categories. Consider his classification of youth who "have an over-early ripeness in their years" in the final sentences, and discuss whether these subcategories still exist today. How might his descriptions be updated?

4. Write your own short and well-balanced essay that contrasts youth and age.

Ben Jonson: *To Write Well*

For a man to write well, there are required three necessaries: to read the best authors, observe the best speakers, and much exercise of his own style. In style to consider what ought to be written, and after what manner; he must first think and excogitate his matter, then choose his words, and examine the weight of either. Then take care in placing and ranking both matter and words, that the composition be comely, and to do this with diligence and often. No matter how slow the style be at first, so it be laboured and accurate; seek the best, and be not glad of the froward conceits, or first words, that offer themselves to us; but judge of what we invent, and order what we approve. Repeat often what we have formerly written; which beside that it helps the consequence, and makes the juncture better, it quickens the heat of imagination, that often cools in the time of setting down, and gives it new strength, as if it grew lustier by the going back. As

From Timber, or Discoveries, Made upon men and matter, as they have flowed each out of his daily readings, or had their reflux to his peculiar notion of the times, *printed in 1740 and containing notes, extracts, and reflections on miscellaneous subjects.*

we see in the contention of leaping, they jump farthest, that fetch their race largest: or, as in throwing a dart or javelin, we force back our arms, to make our loose the stronger. Yet, if we have a fair gale of wind, I forbid not the steering out of our sail, so the favour of the gale deceive us not. For all that we invent doth please us in conception of birth, else we would never set it down. But the safest is to return to our judgement, and handle over again those things, the easiness of which might make them justly suspected. So did the best writers in their beginnings; they imposed upon themselves care and industry; they did nothing rashly: they obtained first to write well, and then custom made it easy and a habit. By little and little their matter shewed itself to them more plentifully; their words answered, their composition followed; and all, as in a well-ordered family, presented itself in the place. So that the sum of all is, ready writing makes not good writing; but good writing brings on ready writing: yet, when we think we have got the faculty, it is even then good to resist it; as to give a horse a check sometimes with a bit, which doth not so much stop his course, as stir his mettle. Again, whether a man's genius is best able to reach thither, it should more and more contend, lift, and dilate itself, as men of low stature raise themselves on their toes, and so oft-times get even, if not eminent. Besides, as it is fit for grown and able writers to stand of themselves, and work with their own strength, to trust and endeavour by their own faculties: so it is fit for the beginner and learner to study others and the best. For the mind and memory are more sharply exercised in comprehending another man's things than our own; and such as accustom themselves, and are familiar with the best authors, shall ever and anon find somewhat of them in themselves, and in the expression of their minds, even when they feel it not, be able to utter something like theirs, which hath an authority above their own. Nay, sometimes it is the reward of a man's study, the praise of quoting another man fitly: and though a man be more prone, and able for one kind of writing than another, yet he must exercise all. For as in an instrument, so in style, there must be a harmony and consent of parts.

Questions

1. Jonson begins by listing three practices necessary to good writing. How does he illustrate these in the rest of the paragraph?

2. Jonson contrasts "good writing" with "ready writing." What is the difference? What is their relationship?

3. Are there aspects of good writing that Jonson fails to consider? Write a paragraph about some aspect of modern writing that you believe is essential to its being *good*.

John Donne: *No Man Is an Island*

No man is an island, entire of itself; every man is a piece of the continent, a part of the main.[1] If a clod be washed away by the sea, Europe is the less, as well as if a promontory were, as well as if a manor of thy friend's or of thine own were. Any man's death diminishes me, because I am involved in mankind; and therefore never send to know for whom the bell tolls; it tolls for thee.[2]

Originally given as a sermon; later published as Meditation 17 *of Donne's* Devotions upon Emergent Occasions *(1623).*

1. Mainland.
2. Church bells were rung to mark the death of parishioners.

Questions

1. The main metaphor, or conceit, of this passage compares a person to a clod of dirt. List the similarities within the passage and add any more that you can. What are the strengths and limitations of this metaphor?
2. Rewrite Donne's second sentence in your own words.

Samuel Johnson: *Against Wicked Characters*

It is justly considered as the greatest excellency of art, to imitate nature; but it is necessary to distinguish those parts of nature, which are most proper for imitation: greater care is still required in representing life, which is so often discoloured by passion, or deformed by wickedness. If the world be promiscuously described, I cannot see of what use it can be to read the account; or why it may not be as safe to turn the eye immediately upon mankind, as upon a mirror which shows all that presents itself without discrimination. . . .

Many writers, for the sake of following nature, so mingle good and bad qualities in their principal personages, that they are both equally conspicuous; and as we accompany them through their adventures with delight, and are led by degrees to interest ourselves in their favour, we lose the abhorrence of their faults, because they do not hinder our pleasure, or, perhaps, regard them with some kindness for being united with so much merit.

There have been men indeed splendidly wicked, whose endowments threw a brightness on their crimes, and whom scarce any villainy made perfectly detestable, because they never could be wholly divested of their excellencies; but such have been in all ages the great corruptors of the world, and their resemblance ought no more to be preserved, than the art of murdering without pain.

Published in Johnson's bi-weekly periodical, The Rambler, *on Saturday, March 31, 1750. Johnson used this periodical as a venue for expressing his literary criticism and moral philosophy.*

QUESTIONS

1. In paragraph 1 Johnson asserts, "If the world be promiscuously described, I cannot see of what use it can be to read the account." On what basis does he make this argument? What relationship does he posit between literature and life?

2. In paragraph 3 Johnson refers to men "splendidly wicked" whose "endowments threw a brightness on their crimes." What does he mean by "endowments"? Can you think of characters in modern novels, film, or television that illustrate his point?

3. Johnson is known for his balanced, periodic sentences. Choose one and analyze how its form supports its argument.

4. Write an argument either defending or criticizing an author or artist who creates characters who "mingle good and bad qualities." State the principles for your judgment (whether social, moral, or artistic), and give examples to support your points.

MARY WOLLSTONECRAFT: from *A Vindication of the Rights of Woman*

The education of women has, of late, been more attended to than formerly; yet they are still reckoned a frivolous sex, and ridiculed or pitied by the writers who endeavour by satire or instruction to improve them. It is acknowledged that they spend many of the first years of their lives in acquiring a smattering of accomplishments; meanwhile strength of body and mind are sacrificed to libertine notions of beauty, to the desire of establishing themselves,—the only way women can rise in the world,—by marriage. And this desire making mere animals of them, when they marry they act as such children may be expected to act:—they dress; they paint, and nickname God's creatures.[1]—Surely these weak beings are only fit for a seraglio!—Can they be expected to govern a family with judgment, or take care of the poor babes whom they bring into the world?

If then it can be fairly deduced from the present conduct of the sex, from the prevalent fondness for pleasure which takes place of ambition and those nobler passions that open and enlarge the soul; that the instruction which women have hitherto received has only tended, with the constitution of civil society, to render them insignificant objects of desire—mere propagators of fools!—if it can be proved that in aiming to accomplish them, without cultivating their understandings, they are taken out of their sphere of duties, and made ridiculous and useless when the short-lived bloom of beauty is over,[2] I presume

From A Vindication of the Rights of Woman *(1792), written after the publication of Thomas Paine's* A Vindication of the Rights of Man *(1790) as an argument for the extension of political, legal, and educational rights to women.*

1. In Shakespeare's *Hamlet* (III.i.143–45), the hero accuses Ophelia: "You jig, you amble, and you lisp, and nickname God's creatures, and make your wantonness your ignorance"—a sequence of feminine faults that Wollstonecraft echoes.

2. "A lively writer, I cannot recollect his name, asks what business women turned of forty have to do in the world?" [Wollstonecraft's note].

that *rational* men will excuse me for endeavouring to persuade them to become more masculine and respectable.

Indeed the word masculine is only a bugbear: there is little reason to fear that women will acquire too much courage or fortitude; for their apparent inferiority with respect to bodily strength, must render them, in some degree, dependent on men in the various relations of life, but why should it be increased by prejudices that give a sex to virtue, and confound simple truths with sensual reveries?

Women are, in fact, so much degraded by mistaken notions of female excellence, that I do not mean to add a paradox when I assert, that this artificial weakness produces a propensity to tyrannize, and gives birth to cunning, the natural opponent of strength, which leads them to play off those contemptible infantine airs that undermine esteem even whilst they excite desire. Let men become more chaste and modest, and if women do not grow wiser in the same ratio, it will be clear that they have weaker understandings. It seems scarcely necessary to say, that I now speak of the sex in general. Many individuals have more sense than their male relatives; and, as nothing preponderates where there is a constant struggle or an equilibrium, without it has[3] naturally more gravity, some women govern their husbands without degrading themselves, because intellect will always govern.

3. Unless it has.

QUESTIONS

1. Educators once justified excluding women from schools on the grounds that they were intellectually inferior. How does Wollstonecraft unravel the logic of this position?

2. In paragraphs 1 and 3, Wollstonecraft poses a rhetorical question. Discuss her tone here. Does she seem to be addressing an audience of men or women? How does she balance skepticism with reassurance?

3. Wollstonecraft concedes that many individual women behave with great intelligence. What is the purpose of this concession?

BENJAMIN FRANKLIN: from *Poor Richard's Almanack*

Light purse, heavy heart. 1733
Love well, whip well.

Hunger never saw bad bread.
Fools make feasts, and wise men eat 'em.

From Poor Richard's Almanack, *the composite name given to the yearly almanacs Franklin printed between 1732 and 1757. From 1732 to 1747 their title was* Poor Richard; *from 1748 on they were called* Poor Richard Improved.

He that lies down with dogs, shall rise up with fleas.
He is ill clothed, who is bare of virtue.

Without justice courage is weak. 1734
Where there's marriage without love, there will be love without marriage.
Do good to thy friend to keep him, to thy enemy to gain him.

Three may keep a secret, if two of them are dead. 1735
To be humble to superiors is duty, to equals courtesy, to inferiors nobleness.

Fish and visitors stink in three days. 1736
God helps them that help themselves.
God heals, and the doctor takes the fees.

Who has deceiv'd thee so oft as thyself? 1738
Read much, but not many books.
Let thy vices die before thee.

An empty bag cannot stand upright. 1740

Death takes no bribes. 1742

He's a fool that cannot conceal his wisdom. 1745
Many complain of their memory, few of their judgment.

When the well's dry, we know the worth of water. 1746

Write injuries in dust, benefits in marble. 1747

Nine men in *ten* are suicides. 1749
A man in a passion rides a mad horse.

He is a governor that governs his passions, and he is a servant that serves them. 1750

Haste makes waste. 1753

QUESTIONS

1. Some of these proverbs are so familiar that it can be startling to learn they were written by Benjamin Franklin. Choose one such proverb, and discuss how it changes for you when imagining it in its historical context.

2. Many of Poor Richard's sayings deal with similar subjects: how to be a good member of a community, how to stay healthy, how to be a good friend, and so on. Choose two or three related proverbs and discuss the values they impart.

3. Write an essay that takes one of these proverbs as its starting point.

William Blake: *Proverbs of Hell*

In seed time learn, in harvest teach, in winter enjoy.
The road of excess leads to the palace of wisdom.
Prudence is a rich, ugly old maid courted by Incapacity.
He who desires but acts not, breeds pestilence.
5 A fool sees not the same tree that a wise man sees.
He whose face gives no light, shall never become a star.
Eternity is in love with the productions of time.
All wholesome food is caught without a net or a trap.
No bird soars too high, if he soars with his own wings.
10 A dead body revenges not injuries.
The most sublime act is to set another before you.
If the fool would persist in his folly he would become wise.
Folly is the cloak of knavery.
Shame is Pride's cloak.
15 Prisons are built with stones of Law, brothels with bricks of Religion.
Excess of sorrow laughs. Excess of joy weeps.
Joys impregnate. Sorrows bring forth.
What is now proved was once only imagin'd.
One thought fills immensity.
20 Everything possible to be believ'd is an image of truth.
The eagle never lost so much time as when he submitted to learn of the crow.
The fox provides for himself; but God provides for the lion.
Think in the morning. Act in the noon. Eat in the evening. Sleep in the night.
The tigers of wrath are wiser than the horses of instruction.
25 Expect poison from the standing water.
You never know what is enough unless you know what is more than enough.
The weak in courage is strong in cunning.
The thankful receiver bears a plentiful harvest.
The soul of sweet delight can never be defil'd.
30 To create a little flower is the labor of ages.
Damn braces. Bless relaxes.
The best wine is the oldest, the best water the newest.
Prayers plough not! Praises reap not!
Joys laugh not! Sorrows weep not!

From The Marriage of Heaven and Hell *(1790), a book in which Blake sets forth his doctrine of contraries.*

35 Exuberance is Beauty.
Improvement makes straight roads; but the crooked roads without improvement are roads of Genius.
Sooner murder an infant in its cradle than nurse unacted desires.
Where man is not, nature is barren.
Enough! or Too much.

QUESTIONS

1. Blake wrote several works that consider opposites, including *The Marriage of Heaven and Hell* from which these proverbs are taken. Choose two or three proverbs and discuss how they express a point of view contrary to conventional wisdom.

2. Many of these proverbs use the simple verb *is* to join the subject and object of the sentence. Analyze how this joining often yokes together contrary ideas or things.

3. Choose one of the proverbs from Benjamin Franklin's *Poor Richard's Almanack* and rewrite it as a Blakean "proverb of hell."

AMBROSE BIERCE: from *The Devil's Dictionary*

abdication, *n.* An act whereby a sovereign attests his sense of the high temperature of the throne.
accident, *n.* An inevitable occurrence due to the action of immutable natural laws.
accordion, *n.* An instrument in harmony with the sentiments of an assassin.
admiration, *n.* Our polite recognition of another's resemblance to ourselves.
alone, *adj.* In bad company.
bore, *n.* A person who talks when you wish him to listen.
cemetery, *n.* An isolated suburban spot where mourners match lies, poets write at a target and stone-cutters spell for a wager.
childhood, *n.* The period of human life intermediate between the idiocy of infancy and the folly of youth—two removes from the sin of manhood and three from the remorse of age.
Christian, *n.* One who believes that the New Testament is a divinely inspired book admirably suited to the spiritual needs of his neighbor. One who follows the teachings of Christ in so far as they are not inconsistent with a life of sin.
conservative, *n.* A statesman who is enamored of existing evils, as distinguished from the Liberal, who wishes to replace them with others.
consult, *v.t.* To seek another's approval of a course already decided on.
coward, *n.* One who in a perilous emergency thinks with his legs.
diplomacy, *n.* The patriotic art of lying for one's country.

From The Devil's Dictionary *(1906).*

distance, *n.* The only thing that the rich are willing for the poor to call theirs and keep.

education, *n.* That which discloses to the wise and disguises from the foolish their lack of understanding.

erudition, *n.* Dust shaken out of a book into an empty skull.

faith, *n.* Belief without evidence in what is told by one who speaks without knowledge, of things without parallel.

genealogy, *n.* An account of one's descent from an ancestor who did not particularly care to trace his own.

hope, *n.* Desire and expectation rolled into one.

impiety, *n.* Your irreverence toward my deity.

logic, *n.* The art of thinking and reasoning in strict accordance with the limitations and incapacities of the human misunderstanding. The basis of logic is the syllogism, consisting of a major and a minor premise and a conclusion—thus:

> *Major Premise:* Sixty men can do a piece of work sixty times as quickly as one man.
>
> *Minor Premise:* One man can dig a post-hole in sixty seconds; therefore—
>
> *Conclusion:* Sixty men can dig a post-hole in one second. This may be called the syllogism arithmetical, in which, by combining logic and mathematics, we obtain a double certainty and are twice blessed.

love, *n.* A temporary insanity curable by marriage or by removal of the patient from the influences under which he incurred the disorder. This disease, like *caries* and many other ailments, is prevalent only among civilized races living under artificial conditions; barbarous nations breathing pure air and eating simple food enjoy immunity from its ravages. It is sometimes fatal, but more frequently to the physician than to the patient.

pray, *v.* To ask that the laws of the universe be annulled in behalf of a single petitioner confessedly unworthy.

presidency, *n.* The greased pig in the field game of American politics.

religion, *n.* A daughter of Hope and Fear, explaining to Ignorance the nature of the Unknowable.

resolute, *adj.* Obstinate in a course that we approve.

saint, *n.* A dead sinner revised and edited.

valor, *n.* A soldierly compound of vanity, duty and the gambler's hope.

Questions

1. Compare one of Bierce's definitions with the definition in a standard dictionary. What aspect of the conventional definition is Bierce satirizing?

2. Write a few entries for a *Devil's Dictionary* of your own.

ABRAHAM LINCOLN: *The Gettysburg Address*

Four score and seven years ago our fathers brought forth on this continent, a new nation, conceived in Liberty, and dedicated to the proposition that all men are created equal.

Now we are engaged in a great civil war, testing whether that nation, or any nation so conceived and so dedicated, can long endure. We are met on a great battlefield of that war. We have come to dedicate a portion of that field, as a final resting place for those who here gave their lives that that nation might live. It is altogether fitting and proper that we should do this.

But, in a larger sense, we can not dedicate—we can not consecrate—we can not hallow—this ground. The brave men, living and dead, who struggled here, have consecrated it, far above our poor power to add or detract. The world will little note, nor long remember what we say here, but it can never forget what they did here. It is for us the living, rather, to be dedicated here to the unfinished work which they who fought here have thus far so nobly advanced. It is rather for us to be here dedicated to the great task remaining before us—that from these honored dead we take increased devotion to that cause for which they gave the last full measure of devotion—that we here highly resolve that these dead shall not have died in vain—that this nation, under God, shall have a new birth of freedom—and that government of the people, by the people, for the people, shall not perish from the earth.

A presidential address delivered on November 19, 1863, during the height of the American Civil War, on the battlefield at Gettysburg, Pennsylvania.

QUESTIONS

1. President Lincoln's speech is famous for recurring cadences, in which he repeats key words to build up to a point. Locate one or two examples and analyze how they work rhetorically.

2. In "How Lincoln Won the War with Metaphors" (pp. 723–35), the historian James McPherson credits Abraham Lincoln with rhetorical power based on his use of vivid figurative language, especially metaphor. Does this speech rely on metaphor? If you think so, explain how the metaphor(s) function; if you think not, offer an alternative explanation of its effectiveness.

ERNEST HEMINGWAY: from *A Farewell to Arms*

I was always embarrassed by the words sacred, glorious, and sacrifice and the expression in vain. We had heard them, sometimes standing in the rain almost out of earshot, so that only the shouted words came through, and had

From A Farewell to Arms *(1929), a novel depicting the tragedy and destructiveness, personal and cultural, of World War I.*

read them, on proclamations that were slapped up by billposters over other proclamations, now for a long time, and I had seen nothing sacred, and the things that were glorious had no glory and the sacrifices were like the stockyards at Chicago if nothing was done with the meat except to bury it. There were many words that you could not stand to hear and finally only the names of places had dignity. Certain numbers were the same way and certain dates and these with the names of places were all you could say and have them mean anything. Abstract words such as glory, honor, courage, or hallow were obscene beside the concrete names of villages, the numbers of roads, the names of rivers, the numbers of regiments and the dates.

Questions

1. According to the introduction to the "Album of Styles" (p. 474), Hemingway's style is typically "dominated by strong nouns and verbs" and "virtually free of adjectives and Latinate diction." Why do you suppose the first sentence includes so many adjectives? What point does Hemingway make?

2. The final sentence of the paragraph contrasts the "abstract" with the "concrete." Why is the "abstract" associated with the "obscene"?

Martin Luther King Jr.: from *I Have a Dream*

It is obvious today that America has defaulted on this promissory note insofar as her citizens of color are concerned. Instead of honoring this sacred obligation, America has given the Negro people a bad check which has come back marked "insufficient funds." But we refuse to believe that the bank of justice is bankrupt. We refuse to believe that there are insufficient funds in the great vaults of opportunity of this nation. So we have come to cash this check—a check that will give us upon demand the riches of freedom and the security of justice. We have also come to this hallowed spot to remind America of the fierce urgency of *now*. This is no time to engage in the luxury of cooling off or to take the tranquilizing drug of gradualism. *Now* is the time to rise from the dark and desolate valley of segregation to the sunlit path of racial justice. *Now* is the time to open the doors of opportunity to all of God's children. *Now* is the time to lift our nation from the quicksand of racial injustice to the solid rock of brotherhood.

For contextual note, see p. 852.

Questions

1. What does King mean by comparing America's promise to African Americans with a bad check? Discuss the connotations of that metaphor and analyze how King develops it through this paragraph.

2. Compare King's conceit (or metaphor) to John Donne's in "No Man Is an Island" (p. 479). Both men were ministers. Why do you suppose conceits continue to be such powerful tools for ministers?

3. The African American sermonic style relies heavily on repetition and call-and-response. How does King employ and adapt that tradition here?

JOAN DIDION: from *On Going Home*

Paralyzed by the neurotic lassitude engendered by meeting one's past at every turn, around every corner, inside every cupboard, I go aimlessly from room to room. I decide to meet it head on and clean out a drawer, and I spread the contents on the bed. A bathing suit I wore the summer I was seventeen. A letter of rejection from *The Nation*, an aerial photograph of the site for a shopping center my father did not build in 1954. Three teacups hand-painted with cabbage roses and signed "E.M.," my grandmother's initials. There is no final solution for letters of rejection from *The Nation* and teacups hand-painted in 1900. Nor is there any answer to snapshots of one's grandfather as a young man on skis, surveying around Donner Pass in the year 1910. I smooth out the snapshot and look into his face, and do and do not see my own. I close the drawer, and have another cup of coffee with my mother. We get along very well, veterans of a guerrilla war we never understood.

For contextual note, see p. 1.

QUESTIONS

1. Didion is known for being a detached observer of events as she experiences them. Where do you find emotions in this paragraph, and how does she separate herself from them?

2. This essay gains momentum through a list of objects. Write a paragraph about your home in which we learn about your family from the objects in a cupboard or drawer.

TOM WOLFE: from *Yeager*

Anyone who travels very much on airlines in the United States soon gets to know the voice of *the airline pilot* . . . coming over the intercom . . . with a particular drawl, a particular folksiness, a particular down-home calmness that is so exaggerated it begins to parody itself (nevertheless!—it's reassuring) . . . the voice that tells you, as the airliner is caught in thunderheads and goes bolting up and down a thousand feet at a single gulp, to check your seat belts because "it might get a little choppy" . . . the voice that tells you (on a flight from Phoenix preparing for its final approach into Kennedy Airport,

New York, just after dawn): "Now, folks, uh . . . this is the captain . . . ummmm . . . We've got a little ol' red light up here on the control panel that's tryin' to tell us that the *lan*din' gears're not . . . uh . . . *lock*in' into position when we lower 'em . . . Now . . . *I* don't believe that little ol' red light knows what it's *talk*in' about—I believe it's that little ol' red light that iddn' workin' right" . . . faint chuckle, long pause, as if to say, *I'm not even sure all this is really worth going into—still, it may amuse you* . . . "*But* . . . I guess to play it by the rules, we oughta *humor* that little ol' light . . . so we're gonna take her down to about, oh, two or three hundred feet over the runway at Kennedy, and the folks down there on the ground are gonna see if they caint give us a *vis*ual inspection of those ol' landin' gears"—with which he is obviously on intimate ol'-buddy terms, as with every other working part of this mighty ship—"and if I'm right . . . they're gonna tell us everything is copa*cet*ic all the way aroun' an' we'll jes take her on in" . . . and, after a couple of low passes over the field, the voice returns: "Well, folks, those folks down there on the ground—it must be too early for 'em or somethin'—I 'spect they still got the *sleep*ers in their eyes . . . 'cause they say they caint tell if those ol' landin' gears are all the way down or not . . . But, you know, up here in the cockpit we're convinced they're all the way down, so we're jes gonna take her on in . . . And oh" . . . *(I almost forgot)* . . . "while we take a little swing out over the ocean an' empty some of that surplus fuel we're not gonna be needin' anymore—that's what you might be seein' comin' out of the wings—our lovely little ladies . . . if they'll be so kind . . . they're gonna go up and down the aisles and show you how we do what we call 'assumin' the position'" . . . another faint chuckle *(We do this so often, and it's so much fun, we even have a funny little name for it)* . . . and the stewardesses, a bit grimmer, by the looks of them, than *that voice*, start telling the passengers to take their glasses off and take the ballpoint pens and other sharp objects out of their pockets, and they show them *the position*, with the head lowered . . . while down on the field at Kennedy the little yellow emergency trucks start roaring across the field—and even though in your pounding heart and your sweating palms and your broiling brainpan you *know* this is a critical moment in your life, you still can't quite bring yourself to *believe* it, because if it were . . . how could *the captain*, the man who knows the actual situation most intimately . . . how could he keep on drawlin' and chucklin' and driftin' and lollygaggin' in that particular voice of his—

For contextual note, see p. 126.

Questions

1. As a New Journalist, Wolfe was famous for his experimental style, especially his ability to engage the five senses. Sound dominates this paragraph. How does Wolfe create the sense of sitting in an airplane and hearing the pilot as he makes an emergency landing?

2. Why does Wolfe use italics, or italics and parentheses, for some phrases and sentences? How do these phrases function differently from the sentences that recreate the pilot's voice?

3. Think carefully about a distinctive speech pattern or regional dialect. Recreate that speech pattern or dialect in a paragraph or two that tells a story or describes an event.

JOHN MCPHEE: from *Under the Snow*

After ten years of bear trapping and biological study, Alt has equipped so many sows with radios that he has been able to conduct a foster-mother program with an amazingly high rate of success. A mother in hibernation will readily accept a foster cub. If the need to place an orphan arises somewhat later, when mothers and their cubs are out and around, a sow will kill an alien cub as soon as she smells it. Alt has overcome this problem by stuffing sows' noses with Vicks VapoRub. One way or another, he has found new families for forty-seven orphaned cubs. Forty-six have survived. The other, which had become accustomed over three weeks to feedings and caresses by human hands, was not content in a foster den, crawled outside, and died in the snow.

For contextual note, see p. 504.

QUESTIONS

1. McPhee is a celebrated naturalist who is based in New Jersey, a state not known for its wilderness. How do the wild and the civilized come together in his style?

2. In the opening of this essay (see p. 504), McPhee reminisces about his children as infants. Where in this very factual paragraph does he reveal himself to be an affectionate father?

3. Write a paragraph describing nature as you can see it from your home now. Do not omit the visible signs of humanity (telephone wires, the porch, a drainage ditch). If you live in a city, describe a nearby park or greenspace.

GLORIA ANZALDÚA: from *How to Tame a Wild Tongue*

Nosotros los Chicanos straddle the borderlands. On one side of us, we are constantly exposed to the Spanish of the Mexicans, on the other side we hear the Anglos' incessant clamoring so that we forget our language. Among ourselves we don't say *nosotros los americanos, o nosotros los españoles, o nosotros los hispanos*. We say *nosotros los mexicanos* (by *mexicanos* we do not mean citizens of Mexico; we do not mean a national identity, but a racial one). We distinguish between *mexicanos del otro lado* and *mexicanos de este lado*. Deep in our hearts we believe that being Mexican has nothing to do with which country one lives in. Being Mexican is a state of soul—not one of mind, not one of citizenship. Neither eagle nor serpent, but both. And like the ocean, neither animal respects borders.

For contextual note, see p. 411.

Questions

1. Translate the Spanish words and phrases in Anzaldúa's prose. How would this passage be different if it were all in English, or if every Spanish word had its English equivalent in parentheses? What would be gained, and what lost?

2. What does Anzaldúa mean by writing that being Mexican is a state of soul?

3. In the longer essay, Anzaldúa lists the multiple Spanishes that she speaks (see p. 413). Does her bilingual style represent a new English? How many Englishes do you speak?

Jamaica Kincaid: from *Sowers and Reapers*

Middleton is a popular destination for Americans who are interested in gardens, garden history, or a whiff of the sweet stench that makes up so much of American history. It is, on the one hand, a series of beautiful rooms in the garden sense: there is a part for roses only, there is a part for azaleas, there is a part for camellias, and so on and so on. The most spectacular part of the garden is a grassy terrace made by human hands, and on the slope of the terrace are small and perfectly regular risings, so that when seen from below they look like stiff pleats in a skirt that has just been disturbed by a faint breeze. At the foot of the terrace are two small lakes that have been fashioned to look like a butterfly stilled by chloroform. It is all very beautiful, even slightly awesome; and then there is the awfulness, for those gardens and that terrace and those lakes were made by slaves.

For contextual note, see p. 139.

Questions

1. Kincaid is an avid gardener as well as a novelist and essayist. Where in this passage does Kincaid most reveal her reverence for the art of gardening?

2. This passage demands that we confront the ugly truth that slaves made this garden. How does Kincaid reconcile these two facts? How can we?

3. Many beautiful things are made in ugly ways—by slaves or underpaid workers, or through the death of an animal. Write an appreciation of an object that celebrates its beauty while also recognizing the struggle through which it came into being.

Molly Ivins: from *Get a Knife, Get a Dog, but Get Rid of Guns*

Let me start this discussion by pointing out that I am not antigun. I'm proknife. Consider the merits of the knife.

In the first place, you have to catch up with someone in order to stab him. A general substitution of knives for guns would promote physical fitness. We'd turn into a whole nation of great runners. Plus, knives don't ricochet. And people are seldom killed while cleaning their knives.

As a civil libertarian, I, of course, support the Second Amendment. And I believe it means exactly what it says:

5 *A well-regulated militia being necessary to the security of a free state, the right of the people to keep and bear arms shall not be infringed.* Fourteen-year-old boys are not part of a well-regulated militia. Members of wacky religious cults are not part of a well-regulated militia. Permitting unregulated citizens to have guns is destroying the security of this free state.

For contextual note, see p. 323.

QUESTIONS

1. As a columnist, Ivins was known for her provocative style and smart-alecky comments. How does this reputation show itself in the first two sentences of the selection? Why does she make the second sentence shorter than the first?

2. Ivins announces that she will "consider the merits of the knife." What "merits" does she offer? How does each implicitly comment on the problem of gun control (or lack of it)?

3. Read another writer's op-ed in the "Op-Eds and Public Arguments" section, and imagine how Ivins might have approached the topic. Write two or three opening paragraphs of this op-ed in Ivins's style.

IAN FRAZIER: from *Take the F*

Everybody, it seems, is here. At Grand Army Plaza, I have seen traffic tie-ups caused by Haitians and others rallying in support of President Aristide, and by St. Patrick's Day parades, and by Jews of the Lubavitcher sect celebrating the birthday of their Grand Rebbe with a slow procession of ninety-three motor homes—one for each year of his life. Local taxis have bumper stickers that say "Allah Is Great"; one of the men who made the bomb that blew up the World Trade Center used an apartment just a few blocks from me. When an election is held in Russia, crowds line up to cast ballots at a Russian polling place in Brighton Beach. A while ago, I volunteer-taught reading at a public elementary school across the park. One of my students, a girl, was part Puerto Rican, part Greek, and part Welsh. Her looks were a lively combination, set off by sea-green eyes. I went to a map store in Manhattan and bought maps of Puerto Rico, Greece, and Wales to read with her, but they didn't interest her. A teacher at the school was directing a group of students to set up chairs for a program in the auditorium, and she said to me, "We have a problem here—each of these kids speaks a different language." She asked the kids to tell me where they were from. One was from Korea, one from Brazil, one from Poland, one from Guyana, one from Taiwan. In the program that followed, a chorus of

For contextual note, see p. 154.

fourth and fifth graders sang "God Bless America," "You're a Grand Old Flag," and "I'm a Yankee-Doodle Dandy."

Questions

1. Like other *New Yorker* staff writers, Frazier reports what he observes in the city of New York with realistic detail. Locate those phrases or sentences that are "reportorial," that present things or facts in a straightforward way.

2. What does Frazier add to the people, places, and things he reports? Where does his "voice" come in? Locate words or phrases that reveal his attitude or his feelings about what he observes.

3. Write a short description of a place in which you primarily report what you see, but occasionally reveal your response in the adjectives or adverbs you use.

H. Bruce Franklin: from *From Realism to Virtual Reality*

Prior to the Civil War, visual images of America's wars were almost without exception expressions of romanticism and nationalism. Paintings, lithographs, woodcuts, and statues displayed a glorious saga of thrilling American heroism from the Revolution through the Mexican War. Drawing on their imagination, artists could picture action-filled scenes of heroic events, such as Emmanuel Leutze's 1851 painting *Washington Crossing the Delaware*.

Literature, however, was the only art form capable of projecting the action of warfare as temporal flow and movement. Using words as a medium, writers had few limitations on how they chose to paint this action, and their visions had long covered a wide spectrum. One of the Civil War's most distinctively modern images was expressed by Herman Melville in his poem "A Utilitarian View of the Monitor's Fight." Melville sees the triumph of "plain mechanic power" placing war "Where War belongs— / Among the trades and artisans," depriving it of "passion": "all went on by crank, / Pivot, and screw, / And calculations of caloric." Since "warriors / Are now but operatives," he hopes that "War's made / Less grand than Peace."

The most profoundly deglamorizing images of that war, however, were produced not by literature but directly by technology itself. The industrial processes and scientific knowledge that created technowar had also brought forth a new means of perceiving its devastation. Industrial chemicals, manufactured metal plates, lenses, mirrors, bellows, and actuating mechanisms—all were essential to the new art and craft of photography. Thus the Civil War was the first truly modern war—both in how it was fought and in how it was imaged. The romantic images of warfare projected by earlier visual arts were now radically threatened by images of warfare introduced by photography.

For contextual note, see p. 761.

QUESTIONS

1. As an academic historian, Franklin must present an original argument, or thesis, and support it with evidence—as he does in these paragraphs. Locate his thesis and explain how he leads up to it.

2. Franklin uses connective words to emphasize time shifts (*prior to, now*) and conceptual shifts (*thus, however*). Underline such words in this selection, and discuss what function they serve.

3. Scholars often use carefully balanced sentences to present key ideas, contrast differences, and project a sense of the writer's logic. In the third paragraph, Franklin uses this structure in sentences 1 and 3. Analyze this sentence construction for its rhetorical purpose.

4. Take two or three paragraphs from a paper you are writing for a class and incorporate some elements of the academic style you have analyzed in Franklin's piece.

BILL MCKIBBEN: from *The Case for Single-Child Families*

I have one child; she is the light of my life; she makes me care far more about the future than I used to. And I have one child; so even after my work I have some time, money and energy left to do other things. I get to work on Adirondack conservation issues and assist those who are fighting global warming. I've helped my wife start a new school in our town; I can teach Sunday school and help run a nationwide effort to decommercialize Christmas and sit on the board of the local college. . . . If I had three kids, I would still do those things, but less of them; either that, or my work would come at their expense. As it is, once in a while I'm stretched too thin and don't see Sophie for a day, and that reminds me to slow down, to find the real center of my life.

For contextual note, see p. 295.

QUESTIONS

1. McKibben's sentences are "complex" in the sense that he links clauses with semicolons. Compare this modern use of the semicolon to create long sentences to the periodic style of Wollstonecraft or Johnson, who are also included in the "Album of Styles."

2. In passages within this "Album," both Joan Didion and Bill McKibben write about their homes. Compare their tones and overall styles.

General Questions on Album of Styles

1. For any selection: What kinds of words does the writer use? From what sources (Anglo-Saxon, Latin, Greek, French, and so on)? (Most collegiate dictionaries list word origins.) What effects are created by the writer's choice of words?

2. For any selection: What types of sentences does the writer prefer? Long or short? Loose or carefully balanced? What effects does the writer achieve with sentence form and length?

3. For any selection: What metaphors or similes does the writer use? Are they fundamental to the argument or primarily ornamental?

4. For any selection: What is the writer's characteristic voice or tone? What kind of person do you imagine this writer to be?

5. Which selection do you like best? Why? Identify and analyze those aspects of style that create this positive impression.

NATURE AND THE ENVIRONMENT

EDWARD ABBEY *The Serpents of Paradise*

THE APRIL MORNINGS are bright, clear and calm. Not until the afternoon does the wind begin to blow, raising dust and sand in funnel-shaped twisters that spin across the desert briefly, like dancers, and then collapse—whirlwinds from which issue no voice or word except the forlorn moan of the elements under stress. After the reconnoitering dust devils comes the real, the serious wind, the voice of the desert rising to a demented howl and blotting out sky and sun behind yellow clouds of dust, sand, confusion, embattled birds, last year's scrub-oak leaves, pollen, the husks of locusts, bark of juniper. . . .

Time of the red eye, the sore and bloody nostril, the sand-pitted windshield, if one is foolish enough to drive his car into such a storm. Time to sit indoors and continue that letter which is never finished—while the fine dust forms neat little windrows under the edge of the door and on the windowsills. Yet the springtime winds are as much a part of the canyon country as the silence and the glamorous distances; you learn, after a number of years, to love them also.

The mornings therefore, as I started to say and meant to say, are all the sweeter in the knowledge of what the afternoon is

From Abbey's classic book Desert Solitaire: A Season in the Wilderness *(1968). Drawings by Peter Parnall were added in the 1990 edition and are included here.*

likely to bring. Before beginning the morning chores I like to sit on the sill of my doorway, bare feet planted on the bare ground and a mug of hot coffee in hand, facing the sunrise. The air is gelid, not far above freezing, but the butane heater inside the trailer keeps my back warm, the rising sun warms the front, and the coffee warms the interior.

Perhaps this is the loveliest hour of the day, though it's hard to choose. Much depends on the season. In midsummer the sweetest hour begins at sundown, after the awful heat of the afternoon. But now, in April, we'll take the opposite, that hour beginning with the sunrise. The birds, returning from wherever they go in winter, seem inclined to agree. The pinyon jays are whirling in garrulous, gregarious flocks from one stunted tree to the next and back again, erratic exuberant games without any apparent practical function. A few big ravens hang around and croak harsh clanking statements of smug satisfaction from the rimrock, lifting their greasy wings now and then to probe for lice. I can hear but seldom see the canyon wrens singing their distinctive song from somewhere up on the cliffs: a flutelike descent—never ascent—of the whole tone scale. Staking out new nesting claims, I understand. Also invisible but invariably present at some indefinable distance are the mourning doves whose plaintive call suggests irresistibly a kind of seeking out, the attempt by separated souls to restore a lost communion:

Hello . . . they seem to cry, *who . . . are . . . you?*

And the reply from a different quarter. *Hello* . . . (pause) *where . . . are . . . you?*

No doubt this line of analogy must be rejected. It's foolish and unfair to impute to the doves, with serious concerns of their own, an interest in questions more appropriate to their human kin. Yet their song, if not a mating call or a warning, must be what it sounds like, a brooding meditation on space, on solitude. The game.

Other birds, silent, which I have not yet learned to identify, are also lurking in the vicinity, watching me. What the ornithologist terms l.g.b.'s—little gray birds—they flit about from point to point on noiseless wings, their origins obscure.

* * * I share the housetrailer with a number of mice. I don't know how many but apparently only a few, perhaps a single family. They don't disturb me and are welcome to my crumbs and leavings. Where they came

from, how they got into the trailer, how they survived before my arrival (for the trailer had been locked up for six months), these are puzzling matters I am not prepared to resolve. My only reservation concerning the mice is that they do attract rattlesnakes.

10 I'm sitting on my doorstep early one morning, facing the sun as usual, drinking coffee, when I happen to look down and see almost between my bare feet, only a couple of inches to the rear of my heels, the very thing I had in mind. No mistaking that wedgelike head, that tip of horny segmented tail peeping out of the coils. He's under the doorstep and in the shade where the ground and air remain very cold. In his sluggish condition he's not likely to strike unless I rouse him by some careless move of my own.

There's a revolver inside the trailer, a huge British Webley .45, loaded, but it's out of reach. Even if I had it in my hands I'd hesitate to blast a fellow creature at such close range, shooting between my own legs at a living target flat on solid rock thirty inches away. It would be like murder; and where would I set my coffee? My cherrywood walking stick leans against the trailerhouse wall only a few feet away, but I'm afraid that in leaning over for it I might stir up the rattler or spill some hot coffee on his scales.

Other considerations come to mind. Arches National Monument[1] is meant to be among other things a sanctuary for wildlife—for all forms of wildlife. It is my duty as a park ranger to protect, preserve and defend all living things within the park boundaries, making no exceptions. Even if this were not the case I have personal convictions to uphold. Ideals, you might say. I prefer not to kill animals. I'm a humanist; I'd rather kill a *man* than a snake.

What to do. I drink some more coffee and study the dormant reptile at my heels. It is not after all the mighty diamondback, *Crotalus atrox,* I'm confronted with but a smaller species known locally as the horny rattler or more precisely as the Faded Midget. An insulting name for a rattlesnake, which may explain the Faded Midget's alleged bad temper. But the name is apt: he is small and dusty-looking, with a little knob above each eye—the horns. His bite though temporarily disabling would not likely kill a full-grown man in normal health. Even so I don't really want him around. Am I to be compelled to put on boots or shoes every time I wish to step outside? The scorpions, tarantulas, centipedes, and black widows are nuisance enough.

I finish my coffee, lean back and swing my feet up and inside the doorway of the trailer. At once there is a buzzing sound from below and the rattler lifts his head from his coils, eyes brightening, and extends his narrow black tongue to test the air.

15 After thawing out my boots over the gas flame I pull them on and come back to the doorway. My visitor is still waiting beneath the doorstep, basking in the sun, fully alert. The trailerhouse has two doors. I leave by the other and get a long-handled spade out of the bed of the government pickup. With this tool I scoop the snake into the open. He strikes, I can hear the click of the fangs

1. Near Moab, Utah, in the spectacular Canyonlands region, where Abbey lived at the time.

against steel, see the stain of venom. He wants to stand and fight, but I am patient; I insist on herding him well away from the trailer. On guard, head aloft—that evil slit-eyed weaving head shaped like the ace of spades—tail whirring, the rattler slithers sideways, retreating slowly before me until he reaches the shelter of a sandstone slab. He backs under it.

You better stay there, cousin, I warn him; if I catch you around the trailer again I'll chop your head off.

A week later he comes back. If not him his twin brother. I spot him one morning under the trailer near the kitchen drain, waiting for a mouse. I have to keep my promise.

This won't do. If there are midget rattlers in the area there may be diamondbacks too—five, six or seven feet long, thick as a man's wrist, dangerous. I don't want them camping under my home. It looks as though I'll have to trap the mice.

However, before being forced to take that step I am lucky enough to capture a gopher snake. Burning garbage one morning at the park dump, I see a long slender yellow-brown snake emerge from a mound of old tin cans and plastic picnic plates and take off down the sandy bed of a gulch. There is a burlap sack in the cab of the truck which I carry when plucking Kleenex flowers from the brush and cactus along the road; I grab that and my stick, run after the snake and corner it beneath the exposed roots of a bush. Making sure it's a gopher snake and not something less useful, I open the neck of the sack and with a great deal of coaxing and prodding get the snake into it. The gopher snake, *Drymarchon corais couperi,* or bull snake, has a reputation as the enemy of rattlesnakes, destroying or driving them away whenever encountered.

Hoping to domesticate this sleek, handsome and docile reptile, I release him inside the trailerhouse and keep him there for several days. Should I attempt to feed him? I decide against it—let him eat mice. What little water he may need can also be extracted from the flesh of his prey. 20

The gopher snake and I get along nicely. During the day he curls up like a cat in the warm corner behind the heater and at night he goes about his business. The mice, singularly quiet for a change, make themselves scarce. The snake is passive, apparently contented, and makes no resistance when I pick him up with my hands and drape him over an arm or around my neck. When I take him outside into the wind and sunshine his favorite place seems to be inside my shirt, where he wraps himself around my waist and rests on my belt. In this position he sometimes sticks his head out between shirt buttons for a survey of the weather, astonishing and delighting any tourists who may happen to be with me at the time. The scales of a snake are dry and smooth, quite pleasant to the touch. Being a cold blooded creature, of course, he takes his temperature from that of the immediate environment—in this case my body.

We are compatible. From my point of view, friends. After a week of close association I turn him loose on the warm sandstone at my doorstep and leave for a patrol of the park. At noon when I return he is gone. I search everywhere beneath, nearby and inside the trailerhouse, but my companion has disappeared. Has he left the area entirely or is he hiding somewhere close by? At any rate I am troubled no more by rattlesnakes under the door.

The snake story is not yet ended.

In the middle of May, about a month after the gopher snake's disappearance, in the evening of a very hot day, with all the rosy desert cooling like a griddle with the fire turned off, he reappears. This time with a mate.

25 I'm in the stifling heat of the trailer opening a can of beer, barefooted, about to go outside and relax after a hard day watching cloud formations. I happen to glance out the little window near the refrigerator and see two gopher snakes on my verandah engaged in what seems to be a kind of ritual dance. Like a living caduceus they wind and unwind about each other in undulant, graceful, perpetual motion, moving slowly across a dome of sandstone. Invisible but tangible as music is the passion which joins them—sexual? combative? both? A shameless *voyeur,* I stare at the lovers, and then to get a closer view run outside and around the trailer to the back. There I get down on hands and knees and creep toward the dancing snakes, not wanting to frighten or disturb them. I crawl to within six feet of them and stop, flat on my belly, watching from the snake's eye level. Obsessed with their ballet, the serpents seem unaware of my presence.

The two gopher snakes are nearly identical in length and coloring; I cannot be certain that either is actually my former household pet. I cannot even be sure that they are male and female, though their performance resembles so strongly a *pas de deux*[2] by formal lovers. They intertwine and separate, glide side by side in perfect congruence, turn like mirror images of each other and glide back again, wind and unwind again. This is the basic pattern but there is a variation: at regular intervals the snakes elevate their heads, facing one another, as high as they can go, as if each is trying to outreach or overawe the other. Their heads and bodies rise, higher and higher, then topple together and the rite goes on.

I crawl after them, determined to see the whole thing. Suddenly and simultaneously they discover me, prone on my belly a few feet away. The dance stops. After a moment's pause the two snakes come straight toward me, still in flawless unison, straight toward my face, the forked tongues flickering, their intense wild yellow eyes staring directly into my eyes. For an instant I am paralyzed by

2. Literally, step for two (French), a dance for two dancers.

wonder; then, stung by a fear too ancient and powerful to overcome I scramble back, rising, to my knees. The snakes veer and turn and race away from me in parallel motion, their lean elegant bodies making a soft hissing noise as they slide over the sand and stone. I follow them for a short distance, still plagued by curiosity, before remembering my place and the requirements of common courtesy. For godsake let them go in peace, I tell myself. Wish them luck and (if lovers) innumerable offspring, a life of happily ever after. Not for their sake alone but for your own.

In the long hot days and cool evenings to come I will not see the gopher snakes again. Nevertheless I will feel their presence watching over me like totemic deities, keeping the rattlesnakes far back in the brush where I like them best, cropping off the surplus mouse population, maintaining useful connections with the primeval. Sympathy, mutual aid, symbiosis, continuity.

How can I descend to such anthropomorphism? Easily—but is it, in this case, entirely false? Perhaps not. I am not attributing human motives to my snake and bird acquaintances. I recognize that when and where they serve purposes of mine they do so for beautifully selfish reasons of their own. Which is exactly the way it should be. I suggest, however, that it's a foolish, simple-minded rationalism which denies any form of emotion to all animals but man and his dog. This is no more justified than the Moslems are in denying souls to women. It seems to me possible, even probable, that many of the nonhuman undomesticated animals experience emotions unknown to us. What do the coyotes mean when they yodel at the moon? What are the dolphins trying so patiently to tell us? Precisely what did those two enraptured gopher snakes have in mind when they came gliding toward my eyes over the naked sandstone? If I had been as capable of trust as I am susceptible to fear I might have learned something new or some truth so very old we have all forgotten it.

> They do not sweat and whine about their condition.
> They do not lie awake in the dark and weep for their sins.[3]

30 All men are brothers, we like to say, half-wishing sometimes in secret it were not true. But perhaps it is true. And is the evolutionary hue from protozoan to Spinoza[4] any less certain? That also may be true. We are obliged, therefore, to spread the news, painful and bitter though it may be for some to hear, that all living things on hand are kindred. . . .

3. From Walt Whitman's *Song of Myself*, sec. 32.

4. Baruch Spinoza (1632–1677), Dutch philosopher known today for his writings on the doctrine of pantheism.

Questions

1. Why is the word "paradise" included in the title? What does it reveal about Abbey's attitude toward the desert in which he lives?

2. "I'd rather kill a *man* than a snake," writes Abbey in paragraph 12; yet several paragraphs later he threatens, "if I catch you around the trailer again I'll chop your head off" (paragraph 16). What are the rhetorical purposes of these statements? How do they articulate the thematic concerns of the essay?

3. Write an essay in which you use your own experience in nature to defend an ecological or environmental cause.

4. Write about your own encounter with an animal, whether domesticated or wild.

Brian Doyle

Joyas Voladoras

Consider the hummingbird for a long moment. A hummingbird's heart beats ten times a second. A hummingbird's heart is the size of a pencil eraser. A hummingbird's heart is a lot of the hummingbird. *Joyas voladoras,* flying jewels, the first white explorers in the Americas called them, and the white men had never seen such creatures, for hummingbirds came into the world only in the Americas, nowhere else in the universe, more than three hundred species of them whirring and zooming and nectaring in hummer time zones nine times removed from ours, their hearts hammering faster than we could clearly hear if we pressed our elephantine ears to their infinitesimal chests.

Each one visits a thousand flowers a day. They can dive at sixty miles an hour. They can fly backward. They can fly more than five hundred miles without pausing to rest. But when they rest they come close to death: on frigid nights, or when they are starving, they retreat into torpor, their metabolic rate slowing to a fifteenth of their normal sleep rate, their hearts sludging nearly to a halt, barely beating, and if they are not soon warmed, if they do not soon find that which is sweet, their hearts grow cold, and they cease to be. Consider for a moment those hummingbirds who did not open their eyes again today, this very day, in the Americas: bearded helmetcrests and booted racket-tails, violet-tailed sylphs and violet-capped woodnymphs, crimson topazes and purple-crowned fairies, red-tailed comets and amethyst woodstars, rain-bow-bearded thornbills and glittering-bellied emeralds, velvet-purple coronets and golden-bellied star-frontlets, fiery-tailed awlbills and Andean hillstars, spatuletails and pufflegs, each the most amazing thing you have never seen, each thunderous wild heart the size of an infant's fingernail, each mad heart silent, a brilliant music stilled.

Hummingbirds, like all flying birds but more so, have incredible enormous immense ferocious metabolisms. To drive those metabolisms they have racecar hearts that eat oxygen at an eye-popping rate. Their hearts are built of thinner, leaner fibers than ours. Their arteries are stiffer and more taut. They have more

First published in the American Scholar *(Autumn 2004) and later chosen for inclusion in* The Best American Essays 2005 *(2005).*

mitochondria in their heart muscles—anything to gulp more oxygen. Their hearts are stripped to the skin for the war against gravity and inertia, the mad search for food, the insane idea of flight. The price of their ambition is a life closer to death; they suffer more heart attacks and aneurysms and ruptures than any other living creature. It's expensive to fly. You burn out. You fry the machine. You melt the engine. Every creature on earth has approximately two billion heartbeats to spend in a lifetime. You can spend them slowly, like a tortoise, and live to be two hundred years old, or you can spend them fast, like a hummingbird, and live to be two years old.

The biggest heart in the world is inside the blue whale. It weighs more than seven tons. It's as big as a room. It *is* a room, with four chambers. A child could walk around in it, head high, bending only to step through the valves. The valves are as big as the swinging doors in a saloon. This house of a heart drives a creature a hundred feet long. When this creature is born it is twenty feet long and weighs four tons. It is waaaaay bigger than your car. It drinks a hundred gallons of milk from its mama every day and gains two hundred pounds a day, and when it is seven or eight years old it endures an unimaginable puberty and then it essentially disappears from human ken, for next to nothing is known of the mating habits, travel patterns, diet, social life, language, social structure, diseases, spirituality, wars, stories, despairs, and arts of the blue whale. There are perhaps ten thousand blue whales in the world, living in every ocean on earth, and of the largest mammal who ever lived we know nearly nothing. But we know this: the animals with the largest hearts in the world generally travel in pairs, and their penetrating moaning cries, their piercing yearning tongue, can be heard underwater for miles and miles.

5

Mammals and birds have hearts with four chambers. Reptiles and turtles have hearts with three chambers. Fish have hearts with two chambers. Insects and mollusks have hearts with one chamber. Worms have hearts with one chamber, although they may have as many as eleven single-chambered hearts. Unicellular bacteria have no hearts at all; but even they have fluid eternally in motion, washing from one side of the cell to the other, swirling and whirling. No living being is without interior liquid motion. We all churn inside.

So much held in a heart in a lifetime. So much held in a heart in a day, an hour, a moment. We are utterly open with no one, in the end—not mother and father, not wife or husband, not lover, not child, not friend. We open windows to each but we live alone in the house of the heart. Perhaps we must. Perhaps we could not bear to be so naked, for fear of a constantly harrowed heart. When young we think there will come one person who will savor and sustain us always; when we are older we know this is the dream of a child, that all hearts finally are bruised and scarred, scored and torn, repaired by time and will, patched by force of character, yet fragile and rickety forevermore, no matter how ferocious the defense and how many bricks you bring to the wall. You can brick up your heart as stout and tight and hard and cold and impregnable as you possibly can and down it comes in an instant, felled by a woman's second glance, a child's apple breath, the shatter of glass in the road, the words "I have something to tell you," a cat with a broken spine dragging itself into the forest to die, the brush of your mother's papery ancient hand in the thicket of your hair, the memory of your father's voice early in the morning echoing from the kitchen where he is making pancakes for his children.

QUESTIONS

1. Brian Doyle considers the hearts of hummingbirds (paragraphs 1–3), blue whales (paragraph 4), and humans (paragraph 6) in this lyric essay, which uses poetic features such as metaphor, contrast, and repetition. What is his purpose in doing so? How does he make a transition from a focus on animals to a focus on humans?

2. Doyle incorporates several lists into this essay. Trace his use of lists throughout the essay. Which list do you find most effective? Why?

3. Write a lyric essay in which you closely consider some element of human and animal nature.

JOHN MCPHEE

Under the Snow

WHEN MY THIRD DAUGHTER was an infant, I could place her against my shoulder and she would stick there like velvet. Only her eyes jumped from place to place. In a breeze, her bright-red hair might stir, but she would not. Even then, there was profundity in her repose.

When my fourth daughter was an infant, I wondered if her veins were full of ants. Placing her against a shoulder was a risk both to her and to the shoulder. Impulsively, constantly, everything about her moved. Her head seemed about to revolve as it followed the bestirring world.

These memories became very much alive some months ago when—one after another—I had bear cubs under my vest. Weighing three, four, 5.6 pounds, they were wild bears, and for an hour or so had been taken from their dens in Pennsylvania. They were about two months old, with fine short brown hair. When they were made to stand alone, to be photographed in the mouth of a den, they shivered. Instinctively, a person would be moved to hold them. Picked up by the scruff of the neck, they splayed their paws like kittens and screamed like baby bears. The cry of a baby bear is muted, like a human infant's heard from her crib down the hall. The first cub I placed on my shoulder stayed there like a piece of velvet. The shivering stopped. Her bright-blue eyes looked about, not seeing much of anything. My hand, cupped against her back, all but

Originally published in the New Yorker *in the section* Department of Amplification *(April 1983) and included in McPhee's essay collection* Table of Contents *(1985).*

encompassed her rib cage, which was warm and calm. I covered her to the shoulders with a flap of down vest and zipped up my parka to hold her in place.

I was there by invitation, an indirect result of work I had been doing nearby. Would I be busy on March 14th? If there had been a conflict—if, say, I had been invited to lunch on that day with the Queen of Scotland and the King of Spain—I would have gone to the cubs. The first den was a rock cavity in a lichen-covered sandstone outcrop near the top of a slope, a couple of hundred yards from a road in Hawley. It was on posted property of the Scrub Oak Hunting Club—dry hardwood forest underlain by laurel and patches of snow—in the northern Pocono woods. Up in the sky was Buck Alt. Not long ago, he was a dairy farmer, and now he was working for the Keystone State, with directional antennae on his wing struts angled in the direction of bears. Many bears in Pennsylvania have radios around their necks as a result of the summer trapping work of Alt's son Gary, who is a wildlife biologist. In winter, Buck Alt flies the country listening to the radio, crissing and crossing until the bears come on. They come on stronger the closer to them he flies. The transmitters are not omnidirectional. Suddenly, the sound cuts out. Buck looks down, chooses a landmark, approaches it again, on another vector. Gradually, he works his way in, until he is flying in ever tighter circles above the bear. He marks a map. He is accurate within two acres. The plane he flies is a Super Cub.

5 The den could have served as a set for a Passion play. It was a small chamber, open on one side, with a rock across its entrance. Between the freestanding rock and the back of the cave was room for one large bear, and she was curled in a corner on a bed of leaves, her broad head plainly visible from the outside, her cubs invisible between the rock and a soft place, chuckling, suckling, in the wintertime tropics of their own mammalian heaven. Invisible they were, yes, but by no means inaudible. What biologists call chuckling sounded like starlings in a tree.

People walking in woods sometimes come close enough to a den to cause the mother to get up and run off, unmindful of her reputation as a fearless defender of cubs. The cubs stop chuckling and begin to cry: possibly three, four cubs—a ward of mewling bears. The people hear the crying. They find the den and see the cubs. Sometimes they pick them up and carry them away, reporting to the state that they have saved the lives of bear cubs abandoned by their mother. Wherever and whenever this occurs, Gary Alt collects the cubs. After ten years of bear trapping and biological study, Alt has equipped so many sows with radios that he has been able to conduct a foster-mother program with an amazingly high rate of success. A mother in hibernation will readily accept a foster cub. If the need to place an orphan arises somewhat later, when mothers and their cubs are out and around, a sow will kill an alien cub as soon as she smells it. Alt has overcome this problem by stuffing sows' noses with Vicks VapoRub. One way or another, he has found new families for forty-seven orphaned cubs. Forty-six have survived. The other, which had become accustomed over three weeks to feedings and caresses by human hands, was not content in a foster den, crawled outside, and died in the snow.

With a hypodermic jab stick, Alt now drugged the mother, putting her to sleep for the duration of the visit. From deeps of shining fur, he fished out cubs. One. Two. A third. A fourth. Five! The fifth was a foster daughter brought earlier in the winter from two hundred miles away. Three of the four others were male—a ratio consistent with the heavy preponderance of males that Alt's studies have shown through the years. To various onlookers he handed the cubs for safekeeping while he and several assistants carried the mother into the open and weighed her with block and tackle. To protect her eyes, Alt had blindfolded her with a red bandanna. They carried her upside down, being extremely careful lest they scrape and damage her nipples. She weighed two hundred and nineteen pounds. Alt had caught her and weighed her some months before. In the den, she had lost ninety pounds. When she was four years old, she had had four cubs; two years later, four more cubs; and now, after two more years, four cubs. He knew all that about her, he had caught her so many times. He referred to her as Daisy. Daisy was as nothing compared with Vanessa, who was sleeping off the winter somewhere else. In ten seasons, Vanessa had given birth to twenty-three cubs and had lost none. The growth and reproductive rates of black bears are greater in Pennsylvania than anywhere else. Black bears in Pennsylvania grow more rapidly than grizzlies in Montana. Eastern black bears are generally much larger than Western ones. A seven-hundred-pound bear is unusual but not rare in Pennsylvania. Alt once caught a big boar like that who had a thirty-seven-inch neck and was a hair under seven feet long.

This bear, nose to tail, measured five feet five. Alt said, "That's a nice long sow." For weighing the cubs, he had a small nylon stuff sack. He stuffed it with bear and hung it on a scale. Two months before, when the cubs were born, each would have weighed approximately half a pound—less than a newborn porcupine. Now the cubs weighed 3.4, 4.1, 4.4, 4.6, 5.6—cute little numbers with soft tan noses and erectile pyramid ears. Bears have sex in June and July, but the mother's system holds the fertilized egg away from the uterus until November, when implantation occurs. Fetal development lasts scarcely six weeks. Therefore, the creatures who live upon the hibernating mother are so small that everyone survives.

The orphan, less winsome than the others, looked like a chocolate-covered possum. I kept her under my vest. She seemed content there and scarcely moved. In time, I exchanged her for 5.6—the big boy in the litter. Lifted by the scruff and held in the air, he bawled, flashed his claws, and curled his lips like a woofing boar. I stuffed him under the vest, where he shut up and nuzzled. His claws were already more than half an inch long. Alt said that the family would come out of the den in a few weeks but that much of the spring would go by before the cubs gained weight. The difference would be that they were no longer malleable and ductile. They would become pugnacious and scratchy, not to say vicious, and would chew up the hand that caressed them. He said, "If you have an enemy, give him a bear cub."

10 Six men carried the mother back to the den, the red bandanna still tied around her eyes. Alt repacked her into the rock. "We like to return her to the

den as close as possible to the way we found her," he said. Someone remarked that one biologist can work a coon, while an army is needed to deal with a bear. An army seemed to be present. Twelve people had followed Alt to the den. Some days, the group around him is four times as large. Alt, who is in his thirties, was wearing a visored khaki cap with a blue-and-gold keystone on the forehead, and a khaki cardigan under a khaki jump suit. A lithe and light-bodied man with tinted glasses and a blond mustache, he looked like a lieutenant in the Ardennes Forest.[1] Included in the retinue were two reporters and a news photographer. Alt encourages media attention, the better to soften the image of the bears. He says, "People fear bears more than they need to, and respect them not enough." Over the next twenty days, he had scheduled four hundred visitors—state senators, representatives, commissioners, television reporters, word processors, biologists, friends—to go along on his rounds of dens. Days before, he and the denned bears had been hosts to the BBC.[2] The Brits wanted snow. God was having none of it. The BBC brought in the snow.

In the course of the day, we made a brief tour of dens that for the time being stood vacant. Most were rock cavities. They had been used before, and in all likelihood would be used again. Bears in winter in the Pocono Plateau are like chocolate chips in a cookie. The bears seldom go back to the same den two years running, and they often change dens in the course of a winter. In a forty-five-hundred-acre housing development called Hemlock Farms are twenty-three dens known to be in current use and countless others awaiting new tenants. Alt showed one that was within fifteen feet of the intersection of East Spur Court and Pommel Drive. He said that when a sow with two cubs was in there he had seen deer browsing by the outcrop and ignorant dogs stopping off to lift a leg. Hemlock Farms is expensive, and full of cantilevered cypress and unencumbered glass. Houses perch on high flat rock. Now and again, there are bears in the rock—in, say, a floor-through cavity just under the porch. The owners are from New York. Alt does not always tell them that their property is zoned for bears. Once, when he did so, a "For Sale" sign went up within two weeks.

Not far away is Interstate 84. Flying over it one day, Buck Alt heard an oddly intermittent signal. Instead of breaking off once and cleanly, it broke off many times. Crossing back over, he heard it again. Soon he was in a tight turn, now hearing something, now nothing, in a pattern that did not suggest anything he had heard before. It did, however, suggest the interstate. Where a big green sign says, "Milford 11, Port Jervis 20," Gary hunted around and found the bear. He took us now to see the den. We went down a steep slope at the side of the highway and, crouching, peered into a culvert. It was about fifty yards long. There was a disc of daylight at the opposite end. Thirty inches in diameter, it was a perfect place to stash a body, and that is what the bear thought, too. On Gary's first visit, the disc of daylight had not been visible. The bear had denned under the eastbound lanes. She had given birth to three cubs. Soon

1. An area of Belgium, Luxembourg, and France where the 1944–1945 Battle of the Bulge took place.

2. British Broadcasting Corporation.

after he found her, heavy rains were predicted. He hauled the family out and off to a vacant den. The cubs weighed less than a pound. Two days later, water a foot deep was racing through the culvert.

Under High Knob, in remote undeveloped forest about six hundred metres above sea level, a slope falling away in an easterly direction contained a classic excavated den: a small entrance leading into an intimate ovate cavern, with a depression in the center for a bed—in all, about twenty-four cubic feet, the size of a refrigerator-freezer. The den had not been occupied in several seasons, but Rob Buss, a district game protector who works regularly with Gary Alt, had been around to check it three days before and had shined his flashlight into a darkness stuffed with fur. Meanwhile, six inches of fresh snow had fallen on High Knob, and now Alt and his team, making preparations a short distance from the den, scooped up snow in their arms and filled a big sack. They had nets of nylon mesh. There was a fifty-fifty likelihood of yearling bears in the den. Mothers keep cubs until their second spring. When a biologist comes along and provokes the occupants to emerge, there is no way to predict how many will appear. Sometimes they keep coming and coming, like clowns from a compact car. As a bear emerges, it walks into the nylon mesh. A drawstring closes. At the same time, the den entrance is stuffed with a bag of snow. That stops the others. After the first bear has been dealt with, Alt removes the sack of snow. Out comes another bear. A yearling weighs about eighty pounds, and may move so fast that it runs over someone on the biological team and stands on top of him sniffing at his ears. Or her ears. Janice Gruttadauria, a research assistant, is a part of the team. Bear after bear, the procedure is repeated until the bag of snow is pulled away and nothing comes out. That is when Alt asks Rob Buss to go inside and see if anything is there.

Now, moving close to the entrance, Alt spread a tarp on the snow, lay down on it, turned on a five-cell flashlight, and put his head inside the den. The beam played over thick black fur and came to rest on a tiny foot. The sack of snow would not be needed. After drugging the mother with a jab stick, he joined her in the den. The entrance was so narrow he had to shrug his shoulders to get in. He shoved the sleeping mother, head first, out of the darkness and into the light.

15 While she was away, I shrugged my own shoulders and had a look inside. The den smelled of earth but not of bear. The walls were dripping with roots. The water and protein metabolism of hibernating black bears has been explored by the Mayo Clinic as a research model for, among other things, human endurance on long flights through space and medical situations closer to home, such as the maintenance of anephric human beings who are awaiting kidney transplants.

Outside, each in turn, the cubs were put in the stuff sack—a male and a female. The female weighed four pounds. Greedily, I reached for her when Alt took her out of the bag. I planted her on my shoulder while I wrote down facts about her mother: weight, a hundred and ninety-two pounds; length, fifty-eight inches; some toes missing; severe frostbite from a bygone winter evidenced along the edges of the ears.

Eventually, with all weighing and tagging complete, it was time to go. Alt went into the den. Soon he called out that he was ready for the mother. It would be a tight fit. Feet first, she was shoved in, like a safe-deposit box. Inside, Alt tugged at her in close embrace, and the two of them gradually revolved until she was at the back and their positions had reversed. He shaped her like a doughnut—her accustomed den position. The cubs go in the center. The male was handed in to him. Now he was asking for the female. For a moment, I glanced around as if looking to see who had her. The thought crossed my mind that if I bolted and ran far enough and fast enough I could flag a passing car and keep her. Then I pulled her from under the flap of my vest and handed her away.

Alt and others covered the entrance with laurel boughs, and covered the boughs with snow. They camouflaged the den, but that was not the purpose. Practicing wildlife management to a fare-thee-well, Alt wanted the den to be even darker than it had been before; this would cause the family to stay longer inside and improve the cubs' chances when at last they faced the world.

In the evening, I drove down off the Pocono Plateau and over the folded mountains and across the Great Valley and up the New Jersey Highlands and down into the basin and home. No amount of intervening terrain, though—and no amount of distance—could remove from my mind the picture of the covered entrance in the Pennsylvania hillside, or the thought of what was up there under the snow.

Questions

1. John McPhee opens with a memory of holding his daughter when she was an infant, saying she would stick to his shoulder "like velvet" (paragraph 1). Two paragraphs later, he writes about holding a bear cub that stayed on his shoulder "like a piece of velvet" (paragraph 3). Why do you think McPhee makes this comparison? What purpose does it serve in this essay?

2. Trace McPhee's use of simile throughout the essay. For example, he compares bears to chocolate chips (paragraph 11), likens their movement to "clowns from a compact car" (paragraph 13), and describes a researcher positioning a bear "like a doughnut" (paragraph 17). What is the effect of such comparisons? What other similes are significant in this essay?

3. What is the purpose of the kind of bear trapping and biological study McPhee describes? What is your position on this interaction between humans and wildlife? Write an argument in which you either defend the kind of research McPhee describes or make a case for leaving wildlife alone. Be sure to use a specific animal (as McPhee uses bears) in making your claim.

Peter Matthiessen *Tigers in the Snow*

The beautiful wild region known as the Russian Far East curves south along the Sea of Japan like a great claw of Siberia, from the vast delta of the Amur River to the North Korean border, and its coast range—the Sikhote-Alin—extending southward some 600 miles between the Ussuri River and the sea is the last redoubt of *Panthera tigris altaica*, the Siberian or Manchurian tiger, which ranged formerly throughout northeastern China (or Manchuria) and the Korean peninsula, and west as far as Mongolia and Lake Baikal. In the past century, its range has been reduced almost entirely to the Amur-Ussuri watershed, and today the most appropriate name for the largest of the world's great cats is the Amur tiger. . . .

With its small wood cottages, zinc green and faded blue, its vegetable gardens and picket fences, outhouses, guard dogs, and trim woodpiles, and its birch-shaded mud lanes twisting uphill and inland toward the mountains, Old Terney, a small logging and fishing community on the coast of the Russian Far East, appeared to have changed little since described in the first years of the last century. Here I met Maurice Hornocker, a weathered wildlife biologist who is probably the world's foremost authority on the great cats. He introduced me to wildlife biologist Dale Miquelle and also to two Russian scientists, Igor Nikolaev and Evgeny Smirnov, who have both had extensive field experience with *P. t. altaica*. Smirnov calls this zapovednik "the Predator Reserve," since tiger and lynx and wolf and brown and black bear are all present, with lesser carnivores of the fierce weasel tribe—sable and mink, wolverine and badger, weasel and the yellow-throated marten—working the edges. (The wild dog known as the *dhole* is now extinct in Russia, although it occurred in southern Ussuria until the 1970s; the peculiar canid called the raccoon dog remains quite common.) When Smirnov first came here from Moscow as a mouse biologist in 1963, the tiger had been extirpated from the reserve for nearly a decade. Within three years, a few wanderers appeared, then one female produced cubs. When a small population became established, Smirnov's interest switched from mice to tigers, and his data and observations from thirty-odd years in the Sikhote-Alin represent the longest continuous study ever undertaken of this animal.

Smirnov's colleague Igor Nikolaev, of the Academy of Sciences in Vladivostok, is also a consultant on the Siberian Tiger Project. Nikolaev worked for many years with the noted tiger biologist A. G. Yudakov, his co-author in *The Ecology of the Amur Tiger.* (A few years ago, pinned by a felled tree while alone in the forest, Dr. Yudakov dug himself out by chipping frozen dirt from beneath his shattered leg, then crawled and dragged himself toward a settlement. Although still alive when found, he died in hospital a few weeks later.) Niko-

Excerpted from Tigers in the Snow *(2000), an account of Matthiessen's quest for the Amur tiger of the Russian Far East.*

laev is rather quiet and speaks shyly, but in the awed opinion of Dale Miquelle, "Igor knows more about the Amur tiger in the wild than any man alive." In the absence of funds for radio telemetry equipment, tiger research in Russia had been largely based on tracking animals on foot in winter. While a good deal of basic information on tiger numbers and travel routes, predation, scent-making, and other behavior had been obtained, data could be gathered only when snow covered the ground. What radio telemetry made possible was the first year-round study of Amur tiger behavior ever undertaken, and also the first "longitudinal studies" following known individuals through the four seasons.

The researchers were en route to the airstrip, and I went along. In an old AN-2 biplane with a 1,000-HP radial engine, we climbed laboriously into the air and headed north over the low coast range, whose highest peak is 6,575 feet.

Ussuria and Heilongjiang, like northern Japan, are composed of what biogeographers know as "Manchu-Japanese mixed forest," and slightly more than 70 percent of both Primorski Krai and southern Khabarovski Krai, which together comprise about 95 percent of *altaica*'s remaining range, have remained forested. From the air, the unbroken wilderness, rising toward the western ridges and descending again into the Ussuri Valley, seemed utterly unspoiled. Dark forests of Korean pine ascend these mountains, with fir and spruce above 2,500 feet; at lower elevations near the coast, a mixed pine and hardwood taiga is dominated by oak and birch.

Using earphones and the radio, the researchers attempted to find their two tigers, nicknamed Olga and Lena.[1] Soon Olga's signal was located north of Terney, and the plane crisscrossed steep wooded slopes and sunny ledges, gold-leafed oak woods with dark islets of pine where the mountains descended to sheer precipice, white surf, and the dark stone blue of the Sea of Japan. The ungulate animals preyed upon by tigers prefer hillside and stream valley habitats near the sea in which hardwoods, pine, and secondary growth provide food and cover. Cone nuts from the Korean pine and acorns from the Mongolian oak are critical mast for the wild pigs and the deer species as well as for other forest creatures, from bears to squirrels. Though Olga remained hidden under the canopy, the signals from her transmitter revealed that she was moving and presumably in good health. (The transmitters broadcast one signal when the tiger is at rest and another when it is active, with a different frequency for each study animal.)

Roaring and shuddering, the biplane swung up and away, recrossing the beautiful Serebryanka River to the region of Lena's capture site in the south of the reserve. Unlike Olga, this tigress was not moving, which is normal in the middle of the day. However, her signal was still coming from a wooded drainage less than a mile from her capture site. Full recovery from the shock of capture may take two to three days, but the biologists were quietly concerned that Lena had not recovered faster and wandered farther.

1. Prior to Matthiessen's trip, the Russian scientists had captured, tagged, and attached radio transmitters to these two tigers; their practice was to "christen" the tigers at the time of tagging.

Next day, in hopes of discovering what ailed her, we trekked into the forest, following the Khanov Creek upstream for several miles through hardwood taiga of oak and birch, basswood and maple, poplar, ash, and elm, with scattered pines. In the fresh airy greenwood of late June, wherever sunlight sifted through the canopy, were violets and buttercups, wild roses and strawberries, iris, lady's slipper, phlox, wild grape—a flora of the Northern Hemisphere that seemed strangely out of place in a haunt of tigers. But on a dim trail all but closed over by ferns were big raw pugmarks, then a fresh scrape. Perhaps these had been made by Lena, perhaps not. . . .

At any rate, awareness that a tiger is close by lends a certain edge to walking in the taiga. Scrapes were numerous among the ferns of the forest floor, and a fine big print in the dried mud sprang at the eye. ("The perfectly distinct and fresh impressions of an immense cat's paw, standing out sharply printed in the muddy track," as Arseniev describes it. The water had not yet found its way into this quite-fresh pugmark.) High up on a tree trunk, deep scratches marked the place where a tiger on hind legs had sharpened its two-inch claws by raking them downward with the powerful foreshoulders that, together with the stabbing action of its canine teeth and its bone-shearing incisors, allow it to overpower much larger prey. A urine scent post on a hard-rubbed elm was another signal to other tigers that this was an established territory. Knowing that such a powerful creature had paused right here in these silent trees, the fire-striped coat rising and falling as it breathed and listened, was exhilarating, to say the least. Besides excellent hearing, tigers have binocular and color vision. In combination with tail lashing, which raises the black tail tuft in warning, a threatened tiger may rotate its ears to show the bold black-ringed white spots on the backs; otherwise their markings have evolved as camouflage adaptations for tall grass, reeds, and woodlands, just as the spots of leopard and jaguar reflect the dappled lights of wind-danced leaves.

Eventually we neared the capture site at the base of a large Tilia, or basswood, tree where the ground was torn up all around and a sapling as thick as a man's arm had been snapped off clean. The snare restricts but does not restrain the tiger's movements, and Lena's captors spoke with awe of the terrible roars and lunging, the ferocity, with which this 252-pound female had made three swift roaring charges on the cable of her snare before being immobilized by two shotgun-fired darts. (Later that year, a large male tiger pulled free of a snare at Dale Miquelle's approach, but fortunately it bounded off without attacking him.)

10

Since her capture, Lena had moved less than a mile upstream. Doubtless agitated by the contraption on her neck, perhaps still footsore or disoriented by the drug, her instinct may have been to remain in hiding in the cool undergrowth. Using rough triangulation to fix her location, we paused at a point that Maurice judged to be no more than a hundred yards from the place where the agitated tiger was switching her long tail in the alders by the brook. At such close quarters, the great head with its broad black nostrils and long, shining whiskers would already be raised and alert, twitching flies from the white-spotted ears, the visage camouflaged in the striped sunlight by the calligraphy of bold black lines inscribed on the white brows and beard and ruff, in that beautiful and terrifying mask of snow and fire.

In *Dersu the Trapper*,[2] V. K. Arseniev translates an inscription he had found in a Chinese joss house in Primorski Krai: "To the Lord Tiger who dwelleth in the Forest and the Mountains. In ancient days . . . He saved the state. Today his spirit brings happiness to man." Being so near this agitated tiger, I could scarcely say that her spirit brought me "happiness," yet on this day in the Kunalaika forest while Lena observed us from her place of hiding, I felt a kindled exaltation very close to joy—joy in the sense that word was used by the poet Elizabeth Bishop when confronted with the enigma of a roadside moose:[3]

Why, why do we feel
(we all feel) this sweet
sensation of joy?

Over the receiver came more rapid beeping, indicating that Lena, although not moving away, was up and moving. She did not roar but nobody believed that she was in good temper.

We kept our eyes fixed on the sunny greenwood. The tigress lay down, then rose again and moved in a tight circuit like a caged animal, her restlessness transmitted by her signal. But even knowing we were there, she remained where she had rested for the past three days. Finally we withdrew quietly and left the forest.

15 A few days later, Lena was still in the same location, although she had long since metabolized the drug and should have resumed her hunting circuit. Possibly she had made a fortuitous kill where she was resting, but the biologists worried that something had gone wrong, that she was ill, that a precious animal of a rare species might have been harmed. Since Maurice and I were leaving the next day, we decided to camp at a cabin in the Kunalaika Valley and make a last reconnaissance before first light.

At daybreak, as the woodland birds awakened, we set off with Dale Miquelle into the forest. Following the dim path through wet ferns, tracking her signal, we approached Lena even closer than before, hoping to disturb her just enough to get her moving. Having crowded her as much as we dared, we kept our vigil for an hour. Soon the sun rising from the Sea of Japan burned the coast ridges with bright fire, and the cuckoos and thrushes ceased their singing in the leafy stillness. There was only a woodpecker's solitary tapping—a hollow tap, a waiting silence, then another. *Tap.*

Dersu, an indigenous hunter-trapper, once told V. K. Arseniev that all Creation was one body, that it was "all same man; also ground, hill, forest . . . all

2. *Dersu the Trapper* (1941), a book by the Russian explorer V. K. Arseniev, who traveled in the Russian Far East in the early twentieth century and mapped the then-unknown area of Siberia in which Matthiessen is traveling. Dersu, an indigenous hunter-trapper, helped Arseniev's team and saved their lives on more than one occasion.

3. A quotation from "The Moose," a poem by Elizabeth Bishop (1911–1979).

same man. Hear him breathe, all same man." I could feel the tigress breathing as I breathed, and perhaps her sharp eyes could see us through the trees. Certainly she heard us, for her radio signal shifted to a rapid *beep-beep-beep* as she rose and circled. Her harlequin mask would have turned in our direction, the striped fur rising and falling with the fetid meaty breath as she stared and listened—I could all but smell her. Even so, her signal slowed and she settled down again. Perhaps she had been pregnant and had given birth prematurely due to the stress of capture. Perhaps she had made a fortuitous kill and was still guarding it beside the brook—we would never know. . . .

In late summer, returning to America, I found word from Dr. Hornocker that within a few days of our departure from Terney, the tigress Lena had resumed hunting in a normal manner. Since then, a third tigress had been snared and collared. In October we would learn from Dale Miquelle that a fourth female and two half-grown cubs (called Maria Ivanovna, Katerina, and Kolya) had been caught in the north part of the reserve, making six "marked" animals altogether. The Siberian Tiger Project was well under way. Elated, Maurice invited me to return in winter, when there was a far better chance to see a tiger, but three years would pass before this came about.

In January 1996, I found my chance to accept Maurice Hornocker's kind invitation to return to Ussuri[4] Land in winter, when tracking a tiger, and even sighting one, might be possible. In the low sun of winter, the silver aircraft from Alaska crossed the bright volcanoes of Kamchatka and descended into the Siberian barrens at an airport of big urine-colored buildings some fifty miles inland from the gold-mining settlement at Magadan. There snow was falling on deep snow, and the temperature was −48°F.

At Vladivostok[5] airport I was met by Howard Quigley and Dale Miquelle, who was now field director of the Siberian Tiger Project, based in this old port city. On the long drive to town, we stopped for supper at the "Vlad Motor Inn," created and shipped piece by piece from Canada in an effort to re-create an "American" atmosphere where Western businessmen might feel at home. As we departed, the receptionist said, "Okay. Good night. All my best." 20

My companions brought me up to date on the progress of the Siberian Tiger Project, which had already acquired a far more precise understanding of tiger predation and predation rates and also a better understanding of home range size for both male and female tigers in Ussuria; these data were crucial in determining the area required for effective protection and for future planning. Much had also been learned about reproduction—birthrates, intervals between litters, cub survival rates—the better to assess the long-term impact of chronic poaching and the resilience and viability of this population. With the first longitudinal studies of individual tigers made possible by radio telemetry, the project was gaining critical information about social habits—how often tiger pairs associated as well as mated, or how many litters a tigress might produce within a lifetime. In these first years of the project, a dozen litters that had produced

4. A river in the Russian Far East and the name Matthiessen gives to this region.
5. A large port city on the Pacific Ocean in the Russian Far East.

almost thirty new tigers had been documented. Yet many questions were still unanswered. For example, a recent increase in tiger numbers had not been accompanied by a decrease in their prey, suggesting that despite local rumor to the contrary, they were not really competing with the local hunters for game.

Thirteen of the thirty-odd tigers using the Sikhote-Alin Reserve had been captured and fitted with radio collars and returned to the wild without a casualty. Of this group, two had been lost to natural causes: one had been crushed by a falling limb, another had wandered out of radio contact. Two others had not been located since early 1995 and had probably been killed by poachers, although a project tiger had been reported about one hundred miles to the south, near the mining settlement at Dalnegorsk. At present, nine "marked" animals were being monitored. . . .

A cold clear daybreak, −4°F. Frozen smoke from a few village chimneys rose against the dark headland of the cliffs as I fetched split logs for our stove and a bucket of water from the pump. The outhouse, despite its stirring view downriver to the sea, was no place for dawdlers in the Siberian winter. But the little house was warm enough, and soon a cold sun rose from Japan, casting a pewter glaze on the rigid river.

At the airstrip, I recognized the crude old AN-2 biplane, faded gray and orange—the sort of crate one might expect to see belly-deep in scrub and weeds off the far end of the farthest Third World airstrip. After strenuous heating by a hot-air blower on the ground, the frozen engine kicked sluggishly and turned over, and the wind and cold accompanied us into its bare metal cabin as, with a great roar, it zigzagged down the airstrip. Inside, the shuddering machine seemed even slower and more noisy than in 1992, and very much colder, too, but it was airborne, more or less—we were aloft. Valeri, the pilot, climbed to a few thousand feet, to make sure none of the tiger signals would be cut off by the mountains, then turned south down the coast toward Blogovatna, a lovely lake behind the dunes where in those cool early-summer days of 1992 I had walked the woods and beach and sea cliffs, looking for birds.

25 The nine "marked" tigers were monitored biweekly from the air, to make sure they were still alive and still transmitting. All but two were female, which was to be expected. Cubs are divided more or less equally between the sexes, but by adulthood, there are apt to be two to four females for each male. This is because the females remain longer with their mothers, then establish themselves not far away in familiar territory, whereas a young male, striking out into unknown, hostile country toward the end of his second year, encounters considerably more risk from hunters and poachers in addition to accidents or injury due to inexperience in making a kill; in attempting to take over a territory and acquire the females whose home ranges that territory overlaps, he must often fight an older, larger male, sustaining injuries that may be fatal.

Tiger #5—the tigress Katia—which had taken over Lena's range two years after her death, had recently been frequenting Blogovatna. So had Tiger #9, a male named Geny, who had been spending too much time in the environs of Terney, making no one happy. It appeared that Katia had been bred by Geny,

Pathera tigris altaica.

who had been with her over a three-day period in early December, a liaison discovered because the pair remained close to the road and were exceptionally noisy—not uncommon among tigers in the throes of mating. To protect them against poachers, the project's new researchers, a young couple named John Goodrich and Linda Kerley, had monitored their caterwauling. Later they were threatened by Katia, when they inadvertently approached her den site in the Kumami drainage; she backed off only when met with a cloud of pepper spray of the sort used in North America to discourage bears. Apparently Katia had lost a first litter to disease or weakness, or to wolves, lynx, bears, or other predators that discovered the den, or to another tiger.

Because his large territory is hard to defend, a male may be driven off by a stronger male after only two or three years; females persist on their territories longer. In a good prey area, under normal conditions, a tigress may produce a litter every two or three years, but when a new male takes over in her home territory, he may kill his predecessor's young in order to bring the tigress into estrus eight months faster; in this way, most male carnivores—and primates, too—clear the way for their own genes as soon as possible, before they are killed or driven off by new contenders. (In monogamous species, which mostly bond for life, the male may devote his energies to helping protect and rear the young instead of eating them.)

Katia's signals were coming from farther west in the Kunalaika Valley, just below the place on the coast road where Lena had been killed. The plane descended into the river bottoms, which were mostly open, scattered with large cottonwoods and birch and poplar, a few spruce, yet scanning from a slow airplane, often no more than 300 feet above the ground, we were unable to find her. With Dale at his elbow, our dauntless pilot made eight or ten close passes, throttling the clanking engine down to a near-stall, so that the vibrating hulk seemed to shudder to a dead halt in midair; he abandoned this folly only when the ancient machine, carving the valley side too close, collided with its own prop wash and was jarred heavily toward the wooded slope. At last the good Valeri had had enough, for the plane roared up and out of the Kunalaika.

Having apparently bred Katia, Geny had left the Terney region and moved far south across the snowbound ridges. The close proximity of their signals told us that he was presently attending Tiger #3 (Natasha) and her two grown cubs, who would probably disperse on their own later this spring. The four tigers were hidden in a grove of spruce in a snowy hollow, and despite all of Valeri's inspired maneuvers, we did not see them. I began to fear that luck was not with us and we would see no tigers.

The plane banked south and west, leaving the reserve as it crossed the Djigit River, then circled back over a tributary stream where Dale picked up a signal. Crisscrossing the valley, it made a wide turn over a logging track, and there I saw the first wild tiger of my life, bounding across the white expanse in bursts of powder. With the low winter sun glancing off the snow, all I could see was that black, bounding silhouette. The image evoked a Tungus belief that stalking tigers use the sun to blind their prey, leaping out of that wild fireball at dawn or sunset like a tongue of flame.

Crossing the track, the tiger plunged toward a big solitary spruce. Yelling at Howard, who turned in time to see it, I jumped up to the cockpit to point out its location to Dale and Valeri. Our intrepid aviator hurled the last scrap of his prudence to the skies, circling the spruce tighter and tighter, as if intent on vanishing in a tight columnar blur of motor oil, much as those circling tigers in *Little Black Sambo* had dissolved in a golden ring of fine ghee butter. But Tiger #21, the tigress Nadia, had abandoned that lone tree and was making a run for a nearby grove of conifers, for on a turn, as the plane banked across the treetops, I saw the warm burnt-orange creature moving toward me among the sunlit evergreens on the white snow. Feeling herself hidden, or at least safe, she did not bother to look up or turn aside, but moved ahead, intent on her own path, on the sparkling white corridor between the pines. Then the plane was past and she was gone and I sat back sighing, with a vast grin of well-being.

Tiger #12, a 400-pound male (called Dale after Dr. Miquelle), was located in a birch copse on a high rock pinnacle. Having no place to run, he must have been lying motionless on the sunny snow, gazing with hauteur at the old airplane that lumbered past at eye level, spoiling his lordly view. Once again, despite Valeri's crazed efforts, we did not spot him in the sparse cover of small trees, and so we turned back toward the north part of the reserve, where Tiger #4 (Maria Ivanovna, also referred to as Marijuana, or Nirvana) was usually found just outside the boundary. Where ravens scattered she appeared to have a kill, but Marijuana was not seen, and neither was Olga, who was accompanied these days by a female cub. The old biplane returned south, passing offshore of the rock coast where, in 1992, Maurice Hornocker and I, fishing for pink salmon with Volodya, had seen two goral on the sea cliffs. . . .

At seven next morning, when we left Terney with Anatoli Astafiev, the coast range was still locked in bitter darkness, and an hour later, though the sun had tipped the treetops on the cliff with ragged fire, the air remained transfixed by Arctic cold.

QUESTIONS

1. Matthiessen shapes his piece as a quest for two tigers named Olga and Lena. Does he succeed in his quest? Why or why not?

2. In paragraph 12, Matthiessen quotes from *Dersu the Trapper*, an account of a nineteenth-century hunter-trapper, and then from Elizabeth Bishop's poem "The Moose." Why does he include these quotations? How do they help express his feelings as he searches for the tigers?

3. Write about your quest for something elusive, whether an animal, person, or dream. Make it clear whether you succeeded in your quest, though not necessarily by direct statement.

Rachel Carson

Tides

> In every country the moon keeps ever the rule of alliance with the sea which it once for all has agreed upon.
>
> —The Venerable Bede[1]

There is no drop of water in the ocean, not even in the deepest parts of the abyss, that does not know and respond to the mysterious forces that create the tide. No other force that affects the sea is so strong. Compared with the tide the wind-created waves are surface movements felt, at most, no more than a hundred fathoms below the surface. So, despite their impressive sweep, are the planetary currents, which seldom involve more than the upper several hundred fathoms. The masses of water affected by the tidal movement are enormous, as will be clear from one example. Into one small bay on the east coast of North America—Passamaquoddy—2 billion tons of water are carried by the tidal currents twice each day; into the whole Bay of Fundy, 100 billion tons.

Here and there we find dramatic illustration of the fact that the tides affect the whole ocean, from its surface to its floor. The meeting of opposing tidal currents in the Strait of Messina creates whirlpools (one of them is Charybdis of classical fame)[2] which so deeply stir the waters of the strait that fish bearing all the marks of abyssal existence, their eyes atrophied or abnormally large, their bodies studded with phosphorescent organs, frequently are cast up on the lighthouse beach, and the whole area yields a rich collection of deep-sea fauna for the Institute of Marine Biology at Messina.

The tides are a response of the mobile waters of the ocean to the pull of the moon and the more distant sun. In theory, there is a gravitational attraction between every drop of sea water and even the outermost star of the universe. In practice, however, the pull of the remote stars is so slight as to be obliterated in the vaster movements by which the ocean yields to the moon and the sun. Anyone who has lived near tidewater knows that the moon, far more than the sun, controls the tides. He has noticed that, just as the moon rises later each day by fifty minutes, on the average, than the day before, so, in most places, the time of high tide is correspondingly later each day. And as the moon waxes and wanes in its monthly cycle, so the height of the tide varies. Twice each month, when the moon is a mere thread of silver in the sky, and

A chapter from Carson's best-selling book The Sea Around Us *(1951), which won the National Book Award and the John Burroughs Medal, the latter awarded annually to a distinguished book of natural history.*

1. British Benedictine monk and scholar (673–735), canonized in 1899.

2. The Strait of Messina lies between Sicily and the Italian mainland; thought to be the original location of Scylla and Charybdis, i.e., the rocks and the whirlpool in Homer's *Odyssey*.

again when it is full, we have the highest of the high tides, called the springs. At these times sun, moon, and earth are directly in line and the pull of the two heavenly bodies is added together to bring the water high on the beaches, and send its surf leaping upward against the sea cliffs, and draw a brimming tide into the harbors so that the boats float high beside their wharfs. And twice each month, at the quarters of the moon, when sun, moon, and earth lie at the apexes of a triangle, and the pull of sun and moon are opposed, we have the least tides of the lunar month, called the neaps.

That the sun, with a mass 27 million times that of the moon, should have less influence over the tides than a small satellite of the earth is at first surprising. But in the mechanics of the universe, nearness counts for more than distant mass, and when all the mathematical calculations have been made we find that the moon's power over the tides is more than twice that of the sun.

5 The tides are enormously more complicated than all this would suggest. The influence of sun and moon is constantly changing, varying with the phases of the moon, with the distance of moon and sun from the earth, and with the position of each to north or south of the equator. They are complicated further by the fact that every body of water, whether natural or artificial, has its own period of oscillation. Disturb its waters and they will move with a seesaw or rocking motion, with the most pronounced movement at the ends of the container, the least motion at the center. Tidal scientists now believe that the ocean contains a number of "basins," each with its own period of oscillation determined by its length and depth. The disturbance that sets the water in motion is the attracting force of the moon and sun. But the kind of motion, that is, the period of the swing of the water, depends upon the physical dimensions of the basin. What this means in terms of actual tides we shall presently see.

The tides present a striking paradox, and the essence of it is this: the force that sets them in motion is cosmic, lying wholly outside the earth and presumably acting impartially on all parts of the globe, but the nature of the tide at any particular place is a local matter, with astonishing differences occurring within a very short geographic distance. When we spend a long summer holiday at the seashore we may become aware that the tide in our cove behaves very differently from that at a friend's place twenty miles up the coast, and is strikingly different from what we may have known in some other locality. If we are summering on Nantucket Island our boating and swimming will be little disturbed by the tides, for the range between high water and low is only about a foot or two. But if we choose to vacation near the upper part of the Bay of Fundy, we must accommodate ourselves to a rise and fall of 40 to 50 feet, although both places are included within the same body of water—the Gulf of Maine. Or if we spend our holiday on Chesapeake Bay we may find that the time of high water each day varies by as much as 12 hours in different places on the shores of the same bay.

The truth of the matter is that local topography is all-important in determining the features that to our minds make "the tide." The attractive force of the heavenly bodies sets the water in motion, but how, and how far, and how strongly it will rise depend on such things as the slope of the bottom, the depth of a channel, or the width of a bay's entrance.

If the history of the earth's tides should one day be written by some observer of the universe, it would no doubt be said that they reached their greatest grandeur and power in the younger days of Earth, and that they slowly grew feebler and less imposing until one day they ceased to be. For the tides were not always as they are today, and as with all that is earthly, their days are numbered.

In the days when the earth was young, the coming in of the tide must have been a stupendous event. If the moon was * * * formed by the tearing away of a part of the outer crust of the earth, it must have remained for a time very close to its parent. Its present position is the consequence of being pushed farther and farther away from the earth for some 2 billion years. When it was half its present distance from the earth, its power over the ocean tides was eight times as great as now, and the tidal range may even then have been several hundred feet on certain shores. But when the earth was only a few million years old, assuming that the deep ocean basins were then formed, the sweep of the tides must have been beyond all comprehension. Twice each day, the fury of the incoming waters would inundate all the margins of the continents. The range of the surf must have been enormously extended by the reach of the tides, so that the waves would batter the crests of high cliffs and sweep inland to erode the continents. The fury of such tides would contribute not a little to the general bleakness and grimness and uninhabitability of the young earth.

Under such conditions, no living thing could exist on the shores or pass beyond them, and, had conditions not changed, it is reasonable to suppose that life would have evolved no further than the fishes. But over the millions of years the moon has receded, driven away by the friction of the tides it creates. The very movement of the water over the bed of the ocean, over the shallow edges of the continents, and over the inland seas carries within itself the power that is slowly destroying the tides, for tidal friction is gradually slowing down the rotation of the earth. In those early days we have spoken of, it took the earth a much shorter time—perhaps only about 4 hours—to make a complete rotation on its axis. Since then, the spinning of the globe has been so greatly slowed that a rotation now requires, as everyone knows, about 24 hours. This retarding will continue, according to mathematicians, until the day is about 50 times as long as it is now.

10

And all the while the tidal friction will be exerting a second effect, pushing the moon farther away, just as it has already pushed it out more than 200,000 miles. As the moon recedes, it will, of course, have less power over the tides and they will grow weaker. It will also take the moon longer to complete its orbit around the earth. When finally the length of the day and of the month coincide, the moon will no longer rotate relatively to the earth, and there will be no lunar tides.

All this, of course, will require time on a scale the mind finds it difficult to conceive, and before it happens it is quite probable that the human race will have vanished from the earth. This may seem, then, like a Wellsian fantasy[3] of a world so remote that we may dismiss it from our thoughts. But already, even in our allotted fraction of earthly time, we can see some of the effects of these cosmic processes. Our day is believed to be several seconds longer than that of Babylonian times. Britain's Astronomer Royal recently called the attention of the American Philosophical Society to the fact that the world will soon have to choose between two kinds of time. The tide-induced lengthening of the day has already complicated the problems of human systems of keeping time. Conventional clocks, geared to the earth's rotation, do not show the effect of the lengthening days. New atomic clocks now being constructed will show actual time and will differ from other clocks.

Although the tides have become tamer, and their range is now measured in tens instead of hundreds of feet, mariners are nevertheless greatly concerned not only with the stages of the tide and the set of the tidal currents, but with the many violent movements and disturbances of the sea that are indirectly related to the tides. Nothing the human mind has invented can tame a tide rip or control the rhythm of the water's ebb and flow, and the most modern instruments cannot carry a vessel over a shoal until the tide has brought a sufficient depth of water over it. Even the *Queen Mary* waits for slack water to come to her pier in New York; otherwise the set of the tidal current might swing her against the pier with enough force to crush it. On the Bay of Fundy, because of the great range of tide, harbor activities follow a pattern as rhythmic as the tides themselves, for vessels can come to the docks to take on or discharge cargo during only a few hours on each tide, leaving promptly to avoid being stranded in mud at low water.

In the confinement of narrow passages or when opposed by contrary winds and swells, the tidal currents often move with uncontrollable violence, creating some of the most dangerous waterways of the world. It is only necessary to read the Coast Pilots and Sailing Directions for various parts of the world to understand the menace of such tidal currents to navigation.

15 "Vessels around the Aleutians are in more danger from tidal currents than from any other cause, save the lack of surveys," says the postwar edition of the *Alaska Pilot*. Through Unalga and Akutan Passes, which are among the most-used routes for vessels entering the Bering Sea from the Pacific, strong tidal currents pour, making their force felt well offshore and setting vessels unexpectedly against the rocks. Through Akun Strait the flood tide has the velocity of a mountain torrent, with dangerous swirls and over-falls. In each of these passes the tide will raise heavy, choppy seas if opposed by wind or swells. "Vessels must be prepared to take seas aboard," warns the *Pilot*, for a 15-foot wave of a tide rip may suddenly rise and sweep across a vessel, and more than one man has been carried off to his death in this way.

On the opposite side of the world, the tide setting eastward from the open Atlantic presses between the islands of the Shetlands and Orkneys into the North Sea, and on the ebb returns through the same narrow passages.

3. H. G. Wells (1866–1946), British author whose works include science fiction.

At certain stages of the tide these waters are dotted with dangerous eddies, with strange upward domings, or with sinister pits or depressions. Even in calm weather boats are warned to avoid the eddies of Pentland Firth, which are known as the Swilkie; and with an ebb tide and a northwest wind the heavy breaking seas of the Swilkie are a menace to vessels "which few, having once experienced, would be rash enough to encounter a second time."

* * *

The influence of the tide over the affairs of sea creatures as well as men may be seen all over the world. The billions upon billions of sessile animals, like oysters, mussels, and barnacles, owe their very existence to the sweep of the tides, which brings them the food which they are unable to go in search of. By marvelous adaptations of form and structure, the inhabitants of the world between the tide lines are enabled to live in a zone where the danger of being dried up is matched against the danger of being washed away, where for every enemy that comes by sea there is another that comes by land, and where the most delicate of living tissues must somehow withstand the assault of storm waves that have the power to shift tons of rock or to crack the hardest granite.

The most curious and incredibly delicate adaptations, however, are the ones by which the breeding rhythm of certain marine animals is timed to coincide with the phases of the moon and the stages of the tide. In Europe it has been well established that the spawning activities of oysters reach their peak on the spring tides, which are about two days after the full or the new moon. In the waters of northern Africa there is a sea urchin that, on the nights when the moon is full and apparently only then, releases its reproductive cells into the sea. And in tropical waters in many parts of the world there are small marine worms whose spawning behavior is so precisely adjusted to the tidal calendar that, merely from observing them, one could tell the month, the day, and often the time of day as well.

Near Samoa in the Pacific, the palolo worm lives out its life on the bottom of the shallow sea, in holes in the rocks and among the masses of corals. Twice each year, during the neap tides of the moon's last quarter in October and November, the worms forsake their burrows and rise to the surface in swarms that cover the water. For this purpose, each worm has literally broken its body in two, half to remain in its rocky tunnel, half to carry the reproductive products to the surface and there to liberate the cells. This happens at dawn on the day before the moon reaches its last quarter, and again on the following day; on the second day of the spawning the quantity of eggs liberated is so great that the sea is discolored.

The Fijians, whose waters have a similar worm, call them "Mbalolo" and have designated the periods of their spawning "Mbalolo lailai" (little) for October and "Mbalolo levu" (large) for November. Similar forms near the Gilbert Islands respond to certain phases of the moon in June and July; in the Malay Archipelago a related worm swarms at the surface on the second and third nights after the full moon of March and April, when the tides are running highest. A Japanese palolo swarms after the new moon and again after the full moon in October and November. 20

Concerning each of these, the question recurs but remains unanswered: is it the state of the tides that in some unknown way supplies the impulse from which springs this behavior, or is it, even more mysteriously, some other influence of the moon? It is easier to imagine that it is the press and the rhythmic movement of the water that in some way brings about this response. But why is it only certain tides of the year, and why for some species is it the fullest tides of the month and for others the least movements of the waters that are related to the perpetuation of the race? At present, no one can answer.

No other creature displays so exquisite an adaptation to the tidal rhythm as the grunion—a small, shimmering fish about as long as a man's hand. Through no one can say what processes of adaptation, extending over no one knows how many millennia, the grunion has come to know not only the daily rhythm of the tides, but the monthly cycle by which certain tides sweep higher on the beaches than others. It has so adapted its spawning habits to the tidal cycle that the very existence of the race depends on the precision of this adjustment.

Shortly after the full moon of the months from March to August, the grunion appear in the surf on the beaches of California. The tide reaches flood stage, slackens, hesitates, and begins to ebb. Now on these waves of the ebbing tide the fish begin to come in. Their bodies shimmer in the light of the moon as they are borne up the beach on the crest of a wave, they lie glittering on the wet sand for a perceptible moment of time, then fling themselves into the wash of the next wave and are carried back to sea. For about an hour after the turn of the tide this continues, thousands upon thousands of grunion coming up onto the beach, leaving the water, returning to it. This is the spawning act of the species.

During the brief interval between successive waves, the male and female have come together in the wet sand, the one to shed her eggs, the other to fertilize them. When the parent fish return to the water, they have left behind a mass of eggs buried in the sand. Succeeding waves on that night do not wash out the eggs because the tide is already ebbing. The waves of the next high tide will not reach them, because for a time after the full of the moon each tide will halt its advance a little lower on the beach than the preceding one. The eggs, then, will be undisturbed for at least a fortnight. In the warm, damp, incubating sand they undergo their development. Within two weeks the magic change from fertilized egg to larval fishlet is completed, the perfectly formed little grunion still confined within the membranes of the egg, still buried in the sand, waiting for release. With the tides of the new moon it comes. Their waves wash over the places where the little masses of the grunion eggs were buried, the swirl and rush of the surf stirring the sand deeply. As the sand is washed away, and the eggs feel the touch of the cool sea water, the membranes rupture, the fishlets hatch, and the waves that released them bear them away to the sea.

25 But the link between tide and living creature I like best to remember is that of a very small worm, flat of body, with no distinction of appearance, but with one unforgettable quality. The name of this worm is *Convoluta roscoffensis*, and it lives on the sandy beaches of northern Brittany and the Channel Islands. Convoluta has entered into a remarkable partnership with a green alga, whose cells inhabit the body of the worm and lend to its tissues their own

green color. The worm lives entirely on the starchy products manufactured by its plant guest, having become so completely dependent upon this means of nutrition that its digestive organs have degenerated. In order that the algal cells may carry on their function of photosynthesis (which is dependent upon sunlight) Convoluta rises from the damp sands of the intertidal zone as soon as the tide has ebbed, the sand becoming spotted with large green patches composed of thousands of the worms. For the several hours while the tide is out, the worms lie thus in the sun, and the plants manufacture their starches and sugars; but when the tide returns, the worms must again sink into the sand to avoid being washed away, out into deep water. So the whole lifetime of the worm is a succession of movements conditioned by the stages of the tide—upward into sunshine on the ebb, downward on the flood.

What I find most unforgettable about Convoluta is this: sometimes it happens that a marine biologist, wishing to study some related problem, will transfer a whole colony of the worms into the laboratory, there to establish them in an aquarium, where there are no tides. But twice each day Convoluta rises out of the sand on the bottom of the aquarium, into the light of the sun. And twice each day it sinks again into the sand. Without a brain, or what we would call a memory, or even any very clear perception, Convoluta continues to live out its life in this alien place, remembering, in every fiber of its small green body, the tidal rhythm of the distant sea.

Questions

1. No one would call Carson's prose style lively. (Look closely, for example, at her verbs.) How, then, does this piece work? What accounts for its overall impact?

2. *The Sea Around Us* was translated into over thirty languages. Do you think it was easy or difficult to translate? On what characteristics of Carson's writing do you base your opinion?

3. Write about a common natural phenomenon like clouds or tides, using research or personal knowledge or both.

John Muir

A Wind-Storm in the Forests

The mountain winds, like the dew and rain, sunshine and snow, are measured and bestowed with love on the forests to develop their strength and beauty. However restricted the scope of other forest influences, that of the winds is universal. The snow bends and trims the upper forests every winter, the lightning strikes a single tree here and there, while avalanches mow down thousands at

From Muir's classic account The Mountains of California *(1894), a book of scientific observation and personal memoir.*

a swoop as a gardener trims out a bed of flowers. But the winds go to every tree, fingering every leaf and branch and furrowed bole; not one is forgotten; the Mountain Pine towering with outstretched arms on the rugged buttresses of the icy peaks, the lowliest and most retiring tenant of the dells; they seek and find them all, caressing them tenderly, bending them in lusty exercise, stimulating their growth, plucking off a leaf or limb as required, or removing an entire tree or grove, now whispering and cooing through the branches like a sleepy child, now roaring like the ocean; the winds blessing the forests, the forests the winds, with ineffable beauty and harmony as the sure result.

After one has seen pines six feet in diameter bending like grasses before a mountain gale, and ever and anon some giant falling with a crash that shakes the hills, it seems astonishing that any, save the lowest thickset trees, could ever have found a period sufficiently stormless to establish themselves; or, once established, that they should not, sooner or later, have been blown down. But when the storm is over, and we behold the same forests tranquil again, towering fresh and unscathed in erect majesty, and consider what centuries of storms have fallen upon them since they were first planted,—hail, to break the tender seedlings; lightning, to scorch and shatter; snow, winds, and avalanches, to crush and overwhelm,—while the manifest result of all this wild storm-culture is the glorious perfection we behold; then faith in Nature's forestry is established, and we cease to deplore the violence of her most destructive gales, or of any other storm-implement whatsoever.

There are two trees in the Sierra forests that are never blown down, so long as they continue in sound health. These are the Juniper and the Dwarf Pine of the summit peaks. Their stiff, crooked roots grip the storm-beaten ledges like eagles' claws, while their lithe, cord-like branches bend round compliantly, offering but slight holds for winds, however violent. The other alpine conifers—the Needle Pine, Mountain Pine, Two-leaved Pine, and Hemlock Spruce—are never thinned out by this agent to any destructive extent, on account of their admirable toughness and the closeness of their growth. In general the same is true of the giants of the lower zones. The kingly Sugar Pine, towering aloft to a height of more than 200 feet, offers a fine mark to storm-winds: but it is not densely foliaged, and its long, horizontal arms swing round

A wind-storm in the California forests (after a sketch by the author)

compliantly in the blast, like tresses of green, fluent algæ in a brook; while the Silver Firs in most places keep their ranks well together in united strength. The Yellow or Silver Pine is more frequently overturned than any other tree on the Sierra, because its leaves and branches form a larger mass in proportion to its height, while in many places it is planted sparsely, leaving open lanes through which storms may enter with full force. Furthermore, because it is distributed along the lower portion of the range, which was the first to be left bare on the breaking up of the ice-sheet at the close of the glacial winter, the soil it is growing upon has been longer exposed to post-glacial weathering, and consequently is in a more crumbling, decayed condition than the fresher soils farther up the range, and therefore offers a less secure anchorage for the roots.

While exploring the forest zones of Mount Shasta, I discovered the path of a hurricane strewn with thousands of pines of this species. Great and small had been uprooted or wrenched off by sheer force, making a clean gap, like that made by a snow avalanche. But hurricanes capable of doing this class of work are rare in the Sierra, and when we have explored the forests from one extremity of the range to the other, we are compelled to believe that they are the most beautiful on the face of the earth, however we may regard the agents that have made them so.

There is always something deeply exciting, not only in the sounds of winds in the woods, which exert more or less influence over every mind, but in their varied waterlike flow as manifested by the movements of the trees, especially those of the conifers. By no other trees are they rendered so extensively and impressively visible, not even by the lordly tropic palms or tree-ferns responsive to the gentlest breeze. The waving of a forest of the giant Sequoias is indescribably impressive and sublime, but the pines seem to me the best interpreters of winds. They are mighty waving goldenrods, ever in tune, singing and writing wind-music all their long century lives. Little, however, of this noble tree-waving and tree-music will you see or hear in the strictly alpine portion of the forests. The burly Juniper, whose girth sometimes more than equals its height, is about as rigid as the rocks on which it grows. The slender lash-like sprays of the Dwarf Pine stream out in wavering ripples, but the tallest and slenderest are far too unyielding to wave even in the heaviest gales. They only shake in quick, short vibrations. The Hemlock Spruce, however, and the Mountain Pine, and some of the tallest thickets of the Two-leaved species bow in storms with considerable scope and gracefulness. But it is only in the lower and middle zones that the meeting of winds and woods is to be seen in all its grandeur.

5

One of the most beautiful and exhilarating storms I ever enjoyed in the Sierra occurred in December, 1874, when I happened to be exploring one of the tributary valleys of the Yuba River. The sky and the ground and the trees had been thoroughly rain-washed and were dry again. The day was intensely pure, one of those incomparable bits of California winter, warm and balmy and full of white sparkling sunshine, redolent of all the purest influences of the spring, and at the same time enlivened with one of the most bracing wind-storms conceivable. Instead of camping out, as I usually do, I then chanced to be stopping at the house of a friend. But when the storm began to sound, I lost no time in pushing out into the woods to enjoy it. For on such occasions Nature has always something rare to show us, and the danger to life and limb is hardly greater than one would experience crouching deprecatingly beneath a roof.

It was still early morning when I found myself fairly adrift. Delicious sunshine came pouring over the hills, lighting the tops of the pines, and setting free a stream of summery fragrance that contrasted strangely with the wild tones of the storm. The air was mottled with pine-tassels and bright green plumes, that went flashing past in the sunlight like birds pursued. But there was not the slightest dustiness, nothing less pure than leaves, and ripe pollen, and flecks of withered bracken and moss. I heard trees falling for hours at the rate of one every two or three minutes; some uprooted, partly on account of the loose, water-soaked condition of the ground; others broken straight across, where some weakness caused by fire had determined the spot. The gestures of the various trees made a delightful study. Young Sugar Pines, light and feathery as squirrel-tails, were bowing almost to the ground; while the grand old patriarchs, whose massive boles had been tried in a hundred storms, waved solemnly above them, their long, arching branches streaming fluently on the gale, and every needle thrilling and ringing and shedding off keen lances of light like a diamond. The Douglas Spruces,[1] with long sprays drawn out in level tresses, and needles massed in a gray, shimmering glow, presented a most striking appearance as they stood in bold relief along the hilltops. The madroños[2] in the dells, with their red bark and large glossy leaves tilted every way, reflected the sunshine in throbbing spangles like those one so often sees on the rippled surface of a glacier lake. But the Silver Pines were now the most impressively beautiful of all. Colossal spires 200 feet in height waved like supple goldenrods chanting and bowing low as if in worship, while the whole mass of their long, tremulous foliage was kindled into one continuous blaze of white sun-fire. The force of the gale was such that the most steadfast monarch of them all rocked down to its roots with a motion plainly perceptible when one leaned against it. Nature was holding high festival, and every fiber of the most rigid giants thrilled with glad excitement.

I drifted on through the midst of this passionate music and motion, across many a glen, from ridge to ridge; often halting in the lee of a rock for shelter, or to gaze and listen. Even when the grand anthem had swelled to its highest pitch, I could distinctly hear the varying tones of individual trees,—Spruce, and Fir, and Pine, and leafless Oak—and even the infinitely gentle rustle of the withered grasses at my feet. Each was expressing itself in its own way,—singing its own song, and making its own peculiar gestures,—manifesting a richness of variety to be found in no other forest I have yet seen. The coniferous woods of Canada, and the Carolinas, and Florida, are made up of trees that resemble one another about as nearly as blades of grass, and grow close together in much the same way. Coniferous trees, in general, seldom possess individual character, such as is manifest among Oaks and Elms. But the Cali-

1. Another name for Douglas fir.
2. A type of evergreen tree.

fornia forests are made up of a greater number of distinct species than any other in the world. And in them we find, not only a marked differentiation into special groups, but also a marked individuality in almost every tree, giving rise to storm effects indescribably glorious.

Toward midday, after a long, tingling scramble through copses of hazel and ceanothus,[3] I gained the summit of the highest ridge in the neighborhood; and then it occurred to me that it would be a fine thing to climb one of the trees to obtain a wider outlook and get my ear close to the Æolian music[4] of its topmost needles. But under the circumstances the choice of a tree was a serious matter. One whose instep was not very strong seemed in danger of being blown down, or of being struck by others in case they should fall; another was branchless to a considerable height above the ground, and at the same time too large to be grasped with arms and legs in climbing; while others were not favorably situated for clear views. After cautiously casting about, I made choice of the tallest of a group of Douglas Spruces that were growing close together like a tuft of grass, no one of which seemed likely to fall unless all the rest fell with it. Though comparatively young, they were about 100 feet high, and their lithe, brushy tops were rocking and swirling in wild ecstasy. Being accustomed to climb trees in making botanical studies, I experienced no difficulty in reaching the top of this one, and never before did I enjoy so noble an exhilaration of motion. The slender tops fairly flapped and swished in the passionate torrent, bending and swirling backward and forward, round and round, tracing indescribable combinations of vertical and horizontal curves, while I clung with muscles firm braced, like a bobolink on a reed.

In its widest sweeps my tree-top described an arc of from twenty to thirty degrees, but I felt sure of its elastic temper, having seen others of the same species still more severely tried—bent almost to the ground indeed, in heavy snows—without breaking a fiber. I was therefore safe, and free to take the wind into my pulses and enjoy the excited forest from my superb outlook. The view from here must be extremely beautiful in any weather. Now my eye roved over the piny hills and dales as over fields of waving grain, and felt the light running in ripples and broad swelling undulations across the valleys from ridge to ridge, as the shining foliage was stirred by corresponding waves of air. Oftentimes these waves of reflected light would break up suddenly into a kind of beaten foam, and again, after chasing one another in regular order, they would seem to bend forward in concentric curves, and disappear on some hillside, like sea-waves on a shelving shore. The quantity of light reflected from the bent needles was so great as to make whole groves appear as if covered with snow, while the black shadows beneath the trees greatly enhanced the effect of the silvery splendor.

Excepting only the shadows there was nothing somber in all this wild sea of pines. On the contrary, notwithstanding this was the winter season, the

3. A type of evergreen shrub.

4. Music made by the wind, from Aeolus, the Greek god of the winds, the strings of whose harp were sounded by the wind.

colors were remarkably beautiful. The shafts of the pine and libocedrus[5] were brown and purple, and most of the foliage was well tinged with yellow; the laurel groves, with the pale undersides of their leaves turned upward, made masses of gray; and then there was many a dash of chocolate color from clumps of manzanita,[6] and jet of vivid crimson from the bark of the madroños, while the ground on the hillsides, appearing here and there through openings between the groves, displayed masses of pale purple and brown.

The sounds of the storm corresponded gloriously with this wild exuberance of light and motion. The profound bass of the naked branches and boles booming like waterfalls; the quick, tense vibrations of the pine-needles, now rising to a shrill, whistling hiss, now falling to a silky murmur; the rustling of laurel groves in the dells, and the keen metallic click of leaf on leaf—all this was heard in easy analysis when the attention was calmly bent.

The varied gestures of the multitude were seen to fine advantage, so that one could recognize the different species at a distance of several miles by this means alone, as well as by their forms and colors, and the way they reflected the light. All seemed strong and comfortable, as if really enjoying the storm, while responding to its most enthusiastic greetings. We hear much nowadays concerning the universal struggle for existence, but no struggle in the common meaning of the word was manifest here; no recognition of danger by any tree; no deprecation; but rather an invincible gladness as remote from exultation as from fear.

I kept my lofty perch for hours, frequently closing my eyes to enjoy the music by itself, or to feast quietly on the delicious fragrance that was streaming past. The fragrance of the woods was less marked than that produced during warm rain, when so many balsamic buds and leaves are steeped like tea; but, from the chafing of resiny branches against each other, and the incessant attrition of myriads of needles, the gale was spiced to a very tonic degree. And besides the fragrance from these local sources there were traces of scents brought from afar. For this wind came first from the sea, rubbing against its fresh, briny waves, then distilled through the redwoods, threading rich ferny gulches, and spreading itself in broad undulating currents over many a flower-enameled ridge of the coast mountains, then across the golden plains, up the purple foothills, and into these piny woods with the varied incense gathered by the way.

15 Winds are advertisements of all they touch, however much or little we may be able to read them; telling their wanderings even by their scents alone. Mariners detect the flowery perfume of land-winds far at sea, and sea-winds carry the fragrance of dulse and tangle far inland, where it is quickly recognized, though mingled with the scents of a thousand land-flowers. As an illustration of this, I may tell here that I breathed sea-air on the Firth of Forth, in Scotland, while a boy; then was taken to Wisconsin, where I remained nineteen years; then, without in all this time having breathed one breath of the sea, I walked

5. A genus of cedar trees. In the Sierra Nevada, *Libocedrus decurans* often reaches a height of 150 feet.

6. A type of evergreen shrub.

quietly, alone, from the middle of the Mississippi Valley to the Gulf of Mexico, on a botanical excursion, and while in Florida, far from the coast, my attention wholly bent on the splendid tropical vegetation about me, I suddenly recognized a sea-breeze, as it came sifting through the palmettos and blooming vine-tangles, which at once awakened and set free a thousand dormant associations, and made me a boy again in Scotland, as if all the intervening years had been annihilated.

Most people like to look at mountain rivers, and bear them in mind; but few care to look at the winds, though far more beautiful and sublime, and though they become at times about as visible as flowing water. When the north winds in winter are making upward sweeps over the curving summits of the High Sierra, the fact is sometimes published with flying snow-banners a mile long. Those portions of the winds thus embodied can scarce be wholly invisible, even to the darkest imagination. And when we look around over an agitated forest, we may see something of the wind that stirs it, by its effects upon the trees. Yonder it descends in a rush of water-like ripples, and sweeps over the bending pines from hill to hill. Nearer, we see detached plumes and leaves, now speeding by on level currents, now whirling in eddies, or, escaping over the edges of the whirls, soaring aloft on grand, upswelling domes of air, or tossing on flame-like crests. Smooth, deep currents, cascades, falls, and swirling eddies, sing around every tree and leaf, and over all the varied topography of the region with telling changes of form, like mountain rivers conforming to the features of their channels.

After tracing the Sierra streams from their fountains to the plains, marking where they bloom white in falls, glide in crystal plumes, surge gray and foam-filled in boulder-choked gorges, and slip through the woods in long, tranquil reaches—after thus learning their language and forms in detail, we may at length hear them chanting all together in one grand anthem, and comprehend them all in clear inner vision, covering the range like lace. But even this spectacle is far less sublime and not a whit more substantial than what we may behold of these storm-streams of air in the mountain woods.

We all travel the milky way together, trees and men; but it never occurred to me until this stormday, while swinging in the wind, that trees are travelers, in the ordinary sense. They make many journeys, not extensive ones, it is true; but our own little journeys, away and back again, are only little more than tree-wavings—many of them not so much.

When the storm began to abate, I dismounted and sauntered down through the calming woods. The storm-tones died away, and, turning toward the east, I beheld the countless hosts of the forests hushed and tranquil, towering above one another on the slopes of the hills like a devout audience. The setting sun filled them with amber light, and seemed to say, while they listened, "My peace I give unto you."

As I gazed on the impressive scene, all the so-called ruin of the storm was forgotten, and never before did these noble woods appear so fresh, so joyous, so immortal.

20

QUESTIONS

1. What preconceptions did you bring to Muir's title, "A Wind-Storm in the Forests"? How does the opening sentence—indeed, the entire opening paragraph—suggest a different perspective?

2. The central adventure in this essay occurs when Muir climbs "a Douglas Spruce" (paragraph 9). Why does Muir undertake this climb? What does he wish to experience?

3. Write about an experience you have had in nature, whether dramatic (as in Muir's essay) or more quiet (as in Mary Oliver's).

CHIEF SEATTLE *Letter to President Pierce, 1855*

WE KNOW THAT the white man does not understand our ways. One portion of the land is the same to him as the next, for he is a stranger who comes in the night and takes from the land whatever he needs. The earth is not his brother, but his enemy, and when he has conquered it, he moves on. He leaves his fathers' graves, and his children's birthright is forgotten. The sight of your cities pains the eyes of the red man. But perhaps it is because the red man is a savage and does not understand.

There is no quiet place in the white man's cities. No place to hear the leaves of spring or the rustle of insects' wings. But perhaps because I am a savage and do not understand, the clatter only seems to insult the ears. The Indian prefers the soft sound of the wind darting over the face of the pond, the smell of the wind itself cleansed by a mid-day rain, or scented with the piñon pine. The air is precious to the red man. For all things share the same breath—the beasts, the trees, the man. Like a man dying for many days, he is numb to the stench.

What is man without the beasts? If all the beasts were gone, men would die from great loneliness of spirit, for whatever happens to the beasts also happens to man. All things are connected. Whatever befalls the earth befalls the sons of the earth.

It matters little where we pass the rest of our days; they are not many. A few more hours, a few more winters, and none of the children of the great tribes that once lived on this earth, or that roamed in small bands in the woods, will be left to mourn the graves of a people once as powerful and hopeful as yours.

5 The whites, too, shall pass—perhaps sooner than other tribes. Continue to contaminate your bed, and you will one night suffocate in your own waste. When the buffalo are all slaughtered, the wild horses all tamed, the secret corners of the forest heavy with the scent of many men, and the view of the ripe

Because of its origin as an oration given in Salish, there are many different versions of Chief Seattle's speech; this one comes from Native American Testimony: An Anthology of Indian and White Relations, *edited by Peter Nabokov (1977).*

hills blotted by talking wires,[1] where is the thicket? Gone. Where is the eagle? Gone. And what is it to say goodby to the swift and the hunt, the end of living and the beginning of survival? We might understand if we knew what it was that the white man dreams, what he describes to his children on the long winter nights, what visions he burns into their minds, so they will wish for tomorrow. But we are savages. The white man's dreams are hidden from us.

1. I.e., the telegraph.

QUESTIONS

1. Chief Seattle repeatedly refers to the red man as "a savage" who "does not understand," yet in the course of this letter he gives evidence of a great deal of understanding. What is the purpose of such ironic comments and apparently self-disparaging remarks?

2. Scholars have recently suggested that Chief Seattle's "Letter" is in fact the creation of a white man, based on Seattle's public oratory. If so, what rhetorical techniques does the white editor associate with Indian speech? Why might he have done so?

3. A surprisingly modern note of ecological awareness resounds in the statement "[W]hatever happens to the beasts also happens to man. All things are connected" (paragraph 3). Locate two or three similar observations, and explain their effectiveness.

4. Chief Seattle says that the red man might understand the white man better "if we knew what it was that the white man dreams, what he describes to his children on the long winter nights, what visions he burns into their minds, so they will wish for tomorrow" (paragraph 5). Write a short essay explaining, either straightforwardly or ironically, how "the white man" might reply. If you prefer, write the reply itself.

WILLIAM CRONON *The Trouble with Wilderness*

PRESERVING WILDERNESS has for decades been a fundamental tenet—indeed, a passion—of the environmental movement, especially in the United States. For many Americans, wilderness stands as the last place where civilization, that all-too-human disease, has not fully infected the earth. It is an island in the polluted sea of urban-industrial modernity, a refuge we must somehow recover to save the planet. As Henry David Thoreau famously declared, "In Wildness is the preservation of the World."

But is it? The more one knows of its peculiar history, the more one realizes that wilderness is not quite what it seems. Far from being the one place

Cronon published a number of versions of this essay, each aimed at a different audience. This version comes from the New York Times *(August 13, 1995); another version appears as the introduction to his book* Uncommon Ground: Toward Reinventing Nature *(1995).*

on earth that stands apart from humanity, it is quite profoundly a human creation—indeed, the creation of very particular human cultures at very particular moments in human history. It is not a pristine sanctuary where the last remnant of an endangered but still transcendent nature can be encountered without the contaminating taint of civilization. Instead, it is a product of that civilization. As we gaze into the mirror it holds up for us, we too easily imagine that what we behold is nature when in fact we see the reflection of our own longings and desires. Wilderness can hardly be the solution to our culture's problematic relationship with the nonhuman world, for wilderness is itself a part of the problem.

To assert the unnaturalness of so natural a place may seem perverse: we can all conjure up images and sensations that seem all the more hauntingly real for having engraved themselves so indelibly on our memories. Remember this? The torrents of mist shooting out from the base of a great waterfall in the depths of a Sierra Nevada canyon, the droplets cooling your face as you listen to the roar of the water and gaze toward the sky through a rainbow that hovers just out of reach. Or this: Looking out across a desert canyon in the evening air, the only sound a lone raven calling in the distance, the rock walls dropping away into a chasm so deep that its bottom all but vanishes as you squint into the amber light of the setting sun. Remember the feelings of such moments, and you will know as well as I do that you were in the presence of something irreducibly nonhuman, something profoundly Other than yourself. Wilderness is made of that too.

And yet: what brought each of us to the places where such memories became possible is entirely a cultural invention.

5 For the Americans who first celebrated it, wilderness was tied to the myth of the frontier. The historian Frederick Jackson Turner wrote the classic academic statement of this myth in 1893, but it had been part of American thought for well over a century. As Turner described the process, Easterners and European immigrants, in moving to the wild lands of the frontier, shed the trappings of civilization and thereby gained an energy, an independence and a creativity that were the sources of American democracy and national character. Seen this way, wilderness became a place of religious redemption and national renewal, the quintessential location for experiencing what it meant to be an American.

Those who celebrate the frontier almost always look backward, mourning an older, simpler world that has disappeared forever. That world and all its attractions, Turner said, depended on free land—on wilderness. It is no accident that the movement to set aside national parks and wilderness areas gained real momentum just as laments about the vanishing frontier reached their peak. To protect wilderness was to protect the nation's most sacred myth of origin.

The decades following the Civil War saw more and more of the nation's wealthiest citizens seeking out wilderness for themselves. The passion for wild land took many forms: enormous estates in the Adirondacks and elsewhere (disingenuously called "camps" despite their many servants and amenities); cattle ranches for would-be roughriders on the Great Plains; guided big-game hunting trips in the Rockies. Wilderness suddenly emerged as the landscape of choice for elite tourists. For them, it was a place of recreation.

In just this way, wilderness came to embody the frontier myth, standing for the wild freedom of America's past and seeming to represent a highly attractive natural alternative to the ugly artificiality of modern civilization. The irony, of course, was that in the process wilderness came to reflect the very civilization its devotees sought to escape. Ever since the nineteenth century, celebrating wilderness has been an activity mainly for well-to-do city folks. Country people generally know far too much about working the land to regard unworked land as their ideal.

There were other ironies as well. The movement to set aside national parks and wilderness areas followed hard on the heels of the final Indian wars, in which the prior human inhabitants of these regions were rounded up and moved onto reservations so that tourists could safely enjoy the illusion that they were seeing their nation in its pristine, original state—in the new morning of God's own creation. Meanwhile, its original inhabitants were kept out by dint of force, their earlier uses of the land redefined as inappropriate or even illegal. To this day, for instance, the Blackfeet continue to be accused of "poaching" on the lands of Glacier National Park, in Montana, that originally belonged to them and that were ceded by treaty only with the proviso that they be permitted to hunt there.

10 The removal of Indians to create an "uninhabited wilderness" reminds us just how invented and how constructed the American wilderness really is. One of the most striking proofs of the cultural invention of wilderness is its thoroughgoing erasure of the history from which it sprang. In virtually all its manifestations, wilderness represents a flight from history. Seen as the original garden, it is a place outside time, from which human beings had to be ejected before the fallen world of history could properly begin.[1] Seen as the frontier, it is a savage world at the dawn of civilization, whose transformation represents the very beginning of the national historical epic. Seen as sacred nature, it is the home of a God who transcends history, untouched by time's arrow. No matter what the angle from which we regard it, wilderness offers us the illusion that we can escape the cares and troubles of the world in which our past has ensnared us. It is the natural, unfallen antithesis of an unnatural civilization that has lost its soul, the place where we can see the world as it really is, and so know ourselves as we really are—or ought to be.

The trouble with wilderness is that it reproduces the very values its devotees seek to reject. It offers the illusion that we can somehow wipe clean the slate of our past and return to the tabula rasa[2] that supposedly existed before we began to leave our marks on the world. The dream of an unworked natural landscape is very much the fantasy of people who have never themselves had to work the land to make a living—urban folk for whom food comes from a supermarket or a restaurant instead of a field, and for whom the wooden houses in which they live and work apparently have no meaningful connection

1. According to the Bible, Adam and Eve were ejected from the Garden of Eden for disobeying God's command.

2. Clean slate (Latin).

to the forests in which trees grow and die. Only people whose relation to the land was already alienated could hold up wilderness as a model for human life in nature, for the romantic ideology of wilderness leaves no place in which human beings can actually make their living from the land.

We live in an urban-industrial civilization, but too often pretend to ourselves that our real home is in the wilderness. We work our nine-to-five jobs, we drive our cars (not least to reach the wilderness), we benefit from the intricate and all too invisible networks with which society shelters us, all the while pretending that these things are not an essential part of who we are. By imagining that our true home is in the wilderness, we forgive ourselves for the homes we actually inhabit. In its flight from history, in its siren song[3] of escape, in its reproduction of the dangerous dualism that sets human beings somehow outside nature—in all these ways, wilderness poses a threat to responsible environmentalism at the end of the twentieth century.

Do not misunderstand me. What I criticize here is not wild nature, but the alienated way we often think of ourselves in relation to it. Wilderness can still teach lessons that are hard to learn anywhere else. When we visit wild places, we find ourselves surrounded by plants and animals and landscapes whose otherness compels our attention. In forcing us to acknowledge that they are not of our making, that they have little or no need for humanity, they recall for us a creation far greater than our own. In wilderness, we need no reminder that a tree has its own reasons for being, quite apart from us—proof that ours is not the only presence in the universe.

We get into trouble only if we see the tree in the garden as wholly artificial and the tree in the wilderness as wholly natural. Both trees in some ultimate sense are wild; both in a practical sense now require our care. We need to reconcile them, to see a natural landscape that is also cultural, in which city, suburb, countryside and wilderness each has its own place. We need to discover a middle ground in which all these things, from city to wilderness, can somehow be encompassed in the word "home." Home, after all, is the place where we live. It is the place for which we take responsibility, the place we try to sustain so we can pass on what is best in it (and in ourselves) to our children.

15 Learning to honor the wild—learning to acknowledge the autonomy of the other—means striving for critical self-consciousness in all our actions. It means that reflection and respect must accompany each act of use, and means we must always consider the possibility of nonuse. It means looking at the part of nature we intend to turn toward our own ends and asking whether we can use it again and again and again—sustainably—without diminishing it in the process. Most of all, it means practicing remembrance and gratitude for the nature, culture and history that have come together to make the world as we know it. If wildness can stop being (just) out there and start being (also) in here, if it can start being as humane as it is natural, then perhaps we can get on with the unending task of

3. In Homer's *Odyssey*, the Sirens use irresistible songs to tempt Odysseus and his crew to steer their ship toward destruction, so a siren song is an alluring but deceptive appeal.

struggling to live rightly in the world—not just in the garden, not just in the wilderness, but in the home that encompasses them both.

Questions

1. In paragraph 12 Cronon writes, "We live in an urban-industrial civilization, but too often pretend to ourselves that our real home is in the wilderness." Cronon gives no examples. What examples might back up Cronon's statement? Can you think of counterexamples as well?

2. Who is Cronon's "we" throughout his essay? Why does he use "we" so frequently?

3. Paragraph 2 raises the issue of whether wilderness provides us with a "mirror." Look through the essay for similar visual imagery; then explain the role that such imagery plays.

4. If you found significant counterexamples in response to Question 1, write a letter to the editor in which you question or object to one aspect of Cronon's argument.

Mary Oliver

Waste Land: An Elegy

At our town's old burn dump, not officially used for years, discarded peppermint and raspberries reconnected their roots to the gravelly earth and went on growing; a couple of apple trees blossomed and bore each year a bushel of green and bumpy fruit. Blackberries drifted up and down the slopes; thistles, Bouncing Bet, everlasting, goldenrod, wild carrot lifted their leaves and then their flowers and then their rafts of seeds. Honeysuckle, in uplifted waves, washed toward some pink roses, no longer a neat and civilized hedge but a thorny ledge, with darkness at its hem. Now the burn dump is no more. The old world had its necessities; presently there are new ones, and they are not so simply met—nor will the old parcels of land suffice. On these few acres of land, and more, will be established the heartland of our town's sewage, where the buried pipes will converge with the waste of our lives. What a sad hilarity! I want to talk about flowers, but the necessity has become, for our visitor-rich town, how to deal with the daily sewage of, it may be, sixty thousand souls. At least that was a weekend estimate a few years ago. They come, to this last town on the long Cape,[1] in good part for the very beauty that their numbers imperil. They come for fellowship, the beaches and the sun, the entertainment, the shops and restaurants. They inhabit old captains' houses turned into inns, or the condominiums ever rising along newly created streets and crowded cul-de-sacs. So, this is an elegy.

Published in Orion *magazine (September/October 2003) just before the appearance of Oliver's book collection,* Long Life: Essays and Other Writings *(2004).*

1. Cape Cod, Massachusetts.

In the summers, black snakes swirled among the creamy blossoms of the honeysuckle and the pink-petaled roses. When I walked through the grass, their black faces appeared, like exotic flowers. There were almost always two of them, sometimes three. One had eyes the color of garnets. It gave no greeting, only a long, motionless gaze. And they were brave, those snakes. Occasionally when I came upon a pair sleeping in the sun, on stones or a heap of old asphalt shingles, one of them would streak toward me and fling itself against my body, before it turned and followed the other away, whipping after it into the shadows under the roses.

Soon they will be off, hunting another place to live. Which may not be so easy, for the world today is nothing if it is not sprawl, and this not only within the residential areas but the seemingly endless facilities such settlements need. And we do need them. (So, this is an elegy.) Box turtles nested here, and painted turtles also. Out of the shallow ponds below the crest of the hill, snapping turtles crawled to lay their pale, leathery eggs. Raccoons aspire to them; many of the nests were ransacked as soon as the turtle had shuffled away. Foxes left their dainty tracks, and in summer the red-coated deer.

The toad was always here, with his gold-rimmed eyes.

5 And, in a certain shaded place nearby, the uncommon, cool and gleaming bunchberry.

For years there were signs posted, prohibitions against leaving trash. In more recent years another sign designated the area a motorcycle and motorbike course. The bikes appeared most often in the afternoons; they snarled over the field, they cut ruts along the trails, they raced with a furious, uncontainable form of boy-energy and noise. I hated it, yet did not resent it. There must be a place for boys and their trappings, though surely it should not have been here, on one of the few town-owned woodlands fresh and untrammeled except for its polluted center. Also it joined seamlessly with the National Seashore, and what young boy hunched over the handlebars of his bike could remember that invisible line? So sections of the park's shady paths also became rutted by tires and besotted by blown trash. But when space is limited for recreations of such different kinds, compatibility is given improbable tasks.

As for the trash, which gathered in spite of the signs, it did what trash does and ever will do; it lay there, and did not grow thin or fade or even, much of it, rot. Old stoves were predominant. And dozens of tires, lining the bike track, the standing water within them breeding uncountable numbers of mosquitoes.

And yet, at certain hours, in the absence of boys and their bikes, I could walk here and see birds I found nowhere else: the indigo bunting, for example, and the black-billed cuckoo. And their more findable associates: goldfinches, catbirds, the brown thrasher, the yellowthroat, palm warblers, the grosbeak. The ruby-throated hummingbird nested here, but even now I will not tell you in precisely what tree. It was a secret to be kept then, so why not keep it still, now that the birds and the tree itself have vanished? And there were daisies, and butter-and-eggs, and milkweed with its mauve pendants, and Black-eyed Susans. There were rugosas, white and red. In the summer light they shot upward heavy with buds and pleated, glossy leaves. Then sagged under their own sweet weight.

But this is an elegy. Now there are buildings to take care of this new and important work. A brick building, neat and Cape Cod enough that it could almost be a bank! And behind it a huge, circular, cement construction—I cannot call it a building—round and thick-walled: not built for beauty, and not yet finished. Piles of pipes are everywhere. The blackberries that climbed up and down the hill, the goldenrod, the honeysuckle are gone; the pink roses are gone; the fox tracks are gone.

The land itself has been capped against the poisons that have been seeping all these years into the ground, from the fires, from the unknown elements cast away: oils and paints and car batteries and a hundred offensive substances more. And, imagine! for what unaware years I picked the blackberries and the raspberries, and thought them sweet and fine—thought them good fortune. And found, on the rubbled hillsides, strange shapes of old jars, glass bent and reshaped by the flames. Nuggets of deep blue from medicine containers; once a glass airplane that originally held candy, with a chip missing from one wing. 10

But, this is an elegy. A part of the book of not-wanting-to-let-go. And, go it must; and go it has. The pink roses and the toad with gold-rimmed eyes. The young boys on bikes who in fact are men now. Even the tires are gone. The town government has made its not unreasonable decision. We cannot continue with failing cesspools; we cannot condone seepage into the water supply, or into the blue harbor that lies along the town's frontage. And, we are so many.

In May the moccasin flowers blossomed, even in this thin soil, extravagantly. They stood in gatherings of six or seven, like small choirs getting ready to sing. Very rarely, one flower would rise pure white.

I do not like what has happened. I do not hold the loss lightly. I wish to be reasonable; I know I must be amenable to what is necessary. But—such few choices! I apologize to the hummingbird. I hope the snakes have found a new home. I hope the new system works. I am glad that I have a good memory; I will not forget the dainty tracks of the fox, or the goldfinches, or the everlasting. I think I know what our manifest, tree-filled, creature-lively world is—our garden and our pasture and our recreation. Also it is our schoolhouse, courthouse, church, graveyard, and the soft breath of eternity.

I walk in the world to love it. Only one question, really, frightens me. I wonder why, in all the years I walked in the old burn dump—this waste place, this secret garden—I never met another soul there, who had come forth for a like reason.

QUESTIONS

1. An elegy is a lament for something lost, often for the death of a person. What losses does Oliver write about in this essay?

2. At the end of a traditional elegy, the poet or writer offers consolation to the bereaved or hope for the future. Does Oliver offer consolation, or does she leave the reader with a sense of loss? Locate the places in the ending (paragraphs 13–14) that support your response.

3. Another author in *The Norton Reader* writes about dumps—Lars Eighner in "On Dumpster Diving" (see "Personal Accounts"). Write an essay in which you compare Oliver's experience and interest in her town dump with Eighner's.

SANDRA STEINGRABER *Tune of the Tuna Fish*

TO COMMEMORATE my daughter's first piano recital last spring, my mother sent a package of old songbooks and sheet music that she had scooped from the bench of my own childhood piano, where they had undoubtedly sat for more than thirty years. Faith immediately seized on *The Red Book,* one of my very first lesson books, and began to sight-read some of the pieces. Her favorite was "Tune of the Tuna Fish" (copyright 1945), which introduces the key of F major. The cartoon drawing accompanying the song depicts a yodeling fish. The lyrics are as follows:

> Tuna fish! Tuna fish! Sing a tune of tuna fish!
> Tuna fish! Tuna fish! It's a favorite dish.
> Everybody likes it so. From New York to Kokomo.
> Tuna fish! Tuna fish! It's a favorite dish.

After we belted the song out a few times together, Faith asked, "Mama, what is a tuna fish? Have I ever eaten one?" In fact, she hadn't. Although tuna salad sandwiches were a mainstay of my own childhood diet, tuna has, during the time period between my childhood and my daughter's, become so contaminated with mercury that I choose not to buy it.

A few weeks later, at a potluck picnic, an elderly woman offered Faith a tuna salad sandwich. She loved it. On the ride home, she announced that she would like tuna sandwiches for her school lunches. She wants to eat one *every day.* I smiled that noncommittal motherly smile and said, "We'll see." She broke into song, "Everybody likes it so. From New York to Kokomo. . . ."

A month after that, Faith walked up to me with an alarmed look. Is it true, she wanted to know, that tuna fish have mercury in them? And mercury poisons children? Will she die from eating that sandwich at the picnic? I was able to reassure her that she was fine, but I was left wondering where she'd heard all this. Then I noticed that I'd left out on my office desk a copy of an article about the impact of mercury on fetal brain growth and development. It was one that I myself had authored. Could she have seen it? At age six, can she read well enough to have figured it out?

Published in Orion *(February 2006), a magazine founded in 1982 to explore "an emerging alternative worldview informed by a growing ecological awareness and the need for cultural change"; the magazine includes photos and paintings as well as essays.*

Other than the twenty-three chromosomes that each of us parents contributes to our offspring during the moment of conception, their growing bodies are entirely made up of rearranged molecules of air, food, and water. Our children are the jet stream, the food web, and the water cycle. Whatever is in the environment is also in them. We know that this now includes hundreds of industrial pollutants. A recent study of umbilical cord blood, collected by the Red Cross from ten newborns and analyzed in two different laboratories, revealed the presence of pesticides, stain removers, wood preservatives, heavy metals, and industrial lubricants, as well as the wastes from burning coal, garbage, and gasoline. Of the 287 chemicals detected, 180 were suspected carcinogens, 217 were toxic to the brain and nervous system, and 208 have been linked to abnormal development and birth defects in lab animals.

5 One of these chemicals was methylmercury, the form of mercury found in fish. Its presence in umbilical cord blood is especially troubling because methylmercury has been shown to paralyze migrating fetal brain cells and halt their cell division. As a result, the architecture of the brain is subtly altered in ways that can lead to learning disabilities, delayed mental development, and shortened attention spans in later childhood. Moreover, the placenta actively pumps methylmercury into the umbilical cord, raising the concentration of mercury in fetal blood above that of the mother's own blood. Most pregnant mothers probably don't realize that when they eat tuna, the mercury within is transferred to and concentrated in the blood of their unborn babies.

Recently, I've been talking with my children about why we buy organically grown food. I've explained to Faith and her younger brother, Elijah, that I like to give my food dollars to farmers who sustain the soil, are kind to their animals, and don't use chemicals that poison birds, fish, and toads. I add that I like to buy food that is grown right here in our own county. It tastes better and doesn't require lots of gasoline to get to our house. I haven't shared with them the results of the 2003 Seattle study, which revealed that children with conventional diets had, on average, nine times more insecticide residues in their urine than those who ate organic produce.

But there is no "organic" option for buying tuna. No mercury-free tuna exists. When mercury from coal-burning power plants rains down from the atmosphere into the world's oceans, ancient anaerobic bacteria found in marine sediments transform this heavy metal into methylmercury, which is quickly siphoned up the food chain. Because tuna is a top-of-the-food chain predator, methylmercury inexorably concentrates in the flesh of its muscle tissue. There is no special way of cleaning or cooking tuna that would lower its body burden. Nor is there any way of keeping mercury from trespassing into a child's brain, once he or she consumes the tuna. Nor is there a way of preventing those molecules of mercury from interfering with brain cell functioning. In that sense, the problem of tuna fish is more akin to the problem of air and water pollution: it is not a problem we can shop our way out of.

Recognizing the potential for methylmercury to create neurological problems in children, the U.S. Food and Drug Administration has now promulgated advisories and guidelines on how much tuna is safe for pregnant women and children—as well as nursing mothers and women who might become pregnant—to eat in a month's time. There is debate about whether these current restrictions are protective enough. But even if they are sufficient, I find them highly impractical. Children do not want to eat a food they like once a month, or even once a week. In my experience, when children discover a new food item to their liking, they want it all the time. They want it for breakfast, lunch, and dinner from here to Sunday. Children's dining habits are, for mysterious reasons, highly ritualized. Elijah, for example, consumed two avocados a day for the better part of his second year. I vaguely recall one summer when I, at about age seven, ate liver sausage on Saltines as part of every meal.

How, then, do you explain to a young child with a tuna jones that she'll have to wait until next month before she can have her favorite dish again? Do you tell her that she's already consumed her monthly quota of a known brain poison, as determined by the federal government? Or do you make up some other excuse?

10 I eventually sat down with Faith and showed her the article I had written. I said that I was working hard to stop the mercury contamination of seafood so that she could someday enjoy tuna without needing to worry. I said that keeping mercury out of tuna required generating electricity in some way other than burning coal, which is why her father and I support solar energy and wind power.

Soon after, we went hiking in the woods near the day camp she had attended earlier in the summer. Faith summarized for me the history of the old stone building where snakes and turtles are housed in one wing and bunk beds fill the other. It was originally built, she explained, as a *pre-ven-tor-i-um*. Children whose parents were sick with tuberculosis were brought there to live so they wouldn't get sick, too. In fact, I already knew the history of the Cayuga Nature Center but was, nonetheless, amazed at my daughter's ability to recount this information. I tried to gauge whether she was worried about the idea of children being separated from their families because of disease. "You know," I said, "we don't have to worry about tuberculosis anymore. We fixed that problem." She said she knew that. That's why the building had been turned into a camp for everyone.

The top of the hill offered a view across Cayuga Lake. On the far bank floated the vaporous emissions from New York State Electric and Gas Corporation's Cayuga Plant, whose coal-burning stacks were plainly visible against an otherwise cloudless sky. It's one of the state's biggest emitters of mercury. In the year my daughter was born, the Cayuga facility released 323 pounds of mercury into the environment. Pointing it out to Faith, I said that's where the mercury comes from that gets inside the fish. I said that I hoped one day we could fix that problem, too. She thought about it a minute and said, then they can do something else with the building.

QUESTIONS

1. Steingraber's essay informs readers of the high levels of mercury in fish and the dangers of eating a tuna fish sandwich. Why, then, does she begin with her daughter's piano playing? What roles do her daughter, Faith, and later her son, Elijah, play in this essay?

2. What facts about industrial pollutants, including methylmercury, does Steingraber provide? Where do they appear in the essay? How do they relate—structurally and conceptually—to the episodes with her daughter?

3. Does Steingraber suggest a solution to the problem of industrial pollutants? In terms of the environment, does the essay end on a hopeful or despairing note?

4. Write an essay about another kind of environmental problem, ideally one with personal or local significance. Interweave facts with examples or short narratives.

TERRY TEMPEST WILLIAMS

The Clan of One-Breasted Women

I BELONG TO a Clan of One-Breasted Women. My mother, my grandmothers, and six aunts have all had mastectomies. Seven are dead. The two who survive have just completed rounds of chemotherapy and radiation.

I've had my own problems: two biopsies for breast cancer and a small tumor between my ribs diagnosed as "a border-line malignancy."

This is my family history.

Most statistics tell us breast cancer is genetic, hereditary, with rising percentages attached to fatty diets, childlessness, or becoming pregnant after thirty. What they don't say is living in Utah may be the greatest hazard of all.

We are a Mormon family with roots in Utah since 1847. The word-of-wisdom, a religious doctrine of health, kept the women in my family aligned with good foods: no coffee, no tea, tobacco, or alcohol. For the most part, these women were finished having their babies by the time they were thirty. And only one faced breast cancer prior to 1960. Traditionally, as a group of people, Mormons have a low rate of cancer. 5

Is our family a cultural anomaly? The truth is we didn't think about it. Those who did, usually the men, simply said, "bad genes." The women's attitude was stoic. Cancer was part of life. On February 16, 1971, the eve before my mother's surgery, I accidently picked up the telephone and overheard her ask my grandmother what she could expect.

From the winter 1989 issue of the Witness, *a small circulation journal that calls itself "a feisty, independent, provocative, intelligent, feminist voice of Christian social conscience"; later included in* Refuge: An Unnatural History of Family and Place *(1991).*

"Diane, it is one of the most spiritual experiences you will ever encounter."

I quietly put down the receiver.

Two days later, my father took my three brothers and me to the hospital to visit her. She met us in the lobby in a wheelchair. No bandages were visible. I'll never forget her radiance, the way she held herself in a purple velour robe and how she gathered us around her.

10 "Children, I am fine. I want you to know I felt the arms of God around me."

We believed her. My father cried. Our mother, his wife, was thirty-eight years old.

Two years ago, after my mother's death from cancer, my father and I were having dinner together. He had just returned from St. George where his construction company was putting in natural gas lines for towns in southern Utah. He spoke of his love for the country: the sandstoned landscape, bare-boned and beautiful. He had just finished hiking the Kolob trail in Zion National Park. We got caught up in reminiscing, recalling with fondness our walk up Angel's Landing on his fiftieth birthday and the years our family had vacationed there. This was a remembered landscape where we had been raised.

Over dessert, I shared a recurring dream of mine. I told my father that for years, as long as I could remember, I saw this flash of light in the night in the desert. That this image had so permeated my being, I could not venture south without seeing it again, on the horizon, illuminating buttes and mesas.

"You did see it," he said.

15 "Saw what?" I asked, a bit tentative.

"The bomb. The cloud. We were driving home from Riverside, California. You were sitting on your mother's lap. She was pregnant. In fact, I remember the date, September 7, 1957. We had just gotten out of the Service. We were driving north, past Las Vegas. It was an hour or so before dawn, when this explosion went off. We not only heard it, but felt it. I thought the oil tanker in front of us had blown up. We pulled over and suddenly, rising from the desert floor, we saw it, clearly, this golden-stemmed cloud, the mushroom. The sky seemed to vibrate with an eerie pink glow. Within a few minutes, a light ash was raining on the car."

I stared at my father. This was new information to me.

"I thought you knew that," my father said. "It was a common occurrence in the fifties."

It was at this moment I realized the deceit I had been living under. Children growing up in the American Southwest, drinking contaminated milk from contaminated cows, even from the contaminated breasts of their mother, my mother—members, years later, of the Clan of One-breasted Women.

20 It is a well-known story in the Desert West, "The Day We Bombed Utah," or perhaps, "The Years We Bombed Utah."[1] Above ground atomic testing in Nevada took place from January 27, 1951, through July 11, 1962. Not only were the winds blowing north, covering "low use segments of the population"

1. Fuller, John G., *The Day We Bombed Utah* (New York: New American Library, 1984) [Williams's note].

with fallout and leaving sheep dead in their tracks, but the climate was right.[2] The United States of the 1950s was red, white, and blue. The Korean War was raging. McCarthyism was rampant. Ike was it and the Cold War was hot.[3] If you were against nuclear testing, you were for a Communist regime.

Much has been written about this "American nuclear tragedy." Public health was secondary to national security. The Atomic Energy Commissioner, Thomas Murray, said, "Gentlemen, we must not let anything interfere with this series of tests, nothing."[4]

Again and again, the American public was told by its government, in spite of burns, blisters, and nausea, "It has been found that the tests may be conducted with adequate assurance of safety under conditions prevailing at the bombing reservations."[5] Assuaging public fears was simply a matter of public relations. "Your best action," an Atomic Energy Commission booklet read, "is not to be worried about fallout." A news release typical of the times stated, "We find no basis for concluding that harm to any individual has resulted from radioactive fallout."[6]

On August 30, 1979, during Jimmy Carter's presidency, a suit was filed entitled "Irene Allen vs. the United States of America." Mrs. Allen was the first to be alphabetically listed with twenty-four test cases, representative of nearly 1200 plaintiffs seeking compensation from the United States government for cancers caused from nuclear testing in Nevada.

Irene Allen lived in Hurricane, Utah. She was the mother of five children and had been widowed twice. Her first husband with their two oldest boys had watched the tests from the roof of the local high school. He died of leukemia in 1956. Her second husband died of pancreatic cancer in 1978.

In a town meeting conducted by Utah Senator Orrin Hatch, shortly before the suit was filed, Mrs. Allen said, "I am not blaming the government, I want you to know that, Senator Hatch. But I thought if my testimony could help in any way so this wouldn't happen again to any of the generations coming up after us . . . I am really happy to be here this day to bear testimony of this."[7] 25

2. Discussion on March 14, 1988, with Carole Gallagher, photographer and author, *American Ground Zero: The Secret Nuclear War*, published by Random House, 1994 [Williams's note].

3. Events and figures of the 1950s: the Korean War (1950–53) pitted the combined forces of the Republic of Korea and the United Nations (primarily the United States) against the invading armies of Communist North Korea; McCarthyism, after Republican senator Joseph S. McCarthy, refers to the Communist "witch-hunt" led by the senator; Ike is the nickname of Dwight D. Eisenhower, president from 1953 to 1961; the Cold War refers to the power struggle between the Western powers and the Communist bloc that began at the end of World War II.

4. Szasz, Ferenc M., "Downwind From the Bomb," *Nevada Historical Society Quarterly*, Fall 1987, Vol. XXX, No. 3, p. 185 [Williams's note].

5. Fradkin, Philip L., *Fallout* (Tucson: University of Arizona Press, 1989), 98 [Williams's note].

6. Ibid., 109 [Williams's note].

7. Town meeting held by Senator Orrin Hatch in St. George, Utah, April 17, 1979, transcript, 26–28 [Williams's note].

God-fearing people. This is just one story in an anthology of thousands.

On May 10, 1984, Judge Bruce S. Jenkins handed down his opinion. Ten of the plaintiffs were awarded damages. It was the first time a federal court had determined that nuclear tests had been the cause of cancers. For the remaining fourteen test cases, the proof of causation was not sufficient. In spite of the split decision, it was considered a landmark ruling.[8] It was not to remain so for long.

In April, 1987, the 10th Circuit Court of Appeals overturned Judge Jenkins' ruling on the basis that the United States was protected from suit by the legal doctrine of sovereign immunity, the centuries-old idea from England in the days of absolute monarchs.[9]

In January, 1988, the Supreme Court refused to review the Appeals Court decision. To our court system, it does not matter whether the United States Government was irresponsible, whether it lied to its citizens or even that citizens died from the fallout of nuclear testing. What matters is that our government is immune. "The King can do no wrong."

30 In Mormon culture, authority is respected, obedience is revered, and independent thinking is not. I was taught as a young girl not to "make waves" or "rock the boat."

"Just let it go—" my mother would say. "You know how you feel, that's what counts."

For many years, I did just that—listened, observed, and quietly formed my own opinions within a culture that rarely asked questions because they had all the answers. But one by one, I watched the women in my family die common, heroic deaths. We sat in waiting rooms hoping for good news, always receiving the bad. I cared for them, bathed their scarred bodies and kept their secrets. I watched beautiful women become bald as cytoxan, cisplatin and adriamycin were injected into their veins. I held their foreheads as they vomited green-black bile and I shot them with morphine when the pain became inhuman. In the end, I witnessed their last peaceful breaths, becoming a midwife to the rebirth of their souls. But the price of obedience became too high.

The fear and inability to question authority that ultimately killed rural communities in Utah during atmospheric testing of atomic weapons was the same fear I saw being held in my mother's body. Sheep. Dead sheep. The evidence is buried.

I cannot prove that my mother, Diane Dixon Tempest, or my grandmothers, Lettie Romney Dixon and Kathryn Blackett Tempest, along with my aunts contracted cancer from nuclear fallout in Utah. But I can't prove they didn't.

35 My father's memory was correct, the September blast we drove through in 1957 was part of Operation Plumbbob, one of the most intensive series of bomb tests to be initiated. The flash of light in the night in the desert I had always thought was a dream developed into a family nightmare. It took four-

8. Fradkin, *Fallout*, 228 [Williams's note].

9. U.S. vs. Allen, 816 Federal Reporter, 2d/1417 (10th Circuit Court 1987), cert. denied, 108 S. CT. 694 (1988) [Williams's note].

teen years, from 1957 to 1971, for cancer to show up in my mother—the same time, Howard L. Andrews, an authority on radioactive fallout at the National Institutes of Health, says radiation cancer requires to become evident.[10] The more I learn about what it means to be a "downwinder," the more questions I drown in.

What I do know, however, is that as a Mormon woman of the fifth generation of "Latter-Day-Saints," I must question everything, even if it means losing my faith, even if it means becoming a member of a border tribe among my own people. Tolerating blind obedience in the name of patriotism or religion ultimately takes our lives.

When the Atomic Energy Commission described the country north of the Nevada Test Site as "virtually uninhabited desert terrain," my family members were some of the "virtual uninhabitants."

One night, I dreamed women from all over the world circling a blazing fire in the desert. They spoke of change, of how they hold the moon in their bellies and wax and wane with its phases. They mocked at the presumption of even-tempered beings and made promises that they would never fear the witch inside themselves. The women danced wildly as sparks broke away from the flames and entered the night sky as stars.

And they sang a song given to them by Shoshoni grandmothers:

Ah ne nah, nah
nin nah nah—
Ah ne nah, nah
nin nah nah—
Nyaga mutzi
oh ne nay—
Nyaga mutzi
oh ne nay—[11]

The women danced and drummed and sang for weeks, preparing themselves for what was to come. They would reclaim the desert for the sake of their children, for the sake of the land. 40

A few miles downwind from the fire circle, bombs were being tested. Rabbits felt the tremors. Their soft leather pads on paws and feet recognized the shaking sands while the roots of mesquite and sage were smoldering. Rocks were hot from the inside out and dust devils hummed unnaturally. And each time there was another nuclear test, ravens watched the desert heave. Stretch marks appeared. The land was losing its muscle.

10. Fradkin, Op. cit., 116 [Williams's note].

11. This song was sung by the Western Shoshone women as they crossed the line at the Nevada Test Site on March 18, 1988, as part of their "Reclaim the Land" action. The translation they gave was: "Consider the rabbits how gently they walk on the earth. Consider the rabbits how gently they walk on the earth. We remember them. We can walk gently also. We remember them. We can walk gently also" [Williams's note].

The women couldn't bear it any longer. They were mothers. They had suffered labor pains but always under the promise of birth. The red hot pains beneath the desert promised death only as each bomb became a stillborn. A contract had been broken between human beings and the land. A new contract was being drawn by the women who understood the fate of the earth as their own.

Under the cover of darkness, ten women slipped under the barbed wire fence and entered the contaminated country. They were trespassing. They walked toward the town of Mercury in moonlight, taking their cues from coyote, kit fox, antelope squirrel, and quail. They moved quietly and deliberately through the maze of Joshua trees. When a hint of daylight appeared they rested, drinking tea and sharing their rations of food. The women closed their eyes. The time had come to protest with the heart, that to deny one's genealogy with the earth was to commit treason against one's soul.

At dawn, the women draped themselves in mylar, wrapping long streamers of silver plastic around their arms to blow in the breeze. They wore clear masks that became the faces of humanity. And when they arrived on the edge of Mercury, they carried all the butterflies of a summer day in their wombs. They paused to allow their courage to settle.

45 The town which forbids pregnant women and children to enter because of radiation risks to their health was asleep. The women moved through the streets as winged messengers, twirling around each other in slow motion, peeking inside homes and watching the easy sleep of men and women. They were astonished by such stillness and periodically would utter a shrill note or low cry just to verify life.

The residents finally awoke to what appeared as strange apparitions. Some simply stared. Others called authorities, and in time, the women were apprehended by wary soldiers dressed in desert fatigues. They were taken to a white, square building on the other edge of Mercury. When asked who they were and why they were there, the women replied, "We are mothers and we have come to reclaim the desert for our children."

The soldiers arrested them. As the ten women were blindfolded and handcuffed, they began singing:

You can't forbid us everything
You can't forbid us to think—
You can't forbid our tears to flow
And you can't stop the songs that we sing.

The women continued to sing louder and louder, until they heard the voices of their sisters moving across the mesa.

Ah ne nah, nah
nin nah nah—
Ah ne nah, nah
nin nah nah—
Nyaga mutzi

oh ne nay—
Nyaga mutzi
oh ne nay—

"Call for re-enforcement," one soldier said.

"We have," interrupted one woman. "We have—and you have no idea of our numbers." 50

On March 18, 1988, I crossed the line at the Nevada Test Site and was arrested with nine other Utahns for trespassing on military lands. They are still conducting nuclear tests in the desert. Ours was an act of civil disobedience. But as I walked toward the town of Mercury, it was more than a gesture of peace. It was a gesture on behalf of the Clan of One-Breasted Women.

As one officer cinched the handcuffs around my wrists, another frisked my body. She found a pen and a pad of paper tucked inside my left boot.

"And these?" she asked sternly.

"Weapons," I replied.

Our eyes met. I smiled. She pulled the leg of my trousers back over my boot. 55

"Step forward, please," she said as she took my arm.

We were booked under an afternoon sun and bussed to Tonapah, Nevada. It was a two-hour ride. This was familiar country to me. The Joshua trees standing their ground had been named by my ancestors who believed they looked like prophets pointing west to the promised land. These were the same trees that bloomed each spring, flowers appearing like white flames in the Mojave. And I recalled a full moon in May when my mother and I had walked among them, flushing out mourning doves and owls.

The bus stopped short of town. We were released. The officials thought it was a cruel joke to leave us stranded in the desert with no way to get home. What they didn't realize is that we were home, soul-centered and strong, women who recognized the sweet smell of sage as fuel for our spirits.

Questions

1. Williams uses a variety of evidence in this essay, including personal memory, family history, government documents, and other sources. List the evidence and the order in which she uses it. Why does Williams present her material in this order?

2. The essay begins with a description of what Williams later calls a "family nightmare" and ends with a dream vision. What is the rhetorical effect of this interactive opening and closing?

3. What does Williams mean by the statement "I must question everything" (paragraph 36)?

4. Do some research on an environmental issue that affects you or your family, and, using Williams as a model, write an essay that combines your personal experience and your research.

Ethics

Mark Twain — *Advice to Youth*

Being told I would be expected to talk here, I inquired what sort of a talk I ought to make. They said it should be something suitable to youth—something didactic, instructive, or something in the nature of good advice. Very well. I have a few things in my mind which I have often longed to say for the instruction of the young; for it is in one's tender early years that such things will best take root and be most enduring and most valuable. First, then, I will say to you, my young friends—and I say it beseechingly, urgingly—

Always obey your parents, when they are present. This is the best policy in the long run, because if you don't they will make you. Most parents think they know better than you do, and you can generally make more by humoring that superstition than you can by acting on your own better judgment.

Be respectful to your superiors, if you have any, also to strangers, and sometimes to others. If a person offend you, and you are in doubt as to whether it was intentional or not, do not resort to extreme measures; simply watch your chance and hit him with a brick. That will be sufficient. If you shall find that he had not intended any offense, come out frankly and confess yourself in the wrong when you struck him; acknowledge it like a man and say you didn't mean to. Yes, always avoid violence; in this age of charity and kindliness, the time has gone by for such things. Leave dynamite to the low and unrefined.

Go to bed early, get up early—this is wise. Some authorities say get up with the sun; some others say get up with one thing, some with another. But a lark is really the best thing to get up with. It gives you a splendid reputation with everybody to know that you get up with the lark; and if you get the right kind of a lark, and work at him right, you can easily train him to get up at half past nine, every time—it is no trick at all.

5 Now as to the matter of lying. You want to be very careful about lying; otherwise you are nearly sure to get caught. Once caught, you can never again be, in the eyes of the good and the pure, what you were before. Many a young person has injured himself permanently through a single clumsy and illfinished lie, the result of carelessness born of incomplete training. Some authorities hold that the young ought not to lie at all. That, of course, is putting it rather stronger than necessary; still, while I cannot go quite so far as that, I do maintain, and I believe I am right, that the young ought to be temperate in the use

Text of a lecture given by Twain (a.k.a. Samuel Clemens) in 1882. The original audience and occasion for this lecture remain unknown.

of this great art until practice and experience shall give them that confidence, elegance, and precision which alone can make the accomplishment graceful and profitable. Patience, diligence, painstaking attention to detail—these are the requirements; these, in time, will make the student perfect; upon these, and upon these only, may he rely as the sure foundation for future eminence. Think what tedious years of study, thought, practice, experience, went to the equipment of that peerless old master who was able to impose upon the whole world the lofty and sounding maxim that "truth is mighty and will prevail"—the most majestic compound fracture of fact which any of woman born has yet achieved. For the history of our race, and each individual's experience, are sown thick with evidence that a truth is not hard to kill and that a lie told well is immortal. There is in Boston a monument of the man who discovered anaesthesia; many people are aware, in these latter days, that that man didn't discover it at all, but stole the discovery from another man. Is this truth mighty, and will it prevail? Ah no, my hearers, the monument is made of hardy material, but the lie it tells will outlast it a million years. An awkward, feeble, leaky lie is a thing which you ought to make it your unceasing study to avoid; such a lie as that has no more real permanence than an average truth. Why, you might as well tell the truth at once and be done with it. A feeble, stupid, preposterous lie will not live two years—except it be a slander upon somebody. It is indestructible, then, of course, but that is no merit of yours. A final word: begin your practice of this gracious and beautiful art early—begin now. If I had begun earlier, I could have learned how.

Never handle firearms carelessly. The sorrow and suffering that have been caused through the innocent but heedless handling of firearms by the young! Only four days ago, right in the next farmhouse to the one where I am spending the summer, a grandmother, old and gray and sweet, one of the loveliest spirits in the land, was sitting at her work, when her young grandson crept in and got down an old, battered, rusty gun which had not been touched for many years and was supposed not to be loaded, and pointed it at her, laughing and threatening to shoot. In her fright she ran screaming and pleading toward the door on the other side of the room; but as she passed him he placed the gun almost against her very breast and pulled the trigger! He had supposed it was not loaded. And he was right—it wasn't. So there wasn't any harm done. It is the only case of that kind I ever heard of. Therefore, just the same, don't you meddle with old unloaded firearms; they are the most deadly and unerring things that have ever been created by man. You don't have to take any pains at all with them; you don't have to have a rest, you don't have to have any sights on the gun, you don't have to take aim, even. No, you just pick out a relative and bang away, and you are sure to get him. A youth who can't hit a cathedral at thirty yards with a Gatling gun in three-quarters of an hour, can take up an old empty musket and bag his grandmother every time, at a hundred. Think what Waterloo[1] would have been if one of the armies had been boys armed

1. The bloody battle (1815) in which Napoleon suffered his final defeat at the hands of English and German troops under the Duke of Wellington.

with old muskets supposed not to be loaded, and the other army had been composed of their female relations. The very thought of it makes one shudder.

There are many sorts of books; but good ones are the sort for the young to read. Remember that. They are a great, an inestimable, an unspeakable means of improvement. Therefore be careful in your selection, my young friends; be very careful; confine yourselves exclusively to Robertson's Sermons, Baxter's *Saint's Rest, The Innocents Abroad,* and works of that kind.[2]

But I have said enough. I hope you will treasure up the instructions which I have given you, and make them a guide to your feet and a light to your understanding. Build your character thoughtfully and painstakingly upon these precepts, and by and by, when you have got it built, you will be surprised and gratified to see how nicely and sharply it resembles everybody else's.

2. The five volumes of sermons by Frederick William Robertson (1816–1853), an English clergyman, and Richard Baxter's *Saints' Everlasting Rest* (1650) were well-known religious works; *The Innocents Abroad* is Twain's own collection of humorous travel sketches.

QUESTIONS

1. Underline the various pieces of "serious" advice that Twain offers and notice where and how he begins to turn each one upside down.

2. Mark Twain was already known as a comic author when he delivered "Advice to Youth" as a lecture in 1882; it was not published until 1923. We do not know the circumstances under which he delivered it or to whom. Using evidence from the text, imagine both the circumstances and the audience.

3. Rewrite "Advice to Youth" for a modern audience, perhaps as a lecture for a school assembly or a commencement address.

STEVEN PINKER

The Moral Instinct

WHICH OF THE FOLLOWING PEOPLE would you say is the most admirable: Mother Teresa, Bill Gates or Norman Borlaug? And which do you think is the least admirable? For most people, it's an easy question. Mother Teresa, famous for ministering to the poor in Calcutta, has been beatified by the Vatican, awarded the Nobel Peace Prize and ranked in an American poll as the most admired person of the 20th century. Bill Gates, infamous for giving us the Microsoft dancing paper clip and the blue screen of death, has been decapitated in effigy in "I Hate

Published in the New York Times Magazine *on January 13, 2008, Pinker's essay draws on the work of many philosophers and cognitive psychologists and from ideas he advanced in* The Blank Slate: The Modern Denial of Human Nature *(2002).*

Gates" Web sites and hit with a pie in the face. As for Norman Borlaug . . . who the heck is Norman Borlaug?

Yet a deeper look might lead you to rethink your answers. Borlaug, father of the "Green Revolution" that used agricultural science to reduce world hunger, has been credited with saving a billion lives, more than anyone else in history. Gates, in deciding what to do with his fortune, crunched the numbers and determined that he could alleviate the most misery by fighting everyday scourges in the developing world like malaria, diarrhea and parasites. Mother Teresa, for her part, extolled the virtue of suffering and ran her well-financed missions accordingly: their sick patrons were offered plenty of prayer but harsh conditions, few analgesics and dangerously primitive medical care.

It's not hard to see why the moral reputations of this trio should be so out of line with the good they have done. Mother Teresa was the very embodiment of saintliness: white-clad, sad-eyed, ascetic and often photographed with the wretched of the earth. Gates is a nerd's nerd and the world's richest man, as likely to enter heaven as the proverbial camel squeezing through the needle's eye. And Borlaug, now 93, is an agronomist who has spent his life in labs and nonprofits, seldom walking onto the media stage, and hence into our consciousness, at all.

I doubt these examples will persuade anyone to favor Bill Gates over Mother Teresa for sainthood. But they show that our heads can be turned by an aura of sanctity, distracting us from a more objective reckoning of the actions that make people suffer or flourish. It seems we may all be vulnerable to moral illusions, the ethical equivalent of the bending lines that trick the eye on cereal boxes and in psychology textbooks. Illusions are a favorite tool of perception scientists for exposing the working of the five senses, and of philosophers for shaking people out of the naïve belief that our minds give us a transparent window onto the world (since if our eyes can be fooled by an illusion, why should we trust them at other times?). Today, a new field is using illusions to unmask a sixth sense, the moral sense. Moral intuitions are being drawn out of people in the lab, on Web sites and in brain scanners, and are being explained with tools from game theory, neuroscience and evolutionary biology.

"Two things fill the mind with ever new and increasing admiration and awe, the oftener and more steadily we reflect on them," wrote Immanuel Kant,[1] "the starry heavens above and the moral law within." These days, the moral law within is being viewed with increasing awe, if not always admiration. The human moral sense turns out to be an organ of considerable complexity, with quirks that reflect its evolutionary history and its neurobiological foundations.

5

These quirks are bound to have implications for the human predicament. Morality is not just any old topic in psychology but close to our conception of the meaning of life. Moral goodness is what gives each of us the sense that we are worthy human beings. We seek it in our friends and mates, nurture it in our children, advance it in our politics and justify it with our religions. A dis-

1. German philosopher (1724–1804) famous for conceptualizing moral action as a "categorical imperative"; the sentence Pinker quotes is inscribed on Kant's tombstone.

respect for morality is blamed for everyday sins and history's worst atrocities. To carry this weight, the concept of morality would have to be bigger than any of us and outside all of us.

So dissecting moral intuitions is no small matter. If morality is a mere trick of the brain, some may fear, our very grounds for being moral could be eroded. Yet as we shall see, the science of the moral sense can instead be seen as a way to strengthen those grounds, by clarifying what morality is and how it should steer our actions.

THE MORALIZATION SWITCH

The starting point for appreciating that there *is* a distinctive part of our psychology for morality is seeing how moral judgments differ from other kinds of opinions we have on how people ought to behave. Moralization is a psychological state that can be turned on and off like a switch, and when it is on, a distinctive mind-set commandeers our thinking. This is the mind-set that makes us deem actions immoral ("killing is wrong"), rather than merely disagreeable ("I hate Brussels sprouts"), unfashionable ("bell-bottoms are out") or imprudent ("don't scratch mosquito bites").

The first hallmark of moralization is that the rules it invokes are felt to be universal. Prohibitions of rape and murder, for example, are felt not to be matters of local custom but to be universally and objectively warranted. One can easily say, "I don't like Brussels sprouts, but I don't care if you eat them," but no one would say, "I don't like killing, but I don't care if you murder someone."

10 The other hallmark is that people feel that those who commit immoral acts deserve to be punished. Not only is it allowable to inflict pain on a person who has broken a moral rule; it is wrong *not* to, to "let them get away with it." People are thus untroubled in inviting divine retribution or the power of the state to harm other people they deem immoral. Bertrand Russell wrote, "The infliction of cruelty with a good conscience is a delight to moralists—that is why they invented hell."

We all know what it feels like when the moralization switch flips inside us—the righteous glow, the burning dudgeon, the drive to recruit others to the cause. The psychologist Paul Rozin has studied the toggle switch by comparing two kinds of people who engage in the same behavior but with different switch settings.[2] Health vegetarians avoid meat for practical reasons, like lowering cholesterol and avoiding toxins. Moral vegetarians avoid meat for ethical reasons: to avoid complicity in the suffering of animals. By investigating their feelings about meat-eating, Rozin showed that the moral motive sets off a cascade of opinions. Moral vegetarians are more likely to treat meat as a contaminant—they refuse, for example, to eat a bowl of soup into which a drop of beef broth has fallen. They are more likely to think that other people ought to be vegetarians, and are

2. Paul Rozin (b. 1936), professor of psychology at the University of Pennsylvania whose 1999 article, "Food Is Fundamental, Fun, Frightening, and Far-Reaching," influences this section of Pinker's essay.

more likely to imbue their dietary habits with other virtues, like believing that meat avoidance makes people less aggressive and bestial.

Much of our recent social history, including the culture wars between liberals and conservatives, consists of the moralization or amoralization of particular kinds of behavior. Even when people agree that an outcome is desirable, they may disagree on whether it should be treated as a matter of preference and prudence or as a matter of sin and virtue. Rozin notes, for example, that smoking has lately been moralized. Until recently, it was understood that some people didn't enjoy smoking or avoided it because it was hazardous to their health. But with the discovery of the harmful effects of secondhand smoke, smoking is now treated as immoral. Smokers are ostracized; images of people smoking are censored; and entities touched by smoke are felt to be contaminated (so hotels have not only nonsmoking rooms but nonsmoking *floors*). The desire for retribution has been visited on tobacco companies, who have been slapped with staggering "punitive damages."

At the same time, many behaviors have been amoralized, switched from moral failings to lifestyle choices. They include divorce, illegitimacy, being a working mother, marijuana use and homosexuality. Many afflictions have been reassigned from payback for bad choices to unlucky misfortunes. There used to be people called "bums" and "tramps"; today they are "homeless." Drug addiction is a "disease"; syphilis was rebranded from the price of wanton behavior to a "sexually transmitted disease" and more recently a "sexually transmitted infection."

This wave of amoralization has led the cultural right to lament that morality itself is under assault, as we see in the group that anointed itself the Moral Majority. In fact there seems to be a Law of Conservation of Moralization, so that as old behaviors are taken out of the moralized column, new ones are added to it. Dozens of things that past generations treated as practical matters are now ethical battlegrounds, including disposable diapers, I.Q. tests, poultry farms, Barbie dolls and research on breast cancer. Food alone has become a minefield, with critics sermonizing about the size of sodas, the chemistry of fat, the freedom of chickens, the price of coffee beans, the species of fish and now the distance the food has traveled from farm to plate.

15 Many of these moralizations, like the assault on smoking, may be understood as practical tactics to reduce some recently identified harm. But whether an activity flips our mental switches to the "moral" setting isn't just a matter of how much harm it does. We don't show contempt to the man who fails to change the batteries in his smoke alarms or takes his family on a driving vacation, both of which multiply the risk they will die in an accident. Driving a gas-guzzling Hummer is reprehensible, but driving a gas-guzzling old Volvo is not; eating a Big Mac is unconscionable, but not imported cheese or crème brûlée. The reason for these double standards is obvious: people tend to align their moralization with their own lifestyles.

Reasoning and Rationalizing

It's not just the content of our moral judgments that is often questionable, but the way we arrive at them. We like to think that when we have a conviction, there are good reasons that drove us to adopt it. That is why an older approach to moral psychology, led by Jean Piaget and Lawrence Kohlberg,[3] tried to document the lines of reasoning that guided people to moral conclusions. But consider these situations, originally devised by the psychologist Jonathan Haidt:[4]

> Julie is traveling in France on summer vacation from college with her brother Mark. One night they decide that it would be interesting and fun if they tried making love. Julie was already taking birth-control pills, but Mark uses a condom, too, just to be safe. They both enjoy the sex but decide not to do it again. They keep the night as a special secret, which makes them feel closer to each other. What do you think about that—was it O.K. for them to make love?
>
> A woman is cleaning out her closet and she finds her old American flag. She doesn't want the flag anymore, so she cuts it up into pieces and uses the rags to clean her bathroom.
>
> A family's dog is killed by a car in front of their house. They heard that dog meat was delicious, so they cut up the dog's body and cook it and eat it for dinner.

Most people immediately declare that these acts are wrong and then grope to justify *why* they are wrong. It's not so easy. In the case of Julie and Mark, people raise the possibility of children with birth defects, but they are reminded that the couple were diligent about contraception. They suggest that the siblings will be emotionally hurt, but the story makes it clear that they weren't. They submit that the act would offend the community, but then recall that it was kept a secret. Eventually many people admit, "I don't know, I can't explain it, I just know it's wrong." People don't generally engage in moral reasoning, Haidt argues, but moral *rationalization*: they begin with the conclusion, coughed up by an unconscious emotion, and then work backward to a plausible justification.

The gap between people's convictions and their justifications is also on display in the favorite new sandbox for moral psychologists, a thought experiment devised by the philosophers Philippa Foot and Judith Jarvis Thomson called the Trolley Problem.[5] On your morning walk, you see a trolley car hurtling down the track, the conductor slumped over the controls. In the path of the trolley are five men working on the track, oblivious to the danger. You are standing at a fork in

3. Jean Piaget (1896–1980), Swiss developmental psychologist; Lawrence Kohlberg (1927–1987), American psychologist who applied Piaget's theories of cognitive development to formulate his own theory of the stages of moral development.

4. Professor of psychology at the University of Virginia who began to formulate these questions at the University of Pennsylvania while working on his Ph.D.

5. Philippa Foot (1920–2010), British ethicist who introduced the "Trolley Problem"; Judith Jarvis Thomson (b. 1929), American moral philosopher and metaphysician, who also extensively studied this ethical problem.

the track and can pull a lever that will divert the trolley onto a spur, saving the five men. Unfortunately, the trolley would then run over a single worker who is laboring on the spur. Is it permissible to throw the switch, killing one man to save five? Almost everyone says "yes."

Consider now a different scene. You are on a bridge overlooking the tracks and have spotted the runaway trolley bearing down on the five workers. Now the only way to stop the trolley is to throw a heavy object in its path. And the only heavy object within reach is a fat man standing next to you. Should you throw the man off the bridge? Both dilemmas present you with the option of sacrificing one life to save five, and so, by the utilitarian standard of what would result in the greatest good for the greatest number, the two dilemmas are morally equivalent. But most people don't see it that way: though they would pull the switch in the first dilemma, they would not heave the fat man in the second. When pressed for a reason, they can't come up with anything coherent, though moral philosophers haven't had an easy time coming up with a relevant difference, either.

20 When psychologists say "most people" they usually mean "most of the two dozen sophomores who filled out a questionnaire for beer money." But in this case it means most of the 200,000 people from a hundred countries who shared their intuitions on a Web-based experiment conducted by the psychologists Fiery Cushman and Liane Young and the biologist Marc Hauser. A difference between the acceptability of switch-pulling and man-heaving, and an inability to justify the choice, was found in respondents from Europe, Asia and North and South America; among men and women, blacks and whites, teenagers and octogenarians, Hindus, Muslims, Buddhists, Christians, Jews and atheists; people with elementary-school educations and people with Ph.D.'s.

Joshua Greene,[6] a philosopher and cognitive neuroscientist, suggests that evolution equipped people with a revulsion to manhandling an innocent person. This instinct, he suggests, tends to overwhelm any utilitarian calculus that would tot up the lives saved and lost. The impulse against roughing up a fellow human would explain other examples in which people abjure killing one to save many, like euthanizing a hospital patient to harvest his organs and save five dying patients in need of transplants, or throwing someone out of a crowded lifeboat to keep it afloat.

By itself this would be no more than a plausible story, but Greene teamed up with the cognitive neuroscientist Jonathan Cohen and several Princeton colleagues to peer into people's brains using functional M.R.I.[7] They sought to find signs of a conflict between brain areas associated with emotion (the ones that recoil from harming someone) and areas dedicated to rational analysis (the ones that calculate lives lost and saved).

6. Assistant professor of psychology at Harvard who has also extensively studied the "Trolley Problem."

7. See, for example, J. D. Greene, L. E. Nystrom, A. D. Engell, J. M. Darley, and J. D. Cohen (2004), "The Neural Bases of Cognitive Conflict and Control in Moral Judgment," *Neuron*, vol. 44, pp. 389–400.

When people pondered the dilemmas that required killing someone with their bare hands, several networks in their brains lighted up. One, which included the medial (inward-facing) parts of the frontal lobes, has been implicated in emotions about other people. A second, the dorsolateral (upper and outer-facing) surface of the frontal lobes, has been implicated in ongoing mental computation (including nonmoral reasoning, like deciding whether to get somewhere by plane or train). And a third region, the anterior cingulated cortex (an evolutionarily ancient strip lying at the base of the inner surface of each cerebral hemisphere), registers a conflict between an urge coming from one part of the brain and an advisory coming from another.

But when the people were pondering a hands-off dilemma, like switching the trolley onto the spur with the single worker, the brain reacted differently: only the area involved in rational calculation stood out. Other studies have shown that neurological patients who have blunted emotions because of damage to the frontal lobes become utilitarians: they think it makes perfect sense to throw the fat man off the bridge. Together, the findings corroborate Greene's theory that our nonutilitarian intuitions come from the victory of an emotional impulse over a cost-benefit analysis.

A Universal Morality?

25 The findings of trolleyology—complex, instinctive and worldwide moral intuitions—led Hauser and John Mikhail (a legal scholar) to revive an analogy from the philosopher John Rawls between the moral sense and language. According to Noam Chomsky,[8] we are born with a "universal grammar" that forces us to analyze speech in terms of its grammatical structure, with no conscious awareness of the rules in play. By analogy, we are born with a universal moral grammar that forces us to analyze human action in terms of its moral structure, with just as little awareness.

The idea that the moral sense is an innate part of human nature is not far-fetched. A list of human universals collected by the anthropologist Donald E. Brown[9] includes many moral concepts and emotions, including a distinction between right and wrong; empathy; fairness; admiration of generosity; rights and obligations; proscription of murder, rape and other forms of violence; redress of wrongs; sanctions for wrongs against the community; shame; and taboos.

The stirrings of morality emerge early in childhood. Toddlers spontaneously offer toys and help to others and try to comfort people they see in distress. And according to the psychologists Elliot Turiel and Judith Smetana, preschoolers have an inkling of the difference between societal conventions and moral principles. Four-year-olds say that it is not O.K. to wear pajamas to

8. American linguist, philosopher, and cognitive scientist (b. 1928) famous for his studies, begun in the 1950s, of "an innate set of linguistic principles shared by all humans," which he called a "universal grammar."

9. Professor of anthropology at the University of California–Santa Barbara; he is quoted at length in Pinker's 2002 book *The Blank Slate: The Modern Denial of Human Nature*, which argues against tabula rasa models.

school (a convention) and also not O.K. to hit a little girl for no reason (a moral principle). But when asked whether these actions would be O.K. if the teacher allowed them, most of the children said that wearing pajamas would now be fine but that hitting a little girl would still not be.

Though no one has identified genes for morality, there is circumstantial evidence they exist. The character traits called "conscientiousness" and "agreeableness" are far more correlated in identical twins separated at birth (who share their genes but not their environment) than in adoptive siblings raised together (who share their environment but not their genes). People given diagnoses of "antisocial personality disorder" or "psychopathy" show signs of morality blindness from the time they are children. They bully younger children, torture animals, habitually lie and seem incapable of empathy or remorse, often despite normal family backgrounds. Some of these children grow up into the monsters who bilk elderly people out of their savings, rape a succession of women or shoot convenience-store clerks lying on the floor during a robbery.

Though psychopathy probably comes from a genetic predisposition, a milder version can be caused by damage to frontal regions of the brain (including the areas that inhibit intact people from throwing the hypothetical fat man off the bridge). The neuroscientists Hanna and Antonio Damasio and their colleagues found that some children who sustain severe injuries to their frontal lobes can grow up into callous and irresponsible adults, despite normal intelligence. They lie, steal, ignore punishment, endanger their own children and can't think through even the simplest moral dilemmas, like what two people should do if they disagreed on which TV channel to watch or whether a man ought to steal a drug to save his dying wife.

30 The moral sense, then, may be rooted in the design of the normal human brain. Yet for all the awe that may fill our minds when we reflect on an innate moral law within, the idea is at best incomplete. Consider this moral dilemma: A runaway trolley is about to kill a schoolteacher. You can divert the trolley onto a sidetrack, but the trolley would trip a switch sending a signal to a class of 6-year-olds, giving them permission to name a teddy bear Muhammad. Is it permissible to pull the lever?

This is no joke. Last month a British woman teaching in a private school in Sudan allowed her class to name a teddy bear after the most popular boy in the class, who bore the name of the founder of Islam. She was jailed for blasphemy and threatened with a public flogging, while a mob outside the prison demanded her death. To the protesters, the woman's life clearly had less value than maximizing the dignity of their religion, and their judgment on whether it is right to divert the hypothetical trolley would have differed from ours. Whatever grammar guides people's moral judgments can't be all *that* universal. Anyone who stayed awake through Anthropology 101 can offer many other examples.

Of course, languages vary, too. In Chomsky's theory, languages conform to an abstract blueprint, like having phrases built out of verbs and objects, while the details vary, like whether the verb or the object comes first. Could we be wired with an abstract spec sheet that embraces all the strange ideas that people in different cultures moralize?

THE VARIETIES OF MORAL EXPERIENCE

When anthropologists like Richard Shweder and Alan Fiske survey moral concerns across the globe, they find that a few themes keep popping up from amid the diversity. People everywhere, at least in some circumstances and with certain other folks in mind, think it's bad to harm others and good to help them. They have a sense of fairness: that one should reciprocate favors, reward benefactors and punish cheaters. They value loyalty to a group, sharing and solidarity among its members and conformity to its norms. They believe that it is right to defer to legitimate authorities and to respect people with high status. And they exalt purity, cleanliness and sanctity while loathing defilement, contamination and carnality.

The exact number of themes depends on whether you're a lumper or a splitter, but Haidt counts five—harm, fairness, community (or group loyalty), authority and purity—and suggests that they are the primary colors of our moral sense.[10] Not only do they keep reappearing in cross-cultural surveys, but each one tugs on the moral intuitions of people in our own culture. Haidt asks us to consider how much money someone would have to pay us to do hypothetical acts like the following:

> Stick a pin into your palm.
>
> Stick a pin into the palm of a child you don't know. (Harm.)
>
> Accept a wide-screen TV from a friend who received it at no charge because of a computer error.
>
> Accept a wide-screen TV from a friend who received it from a thief who had stolen it from a wealthy family. (Fairness.)
>
> Say something bad about your nation (which you don't believe) on a talk-radio show in your nation.
>
> Say something bad about your nation (which you don't believe) on a talk-radio show in a foreign nation. (Community.)
>
> Slap a friend in the face, with his permission, as part of a comedy skit.
>
> Slap your minister in the face, with his permission, as part of a comedy skit. (Authority.)
>
> Attend a performance-art piece in which the actors act like idiots for 30 minutes, including flubbing simple problems and falling down on stage.
>
> Attend a performance-art piece in which the actors act like animals for 30 minutes, including crawling around naked and urinating on stage. (Purity.)

In each pair, the second action feels far more repugnant. Most of the moral illusions we have visited come from an unwarranted intrusion of one of the moral spheres into our judgments. A violation of community led people to

10. Haidt discusses these themes in "The Moral Mind: How 5 Sets of Innate Moral Intuitions Guide the Development of Many Culture-specific Virtues, and Perhaps Even Modules," in *The Innate Mind*, ed. P. Carruthers, S. Laurence, and S. Stich (New York: Oxford University Press), vol. 3, pp. 367–391.

frown on using an old flag to clean a bathroom. Violations of purity repelled the people who judged the morality of consensual incest and prevented the moral vegetarians and nonsmokers from tolerating the slightest trace of a vile contaminant. At the other end of the scale, displays of extreme purity lead people to venerate religious leaders who dress in white and affect an aura of chastity and asceticism.

THE GENEALOGY OF MORALS

The five spheres are good candidates for a periodic table of the moral sense not only because they are ubiquitous but also because they appear to have deep evolutionary roots. The impulse to avoid harm, which gives trolley ponderers the willies when they consider throwing a man off a bridge, can also be found in rhesus monkeys, who go hungry rather than pull a chain that delivers food to them and a shock to another monkey. Respect for authority is clearly related to the pecking orders of dominance and appeasement that are widespread in the animal kingdom. The purity-defilement contrast taps the emotion of disgust that is triggered by potential disease vectors like bodily effluvia, decaying flesh and unconventional forms of meat, and by risky sexual practices like incest. 35

The other two moralized spheres match up with the classic examples of how altruism can evolve that were worked out by sociobiologists in the 1960s and 1970s and made famous by Richard Dawkins in his book "The Selfish Gene."[11] Fairness is very close to what scientists call reciprocal altruism, where a willingness to be nice to others can evolve as long as the favor helps the recipient more than it costs the giver and the recipient returns the favor when fortunes reverse. The analysis makes it sound as if reciprocal altruism comes out of a robotlike calculation, but in fact Robert Trivers, the biologist who devised the theory, argued that it is implemented in the brain as a suite of moral emotions. Sympathy prompts a person to offer the first favor, particularly to someone in need for whom it would go the furthest. Anger protects a person against cheaters who accept a favor without reciprocating, by impelling him to punish the ingrate or sever the relationship. Gratitude impels a beneficiary to reward those who helped him in the past. Guilt prompts a cheater in danger of being found out to repair the relationship by redressing the misdeed and advertising that he will behave better in the future (consistent with Mencken's definition of *conscience* as "the inner voice which warns us that someone might be looking"). Many experiments on who helps whom, who likes whom, who punishes whom and who feels guilty about what have confirmed these predictions.

Community, the very different emotion that prompts people to share and sacrifice without an expectation of payback, may be rooted in nepotistic altruism, the empathy and solidarity we feel toward our relatives (and which evolved because any gene that pushed an organism to aid a relative would have helped copies of itself sitting inside that relative). In humans, of course, communal

11. In *The Selfish Gene* (1976), Richard Dawkins took a gene-centered view of evolution, arguing that selection at the level of organisms almost never overrides selection based on genes.

feelings can be lavished on nonrelatives as well. Sometimes it pays people (in an evolutionary sense) to love their companions because their interests are yoked, like spouses with common children, in-laws with common relatives, friends with common tastes or allies with common enemies. And sometimes it doesn't pay them at all, but their kinship-detectors have been tricked into treating their groupmates as if they were relatives by tactics like kinship metaphors (*blood brothers, fraternities, the fatherland*), origin myths, communal meals and other bonding rituals.

JUGGLING THE SPHERES

All this brings us to a theory of how the moral sense can be universal and variable at the same time. The five moral spheres are universal, a legacy of evolution. But how they are ranked in importance, and which is brought in to moralize which area of social life—sex, government, commerce, religion, diet and so on—depends on the culture. Many of the flabbergasting practices in faraway places become more intelligible when you recognize that the same moralizing impulse that Western elites channel toward violations of harm and fairness (our moral obsessions) is channeled elsewhere to violations in the other spheres. Think of the Japanese fear of nonconformity (community), the holy ablutions and dietary restrictions of Hindus and Orthodox Jews (purity), the outrage at insulting the Prophet among Muslims (authority). In the West, we believe that in business and government, fairness should trump community and try to root out nepotism and cronyism. In other parts of the world this is incomprehensible—what heartless creep would favor a perfect stranger over his own brother?

The ranking and placement of moral spheres also divides the cultures of liberals and conservatives in the United States. Many bones of contention, like homosexuality, atheism and one-parent families from the right, or racial imbalances, sweatshops and executive pay from the left, reflect different weightings of the spheres. In a large Web survey, Haidt found that liberals put a lopsided moral weight on harm and fairness while playing down group loyalty, authority and purity. Conservatives instead place a moderately high weight on all five. It's not surprising that each side thinks it is driven by lofty ethical values and that the other side is base and unprincipled.

40 Reassigning an activity to a different sphere, or taking it out of the moral spheres altogether, isn't easy. People think that a behavior belongs in its sphere as a matter of sacred necessity and that the very act of questioning an assignment is a moral outrage. The psychologist Philip Tetlock has shown that the mentality of taboo—a conviction that some thoughts are sinful to think—is not just a superstition of Polynesians but a mind-set that can easily be triggered in college-educated Americans.[12] Just ask them to think about applying the sphere

12. Philip E. Tetlock, professor of business and political science at the University of California, applies the concept of taboo to matters of business and government in articles such as "The Psychology of the Unthinkable: Taboo Trade-offs, Forbidden Base Rates, and Heretical Counterfactuals," *Journal of Personality and Social Psychology*, vol. 78, pp. 853–870.

of reciprocity to relationships customarily governed by community or authority. When Tetlock asked subjects for their opinions on whether adoption agencies should place children with the couples willing to pay the most, whether people should have the right to sell their organs and whether they should be able to buy their way out of jury duty, the subjects not only disagreed but felt personally insulted and were outraged that anyone would raise the question.

The institutions of modernity often question and experiment with the way activities are assigned to moral spheres. Market economies tend to put everything up for sale. Science amoralizes the world by seeking to understand phenomena rather than pass judgment on them. Secular philosophy is in the business of scrutinizing all beliefs, including those entrenched by authority and tradition. It's not surprising that these institutions are often seen to be morally corrosive.

Is Nothing Sacred?

And "morally corrosive" is exactly the term that some critics would apply to the new science of the moral sense. The attempt to dissect our moral intuitions can look like an attempt to debunk them. Evolutionary psychologists seem to want to unmask our noblest motives as ultimately self-interested—to show that our love for children, compassion for the unfortunate and sense of justice are just tactics in a Darwinian struggle to perpetuate our genes. The explanation of how different cultures appeal to different spheres could lead to a spineless relativism, in which we would never have grounds to criticize the practice of another culture, no matter how barbaric, because "we have our kind of morality and they have theirs." And the whole enterprise seems to be dragging us to an amoral nihilism, in which morality itself would be demoted from a transcendent principle to a figment of our neural circuitry.

In reality, none of these fears are warranted, and it's important to see why not. The first misunderstanding involves the logic of evolutionary explanations. Evolutionary biologists sometimes anthropomorphize DNA for the same reason that science teachers find it useful to have their students imagine the world from the viewpoint of a molecule or a beam of light. One shortcut to understanding the theory of selection without working through the math is to imagine that the genes are little agents that try to make copies of themselves.

Unfortunately, the meme of the selfish gene escaped from popular biology books and mutated into the idea that organisms (including people) are ruthlessly self-serving. And this doesn't follow. Genes are not a reservoir of our dark unconscious wishes. "Selfish" genes are perfectly compatible with selfless organisms, because a gene's metaphorical goal of selfishly replicating itself can be implemented by wiring up the brain of the organism to do unselfish things, like being nice to relatives or doing good deeds for needy strangers. When a mother stays up all night comforting a sick child, the genes that endowed her with that tenderness were "selfish" in a metaphorical sense, but by no stretch of the imagination is *she* being selfish.

Nor does reciprocal altruism—the evolutionary rationale behind fairness— imply that people do good deeds in the cynical expectation of repayment down

45

the line. We all know of unrequited good deeds, like tipping a waitress in a city you will never visit again and falling on a grenade to save platoonmates. These bursts of goodness are not as anomalous to a biologist as they might appear.

In his classic 1971 article, Trivers, the biologist, showed how natural selection could push in the direction of true selflessness.[13] The emergence of tit-for-tat reciprocity, which lets organisms trade favors without being cheated, is just a first step. A favor-giver not only has to avoid blatant cheaters (those who would accept a favor but not return it) but also prefer generous reciprocators (those who return the biggest favor they can afford) over stingy ones (those who return the smallest favor they can get away with). Since it's good to be chosen as a recipient of favors, a competition arises to be the most generous partner around. More accurately, a competition arises to *appear* to be the most generous partner around, since the favor-giver can't literally read minds or see into the future. A reputation for fairness and generosity becomes an asset.

Now this just sets up a competition for potential beneficiaries to inflate their reputations without making the sacrifices to back them up. But it also pressures the favor-giver to develop ever-more-sensitive radar to distinguish the genuinely generous partners from the hypocrites. This arms race will eventually reach a logical conclusion. The most effective way to *seem* generous and fair, under harsh scrutiny, is to be generous and fair. In the long run, then, reputation can be secured only by commitment. At least some agents evolve to be genuinely high-minded and self-sacrificing—they are moral not because of what it brings them but because that's the kind of people they are.

Of course, a theory that predicted that everyone always sacrificed themselves for another's good would be as preposterous as a theory that predicted that no one ever did. Alongside the niches for saints there are niches for more grudging reciprocators, who attract fewer and poorer partners but don't make the sacrifices necessary for a sterling reputation. And both may coexist with outright cheaters, who exploit the unwary in one-shot encounters. An ecosystem of niches, each with a distinct strategy, can evolve when the payoff of each strategy depends on how many players are playing the other strategies. The human social environment does have its share of generous, grudging and crooked characters, and the genetic variation in personality seems to bear the fingerprints of this evolutionary process.

Is Morality a Figment?

So a biological understanding of the moral sense does not entail that people are calculating maximizers of their genes or self-interest. But where does it leave the concept of morality itself?

50 Here is the worry. The scientific outlook has taught us that some parts of our subjective experience are products of our biological makeup and have no objective counterpart in the world. The qualitative difference between red and

13. See R. L. Trivers, "The Evolution of Reciprocal Altruism," *Quarterly Review of Biology*, vol. 46 (1971), pp. 35–57.

green, the tastiness of fruit and foulness of carrion, the scariness of heights and prettiness of flowers are design features of our common nervous system, and if our species had evolved in a different ecosystem or if we were missing a few genes, our reactions could go the other way. Now, if the distinction between right and wrong is also a product of brain wiring, why should we believe it is any more real than the distinction between red and green? And if it is just a collective hallucination, how could we argue that evils like genocide and slavery are wrong for everyone, rather than just distasteful to us?

Putting God in charge of morality is one way to solve the problem, of course, but Plato[14] made short work of it 2,400 years ago. Does God have a good reason for designating certain acts as moral and others as immoral? If not—if his dictates are divine whims—why should we take them seriously? Suppose that God commanded us to torture a child. Would that make it all right, or would some other standard give us reasons to resist? And if, on the other hand, God was forced by moral reasons to issue some dictates and not others—if a command to torture a child was never an option—then why not appeal to those reasons directly?

This throws us back to wondering where those reasons could come from, if they are more than just figments of our brains. They certainly aren't in the physical world like wavelength or mass. The only other option is that moral truths exist in some abstract Platonic realm, there for us to discover, perhaps in the same way that mathematical truths (according to most mathematicians) are there for us to discover. On this analogy, we are born with a rudimentary concept of number, but as soon as we build on it with formal mathematical reasoning, the nature of mathematical reality forces us to discover some truths and not others. (No one who understands the concept of two, the concept of four and the concept of addition can come to any conclusion but that 2+2=4.) Perhaps we are born with a rudimentary moral sense, and as soon as we build on it with moral reasoning, the nature of moral reality forces us to some conclusions but not others.

Moral realism, as this idea is called, is too rich for many philosophers' blood. Yet a diluted version of the idea—if not a list of cosmically inscribed Thou-Shalts, then at least a few If-Thens—is not crazy. Two features of reality point any rational, self-preserving social agent in a moral direction. And they could provide a benchmark for determining when the judgments of our moral sense are aligned with morality itself.

One is the prevalence of nonzero-sum games. In many arenas of life, two parties are objectively better off if they both act in a nonselfish way than if each of them acts selfishly. You and I are both better off if we share our surpluses, rescue each other's children in danger and refrain from shooting at each other, compared with hoarding our surpluses while they rot, letting the other's child drown while we file our nails or feuding like the Hatfields and McCoys. Granted,

14. Greek philosopher (428/427 B.C.E.–348/347 B.C.E.) who discusses this question in his dialogue *Euthyphro*; in it Socrates asks Euthyphro: "Is the pious loved by the gods because it is pious, or is it pious because it is loved by the gods?"

I might be a bit better off if I acted selfishly at your expense and you played the sucker, but the same is true for you with me, so if each of us tried for these advantages, we'd both end up worse off. Any neutral observer, and you and I if we could talk it over rationally, would have to conclude that the state we should aim for is the one in which we both are unselfish. These spreadsheet projections are not quirks of brain wiring, nor are they dictated by a supernatural power; they are in the nature of things.

55 The other external support for morality is a feature of rationality itself: that it cannot depend on the egocentric vantage point of the reasoned. If I appeal to you to do anything that affects me—to get off my foot, or tell me the time or not run me over with your car—then I can't do it in a way that privileges my interests over yours (say, retaining my right to run you over with my car) if I want you to take me seriously. Unless I am Galactic Overlord,[15] I have to state my case in a way that would force me to treat you in kind. I can't act as if my interests are special just because I'm me and you're not, any more than I can persuade you that the spot I am standing on is a special place in the universe just because I happen to be standing on it.

Not coincidentally, the core of this idea—the interchangeability of perspectives—keeps reappearing in history's best-thought-through moral philosophies, including the Golden Rule (itself discovered many times); Spinoza's Viewpoint of Eternity; the Social Contract of Hobbes, Rousseau and Locke; Kant's Categorical Imperative; and Rawls's Veil of Ignorance. It also underlies Peter Singer's theory of the Expanding Circle[16]—the optimistic proposal that our moral sense, though shaped by evolution to overvalue self, kin and clan, can propel us on a path of moral progress, as our reasoning forces us to generalize it to larger and larger circles of sentient beings.

Doing Better by Knowing Ourselves

Morality, then, is still something larger than our inherited moral sense, and the new science of the moral sense does not make moral reasoning and conviction obsolete. At the same time, its implications for our moral universe are profound.

At the very least, the science tells us that even when our adversaries' agenda is most baffling, they may not be amoral psychopaths but in the throes of a moral mind-set that appears to them to be every bit as mandatory and universal as ours does to us. Of course, some adversaries really are psycho-

15. Galactic Overlords appear in the *Star Wars* film epics produced by George Lucas from 1977 to 1995.

16. Pinker cites a historical list—Baruch Spinoza (1632–1677), Dutch Jewish philosopher; Thomas Hobbes (1588–1679), English philosopher; Jean-Jacques Rousseau (1712–1778), Swiss philosopher; John Locke (1632–1704), English philosopher; Immanuel Kant (1724–1804), German philosopher; John Rawls (1921–2002), American philosopher; Peter Singer (b. 1946), Australian philosopher who teaches at Princeton University—to show the persistence of this belief in Western philosophy.

paths, and others are so poisoned by a punitive moralization that they are beyond the pale of reason. (The actor Will Smith had many historians on his side when he recently speculated to the press that Hitler thought he was acting morally.)[17] But in any conflict in which a meeting of the minds is not completely hopeless, a recognition that the other guy is acting from moral rather than venal reasons can be a first patch of common ground. One side can acknowledge the other's concern for community or stability or fairness or dignity, even while arguing that some other value should trump it in that instance. With affirmative action, for example, the opponents can be seen as arguing from a sense of fairness, not racism, and the defenders can be seen as acting from a concern with community, not bureaucratic power. Liberals can ratify conservatives' concern with families while noting that gay marriage is perfectly consistent with that concern.

The science of the moral sense also alerts us to ways in which our psychological makeup can get in the way of our arriving at the most defensible moral conclusions. The moral sense, we are learning, is as vulnerable to illusions as the other senses. It is apt to confuse morality per se with purity, status and conformity. It tends to reframe practical problems as moral crusades and thus see their solution in punitive aggression. It imposes taboos that make certain ideas indiscussible. And it has the nasty habit of always putting the self on the side of the angels.

Though wise people have long reflected on how we can be blinded by our own sanctimony, our public discourse still fails to discount it appropriately. In the worst cases, the thoughtlessness of our brute intuitions can be celebrated as a virtue. In his influential essay "The Wisdom of Repugnance," Leon Kass, former chair of the President's Council on Bioethics, argued that we should disregard reason when it comes to cloning and other biomedical technologies and go with our gut: "We are repelled by the prospect of cloning human beings . . . because we intuit and feel, immediately and without argument, the violation of things that we rightfully hold dear. . . . In this age in which everything is held to be permissible so long as it is freely done . . . repugnance may be the only voice left that speaks up to defend the central core of our humanity. Shallow are the souls that have forgotten how to shudder."[18] 60

There are, of course, good reasons to regulate human cloning, but the shudder test is not one of them. People have shuddered at all kinds of morally irrelevant violations of purity in their culture: touching an untouchable, drinking from the same water fountain as a Negro, allowing Jewish blood to mix with Aryan blood, tolerating sodomy between consenting men. And if our ancestors'

17. Allegedly, Smith said to an interviewer from the Scottish *Daily Record* (December 23, 2007), "Even Hitler didn't wake up going, 'Let me do the most evil thing I can do today.' . . . think he woke up in the morning and using a twisted, backwards logic, he set out to do what he thought was 'good.'"

18. Leon R. Kass, "The Wisdom of Repugnance," *New Republic*, June 2, 1997.

repugnance had carried the day, we never would have had autopsies, vaccinations, blood transfusions, artificial insemination, organ transplants and in vitro fertilization, all of which were denounced as immoral when they were new.

There are many other issues for which we are too quick to hit the moralization button and look for villains rather than bug fixes. What should we do when a hospital patient is killed by a nurse who administers the wrong drug in a patient's intravenous line? Should we make it easier to sue the hospital for damages? Or should we redesign the IV fittings so that it's physically impossible to connect the wrong bottle to the line?

And nowhere is moralization more of a hazard than in our greatest global challenge. The threat of human-induced climate change has become the occasion for a moralistic revival meeting. In many discussions, the cause of climate change is overindulgence (too many S.U.V.'s) and defilement (sullying the atmosphere), and the solution is temperance (conservation) and expiation (buying carbon offset coupons). Yet the experts agree that these numbers don't add up: even if every last American became conscientious about his or her carbon emissions, the effects on climate change would be trifling, if for no other reason than that two billion Indians and Chinese are unlikely to copy our born-again abstemiousness. Though voluntary conservation may be one wedge in an effective carbon-reduction pie, the other wedges will have to be morally boring, like a carbon tax and new energy technologies, or even taboo, like nuclear power and deliberate manipulation of the ocean and atmosphere. Our habit of moralizing problems, merging them with intuitions of purity and contamination, and resting content when we feel the right feelings, can get in the way of doing the right thing.

Far from debunking morality, then, the science of the moral sense can advance it, by allowing us to see through the illusions that evolution and culture have saddled us with and to focus on goals we can share and defend. As Anton Chekhov wrote, "Man will become better when you show him what he is like."[19]

19. Anton Chekhov (1860–1904), Russian playwright and fiction writer, made this statement (in the Russian language) in one of his notebooks.

QUESTIONS

1. Pinker's essay, published for a general American readership, incorporates the work of scholars and scientists. What techniques does he use to create interest in the question of moral judgments for general readers?

2. Where does Pinker "translate" academic research into common language—and where doesn't he? Try to formulate the principle he uses for retaining philosophical language—or not.

3. Near the center of the essay is a section titled "A Universal Morality?" Does Pinker believe that morality is universal, or does he question this concept? How does the remainder of his essay clarify his position?

4. In the section "The Varieties of Moral Experience," Pinker lists five themes that recur in moral systems throughout the world. Choose another essay from this section, and analyze its ethical argument using these five themes.

5. Pinker's essay was published without footnotes, yet it clearly credits the work of many other philosophers and researchers. Choose one reference to another person's scholarly work, find the article on which it is based, and write a brief discussion of how Pinker paraphrases and/or cites the work. You might consider whether Pinker describes the work accurately or whether he oversimplifies or distorts it.

Jonathan Rauch

In Defense of Prejudice

THE WAR ON PREJUDICE is now, in all likelihood, the most uncontroversial social movement in America. Opposition to "hate speech," formerly identified with the liberal left, has become a bipartisan piety. In the past year, groups and factions that agree on nothing else have agreed that the public expression of any and all prejudices must be forbidden. On the left, protesters and editorialists have insisted that Francis L. Lawrence resign as president of Rutgers University for describing blacks as "a disadvantaged population that doesn't have that genetic, hereditary background to have a higher average." On the other side of the ideological divide, Ralph Reed, the executive director of the Christian Coalition, responded to criticism of the religious right by calling a press conference to denounce a supposed outbreak of "name-calling, scapegoating, and religious bigotry." Craig Rogers, an evangelical Christian student at California State University, recently filed a $2.5 million sexual-harassment suit against a lesbian professor of psychology, claiming that anti-male bias in one of her lectures violated campus rules and left him feeling "raped and trapped."

In universities and on Capitol Hill, in workplaces and newsrooms, authorities are declaring that there is no place for racism, sexism, homophobia, Christian-bashing, and other forms of prejudice in public debate or even in private thought. "Only when racism and other forms of prejudice are expunged," say the crusaders for sweetness and light, "can minorities be safe and society be fair." So sweet, this dream of a world without prejudice. But the very last thing society should do is seek to utterly eradicate racism and other forms of prejudice.

I suppose I should say, in the customary I-hope-I-don't-sound-too-defensive tone, that I am not a racist and that this is not an article favoring racism or any other particular prejudice. It is an article favoring intellectual pluralism, which permits the expression of various forms of bigotry and always will. Although we

Originally published in Harper's Magazine *(May 1995) with the subtitle "Why Incendiary Speech Must Be Protected." Articles in* Harper's *focus on current issues in politics, science, and the arts.*

like to hope that a time will come when no one will believe that people come in types and that each type belongs with its own kind, I doubt such a day will ever arrive. By all indications, *Homo sapiens* is a tribal species for whom "us versus them" comes naturally and must be continually pushed back. Where there is genuine freedom of expression, there will be racist expression. There will also be people who believe that homosexuals are sick or threaten children or—especially among teenagers—are rightful targets of manly savagery. Homosexuality will always be incomprehensible to most people, and what is incomprehensible is feared. As for anti-Semitism, it appears to be a hardier virus than influenza. If you want pluralism, then you get racism and sexism and homophobia, and communism and fascism and xenophobia and tribalism, and that is just for a start. If you want to believe in intellectual freedom and the progress of knowledge and the advancement of science and all those other good things, then you must swallow hard and accept this: for as thickheaded and wayward an animal as us, the realistic question is how to make the best of prejudice, not how to eradicate it.

Indeed, "eradicating prejudice" is so vague a proposition as to be meaningless. Distinguishing prejudice reliably and nonpolitically from nonprejudice, or even defining it crisply, is quite hopeless. We all feel we know prejudice when we see it. But do we? At the University of Michigan, a student said in a classroom discussion that he considered homosexuality a disease treatable with therapy. He was summoned to a formal disciplinary hearing for violating the school's policy against speech that "victimizes" people based on "sexual orientation." Now, the evidence is abundant that this particular hypothesis is wrong, and any American homosexual can attest to the harm that the student's hypothesis has inflicted on many real people. But was it a statement of prejudice or of misguided belief? Hate speech or hypothesis? Many Americans who do not regard themselves as bigots or haters believe that homosexuality is a treatable disease. They may be wrong, but are they all bigots? I am unwilling to say so, and if you are willing, beware. The line between a prejudiced belief and a merely controversial one is elusive, and the harder you look the more elusive it becomes. "God hates homosexuals" is a statement of fact, not of bias, to those who believe it; "American criminals are disproportionately black" is a statement of bias, not of fact, to those who disbelieve it.

5 Who is right? You may decide, and so may others, and there is no need to agree. That is the great innovation of intellectual pluralism (which is to say, of post-Enlightenment science, broadly defined). We cannot know in advance or for sure which belief is prejudice and which is truth, but to advance knowledge we don't need to know. The genius of intellectual pluralism lies not in doing away with prejudices and dogmas but in channeling them—making them socially productive by pitting prejudice against prejudice and dogma against dogma, exposing all to withering public criticism. What survives at the end of the day is our base of knowledge.

What they told us in high school about this process is very largely a lie. The Enlightenment tradition taught us that science is orderly, antiseptic, rational, the province of detached experimenters and high-minded logicians. In the popular view, science stands for reason against prejudice, openmindedness against dogma, calm consideration against passionate attachment—all personified by pop-science icons like the magisterially deductive Sherlock Holmes, the coolly analytic Mr. Spock, the genially authoritative Mr. Science (from our junior-high science films). Yet one of science's dirty secrets is that although science as a whole is as unbiased as anything human can be, scientists are just as biased as anyone else, sometimes more so. "One of the strengths of science," writes the philosopher of science David L. Hull, "is that it does not require that scientists be unbiased, only that different scientists have different biases." Another dirty secret is that, no less than the rest of us, scientists can be dogmatic and pigheaded. "Although this pigheadedness often damages the careers of individual scientists," says Hull, "it is beneficial for the manifest goal of science," which relies on people to invest years in their ideas and defend them passionately. And the dirtiest secret of all, if you believe in the antiseptic popular view of science, is that this most ostensibly rational of enterprises depends on the most irrational of motives—ambition, narcissism, animus, even revenge. "Scientists acknowledge that among their motivations are natural curiosity, the love of truth, and the desire to help humanity, but other inducements exist as well, and one of them is to 'get that son of a bitch,'" says Hull. "Time and again, scientists whom I interviewed described the powerful spur that 'showing that son of a bitch' supplied to their own research."

Many people, I think, are bewildered by this unvarnished and all too human view of science. They believe that for a system to be unprejudiced, the people in it must also be unprejudiced. In fact, the opposite is true. Far from eradicating ugly or stupid ideas and coarse or unpleasant motives, intellectual pluralism relies upon them to excite intellectual passion and redouble scientific effort. I know of no modern idea more ugly and stupid than that the Holocaust never happened, nor any idea more viciously motivated. Yet the deniers' claims that the Auschwitz gas chambers could not have worked led to closer study and, in 1993, research showing, at last, how they actually did work. Thanks to prejudice and stupidity, another opening for doubt has been shut.

An enlightened and efficient intellectual regime lets a million prejudices bloom, including many that you or I may regard as hateful or grotesque. It avoids any attempt to stamp out prejudice, because stamping out prejudice really means forcing everyone to share the same prejudice, namely that of whoever is in authority. The great American philosopher Charles Sanders Peirce wrote in 1877: "When complete agreement could not otherwise be reached, a general massacre of all who have not thought in a certain way has proved a very effective means of settling opinion in a country." In speaking of "settling opinion," Peirce was writing about one of the two or three most fundamental problems that any human society must confront and solve. For most societies down through the centuries, this problem was dealt with in the manner he described: errors were identified by the authorities—priests, politburos, dictators—or by mass opinion, and then the error-makers were eliminated along with their putative mistakes. "Let all men who reject the established belief be terrified into silence," wrote Peirce, describing this system. "This method has, from the earliest times, been one of the chief means of upholding correct theological and political doctrines."

Intellectual pluralism substitutes a radically different doctrine: we kill our mistakes rather than each other. Here I draw on another great philosopher, the late Karl Popper, who pointed out that the critical method of science "consists in letting our hypotheses die in our stead." Those who are in error are not (or are not supposed to be) banished or excommunicated or forced to sign a renunciation or required to submit to "rehabilitation" or sent for psychological counseling. It is the error we punish, not the errant. By letting people make errors—even mischievous, spiteful errors (as, for instance, Galileo's insistence on Copernicanism was taken to be in 1633)—pluralism creates room to challenge orthodoxy, think imaginatively, experiment boldly. Brilliance and bigotry are empowered in the same stroke.

10 Pluralism is the principle that protects and makes a place in human company for that loneliest and most vulnerable of all minorities, the minority who is hounded and despised among blacks and whites, gays and straights, who is suspect or criminal among every tribe and in every nation of the world, and yet on whom progress depends: the dissident. I am not saying that dissent is always or even usually enlightened. Most of the time it is foolish and self-serving. No dissident has the right to be taken seriously, and the fact that Aryan Nation[1] racists or Nation of Islam[2] anti-Semites are unorthodox does not entitle them to respect. But what goes around comes around. As a supporter of gay marriage, for example, I reject the majority's view of family, and as a Jew I reject its view of God. I try to be civil, but the fact is that most Americans regard my views on marriage as a reckless assault on the most fundamental of all institutions, and many people are more than a little discomfited by the statement, "Jesus Christ was no more divine than anybody else" (which is why so few people ever say it). Trap the racists and anti-Semites, and you lay a trap for me too. Hunt for them with eradication in your mind, and you have brought dissent itself within your sights.

The new crusade against prejudice waves aside such warnings. Like earlier crusades against antisocial ideas, the mission is fueled by good (if cocksure) intentions and a genuine sense of urgency. Some kinds of error are held to be intolerable, like pollutants that even in small traces poison the water for a whole town. Some errors are so pernicious as to damage real people's lives, so wrongheaded that no person of right mind or goodwill could support them. Like their forebears of other stripe—the Church in its campaigns against heretics, the McCarthyites in their campaigns against Communists[3]—the modern anti-racist

1. A white separatist religious group in the United States.

2. An African American religious organization in the United States that combines some of the practices and beliefs of Islam with a philosophy of black separatism.

3. In the early 1950s, Senator Joseph McCarthy pursued suspected Communists in the government and throughout the nation. Although his "Fight for America" did not result in a single conviction, he and his followers ruined the lives and careers of many they investigated. McCarthy was later condemned for "conduct contrary to Senatorial traditions."

and anti-sexist and anti-homophobic campaigners are totalists, demanding not that misguided ideas and ugly expressions be corrected or criticized but that they be eradicated. They make war not on errors but on error, and like other totalists they act in the name of public safety—the safety, especially, of minorities.

The sweeping implications of this challenge to pluralism are not, I think, well enough understood by the public at large. Indeed, the new brand of totalism has yet even to be properly named. "Multiculturalism," for instance, is much too broad. "Political correctness" comes closer but is too trendy and snide. For lack of anything else, I will call the new anti-pluralism "purism," since its major tenet is that society cannot be just until the last traces of invidious prejudice have been scrubbed away. Whatever you call it, the purists' way of seeing things has spread through American intellectual life with remarkable speed, so much so that many people will blink at you uncomprehendingly or even call you a racist (or sexist or homophobe, etc.) if you suggest that expressions of racism should be tolerated or that prejudice has its part to play.

The new purism sets out, to begin with, on a campaign against words, for words are the currency of prejudice, and if prejudice is hurtful then so must be prejudiced words. "We are not safe when these violent words are among us," wrote Mari Matsuda, then a UCLA law professor. Here one imagines gangs of racist words swinging chains and smashing heads in back alleys. To suppress bigoted language seems, at first blush, reasonable, but it quickly leads to a curious result. A peculiar kind of verbal shamanism takes root, as though certain expressions, like curses or magical incantations, carry in themselves the power to hurt or heal—as though words were bigoted rather than people. "Context is everything," people have always said. The use of the word "nigger" in *Huckleberry Finn*[4] does not make the book an "act" of hate speech—or does it? In the new view, this is no longer so clear. The very utterance of the word "nigger" (at least by a non-black) is a racist act. When a *Sacramento Bee* cartoonist put the word "nigger" mockingly in the mouth of a white supremacist, there were howls of protest and 1,400 canceled subscriptions and an editorial apology, even though the word was plainly being invoked against racists, not against blacks.

Faced with escalating demands of verbal absolutism, newspapers issue lists of forbidden words. The expressions "gyp" (derived from "Gypsy") and "Dutch treat" were among the dozens of terms stricken as "offensive" in a much-ridiculed (and later withdrawn) *Los Angeles Times* speech code. The University of Missouri journalism school issued a *Dictionary of Cautionary Words and Phrases*, which included "*Buxom*: Offensive reference to a woman's chest. Do not use. See 'Woman.' *Codger*: Offensive reference to a senior citizen."

15 As was bound to happen, purists soon discovered that chasing around after words like "gyp" or "buxom" hardly goes to the roots of the problem. As long as they remain bigoted, bigots will simply find other words. If they can't call you a kike then they will say Jewboy, Judas, or Hebe, and when all those are banned they will press words like "oven" and "lampshade" into their service.

4. Mark Twain's 1889 novel includes coarse language, some of it now called racist.

The vocabulary of hate is potentially as rich as your dictionary, and all you do by banning language used by cretins is to let them decide what the rest of us may say. The problem, some purists have concluded, must therefore go much deeper than laws: it must go to the deeper level of ideas. Racism, sexism, homophobia, and the rest must be built into the very structure of American society and American patterns of thought, so pervasive yet so insidious that, like water to a fish, they are both omnipresent and unseen. The mere existence of prejudice constructs a society whose very nature is prejudiced.

This line of thinking was pioneered by feminists, who argued that pornography, more than just being expressive, is an act by which men construct an oppressive society. Racial activists quickly picked up the argument. Racist expressions are themselves acts of oppression, they said. "All racist speech constructs the social reality that constrains the liberty of nonwhites because of their race," wrote Charles R. Lawrence III, then a law professor at Stanford. From the purist point of view, a society with even one racist is a racist society, because the idea itself threatens and demeans its targets. They cannot feel wholly safe or wholly welcome as long as racism is present. Pluralism says: There will always be some racists. Marginalize them, ignore them, exploit them, ridicule them, take pains to make their policies illegal, but otherwise leave them alone. Purists say: That's not enough. Society cannot be just until these pervasive and oppressive ideas are searched out and eradicated.

And so what is now under way is a growing drive to eliminate prejudice from every corner of society. I doubt that many people have noticed how far-reaching this anti-pluralist movement is becoming.

In universities: Dozens of universities have adopted codes proscribing speech or other expression that (this is from Stanford's policy, which is more or less representative) "is intended to insult or stigmatize an individual or a small number of individuals on the basis of their sex, race, color, handicap, religion, sexual orientation or national and ethnic origin." Some codes punish only persistent harassment of a targeted individual, but many, following the purist doctrine that even one racist is too many, go much further. At Penn, an administrator declared: "We at the University of Pennsylvania have guaranteed students and the community that they can live in a community free of sexism, racism, and homophobia." Here is the purism that gives "political correctness" its distinctive combination of puffy high-mindedness and authoritarian zeal.

In school curricula: "More fundamental than eliminating racial segregation has to be the removal of racist thinking, assumptions, symbols, and materials in the curriculum," writes theorist Molefi Kete Asante. In practice, the effort to "remove racist thinking" goes well beyond striking egregious references from textbooks. In many cases it becomes a kind of mental engineering in which students are encouraged to see prejudice.

20 Ah, but the task of scouring minds clean is Augean.[5] "Nobody escapes," said a Rutgers University report on campus prejudice. Bias and prejudice, it

5. In Greek mythology, Heracles was assigned twelve difficult and dangerous tasks, referred to as the Labors of Heracles. One task required cleaning the enormous stables

found, cross every conceivable line, from sex to race to politics: "No matter who you are, no matter what the color of your skin, no matter what your gender or sexual orientation, no matter what you believe, no matter how you behave, there is somebody out there who doesn't like people of your kind." Charles Lawrence writes: "Racism is ubiquitous. We are all racists." If he means that most of us think racist thoughts of some sort at one time or another, he is right. If we are going to "eliminate prejudices and biases from our society," then the work of the prejudice police is unending. They are doomed to hunt and hunt, scour and scour and scour.

What is especially dismaying is that the purists pursue prejudice in the name of protecting minorities. In order to protect people like me (homosexual), they must pursue people like me (dissident). In order to bolster minority self-esteem, they suppress minority opinion. There are, of course, all kinds of practical and legal problems with the purists' campaign: the incursions against the First Amendment; the inevitable abuses by prosecutors and activists who define as "hateful" or "violent" whatever speech they dislike or can score points off of; the lack of any evidence that repressing prejudice eliminates rather than inflames it. But minorities, of all people, ought to remember that by definition we cannot prevail by numbers, and we generally cannot prevail by force. Against the power of ignorant mass opinion and group prejudice and superstition, we have only our voices. If you doubt that minorities' voices are powerful weapons, think of the lengths to which Southern officials went to silence the Reverend Martin Luther King Jr. (recall that the city commissioner of Montgomery, Alabama, won a $500,000 libel suit, later overturned in *New York Times v. Sullivan* [1964], regarding an advertisement in the *Times* placed by civil-rights leaders who denounced the Montgomery police). Think of how much gay people have improved their lot over twenty-five years simply by refusing to remain silent. Recall the Michigan student who was prosecuted for saying that homosexuality is a treatable disease, and notice that he was black. Under that Michigan speech code, more than twenty blacks were charged with racist speech, while no instance of racist speech by whites was punished. In Florida, the hate-speech law was invoked against a black man who called a policeman a "white cracker"; not so surprisingly, in the first hate-crimes case to reach the Supreme Court, the victim was white and the defendant black.

In the escalating war against "prejudice," the right is already learning to play by the rules that were pioneered by the purist activists of the left. Last year leading Democrats, including the President, criticized the Republican Party for being increasingly in the thrall of the Christian right. Some of the rhetoric was harsh ("fire-breathing Christian radical right"), but it wasn't vicious or even clearly wrong. Never mind: when Democratic Representative Vic Fazio said Republicans were "being forced to the fringes by the aggressive political tactics of the religious right," the chairman of the Republican National Committee,

---

of Augeas, king of Elis, which Heracles did by diverting the rivers Alpheus and Peneus so that they flowed through the stables and swept them clean.

Haley Barbour, said, "Christian-bashing" was "the left's preferred form of religious bigotry." Bigotry! Prejudice! "Christians active in politics are now on the receiving end of an extraordinary campaign of bias and prejudice," said the conservative leader William J. Bennett. One discerns, here, where the new purism leads. Eventually, any criticism of any group will be "prejudice."

Here is the ultimate irony of the new purism: words, which pluralists hope can be substituted for violence, are redefined by purists *as* violence. "The experience of being called 'nigger,' 'spic,' 'Jap,' or 'kike' is like receiving a slap in the face," Charles Lawrence wrote in 1990. "Psychic injury is no less an injury than being struck in the face, and it often is far more severe." This kind of talk is commonplace today. Epithets, insults, often even polite expressions of what's taken to be prejudice are called by purists "assaultive speech," "words that wound," "verbal violence." "To me, racial epithets are not speech," one University of Michigan law professor said. "They are bullets." In her speech accepting the 1993 Nobel Prize for Literature in Stockholm, Sweden, the author Toni Morrison[6] said this: "Oppressive language does more than represent violence; it is violence."

It is not violence. I am thinking back to a moment on the subway in Washington, a little thing. I was riding home late one night and a squad of noisy kids, maybe seventeen or eighteen years old, noisily piled into the car. They yelled across the car and a girl said, "Where do we get off?"

25 A boy said, "Farragut North."

The girl: "*Faggot* North!"

The boy: "Yeah! Faggot North!"

General hilarity.

First, before the intellect resumes control, there is a moment of fear, an animal moment. Who are they? How many of them? How dangerous! Where is the way out? All of these things are noted preverbally and assessed by the gut. Then the brain begins an assessment: they are sober, this is probably too public a place for them to do it, there are more girls than boys, they were just talking, it is probably nothing.

30 They didn't notice me and there was no incident. The teenage babble flowed on, leaving me to think. I became interested in my own reaction: the jump of fear out of nowhere like an alert animal, the sense for a brief time that one is naked and alone and should hide or run away. For a time, one ceases to be a human being and becomes instead a faggot.

The fear engendered by these words is real. The remedy is as clear and as imperfect as ever: protect citizens against violence. This, I grant, is something that American society has never done very well and now does quite poorly. It is no solution to define words as violence or prejudice as oppression, and then by cracking down on words or thoughts pretend that we are doing something about violence and oppression. No doubt it is easier to pass a speech code or hate-crimes law and proclaim the streets safer than actually to make the streets

6. African American author (b. 1931).

safer, but the one must never be confused with the other. Every cop or prosecutor chasing words is one fewer chasing criminals. In a world rife with real violence and oppression, full of Rwandas and Bosnias and eleven-year-olds spraying bullets at children in Chicago and in turn being executed by gang lords, it is odious of Toni Morrison to say that words are violence.

Indeed, equating "verbal violence" with physical violence is a treacherous, mischievous business. Not long ago a writer was charged with viciously and gratuitously wounding the feelings and dignity of millions of people. He was charged, in effect, with exhibiting flagrant prejudice against Muslims and outrageously slandering their beliefs. "What is freedom of expression?" mused Salman Rushdie[7] a year after the ayatollahs sentenced him to death and put a price on his head. "Without the freedom to offend, it ceases to exist." I can think of nothing sadder than that minority activists, in their haste to make the world better, should be the ones to forget the lesson of Rushdie's plight: for minorities, pluralism, not purism, is the answer. The campaigns to eradicate prejudice—all of them, the speech codes and workplace restrictions and mandatory therapy for accused bigots and all the rest—should stop, now. The whole objective of eradicating prejudice, as opposed to correcting and criticizing it, should be repudiated as a fool's errand. Salman Rushdie is right, Toni Morrison wrong, and minorities belong at his side, not hers.

7. British novelist of Indian descent (b. 1947). Muslims condemned Rushdie's novel *The Satanic Verses* (1988) as an attack on the Islamic faith; in 1989, Iran's Ayatollah Khomeini declared that Rushdie and everyone involved in the book's publication should be put to death; the death sentence was lifted in 1998.

Questions

1. Rauch advances a controversial argument: that we should allow prejudice to be expressed rather than seek to repress or eradicate it. How, in the opening paragraphs, does he establish himself as a reasonable, even likable person whose views should be heard? Where else in the essay does he create this persona? Why is persona (or *ethos*) important in ethical argument?

2. What does Rauch mean by "intellectual pluralism" (paragraph 3)? Where does he come closest to giving a definition? How does he use examples to imply a definition?

3. In the third section of the essay (paragraphs 12–20), Rauch defines the position antithetical to his own as "purism." Why does he choose this term rather than another? What does it mean?

4. What are some counterarguments to Rauch's position? How many of these arguments does Rauch himself raise and refute? How effective is he at refuting them?

5. Rauch ends with quotations from Toni Morrison and Salman Rushdie. Why? What do their experiences as writers add to his argument?

Peter Singer

What Should a Billionaire Give—and What Should You?

What is a human life worth? You may not want to put a price tag on it. But if we really had to, most of us would agree that the value of a human life would be in the millions. Consistent with the foundations of our democracy and our frequently professed belief in the inherent dignity of human beings, we would also agree that all humans are created equal, at least to the extent of denying that differences of sex, ethnicity, nationality, and place of residence change the value of a human life.

With Christmas approaching, and Americans writing checks to their favorite charities, it's a good time to ask how these two beliefs—that a human life, if it can be priced at all, is worth millions, and that the factors I have mentioned do not alter the value of a human life—square with our actions. Perhaps this year such questions lurk beneath the surface of more family discussions than usual, for it has been an extraordinary year for philanthropy, especially philanthropy to fight global poverty.

For Bill Gates,[1] the founder of Microsoft, the ideal of valuing all human life equally began to jar against reality some years ago, when he read an article about diseases in the developing world and came across the statistic that half a million children die every year from rotavirus, the most common cause of severe diarrhea in children. He had never heard of rotavirus. "How could I never have heard of something that kills half a million children every year?" he asked himself. He then learned that in developing countries, millions of children die from diseases that have been eliminated, or virtually eliminated, in the United States. That shocked him because he assumed that, if there are vaccines and treatments that could save lives, governments would be doing everything possible to get them to the people who need them. As Gates told a meeting of the World Health Assembly in Geneva last year, he and his wife, Melinda, "couldn't escape the brutal conclusion that—in our world today—some lives are seen as worth saving and others are not." They said to themselves, "This can't be true." But they knew it was.

Gates's speech to the World Health Assembly concluded on an optimistic note, looking forward to the next decade when "people will finally accept that the death of a child in the developing world is just as tragic as the death of a

Originally published in the New York Times Magazine, *a Sunday supplement of the daily newspaper; later included in* Best American Essays *(2007), edited by David Foster Wallace.*

1. William Gates (b. 1955) began the William H. Gates Foundation in 1994; it was renamed and expanded in 1999 as the Bill and Melissa Gates Foundation; its guiding principles, which can be read at gatesfoundation.org, include this: "We demand ethical behavior of ourselves."

child in the developed world." That belief in the equal value of all human life is also prominent on the website of the Bill and Melinda Gates Foundation, where under "Our Values" we read: "All lives—no matter where they are being led—have equal value."

We are very far from acting in accordance with that belief. In the same world in which more than a billion people live at a level of affluence never previously known, roughly a billion other people struggle to survive on the purchasing power equivalent of less than one U.S. dollar per day. Most of the world's poorest people are undernourished, lack access to safe drinking water or even the most basic health services, and cannot send their children to school. According to UNICEF,[2] more than 10 million children die every year—about 30,000 per day—from avoidable, poverty-related causes. 5

Last June the investor Warren Buffett[3] took a significant step toward reducing those deaths when he pledged $31 billion to the Gates Foundation and another $6 billion to other charitable foundations. Buffett's pledge, set alongside the nearly $30 billion given by Bill and Melinda Gates to their foundation, has made it clear that the first decade of the twenty-first century is a new "golden age of philanthropy." On an inflation-adjusted basis, Buffett has pledged to give more than double the lifetime total given away by two of the philanthropic giants of the past, Andrew Carnegie and John D. Rockefeller,[4] put together. Bill and Melinda Gates's gifts are not far behind.

Gates's and Buffett's donations will now be put to work primarily to reduce poverty, disease, and premature death in the developing world. According to the Global Forum for Health Research, less than 10 percent of the world's health research budget is spent on combating conditions that account for 90 percent of the global burden of disease. In the past, diseases that affect only the poor have been of no commercial interest to pharmaceutical manufacturers, because the poor cannot afford to buy their products. The Global Alliance for Vaccines and Immunization (GAVI), heavily supported by the Gates Foundation, seeks to change this by guaranteeing to purchase millions of doses of vaccines, when they are developed, that can prevent diseases like malaria. GAVI has also assisted developing countries to immunize more people with existing vaccines: 99 million additional children have been reached to date. By doing this, GAVI claims to have already averted nearly 1.7 million future deaths.

2. Acronym for United Nations International Children's Emergency Fund (now United Nations Children's Fund).

3. American industrialist and investor-genius (b. 1930) said to be the third wealthiest person in the world.

4. Andrew Carnegie (1835–1919), millionaire owner of Carnegie Steel Company, argued in "The Gospel of Wealth" that the life of a wealthy person has two parts: accumulating wealth and then distributing this wealth to benevolent causes; after his retirement from business, Carnegie devoted his final two decades to philanthropy. John D. Rockefeller (1839–1937), American oil magnate, spent the last forty years of his life using his fortune to aid good causes and developed a systematic approach to philanthropy, creating foundations that focused on medicine, education, and scientific research.

Philanthropy on this scale raises many ethical questions: Why are the people who are giving doing so? Does it do any good? Should we praise them for giving so much or criticize them for not giving still more? Is it troubling that such momentous decisions are made by a few extremely wealthy individuals? And how do our judgments about them reflect on our own way of living?

Let's start with the question of motives. The rich must—or so some of us with less money like to assume—suffer sleepless nights because of their ruthlessness in squeezing out competitors, firing workers, shutting down plants, or whatever else they have to do to acquire their wealth. When wealthy people give away money, we can always say that they are doing it to ease their consciences or generate favorable publicity. It has been suggested—by, for example, David Kirkpatrick, a senior editor at *Fortune* magazine—that Bill Gates's turn to philanthropy was linked to the antitrust problems Microsoft had in the United States and the European Union. Was Gates, consciously or subconsciously, trying to improve his own image and that of his company?

10 This kind of sniping tells us more about the attackers than the attacked. Giving away large sums, rather than spending the money on corporate advertising or developing new products, is not a sensible strategy for increasing personal wealth. When we read that someone has given away a lot of their money, or time, to help others, it challenges us to think about our own behavior. Should we be following their example, in our own modest way? But if the rich just give their money away to improve their image, or to make up for past misdeeds—misdeeds quite unlike any we have committed, of course—then, conveniently, what they are doing has no relevance to what we ought to do.

A famous story is told about Thomas Hobbes, the seventeenth-century English philosopher, who argued that we all act in our own interests. On seeing him give alms to a beggar, a cleric asked Hobbes if he would have done this if Christ had not commanded us to do so. Yes, Hobbes replied, he was in pain to see the miserable condition of the old man, and his gift, by providing the man with some relief from that misery, also eased Hobbes's pain. That reply reconciles Hobbes's charity with his egoistic theory of human motivation, but at the cost of emptying egoism of much of its bite. If egoists suffer when they see a stranger in distress, they are capable of being as charitable as any altruist.

Followers of the eighteenth-century German philosopher Immanuel Kant would disagree. They think an act has moral worth only if it is done out of a sense of duty. Doing something merely because you enjoy doing it, or enjoy seeing its consequences, they say, has no moral worth, because if you happened not to enjoy doing it, then you wouldn't do it, and you are not responsible for your likes and dislikes, whereas you are responsible for your obedience to the demands of duty.

Perhaps some philanthropists are motivated by their sense of duty. Apart from the equal value of all human life, the other "simple value" that lies at the core of the work of the Gates Foundation, according to its website, is "To whom much has been given, much is expected." That suggests the view that those who have great wealth have a duty to use it for a larger purpose than their own interests. But while such questions of motive may be relevant to our assessment of Gates's or Buffett's character, they pale into insignificance when we consider the effect of what Gates and Buffett are doing. The parents whose children could die from rotavirus care more about getting the help that will save their children's lives than about the motivations of those who make that possible.

Interestingly, neither Gates nor Buffett seems motivated by the possibility of being rewarded in heaven for his good deeds on earth. Gates told a *Time* interviewer, "There's a lot more I could be doing on a Sunday morning" than going to church. Put them together with Andrew Carnegie, famous for his freethinking, and three of the four greatest American philanthropists have been atheists or agnostics. (The exception is John D. Rockefeller.) In a country in which 96 percent of the population say they believe in a supreme being, that's a striking fact. It means that in one sense, Gates and Buffett are probably less self-interested in their charity than someone like Mother Teresa,[5] who as a pious Roman Catholic believed in reward and punishment in the afterlife.

More important than questions about motives are questions about whether there is an obligation for the rich to give, and if so, how much they should give. A few years ago, an African-American cabdriver taking me to the Inter-American Development Bank in Washington asked me if I worked at the bank. I told him I did not but was speaking at a conference on development and aid. He then assumed that I was an economist, but when I said no, my training was in philosophy, he asked me if I thought the United States should give foreign aid. When I answered affirmatively, he replied that the government shouldn't tax people in order to give their money to others. That, he thought, was robbery. When I asked if he believed that the rich should voluntarily donate some of what they earn to the poor, he said that if someone had worked for his money, he wasn't going to tell him what to do with it. 15

At that point we reached our destination. Had the journey continued, I might have tried to persuade him that people can earn large amounts only when they live under favorable social circumstances, and that they don't create those circumstances by themselves. I could have quoted Warren Buffett's acknowledgment that society is responsible for much of his wealth. "If you stick me down in the middle of Bangladesh or Peru," he said, "you'll find out how much this talent is going to produce in the wrong kind of soil." The Nobel Prize–winning economist and social scientist Herbert Simon[6] estimated that "social capital" is

5. Agnes Gonxha Bojaxhiu (1910–1997), known as Mother Teresa, founded the Missionaries of Charity in Kolkata, India, at the age of forty and devoted the rest of her life to caring for the poor, orphaned, sick, and dying.

6. Throughout his professional career Herbert Simon (1916–2001) advocated a basic income guarantee; in a 2001 *Boston Review* article, "UBI (Universal Basic Income) and the Flat Tax," he argued that a 70 percent flat income tax could support all government spending with enough left to supply an $8,000 basic income for every adult and every child in the United States.

responsible for at least 90 percent of what people earn in wealthy societies like those of the United States or northwestern Europe. By social capital Simon meant not only natural resources but, more important, the technology and organizational skills in the community, and the presence of good government. These are the foundation on which the rich can begin their work. "On moral grounds," Simon added, "we could argue for a flat income tax of 90 percent." Simon was not, of course, advocating so steep a rate of tax, for he was well aware of disincentive effects. But his estimate does undermine the argument that the rich are entitled to keep their wealth because it is all a result of their hard work. If Simon is right, that is true of at most 10 percent of it.

In any case, even if we were to grant that people deserve every dollar they earn, that doesn't answer the question of what they should do with it. We might say that they have a right to spend it on lavish parties, private jets, and luxury yachts, or, for that matter, to flush it down the toilet. But we could still think that for them to do these things while others die from easily preventable diseases is wrong. In an article I wrote more than three decades ago, at the time of a humanitarian emergency in what is now Bangladesh, I used the example of walking by a shallow pond and seeing a small child who has fallen in and appears to be in danger of drowning. Even though we did nothing to cause the child to fall into the pond, almost everyone agrees that if we can save the child at minimal inconvenience or trouble to ourselves, we ought to do so. Anything else would be callous, indecent, and, in a word, wrong. The fact that in rescuing the child we may, for example, ruin a new pair of shoes is not a good reason for allowing the child to drown. Similarly if for the cost of a pair of shoes we can contribute to a health program in a developing country that stands a good chance of saving the life of a child, we ought to do so.

Perhaps, though, our obligation to help the poor is even stronger than this example implies, for we are less innocent than the passerby who did nothing to cause the child to fall into the pond. Thomas Pogge, a philosopher at Columbia University, has argued that at least some of our affluence comes at the expense of the poor. He bases this claim not simply on the usual critique of the barriers that Europe and the United States maintain against agricultural imports from developing countries but also on less familiar aspects of our trade with developing countries. For example, he points out that international corporations are willing to make deals to buy natural resources from any government, no matter how it has come to power. This provides a huge financial incentive for groups to try to overthrow the existing government. Successful rebels are rewarded by being able to sell off the nation's oil, minerals, or timber.

In their dealings with corrupt dictators in developing countries, Pogge asserts, international corporations are morally no better than someone who knowingly buys stolen goods—with the difference that the international legal and political order recognizes the corporations, not as criminals in possession of stolen goods but as the legal owners of the goods they have bought. This situation is, of course, beneficial for the industrial nations, because it enables us to obtain the raw materials we need to maintain our prosperity, but it is a disaster for resource-rich developing countries, turning the wealth that should benefit them into a curse that leads to a cycle of coups, civil wars, and corruption, and is of little benefit to the people as a whole.

20 In this light, our obligation to the poor is not just one of providing assistance to strangers but one of compensation for harms that we have caused and are still causing them. It might be argued that we do not owe the poor compensation, because our affluence actually benefits them. Living luxuriously, it is said, provides employment, and so wealth trickles down, helping the poor more effectively than aid does. But the rich in industrialized nations buy virtually nothing that is made by the very poor. During the past twenty years of economic globalization, although expanding trade has helped lift many of the world's poor out of poverty, it has failed to benefit the poorest 10 percent of the world's population. Some of the extremely poor, most of whom live in sub-Saharan Africa, have nothing to sell that rich people want, while others lack the infrastructure to get their goods to market. If they can get their crops to a port, European and U.S. subsidies often mean that they cannot sell them, despite—as for example in the case of West African cotton growers who compete with vastly larger and richer U.S. cotton producers—having a lower production cost than the subsidized producers in the rich nations.

The remedy to these problems, it might reasonably be suggested, should come from the state, not from private philanthropy. When aid comes through the government, everyone who earns above the tax-free threshold contributes something, with more collected from those with greater ability to pay. Much as we may applaud what Gates and Buffett are doing, we can also be troubled by a system that leaves the fate of hundreds of millions of people hanging on the decisions of two or three private citizens. But the amount of foreign development aid given by the U.S. government is, at 22 cents for every $100 the nation earns, about the same, as a percentage of gross national income, as Portugal gives and about half that of the United Kingdom. Worse still, much of it is directed where it best suits U.S. strategic interests—Iraq is now by far the largest recipient of U.S. development aid, and Egypt, Jordan, Pakistan, and Afghanistan all rank in the top ten. Less than a quarter of official U.S. development aid—barely a nickel in every $100 of our GNI[7]—goes to the world's poorest nations.

Adding private philanthropy to U.S. government aid improves this picture, because Americans privately give more per capita to international philanthropic causes than the citizens of almost any other nation. Even when private donations are included, however, countries like Norway, Denmark, Sweden, and the Netherlands give three or four times as much foreign aid, in proportion to the size of their economies, as the United States gives—with a much larger percentage going to the poorest nations. At least as things now stand, the case for philanthropic efforts to relieve global poverty is not susceptible to the argument that the government has taken care of the problem. And even if official U.S. aid were better directed and comparable, relative to our gross domestic product, with that of the most generous nations, there would still be a role for private

7. Gross national income.

philanthropy. Unconstrained by diplomatic considerations or the desire to swing votes at the United Nations, private donors can more easily avoid dealing with corrupt or wasteful governments. They can go directly into the field, working with local villages and grass-roots organizations.

Nor are philanthropists beholden to lobbyists. As the *New York Times* reported recently, billions of dollars of U.S. aid is tied to domestic goods. Wheat for Africa must be grown in America, although aid experts say this often depresses local African markets, reducing the incentive for farmers there to produce more. In a decision that surely costs lives, hundreds of millions of condoms intended to stop the spread of AIDS in Africa and around the world must be manufactured in the United States, although they cost twice as much as similar products made in Asia.

In other ways, too, private philanthropists are free to venture where governments fear to tread. Through a foundation named for his wife, Susan Thompson Buffett, Warren Buffett has supported reproductive rights, including family planning and prochoice organizations. In another unusual initiative, he has pledged $50 million for the International Atomic Energy Agency's plan to establish a "fuel bank" to supply nuclear-reactor fuel to countries that meet their nuclear-nonproliferation commitments. The idea, which has been talked about for many years, is widely agreed to be a useful step toward discouraging countries from building their own facilities for producing nuclear fuel, which could then be diverted to weapons production. It is, Buffett said, "an investment in a safer world." Though it is something that governments could and should be doing, no government had taken the first step.

25 Aid has always had its critics. Carefully planned and intelligently directed private philanthropy may be the best answer to the claim that aid doesn't work. Of course, as in any large-scale human enterprise, some aid can be ineffective. But provided that aid isn't actually counterproductive, even relatively inefficient assistance is likely to do more to advance human well-being than luxury spending by the wealthy.

The rich, then, should give. But how much should they give? Gates may have given away nearly $30 billion, but that still leaves him sitting at the top of the Forbes list of the richest Americans, with $53 billion. His 66,000-square-foot high-tech lakeside estate near Seattle is reportedly worth more than $100 million. Property taxes are about $1 million. Among his possessions is the Leicester Codex, the only handwritten book by Leonardo da Vinci still in private hands, for which he paid $30.8 million in 1994. Has Bill Gates done enough? More pointedly, you might ask: If he really believes that all lives have equal value, what is he doing living in such an expensive house and owning a Leonardo codex? Are there no more lives that could be saved by living more modestly and adding the money thus saved to the amount he has already given?

Yet we should recognize that, if judged by the proportion of his wealth that he has given away, Gates compares very well with most of the other people on the *Forbes* 400 list, including his former colleague and Microsoft cofounder, Paul Allen. Allen, who left the company in 1983, has given, over his lifetime, more than $800 million to philanthropic causes. That is far more than nearly any of us will ever be able to give. But *Forbes* lists Allen as the fifth-richest American, with a net worth of $16 billion. He owns the Seattle Seahawks, the Portland Trailblazers, a 413-foot oceangoing yacht that carries two helicopters and a 60-foot submarine. He has given only about 5 percent of his total wealth.

Is there a line of moral adequacy that falls between the 5 percent that Allen has given away and the roughly 35 percent that Gates has donated? Few people have set a personal example that would allow them to tell Gates that he has not given enough, but one who could is Zell Kravinsky. A few years ago, when he was in his mid-forties, Kravinsky gave almost all of his $45 million real estate fortune to health-related charities, retaining only his modest family home in Jenkintown, near Philadelphia, and enough to meet his family's ordinary expenses. After learning that thousands of people with failing kidneys die each year while waiting for a transplant, he contacted a Philadelphia hospital and donated one of his kidneys to a complete stranger.

After reading about Kravinsky in *The New Yorker*, I invited him to speak to my classes at Princeton. He comes across as anguished by the failure of others to see the simple logic that lies behind his altruism. Kravinsky has a mathematical mind—a talent that obviously helped him in deciding what investments would prove profitable—and he says that the chances of dying as a result of donating a kidney are about one in four thousand. For him this implies that to withhold a kidney from someone who would otherwise die means valuing one's own life at four thousand times that of a stranger, a ratio Kravinsky considers "obscene."

30

What marks Kravinsky from the rest of us is that he takes the equal value of all human life as a guide to life, not just as a nice piece of rhetoric. He acknowledges that some people think he is crazy, and even his wife says she believes that he goes too far. One of her arguments against the kidney donation was that one of their children may one day need a kidney, and Zell could be the only compatible donor. Kravinsky's love for his children is, as far as I can tell, as strong as that of any normal parent. Such attachments are part of our nature, no doubt the product of our evolution as mammals who give birth to children, who for an unusually long time require our assistance in order to survive. But that does not, in Kravinsky's view, justify our placing a value on the lives of our children that is thousands of times greater than the value we place on the lives of the children of strangers. Asked if he would allow his child to die if it would enable a thousand children to live, Kravinsky said yes. Indeed, he has said he would permit his child to die even if this enabled only two other children to live. Nevertheless, to appease his wife, he recently went back into real estate, made some money, and bought the family a larger home. But he still remains committed to giving away as much as possible, subject only to keeping his domestic life reasonably tranquil.

Buffett says he believes in giving his children "enough so they feel they could do anything, but not so much that they could do nothing." That means, in his judgment, "a few hundred thousand" each. In absolute terms, that is far more than most Americans are able to leave their children and, by Kravinsky's standard, certainly too much. (Kravinsky says that the hard part is not giving away the first $45 million but the last $10,000, when you have to live so cheaply that you can't function in the business world.) But even if Buffett left each of his three children a million dollars each, he would still have given away more than 99.99 percent of his wealth. When someone does that much—especially in a society in which the norm is to leave most of your wealth to your children—it is better to praise them than to cavil about the extra few hundred thousand dollars they might have given.

Philosophers like Liam Murphy of New York University and my colleague Kwame Anthony Appiah at Princeton contend that our obligations are limited to carrying our fair share of the burden of relieving global poverty. They would have us calculate how much would be required to ensure that the world's poorest people have a chance at a decent life, and then divide this sum among the affluent. That would give us each an amount to donate, and having given that, we would have fulfilled our obligations to the poor.

What might that fair amount be? One way of calculating it would be to take as our target, at least for the next nine years, the Millennium Development Goals, set by the United Nations Millennium Summit in 2000. On that occasion, the largest gathering of world leaders in history jointly pledged to meet, by 2015, a list of goals that include:

- Reducing by half the proportion of the world's people in extreme poverty (defined as living on less than the purchasing-power equivalent of one U.S. dollar per day).
- Reducing by half the proportion of people who suffer from hunger.
- Ensuring that children everywhere are able to take a full course of primary schooling.
- Ending sex disparity in education.
- Reducing by two thirds the mortality rate among children under five.
- Reducing by three quarters the rate of maternal mortality.
- Halting and beginning to reverse the spread of HIV / AIDS and halting and beginning to reduce the incidence of malaria and other major diseases.
- Reducing by half the proportion of people without sustainable access to safe drinking water.

Last year a United Nations task force, led by the Columbia University economist Jeffrey Sachs, estimated the annual cost of meeting these goals to be $121 billion in 2006, rising to $189 billion by 2015. When we take account of existing official development aid promises, the additional amount needed each year to meet the goals is only $48 billion for 2006 and $74 billion for 2015.

Now let's look at the incomes of America's rich and superrich and ask how much they could reasonably give. The task is made easier by statistics recently provided by Thomas Piketty and Emmanuel Saez, economists at the École Normale Supérieure, Paris-Jourdan, and the University of California, Berkeley, respectively, based on U.S. tax data for 2004. Their figures are for pretax income, excluding income from capital gains, which for the very rich are nearly always substantial. For simplicity I have rounded the figures, generally downward. Note too that the numbers refer to "tax units"—that is, in many cases, families rather than individuals.

Piketty and Saez's top bracket comprises 0.01 percent of U.S. taxpayers. There are 14,400 of them, earning an average of $12,775,000, with total earnings of $184 billion. The minimum annual income in this group is more than $5 million, so it seems reasonable to suppose that they could, without much hardship, give away a third of their annual income, an average of $4.3 million each, for a total of around $61 billion. That would still leave each of them with an annual income of at least $3.3 million. 35

Next comes the rest of the top 0.1 percent (excluding the category just described, as I shall do henceforth). There are 129,600 in this group, with an average income of just over $2 million and a minimum income of $1.1 million. If they were each to give a quarter of their income, that would yield about $65 billion and leave each of them with at least $846,000 annually.

The top 0.5 percent consists of 575,900 taxpayers, with an average income of $623,000 and a minimum of $407,000. If they were to give one fifth of their income, they would still have at least $325,000 each, and they would be giving a total of $72 billion.

Coming down to the level of those in the top 1 percent, we find 719,900 taxpayers with an average income of $327,000 and a minimum of $276,000. They could comfortably afford to give 15 percent of their income. That would yield $35 billion and leave them with at least $234,000.

Finally, the remainder of the nation's top 10 percent earn at least $92,000 annually, with an average of $132,000. There are nearly 13 million in this group. If they gave the traditional tithe—10 percent of their income, or an average of $13,200 each—this would yield about $171 billion and leave them a minimum of $83,000.

You could spend a long time debating whether the fractions of income I have suggested for donation constitute the fairest possible scheme. Perhaps the sliding scale should be steeper, so that the superrich give more and the merely comfortable give less. And it could be extended beyond the top 10 percent of American families, so that everyone able to afford more than the basic necessities of life gives something, even if it is as little as 1 percent. Be that as it may, the remarkable thing about these calculations is that a scale of donations that is unlikely to impose significant hardship on anyone yields a total of $404 billion—from just 10 percent of American families. 40

Obviously, the rich in other nations should share the burden of relieving global poverty. The United States is responsible for 36 percent of the gross domestic product of all Organization for Economic Cooperation and Development nations. Arguably, because the United States is richer than all other major nations, and its wealth is more unevenly distributed than wealth in almost any other industrialized country, the rich in the United States should contribute more than 36 percent of total global donations. So somewhat more than 36 percent of all aid to relieve global poverty should come from this country. For simplicity, let's take half as a fair share for the United States. On that basis, extending the scheme I have suggested worldwide would provide $808 billion annually for development aid. That's more than six times what the task force chaired by Sachs estimated would be required for 2006 in order to be on track to meet the Millennium Development Goals, and more than sixteen times the shortfall between that sum and existing official development aid commitments.

If we are obliged to do no more than our fair share of eliminating global poverty, the burden will not be great. But is that really all we ought to do? Since we all agree that fairness is a good thing, and none of us like doing more because others don't pull their weight, the fair-share view is attractive. In the end, however, I think we should reject it. Let's return to the drowning child in the shallow pond. Imagine it is not one small child who has fallen in, but fifty children. We are among fifty adults, unrelated to the children, picnicking on the lawn around the pond. We can easily wade into the pond and rescue the children, and the fact that we would find it cold and unpleasant sloshing around in the knee-deep muddy water is no justification for failing to do so. The "fair share" theorists would say that if we each rescue one child, all the children will be saved, and so none of us have an obligation to save more than one. But what if half the picnickers prefer staying clean and dry to rescuing any children at all? Is it acceptable if the rest of us stop after we have rescued just one child, knowing that we have done our fair share, but that half the children will drown? We might justifiably be furious with those who are not doing their fair share, but our anger with them is not a reason for letting the children die. In terms of praise and blame, we are clearly right to condemn, in the strongest terms, those who do nothing. In contrast, we may withhold such condemnation from those who stop when they have done their fair share. Even so, they have let children drown when they could easily have saved them, and that is wrong.

Similarly, in the real world, it should be seen as a serious moral failure when those with ample income do not do their fair share toward relieving global poverty. It isn't so easy, however, to decide on the proper approach to take to those who limit their contribution to their fair share when they could easily do more and when, because others are not playing their part, a further donation would assist many in desperate need. In the privacy of our own judgment, we should believe that it is wrong not to do more. But whether we should actually criticize people who are doing their fair share, but no more than that, depends on the psychological impact that such criticism will have on them, and on others. This in turn may depend on social practices. If the majority are doing little or nothing, setting a standard higher than the fair-share level may seem so demanding that it discourages people who are willing to make an equitable contribution from doing even that. So it may be best to refrain from criticizing those who achieve the fair-share level. In moving our society's standards forward, we may have to progress one step at a time.

For more than thirty years, I've been reading, writing, and teaching about the ethical issue posed by the juxtaposition, on our planet, of great abundance and life-threatening poverty. Yet it was not until, in preparing this article, I calculated how much America's top 10 percent of income earners actually make that I fully understood how easy it would be for the world's rich to eliminate, or virtually eliminate, global poverty. (It has actually become much easier over the past thirty years, as the rich have grown significantly richer.) I found the result astonishing. I double-checked the figures and asked a research assistant to check them as well. But they were right. Measured against our capacity, the Millennium Development Goals are indecently, shockingly modest. If we fail to achieve them—as on present indications we well might—we have no excuses. The target we should be setting for ourselves is not halving the proportion of people living in extreme poverty, and without enough to eat, but ensuring that no one, or virtually no one, needs to live in such degrading conditions. That is a worthy goal, and it is well within our reach.

Questions

1. Singer's title poses a two-part question: What should a billionaire give—and what should you? At the end of his essay, he gives an answer. Discuss the pros and cons of his proposal, including the effects it would have on the givers and the receivers.

2. What ethical arguments does Singer make before presenting his proposal? What facts and principles underlie his position that all Americans in the top 10 percent income bracket should give a specific percentage to alleviate the plight of the poor?

3. Singer's essay depends on anecdotes as well as facts. Choose one anecdote you consider highly effective, and suggest the reasons it succeeds rhetorically.

4. It is possible to read online statements by many of the philanthropists Singer interviews or cites. Choose one whose ideas interest you, read more about his or her philanthropy, and write a brief account of what he or she has contributed and why.

Atul Gawande *When Doctors Make Mistakes*

I—Crash Victim

At 2 a.m. on a crisp Friday in winter, I was in sterile gloves and gown, pulling a teenage knifing victim's abdomen open, when my pager sounded. "Code Trauma, three minutes," the operating-room nurse said, reading aloud from my pager display. This meant that an ambulance would be bringing another trauma patient to the hospital momentarily, and, as the surgical resident on duty for emergencies, I would have to be present for the patient's arrival. I stepped back from the table and took off my gown. Two other surgeons were working on the knifing victim: Michael Ball, the attending (the staff surgeon in charge of the case), and David Hernandez, the chief resident (a general surgeon in his last of five years of training). Ordinarily, these two would have come later to help with the trauma, but they were stuck here. Ball, a dry, imperturbable forty-two-year-old Texan, looked over to me as I headed for the door. "If you run into any trouble, you call, and one of us will peel away," he said.

I did run into trouble. In telling this story, I have had to change significant details about what happened (including the names of the participants and aspects of my role), but I have tried to stay as close to the actual events as I could while protecting the patient, myself, and the rest of the staff. The way that things go wrong in medicine is normally unseen and, consequently, often misunderstood. Mistakes do happen. We think of them as aberrant; they are anything but.

The emergency room was one floor up, and, taking the stairs two at a time, I arrived just as the emergency medical technicians wheeled in a woman who appeared to be in her thirties and to weigh more than two hundred pounds. She lay motionless on a hard orange plastic spinal board—eyes closed, skin pale, blood running out of her nose. A nurse directed the crew into Trauma Bay 1, an examination room outfitted like an O.R., with green tiles on the wall, monitoring devices, and space for portable X-ray equipment. We lifted her onto the bed and then went to work. One nurse began cutting off the woman's clothes. Another took vital signs. A third inserted a large-bore intravenous line into her right arm. A surgical intern put a Foley catheter[1] into her bladder. The emergency-medicine attending was Samuel Johns, a gaunt, Ichabod Crane–like[2]

First published in the "Annals of Medicine" section of the New Yorker *(February 1, 1999), then in Gawande's first book,* Complications: A Surgeon's Notes on an Imperfect Science *(2002). He has continued the theme of medical error in* Better: A Surgeon's Notes on Performance *(2007) and* The Checklist Manifesto: How to Get Things Right *(2009).*

1. A thin tube inserted into the bladder to drain urine.

2. Ichabod Crane, the fictional hero of Washington Irving's "Legend of Sleepy Hollow," is described as "tall, but exceedingly lank, with narrow shoulders, long arms and legs, hands that dangled a mile out of his sleeves, feet that might have served for shovels, and his whole frame most loosely hung together."

man in his fifties. He was standing to one side with his arms crossed, observing, which was a sign that I could go ahead and take charge.

If you're in a hospital, most of the "moment to moment" doctoring you get is from residents—physicians receiving specialty training and a small income in exchange for their labor. Our responsibilities depend on our level of training, but we're never entirely on our own: there's always an attending, who oversees our decisions. That night, since Johns was the attending and was responsible for the patient's immediate management, I took my lead from him. But he wasn't a surgeon, and so he relied on me for surgical expertise.

"What's the story?" I asked.

An E.M.T. rattled off the details: "Unidentified white female unrestrained driver in high-speed rollover. Ejected from the car. Found unresponsive to pain. Pulse a hundred, B.P. a hundred over sixty, breathing at thirty on her own . . ."

As he spoke, I began examining her. The first step in caring for a trauma patient is always the same. It doesn't matter if a person has been shot eleven times or crushed by a truck or burned in a kitchen fire. The first thing you do is make sure that the patient can breathe without difficulty. This woman's breaths were shallow and rapid. An oximeter, by means of a sensor placed on her finger, measured the oxygen saturation of her blood. The "O_2 sat" is normally more than ninety-five percent for a patient breathing room air. The woman was wearing a face mask with oxygen turned up full blast, and her sat was only ninety percent.

"She's not oxygenating well," I announced in the flattened-out, wake-me-up-when-something-interesting-happens tone that all surgeons have acquired by about three months into residency. With my fingers, I verified that there wasn't any object in her mouth that would obstruct her airway; with a stethoscope, I confirmed that neither lung had collapsed. I got hold of a bag mask, pressed its clear facepiece over her nose and mouth, and squeezed the bellows, a kind of balloon with a one-way valve, shooting a litre of air into her with each compression. After a minute or so, her oxygen came up to a comfortable ninety-eight percent. She obviously needed our help with breathing. "Let's tube her," I said. That meant putting a tube down through her vocal cords and into her trachea, which would insure a clear airway and allow for mechanical ventilation.

Johns, the attending, wanted to do the intubation. He picked up a Mac 3 laryngoscope, a standard but fairly primitive-looking L-shaped metal instrument for prying open the mouth and throat, and slipped the shoehornlike blade deep into her mouth and down to her larynx. Then he yanked the handle up toward the ceiling to pull her tongue out of the way, open her mouth and throat, and reveal the vocal cords, which sit like fleshy tent flaps at the entrance to the trachea. The patient didn't wince or gag: she was still out cold.

"Suction!" he called. "I can't see a thing."

He sucked out about a cup of blood and clot. Then he picked up the endotracheal tube—a clear rubber pipe about the diameter of an index finger and three times as long—and tried to guide it between her cords. After a minute, her sat[3] started to fall.

3. Abbreviation for saturation, as in O_2 sat.

"You're down to seventy percent," a nurse announced.

Johns kept struggling with the tube, trying to push it in, but it banged vainly against the cords. The patient's lips began to turn blue.

"Sixty percent," the nurse said.

15 Johns pulled everything out of the patient's mouth and fitted the bag mask back on. The oximeter's luminescent-green readout hovered at sixty for a moment and then rose steadily, to ninety-seven percent. After a few minutes, he took the mask off and again tried to get the tube in. There was more blood, and there may have been some swelling, too: all the poking down the throat was probably not helping. The sat fell to sixty percent. He pulled out and bagged her until she returned to ninety-five percent.

When you're having trouble getting the tube in, the next step is to get specialized expertise. "Let's call anesthesia," I said, and Johns agreed. In the meantime, I continued to follow the standard trauma protocol: completing the examination and ordering fluids, lab tests, and X-rays. Maybe five minutes passed as I worked.

The patient's sats drifted down to ninety-two percent—not a dramatic change but definitely not normal for a patient who is being manually ventilated. I checked to see if the sensor had slipped off her finger. It hadn't. "Is the oxygen up full blast?" I asked a nurse.

"It's up all the way," she said.

I listened again to the patient's lungs—no collapse. "We've got to get her tubed," Johns said. He took off the oxygen mask and tried again.

20 Somewhere in my mind, I must have been aware of the possibility that her airway was shutting down because of vocal-cord swelling or blood. If it was, and we were unable to get a tube in, then the only chance she'd have to survive would be an emergency tracheostomy: cutting a hole in her neck and inserting a breathing tube into her trachea. Another attempt to intubate her might even trigger a spasm of the cords and a sudden closure of the airway—which is exactly what did happen.

If I had actually thought this far along, I would have recognized how ill-prepared I was to do an emergency "trache." Of the people in the room, it's true, I had the most experience doing tracheostomies, but that wasn't saying much. I had been the assistant surgeon in only about half a dozen, and all but one of them had been non-emergency cases, employing techniques that were not designed for speed. The exception was a practice emergency trache I had done on a goat. I should have immediately called Dr. Ball for backup. I should have got the trache equipment out—lighting, suction, sterile instruments—just in case. Instead of hurrying the effort to get the patient intubated because of a mild drop in saturation, I should have asked Johns to wait until I had help nearby. I might even have recognized that she was already losing her airway. Then I could have grabbed a knife and started cutting her a tracheostomy while things were still relatively stable and I had time to proceed slowly. But for whatever reasons—hubris, inattention, wishful thinking, hesitation, or the uncertainty of the moment—I let the opportunity pass.

Johns hunched over the patient, intently trying to insert the tube through her vocal cords. When her sat once again dropped into the sixties, he stopped and put the mask back on. We stared at the monitor. The numbers weren't coming up. Her lips were still blue. Johns squeezed the bellows harder to blow more oxygen in.

"I'm getting resistance," he said.

The realization crept over me: this was a disaster. "Damn it, we've lost her airway," I said. "Trache kit! Light! Somebody call down to O.R. 25 and get Ball up here!"

People were suddenly scurrying everywhere. I tried to proceed deliberately, and not let panic take hold. I told the surgical intern to get a sterile gown and gloves on. I took a bactericidal solution off a shelf and dumped a whole bottle of yellow-brown liquid on the patient's neck. A nurse unwrapped the tracheostomy kit—a sterilized set of drapes and instruments. I pulled on a gown and a new pair of gloves while trying to think through the steps. This is simple, really, I tried to tell myself. At the base of the thyroid cartilage, the Adam's apple, is a little gap in which you find a thin, fibrous covering called the cricothyroid membrane. Cut through that and—voilà! You're in the trachea. You slip through the hole a four-inch plastic tube shaped like a plumber's elbow joint, hook it up to oxygen and a ventilator, and she's all set. Anyway, that was the theory.

I threw some drapes over her body, leaving the neck exposed. It looked as thick as a tree. I felt for the bony prominence of the thyroid cartilage. But I couldn't feel anything through the rolls of fat. I was beset by uncertainty—where should I cut? should I make a horizontal or a vertical incision?—and I hated myself for it. Surgeons never dithered, and I was dithering.

"I need better light," I said.

Someone was sent out to look for one.

"Did anyone get Ball?" I asked. It wasn't exactly an inspiring question.

"He's on his way," a nurse said.

There wasn't time to wait. Four minutes without oxygen would lead to permanent brain damage, if not death. Finally, I took the scalpel and cut. I just cut. I made a three-inch left-to-right swipe across the middle of the neck, following the procedure I'd learned for elective cases. I figured that if I worked through the fat I might be able to find the membrane in the wound. Dissecting down with scissors while the intern held the wound open with retractors, I hit a vein. It didn't let loose a lot of blood, but there was enough to fill the wound: I couldn't see anything. The intern put a finger on the bleeder. I called for suction. But the suction wasn't working; the tube was clogged with the clot from the intubation efforts.

"Somebody get some new tubing," I said. "And where's the light?"

Finally, an orderly wheeled in a tall overhead light, plugged it in, and flipped on the switch. It was still too dim; I could have done better with a flashlight.

I wiped up the blood with gauze, then felt around in the wound with my fingertips. This time, I thought I could feel the hard ridges of the thyroid cartilage and, below it, the slight gap of the cricothyroid membrane, though I couldn't be sure. I held my place with my left hand.

35 James O'Connor, a silver-haired, seen-it-all anesthesiologist, came into the room. Johns gave him a quick rundown on the patient and let him take over bagging her.

Holding the scalpel in my right hand like a pen, I stuck the blade down into the wound at the spot where I thought the thyroid cartilage was. With small, sharp strokes—working blindly, because of the blood and the poor light—I cut down through the overlying fat and tissue until I felt the blade scrape against the almost bony cartilage. I searched with the tip of the knife, walking it along until I felt it reach a gap. I hoped it was the cricothyroid membrane, and pressed down firmly. Then I felt the tissue suddenly give, and I cut an inch-long opening.

When I put my index finger into it, it felt as if I were prying open the jaws of a stiff clothespin. Inside, I thought I felt open space. But where were the sounds of moving air that I expected? Was this deep enough? Was I even in the right place?

"I think I'm in," I said, to reassure myself as much as anyone else.

"I hope so," O'Connor said. "She doesn't have much longer."

40 I took the tracheostomy tube and tried to fit it in, but something seemed to be blocking it. I twisted it and turned it, and finally jammed it in. Just then, Ball, the surgical attending, arrived. He rushed up to the bed and leaned over for a look. "Did you get it?" he asked. I said that I thought so. The bag mask was plugged onto the open end of the trache tube. But when the bellows were compressed the air just gurgled out of the wound. Ball quickly put on gloves and a gown.

"How long has she been without an airway?" he asked.

"I don't know. Three minutes."

Ball's face hardened as he registered that he had about a minute in which to turn things around. He took my place and summarily pulled out the trache tube. "God, what a mess," he said. "I can't see a thing in this wound. I don't even know if you're in the right place. Can we get better light and suction?" New suction tubing was found and handed to him. He quickly cleaned up the wound and went to work.

The patient's sat had dropped so low that the oximeter couldn't detect it anymore. Her heart rate began slowing down—first to the sixties and then to the forties. Then she lost her pulse entirely. I put my hands together on her chest, locked my elbows, leaned over her, and started doing chest compressions.

45 Ball looked up from the patient and turned to O'Connor. "I'm not going to get her an airway in time," he said. "You're going to have to try from above." Essentially, he was admitting my failure. Trying an oral intubation again was pointless—just something to do instead of watching her die. I was stricken, and concentrated on doing chest compressions, not looking at anyone. It was over, I thought.

And then, amazingly, O'Connor: "I'm in." He had managed to slip a pediatric-size endotracheal tube through the vocal cords. In thirty seconds, with oxygen being manually ventilated through the tube, her heart was back, racing at a hundred and twenty beats a minute. Her sat registered at sixty and then climbed. Another thirty seconds and it was at ninety-seven percent. All the people in the room exhaled, as if they, too, had been denied their breath. Ball and I said little except to confer about the next steps for her. Then he went back downstairs to finish working on the stab-wound patient still in the O.R.

We eventually identified the woman, whom I'll call Louise Williams; she was thirty-four years old and lived alone in a nearby suburb. Her alcohol level on arrival had been three times the legal limit, and had probably contributed to her unconsciousness. She had a concussion, several lacerations, and significant soft-tissue damage. But X-rays and scans revealed no other injuries from the crash. That night, Ball and Hernandez brought her to the O.R. to fit her with a proper tracheostomy. When Ball came out and talked to family members, he told them of the dire condition she was in when she arrived, the difficulties "we" had had getting access to her airway, the disturbingly long period of time that she had gone without oxygen, and thus his uncertainty about how much brain function she still possessed. They listened without protest; there was nothing for them to do but wait.

II—The Banality of Error

To much of the public—and certainly to lawyers and the media—medical error is a problem of bad physicians. Consider some other surgical mishaps. In one, a general surgeon left a large metal instrument in a patient's abdomen, where it tore through the bowel and the wall of the bladder. In another, a cancer surgeon biopsied the wrong part of a woman's breast and thereby delayed her diagnosis of cancer for months. A cardiac surgeon skipped a small but key step during a heart-valve operation, thereby killing the patient. A surgeon saw a man racked with abdominal pain in the emergency room and, without taking a C.T. scan, assumed that the man had a kidney stone; eighteen hours later, a scan showed a rupturing abdominal aortic aneurysm, and the patient died not long afterward.

How could anyone who makes a mistake of that magnitude be allowed to practice medicine? We call such doctors "incompetent," "unethical," and "negligent." We want to see them punished. And so we've wound up with the public system we have for dealing with error: malpractice lawsuits, media scandal, suspensions, firings.

There is, however, a central truth in medicine that complicates this tidy vision of misdeeds and misdoers: *All* doctors make terrible mistakes. Consider the cases I've just described. I gathered them simply by asking respected surgeons I know—surgeons at top medical schools—to tell me about mistakes they had made just in the past year. Every one of them had a story to tell. 50

In 1991, *The New England Journal of Medicine* published a series of landmark papers from a project known as the Harvard Medical Practice Study—a review of more than thirty thousand hospital admissions in New York State. The study found that nearly four percent of hospital patients suffered complications from treatment which prolonged their hospital stay or resulted in disability or death, and that two-thirds of such complications were due to errors in care. One in four, or one percent of admissions, involved actual negligence. It was estimated that, nationwide, a hundred and twenty thousand patients die each year at least partly as a result of errors in care. And subsequent investigations around the country have confirmed the ubiquity of error. In one small study of how clinicians perform when patients have a sudden cardiac arrest, twenty-seven of thirty clinicians made an error in using the defibrillator; they may have charged it incorrectly or lost valuable time trying to figure out how to work a particular model. According to a 1995 study, mistakes in administering drugs—giving the wrong drug or the wrong dose, say—occur, on the average, about once for every hospital admission, mostly without ill effects, but one percent of the time with serious consequences.

If error were due to a subset of dangerous doctors, you might expect malpractice cases to be concentrated among a small group, but in fact they follow a uniform, bell-shaped distribution. Most surgeons are sued at least once in the course of their careers. Studies of specific types of error, too, have found that repeat offenders are not the problem. The fact is that virtually everyone who cares for hospital patients will make serious mistakes, and even commit acts of negligence, every year. For this reason, doctors are seldom outraged when the press reports yet another medical horror story. They usually have a different reaction: *That could be me*. The important question isn't how to keep bad physicians from harming patients; it's how to keep good physicians from harming patients.

Medical-malpractice suits are a remarkably ineffective remedy. Troyen Brennan, a Harvard professor of law and public health, points out that research has consistently failed to find evidence that litigation reduces medical-error rates. In part, this may be because the weapon is so imprecise. Brennan led several studies following up on the patients in the Harvard Medical Practice Study. He found that fewer than two percent of the patients who had received substandard care ever filed suit. Conversely, only a small minority among the patients who did sue had in fact been the victims of negligent care. And a patient's likelihood of winning a suit depended primarily on how poor his or her outcome was, regardless of whether that outcome was caused by disease or unavoidable risks of care.

The deeper problem with medical-malpractice suits, however, is that by demonizing errors they prevent doctors from acknowledging and discussing them publicly. The tort system makes adversaries of patient and physician, and pushes each to offer a heavily slanted version of events. When things go wrong, it's almost impossible for a physician to talk to a patient honestly about mistakes. Hospital lawyers warn doctors that, although they must, of course, tell patients about complications that occur, they are never to intimate that they were at fault, lest the "confession" wind up in court as damning evidence in a black-and-white morality tale. At most, a doctor might say, "I'm sorry that things didn't go as well as we had hoped."

There is one place, however, where doctors can talk candidly about their mistakes, if not with patients, then at least with one another. It is called the Morbidity and Mortality Conference—or, more simply, M. & M.—and it takes place, usually once a week, at nearly every academic hospital in the country. This institution survives because laws protecting its proceedings from legal discovery have stayed on the books in most states, despite frequent challenges. Surgeons, in particular, take the M. & M. seriously. Here they can gather behind closed doors to review the mistakes, complications, and deaths that occurred on their watch, determine responsibility, and figure out what to do differently next time. 55

III—Show and Tell

At my hospital, we convene every Tuesday at five o'clock in a steep, plush amphitheatre lined with oil portraits of the great doctors whose achievements we're meant to live up to. All surgeons are expected to attend, from the interns to the chairman of surgery; we're also joined by medical students doing their surgery "rotation." An M. & M. can include almost a hundred people. We file in, pick up a photocopied list of cases to be discussed, and take our seats. The front row is occupied by the most senior surgeons: terse, serious men, now out of their scrubs and in dark suits, lined up like a panel of senators at a hearing. The chairman is a leonine presence in the seat closest to the plain wooden podium from which each case is presented. In the next few rows are the remaining surgical attending; these tend to be younger, and several of them are women. The chief residents have put on long white coats and usually sit in the side rows. I join the mass of other residents, all of us in short white coats and green scrub pants, occupying the back rows.

For each case, the chief resident from the relevant service—cardiac, vascular, trauma, and so on—gathers the information, takes the podium, and tells the story. Here's a partial list of cases from a typical week (with a few changes to protect confidentiality): a sixty-eight-year-old man who bled to death after heart-valve surgery; a forty-seven-year-old woman who had to have a reoperation because of infection following an arterial bypass done in her left leg; a forty-four-year-old woman who had to have bile drained from her abdomen after gall-bladder surgery; three patients who had to have reoperations for bleeding following surgery; a sixty-three-year-old man who had a cardiac arrest following heart-bypass surgery; a sixty-six-year-old woman whose sutures suddenly gave way in an abdominal wound and nearly allowed her intestines to spill out. Ms. Williams's case, my failed tracheostomy, was just one case on a list like this. David Hernandez, the chief trauma resident, had subsequently reviewed the records and spoken to me and others involved. When the time came, it was he who stood up front and described what had happened.

Hernandez is a tall, rollicking, good old boy who can tell a yarn, but M. & M. presentations are bloodless and compact. He said something like: "This was a thirty-four-year-old female unrestrained driver in a high-speed rollover. The patient apparently had stable vitals at the scene but was unresponsive, and brought in by ambulance unintubated. She was G.C.S. 7 on arrival." G.C.S. stands for the Glasgow Coma Scale, which rates the severity of head injuries, from three to fifteen. G.C.S. 7 is in the comatose range. "Attempts to intubate were made without success in the E.R. and may have contributed to airway closure. A cricothyroidotomy[4] was attempted without success."

These presentations can be awkward. The chief residents, not the attendings, determine which cases to report. That keeps the attending honest—no one can cover up mistakes—but it puts the chief residents, who are, after all, underlings, in a delicate position. The successful M. & M. presentation inevitably involves a certain elision of detail and a lot of passive verbs. No one screws up a cricothyroidotomy. Instead, "a cricothyroidotomy was attempted without success." The message, however, was not lost on anyone.

60 Hernandez continued, "The patient arrested and required cardiac compressions. Anesthesia was then able to place a pediatric E.T. tube and the patient recovered stable vitals. The tracheostomy was then completed in the O.R."

So Louise Williams had been deprived of oxygen long enough to go into cardiac arrest, and everyone knew that meant she could easily have suffered a disabling stroke or been left a vegetable. Hernandez concluded with the fortunate aftermath: "Her workup was negative for permanent cerebral damage or other major injuries. The tracheostomy was removed on Day 2. She was discharged to home in good condition on Day 3." To the family's great relief, and mine, she had woken up in the morning a bit woozy but hungry, alert, and mentally intact. In a few weeks, the episode would heal to a scar.

But not before someone was called to account. A front-row voice immediately thundered, "What do you mean, 'A cricothyroidotomy was attempted without success?'" I sank into my seat, my face hot.

"This was my case," Dr. Ball volunteered from the front row. It is how every attending begins, and that little phrase contains a world of surgical culture. For all the talk in business schools and in corporate America about the virtues of "flat organizations," surgeons maintain an old-fashioned sense of hierarchy. When things go wrong, the attending is expected to take full responsibility. It makes no difference whether it was the resident's hand that slipped and lacerated an aorta; it doesn't matter whether the attending was at home in bed when a nurse gave a wrong dose of medication. At the M. & M., the burden of responsibility falls on the attending.

Ball went on to describe the emergency attending's failure to intubate Williams and his own failure to be at her bedside when things got out of control. He described the bad lighting and her extremely thick neck, and was careful to make those sound not like excuses but merely like complicating factors. Some

4. An emergency incision through the cricothyroid membrane to secure a patient's airway during an emergency—described in paragraphs 31–46.

attending shook their heads in sympathy. A couple of them asked questions to clarify certain details. Throughout, Ball's tone was objective, detached. He had the air of a CNN newscaster describing unrest in Kuala Lumpur.[5]

As always, the chairman, responsible for the over-all quality of our surgery service, asked the final question. What, he wanted to know, would Ball have done differently? Well, Ball replied, it didn't take long to get the stab-wound patient under control in the O.R., so he probably should have sent Hernandez up to the E.R. at that point or let Hernandez close the abdomen while he himself came up. People nodded. Lesson learned. Next case. 65

At no point during the M. & M. did anyone question why I had not called for help sooner or why I had not had the skill and knowledge that Williams needed. This is not to say that my actions were seen as acceptable. Rather, in the hierarchy, addressing my errors was Ball's role. The day after the disaster, Ball had caught me in the hall and taken me aside. His voice was more wounded than angry as he went through my specific failures. First, he explained, in an emergency tracheostomy it might have been better to do a vertical neck incision; that would have kept me out of the blood vessels, which run up and down—something I should have known at least from my reading. I might have had a much easier time getting her an airway then, he said. Second, and worse to him than mere ignorance, he didn't understand why I hadn't called him when there were clear signs of airway trouble developing. I offered no excuses. I promised to be better prepared for such cases and to be quicker to ask for help.

Even after Ball had gone down the fluorescent-lit hallway, I felt a sense of shame like a burning ulcer. This was not guilt: guilt is what you feel when you have done something wrong. What I felt was shame: *I* was what was wrong. And yet I also knew that a surgeon can take such feelings too far. It is one thing to be aware of one's limitations. It is another to be plagued by self-doubt. One surgeon with a national reputation told me about an abdominal operation in which he had lost control of bleeding while he was removing what turned out to be a benign tumor and the patient had died. "It was a clean kill," he said. Afterward, he could barely bring himself to operate. When he did operate, he became tentative and indecisive. The case affected his performance for months.

Even worse than losing self-confidence, though, is reacting defensively. There are surgeons who will see faults everywhere except in themselves. They have no questions and no fears about their abilities. As a result, they learn nothing from their mistakes and know nothing of their limitations. As one surgeon told me, it is a rare but alarming thing to meet a surgeon without fear. "If you're not a little afraid when you operate," he said, "you're bound to do a patient a grave disservice."

The atmosphere at the M. & M. is meant to discourage both attitudes—self-doubt and denial—for the M. & M. is a cultural ritual that inculcates in surgeons a "correct" view of mistakes. "What would you do differently?" a

5. The capital of Malaysia; it was hit by economic crisis and political unrest in the late 1990s when the deputy prime minister, Dato' Seri Anwar Ibrahim, was fired.

chairman asks concerning cases of avoidable complications. "Nothing" is seldom an acceptable answer.

70 In its way, the M. & M. is an impressively sophisticated and human institution. Unlike the courts or the media, it recognizes that human error is generally not something that can be deterred by punishment. The M. & M. sees avoiding error as largely a matter of will—of staying sufficiently informed and alert to anticipate the myriad ways that things can go wrong and then trying to head off each potential problem before it happens. Why do things go wrong? Because, doctors say, making them go right is hard stuff. It isn't damnable that an error occurs, but there is some shame to it. In fact, the M. & M.'s ethos can seem paradoxical. On the one hand, it reinforces the very American idea that error is intolerable. On the other hand, the very existence of the M. & M., its place on the weekly schedule, amounts to an acknowledgment that mistakes are an inevitable part of medicine.

But why do they happen so often? Lucian Leape, medicine's leading expert on error, points out that many other industries—whether the task is manufacturing semiconductors or serving customers at the Ritz-Carlton—simply wouldn't countenance error rates like those in hospitals. The aviation industry has reduced the frequency of operational errors to one in a hundred thousand flights, and most of those errors have no harmful consequences. The buzzword at General Electric these days is "Six Sigma," meaning that its goal is to make product defects so rare that in statistical terms they are more than six standard deviations away from being a matter of chance—almost a one-in-a-million occurrence.

Of course, patients are far more complicated and idiosyncratic than airplanes, and medicine isn't a matter of delivering a fixed product or even a catalogue of products; it may well be more complex than just about any other field of human endeavor. Yet everything we've learned in the past two decades—from cognitive psychology, from "human factors" engineering, from studies of disasters like Three Mile Island and Bhopal[6]—has yielded the same insights: not only do all human beings err but they err frequently and in predictable, patterned ways. And systems that do not adjust for these realities can end up exacerbating rather than eliminating error.

The British psychologist James Reason argues, in his book *Human Error*, that our propensity for certain types of error is the price we pay for the brain's remarkable ability to think and act intuitively—to sift quickly through the sensory information that constantly bombards us without wasting time trying to work through every situation anew. Thus systems that rely on human perfection present what Reason calls "latent errors"—errors waiting to happen. Medi-

6. In 1979 there was a partial meltdown of a pressurized water reactor at Three Mile Island Nuclear Generating Station near Harrisburg, Pennsylvania; the Bhopal Gas disaster occurred in December 1984 at the Union Carbide pesticide plant in Bhopal, Madhya Pradesh, India, exposing 500,000 people to dangerous chemicals.

cine teems with examples. Take writing out a prescription, a rote procedure that relies on memory and attention, which we know are unreliable. Inevitably, a physician will sometimes specify the wrong dose or the wrong drug. Even when the prescription is written correctly, there's a risk that it will be misread. (Computerized ordering systems can almost eliminate errors of this kind, but only a small minority of hospitals have adopted them.) Medical equipment, which manufacturers often build without human operators in mind, is another area rife with latent errors: one reason physicians are bound to have problems when they use cardiac defibrillators is that the devices have no standard design. You can also make the case that onerous workloads, chaotic environments, and inadequate team communication all represent latent errors in the system.

James Reason makes another important observation: disasters do not simply occur; they evolve. In complex systems, a single failure rarely leads to harm. Human beings are impressively good at adjusting when an error becomes apparent, and systems often have built-in defenses. For example, pharmacists and nurses routinely check and counter-check physicians' orders. But errors do not always become apparent, and backup systems themselves often fail as a result of latent errors. A pharmacist forgets to check one of a thousand prescriptions. A machine's alarm bell malfunctions. The one attending trauma surgeon available gets stuck in the operating room. When things go wrong, it is usually because a series of failures conspire to produce disaster.

The M. & M. takes none of this into account. For that reason, many experts see it as a rather shabby approach to analyzing error and improving performance in medicine. It isn't enough to ask what a clinician could or should have done differently so that he and others may learn for next time. The doctor is often only the final actor in a chain of events that set him or her up to fail. Error experts, therefore, believe that it's the process, not the individuals in it, which requires closer examination and correction. In a sense, they want to industrialize medicine. And they can already claim one success story: the specialty of anesthesiology, which has adopted their precepts and seen extraordinary results. 75

IV—Nearly Perfect

At the center of the emblem of the American Society of Anesthesiologists is a single word: "Vigilance." When you put a patient to sleep under general anesthesia, you assume almost complete control of the patient's body. The body is paralyzed, the brain rendered unconscious, and machines are hooked up to control breathing, heart rate, blood pressure—all the vital functions. Given the complexity of the machinery and of the human body, there are a seemingly infinite number of ways in which things can go wrong, even in minor surgery. And yet anesthesiologists have found that if problems are detected they can usually be solved. In the nineteen-forties, there was only one death resulting from anesthesia in every twenty-five hundred operations, and between the nineteen-sixties and the nineteen-eighties the rate had stabilized at one or two in every ten thousand operations.

But Ellison (Jeep) Pierce had always regarded even that rate as unconscionable. From the time he began practicing, in 1960, as a young anesthesiologist out of North Carolina and the University of Pennsylvania, he had maintained a case file of details from all the deadly anesthetic accidents he had come across or participated in. But it was one case in particular that galvanized him. Friends of his had taken their eighteen-year-old daughter to the hospital to have her wisdom teeth pulled, under general anesthesia. The anesthesiologist inserted the breathing tube into her esophagus instead of her trachea, which is a relatively common mishap, and then failed to spot the error, which is not. Deprived of oxygen, she died within minutes. Pierce knew that a one-in-ten-thousand death rate, given that anesthesia was administered in the United States an estimated thirty-five million times each year, meant thirty-five hundred avoidable deaths like that one.

In 1982, Pierce was elected vice-president of the American Society of Anesthesiologists and got an opportunity to do something about the death rate. The same year, ABC's "20/20" aired an exposé that caused a considerable stir in his profession. The segment began, "If you are going to go into anesthesia, you are going on a long trip, and you should not do it if you can avoid it in any way. General anesthesia [is] safe most of the time, but there are dangers from human error, carelessness, and a critical shortage of anesthesiologists. This year, six thousand patients will die or suffer brain damage." The program presented several terrifying cases from around the country. Between the small crisis that the show created and the sharp increases in physicians' malpractice-insurance premiums at that time, Pierce was able to mobilize the Society of Anesthesiologists around the problem of error.

He turned for ideas not to a physician but to an engineer named Jeffrey Cooper, the lead author of a ground-breaking 1978 paper entitled "Preventable Anesthesia Mishaps: A Study of Human Factors." An unassuming, fastidious man, Cooper had been hired in 1972, when he was twenty-six years old, by the Massachusetts General Hospital bioengineering unit, to work on developing machines for anesthesiology researchers. He gravitated toward the operating room, however, and spent hours there observing the anesthesiologists, and one of the first things he noticed was how poorly the anesthesia machines were designed. For example, a clockwise turn of a dial decreased the concentration of potent anesthetics in about half the machines but increased the concentration in the other half. He decided to borrow a technique called "critical incident analysis"—which had been used since the nineteen-fifties to analyze mishaps in aviation—in an effort to learn how equipment might be contributing to errors in anesthesia. The technique is built around carefully conducted interviews, designed to capture as much detail as possible about dangerous incidents: how specific accidents evolved and what factors contributed to them. This information is then used to look for patterns among different cases.

80 Getting open, honest reporting is crucial. The Federal Aviation Administration has a formalized system for analyzing and reporting dangerous aviation

incidents, and its enormous success in improving airline safety rests on two cornerstones. Pilots who report an incident within ten days have automatic immunity from punishment, and the reports go to a neutral, outside agency, NASA, which has no interest in using the information against individual pilots. For Jeffrey Cooper, it was probably an advantage that he was an engineer, and not a physician, so that anesthesiologists regarded him as a discreet, unthreatening interviewer.

The result was the first in-depth, scientific look at errors in medicine. His detailed analysis of three hundred and fifty-nine errors provided a view of the profession unlike anything that had been seen before. Contrary to the prevailing assumption that the start of anesthesia ("takeoff") was the most dangerous part, anesthesiologists learned that incidents tended to occur in the middle of anesthesia, when vigilance waned. The most common kind of incident involved errors in maintaining the patient's breathing, and these were usually the result of an undetected disconnection or misconnection of the breathing tubing, mistakes in managing the airway, or mistakes in using the anesthesia machine. Just as important, Cooper enumerated a list of contributory factors, including inadequate experience, inadequate familiarity with equipment, poor communication among team members, haste, inattention, and fatigue.

The study provoked widespread debate among anesthesiologists, but there was no concerted effort to solve the problems until Jeep Pierce came along. Through the anesthesiology society at first, and then through a foundation that he started, Pierce directed funding into research on how to reduce the problems Cooper had identified, sponsored an international conference to gather ideas from around the world, and brought anesthesia-machine designers into safety discussions.

It all worked. Hours for anesthesiology residents were shortened. Manufacturers began redesigning their machines with fallible human beings in mind. Dials were standardized to turn in a uniform direction; locks were put in to prevent accidental administration of more than one anesthetic gas; controls were changed so that oxygen delivery could not be turned down to zero.

Where errors could not be eliminated directly, anesthesiologists began looking for reliable means of detecting them earlier. For example, because the trachea and the esophagus are so close together, it is almost inevitable that an anesthesiologist will sometimes put the breathing tube down the wrong pipe. Anesthesiologists had always checked for this by listening with a stethoscope for breath sounds over both lungs. But Cooper had turned up a surprising number of mishaps—like the one that befell the daughter of Pierce's friends—involving undetected esophageal intubations. Something more effective was needed. In fact, monitors that could detect this kind of error had been available for years, but, in part because of their expense, relatively few anesthesiologists used them. One type of monitor could verify that the tube was in the trachea by detecting carbon dioxide being exhaled from the lungs. Another type, the pulse oximeter, tracked blood-oxygen levels, thereby providing an early warning that something was wrong with the patient's breathing system. Prodded by Pierce and others, the anesthesiology society made the use of both types of monitor for every patient receiving general anesthesia an official standard. Today, anesthesia deaths from misconnecting the breathing system or intubating the esophagus rather than the trachea are virtually unknown. In a decade, the over-all death rate dropped to just one in more than two hundred thousand cases—less than a twentieth of what it had been.

85 And the reformers have not stopped there. David Gaba, a professor of anesthesiology at Stanford, has focused on improving human performance. In aviation, he points out, pilot experience is recognized to be invaluable but insufficient: pilots seldom have direct experience with serious plane malfunction anymore. They are therefore required to undergo yearly training in crisis simulators. Why not doctors, too?

Gaba, a physician with training in engineering, led in the design of an anesthesia-simulation system known as the Eagle Patient Simulator. It is a life-size, computer-driven mannequin that is capable of amazingly realistic behavior. It has a circulation, a heartbeat, and lungs that take in oxygen and expire carbon dioxide. If you inject drugs into it or administer inhaled anesthetics, it will detect the type and amount, and its heart rate, its blood pressure, and its oxygen levels will respond appropriately. The "patient" can be made to develop airway swelling, bleeding, and heart disturbances. The mannequin is laid on an operating table in a simulation room equipped exactly like the real thing. Here both residents and experienced attending physicians learn to perform effectively in all kinds of dangerous, and sometimes freak, scenarios: an anesthesia-machine malfunction, a power outage, a patient who goes into cardiac arrest during surgery, and even a cesarean-section patient whose airway shuts down and who requires an emergency tracheostomy.

Though anesthesiology has unquestionably taken the lead in analyzing and trying to remedy "systems" failures, there are signs of change in other quarters. The American Medical Association, for example, set up its National Patient Safety Foundation in 1997 and asked Cooper and Pierce to serve on the board of directors. The foundation is funding research, sponsoring conferences, and attempting to develop new standards for hospital drug-ordering systems that could substantially reduce medication mistakes—the single most common type of medical error.

Even in surgery there have been some encouraging developments. For instance, operating on the wrong knee or foot or other body part of a patient has been a recurrent, if rare, mistake. A typical response has been to fire the surgeon. Recently, however, hospitals and surgeons have begun to recognize that the body's bilateral symmetry makes these errors predictable. Last year, the American Academy of Orthopedic Surgeons endorsed a simple way of preventing them: make it standard practice for surgeons to initial, with a marker, the body part to be cut before the patient comes to surgery.

The Northern New England Cardiovascular Disease Study Group, based at Dartmouth, is another success story. Though the group doesn't conduct the sort of in-depth investigation of mishaps that Jeffrey Cooper pioneered, it has shown what can be done simply through statistical monitoring. Six hospitals belong to this consortium, which tracks deaths and complications (such as wound infections, uncontrolled bleeding, and stroke) arising from heart surgery and tries to identify various risk factors. Its researchers found, for example, that there were relatively high death rates among patients who developed anemia after bypass surgery, and that anemia developed most often in small patients. The fluid used to "prime" the heart-lung machine caused the anemia, because it diluted a patient's blood, so the smaller the patient (and his or her blood supply) the greater the effect. Members of the consortium now have several promising solutions to the problem. Another study found that a group at one hospital had made mistakes in "handoffs"—say, in passing preoperative lab results to the people in the operating room. The study group solved the problem by developing a pilot's checklist for all patients coming to the O.R. These efforts have introduced a greater degree of standardization, and so reduced the death rate in those six hospitals from four percent to three percent between 1991 and 1996. That meant two hundred and ninety-three fewer deaths. But the Northern New England cardiac group, even with its narrow focus and techniques, remains an exception; hard information about how things go wrong is still scarce. There is a hodgepodge of evidence that latent errors and systemic factors may contribute to surgical errors: the lack of standardized protocols, the surgeon's inexperience, the hospital's inexperience, inadequately designed technology and techniques, thin staffing, poor teamwork, time of day, the effects of managed care and corporate medicine, and so on and so on. But which are the major risk factors? We still don't know. Surgery, like most of medicine, awaits its Jeff Cooper.

V—Getting It Right

It was a routine gallbladder operation, on a routine day: on the operating table was a mother in her forties, her body covered by blue paper drapes except for her round, antiseptic-coated belly. The gallbladder is a floppy, finger-length sac of bile like a deflated olive-green balloon tucked under the liver, and when gallstones form, as this patient had learned, they can cause excruciating bouts of pain. Once we removed her gallbladder, the pain would stop. 90

There are risks to this surgery, but they used to be much greater. Just a decade ago, surgeons had to make a six-inch abdominal incision that left patients in the hospital for the better part of a week just recovering from the wound. Today, we've learned to take out gallbladders with a minute camera and instruments that we manipulate through tiny incisions. The operation, often done as day surgery, is known as laparoscopic cholecystectomy, or "lap chole." Half a million Americans a year now have their gallbladders removed this way; at my hospital alone, we do several hundred lap choles annually.

When the attending gave me the go-ahead, I cut a discreet inch-long semicircle in the wink of skin just above the belly button. I dissected through fat and fascia until I was inside the abdomen, and dropped into place a "port," a half-inch-wide sheath for slipping instruments in and out. We hooked gas tubing up to a side vent on the port, and carbon dioxide poured in, inflating the abdomen until it was distended like a tire. I inserted the miniature camera. On a video monitor a few feet away, the woman's intestines blinked into view. With the abdomen inflated, I had room to move the camera, and I swung it around to look at the liver. The gallbladder could be seen poking out from under the edge.

We put in three more ports through even tinier incisions, spaced apart to complete the four corners of a square. Through the ports on his side, the attending put in two long "graspers," like small-scale versions of the device that a department-store clerk might use to get a hat off the top shelf. Watching the screen as he maneuvered them, he reached under the edge of the liver, clamped onto the gallbladder, and pulled it up into view. We were set to proceed.

Removing the gallbladder is fairly straightforward. You sever it from its stalk and from its blood supply, and pull the rubbery sac out of the abdomen through the incision near the belly button. You let the carbon dioxide out of the belly, pull out the ports, put a few stitches in the tiny incisions, slap some Band-Aids on top, and you're done. There's one looming danger, though: the stalk of the gallbladder is a branch off the liver's only conduit for sending bile to the intestines for the digestion of fats. And if you accidentally injure this main bile duct, the bile backs up and starts to destroy the liver. Between ten and twenty percent of the patients to whom this happens will die. Those who survive often have permanent liver damage and can go on to require liver transplantation. According to a standard textbook, "injuries to the main bile duct are nearly always the result of misadventure during operation and are therefore a serious reproach to the surgical profession." It is a true surgical error, and, like any surgical team doing a lap chole, we were intent on avoiding this mistake.

95 Using a dissecting instrument, I carefully stripped off the fibrous white tissue and yellow fat overlying and concealing the base of the gallbladder. Now we could see its broad neck and the short stretch where it narrowed down to a duct—a tube no thicker than a strand of spaghetti peeking out from the surrounding tissue, but magnified on the screen to the size of major plumbing. Then, just to be absolutely sure we were looking at the gallbladder duct and not the main bile duct, I stripped away some more of the surrounding tissue. The attending and I stopped at this point, as we always do, and discussed the anatomy. The neck of the gallbladder led straight into the tube we were eying. So it had to be the right duct. We had exposed a good length of it without a sign of the main bile duct. Everything looked perfect, we agreed. "Go for it," the attending said.

I slipped in the clip applier, an instrument that squeezes V-shaped metal clips onto whatever you put in its jaws. I got the jaws around the duct and was about to fire when my eye caught, on the screen, a little globule of fat lying on top of the duct. That wasn't necessarily anything unusual, but somehow it didn't look right. With the tip of the clip applier, I tried to flick it aside, but, instead of a little globule, a whole layer of thin unseen tissue came up, and, underneath, we saw that the duct had a fork in it. My stomach dropped. If not for that little extra fastidiousness, I would have clipped off the main bile duct.

Here was the paradox of error in medicine. With meticulous technique and assiduous effort to insure that they have correctly identified the anatomy, surgeons need never cut the main bile duct. It is a paradigm of an avoidable error. At the same time, studies show that even highly experienced surgeons inflict this terrible injury about once in every two hundred lap choles. To put it another way, I may have averted disaster this time, but a statistician would say that, no matter how hard I tried, I was almost certain to make this error at least once in the course of my career.

But the story doesn't have to end here, as the cognitive psychologists and industrial-error experts have demonstrated. Given the results they've achieved in anesthesiology, it's clear that we can make dramatic improvements by going after the process, not the people. But there are distinct limitations to the industrial cure, however necessary its emphasis on systems and structures. It would be deadly for us, the individual actors, to give up our belief in human perfectibility. The statistics may say that someday I will sever someone's main bile duct, but each time I go into a gallbladder operation I believe that with enough will and effort I can beat the odds. This isn't just professional vanity. It's a necessary part of good medicine, even in superbly "optimized" systems. Operations like that lap chole have taught me how easily error can occur, but they've also showed me something else: effort does matter; diligence and attention to the minutest details can save you.

This may explain why many doctors take exception to talk of "systems problems," "continuous quality improvement," and "process reëngineering." It is the dry language of structures, not people. I'm no exception: something in me, too, demands an acknowledgment of my autonomy, which is also to say my ultimate culpability. Go back to that Friday night in the E.R., to the moment when I stood, knife in hand, over Louise Williams, her lips blue, her throat a swollen, bloody, and suddenly closed passage. A systems engineer might have proposed some useful changes. Perhaps a backup suction device should always be at hand, and better light more easily available. Perhaps the institution could have trained me better for such crises, could have required me to have operated on a few more goats. Perhaps emergency tracheostomies are so difficult under any circumstances that an automated device could have been designed to do a better job. But the could-haves are infinite, aren't they? Maybe Williams could have worn her seat belt, or had one less beer that night. We could call any or all of these factors latent errors, accidents waiting to happen.

But although they put the odds against me, it wasn't as if I had no chance of succeeding. Good doctoring is all about making the most of the hand you're dealt, and I failed to do so. The indisputable fact was that I hadn't called for help when I could have, and when I plunged the knife into her neck and made my horizontal slash my best was not good enough. It was just luck, hers and mine, that Dr. O'Connor somehow got a breathing tube into her in time.

There are all sorts of reasons that it would be wrong to take my license away or to take me to court. These reasons do not absolve me. Whatever the limits of the M. & M., its fierce ethic of personal responsibility for errors is a formidable virtue. No matter what measures are taken, medicine will sometimes falter, and it isn't reasonable to ask that it achieve perfection. What's reasonable is to ask that medicine never cease to aim for it.

QUESTIONS

1. Gawande states flatly: "*All* doctors make terrible mistakes" (paragraph 50), and then proceeds to analyze why. What are the main reasons he offers?

2. In section IV, "Nearly Perfect," Gawande discusses attempts by different medical groups to eliminate or reduce error. What approaches have been effective? What are the limits of these approaches?

3. Although it incorporates significant research, this essay fits the genre of the personal narrative. At the beginning and end, Gawande narrates two of his experiences in the operating room. Are these examples similar or different? Does the rhetorical purpose of the anecdote stay the same, or does it change as Gawande moves through his discussion of medical error? Explain.

4. Narrate a personal experience in which you made a serious error. Try, like Gawande, to incorporate the research or advice of others who might help you understand the reasons for your error.

TOM REGAN *The Case for Animal Rights*

I REGARD MYSELF as an advocate of animal rights—as a part of the animal rights movement. That movement, as I conceive it, is committed to a number of goals, including:

- the total abolition of the use of animals in science;
- the total dissolution of commercial animal agriculture;
- the total elimination of commercial and sport hunting and trapping.

There are, I know, people who profess to believe in animal rights but do not avow these goals. Factory farming, they say, is wrong—it violates animals' rights—but traditional animal agriculture is all right. Toxicity tests of cosmetics on animals violates their rights, but important medical research—cancer research, for example—does not. The clubbing of baby seals is abhorrent, but not the harvesting of adult seals. I used to think I understood this reasoning. Not any more. You don't change unjust institutions by tidying them up.

From In Defense of Animals *(1985), one of several books Regan has published on this ethical issue. Others include* The Case for Animal Rights *(1983) and* Defending Animal Rights *(2001).*

What's wrong—fundamentally wrong—with the way animals are treated isn't the details that vary from case to case. It's the whole system. The forlornness of the veal calf is pathetic, heart-wrenching; the pulsing pain of the chimp with electrodes planted deep in her brain is repulsive; the slow, tortuous death of the racoon caught in the leg-hold trap is agonizing. But what is wrong isn't the pain, isn't the suffering, isn't the deprivation. These compound what's wrong. Sometimes—often—they make it much, much worse. But they are not the fundamental wrong.

The fundamental wrong is the system that allows us to view animals as *our resources,* here for *us*—to be eaten, or surgically manipulated, or exploited for sport or money. Once we accept this view of animals—as our resources—the rest is as predictable as it is regrettable. Why worry about their loneliness, their pain, their death? Since animals exist for us, to benefit us in one way or another, what harms them really doesn't matter—or matters only if it starts to bother us, makes us feel a trifle uneasy when we eat our veal escalope, for example. So, yes, let us get veal calves out of solitary confinement, give them more space, a little straw, a few companions. But let us keep our veal escalope.

But a little straw, more space and a few companions won't eliminate—won't even touch—the basic wrong that attaches to our viewing and treating these animals as our resources. A veal calf killed to be eaten after living in close confinement is viewed and treated in this way: but so, too, is another who is raised (as they say) "more humanely." To right the wrong of our treatment of farm animals requires more than making rearing methods "more humane"; it requires the total dissolution of commercial animal agriculture.

5 How we do this, whether we do it or, as in the case of animals in science, whether and how we abolish their use—these are to a large extent political questions. People must change their beliefs before they change their habits. Enough people, especially those elected to public office, must believe in change—must want it—before we will have laws that protect the rights of animals. This process of change is very complicated, very demanding, very exhausting, calling for the efforts of many hands in education, publicity, political organization and activity, down to the licking of envelopes and stamps. As a trained and practicing philosopher, the sort of contribution I can make is limited but, I like to think, important. The currency of philosophy is ideas—their meaning and rational foundation—not the nuts and bolts of the legislative process, say, or the mechanics of community organization. That's what I have been exploring over the past ten years or so in my essays and talks and, most recently, in my book, *The Case for Animal Rights.* I believe the major conclusions I reach in the book are true because they are supported by the weight of the best arguments. I believe the idea of animal rights has reason, not just emotion, on its side.

In the space I have at my disposal here I can only sketch, in the barest outline, some of the main features of the book. Its main themes—and we should not be surprised by this—involve asking and answering deep, foundational moral questions about what morality is, how it should be understood and what is the best moral theory, all considered. I hope I can convey something of the shape I think this theory takes. The attempt to do this will be (to use a word a friendly critic once used to describe my work) cerebral, perhaps too cerebral. But this is misleading. My feelings about how animals are sometimes treated run just as deep and just as strong as those of my more volatile compatriots. Philosophers do—to use the jargon of the day—have a right side to their brains. If it's the left side we contribute (or mainly should), that's because what talents we have reside there.

How to proceed? We begin by asking how the moral status of animals has been understood by thinkers who deny that animals have rights. Then we test the mettle of their ideas by seeing how well they stand up under the heat of fair criticism. If we start our thinking in this way, we soon find that some people believe that we have no duties directly to animals, that we owe nothing to them, that we can do nothing that wrongs them. Rather, we can do wrong acts that involve animals, and so we have duties regarding them, though none to them. Such views may be called indirect duty views. By way of illustration: suppose your neighbor kicks your dog. Then your neighbor has done something wrong. But not to your dog. The wrong that has been done is a wrong to you. After all, it is wrong to upset people, and your neighbor's kicking your dog upsets you. So you are the one who is wronged, not your dog. Or again: by kicking your dog your neighbor damages your property. And since it is wrong to damage another person's property, your neighbor has done something wrong—to you, of course, not to your dog. Your neighbor no more wrongs your dog than your car would be wronged if the windshield were smashed. Your neighbor's duties involving your dog are indirect duties to you. More generally, all of our duties regarding animals are indirect duties to one another—to humanity.

How could someone try to justify such a view? Someone might say that your dog doesn't feel anything and so isn't hurt by your neighbor's kick, doesn't care about the pain since none is felt, is as unaware of anything as is your windshield. Someone might say this, but no rational person will, since, among other considerations, such a view will commit anyone who holds it to the position that no human being feels pain either—that human beings also don't care about what happens to them. A second possibility is that though both humans and your dog are hurt when kicked, it is only human pain that matters. But, again, no rational person can believe this. Pain is pain wherever it occurs. If your neighbor's causing you pain is wrong because of the pain that is caused, we cannot rationally ignore or dismiss the moral relevance of the pain that your dog feels.

Philosophers who hold indirect duty views—and many still do—have come to understand that they must avoid the two defects just noted: that is, both the view that animals don't feel anything as well as the idea that only human pain can be morally relevant. Among such thinkers the sort of view now favored is one or other form of what is called *contractarianism*.

10 Here, very crudely, is the root idea: morality consists of a set of rules that individuals voluntarily agree to abide by, as we do when we sign a contract (hence the name contractarianism). Those who understand and accept the terms of the contract are covered directly; they have rights created and recognized by, and protected in, the contract and these contractors can also have

protection spelled out for others who, though they lack the ability to understand morality and so cannot sign the contract themselves, are loved or cherished by those who can. Thus young children, for example, are unable to sign contracts and lack rights. But they are protected by the contract none the less because of the sentimental interests of others, most notably their parents. So we have, then, duties involving these children, duties regarding them, but no duties to them. Our duties in their case are indirect duties to other human beings, usually their parents.

As for animals, since they cannot understand contracts, they obviously cannot sign; and since they cannot sign, they have no rights. Like children, however, some animals are the objects of the sentimental interest of others. You, for example, love your dog or cat. So those animals that enough people care about (companion animals, whales, baby seals, the American bald eagle), though they lack rights themselves, will be protected because of the sentimental interests of people. I have, then, according to contractarianism, no duty directly to your dog or any other animal, not even the duty not to cause them pain or suffering; my duty not to hurt them is a duty I have to those people who care about what happens to them. As for other animals, where no or little sentimental interest is present—in the case of farm animals, for example, or laboratory rats—what duties we have grow weaker and weaker, perhaps to vanishing point. The pain and death they endure, though real, are not wrong if no one cares about them.

When it comes to the moral status of animals, contractarianism could be a hard view to refute if it were an adequate theoretical approach to the moral status of human beings. It is not adequate in this latter respect, however, which makes the question of its adequacy in the former case, regarding animals, utterly moot. For consider: morality, according to the (crude) contractarian position before us, consists of rules that people agree to abide by. What people? Well, enough to make a difference—enough, that is, *collectively* to have the power to enforce the rules that are drawn up in the contract. This is very well and good for the signatories but not so good for anyone who is not asked to sign. And there is nothing in contractarianism of the sort we are discussing that guarantees or requires that everyone will have a chance to participate equally in framing the rules of morality. The result is that this approach to ethics could sanction the most blatant forms of social, economic, moral and political injustice, ranging from a repressive caste system to systematic racial or sexual discrimination. Might, according to this theory, does make right. Let those who are the victims of injustice suffer as they will. It matters not so long as no one else—no contractor, or too few of them—cares about it. Such a theory takes one's moral breath away . . . as if, for example, there would be nothing wrong with apartheid in South Africa if few white South Africans were upset by it. A theory with so little to recommend it at the level of the ethics of our treatment of our fellow humans cannot have anything more to recommend it when it comes to the ethics of how we treat our fellow animals.

The version of contractarianism just examined is, as I have noted, a crude variety, and in fairness to those of a contractarian persuasion it must be noted that much more refined, subtle and ingenious varieties are possible.

For example, John Rawls,[1] in his *A Theory of Justice,* sets forth a version of contractarianism that forces contractors to ignore the accidental features of being a human being—for example, whether one is white or black, male or female, a genius or of modest intellect. Only by ignoring such features, Rawls believes, can we ensure that the principles of justice that contractors would agree upon are not based on bias or prejudice. Despite the improvement a view such as Rawls's represents over the cruder forms of contractarianism, it remains deficient: it systematically denies that we have direct duties to those human beings who do not have a sense of justice—young children, for instance, and many mentally retarded humans. And yet it seems reasonably certain that, were we to torture a young child or a retarded elder, we would be doing something that wronged him or her, not something that would be wrong if (and only if) other humans with a sense of justice were upset. And since this is true in the case of these humans, we cannot rationally deny the same in the case of animals.

Indirect duty views, then, including the best among them, fail to command our rational assent. Whatever ethical theory we should accept rationally, therefore, it must at least recognize that we have some duties directly to animals, just as we have some duties directly to each other. The next two theories I'll sketch attempt to meet this requirement.

15 The first I call the cruelty-kindness view. Simply stated, this says that we have a direct duty to be kind to animals and a direct duty not to be cruel to them. Despite the familiar, reassuring ring of these ideas, I do not believe that this view offers an adequate theory. To make this clearer, consider kindness. A kind person acts from a certain kind of motive—compassion or concern, for example. And that is a virtue. But there is no guarantee that a kind act is a right act. If I am a generous racist, for example, I will be inclined to act kindly towards members of my own race, favoring their interests above those of others. My kindness would be real and, so far as it goes, good. But I trust it is too obvious to require argument that my kind acts may not be above moral reproach—may, in fact, be positively wrong because rooted in injustice. So kindness, notwithstanding its status as a virtue to be encouraged, simply will not carry the weight of a theory of right action.

Cruelty fares no better. People or their acts are cruel if they display either a lack of sympathy for or, worse, the presence of enjoyment in another's suffering. Cruelty in all its guises is a bad thing, a tragic human failing. But just as a person's being motivated by kindness does not guarantee that he or she does what is right, so the absence of cruelty does not ensure that he or she avoids doing what is wrong. Many people who perform abortions, for example, are not cruel, sadistic people. But that fact alone does not settle the terribly difficult question of the morality of abortion. The case is no different when we examine the ethics of our treatment of animals. So, yes, let us be for kindness and against cruelty. But let us not suppose that being for the one and against the other answers questions about moral right and wrong.

1. American philosopher (1921–2002).

Some people think that the theory we are looking for is utilitarianism. A utilitarian accepts two moral principles. The first is that of equality: everyone's interests count, and similar interests must be counted as having similar weight or importance. White or black, American or Iranian, human or animal—everyone's pain or frustration matter, and matter just as much as the equivalent pain or frustration of anyone else. The second principle a utilitarian accepts is that of utility: do the act that will bring about the best balance between satisfaction and frustration for everyone affected by the outcome.

As a utilitarian, then, here is how I am to approach the task of deciding what I morally ought to do: I must ask who will be affected if I choose to do one thing rather than another, how much each individual will be affected, and where the best results are most likely to lie—which option, in other words, is most likely to bring about the best results, the best balance between satisfaction and frustration. That option, whatever it may be, is the one I ought to choose. That is where my moral duty lies.

The great appeal of utilitarianism rests with its uncompromising *egalitarianism:* everyone's interests count and count as much as the like interests of everyone else. The kind of odious discrimination that some forms of contractarianism can justify—discrimination based on race or sex, for example—seems disallowed in principle by utilitarianism, as is speciesism, systematic discrimination based on species membership.

The equality we find in utilitarianism, however, is not the sort an advocate of animal or human rights should have in mind. Utilitarianism has no room for the equal moral rights of different individuals because it has no room for their equal inherent value or worth. What has value for the utilitarian is the satisfaction of an individual's interests, not the individual whose interests they are. A universe in which you satisfy your desire for water, food and warmth is, other things being equal, better than a universe in which these desires are frustrated. And the same is true in the case of an animal with similar desires. But neither you nor the animal have any value in your own right. Only your feelings do. 20

Here is an analogy to help make the philosophical point clearer: a cup contains different liquids, sometimes sweet, sometimes bitter, sometimes a mix of the two. What has value are the liquids: the sweeter the better, the bitterer the worse. The cup, the container, has no value. It is what goes into it, not what they go into, that has value. For the utilitarian you and I are like the cup; we have no value as individuals and thus no equal value. What has value is what goes into us, what we serve as receptacles for; our feelings of satisfaction have positive value, our feelings of frustration negative value.

Serious problems arise for utilitarianism when we remind ourselves that it enjoins us to bring about the best consequences. What does this mean? It doesn't mean the best consequences for me alone, or for my family or friends, or any other person taken individually. No, what we must do is, roughly, as follows: we must add up (somehow!) the separate satisfactions and frustrations of everyone likely to be affected by our choice, the satisfactions in one column, the frustrations in the other. We must total each column for each of the options before us. That is what it means to say the theory is aggregative. And then we must choose that option which is most likely to bring about the best balance of totaled satisfactions over totaled frustrations. Whatever act would lead to this outcome is the one we ought morally to perform—it is where our moral duty lies. And that act quite clearly might not be the same one that would bring about the best results for me personally, or for my family or friends, or for a lab animal. The best aggregated consequences for everyone concerned are not necessarily the best for each individual.

That utilitarianism is an aggregative theory—different individuals' satisfactions or frustrations are added, or summed, or totaled—is the key objection to this theory. My Aunt Bea is old, inactive, a cranky, sour person, though not physically ill. She prefers to go on living. She is also rather rich. I could make a fortune if I could get my hands on her money, money she intends to give me in any event, after she dies, but which she refuses to give me now. In order to avoid a huge tax bite, I plan to donate a handsome sum of my profits to a local children's hospital. Many, many children will benefit from my generosity, and much joy will be brought to their parents, relatives and friends. If I don't get the money rather soon, all these ambitions will come to naught. The once-in-a-lifetime opportunity to make a real killing will be gone. Why, then, not kill my Aunt Bea? Oh, of course I *might* get caught. But I'm no fool and, besides, her doctor can be counted on to cooperate (he has an eye for the same investment and I happen to know a good deal about his shady past). The deed can be done . . . professionally, shall we say. There is *very* little chance of getting caught. And as for my conscience being guilt-ridden, I am a resourceful sort of fellow and will take more than sufficient comfort—as I lie on the beach at Acapulco—in contemplating the joy and health I have brought to so many others.

Suppose Aunt Bea is killed and the rest of the story comes out as told. Would I have done anything wrong? Anything immoral? One would have thought that I had. Not according to utilitarianism. Since what I have done has brought about the best balance between totaled satisfaction and frustration for all those affected by the outcome, my action is not wrong. Indeed, in killing Aunt Bea the physician and I did what duty required.

25 This same kind of argument can be repeated in all sorts of cases, illustrating, time after time, how the utilitarian's position leads to results that impartial people find morally callous. It *is* wrong to kill my Aunt Bea in the name of bringing about the best results for others. A good end does not justify an evil means. Any adequate moral theory will have to explain why this is so. Utilitarianism fails in this respect and so cannot be the theory we seek.

What to do? Where to begin anew? The place to begin, I think, is with the utilitarian's view of the value of the individual—or, rather, lack of value. In its place, suppose we consider that you and I, for example, do have value as individuals—what we'll call *inherent value.* To say we have such value is to say that we are something more than, something different from, mere receptacles. Moreover, to ensure that we do not pave the way for such injustices as slavery or sexual discrimination, we must believe that all who have inherent value have it equally, regardless of their sex, race, religion, birthplace and so on. Similarly to be discarded as irrelevant are one's talents or skills, intelligence and wealth, personality or pathology, whether one is loved and admired or despised and loathed. The genius and the retarded child, the prince and the pauper, the brain surgeon and the fruit vendor, Mother Teresa[2] and the most unscrupulous used-car salesman—all have inherent value, all possess it equally, and all have an equal right to be treated with respect, to be treated in ways that do not reduce them to the status of things, as if they existed as resources for others. My value as an individual is independent of my usefulness to you. Yours is not dependent on your usefulness to me. For either of us to treat the other in ways that fail to show respect for the other's independent value is to act immorally, to violate the individual's rights.

Some of the rational virtues of this view—what I call the rights view—should be evident. Unlike (crude) contractarianism, for example, the rights view *in principle* denies the moral tolerability of any and all forms of racial, sexual or social discrimination; and unlike utilitarianism, this view *in principle* denies that we can justify good results by using evil means that violate an individual's rights—denies, for example, that it could be moral to kill my Aunt Bea to harvest beneficial consequences for others. That would be to sanction the disrespectful treatment of the individual in the name of the social good, something the rights view will not—categorically will not—ever allow.

The rights view, I believe, is rationally the most satisfactory moral theory. It surpasses all other theories in the degree to which it illuminates and explains the foundation of our duties to one another—the domain of human morality. On this score it has the best reasons, the best arguments, on its side. Of course, if it were possible to show that only human beings are included within its scope, then a person like myself, who believes in animal rights, would be obliged to look elsewhere.

But attempts to limit its scope to humans only can be shown to be rationally defective. Animals, it is true, lack many of the abilities humans possess. They can't read, do higher mathematics, build a bookcase or make *baba ghanoush.*[3] Neither can many human beings, however, and yet we don't (and shouldn't) say that they (these humans) therefore have less inherent value, less of a right to be treated with respect, than do others. It is the *similarities* between those human beings who most clearly, most noncontroversially have such value (the people reading this, for example), not our differences, that matter most. And the really crucial, the basic similarity is simply this: we are each of us the experiencing subject of a life, a conscious creature having an individual welfare that has importance to us whatever our usefulness to others. We want and prefer things, believe and feel things, recall and expect things. And all these dimensions of our life, including our pleasure and pain, our enjoyment and suffering, our satisfaction and frustration, our continued existence or our untimely death—all make a difference to the quality of our life as lived, as experienced, by us as individuals. As the same is true of those animals that concern us (the ones that

2. Nun (1910–1997) who founded the Missionaries of Charity in Kolkata, India, and is now proverbially known as the ultimate good person.

3. An eggplant-sesame spread or dip popular in the Middle East.

are eaten and trapped, for example), they too must be viewed as the experiencing subjects of a life, with inherent value of their own.

30 Some there are who resist the idea that animals have inherent value. "Only humans have such value," they profess. How might this narrow view be defended? Shall we say that only humans have the requisite intelligence, or autonomy, or reason? But there are many, many humans who fail to meet these standards and yet are reasonably viewed as having value above and beyond their usefulness to others. Shall we claim that only humans belong to the right species, the species *Homo sapiens*?[4] But this is blatant speciesism. Will it be said, then, that all—and only—humans have immortal souls? Then our opponents have their work cut out for them. I am myself not ill-disposed to the proposition that there are immortal souls. Personally, I profoundly hope I have one. But I would not want to rest my position on a controversial ethical issue on the even more controversial question about who or what has an immortal soul. That is to dig one's hole deeper, not to climb out. Rationally, it is better to resolve moral issues without making more controversial assumptions than are needed. The question of who has inherent value is such a question, one that is resolved more rationally without the introduction of the idea of immortal souls than by its use.

Well, perhaps some will say that animals have some inherent value, only less than we have. Once again, however, attempts to defend this view can be shown to lack rational justification. What could be the basis of our having more inherent value than animals? Their lack of reason, or autonomy, or intellect? Only if we are willing to make the same judgment in the case of humans who are similarly deficient. But it is not true that such humans—the retarded child, for example, or the mentally deranged—have less inherent value than you or I. Neither, then, can we rationally sustain the view that animals like them in being the experiencing subjects of a life have less inherent value. *All* who have inherent value have it *equally,* whether they be human animals or not.

Inherent value, then, belongs equally to those who are the experiencing subjects of a life. Whether it belongs to others—to rocks and rivers, trees and glaciers, for example—we do not know and may never know. But neither do we need to know, if we are to make the case for animal rights. We do not need to know, for example, how many people are eligible to vote in the next presidential election before we can know whether I am. Similarly, we do not need to know how many individuals have inherent value before we can know that some do. When it comes to the case for animal rights, then, what we need to know is whether the animals that, in our culture, are routinely eaten, hunted and used in our laboratories, for example, are like us in being subjects of a life. And we do know this. We do know that many—literally, billions and billions—of these animals are the subjects of a life in the sense explained and so have inherent value if we do. And since, in order to arrive at the best theory of our duties to one another, we must recognize our equal inherent value as individuals,

4. Latin for "man with intellect," the taxonomic designation for the modern human species.

reason—not sentiment, not emotion—reason compels us to recognize the equal inherent value of these animals and, with this, their equal right to be treated with respect.

That, *very* roughly, is the shape and feel of the case for animal rights. Most of the details of the supporting argument are missing. They are to be found in the book to which I alluded earlier. Here, the details go begging, and I must, in closing, limit myself to four final points.

The first is how the theory that underlies the case for animal rights shows that the animal rights movement is a part of, not antagonistic to, the human rights movement. The theory that rationally grounds the rights of animals also grounds the rights of humans. Thus those involved in the animal rights movement are partners in the struggle to secure respect for human rights—the rights of women, for example, or minorities, or workers. The animal rights movement is cut from the same moral cloth as these.

35 Second, having set out the broad outlines of the rights view, I can now say why its implications for farming and science, among other fields, are both clear and uncompromising. In the case of the use of animals in science, the rights view is categorically abolitionist. Lab animals are not our tasters; we are not their kings. Because these animals are treated routinely, systematically as if their value were reducible to their usefulness to others, they are routinely, systematically treated with a lack of respect, and thus are their rights routinely, systematically violated. This is just as true when they are used in trivial, duplicative, unnecessary or unwise research as it is when they are used in studies that hold out real promise of human benefits. We can't justify harming or killing a human being (my Aunt Bea, for example) just for these sorts of reason. Neither can we do so even in the case of so lowly a creature as a laboratory rat. It is not just refinement or reduction that is called for, not just larger, cleaner cages, not just more generous use of anaesthetic or the elimination of multiple surgery, not just tidying up the system. It is complete replacement. The best we can do when it comes to using animals in science is—not to use them. That is where our duty lies, according to the rights view.

As for commercial animal agriculture, the rights view takes a similar abolitionist position. The fundamental moral wrong here is not that animals are kept in stressful close confinement or in isolation, or that their pain and suffering, their needs and preferences are ignored or discounted. All these *are* wrong, of course, but they are not the fundamental wrong. They are symptoms and effects of the deeper, systematic wrong that allows these animals to be viewed and treated as lacking independent value, as resources for us—as, indeed, a renewable resource. Giving farm animals more space, more natural environments, more companions does not right the fundamental wrong, any more than giving lab animals more anaesthesia or bigger, cleaner cages would right the fundamental wrong in their case. Nothing less than the total dissolution of commercial animal agriculture will do this, just as, for similar reasons I won't develop at length here, morality requires nothing less than the total elimination of hunting and trapping for commercial and sporting ends. The rights view's implications, then, as I have said, are clear and uncompromising.

My last two points are about philosophy, my profession. It is, most obviously, no substitute for political action. The words I have written here and in other places by themselves don't change a thing. It is what we do with the thoughts that the words express—our acts, our deeds—that changes things. All that philosophy can do, and all I have attempted, is to offer a vision of what our deeds should aim at. And the why. But not the how.

Finally, I am reminded of my thoughtful critic, the one I mentioned earlier, who chastised me for being too cerebral. Well, cerebral I have been: indirect duty views, utilitarianism, contractarianism—hardly the stuff deep passions are made of. I am also reminded, however, of the image another friend once set before me—the image of the ballerina as expressive of disciplined passion. Long hours of sweat and toil, of loneliness and practice, of doubt and fatigue: those are the discipline of her craft. But the passion is there too, the fierce drive to excel, to speak through her body, to do it right, to pierce our minds. That is the image of philosophy I would leave with you, not "too cerebral" but *disciplined passion.* Of the discipline enough has been seen. As for the passion: there are times, and these not infrequent, when tears come to my eyes when I see, or read, or hear of the wretched plight of animals in the hands of humans. Their pain, their suffering, their loneliness, their innocence, their death. Anger. Rage. Pity. Sorrow. Disgust. The whole creation groans under the weight of the evil we humans visit upon these mute, powerless creatures. It *is* our hearts, not just our heads, that call for an end to it all, that demand of us that we overcome, for them, the habits and forces behind their systematic oppression. All great movements, it is written, go through three stages: ridicule, discussion, adoption. It is the realization of this third stage, adoption, that requires both our passion and our discipline, our hearts and our heads. The fate of animals is in our hands. God grant we are equal to the task.

Questions

1. Regan argues against four views that deny rights to animals: indirect duty, contractarianism, cruelty-kindness, and utilitarianism. Locate his account of each and explain his objections to it.

2. Regan then argues for what he calls a "rights view," which is, he claims, "rationally the most satisfactory moral theory" (paragraph 28). Explain both his view and his claim.

3. What are the advantages of arguing for views that conflict with one's own before arguing for one's own? What are the disadvantages?

4. Regan includes among his goals "the total dissolution of commercial animal agriculture" and "the total elimination of commercial and sport hunting and trapping" (paragraph 1). Do these goals include vegetarianism? If so, why does he not use the word "vegetarian"?

5. Write an essay in which you take a position on an issue about which you have strong feelings. Following Regan's example, focus on your argument while both acknowledging and excluding your feelings.

Michael Pollan *An Animal's Place*

THE FIRST TIME I opened Peter Singer's *Animal Liberation*, I was dining alone at the Palm,[1] trying to enjoy a rib-eye steak cooked medium-rare. If this sounds like a good recipe for cognitive dissonance (if not indigestion), that was sort of the idea. Preposterous as it might seem, to supporters of animal rights, what I was doing was tantamount to reading *Uncle Tom's Cabin* on a plantation in the Deep South in 1852.

Singer and the swelling ranks of his followers ask us to imagine a future in which people will look back on my meal, and this steakhouse, as relics of an equally backward age. Eating animals, wearing animals, experimenting on animals, killing animals for sport: all these practices, so resolutely normal to us, will be seen as the barbarities they are, and we will come to view "speciesism"—a neologism I had encountered before only in jokes—as a form of discrimination as indefensible as racism or anti-Semitism.

Even in 1975, when *Animal Liberation* was first published, Singer, an Australian philosopher now teaching at Princeton, was confident that he had the wind of history at his back. The recent civil rights past was prologue, as one liberation movement followed on the heels of another. Slowly but surely, the white man's circle of moral consideration was expanded to admit first blacks, then women, then homosexuals. In each case, a group once thought to be so different from the prevailing "we" as to be undeserving of civil rights was, after a struggle, admitted to the club. Now it was animals' turn.

That animal liberation is the logical next step in the forward march of moral progress is no longer the fringe idea it was back in 1975. A growing and increasingly influential group of philosophers, ethicists, law professors and activists are convinced that the great moral struggle of our time will be for the rights of animals.

5 So far the movement has scored some of its biggest victories in Europe. Earlier this year, Germany became the first nation to grant animals a constitutional right: the words "and animals" were added to a provision obliging the state to respect and protect the dignity of human beings. The farming of animals for fur was recently banned in England. In several European nations, sows may no longer be confined to crates nor laying hens to "battery cages"—stacked wired cages so small the birds cannot stretch their wings. The Swiss are amending their laws to change the status of animals from "things" to "beings."

Though animals are still very much "things" in the eyes of American law, change is in the air. Thirty-seven states have recently passed laws making some forms of animal cruelty a crime, twenty-one of them by ballot initiative.

Published on November 10, 2002, in the New York Times Magazine, *a supplement to the Sunday newspaper.*

1. Famous New York City steakhouse.

Following protests by activists, McDonald's and Burger King forced significant improvements in the way the U.S. meat industry slaughters animals. Agribusiness and the cosmetics and apparel industries are all struggling to defuse mounting public concerns over animal welfare.

Once thought of as a left-wing concern, the movement now cuts across ideological lines. Perhaps the most eloquent recent plea on behalf of animals, a new book called *Dominion*, was written by a former speechwriter for President Bush. And once outlandish ideas are finding their way into mainstream opinion. A recent Zogby poll found that fifty-one percent of Americans believe that primates are entitled to the same rights as human children.

What is going on here? A certain amount of cultural confusion, for one thing. For at the same time many people seem eager to extend the circle of our moral consideration to animals, in our factory farms and laboratories we are inflicting more suffering on more animals than at any time in history. One by one, science is dismantling our claims to uniqueness as a species, discovering that such things as culture, toolmaking, language and even possibly self-consciousness are not the exclusive domain of *Homo sapiens*. Yet most of the animals we kill lead lives organized very much in the spirit of Descartes,[2] who famously claimed that animals were mere machines, incapable of thought or feeling. There's a schizoid quality to our relationship with animals, in which sentiment and brutality exist side by side. Half the dogs in America will receive Christmas presents this year, yet few of us pause to consider the miserable life of the pig—an animal easily as intelligent as a dog—that becomes the Christmas ham.

We tolerate this disconnect because the life of the pig has moved out of view. When's the last time you saw a pig? (Babe doesn't count.) Except for our pets, real animals—animals living and dying—no longer figure in our everyday lives. Meat comes from the grocery store, where it is cut and packaged to look as little like parts of animals as possible. The disappearance of animals from our lives has opened a space in which there's no reality check, either on the sentiment or the brutality. This is pretty much where we live now, with respect to animals, and it is a space in which the Peter Singers and Frank Perdues of the world can evidently thrive equally well.

10 Several years ago, the English critic John Berger wrote an essay, "Why Look at Animals?," in which he suggested that the loss of everyday contact between ourselves and animals—and specifically the loss of eye contact—has left us deeply confused about the terms of our relationship to other species. That eye contact, always slightly uncanny, had provided a vivid daily reminder that animals were at once crucially like and unlike us; in their eyes we glimpsed something unmistakably familiar (pain, fear, tenderness) and something irretrievably alien. Upon this paradox people built a relationship in which they felt they could both honor and eat animals without looking away. But that accommodation has pretty much broken down; nowadays, it seems, we either look away or become vegetarians. For my own part, neither option seemed especially appetizing.

2. René Descartes (1596–1650), French philosopher.

Which might explain how I found myself reading *Animal Liberation* in a steakhouse.

This is not something I'd recommend if you're determined to continue eating meat. Combining rigorous philosophical argument with journalistic description, *Animal Liberation* is one of those rare books that demand that you either defend the way you live or change it. Because Singer is so skilled in argument, for many readers it is easier to change. His book has converted countless thousands to vegetarianism, and it didn't take long for me to see why: within a few pages, he had succeeded in throwing me on the defensive.

Singer's argument is disarmingly simple and, if you accept its premises, difficult to refute. Take the premise of equality, which most people readily accept. Yet what do we really mean by it? People are not, as a matter of fact, equal at all—some are smarter than others, better looking, more gifted. "Equality is a moral idea," Singer points out, "not an assertion of fact." The moral idea is that everyone's interests ought to receive equal consideration, regardless of "what abilities they may possess." Fair enough; many philosophers have gone this far. But fewer have taken the next logical step. "If possessing a higher degree of intelligence does not entitle one human to use another for his or her own ends, how can it entitle humans to exploit nonhumans for the same purpose?"

This is the nub of Singer's argument, and right around here I began scribbling objections in the margin. *But humans differ from animals in morally significant ways.* Yes they do, Singer acknowledges, which is why we shouldn't treat pigs and children alike. Equal consideration of interests is not the same as equal treatment, he points out: children have an interest in being educated; pigs, in rooting around in the dirt. But where their interests are the same, the principle of equality demands they receive the same consideration. And the one all-important interest that we share with pigs, as with all sentient creatures, is an interest in avoiding pain.

Here Singer quotes a famous passage from Jeremy Bentham, the eighteenth-century utilitarian philosopher, that is the wellspring of the animal rights movement. Bentham was writing in 1789, soon after the French colonies freed black slaves, granting them fundamental rights. "The day *may* come," he speculates, "when the rest of the animal creation may acquire those rights." Bentham then asks what characteristic entitles any being to moral consideration. "Is it the faculty of reason or perhaps the faculty of discourse?" Obviously not, since "a full-grown horse or dog is beyond comparison a more rational, as well as a more conversable animal, than an infant." He concludes: "The question is not, Can they *reason*? nor, Can they *talk*? but, Can they *suffer*?"

15 Bentham here is playing a powerful card philosophers call the "argument from marginal cases," or AMC for short. It goes like this: There are humans—infants, the severely retarded, the demented—whose mental function cannot match that of a chimpanzee. Even though these people cannot reciprocate our moral attentions, we nevertheless include them in the circle of our moral consideration. So on what basis do we exclude the chimpanzee?

Because he's a chimp, I furiously scribbled in the margin, *and they're human!* For Singer that's not good enough. To exclude the chimp from moral consideration simply because he's not human is no different from excluding the slave simply because he's not white. In the same way we'd call that exclusion racist, the animal rightist contends that it is speciesist to discriminate against the chimpanzee solely because he's not human.

But the differences between blacks and whites are trivial compared with the differences between my son and a chimp. Singer counters by asking us to imagine a hypothetical society that discriminates against people on the basis of something nontrivial—say, intelligence. If that scheme offends our sense of equality, then why is the fact that animals lack certain human characteristics any more just as a basis for discrimination? Either we do not owe any justice to the severely retarded, he concludes, or we do owe it to animals with higher capabilities.

This is where I put down my fork. If I believe in equality, and equality is based on interests rather than characteristics, then I have to either take the interests of the steer I'm eating into account or concede that I am a speciesist. For the time being, I decided to plead guilty as charged. I finished my steak.

But Singer had planted a troubling notion, and in the days afterward, it grew and grew, watered by the other animal rights thinkers I began reading: the philosophers Tom Regan and James Rachels; the legal theorist Steven M. Wise; the writers Joy Williams and Matthew Scully. I didn't *think* I minded being a speciesist, but could it be, as several of these writers suggest, that we will someday come to regard speciesism as an evil comparable to racism? Will history someday judge us as harshly as it judges the Germans who went about their ordinary lives in the shadow of Treblinka? Precisely that question was recently posed by J. M. Coetzee, the South African novelist, in a lecture delivered at Princeton; he answered it in the affirmative. If animal rightists are right, "a crime of stupefying proportions" (in Coetzee's words) is going on all around us every day, just beneath our notice.

20 It's an idea almost impossible to entertain seriously, much less to accept, and in the weeks following my restaurant face-off between Singer and the steak, I found myself marshaling whatever mental power I could muster to try to refute it. Yet Singer and his allies managed to trump almost all my objections.

My first line of defense was obvious. *Animals kill one another all the time. Why treat animals more ethically than they treat one another?* (Ben Franklin tried this one long before me: during a fishing trip, he wondered, "If you eat one another, I don't see why we may not eat you." He admits, however, that the rationale didn't occur to him until the fish were in the frying pan, smelling "admirably well." The advantage of being a "reasonable creature," Franklin remarks, is that you can find a reason for whatever you want to do.) To the "they do it too" defense, the animal rightist has a devastating reply: Do you really want to base your morality on the natural order? Murder and rape are natural too. Besides, humans don't need to kill other creatures in order to survive; animals do. (Though if my cat, Otis, is any guide, animals sometimes kill for sheer pleasure.)

This suggests another defense. *Wouldn't life in the wild be worse for these farm animals?* "Defenders of slavery imposed on black Africans often made a similar point," Singer retorts. "The life of freedom is to be preferred."

But domesticated animals can't survive in the wild; in fact, without us they wouldn't exist at all. Or as one nineteenth-century political philosopher put it, "The pig has a stronger interest than anyone in the demand for bacon. If all the world were Jewish, there would be no pigs at all." But it turns out that this would be fine by the animal rightists: for if pigs don't exist, they can't be wronged.

Animals on factory farms have never known any other life. Singer replies that "animals feel a need to exercise, stretch their limbs or wings, groom themselves and turn around, whether or not they have ever lived in conditions that permit this." The measure of their suffering is not their prior experiences but the unremitting daily frustration of their instincts.

25 *OK, the suffering of animals is a legitimate problem, but the world is full of problems, and surely human problems must come first!* Sounds good, and yet all the animal people are asking me to do is to stop eating meat and wearing animal furs and hides. There's no reason I can't devote myself to solving humankind's problems while being a vegetarian who wears synthetics.

But doesn't the fact that we could choose to forgo meat for moral reasons point to a crucial moral difference between animals and humans? As Kant pointed out, the human being is the only moral animal, the only one even capable of entertaining a concept of "rights." What's wrong with reserving moral consideration for those able to reciprocate it? Right here is where you run smack into the AMC: the moral status of the retarded, the insane, the infant and the Alzheimer's patient. Such "marginal cases," in the detestable argot of modern moral philosophy, cannot participate in moral decision-making any more than a monkey can, yet we nevertheless grant them rights.

That's right, I respond, for the simple reason that they're one of us. And all of us have been, and will probably once again be, marginal cases ourselves. What's more, these people have fathers and mothers, daughters and sons, which makes our interest in their welfare deeper than our interest in the welfare of even the most brilliant ape.

Alas, none of these arguments evade the charge of speciesism; the racist, too, claims that it's natural to give special consideration to one's own kind. A utilitarian like Singer would agree, however, that the feelings of relatives do count for something. Yet the principle of equal consideration of interests demands that, given the choice between performing a painful medical experiment on a severely retarded orphan and on a normal ape, we must sacrifice the child. Why? Because the ape has a greater capacity for pain.

Here in a nutshell is the problem with the AMC: it can be used to help the animals, but just as often it winds up hurting the marginal cases. Giving up our speciesism will bring us to a moral cliff from which we may not be prepared to jump, even when logic is pushing us.

30 And yet this isn't the moral choice I am being asked to make. (Too bad; it would be so much easier!) In everyday life, the choice is not between babies and chimps but between the pork and the tofu. Even if we reject the "hard

utilitarianism" of a Peter Singer, there remains the question of whether we owe animals that can feel pain *any* moral consideration, and this seems impossible to deny. And if we do owe them moral consideration, how can we justify eating them?

This is why killing animals for meat (and clothing) poses the most difficult animal rights challenge. In the case of animal testing, all but the most radical animal rightists are willing to balance the human benefit against the cost to the animals. That's because the unique qualities of human consciousness carry weight in the utilitarian calculus: human pain counts for more than that of a mouse, since our pain is amplified by emotions like dread; similarly, our deaths are worse than an animal's because we understand what death is in a way they don't. So the argument over animal testing is really in the details: Is this particular procedure or test *really* necessary to save human lives? (Very often it's not, in which case we probably shouldn't do it.) But if humans no longer need to eat meat or wear skins, then what exactly are we putting on the human side of the scale to outweigh the interests of the animal?

I suspect that this is finally why the animal people managed to throw me on the defensive. It's one thing to choose between the chimp and the retarded child or to accept the sacrifice of all those pigs surgeons practiced on to develop heart-bypass surgery. But what happens when the choice is between "a lifetime of suffering for a nonhuman animal and the gastronomic preference of a human being?" You look away—or you stop eating animals. And if you don't want to do either? Then you have to try to determine if the animals you're eating have really endured "a lifetime of suffering."

Whether our interest in eating animals outweighs their interest in not being eaten (assuming for the moment that is their interest) turns on the vexed question of animal suffering. Vexed, because it is impossible to know what really goes on in the mind of a cow or a pig or even an ape. Strictly speaking, this is true of other humans, too, but since humans are all basically wired the same way, we have excellent reason to assume that other people's experience of pain feels much like our own. Can we say that about animals? Yes and no.

I have yet to find anyone who still subscribes to Descartes's belief that animals cannot feel pain because they lack a soul. The general consensus among scientists and philosophers is that when it comes to pain, the higher animals are wired much the way we are for the same evolutionary reasons, so we should take the writhings of the kicked dog at face value. Indeed, the very premise of a great deal of animal testing—the reason it has value—is that animals' experience of physical and even some psychological pain closely resembles our own. Otherwise, why would cosmetics testers drip chemicals into the eyes of rabbits to see if they sting? Why would researchers study head trauma by traumatizing chimpanzee heads? Why would psychologists attempt to induce depression and "learned helplessness" in dogs by exposing them to ceaseless random patterns of electrical shock?

35 That said, it can be argued that human pain differs from animal pain by an order of magnitude. This qualitative difference is largely the result of our

possession of language and, by virtue of language, an ability to have thoughts about thoughts and to imagine alternatives to our current reality. The philosopher Daniel C. Dennett suggests that we would do well to draw a distinction between pain, which a great many animals experience, and suffering, which depends on a degree of self-consciousness only a few animals appear to command. Suffering, in this view, is not just lots of pain but pain intensified by human emotions like loss, sadness, worry, regret, self-pity, shame, humiliation and dread.

Consider castration. No one would deny the procedure is painful to animals, yet animals appear to get over it in a way humans do not. (Some rhesus monkeys competing for mates will bite off a rival's testicle; the very next day the victim may be observed mating, seemingly little the worse for wear.) Surely the suffering of a man able to comprehend the full implications of castration, to anticipate the event and contemplate its aftermath, represents an agony of another order.

By the same token, however, language and all that comes with it can also make certain kinds of pain *more* bearable. A trip to the dentist would be a torment for an ape that couldn't be made to understand the purpose and duration of the procedure.

As humans contemplating the pain and suffering of animals, we do need to guard against projecting onto them what the same experience would feel like to us. Watching a steer force-marched up the ramp to the kill-floor door, as I have done, I need to remind myself that this is not Sean Penn in *Dead Man Walking*, that in a bovine brain the concept of nonexistence is blissfully absent. "If we fail to find suffering in the [animal] lives we can see," Dennett writes in *Kinds of Minds*, "we can rest assured there is no invisible suffering somewhere in their brains. If we find suffering, we will recognize it without difficulty."

Which brings us—reluctantly, necessarily—to the American factory farm, the place where all such distinctions turn to dust. It's not easy to draw lines between pain and suffering in a modern egg or confinement hog operation. These are places where the subtleties of moral philosophy and animal cognition mean less than nothing, where everything we've learned about animals at least since Darwin has been simply . . . set aside. To visit a modern CAFO (Confined Animal Feeding Operation) is to enter a world that, for all its technological sophistication, is still designed according to Cartesian principles: animals are machines incapable of feeling pain. Since no thinking person can possibly believe this anymore, industrial animal agriculture depends on a suspension of disbelief on the part of the people who operate it and a willingness to avert your eyes on the part of everyone else.

40 From everything I've read, egg and hog operations are the worst. Beef cattle in America at least still live outdoors, albeit standing ankle deep in their own waste, eating a diet that makes them sick. And broiler chickens, although they do get their beaks snipped off with a hot knife to keep them from cannibalizing one another under the stress of their confinement, at least don't spend their eight-week lives in cages too small to ever stretch a wing. That fate is reserved

for the American laying hen, who passes her brief span piled together with a half-dozen other hens in a wire cage whose floor a single page of this magazine could carpet. Every natural instinct of this animal is thwarted, leading to a range of behavioral "vices" that can include cannibalizing her cagemates and rubbing her body against the wire mesh until it is featherless and bleeding. Pain? Suffering? Madness? The operative suspension of disbelief depends on more neutral descriptors, like "vices" and "stress." Whatever you want to call what's going on in those cages, the ten percent or so of hens that can't bear it and simply die is built into the cost of production. And when the output of the others begins to ebb, the hens will be "force-molted"—starved of food and water and light for several days in order to stimulate a final bout of egg-laying before their life's work is done.

Simply reciting these facts, most of which are drawn from poultry-trade magazines, makes me sound like one of those animal people, doesn't it? I don't mean to, but this is what can happen when . . . you look. It certainly wasn't my intention to ruin anyone's breakfast. But now that I probably have spoiled the eggs, I do want to say one thing about the bacon, mention a single practice (by no means the worst) in modern hog production that points to the compound madness of an impeccable industrial logic.

Piglets in confinement operations are weaned from their mothers ten days after birth (compared with thirteen weeks in nature) because they gain weight faster on their hormone- and antibiotic-fortified feed. This premature weaning leaves the pigs with a life-long craving to suck and chew, a desire they gratify in confinement by biting the tail of the animal in front of them. A normal pig would fight off his molester, but a demoralized pig has stopped caring. "Learned helplessness" is the psychological term, and it's not uncommon in confinement operations, where tens of thousands of hogs spend their entire lives ignorant of sunshine or earth or straw, crowded together beneath a metal roof upon metal slats suspended over a manure pit. So it's not surprising that an animal as sensitive and intelligent as a pig would get depressed, and a depressed pig will allow his tail to be chewed on to the point of infection. Sick pigs, being underperforming "production units," are clubbed to death on the spot. The USDA's recommended solution to the problem is called "tail docking." Using a pair of pliers (and no anesthetic), most but not all of the tail is snipped off. Why the little stump? Because the whole point of the exercise is not to remove the object of tail-biting so much as to render it *more* sensitive. Now, a bite on the tail is so painful that even the most demoralized pig will mount a struggle to avoid it.

Much of this description is drawn from *Dominion*, Matthew Scully's recent book in which he offers a harrowing description of a North Carolina hog operation. Scully, a Christian conservative, has no patience for lefty rights talk, arguing instead that while God did give man "dominion" over animals ("Every moving thing that liveth shall be meat for you"), he also admonished us to show them mercy. "We are called to treat them with kindness, not because they have rights or power or some claim to equality but . . . because they stand unequal and powerless before us."

Scully calls the contemporary factory farm "our own worst nightmare" and, to his credit, doesn't shrink from naming the root cause of this evil:

unfettered capitalism. (Perhaps this explains why he resigned from the Bush administration just before his book's publication.) A tension has always existed between the capitalist imperative to maximize efficiency and the moral imperatives of religion or community which have historically served as a counterweight to the moral blindness of the market. This is one of "the cultural contradictions of capitalism"—the tendency of the economic impulse to erode the moral underpinnings of society. Mercy toward animals is one such casualty.

More than any other institution, the American industrial animal farm offers a nightmarish glimpse of what capitalism can look like in the absence of moral or regulatory constraint. In these places life itself is redefined—as protein production—and with it suffering. *That* venerable word becomes "stress," an economic problem in search of a cost-effective solution, like tail-docking or beak-clipping or, in the industry's latest plan, by simply engineering the "stress gene" out of pigs and chickens. "Our own worst nightmare" such a place may well be; it is also real life for the billions of animals unlucky enough to have been born beneath these grim steel roofs, into the brief, pitiless life of a "production unit" in the days before the suffering gene was found. 45

Vegetarianism doesn't seem an unreasonable response to such an evil. Who would want to be made complicit in the agony of these animals by eating them? You want to throw *something* against the walls of those infernal sheds, whether it's the Bible, a new constitutional right or a whole platoon of animal rightists bent on breaking in and liberating the inmates. In the shadow of these factory farms, Coetzee's notion of a "stupefying crime" doesn't seem far-fetched at all.

But before you swear off meat entirely, let me describe a very different sort of animal farm. It is typical of nothing, and yet its very existence puts the whole moral question of animal agriculture in a different light. Polyface Farm occupies 550 acres of rolling grassland and forest in the Shenandoah Valley of Virginia. Here, Joel Salatin and his family raise six different food animals—cattle, pigs, chickens, rabbits, turkeys and sheep—in an intricate dance of symbiosis designed to allow each species, in Salatin's words, "to fully express its physiological distinctiveness."

What this means in practice is that Salatin's chickens live like chickens; his cows, like cows; pigs, pigs. As in nature, where birds tend to follow herbivores, once Salatin's cows have finished grazing a pasture, he moves them out and tows in his "eggmobile," a portable chicken coop that houses several hundred laying hens—roughly the natural size of a flock. The hens fan out over the pasture, eating the short grass and picking insect larvae out of the cowpats—all the while spreading the cow manure and eliminating the farm's parasite problem. A diet of grubs and grass makes for exceptionally tasty eggs and contented chickens, and their nitrogenous manure feeds the pasture. A few weeks later, the chickens move out and the sheep come in, dining on the lush new growth as well as on the weed species (nettles, nightshade) that the cattle and chickens won't touch.

Meanwhile, the pigs are in the barn turning the compost. All winter long, while the cattle were indoors, Salatin layered their manure with straw, wood chips—and corn. By March, this steaming compost layer cake stands three feet high, and the pigs, whose powerful snouts can sniff out and retrieve the fermented corn at the bottom, get to spend a few happy weeks rooting through the pile, aerating it as they work. All you can see of these pigs, intently nosing out the tasty alcoholic morsels, are their upturned pink hams and corkscrew tails churning the air. The finished compost will go to feed the grass; the grass, the cattle; the cattle, the chickens; and eventually all of these animals will feed us.

50 I thought a lot about vegetarianism and animal rights during the day I spent on Joel Salatin's extraordinary farm. So much of what I'd read, so much of what I'd accepted, looked very different from here. To many animal rightists, even Polyface Farm is a death camp. But to look at these animals is to see this for the sentimental conceit it is. In the same way that we can probably recognize animal suffering when we see it, animal happiness is unmistakable, too, and here I was seeing it in abundance.

For any animal, happiness seems to consist in the opportunity to express its creaturely character—its essential pigness or wolfness or chickenness. Aristotle speaks of each creature's "characteristic form of life." For domesticated species, the good life, if we can call it that, cannot be achieved apart from humans—apart from our farms and, therefore, our meat-eating. This, it seems to me, is where animal rightists betray a profound ignorance about the workings of nature. To think of domestication as a form of enslavement or even exploitation is to misconstrue the whole relationship, to project a human idea of power onto what is, in fact, an instance of mutualism between species. Domestication is an evolutionary, rather than a political, development. It is certainly not a regime humans imposed on animals some ten thousand years ago.

Rather, domestication happened when a small handful of especially opportunistic species discovered through Darwinian trial and error that they were more likely to survive and prosper in an alliance with humans than on their own. Humans provided the animals with food and protection, in exchange for which the animals provided the humans their milk and eggs and—yes—their flesh. Both parties were transformed by the relationship: animals grew tame and lost their ability to fend for themselves (evolution tends to edit out unneeded traits), and humans gave up their hunter-gatherer ways for the settled life of agriculturists. (Humans changed biologically too, evolving such new traits as a tolerance for lactose as adults.)

From the animals' point of view, the bargain with humanity has been a great success, at least until our own time. Cows, pigs, dogs, cats and chickens have thrived, while their wild ancestors have languished. (There are ten thousand wolves in North America, fifty million dogs.) Nor does their loss of autonomy seem to trouble these creatures. It is wrong, the rightists say, to treat animals as "means" rather than "ends," yet the happiness of a working animal like the dog consists precisely in serving as a "means." Liberation is the last thing such a creature wants. To say of one of Joel Salatin's caged chickens that "the life of freedom is to be preferred" betrays an ignorance about chicken preferences—which on this farm are heavily focused on not getting their heads bitten off by weasels.

But haven't these chickens simply traded one predator for another—weasels for humans? True enough, and for the chickens this is probably not a bad deal. For brief as it is, the life expectancy of a farm animal would be considerably briefer in the world beyond the pasture fence or chicken coop. A sheep farmer told me that a bear will eat a lactating ewe alive, starting with her udders. "As a rule," he explained, "animals don't get 'good deaths' surrounded by their loved ones."

55 The very existence of predation—animals eating animals—is the cause of much anguished hand-wringing in animal rights circles. "It must be admitted," Singer writes, "that the existence of carnivorous animals does pose one problem for the ethics of Animal Liberation, and that is whether we should do anything about it." Some animal rightists train their dogs and cats to become vegetarians. (Note: cats will require nutritional supplements to stay healthy.) Matthew Scully calls predation "the intrinsic evil in nature's design . . . among the hardest of all things to fathom." *Really?* A deep Puritan streak pervades animal rights activists, an abiding discomfort not only with our animality but with the animals' animality too.

However it may appear to us, predation is not a matter of morality or politics; it, also, is a matter of symbiosis. Hard as the wolf may be on the deer he eats, the herd depends on him for its well-being; without predators to cull the herd, deer overrun their habitat and starve. In many places, human hunters have taken over the predator's ecological role. Chickens also depend for their continued well-being on their human predators—not individual chickens, but chickens as a species. The surest way to achieve the extinction of the chicken would be to grant chickens a "right to life."

Yet here's the rub: the animal rightist is not concerned with species, only individuals. Tom Regan, author of *The Case for Animal Rights*, bluntly asserts that because "species are not individuals . . . the rights view does not recognize the moral rights of species to anything, including survival." Singer concurs, insisting that only sentient individuals have interests. But surely a species can have interests—in its survival, say—just as a nation or community or a corporation can. The animal rights movement's exclusive concern with individual animals makes perfect sense given its roots in a culture of liberal individualism, but does it make any sense in nature?

Consider this hypothetical episode: In 1611 Juan da Goma (a.k.a. Juan the Disoriented) made accidental landfall on Wrightson Island, a six-square-mile rock in the Indian Ocean. The island's sole distinction is as the only known home of the Arcania tree and the bird that nests in it, the Wrightson giant sea sparrow. Da Goma and his crew stayed a week, much of that time spent in a failed bid to recapture the ship's escaped goat—who happened to be pregnant. Nearly four centuries later, Wrightson Island is home to 380 goats that have consumed virtually every scrap of vegetation in their reach. The youngest Arcania tree on the island is more than three hundred years old, and only fifty-two sea sparrows remain. In the animal rights view, any one of those goats have at least as much right to life as the last Wrightson sparrow on earth, and the trees, because they are not sentient, warrant no moral consideration whatsoever.

(In the mid-1980s a British environmental group set out to shoot the goats, but was forced to cancel the expedition after the Mammal Liberation Front bombed its offices.)

The story of Wrightson Island (invented by the biologist David Ehrenfeld in *Beginning Again*) suggests at the very least that a human morality based on individual rights makes for an awkward fit when applied to the natural world. This should come as no surprise: morality is an artifact of human culture, devised to help us negotiate social relations. It's very good for that. But just as we recognize that nature doesn't provide an adequate guide for human social conduct, isn't it anthropocentric to assume that our moral system offers an adequate guide for nature? We may require a different set of ethics to guide our dealings with the natural world, one as well suited to the particular needs of plants and animals and habitats (where sentience counts for little) as rights suit us humans today.

60 To contemplate such questions from the vantage of a farm is to appreciate just how parochial and urban an ideology animal rights really is. It could thrive only in a world where people have lost contact with the natural world, where animals no longer pose a threat to us and human mastery of nature seems absolute. "In our normal life," Singer writes, "there is no serious clash of interests between human and nonhuman animals." Such a statement assumes a decidedly urbanized "normal life," one that certainly no farmer would recognize.

The farmer would point out that even vegans have a "serious clash of interests" with other animals. The grain that the vegan eats is harvested with a combine that shreds field mice, while the farmer's tractor crushes woodchucks in their burrows, and his pesticides drop songbirds from the sky. Steve Davis, an animal scientist at Oregon State University, has estimated that if America were to adopt a strictly vegetarian diet, the total number of animals killed every year would actually *increase*, as animal pasture gave way to row crops. Davis contends that if our goal is to kill as few animals as possible, then people should eat the largest possible animal that can live on the least intensively cultivated land: grass-fed beef for everybody. It would appear that killing animals is unavoidable no matter what we choose to eat.

When I talked to Joel Salatin about the vegetarian utopia, he pointed out that it would also condemn him and his neighbors to importing their food from distant places, since the Shenandoah Valley receives too little rainfall to grow many row crops. Much the same would hold true where I live, in New England. We get plenty of rain, but the hilliness of the land has dictated an agriculture based on animals since the time of the Pilgrims. The world is full of places where the best, if not the only, way to obtain food from the land is by grazing animals on it—especially ruminants, which alone can transform grass into protein and whose presence can actually improve the health of the land.

The vegetarian utopia would make us even more dependent than we already are on an industrialized national food chain. That food chain would in turn be even more dependent than it already is on fossil fuels and chemical fertilizer, since food would need to travel farther and manure would be in short supply. Indeed, it is doubtful that you can build a more sustainable agriculture without animals to cycle nutrients and support local food production. If our concern is for the health of nature—rather than, say, the internal consistency of our moral code or the condition of our souls—then eating animals may sometimes be the most ethical thing to do.

There is, too, the fact that we humans have been eating animals as long as we have lived on this earth. Humans may not need to eat meat in order to survive, yet doing so is part of our evolutionary heritage, reflected in the design of our teeth and the structure of our digestion. Eating meat helped make us what we are, in a social and biological sense. Under the pressure of the hunt, the human brain grew in size and complexity, and around the fire where the meat was cooked, human culture first flourished. Granting rights to animals may lift us up from the brutal world of predation, but it will entail the sacrifice of part of our identity—our own animality.

65 Surely this is one of the odder paradoxes of animal rights doctrine. It asks us to recognize all that we share with animals and then demands that we act toward them in a most unanimalistic way. Whether or not this is a good idea, we should at least acknowledge that our desire to eat meat is not a trivial matter, no mere "gastronomic preference." We might as well call sex—also now technically unnecessary—a mere "recreational preference." Whatever else it is, our meat-eating is something very deep indeed.

Are any of these good enough reasons to eat animals? I'm mindful of Ben Franklin's definition of the reasonable creature as one who can come up with reasons for whatever he wants to do. So I decided I would track down Peter Singer and ask him what he thought. In an e-mail message, I described Polyface and asked him about the implications for his position of the Good Farm—one where animals got to live according to their nature and to all appearances did not suffer.

"I agree with you that it is better for these animals to have lived and died than not to have lived at all," Singer wrote back. Since the utilitarian is concerned exclusively with the sum of happiness and suffering and the slaughter of an animal that doesn't comprehend that death need not involve suffering, the Good Farm adds to the total of animal happiness, provided you replace the slaughtered animal with a new one. However, he added, this line of thinking doesn't obviate the wrongness of killing an animal that "has a sense of its own existence over time and can have preferences for its own future." In other words, it's OK to eat the chicken, but he's not so sure about the pig. Yet, he wrote, "I would not be sufficiently confident of my arguments to condemn someone who purchased meat from one of these farms."

Singer went on to express serious doubts that such farms could be practical on a large scale, since the pressures of the marketplace will lead their owners to cut costs and corners at the expense of the animals. He suggested, too, that killing animals is not conducive to treating them with respect. Also, since humanely raised food will be more expensive, only the well-to-do can afford morally defensible animal protein. These are important considerations, but they don't alter my essential point: what's wrong with animal agriculture—with eating animals—is the practice, not the principle.

What this suggests to me is that people who care should be working not for animal rights but animal welfare—to ensure that farm animals don't suffer and that their deaths are swift and painless. In fact, the decent-life-merciful-death line is how Jeremy Bentham justified his own meat-eating. Yes, the philosophical father of animal rights was himself a carnivore. In a passage rather less frequently quoted by animal rightists, Bentham defended eating animals on the grounds that "we are the better for it, and they are never the worse . . . The death they suffer in our hands commonly is, and always may be, a speedier and, by that means, a less painful one than that which would await them in the inevitable course of nature."

70 My guess is that Bentham never looked too closely at what happens in a slaughterhouse, but the argument suggests that, in theory at least, a utilitarian can justify the killing of humanely treated animals—for meat or, presumably, for clothing. (Though leather and fur pose distinct moral problems. Leather is a byproduct of raising domestic animals for food, which can be done humanely. However, furs are usually made from wild animals that die brutal deaths—usually in leg-hold traps—and since most fur species aren't domesticated, raising them on farms isn't necessarily more humane.) But whether the issue is food or fur or hunting, what should concern us is the suffering, not the killing. All of which I was feeling pretty good about—until I remembered that utilitarians can also justify killing retarded orphans. Killing just isn't the problem for them that it is for other people, including me.

During my visit to Polyface Farm, I asked Salatin where his animals were slaughtered. He does the chickens and rabbits right on the farm, and would do the cattle, pigs and sheep there too if only the USDA would let him. Salatin showed me the open-air abattoir he built behind the farmhouse—a sort of outdoor kitchen on a concrete slab, with stainless-steel sinks, scalding tanks, a feather-plucking machine and metal cones to hold the birds upside down while they're being bled. Processing chickens is not a pleasant job, but Salatin insists on doing it himself because he's convinced he can do it more humanely and cleanly than any processing plant. He slaughters every other Saturday through the summer. Anyone's welcome to watch.

I asked Salatin how he could bring himself to kill a chicken.

"People have a soul; animals don't," he said. "It's a bedrock belief of mine." Salatin is a devout Christian. "Unlike us, animals are not created in God's image, so when they die, they just die."

The notion that only in modern times have people grown uneasy about killing animals is a flattering conceit. Taking a life is momentous, and people have been working to justify the slaughter of animals for thousands of years. Religion and especially ritual has played a crucial part in helping us reckon the moral costs. Native Americans and other hunter-gatherers would give thanks to their prey for giving up its life so the eater might live (sort of like saying grace).

Many cultures have offered sacrificial animals to the gods, perhaps as a way to convince themselves that it was the gods' desires that demanded the slaughter, not their own. In ancient Greece, the priests responsible for the slaughter (priests!—now we entrust the job to minimum-wage workers) would sprinkle holy water on the sacrificial animal's brow. The beast would promptly shake its head, and this was taken as a sign of assent. Slaughter doesn't necessarily preclude respect. For all these people, it was the ceremony that allowed them to look, then to eat.

75 Apart from a few surviving religious practices, we no longer have any rituals governing the slaughter or eating of animals, which perhaps helps to explain why we find ourselves where we do, feeling that our only choice is to either look away or give up meat. Frank Perdue is happy to serve the first customer; Peter Singer, the second.

Until my visit to Polyface Farm, I had assumed these were the only two options. But on Salatin's farm, the eye contact between people and animals whose loss John Berger mourned is still a fact of life—and of death, for neither the lives nor the deaths of these animals have been secreted behind steel walls. "Food with a face," Salatin likes to call what he's selling, a slogan that probably scares off some customers. People see very different things when they look into the eyes of a pig or a chicken or a steer—a being without a soul, a "subject of a life" entitled to rights, a link in a food chain, a vessel for pain and pleasure, a tasty lunch. But figuring out what we do think, and what we can eat, might begin with the looking.

We certainly won't philosophize our way to an answer. Salatin told me the story of a man who showed up at the farm one Saturday morning. When Salatin noticed a PETA bumper sticker on the man's car, he figured he was in for it. But the man had a different agenda. He explained that after sixteen years as a vegetarian, he had decided that the only way he could ever eat meat again was if he killed the animal himself. He had come to *look*.

"Ten minutes later we were in the processing shed with a chicken," Salatin recalled. "He slit the bird's throat and watched it die. He saw that the animal did not look at him accusingly, didn't do a Disney double take. The animal had been treated with respect when it was alive, and he saw that it could also have a respectful death—that it wasn't being treated as a pile of protoplasm."

Salatin's open-air abattoir is a morally powerful idea. Someone slaughtering a chicken in a place where he can be watched is apt to do it scrupulously, with consideration for the animal as well as for the eater. This is going to sound quixotic, but maybe all we need to do to redeem industrial animal agriculture in this country is to pass a law requiring that the steel and concrete walls of the CAFOs and slaughterhouses be replaced with . . . glass. If there's any new "right" we need to establish, maybe it's this one: the right to look.

80 No doubt the sight of some of these places would turn many people into vegetarians. Many others would look elsewhere for their meat, to farmers like Salatin. There are more of them than I would have imagined. Despite the relentless consolidation of the American meat industry, there has been a revival of small farms where animals still live their "characteristic form of life." I'm

thinking of the ranches where cattle still spend their lives on grass, the poultry farms where chickens still go outside and the hog farms where pigs live as they did fifty years ago—in contact with the sun, the earth and the gaze of a farmer.

For my own part, I've discovered that if you're willing to make the effort, it's entirely possible to limit the meat you eat to nonindustrial animals. I'm tempted to think that we need a new dietary category, to go with the vegan and lactovegetarian and piscatorian. I don't have a catchy name for it yet (humanocarnivore?), but this is the only sort of meat-eating I feel comfortable with these days. I've become the sort of shopper who looks for labels indicating that his meat and eggs have been humanely grown (the American Humane Association's new "Free Farmed" label seems to be catching on), who visits the farms where his chicken and pork come from and who asks kinky-sounding questions about touring slaughterhouses. I've actually found a couple of small processing plants willing to let a customer onto the kill floor, including one, in Cannon Falls, Minnesota, with a glass abattoir.

The industrialization—and dehumanization—of American animal farming is a relatively new, evitable and local phenomenon: no other country raises and slaughters its food animals quite as intensively or as brutally as we do. Were the walls of our meat industry to become transparent, literally or even figuratively, we would not long continue to do it this way. Tail-docking and sow crates and beak-clipping would disappear overnight, and the days of slaughtering four hundred head of cattle an hour would come to an end. For who could stand the sight? Yes, meat would get more expensive. We'd probably eat less of it, too, but maybe when we did eat animals, we'd eat them with the consciousness, ceremony and respect they deserve.

QUESTIONS

1. Precisely how much of the Animal Liberation approach has Pollan accepted? How can you tell?

2. Things change when Pollan visits Polyface Farm, the humane operation run by Joel Salatin. What about the farm convinces Pollan that it represents an alternative to Peter Singer's approach?

3. Describe the structure of Pollan's essay. How does he introduce Animal Liberation and how does he argue against it?

David Foster Wallace *Consider the Lobster*

The enormous, pungent, and extremely well marketed Maine Lobster Festival is held every late July in the state's midcoast region, meaning the western side of Penobscot Bay, the nerve stem of Maine's lobster industry. What's called the midcoast runs from Owl's Head and Thomaston in the south to Belfast in the north. * * * The region's two main communities are Camden, with its very old money and yachty harbor and five-star restaurants and phenomenal B&Bs, and Rockland, a serious old fishing town that hosts the Festival every summer in historic Harbor Park, right along the water.[1]

Tourism and lobster are the midcoast region's two main industries, and they're both warm-weather enterprises, and the Maine Lobster Festival represents less an intersection of the industries than a deliberate collision, joyful and lucrative and loud. * * * Festival highlights: concerts by Lee Ann Womack and Orleans, annual Maine Sea Goddess beauty pageant, Saturday's big parade, Sunday's William G. Atwood Memorial Crate Race, annual Amateur Cooking Competition, carnival rides and midway attractions and food booths, and the MLF's Main Eating Tent, where something over 25,000 pounds of fresh-caught Maine lobster is consumed after preparation in the World's Largest Lobster Cooker near the grounds' north entrance. Also available are lobster rolls, lobster turnovers, lobster sauté, Down East lobster salad, lobster bisque, lobster ravioli, and deep-fried lobster dumplings. Lobster Thermidor is obtainable at a sit-down restaurant called The Black Pearl on Harbor Park's northwest wharf. A large all-pine booth sponsored by the Maine Lobster Promotion Council has free pamphlets with recipes, eating tips, and Lobster Fun Facts. The winner of Friday's Amateur Cooking Competition prepares Saffron Lobster Ramekins, the recipe for which is available for public downloading at www.mainelobsterfestival.com. There are lobster T-shirts and lobster bobblehead dolls and inflatable lobster pool toys and clamp-on lobster hats with big scarlet claws that wobble on springs. Your assigned correspondent saw it all, accompanied by one girlfriend and both his own parents—one of which parents was actually born and raised in Maine, albeit in the extreme northern inland part, which is potato country and a world away from the touristic midcoast.[2]

For practical purposes, everyone knows what a lobster is. As usual, though, there's much more to know than most of us care about—it's all a matter of what your interests are. Taxonomically speaking, a lobster is a marine crustacean of

First published in Gourmet *(August 2004), a magazine for food lovers; later included in Wallace's collection* Consider the Lobster, and Other Essays *(2005).*

1. There's a comprehensive native apothegm: "Camden by the sea, Rockland by the smell" [Wallace's note].

2. N.B. All personally connected parties have made it clear from the start that they do not want to be talked about in this article. [Wallace's note].

the family Homaridae, characterized by five pairs of jointed legs, the first pair terminating in large pincerish claws used for subduing prey. Like many other species of benthic[3] carnivore, lobsters are both hunters and scavengers. They have stalked eyes, gills on their legs, and antennae. There are dozens of different kinds worldwide, of which the relevant species here is the Maine lobster, *Homarus americanus*. The name "lobster" comes from the Old English *loppestre*, which is thought to be a corrupt form of the Latin word for locust combined with the Old English *loppe*, which meant spider.

Moreover, a crustacean is an aquatic arthropod of the class Crustacea, which comprises crabs, shrimp, barnacles, lobsters, and freshwater crayfish. All this is right there in the encyclopedia. And an arthropod is an invertebrate member of the phylum Arthropoda, which phylum covers insects, spiders, crustaceans, and centipedes/millipedes, all of whose main commonality, besides the absence of a centralized brain-spine assembly, is a chitinous[4] exoskeleton composed of segments, to which appendages are articulated in pairs.

5 The point is that lobsters are basically giant sea-insects.[5] Like most arthropods, they date from the Jurassic period, biologically so much older than mammalia that they might as well be from another planet. And they are—particularly in their natural brown-green state, brandishing their claws like weapons and with thick antennae awhip—not nice to look at. And it's true that they are garbagemen of the sea, eaters of dead stuff,[6] although they'll also eat some live shellfish, certain kinds of injured fish, and sometimes each other.

But they are themselves good eating. Or so we think now. Up until sometime in the 1800s, though, lobster was literally low-class food, eaten only by the poor and institutionalized. Even in the harsh penal environment of early America, some colonies had laws against feeding lobsters to inmates more than once a week because it was thought to be cruel and unusual, like making people eat rats. One reason for their low status was how plentiful lobsters were in old New England. "Unbelievable abundance" is how one source describes the situation, including accounts of Plymouth pilgrims wading out and capturing all they wanted by hand, and of early Boston's seashore being littered with lobsters after hard storms—these latter were treated as a smelly nuisance and ground up for fertilizer. There is also the fact that premodern lobster was often cooked dead and then preserved, usually packed in salt or crude hermetic containers. Maine's earliest lobster industry was based around a dozen such seaside canneries in the 1840s, from which lobster was shipped as far away as California, in demand only because it was cheap and high in protein, basically chewable fuel.

Now, of course, lobster is posh, a delicacy, only a step or two down from caviar. The meat is richer and more substantial than most fish, its taste subtle

3. Related to the bottom of a body of water.

4. A tough, protective semitransparent substance, related to cellulose.

5. Midcoasters' native term for a lobster is, in fact, "bug," as in "Come around on Sunday and we'll cook up some bugs" [Wallace's note].

6. Factoid: Lobster traps are usually baited with dead herring [Wallace's note].

compared to the marine-gaminess of mussels and clams. In the U.S. pop-food imagination, lobster is now the seafood analog to steak, with which it's so often twinned as Surf 'n' Turf on the really expensive part of the chain steak house menu.

In fact, one obvious project of the MLF, and of its omnipresently sponsorial Maine Lobster Promotion Council, is to counter the idea that lobster is unusually luxe or rich or unhealthy or expensive, suitable only for effete palates or the occasional blow-the-diet treat. It is emphasized over and over in presentations and pamphlets at the Festival that Maine lobster meat has fewer calories, less cholesterol, and less saturated fat than chicken.[7] And in the Main Eating Tent, you can get a "quarter" (industry shorthand for a 1¼-pound lobster), a 4-ounce cup of melted butter, a bag of chips, and a soft roll w/ butter-pat for around $12.00, which is only slightly more expensive than supper at McDonald's.

* * *

Lobster is essentially a summer food. This is because we now prefer our lobsters fresh, which means they have to be recently caught, which for both tactical and economic reasons takes place at depths of less than 25 fathoms. Lobsters tend to be hungriest and most active (i.e., most trappable) at summer water temperatures of 45–50°F. In the autumn, some Maine lobsters migrate out into deeper water, either for warmth or to avoid the heavy waves that pound New England's coast all winter. Some burrow into the bottom. They might hibernate; nobody's sure. Summer is also lobsters' molting season—specifically early- to mid-July. Chitinous arthropods grow by molting, rather the way people have to buy bigger clothes as they age and gain weight. Since lobsters can live to be over 100, they can also get to be quite large, as in 20 pounds or more—though truly senior lobsters are rare now, because New England's waters are so heavily trapped.[8] Anyway, hence the culinary distinction between hard- and soft-shell lobsters, the latter sometimes a.k.a. shedders. A soft-shell lobster is one that has recently molted. In midcoast restaurants, the summer menu often offers both kinds, with shedders being slightly cheaper even though they're easier to dismantle and the meat is allegedly sweeter. The reason for the discount is that a molting lobster uses a layer of seawater for insulation while its new shell is hardening, so there's slightly less actual meat when you crack open a shedder, plus a redolent gout of water that gets all over everything and can sometimes jet out lemonlike and catch a tablemate right in the eye. If it's winter or you're buying lobster someplace far from New England, on the other hand, you can almost bet that the lobster is a hard-shell, which for obvious reasons travel better.

7. Of course, the common practice of dipping the lobster meat in melted butter torpedoes all these happy fat-specs, which none of the Council's promotional stuff ever mentions, any more than potato-industry PR talks about sour cream and bacon bits [Wallace's note].

8. Datum: in a good year, the U.S. industry produces around 80 million pounds of lobster, and Maine accounts for more than half of that total [Wallace's note].

10 As an à la carte entrée, lobster can be baked, broiled, steamed, grilled, sautéed, stir-fried, or microwaved. The most common method, though, is boiling. If you're someone who enjoys having lobster at home, this is probably the way you do it, since boiling is so easy. You need a large kettle w/ cover, which you fill about half full with water (the standard advice is that you want 2.5 quarts of water per lobster). Seawater is optimal, or you can add two tbsp salt per quart from the tap. It also helps to know how much your lobsters weigh. You get the water boiling, put in the lobsters one at a time, cover the kettle, and bring it back up to a boil. Then you bank the heat and let the kettle simmer—ten minutes for the first pound of lobster, then three minutes for each pound after that. (This is assuming you've got hard-shell lobsters, which, again, if you don't live between Boston and Halifax, is probably what you've got. For shedders, you're supposed to subtract three minutes from the total.) The reason the kettle's lobsters turn scarlet is that boiling somehow suppresses every pigment in their chitin but one. If you want an easy test of whether the lobsters are done, you try pulling on one of their antennae—if it comes out of the head with minimal effort, you're ready to eat.

A detail so obvious that most recipes don't even bother to mention it is that each lobster is supposed to be alive when you put it in the kettle. This is part of lobster's modern appeal: It's the freshest food there is. There's no decomposition between harvesting and eating. And not only do lobsters require no cleaning or dressing or plucking (though the mechanics of actually eating them are a different matter), but they're relatively easy for vendors to keep alive. They come up alive in the traps, are placed in containers of seawater, and can, so long as the water's aerated and the animals' claws are pegged or banded to keep them from tearing one another up under the stresses of captivity,[9] survive right up until they're boiled. Most of us have been in supermarkets or restaurants that feature tanks of live lobster, from which you can pick out your supper while it watches you point. And part of the overall spectacle of the Maine Lobster Festival is that you can see actual lobstermen's vessels docking at the wharves along the northeast grounds and unloading freshly caught product, which is transferred by hand or cart 100 yards to the great clear tanks stacked up around the Festival's cooker—which is, as mentioned, billed as the World's Largest Lobster Cooker and can process over 100 lobsters at a time for the Main Eating Tent.

9. N.B. Similar reasoning underlies the practice of what's termed "debeaking" broiler chickens and brood hens in modern factory farms. Maximum commercial efficiency requires that enormous poultry populations be confined in unnaturally close quarters, under which conditions many birds go crazy and peck one another to death. As a purely observational side-note, be apprised that debeaking is usually an automated process and that the chickens receive no anesthetic. It's not clear to me whether most *Gourmet* readers know about debeaking, or about related practices like dehorning cattle in commercial feedlots, cropping swine's tails in factory hog farms to keep psychotically bored neighbors from chewing them off, and so forth. It so happens that your assigned correspondent knew almost nothing about standard meat-industry operations before starting work on this article [Wallace's note].

So then here is a question that's all but unavoidable at the World's Largest Lobster Cooker, and may arise in kitchens across the U.S.: Is it all right to boil a sentient creature alive just for our gustatory pleasure? A related set of concerns: Is the previous question irksomely PC or sentimental? What does "all right" even mean in this context? Is it all just a matter of individual choice?

As you may or may not know, a certain well-known group called People for the Ethical Treatment of Animals thinks that the morality of lobster-boiling is not just a matter of individual conscience. In fact, one of the very first things we hear about the MLF . . . well, to set the scene: We're coming in by cab from the almost indescribably odd and rustic Knox County Airport[10] very late on the night before the Festival opens, sharing the cab with a wealthy political consultant who lives on Vinalhaven Island in the bay half the year (he's headed for the island ferry in Rockland). The consultant and cabdriver are responding to informal journalistic probes about how people who live in the midcoast region actually view the MLF, as in is the Festival just a big-dollar tourist thing or is it something local residents look forward to attending, take genuine civic pride in, etc. The cabdriver—who's in his seventies, one of apparently a whole platoon of retirees the cab company puts on to help with the summer rush, and wears a U.S.-flag lapel pin, and drives in what can only be called a very deliberate way—assures us that locals do endorse and enjoy the MLF, although he himself hasn't gone in years, and now come to think of it no one he and his wife know has, either. However, the demilocal consultant's been to recent Festivals a couple times (one gets the impression it was at his wife's behest), of which his most vivid impression was that "you have to line up for an ungodly long time to get your lobsters, and meanwhile there are all these ex–flower children coming up and down along the line handing out pamphlets that say the lobsters die in terrible pain and you shouldn't eat them."

And it turns out that the post-hippies of the consultant's recollection were activists from PETA. There were no PETA people in obvious view at the 2003 MLF,[11] but they've been conspicuous at many of the recent Festivals. Since at

10. The terminal used to be somebody's house, for example, and the lost-luggage-reporting room was clearly once a pantry [Wallacer's note].

11. It turned out that Mr. William R. Rivas-Rivas, a high-ranking PETA official out of the group's Virginia headquarters, was indeed there this year, albeit solo, working the Festival's main and side entrances on Saturday, August 2, handing out pamphlets and adhesive stickers emblazoned with "Being Boiled Hurts," which is the tagline in most of PETA's published material about lobster. I learned that he'd been there only later, when speaking with Mr. Rivas-Rivas on the phone. I'm not sure how we missed seeing him *in situ* at the Festival, and I can't see much to do except apologize for the oversight—although it's also true that Saturday was the day of the big MLF parade through Rockland, which basic journalistic responsibility seemed to require going to (and which, with all due respect, meant that Saturday was maybe not the best day for PETA to work the Harbor Park grounds, especially if it was going to be just one person for one day, since a lot of diehard MLF partisans were off-site watching the parade (which, again with no offense intended, was in truth kind of cheesy and boring, consisting mostly of slow homemade flats and vari-

least the mid-1990s, articles in everything from *The Camden Herald* to *The New York Times* have described PETA urging boycotts of the MLF, often deploying celebrity spokespeople like Mary Tyler Moore for open letters and ads saying stuff like "Lobsters are extraordinarily sensitive" and "To me, eating a lobster is out of the question." More concrete is the oral testimony of Dick, our florid and extremely gregarious rental-car guy, to the effect that PETA's been around so much in recent years that a kind of brittlely tolerant homeostasis now obtains between the activists and the Festival's locals, e.g.: "We had some incidents a couple years ago. One lady took most of her clothes off and painted herself like a lobster, almost got herself arrested. But for the most part they're let alone. [Rapid series of small ambiguous laughs, which with Dick happens a lot.] They do their thing and we do our thing."

15 This whole interchange takes place on Route 1, 30 July, during a four-mile, 50-minute ride from the airport[12] to the dealership to sign car-rental papers. Several irreproducible segues down the road from the PETA anecdotes, Dick—whose son-in-law happens to be a professional lobsterman and one of the Main Eating Tent's regular suppliers—articulates what he and his family feel is the crucial mitigating factor in the whole morality-of-boiling-lobsters-alive issue: "There's a part of the brain in people and animals that lets us feel pain, and lobsters' brains don't have this part."

Besides the fact that it's incorrect in about 11 different ways, the main reason Dick's statement is interesting is that its thesis is more or less echoed by the Festival's own pronouncement on lobsters and pain, which is part of a Test Your Lobster IQ quiz that appears in the 2003 MLF program courtesy of the Maine Lobster Promotion Council: "The nervous system of a lobster is very simple, and is in fact most similar to the nervous system of the grasshopper. It is decentralized with no brain. There is no cerebral cortex, which in humans is the area of the brain that gives the experience of pain."

Though it sounds more sophisticated, a lot of the neurology in this latter claim is still either false or fuzzy. The human cerebral cortex is the brain-part that deals with higher faculties like reason, metaphysical self-awareness, language, etc. Pain reception is known to be part of a much older and more primitive system of nociceptors and prostaglandins that are managed by the brain stem and thalamus.[13] On the other hand, it is true that the cerebral cortex is

ous midcoast people waving at one another, and with an extremely annoying man dressed as Blackbeard ranging up and down the length of the crowd saying "Arrr" over and over and brandishing a plastic sword at people, etc.; plus it rained)) [Wallace's note].

12. The short version regarding why we were back at the airport after already arriving the previous night involves lost luggage and a miscommunication about where and what the local National Car Rental franchise was—Dick came out personally to the airport and got us, out of no evident motive but kindness. (He also talked nonstop the entire way, with a very distinctive speaking style that can be described only as manically laconic; the truth is that I now know more about this man than I do about some members of my own family) [Wallace's note].

13. To elaborate by way of example: The common experience of accidentally touching a hot stove and taking your hand back before you're even aware that anything's going

involved in what's variously called suffering, distress, or the emotional experience of pain—i.e., experiencing painful stimuli as unpleasant, very unpleasant, unbearable, and so on.

Before we go any further, let's acknowledge that the questions of whether and how different kinds of animals feel pain, and of whether and why it might be justifiable to inflict pain on them in order to eat them, turn out to be extremely complex and difficult. And comparative neuroanatomy is only part of the problem. Since pain is a totally subjective mental experience, we do not have direct access to anyone or anything's pain but our own; and even just the principles by which we can infer that others experience pain and have a legitimate interest in not feeling pain involve hard-core philosophy—metaphysics, epistemology, value theory, ethics. The fact that even the most highly evolved nonhuman mammals can't use language to communicate with us about their subjective mental experience is only the first layer of additional complication in trying to extend our reasoning about pain and morality to animals. And everything gets progressively more abstract and convolved as we move farther and farther out from the higher-type mammals into cattle and swine and dogs and cats and rodents, and then birds and fish, and finally invertebrates like lobsters.

The more important point here, though, is that the whole animal-cruelty-and-eating issue is not just complex, it's also uncomfortable. It is, at any rate, uncomfortable for me, and for just about everyone I know who enjoys a variety of foods and yet does not want to see herself as cruel or unfeeling. As far as I can tell, my own main way of dealing with this conflict has been to avoid thinking about the whole unpleasant thing. I should add that it appears to me unlikely that many readers of GOURMET wish to think hard about it, either, or to be queried about the morality of their eating habits in the pages of a culinary monthly. Since, however, the assigned subject of this article is what it was like to attend the 2003 MLF, and thus to spend several days in the midst of a great mass of Americans all eating lobster, and thus to be more or less impelled to think hard about lobster and the experience of buying and eating lobster, it turns out that there is no honest way to avoid certain moral questions.

20 There are several reasons for this. For one thing, it's not just that lobsters get boiled alive, it's that you do it yourself—or at least it's done specifically for you, on-site.[14] As mentioned, the World's Largest Lobster Cooker, which is high-

on is explained by the fact that many of the processes by which we detect and avoid painful stimuli do not involve the cortex. In the case of the hand and stove, the brain is bypassed altogether; all the important neurochemical action takes place in the spine [Wallace's note].

14. Morality-wise, let's concede that this cuts both ways. Lobster-eating is at least not abetted by the system of corporate factory farms that produces most beef, pork, and chicken. Because, if nothing else, of the way they're marketed and packaged for sale, we eat these latter meats without having to consider that they were once conscious, sentient creatures to whom horrible things were done. (N.B. PETA distributes a certain video—the title of which is being omitted as part of the elaborate editorial compromise by which this note appears at all—in which you can see just about everything meat-

lighted as an attraction in the Festival's program, is right out there on the MLF's north grounds for everyone to see. Try to imagine a Nebraska Beef Festival[15] at which part of the festivities is watching trucks pull up and the live cattle get driven down the ramp and slaughtered right there on the World's Largest Killing Floor or something—there's no way.

The intimacy of the whole thing is maximized at home, which of course is where most lobster gets prepared and eaten (although note already the semi-conscious euphemism "prepared," which in the case of lobsters really means killing them right there in our kitchens). The basic scenario is that we come in from the store and make our little preparations like getting the kettle filled and boiling, and then we lift the lobsters out of the bag or whatever retail container they came home in . . . whereupon some uncomfortable things start to happen. However stuporous the lobster is from the trip home, for instance, it tends to come alarmingly to life when placed in boiling water. If you're tilting it from a container into the steaming kettle, the lobster will sometimes try to cling to the container's sides or even to hook its claws over the kettle's rim like a person trying to keep from going over the edge of a roof. And worse is when the lobster's fully immersed. Even if you cover the kettle and turn away, you can usually hear the cover rattling and clanking as the lobster tries to push it off. Or the creature's claws scraping the sides of the kettle as it thrashes around. The lobster, in other words, behaves very much as you or I would behave if we were plunged into boiling water (with the obvious exception of screaming).[16] A blunter way to say this is that the lobster acts as if it's in terrible pain, causing some cooks to leave the kitchen altogether and to take one of those little lightweight plastic oven timers with them into another room and wait until the whole process is over.

---

related you don't want to see or think about. (N.B. 2. Not that PETA's any sort of font of unspoken truth. Like many partisans in complex moral disputes, the PETA people are fanatics, and a lot of their rhetoric seems simplistic and self-righteous. Personally, though, I have to say that I found this unnamed video both credible and deeply upsetting.)) [Wallace's note].

15. Is it significant that "lobster," "fish," and "chicken" are our culture's words for the animal and the meat, whereas most mammals seem to require euphemisms like "beef" and "pork" that help us separate the meat we eat from the living creature the meat once was? Is this evidence that some kind of deep unease about eating higher animals is endemic enough to show up in the English usage, but that the unease diminishes as we move out of the mammalian order? (And is "lamb"/"lamb" the counterexample that sinks the whole theory, or are there special, biblico-historical reasons for that equivalence?) [Wallace's note].

16. There's a relevant populist myth about the high-pitched whistling sound that sometimes issues from a pot of boiling lobster. The sound is really vented steam from the layer of seawater between the lobster's flesh and its carapace (this is why shedders whistle more than hard-shells), but the pop version has it that the sound is the lobster's rabbitlike death scream. Lobsters communicate via pheromones in their urine and don't have anything close to the vocal equipment for screaming, but the myth's very persistent—which might, once again, point to a low-level cultural unease about boiling the thing [Wallace's note].

There happen to be two main criteria that most ethicists agree on for determining whether a living creature has the capacity to suffer and so has genuine interests that it may or may not be our moral duty to consider.[17] One is how much of the neurological hardware required for pain-experience the animal comes equipped with—nociceptors, prostaglandins, neuronal opioid receptors, etc. The other criterion is whether the animal demonstrates behavior associated with pain. And it takes a lot of intellectual gymnastics and behaviorist hairsplitting not to see struggling, thrashing, and lid-clattering as just such pain-behavior. According to marine zoologists, it usually takes lobsters between 35 and 45 seconds to die in boiling water. (No source I could find talked about how long it takes them to die in superheated steam; one rather hopes it's faster.)

There are, of course, other fairly common ways to kill your lobster on-site and so achieve maximum freshness. Some cooks' practice is to drive a sharp heavy knife point-first into a spot just above the midpoint between the lobster's eyestalks (more or less where the Third Eye is in human foreheads). This is alleged either to kill the lobster instantly or to render it insensate—and is said at least to eliminate the cowardice involved in throwing a creature into boiling water and then fleeing the room. As far as I can tell from talking to proponents of the knife-in-the-head method, the idea is that it's more violent but ultimately more merciful, plus that a willingness to exert personal agency and accept responsibility for stabbing the lobster's head honors the lobster somehow and entitles one to eat it. (There's often a vague sort of Native American spirituality-of-the-hunt flavor to pro-knife arguments.) But the problem with the knife method is basic biology: Lobsters' nervous systems operate off not one but several ganglia, a.k.a. nerve bundles, which are sort of wired in series and distributed all along the lobster's underside, from stem to stern. And disabling only the frontal ganglion does not normally result in quick death or unconsciousness. Another alternative is to put the lobster in cold salt water and then very slowly bring it up to a full boil. Cooks who advocate this method are going mostly on the analogy to a frog, which can supposedly be kept from jumping out of a boiling pot by heating the water incrementally. In order to save a lot of research-summarizing, I'll simply assure you that the analogy between frogs and lobsters turns out not to hold.

Ultimately, the only certain virtues of the home-lobotomy and slow-heating methods are comparative, because there are even worse/crueler ways people prepare lobster. Time-thrifty cooks sometimes microwave them alive (usually after poking several extra vent holes in the carapace, which is a precaution

17. "Interests" basically means strong and legitimate preferences, which obviously require some degree of consciousness, responsiveness to stimuli, etc. See, for instance, the utilitarian philosopher Peter Singer, whose 1974 *Animal Liberation* is more or less the bible of the modern animal-rights movement: "It would be nonsense to say that it was not in the interests of a stone to be kicked along the road by a schoolboy. A stone does not have interests because it cannot suffer. Nothing that we can do to it could possibly make any difference to its welfare. A mouse, on the other hand, does have an interest in not being kicked along the road, because it will suffer if it is" [Wallace's note].

most shellfish-microwavers learn about the hard way). Live dismemberment, on the other hand, is big in Europe: Some chefs cut the lobster in half before cooking; others like to tear off the claws and tail and toss only these parts in the pot.

25 And there's more unhappy news respecting suffering-criterion number one. Lobsters don't have much in the way of eyesight or hearing, but they do have an exquisite tactile sense, one facilitated by hundreds of thousands of tiny hairs that protrude through their carapace. "Thus," in the words of T. M. Prudden's industry classic *About Lobster*, "it is that although encased in what seems a solid, impenetrable armor, the lobster can receive stimuli and impressions from without as readily as if it possessed a soft and delicate skin." And lobsters do have nociceptors,[18] as well as invertebrate versions of the prostaglandins and major neurotransmitters via which our own brains register pain.

Lobsters do not, on the other hand, appear to have the equipment for making or absorbing natural opioids like endorphins and enkephalins, which are what more advanced nervous systems use to try to handle intense pain. From this fact, though, one could conclude either that lobsters are maybe even *more* vulnerable to pain, since they lack mammalian nervous systems' built-in analgesia, or, instead, that the absence of natural opioids implies an absence of the really intense pain-sensations that natural opioids are designed to mitigate. I for one can detect a marked upswing in mood as I contemplate this latter possibility: It could be that their lack of endorphin/enkephalin hardware means that lobsters' raw subjective experience of pain is so radically different from mammals' that it may not even deserve the term *pain*. Perhaps lobsters are more like those frontal-lobotomy patients one reads about who report experiencing pain in a totally different way than you and I. These patients evidently do feel physical pain, neurologically speaking, but don't dislike it—though neither do they like it; it's more that they feel it but don't feel anything *about* it—the point being that the pain is not distressing to them or something they want to get away from. Maybe lobsters, who are also without frontal lobes, are detached from the neurological-registration-of-injury-or-hazard we call pain in just the same way. There is, after all, a difference between (1) pain as a purely neurological event, and (2) actual suffering, which seems crucially to involve an emotional component, an awareness of pain as unpleasant, as something to fear/dislike/want to avoid.

Still, after all the abstract intellection, there remain the facts of the frantically clanking lid, the pathetic clinging to the edge of the pot. Standing at the stove, it is hard to deny in any meaningful way that this is a living creature experiencing pain and wishing to avoid/escape the painful experience. To my lay mind, the lobster's behavior in the kettle appears to be the expression of a *preference*; and it may well be that an ability to form preferences is the decisive

18. This is the neurological term for special pain receptors that are (according to Jane A. Smith and Kenneth M. Boyd's *Lives in the Balance*) "sensitive to potentially damaging extremes of temperature, to mechanical forces, and to chemical substances which are released when body tissues are damaged" [Wallace's note].

criterion for real suffering.[19] The logic of this (preference → suffering) relation may be easiest to see in the negative case. If you cut certain kinds of worms in half, the halves will often keep crawling around and going about their vermiform business as if nothing had happened. When we assert, based on their post-op behavior, that these worms appear not to be suffering, what we're really saying is that there's no sign that the worms know anything bad has happened or would *prefer* not to have gotten cut in half.

Lobsters, however, are known to exhibit preferences. Experiments have shown that they can detect changes of only a degree or two in water temperature; one reason for their complex migratory cycles (which can often cover 100-plus miles a year) is to pursue the temperatures they like best.[20] And, as mentioned, they're bottom-dwellers and do not like bright light: If a tank of food lobsters is out in the sunlight or a store's fluorescence, the lobsters will always congregate in whatever part is darkest. Fairly solitary in the ocean, they also clearly dislike the crowding that's part of their captivity in tanks, since (as also mentioned) one reason why lobsters' claws are banded on capture is to keep them from attacking one another under the stress of close-quarter storage.

In any event, at the Festival, standing by the bubbling tanks outside the World's Largest Lobster Cooker, watching the fresh-caught lobsters pile over one another, wave their hobbled claws impotently, huddle in the rear corners, or scrabble frantically back from the glass as you approach, it is difficult not to sense that they're unhappy, or frightened, even if it's some rudimentary version

19. "Preference" is maybe roughly synonymous with "interest," but it is a better term for our purposes because it's less abstractly philosophical—"preference" seems more personal, and it's the whole idea of a living creature's personal experience that's at issue [Wallace's note].

20. Of course, the most common sort of counterargument here would begin by objecting that "like best" is really just a metaphor, and a misleadingly anthropomorphic one at that. The counterarguer would posit that the lobster seeks to maintain a certain optimal ambient temperature out of nothing but unconscious instinct (with a similar explanation for the low-light affinities about to be mentioned in the main text). The thrust of such a counterargument will be that the lobster's thrashings and clankings in the kettle express not unpreferred pain but involuntary reflexes, like your leg shooting out when the doctor hits your knee. Be advised that there are professional scientists, including many researchers who use animals in experiments, who hold to the view that nonhuman creatures have no real feelings at all, only "behaviors." Be further advised that this view has a long history that goes all the way back to Descartes, although its modern support comes mostly from behaviorist psychology.

To these what-look-like-pain-are-really-only-reflexes counterarguments, however, there happen to be all sorts of scientific and pro-animal-rights counter-counterarguments. And then further attempted rebuttals and redirects, and so on. Suffice to say that both the scientific and the philosophical arguments on either side of the animal-suffering issue are involved, abstruse, technical, often informed by self-interest or ideology, and in the end so totally inconclusive that as a practical matter, in the kitchen or restaurant, it all still seems to come down to individual conscience, going with (no pun) your gut [Wallace's note].

of these feelings . . . and, again, why does rudimentariness even enter into it? Why is a primitive, inarticulate form of suffering less urgent or uncomfortable for the person who's helping to inflict it by paying for the food it results in? I'm not trying to give you a PETA-like screed here—at least I don't think so. I'm trying, rather, to work out and articulate some of the troubling questions that arise amid all the laughter and saltation and community pride of the Maine Lobster Festival. The truth is that if you, the Festival attendee, permit yourself to think that lobsters can suffer and would rather not, the MLF can begin to take on aspects of something like a Roman circus or medieval torture-fest.

30 Does that comparison seem a bit much? If so, exactly why? Or what about this one: Is it not possible that future generations will regard our own present agribusiness and eating practices in much the same way we now view Nero's entertainments or Aztec sacrifices? My own immediate reaction is that such a comparison is hysterical, extreme—and yet the reason it seems extreme to me appears to be that I believe animals are less morally important than human beings;[21] and when it comes to defending such a belief, even to myself, I have to acknowledge that (a) I have an obvious selfish interest in this belief, since I like to eat certain kinds of animals and want to be able to keep doing it, and (b) I have not succeeded in working out any sort of personal ethical system in which the belief is truly defensible instead of just selfishly convenient.

Given this article's venue and my own lack of culinary sophistication, I'm curious about whether the reader can identify with any of these reactions and acknowledgments and discomforts. I am also concerned not to come off as shrill or preachy when what I really am is confused. Given the (possible) moral status and (very possible) physical suffering of the animals involved, what ethical convictions do gourmets evolve that allow them not just to eat but to savor and enjoy flesh-based viands (since of course refined *enjoyment*, rather than just ingestion, is the whole point of gastronomy)? And for those gourmets who'll have no truck with convictions or rationales and who regard stuff like the previous paragraph as just so much pointless navel-gazing, what makes it feel okay, inside, to dismiss the whole issue out of hand? That is, is their refusal to think about any of this the product of actual thought, or is it just that they don't want to think about it? Do they ever think about their reluctance to think about it? After all, isn't being extra aware and attentive and thoughtful about one's food and its overall context part of what distinguishes a real gourmet? Or is all the gourmet's extra attention and sensibility just supposed to be aesthetic, gustatory?

These last couple queries, though, while sincere, obviously involve much larger and more abstract questions about the connections (if any) between aesthetics and morality, and these questions lead straightaway into such deep

21. Meaning a *lot* less important, apparently, since the moral comparison here is not the value of one human's life vs. the value of one animal's life, but rather the value of one animal's life vs. the value of one human's taste for a particular kind of protein. Even the most diehard carniphile will acknowledge that it's possible to live and eat well without consuming animals [Wallace's note].

and treacherous waters that it's probably best to stop the public discussion right here. There are limits to what even interested persons can ask of each other.

QUESTIONS

1. Wallace finally admits to being "confused" (paragraph 31) about the morality of eating lobsters. After reading his essay, what are your feelings? Are they changed from what they were before you read his essay?

2. Comment on Wallace's footnotes, which sometimes add information but at other times seem to carry on another argument on the bottom of the page. Why do you think he includes both kinds?

3. Why do you think *Gourmet* published Wallace's essay?

4. Write about some festival you have attended, trying for Wallace's mode of outsider observation.

MICHAEL LEVIN

The Case for Torture

IT IS GENERALLY assumed that torture is impermissible, a throwback to a more brutal age. Enlightened societies reject it outright, and regimes suspected of using it risk the wrath of the United States.

I believe this attitude is unwise. There are situations in which torture is not merely permissible but morally mandatory. Moreover, these situations are moving from the realm of imagination to fact.

Death: Suppose a terrorist has hidden an atomic bomb on Manhattan Island which will detonate at noon on July 4 unless . . . (here follow the usual demands for money and release of his friends from jail). Suppose, further, that he is caught at 10 a.m. of the fateful day, but—preferring death to failure—won't disclose where the bomb is. What do we do? If we follow due process—wait for his lawyer, arraign him—millions of people will die. If the only way to save those lives is to subject the terrorist to the most excruciating possible pain, what grounds can there be for not doing so? I suggest there are none. In any case, I ask you to face the question with an open mind.

Torturing the terrorist is unconstitutional? Probably. But millions of lives surely outweigh constitutionality. Torture is barbaric? Mass murder is far more barbaric. Indeed, letting millions of innocents die in deference to one who

Originally published in Newsweek *in the "My Turn" column on June 7, 1982. The magazine introduced the column in 1972 to encourage members of the general public, as well as professional writers, to voice their views on current events and issues.*

flaunts his guilt is moral cowardice, an unwillingness to dirty one's hands. If *you* caught the terrorist, could you sleep nights knowing that millions died because you couldn't bring yourself to apply the electrodes?

5 Once you concede that torture is justified in extreme cases, you have admitted that the decision to use torture is a matter of balancing innocent lives against the means needed to save them. You must now face more realistic cases involving more modest numbers. Someone plants a bomb on a jumbo jet. He alone can disarm it, and his demands cannot be met (or if they can, we refuse to set a precedent by yielding to his threats). Surely we can, we must, do anything to the extortionist to save the passengers. How can we tell 300, or 100, or 10 people who never asked to be put in danger, "I'm sorry, you'll have to die in agony, we just couldn't bring ourselves to . . ."

Here are the results of an informal poll about a third, hypothetical, case. Suppose a terrorist group kidnapped a newborn baby from a hospital. I asked four mothers if they would approve of torturing kidnappers if that were necessary to get their own newborns back. All said yes, the most "liberal" adding that she would like to administer it herself.

I am not advocating torture as punishment. Punishment is addressed to deeds irrevocably past. Rather, I am advocating torture as an acceptable measure for preventing future evils. So understood, it is far less objectionable than many extant punishments. Opponents of the death penalty, for example, are forever insisting that executing a murderer will not bring back his victim (as if the purpose of capital punishment were supposed to be resurrection, not deterrence or retribution). But torture, in the cases described, is intended not to bring anyone back but to keep innocents from being dispatched. The most powerful argument against using torture as a punishment or to secure confessions is that such practices disregard the rights of the individual. Well, if the individual is all that important—and he is—it is correspondingly important to protect the rights of individuals threatened by terrorists. If life is so valuable that it must never be taken, the lives of the innocents must be saved even at the price of hurting the one who endangers them.

Better precedents for torture are assassination and pre-emptive attack. No Allied leader would have flinched at assassinating Hitler, had that been possible. (The Allies did assassinate Heydrich.)[1] Americans would be angered to learn that Roosevelt could have had Hitler killed in 1943—thereby shortening the war and saving millions of lives—but refused on moral grounds. Similarly, if nation A learns that nation B is about to launch an unprovoked attack, A has a right to save itself by destroying B's military capability first. In the same way, if the police can by torture save those who would otherwise die at the hands of kidnappers or terrorists, they must.

Idealism: There is an important difference between terrorists and their victims that should mute talk of the terrorists' "rights." The terrorist's victims

1. Reinhard Heydrich (1904–1942), German head of the Nazi SS who was shot by Czech resistance fighters.

are at risk unintentionally, not having asked to be endangered. But the terrorist knowingly initiated his actions. Unlike his victims, he volunteered for the risks of his deed. By threatening to kill for profit or idealism, he renounces civilized standards, and he can have no complaint if civilization tries to thwart him by whatever means necessary.

10 Just as torture is justified only to save lives (not extort confessions or recantations), it is justifiably administered only to those *known* to hold innocent lives in their hands. Ah, but how can the authorities ever be sure they have the right malefactor? Isn't there a danger of error and abuse? Won't We turn into Them?

Questions like these are disingenuous in a world in which terrorists proclaim themselves and perform for television. The name of their game is public recognition. After all, you can't very well intimidate a government into releasing your freedom fighters unless you announce that it is your group that has seized its embassy. "Clear guilt" is difficult to define, but when 40 million people see a group of masked gunmen seize an airplane on the evening news, there is not much question about who the perpetrators are. There will be hard cases where the situation is murkier. Nonetheless, a line demarcating the legitimate use of torture can be drawn. Torture only the obviously guilty, and only for the sake of saving innocents, and the line between Us and Them will remain clear.

There is little danger that the Western democracies will lose their way if they choose to inflict pain as one way of preserving order. Paralysis in the face of evil is the greater danger. Some day soon a terrorist will threaten tens of thousands of lives, and torture will be the only way to save them. We had better start thinking about this.

Questions

1. On what assumptions about torture (and its efficacy) does Levin's argument rest? Do you agree with his assumptions? Why or why not?

2. What support does Levin provide for his position? List the key evidence that Levin gives, and analyze how it is or is not compelling.

3. Write your own argument about the use of torture. Be sure to consider how you will support your position and how you will answer readers who hold a different view.

Sallie Tisdale

We Do Abortions Here: A Nurse's Story

We do abortions here; that is all we do. There are weary, grim moments when I think I cannot bear another basin of bloody remains, utter another kind phrase of reassurance. So I leave the procedure room in the back and reach for a new chart. Soon I am talking to an eighteen-year-old woman pregnant for the fourth time. I push up her sleeve to check her blood pressure and find row upon row of needle marks, neat and parallel and discolored. She has been so hungry for her drug for so long that she has taken to using the loose skin of her upper arms; her elbows are already a permanent ruin of bruises. She is surprised to find herself nearly four months pregnant. I suspect she is often surprised, in a mild way, by the blows she is dealt. I prepare myself for another basin, another brief and chafing loss.

"How can you stand it?" Even the clients ask. They see the machine, the strange instruments, the blood, the final stroke that wipes away the promise of pregnancy. Sometimes I see that too: I watch a woman's swollen abdomen sink to softness in a few stuttering moments and my own belly flip-flops with sorrow. But all it takes for me to catch my breath is another interview, one more story that sounds so much like the last one. There is a numbing sameness lurking in this job: the same questions, the same answers, even the same trembling tone in the voices. The worst is the sameness of human failure, of inadequacy in the face of each day's dull demands.

In describing this work, I find it difficult to explain how much I enjoy it most of the time. We laugh a lot here, as friends and as professional peers. It's nice to be with women all day. I like the sudden, transient bonds I forge with some clients: moments when I am in my strength, remembering weakness, and a woman in weakness reaches out for my strength. What I offer is not power, but solidness, offered almost eagerly. Certain clients waken in me every tender urge I have—others make me wince and bite my tongue. Both challenge me to find a balance. It is a sweet brutality we practice here, a stark and loving dispassion.

I look at abortion as if I am standing on a cliff with a telescope, gazing at some great vista. I can sweep the horizon with both eyes, survey the scene in all its distance and size. Or I can put my eye to the lens and focus on the small details, suddenly so close. In abortion the absolute must always be tempered by the contextual, because both are real, both valid, both hard. How can we do this? How can we refuse? Each abortion is a measure of our failure to protect, to nourish our own. Each basin I empty is a promise—but a promise broken a long time ago.

From Harper's Magazine *(October 1990), a monthly that includes fiction, essays, reviews, and commentary on American politics and culture.*

I grew up on the great promise of birth control. Like many women my age, I took the pill as soon as I was sexually active. To risk pregnancy when it was so easy to avoid seemed stupid, and my contraceptive success, as it were, was part of the promise of social enlightenment. But birth control fails, far more frequently than laboratory trials predict. Many of our clients take the pill; its failure to protect them is a shocking realization. We have clients who have been sterilized, whose husbands have had vasectomies; each one is a statistical misfit, fine print come to life. The anger and shame of these women I hold in one hand, and the basin in the other. The distance between the two, the length I pace and try to measure, is the size of an abortion. 5

The procedure is disarmingly simple. Women are surprised, as though the mystery of conception, a dark and hidden genesis, requires an elaborate finale. In the first trimester of pregnancy, it's a mere few minutes of vacuuming, a neat tidying up. I give a woman a small yellow Valium, and when it has begun to relax her, I lead her into the back, into bareness, the stirrups. The doctor reaches in her, opening the narrow tunnel to the uterus with a succession of slim, smooth bars of steel. He inserts a plastic tube and hooks it to a hose on the machine. The woman is framed against white paper that crackles as she moves, the light bright in her eyes. Then the machine rumbles low and loud in the small windowless room; the doctor moves the tube back and forth with an efficient rhythm, and the long tail of it fills with blood that spurts and stumbles along into a jar. He is usually finished in a few minutes. They are long minutes for the woman; her uterus frequently reacts to its abrupt emptying with a powerful, unceasing cramp, which cuts off the blood vessels and enfolds the irritated, bleeding tissue.

I am learning to recognize the shadows that cross the faces of the women I hold. While the doctor works between her spread legs, the paper drape hiding his intent expression, I stand beside the table. I hold the woman's hands in mine, resting them just below her ribs. I watch her eyes, finger her necklace, stroke her hair. I ask about her job, her family; in a haze she answers me; we chatter, faces close, eyes meeting and sliding apart.

I watch the shadows that creep up unnoticed and suddenly darken her face as she screws up her features and pushes a tear out each side to slide down her cheeks. I have learned to anticipate the quiver of chin, the rapid intake of breath and the surprising sobs that rise soon after the machine starts to drum. I know this is when the cramp deepens, and the tears are partly the tears that follow pain—the sharp, childish crying when one bumps one's head on a cabinet door. But a well of woe seems to open beneath many women when they hear that thumping sound. The anticipation of the moment has finally come to fruit; the moment has arrived when the loss is no longer an imagined one. It has come true.

I am struck by the sameness and I am struck every day by the variety here—how this commonplace dilemma can so display the differences of women. A twenty-one-year-old woman, unemployed, uneducated, without family, in the fifth month of her fifth pregnancy. A forty-two-year-old mother of teenagers, shocked by her condition, refusing to tell her husband. A twenty-three-year-old mother of two having her seventh abortion, and many women in their thirties having their first. Some are stoic, some hysterical, a few giggle uncontrollably, many cry.

10 I talk to a sixteen-year-old uneducated girl who was raped. She has gonorrhea. She describes blinding headaches, attacks of breathlessness, nausea. "Sometimes I feel like two different people," she tells me with a calm smile, "and I talk to myself."

I pull out my plastic models. She listens patiently for a time, and then holds her hands wide in front of her stomach.

"When's the baby going to go up into my stomach?" she asks.

I blink. "What do you mean?"

"Well," she says, still smiling, "when women get so big, isn't the baby in your stomach? Doesn't it hatch out of an egg there?"

15 My first question in an interview is always the same. As I walk down the hall with the woman, as we get settled in chairs and I glance through her files, I am trying to gauge her, to get a sense of the words, and the tone, I should use. With some I joke, with others I chat, sometimes I fall into a brisk, business-like patter. But I ask every woman, "Are you sure you want to have an abortion?" Most nod with grim knowing smiles. "Oh, yes," they sigh. Some seek forgiveness, offer excuses. Occasionally a woman will flinch and say, "Please don't use that word."

Later I describe the procedure to come, using care with my language. I don't say "pain" any more than I would say "baby." So many are afraid to ask how much it will hurt. "My sister told me—" I hear. "A friend of mine said—" and the dire expectations unravel. I prick the index finger of a woman for a drop of blood to test, and as the tiny lancet approaches the skin she averts her eyes, holding her trembling hand out to me and jumping at my touch.

It is when I am holding a plastic uterus in one hand, a suction tube in the other, moving them together in imitation of the scrubbing to come, that women ask the most secret question. I am speaking in a matter-of-fact voice about "the tissue" and "the contents" when the woman suddenly catches my eye and asks, "How big is the baby now?" These words suggest a quiet need for a definition of the boundaries being drawn. It isn't so odd, after all, that she feels relief when I describe the growing bud's bulbous shape, its miniature nature. Again I gauge, and sometimes lie a little, weaseling around its infantile features until its clinging power slackens.

But when I look in the basin, among the curdlike blood clots, I see an elfin thorax, attenuated, its pencilline ribs all in parallel rows with tiny knobs of spine rounding upwards. A translucent arm and hand swim beside.

A sleepy-eyed girl, just fourteen, watched me with a slight and goofy smile all through her abortion. "Does it have little feet and little fingers and all?" she'd asked earlier. When the suction was over she sat up woozily at the end of the table and murmured, "Can I see it?" I shook my head firmly.

20 "It's not allowed," I told her sternly, because I knew she didn't really want to see what was left. She accepted this statement of authority, and a shadow of confused relief crossed her plain, pale face.

Privately, even grudgingly, my colleagues might admit the power of abortion to provoke emotion. But they seem to prefer the broad view and disdain the telescope. Abortion is a matter of choice, privacy, control. Its uncertainty lies in specific cases: retarded women and girls too young to give consent for surgery, women who are ill or hostile or psychotic. Such common dilemmas are met with both compassion and impatience: they slow things down. We are too busy to chew over ethics. One person might discuss certain concerns, behind closed doors, or describe a particularly disturbing dream. But generally there is to be no ambivalence.

Every day I take calls from women who are annoyed that we cannot see them, cannot do their abortion today, this morning, now. They argue the price, demand that we stay after hours to accommodate their job or class schedule. Abortion is so routine that one expects it to be like a manicure: quick, cheap, and painless.

Still, I've cultivated a certain disregard. It isn't negligence, but I don't always pay attention. I couldn't be here if I tried to judge each case on its merits; after all, we do over a hundred abortions a week. At some point each individual in this line of work draws a boundary and adheres to it. For one physician the boundary is a particular week of gestation; for another, it is a certain number of repeated abortions. But these boundaries can be fluid too: one physician overruled his own limit to abort a mature but severely malformed fetus. For me, the limit is allowing my clients to carry their own burden, shoulder the responsibility themselves. I shoulder the burden of trying not to judge them.

This city has several "crisis pregnancy centers" advertised in the Yellow Pages. They are small offices staffed by volunteers, and they offer free pregnancy testing, glossy photos of dead fetuses, and movies. I had a client recently whose mother is active in the anti-abortion movement. The young woman went to the local crisis center and was told that the doctor would make her touch her dismembered baby, that the pain would be the most horrible she could imagine, and that she might, after an abortion, never be able to have children. All lies. They called her at home and at work, over and over and over, but she had been wise enough to give a false name. She came to us a fugitive. We who do abortions are marked, by some, as impure. It's dirty work.

When a deliveryman comes to the sliding glass window by the reception desk and tilts a box toward me, I hesitate. I read the packing slip, assess the shape and weight of the box in light of its supposed contents. We request familiar faces. The doors are carefully locked; I have learned to half glance around at bags and boxes, looking for a telltale sign. I register with security when I arrive, and I am careful not to bang a door. We are all a little on edge here. 25

Concern about size and shape seem to be natural, and so is the relief that follows. We make the powerful assumption that the fetus is different from us, and even when we admit the similarities, it is too simplistic to be seduced by form alone. But the form is enormously potent—humanoid, powerless, palm-sized, and pure, it evokes an almost fierce tenderness when viewed simply as what it appears to be. But appearance, and even potential, aren't enough. The fetus, in becoming itself, can ruin others; its utter dependence has a sinister side. When I am struck in the moment by the contents in the basin, I am careful to remember the context, to note the tearful teenager and the woman sighing with something more than relief. One kind of question, though, I find considerably trickier.

"Can you tell what it is?" I am asked, and this means gender. This question is asked by couples, not women alone. Always couples would abort a girl and keep a boy. I have been asked about twins, and even if I could tell what race the father was.

An eighteen-year-old woman with three daughters brought her husband to the interview. He glared first at me, then at his wife, as he sank lower and lower in the chair, picking his teeth with a toothpick. He interrupted a conversation with his wife to ask if I could tell whether the baby would be a boy or a girl. I told him I could not.

"Good," he replied in a slow and strangely malevolent voice, "'cause if it was a boy I'd wring her neck."

30 In a literal sense, abortion exists because we are able to ask such questions, able to assign a value to the fetus which can shift with changing circumstances. If the human bond to a child were as primitive and unflinchingly narrow as that of other animals, there would be no abortion. There would be no abortion because there would be nothing more important than caring for the young and perpetuating the species, no reason for sex but to make babies. I sense this sometimes, this wordless organic duty, when I do ultrasounds.

We do ultrasound, a sound-wave test that paints a faint, gray picture of the fetus, whenever we're uncertain of gestation. Age is measured by the width of the skull and confirmed by the length of the femur or thighbone; we speak of a pregnancy as being a certain "femur length" in weeks. The usual concern is whether a pregnancy is within the legal limit for an abortion. Women this far along have bellies which swell out round and tight like trim muscles. When they lie flat, the mound rises softly above the hips, pressing the umbilicus upward.

It takes practice to read an ultrasound picture, which is grainy and etched as though in strokes of charcoal. But suddenly a rapid rhythmic motion appears—the beating heart. Nearby is a soft oval, scratched with lines—the skull. The leg is harder to find, and then suddenly the fetus moves, bobbing in the surf. The skull turns away, an arm slides across the screen, the torso rolls. I know the weight of a baby's head on my shoulder, the whisper of lips on ears, the delicate curve of a fragile spine in my hand. I know how heavy and correct a newborn cradled feels. The creature I watch in secret requires nothing from me but to be left alone, and that is precisely what won't be done.

These inadvertently made beings are caught in a twisting web of motive and desire. They are at least inconvenient, sometimes quite literally dangerous in the womb, but most often they fall somewhere in between—consequences never quite believed in come to roost. Their virtue rises and falls outside their own nature: they become only what we make them. A fetus created by accident is the most absolute kind of surprise. Whether the blame lies in a failed IUD, a slipped condom, or a false impression of safety, that fetus is a thing whose creation has been actively worked against. Its existence is an error. I think this is why so few women, even late in a pregnancy, will consider giving a baby up for adoption. To do so means making the fetus real—imagining it as something whole and outside oneself. The decision to terminate a pregnancy is sometimes so difficult and confounding that it creates an enormous demand for immediate action. The decision is a rejection; the pregnancy has become something to be rid of, a condition to be ended. It is a burden, a weight, a thing separate.

Women have abortions because they are too old, and too young, too poor, and too rich, too stupid, and too smart. I see women who berate themselves with violent emotions for their first and only abortion, and others who return three times, five times, hauling two or three children, who cannot remember to take a pill or where they put the diaphragm. We talk glibly about choice. But the choice for what? I see all the broken promises in lives lived like a series of impromptu obstacles. There are the sweet, light promises of love and intimacy, the glittering promise of education and progress, the warm promise of safe families, long years of innocence and community. And there is the promise of freedom: freedom from failure, from faithlessness. Freedom from biology. The early feminist defense of abortion asked many questions, but the one I remember is this: Is biology destiny? And the answer is yes, sometimes it is. Women who have the fewest choices of all exercise their right to abortion the most.

35 Oh, the ignorance. I take a woman to the back room and ask her to undress; a few minutes later I return and find her positioned discreetly behind a drape, still wearing underpants. "Do I have to take these off too?" she asks, a little shocked. Some swear they have not had sex, many do not know what a uterus is, how sperm and egg meet, how sex makes babies. Some late seekers do not believe themselves pregnant; they believe themselves *impregnable.* I was chastised when I began this job for referring to some clients as girls: it is a feminist heresy. They come so young, snapping gum, sockless and sneakered, and their shakily applied eyeliner smears when they cry. I call them girls with maternal benignity. I cannot imagine them as mothers.

The doctor seats himself between the woman's thighs and reaches into the dilated opening of a five-month pregnant uterus. Quickly he grabs and crushes the fetus in several places, and the room is filled with a low clatter and snap of forceps, the click of the tanaculum, and a pulling, sucking sound. The paper crinkles as the drugged and sleepy woman shifts, the nurse's low, honey-brown voice explains each step in delicate words.

I have fetus dreams, we all do here: dreams of abortions one after the other; of buckets of blood splashed on the walls; trees full of crawling fetuses. I dreamed that two men grabbed me and began to drag me away. "Let's do an abortion," they said with a sickening leer, and I began to scream, plunged into a vision of sucking, scraping pain, of being spread and torn by impartial instruments that do only what they are bidden. I woke from this dream barely able to breathe and thought of kitchen tables and coat hangers, knitting needles striped with blood, and women all alone clutching a pillow in their teeth to keep the screams from piercing the apartment-house walls. Abortion is the narrowest edge between kindness and cruelty. Done as well as it can be, it is still violence—merciful violence, like putting a suffering animal to death.

Maggie, one of the nurses, received a call at midnight not long ago. It was a woman in her twentieth week of pregnancy; the necessarily gradual process of cervical dilation begun the day before had stimulated labor, as it sometimes does. Maggie and one of the doctors met the woman at the office in the night. Maggie helped her onto the table, and as she lay down the fetus was delivered into Maggie's hands. When Maggie told me about it the next day, she cupped her hands into a small bowl—"It was just like a little kitten," she said softly, wonderingly. "Everything was still attached."

At the end of the day I clean out the suction jars, pouring blood into the sink, splashing the sides with flecks of tissue. From the sink rises a rich and humid smell, hot, earthy, and moldering; it is the smell of something recently alive beginning to decay. I take care of the plastic tub on the floor, filled with pieces too big to be trusted to the trash. The law defines the contents of the bucket I hold protectively against my chest as "tissue." Some would say my complicity in filling that bucket gives me no right to call it anything else. I slip the tissue gently into a bag and place it in the freezer, to be burned at another time. Abortion requires of me an entirely new set of assumptions. It requires a willingness to live with conflict, fearlessness, and grief. As I close the freezer door, I imagine a world where this won't be necessary, and then return to the world where it is.

QUESTIONS

1. Tisdale speaks of taking both broad views—"as if I am standing on a cliff with a telescope"—and narrow views—"I can put my eye to the lens and focus on the small details" (paragraph 4). Choose one section of this essay and mark the passages you would describe as taking broad views and the passages you would describe as taking narrow views. What is the effect of Tisdale's going back and forth between them? How does she manage transitions?

2. "We are too busy to chew over ethics" (paragraph 21), Tisdale observes. What does she mean by ethics? Does she engage with what you consider ethical issues in this essay? Explain.

3. Although Tisdale takes a pro-choice position, a pro-lifer could use parts of her essay against her. What parts? What are the advantages and disadvantages of including material that could be used in support of the opposition?

4. Write a pro-choice or pro-life essay of your own. Include material that could be used in support of the opposition. You may use Tisdale's essay, but you need not.

Nora Ephron *The Boston Photographs*

"I made all kinds of pictures because I thought it would be a good rescue shot over the ladder . . . never dreamed it would be anything else. . . . I kept having to move around because of the light set. The sky was bright and they were in deep shadow. I was making pictures with a motor drive and he, the fire fighter, was reaching up and, I don't know, everything started falling. I followed the girl down taking pictures . . . I made three or four frames. I realized what was going on and I completely turned around, because I didn't want to see her hit."

You probably saw the photographs. In most newspapers, there were three of them. The first showed some people on a fire escape—a fireman, a woman and a child. The fireman had a nice strong jaw and looked very brave. The woman was holding the child. Smoke was pouring from the building behind them. A rescue ladder was approaching, just a few feet away, and the fireman had one arm around the woman and one arm reaching out toward the ladder. The second picture showed the fire escape slipping off the building. The child had fallen on the escape and seemed about to slide off the edge. The woman was grasping desperately at the legs of the fireman, who had managed to grab the ladder. The third picture showed the woman and child in midair, falling to the ground. Their arms and legs were outstretched, horribly distended. A potted plant was falling too. The caption said that the woman, Diana Bryant, nineteen, died in the fall. The child landed on the woman's body and lived.

The pictures were taken by Stanley Forman, thirty, of the *Boston Herald American*. He used a motor-driven Nikon F set at 1/250, f 5.6–8. Because of the motor, the camera can click off three frames a second. More than four hundred newspapers in the United States alone carried the photographs; the tear sheets from overseas are still coming in. The *New York Times* ran them on the first page of its second section; a paper in south Georgia gave them nineteen columns; the *Chicago Tribune*, the *Washington Post* and the *Washington Star* filled almost half their front pages, the *Star* under a somewhat redundant headline that read: SENSATIONAL PHOTOS OF RESCUE ATTEMPT THAT FAILED.

The photographs are indeed sensational. They are pictures of death in action, of that split second when luck runs out, and it is impossible to look at them without feeling their extraordinary impact and remembering, in an almost subconscious way, the morbid fantasy of falling, falling off a building, falling to one's death. Beyond that, the pictures are classics, old-fashioned but perfect examples of photojournalism at its most spectacular. They're throwbacks, really, fire pictures, 1930s tabloid shots; at the same time they're technically superb and thoroughly modern—the sequence could not have been taken at all until the development of the motor-driven camera some sixteen years ago.

Originally written for Ephron's column on the media in Esquire *(November 1975), this essay later appeared in her collection* Scribble, Scribble: Notes on the Media *(1978).*

5 Most newspaper editors anticipate some reader reaction to photographs like Forman's; even so, the response around the country was enormous, and almost all of it was negative. I have read hundreds of the letters that were printed in letters-to-the-editor sections, and they repeat the same points. "Invading the privacy of death." "Cheap sensationalism." "I thought I was reading the *National Enquirer*." "Assigning the agony of a human being in terror of imminent death to the status of a side-show act." "A tawdry way to sell newspapers." The *Seattle Times* received sixty letters and calls; its managing editor even got a couple of them at home. A reader wrote the *Philadelphia Inquirer*: "*Jaws* and *Towering Inferno* are playing downtown; don't take business away

from people who pay good money to advertise in your own paper." Another reader wrote the *Chicago Sun-Times*: "I shall try to hide my disappointment that Miss Bryant wasn't wearing a skirt when she fell to her death. You could have had some award-winning photographs of her underpants as her skirt billowed over her head, you voyeurs." Several newspaper editors wrote columns defending the pictures: Thomas Keevil of the *Costa Mesa* (California) *Daily Pilot* printed a ballot for readers to vote on whether they would have printed the pictures; Marshall L. Stone of Maine's *Bangor Daily News*, which refused to print the famous assassination picture of the Vietcong prisoner in Saigon, claimed that the Boston pictures showed the dangers of fire escapes

and raised questions about slumlords. (The burning building was a five-story brick apartment house on Marlborough Street in the Back Bay section of Boston.)[1]

For the last five years, the *Washington Post* has employed various journalists as ombudsmen, whose job is to monitor the paper on behalf of the public. The *Post*'s current ombudsman is Charles Seib, former managing editor of the *Washington Star*; the day the Boston photographs appeared, the paper received

1. Since 1975 Marlborough Street has been gentrified; it is now one of Boston's most sought-after addresses.

over seventy calls in protest. As Seib later wrote in a column about the pictures, it was "the largest reaction to a published item that I have experienced in eight months as the *Post*'s ombudsman. . . .

"In the *Post*'s newsroom, on the other hand, I found no doubts, no second thoughts . . . the question was not whether they should be printed but how they should be displayed. When I talked to editors . . . they used words like 'interesting' and 'riveting' and 'gripping' to describe them. The pictures told something about life in the ghetto, they said (although the neighborhood where the tragedy occurred is not a ghetto, I am told). They dramatized the need to check on the safety of fire escapes. They dramatically conveyed something that had happened, and that is the business we're in. They were news. . . .

"Was publication of that [third] picture a bow to the same taste for the morbidly sensational that makes gold mines of disaster movies? Most papers will not print the picture of a dead body except in the most unusual circumstances. Does the fact that the final picture was taken a millisecond before the young woman died make a difference? Most papers will not print a picture of a bare female breast. Is that a more inappropriate subject for display than the picture of a human being's last agonized instant of life?" Seib offered no answers to the questions he raised, but he went on to say that although as an editor he would probably have run the pictures, as a reader he was "revolted by them."

In conclusion, Seib wrote: "Any editor who decided to print those pictures without giving at least a moment's thought to what purpose they served and what their effect was likely to be on the reader should ask another question: Have I become so preoccupied with manufacturing a product according to professional traditions and standards that I have forgotten about the consumer, the reader?"

10 It should be clear that the phone calls and letters and Seib's own reaction were occasioned by one factor alone: the death of the woman. Obviously, had she survived the fall, no one would have protested; the pictures would have had a completely different impact. Equally obviously, had the child died as well—or instead—Seib would undoubtedly have received ten times the phone calls he did. In each case, the pictures would have been exactly the same—only the captions, and thus the responses, would have been different.

But the questions Seib raises are worth discussing—though not exactly for the reasons he mentions. For it may be that the real lesson of the Boston photographs is not the danger that editors will be forgetful of reader reaction, but that they will continue to censor pictures of death precisely because of that reaction. The protests Seib fielded were really a variation on an old theme—and we saw plenty of it during the Nixon-Agnew years—the "Why doesn't the press print the good news?" argument. In this case, of course, the objections were all dressed up and cleverly disguised as righteous indignation about the privacy of death. This is a form of puritanism that is often justifiable; just as often it is merely puritanical.

Seib takes it for granted that the widespread though fairly recent newspaper policy against printing pictures of dead bodies is a sound one; I don't know that it makes any sense at all. I recognize that printing pictures of corpses raises all sorts of problems about taste and titillation and sensationalism; the fact is, however, that people die. Death happens to be one of life's main events. And it is irresponsible—and more than that, inaccurate—for newspapers to fail to show it, or to show it only when an astonishing set of photos comes in over the Associated Press wire. Most papers covering fatal automobile accidents will print pictures of mangled cars. But the significance of fatal automobile accidents is not that a great deal of steel is twisted but that people die. Why not show it? That's what accidents are about. Throughout the Vietnam war, editors were reluctant to print atrocity pictures. Why *not* print them? That's what that war was about. Murder victims are almost never photographed; they are granted their privacy. But their relatives are relentlessly pictured on their way in and out of hospitals and morgues and funerals.

I'm not advocating that newspapers print these things in order to teach their readers a lesson. The *Post* editors justified their printing of the Boston pictures with several arguments in that direction; every one of them is irrelevant. The pictures don't show anything about slum life; the incident could have happened anywhere, and it did. It is extremely unlikely that anyone who saw them rushed out and had his fire escape strengthened. And the pictures were not news—at least they were not national news. It is not news in Washington, or New York, or Los Angeles that a woman was killed in a Boston fire. The only newsworthy thing about the pictures is that they were taken. They deserve to be printed because they are great pictures, breathtaking pictures of something that happened. That they disturb readers is exactly as it should be: that's why photojournalism is often more powerful than written journalism.

QUESTIONS

1. Why does Ephron begin with the words of the photographer Stanley Forman? What information—as well as perspective—does her opening paragraph convey?

2. What was public reaction to the publication of the Boston photographs? What reasons did newspeople give for printing them? How does Ephron arrange these responses?

3. What conclusions does Ephron reach about the ethics of publishing sensational photographs? Does she offer ethical guidelines?

4. Find a startling photograph recently printed in a newspaper or magazine, and argue for or against its publication, using Ephron's terms and your own.

5. Examine the Vietcong assassination photo (p. 770) in H. Bruce Franklin's "From Realism to Virtual Reality". Were the issues about publishing this photo the same as those for the Boston photographs Ephron discusses? Were they different? Or different enough? Write an essay about the issues surrounding the two photo publications.

Michael Dirda *In Wildness Is the Preservation of the World*

Humankind, noted the dour T. S. Eliot,[1] cannot bear very much reality. One way people avoid it is to imagine a time when society was truly courtly, genteel, or comradely. If only we could, say, reinspire our children with noble ideals, they—never us parents—could build again a golden age and become its heroes, light-bringers, Nobel laureates. (We do tend to forget, as the poet Randall Jarrell quipped,[2] that the people who lived in a golden age probably went around complaining how yellow everything was.)

The matter of ideals lies at the heart of education: What, finally, are the values we wish to impart? In some compendia of moral wisdom—such as William Bennett's *Book of Virtues*[3]—we are bludgeoned with powerful accounts of good and evil, where virtue is nearly always triumphant. To endure times of crisis and doubt, we are told, people require strong, clear lessons, with unambiguous moral points. This is pure Aristotle,[4] by the way, who felt that virtuous behavior was largely the product of habit and practice.

Certainly, such an approach will create a citizenry assured of itself, anchored in its convictions. Yet do we want a nation of true believers? Moralists tend to promulgate creeds of rationalism, individual self-discipline, faith—all the sturdy yeoman traits. But what of ecstasy, community, and doubt? Surely, as the poet Yeats[5] said, body should not be bruised to pleasure soul. Ought our schools to produce young fogeys, ten-year-old saints and cautious teenagers who never jaywalk or drive too fast? Civility and courtesy are crucially important, yet, deep down, Americans seldom demonstrate any high regard for an obedient Little Lord Fauntleroy or Goody Two-shoes.[6] Our heroes don't follow

Included in Dirda's Pulitzer Prize–winning collection, Book by Book: Notes on Reading and Life *(2005), which emphasizes the importance of "books as life-teachers." Dirda's title comes from Henry David Thoreau's 1861 essay "Walking," about which Dirda wrote in "The Pleasures and Provocations of America's Most Famous Naturalist" for the* Washington Post *(April 22, 2001).*

1. Thomas Sterns Eliot (1888–1965), American poet and literary critic.

2. Jarrell (1914–1965), American poet, made this statement in "The Taste of the Age," a column in the *Saturday Evening Post* (July 26, 1958).

3. William Bennett (b. 1943) published *The Book of Virtues: A Treasury of Great Moral Stories* in 1993 after completing his term as chairman of the National Endowment for the Humanities under Ronald Reagan.

4. Greek philosopher (384 B.C.E.–322 B.C.E.).

5. William Butler Yeats (1865–1939), Irish poet, wrote "The body is not bruised to pleasure soul" in his poem "Among School Children."

6. *Little Lord Fauntleroy* (1886) by Frances Hodgson Burnett and the anonymous *The History of Goody Two-Shoes* (1765) are didactic children's stories; the phrase "goody-two shoes" now means an excessively (and irritatingly) virtuous person.

the rules; they flout them. We admire rebels, mavericks, drifters, scoundrels, and outcasts. The most archetypal Americans are, after all, Huckleberry Finn, Scarlett O'Hara, Malcolm X, and Bart Simpson.[7] We need to learn from them as well as from noble George Washington and Clara Barton.[8]

In short, if you are given lined paper, write crosswise. At least occasionally.

7. Huckleberry Finn, hero of Mark Twain's novel *The Adventures of Huckleberry Finn* (1885); Scarlett O'Hara, heroine of Margaret Mitchell's *Gone with the Wind* (1936); Malcolm X (1925–1965), a real person born as Malcolm Little and later named El-Hajj Malik El-Shabazz; and Bart Simpson, main character of the television comic series *The Simpsons*—all are American characters with a rebellious streak.
8. George Washington (1732–1799), first U.S. president; Clara Barton (1821–1912), founder of the American Red Cross.

QUESTIONS

1. Consider Dirda's title, which derives from Thoreau's essay "Walking," and refers to wild things in nature. How does Dirda extend the concept of *wildness* to American character?
2. What is Dirda's implicit attitude to books like William Bennett's *The Book of Virtues*? What verbal clues reveal that attitude?
3. Read three selections of proverbs by authors in the "Album of Styles": Ben Franklin (p. 481), William Blake (p. 483), and Ambrose Bierce (p. 484). Which author's proverbs do you think Dirda would most approve of? Why?
4. Dirda lists several possible models for Americans in his final paragraph. Choose one that you believe to be a good model, and argue your case in a brief essay.

PAUL FUSSELL

Thank God for the Atom Bomb

MANY YEARS AGO in New York I saw on the side of a bus a whiskey ad I've remembered all this time. It's been for me a model of the short poem, and indeed I've come upon few short poems subsequently that exhibited more poetic talent. The ad consisted of two eleven-syllable lines of "verse," thus:

> In life, experience is the great teacher.
> In Scotch, Teacher's is the great experience.

For present purposes we must jettison the second line (licking our lips, to be sure, as it disappears), leaving the first to register a principle whose banality suggests that it enshrines a most useful truth. I bring up the matter because,

Originally published as an article in the New Republic *(August 22, 1981); later included in Fussell's* Thank God for the Atom Bomb, and Other Essays *(1988).*

writing on the forty-second anniversary of the atom-bombing of Hiroshima and Nagasaki, I want to consider something suggested by the long debate about the ethics, if any, of that ghastly affair. Namely, the importance of experience, sheer, vulgar experience, in influencing, if not determining, one's views about that use of the atom bomb.

The experience I'm talking about is having to come to grips, face to face, with an enemy who designs your death. The experience is common to those in the marines and the infantry and even the line navy, to those, in short, who fought the Second World War mindful always that their mission was, as they were repeatedly assured, "to close with the enemy and destroy him." *Destroy*, notice: not hurt, frighten, drive away, or capture. I think there's something to be learned about that war, as well as about the tendency of historical memory unwittingly to resolve ambiguity and generally clean up the premises, by considering the way testimonies emanating from real war experience tend to complicate attitudes about the most cruel ending of that most cruel war.

"What did you do in the Great War, Daddy?" The recruiting poster deserves ridicule and contempt, of course, but here its question is embarrassingly relevant, and the problem is one that touches on the dirty little secret of social class in America. Arthur T. Hadley said recently that those for whom the use of the A-bomb was "wrong" seem to be implying "that it would have been better to allow thousands on thousands of American and Japanese infantrymen to die in honest hand-to-hand combat on the beaches than to drop those two bombs." People holding such views, he notes, "do not come from the ranks of society that produce infantrymen or pilots." And there's an eloquence problem: most of those with firsthand experience of the war at its worst were not elaborately educated people. Relatively inarticulate, most have remained silent about what they know. That is, few of those destined to be blown to pieces if the main Japanese islands had been invaded went on to become our most effective men of letters or impressive ethical theorists or professors of contemporary history or of international law. The testimony of experience has tended to come from rough diamonds—James Jones[1] is an example—who went through the war as enlisted men in the infantry or the Marine Corps.

Anticipating objections from those without such experience, in his book *WWII* Jones carefully prepares for his chapter on the A-bombs by detailing the plans already in motion for the infantry assaults on the home islands of Kyushu (thirteen divisions scheduled to land in November 1945) and ultimately Honshu (sixteen divisions scheduled for March 1946). Planners of the invasion assumed that it would require a full year, to November 1946, for the Japanese to be sufficiently worn down by land-combat attrition to surrender. By that time, one million American casualties was the expected price. Jones observes that the forthcoming invasion of Kyushu "was well into its collecting and stockpiling stages before the war ended." (The island of Saipan was designated a main ammunition and supply base for the invasion, and if you go there today you can see some of the assembled stuff still sitting there.) "The assault troops were

1. American novelist (1921–1977), author of *From Here to Eternity* (1951), the first volume in a trilogy about World War II.

chosen and already in training," Jones reminds his readers, and he illuminates by the light of experience what this meant:

> What it must have been like to some old-timer buck sergeant or staff sergeant who had been through Guadalcanal or Bougainville or the Philippines, to stand on some beach and watch this huge war machine beginning to stir and move all around him and know that he very likely had survived this far only to fall dead on the dirt of Japan's home islands, hardly bears thinking about.

5 Another bright enlisted man, this one an experienced marine destined for the assault on Honshu, adds his testimony. Former Pfc. E. B. Sledge, author of the splendid memoir *With the Old Breed at Peleliu and Okinawa*, noticed at the time that the fighting grew "more vicious the closer we got to Japan," with the carnage of Iwo Jima and Okinawa worse than what had gone before. He points out that

> what we had *experienced* [my emphasis] in fighting the Japs (pardon the expression) on Peleliu and Okinawa caused us to formulate some very definite opinions that the invasion . . . would be a ghastly bloodletting. . . . It would shock the American public and the world. [Every Japanese] soldier, civilian, woman, and child would fight to the death with whatever weapons they had, rifle, grenade, or bamboo spear.

The Japanese pre-invasion patriotic song, "One Hundred Million Souls for the Emperor," says Sledge, "meant just that." Universal national kamikaze was the point. One kamikaze pilot, discouraged by his unit's failure to impede the Americans very much despite the bizarre casualties it caused, wrote before diving his plane onto an American ship, "I see the war situation becoming more desperate. All Japanese must become soldiers and die for the Emperor." Sledge's First Marine Division was to land close to the Yokosuka Naval Base, "one of the most heavily defended sectors of the island." The marines were told, he recalls, that

> due to the strong beach defenses, caves, tunnels, and numerous Jap suicide torpedo boats and manned mines, few Marines in the first five assault waves would get ashore alive—my company was scheduled to be in the first and second waves. The veterans in the outfit felt we had already run out of luck anyway. . . . We viewed the invasion with complete resignation that we would be killed—either on the beach or inland.

And the invasion was going to take place: there's no question about that. It was not theoretical or merely rumored in order to scare the Japanese. By July 10, 1945, the prelanding naval and aerial bombardment of the coast had begun, and the battleships *Iowa, Missouri, Wisconsin,* and *King George V* were steaming up and down the coast, softening it up with their sixteen-inch shells.

On the other hand, John Kenneth Galbraith[2] is persuaded that the Japanese would have surrendered surely by November without an invasion. He

2. American economist and professor of economics at Harvard University (1908–2006). During World War II he was in charge of wartime price control, and after the war he went to Japan with other economists to study the economic and social conditions.

thinks the A-bombs were unnecessary and unjustified because the war was ending anyway. The A-bombs meant, he says, "a difference, at most, of two or three weeks." But at the time, with no indication that surrender was on the way, the kamikazes were sinking American vessels, the *Indianapolis* was sunk (880 men killed), and Allied casualties were running to over 7,000 per week. "Two or three weeks," says Galbraith. Two weeks more means 14,000 more killed and wounded, three weeks more, 21,000. Those weeks mean the world if you're one of those thousands or related to one of them. During the time between the dropping of the Nagasaki bomb on August 9 and the actual surrender on the fifteenth, the war pursued its accustomed course: on the twelfth of August eight captured American fliers were executed (heads chopped off); the fifty-first United States submarine, *Bonefish*, was sunk (all aboard drowned); the destroyer *Callaghan* went down, the seventieth to be sunk, and the Destroyer Escort *Underhill* was lost. That's a bit of what happened in six days of the two or three weeks posited by Galbraith. What did he do in the war? He worked in the Office of Price Administration in Washington. I don't demand that he experience having his ass shot off. I merely note that he didn't.

Likewise, the historian Michael Sherry, author of a recent book on the rise of the American bombing mystique, *The Creation of Armageddon*, argues that we didn't delay long enough between the test explosion in New Mexico and the mortal explosions in Japan. More delay would have made possible deeper moral considerations and perhaps laudable second thoughts and restraint. "The risks of delaying the bomb's use," he says, "would have been small—not the thousands of casualties expected of invasion but only a few days or weeks of relatively routine operations." While the mass murders represented by these "relatively routine operations" were enacting, Michael Sherry was safe at home. Indeed, when the bombs were dropped he was going on eight months old, in danger only of falling out of his pram. In speaking thus of Galbraith and Sherry, I'm aware of the offensive implications *ad hominem*.[3] But what's at stake in an infantry assault is so entirely unthinkable to those without the experience of one, or several, or many, even if they possess very wide-ranging imaginations and warm sympathies, that experience is crucial in this case.

In general, the principle is, the farther from the scene of horror, the easier the talk. One young combat naval officer close to the action wrote home in the fall of 1943, just before the marines underwent the agony of Tarawa: "When I read that we will fight the Japs for years if necessary and will sacrifice hundreds of thousands if we must, I always like to check from where he's talking: it's seldom out here." That was Lieutenant (j.g.) John F. Kennedy. And Winston Churchill, with an irony perhaps too broad and easy, noted in Parliament that the people who preferred invasion to A-bombing seemed to have "no intention of proceeding to the Japanese front themselves." 10

A remoteness from experience like Galbraith's and Sherry's, and a similar rationalistic abstraction from actuality, seem to motivate the reaction of an anonymous reviewer of William Manchester's *Goodbye Darkness: A Memoir of*

3. Marked by an attack on an opponent's character; literally, to the man (Latin).

the Pacific War for *The New York Review of Books*. The reviewer naturally dislikes Manchester's still terming the enemy Nips or Japs, but what really shakes him (her?) is this passage of Manchester's:

> After Biak the enemy withdrew to deep caverns. Rooting them out became a bloody business which reached its ultimate horrors in the last months of the war. You think of the lives which would have been lost in an invasion of Japan's home islands—a staggering number of Americans but millions more of Japanese—and you thank God for the atomic bomb.

Thank God for the atom bomb. From this, "one recoils," says the reviewer. One does, doesn't one?

And not just a staggering number of Americans would have been killed in the invasion. Thousands of British assault troops would have been destroyed too, the anticipated casualties from the almost 200,000 men in the six divisions (the same number used to invade Normandy) assigned to invade the Malay Peninsula on September 9. Aimed at the reconquest of Singapore, this operation was expected to last until about March 1946—that is, seven more months of infantry fighting. "But for the atomic bombs," a British observer intimate with the Japanese defenses notes, "I don't think we would have stood a cat in hell's chance. We would have been murdered in the biggest massacre of the war. They would have annihilated the lot of us."

The Dutchman Laurens van der Post had been a prisoner of the Japanese for three and a half years. He and thousands of his fellows, enfeebled by beriberi and pellagra, were being systematically starved to death, the Japanese rationalizing this treatment not just because the prisoners were white men but because they had allowed themselves to be captured at all and were therefore moral garbage. In the summer of 1945 Field Marshal Terauchi issued a significant order: at the moment the Allies invaded the main islands, all prisoners were to be killed by the prison-camp commanders. But thank God that did not happen. When the A-bombs were dropped, van der Post recalls, "This cataclysm I was certain would make the Japanese feel that they could withdraw from the war without dishonor, because it would strike them, as it had us in the silence of our prison night, as something supernatural."

In an exchange of views not long ago in *The New York Review of Books*, Joseph Alsop and David Joravsky set forth the by now familiar argument on both sides of the debate about the "ethics" of the bomb. It's not hard to guess which side each chose once you know that Alsop experienced capture by the Japanese at Hong Kong early in 1942, while Joravsky came into no deadly contact with the Japanese: a young, combat-innocent soldier, he was on his way to the Pacific when the war ended. The editors of *The New York Review* gave the debate the tendentious title "Was the Hiroshima Bomb Necessary?" surely an unanswerable question (unlike "Was It Effective?") and one precisely indicating the intellectual difficulties involved in imposing *ex post facto*[4] a rational and even a

4. After the fact (Latin).

genteel ethics on this event. In arguing the acceptability of the bomb, Alsop focuses on the power and fanaticism of War Minister Anami, who insisted that Japan fight to the bitter end, defending the main islands with the same techniques and tenacity employed at Iwo and Okinawa. Alsop concludes: "Japanese surrender could never have been obtained, at any rate without the honor-satisfying bloodbath envisioned by . . . Anami, if the hideous destruction of Hiroshima and Nagasaki had not finally galvanized the peace advocates into tearing up the entire Japanese book of rules." The Japanese plan to deploy the undefeated bulk of their ground forces, over two million men, plus 10,000 kamikaze planes, plus the elderly and all the women and children with sharpened spears they could muster in a suicidal defense makes it absurd, says Alsop, to "hold the common view, by now hardly challenged by anyone, that the decision to drop the two bombs on Japan was wicked in itself, and that President Truman and all others who joined in making or who [like Robert Oppenheimer][5] assented to this decision shared in the wickedness." And in explanation of "the two bombs," Alsop adds: "The true, climactic, and successful effort of the Japanese peace advocates . . . did not begin in deadly earnest until *after* the second bomb had destroyed Nagasaki. The Nagasaki bomb was thus the trigger to all the developments that led to peace." At this time the army was so unready for surrender that most looked forward to the forthcoming invasion as an indispensable opportunity to show their mettle, enthusiastically agreeing with the army spokesman who reasoned early in 1945, "Since the retreat from Guadalcanal, the Army has had little opportunity to engage the enemy in land battles. But when we meet in Japan proper, our Army will demonstrate its invincible superiority." This possibility foreclosed by the Emperor's post-A-bomb surrender broadcast, the shocked, disappointed officers of one infantry battalion, anticipating a professionally impressive defense of the beaches, killed themselves in the following numbers: one major, three captains, ten first lieutenants, and twelve second lieutenants.

15 David Joravsky, now a professor of history at Northwestern, argued on the other hand that those who decided to use the A-bombs on cities betray defects of "reason and self-restraint." It all needn't have happened, he says, "if the U.S. government had been willing to take a few more days and to be a bit more thoughtful in opening up the age of nuclear warfare." I've already noted what "a few more days" would mean to the luckless troops and sailors on the spot, and as to being thoughtful when "opening up the age of nuclear warfare," of course no one was focusing on anything as portentous as that, which reflects a historian's tidy hindsight. The U.S. government was engaged not in that sort of momentous thing but in ending the war conclusively, as

5. J. Robert Oppenheimer (1904–1967), American physicist and organizer of the research station at Los Alamos, New Mexico, that developed the atomic bomb, and after World War II, chair of the U.S. Atomic Energy Commission. As chair of the AEC, he opposed developing even more powerful hydrogen bombs but conceded when President Truman approved the legislation to do so.

well as irrationally Remembering Pearl Harbor with a vengeance. It didn't know then what everyone knows now about leukemia and various kinds of carcinoma and birth defects. Truman was not being sly or coy when he insisted that the bomb was "only another weapon." History, as Eliot's "Gerontion" notes,

> . . . has many cunning passages, contrived corridors
> And issues, deceives with whispering ambitions,
> Guides us by vanities. . . .
>   Think
> Neither fear nor courage saves us.
>   Unnatural vices
> Are fathered by our heroism. Virtues
> Are forced upon us by our impudent crimes.

Understanding the past requires pretending that you don't know the present. It requires feeling its own pressure on your pulses without any *ex post facto* illumination. That's a harder thing to do than Joravsky seems to think.

The Alsop-Joravsky debate, reduced to a collision between experience and theory, was conducted with a certain civilized respect for evidence. Not so the way the scurrilous, agitprop *New Statesman* conceives those justifying the dropping of the bomb and those opposing. They are, on the one hand, says Bruce Page, "the imperialist class-forces acting through Harry Truman" and, on the other, those representing "the humane, democratic virtues"—in short, "fascists" as opposed to "populists." But ironically the bomb saved the lives not of any imperialists but only of the low and humble, the quintessentially democratic huddled masses—the conscripted enlisted men manning the fated invasion divisions and the sailors crouching at their gun-mounts in terror of the Kamikazes. When the war ended, Bruce Page was nine years old. For someone of his experience, phrases like "imperialist class forces" come easily, and the issues look perfectly clear.

He's not the only one to have forgotten, if he ever knew, the unspeakable savagery of the Pacific war. The dramatic postwar Japanese success at hustling and merchandising and tourism has (happily, in many ways) effaced for most people the vicious assault context in which the Hiroshima horror should be viewed. It is easy to forget, or not to know, what Japan was like before it was first destroyed, and then humiliated, tamed, and constitutionalized by the West. "Implacable, treacherous, barbaric"—those were Admiral Halsey's characterizations of the enemy, and at the time few facing the Japanese would deny that they fit to a T. One remembers the captured American airmen—the lucky ones who escaped decapitation—locked for years in packing crates. One remembers the gleeful use of bayonets on civilians, on nurses and the wounded, in Hong Kong and Singapore. Anyone who actually fought in the Pacific recalls the Japanese routinely firing on medics, killing the wounded (torturing them first, if possible), and cutting off the penises of the dead to stick in the corpses' mouths. The degree to which Americans register shock and extraordinary shame about the Hiroshima bomb correlates closely with lack of information about the Pacific war.

And of course the brutality was not just on one side. There was much sadism and cruelty, undeniably racist, on ours. (It's worth noting in passing how few hopes blacks could entertain of desegregation and decent treatment when the U.S. Army itself slandered the enemy as "the little brown Jap.") Marines and soldiers could augment their view of their own invincibility by possessing a well-washed Japanese skull, and very soon after Guadalcanal it was common to treat surrendering Japanese as handy rifle targets. Plenty of Japanese gold teeth were extracted—some from still living mouths—with Marine Corps Ka-Bar Knives,[6] and one of E. B. Sledge's fellow marines went around with a cut-off Japanese hand. When its smell grew too offensive and Sledge urged him to get rid of it, he defended his possession of this trophy thus: "How many Marines you reckon that hand pulled the trigger on?" (It's hardly necessary to observe that a soldier in the ETO would probably not have dealt that way with a German or Italian—that is, a "white person's"—hand.) In the Pacific the situation grew so public and scandalous that in September 1942, the Commander in Chief of the Pacific Fleet issued this order: "No part of the enemy's body may be used as a souvenir. Unit Commanders will take stern disciplinary action. . . ."

Among Americans it was widely held that the Japanese were really subhuman, little yellow beasts, and popular imagery depicted them as lice, rats, bats, vipers, dogs, and monkeys. What was required, said the Marine Corps journal *The Leatherneck* in May 1945, was "a gigantic task of extermination." The Japanese constituted a "pestilence," and the only appropriate treatment was "annihilation." Some of the marines landing on Iwo Jima had "Rodent Exterminator" written on their helmet covers, and on one American flagship the naval commander had erected a large sign enjoining all to "KILL JAPS! KILL JAPS! KILL MORE JAPS!" Herman Wouk remembers the Pacific war scene correctly while analyzing Ensign Keith in *The Caine Mutiny*: "Like most of the naval executioners of Kwajalein, he seemed to regard the enemy as a species of animal pest." And the feeling was entirely reciprocal: "From the grim and desperate taciturnity with which the Japanese died, they seemed on their side to believe that they were contending with an invasion of large armed ants." Hiroshima seems to follow in natural sequence: "This obliviousness of both sides to the fact that the opponents were human beings may perhaps be cited as the key to the many massacres of the Pacific war." Since the Jap vermin resist so madly and have killed so many of us, let's pour gasoline into their bunkers and light it and then shoot those afire who try to get out. Why not? Why not blow them all up, with satchel charges or with something stronger? Why not, indeed, drop a new kind of bomb on them, and on the un-uniformed ones too, since the Japanese government has announced that women from ages of seventeen to forty are being called up to repel the invasion? The intelligence officer of the U.S. Fifth Air Force declared on July 21, 1945, that "the entire population of Japan

6. High-carbon steel knives carried by Marines (officers and gunners) who did not carry bayonet-bearing rifles.

is a proper military target," and he added emphatically, "*There are no civilians in Japan.*" Why delay and allow one more American high school kid to see his own intestines blown out of his body and spread before him in the dirt while he screams and screams when with the new bomb we can end the whole thing just like that?

20 On Okinawa, only weeks before Hiroshima, 123,000 Japanese and Americans *killed* each other. (About 140,000 Japanese died at Hiroshima.) "Just awful" was the comment on the Okinawa slaughter not of some pacifist but of General MacArthur. On July 14, 1945, General Marshall sadly informed the Combined Chiefs of Staff—he was not trying to scare the Japanese—that it's "now clear . . . that in order to finish with the Japanese quickly, it will be necessary to invade the industrial heart of Japan." The invasion was definitely on, as I know because I was to be in it.

When the atom bomb ended the war, I was in the Forty-fifth Infantry Division, which had been through the European war so thoroughly that it had needed to be reconstituted two or three times. We were in a staging area near Rheims, ready to be shipped back across the United States for refresher training at Fort Lewis, Washington, and then sent on for final preparation in the Philippines. My division, like most of the ones transferred from Europe, was to take part in the invasion of Honshu. (The earlier landing on Kyushu was to be carried out by the 700,000 infantry already in the Pacific, those with whom James Jones has sympathized.) I was a twenty-one-year-old second lieutenant of infantry leading a rifle platoon. Although still officially fit for combat, in the German war I had already been wounded in the back and the leg badly enough to be adjudged, after the war, 40 percent disabled. But even if my leg buckled and I fell to the ground whenever I jumped out of the back of a truck, and even if the very idea of more combat made me breathe in gasps and shake all over, my condition was held to be adequate for the next act. When the atom bombs were dropped and news began to circulate that "Operation Olympic" would not, after all, be necessary, when we learned to our astonishment that we would not be obliged in a few months to rush up the beaches near Tokyo assault-firing while being machine-gunned, mortared, and shelled, for all the practiced phlegm of our tough façades we broke down and cried with relief and joy. We were going to live. We were going to grow to adulthood after all. The killing was all going to be over, and peace was actually going to be the state of things. When the *Enola Gay* dropped its package, "There were cheers," says John Toland, "over the intercom; it meant the end of the war." Down on the ground the reaction of Sledge's marine buddies when they heard the news was more solemn and complicated. They heard about the end of the war

> with quiet disbelief coupled with an indescribable sense of relief. We thought the Japanese would never surrender. Many refused to believe it. . . . Sitting in stunned silence, we remembered our dead. So many dead. So many maimed. So many bright futures consigned to the ashes of the past. So many dreams lost in the madness that had engulfed us. Except for a few widely scattered shouts of joy, the survivors of the abyss sat hollow-eyed and silent, trying to comprehend a world without war.

These troops who cried and cheered with relief or who sat stunned by the weight of their experience are very different from the high-minded, guilt-ridden GIs we're told about by J. Glenn Gray in his sensitive book *The Warriors*. During the war in Europe Gray was an interrogator in the Army Counterintelligence Corps, and in that capacity he experienced the war at Division level. There's no denying that Gray's outlook on everything was admirably noble, elevated, and responsible. After the war he became a much-admired professor of philosophy at Colorado College and an esteemed editor of Heidegger.[7] But *The Warriors*, his meditation on the moral and psychological dimensions of modern soldiering, gives every sign of error occasioned by remoteness from experience. Division headquarters is miles—*miles*—behind the line where soldiers experience terror and madness and relieve those pressures by crazy brutality and sadism. Indeed, unless they actually encountered the enemy during the war, most "soldiers" have very little idea what "combat" was like. As William Manchester says, "All who wore uniforms are called veterans, but more than 90 percent of them are as uninformed about the killing zones as those on the home front." Manchester's fellow marine E. B. Sledge thoughtfully and responsibly invokes the terms *drastically* and *totally* to underline the differences in experience between front and rear, and not even the far rear, but the close rear. "Our code of conduct toward the enemy," he notes, "differed drastically from that prevailing back at the division CP." (He's describing gold-tooth extraction from still-living Japanese.) Again he writes: "We existed in an environment totally incomprehensible to men behind the lines . . . ," even, he would insist, to men as intelligent and sensitive as Glenn Gray, who missed seeing with his own eyes Sledge's marine friends sliding under fire down a shell-pocked ridge slimy with mud and liquid dysentery shit into the maggoty Japanese and USMC corpses at the bottom, vomiting as the maggots burrowed into their own foul clothing. "We didn't talk about such things," says Sledge. "They were too horrible and obscene even for hardened veterans. . . . Nor do authors normally write about such vileness; unless they have seen it with their own eyes, it is too preposterous to think that men could actually live and fight for days and nights on end under such terrible conditions and not be driven insane." And Sledge has added a comment on such experience and the insulation provided by even a short distance: "Often people just behind our rifle companies couldn't understand what we knew." Glenn Gray was not in a rifle company, or even just behind one. "When the news of the atomic bombing of Hiroshima and Nagasaki came," he asks us to believe, "many an American soldier felt shocked and ashamed." Shocked, OK, but why ashamed? Because we'd destroyed civilians? We'd been doing that for years, in raids on Hamburg and Berlin and Cologne and Frankfurt and Mannheim and Dresden, and Tokyo, and besides, the two A-bombs wiped out 10,000 Japanese troops, not often thought of now, John Hersey's[8] kindly physicians and Jesuit priests being more touching. If around division headquarters some of the people Gray talked

7. Martin Heidegger (1889–1976), German existentialist philosopher.

8. American fiction and nonfiction writer (1914–1993), author of *Hiroshima* (1946), a moving account of the devastation and human suffering caused by the atomic bomb.

to felt ashamed, down in the rifle companies no one did, despite Gray's assertions. "The combat soldier," he says,

> knew better than did Americans at home what those bombs meant in suffering and injustice. The man of conscience realized intuitively that the vast majority of Japanese in both cities were no more, if no less, guilty of the war than were his own parents, sisters, or brothers.

I find this canting nonsense. The purpose of the bombs was not to "punish" people but to stop the war. To intensify the shame Gray insists we feel, he seems willing to fiddle the facts. The Hiroshima bomb, he says, was dropped "without any warning." But actually, two days before, 720,000 leaflets were dropped on the city urging everyone to get out and indicating that the place was going to be (as the Potsdam Declaration[9] had promised) obliterated. Of course few left.

Experience whispers that the pity is not that we used the bomb to end the Japanese war but that it wasn't ready in time to end the German one. If only it could have been rushed into production faster and dropped at the right moment on the Reich Chancellery or Berchtesgaden or Hitler's military headquarters in East Prussia (where Colonel Stauffenberg's July 20 bomb didn't do the job because it wasn't big enough), much of the Nazi hierarchy could have been pulverized immediately, saving not just the embarrassment of the Nuremberg trials but the lives of around four million Jews, Poles, Slavs, and gypsies, not to mention the lives and limbs of millions of Allied and German soldiers. If the bomb had only been ready in time, the young men of my infantry platoon would not have been so cruelly killed and wounded.

25 All this is not to deny that like the Russian Revolution, the atom-bombing of Japan was a vast historical tragedy, and every passing year magnifies the dilemma into which it has lodged the contemporary world. As with the Russian Revolution, there are two sides—that's why it's a tragedy instead of a disaster—and unless we are, like Bruce Page, simple-mindedly unimaginative and cruel, we will be painfully aware of both sides at once. To observe that from the viewpoint of the war's victims-to-be the bomb seemed precisely the right thing to drop is to purchase no immunity from horror. To experience both sides, one might study the book *Unforgettable Fire: Pictures Drawn by Atomic Bomb Survivors,* which presents a number of amateur drawings and watercolors of the Hiroshima scene made by middle-aged and elderly survivors for a peace exhibition in 1975. In addition to the almost unbearable pictures, the book offers brief moments of memoir not for the weak-stomached:

9. An agreement signed on July 26, 1945, by the president of the United States and the prime minister of Great Britain, with the concurrence of Generalissimo Chiang Kai-shek of Nationalist China, that mandated Japanese surrender, offering them a choice between unconditional surrender and total destruction, and that set forth the principles under which the defeated Axis territories would be governed and rebuilt.

> While taking my severely wounded wife out to the river bank . . . , I was horrified indeed at the sight of a stark naked man standing in the rain with his eyeball in his palm. He looked to be in great pain but there was nothing that I could do for him. I wonder what became of him. Even today, I vividly remember the sight. I was simply miserable.

These childlike drawings and paintings are of skin hanging down, breasts torn off, people bleeding and burning, dying mothers nursing dead babies. A bloody woman holds a bloody child in the ruins of a house, and the artist remembers her calling, "Please help this child! Someone, please help this child. Please help! Someone, please." As Samuel Johnson said of the smothering of Desdemona, the innocent in another tragedy, "It is not to be endured." Nor, it should be noticed, is an infantryman's account of having his arm blown off in the Arno Valley in Italy in 1944:

> I wanted to die and die fast. I wanted to forget this miserable world. I cursed the war, I cursed the people who were responsible for it, I cursed God for putting me here . . . to suffer for something I never did or knew anything about.

(A good place to interrupt and remember Glenn Gray's noble but hopelessly one-sided remarks about "injustice," as well as "suffering.")

"For this was hell," the soldier goes on,

> and I never imagined anything or anyone could suffer so bitterly. I screamed and cursed. Why? What had I done to deserve this? But no answer came. I yelled for medics, because subconsciously I wanted to live. I tried to apply my right hand over my bleeding stump, but I didn't have the strength to hold it. I looked to the left of me and saw the bloody mess that was once my left arm; its fingers and palm were turned upward, like a flower looking to the sun for its strength.

The future scholar-critic who writes *The History of Canting in the Twentieth Century* will find much to study and interpret in the utterances of those who dilate on the special wickedness of the A-bomb-droppers. He will realize that such utterance can perform for the speaker a valuable double function. First, it can display the fineness of his moral weave. And second, by implication it can also inform the audience that during the war he was not socially so unfortunate as to find himself down there with the ground forces, where he might have had to compromise the purity and clarity of his moral system by the experience of weighing his own life against someone else's. Down there, which is where the other people were, is the place where coarse self-interest is the rule. When the young soldier with the wild eyes comes at you, firing, do you shoot him in the foot, hoping he'll be hurt badly enough to drop or mis-aim the gun with which he's going to kill you, or do you shoot him in the chest (or, if you're a prime shot, in the head) and make certain that you and not he will be the survivor of that mortal moment?

It would be not just stupid but would betray a lamentable want of human experience to expect soldiers to be very sensitive humanitarians. The Glenn 30

Grays of this world need to have their attention directed to the testimony of those who know, like, say, Admiral of the Fleet Lord Fisher, who said, "Moderation in war is imbecility," or Sir Arthur Harris, director of the admittedly wicked aerial-bombing campaign designed, as Churchill put it, to "dehouse" the German civilian population, who observed that "War is immoral," or our own General W. T. Sherman: "War is cruelty, and you cannot refine it." Lord Louis Mountbatten, trying to say something sensible about the dropping of the A-bomb, came up only with "War is crazy." Or rather, it requires choices among crazinesses. "It would seem even more crazy," he went on, "if we were to have more casualties on our side to save the Japanese." One of the unpleasant facts for anyone in the ground armies during the war was that you had to become pro tem[10] a subordinate of the very uncivilian George S. Patton[11] and respond somehow to his unremitting insistence that you embrace his view of things. But in one of his effusions he was right, and his observation tends to suggest the experimental dubiousness of the concept of "just wars." "War is not a contest with gloves," he perceived. "It is resorted to only when laws, which are rules, have failed." Soldiers being like that, only the barest decencies should be expected of them. They did not start the war, except in the terrible sense hinted at in Frederic Manning's observation based on his front-line experience in the Great War: "War is waged by men; not by beasts, or by gods. It is a peculiarly human activity. To call it a crime against mankind is to miss at least half its significance; it is also the punishment of a crime." Knowing that unflattering truth by experience, soldiers have every motive for wanting a war stopped, by any means.

The stupidity, parochialism, and greed in the international mismanagement of the whole nuclear challenge should not tempt us to misimagine the circumstances of the bomb's first "use." Nor should our well-justified fears and suspicions occasioned by the capture of the nuclear-power trade by the inept and the mendacious (who have fucked up the works at Three Mile Island, Chernobyl, etc.)[12] tempt us to infer retrospectively extraordinary corruption, imbecility, or motiveless malignity in those who decided, all things considered, to drop the bomb. Times change. Harry Truman * * * knew war, and he knew better than some of his critics then and now what he was doing and why he was doing it. "Having found the bomb," he said, "we have used it. . . . We have used it to shorten the agony of young Americans."

The past, which as always did not know the future, acted in ways that ask to be imagined before they are condemned. Or even simplified.

10. Short for *pro tempore*: temporarily; literally, for the time being (Latin).

11. American general (1885–1945) who served in North Africa and Sicily in World War II before becoming commander of the Third Army, which drove the Nazis from France and back into Germany.

12. Two disasters at nuclear power plants: the first, near Harrisburg, Pennsylvania, occurred in the spring of 1979; the second, in the Soviet Union, occurred in the spring of 1986.

Questions

1. Note the places where Fussell includes personal experience in this essay. How much is his own, how much belongs to others? Why does he include both kinds?

2. Fussell dismisses with contempt those who disagree with him. Locate some examples. How do you respond to them? Would you use Fussell's strategies to dismiss those who disagree with you? Explain.

3. Mark some instances of Fussell's "voice." What kind of voice does he adopt? What kind of person does he present himself as?

4. Write a similarly argumentative essay in which you take a strong position. Include your own experience and the experiences of others if appropriate.

History

Laurel Thatcher Ulrich *The Slogan: "Well-Behaved Women Seldom Make History"*

Some time ago a former student e-mailed me from California: "You'll be delighted to know that you are quoted frequently on bumpers in Berkeley." Through a strange stroke of fate I've gotten used to seeing my name on bumpers. And on T-shirts, tote bags, coffee mugs, magnets, buttons, greeting cards, and websites.

I owe this curious fame to a single line from a scholarly article I published in 1976. In the opening paragraph, I wrote: "Well-behaved women seldom make history." That sentence, slightly altered, escaped into popular culture in 1995, when journalist Kay Mills used it as an epigraph for her informal history of American women, *From Pocahontas to Power Suits.* Perhaps by accident, she changed the word *seldom* to *rarely.* Little matter. According to my dictionary, *seldom* and *rarely* mean the same thing: "Well-behaved women *infrequently*, or *on few occasions*, make history."[1] This may be one of those occasions. My original article was a study of the well-behaved women celebrated in Puritan funeral sermons.

In 1996, a young woman named Jill Portugal found the "rarely" version of the quote in her roommate's copy of *The New Beacon Book of Quotations by Women.*[2] She wrote me from Oregon asking permission to print it on T-shirts. I was amused by her request and told her to go ahead; all I asked was that she send me a T-shirt. The success of her enterprise surprised both of us. A plain white shirt with the words "Well-behaved women rarely make history" printed in black roman type became a best-selling item. Portugal calls her company

Published as the title essay of her book Well-Behaved Women Seldom Make History *(2007), Ulrich's personal narrative reflects on her early scholarship in "Vertuous Women Found: New England Ministerial Literature, 1668–1735"* (American Quarterly, *1976) and on her continuing interest in discovering women's roles in history.*

1. *The Oxford English Dictionary* says that *seldom* was present in Old English by the ninth century C.E. *Rarely* came along five or six hundred years later as a borrowing from French or Latin [Ulrich's note].

2. *The New Beacon Book of Quotations by Women* (1996) brings together the "wisdom of women" which has, "through the years, been underappreciated," according to its editor Rosalie Maggio.

"one angry girl designs." Committed to "taking over the world, one shirt at a time," she fights sexual harassment, rape, pornography, and what she calls "fascist beauty standards."[3]

Her success inspired imitators, only a few of whom bothered to ask permission. My runaway sentence now keeps company with anarchists, hedonists, would-be witches, political activists of many descriptions, and quite a few well-behaved women. It has been featured in *Cosmo Girl*, the *Christian Science Monitor*, and *Creative Keepsake Scrapbooking Magazine*. According to news reports, it was a favorite of the pioneering computer scientist Anita Borg. The Sweet Potato Queens of Jackson, Mississippi, have adopted it as an "official maxim," selling their own pink-and-green T-shirt alongside another that reads "Never Wear Panties to a Party."

5 My accidental fame has given me a new perspective on American popular culture. While some women contemplate the demise of feminism, others seem to have only just discovered it. A clerk in the Amtrak ticket office in D.C.'s Union Station told a fellow historian that all the women in her office wore the button. "I couldn't resist telling her that I was acquainted with you, and she just lit right up, and made me promise to tell you that the women at the Amtrak office thank you for all your 'words of wisdom.'"

I do, in fact, get quite a bit of fan mail. Recently a woman I had never met wrote to tell me she had seen someone wearing the T-shirt in a New York City subway. She wanted to know where to buy a shirt for herself, since she was one of the named plaintiffs in a gender discrimination suit against a major corporation. I have had notes thanking me for the slogan from a biology instructor at a community college on the White Mountain Apache Reservation in Arizona, from the program coordinator in a Massachusetts nursing home who started a "Wild Women's Group" for the residents there, and from the director of an Ohio homeless legal assistance program. A Massachusetts educator wrote to tell me she had painted my words and other inspiring quotations on the front hood of her 1991 Honda Civic, then covered the body of the car with the names of high-achieving women throughout history.

One of the most amusing e-mails was from an undergraduate who asked if I could give her the original source of the quotation. She wanted to use it in her honors thesis, and she didn't think her adviser would approve of a footnote to a T-shirt. The most surprising, given the origins of the quote, was from a woman named Lori Pearson who told me that my words had helped her write a funeral eulogy for her best friend, Kathy Thill, who was the first woman to become an electric designer for a public utility in Minnesota. She said Thill "was spunky, courageous, and just a helluva lot of fun."[4]

Other uses of the quote have been less inspiring. While standing at the check-out counter of an independent bookstore, I discovered my name and sentence on a dusky blue magnet embellished with one leopard-print stiletto-

3. See her website at http://www.oneangrygirl.net/ [Ulrich's note].

4. Lori Pearson to Laurel Ulrich, January 23, 2004, copy of e-mail in my possession, used by permission [Ulrich's note].

heeled shoe above a smoldering cigarette in a long black holder. Even more unsettling was finding a website selling T-shirts printed with both my name and a grainy photograph of me standing at a lectern. When I e-mailed to ask why the proprietors were selling my picture without permission, they responded, "I guess we are not very well-behaved girls."

The ambiguity of the slogan surely accounts for its appeal. To the public-spirited, it is a provocation to action, a less pedantic way of saying that if you want to make a difference in the world, you can't worry too much about what people think. To a few it may say, "Good girls get no credit." To a lot more, "Bad girls have more fun." Its popularity proves its point. Nobody has proposed printing T-shirts with any of the other one-liners in my article on funeral sermons. It is hard to imagine the women of Amtrak voluntarily wearing buttons that read, "The real drama is in the humdrum." Nor do I think the "Wild Women" of that Massachusetts nursing home would be cheered up by "They never asked to be remembered on earth. And they haven't been." Kay Mills certainly knew what she was doing when she picked one snappy sentence from that article about sermons.

10 But because I am a historian, I can't quite leave it at that. For some time now I've been collecting responses to the slogan, puzzling over the contradictory answers I have received, and wondering why misbehavior is such an appealing theme. It is hard to tell whether this is about feminism, post-feminism, or something much older. One thing it doesn't appear to have a lot to do with is history, at least not the kind that comes in books. For most people, the struggle is with the here and now, and with norms of good behavior that seem outdated yet will not go away.

Connie Schultz, a columnist for the *Cleveland Plain Dealer*, keeps a bumper sticker on her desk. She says that when men pass her desk, they "sometimes smile, sometimes snicker." One man read the words aloud, frowned, then pointed to a photo Schultz had on her desk of a friend with a newborn baby. "'That's how women make history,' he huffed, then walked away." In contrast, women visiting her office usually have "an *a-ha* response." Schultz thinks they are remembering the lessons in good behavior they learned in girlhood, lessons she herself experienced: "Considerate meant deferential. Respectful was obedient. Polite was silent. 'No one likes a know-it-all,' we were told. And so we acted as if we knew nothing at all." As a journalist, Schultz had to overcome that conditioning to take on gritty topics usually reserved for male reporters. In 2005, her columns "in support of the weak, the oppressed, the underdog" won her a Pulitzer Prize.[5]

Jeanne Coverdale, the owner of an Iowa shop that sells quilting supplies both locally and online, was attending a conference in Puyallup, Washington, when she heard somebody use the "seldom" version of the quote. She immediately wrote it down, then went home and produced a snazzy blue-and-purple

5. "Inciteful insight: Wisdom of a simple phrase, challenges, inspires women," *Cleveland Plain Dealer*, May 1, 2003, Section F, pp. 1, 5; Chris Sheper, "Plain Dealer's Connie Schultz wins Pulitzer," ibid., April 5, 2005, Section A, p. 1 [Ulrich's note].

tie-dyed T-shirt. The shirt was so popular she eventually created a whole line of products featuring the slogan, including a "leash" for keeping runaway scissors at home. When she wrote to thank me for the quotation, I was surprised: Hand-quilters hardly seem like candidates for rebellion. When I asked her about it, she responded that though most of her customers are indeed "salt-of-the-earth types, they like to see themselves as a little outrageous and naughty and out-of-control with their hobby."[6]

For the Sweet Potato Queens, being "outrageous and naughty and out-of-control" *is* a hobby. They adopt red wigs, false eyelashes, and sequined green dresses for the annual St. Patrick's Day parade in Jackson, Mississippi. Singer Kacey Jones recently performed their theme song on Garrison Keillor's radio show *Prairie Home Companion*. The first verse and the refrain go this way:

> *Now, I've been gettin' in trouble ever since I was a child*
> *Mama told me, "Girls like you turn into women that run wild"*
> *But if I didn't do what I'd done, I wouldn't of had me so much fun*
> *And Mama, life's too short to live it any other way*
>
> *Well-behaved women don't drink shots and beers*
> *That's why well-behaved women bore us all to tears*
> *They're politically correct but we invite them to defect*
> *'Cuz well-behaved women rarely make history.*[7]

The song continues with a rollicking roster of "historical chicks," mostly sirens of the stage and screen like Mae West, Sophia Loren, and Brigitte Bardot, though Golda Meir[8] got into one verse because her name is a rough rhyme for Cher.[9]

At first glance, there is a chasm between the purposeful professionalism of Connie Schultz and the raucous "misbehavior" of the SPQs. But some people see a connection. In May 2001, a reporter for a daily newspaper in South Carolina wrote to ask me if I was the author of the slogan. When I asked him why he wanted to know, he explained that a state Supreme Court justice, a woman "who has a historic career in public service here, hit a parked car, drove away, and later admitted she was drinking." When the reporter asked for a com-

6. Jeanne Coverdale to Laurel Ulrich, October 2, 2003, copy of e-mail in my possession, used by permission [Ulrich's note].

7. Kacey Jones and Jill Conner Browne, "Well-Behaved Women Rarely Make History," on *The Sweet Potato Queens Big Ass Box of Music* (Igo Records, 2003) [Ulrich's note].

8. Mae West (1893–1980), American actress; Sophia Loren (b. 1934), Italian actress; Brigitte Bardot (b. 1934), French actress; all three were sex symbols. Golda Meir (1898–1978) served as prime minister of Israel from 1969 to 1974. Cherilyn Sarkisian (b. 1946), known as "Cher," is a popular singer-songwriter and actress.

9. Kacey Jones to Laurel Ulrich, January 19, 2004, copy of e-mail in my possession, used by permission [Ulrich's note].

ment from one of the judge's supporters, a local leader famous for his wit, the man responded, "Well-behaved women seldom make history. Any further explanation is superfluous." To him it seemed obvious that any woman spunky enough to rise to the top of her profession was also likely to break other social norms.

15 Not long afterward, a friend sent me a clipping from the *Denver Post* that described the opposite case, a woman with a wild reputation who ended up in a responsible position. The newspaper reporter played the contrast for all it was worth, beginning with a description of Kathy "Cargo" Rodeman in a bar.[10] The man sitting on the stool next to her did not know that she had once beaten her drunken father with a chair and a fireplace poker. So when he jabbed her one time too many, "she turned, hooked one long wiry arm around the guy's waist, and took him down." Weeks later, the town of Oak Creek, Colorado, elected her mayor. Some people wondered how a woman who had been arrested more than a dozen times and who was so poor her phone was about to be turned off could end up in such an office. "She's wild and crazy," said the local police chief, her major political rival. Rodeman doesn't deny it. "My momma started buyin' me cigarettes when I was 8 so I'd stop stealin' hers," she told the reporter. She said that when she was eighteen she tried hard drugs, but quit because she liked it too much. Rodeman may be wild, but according to the *Denver Post* she takes pride in two things: "I am a hard worker and a good mother." Her car, which is her second office, carries a familiar slogan. "That bumper sticker gets me in more trouble," she says.[11]

So what do people see when they read that well-behaved women rarely make history? Do they imagine good-time girls in stiletto heels or do-good girls carrying clipboards and passing petitions? Do they envision an out-of-control hobbyist or a single mother taking down a drunk in a bar? I suspect that it depends on where they stand themselves.

A manager in a Los Angeles development firm wrote to tell me that she and other members of the staff were outraged when the editor of their company magazine printed my sentence on T-shirts and coffee mugs distributed at a trade show. They thought the slogan was "disrespectful to women," that it was "sexist," "immoral and unethical," and a "horrible representation for our company." After a little research my correspondent discovered more positive implications of the slogan, but she still worried about its impact on the general public. "The ugly truth is, a regular joe would not know what your phrase means. People who are surrounded and involved in woman's issues and working to break the barriers women experience in the business world and in life in general, would be far more likely to look at your phrase in a different light," she

10. Rodeman, mayor of Oak Creek, California, from 2002 to 2006, was also arrested for drunk driving, as was the unnamed state supreme court justice mentioned in the previous paragraph.

11. "Mayor Cargo's baggage riles foes," *Denver Post*, September 22, 2002, Section A, pp. 1, 18 [Ulrich's note].

wrote. In this case, history came to the rescue. Her company decided to keep the slogan but print it with a picture of a historical figure "such as Queen Elizabeth or Joan of Arc."[12]

For some, history is a repository of edifying examples, for others a source of—if vague—vicarious rebellion. A custom-designed T-shirt for a women's camp-out in New England featured a cartoon of a long-lashed Lady Godiva perched on a bemused horse.[13] When I asked the designer whether her drawing alluded to some forbidden activity, skinny-dipping perhaps, or an addiction to Belgian chocolate, she laughed and said she had no idea. It was just the first image that popped into her mind when she thought about the slogan.

A "Misbehaving Women Quilt" displayed at a national fiber arts festival in Nashua, New Hampshire, in the fall of 2002, featured nineteen meticulously embroidered and appliquéd mythical and historical figures ranging from Mother Eve to Gloria Steinem.[14] Suzanne Bruno, who organized the project, admits that "the 'misbehaving' guidelines were pretty loose." One quilter featured her suffragist grandmother carrying a 1918 Armistice Day banner reading, WE MADE THEM SURRENDER. Another portrayed Katharine Lee Bates, the author of "America the Beautiful." The printed guide did not explain what qualified Bates as a misbehaving woman, but it must have been her lifelong partnership with fellow Wellesley College professor Katharine Coman. Bruno's own square featured Lizzie Borden with an ax and her favorite flower, a pansy.[15]

20 The historical content in *Cool Women: The Thinking Girl's Guide to the Hippest Women in History* is even more eclectic. The product of Girl Press, self-described publishers of "slightly dangerous books for girl mavericks," it splashes a green strip and the words "Well-behaved women rarely make history" across an orange cover filled with the names of famous—and infamous—women. There are lady pirates, suffragists, sports champions, Apache warriors, and samurai, as well as the "Fearless Flying WASPs" (female pilots) of World War II. The book is commendably multicultural, giving as much space to Queen Njinga

12. Either Queen Elizabeth I (1533–1603) or Queen Elizabeth II (b. 1926), both reigning monarchs of England; Joan of Arc (1412–1431), who led the French army to victory against the English during the Hundred Years' War, was captured and tried by an English ecclesiastical court for heresy, and burned at the stake. See paragraph 26 for Ulrich's discussion of Joan of Arc's historical significance.

13. Lady Godiva rode naked on a horse through the streets of Coventry to urge her husband to reduce taxes on the poor; see paragraph 27 for Ulrich's discussion.

14. American feminist (b. 1934) who became a leading spokesperson for the Women's Liberation Movement in the 1960s and 70s.

15. Suzanne Bruno, *The Misbehaving Women Quilt Companion Booklet* (Raymond, Me., 2002). On Bates, see Judith Schwarz, "'Yellow Clover': Katharine Lee Bates and Katharine Coman," *Frontiers: A Journal of Women Studies* 4 (1979): 59–67; and a brief biography on the Wellesley College website, http://www.wellesley.edu/Anniversary/bates.html [Ulrich's note].

of Angola[16] as to Joan of Arc—though, unlike the edifying biographies parents and teachers might prefer, it does not discriminate between bandit queens and tennis greats, and it pays as much attention to fictional characters like Scarlett O'Hara as to historical figures like Harriet Tubman.[17] An acknowledgment on the inside says the authors donate part of their royalties to Girls Inc. of Greater Santa Barbara, a "nonprofit organization dedicated to empowering girls to be strong, smart, and bold." The pervasive theme is rebellion. When deviance isn't apparent, the prose creates it. Georgia O'Keeffe was a "renegade artist." Martha Graham was the "ultimate wild girl of dance." Marie Curie[18] "walked into the boys' club of the science world and basically tore the place apart."[19]

Cool Women suggests that "empowered" women are by definition "wild" women. That is a very old idea. Since antiquity, misogynists have insisted that females, being more emotional than males, are less stable, more likely to swing between extremes. Think of the old nursery rhyme that says, *when she was good, she was very, very good, but when she was bad she* . . . made history?

So how does a woman make history? Obviously, Marie Curie didn't win two Nobel Prizes by throwing tantrums in the lab. True, after her husband's death French tabloids pilloried her for having an affair with a married collaborator.[20] But she isn't remembered today because she was "bad" but because she was "very, very good" at what she did. So why doesn't high achievement in science qualify a woman as "well-behaved"? Could it be because some people still assume women aren't supposed to stand out in a crowd?

The "well-behaved women" quote works because it plays into longstanding stereotypes about the invisibility and the innate decorum of the female sex. Many people think women are less visible in history than men because their bodies impel them to nurture. Their job is to bind the wounds, stir the soup, and

16. Queen Njína (or Nzinga) of Angola (1583–1663) resisted the Portuguese conquest of her country; see paragraph 27 for Ulrich's discussion of her significance.

17. Scarlett O'Hara is the fictional heroine of the novel *Gone with the Wind*, set during the American Civil War; Harriet Tubman (c. 1820–1913) was an African American abolitionist and Union spy during the Civil War.

18. Georgia O'Keeffe (1887–1986), American artist; Martha Graham (1894–1991), American dancer and choreographer; Marie Curie (1867–1934), Polish-born French chemist and physicist who pioneered in the field of radioactivity, was awarded two Nobel prizes for her research.

19. *Cool Women* was written by Dawn Chipman, Mari Florence, and Naomi Wax, and edited by Pam Nelson (Chicago: Girl Press, 1998) [Ulrich's note].

20. Nor have Curie's scientific contributions gone unquestioned. When she was nominated to the French Academy in 1911, opponents argued that she was a mere assistant, though a good one, to her husband. *Le Journal des Débats*, in its issue of January 20, 1911, found it a "very delicate problem to determine with certainty . . . what part was really played by Mme Curie." See J. L. Davis, "The Research School of Marie Curie in the Paris Faculty, 1907–14," *Annals of Science* 52 (1995): 348. For a fascinating account of the tabloid accusations and their significance, see Susan Quinn, *Marie Curie: A Life* (New York: Simon & Schuster, 1994), Chapter 14. As Quinn points out, Curie's fame made her an easy target [Ulrich's note].

bear the children of those whose mission it is to fight wars, rule nations, and define the cosmos. Not all those who make this argument consider women unimportant—on the contrary, they often revere the contributions of women as wives, mothers, and caregivers—or at least they say so. But they also assume that domestic roles haven't changed much over the centuries, and that women who perform them have no history. A New Hampshire pastor captured this notion when he wrote in his commonplace book in 1650, "Woman's the center & lines are men." If women occupy the fixed center of life, and if history is seen as a linear progression of public events, a changing panorama of wars and kingdoms, then only those who through outrageous behavior, divine intervention, or sheer genius step into the stream of public consequence have a history.

The problem with this argument is not only that it limits women. It also limits history. Good historians are concerned not only with famous people and public events but with broad transformations in human behavior, things like falling death rates or transatlantic migration. Here seemingly small actions by large numbers of people can bring about profound change. But this approach runs up against another imperative of history—its reliance on written sources. Until recent times most women (and a great many men) were illiterate. As a consequence their activities were recorded, if at all, in other people's writing. People who caused trouble might show up in court records, newspapers, or their masters' diaries. Those who quietly went about their lives were either forgotten, seen at a distance, or idealized into anonymity. Even today, publicity favors those who make—or break—laws.

But the difficulty is bigger than that. History is an account of the past based on surviving sources, but it is also a way of making sense out of the present. In the heat and confusion of events, people on all sides of an issue mine old stories for inspiration, enlightenment, or confirmation. Their efforts add to the layers of understanding attached to the original events, shaping what later generations know and care about. Scholars sometimes call these popular reconstructions of the past "memory" to distinguish them from formal history. But serious history is also forged in the tumult of change. History is not just what happened in the past. It is what later generations choose to remember. 25

The figure of Joan of Arc can rescue a controversial coffee mug today because office workers in Los Angeles in 2004 are no longer obsessed with the issues that fractured France and England when Joan put on her armor in 1429. Was she a saint, a witch, a virgin, a whore, a transvestite, or a simple peasant? Over time, she has been all these things. She was burned as a heretic in 1431, then posthumously reprieved in 1456. She was alternately venerated and vilified for the next four centuries. In *Henry VI*, Shakespeare portrayed her as a witch, a "dolphin or dogfish," a "Devil, or Devil's dam." In the introduction to his play *Saint Joan*, George Bernard Shaw called her "the most notable Warrior Saint in the Christian calendar, and the queerest fish among the eccentric worthies of the Middle Ages." Although the case for her beatification was first put forward in 1869, she wasn't canonized until 1920. Even then her meaning would not stay fixed. On one side of the English Channel, she inspired women suffragists; on the other, she became an icon of Catholic conservatism.[21] Clearly notions of good behavior vary from place to place, and they change over time.

The Angolan heroine Njinga Mbandi, known in some accounts as Queen Zhinga or Jinga, has gone through a similar transformation. In seventeenth-century sources, she spanned the spectrum from devout Christian to savage warrior. Portuguese missionaries were happy to claim her as an early convert, but changed their minds when she recanted and established a rebel kingdom. A book published in England in 1670 described her as dressed in animal skins with a feather stuck "through the holes of her bored Nose," hacking off a victim's head, then drinking "a great draught of his blood."[22] But all that had changed by the 1830s, when the American abolitionist Lydia Maria Child used her achievements to refute proslavery arguments about the incapacity of Africans for self-rule. "History furnishes very few instances of bravery, intelligence and perseverance equal to the famous Zhinga, the Negro queen of Angola," Child wrote. In the twentieth century, after Angolans once again won their independence from Portugal, Njinga became a national heroine. Today, some accounts refer to her as "an African Joan of Arc."[23] So she was, in more ways than one.

Sometimes fiction overwhelms history and people get remembered for things they didn't do. Consider that edifying, outrageous, and amusing character Lady Godiva. Historians still wonder how a pious eleventh-century Anglo-Saxon woman named Godgifu became known as an equestrian streaker. In her own lifetime, she was a well-behaved woman who endowed Christian monasteries and cathedrals. The story of her ride first appeared nearly two centuries after her death in the chronicle of an English monk, who portrayed her as a dutiful wife who undertook to ride unclothed only because her husband, as a cruel joke, said he would reduce taxes on his subjects on the day she rode naked through the streets of Coventry. Since Godgifu herself owned the lands around Coventry, she would have had no need for such a stratagem. But the monk's story prevailed. The story of an imagined woman devoted both to her people

21. Marina Warner, *Joan of Arc: The Image of Female Heroism* (New York: Alfred A. Knopf, 1981), is the essential study. Also see Deborah Fraioli, "The Literary Image of Joan of Arc: Prior Influences," *Speculum* 56 (1981): 811–83; Eric Jennings, "'Reinventing Jeanne': The Iconology of Joan of Arc in Vichy Schoolbooks, 1940–44," *Journal of Contemporary History* 29 (1994): 711–34; Lisa Tickner, *The Spectacle of Women: Imagery of the Suffrage Campaign 1907–1914* (London: Chatto & Windus, 1987), pp. 208–11, 234 [Ulrich's note].

22. John Ogilby, *Africa . . . collected and translated from the most authentick authors* (London: T. Johnson, 1970), quoted in Antonia Fraser, *The Warrior Queens* (New York: Alfred A. Knopf, 1989), pp. 241–42 [Ulrich's note].

23. Fraser, *Warrior Queens*, pp. 242–43; Heinrich Loth, *Woman in Ancient Africa*, trans. Sheila Marnie (Westport, Conn.: Lawrence Hill, 1987), p. 58; Joseph C. Miller, "Nzinga of Matamba in a New Perspective," *Journal of African History* (1975): 201–16. Africanists Linda Heywood and Catherine Skidmore-Hess are now engaged in full-length studies of Njinga. I thank them both for telling me about their projects [Ulrich's note].

and obedient to her husband so entranced Queen Victoria that she gave Prince Albert a silver statue of the nude rider for his forty-eighth birthday. A re-enactment of Godiva's ride is the centerpiece of a popular festival in Coventry, England, to this day. Elsewhere the legend is losing its power, perhaps because nudity has become so commonplace. Perhaps in another generation Godgifu will be reincarnated as a wealthy philanthropist.[24]

Historians don't own history. But we do have a lot of experience sifting through competing evidence. Historical research is a bit like detective work. We re-create past events from fragments of information, trying hard to distinguish credible accounts from wishful thinking. One of our jobs is to explore the things that get left out when a person becomes an icon. Recent scholarship on the Sweet Potato Queens' heroine, Mae West, is a good example. There is no question about West's reputation for misbehavior. She said it herself: "When I'm bad, I'm better." Beginning her stage career at the age of six, she moved from playing the saintly Little Eva in *Uncle Tom's Cabin* to shimmying her way to fame. In uptight Boston, theater owners cut off the lights "with West's first ripple." But in New York she was the darling of urban sophisticates who wanted to explore the seamy side of life without leaving their theater seats. When she moved to Hollywood in the 1930s, censors tried to clean up her scripts, but she knew how to fill even the blandest lines with sexual innuendo. *Variety* complained that "Mae couldn't sing a lullaby without making it sexy."[25]

That is how Mae West made history. But what sort of history did she make? Some recent studies focus on her debts to the male homosexuals whose outrageous impersonations defined *camp* in the 1920s. Others claim that her largest debt was to African American entertainers. West's shimmy, for example, ultimately derived from West African traditions adapted in rural dance halls, or "jooks." Her ballad "Honey let yo' drawers hang down low" (which may have inspired the Sweet Potato Queens' "Never Wear Panties to a Party") was a favorite in southern jooks. In the early twentieth century, West, the sexually active, streetwise girl from Brooklyn, gave middle-class audiences a glimpse of worlds that both fascinated and repelled. Like the legendary Godiva, she allowed people to imagine the unimaginable. Because she was also a savvy businesswoman, she was able to live off other people's fantasies.[26]

30

24. Daniel Donoghue, *Lady Godiva: A Literary History of the Legend* (Malden, Mass., and Oxford: Blackwell, 2003), pp. 1–25, 45, 81, 104–5 [Ulrich's note].

25. Jill Watts, *Mae West: An Icon in Black and White* (New York: Oxford University Press, 2001), pp. 21, 56, 156 [Ulrich's note].

26. Marybeth Hamilton, *When I'm Bad, I'm Better: Mae West, Sex, and American Entertainment* (New York: HarperCollins, 1995), pp. 2, 236–37, 248–50, 254; Watts, *Mae West*, pp. 70–92; Emily Wortis Leider, *Becoming Mae West* (New York: Farrar, Straus & Giroux, 1997), p. 351. Watts suggests that one of West's grandfathers may have been black. On this point, see Heather O'Donnell, "Signifying Sex," *American Quarterly* 54 (2002): 499–505 [Ulrich's note].

A first-year student at a California university told me that to make history, people need to do the unexpected. She offered the example of civil rights activist Rosa Parks, "who would not leave her seat."[27] I like her emphasis on the unexpected. It not only captures the sense of history as the study of how things change, it offers a somewhat more complex way of understanding the contribution of a woman like Parks.

Was Parks a well-behaved woman? The Montgomery, Alabama, bus company did not think so. As the student from California recognized, Parks made history precisely because she dared to challenge both social norms and the law. Her refusal to obey the statute that required her to give up her seat to a white passenger sparked the 361-day-long boycott that thrust Martin Luther King into the public eye and led to a historic Supreme Court decision outlawing segregation on public transportation.[28] Yet Parks became an icon for the civil rights movement not only for her courage but because the media identified her as a hard-working seamstress who simply got tired of moving to the back of the bus. Few people outside Montgomery knew her as the politically conscious secretary of the local NAACP, nor understood how many years she and her husband had been working for social justice before that fateful day on the bus. In 1954 and 1955, Parks had attended workshops on desegregation sponsored by the radical Highlander Folk School in Tennessee, a public education project that Mississippi's Senator James Eastland excoriated as a "front for a conspiracy to overthrow this country."[29]

Nor has popular history recorded the names of other Montgomery women—teenagers—whose arrests that year for refusing to give up their seats failed to ignite a movement. Years later, E. D. Nixon, president of the Montgomery NAACP, explained why he hadn't chosen any of these other women to make a historic stand against segregation. "OK, the case of Louise Smith. I found her daddy in front of his shack, barefoot, drunk. Always drunk. Couldn't use her. In that year's second case, the girl, very brilliant but she'd had an illegitimate baby. Couldn't use her. The last case before Rosa was the daughter of a preacher who headed a reform school for years. My interview of her convinced me that she wouldn't stand up to pressure. She were even afraid of me. When Rosa Parks was arrested, I thought, 'This is it!' 'Cause she's morally clean, she's reliable, nobody had nothing on her, she had the courage of her convictions."[30] Parks's publicly acknowledged good behavior helped to justify her rebellion and win

27. Shana Pearson to Laurel Ulrich, August 4, 2003, copy of e-mail in my possession, used by permission [Ulrich's note].

28. Robert Hughes Wright, *The Birth of the Montgomery Bus Boycott* (Southfield, Mich.: Charro Press, 1991), p. 27; Rita Dove, "Rosa Parks: Her simple act of protest galvanized America's civil rights revolution," http://www.time.com/time/time100/heroes/profile/parks01.html [Ulrich's note].

29. C. Alvin Hughes, "A New Agenda for the South: The Role and Influence of the Highlander Folk School, 1953–1961," *Phylon* 46 (1985): 242–50 [Ulrich's note].

30. David J. Garrow, ed., *The Walking City: The Montgomery Bus Boycott, 1955–1956* (Brooklyn, N.Y.: Carlson, 1989), p. 546 [Ulrich's note].

support for her cause. As one friend recalled, she "was too sweet to even say 'damn' in anger."[31]

After Parks's death in the fall of 2005, the airways were filled with tributes celebrating the life of the "humble seamstress," the "simple woman" who sparked a revolution because her feet were tired. Reviewing these eulogies, syndicated columnist Ellen Goodman asked, "Is it possible we prefer our heroes to be humble? Or is it just our heroines?" She wondered if it wasn't time Americans got over the notion that women are "accidental heroines," unassuming creatures thrust into the public eye by circumstances beyond their control. Goodman noted that Parks and her compatriots spent years preparing for just such an opportunity. She concluded: "Rosa Parks was 'unassuming'—except that she rejected all the assumptions about her place in the world. Rosa Parks was a 'simple woman'—except for a mind made up and fed up. She was 'quiet'—except, of course, for one thing. Her willingness to say 'no' changed the world."[32]

The California student said that in contrast to Parks a "well-behaved woman" is "a quiet, subservient, polite, indoors, cooking, cleaning type of girl who would never risk shame by voicing her own opinion." There is a delicious irony in this part of her definition. Notice that it associates a particular kind of work—cooking and cleaning—with subservience and passivity. Yet the boycott that made Parks famous was sustained by hundreds of African American domestic servants—cooks and maids—who walked to work rather than ride segregated buses. They too did the unexpected.[33]

35

Serious history talks back to slogans. But in the contest for public attention, slogans usually win. Consider my simple sentence. It sat quietly for years in the folds of a scholarly journal. Now it honks its ambiguous wisdom from coffee mugs and tailgates.

* * *

In my scholarly work, my form of misbehavior has been to care about things that other people find predictable or boring. My second book is a case in point.[34]

31. Steven M. Millner, "The Montgomery Bus Boycott: A Case Study in the Emergence and Career of a Social Movement," in Garrow, *Walking City*, p. 443 [Ulrich's note].

32. Ellen Goodman, "The mythology of Rosa Parks," *Boston Globe*, October 28, 2005, p. E10 [Ulrich's note].

33. Awele Makeba's powerful one-woman show, "Rage Is Not a 1-Day Thing," dramatizes the lives of sixteen little-known participants, male and female, black and white. For details see her website, http://www.awele.com/programs.htm. For a list of resources prepared for the fiftieth anniversary of the boycott in 2005, see http://www.teachingforchange.org/busboycott/busboycott.htm. Additional document can be found in Stewart Burns, ed., *Daybreak of Freedom: The Montgomery Bus Boycott* (Chapel Hill and London: University of North Carolina Press, 1997). Herbert Kohl, *She Would Not Be Moved: How We Tell the Story of Rosa Parks and the Montgomery Bus Boycott* (New York and London: The New Press, 2005), urges teachers to move from the theme "Rosa Was Tired" to the more historically accurate concept "Rosa Was Ready" [Ulrich's note].

34. This book, *A Midwife's Tale: The Life of Martha Ballard based on her diary, 1785–1812* (1990), won the Pulitzer Prize for history.

At a distance, the life of Martha Moore Ballard was the stuff from which funeral sermons were made. She was a "good wife" in every sense of the word, indistinguishable from all the self-sacrificing and pious women celebrated in Puritan eulogies. In conventional terms, she did not make history. She cherished social order, respected authority, and abhorred violence. As a midwife and healer, she relied on home-grown medicines little different from those found in English herbals a century before her birth. Her religious sentiments were conventional; her reading was limited to the Bible, edifying pamphlets, and newspapers. Although she lived through the American Revolution, she had little interest in politics. She was a caregiver and a sustainer rather than a mover and shaker.

Ballard made history by performing a methodical and seemingly ordinary act—writing a few words in her diary every day. Through the diary we know her as a pious herbalist whose curiosity about the human body led her to observe and record autopsies as well as nurse the sick, whose integrity allowed her to testify in a sensational rape trial against a local judge who was her husband's employer, and whose sense of duty took her out of bed at night not only to deliver babies but to care for the bodies of a wife and children murdered by their own husband and father. The power of the diary is not only in its sensational stories, however, but in its patient, daily recording of seemingly inconsequential events, struggles with fatigue and discouragement, conflicts with her son, and little things—like the smell of a room where a dead body lay. In Ballard's case, the drama really was in the humdrum. The steadiness of the diary provided the frame for everything else that happened.

But it took at least two feminist movements to give significance to her life. Nineteenth-century feminism sent her great-great-granddaughter Mary Hobart to medical school in 1882. Hobart, who believed she had inherited the mantle of her "gifted ancestor," lovingly cared for the diary, and shortly before her death, gave it to the Maine State Library at Augusta. There it sat, of interest mainly to local historians and genealogists, until a second women's movement launched a renaissance in history. I found it there in the summer of 1981 when I went to the Maine State Archives to research an entirely different topic.[35]

40 To all appearances, Martha Ballard was a well-behaved woman. Had she been better-behaved, however—more protective of her own and others' reputations—she would have inked out the family conflicts and neighborhood scandals that leaked into her record despite her best efforts to remain circumspect. Or she might never have kept a diary at all. Her occupation gave her a reason to keep records, but something else drove her to transform a list of births into a daily journal and a journal into a powerful assertion of her own presence and weight in the world. Most well-behaved women are too busy living

35. Earlier I had made a systematic search of Andrea Hinding's then newly published *Women's History Sources: A Guide to Archives and Manuscript Collections in the United States* (New York: R. R. Bowker, 1979). If I hadn't already noted the existence of two eighteenth-century diaries at the Maine State Library, housed in the same building as the archives, I might not have discovered the Ballard diary. The Maine State Library is generally off the beaten track for scholars [Ulrich's note].

their lives to think about recording what they do and too modest about their own achievements to think anybody else will care. Ballard was different. She was not a mover and shaker, but neither did she choose invisibility.

Although I have received mail addressed to Martha Ballard and have been identified on at least one college campus as a midwife, I am only a little bit like my eighteenth-century subject. Like her, I was raised to be an industrious housewife and a self-sacrificing and charitable neighbor, but sometime in my thirties I discovered that writing about women's work was a lot more fun than doing it. I remember thinking one winter day how ironic it was that I was wrapped in a bathrobe with the heat of a wood stove rising toward my loft as I wrote about a courageous woman who braved snowstorms and crossed a frozen river on a cake of ice to care for mothers in labor. I felt selfish, pampered, and decadent. But I did not stop what I was doing. I did not know why I needed to write Martha's story, and I could not imagine that anybody else would ever want to follow me through my meandering glosses on her diary. I was astonished at the reception of the book. Even more important than the prizes was the discovery of how important this long-dead midwife's story was to nurses, midwives, and anonymous caregivers dealing with quite different circumstances today. These readers helped me to see that history is more than an engaging enterprise. It is a primary way of creating meaning. The meaning I found in Martha Ballard's life had something to do with my own life experience, but perhaps a lot more to do with the collective experiences of a generation of Americans coping with dramatic changes in their own lives.

When I wrote that "well-behaved women seldom make history," I was making a commitment to help recover the lives of otherwise obscure women. I had no idea that thirty years later, my own words would come back to me transformed. While I like some of the uses of the slogan more than others, I wouldn't call it back even if I could. I applaud the fact that so many people—students, teachers, quilters, nurses, newspaper columnists, old ladies in nursing homes, and mayors of western towns—think they have the right to make history.

Questions

1. Ulrich follows the after-effects of one sentence she wrote for a scholarly article: "Well-behaved women seldom make history." Make a list of ten different popular interpretations of her statement. Which ones do you think come closest to what she intended? Which ones misinterpret her original meaning?

2. Midway through her essay (paragraph 24) Ulrich begins to address the problem of misinterpreting her statement because it "limits history." What does Ulrich consider "good history"? How would "good historians" treat the lives of women from past ages?

3. Why does Ulrich end with a brief account of the life of Martha Moore Ballard, a Puritan woman about whom she wrote an entire book? What point does this final example make?

4. Could you alter Ulrich's statement to read "Well-behaved *men* seldom make history" or "Well-behaved *people* seldom make history"? Write an argument for or against such an alteration. Incorporate examples from the lives of historical figures or people you know.

Barbara Tuchman *"This Is the End of the World": The Black Death*

In October 1347, two months after the fall of Calais,[1] Genoese trading ships put into the harbor of Messina in Sicily with dead and dying men at the oars. The ships had come from the Black Sea port of Caffa (now Feodosiya) in the Crimea, where the Genoese maintained a trading post. The diseased sailors showed strange black swellings about the size of an egg or an apple in the armpits and groin. The swellings oozed blood and pus and were followed by spreading boils and black blotches on the skin from internal bleeding. The sick suffered severe pain and died quickly within five days of the first symptoms. As the disease spread, other symptoms of continuous fever and spitting of blood appeared instead of the swellings or buboes. These victims coughed and sweated heavily and died even more quickly, within three days or less, sometimes in 24 hours. In both types everything that issued from the body—breath, sweat, blood from the buboes and lungs, bloody urine, and blood-blackened excrement—smelled foul. Depression and despair accompanied the physical symptoms, and before the end "death is seen seated on the face."

The disease was bubonic plague, present in two forms: one that infected the bloodstream, causing the buboes and internal bleeding, and was spread by contact; and a second, more virulent pneumonic type that infected the lungs and was spread by respiratory infection. The presence of both at once caused the high mortality and speed of contagion. So lethal was the disease that cases were known of persons going to bed well and dying before they woke, of doctors catching the illness at a bedside and dying before the patient. So rapidly did it spread from one to another that to a French physician, Simon de Covino, it seemed as if one sick person "could infect the whole world." The malignity of the pestilence appeared more terrible because its victims knew no prevention and no remedy.

The physical suffering of the disease and its aspect of evil mystery were expressed in a strange Welsh lament which saw "death coming into our midst like black smoke, a plague which cuts off the young, a rootless phantom which has no mercy for fair countenance. Woe is me of the shilling in the armpit! It is seething, terrible . . . a head that gives pain and causes a loud cry . . . a painful angry knob . . . Great is its seething like a burning cinder . . . a grievous thing of ashy color." Its eruption is ugly like the "seeds of black peas, broken fragments of brittle sea-coal . . . the early ornaments of black death, cinders of the

From A Distant Mirror: The Calamitous Fourteenth Century *(1978), in which Tuchman presents a vivid picture of life in medieval France and draws parallels between the disasters of that time and those in our own.*

1. After a year-long siege, the French citizens of Calais surrendered to Edward III, king of England and self-declared king of France.

The Triumph of Death. A detail from a fresco by Francesco Traini in the Camposanto, Pisa, c. 1350.

peelings of the cockle weed, a mixed multitude, a black plague like halfpence, like berries. . . ."

Rumors of a terrible plague supposedly arising in China and spreading through Tartary (Central Asia) to India and Persia, Mesopotamia, Syria, Egypt, and all of Asia Minor had reached Europe in 1346. They told of a death toll so devastating that all of India was said to be depopulated, whole territories covered by dead bodies, other areas with no one left alive. As added up by Pope Clement VI at Avignon, the total of reported dead reached 23,840,000. In the absence of a concept of contagion, no serious alarm was felt in Europe until the trading ships brought their black burden of pestilence into Messina while other infected ships from the Levant carried it to Genoa and Venice.

5 By January 1348 it penetrated France via Marseille, and North Africa via Tunis. Shipborne along coasts and navigable rivers, it spread westward from Marseille through the ports of Languedoc to Spain and northward up the Rhône to Avignon, where it arrived in March. It reached Narbonne, Montpellier, Carcassonne, and Toulouse between February and May, and at the same time in Italy spread to Rome and Florence and their hinterlands. Between June and August it reached Bordeaux, Lyon, and Paris, spread to Burgundy and Normandy, and crossed the Channel from Normandy into southern England. From Italy during the same summer it crossed the Alps into Switzerland and reached eastward to Hungary.

Burial of the plague victim. From *Annales de Gilles li Muisis.*

In a given area the plague accomplished its kill within four to six months and then faded, except in the larger cities, where, rooting into the close-quartered population, it abated during the winter, only to reappear in spring and rage for another six months.

In 1349 it resumed in Paris, spread to Picardy, Flanders, and the Low Countries, and from England to Scotland and Ireland as well as to Norway, where a ghost ship with a cargo of wool and a dead crew drifted offshore until it ran aground near Bergen. From there the plague passed into Sweden, Denmark, Prussia, Iceland, and as far as Greenland. Leaving a strange pocket of immunity in Bohemia, and Russia unattacked until 1351, it had passed from most of Europe by mid-1350. Although the mortality rate was erratic, ranging from one fifth in some places to nine tenths or almost total elimination in others, the overall estimate of modern demographers has settled—for the area extending from India to Iceland—around the same figure expressed in Froissart's casual words: "a third of the world died." His estimate, the common one at the time, was not an inspired guess but a borrowing of St. John's figure for mortality from plague in Revelation, the favorite guide to human affairs of the Middle Ages.

A third of Europe would have meant about 20 million deaths. No one knows in truth how many died. Contemporary reports were an awed impression, not an accurate count. In crowded Avignon, it was said, 400 died daily; 7,000 houses emptied by death were shut up; a single graveyard received 11,000 corpses in six weeks; half the city's inhabitants reportedly died, including 9 cardinals or one third of the total, and 70 lesser prelates. Watching the endlessly passing death carts, chroniclers let normal exaggeration take wings and put the Avignon death toll at 62,000 and even at 120,000, although the city's total population was probably less than 50,000.

When graveyards filled up, bodies at Avignon were thrown into the Rhône until mass burial pits were dug for dumping the corpses. In London in such pits corpses piled up in layers until they overflowed. Everywhere reports speak of the sick dying too fast for the living to bury. Corpses were dragged out of homes and left in front of doorways. Morning light revealed new piles of bodies. In Florence the dead were gathered up by the Compagnia della Misericordia—founded in 1244 to care for the sick—whose members wore red robes and hoods masking the face except for the eyes. When their efforts failed, the dead lay putrid in the streets for days at a time. When no coffins were to be had, the bodies were laid on boards, two or three at once, to be carried to graveyards or common pits. Families dumped their own relatives into the pits, or buried them so hastily and thinly "that dogs dragged them forth and devoured their bodies."

Amid accumulating death and fear of contagion, people died without last rites and were buried without prayers, a prospect that terrified the last hours of the stricken. A bishop in England gave permission to laymen to make confession to each other as was done by the Apostles, "or if no man is present then even to a woman," and if no priest could be found to administer extreme unction, "then faith must suffice." Clement VI found it necessary to grant remissions of sin to all who died of the plague because so many were unattended by priests. "And no bells tolled," wrote a chronicler of Siena, "and nobody wept no matter what his loss because almost everyone expected death. . . . And people said and believed, 'This is the end of the world.'" 10

In Paris, where the plague lasted through 1349, the reported death rate was 800 a day, in Pisa 500, in Vienna 500 to 600. The total dead in Paris numbered 50,000 or half the population. Florence, weakened by the famine of 1347, lost three to four fifths of its citizens, Venice two thirds, Hamburg and Bremen, though smaller in size, about the same proportion. Cities, as centers of transportation, were more likely to be affected than villages, although once a village was infected, its death rate was equally high. At Givry, a prosperous village in Burgundy of 1,200 to 1,500 people, the parish register records 615 deaths in the space of fourteen weeks, compared to an average of thirty deaths a year in the previous decade. In three villages of Cambridgeshire, manorial records show a death rate of 47 percent, 57 percent, and in one case 70 percent. When the last survivors, too few to carry on, moved away, a deserted village sank back into the wilderness and disappeared from the map altogether, leaving only a grass-covered ghostly outline to show where mortals once had lived.

In enclosed places such as monasteries and prisons, the infection of one person usually meant that of all, as happened in the Franciscan convents of Carcassonne and Marseille, where every inmate without exception died. Of the 140 Dominicans at Montpellier only seven survived. Petrarch's[2] brother Gherardo, member of a Carthusian monastery, buried the prior and 34 fellow monks one by one, sometimes three a day, until he was left alone with his dog and fled

2. Francesco Petrarch (1304–1374), Italian writer whose sonnets to "my lady Laura" influenced a tradition of European love poetry for centuries.

to look for a place that would take him in. Watching every comrade die, men in such places could not but wonder whether the strange peril that filled the air had not been sent to exterminate the human race. In Kilkenny, Ireland, Brother John Clyn of the Friars Minor, another monk left alone among dead men, kept a record of what had happened lest "things which should be remembered perish with time and vanish from the memory of those who come after us." Sensing "the whole world, as it were, placed within the grasp of the Evil One," and waiting for death to visit him too, he wrote, "I leave parchment to continue this work, if perchance any man survive and any of the race of Adam escape this pestilence and carry on the work which I have begun." Brother John, as noted by another hand, died of the pestilence, but he foiled oblivion.

The largest cities of Europe, with populations of about 100,000, were Paris and Florence, Venice and Genoa. At the next level, with more than 50,000, were Ghent and Bruges in Flanders, Milan, Bologna, Rome, Naples, and Palermo, and Cologne. London hovered below 50,000, the only city in England except York with more than 10,000. At the level of 20,000 to 50,000 were Bordeaux, Toulouse, Montpellier, Marseille, and Lyon in France, Barcelona, Seville, and Toledo in Spain, Siena, Pisa, and other secondary cities in Italy, and the Hanseatic trading cities of the Empire. The plague raged through them all, killing anywhere from one third to two thirds of their inhabitants. Italy, with a total population of 10 to 11 million, probably suffered the heaviest toll. Following the Florentine bankruptcies, the crop failures and workers' riots of 1346–47, the revolt of Cola di Rienzi that plunged Rome into anarchy, the plague came as the peak of successive calamities. As if the world were indeed in the grasp of the Evil One, its first appearance on the European mainland in January 1348 coincided with a fearsome earthquake that carved a path of wreckage from Naples up to Venice. Houses collapsed, church towers toppled, villages were crushed, and the destruction reached as far as Germany and Greece. Emotional response, dulled by horrors, underwent a kind of atrophy epitomized by the chronicler who wrote, "And in these days was burying without sorrowe and wedding without friendschippe."

In Siena, where more than half the inhabitants died of the plague, work was abandoned on the great cathedral, planned to be the largest in the world, and never resumed, owing to loss of workers and master masons and "the melancholy and grief" of the survivors. The cathedral's truncated transept still stands in permanent witness to the sweep of death's scythe. Agnolo di Tura, a chronicler of Siena, recorded the fear of contagion that froze every other instinct. "Father abandoned child, wife husband, one brother another," he wrote, "for this plague seemed to strike through the breath and sight. And so they died. And no one could be found to bury the dead for money or friendship. . . . And I, Agnolo di Tura, called the Fat, buried my five children with my own hands, and so did many others likewise."

15 There were many to echo his account of inhumanity and few to balance it, for the plague was not the kind of calamity that inspired mutual help. Its loathsomeness and deadliness did not herd people together in mutual distress, but only prompted their desire to escape each other. "Magistrates and notaries

refused to come and make the wills of the dying," reported a Franciscan friar of Piazza in Sicily; what was worse, "even the priests did not come to hear their confessions." A clerk of the Archbishop of Canterbury reported the same of English priests who "turned away from the care of their benefices from fear of death." Cases of parents deserting children and children their parents were reported across Europe from Scotland to Russia. The calamity chilled the hearts of men, wrote Boccaccio[3] in his famous account of the plague in Florence that serves as introduction to the *Decameron.* "One man shunned another . . . kinsfolk held aloof, brother was forsaken by brother, oftentimes husband by wife; nay, what is more, and scarcely to be believed, fathers and mothers were found to abandon their own children to their fate, untended, unvisited as if they had been strangers." Exaggeration and literary pessimism were common in the 14th century, but the Pope's physician, Guy de Chauliac, was a sober, careful observer who reported the same phenomenon: "A father did not visit his son, nor the son his father. Charity was dead."

Yet not entirely. In Paris, according to the chronicler Jean de Venette, the nuns of the Hôtel Dieu or municipal hospital, "having no fear of death, tended the sick with all sweetness and humility." New nuns repeatedly took the places of those who died, until the majority "many times renewed by death now rest in peace with Christ as we may piously believe."

When the plague entered northern France in July 1348, it settled first in Normandy and, checked by winter, gave Picardy a deceptive interim until the next summer. Either in mourning or warning, black flags were flown from church towers of the worst-stricken villages of Normandy. "And in that time," wrote a monk of the abbey of Fourcarment, "the mortality was so great among the people of Normandy that those of Picardy mocked them." The same unneighborly reaction was reported of the Scots, separated by a winter's immunity from the English. Delighted to hear of the disease that was scourging the "southrons," they gathered forces for an invasion, "laughing at their enemies." Before they could move, the savage mortality fell upon them too, scattering some in death and the rest in panic to spread the infection as they fled.

In Picardy in the summer of 1349 the pestilence penetrated the castle of Coucy to kill Enguerrand's[4] mother, Catherine, and her new husband. Whether her nine-year-old son escaped by chance or was perhaps living elsewhere with one of his guardians is unrecorded. In nearby Amiens, tannery workers, responding quickly to losses in the labor force, combined to bargain for higher wages. In another place villagers were seen dancing to drums and trumpets, and on being asked the reason, answered that, seeing their neighbors die day by day while their village remained immune, they believed they could keep the plague from entering "by the jollity that is in us. That is why we dance." Further

3. Giovanni Boccaccio (1313–1375), Italian writer best known for his collection of stories, *The Decameron*, in which seven young ladies and three young men flee from Florence to escape the Black Death and tell stories to while away the time.

4. Enguerrand de Coucy, a French nobleman, is the historical figure around whom Tuchman constructs her account of the fourteenth century.

north in Tournai on the border of Flanders, Gilles li Muisis, Abbot of St. Martin's, kept one of the epidemic's most vivid accounts. The passing bells rang all day and all night, he recorded, because sextons were anxious to obtain their fees while they could. Filled with the sound of mourning, the city became oppressed by fear, so that the authorities forbade the tolling of bells and the wearing of black and restricted funeral services to two mourners. The silencing of funeral bells and of criers' announcements of deaths was ordained by most cities. Siena imposed a fine on the wearing of mourning clothes by all except widows.

Flight was the chief recourse of those who could afford it or arrange it. The rich fled to their country places like Boccaccio's young patricians of Florence, who settled in a pastoral palace "removed on every side from the roads" with "wells of cool water and vaults of rare wines." The urban poor died in their burrows, "and only the stench of their bodies informed neighbors of their death." That the poor were more heavily afflicted than the rich was clearly remarked at the time, in the north as in the south. A Scottish chronicler, John of Fordun, stated flatly that the pest "attacked especially the meaner sort and common people—seldom the magnates." Simon de Covino of Montpellier made the same observation. He ascribed it to the misery and want and hard lives that made the poor more susceptible, which was half the truth. Close contact and lack of sanitation was the unrecognized other half. It was noticed too that the young died in greater proportion than the old; Simon de Covino compared the disappearance of youth to the withering of flowers in the fields.

In the countryside peasants dropped dead on the roads, in the fields, in their houses. Survivors in growing helplessness fell into apathy, leaving ripe wheat uncut and livestock untended. Oxen and asses, sheep and goats, pigs and chickens ran wild and they too, according to local reports, succumbed to the pest. English sheep, bearers of the precious wool, died throughout the country. The chronicler Henry Knighton, canon of Leicester Abbey, reported 5,000 dead in one field alone, "their bodies so corrupted by the plague that neither beast nor bird would touch them," and spreading an appalling stench. In the Austrian Alps wolves came down to prey upon sheep and then, "as if alarmed by some invisible warning, turned and fled back into the wilderness." In remote Dalmatia bolder wolves descended upon a plague-stricken city and attacked human survivors. For want of herdsmen, cattle strayed from place to place and died in hedgerows and ditches. Dogs and cats fell like the rest.

The dearth of labor held a fearful prospect because the 14th century lived close to the annual harvest both for food and for next year's seed. "So few servants and laborers were left," wrote Knighton, "that no one knew where to turn for help." The sense of a vanishing future created a kind of dementia of despair. A Bavarian chronicler of Neuberg on the Danube recorded that "Men and women . . . wandered around as if mad" and let their cattle stray "because no one had any inclination to concern themselves about the future." Fields went uncultivated, spring seed unsown. Second growth with nature's awful energy crept back over cleared land, dikes crumbled, salt water reinvaded and soured the lowlands. With so few hands remaining to restore the work of centuries, people felt, in Walsingham's words, that "the world could never again regain its former prosperity."

Though the death rate was higher among the anonymous poor, the known and the great died too. King Alfonso XI of Castile was the only reigning monarch killed by the pest, but his neighbor King Pedro of Aragon lost his wife, Queen Leonora, his daughter Marie, and a niece in the space of six months. John Cantacuzene, Emperor of Byzantium, lost his son. In France the lame Queen Jeanne and her daughter-in-law Bonne de Luxemburg, wife of the Dauphin, both died in 1349 in the same phase that took the life of Enguerrand's mother. Jeanne, Queen of Navarre, daughter of Louis X, was another victim. Edward III's second daughter, Joanna, who was on her way to marry Pedro, the heir of Castile, died in Bordeaux. Women appear to have been more vulnerable than men, perhaps because, being more housebound, they were more exposed to fleas. Boccaccio's mistress Fiammetta, illegitimate daughter of the King of Naples, died, as did Laura, the beloved—whether real or fictional—of Petrarch. Reaching out to us in the future, Petrarch cried, "Oh happy posterity who will not experience such abysmal woe and will look upon our testimony as a fable."

In Florence Giovanni Villani, the great historian of his time, died at 68 in the midst of an unfinished sentence: "*. . . e dure questo pistolenza fino a . . .* (in the midst of this pestilence there came to an end . . .)." Siena's master painters, the brothers Ambrogio and Pietro Lorenzetti, whose names never appear after 1348, presumably perished in the plague, as did Andrea Pisano, architect and sculptor of Florence. William of Ockham and the English mystic Richard Rolle of Hampole both disappear from mention after 1349. Francisco Datini, merchant of Prato, lost both his parents and two siblings. Curious sweeps of mortality afflicted certain bodies of merchants in London. All eight wardens of the Company of Cutters, all six wardens of the Hatters, and four wardens of the Goldsmiths died before July 1350. Sir John Pulteney, master draper and four times Mayor of London, was a victim, likewise Sir John Montgomery, Governor of Calais.

Among the clergy and doctors the mortality was naturally high because of the nature of their professions. Out of 24 physicians in Venice, 20 were said to have lost their lives in the plague, although, according to another account, some were believed to have fled or to have shut themselves up in their houses. At Montpellier, site of the leading medieval medical school, the physician Simon de Covino reported that, despite the great number of doctors, "hardly one of them escaped." In Avignon, Guy de Chauliac confessed that he performed his medical visits only because he dared not stay away for fear of infamy, but "I was in continual fear." He claimed to have contracted the disease but to have cured himself by his own treatment; if so, he was one of the few who recovered.

Clerical mortality varied with rank. Although the one-third toll of cardinals reflects the same proportion as the whole, this was probably due to their concentration in Avignon. In England, in strange and almost sinister procession, the Archbishop of Canterbury, John Stratford, died in August 1348, his appointed successor died in May 1349, and the next appointee three months later, all three within a year. Despite such weird vagaries, prelates in general managed to sustain a higher survival rate than the lesser clergy. Among bishops the deaths have been estimated at about one in twenty. The loss of priests, even if many avoided their fearful duty of attending the dying, was about the same as among the population as a whole.

Government officials, whose loss contributed to the general chaos, found, on the whole, no special shelter. In Siena four of the nine members of the governing oligarchy died, in France one third of the royal notaries, in Bristol 15 out of the 52 members of the Town Council or almost one third. Tax-collecting obviously suffered, with the result that Philip VI was unable to collect more than a fraction of the subsidy granted him by the Estates in the winter of 1347–48.

Lawlessness and debauchery accompanied the plague as they had during the great plague of Athens of 430 B.C., when according to Thucydides, men grew bold in the indulgence of pleasure: "For seeing how the rich died in a moment and those who had nothing immediately inherited their property, they reflected that life and riches were alike transitory and they resolved to enjoy themselves while they could." Human behavior is timeless. When St. John had his vision of plague in Revelation, he knew from some experience or race memory that those who survived "repented not of the work of their hands. . . . Neither repented they of their murders, nor of their sorceries, nor of their fornication, nor of their thefts."

Ignorance of the cause augmented the sense of horror. Of the real carriers, rats and fleas, the 14th century had no suspicion, perhaps because they were so familiar. Fleas, though a common household nuisance, are not once mentioned in contemporary plague writings, and rats only incidentally, although folklore commonly associated them with pestilence. The legend of the Pied Piper arose from an outbreak of 1284. The actual plague bacillus, *Pasturella pestis,* remained undiscovered for another 500 years. Living alternately in the stomach of the flea and the bloodstream of the rat who was the flea's host, the bacillus in its bubonic form was transferred to humans and animals by the bite of either rat or flea. It traveled by virtue of *Rattus rattus,* the small medieval black rat that lived on ships, as well as by the heavier brown or sewer rat. What precipitated the turn of the bacillus from innocuous to virulent form is unknown, but the occurrence is now believed to have taken place not in China but somewhere in central Asia and to have spread along the caravan routes. Chinese origin was a mistaken notion of the 14th century based on real but belated reports of huge death tolls in China from drought, famine, and pestilence which have since been traced to the 1330s, too soon to be responsible for the plague that appeared in India in 1346.

The phantom enemy had no name. Called the Black Death only in later recurrences, it was known during the first epidemic simply as the Pestilence or Great Mortality. Reports from the East, swollen by fearful imaginings, told of strange tempests and "sheets of fire" mingled with huge hailstones that "slew almost all," or a "vast rain of fire" that burned up men, beasts, stones, trees, villages, and cities. In another version, "foul blasts of wind" from the fires carried the infection to Europe "and now as some suspect it cometh round the seacoast." Accurate observation in this case could not make the mental jump to ships and rats because no idea of animal- or insect-borne contagion existed.

The earthquake was blamed for releasing sulfurous and foul fumes from the earth's interior, or as evidence of a titanic struggle of planets and oceans causing waters to rise and vaporize until fish died in masses and corrupted the air. All these explanations had in common a factor of poisoned air, of miasmas and thick, stinking mists traced to every kind of natural or imagined agency from stagnant lakes to malign conjunction of the planets, from the hand of the Evil One to the wrath of God. Medical thinking, trapped in the theory of astral influences, stressed air as the communicator of disease, ignoring sanitation or visible carriers. The existence of two carriers confused the trail, the more so because the flea could live and travel independently of the rat for as long as a month and, if infected by the particularly virulent septicemic form of the bacillus, could infect humans without reinfecting itself from the rat. The simultaneous presence of the pneumonic form of the disease, which was indeed communicated through the air, blurred the problem further.

The mystery of the contagion was "the most terrible of all the terrors," as an anonymous Flemish cleric in Avignon wrote to a correspondent in Bruges. Plagues had been known before, from the plague of Athens (believed to have been typhus) to the prolonged epidemic of the 6th century A.D., to the recurrence of sporadic outbreaks in the 12th and 13th centuries, but they had left no accumulated store of understanding. That the infection came from contact with the sick or with their houses, clothes, or corpses was quickly observed but not comprehended. Gentile da Foligno, renowned physician of Perugia and doctor of medicine at the universities of Bologna and Padua, came close to respiratory infection when he surmised that poisonous material was "communicated by means of air breathed out and in." Having no idea of microscopic carriers, he had to assume that the air was corrupted by planetary influences. Planets, however, could not explain the ongoing contagion. The agonized search for an answer gave rise to such theories as transference by sight. People fell ill, wrote Guy de Chauliac, not only by remaining with the sick but "even by looking at them." Three hundred years later Joshua Barnes, the 17th century biographer of Edward III, could write that the power of infection had entered into beams of light and "darted death from the eyes."

Doctors struggling with the evidence could not break away from the terms of astrology, to which they believed all human physiology was subject. Medicine was the one aspect of medieval life, perhaps because of its links with the Arabs, not shaped by Christian doctrine. Clerics detested astrology, but could not dislodge its influence. Guy de Chauliac, physician to three popes in succession, practiced in obedience to the zodiac. While his *Cirurgia* was the major treatise on surgery of its time, while he understood the use of anesthesia made from the juice of opium, mandrake, or hemlock, he nevertheless prescribed bleeding and purgatives by the planets and divided chronic from acute diseases on the basis of one being under the rule of the sun and the other of the moon.

In October 1348 Philip VI asked the medical faculty of the University of Paris for a report on the affliction that seemed to threaten human survival.

With careful thesis, antithesis, and proofs, the doctors ascribed it to a triple conjunction of Saturn, Jupiter, and Mars in the 40th degree of Aquarius said to have occurred on March 20, 1345. They acknowledged, however, effects "whose cause is hidden from even the most highly trained intellects." The verdict of the masters of Paris became the official version. Borrowed, copied by scribes, carried abroad, translated from Latin into various vernaculars, it was everywhere accepted, even by the Arab physicians of Cordova and Granada, as the scientific if not the popular answer. Because of the terrible interest of the subject, the translations of the plague tracts stimulated use of national languages. In that one respect, life came from death.

To the people at large there could be but one explanation—the wrath of God. Planets might satisfy the learned doctors, but God was closer to the average man. A scourge so sweeping and unsparing without any visible cause could only be seen as Divine punishment upon mankind for its sins. It might even be God's terminal disappointment in his creature. Matteo Villani compared the plague to the Flood in ultimate purpose and believed he was recording "the extermination of mankind." Efforts to appease Divine wrath took many forms, as when the city of Rouen ordered that everything that could anger God, such as gambling, cursing, and drinking, must be stopped. More general were the penitent processions authorized at first by the Pope, some lasting as long as three days, some attended by as many as 2,000, which everywhere accompanied the plague and helped to spread it.

35 Barefoot in sackcloth, sprinkled with ashes, weeping, praying, tearing their hair, carrying candles and relics, sometimes with ropes around their necks or beating themselves with whips, the penitents wound through the streets, imploring the mercy of the Virgin and saints at their shrines. In a vivid illustration for the *Très Riches Heures* of the Duc de Berry, the Pope is shown in a penitent procession attended by four cardinals in scarlet from hat to hem. He raises both arms in supplication to the angel on top of the Castel Sant' Angelo, while white-robed priests bearing banners and relics in golden cases turn to look as one of their number, stricken by the plague, falls to the ground, his face contorted with anxiety. In the rear, a gray-clad monk falls beside another victim already on the ground as the townspeople gaze in horror. (Nominally the illustration represents a 6th century plague in the time of Pope Gregory the Great, but as medieval artists made no distinction between past and present, the scene is shown as the artist would have seen it in the 14th century.) When it became evident that these processions were sources of infection, Clement VI had to prohibit them.

In Messina, where the plague first appeared, the people begged the Archbishop of neighboring Catania to lend them the relics of St. Agatha. When the Catanians refused to let the relics go, the Archbishop dipped them in holy water and took the water himself to Messina, where he carried it in a procession with prayers and litanies through the streets. The demonic, which shared the medieval cosmos with God, appeared as "demons in the shape of dogs" to terrify the people. "A black dog with a drawn sword in his paws appeared among them,

Penitential procession led by the Pope during the plague (pictured in 14th century Rome although it purports to illustrate the 6th century plague under Gregory the Great). By Pol de Limbourg for the *Très Riches Heures* of the Duc de Berry, c. 1410.

gnashing his teeth and rushing upon them and breaking all the silver vessels and lamps and candlesticks on the altars and casting them hither and thither. . . . So the people of Messina, terrified by this prodigious vision, were all strangely overcome by fear."

The apparent absence of earthly cause gave the plague a supernatural and sinister quality. Scandinavians believed that a Pest Maiden emerged from the mouth of the dead in the form of a blue flame and flew through the air to infect the next house. In Lithuania the Maiden was said to wave a red scarf through the door or window to let in the pest. One brave man, according to legend, deliberately waited at his open window with drawn sword and, at the fluttering of the scarf, chopped off the hand. He died of his deed, but his village was spared and the scarf long preserved as a relic in the local church.

Beyond demons and superstition the final hand was God's. The Pope acknowledged it in a Bull of September 1348, speaking of the "pestilence with which God is afflicting the Christian people." To the Emperor John Cantacuzene it was manifest that a malady of such horrors, stenches, and agonies, and especially one bringing the dismal despair that settled upon its victims before they died, was not a plague "natural" to mankind but "a chastisement from Heaven." To Piers Plowman[5] "these pestilences were for pure sin."

The general acceptance of this view created an expanded sense of guilt, for if the plague were punishment there had to be terrible sin to have occasioned it. What sins were on the 14th century conscience? Primarily greed, the sin of avarice, followed by usury, worldliness, adultery, blasphemy, falsehood, luxury, irreligion. Giovanni Villani, attempting to account for the cascade of calamity that had fallen upon Florence, concluded that it was retribution for the sins of avarice and usury that oppressed the poor. Pity and anger about the condition of the poor, especially victimization of the peasantry in war, was often expressed by writers of the time and was certainly on the conscience of the century. Beneath it all was the daily condition of medieval life, in which hardly an act or thought, sexual, mercantile, or military, did not contravene the dictates of the Church. Mere failure to fast or attend mass was sin. The result was an underground lake of guilt in the soul that the plague now tapped.

40 That the mortality was accepted as God's punishment may explain in part the vacuum of comment that followed the Black Death. An investigator has noticed that in the archives of Périgord references to the war are innumerable, to the plague few. Froissart mentions the great death but once, Chaucer gives it barely a glance. Divine anger so great that it contemplated the extermination of man did not bear close examination.

5. The main character (and title) of a fourteenth-century poem by the English poet William Langland (c. 1330–c. 1386).

QUESTIONS

1. Why does Tuchman begin with the account of the Genoese trading ships?

2. What ways does Tuchman find to group related facts together—in other words, what categories does she develop? Suggest other categories that Tuchman might have used in arranging her facts. What would she have gained or lost by using such categories?

3. Can you determine a basis for Tuchman's decision sometimes to quote a source, sometimes to recount it in her own words?

4. Write a brief account of a modern disaster, based on research from several sources.

Philip Alcabes

The Bioterrorism Scare: A Historical Perspective

Since the fall of 2001, when America embarked on a "war on terrorism" and federal officials started warning us about the next plague, here are some events that have not happened: a U.S. epidemic of sudden acute respiratory syndrome (SARS),[1] a widespread anthrax outbreak, any smallpox attack, the discovery of hard evidence of a biological weapons program in Iraq. Yet the talk about "biopreparedness" continues. Some people in Washington want the Centers for Disease Control and Prevention to be transferred from the Department of Health and Human Services to Homeland Security. There is even a professional journal, *Biosecurity and Bioterrorism*, devoted to learned discussions of the topic. Is it sound public policy to rush to protect the country against the threat of attack with germs that could cause an epidemic? Does the bio in biosecurity mean that we should turn our public health into a matter of civil defense? Or have we Americans been sold a bill of goods?

Throughout history, the responses to both actual communicable disease and the threat of it have been guided by the metaphor of the stranger as the spreader of contagion. Allegations that epidemic disease was caused by foreigners are ancient. Thucydides[2] reported that his contemporaries, in the fifth century B.C., attributed the Plague of Athens[3] to Ethiopians. Later on, such thinking was refined to impute causation specifically to enemy foreigners. Many European and American authors still believe that the Black Death[4] entered western Europe after the Mongols, besieging the city of Kefe (or Kaffa, now Feodosiya in Ukraine) in 1346, catapulted into the European-held city the corpses of comrades who had died of plague. When the siege was lifted, the theory goes, the disease reached Genoa aboard ships. Although Kefe clearly experienced plague in 1346, the story of its source is almost certainly apocryphal: Xenopsylla cheopis, the flea that usually carries the plague bacillus, has affinity only for warm bodies and will desert a corpse within hours of death. But the myth's persistence attests to the readiness of some, even centuries later, to believe that epidemics were caused by enemies.

Published in the American Scholar, *the magazine of the Phi Beta Kappa Society (Spring 2004).*

1. Severe Acute Respiratory Syndrome, a pneumonia-like condition that broke out in Singapore and China in 2002.
2. Greek historian (c. 460–400 B.C.E.).
3. An epidemic that struck Athens in 430 B.C.E. during the second year of the Peloponnesian War against Sparta.
4. An epidemic of bubonic plague that struck Europe in the fourteenth century, killing approximately one-third of the population.

Similarly, Londoners believed that the Great Plague of 1665[5] was brought by the Dutch, with whom England was then at war (echoes of that belief appear in both Defoe's *Journal of the Plague Year* and Samuel Pepys's *Diary*),[6] although there is no evidence that plague in fact came to England from Holland. The great influenza pandemic of 1918–19, which killed more than 20 million people—possibly as many as 40 million—in a world at war, was attributed to various enemies. In fact, the name by which we remember this epidemic, "Spanish Flu," seems to have been a compromise acceptable to the warring parties (Spain was neutral in the war). And in a telling instance, very shortly after Germany broke its pact with the Soviet Union and invaded its former ally, Hitler[7] used the term Pestherd—"plague focus"—to refer to Russia, accusing the Soviets of infecting Europe with Jewish "bacilli." It was the metaphor of foreign culpability for disease turned inside out, Hitler imputing pathogenic properties to Jews and creating a new enemy by alleging that it was Russia that had spawned them. More recently, Tanzanians attributed the high death rate from AIDS in their Kagera province to HIV infections brought by Idi Amin's[8] Ugandan troops, who crossed the border into Tanzania in the late 1970s. "It made sense, then," Laurie Garrett[9] writes in *The Coming Plague*, "to assume that the new disease came from old enemies." When West Nile encephalitis made its Western hemisphere debut in New York in 1999, epidemiologists received calls from the FBI; they (and the CIA, too) were concerned that it might be the work of foreign bioterrorists.

The Stranger Spreading Germs shows up often in literature and film. Alessandro Manzoni's[10] 1821 novel, *I Promessi Sposi*, attributes the advance of plague in 1629 to the German army, then campaigning through the valleys of northern Italy in the Thirty Years' War. In the novel, foreigners, particularly the French, come under suspicion in plague-ridden Milan, where they are accused of "daubing" plague-inducing substances on walls or sprinkling plague powders on the streets; those found guilty of such felonious behavior are tortured to death. In F. W. Murnau's[11] classic silent film *Nosferatu*, plague arrives in

5. An epidemic of bubonic plague that hit London in the seventeenth century, killing up to a fifth of the population.

6. Daniel Defoe (1660–1731), British writer best known for his novel *Robinson Crusoe* (1719); Pepys (1633–1703), British naval administrator and politician known for his diary written in code.

7. Adolf Hitler (1889–1945), Austrian-born Chancellor of Germany, leader of the Nazi party, and perpetrator of World War II.

8. Dictatorial Ugandan president (1924–2003) who ruled during the 1970s.

9. Pulitzer Prize–winning science writer and author of *The Coming Plague* (1994) and *Betrayal of Trust: The Collapse of Global Public Health* (2000).

10. Italian writer (1775–1883) whose novel *I Promessi Sposi* (translated into English as "The Betrothed") includes a detailed description of the plague that Milan suffered in 1630.

11. German film director (1888–1931) who based his film *Nosferatu* (1922) on Bram Stoker's novel *Dracula* (1897).

Bremen by sea, brought from the East by the odious Other, the undead Nosferatu. In 1922, just after the carnage of World War I and the far greater mortality of the Spanish Flu pandemic, Murnau depicted Evil as the man who was beyond death, the inscrutable and indomitable being who brings pestilence from the benighted Ausland.[12]

Sometimes, of course, epidemics have come from the enemy foreigner. Clearly, Cortes[13] was able to conquer Mexico because of smallpox. The disease appeared among the Taino[14] on Hispaniola in 1518, brought by Spaniards who had colonized the island; later, it would contribute to the Taino's extinction. By 1519 smallpox was in Cuba. Cortes, who was secretary to the governor of Cuba, left to take Tenochtitlan from the Aztec chief Montezuma;[15] either Cortes's Spanish troops or those of Narvaez,[16] who led a relief expedition against the Aztecs after they repulsed Cortes's initial sallies, brought smallpox to the Aztecs. The disease, to which the Aztecs were immunologically naive, so diminished their numbers that Cortes had only to finish them off. Smallpox thence spread southward, killing the Incan emperor Huayna Capac[17] and then his son in 1524–25, and plunging their people into civil war. Francisco Pizarro had little more to do to vanquish the Incas than march into Cuzco.[18]

5

It is unlikely that the Spaniards infected the American natives deliberately—and the Aztecs, at least, seemed to interpret the devastation as evidence of divine disfavor, not treachery on the part of Spain. But in the French and Indian War, in the early 1760s, smallpox does seem to have been spread deliberately. During the conflict known as Pontiac's Rebellion, Sir Jeffrey Amherst, the British commanding general, approved a plan to distribute smallpox-contaminated blankets "to innoculate the Indians" besieging Fort Pitt, at the fork of the Ohio River. That epidemic smallpox occurred in the Ohio Valley at the time is an established fact.

Around the same time, the Polish army considered producing cannon shells filled with the saliva of rabid dogs, in an attempt to poison the air the enemy breathed. Later, during World War I, the German biological warfare program sought to create animal epidemics—epizootics, in the lingo of epidemiology—that would diminish their enemies' ability to fight. German agents deliberately infected their neutral trading partners' livestock and animal feed with the

12. German for "foreign country."

13. Hernando Cortes (1485–1547), Spanish conquistador who brought about the demise of the Aztec Empire in present-day Mexico.

14. Natives of Cuba, Haiti, the Dominican Republic, Puerto Rico, and Jamaica, whom Columbus encountered upon his arrival in the Americas.

15. Tenochtitlan: capital of the Aztec Empire, which was destroyed by conquering Spaniards and became the site of present-day Mexico City; Montezuma (c. 1466–1520), emperor of the Aztecs at the beginning of the Spanish conquest.

16. Panfilo de Narvaez (1470–1528), Spanish conquistador.

17. Chief of the Incas (1493–1527), a people native to South America.

18. Pizarro (1475–1541), Spanish conquistador who helped bring about the demise of the Inca Empire; Cuzco was its capital.

agents of glanders (principally an equine disease) and anthrax. Romanian sheep were infected with both microbes in 1916 before export to Russia; more than two hundred Argentine mules intended as dray animals[19] for Allied forces died after being inoculated with both bacteria; French cavalry horses were infected with glanders; and attempts were made to contaminate animal feed in the United States. During World War II, the Third Reich avowedly eschewed use of biological warfare, but one report holds that Colorado beetles were dropped by German airplanes on potato crops in southern England. The U.S. Army claims that the retreating Wehrmacht[20] contaminated a reservoir in Bohemia with sewage, presumably to produce disease in the advancing Soviet army.

The best documented, and most successful, deliberately caused human epidemic was set by the infamous Unit 731 of the Japanese Imperial Army, stationed in conquered China during World War II. In addition to numerous heinous medical "experiments"—tortures, really—the unit dropped plague-carrying fleas on eleven Chinese towns. The number of Chinese who died of plague was probably about seven hundred. Unit 731 also produced cholera. In fact, Japanese soldiers, whom the unit had failed to warn or prepare, died in large numbers after entering Chinese areas seeded with Vibrio cholerae.[21] Some historians put the total number of deaths attributable to the unit's intentional contaminations, including others involving anthrax and typhoid, in the thousands.

In connection with humans deliberately causing epidemics, the smallpox germ, variola virus, is the one we hear most about. It enjoyed a five-hundred-year career as a natural epidemic pathogen, from roughly the late fifteenth century until the late twentieth. Then smallpox was eradicated from the earth. Variola killed several hundred million people in the first half of the twentieth century alone—a public-health menace to be reckoned with. No doubt because of its fearsome reputation, it is the subject of a great number of speculative scenarios about how it might be resurrected as an epidemic scourge.

10 In fact, though, none of those scenarios is even remotely likely. First, not many people have access to viable smallpox stocks. Second, the disease that variola virus produces is fairly easy to diagnose. Third, vaccination will prevent disease even in already-infected contacts of smallpox cases, and vaccine stocks are reasonably large nowadays. The hubbub about smallpox has had the effect of sharpening physicians' diagnostic skills (indeed, so much so that instances of overdiagnosis produce false alarms) and expanding the supply of available vaccine. At this point, standard public-health procedures, including case diagnosis, contact investigation, and immunization of possibly infected individuals, would be adequate to prevent an outbreak in the unlikely event that some individuals were deliberately infected.

Anthrax is the second most popular topic of bioterrorism conversation. We have seen intentional anthrax infection—the much-ballyhooed postal anthrax events that took place in the fall of 2001. Three characteristics of that

19. Animals used to move wagons, such as horses, oxen, and mules.

20. German for "defense force," the name of the German army under Adolf Hitler.

21. The bacterium that causes cholera.

outbreak are of note: very few people became ill; very, very few died; and it was almost certainly not produced by a stranger. Environmental studies in mailrooms indicated that many hundreds of people were probably exposed to anthrax spores that fall, yet only twenty-two people got sick. And of those twenty-two, half had cutaneous anthrax, the rarely-life-threatening skin form of the disease. Only five died. In the jargon of epidemiology, anthrax turned out to be neither very infectious nor very pathogenic. That experience should tell us that spraying anthrax spores from crop dusters or releasing them from aerosol cans into the subway is highly unlikely to make many people ill. Speculation about subway attacks stems from a real event in March 1995, when the Japanese religious cult Aum Shinrikyo released the nerve toxin sarin in the Tokyo subway system. Twelve people died. Two subsequent attempts to release toxins in the Tokyo subways were foiled. Note that Aum was using a gas, which does not have to be sprayed; it diffuses by itself. This is not how germs are disseminated, and it is a distinction worth bearing in mind. And even that ignores the more central question of likelihood. Large-scale poisonings are not easy to carry out well. The light death toll from mailed anthrax was a result of the low pathogenicity of the bacteria—half the cases were not pulmonary and were therefore unlikely to be fatal—and the comparative treatability of anthrax disease once detected. Do five deaths constitute a public-health crisis? Along with his colleagues, Victor Sidel, Distinguished Professor of Social Medicine at Albert Einstein College of Medicine in New York, has noted that a fraction of our nation's expenditure on biopreparedness would pay for effective treatment of tuberculosis for all of the two million people who get TB each year in India, thereby preventing close to half a million deaths a year. Half a million deaths because commonly available antibiotics are not affordable—now there's a public-health problem.

The other microbe that is on the lists of virtually all the bioterrorism watchers is the plague bacillus. It is true that Unit 731 produced plague outbreaks in China by dropping infected fleas on towns. But at that time plague was a recurring problem in Asia: a ferocious epidemic struck Manchuria in 1910, and another occurred in 1921. (It still is a problem: a large outbreak caused many deaths in India as recently as 1994.) By contrast, despite the presence of Yersinia pestis, the plague bacterium, in wild rodents in the Western Hemisphere, there has never been an extensive epidemic of human plague in this country. Even when plague epidemics moved out of Asia through much of South America, circa 1900, the U.S. saw only a small outbreak in San Francisco's Chinatown. The reason is not that Americans are immune to plague; it is that the urban arrangements that we have been accustomed to for the past two hundred years are inhospitable to the rat-flea-bacillus ecosystem. Such reforms as garbage removal, pest control, and better housing explain why plague disappeared from eastern Europe in the early 1700s and has never troubled us seriously here. Since epidemics of plague are unlikely, should we then worry that terrorists will produce isolated cases? Perhaps, but garden-variety antibiotics are very effective at treating the disease and interrupting transmission. There is no potential for the next catastrophe there.

Other pathogens have been mentioned as possible bioweapons—for example, the agents of tularemia, botulism, and Q fever.[22] These organisms are not generally transmitted from person to person, so they carry little or no outbreak potential. Hemorrhagic fever viruses are sometimes transmitted by mosquitoes or by the bite of infected animals. It has never been shown that they can be manipulated into transportable weapons and then elude standard mosquito- and animal-control programs.

All in all, there is little evidence that terrorists are more likely, or better able, to use microbes as part of their armamentarium than ever before. If there were evidence, would editorialists in the nation's most prestigious medical journal need to argue, as they did in the context of the purported smallpox threat, that public-health decisions should rely on "theoretical data"? Consider the ratio of known success to attempts at bioterrorism. Jessica Stern reports in *The Ultimate Terrorists* that the Aura Shinrikyo cult drove three trucks set up to spray botulinum toxin through Tokyo in 1990, but no cases of botulism resulted. Judith Miller, William Broad, and Stephen Engelberg report in their book, *Germs*, that Aura sprayed anthrax spores from the roof of its building in Tokyo in 1993. This apparently killed some birds, but no humans got sick. Aum members also reportedly tried to procure Ebola virus in the 1990s from what was then Zaire, but if they were able to get the virus, they were unable to produce any cases of Ebola.

15 In the 1960s, a Japanese researcher purposely contaminated food with Salmonella typhi,[23] producing outbreaks of typhoid fever and dysentery, but no deaths. In 1970, four Canadian students got sick after eating food that had been deliberately contaminated with pig ringworm ova. A neo-Nazi group in the U.S. stockpiled the typhoid bacterium in 1972, with the intent of contaminating the water supplies of midwestern cities. They failed. In 1984, members of the Rajneeshee cult[24] contaminated ten Oregon salad bars with Salmonella typhimurium, which causes diarrhea. Federal investigators located 751 cases of salmonellosis, but no deaths occurred. In 1996, twelve people in Texas developed dysentery after eating doughnuts or muffins purposely contaminated with shigella bacteria[25] by a disgruntled lab worker. Again, no deaths.

Presumably, these initiatives represent only a small subset—the known ones—of all attempts to cause mayhem by deliberately introducing germs into a population. Indeed, one systematic study uncovered twenty-nine such attempts to use germs to harm others, although a large proportion seemed to have been

22. Tularemia: highly infectious disease with flulike symptoms; botulism: an often food-borne illness that can cause paralysis; Q fever: short for "Query Fever," an extremely infectious illness that can be contracted through inhalation of bacteria, so called because its discoverer could not recognize it.

23. The bacterium responsible for typhoid fever and salmonellosis.

24. Followers of the controversial cult leader Rajneesh Chandra Mohan Jain.

25. A family of bacteria, named for the Japanese scientist Shiga who discovered it, that causes diarrhea, fever, and stomach cramps.

perpetrated by single individuals whose aims were against other individuals rather than the population. No doubt there are still more instances, unknown because they were unsuccessful. And yet we can enumerate on the fingers of one hand the deadly epidemics that have in fact been caused deliberately. In the creation of epidemics, the gap between intention and the deed itself is a wide one.

Americans began looking at new infectious diseases as a grave social menace in the early 1990s, and that anxiety resonated loudly after the publication of Laurie Garrett's *Coming Plague* in 1994. In a sense, the relatively recent worry about bioterrorism is a spin-off of the past decade's concern about the "coming plague." In reality, the intensity of even naturally occurring new epidemics never matches that anticipation.

Our most recent experience with so-called emerging infections has been SARS. It appeared suddenly in southern China in late 2002, the causative virus probably having entered the human population through people who had substantial contact with domestic animals. Although SARS affected more than 8,000 people worldwide and killed more than 700, it was a negligible problem in the U.S. (eight cases, no deaths) and produced no more than a mild epidemic in most other countries: despite the high case-fatality ratio (people diagnosed with SARS had about one chance in ten of dying from the disease), only in China, Hong Kong, Singapore, and Canada were there more than five SARS deaths. Only nineteen countries saw more than a single SARS case. In all the affected areas, the outbreak was brought under control within about six months of its onset.

Two aspects of the SARS experience are important. First, though it is easy to acquire the virus by inhaling respiratory secretions from a SARS sufferer, it also turns out to be easy to prevent or control an outbreak. The key is to use standard infectious-disease-control measures, including case finding and reporting, active surveillance at points of entry to the country, isolation of possible cases, and recommendations against travel to heavily affected regions. None of these measures requires cutting-edge technology; all have been used in controlling communicable disease for well over a century.

Second, SARS made news partly because it was not the expected epidemic. 20
For six months before the advent of SARS, Americans had been worrying very publicly about smallpox. Urged toward apprehension by the federal government, we had alarmed ourselves about the possibility that the long-defunct disease would be reborn in the hands of bioterrorists. The administration made ready, in mid-2002, to vaccinate half a million armed-services personnel and half a million health-care workers. The former plan it came close to accomplishing; the latter was abandoned because so many health-care workers refused to show up for vaccination. All of it repeatedly made the headlines and the evening news reports. Yet what happened in the end was not smallpox, or smallpox prevention; it was SARS. Had our faces not already been turned toward epidemic disease and our anxieties about infection elevated, had the news hours not been hungry for new news after a month of relentless coverage of the Iraq war, SARS might not have made such big headlines.

The lesson we should learn from our experience with SARS is that if we are vigilant about spotting new disease outbreaks and equally vigilant about applying public-health programs to curtail their spread, we can limit them, although we cannot ward them off completely. We cannot make life risk-free. Had we dealt with AIDS and West Nile encephalitis the way we dealt with SARS (which, of course, may return in the future and therefore requires continued vigilance), their course might have been different. West Nile, ending only its fifth season in the U.S. as I write, is already virtually a national epidemic; AIDS went national within six or seven years of its appearance. But in its initial season, 1999, in New York City, West Nile virus caused forty-six cases of encephalitis and seven deaths: not negligible, but a public-health problem more minor than Lyme disease (and far less extensive, in New York, than asthma or lead poisoning). AIDS began with a handful of cases—there were only a few hundred in 1981, the first year it was recognized—and the U.S. might have kept the toll fairly small had we had the political nerve to do something about it at the time. The point is that, at the outset, none of these "plagues" were cataclysmic. Epidemics do not work that way. Errant microbes do not find their way into the human ecosystem and wipe out most of the population unannounced. The Andromeda Strain[26] is fantasy.

The crystal ball with which we divine epidemic mayhem is no clearer now than it used to be, and no clearer than the vision with which we try to foresee the coming plague. No one can dispute, after the events of September 11, 2001, that some people wish us harm. However, that harm is not likely to come from bioterrorism. To worry that the Middle Easterner, the Arab, or any Muslim—however the Stranger is configured—will use germs to attack us would be to pretend that we can indeed foresee great epidemics. For two reasons, that is certainly not the case. First, humans, even ill-tempered and badly behaved humans, have never been able to use germs or weapons to the terrible degree of mortal effect that nature always has been able to use germs. Just four communicable diseases—malaria, smallpox, AIDS, and tuberculosis—killed well over half a billion people in the twentieth century, or about ten times the combined tolls of World Wars I and II, history's bloodiest conflicts. Even today, with good vaccines and effective antibiotics to stop them, infectious diseases kill about 10 million people each year.

The worst catastrophes the world has seen have been not the genocides, however gruesome, but the cataclysmic disease outbreaks. When a few million people are killed by design with Zyklon B,[27] the machete, or the machine gun, it is a horror and an outrage; it shakes our moral faith. But the Black Death killed a third of Europe's population in just four years in the mid-1300s. Smallpox wiped out entire tribes of American natives after Europeans arrived in the 1500s. Plague killed over 50,000 in Moscow alone in just a few months in 1771.

26. A contagious illness of extraterrestrial origin and boundless danger, invented by novelist Michael Crichton in his book of the same title.

27. A cyanide-based insecticide with which the Nazis killed millions in gas chambers.

The Spanish Flu killed between 20 and 40 million in sixteen months in 1918–19.

And that suddenness is the second point. Prevision is of little help against epidemic disasters. Each of the disasters I just mentioned, and every other great epidemic of history, was unimaginable until the moment it began. But neither is prescience necessary: each epidemic, even the ones that turned out to be most terrible, began slowly, percolated a while, and could have been stopped with conventional public-health responses had anyone acted in time. SARS reminded us of that.

Whether or not the Stranger is an enemy avowedly bent on terror, casting him in the role of microbial evildoer has the perilous effect of distracting us from realizing two truths: the disheartening one that the epidemic crystal ball is always cloudy, and the uncomfortable one that it is usually social circumstances that make epidemics possible and public-health funding that stops them. 25

Worrying about the germ-bearing Stranger, we forgo the upkeep of a workaday public-health apparatus in favor of fabricating modern wonders. The CDC[28] now operates what it calls a "war room." From there, it can coordinate activities around SARS, West Nile virus, and other infections, as well as bioterrorism—if it can be found—using high-tech communications equipment. The war room is in an "undisclosed location." Once, CDC officials knew they were running a public-health agency. Now, apparently, they must act as if they are in charge of national defense. After the U.S. Department of Health and Human Services scotched the 2002 plan to vaccinate health-care workers, the CDC announced it would continue its effort to vaccinate police officers and firefighters, despite numerous reasons to stop: several deaths directly attributable to the vaccine; several more possibly attributable; evidence that people who might be predisposed to heart disease (something like 10 or 15 percent of the middle-aged population) can be harmed by the vaccination; certainty that people with HIV infection (a sizable percentage of the adult population in some big-city neighborhoods) must not be vaccinated; and of course the complete absence of natural smallpox infection anywhere in the world for the past twenty-five years.

Federal grant money, under President Bush's multimillion-dollar Project BioShield program, has been allocated to technologic innovation for bioterrorism prevention. By 2003, according to *The Chronicle of Higher Education*, the National Institutes of Health were supporting almost seventy extramural research projects on anthrax alone. The NIH has funded two new National Biocontainment Laboratories and new facilities at Regional Biocontainment Laboratories, most at major universities, to the tune of $360 million in start-up costs. The University of Pittsburgh just lured the top staff of the Center for Civilian Biodefense Strategies away from Johns Hopkins by offering to set up a Center for Biosecurity with a $12 million endowment. The University of South Florida recently received $5 million in federal grant money for its Center for Biological Defense, which has projects like "Photocatalytic Air Disinfection" and

28. Centers for Disease Control and Prevention.

"Aquatic Real-time Monitoring System (ARMS) for Bioterrorism Events." And Auburn University received a million-dollar federal biopreparedness grant for something called a Canine Detection Center. When Harvard received a $1.2 million federal grant in 2002 to set up a program for detecting "events possibly related to bioterrorism" by electronically linking 20 million patient-care records from around the country (an endeavor called syndromic surveillance), the grant was a mere drop in the bucket: Congress soon allotted $420 million to Homeland Security for a larger linked health-monitoring network. A consortium led by the New York Academy of Medicine then developed software for syndromic surveillance. The new software allows public health officials to monitor what are called "aberrant clusters health events"—translation: more than the expected number of cases of some symptom that might be related to a disease that might be produced by an organism that might be in the possession of terrorists. Syndromic surveillance works fine if someone knows what to look for. But it is of no help at all with the unexpected. When there really was bioterrorism in the U.S.—the anthrax attacks in fall 2001—linked databases were useless; it took a smart clinician to figure out that anthrax was around, and old-fashioned shoe-leather epidemiology quickly worked out which people had been affected. West Nile virus, ditto. A friend who is an official of a local health department tells me that the syndromic surveillance experts find it works well for predicting the first influenza outbreak each year. But anyone's grandmother can predict the first influenza outbreak where I live, in the New York City area, since the symptoms are always the same and flu always starts here in the two weeks preceding Thanksgiving. For all its meager productivity, the syndromic surveillance software also throws out plenty of false-positive "clusters" that waste investigators' time. It is our new and expensive white elephant, justified by the fear of evildoers and germs.

It all sounds a little phantasmagoric.

In "The Expose of 1935," Walter Benjamin[29] identified certain phantasmagorias of modern life as Wunschbilder, "wish symbols," that seek to "transfigure the . . . inadequacies in the social organization." Benjamin was concerned with phantasmagorias as magical images, as he put it in his Passagen-Werk, "residues of a dream world," revelations of unfulfilled wishes. In this sense we might ask whether the many projects of the Bioshield—the electronic anthrax detectors, the hyperdatabanks, the supersecure biohazard-level-4 labs, the men and women in full-body protective suits, the urban-evacuation exercises, whatever it is they are doing with dogs at Auburn University, and so on—are emblems of some shared desire to feel that all the effort America expends on technology development protects us from something. We might ask whether the something is the Stranger Spreading Germs. And we must ask what the cost is.

30 The core issue here is that the Stranger Spreading Germs is a metaphor, and largely an empty one. Bioterrorism is not a public-health problem, and will not become one. The next plague, whatever it is, will not decimate us unheralded.

29. German literary critic and philosopher (1892–1940).

In signing the contract on biopreparedness, we have bought a confection, a defense against the chimeric stranger with the metaphorical germs.

And the costs of buy-in? When our public-health "leaders" corroborate government rhetoric about bioterrorists by reassuring us that our state or municipal health department is ready for any smallpox, anthrax, or plague attack, they legitimate both their own efforts and the standing of their offices. The planned result is that we will not question spending tax dollars so those officials can continue to defend us, even when it means closing down municipal clinics or shortchanging programs for the poor, and even if such biodefense is not what we most need or want.

The biopreparedness campaign goes to work. It discredits the simple logic of public health. Lose the distinction between the minuscule risk of dying in an intentional outbreak and the millionfold-higher chance of dying in a natural pandemic, it says. Ignore the hundredfold-higher-still chance of dying of cancer or heart disease. Defund the prenatal-care clinics, the chest clinics, the exercise and cancer screening and lead abatement programs. Ignore the lessons of history: forget that human attempts to create epidemics have almost always failed, and dismiss the repeated ability of a well-funded public-health apparatus to control epidemic disease with time-tested measures. Just think about germs, and tremble.

The lesson of history that we ignore at our peril is this: nobody can tell us how the next epidemic will happen. New germs come and go, epidemics wax and wane, but national catastrophes happen rarely. And when they do, it is never because of a stranger spreading germs. Anyone who promises certain protection from the next plague is selling us a bill of goods.

QUESTIONS

1. Philip Alcabes argues that, historically, most plagues and epidemics have been wrongly interpreted in terms of "the stranger as the spreader of contagion" (paragraph 2). What historical evidence does he supply to support this claim in the opening paragraphs (1–9)? Why does he wish to refute the belief that strangers are the source of disease, plagues, epidemics, and other such biological invasions?

2. What role have books, films, and other fictional media played in past and current "bioterrorism scares"? Locate Alcabes's examples of fictional scare tactics, and analyze his treatment of these media.

3. Instead of buying into the "bioterrorism scare," what does Alcabes suggest Americans do? What does he, as a professor of urban public health, advance as an appropriate set of actions?

4. Test Alcabes's claim that a "core issue [in the bioterrorism scare] is that the Stranger Spreading Germs is a metaphor, and largely an empty one" (paragraph 30) by examining newspaper and magazine articles about SARS, anthrax, or other scares. Write up what you find about the use of this metaphor and/or other metaphors in these articles.

WALT WHITMAN

Death of Abraham Lincoln

I SHALL NOT easily forget the first time I ever saw Abraham Lincoln. It must have been about the 18th or 19th of February, 1861. It was rather a pleasant afternoon, in New York City, as he arrived there from the West, to remain a few hours, and then pass on to Washington, to prepare for his inauguration. I saw him in Broadway, near the site of the present Post-office. He came down, I think from Canal street, to stop at the Astor House. The broad spaces, sidewalks, and streets in the neighborhood, and for some distance, were crowded with solid masses of people, many thousands. The omnibuses and other vehicles had all been turn'd off, leaving an unusual hush in that busy part of the city. Presently two or three shabby hack barouches made their way with some difficulty through the crowd, and drew up at the Astor House entrance. A tall figure stepp'd out of the centre of these barouches, paus'd leisurely on the sidewalk, look'd up at the granite walls and looming architecture of the grand old hotel—then, after a relieving stretch of arms and legs, turn'd round for over a minute to slowly and good-humoredly scan the appearance of the vast and silent crowds. There were no speeches—no compliments—no welcome—as far as I could hear, not a word said. Still much anxiety was conceal'd in the quiet. Cautious persons had fear'd some mark'd insult or indignity to the President-elect—for he possess'd no personal popularity at all in New York City, and very little political. But it was evidently tacitly agreed that if the few political supporters of Mr. Lincoln present would entirely abstain from any demonstration on their side, the immense majority, who were anything but supporters, would abstain on their sides also. The result was a sulky, unbroken silence, such as certainly never before characterized so great a New York crowd.

Almost in the same neighborhood I distinctly remember'd seeing Lafayette on his visit to America in 1825. I had also personally seen and heard, various years afterward, how Andrew Jackson, Clay, Webster, Hungarian Kossuth, Filibuster Walker, the Prince of Wales[1] on his visit, and other *célèbres,* native and foreign, had been welcom'd there—all that indescribable human roar and magnetism, unlike any other sound in the universe—the glad exulting thunder-shouts of countless unloos'd throats of men! But on this occasion, not a voice—not a sound. From the top of an omnibus, (driven up one side, close by, and block'd by the curbstone and the crowds), I had, I say, a capital view of it all,

From Whitman's collection of prose writings, Specimen Days *(1882).*

1. Marquis de Lafayette (1757–1834), French statesman and general who fought for the United States in the War of Independence; Jackson (1767–1845), seventh president of the United States, 1829–1837; Henry Clay (1777–1852), American statesman and orator; Daniel Webster (1782–1852), American statesman and orator; Lajos Kossuth (1802–1894), Hungarian patriot and statesman; William Walker (1824–1860), an American who filibustered (i.e., undertook unsanctioned revolutionary activities) in Central America; the future Edward VII (1841–1910), Queen Victoria's son.

and especially of Mr. Lincoln, his look and gait—his perfect composure and coolness—his unusual and uncouth height, his dress of complete black, stove-pipe hat push'd back on the head, dark-brown complexion, seam'd and wrinkled yet canny-looking face, black, bushy head of hair, disproportionately long neck, and his hands held behind as he stood observing the people. He look'd with curiosity upon that immense sea of faces, and the sea of faces return'd the look with similar curiosity. In both there was a dash of comedy, almost farce, such as Shakspere puts in his blackest tragedies. The crowd that hemm'd around consisted I should think of thirty to forty thousand men, not a single one his personal friend—while I have no doubt, (so frenzied were the ferments of the time,) many an assassin's knife and pistol lurk'd in hip or breast-pocket there, ready, soon as break and riot came.

But no break or riot came. The tall figure gave another relieving stretch or two of arms and legs; then with moderate pace, and accompanied by a few unknown-looking persons, ascended the portico-steps of the Astor House, disappear'd through its broad entrance—and the dumb-show ended.

I saw Abraham Lincoln often the four years following that date. He changed rapidly and much during his Presidency—but this scene, and him in it, are indelibly stamp'd upon my recollection. As I sat on the top of my omnibus, and had a good view of him, the thought, dim and inchoate then, has since come out clear enough, that four sorts of genius, four mighty and primal hands, will be needed to the complete limning of this man's future portrait—the eyes and brains and finger-touch of Plutarch and Eschylus and Michel Angelo, assisted now by Rabelais.[2]

And now—(Mr. Lincoln passing on from this scene to Washington, where he was inaugurated, amid armed cavalry, and sharpshooters at every point—the first instance of the kind in our history—and I hope it will be the last)—now the rapid succession of well-known events, (too well-known—I believe, these days, we almost hate to hear them mention'd)—the national flag fired on at Sumter—the uprising of the North, in paroxysms of astonishment and rage—the chaos of divided councils—the call for troops—the first Bull Run—the stunning cast-down, shock, and dismay of the North—and so in full flood the Secession war. Four years of lurid, bleeding, murky, murderous war. Who paint those years, with all their scenes?—the hard-fought engagements—the defeats, plans, failures—the gloomy hours, days, when our Nationality seem'd hung in pall of doubt, perhaps death—the Mephistophelean sneers of foreign lands and attachés—the dreaded Scylla of European interference, and the Charybdis of the tremendously dangerous latent strata of secession sympathizers throughout the free States,[3] (far more numerous than is supposed)—the

2. Plutarch (46?–120 C.E.), Greek author who wrote the histories of famous Greeks and Romans; Aeschylus (525–456 B.C.E.), Greek tragic dramatist; Michelangelo Buonarroti (1475–1574), Italian architect, painter, sculptor, and poet; François Rabelais (1493–1553), French author who created the giants Gargantua and Pantagruel.

3. Mephistopheles is the name of an evil spirit to whom men legendarily sell their souls in exchange for something they desire; the character appears in European litera-

long marches in summer—the hot sweat, and many a sunstroke, as on the rush to Gettysburg in '63—the night battles in the woods, as under Hooker at Chancellorsville—the camps in winter—the military prisons—the hospitals—(alas! alas! the hospitals.)

The Secession war? Nay, let me call it the Union war. Though whatever call'd, it is even yet too near us—too vast and too closely overshadowing—its branches unform'd yet, (but certain,) shooting too far into the future—and the most indicative and mightiest of them yet ungrown. A great literature will yet arise out of the era of those four years, those scenes—era compressing centuries of native passion, first-class pictures, tempests of life and death—an inexhaustible mine for the histories, drama, romance, and even philosophy, of peoples to come—indeed the verteber[4] of poetry and art, (of personal character too,) for all future America—far more grand, in my opinion, to the hands capable of it, than Homer's siege of Troy, or the French wars to Shakspere.[5]

But I must leave these speculations, and come to the theme I have assign'd and limited myself to. Of the actual murder of President Lincoln, though so much has been written, probably the facts are yet very indefinite in most persons' minds. I read from my memoranda, written at the time, and revised frequently and finally since.

The day, April 14, 1865, seems to have been a pleasant one throughout the whole land—the moral atmosphere pleasant too—the long storm, so dark, so fratricidal, full of blood and doubt and gloom, over and ended at last by the sunrise of such an absolute National victory, and utter break-down of Secessionism—we almost doubted our own senses! Lee had capitulated beneath the apple-tree of Appomattox. The other armies, the flanges of the revolt, swiftly follow'd. And could it really be, then? Out of all the affairs of this world of woe and failure and disorder, was there really come the confirm'd, unerring sign of plan, like a shaft of pure light—of rightful rule—of God? So the day, as I say, was propitious. Early herbage, early flowers, were out. (I remember where I was stopping at the time, the season being advanced, there were many lilacs in full bloom. By one of those caprices that enter and give tinge to events without being at all a part of them, I find myself always reminded of the great tragedy of that day by the sight and odor of these blossoms.[6] It never fails.)

But I must not dwell on accessories. The deed hastens. The popular afternoon paper of Washington, the little *Evening Star,* has spatter'd all over its third page, divided among the advertisements in a sensational manner, in a hundred different places, "*The President and his Lady will be at the Theatre this evening. . . .*" (Lincoln was fond of the theatre. I have myself seen him there

---

ture most frequently in tales and drama about Faust, a German conjurer who lived from about 1488 to 1541. In Homer's *Odyssey,* Scylla and Charybdis are the rocks and the whirlpool between which Odysseus must navigate.

4. Vertebra.

5. In the *Iliad* and in Shakespeare's history plays.

6. Cf. Whitman's elegy on Lincoln, "When Lilacs Last in the Dooryard Bloom'd" (1865–66).

several times. I remember thinking how funny it was that he, in some respects the leading actor in the stormiest drama known to real history's stage through centuries, should sit there and be so completely interested and absorb'd in those human jackstraws, moving about with their silly little gestures, foreign spirit, and flatulent text.)

On this occasion the theatre was crowded, many ladies in rich and gay costumes, officers in their uniforms, many well-known citizens, young folks, the usual clusters of gas-lights, the usual magnetism of so many people, cheerful, with perfumes, music of violins and flutes—(and over all, and saturating all, that vast, vague wonder, *Victory,* the nation's victory, the triumph of the Union, filling the air, the thought, the sense, with exhilaration more than all music and perfumes.)

The President came betimes, and, with his wife, witness'd the play from the large stage-boxes of the second tier, two thrown into one, and profusely drap'd with the national flag. The acts and scenes of the piece—one of those singularly written compositions which have at least the merit of giving entire relief to an audience engaged in mental action or business excitements and cares during the day, as it makes not the slightest call on either the moral, emotional, esthetic, or spiritual nature—a piece, (*Our American Cousin,*)[7] in which, among other characters so call'd, a Yankee, certainly such a one as was never seen, or the least like it ever seen, in North America, is introduced in England, with a varied fol-de-rol of talk, plot, scenery, and such phantasmagoria as goes to make up a modern popular drama—had progress'd through perhaps a couple of its acts, when in the midst of this comedy, or non-such, or whatever it is to be call'd, and to offset it, or finish it out, as if in Nature's and the great Muse's mockery of those poor mimes, came interpolated that scene, not really or exactly to be described at all, (for on the many hundreds who were there it seems to this hour to have left a passing blur, a dream, a blotch)—and yet partially to be described as I now proceed to give it. There is a scene in the play representing a modern parlor, in which two unprecedented English ladies are inform'd by the impossible Yankee that he is not a man of fortune, and therefore undesirable for marriage-catching purposes; after which, the comments being finish'd, the dramatic trio make exit, leaving the stage clear for a moment. At this period came the murder of Abraham Lincoln. Great as all its manifold train, circling round it, and stretching into the future for many a century, in the politics, history, art &c., of the New World, in point of fact the main thing, the actual murder, transpired with the quiet and simplicity of any commonest occurrence—the bursting of a bud or pod in the growth of vegetation, for instance. Through the general hum following the stage pause, with the change of positions, came the muffled sound of a pistol-shot, which not one-hundredth part of the audience heard at the time—and yet a moment's hush—somehow, surely, a vague startled thrill—and then, through the ornamented, draperied, starr'd and striped space-way of the President's box, a sudden figure, a man, raises himself with hands and feet, stands a moment on the railing, leaps below

7. By the British playwright Tom Taylor (1817–1880).

to the stage, (a distance of perhaps fourteen or fifteen feet), falls out of position, catching his boot-heel in the copious drapery, (the American flag,) falls on one knee, quickly recovers himself, rises as if nothing had happen'd, (he really sprains his ankle, but unfelt then)—and so the figure, Booth,[8] the murderer, dress'd in plain black broadcloth, bareheaded, with full, glossy, raven hair, and his eyes like some mad animal's flashing with light and resolution, yet with a certain strange calmness, holds aloft in one hand a large knife—walks along not much back from the footlights—turns fully toward the audience his face of statuesque beauty, lit by those basilisk eyes, flashing with desperation, perhaps insanity—launches out in a firm and steady voice the words *Sic semper tyrannis*[9]—and then walks with neither slow nor very rapid pace diagonally across to the back of the stage, and disappears. (Had not all this terrible scene—making the mimic ones preposterous—had it not all been rehears'd, in blank, by Booth, beforehand?)

A moment's hush—a scream—the cry of "*murder*"—Mrs. Lincoln leaning out of the box, with ashy cheeks and lips, with involuntary cry, pointing to the retreating figure, "*He has kill'd the President.*" And still a moment's strange, incredulous suspense—and then the deluge! then that mixture of horror, noises, uncertainty—(the sound, somewhere back, of a horse's hoofs clattering with speed)—the people burst through chairs and railings, and break them up—there is inextricable confusion and terror—women faint—quite feeble persons fall, and are trampl'd on—many cries of agony are heard—the broad stage suddenly fills to suffocation with a dense and motley crowd, like some horrible carnival—the audience rush generally upon it, at least the strong men do—the actors and actresses are all there in their playcostumes and painted faces, with mortal fright showing through the rouge—the screams and calls, confused talk—redoubled, trebled—two or three manage to pass up water from the stage to the President's box—others try to clamber up—&c., &c.

In the midst of all this, the soldiers of the President's guard, with others, suddenly drawn to the scene, burst in—(some two hundred altogether)—they storm the house, through all the tiers, especially the upper ones, inflam'd with fury, literally charging the audience with fix'd bayonets, muskets, and pistols, shouting "*Clear out! clear out! you sons of* ———". . . . Such a wild scene, or a suggestion of it rather, inside the play-house that night.

Outside, too, in the atmosphere of shock and craze, crowds of people, fill'd with frenzy, ready to seize any outlet for it, come near committing murder several times on innocent individuals. One such case was especially exciting. The infuriated crowd, through some chance, got started against one man, either for words he utter'd, or perhaps without any cause at all, and were proceeding at once to actually hang him on a neighboring lamp-post, when he was rescued by a few heroic policemen, who placed him in their midst, and fought their way slowly and amid great peril toward the station-house. It was a fitting episode of the whole affair. The crowd rushing and eddying to and fro—the night, the

8. John Wilkes Booth (1835–1865).

9. "Thus always to tyrants," the motto of the state of Virginia.

yells, the pale faces, many frighten'd people trying in vain to extricate themselves—the attack'd man, not yet freed from the jaws of death, looking like a corpse—the silent, resolute, half-dozen policemen, with no weapons but their little clubs, yet stern and steady through all those eddying swarms—made a fitting side-scene to the grand tragedy of the murder. They gain'd the station house with the protected man, whom they placed in security for the night, and discharged him in the morning.

And in the midst of that pandemonium, infuriated soldiers, the audience and the crowd, the stage, and all its actors and actresses, its paint-pots, spangles, and gas-lights—the life blood from those veins, the best and sweetest of the land, drips slowly down, and death's ooze already begins its little bubbles on the lips. 15

Thus the visible incidents and surroundings of Abraham Lincoln's murder, as they really occur'd. Thus ended the attempted secession of these States: thus the four years' war. But the main things come subtly and invisibly afterward, perhaps long afterward—neither military, political, nor (great as those are,) historical. I say, certain secondary and indirect results, out of the tragedy of this death, are, in my opinion, greatest. Not the event of the murder itself. Not that Mr. Lincoln strings the principal points and personages of the period, like beads, upon the single string of his career. Not that his idiosyncrasy, in its sudden appearance and disappearance, stamps this Republic with a stamp more mark'd and enduring than any yet given by any one man—(more even than Washington's;)—but, join'd with these, the immeasurable value and meaning of that whole tragedy lies, to me, in senses finally dearest to a nation, (and here all our own)—the imaginative and artistic senses—the literary and dramatic ones. Not in any common or low meaning of those terms, but a meaning precious to the race, and to every age. A long and varied series of contradictory events arrives at last at its highest poetic, single, central, pictorial *dénouement.* The whole involved, baffling, multiform whirl of the secession period comes to a head, and is gather'd in one brief flash of lightning-illumination—one simple, fierce deed. Its sharp culmination, and as it were solution, of so many bloody and angry problems, illustrates those climax-moments on the stage of universal Time, where the historic Muse at one entrance, and the tragic Muse at the other, suddenly ringing down the curtain, close an immense act in the long drama of creative thought, and give it radiation, tableau, stranger than fiction. Fit radiation—fit close! How the imagination—how the student loves these things! America, too, is to have them. For not in all great deaths, not far or near—not Caesar in the Roman senate-house, or Napoleon passing away in the wild night-storm at St. Helena—not Paleologus,[10] falling, desperately fighting, piled over dozens deep with Grecian corpses—not calm old Socrates, drinking the hemlock—outvies that terminus of the secession war, in one man's life, here in our midst, in our time—that seal of the emancipation of three million slaves—that parturition and delivery of our at last really free Republic, born

10. Emperor Constantine XI, who yielded Constantinople to the Turks in 1453.

again, henceforth to commence its career of genuine homogeneous Union, compact, consistent with itself.

Nor will ever future American Patriots and Unionists, indifferently over the whole land, or North or South, find a better moral to their lesson. The final use of the greatest men of a Nation is, after all, not with reference to their deeds in themselves, or their direct bearing on their times or lands. The final use of a heroic-eminent life—especially of a heroic-eminent death—is its indirect filtering into the nation and the race, and to give, often at many removes, but unerringly, age after age, color and fibre to the personalism of the youth and maturity of that age, and of mankind. Then, there is a cement to the whole people, subtler, more underlying, than any thing in written constitution, or courts or armies—namely, the cement of a death identified thoroughly with that people, at its head, and for its sake. Strange, (is it not?) that battles, martyrs, agonies, blood, even assassination, should so condense—perhaps only really, lastingly condense—a Nationality.

I repeat it—the grand deaths of the race—the dramatic deaths of every nationality—are its most important inheritance-value—in some respects beyond its literature and art—(as the hero is beyond his finest portrait, and the battle itself beyond its choicest song or epic.) Is not here indeed the point underlying all tragedy? the famous pieces of the Grecian masters—and all masters? Why, if the old Greeks had had this man, what trilogies of plays—what epics—would have been made out of him! How the rhapsodes would have recited him! How quickly that quaint tall form would have enter'd into the region where men vitalize gods, and gods divinify men! But Lincoln, his times, his death—great as any, any age—belong altogether to our own, and are autochthonic.[11] (Sometimes indeed I think our American days, our own stage—the actors we know and have shaken hands, or talk'd with—more fateful than any thing in Eschylus—more heroic than the fighters around Troy—afford kings of men for our Democracy prouder than Agamemnon—models of character cute and hardy as Ulysses—deaths more pitiful than Priam's.)[12]

When centuries hence, (as it must, in my opinion, be centuries hence before the life of these States, or of Democracy, can be really written and illustrated,) the leading historians and dramatists seek for some personage, some special event, incisive enough to mark with deepest cut, and mnemonize, this turbulent nineteenth century of ours, (not only these States, but all over the political and social world)—something, perhaps, to close that gorgeous procession of European feudalism, with all its pomp and caste-prejudices, (of whose long train we in America are yet so inextricably the heirs)—something to identify with terrible identification, by far the greatest revolutionary step in the history of the United States, (perhaps the greatest of the world, our century)—the

11. Native, indigenous.

12. Eschylus (i.e., Aeschylus), Greek tragic dramatist (525–456 B.C.E.) whose plays, like Homer's epics, deal with such figures of the Trojan War as Agamemnon, leader of the Greek forces; Ulysses (Odysseus), whose return to Ithaca after the war took ten years; and Priam, slaughtered king of Troy. "Cute" here means "acute."

absolute extirpation and erasure of slavery from the States—those historians will seek in vain for any point to serve more thoroughly their purpose, than Abraham Lincoln's death.

Dear to the Muse—thrice dear to Nationality—to the whole human race—precious to this Union—precious to Democracy—unspeakably and forever precious—their first great Martyr Chief. 20

Questions

1. Whitman delivered this piece as a lecture. What features suggest a lecture? How might it have differed if he had composed it as an essay to be read rather than a lecture to be heard?

2. The events of the assassination lead Whitman to mention his perception of Lincoln's fondness for the theater. How does he make this observation serve a larger purpose?

3. At the end of this speech, Whitman speaks grandly of Lincoln's significance for far more than the citizens of the United States. As he sees it, what do all these people have in common that allows for Lincoln's more-than-national significance?

4. How does Whitman convey the sense of horror and confusion in the scene when Lincoln is shot? Using some of Whitman's techniques, write an account of a similar scene that produces a strong emotional effect.

James M. McPherson *How Lincoln Won the War with Metaphors*

In an essay on the reasons for Confederate defeat in the Civil War, southern historian David M. Potter made a striking assertion: "If the Union and Confederacy had exchanged presidents with one another, the Confederacy might have won its independence." Is this rather dramatic conclusion justified? Most historians would probably agree with Potter's general point that Davis's shortcomings as a leader played a role in Confederate defeat.[1] They would also agree that one of Davis's principal failures was an inability to communicate effec-

Published as a chapter of McPherson's study of the Civil War, Abraham Lincoln and the Second American Revolution *(1991).*

1. Jefferson Davis (1808–1889) served as president of the Confederate States of America from its inception in 1861 to its defeat in 1865; prior to the Civil War, he had served in the U.S. government as secretary of war (1853–57) and as senator from Mississippi (1847–1851, 1857–1861).

tively with other Confederate leaders and with the southern people. As Potter put it, Davis "seemed to think in abstractions and to speak in platitudes."[2]

Lincoln, by contrast, most emphatically did *not* think in abstractions and rarely spoke in platitudes. We have not had another president—except perhaps Franklin D. Roosevelt[3]—who expressed himself in such a clear, forceful, logical manner as Lincoln. It is no coincidence that Lincoln and Roosevelt were great war presidents who led the United States to its most decisive victories in its most important wars. Their pre-eminent quality as leaders was an ability to communicate the meaning and purpose of these wars in an intelligible, inspiring manner that helped energize and mobilize their people to make the sacrifices necessary for victory. By contrast, Jefferson Davis, as another historian has concluded, failed to do a good job "in eliciting the enthusiasm and energies of the people."[4]

Wherein lay Lincoln's advantage over Davis in this matter? It certainly did not derive from a better education. Davis had received one of the best educations that money could buy in his day. He attended one "college" in Kentucky and another in Mississippi, which were really secondary schools or academies; he went to Transylvania University in Kentucky, which was one of the best genuine colleges west of the Appalachians at that time; and he graduated from the military academy at West Point, the best American school for engineering as well as for military science in that era. From his education Davis acquired excellent training in the classics, in rhetoric, logic, literature, and science. He should have been a superb communicator. And in many respects he was, by the standards of the time. He could write with vigorous logic, turn a classical phrase, quote the leading authorities on many a subject, and close with a rhetorical flourish.

Lincoln had only a year or so of formal schooling in the typical rote-learning "blab schools" of the day, schooling that he obtained, as he later put it, "by littles"—a month here, a couple of months there, spread out over a period of a few years. Lincoln was basically a self-taught man. Of course he later read law, which along with the practice of that profession helped to give him an ability to write and speak with clarity, a skill in logical analysis, and a knack for finding exactly the right word or phrase to express his meaning. But Jefferson Davis also possessed most of these skills of expository writing and speaking. So we are still left with the question: wherein lay Lincoln's superiority?

5 The answer may be found in a paradox: perhaps the defects of Lincoln's education proved a benefit. Instead of spending years inside the four walls of a classroom, Lincoln worked on frontier dirt farms most of his youth, he split

2. David M. Potter, "Jefferson Davis and the Political Factors in Confederate Defeat," in David Donald, ed., *Why the North Won the Civil War* (Baton Rouge, 1960), 112, 104 [McPherson's note].

3. Thirty-second president of the United States (1882–1945), serving from 1933 to 1945.

4. Paul D. Escott, *After Secession: Jefferson Davis and the Failure of Confederate Nationalism* (Baton Rouge, 1978), 269 [McPherson's note].

rails, he rafted down the Mississippi on a flatboat, he surveyed land, he worked in a store where he learned to communicate with the farmers and other residents of a rural community. Lincoln grew up close to the rhythms of nature, of wild beasts and farm animals, of forest and running water, of seasons and crops and of people who got their meager living from the land. These things, more than books, furnished his earliest education. They infused his speech with the images of nature. And when he turned to books, what were his favorites? They were the King James Bible, *Aesop's Fables, Pilgrim's Progress,*[5] and Shakespeare's plays. What do these four have in common? They are rich in figurative language—in allegory, parable, fable, metaphor—in words and stories that seem to say one thing but mean another, in images that illustrate something more profound than their surface appearance.

Here lies one of the secrets of Lincoln's success as a communicator: his skill in the use of figurative language, of which metaphor is the most common example. We all use metaphors every day. We tell someone to stop beating around the bush; we say that we have too many irons in the fire; we express a desire to get to the heart of the matter; we worry about fitting square pegs in round holes; we see light at the end of the tunnel; and so on. Most of these examples are "dead" metaphors—that is, they are so commonplace that we often do not realize that they are metaphors, and they thus lose their power to evoke a vivid image in our minds. The best "live" metaphors are those that use a simple, concrete figure to illustrate a complex and perhaps abstract concept, thereby giving life and tangible meaning to something that might otherwise escape comprehension.

One of the first things that strikes a student of Lincoln's speeches and writings is his frequent use of images and figurative language. His speeches and letters abound with metaphors. Many of them are extraordinarily well chosen and apt; they have the persuasive power of concreteness and clarity. By contrast, Jefferson Davis's prose contains few metaphors or images of any kind. It is relentlessly literal. It is formal, precise, logical, but also stiff, cold, and abstract. Davis's wartime letters and speeches bristle with anger and bitterness toward Yankees and toward Davis's critics and adversaries within the Confederacy. But the few metaphors he used to illustrate his points are quite dead—references to sowing the seeds of discontent and thereby harvesting defeat, and the like.

To be sure, a number of Lincoln's metaphors were dead on arrival. He complained of dealing with people who had axes to grind; he said more than once that he wanted everyone to have a fair start in the race of life; he referred to the ship of state and its navigational problems during his presidency; and so on. But Lincoln could neatly turn a seemingly dead metaphor into a live one. In his first message to a special session of Congress that met three months after

5. *Aesop's Fables* are didactic stories credited to Aesop (620–560 B.C.E.), a slave who lived in ancient Greece; *The Pilgrim's Progress,* subtitled "from This World to That Which Is to Come," is a Christian allegory written by John Bunyan, published in 1678, and frequently reprinted with illustrations throughout the nineteenth century.

the war began, Lincoln critically reviewed the long and, as he put it, sophistic attempt by southern leaders to legitimize their actions by arguments for state sovereignty and the constitutional right of secession. "With rebellion thus sugar-coated," said the president, "they have been drugging the public mind of their section for more than thirty years," and this war was the result. Here Lincoln injected life into a rather tired metaphor, "sugar-coated," and used it to clinch his point in a luminous manner. This occasion also gave Lincoln an opportunity to define his philosophy of communication with the public. When the government printer set the message in type he objected to the phrase about sugar-coating the rebellion. "You have used an undignified expression in the message," the printer told the president. "A message to Congress [is] a different affair from a speech at a mass-meeting in Illinois. . . . The messages [become] a part of history, and should be written accordingly. . . . I would alter the structure of that, if I were you." Lincoln replied with a twinkle in his eye: "That word expresses precisely my idea, and I am not going to change it. The time will never come in this country when the people won't know exactly what *sugar-coated* means![6] Lincoln was right; people knew exactly what he meant then, and his metaphor retains its pithiness today.

Lincoln used a different but equally expressive metaphor to describe the threat of secession on another important occasion, his speech at Cooper Institute in New York in February 1860, a speech that gave him great visibility among eastern Republicans and helped launch him toward the presidential nomination three months later. This time he discussed southern warnings to the North of the dire consequences if a Republican president was elected. "In that supposed event," said Lincoln directing his words to the South, "you say, you will destroy the Union; and then, you say, the great crime of having destroyed it will be upon us! That is cool. A highwayman holds a pistol to my ear, and mutters through his teeth, 'Stand and deliver, or I shall kill you, and then you will be a murderer!'"[7]

10 No one could fail to understand Lincoln's point. And through his whole life one of his main concerns was that everyone understand precisely what he was saying. A colleague who praised this quality once asked Lincoln where his concern with exact clarity came from. "Among my earliest recollections," replied Lincoln, "I remember how, when a mere child, I used to get irritated when anybody talked to me in a way I could not understand. I don't think I ever got angry at anything else in my life. . . . I can remember going to my little bedroom, after hearing the neighbors talk of an evening with my father, and spending the night walking up and down, and trying to make out what was the exact meaning of some of their, to me, dark sayings. I could not sleep . . . when I got on such a hunt after an idea, until I had caught it; and when I thought I had

6. The metaphor can be found in Roy P. Basler, ed., *The Collected Works of Abraham Lincoln,* 9 vols. (New Brunswick, N.J., 1953–55), IV, 433; the exchange between Lincoln and the government printer was recounted in Francis B. Carpenter, *Six Months at the White House with Abraham Lincoln* (New York, 1866), 126–27 [McPherson's note].

7. *Collected Works of Lincoln*, III, 546–47 [McPherson's note].

got it, I was not satisfied . . . until I had put it in language plain enough, as I thought, for any boy I knew to comprehend. This was a kind of passion with me, and it has stuck by me."[8]

Many contemporaries testified to this Lincolnian passion, and to his genius for using everyday metaphors to achieve it. Francis Carpenter,[9] the artist who spent six months at the White House during 1864 painting a picture of Lincoln and his cabinet, noted that the president's "lightest as well as his most powerful thought almost invariably took on the form of a figure of speech, which drove the point *home*, and *clinched* it, as few abstract reasoners are able to do." Lincoln was also famous for telling stories. Many of them were parables intended to make or illustrate a point; and a parable is an extended metaphor. "It is not the story itself," Lincoln once said, "but its purpose, or effect, that interests me."[10]

When Lincoln said, "Now that reminds me of a story," his listeners knew that they could expect a parable. Take for example this story that Lincoln told soon after he had gotten rid of his controversial Secretary of War Simon Cameron.[11] Since some other cabinet members had also made enemies among one faction or another, a delegation of politicians called on the president and advised him that this might be a good time to make a wholesale change in the cabinet. Lincoln shook his head and replied, "This reminds me of a story. When I was a boy I knew a farmer named Joe Wilson who was proud of his prize chickens. But he started to lose some of them to raids by skunks on the henhouse. One night he heard a loud cackling from the chickens and crept out with his shotgun to find a half-dozen of the black and white critters running in and out of the shed. Thinking to clean out the whole tribe, he put a double charge in the gun and fired away. Somehow he hit only one, and the rest scampered off." At this point in the story, Lincoln would act it out by holding his nose and screwing up his face in a pained expression, while he continued. "The neighbors asked Joe why he didn't follow up the skunks and kill the rest. 'Blast it,' said Joe, 'it was eleven weeks before I got over killin' one. If you want any more skirmishing in that line you can just do it yourselves!' "[12]

Nobody could fail to get Lincoln's point. But not everyone approved of his habit of telling stories—some of which were a good bit more earthy than this one. Some people considered it undignified for the president of the United States to carry on in such a fashion. But Lincoln had a reply for them, as related

8. Carpenter, *Six Months at the White House*, 312–13 [McPherson's note].

9. Francis Bicknell Carpenter (1830–1900) painted the famous *First Reading of the Emancipation Proclamation of President Lincoln*, showing Lincoln surrounded by cabinet members.

10. *Ibid.*, 235–36; Paul M. Zall, *Abe Lincoln Laughing: Humorous Anecdotes from Original Sources by and about Abraham Lincoln* (Berkeley, 1982), 3 [McPherson's note].

11. Simon Cameron (1799–1889) served as secretary of war under Lincoln for less than a year (March 5, 1861–January 14, 1862).

12. Paraphrased from Carpenter, *Six Months at the White House*, 138–39 [McPherson's note].

by Chauncey Depew, a prominent lawyer, railroad president, and New York Republican leader. "I heard him tell a great many stories," said Depew, "many of which would not do exactly for the drawing room, but for the person he wished to reach, and the object he desired to accomplish with the individual, the story did more than any argument could have done. He once said to me, in reference to some sharp criticism which had been made upon his story-telling: . . . 'I have found in the course of a long experience that common people'—and, repeating it—'common people, take them as they run, are more easily influenced and informed through the medium of a broad illustration than in any other way, and as to what the hypercritical few may think, I don't care.' "[13]

This was something that Jefferson Davis never understood. He would never be caught telling a story about skunks to make a point about political timing and leadership. He did not have Lincoln's concern for reaching the common people or his knack for doing so. Lincoln was especially fond of animal metaphors and parables, as in the case of the skunk story. This derived in part from his own rural background. It also undoubtedly derived from the many boyhood hours he spent with *Aesop's Fables*. During one of those hours his cousin Dennis Hanks said to him: "Abe, them yarns is all lies." Lincoln looked up for a moment, and replied: "Mighty darn good lies, Denny."[14] And as an adult Lincoln knew that these "lies," these fables about animals, provided an excellent way to communicate with a people who were still close to their rural roots and understood the idioms of the forest and barnyard.

15 Some of Lincoln's most piquant animal metaphors occurred in his comments about or communications with commanding generals during the war. General George B. McClellan clamored repeatedly for reinforcements and understated his own strength while overstating that of the enemy. On one of these occasions Lincoln, who had already reinforced McClellan and knew that Union forces outnumbered the Confederates, said in exasperation that sending troops to McClellan was like shoveling flies across the barnyard—most of them never seemed to get there. Later on, when Joseph Hooker had become commander of the Army of the Potomac, Lincoln visited him at the front. Hooker boasted that he had built this force into "the finest army on the planet." He added that he hoped God Almighty would have mercy on Bobby Lee because he, Joe Hooker, would have none. Lincoln listened to this and commented that "the hen is the wisest of all the animal creation because she never cackles until the egg is laid."[15] And to be sure, it was Lee who laid the egg by beating Hooker decisively at Chancellorsville.[16] Lee then invaded the North in the campaign

13. Quoted in Herbert Joseph Edwards and John Erskine Hankins, *Lincoln the Writer: The Development of His Literary Style* (Orono, Maine, 1962), 26 [McPherson's note].

14. Keith Jennison, *The Humorous Mr. Lincoln* (New York, 1965), 26 [McPherson's note].

15. James M. McPherson, *Ordeal By Fire: The Civil War and Reconstruction* (New York, 1982), 319 [McPherson's note].

16. In the battle of Chancellorsville, fought from April 30 to May 6, 1863, General Robert E. Lee had an army half the size of Hooker's.

that led to Gettysburg. As Lee began to move north, Hooker proposed to cross the Rappahannock River and attack his rear guard. Lincoln disapproved with these words in a telegram to Hooker: "I would not take any risk of being entangled upon the river, like an ox jumped half over a fence, and liable to be torn by dogs, front and rear, without a fair chance to gore one way or kick the other." Napoleon himself could not have given better tactical advice or phrased it half so well. A week later, when the Confederate invasion force was strung out over nearly a hundred miles of Virginia roads, Lincoln telegraphed Hooker: "If the head of Lee's army is at Martinsburg and the tail of it on the Plank road between Fredericksburg and Chancellorsville, the animal must be very slim somewhere. Could you not break him?"[17] But Hooker seemed reluctant to fight Lee again, so Lincoln replaced him with George G. Meade who won the battle of Gettysburg but proved to be cautious and defensive afterward.

Thus in 1864 Lincoln brought to the East his most successful commander, Ulysses S. Grant, to become general in chief. In a private conference with Grant soon after he arrived in Washington, Lincoln referred to the military situation and told Grant he could best illustrate what he wanted to say by a story. There was once a great war among the animals, said the president, and one side had great difficulty finding a commander who had enough confidence in himself to fight. Finally they found a monkey, by the name of Jocko, who said he could command the army if his tail could be made a little longer. So the other animals found more tail and spliced it onto Jocko's. He looked at it admiringly, but said he thought he needed just a little more. So they found some more and spliced it on. This process was repeated many times until Jocko's tail was so long that when coiled it filled the whole room. Still he called for more tail, and they kept adding by coiling it around his shoulders and then around his whole body until he suffocated. Grant understood the point; unlike McClellan and other generals, he would not keep calling for more troops as an excuse for not fighting.[18]

Instead, the new general in chief worked out a plan for the two main Union armies, in Virginia and Georgia, to advance simultaneously against the two principal Confederate armies while smaller Union forces elsewhere pinned down Confederate detachments to prevent them from reinforcing the main armies. This was the kind of coordinated offensive that Lincoln had been urging on his generals for two years, and he was delighted finally to have a commander who would do it. Lincoln's expressive description of the auxiliary role of the smaller armies on the periphery was: "Those not skinning can hold a leg."[19] Grant liked this phrase so much that he used it in his own dispatches.

Later on, when Grant had Lee's army under siege at Petersburg while Sherman was marching through Georgia and South Carolina destroying everything in his path, Lincoln described Union strategy in this fashion: "Grant has the bear by the hind leg while Sherman takes off the hide." On another occasion

17. *Collected Works of Lincoln*, VI, 249, 273 [McPherson's note].

18. Zall, *Abe Lincoln Laughing,* 86 [McPherson's note].

19. Tyler Dennett, ed., *Lincoln and the Civil War in the Diaries and Letters of John Hay* (New York, 1939), 179 [McPherson's note].

Lincoln changed the metaphor in an official telegram to Grant: "I have seen your despatch expressing your unwillingness to break your hold where you are. Neither am I willing. Hold on with a bull-dog grip, and chew & choke, as much as possible."[20] In the end it was Grant's chewing and choking while Sherman took off the hide that won the war.

The principal cause of this war was slavery and one of its main consequences was the abolition of slavery. This peculiar institution gave rise to many Lincolnian metaphors, animal and otherwise. One of them was a metaphor of snakes and children that Lincoln used in several speeches during his tour of New England in the late winter of 1860. The central tenet of the Republican party's policy was to restrict the spread of slavery into new territories while pledging not to interfere with it in states where it already existed and was therefore protected by the Constitution. Lincoln considered slavery a moral wrong and a social evil. He hoped that the South would eventually take steps to end it voluntarily and peacefully. In the meantime, he said, we must not introduce this evil where it does not now exist. "If I saw a venomous snake crawling in the road," said Lincoln in illustration of his point, "any man would say I might seize the nearest stick and kill it; but if I found that snake in bed with my children, that would be another question. I might hurt the children more than the snake, and it might bite them. . . . But if there was a bed newly made up, to which the children were to be taken, and it was proposed to take a batch of young snakes and put them there with them, I take it no man would say there was any question how I ought to decide. . . . The new Territories are the newly made bed to which our children are to go, and it lies with the nation to say whether they shall have snakes mixed up with them or not."[21]

20 In our day of 30-second political spot commercials on television, this metaphor seems long and involved. But Lincoln's audiences understood it perfectly and appreciated it boisterously. The stenographic report of this speech at New Haven indicates prolonged applause, laughter, and cheering as he spun out the metaphor. A professor of rhetoric at Yale was so taken with Lincoln's speech that he followed him to another town to hear him speak again and then gave a lecture on Lincoln's techniques to his class. After Lincoln spoke at Norwich, Connecticut, the town's leading clergyman happened to travel on the same train with Lincoln next day and talked with him, praising his style, "especially your illustrations, which were romance and pathos, and fun and logic all welded together. That story about the snakes, for example . . . was at once queer and comical, and tragic and argumentative. It broke through all the barriers of a man's previous opinions and prejudices at a crash, and blew up the citadel of his false theories before he could know what had hurt him."[22]

Lincoln used a number of other metaphors to describe slavery, including that of a cancer which must be prevented from spreading lest it kill the body

20. Shelby Foote, *The Civil War: A Narrative. Red River to Appomattox* (New York, 1974), 864; *Collected Works of Lincoln,* VII, 499 [McPherson's note].

21. *Collected Works of Lincoln,* IV, 18 [McPherson's note].

22. Carpenter, *Six Months at the White House*, 310–11 [McPherson's note].

politic. His best-known slavery metaphor formed the central theme of the most famous speech he gave before the Civil War, the House Divided address in 1858. Here the house was a metaphor for the Union, which had been divided against itself by slavery and could not continue to be so divided forever without collapsing. Therefore the Republicans wanted to stop the further spread of slavery as a first step toward what Lincoln called its "ultimate extinction." This metaphor of a house divided became probably the single most important image of the relationship between slavery and the Union, and remains so today. It provided an instant mental picture of what Republicans stood for. It also helped provoke the South into secession when Lincoln was elected president, because no matter how much Lincoln professed his intention to tolerate slavery where it already existed, had not this Black Republican Yankee also called slavery a moral wrong and looked forward to its ultimate extinction?

In that same speech, Lincoln elaborated the house metaphor to illustrate another of the Republican party's favorite themes—that the Democrats were dominated by a "slave power conspiracy" to expand the institution of bondage over the whole country. "When we see a lot of framed timbers," said Lincoln, "different portions of which we know have been gotten out at different times and places by different workmen—Stephen, Franklin, Roger and James, for instance—and when we see these timbers joined together, and see they exactly make the frame of a house . . . we find it impossible not to *believe* that Stephen and Franklin and Roger and James all understood one another from the beginning, and all worked upon a common *plan* or *draft*."[23] The point of this rather elaborate metaphor seems obscure today. But Lincoln's audience knew exactly what he was talking about. The four men he named were Stephen Douglas, leader of the Democratic party, Franklin Pierce and James Buchanan, the previous and current presidents of the United States, both Democrats, and Roger Taney, chief justice of the Supreme Court, also a Democrat. The house for which each of them separately framed timbers, but with a secret understanding to make everything fit together, was a conspiracy to expand slavery. The timbers were the Kansas-Nebraska Act that repealed the Missouri Compromise and made possible the expansion of slavery north of latitude 36° 30' where it had previously been prohibited; the Dred Scott decision that legalized slavery in all territories; the Democratic pledge to acquire Cuba as a new slave territory; and other items.

After the Civil War broke out, Lincoln's main problem—next to winning the war—was what to do about slavery. And by the second year of war the slavery issue became bound up with the fate of the Union itself as Lincoln gradually came to the conclusion that he could not win the war without striking down slavery.

In his public and private communications concerning slavery during the war, Lincoln used a number of telling metaphors and similes. His first effort was to persuade the loyal border states to accept a policy of gradual, compensated emancipation. This proposal, he said in an appeal to the people of the

23. *Collected Works of Lincoln,* II, 465–66 [McPherson's note].

border states in May 1862, "makes common cause for a common object, casting no reproaches on any. It acts not the pharisee. The change it contemplates would come gently as the dews of heaven, not rending or wrecking anything. Will you not embrace it?" When the border states did not respond, Lincoln shifted from soft blandishment to blunt warning. In July 1862 he called border-state congressmen to the White House. By then the war had taken a harder turn. Republican congressmen had passed a bill to confiscate the property of rebels against the government, including their slave property. Lincoln himself had just about decided to issue an emancipation proclamation to apply to the Confederate states. The impact of these measures was bound to spill over into the Unionist border states. Slaves there were already emancipating themselves by running away to Union army lines. In these circumstances Lincoln now told border-state congressmen that his plan of gradual emancipation with compensation from the federal government was the best they could get. Otherwise, as the war continued to escalate in intensity, "the institution in your states will be extinguished by mere friction and abrasion."[24] The image of friction and abrasion was a most appropriate one, but it left the border-state congressmen unmoved. Most of them voted against Lincoln's offer—and three more years of war did extinguish slavery by friction and abrasion, in the border states as well as in the Confederate states.

25 After his unsuccessful appeal to the border states, Lincoln made up his mind to issue an emancipation proclamation. He used a variety of metaphors to explain his reasons for doing so. "It had got to midsummer 1862," the president later summarized. "Things had gone on from bad to worse, until I felt that we had reached the end of our rope on the plan of operations we had been pursuing; that we had about played our last card, and must change our tactics, or lose the game!"[25] Both metaphors here—the end of our rope and played our last card—are rather tired, almost dead, but nevertheless the context and the importance of the issue bring them alive and make them work. Lincoln liked the card-playing metaphor; in letters to conservatives who objected to the government's total-war policy of confiscation and emancipation, Lincoln wrote with some asperity that "this government cannot much longer play a game in which it stakes all, and its enemies stake nothing. . . . It may as well be understood, once for all, that I shall not surrender this game leaving any available card unplayed."[26]

Lincoln used other, more original and expressive metaphors at the same time, asking one conservative if he expected the government to wage this war "with elder-stalk squirts, charged with rose water." To a southern Unionist who had complained that emancipation of slaves owned by rebels would inevitably expand into emancipation of slaves owned by loyal Unionists as well, Lincoln replied with an angry letter denouncing those Unionists who did nothing to help the North win the war and who expected the government to take time out

24. *Ibid.*, V, 223, 318 [McPherson's note].

25. Carpenter, *Six Months at the White House*, 20–21 [McPherson's note].

26. *Collected Works of Lincoln*, V, 350, 343 [McPherson's note].

to protect their property while it was struggling for its very survival. The president spun out a metaphor of a ship in a storm to clinch the point. Do southern Unionists expect, he asked, "to touch neither a sail nor a pump, but to be merely passengers,—deadheads at that—to be carried snug and dry, throughout the storm, and safely landed right side up[?] Nay, more; even a mutineer is to go untouched lest these sacred passengers receive an accidental wound."[27]

When the constitutionality of the emancipation proclamation was questioned, Lincoln defended it not only by citing his military powers as commander in chief in time of war to seize enemy property, but he also used an apt metaphor to illustrate how a lesser constitutional right—of property in slaves—might have to be sacrificed in the interests of a greater constitutional duty—that of preserving the nation's life. "Often a limb must be amputated to save a life," Lincoln pointed out in this age without antibiotics when everyone knew of wounded soldiers who had lost an arm or leg to stop the spread of fatal infections. "The surgeon," Lincoln continued, "is solemnly bound to try to save both life and limb; but when the crisis comes, and the limb must be sacrificed as the only chance of saving the life, no honest man will hesitate. . . . In our case, the moment came when I felt that slavery must die that the nation might live!"[28]

One final metaphor that Lincoln used to illustrate a point about slavery is particularly striking. This one concerned the definition of liberty. The South professed to have seceded and gone to war in defense of its rights and liberties. The chief liberty that southerners believed to be threatened by the election of Lincoln was their right to own slaves. In a public speech in 1864 at Baltimore, in a border state where the frictions and abrasions of war had by then just about ground up slavery, Lincoln illustrated the paradox of conflicting definitions of liberty with an Aesopian fable. "The shepherd drives the wolf from the sheep's throat, for which the sheep thanks the shepherd as a *liberator,* while the wolf denounces him for the same act as a destroyer of liberty, especially as the sheep was a black one."[29] This image leaves no doubt which definition of liberty Lincoln subscribed to, or whose cause in this war—the northern shepherd's or the southern wolf's—was the nobler one. This passage comes as close to a lyrical expression of northern purpose as anything short of poetry could.* * *

It was when he defined the *purpose* of that war—the meaning of Union and why it was worth fighting for—that he soared to his greatest poetic eloquence. "Union" was something of an abstraction that required concrete symbols to make its meaning clear to the people who would have to risk their lives for it. The flag was the most important such symbol. But Lincoln wanted to go beyond the flag and strike deeper symbolic chords of patriotism. And in so doing he furnished some of the finest examples of poetic metaphor in our national literature.

27. *Ibid.*, V, 345–46 [McPherson's note].

28. *Ibid.*, VII, 281; Carpenter, *Six Months at the White House*, 76–77 [McPherson's note].

29. *Collected Works of Lincoln,* VII, 302 [McPherson's note].

30 In the peroration of his first inaugural address, Lincoln appealed to the South with an evocation of the symbols of a common history and shared memories as metaphors for the Union. "We must not be enemies," he declared. "Though passion may have strained, it must not break our bonds of affection. The mystic chords of memory, stretching from every battle-field, and patriot grave, to every living heart and hearthstone, all over this broad land, will yet swell the chorus of the Union, when again touched, as surely they will be, by the better angels of our nature."[30]

Having here summoned forth the past as a metaphor for Union, Lincoln invoked the future in the peroration of his message to Congress in December 1862. Now he added emancipation to Union as the legacy which the people of that generation would leave to their children's children. "Fellow-citizens, we cannot escape history. . . . The fiery trial through which we pass, will light us down, in honor or dishonor, to the latest generation. . . . We shall nobly save, or meanly lose, the last best, hope of earth. . . . In *giving* freedom to the *slave*, we *assure* freedom to the *free*."[31]

Lincoln put these symbolic themes of past, present, and future together in the most famous of his poems, the Gettysburg Address.[32] In this elegy there are no metaphors in a conventional sense; rather there are what two literary scholars have called "concealed" or "structural" metaphors—that is, metaphors that are built into the structure of the address in such a way that they are not visible but are essential to its meaning.[33] The Gettysburg Address contains three parallel sets of three images each that are intricately interwoven: past, present, future; continent, nation, battlefield; and birth, death, rebirth. Let us disaggregate these metaphors for purposes of analysis, even though in the process we destroy their poetic qualities. Four score and seven years in the *past* our fathers *conceived* and *brought forth* on this *continent* a *nation* that stood for something important in the world: the proposition that all men are created equal. *Now,* our generation faces a great war testing whether such a nation standing for such an ideal can survive. In dedicating the cemetery on this *battlefield*, the living must take inspiration to finish the task that those who lie buried here nobly advanced by giving the last full measure of their devotion. Life and death in this passage have a paradoxical but metaphorical relationship: men died that the nation might live, yet metaphorically the old Union also died, and with it died the institution of slavery. After these deaths, the nation must have a "new birth of freedom" so that the government of, by, and for the people that our fathers conceived and brought forth in the past "shall not perish from the earth" but be preserved as a legacy for the *future*.[34]

30. *Ibid.*, IV, 271 [McPherson's note].

31. *Ibid.*, V, 537 [McPherson's note].

32. For the "Gettysburg Address," see p. 485.

33. Edwards and Hankins, *Lincoln the Writer*, p. 89 [McPherson's note].

34. James Hurt, "All the Living and the Dead: Lincoln's Imagery," *American Literature* 52 (1980–81): 379 [McPherson's note].

Contrary to common impression, Lincoln's Gettysburg Address was not ignored or unappreciated at the time. Lincoln himself may have contributed to this legend, for he reportedly told his friend and bodyguard, Ward Hill Lamon, that the speech was "a flat failure." Mixing a live metaphor with a dead simile (as Lamon remembered it a quarter-century later), Lincoln said that the address "won't scour"; it "fell upon the audience like a wet blanket."[35] It is true that admiration for the Gettysburg Address grew over the years. But many auditors and readers immediately recognized its greatness; one of them was Edward Everett, the main orator of the day, who wrote to Lincoln the next day: "I should be glad, if I could flatter myself, that I came as near to the central idea of the occasion, in two hours, as you did in two minutes."[36]

Jefferson Davis did not—and probably could not—write anything like the Gettysburg Address, or like anything else in the way of images and metaphors that Lincoln used to illustrate his points both great and small. Communication and inspiration are two of the most important functions of a president in times of crisis. Thus perhaps David Potter's suggestion that if the Union and Confederacy had exchanged presidents the South might have won the Civil War does not seem so farfetched after all.

35. Ward Hill Lamon, *Recollections of Abraham Lincoln, 1847–1865* (Chicago, 1895), 171, 175 [McPherson's note].

36. *Collected Works of Lincoln*, VII, 24–25 [McPherson's note].

Questions

1. McPherson credits Abraham Lincoln with rhetorical power based on his use of vivid figurative language, including allegory, parable, fable, and metaphor. Choose three examples that McPherson offers, and explain why they are effective.

2. Can a president actually win a war by using effective metaphors, or is McPherson's title an over-simplification of his argument? What examples come closest to demonstrating that Lincoln's speech altered the course of the Civil War? What other examples of Lincoln's speech does McPherson offer—and why?

3. Early in his essay (paragraphs 1–5) McPherson compares the educations of Jefferson Davis and Abraham Lincoln, pointing out that the former had a superior education and yet was inferior as a speaker and writer. Does McPherson intend to denigrate formal education? What is the purpose of this compare/contrast section?

4. Read one of Lincoln's speeches either online or in *The Norton Reader* (see "Gettysburg Address," p. 486, or "Second Inaugural Address," pp. 813–815), and analyze its primary metaphors. Do the metaphors support McPherson's argument or require you to modify it? Write a brief analysis of the speech, including its rhetorical purpose and use of metaphor.

Hannah Arendt *Deportations from Western Europe*

At the Wannsee Conference,[1] Martin Luther, of the Foreign Office, warned of great difficulties in the Scandinavian countries, notably in Norway and Denmark. (Sweden was never occupied, and Finland, though in the war on the side of the Axis, was one country the Nazis never even approached on the Jewish question. This surprising exception of Finland, with some two thousand Jews, may have been due to Hitler's great esteem for the Finns, whom perhaps he did not want to subject to threats and humiliating blackmail.) Luther proposed postponing evacuations from Scandinavia for the time being, and as far as Denmark was concerned, this really went without saying, since the country retained its independent government, and was respected as a neutral state, until the fall of 1943, although it, along with Norway, had been invaded by the German Army in April, 1940. There existed no Fascist or Nazi movement in Denmark worth mentioning, and therefore no collaborators. In Norway, however, the Germans had been able to find enthusiastic supporters; indeed, Vidkun Quisling, leader of the pro-Nazi and anti-Semitic Norwegian party, gave his name to what later became known as a "quisling government." The bulk of Norway's seventeen hundred Jews were stateless, refugees from Germany; they were seized and interned in a few lightning operations in October and November, 1942. When Eichmann's[2] office ordered their deportation to Auschwitz, some of Quisling's own men resigned their government posts. This may not have come as a surprise to Mr. Luther and the Foreign Office, but what was much more serious, and certainly totally unexpected, was that Sweden immediately offered asylum, and even Swedish nationality, to all who were persecuted. Dr. Ernst von Weizsäcker, Undersecretary of State of the Foreign Office, who received the proposal, refused to discuss it, but the offer helped nevertheless. It is always relatively easy to get out of a country illegally, whereas it is nearly impossible to enter the place of refuge without permission and to dodge the immigration authorities. Hence, about nine hundred people, slightly more than half of the small Norwegian community, could be smuggled into Sweden.

It was in Denmark, however, that the Germans found out how fully justified the Foreign Office's apprehensions had been. The story of the Danish

Originally published in the "Reporter at Large" section of the New Yorker *(February–March 1963), Arendt's articles covered the trial of Adolf Eichmann, the Nazi lieutenant colonel responsible for transporting countless Jews to concentration camps. This selection comes from the book version of her account,* Eichmann in Jerusalem: A Report on the Banality of Evil *(1963), which, beyond reportage, raises larger questions about the crime of genocide and the nature of totalitarianism.*

1. A meeting of German officials on "the Jewish question."

2. Adolf Eichmann (1906–1962), German Nazi in charge of the execution of Jews (1942–45).

Jews is *sui generis*,[3] and the behavior of the Danish people and their government was unique among all the countries in Europe—whether occupied, or a partner of the Axis, or neutral and truly independent. One is tempted to recommend the story as required reading in political science for all students who wish to learn something about the enormous power potential inherent in non-violent action and in resistance to an opponent possessing vastly superior means of violence. To be sure, a few other countries in Europe lacked proper "understanding of the Jewish question," and actually a majority of them were opposed to "radical" and "final" solutions. Like Denmark, Sweden, Italy, and Bulgaria proved to be nearly immune to anti-Semitism, but of the three that were in the German sphere of influence, only the Danes dared speak out on the subject to their German masters. Italy and Bulgaria sabotaged German orders and indulged in a complicated game of double-dealing and double-crossing, saving their Jews by a tour de force of sheer ingenuity, but they never contested the policy as such. That was totally different from what the Danes did. When the Germans approached them rather cautiously about introducing the yellow badge, they were simply told that the King would be the first to wear it, and the Danish government officials were careful to point out that anti-Jewish measures of any sort would cause their own immediate resignation. It was decisive in this whole matter that the Germans did not even succeed in introducing the vitally important distinction between native Danes of Jewish origin, of whom there were about sixty-four hundred, and the fourteen hundred German Jewish refugees who had found asylum in the country prior to the war and who now had been declared stateless by the German government. This refusal must have surprised the Germans no end, since it appeared so "illogical" for a government to protect people to whom it had categorically denied naturalization and even permission to work. (Legally, the prewar situation of refugees in Denmark was not unlike that in France, except that the general corruption in the Third Republic's civil services enabled a few of them to obtain naturalization papers, through bribes or "connections," and most refugees in France could work illegally, without a permit. But Denmark, like Switzerland, was no country *pour se débrouiller.*)[4] The Danes, however, explained to the German officials that because the stateless refugees were no longer German citizens, the Nazis could not claim them without Danish assent. This was one of the few cases in which statelessness turned out to be an asset, although it was of course not statelessness per se that saved the Jews but, on the contrary, the fact that the Danish government had decided to protect them. Thus, none of the preparatory moves, so important for the bureaucracy of murder, could be carried out, and operations were postponed until the fall of 1943.

What happened then was truly amazing; compared with what took place in other European countries, everything went topsy-turvey. In August, 1943—after the German offensive in Russia had failed, the Afrika Korps had surrendered in Tunisia, and the Allies had invaded Italy—the Swedish government

3. Unique; literally, of its own kind (Latin).

4. For wangling—using bribery to circumvent bureaucratic regulations.

canceled its 1940 agreement with Germany which had permitted German troops the right to pass through the country. Thereupon, the Danish workers decided that they could help a bit in hurrying things up; riots broke out in Danish shipyards, where the dock workers refused to repair German ships and then went on strike. The German military commander proclaimed a state of emergency and imposed martial law, and Himmler[5] thought this was the right moment to tackle the Jewish question, whose "solution" was long overdue. What he did not reckon with was that—quite apart from Danish resistance—the German officials who had been living in the country for years were no longer the same. Not only did General von Hannecken, the military commander, refuse to put troops at the disposal of the Reich plenipotentiary, Dr. Werner Best; the special S.S. units (*Einsatzkommandos*) employed in Denmark very frequently objected to "the measures they were ordered to carry out by the central agencies"—according to Best's testimony of Nuremberg. And Best himself, an old Gestapo man and former legal adviser to Heydrich, author of a then famous book on the police, who had worked for the military government in Paris to the entire satisfaction of his superiors, could no longer be trusted, although it is doubtful that Berlin ever learned the extent of his unreliability. Still, it was clear from the beginning that things were not going well, and Eichmann's office sent one of its best men to Denmark—Rolf Günther, whom no one had ever accused of not possessing the required "ruthless toughness." Günther made no impression on his colleagues in Copenhagen, and now von Hannecken refused even to issue a decree requiring all Jews to report for work.

Best went to Berlin and obtained a promise that all Jews from Denmark would be sent to Theresienstadt[6] regardless of their category—a very important concession, from the Nazis' point of view. The night of October 1 was set for their seizure and immediate departure—ships were ready in the harbor—and since neither the Danes nor the Jews nor the German troops stationed in Denmark could be relied on to help, police units arrived from Germany for a door-to-door search. At the last moment, Best told them that they were not permitted to break into apartments, because the Danish police might then interfere, and they were not supposed to fight it out with the Danes. Hence they could seize only those Jews who voluntarily opened their doors. They found exactly 477 people, out of a total of more than 7,800, at home and willing to let them in. A few days before the date of doom, a German shipping agent, Georg F. Duckwitz, having probably been tipped off by Best himself, had revealed the whole plan to Danish government officials, who, in turn, had hurriedly informed the heads of the Jewish community. They, in marked contrast to Jewish leaders in other countries, had then communicated the news openly in the synagogues on the occasion of the New Year services. The Jews had just time enough to leave their apartments and go into hiding, which was very easy in Denmark, because,

5. Heinrich Himmler (1900–1945), high-ranking official in Nazi Germany who organized the SS (*Schutzstaffel*, Elite Guard) in 1929 and the Gestapo in 1933.

6. A camp for certain classes of prisoners who were supposed to receive special treatment.

in the words of the judgment, "all sections of the Danish people, from the King down to simple citizens," stood ready to receive them.

They might have remained in hiding until the end of the war if the Danes had not been blessed with Sweden as a neighbor. It seemed reasonable to ship the Jews to Sweden, and this was done with the help of the Danish fishing fleet. The cost of transportation for people without means—about a hundred dollars per person—was paid largely by wealthy Danish citizens, and that was perhaps the most astounding feat of all, since this was a time when Jews were paying for their own deportation, when the rich among them were paying fortunes for exit permits (in Holland, Slovakia, and, later, in Hungary) either by bribing the local authorities or by negotiating "legally" with the S.S., who accepted only hard currency and sold exit permits, in Holland, to the tune of five or ten thousand dollars per person. Even in places where Jews met with genuine sympathy and a sincere willingness to help, they had to pay for it, and the chances poor people had of escaping were nil.

It took the better part of October to ferry all the Jews across the five to fifteen miles of water that separates Denmark from Sweden. The Swedes received 5,919 refugees, of whom at least 1,000 were of German origin, 1,310 were half-Jews, and 686 were non-Jews married to Jews. (Almost half the Danish Jews seem to have remained in the country and survived the war in hiding.) The non-Danish Jews were better off than ever before; they all received permission to work. The few hundred Jews whom the German police had been able to arrest were shipped to Theresienstadt. They were old or poor people, who either had not received the news in time or had not been able to comprehend its meaning. In the ghetto, they enjoyed greater privileges than any other group because of the never-ending "fuss" made about them by Danish institutions and private persons. Forty-eight persons died, a figure that was not particularly high, in view of the average age of the group. When everything was over, it was the considered opinion of Eichmann that "for various reasons the action against the Jews in Denmark has been a failure," whereas the curious Dr. Best declared that "the objective of the operation was not to seize a great number of Jews but to clean Denmark of Jews, and this objective has now been achieved."

Politically and psychologically, the most interesting aspect of this incident is perhaps the role played by the German authorities in Denmark, their obvious sabotage of orders from Berlin. It is the only case we know of in which the Nazis met with *open* native resistance, and the result seems to have been that those exposed to it changed their minds. They themselves apparently no longer looked upon the extermination of a whole people as a matter of course. They had met resistance based on principle, and their "toughness" had melted like butter in the sun; they had even been able to show a few timid beginnings of genuine courage. That the ideal of "toughness," except, perhaps, for a few half-demented brutes, was nothing but a myth of self-deception, concealing a ruthless desire for conformity at any price, was clearly revealed at the Nuremberg Trials, where the defendants accused and betrayed each other and assured the world that they "had always been against it" or claimed, as Eichmann was to do, that their best qualities had been "abused" by their superiors. (In Jerusalem, he accused "those in power" of having abused his "obedience." "The subject of a good government is lucky, the subject of a bad government is unlucky. I had no luck.") The atmosphere had changed, and although most of them must have known that they were doomed, not a single one of them had the guts to defend the Nazi ideology. Werner Best claimed at Nuremberg that he had played a complicated double role and that it was thanks to him that the Danish officials had been warned of the impending catastrophe; documentary evidence showed, on the contrary, that he himself had proposed the Danish operation in Berlin, but he explained that this was all part of the game. He was extradited to Denmark and there condemned to death, but he appealed the sentence, with surprising results; because of "new evidence," his sentence was commuted to five years in prison, from which he was released soon afterward. He must have been able to prove to the satisfaction of the Danish court that he really had done his best.

QUESTIONS

1. Why do you think the Danes spoke out against anti-Semitism when other countries under German influence chose different methods of response or resistance? What details or hints does Arendt provide?

2. In paragraph 7, Arendt writes about Nazis who, when "met with open native resistance," changed their minds. What possible reasons does Arendt offer for this change? Are there other reasons you can think of for such change?

3. In paragraph 2, Arendt writes about "the enormous power potential inherent in nonviolent action and in resistance to an opponent possessing vastly superior means of violence." Research a more recent political situation in which you think a government or group of people could productively respond in a nonviolent manner and write about it.

ALBERTO MANGUEL The Library as Survival

I lived off art, I lived off love,
I never harmed a living soul. . . .
Why then, Lord,
Why do You reward me thus?

PUCCINI, *Tosca*, ACT II

LIKE THE DEAD SEA SCROLLS, like every book that has come down to us from the hands of distant readers, each of my books holds the history of its survival. From fire, water, the passage of time, neglectful readers and the hand of the censor, each of my books has escaped to tell me its story.

A few years ago, in a stand at the Berlin flea market, I found a thin black book bound in hard cloth covers that bore no inscription whatsoever. The title page, in fine Gothic lettering, declared it to be a *Gebet-Ordnung für den Jugend-gottesdienst in der jüdißchen Gemeinde zu Berlin (Sabbath-Nachmittag)* [Order of Prayer for Youth Service in the Jewish Community of Berlin (Sabbath-Evening)]. Among the prayers is included one "for our king, Wilhelm II, Kaiser of the German Realm" and his "Empress and Queen Auguste-Victoria." This was the eighth edition, printed by Julius Gittenfeld in Berlin in 1908, and had been bought at the bookstore of C. Boas Nachf. on Neue Friedrichstraße 69, "at the corner of Klosterstraße," a corner that no longer exists. There was no indication of the name of the owner.

A year before the book was printed, Germany had refused the armament limitations proposed by the Hague Peace Conference;[1] a few months later, the expropriation law decreed by Reichskanzler and Preußischer Ministerpräsident Fürst Bernhard von Bülow authorized further German settlements in Poland; in spite of hardly ever being used against Polish landowners, this law granted Germany early territorial rights that in turn, in June 1940, allowed the establishment of a concentration camp in Auschwitz.[2] The original owner of the *Gebet-Ordnung* probably bought or was given the book when he was thirteen years old, the age at which he would have his bar mitzvah and be permitted to join in synagogue prayers. If he survived the First World War, he would have been thirty-eight on the birth of the Third Reich in 1933; if he stayed on in

Published as a chapter of Manguel's book, The Library at Night *(2006), which interweaves stories of the author's personal library with accounts of great libraries throughout the world.*

1. There were two Hague Peace Conferences (1899 and 1907), officially called "Convention for the Pacific Settlement of International Disputes." Manguel refers to the 1907 conference, which began with the participants' resolve "to work for the maintenance of general peace" and "to promote by all the efforts in their power the friendly settlement of international disputes."

2. Auschwitz is the name for a network of concentration camps in Poland during the Nazi occupation.

The German prayer book printed in Berlin in 1908.

Berlin, it is likely that he was deported, like so many other Berlin Jews, to Poland.[3] Perhaps he had time to give the prayer book to someone before being taken away; perhaps he hid it, or left it behind with other books he had collected.

After the Nazis began their looting and destruction of the Jewish libraries, the librarian in charge of the Sholem Aleichem Library in Biala Podlaska decided to save the books by carting away, day after day, as many as he and a colleague could manage, even though he believed that very soon "there would be no readers left." After two weeks the holdings had been moved to a secret attic, where they were discovered by the historian Tuvia Borzykowski long after the war ended. Writing about the librarian's action, Borzykowski remarked that it was carried out "without any consideration as to whether anyone would ever need the saved books":[4] it was an act of rescuing memory per se. The universe, the ancient cabbalists believed, is not contingent on our reading it; only on the possibility of our reading it.

5 With the emblematic book-burning in a square on Unter den Linden, opposite the University of Berlin, on the evening of 10 May, 1933, books became a specific target of the Nazis. Less than five months after Hitler became chancellor,

3. Philip Friedman, *Roads to Extinction: Essays on the Holocaust*, ed. Ada June Friedman (New York and Philadelphia: The Jewish Publication Society of America, 1980) [Manguel's note].

4. Tuvia Borzykowski, *Ben kirot noflim*, trans. Mosheh Basok (Tel Aviv: Ha-Kibbuts ha-Meuhad, 1964) [Manguel's note].

the new propaganda minister of the Reich, Dr. Joseph Goebbels, declared that the public burning of books by authors such as Heinrich Mann, Stefan Zweig, Freud, Zola, Proust, Gide, Helen Keller and H.G. Wells allowed "the soul of the German people again to express itself. These flames not only illuminate the final end of an old era; they also light up the new."[5] The new era proscribed the sale or circulation of thousands of books, in either shops or libraries, as well as the publishing of new ones. Volumes commonly kept on sitting-room shelves because they were prestigious or entertaining became suddenly dangerous. Private holdings of the indexed books were prohibited; many books were confiscated and destroyed. Hundreds of Jewish libraries throughout Europe were burnt down, both personal collections and public treasure-houses. A Nazi correspondent gleefully reported the destruction of the famous library of the Lublin Yeshiva in 1939:

> For us it was a matter of special pride to destroy the Talmudic Academy, which was known as the greatest in Poland . . . We threw the huge talmudic library out of the building and carried the books to the market place, where we set fire to them. The fire lasted twenty hours. The Lublin Jews assembled around and wept bitterly, almost silencing us with their cries. We summoned the military band, and with joyful shouts the soldiers drowned out the sounds of the Jewish cries.[6]

At the same time, the Nazis decided to spare a number of books for commercial and archival purposes. In 1938 Alfred Rosenberg, one of the principal Nazi theoreticians, proposed that Jewish collections, including both secular and religious literature, should be preserved in an institute set up to study "the Jewish question." Two years later, the Institut zur Erforschung der Judenfrage was opened in Frankfurt am Main. To procure the necessary material, Hitler himself authorized Rosenberg to create a task force of expert German librarians, the notorious ERR, Einsatzstab Reichsleiter Rosenberg.[7] Among the confiscated collections incorporated to the institute were those of the rabbinical seminaries of Breslau and Vienna, the Hebraica and Judaica departments of the Frankfurt Municipal Library, the Collegio Rabbinico in Rome, the Societas Spinoziana in The Hague and the Spinoza Home in Rijnsburg, the Dutch publishing companies Querido, Pegazus and Fischer-Berman,[8] the International Institute of Social History in Amsterdam, Beth Maidrash Etz Hayim, the Israelitic seminary of Amsterdam, the Portuguese Israelitic seminary and the Rosenthaliana, Rabbi Moshe Pessah in Volos, the Strashun Library in Vilna (the grandson of the founder committed

5. William L. Shirer, *The Rise and Fall of the Third Reich: A History of Nazi Germany* (New York: Simon and Schuster, 1960) [Manguel's note].

6. Quoted in Friedman, "The Fate of the Jewish Book," in *Roads to Extinction* [Manguel's note].

7. Donald E. Collins and Herbert P. Rothfeder, "The Einsatzstab Reichsleiter Rosenberg and the Looting of Jewish and Masonic Libraries During World War II," in *Journal of Library History* 18, 1983 [Manguel's note].

8. Founded by the exiled son-in-law of Samuel Fischer, the celebrated German publisher [Manguel's note].

suicide when ordered to assist with the cataloguing), libraries in Hungary (a parallel institute on "the Jewish question" was set up in Budapest), libraries in Denmark and Norway and dozens of libraries in Poland (especially the great library of the Warsaw synagogue and of the Institute for Jewish Studies). From these vast hoards, Rosenberg's henchmen selected the books to be sent to his institute; all others were destroyed. In February 1943 the institute issued the following directives for the selection of library material: "all writings which deal with the history, culture, and nature of Judaism, as well as books written by Jewish authors in languages other than Hebrew and Yiddish, must be shipped to Frankfurt." But "books in Hebrew script (Hebrew or Yiddish) of recent date, later than the year 1800, may be turned to pulp; this applies also to prayer books, *Memorbücher*, and other religious works in the German language."[9] Regarding the many Torah scrolls, it was suggested that "perhaps the leather can be put to use for bookbinding." Miraculously, my prayer book escaped.

Seven months after these directives were given, in September 1943, the Nazis set up a "family camp" as an extension of the Auschwitz precinct, in the birch forest of Birkenau, which included a separate block, "number 31," built especially for children. It was designed to serve as proof to the world that Jews deported to the east were not being killed. In fact, they were allowed to live six months before being sent on to the same fate as the other deported victims. Eventually, having served its purpose as propaganda, the "family camp" was permanently closed.[10]

While it lasted, Block 31 housed up to five hundred children together with several prisoners appointed "counsellors," and in spite of the severe surveillance it possessed, against all expectations, a clandestine children's library. The library was minuscule; it consisted of eight books, which included H.G. Well's *A Short History of the World*,[11] a Russian school textbook and an analytical geometry text. Once or twice an inmate from another camp managed to smuggle in a new book, so that the number of holdings rose to nine or ten. At the end of each day, the books, together with other valuables such as medicines and bits of food, would be entrusted to one of the older girls, whose responsibility it was to hide them in a different place every night. Paradoxically, books that were banned throughout the Reich (those by H. G. Wells, for instance) were sometimes available in concentration camp libraries.

Although eight or ten books made up the physical collection of the Birkenau children's library, there were others that circulated through word of mouth

9. Quoted in Friedman, "The Fate of the Jewish Book," in *Roads to Extinction* [Manguel's note].

10. Nili Keren, "The Family Camp" in *Anatomy of the Auschwitz Death Camp*, ed. Yisrael Gutman and Michael Birnbaum (Bloomington, IN: Indiana University Press, 1994), quoted in David Shavit, *Hunger for the Printed Word: Books and Libraries in the Jewish Ghettos of Nazi-Occupied Europe* (Jefferson, NC, and London: McFarland & Co., 1997) [Manguel's note].

11. H. G. Wells's *A Short History of the World* (1922), like his earlier three-volume *Outline of History* (1920), approached history on an evolutionary, sociological, and anthropological basis.

Liberation of the survivors of the Birkenau Concentration Camp.

alone. Whenever they could escape surveillance, the counsellors would recite to the children books they had themselves learned by heart in earlier days, taking turns so that different counsellors "read" to different children every time; this rotation was known as "exchanging books in the library."[12]

It is almost impossible to imagine that under the unbearable conditions imposed by the Nazis, intellectual life could still continue. The historian Yitzhak Schipper, who was writing a book on the Khazars while he was an inmate of the Warsaw ghetto, was asked how he did his work without being able to sit and research in the appropriate libraries. "To write history," he answered, "you need a head, not an ass."[13]

There was even a continuation of the common, everyday routines of reading. This persistence adds to both the wonder and the horror: that in such nightmarish circumstances men and women would still read about Hugo's Jean Valjean and Tolstoy's Natasha,[14] would fill in request cards and pay fines 10

12. Shavit, *Hunger for the Printed Word* [Manguel's note].

13. *"Mensh, oyf tsu shraybn geshikhte darf men hobn a kop un nisht keyn tukhes,"* quoted in Yitzhak Zuckerman, "Antek," in *A Surplus of Memory: Chronicle of the Warsaw Ghetto Uprising*, trans. and ed. Barbara Harshav (Berkeley and Los Angeles: University of California Press, 1993) [Manguel's note].

14. Jean Valjean, a peasant character in Victor Hugo's *Les Misérables* (1862), struggles with the law for stealing bread during a period of famine; Natasha, the heroine of Leo Tolstoy's *War and Peace* (1869), suffers a romantic seduction and broken engagement.

for late returns, would discuss the merits of a modern author or follow once again the cadenced verses of Heine. Reading and its rituals became acts of resistance; as the Italian psychologist Andrea Devoto noted, "everything could be treated as resistance because everything was prohibited."[15]

In the concentration camp of Bergen-Belsen, a copy of Thomas Mann's *The Magic Mountain* was passed around among the inmates. One boy remembered the time he was allotted to hold the book in his hands as "one of the highlights of the day, when someone passed it to me. I went into a corner to be at peace and then I had an hour to read it."[16] Another young Polish victim, recalling the days of fear and discouragement, had this to say: "The book was my best friend, it never betrayed me; it comforted me in my despair; it told me that I was not alone."[17]

"Any victim demands allegiance," wrote Graham Greene,[18] who believed it was the writer's task to champion victims, to restore their visibility, to set up warnings that, by means of an inspired craft, will act as touchstones for something approaching understanding. The authors of the books on my shelves cannot have known who would read them, but the stories they tell foresee or imply or witness experiences that may not yet have taken place.

Because the victim's voice is all-important, oppressors often attempt to silence their victims: by literally cutting out their tongues, as in the case of the raped Philomela in Ovid, and Lavinia in *Titus Andronicus*, or by secreting them away, as the king does with Segismundo in Calderón's *Life Is a Dream*, or as Mr. Rochester does to his mad wife in *Jane Eyre*, or by simply denying their stories, as in the professorial addendum in Margaret Atwood's *The Handmaid's Tale*.[19] In real life, victims are "disappeared," locked up in a ghetto, sent to prison or a torture camp, denied credibility. The literature on my shelves tells over and over again the victim's story, from Job to Desdemona, from Goethe's Gretchen to Dante's Francesca,[20] not as mirror (the German surgeon Johann Paul Kremer warned in his Auschwitz diary, "By comparison, Dante's

15. Quoted in Shavit, *Hunger for the Printed Word* [Manguel's note].

16. Deborah Dwork, *Children with a Star: Jewish Youth in Nazi Europe* (New Haven, CT: Yale University Press, 1991) [Manguel's note].

17. Moshe Kligsberg, *"Die yidishe yugent-bavegnung in Polyn tsvishn beyde vel-milkhumes (a sotsyologishe shtudie),"* in *Studies in Polish Jewry 1919–1939*, ed. Joshua A. Fishman (New York: YIVO Institute for Jewish Research, 1974) [Manguel's note].

18. Graham Greene, *The Heart of the Matter* (London: Heinemann, 1948) [Manguel's note].

19. Manguel gives a historical sequence of plays and novels in which characters are prevented from testifying to their plight—William Shakespeare's *Titus Andronicus* (c. 1590); Pedro Calderón de la Barca's *Life Is a Dream* (1635); Charlotte Brontë's *Jane Eyre* (1847), and Margaret Atwood's *A Handmaid's Tale* (1985)—to show the abiding problem of victimization.

20. These characters, mostly women, suffer unmerited punishment or death: Job in the Hebrew Bible; Desdemona in Shakespeare's *Othello*; Gretchen in Johann Wolfgang von Goethe's *Faust*; Francesco in Dante's *Inferno*, the first part of *The Divine Comedy*.

inferno seems almost a comedy"[21]) but as metaphor. Most of these stories would have been found in the library of any educated German in the 1930s. What lessons were learned from those books is another matter.

In Western culture, the archetypal victim is the Trojan princess Polyxena. The daughter of Priam and Hecuba, she was supposed to marry Achilles but her brother Hector opposed the union. Achilles stole into the temple of Apollo to catch sight of her, but was discovered there and murdered. According to Ovid, after the destruction of Troy the spirit of Achilles appeared to the victorious Greeks as they were about to embark, and demanded that the princess be sacrificed to him. Accordingly, she was dragged to Achilles' tomb and killed by Achilles' son Neoptolemus. Polyxena is perfect for the victim's role: innocent of cause, innocent of blame, innocent of benefiting others with her death, a blank page haunting the reader with unanswered questions. Arguments, however specious, were made by the Greeks to find reasons for the ghost's request, to justify compliance with the sacrifice, to excuse the blade that Achilles' son drove into her bared breast. But no argument can convince us that Polyxena's death was merited. The essence of her victimhood—as of all victimhood—is injustice.

My library witnesses the injustice suffered by Polyxena, and all fictional phantoms who lend voice to countless ghosts who were once solid flesh. It does not clamour for revenge, another constant subject of our literatures. It argues that the strictures that define us as a social group must be constructive or cautionary, not willfully destructive, if they are to have any sane collective meaning—if the injury to a victim is to be seen as an injury to society as a whole, in recognition of our common humanity. Justice, as the English dictum has it, must not only be done, it must be seen to be done. Justice must not seek a private sense of satisfaction, but must publicly lend strength to society's self-healing impulse to learn. If justice takes place, there may be hope, even in the face of a seemingly capricious divinity.

A Hasidic legend collected by Martin Buber[22] tells of a man who took God to trial. In Vienna, a decree was issued that would make the difficult life of the Jews of Polish Galicia even harder. The man argued that God should not turn his people into victims, but should allow them to toil for him in freedom. A tribunal of rabbis agreed to consider the man's arguments, and considered, as was proper, that both plaintiff and defendant retire during their deliberations. "The plaintiff will wait outside; we cannot ask You, Lord of the Universe, to withdraw, since your glory is omnipresent. But we will not allow You to influence us." The rabbis deliberated in silence and with their eyes closed. Later that evening, they called the man and told him their verdict: his argument was just. At that very same hour, the decree was cancelled.[23]

21. Diary of Johann Paul Kremer (entry for 2 September, 1942), ed. Kazimierz Smolen, in *KL Auschwitz seen by the SS*, second edition (O'swieçim, 1978), quoted in Martin Gilbert, *The Holocaust* (London: William Collins, 1986) [Manguel's note].

22. Jewish philosopher (1878–1965), known for his religious existentialism.

23. Martin Buber, *Die Erzählungen der Chassidim* (Frankfurt am Main: Manesse Verlag, 1949) [Manguel's note].

In Polyxena's world, the outcome is less happy. God, the gods, the Devil, nature, the social system, the world, the *primum mobile*, refuses to acknowledge guilt or responsibility. My library repeats again and again the same question: Who makes Job endure so much pain and loss? Who is to blame for Winnie's sinking in Beckett's *Happy Days*? Who relentlessly destroys the life of Gervaise Macquart in Zola's *L'assommoir*? Who victimizes the protagonists of Rohinton Mistry's *A Fine Balance*?

Throughout history, those confronted with the unbearable account of the horrors they have committed—torturers, murderers, merciless wielders of power, shamelessly obedient bureaucrats—seldom answer the question "why?" Their impassive faces reject any admission of guilt, reflect nothing but a refusal to move from the past of their deeds into the consequences. Yet the books on my shelves can help me imagine their future. According to Victor Hugo, hell takes on different shapes for its different inhabitants: for Cain it has the face of Abel, for Nero that of Agrippina.[24] For Macbeth, hell bears the face of Banquo; for Medea, that of her children. Romain Gary dreamt of a certain Nazi officer condemned to the constant presence of the ghost of a murdered Jewish clown.[25]

If time flows endlessly, as the mysterious connections between my books suggest, repeating its themes and discoveries throughout the centuries, then every misdeed, every treason, every evil act will eventually find its true consequences. After the story has stopped, just beyond the threshold of my library, Carthage will rise again from the strewn Roman salt. Don Juan will confront the anguish of Doña Elvira. Brutus will look again on Caesar's ghost,[26] and every torturer will have to beg his victim's pardon in order to complete time's inevitable circle.

20 My library allows me this unrealizable hope. But for the victims, of course, no reasons, literary or other, can excuse or expiate the deeds of their torturers. Nick Caistor, in his introduction to the English edition of *Nunca más*, the report on the "disappeared" during the Argentinian military dictatorship, reminds us that the stories that ultimately reach us are but the reports of the survivors. "One can only speculate," says Caistor, "as to what accounts of atrocity the thousands of dead took with them to their unmarked graves."[27]

It is difficult to understand how people continue to carry out the human gestures of everyday life when life itself has become inhuman; how, in the midst of starving and sickness, beatings and slaughter, men and women persist in civilized rituals of courtesy and kindness, inventing stratagems of survival for the sake of a speck of something loved, for one book rescued out of thousands, one reader out of tens of thousands, for a voice that will echo until the

24. Victor Hugo, *Inferi: La légend des siècles* (Paris, 1883) [Manguel's note].

25. Romain Gary, *La danse de Genghis Cohn* (Paris: Gallimard, 1967) [Manguel's note].

26. The Romans not only defeated Carthage but then spread salt on the land to prevent future crops from growing; Doña Elvira is an abandoned woman in Lord Byron's *Don Juan* (1819–1824); Brutus assassinated Julius Caesar in 44 B.C.E.

27. *Nunca Más: A Report by Argentina's National Commission on Disappeared People* (London and Boston: Faber & Faber in association with Index on Censorship, 1986) [Manguel's note].

end of time the words of Job's servant: "And I only am escaped alone to tell thee." Throughout history, the victor's library stands as an emblem of power, repository of the official version, but the version that haunts us is the other, the version in the library of ashes. The victim's library, abandoned or destroyed, keeps on asking, "How were such acts possible?" My prayer book belongs to that questioning library.

After the European crusaders, following a forty-day siege, took the city of Jerusalem on 15 July, 1099, slaughtering the Muslim men, women and children and burning alive the entire Jewish community inside the locked synagogue, a handful of Arabs who had managed to escape arrived in Damascus, bringing with them the Koran of 'Uthman, one of the oldest existing copies of the holy book. They believed that their fate had been foretold in its pages (since God's word must necessarily hold all past, present and future events), and that, if only they had been able to read the text clearly, they would have known the outcome of their own narrative.[28] History was, for these readers, nothing but "the unfolding of God's will for the world."[29] As our libraries teach us, books can sometimes help us phrase our questions, but they do not necessarily enable us to decipher the answers. Through reported voices and imagined stories, books merely allow us to remember what we have never suffered and have never known. The suffering itself belongs only to the victims. Every reader is, in this sense, an outsider.

Emerging from hell, travelling against Lethe's current[30] towards recollection, Dante carries with him the sounds of the suffering souls, but also the knowledge that those souls are being punished for their own avowed sins.[31] The souls whose voices resound in our present are, unlike Dante's damned, blameless. They were tortured and killed for no other reason than their existence, and maybe not even that. Evil requires no reason. How can we contain, between the covers of a book, a useful representation of something that, in its very essence, refuses to be contained, whether in Mann's *The Magic Mountain* or in an ordinary prayer book? How can we, as readers, hope to hold in our hands the circle of the world and time, when the world will always exceed the

Portrait of Jacob Edelstein

28. Amin Maalouf, *Les croisades vues par les Arabes* (Paris: Editions Jean-Claude Lattès, 1983) [Manguel's note].

29. Carole Hillenbrand, *The Crusades: Islamic Perspectives* (New York: Routledge, 2000) [Manguel's note].

30. The river of forgetfulness in classical myth, used by Dante in the *Purgatorio*, the second part of *The Divine Comedy*.

31. Dante, *Inferno*, XXXIV, 129–132 [Manguel's note].

A sketch of the library in the Theresienstadt Ghetto, by Alfred Bergel, dated 27 November 1943.

margins of a page, and all we can witness is the moment defined by a paragraph or a verse, "choosing," as Blake said, "forms of worship from poetic tales"? And so we return to the question of whether a book, any book, can serve its impossible purpose.

Perhaps. One day in June 1944, Jacob Edelstein, former elder of the Theresienstadt ghetto, who had been taken to Birkenau, was in his barracks, wrapped in his ritual shawl, saying the morning prayers he had learned long ago from a book no doubt similar to my *Gebet-Ordnung*. He had only just begun when SS Lieutenant Franz Hoessler entered the barracks to take Edelstein away. A fellow prisoner, Yossl Rosensaft, recalled the scene a year later:

25 Suddenly the door burst open and Hoessler strutted in, accompanied by three SS men. He called out Jacob's name. Jacob did not move. Hoessler screamed: "I am waiting for you, hurry up!" Jacob turned round very slowly, faced Hoessler and said: "Of my last moments on this earth, allotted to me by the Almighty, I am the master, not you." Whereupon he turned back to face the wall and finished his prayers. He then folded his prayer shawl unhurriedly, handed it to one of the inmates and said to Hoessler: "I am now ready."[32]

32. Quoted in Gilbert, *The Holocaust* [Manguel's note].

Questions

1. Manguel begins each chapter with a variation on the title, "The Library as . . ." Explain his choice for this selection: "The Library as Survival." Given that he tells so many stories of death and destruction, why does he choose "survival" for his account of Jewish books and libraries in World War II?

2. Perhaps because he is writing about books, Manguel frequently alludes to literary stories and myths (paragraphs 10, 11, 13, 14, 19, 23). Choose one or two, do research on the story or myth, and explain how Manguel uses the allusion to make his argument about survival.

3. Can a book help a person survive? Consider the closing example of Jacob Edelstein or some example from your own experience. Speculate on possible answers to this question that Manguel raises.

4. Write a brief account of a book that has survived in your family's library or in your personal collection. Where did the book originate? Who has owned it? What trials or mishaps has it endured? Think of your account as a history of a book.

PHILIP GOUREVITCH *After the Genocide*

IN THE PROVINCE of Kibungo, in eastern Rwanda, in the swamp- and pasture-land near the Tanzanian border, there's a rocky hill called Nyarubuye with a church where many Tutsis were slaughtered in mid-April of 1994. A year after the killing I went to Nyarubuye with two Canadian military officers. We flew in a United Nations helicopter, traveling low over the hills in the morning mists, with the banana trees like green starbursts dense over the slopes. The uncut grass blew back as we dropped into the center of the parish schoolyard. A lone soldier materialized with his Kalashnikov, and shook our hands with stiff, shy formality. The Canadians presented the paperwork for our visit, and I stepped up into the open doorway of a classroom.

At least fifty mostly decomposed cadavers covered the floor, wadded in clothing, their belongings strewn about and smashed. Macheted skulls had rolled here and there.

The dead looked like pictures of the dead. They did not smell. They did not buzz with flies. They had been killed thirteen months earlier, and they hadn't been moved. Skin stuck here and there over the bones, many of which lay scattered away from the bodies, dismembered by the killers, or by scavengers—birds, dogs, bugs. The more complete figures looked a lot like people, which they were once. A woman in a cloth wrap printed with flowers lay near the door. Her fleshless hip bones were high and her legs slightly spread, and a child's skeleton extended between them. Her torso was hollowed out. Her ribs and spinal column poked through the rotting cloth. Her head was tipped back and her mouth was open: a strange image—half agony, half repose.

I had never been among the dead before. What to do? Look? Yes. I wanted to see them, I suppose; I had come to see them—the dead had been left unburied at Nyarubuye for memorial purposes—and there they were, so intimately exposed. I didn't need to see them. I already knew, and believed, what had happened in Rwanda. Yet looking at the buildings and the bodies, and hearing the silence of the place, with the grand Italianate basilica standing there deserted, and beds of exquisite, decadent, death-fertilized flowers blooming over the corpses, it was still strangely unimaginable. I mean one still had to imagine it.

5 Those dead Rwandans will be with me forever, I expect. That was why I had felt compelled to come to Nyarubuye: to be stuck with them—not with their experience, but with the experience of looking at them. They had been killed there, and they were dead there. What else could you really see at first? The Bible bloated with rain lying on top of one corpse or, littered about, the little woven wreaths of thatch which Rwandan women wear as crowns to

Gourevitch spent nine months in Rwanda chronicling the 1994 massacre of over 800,000 people. His resulting New Yorker *article, "After the Genocide" (December 18, 1995), was a finalist for the Overseas Press Club Award.*

balance the enormous loads they carry on their heads, and the water gourds, and the Converse tennis sneaker stuck somehow in a pelvis.

The soldier with the Kalashnikov—Sergeant Francis of the Rwandese Patriotic Army, a Tutsi whose parents had fled to Uganda with him when he was a boy, after similar but less extensive massacres in the early 1960s, and who had fought his way home in 1994 and found it like this—said that the dead in this room were mostly women who had been raped before being murdered. Sergeant Francis had high, rolling girlish hips, and he walked and stood with his butt stuck out behind him, an oddly purposeful posture, tipped forward, driven. He was, at once, candid and briskly official. His English had the punctilious clip of military drill, and after he told me what I was looking at I looked instead at my feet. The rusty head of a hatchet lay beside them in the dirt.

A few weeks earlier, in Bukavu, Zaire, in the giant market of a refugee camp that was home to many Rwandan Hutu militiamen, I had watched a man butchering a cow with a machete. He was quite expert at his work, taking big precise strokes that made a sharp hacking noise. The rallying cry to the killers during the genocide was "Do your work!" And I saw that it *was* work, this butchery; hard work. It took many hacks—two, three, four, five hard hacks—to chop through the cow's leg. How many hacks to dismember a person?

Considering the enormity of the task, it is tempting to play with theories of collective madness, mob mania, a fever of hatred erupted into a mass crime of passion, and to imagine the blind orgy of the mob, with each member killing one or two people. But at Nyarubuye, and at thousands of other sites in this tiny country, on the same days of a few months in 1994, hundreds of thousands of Hutus had worked as killers in regular shifts. There was always the next victim, and the next. What sustained them, beyond the frenzy of the first attack, through the plain physical exhaustion and mess of it?

The pygmy in Gikongoro said that humanity is part of nature and that we must go against nature to get along and have peace. But mass violence, too, must be organized; it does not occur aimlessly. Even mobs and riots have a design, and great and sustained destruction requires great ambition. It must be conceived as the means toward achieving a new order, and although the idea behind that new order may be criminal and objectively very stupid, it must also be compellingly simple and at the same time absolute. The ideology of genocide is all of those things, and in Rwanda it went by the bald name of Hutu Power. For those who set about systematically exterminating an entire people—even a fairly small and unresisting subpopulation of perhaps a million and a quarter men, women, and children, like the Tutsis in Rwanda—blood lust surely helps. But the engineers and perpetrators of a slaughter like the one just inside the door where I stood need not enjoy killing, and they may even find it unpleasant. What is required above all is that they want their victims dead. They have to want it so badly that they consider it a necessity.

So I still had much to imagine as I entered the classroom and stepped carefully between the remains. These dead and their killers had been neighbors, schoolmates, colleagues, sometimes friends, even in-laws. The dead had seen their killers training as militias in the weeks before the end, and it was 10 well known that they were training to kill Tutsis; it was announced on the radio, it was in the newspapers, people spoke of it openly. The week before the massacre at Nyarubuye, the killing began in Rwanda's capital, Kigali. Hutus who opposed the Hutu Power ideology were publicly denounced as "accomplices" of the Tutsis and were among the first to be killed as the extermination got under way. In Nyarubuye, when Tutsis asked the Hutu Power mayor how they might be spared, he suggested that they seek sanctuary at the church. They did, and a few days later the mayor came to kill them. He came at the head of a pack of soldiers, policemen, militiamen, and villagers; he gave out arms and orders to complete the job well. No more was required of the mayor, but he was also said to have killed a few Tutsis himself.

The killers killed all day at Nyarubuye. At night they cut the Achilles tendons of survivors and went off to feast behind the church, roasting cattle looted from their victims in big fires, and drinking beer. (Bottled beer, banana beer—Rwandans may not drink more beer than other Africans, but they drink prodigious quantities of it around the clock.) And, in the morning, still drunk after whatever sleep they could find beneath the cries of their prey, the killers at Nyarubuye went back and killed again. Day after day, minute to minute, Tutsi by Tutsi: all across Rwanda, they worked like that. "It was a process," Sergeant Francis said. I can see that it happened, I can be told how, and after nearly three years of looking around Rwanda and listening to Rwandans, I can tell you how, and I will. But the horror of it—the idiocy, the waste, the sheer wrongness—remains uncircumscribable.

Like Leontius, the young Athenian in Plato,[1] I presume that you are reading this because you desire a closer look, and that you, too, are properly disturbed by your curiosity. Perhaps, in examining this extremity with me, you hope for some understanding, some insight, some flicker of self-knowledge—a moral, or a lesson, or a clue about how to behave in this world: some such information. I don't discount the possibility, but when it comes to genocide, you already know right from wrong. The best reason I have come up with for looking closely into Rwanda's stories is that ignoring them makes me even more uncomfortable about existence and my place in it. The horror, as horror, interests me only insofar as a precise memory of the offense is necessary to understand its legacy.

The dead at Nyarubuye were, I'm afraid, beautiful. There was no getting around it. The skeleton is a beautiful thing. The randomness of the fallen forms, the strange tranquillity of their rude exposure, the skull here, the arm bent in some uninterpretable gesture there—these things were beautiful, and their beauty only added to the affront of the place. I couldn't settle on any meaningful response: revulsion, alarm, sorrow, grief, shame, incomprehension, sure, but nothing truly meaningful. I just looked, and I took photographs,

1. In Plato's *Republic*, Leontius struggles over whether to stare at corpses left by the executioner. He wants to look but knows that his curiosity is wrong. He gives in to the temptation.

because I wondered whether I could really see what I was seeing while I saw it, and I wanted also an excuse to look a bit more closely.

We went on through the first room and out the far side. There was another room and another and another and another. They were all full of bodies, and more bodies were scattered in the grass and there were stray skulls in the grass, which was thick and wonderfully green. Standing outside, I heard a crunch. The old Canadian colonel stumbled in front of me, and I saw, though he did not notice, that his foot had rolled on a skull and broken it. For the first time at Nyarubuye my feelings focused, and what I felt was a small but keen anger at this man. Then I heard another crunch, and felt a vibration underfoot. I had stepped on one, too.

Rwanda is spectacular to behold. Throughout its center, a winding succession of steep, tightly terraced slopes radiates out from small roadside settlements and solitary compounds. Gashes of red clay and black loam mark fresh hoe work; eucalyptus trees flash silver against brilliant green tea plantations; banana trees are everywhere. On the theme of hills, Rwanda produces countless variations: jagged rain forests, round-shouldered buttes, undulating moors, broad swells of savanna, volcanic peaks sharp as filed teeth. During the rainy season, the clouds are huge and low and fast, mists cling in highland hollows, lightning flickers through the nights, and by day the land is lustrous. After the rains, the skies lift, the terrain takes on a ragged look beneath the flat unvarying haze of the dry season, and in the savannas of the Akagera Park wildlife blackens the hills. 15

One day, when I was returning to Kigali from the south, the car mounted a rise between two winding valleys, the windshield filled with purple-bellied clouds, and I asked Joseph, the man who was giving me a ride, whether Rwandans realize what a beautiful country they have. "Beautiful?" he said. "You think so? After the things that happened here? The people aren't good. If the people were good, the country might be OK." Joseph told me that his brother and sister had been killed, and he made a soft hissing click with his tongue against his teeth. "The country is empty," he said. "Empty!"

It was not just the dead who were missing. The genocide had been brought to a halt by the Rwandese Patriotic Front, a rebel army led by Tutsi refugees from past persecutions, and as the RPF advanced through the country in the summer of 1994, some two million Hutus had fled into exile at the behest of the same leaders who had urged them to kill. Yet except in some rural areas in the south, where the desertion of Hutus had left nothing but bush to reclaim the fields around crumbling adobe houses, I, as a newcomer, could not see the emptiness that blinded Joseph to Rwanda's beauty. Yes, there were grenade-flattened buildings, burnt homesteads, shot-up facades, and mortar-pitted roads. But these were the ravages of war, not of genocide, and by the summer of 1995, most of the dead had been buried. Fifteen months earlier, Rwanda had been the most densely populated country in Africa. Now the work of the killers looked just as they had intended: invisible.

From time to time, mass graves were discovered and excavated, and the remains would be transferred to new, properly consecrated mass graves. Yet even the occasionally exposed bones, the conspicuous number of amputees and people with deforming scars, and the superabundance of packed orphanages could not be taken as evidence that what had happened to Rwanda was an attempt to eliminate a people. There were only people's stories.

"Every survivor wonders why he is alive," Abbé Modeste, a priest at the cathedral in Butare, Rwanda's second-largest city, told me. Abbé Modeste had hidden for weeks in his sacristy, eating communion wafers, before moving under the desk in his study, and finally into the rafters at the home of some neighboring nuns. The obvious explanation of his survival was that the RPF had come to the rescue. But the RPF didn't reach Butare till early July, and roughly seventy-five percent of the Tutsis in Rwanda had been killed by early May. In this regard, at least, the genocide had been entirely successful: to those who were targeted, it was not death but life that seemed an accident of fate.

20 "I had eighteen people killed at my house," said Etienne Niyonzima, a former businessman who had become a deputy in the National Assembly. "Everything was totally destroyed—a place of fifty-five meters by fifty meters. In my neighborhood they killed six hundred and forty-seven people. They tortured them, too. You had to see how they killed them. They had the number of everyone's house, and they went through with red paint and marked the homes of all the Tutsis and of the Hutu moderates. My wife was at a friend's, shot with two bullets. She is still alive, only"—he fell quiet for a moment—"she has no arms. The others with her were killed. The militia left her for dead. Her whole family of sixty-five in Gitarama were killed." Niyonzima was in hiding at the time. Only after he had been separated from his wife for three months did he learn that she and four of their children had survived. "Well," he said, "one son was cut in the head with a machete. I don't know where he went." His voice weakened, and caught. "He disappeared." Niyonzima clicked his tongue, and said, "But the others are still alive. Quite honestly, I don't understand at all how I was saved."

Laurent Nkongoli attributed his survival to "Providence, and also good neighbors, an old woman who said, 'Run away, we don't want to see your corpse.'" Nkongoli, a lawyer, who had become the vice president of the National Assembly after the genocide, was a robust man, with a taste for double-breasted suit jackets and lively ties, and he moved, as he spoke, with a brisk determination. But before taking his neighbor's advice, and fleeing Kigali in late April of 1994, he said, "I had accepted death. At a certain moment this happens. One hopes not to die cruelly, but one expects to die anyway. Not death by machete, one hopes, but with a bullet. If you were willing to pay for it, you could often ask for a bullet. Death was more or less normal, a resignation. You lose the will to fight. There were four thousand Tutsis killed here at Kacyiru"—a neighborhood of Kigali. "The soldiers brought them here, and told them to sit down because they were going to throw grenades. And they sat.

"Rwandan culture is a culture of fear," Nkongoli went on. "I remember what people said." He adopted a pipey voice, and his face took on a look of disgust: "'Just let us pray, then kill us,' or 'I don't want to die in the street, I want to die at home.'" He resumed his normal voice. "When you're that resigned and oppressed you're already dead. It shows the genocide was prepared for too long. I detest this fear. These victims of genocide had been psychologically prepared to expect death just for being Tutsi. They were being killed for so long that they were already dead."

I reminded Nkongoli that, for all his hatred of fear, he had himself accepted death before his neighbor urged him to run away. "Yes," he said. "I got tired in the genocide. You struggle so long, then you get tired."

Every Rwandan I spoke with seemed to have a favorite, unanswerable question. For Nkongoli, it was how so many Tutsis had allowed themselves to be killed. For François Xavier Nkurunziza, a Kigali lawyer, whose father was Hutu and whose mother and wife were Tutsi, the question was how so many Hutus had allowed themselves to kill. Nkurunziza had escaped death only by chance as he moved around the country from one hiding place to another, and he had lost many family members. "Conformity is very deep, very developed here," he told me. "In Rwandan history, everyone obeys authority. People revere power, and there isn't enough education. You take a poor, ignorant population, and give them arms, and say, 'It's yours. Kill.' They'll obey. The peasants, who were paid or forced to kill, were looking up to people of higher socio-economic standing to see how to behave. So the people of influence, or the big financiers, are often the big men in the genocide. They may think they didn't kill because they didn't take life with their own hands, but the people were looking to them for their orders. And, in Rwanda, an order can be given very quietly."

As I traveled around the country, collecting accounts of the killing, it almost seemed as if, with the machete, the *masu*—a club studded with nails—a few well-placed grenades, and a few bursts of automatic-rifle fire, the quiet orders of Hutu Power had made the neutron bomb[2] obsolete. 25

"Everyone was called to hunt the enemy," said Theodore Nyilinkwaya, a survivor of the massacres in his home village of Kimbogo, in the southwestern province of Cyangugu. "But let's say someone is reluctant. Say that guy comes with a stick. They tell him, 'No, get a *masu*.' So, OK, he does, and he runs along with the rest, but he doesn't kill. They say, 'Hey, he might denounce us later. He must kill. Everyone must help to kill at least one person.' So this person who is not a killer is made to do it. And the next day it's become a game for him. You don't need to keep pushing him."

At Nyarubuye, even the little terracotta votive statues in the sacristy had been methodically decapitated. "They were associated with Tutsis," Sergeant Francis explained.

2. A nuclear device designed to kill people while leaving structures relatively intact.

Questions

1. In paragraph 10 Gourevitch says, "So I still had much to imagine . . ." What does he believe he needs to imagine? And why do you think an act of imagination is so important to him?

2. As paragraph 12 opens, the pronouns change, moving from the first person "I" to the second person "you," in a direct address to us, the readers. What is the effect of this pronoun shift here? Can the author "presume" to know why we are reading?

3. This essay has two sections separated by a white space. How can the two sections be compared? What do they have in common? Do you note any parallels?

4. Plan and then write two different descriptive paragraphs that both lead up to highly significant last lines, as in Gourevitch's paragraphs 14 and 27. Consider what kinds of writing such conclusions might be best suited for.

HENRY DAVID THOREAU *The Battle of the Ants*

ONE DAY WHEN I went out to my wood-pile, or rather my pile of stumps, I observed two large ants, the one red, the other much larger, nearly half an inch long, and black, fiercely contending with one another. Having once got hold they never let go, but struggled and wrestled and rolled on the chips incessantly. Looking farther, I was surprised to find that the chips were covered with such combatants, that it was not a *duellum*, but a *bellum*, a war between two races of ants, the red always pitted against the black, and frequently two red ones to one black. The legions of these Myrmidons[1] covered all the hills and vales in my wood-yard, and the ground was already strewn with the dead and dying, both red and black. It was the only battle which I have ever witnessed, the only battle-field I ever trod while the battle was raging; internecine war; the red republicans on the one hand, and the black imperialists on the other. On every side they were engaged in deadly combat, yet without any noise that I could hear, and human soldiers never fought so resolutely. I watched a couple that were fast locked in each other's embraces, in a little sunny valley amid the chips, now at noonday prepared to fight till the sun went down, or life went out. The smaller red champion had fastened himself like a vice to his adversary's front, and through all the tumblings on that field never for an instant ceased to gnaw at one of his feelers near the root, having already caused the other to go by the board; while the stronger black one dashed him from side to side, and, as I saw on looking nearer, had already divested him of several of his members. They fought with more pertinacity than bulldogs. Neither manifested the least disposition to retreat. It was evident that their battle-cry was "Conquer or die." In the meanwhile there came along a single red ant on the hillside of this valley, evidently full of excitement, who either had despatched his foe, or had not yet taken part in the battle; probably the latter, for he had

From Thoreau's most famous book, Walden *(1854), an account of his life in a small cabin on Walden Pond, outside the village of Concord, Massachusetts.*

1. The reference is to the powerful soldiers of Achilles in Homer's *Iliad.*

lost none of his limbs; whose mother had charged him to return with his shield or upon it. Or perchance he was some Achilles, who had nourished his wrath apart, and had now come to avenge or rescue his Patroclus.[2] He saw this unequal combat from afar—for the blacks were nearly twice the size of the red—he drew near with rapid pace till he stood on his guard within half an inch of the combatants; then, watching his opportunity, he sprang upon the black warrior, and commenced his operations near the root of his right fore leg, leaving the foe to select among his own members; and so there were three united for life, as if a new kind of attraction had been invented which put all other locks and cements to shame. I should not have wondered by this time to find that they had their respective musical bands stationed on some eminent chip, and playing their national airs the while, to excite the slow and cheer the dying combatants. I was myself excited somewhat even as if they had been men. The more you think of it, the less the difference. And certainly there is not the fight recorded in Concord history, at least, if in the history of America, that will bear a moment's comparison with this, whether for the numbers engaged in it, or for the patriotism and heroism displayed. For numbers and for carnage it was an Austerlitz or Dresden.[3] Concord Fight! Two killed on the patriots' side, and Luther Blanchard wounded! Why here every ant was a Buttrick—"Fire! for God's sake fire!"—and thousands shared the fate of Davis and Hosmer. There was not one hireling there. I have no doubt that it was a principle they fought for, as much as our ancestors, and not to avoid a three-penny tax on their tea; and the results of this battle will be as important and memorable to those whom it concerns as those of the battle of Bunker Hill, at least.

I took up the chip on which the three I have particularly described were struggling, carried into my house, and placed it under a tumbler on my window-sill, in order to see the issue. Holding a microscope to the first-mentioned red ant, I saw that, though he was assiduously gnawing at the near fore leg of his enemy, having severed his remaining feeler, his own breast was all torn away, exposing what vitals he had there to the jaws of the black warrior, whose breast-plate was apparently too thick for him to pierce; and the dark carbuncles of the sufferer's eyes shone with ferocity such as war only could excite. They struggled half an hour longer under the tumbler, and when I looked again the black soldier had severed the heads of his foes from their bodies, and the still living heads were hanging on either side of him like ghastly trophies at his saddle-bow, still apparently as firmly fastened as ever, and he was endeavoring with feeble struggles, being without feelers, and with only the remnant of a leg, and I know not how many other wounds, to divest himself of them; which at length, after half

2. In the *Iliad*, the Greek warrior and friend whose death Achilles avenges. Achilles had previously refused to fight after a falling-out with Agamemnon, the leader of the Greek army.

3. Austerlitz and Dresden were bloody Napoleonic victories. The battles at Lexington and Concord, opening the American Revolution, took place on April 19, 1775; the names that follow are those of men who took part, and the words "Fire! for God's sake fire!" were those that, by popular account, started the war.

an hour more, he accomplished. I raised the glass, and he went off over the window-sill in that crippled state. Whether he finally survived that combat, and spent the remainder of his days in some Hôtel des Invalides,[4] I do not know; but I thought that his industry would not be worth much thereafter. I never learned which party was victorious, nor the cause of the war, but I felt for the rest of that day as if I had my feelings excited and harrowed by witnessing the struggle, the ferocity and carnage, of a human battle before my door.

Kirby and Spence tell us that the battles of ants have long been celebrated and the date of them recorded, though they say that Huber[5] is the only modern author who appears to have witnessed them. "Aeneas Sylvius," say they, "after giving a very circumstantial account of one contested with great obstinacy by a great and small species on the trunk of a pear tree," adds that " 'this action was fought in the pontificate of Eugenius the Fourth, in the presence of Nicholas Pistoriensis, an eminent lawyer, who related the whole history of the battle with the greatest fidelity.' A similar engagement between great and small ants is recorded by Olaus Magnus, in which the small ones, being victorious, are said to have buried the bodies of their own soldiers, but left those of their giant enemies a prey to the birds. This event happened previous to the expulsion of the tyrant Christiern the Second from Sweden." The battle which I witnessed took place in the Presidency of Polk, five years before the passage of Webster's Fugitive-Slave Bill.[6]

4. A French hospital for wounded soldiers and sailors.

5. Kirby and Spence were nineteenth-century American entomologists; François Huber (1750–1831) was a great Swiss entomologist.

6. Passed in 1851.

QUESTIONS

1. Thoreau uses the Latin word *bellum* to describe the battle of the ants and follows it with a reference to the Myrmidons, the soldiers of Achilles in Homer's *Iliad*. Locate additional examples of this kind of allusion. How does it work? Why does Thoreau compare the ants to Greek soldiers?

2. Ordinarily we speak of accounts of natural events as "natural history" and accounts of human events as "history." How does Thoreau, in this selection, blur the distinction? To what effect?

3. Look up a description of the behavior of ants in a book by one of the entomologists Thoreau refers to or in another scientific text. Compare the scientist's style with Thoreau's. Take another event in nature and describe it twice, once in scientific and once in allusive language. Or write an essay in which you describe and analyze the differences between the scientist's style and Thoreau's.

H. Bruce Franklin

From Realism to Virtual Reality: Images of America's Wars

The Industrial Revolution was only about one century old when modern technological warfare burst upon the world in the US Civil War. During that century human progress had already been manifested in the continually increasing deadliness and range of weapons, as well as in other potential military benefits of industrial capitalism. But it was the Civil War that actually demonstrated industrialism's ability to produce carnage and devastation on an unprecedented scale, thus foreshadowing a future more and more dominated by what we have come to call *technowar.* For the first time, immense armies had been transported by railroad, coordinated by telegraph, and equipped with an ever-evolving arsenal of mass-produced weapons designed by scientists and engineers. The new machines of war—such as the repeating rifle, the primitive machine gun, the submarine, and the steam-powered, ironclad warship—were being forged by other machines. Industrial organization was essential, therefore, not only in the factories where the technoweapons were manufactured but also on the battlefields and waters where these machines destroyed each other and slaughtered people.

Prior to the Civil War, visual images of America's wars were almost without exception expressions of romanticism and nationalism. Paintings, lithographs, woodcuts, and statues displayed a glorious saga of thrilling American heroism from the Revolution through the Mexican War. Drawing on their imagination, artists could picture action-filled scenes of heroic events, such as Emmanuel Leutze's 1851 painting *Washington Crossing the Delaware.*[1]

Literature, however, was the only art form capable of projecting the action of warfare as temporal flow and movement. Using words as a medium, writers had few limitations on how they chose to paint this action, and their visions had long covered a wide spectrum. One of the Civil War's most distinctively modern images was expressed by Herman Melville in his poem "A Utilitarian View of the Monitor's Fight." Melville sees the triumph of "plain mechanic power" placing war "Where War belongs— / Among the trades and artisans," depriving it of "passion": "all went on by crank, / Pivot, and screw, / And calculations of caloric." Since "warriors / Are now but operatives," he hopes that "War's made / Less grand than Peace."

From Georgia Review *(Spring 1994), a small circulation quarterly published by the University of Georgia.*

1. See especially Alan Trachtenberg, *Reading American Photographs: Images as History, Mathew Brady to Walker Evans* (New York: Hill and Wang, 1989), p. 74; and William A. Frassanito, *Antietam: The Photographic Legacy of America's Bloodiest Day* (New York: Charles Scribner's Sons, 1978), pp. 27–28 [Franklin's note].

Figure 1. "A Harvest of Death, Gettysburg," 1863 photograph by Timothy O'Sullivan.

The most profoundly deglamorizing images of that war, however, were produced not by literature but directly by technology itself. The industrial processes and scientific knowledge that created technowar had also brought forth a new means of perceiving its devastation. Industrial chemicals, manufactured metal plates, lenses, mirrors, bellows, and actuating mechanisms—all were essential to the new art and craft of photography. Thus the Civil War was the first truly modern war—both in how it was fought and in how it was imaged. The romantic images of warfare projected by earlier visual arts were now radically threatened by images of warfare introduced by photography.

5 Scores of commercial photographers, seeking authenticity and profits, followed the Union armies into battle. Although evidently more than a million photographs of the Civil War were taken, hardly any show actual combat or other exciting action typical of the earlier paintings.[2] The photographers' need to stay close to their cumbersome horse-drawn laboratory wagons usually kept them from the thick of battle, and the collodion wet-plate process, which demanded long exposures, forced them to focus on scenes of stillness rather than action. Among all human subjects, those who stayed most perfectly still for the camera were the dead. Hence Civil War photography, dominated by images of death, inaugurated a grim, profoundly antiromantic realism.

Perhaps the most widely reproduced photo from the war, Timothy O'Sullivan's "A Harvest of Death, Gettysburg," contains numerous corpses of Confederate soldiers, rotting after lying two days in the rain (see *Figure 1*). Stripped of their shoes and with their pockets turned inside out, the bodies

2. William C. Davis, "Finding the Hidden Images of the Civil War," *Civil War Times Illustrated*, 21 (1982, #2), 9 [Franklin's note].

stretch into the distance beyond the central corpse, whose mouth gapes gruesomely.

The first of such new images of war were displayed for sale to the public by Mathew Brady at his Broadway gallery in October 1862. Brady entitled his show "The Dead of Antietam." *The New York Times* responded in an awed editorial:

> The living that throng Broadway care little perhaps for the Dead at Antietam, but we fancy they would jostle less carelessly down the great thoroughfare . . . were a few dripping bodies, fresh from the field, laid along the pavement. . . .
>
> Mr. Brady has done something to bring home to us the terrible reality and earnestness of war. If he has not brought bodies and laid them in our dooryards and along the streets, he has done something very like it. At the door of his gallery hangs a little placard, "The Dead of Antietam." Crowds of people are constantly going up the stairs; follow them, and you find them bending over photographic views of that fearful battle-field, taken immediately after the action. . . . You will see hushed, reverent groups standing around these weird copies of carnage, bending down to look in the pale faces of the dead, chained by the strange spell that dwells in dead men's eyes.[3]

Oliver Wendell Holmes went further in explicating the meaning of the exhibition, which gives "some conception of what a repulsive, brutal, sickening, hideous thing it is, this dashing together of two frantic mobs to which we give the name of armies." He continues: "Let him who wishes to know what war is look at this series of illustrations. These wrecks of manhood thrown together in careless heaps or ranged in ghastly rows for burial were alive but yesterday. . . ."[4]

Nevertheless, three decades after the end of the Civil War the surging forces of militarism and imperialism were reimaging the conflict as a glorious episode in America's history. The disgust, shame, guilt, and deep national divisions that had followed this war—just like those a century later that followed the Vietnam War—were being buried under an avalanche of jingoist culture, the equivalent of contemporary Ramboism, even down to the cult of muscularism promulgated by Teddy Roosevelt.

It was in this historical context that Stephen Crane used realism, then flourishing as a literary mode, to assault just such treacherous views of war. Although *The Red Badge of Courage* is generally viewed as the great classic novel of the Civil War, it can be read much more meaningfully as Crane's response to the romantic militarism that was attempting to erase from the nation's memory the horrifying lessons taught by the war's realities.[5] Crane,

3. "Brady's Photographs: Pictures of the Dead at Antietam," *The New York Times*, 20 October 1862 [Franklin's note].

4. Oliver Wendell Holmes's "Doings of the Sunbeam," *Atlantic Monthly* (July 1863), p. 12 [Franklin's note]. Holmes (1809–1894) was an American physician, writer, and frequent contributor to the *Atlantic Monthly*, an American magazine founded in 1857 and still famous for its coverage of politics and the arts.

5. This concept is developed most effectively by Amy Kaplan in "The Spectacle of War in Crane's Revision of History," *New Essays on "The Red Badge of Courage,"* ed. Lee

not subject to the technological limitations of the slow black-and-white photographs that had brought home glimpses of the war's sordid repulsiveness, was able to image the animal frenzy that masqueraded as heroic combat and even to add color and tiny moving details to his pictures of the dead:

> The corpse was dressed in a uniform that once had been blue but was now faded to a melancholy shade of green. The eyes, staring at the youth, had changed to the dull hue to be seen on the side of a dead fish. The mouth was opened. Its red had changed to an appalling yellow. Over the grey skin of the face ran little ants. One was trundling some sort of a bundle along the upper lip.[6]

10 Other literary reactions to the new militarism looked even further backward to project images of a future dominated by war. Melville's *Billy Budd,* completed in 1891, envisions this triumph of violence in the aftermath of the American Revolution on the (aptly named) British warship HMS *Bellipotent,* where the best of humanity is hanged to death by the logic of war, the common people are turned into automatons "dispersed to the places allotted them when not at the guns," and the final image is of a sterile, lifeless, inorganic mass of "smooth white marble."[7]

In *A Connecticut Yankee in King Arthur's Court* (1889), Mark Twain recapitulates the development of industrial capitalism and extrapolates its future in a vision of apocalyptic technowar. Hank Morgan and his young disciples have run "secret wires" to dynamite deposits under all their "vast factories, mills, workshops, magazines, etc." and have connected them to a single command button so that nothing can stop them "when we want to blow up our civilization." When Hank does initiate this instantaneous push-button war, "In that explosion all our noble civilization-factories went up in the air and disappeared from the earth." Beyond an electrified fence, the technowarriors have prepared a forty-foot-wide belt of land mines. The first wave of thousands of knights triggers a twentieth-century-style explosion: "As to destruction of life, it was amazing. Moreover, it was beyond estimate. Of course we could not *count* the dead, because they did not exist as individuals, but merely as homogeneous protoplasm, with alloys of iron and buttons."

After Hank and his boys trap the rest of the feudal army inside their electric fence, Hank electrocutes the first batch, a flood is released on the survivors, and the boys man machine guns that "vomit death" into their ranks: "Within ten short minutes after we had opened fire, armed resistance was

Clark Mitchell (Cambridge: Cambridge University Press, 1986), pp. 77–108 [Franklin's note].

6. Stephen Crane, *"The Red Badge of Courage": An Episode in the American Civil War,* ed. Henry Binder (New York: Avon Books, 1983), p. 37 [Franklin's note].

7. H. Bruce Franklin, "From Empire to Empire: *Billy Budd, Sailor,"* in *Herman Melville: Reassessments,* ed. A. Robert Lee (London: Vision Press, 1984), pp. 199–216 [Franklin's note].

totally annihilated. . . . Twenty-five thousand men lay dead around us."[8] That number of dead, it is worth noting, matches exactly the total casualties in America's costliest day of war, the battle of Antietam, and thus recalls Brady's exhibition, "The Dead of Antietam." Twain's vision is even more horrific, for the victors themselves are conquered by "the poisonous air bred by those dead thousands." All that remains of this first experiment in industrialized warfare is a desolate landscape pockmarked by craters and covered with unburied, rotting corpses.

Twain's vision of the future implicit in industrial capitalism began to materialize in the First World War, when armies slaughtered each other on an unprecedented scale, sections of Europe were turned into a wasteland, and weapons of mass destruction first seemed capable of actually destroying civilization. Meanwhile, the scientific, engineering, and organizational progress that had produced the modern machine gun, long-range artillery, poison gas, and fleets of submarines and warplanes had also created a new image-making technology that broke through the limits of still photography. Just as the Civil War was the first to be extensively photographed, the "War to End All Wars" was the first to be extensively imaged in motion pictures.[9]

World War I, of course, generated millions of still photographs, many showing scenes at least as ghastly as the corpse-strewn battlefields of the Civil War, and now there was also authentic documentary film of live action. But for various reasons the most influential photographic images from World War I, though realistic in appearance, displayed not reality but fantasy. Filmmakers who wished to record actual combat were severely restricted by the various governments and military authorities. At the same time, powerful forces were making a historic discovery: the tremendous potential of movies for propaganda and for profits. This was the dawn of twentieth-century image-making.

15 In the United States the most important photographic images were movies designed to inflame the nation, first to enter the war and then to support it. Probably the most influential was *The Battle Cry of Peace*, a 1915 smash hit that played a crucial role in rousing the public against Germany by showing realistic scenes of the invasion and devastation of America by a rapacious Germanic army. Once the US entered the war, the American public got to view an endless series of feature movies, such as *To Hell with the Kaiser; The Kaiser, the Beast of Berlin*; and *The Claws of the Hun*—each outdoing its predecessors in picturing German bestiality. Erich von Stroheim's career began with his portrayal of the archetypal sadistic German officer in films like *The Unbeliever* and *Heart of Humanity*, where in his lust to rape innocent young women he murders anyone who gets in the way—even the crying baby of one intended

8. Mark Twain, *A Connecticut Yankee in King Arthur's Court*, ed. Bernard L. Stein (Berkeley: University of California Press, 1979), pp. 466–86 [Franklin's note].

9. During the Spanish-American War, the Edison Company had recorded some motion pictures of the embarking troops but was unable to obtain any battle footage. Later the company re-created battle scenes in a mountain reservation near Edison's headquarters in Essex County, New Jersey. See "Historian Remembers the Maine, Spain-America Conflict," Newark (NJ) *Star Ledger* 11 February 1992 [Franklin's note].

victim. This genre is surveyed by Larry Wayne Ward, who describes the 1918 Warner Brothers hit *My Four Years in Germany*, which opens with a title card telling the audience they are seeing "Fact Not Fiction":

> After the brutal conquest of Belgium, German troops are shown slaughtering innocent refugees and tormenting prisoners of war. Near the end of the film one of the German officials boasts that "America Won't Fight," a title which dissolves into newsreel footage of President Wilson and marching American soldiers. Soon American troops are seen fighting their way across the European battlefields. As he bayonets another German soldier, a young American doughboy turns to his companions and says, "I promised Dad I'd get six."[10]

Before the end of World War I, the motion picture had already proved to be a more effective vehicle for romanticizing and popularizing war than the antebellum school of heroic painting that had been partly debunked by Civil War photography. Indeed, the audiences that thronged to *My Four Years in Germany* frequently burned effigies of the kaiser outside the theaters and in some cases turned into angry mobs that had to be dispersed by police.

To restore the glamour of preindustrial war, however, it would take more than glorifying the men fighting on the ground or even the aviators supposedly dueling like medieval knights high above the battlefield. What was necessary to reverse Melville's "utilitarian" view of industrial warfare was the romanticizing of machines of war themselves.

The airplane was potentially an ideal vehicle for this romance. But photographic technology had to develop a bit further to bring home the thrills generated by destruction from the sky, because it needed to be seen *from* the sky, not from the ground where its reality was anything but glamorous. The central figure in America's romance with warplanes (as I have discussed at length elsewhere)[11] was Billy Mitchell, who also showed America and the world how to integrate media imagery with technowar.

In 1921, Mitchell staged a historic event by using bombers to sink captured German warships and turning the action into a media bonanza. His goal was to hit the American public with immediate, nationwide images of the airplane's triumph over the warship. The audacity of this enterprise in 1921 was remarkable. There were no satellites to relay images, and no television; in fact, the first experimental radio broadcast station had begun operation only in November 1920.

Back in 1919, Mitchell had given the young photographer George Goddard his own laboratory where, with assistance from Eastman Kodak, Goddard developed high-resolution aerial photography. As soon as Mitchell won the opportunity to bomb the German ships, he put Goddard in command of a key unit: a

10. Larry Wayne Ward, *The Motion Picture Goes to War: The U.S. Government Film Effort during World War I* (Ann Arbor: UMI Research Press, 1985), pp. 55–56 [Franklin's note].

11. H. Bruce Franklin, *War Stars: The Superweapon and the American Imagination* (New York: Oxford University Press, 1988), chapter 15 [Franklin's note].

team of aerial photographers provided with eighteen airplanes and a dirigible. Mitchell's instructions were unambiguous: "I want newsreels of those sinking ships in every theater in the country, just as soon as we can get 'em there." This demanded more than mere picture taking. With his flair for public relations, Mitchell explained to Goddard: "Most of all I need you to handle the newsreel and movie people. They're temperamental, and we've got to get all we can out of them."[12] Goddard had to solve unprecedented logistical problems, flying the film first to Langley Field and thence to Bolling Field for pickup by the newsreel people who would take it to New York for development and national distribution. The sinking of each ship, artfully filmed by relays of Goddard's planes, was screened the very next day in big-city theaters across the country.

This spectacular media coup implanted potent images of the warplane in the public mind, and Mitchell himself became an overnight national hero as millions watched the death of great warships on newsreel screens. Mitchell was a prophet. The battleship was doomed. The airplane would rule the world.

America was now much closer to the 1990 media conception of the Gulf War than to Melville's "Utilitarian View of the Monitor's Fight." Melville's vision of technowar as lacking "passion" was becoming antiquated, for what could be more thrilling—even erotic—than aerial war machines? The evidence is strewn throughout modern America: the warplane models assembled by millions of boys and young men during World War II; the thousands of warplane magazines and books filled with glossy photographs that some find as stimulating as those in "men's" magazines; and Hollywood's own warplane romances, such as *Top Gun*—one of the most popular movies of the 1980's—or *Strategic Air Command*, in which Jimmy Stewart's response to his first sight of a B-47 nuclear bomber is, "She's the most beautiful thing I've ever seen in my life."

One of the warplane's great advantages as a vehicle of romance is its distance from its victims. From the aircraft's perspective, even the most grotesque slaughter it inflicts is sufficiently removed so that it can be imaged aesthetically. The aesthetics of aerial bombing in World War II were prefigured in 1937 by Mussolini's son Vittorio, whose ecstasy about his own experience bombing undefended Ethiopian villages was expressed in his image of his victims "bursting out like a rose after I had landed a bomb in the middle of them."[13] These aesthetics were consummated at the end of World War II by the mushroom clouds that rose over Hiroshima and Nagasaki.

Bracketed by these images, the aerial bombing of World War II has been most insightfully explored in *Catch-22* by Joseph Heller, a bombardier with sixty combat missions. The novel envisions the political and cultural triumph of fascism through the very means used to defeat it militarily. The turning point

12. Burke Davis, *The Billy Mitchell Affair* (New York: Random House, 1967), p. 16 [Franklin's note].

13. *Voli sulle ambe* (Florence, 1937), a book Vittorio Mussolini wrote to convince Italian boys they should all try war, "the most beautiful and complete of all sports." Quoted by Denis Mack Smith, *Mussolini's Roman Empire* (New York: Viking, 1976), p. 75 [Franklin's note].

in Heller's work is the annihilation of an insignificant antifascist Italian mountain village, an event which allows fascist forces, embodied by US Air Corps officers, to gain total control.[14] The sole purpose of the American bombing of the village is image-making. The novel's General Peckem privately admits that bombing this "tiny undefended village, reducing the whole community to rubble" is "entirely unnecessary," but it will allow him to extend his power over the bombing squadrons. He has convinced them that he will measure their success by "a neat aerial photograph" of their *bomb pattern*—"a term I dreamed up," he confides, that "means nothing." The briefing officer tells the crews:

> Colonel Cathcart wants to come out of this mission with a good clean aerial photograph he won't be ashamed to send through channels. Don't forget that General Peckem will be here for the full briefing, and you know how he feels about bomb patterns.[15]

25 Pictures of bomb patterns were not, of course, the most influential American photographic image-making in World War II. The still photos published in *Life* alone could be the subject of several dissertations, and World War II feature movies about strategic bombing have been discussed at length by myself and many others. Indeed, in 1945 one might have wondered how the camera could possibly play a more important role in war.

The answer came in Vietnam, the first war to be televised directly into tens of millions of homes.[16] Television's glimpses of the war's reality were so horrendous and so influential that these images have been scapegoated as one of the main causes of the United States' defeat. Indeed, the Civil War still photographs of corpses seem innocuous when compared to the Vietnam War's on-screen killings, as well as live-action footage of the bulldozing of human carcasses into mass graves, the napalming of children, and the ravaging of villages by American soldiers.

As appalling as these public images were, however, few had meanings as loathsome as the pictures that serve as the central metaphor of Stephen Wright's novel *Meditations in Green.* The hero of the novel has the job that the author had in Vietnam: he works as a photoanalyst in an intelligence unit whose mission is to aid the torture and assassination campaign known as Operation Phoenix, the ecocidal defoliation campaign originally designated Operation Hades, and the genocidal bombing. His official job as "image interpreter" is to scrutinize reconnaissance films to find evidence of life so that it can be eliminated. Not

14. For extended analyses of the significance of this event, see Franklin, *War Stars,* pp. 123–27, and Clinton Burhans Jr., "Spindrift and the Sea: Structural Patterns and Unifying Elements in *Catch-22,*" *Twentieth Century Literature,* 19 (1973), 239–50 [Franklin's note].

15. Joseph Heller, *Catch-22* (New York: Dell, 1962), pp. 334–37 [Franklin's note].

16. When the Korean War began in mid-1950, there were fewer than ten million television sets in the United States. Americans' principal visual images of that war came from newsreels shown before feature films in movie theaters and from still photos in magazines [Franklin's note].

just humans are targets to be erased by bombing; trees themselves become the enemy. Anyone in the unit who has qualms about such genocide and ecocide is defined—in a revealing term—as a "smudge," thus becoming another target for elimination. The perfect image, it is implied, should have nothing left of the human or the natural. From the air, the unit's own base looks like "a concentration camp or a movie lot." The climax of the novel comes when the base is devastated by an enemy attack intercut with scenes from *Night of the Living Dead*, that ghoulish 1968 vision of America which is simultaneously being screened as entertainment.[17]

One of the most influential and enduring single images from the Vietnam War—certainly the most contested—exploded into the consciousness of millions of Americans in February 1968 when they actually watched, within the comfort of their own homes, as the chief of the Saigon national police executed a manacled NLF[18] prisoner. In a perfectly framed sequence, the notorious General Nguyen Ngoc Loan unholsters a snub-nosed revolver and places its muzzle to the prisoner's right temple. The prisoner's head jolts, a sudden spurt of blood gushes straight out of his right temple, and he collapses in death. The next morning, newspaper readers were confronted with AP photographer Eddie Adams' potent stills of the execution (see *Figure* 2). The grim ironies of the scene were accentuated by the cultural significance of the weapon itself: a revolver, a somewhat archaic handgun, symbolic of the American West.

Precisely one decade later this image, with the roles now reversed, was transformed into the dominant metaphor of a Hollywood production presenting a new version of the Vietnam War: *The Deer Hunter.* This lavishly financed movie, which the New York Film Critics' Circle designated the best English-language film of 1978 and which received four Academy Awards, including Best Picture of 1978, succeeded not only in radically reimaging the war but in transforming prisoners of war (POW's) into central symbols of American manhood for the 1980's and 1990's.

The manipulation of familiar images—some already accruing symbolic power—was blatant, though most critics at the time seemed oblivious to it. The basic technique was to take images of the war that had become deeply embedded in America's consciousness and transform them into their opposites. For example, in the film's first scene in Vietnam, a uniformed soldier throws a grenade into an underground village shelter harboring women and children, and then with his automatic rifle mows down a woman and her baby. Although the scene resembles the familiar TV sequence of GI's in Vietnamese villages (as well as *Life*'s photographs of the My Lai massacre), the soldier turns out to be not American but North Vietnamese. In turn he is killed by a lone guerrilla—who is not a Viet Cong but our Special Forces hero, played by Robert DeNiro. Later, when two men plummet from a helicopter, the images replicate a familiar telephotographic sequence showing an NLF prisoner being pushed from a helicop- 30

17. Stephen Wright, *Meditations in Green* (New York: Bantam, 1984) [Franklin's note].

18. National Liberation Front, opponents of the government of South Vietnam who were allied with the North Vietnamese.

Figure 2. General Nguyen Ngoc Loan, head of South Vietnam's police and intelligence, executing a prisoner: 1968 photograph by Eddie Adams.

ter to make other prisoners talk;[19] but the falling men in the movie are American POW's attempting to escape from their murderous North Vietnamese captors.

The structuring metaphor of the film is the Russian roulette that the sadistic Asian Communists force their prisoners to play. The crucial torture scene consists of sequence after sequence of images replicating and replacing the infamous killing of the NLF prisoner by General Nguyen Ngoc Loan. Prisoner after prisoner is hauled out of the tiger cages (which also serve as a substitute image for the tiger cages of the Saigon government) and then forced by the demonic North Vietnamese officer in charge (who always stands to the prisoner's right, our left) to place a revolver to his own right temple. Then the image is framed to eliminate the connection between the prisoner's body and the arm holding the revolver, thus bringing the image closer to the famous execution image (see *Figure* 3). One sequence even replicates the blood spurting out of the victim's right temple.

19. "How Helicopter Dumped a Viet Captive to Death," *Chicago Sun-Times*, 29 November 1969; "Death of a Prisoner," *San Francisco Chronicle*, 29 November 1969 [Franklin's note].

Figure 3. In *The Deer Hunter* (1978), General Loan's revolver metamorphoses into a North Vietnamese revolver, and his NLF prisoner is replaced by South Vietnamese and US prisoners forced to play Russian roulette.

The Deer Hunter's manipulation of this particular image to reverse the roles of victim and victimizer was used again and again in the 1980's by other vehicles of the militarization of American culture from movies to comic books. Take, for example, *P.O.W.: The Escape*, an overtly militaristic 1986 POW rescue movie, inspired by *Rambo* and starring David Carradine as superhero. The bestiality of the Asian Communists is here embodied by a North Vietnamese prison-camp commander who executes an American prisoner with a revolver shot to the right temple in a tableau modeled even more precisely than *The Deer Hunter*'s on the original execution of the NLF prisoner in Saigon (see *Figure 4*). Then—just in case viewers missed it—this scene is replayed later as the movie's only flashback.

Toward the end of the 1980's, however, the infamous execution got manipulated incredibly further, actually shifting the role of the most heartless shooter (originally a South Vietnamese official) from the Vietnamese Communists to the photographers themselves! For example, the cover story of the November 1988 issue of the popular comic book *The 'Nam* portrays the photojournalists, both still photographers and TV cameramen, as the real enemies because they had placed the image on the "front page of every newspaper in the states!" The cover literally reverses the original image by showing the execution scene from a position behind the participants (*Figure 5*). This offers a frontal view of the photographer, whose deadly camera conceals his face and occupies the exact

Figure 4. *P.O.W.: The Escape* (1986) transforms the South Vietnamese execution of a prisoner into a North Vietnamese prison commander's murder of a U.S. prisoner.

center of the picture. The prisoner appears merely as an arm, shoulder, and sliver of a body on the left. The only face shown belongs to the chief of the security police, who displays the righteous—even heroic—indignation that has led him to carry out this justifiable revenge against the treacherous actions of the "Viet Cong" pictured in the story. The climactic image (*Figure 6*) is a full page in which the execution scene appears as a reflection in the gigantic lens of the camera above the leering mouth of the photographer, from which comes a bubble with his greedy words, "Keep shooting! Just keep shooting!" "Shooting" a picture here has become synonymous with murder and treason. In the next panel, two GI's register their shock—not at the execution, but at a TV cameraman focusing on the dead body:

> "Front page of every newspaper in the states!"
> "Geez . . ."

One can hardly imagine a more complete reversal of the acclaim accorded to Civil War photographers for bringing the reality of war and death home to the American people.

The logic of this comic-book militarism, put into practice for each of America's wars since Vietnam, is inescapable: photographers must be allowed to image for the public only what the military deems suitable. Non-military photographers and all journalists were simply banished from the entire war zone during the 1983 invasion of Grenada. Partly as a result of this treatment, the major media accepted a pool system for the 1989 invasion of Panama—and meekly went along with the military's keeping even these selected journalists

Figure 5. Cover story of the November 1988 issue of *The 'Nam,* glorifying General Nguyen Ngoc Loan and making the photographer into the villain.

confined to a US base throughout most of the conflict. (A European reporter who attempted to report directly from the scene was actually shot to death when the military unit sent to arrest him became involved in "friendly fire" with another group of US soldiers.)

The almost complete absence of photographic images was quite convenient for the Grenada and Panama invasions, which were carried out so swiftly and with such minimal military risk that they required no Congressional or public endorsement. And for the first several days after US troops had been dispatched to confront Iraq in August 1990, Secretary of Defense Dick Cheney refused to allow journalists to accompany them. The Pentagon seemed to be operating under the belief that photographic and televised images had helped bring about the US defeat in Vietnam. But for the Gulf War, with its long buildup, its potential for significant casualties, and its intended international and domestic political purposes, *some* effective images proved to be essential.

Figure 6. *The 'Nam* images the photographer as the shooter—and the camera as the most destructive weapon.

To control these images, the US government set up pools of selected reporters and photographers, confined them to certain locations, required them to have military escorts when gathering news, established stringent guidelines limiting what could be reported or photographed, and subjected all written copy, photographs, and videotape to strict censorship.[20] Most of those admitted to the pools, it is interesting to note, represented the very newspapers and TV networks that were simultaneously mounting a major campaign to build support for the war. Journalists were forced to depend on military briefings, where they were often fed deliberately falsified information. Immediately after the ground offensive began, all press briefings and pool reports were indefinitely suspended. In a most revealing negation of the achievement of Civil War photography, with its shocking disclosure of the reality of death, the Pentagon banned the press entirely from Dover Air Force Base during the arrival of the bodies of those killed in the war. Responding to an ACLU legal argument that it was attempting to shield the public from disturbing images, the Pentagon replied that it was merely protecting the privacy of grieving relatives.[21]

Although the media were largely denied access to the battlefields, the Gulf War nevertheless gained the reputation of the first "real-time" television

20. Everette E. Dennis et al., *The Media at War: The Press and the Persian Gulf Conflict* (New York: Gannett Foundation, 1991), pp. 17–18 [Franklin's note].

21. Dennis, pp. 21–22 [Franklin's note].

war, and the images projected into American homes helped to incite the most passionate war fever since World War II. These screened images ranged from the most traditional to the most innovative modes of picturing America's wars. Even the antiquated icon of the heroic commanding general, missing for about forty years, was given new life. Although hardly as striking a figure as the commander in Leutze's *Washington Crossing the Delaware* or the posed picture of General Douglas MacArthur returning to the Philippines during World War II, a public idol took shape in the corpulent form of General Norman Schwarzkopf in his fatigues, boots, and jaunty cap.

But perhaps the most potent images combined techniques pioneered by Billy Mitchell with General Peckem's quest for aerial photos of perfect bomb patterns, the medium of television, and the technological capabilities of the weapons themselves. After all, since one of the main goals of the warmakers was to create the impression of a "clean" technowar—almost devoid of human suffering and death, conducted with surgical precision by wondrous mechanisms—why not project the war from the point of view of the weapons? And so the most thrilling images were transmitted directly by the laser-guidance systems of missiles and by those brilliant creations, "smart" bombs. Fascinated and excited, tens of millions of Americans stared at their screens, sharing the experience of these missiles and bombs unerringly guided by the wonders of American technology to a target identified by a narrator as an important military installation. The generation raised in video arcades and on

Figure 7. Technowar triumphs in TV sequence of a smart bomb destroying an Iraqi building.

Nintendo could hardly be more satisfied. The target got closer and closer, larger and larger (*Figure* 7). And then everything ended with the explosion. There were no bloated human bodies, as in the photographs of the battlefields of Antietam and Gettysburg—and none of the agony of the burned and wounded glimpsed on television relays from Vietnam. There was just nothing at all. In this magnificent triumph of technowar, America's images of its wars had seemingly reached perfection.

QUESTIONS

1. Franklin tells a double story of technological advances in making war and in making images. Trace each stage of both narratives. Explain, at each stage, how he links them.

2. Franklin includes seven illustrations in this essay. Explain his choice of each. Are there others he mentions that you wish he had included? Why? (Locating them might be a class project.)

3. Franklin includes references to literature (fiction, primarily, but also poetry), films, television, and comic books. How does he present the differences among them? Compare the powers he attributes to words and the powers he attributes to images.

4. Take one of the illustrations in this essay and write an essay in which you offer an alternative interpretation of it as a counterargument to Franklin's interpretation.

5. Choose a recent U.S. war (or military action) and reconstruct your sense of it and how you acquired that sense. Locate some of the images you remember, and write an essay comparing your memory of them with the images as you see them now. Or, if you had no sense of the event when it occurred, locate some of the important images of it, and write an essay comparing how you think you would have seen them then and how you see them now.

FRANCES FITZGERALD *Rewriting American History*

THOSE OF US who grew up in the fifties believed in the permanence of our American-history textbooks. To us as children, those texts were the truth of things: they were American history. It was not just that we read them before we understood that not everything that is printed is the truth, or the whole truth. It was that they, much more than other books, had the demeanor and trappings of authority. They were weighty volumes. They spoke in measured cadences: imperturbable, humorless, and as distant as Chinese emperors. Our

From America Revised: History Schoolbooks in the Twentieth Century *(1979), FitzGerald's analysis of how textbook interpretations of key moments in American history have changed over time.*

teachers treated them with respect, and we paid them abject homage by memorizing a chapter a week. But now the textbook histories have changed, some of them to such an extent that an adult would find them unrecognizable.

One current junior-high-school American history begins with a story about a Negro cowboy called George McJunkin. It appears that when McJunkin was riding down a lonely trail in New Mexico one cold spring morning in 1925 he discovered a mound containing bones and stone implements, which scientists later proved belonged to an Indian civilization ten thousand years old. The book goes on to say that scientists now believe there were people in the Americas at least twenty thousand years ago. It discusses the Aztec, Mayan, and Incan civilizations and the meaning of the word "culture" before introducing the European explorers.

Another history text—this one for the fifth grade—begins with the story of how Henry B. Gonzalez, who is a member of Congress from Texas, learned about his own nationality. When he was ten years old, his teacher told him he was an American because he was born in the United States. His grandmother, however, said, "The cat was born in the oven. Does that make him bread?" After reporting that Mr. Gonzalez eventually went to college and law school, the book explains that "the melting pot idea hasn't worked out as some thought it would," and that now "some people say that the people of the United States are more like a salad bowl than a melting pot."

Poor Columbus! He is a minor character now, a walk-on in the middle of American history. Even those books that have not replaced his picture with a Mayan temple or an Iroquois mask do not credit him with discovering America—even for the Europeans. The Vikings, they say, preceded him to the New World, and after that the Europeans, having lost or forgotten their maps, simply neglected to cross the ocean again for five hundred years. Columbus is far from being the only personage to have suffered from time and revision. Captain John Smith, Daniel Boone, and Wild Bill Hickok—the great self-promoters of American history—have all but disappeared, taking with them a good deal of the romance of the American frontier. General Custer has given way to Chief Crazy Horse; General Eisenhower no longer liberates Europe single-handed; and, indeed, most generals, even to Washington and Lee, have faded away, as old soldiers do, giving place to social reformers such as William Lloyd Garrison and Jacob Riis. A number of black Americans have risen to prominence: not only George Washington Carver but Frederick Douglass and Martin Luther King, Jr. W. E. B. Du Bois now invariably accompanies Booker T. Washington. In addition, there is a mystery man called Crispus Attucks, a fugitive slave about whom nothing seems to be known for certain except that he was a victim of the Boston Massacre and thus became one of the first casualties of the American Revolution. Thaddeus Stevens[1] has been reconstructed—his character changed, as it were, from black to white, from cruel and vindictive to persistent and sincere. As for Teddy Roosevelt, he now champions the issue

1. Congressman (1792–1868) who urged Lincoln to emancipate the slaves during the Civil War and advocated strict federal control of the South after the war.

of conservation instead of charging up San Juan Hill. No single President really stands out as a hero, but all Presidents—except certain unmentionables in the second half of the nineteenth century—seem to have done as well as could be expected, given difficult circumstances.

5 Of course, when one thinks about it, it is hardly surprising that modern scholarship and modern perspectives have found their way into children's books. Yet the changes remain shocking. Those who in the sixties complained of the bland optimism, the chauvinism, and the materialism of their old civics text did so in the belief that, for all their protests, the texts would never change. The thought must have had something reassuring about it, for that generation never noticed when its complaints began to take effect and the songs about radioactive rainfall and houses made of ticky-tacky began to appear in the textbooks. But this is what happened.

The history texts now hint at a certain level of unpleasantness in American history. Several books, for instance, tell the story of Ishi, the last "wild" Indian in the continental United States, who, captured in 1911 after the massacre of his tribe, spent the final four and a half years of his life in the University of California's museum of anthropology, in San Francisco. At least three books show the same stunning picture of the breaker boys, the child coal miners of Pennsylvania—ancient children with deformed bodies and blackened faces who stare stupidly out from the entrance to a mine. One book quotes a soldier on the use of torture in the American campaign to pacify the Philippines at the beginning of the century. A number of books say that during the American Revolution the patriots tarred and feathered those who did not support them, and drove many of the loyalists from the country. Almost all the present-day history books note that the United States interned Japanese-Americans in detention camps during the Second World War.

Ideologically speaking, the histories of the fifties were implacable, seamless. Inside their covers, America was perfect: the greatest nation in the world, and the embodiment of democracy, freedom, and technological progress. For them, the country never changed in any important way: its values and its political institutions remained constant from the time of the American Revolution. To my generation—the children of the fifties—these texts appeared permanent just because they were so self-contained. Their orthodoxy, it seemed, left no handholds for attack, no lodging for decay. Who, after all, would dispute the wonders of technology or the superiority of the English colonists over the Spanish? Who would find fault with the pastorale of the West or the Old South? Who would question the anti-Communist crusade? There was, it seemed, no point in comparing these visions with reality, since they were the public truth and were thus quite irrelevant to what existed and to what anyone privately believed. They were—or so it seemed—the permanent expression of mass culture in America.

But now the texts have changed, and with them the country that American children are growing up into. The society that was once uniform is now a patchwork of rich and poor, old and young, men and women, blacks, whites, Hispanics, and Indians. The system that ran so smoothly by means of the

Constitution under the guidance of benevolent conductor Presidents is now a rattletrap affair. The past is no highway to the present; it is a collection of issues and events that do not fit together and that lead in no single direction. The word "progress" has been replaced by the word "change": children, the modern texts insist, should learn history so that they can adapt to the rapid changes taking place around them. History is proceeding in spite of us. The present, which was once portrayed in the concluding chapters as a peaceful haven of scientific advances and Presidential inaugurations, is now a tangle of problems: race problems, urban problems, foreign-policy problems, problems of pollution, poverty, energy depletion, youthful rebellion, assassination, and drugs. Some books illustrate these problems dramatically. One, for instance, contains a picture of a doll half buried in a mass of untreated sewage; the caption reads, "Are we in danger of being overwhelmed by the products of our society and wastage created by their production? Would you agree with this photographer's interpretation?" Two books show the same picture of an old black woman sitting in a straight chair in a dingy room, her hands folded in graceful resignation; the surrounding text discusses the problems faced by the urban poor and by the aged who depend on Social Security. Other books present current problems less starkly. One of the texts concludes sagely:

> Problems are part of life. Nations face them, just as people face them, and try to solve them. And today's Americans have one great advantage over past generations. Never before have Americans been so well equipped to solve their problems. They have today the means to conquer poverty, disease, and ignorance. The technetronic age has put that power into their hands.

Such passages have a familiar ring. Amid all the problems, the deus ex machina[2] of science still dodders around in the gloaming of pious hope.

Even more surprising than the emergence of problems is the discovery that the great unity of the texts has broken. Whereas in the fifties all texts represented the same political view, current texts follow no pattern of orthodoxy. Some books, for instance, portray civil-rights legislation as a series of actions taken by a wise, paternal government; others convey some suggestion of the social upheaval involved and make mention of such people as Stokely Carmichael and Malcolm X.[3] In some books, the Cold War has ended; in others, it continues, with Communism threatening the free nations of the earth.

10 The political diversity in the books is matched by a diversity of pedagogical approach. In addition to the traditional narrative histories, with their endless streams of facts, there are so-called "discovery," or "inquiry," texts, which deal with a limited number of specific issues in American history. These texts do not pretend to cover the past; they focus on particular topics, such as "stratification

2. God from a machine. A reference to early plays in which a god, lowered to the stage by mechanical means, solved the drama's problems; thus, an artificial solution to a difficulty.

3. Carmichael (1941–1998) and Malcolm X (1925–1965) were radical black leaders of the 1960s.

in Colonial society" or "slavery and the American Revolution," and illustrate them with documents from primary and secondary sources. The chapters in these books amount to something like case studies, in that they include testimony from people with different perspectives or conflicting views on a single subject. In addition, the chapters provide background information, explanatory notes, and a series of questions for the student. The questions are the heart of the matter, for when they are carefully selected they force students to think much as historians think: to define the point of view of the speaker, analyze the ideas presented, question the relationship between events, and so on. One text, for example, quotes Washington, Jefferson, and John Adams on the question of foreign alliances and then asks, "What did John Adams assume that the international situation would be after the American Revolution? What did Washington's attitude toward the French alliance seem to be? How do you account for his attitude?" Finally, it asks, "Should a nation adopt a policy toward alliances and cling to it consistently, or should it vary its policies toward other countries as circumstances change?" In these books, history is clearly not a list of agreed-upon facts or a sermon on politics but a babble of voices and a welter of events which must be ordered by the historian.

In matters of pedagogy, as in matters of politics, there are not two sharply differentiated categories of books; rather, there is a spectrum. Politically, the books run from moderate left to moderate right; pedagogically, they run from the traditional history sermons, through a middle ground of narrative texts with inquiry-style questions and of inquiry texts with long stretches of narrative, to the most rigorous of case-study books. What is common to the current texts—and makes all of them different from those of the fifties—is their engagement with the social sciences. In eighth-grade histories, the "concepts" of social sciences make fleeting appearances. But these "concepts" are the very foundation stones of various elementary-school social-studies series. The 1970 Harcourt Brace Jovanovich[4] series, for example, boasts in its preface of "a horizontal base or ordering of conceptual schemes" to match its "vertical arm of behavioral themes." What this means is not entirely clear, but the books do proceed from easy questions to hard ones, such as—in the sixth-grade book—"How was interaction between merchants and citizens different in the Athenian and Spartan social systems?" Virtually all the American-history texts for older children include discussions of "role," "status," and "culture." Some of them stage debates between eminent social scientists in roped-off sections of the text; some include essays on economics or sociology; some contain pictures and short biographies of social scientists of both sexes and of diverse races. Many books seem to accord social scientists a higher status than American Presidents.

Quite as striking as these political and pedagogical alterations is the change in the physical appearance of the texts. The schoolbooks of the fifties showed some effort in the matter of design: they had maps, charts, cartoons, photographs, and an occasional four-color picture to break up the columns of print. But beside the current texts they look as naïve as Soviet fashion magazines. The

4. Major textbook publisher.

print in the fifties books is heavy and far too black, the colors muddy. The photographs are conventional news shots—portraits of Presidents in three-quarters profile, posed "action" shots of soldiers. The other illustrations tend to be Socialist-realist-style[5] drawings (there are a lot of hefty farmers with hoes in the Colonial-period chapters) or incredibly vulgar made-for-children paintings of patriotic events. One painting shows Columbus standing in full court dress on a beach in the New World from a perspective that could have belonged only to the Arawaks.[6] By contrast, the current texts are paragons of sophisticated modern design. They look not like *People* or *Family Circle* but, rather, like *Architectural Digest* or *Vogue*. * * * The amount of space given to illustrations is far greater than it was in the fifties; in fact, in certain "slow-learner" books the pictures far outweigh the text in importance. However, the illustrations have a much greater historical value. Instead of made-up paintings or anachronistic sketches, there are cartoons, photographs, and paintings drawn from the periods being treated. The chapters on the Colonial period will show, for instance, a ship's carved prow, a Revere bowl, a Copley painting[7]—a whole gallery of Early Americana. The nineteenth century is illustrated with nineteenth-century cartoons and photographs—and the photographs are all of high artistic quality. As for the twentieth-century chapters, they are adorned with the contents of a modern-art museum.

The use of all this art and high-quality design contains some irony. The nineteenth-century photographs of child laborers or urban slum apartments are so beautiful that they transcend their subjects. To look at them, or at the Victor Gatto painting of the Triangle shirtwaist-factory fire,[8] is to see not misery or ugliness but an art object. In the modern chapters, the contrast between style and content is just as great: the color photographs of junk yards or polluted rivers look as enticing as *Gourmet*'s photographs of food. The book that is perhaps the most stark in its description of modern problems illustrates the horrors of nuclear testing with a pretty Ben Shahn picture of the Bikini explosion,[9] and the potential for global ecological disaster with a color photograph of the planet swirling its mantle of white clouds. Whereas in the nineteen-fifties the texts were childish in the sense that they were naïve and clumsy, they are now child-

5. Socialist realism, which originated in the Soviet Union, is a style of art that glorifies the communal labor of farmers and industrial workers in works of posterlike simplicity.

6. A Native American tribe, then inhabiting the Caribbean area.

7. Paul Revere (1735–1818), American craftsman and patriot, known both for his fine silver bowls and for his famous midnight ride from Boston to Lexington, on April 18–19, 1775, on the eve of the American Revolutionary War. John Singleton Copley (1738–1815), greatest of the American old masters; he specialized in portraits and historical paintings.

8. In 1941 Victor Joseph Gatto (1893–1965) painted this fire, which occurred on March 25, 1911, when he was eighteen.

9. Ben Shahn (1898–1969) was an American painter and graphic artist with strong social and political concerns; the Bikini atoll, part of the Marshall Islands in the Pacific, was the site of American nuclear bomb testing from 1946 to 1958.

ish in the sense that they are polymorphous-perverse. American history is not dull any longer; it is a sensuous experience.

The surprise that adults feel in seeing the changes in history texts must come from the lingering hope that there is, somewhere out there, an objective truth. The hope is, of course, foolish. All of us children of the twentieth century know, or should know, that there are no absolutes in human affairs, and thus there can be no such thing as perfect objectivity. We know that each historian in some degree creates the world anew and that all history is in some degree contemporary history. But beyond this knowledge there is still a hope for some reliable authority, for some fixed stars in the universe. We may know that journalists cannot be wholly unbiased and that "balance" is an imaginary point between two extremes, and yet we hope that Walter Cronkite[10] will tell us the truth of things. In the same way, we hope that our history will not change—that we learned the truth of things as children. The texts, with their impersonal voices, encourage this hope, and therefore it is particularly disturbing to see how they change, and how fast.

15 Slippery history! Not every generation but every few years the content of American-history books for children changes appreciably. Schoolbooks are not, like trade books,[11] written and left to their fate. To stay in step with the cycles of "adoption"[12] in school districts across the country, the publishers revise most of their old texts or substitute new ones every three or four years. In the process of revision, they not only bring history up to date but make changes—often substantial changes—in the body of the work. History books for children are thus more contemporary than any other form of history. How should it be otherwise? Should students read histories written ten, fifteen, thirty years ago? In theory, the system is reasonable—except that each generation of children reads only one generation of schoolbooks. The transient history is those children's history forever—their particular version of America.

10. Anchor (1916–2009) of the *CBS Evening News* from 1952 to 1981.

11. Books written for a general audience, as opposed to textbooks.

12. The choosing of required textbooks by teachers and school boards.

QUESTIONS

1. What differences does FitzGerald find between the American history textbooks of the 1950s and those of the 1970s? In what ways—according to what she states or implies—have they been improved? Does she see any changes for the worse?

2. FitzGerald's *America Revised* was published in 1979, and textbooks, she argues, change rapidly (paragraph 15). Have American history textbooks changed since the late 1970s and, if so, in what ways? What do you remember of the American history textbooks you used in school—and when did you use them? What kind of American history textbooks are being used today? On your own or in a group, write a brief essay updating FitzGerald's piece.

3. By "rewriting," FitzGerald does not mean changing the facts of American history. What is the relationship between the facts of history and history textbooks?

4. FitzGerald says that in the new texts "the word 'progress' has been replaced by the word 'change'" (paragraph 8). Write an essay in which you consider the difference between these two words and the changes that the replacement of one by the other reflects.

Politics and Government

George Orwell — *Shooting an Elephant*

In Moulmein, in Lower Burma, I was hated by large numbers of people—the only time in my life that I have been important enough for this to happen to me. I was sub-divisional police officer of the town, and in an aimless, petty kind of way anti-European feeling was very bitter. No one had the guts to raise a riot, but if a European woman went through the bazaars alone somebody would probably spit betel juice over her dress. As a police officer I was an obvious target and was baited whenever it seemed safe to do so. When a nimble Burman tripped me up on the football field and the referee (another Burman) looked the other way, the crowd yelled with hideous laughter. This happened more than once. In the end the sneering yellow faces of young men that met me everywhere, the insults hooted after me when I was at a safe distance, got badly on my nerves. The young Buddhist priests were the worst of all. There were several thousands of them in the town and none of them seemed to have anything to do except stand on street corners and jeer at Europeans.

All this was perplexing and upsetting. For at that time I had already made up my mind that imperialism was an evil thing and the sooner I chucked up my job and got out of it the better. Theoretically—and secretly, of course—I was all for the Burmese and all against their oppressors, the British. As for the job I was doing, I hated it more bitterly than I can perhaps make clear. In a job like that you see the dirty work of Empire at close quarters. The wretched prisoners huddling in the stinking cages of the lock-ups, the grey, cowed faces of the long-term convicts, the scarred buttocks of the men who had been flogged with bamboos—all these oppressed me with an intolerable sense of guilt. But I could get nothing into perspective. I was young and ill-educated and I had had to think out my problems in the utter silence that is imposed on every Englishman in the East. I did not even know that the British Empire is dying, still less did I know that it is a great deal better than the younger empires that are going to supplant it. All I knew was that I was stuck between my hatred of the empire I served and my rage against the evil-spirited little beasts who tried to make my job impossible. With one part of my mind I thought of

First published in the periodical New Writing *(Fall 1936), at the beginning of Orwell's writing career and soon after his novel* Burmese Days *(1934) appeared. The essay later became the title piece in a collection,* Shooting an Elephant, and Other Essays *(1950).*

the British Raj[1] as an unbreakable tyranny, as something clamped down, in *saecula saeculorum*,[2] upon the will of prostrate peoples; with another part I thought that the greatest joy in the world would be to drive a bayonet into a Buddhist priest's guts. Feelings like these are the normal by-products of imperialism; ask any Anglo-Indian official, if you can catch him off duty.

One day something happened which in a roundabout way was enlightening. It was a tiny incident in itself, but it gave me a better glimpse than I had had before of the real nature of imperialism—the real motives for which despotic governments act. Early one morning the sub-inspector at a police station the other end of the town rang me up on the 'phone and said that an elephant was ravaging the bazaar. Would I please come and do something about it? I did not know what I could do, but I wanted to see what was happening and I got on to a pony and started out. I took my rifle, an old .44 Winchester and much too small to kill an elephant, but I thought the noise might be useful *in terrorem*. Various Burmans stopped me on the way and told me about the elephant's doings. It was not, of course, a wild elephant, but a tame one which had gone "must."[3] It had been chained up, as tame elephants always are when their attack of "must" is due, but on the previous night it had broken its chain and escaped. Its mahout, the only person who could manage it when it was in that state, had set out in pursuit, but had taken the wrong direction and was now twelve hours' journey away, and in the morning the elephant had suddenly reappeared in the town. The Burmese population had no weapons and were quite helpless against it. It had already destroyed somebody's bamboo hut, killed a cow and raided some fruit-stalls and devoured the stock; also it had met the municipal rubbish van and, when the driver jumped out and took to his heels, had turned the van over and inflicted violences upon it.

The Burmese sub-inspector and some Indian constables were waiting for me in the quarter where the elephant had been seen. It was a very poor quarter, a labyrinth of squalid bamboo huts, thatched with palm-leaf, winding all over a steep hillside. I remember that it was a cloudy, stuffy morning at the beginning of the rains. We began questioning the people as to where the elephant had gone and, as usual, failed to get any definite information. That is invariably the case in the East; a story always sounds clear enough at a distance, but the nearer you get to the scene of events the vaguer it becomes. Some of the people said that the elephant had gone in one direction, some said that he had gone in another, some professed not even to have heard of any elephant. I had almost made up my mind that the whole story was a pack of lies, when we heard yells a little distance away. There was a loud, scandalized cry of "Go away, child! Go away this instant!" and an old woman with a switch in her hand came round the corner of a hut, violently shooing away a crowd of naked children. Some more women followed, clicking their tongues and exclaiming; evidently there was something that the children ought not to have seen. I rounded the hut and saw

1. The imperial government of British India and Burma.
2. Forever and ever.
3. Gone into sexual heat.

a man's dead body sprawling in the mud. He was an Indian, a black Dravidian coolie,[4] almost naked, and he could not have been dead many minutes. The people said that the elephant had come suddenly upon him round the corner of the hut, caught him with its trunk, put its foot on his back and ground him into the earth. This was the rainy season and the ground was soft, and his face had scored a trench a foot deep and a couple of yards long. He was lying on his belly with arms crucified and head sharply twisted to one side. His face was coated with mud, the eyes wide open, the teeth bared and grinning with an expression of unendurable agony. (Never tell me, by the way, that the dead look peaceful. Most of the corpses I have seen looked devilish.) The friction of the great beast's foot had stripped the skin from his back as neatly as one skins a rabbit. As soon as I saw the dead man I sent an orderly to a friend's house nearby to borrow an elephant rifle. I had already sent back the pony, not wanting it to go mad with fright and throw me if it smelt the elephant.

5 The orderly came back in a few minutes with a rifle and five cartridges, and meanwhile some Burmans had arrived and told us that the elephant was in the paddy fields below, only a few hundred yards away. As I started forward practically the whole population of the quarter flocked out of the houses and followed me. They had seen the rifle and were all shouting excitedly that I was going to shoot the elephant. They had not shown much interest in the elephant when he was merely ravaging their homes, but it was different now that he was going to be shot. It was a bit of fun to them, as it would be to an English crowd; besides they wanted the meat. It made me vaguely uneasy. I had no intention of shooting the elephant—I had merely sent for the rifle to defend myself if necessary—and it is always unnerving to have a crowd following you. I marched down the hill, looking and feeling a fool, with the rifle over my shoulder and an ever-growing army of people jostling at my heels. At the bottom, when you got away from the huts, there was a metalled road and beyond that a miry waste of paddy fields a thousand yards across, not yet ploughed but soggy from the first rains and dotted with coarse grass. The elephant was standing eight yards from the road, his left side towards us. He took not the slightest notice of the crowd's approach. He was tearing up bunches of grass, beating them against his knees to clean them and stuffing them into his mouth.

I had halted on the road. As soon as I saw the elephant I knew with perfect certainty that I ought not to shoot him. It is a serious matter to shoot a working elephant—it is comparable to destroying a huge and costly piece of machinery—and obviously one ought not to do it if it can possibly be avoided. And at that distance, peacefully eating, the elephant looked no more dangerous than a cow. I thought then and I think now that his attack of "must" was already passing off; in which case he would merely wander harmlessly about until the mahout came back and caught him. Moreover, I did not in the least want to shoot him. I decided that I would watch him for a little while to make sure that he did not turn savage again, and then go home.

4. A hired worker from southern India, one speaking a Dravidian language. The word "coolie" comes from Koli, or Kuli, the name of an aboriginal race of western India.

But at that moment I glanced round at the crowd that had followed me. It was an immense crowd, two thousand at the least and growing every minute. It blocked the road for a long distance on either side. I looked at the sea of yellow faces above the garish clothes—faces all happy and excited over this bit of fun, all certain that the elephant was going to be shot. They were watching me as they would watch a conjurer about to perform a trick. They did not like me, but with the magical rifle in my hands I was momentarily worth watching. And suddenly I realized that I should have to shoot the elephant after all. The people expected it of me and I had got to do it; I could feel their two thousand wills pressing me forward, irresistibly. And it was at this moment, as I stood there with the rifle in my hands, that I first grasped the hollowness, the futility of the white man's dominion in the East. Here was I, the white man with his gun, standing in front of the unarmed native crowd—seemingly the leading actor of the piece; but in reality I was only an absurd puppet pushed to and fro by the will of those yellow faces behind. I perceived in this moment that when the white man turns tyrant it is his own freedom that he destroys. He becomes a sort of hollow, posing dummy, the conventionalized figure of a sahib. For it is the condition of his rule that he shall spend his life in trying to impress the "natives," and so in every crisis he has got to do what the "natives" expect of him. He wears a mask, and his face grows to fit it. I had got to shoot the elephant. I had committed myself to doing it when I sent for the rifle. A sahib has got to act like a sahib; he has got to appear resolute, to know his own mind and do definite things. To come all that way, rifle in hand, with two thousand people marching at my heels, and then to trail feebly away, having done nothing—no, that was impossible. The crowd would laugh at me. And my whole life, every white man's life in the East, was one long struggle not to be laughed at.

But I did not want to shoot the elephant. I watched him beating his bunch of grass against his knees, with that preoccupied grandmotherly air that elephants have. It seemed to me that it would be murder to shoot him. At that age I was not squeamish about killing animals, but I had never shot an elephant and never wanted to. (Somehow it always seems worse to kill a *large* animal.) Besides, there was the beast's owner to be considered. Alive, the elephant was worth at least a hundred pounds; dead, he would only be worth the value of his tusks, five pounds, possibly. But I had got to act quickly. I turned to some experienced-looking Burmans who had been there when we arrived, and asked them how the elephant had been behaving. They all said the same thing: he took no notice of you if you left him alone, but he might charge if you went too close to him.

It was perfectly clear to me what I ought to do. I ought to walk up to within, say, twenty-five yards of the elephant and test his behavior. If he charged, I could shoot; if he took no notice of me, it would be safe to leave him until the mahout came back. But also I knew that I was going to do no such thing. I was a poor shot with a rifle and the ground was soft mud into which one would sink at every step. If the elephant charged and I missed him, I should have about as much chance as a toad under a steam-roller. But even then I was not thinking particularly of my own skin, only of the watchful yellow faces behind. For at that moment, with the crowd watching me, I was not afraid in the ordinary sense, as I would have been if I had been alone. A white man mustn't be frightened in front of "natives"; and so, in general, he isn't frightened. The sole thought in my mind was that if anything went wrong those two thousand Burmans would see me pursued, caught, trampled on and reduced to a grinning corpse like that Indian up the hill. And if that happened it was quite probable that some of them would laugh. That would never do. There was only one alternative. I shoved the cartridges into the magazine and lay down on the road to get a better aim.

10 The crowd grew very still, and a deep, low, happy sigh, as of people who see the theatre curtain go up at last, breathed from innumerable throats. They were going to have their bit of fun after all. The rifle was a beautiful German thing with cross-hair sights. I did not then know that in shooting an elephant one would shoot to cut an imaginary bar running from ear-hole to ear-hole. I ought, therefore, as the elephant was sideways on, to have aimed straight at his ear-hole; actually I aimed several inches in front of this, thinking the brain would be further forward.

When I pulled the trigger I did not hear the bang or feel the kick—one never does when a shot goes home—but I heard the devilish roar of glee that went up from the crowd. In that instant, in too short a time, one would have thought, even for the bullet to get there, a mysterious, terrible change had come over the elephant. He neither stirred nor fell, but every line of his body had altered. He looked suddenly stricken, shrunken, immensely old, as though the frightful impact of the bullet had paralysed him without knocking him down. At last, after what seemed a long time—it might have been five seconds, I dare say—he sagged flabbily to his knees. His mouth slobbered. An enormous senility seemed to have settled upon him. One could have imagined him thousands of years old. I fired again into the same spot. At the second shot he did not collapse but climbed with desperate slowness to his feet and stood weakly upright, with legs sagging and head drooping. I fired a third time. That was the shot that did for him. You could see the agony of it jolt his whole body and knock the last remnant of strength from his legs. But in falling he seemed for a moment to rise, for as his hind legs collapsed beneath him he seemed to tower upward like a huge rock toppling, his trunk reaching skywards like a tree. He trumpeted, for the first and only time. And then down he came, his belly towards me, with a crash that seemed to shake the ground even where I lay.

I got up. The Burmans were already racing past me across the mud. It was obvious that the elephant would never rise again, but he was not dead. He was breathing very rhythmically with long rattling gasps, his great mound of a side painfully rising and falling. His mouth was wide open—I could see far down into caverns of pale pink throat. I waited a long time for him to die, but his breathing did not weaken. Finally I fired my two remaining shots into the spot where I thought his heart must be. The thick blood welled out of him like red velvet, but still he did not die. His body did not even jerk when the shots hit him, the tortured breathing continued without a pause. He was dying, very slowly and in great agony, but in some world remote from me where not even a bullet could damage him further. I felt that I had got to put an end to that dreadful noise. It seemed dreadful to see the great beast lying there, powerless to move and yet powerless to die, and not even to be able to finish him. I sent back for my small rifle and poured shot after shot into his heart and down his throat. They seemed to make no impression. The tortured gasps continued as steadily as the ticking of a clock.

In the end I could not stand it any longer and went away. I heard later that it took him half an hour to die. Burmans were bringing dahs[5] and baskets even before I left, and I was told they had stripped his body almost to the bones by the afternoon.

Afterwards, of course, there were endless discussions about the shooting of the elephant. The owner was furious, but he was only an Indian and could do nothing. Besides, legally I had done the right thing, for a mad elephant has to be killed, like a mad dog, if its owner fails to control it. Among the Europeans opinion was divided. The older men said I was right, the younger men said it was a damn shame to shoot an elephant for killing a coolie, because an elephant was worth more than any damn Coringhee coolie.[6] And afterwards I was very glad that the coolie had been killed; it put me legally in the right and it gave me a sufficient pretext for shooting the elephant. I often wondered whether any of the others grasped that I had done it solely to avoid looking a fool.

5. Butcher knives.

6. A hired worker from the seaport of Coringa, in Madras, India.

Questions

1. Why did Orwell shoot the elephant? Account for the motives that led him to shoot, and then categorize them as personal motives, circumstantial motives, social motives, or political motives. Is it easy to assign his motives to categories? Why or why not?

2. In this essay the proportion of narrative to analysis is high. Mark each paragraph as narrative or analytic, and note, in particular, how much analysis Orwell places in the middle of the essay. What are the advantages and disadvantages of having it there rather than at the beginning or the end of the essay?

3. Facts ordinarily do not speak for themselves. How does Orwell present his facts to make them speak in support of his analytic points? Look, for example, at the death of the elephant (paragraphs 11 to 13).

4. Write an essay in which you present a personal experience that illuminates a larger issue: schooling, affirmative action, homelessness, law enforcement, taxes, or some other local or national issue.

JONATHAN SWIFT *A Modest Proposal*

FOR PREVENTING THE CHILDREN OF POOR PEOPLE IN IRELAND FROM BEING A BURDEN TO THEIR PARENTS OR COUNTRY, AND FOR MAKING THEM BENEFICIAL TO THE PUBLIC

IT IS A MELANCHOLY OBJECT to those who walk through this great town[1] or travel in the country, when they see the streets, the roads, and cabin doors, crowded with beggars of the female-sex, followed by three, four, or six children, all in rags and importuning every passenger for an alms. These mothers, instead of being able to work for their honest livelihood, are forced to employ all their time in strolling to beg sustenance for their helpless infants, who, as they grow up, either turn thieves for want of work, or leave their dear native country to fight for the Pretender in Spain, or sell themselves to the Barbadoes.[2]

I think it is agreed by all parties that this prodigious number of children in the arms, or on the backs, or at the heels of their mothers, and frequently of their fathers, is in the present deplorable state of the kingdom a very great additional grievance; and therefore whoever could find out a fair, cheap, and easy method of making these children sound, useful members of the commonwealth would deserve so well of the public as to have his statue set up for a preserver of the nation.

But my intention is very far from being confined to provide only for the children of professed beggars; it is of a much greater extent, and shall take in the whole number of infants at a certain age who are born of parents in effect as little able to support them as those who demand our charity in the streets.

As to my own part, having turned my thoughts for many years upon this important subject, and maturely weighed the several schemes of other projectors,[3] I have always found them grossly mistaken in their computation. It is true, a child just dropped from its dam may be supported by her milk for a solar year, with little other nourishment; at most not above the value of two

Printed in 1729 as a pamphlet, a form commonly used for political debate in the eighteenth century.

1. Dublin.

2. Many poor Irish sought to escape poverty by emigrating to the Barbados and other western English colonies, paying for transport by binding themselves to work for a landowner there for a period of years. The Pretender, James Francis Edward Stuart (1688–1766), was a claimant to the English throne. He was barred from succession after his father, King James II, was deposed in a Protestant revolution; thereafter, many Irish Catholics joined the Pretender in his exile in France and Spain and in his unsuccessful attempts at counterrevolution.

3. People with projects; schemers.

shillings,[4] which the mother may certainly get, or the value in scraps, by her lawful occupation of begging; and it is exactly at one year old that I propose to provide for them in such a manner as instead of being a charge upon their parents or the parish, or wanting food and raiment for the rest of their lives, they shall on the contrary contribute to the feeding, and partly to the clothing, of many thousands.

There is likewise another great advantage in my scheme, that it will prevent those voluntary abortions, and that horrid practice of women murdering their bastard children, alas, too frequent among us, sacrificing the poor innocent babes, I doubt, more to avoid the expense than the shame, which would move tears and pity in the most savage and inhuman breast. 5

The number of souls in this kingdom being usually reckoned one million and a half, of these I calculate there may be about two hundred thousand couple whose wives are breeders; from which number I subtract thirty thousand couples who are able to maintain their own children, although I apprehend there cannot be so many under the present distresses of the kingdom; but this being granted, there will remain an hundred and seventy thousand breeders. I again subtract fifty thousand for those women who miscarry, or whose children die by accident or disease within the year. There only remain an hundred and twenty thousand children of poor parents annually born. The question therefore is, how this number shall be reared and provided for, which, as I have already said, under the present situation of affairs, is utterly impossible by all the methods hitherto proposed. For we can neither employ them in handicraft or agriculture; we neither build houses (I mean in the country) nor cultivate land. They can very seldom pick up a livelihood by stealing till they arrive at six years old, except where they are of towardly parts;[5] although I confess they learn the rudiments much earlier, during which time they can however be looked upon only as probationers, as I have been informed by a principal gentleman in the county of Cavan, who protested to me that he never knew above one or two instances under the age of six, even in a part of the kingdom so renowned for the quickest proficiency in that art.

I am assured by our merchants that a boy or a girl before twelve years old is no salable commodity; and even when they come to this age they will not yield above three pounds, or three pounds and half a crown[6] at most on the Exchange; which cannot turn to account either to the parents or the kingdom, the charge of nutriment and rags having been at least four times that value.

I shall now therefore humbly propose my own thoughts, which I hope will not be liable to the least objection.

I have been assured by a very knowing American of my acquaintance in London, that a young healthy child well nursed is at a year old a most delicious, nourishing, and wholesome food, whether stewed, roasted, baked, or boiled; and I make no doubt that it will equally serve in a fricassee or a ragout.

4. A shilling used to be worth about twenty-five cents.

5. Promising abilities.

6. A crown was one quarter of a pound.

10 I do therefore humbly offer it to public consideration that of the hundred and twenty thousand children, already computed, twenty thousand may be reserved for breed, whereof only one fourth part to be males, which is more than we allow to sheep, black cattle, or swine; and my reason is that these children are seldom the fruits of marriage, a circumstance not much regarded by our savages, therefore one male will be sufficient to serve four females. That the remaining hundred thousand may at a year old be offered in sale to the persons of quality and fortune through the kingdom, always advising the mother to let them suck plentifully in the last month, so as to render them plump and fat for a good table. A child will make two dishes at an entertainment for friends; and when the family dines alone, the fore or hind quarter will make a reasonable dish, and seasoned with a little pepper or salt will be very good boiled on the fourth day, especially in winter.

I have reckoned upon a medium that a child just born will weigh twelve pounds, and in a solar year if tolerably nursed increaseth to twenty-eight pounds.

I grant this food will be somewhat dear, and therefore very proper for landlords, who, as they have already devoured most of the parents, seem to have the best title to the children.

Infant's flesh will be in season throughout the year, but more plentiful in March, and a little before and after. For we are told by a grave author, an eminent French physician,[7] that fish being a prolific diet, there are more children born in Roman Catholic countries about nine months after Lent than at any other season; therefore, reckoning a year after Lent, the markets will be more glutted than usual, because the number of popish infants is at least three to one in this kingdom; and therefore it will have one other collateral advantage, by lessening the number of Papists among us.[8]

I have already computed the charge of nursing a beggar's child (in which list I reckon all cottagers, laborers, and four fifths of the farmers) to be about two shillings per annum, rags included; and I believe no gentleman would repine to give ten shillings for the carcass of a good fat child, which, as I have said, will make four dishes of excellent nutritive meat, when he hath only some particular friend or his own family to dine with him. Thus the squire will learn to be a good landlord, and grow popular among the tenants; the mother will have eight shillings net profit, and be fit for work till she produces another child.

15 Those who are more thrifty (as I must confess the times require) may flay the carcass; the skin of which artificially[9] dressed will make admirable gloves for ladies, and summer boots for fine gentlemen.

As to our city of Dublin, shambles[10] may be appointed for this purpose in the most convenient parts of it, and butchers we may be assured will not be

7. The comic writer François Rabelais (1483–1553).

8. The speaker is addressing Protestant Anglo-Irish, who were the chief landowners and administrators, and his views of Catholicism in Ireland and abroad echo theirs.

9. Skillfully.

10. Slaughterhouses.

wanting; although I rather recommend buying the children alive, and dressing them hot from the knife as we do roasting pigs.

A very worthy person, a true lover of his country, and whose virtues I highly esteem, was lately pleased in discoursing on this matter to offer a refinement upon my scheme. He said that many gentlemen of this kingdom, having of late destroyed their deer, he conceived that the want of venison might be well supplied by the bodies of young lads and maidens, not exceeding fourteen years of age nor under twelve, so great a number of both sexes in every county being now ready to starve for want of work and service; and these to be disposed of by their parents, if alive, or otherwise by their nearest relations. But with due deference to so excellent a friend and so deserving a patriot, I cannot be altogether in his sentiments; for as to the males, my American acquaintance assured me from frequent experience that their flesh was generally tough and lean, like that of our schoolboys, by continual exercise, and their taste disagreeable; and to fatten them would not answer the charge. Then as to the females, it would, I think with humble submission, be a loss to the public, because they soon would become breeders themselves: and besides, it is not improbable that some scrupulous people might be apt to censure such a practice (although indeed very unjustly) as a little bordering upon cruelty; which, I confess, hath always been with me the strongest objection against any project, how well soever intended.

But in order to justify my friend, he confessed that this expedient was put into his head by the famous Psalmanazar, a native of the island Formosa,[11] who came from thence to London above twenty years ago, and in conversation told my friend that in his country when any young person happened to be put to death, the executioner sold the carcass to persons of quality as a prime dainty; and that in his time the body of a plump girl of fifteen, who was crucified for an attempt to poison the emperor, was sold to his Imperial Majesty's prime minister of state, and other great mandarins of the court, in joints from the gibbet, at four hundred crowns. Neither indeed can I deny that if the same use were made of several plump young girls in this town, who without one single groat[12] to their fortunes cannot stir abroad without a chair,[13] and appear at the playhouse and assemblies in foreign fineries which they never will pay for, the kingdom would not be the worse.

Some persons of a desponding spirit are in great concern about that vast number of poor people who are aged, diseased, or maimed, and I have been desired to employ my thoughts what course may be taken to ease the nation of so grievous an encumbrance. But I am not in the least pain upon that matter, because it is very well known that they are every day dying and rotting by cold and famine, and filth and vermin, as fast as can be reasonably expected. And

11. Actually a Frenchman, George Psalmanazar had passed himself off as from Formosa (now Taiwan) and had written a fictitious book about his "homeland," with descriptions of human sacrifice and cannibalism.

12. A coin worth about four English pennies.

13. A sedan chair.

as to the younger laborers, they are now in almost as hopeful a condition. They cannot get work, and consequently pine away for want of nourishment to a degree that if at any time they are accidentally hired to common labor, they have not strength to perform it; and thus the country and themselves are happily delivered from the evils to come.

20 I have too long digressed, and therefore shall return to my subject. I think the advantages by the proposal which I have made are obvious and many, as well as of the highest importance.

For first, as I have already observed, it would greatly lessen the number of Papists, with whom we are yearly overrun, being the principal breeders of the nation as well as our most dangerous enemies; and who stay at home on purpose to deliver the kingdom to the Pretender, hoping to take their advantage by the absence of so many good Protestants, who have chosen rather to leave their country than to stay at home and pay tithes against their conscience to an Episcopal curate.

Secondly, the poorer tenants will have something valuable of their own, which by law may be made liable to distress,[14] and help to pay their landlord's rent, their corn and cattle being already seized and money a thing unknown.

Thirdly, whereas the maintenance of an hundred thousand children, from two years old and upwards, cannot be computed at less than ten shillings a piece per annum, the nation's stock will be thereby increased fifty thousand pounds per annum, besides the profit of a new dish introduced to the tables of all gentlemen of fortune in the kingdom who have any refinement in taste. And the money will circulate among ourselves, the goods being entirely of our own growth and manufacture.

Fourthly, the constant breeders, besides the gain of eight shillings sterling per annum by the sale of their children, will be rid of the charge of maintaining them after the first year.

25 Fifthly, this food would likewise bring great custom to taverns, where the vintners will certainly be so prudent as to procure the best receipts for dressing it to perfection, and consequently have their houses frequented by all the fine gentlemen, who justly value themselves upon their knowledge in good eating; and a skillful cook, who understands how to oblige his guests, will contrive to make it as expensive as they please.

Sixthly, this would be a great inducement to marriage, which all wise nations have either encouraged by rewards or enforced by laws and penalties. It would increase the care and tenderness of mothers toward their children, when they were sure of a settlement for life to the poor babes, provided in some sort by the public, to their annual profit instead of expense. We should see an honest emulation among the married women, which of them could bring the fattest child to the market. Men would become as fond of their wives during the time of their pregnancy as they are now of their mares in foal, their cows in calf, or sows when they are ready to farrow; nor offer to beat or kick them (as is too frequent a practice) for fear of a miscarriage.

14. Seizure for the payment of debts.

Many other advantages might be enumerated. For instance, the addition of some thousand carcasses in our exportation of barreled beef, the propagation of swine's flesh, and improvement in the art of making good bacon, so much wanted among us by the great destruction of pigs, too frequent at our tables, which are no way comparable in taste or magnificence to a well-grown, fat, yearling child, which roasted whole will make a considerable figure at a lord mayor's feast or any other public entertainment. But this and many others I omit, being studious of brevity.

Supposing that one thousand families in this city would be constant customers for infants' flesh, besides others who might have it at merry meetings, particularly weddings and christenings, I compute that Dublin would take off annually about twenty thousand carcasses, and the rest of the kingdom (where probably they will be sold somewhat cheaper) the remaining eighty thousand.

I can think of no one objection that will possibly be raised against this proposal, unless it should be urged that the number of people will be thereby much lessened in the kingdom. This I freely own, and it was indeed one principal design in offering it to the world. I desire the reader will observe, that I calculate my remedy for this one individual kingdom of Ireland and for no other that ever was, is, or I think ever can be upon earth. Therefore let no man talk to me of other expedients: of taxing our absentees at five shillings a pound: of using neither clothes nor household furniture except what is of our own growth and manufacture: of utterly rejecting the materials and instruments that promote foreign luxury: of curing the expensiveness of pride, vanity, idleness, and gaming in our women: of introducing a vein of parsimony, prudence, and temperance: of learning to love our country, in the want of which we differ even from Laplanders and the inhabitants of Topinamboo:[15] of quitting our animosities and factions, nor acting any longer like the Jews, who were murdering one another at the very moment their city was taken: of being a little cautious not to sell our country and conscience for nothing: of teaching landlords to have at least one degree of mercy toward their tenants: lastly, of putting a spirit of honesty, industry, and skill into our shopkeepers; who, if a resolution could now be taken to buy only our native goods, would immediately unite to cheat and exact upon us in the price, the measure, and the goodness, nor could ever yet be brought to make one fair proposal of just dealing, though often and earnestly invited to it.[16]

Therefore I repeat, let no man talk to me of these and the like expedients, 30 till he hath at least some glimpse of hope that there will ever be some hearty and sincere attempt to put them in practice.

But as to myself, having been wearied out for many years with offering vain, idle, visionary thoughts, and at length utterly despairing of success, I fortunately fell upon this proposal, which, as it is wholly new, so it hath something solid and real, of no expense and little trouble, full in our own power, and

15. A district in Brazil.

16. Swift himself had made these proposals seriously in various previous works, but to no avail.

whereby we can incur no danger in disobliging England. For this kind of commodity will not bear exportation, the flesh being of too tender a consistence to admit a long continuance in salt, although perhaps I could name a country[17] which would be glad to eat up our whole nation without it.

After all, I am not so violently bent upon my own opinion as to reject any offer proposed by wise men, which shall be found equally innocent, cheap, easy, and effectual. But before something of that kind shall be advanced in contradiction to my scheme, and offering a better, I desire the author or authors will be pleased maturely to consider two points. First, as things now stand, how they will be able to find food and raiment for an hundred thousand useless mouths and backs. And secondly, there being a round million of creatures in human figure throughout this kingdom, whose sole subsistence put into a common stock would leave them in debt two millions of pounds sterling, adding those who are beggars by profession to the bulk of farmers, cottagers, and laborers, with their wives and children who are beggars in effect; I desire those politicians who dislike my overture, and may perhaps be so bold to attempt an answer, that they will first ask the parents of these mortals whether they would not at this day think it a great happiness to have been sold for food at a year old in the manner I prescribe, and thereby have avoided such a perpetual scene of misfortunes as they have since gone through by the oppression of landlords, the impossibility of paying rent without money or trade, the want of common sustenance, with neither house nor clothes to cover them from the inclemencies of the weather, and the most inevitable prospect of entailing the like or greater miseries upon their breed forever.

I profess, in the sincerity of my heart, that I have not the least personal interest in endeavoring to promote this necessary work, having no other motive than the public good of my country, by advancing our trade, providing for infants, relieving the poor, and giving some pleasure to the rich. I have no children by which I can propose to get a single penny; the youngest being nine years old, and my wife past childbearing.

17. England.

Questions

1. Identify examples of the reasonable voice of Swift's authorial persona, such as the title of the essay itself.

2. Look, in particular, at instances in which Swift's authorial persona proposes shocking things. How does the style of the "Modest Proposal" affect its content?

3. Verbal irony consists of saying one thing and meaning another. At what point in this essay do you begin to suspect that Swift is using irony? What additional evidence of irony can you find?

4. Write a modest proposal of your own in the manner of Swift to remedy a real problem; that is, propose an outrageous remedy in a reasonable voice.

Niccolò Machiavelli *The Morals of the Prince*

On the Reasons Why Men Are Praised or Blamed—Especially Princes

It remains now to be seen what style and principles a prince ought to adopt in dealing with his subjects and friends. I know the subject has been treated frequently before, and I'm afraid people will think me rash for trying to do so again, especially since I intend to differ in this discussion from what others have said. But since I intend to write something useful to an understanding reader, it seemed better to go after the real truth of the matter than to repeat what people have imagined. A great many men have imagined states and princedoms such as nobody ever saw or knew in the real world, for there's such a difference between the way we really live and the way we ought to live that the man who neglects the real to study the ideal will learn how to accomplish his ruin, not his salvation. Any man who tries to be good all the time is bound to come to ruin among the great number who are not good. Hence a prince who wants to keep his post must learn how not to be good, and use that knowledge, or refrain from using it, as necessity requires.

Putting aside, then, all the imaginary things that are said about princes, and getting down to the truth, let me say that whenever men are discussed (and especially princes because they are prominent), there are certain qualities that bring them either praise or blame. Thus some are considered generous, others stingy (I use a Tuscan term, since "greedy" in our speech means a man who wants to take other people's goods. We call a man "stingy" who clings to his own); some are givers, others grabbers; some cruel, others merciful; one man is treacherous, another faithful; one is feeble and effeminate, another fierce and spirited; one humane, another proud; one lustful, another chaste; one straightforward, another sly; one harsh, another gentle; one serious, another playful; one religious, another skeptical, and so on. I know everyone will agree that among these many qualities a prince certainly ought to have all those that are considered good. But since it is impossible to have and exercise them all, because the conditions of human life simply do not allow it, a prince must be shrewd enough to avoid the public disgrace of those vices that would lose him his state. If he possibly can, he should also guard against vices that will not lose him his state; but if he cannot prevent them, he should not be too worried about indulging them. And furthermore, he should not be too worried about incurring blame for any vice without which he would find it hard to save his state. For if you look at matters carefully, you will see that something resem-

From The Prince *(1513), a book on statecraft written for Giuliano de' Medici (1479–1516), a member of one of the most famous and powerful families of Renaissance Italy. Excerpted from an edition translated and edited by Robert M. Adams (1977).*

bling virtue, if you follow it, may be your ruin, while something else resembling vice will lead, if you follow it, to your security and well-being.

On Liberality and Stinginess

Let me begin, then, with the first of the qualities mentioned above, by saying that a reputation for liberality is doubtless very fine; but the generosity that earns you that reputation can do you great harm. For if you exercise your generosity in a really virtuous way, as you should, nobody will know of it, and you cannot escape the odium of the opposite vice. Hence if you wish to be widely known as a generous man, you must seize every opportunity to make a big display of your giving. A prince of this character is bound to use up his entire revenue in works of ostentation. Thus, in the end, if he wants to keep a name for generosity, he will have to load his people with exorbitant taxes and squeeze money out of them in every way he can. This is the first step in making him odious to his subjects; for when he is poor, nobody will respect him. Then, when his generosity has angered many and brought rewards to a few, the slightest difficulty will trouble him, and at the first approach of danger, down he goes. If by chance he foresees this, and tries to change his ways, he will immediately be labeled a miser.

Since a prince cannot use this virtue of liberality in such a way as to become known for it unless he harms his own security, he won't mind, if he judges prudently of things, being known as a miser. In due course he will be thought the more liberal man, when people see that his parsimony enables him to live on his income, to defend himself against his enemies, and to undertake major projects without burdening his people with taxes. Thus he will be acting liberally toward all those people from whom he takes nothing (and there are an immense number of them), and in a stingy way toward those people on whom he bestows nothing (and they are very few). In our times, we have seen great things being accomplished only by men who have had the name of misers; all the others have gone under. Pope Julius II, though he used his reputation as a generous man to gain the papacy, sacrificed it in order to be able to make war; the present king of France has waged many wars without levying a single extra tax on his people, simply because he could take care of the extra expenses out of the savings from his long parsimony. If the present king of Spain had a reputation for generosity, he would never have been able to undertake so many campaigns, or win so many of them.

5 Hence a prince who prefers not to rob his subjects, who wants to be able to defend himself, who wants to avoid poverty and contempt, and who doesn't want to become a plunderer, should not mind in the least if people consider him a miser; this is simply one of the vices that enable him to reign. Someone may object that Caesar used a reputation for generosity to become emperor, and many other people have also risen in the world, because they were generous or were supposed to be so. Well, I answer, either you are a prince already, or you are in the process of becoming one; in the first case, this reputation for generosity is harmful to you, in the second case it is very necessary. Caesar

was one of those who wanted to become ruler in Rome; but after he had reached his goal, if he had lived, and had not cut down on his expenses, he would have ruined the empire itself. Someone may say: there have been plenty of princes, very successful in warfare, who have had a reputation for generosity. But I answer: either the prince is spending his own money and that of his subjects, or he is spending someone else's. In the first case, he ought to be sparing; in the second case, he ought to spend money like water. Any prince at the head of his army, which lives on loot, extortion, and plunder, disposes of other people's property, and is bound to be very generous; otherwise, his soldiers would desert him. You can always be a more generous giver when what you give is not yours or your subjects'; Cyrus, Caesar, and Alexander[1] were generous in this way. Spending what belongs to other people does no harm to your reputation, rather it enhances it; only spending your own substance harms you. And there is nothing that wears out faster than generosity; even as you practice it, you lose the means of practicing it, and you become either poor and contemptible or (in the course of escaping poverty) rapacious and hateful. The thing above all against which a prince must protect himself is being contemptible and hateful; generosity leads to both. Thus, it's much wiser to put up with the reputation of being a miser, which brings you shame without hate, than to be forced—just because you want to appear generous—into a reputation for rapacity, which brings shame on you and hate along with it.

On Cruelty and Clemency: Whether It Is Better to Be Loved or Feared

Continuing now with our list of qualities, let me say that every prince should prefer to be considered merciful rather than cruel, yet he should be careful not to mismanage this clemency of his. People thought Cesare Borgia[2] was cruel, but that cruelty of his reorganized the Romagna, united it, and established it in peace and loyalty. Anyone who views the matter realistically will see that this prince was much more merciful than the people of Florence, who, to avoid the reputation of cruelty, allowed Pistoia to be destroyed.[3] Thus, no prince should mind being called cruel for what he does to keep his subjects united and loyal; he may make examples of a very few, but he will be more merciful in reality than those who, in their tenderheartedness, allow disorders to occur, with their attendant murders and lootings. Such turbulence brings harm to an entire community, while the executions ordered by a prince affect only one individual at a time. A new prince, above all others, cannot possibly avoid a name for cruelty, since new states are always in danger. And Virgil, speaking through the mouth of Dido,[4] says:

1. Persian, Roman, and Macedonian conquerors and rulers in ancient times.

2. The son of Pope Alexander VI; he was duke of Romagna, which he subjugated in 1499–1502.

3. By unchecked rioting between opposing factions in 1502.

4. Queen of Carthage and tragic heroine of Virgil's epic, the *Aeneid*.

My cruel fate
And doubts attending an unsettled state
Force me to guard my coast from foreign foes.

Yet a prince should be slow to believe rumors and to commit himself to action on the basis of them. He should not be afraid of his own thoughts; he ought to proceed cautiously, moderating his conduct with prudence and humanity, allowing neither overconfidence to make him careless, nor overtimidity to make him intolerable.

Here the question arises: is it better to be loved than feared, or vice versa? I don't doubt that every prince would like to be both; but since it is hard to accommodate these qualities, if you have to make a choice, to be feared is much safer than to be loved. For it is a good general rule about men, that they are ungrateful, fickle, liars and deceivers, fearful of danger and greedy for gain. While you serve their welfare, they are all yours, offering their blood, their belongings, their lives, and their children's lives, as we noted above—so long as the danger is remote. But when the danger is close at hand, they turn against you. Then, any prince who has relied on their words and has made no other preparations will come to grief; because friendships that are bought at a price, and not with greatness and nobility of soul, may be paid for but they are not acquired, and they cannot be used in time of need. People are less concerned with offending a man who makes himself loved than one who makes himself feared: the reason is that love is a link of obligation which men, because they are rotten, will break any time they think doing so serves their advantage; but fear involves dread of punishment, from which they can never escape.

Still, a prince should make himself feared in such a way that, even if he gets no love, he gets no hate either; because it is perfectly possible to be feared and not hated, and this will be the result if only the prince will keep his hands off the property of his subjects or citizens, and off their women. When he does have to shed blood, he should be sure to have a strong justification and manifest cause; but above all, he should not confiscate people's property, because men are quicker to forget the death of a father than the loss of a patrimony. Besides, pretexts for confiscation are always plentiful, it never fails that a prince who starts living by plunder can find reasons to rob someone else. Excuses for proceeding against someone's life are much rarer and more quickly exhausted.

But a prince at the head of his armies and commanding a multitude of soldiers should not care a bit if he is considered cruel; without such a reputation, he could never hold his army together and ready for action. Among the marvelous deeds of Hannibal,[5] this was prime: that, having an immense army, which included men of many different races and nations, and which he led to battle in distant countries, he never allowed them to fight among themselves or to rise against him, whether his fortune was good or bad. The reason for this could only be his inhuman cruelty, which, along with his countless other

5. Carthaginian general who led a massive but unsuccessful invasion of Rome in 218–203 B.C.E.

talents, made him an object of awe and terror to his soldiers; and without the cruelty, his other qualities would never have sufficed. The historians who pass snap judgments on these matters admire his accomplishments and at the same time condemn the cruelty which was their main cause.

When I say, "His other qualities would never have sufficed," we can see that this is true from the example of Scipio,[6] an outstanding man not only among those of his own time, but in all recorded history; yet his armies revolted in Spain, for no other reason than his excessive leniency in allowing his soldiers more freedom than military discipline permits. Fabius Maximus rebuked him in the senate for this failing, calling him the corrupter of the Roman armies. When a lieutenant of Scipio's plundered the Locrians,[7] he took no action in behalf of the people, and did nothing to discipline that insolent lieutenant; again, this was the result of his easygoing nature. Indeed, when someone in the senate wanted to excuse him on this occasion, he said there are many men who knew better how to avoid error themselves than how to correct error in others. Such a soft temper would in time have tarnished the fame and glory of Scipio, had he brought it to the office of emperor; but as he lived under the control of the senate, this harmful quality of his not only remained hidden but was considered creditable.

Returning to the question of being feared or loved, I conclude that since men love at their own inclination but can be made to fear at the inclination of the prince, a shrewd prince will lay his foundations on what is under his own control, not on what is controlled by others. He should simply take pains not to be hated, as I said.

THE WAY PRINCES SHOULD KEEP THEIR WORD

How praiseworthy it is for a prince to keep his word and live with integrity rather than by craftiness, everyone understands; yet we see from recent experience that those princes have accomplished most who paid little heed to keeping their promises, but who knew how craftily to manipulate the minds of men. In the end, they won out over those who tried to act honestly.

You should consider then, that there are two ways of fighting, one with laws and the other with force. The first is properly a human method, the second belongs to beasts. But as the first method does not always suffice, you sometimes have to turn to the second. Thus a prince must know how to make good use of both the beast and the man. Ancient writers made subtle note of this fact when they wrote that Achilles and many other princes of antiquity were sent to be reared by Chiron the centaur, who trained them in his disci-

6. The Roman general whose successful invasion of Carthage in 203 B.C.E. caused Hannibal's army to be recalled from Rome. The episode described here occurred in 206 B.C.E.

7. Fabius Maximus, not only a senator but also a high public official and general who had fought against Hannibal in Italy; Locrians, people of Sicily defeated by Scipio in 205 B.C.E. and placed under Q. Pleminius.

pline.[8] Having a teacher who is half man and half beast can only mean that a prince must know how to use both these two natures, and that one without the other has no lasting effect.

Since a prince must know how to use the character of beasts, he should pick for imitation the fox and the lion. As the lion cannot protect himself from traps, and the fox cannot defend himself from wolves, you have to be a fox in order to be wary of traps, and a lion to overawe the wolves. Those who try to live by the lion alone are badly mistaken. Thus a prudent prince cannot and should not keep his word when to do so would go against his interest, or when the reasons that made him pledge it no longer apply. Doubtless if all men were good, this rule would be bad; but since they are a sad lot, and keep no faith with you, you in your turn are under no obligation to keep it with them.

15 Besides, a prince will never lack for legitimate excuses to explain away his breaches of faith. Modern history will furnish innumerable examples of this behavior, showing how many treaties and promises have been made null and void by the faithlessness of princes, and how the man succeeded best who knew best how to play the fox. But it is a necessary part of this nature that you must conceal it carefully; you must be a great liar and hypocrite. Men are so simple of mind, and so much dominated by their immediate needs, that a deceitful man will always find plenty who are ready to be deceived. One of many recent examples calls for mention. Alexander VI[9] never did anything else, never had another thought, except to deceive men, and he always found fresh material to work on. Never was there a man more convincing in his assertions, who sealed his promises with more solemn oaths, and who observed them less. Yet his deceptions were always successful, because he knew exactly how to manage this sort of business.

In actual fact, a prince may not have all the admirable qualities we listed, but it is very necessary that he should seem to have them. Indeed, I will venture to say that when you have them and exercise them all the time, they are harmful to you; when you just seem to have them, they are useful. It is good to appear merciful, truthful, humane, sincere, and religious; it is good to be so in reality. But you must keep your mind so disposed that, in case of need, you can turn to the exact contrary. This has to be understood: a prince, and especially a new prince, cannot possibly exercise all those virtues for which men are called "good." To preserve the state, he often has to do things against his word, against charity, against humanity, against religion. Thus he has to have a mind ready to shift as the winds of fortune and the varying circumstances of life may dictate. And as I said above, he should not depart from the good if he can hold to it, but he should be ready to enter on evil if he has to.

Hence a prince should take great care never to drop a word that does not seem imbued with the five good qualities noted above; to anyone who sees or

8. Achilles was foremost among the Greek heroes in the Trojan War. Half man and half horse, the mythical Chiron was said to have taught the arts of war and peace, including hunting, medicine, music, and prophecy.

9. Pope from 1492 to 1503.

hears him, he should appear all compassion, all honor, all humanity, all integrity, all religion. Nothing is more necessary than to seem to have this last virtue. Men in general judge more by the sense of sight than by the sense of touch, because everyone can see but only a few can test by feeling. Everyone sees what you seem to be, few know what you really are; and those few do not dare take a stand against the general opinion, supported by the majesty of the government. In the actions of all men, and especially of princes who are not subject to a court of appeal, we must always look to the end. Let a prince, therefore, win victories and uphold his state; his methods will always be considered worthy, and everyone will praise them, because the masses are always impressed by the superficial appearance of things, and by the outcome of an enterprise. And the world consists of nothing but the masses; the few who have no influence when the many feel secure. A certain prince of our own time, whom it's just as well not to name,[10] preaches nothing but peace and mutual trust, yet he is the determined enemy of both; and if on several different occasions he had observed either, he would have lost both his reputation and his throne.

10. Probably Ferdinand of Spain, then allied with the house of Medici.

Questions

1. This selection contains four sections of *The Prince*: "On the Reasons Why Men Are Praised or Blamed—Especially Princes"; "On Liberality and Stinginess"; "On Cruelty and Clemency: Whether It Is Better to Be Loved or Feared"; and "The Way Princes Should Keep Their Word." How, in each section, does Machiavelli contrast the real and the ideal, what he calls "the way we really live and the way we ought to live" (paragraph 1)? Mark some of the sentences in which he expresses these contrasts.

2. Rewrite some of Machiavelli's advice to princes less forcibly and shockingly, and more palatably. For example, "Any man who tries to be good all the time is bound to come to ruin among the great number who are not good" (paragraph 1) might be rewritten as "Good men are often taken advantage of and harmed by men who are not good."

3. Describe Machiavelli's view of human nature. How do his views of government follow from it?

4. Machiavelli might be described as a sixteenth-century spin doctor teaching a ruler how to package himself. Adapt his advice to a current figure in national, state, or local politics, and write about that figure in a brief essay.

Thomas Jefferson and Others *The Declaration of Independence*

In Congress, July 4, 1776
The unanimous Declaration of the
Thirteen United States of America

When in the course of human events it becomes necessary for one people to dissolve the political bands which have connected them with another, and to assume among the powers of the earth, the separate and equal station to which the Laws of Nature and of Nature's God entitle them, a decent respect to the opinions of mankind requires that they should declare the causes which impel them to the separation.

We hold these truths to be self-evident, that all men are created equal, that they are endowed by their Creator with certain unalienable Rights, that among these are Life, Liberty and the pursuit of Happiness. That to secure these rights, Governments are instituted among Men, deriving their just powers from the consent of the governed. That whenever any Form of Government becomes destructive of these ends, it is the Right of the People to alter or to abolish it, and to institute new Government, laying its foundation on such principles and organizing its powers in such form, as to them shall seem most likely to effect their Safety and Happiness. Prudence, indeed, will dictate that Governments long established should not be changed for light and transient causes; and accordingly all experience hath shewn that mankind are more disposed to suffer, while evils are sufferable, than to right themselves by abolishing the forms to which they are accustomed. But when a long train of abuses and usurpations, pursuing invariably the same Object evinces a design to reduce them under absolute Despotism, it is their right, it is their duty, to throw off such Government, and to provide new Guards for their future security. Such has been the patient sufferance of these Colonies; and such is now the necessity which constrains them to alter their former Systems of Government. The history of the present King of Great Britain is a history of repeated injuries and usurpations, all having in direct object the establishment of an absolute Tyranny over these States. To prove this, let Facts be submitted to a candid world.

He has refused his Assent to Laws, the most wholesome and necessary for the public good.

He has forbidden his Government to pass laws of immediate and pressing importance, unless suspended in their operation till his Assent should be obtained; and when so suspended, he has utterly neglected to attend to them.

This final version of the Declaration of Independence resulted from revisions made to Jefferson's original draft by members of the committee to draft the declaration, including John Adams and Benjamin Franklin, and by members of the Continental Congress.

He has refused to pass other Laws for the accommodation of large districts of people, unless those people would relinquish the right of Representation in the Legislature, a right inestimable to them and formidable to tyrants only. 5

He has called together legislative bodies at places unusual, uncomfortable, and distant from the depository of their Public Records, for the sole purpose of fatiguing them into compliance with his measures.

He has dissolved Representative Houses repeatedly, for opposing with manly firmness his invasions on the rights of the people.

He has refused for a long time, after such dissolutions, to cause others to be elected; whereby the Legislative Powers, incapable of Annihilation, have returned to the People at large for their exercise; the State remaining in the mean time exposed to all the dangers of invasion from without, and convulsions within.

He has endeavored to prevent the population of these States; for that purpose obstructing the Laws for Naturalization of Foreigners; refusing to pass others to encourage their migration hither, and raising the conditions of new Appropriations of Lands.

He has obstructed the Administration of Justice, by refusing his Assent to Laws for establishing Judiciary Powers. 10

He has made Judges dependent on his Will alone, for the tenure of their offices, and the amount and payment of their salaries.

He has erected a multitude of New Offices, and sent hither swarms of Officers to harass our people, and eat out their substance.

He has kept among us, in times of peace, Standing Armies without the Consent of our legislatures.

He has affected to render the Military independent of and superior to the Civil Power.

He has combined with others to subject us to a jurisdiction foreign to our constitution, and unacknowledged by our laws; giving his Assent to their Acts of pretended Legislation: For quartering large bodies of armed troops among us: For protecting them, by a mock Trial, from punishment for any Murders which they should commit on the Inhabitants of these States: For cutting off our Trade with all parts of the world: For imposing Taxes on us without our Consent: For depriving us in many cases, of the benefits of Trial by Jury: For transporting us beyond Seas to be tried for pretended offenses: For abolishing the free System of English Laws in a neighboring Province, establishing therein an Arbitrary government, and enlarging its Boundaries so as to render it at once an example and fit instrument for introducing the same absolute rule into these Colonies: For taking away our Charters, abolishing our most valuable Laws, and altering fundamentally the Forms of our Governments: For suspending our own Legislatures, and declaring themselves invested with power to legislate for us in all cases whatsoever. 15

He has abdicated Government here, by declaring us out of his Protection and waging War against us.

He has plundered our seas, ravaged our Coasts, burnt our towns, and destroyed the lives of our people.

He is at this time transporting large Armies of foreign Mercenaries to complete the works of death, desolation and tyranny, already begun with circumstances of Cruelty & Perfidy scarcely paralleled in the most barbarous ages, and totally unworthy the Head of a civilized nation.

He has constrained our fellow Citizens taken Captive on the high Seas to bear Arms against their Country, to become the executioners of their friends and Brethren, or to fall themselves by their Hands.

20 He has excited domestic insurrections amongst us, and has endeavored to bring on the inhabitants of our frontiers, the merciless Indian Savages, whose known rule of warfare, is an undistinguished destruction of all ages, sexes, and conditions.

In every stage of these Oppressions We have Petitioned for Redress in the most humble terms: Our repeated Petitions have been answered only by repeated injury. A Prince, whose character is thus marked by every act which may define a Tyrant, is unfit to be the ruler of a free people.

Nor have We been wanting in attention to our British brethren. We have warned them from time to time of attempts by their legislature to extend an unwarrantable jurisdiction over us. We have reminded them of the circumstances of our emigration and settlement here. We have appealed to their native justice and magnanimity, and we have conjured them by the ties of our common kindred to disavow these usurpations, which would inevitably interrupt our connections and correspondence. They too have been deaf to the voice of justice and of consanguinity. We must, therefore, acquiesce in the necessity, which denounces our Separation, and hold them, as we hold the rest of mankind, Enemies in War, in Peace Friends.

We, THEREFORE the Representatives of the UNITED STATES OF AMERICA, in General Congress, Assembled, appealing to the Supreme Judge of the world for the rectitude of our intentions, do, in the Name, and by Authority of the good People of these Colonies, solemnly publish and declare, That these United Colonies are, and of Right ought to be FREE AND INDEPENDENT STATES; that they are Absolved from all Allegiance to the British Crown, and that all political connection between them and the State of Great Britain, is and ought to be totally dissolved; and that as Free and Independent States, they have full Power to levy War, conclude Peace, contract Alliances, establish Commerce, and to do all other Acts and Things which Independent States may of right do. And for the support of this Declaration, with a firm reliance on the protection of Divine Providence, we mutually pledge to each other our Lives, our Fortunes, and our sacred Honor.

QUESTIONS

1. The Declaration of Independence is an example of deductive argument: Jefferson sets up general principles, details particular instances, and then draws conclusions. In both the original (reprinted on the following page) and the final drafts, locate the three sections of the Declaration that use deduction. Explain how they work as arguments.

2. Locate the general principles (or "truths") that Jefferson sets up in the first section of both the original and final drafts. Mark the language he uses to describe them: for example, he calls them "sacred & undeniable" in the original draft, "self-evident" in the final draft. What kinds of authority does his language appeal to? Why might he or others have revised the language?

3. Write an essay explaining Jefferson's views on the nature of humankind, the function of government, and the relationship between morality and political life, as expressed in the Declaration of Independence. What assumptions are necessary to make these views, as he says in the final draft, "self-evident"?

Thomas Jefferson *Original Draft of the Declaration of Independence*

A Declaration of the Representatives of the UNITED STATES OF AMERICA, in General Congress Assembled.

When in the course of human events it becomes necessary for a people to advance from that subordination in which they have hitherto remained, & to assume among the powers of the earth the equal & independant station to which the laws of nature & of nature's god entitle them, a decent respect to the opinions of mankind requires that they should declare the causes which impel them to the change.

We hold these truths to be sacred & undeniable; that all men are created equal & independant, that from that equal creation they derive rights inherent & inalienable, among which are the preservation of life, & liberty, & the spirit of happiness; that to secure these ends, governments are instituted among men, deriving their just powers from the consent of the governed; that whenever any form of government shall become destructive of these ends, it is the right of the people to alter or to abolish it, & to institute new government, laying it's foundation on such principles & organising its powers in such form, as to them shall seem most likely to effect their safety & happiness. Prudence indeed will dictate that governments long established should not be changed for light & transient causes: and accordingly all experience hath shewn that mankind are more disposed to suffer while evils are sufferable, than to right themselves by abolishing the forms to which they are accustomed. but when a long train of abuses & usurpations, begun at a distinguished period, & pursuing invariably

On June 11, 1776, Jefferson was elected by the Second Continental Congress to join John Adams, Benjamin Franklin, Roger Sherman, and Robert Livingston in drafting a declaration of independence. The draft presented to Congress on June 28 was primarily the work of Jefferson.

the same object, evinces a design to subject them to arbitrary power, it is their right, it is their duty, to throw off such government & to provide new guards for their future security. such has been the patient sufferance of these colonies; & such is now the necessity which constrains them to expunge their former systems of government. The history of his present majesty, is a history of unremitting injuries and usurpations, among which no one fact stands single or solitary to contradict the uniform tenor of the rest, all of which have in direct object the establishment of an absolute tyranny over these states. to prove this, let facts be submitted to a candid world, for the truth of which we pledge a faith yet unsullied by falsehood.

he has refused his assent to laws the most wholesome and necessary for the public good:

he has forbidden his governors to pass laws of immediate & pressing importance, unless suspended in their operation till his assent should be obtained; and when so suspended, he has neglected utterly to attend to them.

5 he has refused to pass other laws for the accommodation of large districts of people unless those people would relinquish the right of representation, a right inestimable to them, & formidable to tyrants alone:[1]

he has dissolved Representative houses repeatedly & continually, for opposing with manly firmness his invasions on the rights of the people:

he has refused for a long space of time to cause others to be elected, whereby the legislative powers, incapable of annihilation, have returned to the people at large for their exercise, the state remaining in the mean time exposed to all the dangers of invasion from without, &, convulsions within:

he has suffered the administration of justice totally to cease in some of these colonies, refusing his assent to laws for establishing judiciary powers:

he has made our judges dependant on his will alone, for the tenure of their offices, and amount of their salaries:

10 he has erected a multitude of new offices by a self-assumed power, & sent hither swarms of officers to harrass our people & eat out their substance:

he has kept among us in times of peace standing armies & ships of war:

he has affected[2] to render the military, independent of & superior to the civil power:

1. At this point in the manuscript a strip containing the following clause is inserted: "He called together legislative bodies at places unusual, unco[mfortable, & distant from] the depository of their public records for the sole purpose of fatiguing [them into compliance] with his measures." Missing parts in the Library of Congress text are supplied from the copy made by Jefferson for George Wythe. This copy is in the New York Public Library. The fact that this passage was omitted from John Adams's transcript suggests that it was not a part of Jefferson's original rough draft.

2. Tried.

he has combined with others to subject us to a jurisdiction foreign to our constitutions and unacknowledged by our laws; giving his assent to their pretended acts of legislation, for quartering large bodies of armed troops among us;
for protecting them by a mock-trial from punishment for any murders they should commit on the inhabitants of these states;
for cutting off our trade with all parts of the world;
for imposing taxes on us without our consent;
for depriving us of the benefits of trial by jury
he has endeavored to prevent the population of these states; for that purpose obstructing the laws for naturalization of foreigners; refusing to pass others to encourage their migrations hither; & raising the conditions of new appropriations of lands;
for transporting us beyond seas to be tried for pretended offences:
for taking away our charters & altering fundamentally the forms of our governments;
for suspending our own legislatures & declaring themselves invested with power to legislate for us in all cases whatsoever:
he has abdicated government here, withdrawing his governors, & declaring us out of his allegiance & protection:
he has plundered our seas, ravaged our coasts, burnt our towns & destroyed the lives of our people: 15
he is at this time transporting large armies of foreign mercenaries to compleat the works of death, desolation & tyranny, already begun with circumstances of cruelty & perfidy unworthy the head of a civilized nation:
he has endeavored to bring on the inhabitants of our frontiers the merciless Indian savages, whose known rule of warfare is an undistinguished destruction of all ages, sexes, & conditions of existence:
he has incited treasonable insurrections of our fellow-citizens, with the allurements of forfeiture & confiscation of our property:
he has waged cruel war against human nature itself, violating it's most sacred rights of life & liberty in the persons of a distant people who never offended him, captivating & carrying them into slavery in another hemisphere, or to incur miserable death in their transportation thither. this piratical warfare, the opprobrium of *infidel* powers, is the warfare of the CHRISTIAN king of Great Britain. determined to keep open a market where MEN should be bought & sold; he has prostituted his negative for suppressing every legislative attempt to prohibit or to restrain this execrable commerce: and that this assemblage of horrors might want no fact of distinguished die, he is now exciting those very people to rise in arms among us, and to purchase that liberty of which *he* has deprived them, by murdering the people upon whom *he* also obtruded them; thus paying off former crimes committed against the *liberties* of one people, with crimes which he urges them to commit against the *lives* of another.

20 in every stage of these oppressions we have petitioned for redress in the most humble terms; our repeated petitions have been answered by repeated injury. a prince whose character is thus marked by every act which may define a tyrant, is unfit to be the ruler of a people who mean to be free. future ages will scarce believe that the hardiness of one man, adventured within the short compass of twelve years only, on so many acts of tyranny without a mask, over a people fostered & fixed in principles of liberty.

Nor have we been wanting in attentions to our British brethren. we have warned them from time to time of attempts by their legislature to extend a jurisdiction over these our states. we have reminded them of the circumstances of our emigration & settlement here, no one of which could warrant so strange a pretension: that these were effected at the expence of our own blood & treasure, unassisted by the wealth or the strength of Great Britain: that in constituting indeed our several forms of government, we had adopted one common king, thereby laying a foundation for perpetual league & amity with them; but that submission to their [Parliament, was no Part of our Constitution, nor ever in Idea, if History may be][3] credited: and we appealed to their native justice & magnanimity, as to the ties of our common kindred to disavow these usurpations which were likely to interrupt our correspondence & connection. they too have been deaf to the voice of justice & of consanguinity, & when occasions have been given them, by the regular course of their laws, of removing from their councils the disturbers of our harmony, they have by their free election re-established them in power. at this very time too they are permitting their chief magistrate to send over not only soldiers of our common blood, but Scotch & foreign mercenaries to invade & deluge us in blood. these facts have given the last stab to agonizing affection, and manly spirit bids us to renounce for ever these unfeeling brethren. we must endeavor to forget our former love for them, and to hold them as we hold the rest of mankind, enemies in war, in peace friends. we might have been a free & a great people together; but a communication of grandeur & of freedom it seems is below their dignity. be it so, since they will have it: the road to glory & happiness is open to us too; we will climb it in a separate state, and acquiesce in the necessity which pronounces our everlasting Adieu!

We therefore the representatives of the United States of America in General Congress assembled do, in the name & by authority of the good people of these states, reject and renounce all allegiance & subjection to the kings of Great Britain & all others who may hereafter claim by, through, or under them; we utterly dissolve & break off all political connection which may have heretofore subsisted between us & the people or parliament of Great Britain; and finally we do assert and declare these colonies to be free and independant states, and that as free & independant states they shall hereafter have power to levy war, conclude peace, contract alliances, establish commerce, & to do all other acts and things which independant states may of right do. And for the

3. A passage illegible in the original is supplied from John Adams' transcription.

support of this declaration we mutually pledge to each other our lives, our fortunes, & our sacred honour.

Questions

1. Note the stylistic differences (including choices of grammar and punctuation) between the original draft of the Declaration of Independence and the revised draft. What effect do those differences have?

2. Choose one or two significant revisions that Jefferson made between the draft and the final version of the Declaration, and explain why they are significant in a short essay.

Elizabeth Cady Stanton *Declaration of Sentiments and Resolutions*

When, in the course of human events, it becomes necessary for one portion of the family of man to assume among the people of the earth a position different from that which they have hitherto occupied, but one to which the laws of nature and of nature's God entitle them, a decent respect to the opinions of mankind requires that they should declare the causes that impel them to such a course.

We hold these truths to be self-evident: that all men and women are created equal; that they are endowed by their Creator with certain inalienable rights; that among these are life, liberty, and the pursuit of happiness; that to secure these rights governments are instituted, deriving their just powers from the consent of the governed. Whenever any form of government becomes destructive of these ends, it is the right of those who suffer from it to refuse allegiance to it, and to insist upon the institution of a new government, laying its foundation on such principles, and organizing its powers in such form, as to them shall seem most likely to effect their safety and happiness. Prudence indeed, will dictate that governments long established should not be changed for light and transient causes; and accordingly all experience hath shown that mankind are more disposed to suffer, while evils are sufferable, than to right themselves by abolishing the forms to which they were accustomed. But when a long train of abuses and usurpations, pursuing invariably the same object evinces a design to reduce them under absolute despotism, it is their duty to throw off such government, and to provide new guards for their future security.

Written and presented at the first U.S. women's rights convention in Seneca Falls, New York, in 1848. Stanton published this version in A History of Woman Suffrage *(1881), edited by herself, Susan B. Anthony, and Matilda Joslyn Gage, all prominent leaders of the American women's movement.*

Such has been the patient sufferance of the women under this government, and such is now the necessity which constrains them to demand the equal station to which they are entitled.

The history of mankind is a history of repeated injuries and usurpations on the part of man toward woman, having in direct object the establishment of an absolute tyranny over her. To prove this, let facts be submitted to a candid world.

He has never permitted her to exercise her inalienable right to the elective franchise.

5 He has compelled her to submit to laws, in the formation of which she had no voice.

He has withheld from her rights which are given to the most ignorant and degraded men—both natives and foreigners.

Having deprived her of this first right of a citizen, the elective franchise, thereby leaving her without representation in the halls of legislation, he has oppressed her on all sides.

He has made her, if married, in the eye of the law, civilly dead.

He has taken from her all right in property, even to the wages she earns.

10 He has made her, morally, an irresponsible being, as she can commit many crimes with impunity, provided they be done in the presence of her husband. In the covenant of marriage, she is compelled to promise obedience to her husband, he becoming, to all intents and purposes, her master—the law giving him power to deprive her of her liberty, and to administer chastisement.

He has so framed the laws of divorce, as to what shall be the proper causes, and in case of separation, to whom the guardianship of the children shall be given, as to be wholly regardless of the happiness of women—the law, in all cases, going upon a false supposition of the supremacy of man, and giving all power into his hands.

After depriving her of all rights as a married woman, if single, and the owner of property, he has taxed her to support a government which recognizes her only when her property can be made profitable to it.

He has monopolized nearly all the profitable employments, and from those she is permitted to follow, she receives but a scanty remuneration. He closes against her all the avenues to wealth and distinction which he considers most honorable to himself. As a teacher of theology, medicine, or law, she is not known.

He has denied her the facilities for obtaining a thorough education, all colleges being closed against her.

15 He allows her in Church, as well as State, but a subordinate position, claiming Apostolic authority for her exclusion from the ministry, and, with some exceptions, from any public participation in the affairs of the Church.

He has created a false public sentiment by giving to the world a different code of morals for men and women, by which moral delinquencies which exclude women from society, are not only tolerated, but deemed of little account in man.

He has usurped the prerogative of Jehovah himself, claiming it as his right to assign for her a sphere of action, when that belongs to her conscience and to her God.

He has endeavored, in every way that he could, to destroy her confidence in her own powers, to lessen her self-respect, and to make her willing to lead a dependent and abject life.

Now, in view of this entire disfranchisement of one-half the people of this country, their social and religious degradation—in view of the unjust laws above mentioned, and because women do feel themselves aggrieved, oppressed, and fraudulently deprived of their most sacred rights, we insist that they have immediate admission to all the rights and privileges which belong to them as citizens of the United States.

In entering upon the great work before us, we anticipate no small amount of misconception, misrepresentation, and ridicule; but we shall use every instrumentality within our power to effect our object. We shall employ agents, circulate tracts, petition the State and National legislatures, and endeavor to enlist the pulpit and the press in our behalf. We hope this Convention will be followed by a series of Conventions embracing every part of the country. 20

QUESTIONS

1. Stanton imitates both the argument and the style of the Declaration of Independence. Where does her declaration diverge from Jefferson's? For what purpose?

2. Stanton's declaration was presented at the first conference on women's rights in Seneca Falls, New York, in 1848. Using books or web resources, do research on this conference; then use your research to explain the political aims of one of the resolutions.

3. Write your own "declaration" of political, educational, or social rights, using the declarations of Jefferson and Stanton as models.

ABRAHAM LINCOLN *Second Inaugural Address*

AT THIS SECOND appearing to take the oath of the presidential office, there is less occasion for an extended address than there was at the first. Then a statement, somewhat in detail, of a course to be pursued, seemed fitting and proper. Now, at the expiration of four years, during which public declarations have been constantly called forth on every point and phase of the great contest which still absorbs the attention, and engrosses the energies of the nation, little that is new could be presented. The progress of our arms, upon which all else chiefly depends, is as well known to the public as to myself; and it is, I trust,

Delivered on March 4, 1865, as Lincoln took office for a second term as America's sixteenth president. In the nineteenth century U.S. presidents took office in March, not in January as they do today.

reasonably satisfactory and encouraging to all. With high hope for the future, no prediction in regard to it is ventured.

On the occasion corresponding to this four years ago, all thoughts were anxiously directed to an impending civil war. All dreaded it—all sought to avert it. While the inaugural address was being delivered from this place, devoted altogether to *saving* the Union without war, insurgent agents were in the city seeking to *destroy* it without war—seeking to dissolve the Union, and divide effects, by negotiation. Both parties deprecated war; but one of them would *make* war rather than let the nation survive; and the other would *accept* war rather than let it perish. And the war came.

One-eighth of the whole population were colored slaves, not distributed generally over the Union, but localized in the Southern part of it. These slaves constituted a peculiar and powerful interest. All knew that this interest was, somehow, the cause of the war. To strengthen, perpetuate, and extend this interest was the object for which the insurgents would rend the Union, even by war; while the government claimed no right to do more than to restrict the territorial enlargement of it. Neither party expected for the war, the magnitude, or the duration, which it has already attained. Neither anticipated that the *cause* of the conflict might cease with, or even before, the conflict itself should cease. Each looked for an easier triumph, and a result less fundamental and astounding. Both read the same Bible, and pray to the same God; and each invokes His aid against the other. It may seem strange that any men should dare to ask a just God's assistance in wringing their bread from the sweat of other men's faces; but let us judge not that we be not judged.[1] The prayers of both could not be answered; that of neither has been answered fully. The Almighty has His own purposes. "Woe unto the world because of offenses! for it must needs be that offenses come; but woe to that man by whom the offense cometh!"[2] If we shall suppose that American slavery is one of those offenses which, in the providence of God, must needs come, but which, having continued through His appointed time, He now wills to remove, and that He gives to both North and South, this terrible war, as the woe due to those by whom the offense came, shall we discern therein any departure from those divine attributes which the believers in a Living God always ascribe to Him? Fondly do we hope—fervently do we pray—that this mighty scourge of war may speedily pass away. Yet, if God wills that it continue, until all the wealth piled by the bondman's two hundred and fifty years of unrequited toil shall be sunk, and until every drop of blood drawn with the lash, shall be paid by another drawn with the sword, as was said three thousand years ago, so still it must be said "the judgments of the Lord are true and righteous altogether."[3]

1. Lincoln alludes to Jesus's statement in the Sermon on the Mount—"Judge not, that ye be not judged" (Matthew 7.1)—and to God's curse on Adam—"In the sweat of thy face shalt thou eat bread, till thou return unto the ground" (Genesis 3.19).

2. From Jesus' speech to his disciples (Matthew 18.7).

3. Psalms 19.9.

With malice toward none; with charity for all; with firmness in the right, as God gives us to see the right, let us strive on to finish the work we are in; to bind up the nation's wounds; to care for him who shall have borne the battle, and for his widow, and his orphan—to do all which may achieve and cherish a just, and a lasting peace, among ourselves, and with all nations.

Questions

1. Lincoln's speech includes both allusions to and direct quotations from the Bible. What argument does he use these references to support? Why are biblical references important as a persuasive technique?

2. In paragraphs 1–2, Lincoln reflects on his first inaugural speech in order to set the stage for his present speech. Find a copy of the first inaugural speech online or in the library. In what ways does that thirty-five-paragraph speech help inform this four-paragraph speech? What aspects of the Second Inaugural Address does it clarify?

3. Read the text of a more recent presidential address and compare or contrast it to Lincoln's address. (John F. Kennedy's inaugural address follows below; others can be found online.) Does the more recent address use a similar style, language, or set of allusions? How does it differ?

John F. Kennedy *Inaugural Address*

We observe today not a victory of a party but a celebration of freedom—symbolizing an end as well as a beginning—signifying renewal as well as change. For I have sworn before you and Almighty God the same solemn oath our forebears prescribed nearly a century and three quarters ago.

The world is very different now. For man holds in his mortal hands the power to abolish all forms of human poverty and all forms of human life. And yet the same revolutionary beliefs for which our forebears fought are still at issue around the globe—the belief that the rights of man come not from the generosity of the state but from the hand of God.

We dare not forget today that we are the heirs of that first revolution. Let the word go forth from this time and place, to friend and foe alike, that the torch has been passed to a new generation of Americans—born in this century, tempered by war, disciplined by a hard and bitter peace, proud of our ancient heritage—and unwilling to witness or permit the slow undoing of those human rights to which this nation has always been committed, and to which we are committed today at home and around the world.

The inaugural address of John F. Kennedy (1917–1963), America's thirty-fifth president, delivered on January 21, 1961.

Let every nation know, whether it wishes us well or ill, that we shall pay any price, bear any burden, meet any hardship, support any friend, oppose any foe to assure the survival and success of liberty.

5 This much we pledge—and more.

To those old allies whose cultural and spiritual origins we share, we pledge the loyalty of faithful friends. United, there is little we cannot do in a host of cooperative ventures. Divided, there is little we can do—for we dare not meet a powerful challenge at odds and split asunder.

To those new states whom we welcome to the ranks of the free, we pledge our word that one form of colonial control shall not have passed away merely to be replaced by a far more iron tyranny. We shall not always expect to find them supporting our view. But we shall always hope to find them strongly supporting their own freedom—and to remember that, in the past, those who foolishly sought power by riding the back of the tiger ended up inside.

To those peoples in the huts and villages of half the globe struggling to break the bonds of mass misery, we pledge our best efforts to help them help themselves, for whatever period is required—not because the Communists may be doing it, not because we seek their votes, but because it is right. If a free society cannot help the many who are poor, it cannot save the few who are rich.

To our sister republics south of our border,[1] we offer a special pledge—to convert our good words into good deeds—in a new alliance for progress—to assist free men and free governments in casting off the chains of poverty. But this peaceful revolution of hope cannot become the prey of hostile powers. Let all our neighbors know that we shall join with them to oppose aggression or subversion anywhere in the Americas. And let every other power know that this hemisphere intends to remain the master of its own house.

10 To that world assembly of sovereign states, the United Nations, our last best hope in an age where the instruments of war have far outpaced the instruments of peace, we renew our pledge of support—to prevent it from becoming merely a forum for invective—to strengthen its shield of the new and the weak—and to enlarge the area in which its writ may run.

Finally, to those nations who would make themselves our adversary, we offer not a pledge but a request: that both sides begin anew the quest for peace, before the dark powers of destruction unleashed by science[2] engulf all humanity in planned or accidental self-destruction.

We dare not tempt them with weakness. For only when our arms are sufficient beyond doubt can we be certain beyond doubt that they will never be employed.

But neither can two great and powerful groups of nations take comfort from our present course—both sides overburdened by the cost of modern weapons, both rightly alarmed by the steady spread of the deadly atom, yet

1. This paragraph is laced with references to Cuba, which by 1961 had turned to communism under Fidel Castro and had allied itself with the Soviet Union.

2. A reference to atomic weapons.

both racing to alter that uncertain balance of terror that stays the hand of mankind's final war.

So let us begin anew—remembering on both sides that civility is not a sign of weakness, and sincerity is always subject to proof. Let us never negotiate out of fear. But let us never fear to negotiate.

Let both sides explore what problems unite us instead of belaboring those problems which divide us. Let both sides, for the first time, formulate serious and precise proposals for the inspection and control of arms—and bring the absolute power to destroy other nations under the absolute control of all nations. 15

Let both sides seek to invoke the wonders of science instead of its terrors. Together let us explore the stars, conquer the deserts, eradicate disease, tap the ocean depths, and encourage the arts and commerce.

Let both sides unite to heed in all corners of the earth the command of Isaiah—to "undo the heavy burdens and to let the oppressed go free."[3]

And if a beachhead of cooperation may push back the jungle of suspicion, let both sides join in creating a new endeavor—not a new balance of power but a new world of law, where the strong are just and the weak secure and the peace preserved.

All this will not be finished in the first one hundred days. Nor will it be finished in the first one thousand days, nor in the life of this administration, nor even perhaps in our lifetime on this planet. But let us begin.

In your hands, my fellow citizens, more than mine, will rest the final success or failure of our course. Since this country was founded, each generation of Americans has been summoned to give testimony to its national loyalty. The graves of young Americans who answered the call to service surround the globe. 20

Now the trumpet summons us again—not as a call to bear arms, though arms we need—not as a call to battle, though embattled we are—but a call to bear the burden of a long twilight struggle, year in and year out, "rejoicing in hope, patient in tribulation"[4]—a struggle against the common enemies of man: tyranny, poverty, disease, and war itself.

Can we forge against these enemies a grand and global alliance, North and South, East and West, that can assure a more fruitful life for all mankind? Will you join in that historic effort?

In the long history of the world, only a few generations have been granted the role of defending freedom in its hour of maximum danger. I do not shrink from this responsibility—I welcome it. I do not believe that any of us would exchange places with any other people or any other generation. The energy, the faith, the devotion which we bring to this endeavor will light our country and all who serve it—and the glow from that fire can truly light the world.

And so, my fellow Americans, ask not what your country can do for you—ask what you can do for your country.

My fellow citizens of the world, ask not what America will do for you, but what together we can do for the freedom of man. 25

3. Isaiah 58.6.

4. Romans 12.12.

Finally, whether you are citizens of America or citizens of the world, ask of us here the same high standards of strength and sacrifice which we ask of you. With a good conscience our only sure reward, with history the final judge of our deeds, let us go forth to lead the land we love, asking His blessing and His help, but knowing that here on earth God's work must truly be our own.

QUESTIONS

1. Choose three rhetorical devices from this speech and show how they are constructed. What are their common elements? Their differences?

2. On what level of generality is Kennedy operating? When does he get specific?

3. Kennedy was the youngest man to be elected president. Speculate on how that fact might be reflected in this speech.

MARTIN LUTHER KING JR. *Letter from Birmingham Jail*[1]

MY DEAR FELLOW CLERGYMEN:

While confined here in the Birmingham city jail, I came across your recent statement calling my present activities "unwise and untimely." Seldom do I pause to answer criticism of my work and ideas. If I sought to answer all the criticisms that cross my desk, my secretaries would have little time for anything other than such correspondence in the course of the day, and I would have no time for constructive work. But since I feel that you are men of genuine good will and that your criticisms are sincerely set forth, I want to try to answer your statement in what I hope will be patient and reasonable terms.

I think I should indicate why I am here in Birmingham, since you have been influenced by the view which argues against "outsiders coming in." I have the honor of serving as president of the Southern Christian Leadership Conference, an organization operating in every southern state, with headquarters in Atlanta, Georgia. We have some eighty-five affiliated organizations across

Written on April 16, 1963, while King was jailed for civil disobedience; subsequently published in Why We Can't Wait *(1964).*

1. This response to a published statement by eight fellow clergymen from Alabama (Bishop C. C. J. Carpenter, Bishop Joseph A. Durick, Rabbi Milton L. Grafman, Bishop Paul Hardin, Bishop Holan B. Harmon, the Reverend George M. Murray, the Reverend Edward V. Ramage and the Reverend Earl Stallings) was composed under somewhat constricting circumstances. Begun on the margins of the newspaper in which the statement appeared while I was in jail, the letter was continued on scraps of writing paper supplied by a friendly Negro trusty, and concluded on a pad my attorneys were eventually permitted to leave me. Although the text remains in substance unaltered, I have indulged in the author's prerogative of polishing it for publication [King's note].

the South, and one of them is the Alabama Christian Movement for Human Rights. Frequently we share staff, educational, and financial resources with our affiliates. Several months ago the affiliate here in Birmingham asked us to be on call to engage in a nonviolent direct-action program if such were deemed necessary. We readily consented, and when the hour came we lived up to our promise. So I, along with several members of my staff, am here because I was invited here. I am here because I have organizational ties here.

But more basically, I am in Birmingham because injustice is here. Just as the prophets of the eighth century B.C. left their villages and carried their "thus saith the Lord" far beyond the boundaries of their home towns, and just as the Apostle Paul left his village of Tarsus and carried the gospel of Jesus Christ to the far corners of the Greco-Roman world, so am I compelled to carry the gospel of freedom beyond my own home town. Like Paul, I must constantly respond to the Macedonian call for aid.

Moreover, I am cognizant of the interrelatedness of all communities and states. I cannot sit idly by in Atlanta and not be concerned about what happens in Birmingham. Injustice anywhere is a threat to justice everywhere. We are caught in an inescapable network of mutuality, tied in a single garment of destiny. Whatever affects one directly, affects all indirectly. Never again can we afford to live with the narrow, provincial "outside agitator" idea. Anyone who lives inside the United States can never be considered an outsider anywhere within its bounds.

You deplore the demonstrations taking place in Birmingham. But your statement, I am sorry to say, fails to express a similar concern for the conditions that brought about the demonstrations. I am sure that none of you would want to rest content with the superficial kind of social analysis that deals merely with effects and does not grapple with underlying causes. It is unfortunate that demonstrations are taking place in Birmingham, but it is even more unfortunate that the city's white power structure left the Negro community with no alternative. 5

In any nonviolent campaign there are four basic steps: collection of the facts to determine whether injustices exist; negotiation; self-purification; and direct action. We have gone through all these steps in Birmingham. There can be no gainsaying the fact that racial injustice engulfs this community. Birmingham is probably the most thoroughly segregated city in the United States. Its ugly record of brutality is widely known. Negroes have experienced grossly unjust treatment in the courts. There have been more unsolved bombings of Negro homes and churches in Birmingham than in any other city in the nation. These are the hard, brutal facts of the case. On the basis of these conditions, Negro leaders sought to negotiate with the city fathers. But the latter consistently refused to engage in good-faith negotiation.

Then, last September, came the opportunity to talk with leaders of Birmingham's economic community. In the course of the negotiations, certain promises were made by the merchants—for example, to remove the stores' humiliating racial signs. On the basis of these promises, the Reverend Fred Shuttlesworth and the leaders of the Alabama Christian Movement for Human

Rights agreed to a moratorium on all demonstrations. As the weeks and months went by, we realized that we were the victims of a broken promise. A few signs, briefly removed, returned; the others remained.

As in so many past experiences, our hopes had been blasted, and the shadow of deep disappointment settled upon us. We had no alternative except to prepare for direct action, whereby we would present our very bodies as a means of laying our case before the conscience of the local and the national community. Mindful of the difficulties involved, we decided to undertake a process of self-purification. We began a series of workshops on nonviolence, and we repeatedly asked ourselves: "Are you able to accept blows without retaliating?" "Are you able to endure the ordeal of jail?" We decided to schedule our direct-action program for the Easter season, realizing that except for Christmas, this is the main shopping period of the year. Knowing that a strong economic-withdrawal program would be the by-product of direct action, we felt that this would be the best time to bring pressure to bear on the merchants for the needed change.

Then it occurred to us that Birmingham's mayoral election was coming up in March, and we speedily decided to postpone action until after election day. When we discovered that the Commissioner of Public Safety, Eugene "Bull" Connor, had piled up enough votes to be in the run-off, we decided again to postpone action until the day after the run-off so that the demonstrations could not be used to cloud the issues. Like many others, we wanted to see Mr. Connor defeated, and to this end we endured postponement after postponement. Having aided in this community need, we felt that our direct-action program could be delayed no longer.

10 You may well ask, "Why direct action? Why sit-ins, marches, and so forth? Isn't negotiation a better path?" You are quite right in calling for negotiation. Indeed, this is the very purpose of direct action. Nonviolent direct action seeks to create such a crisis and foster such a tension that a community which has constantly refused to negotiate is forced to confront the issue. It seeks so to dramatize the issue that it can no longer be ignored. My citing the creation of tension as part of the work of the nonviolent-resister may sound rather shocking. But I must confess that I am not afraid of the word "tension." I have earnestly opposed violent tension, but there is a type of constructive, nonviolent tension which is necessary for growth. Just as Socrates felt that it was necessary to create a tension in the mind so that individuals could rise from the bondage of myths and half-truths to the unfettered realm of creative analysis and objective appraisal, so must we see the need for nonviolent gadflies to create the kind of tension in society that will help men rise from the dark depths of prejudice and racism to the majestic heights of understanding and brotherhood.

The purpose of our direct-action program is to create a situation so crisis-packed that it will inevitably open the door to negotiation. I therefore concur with you in your call for negotiation. Too long has our beloved Southland been bogged down in a tragic effort to live in monologue rather than dialogue.

One of the basic points in your statement is that the action that I and my associates have taken in Birmingham is untimely. Some have asked: "Why didn't you give the new city administration time to act?" The only answer that

I can give to this query is that the new Birmingham administration must be prodded about as much as the outgoing one, before it will act. We are sadly mistaken if we feel that the election of Albert Boutwell as mayor will bring the millennium to Birmingham. While Mr. Boutwell is a much more gentle person than Mr. Connor, they are both segregationists, dedicated to maintenance of the status quo. I have hoped that Mr. Boutwell will be reasonable enough to see the futility of massive resistance to desegregation. But he will not see this without pressure from devotees of civil rights. My friends, I must say to you that we have not made a single gain in civil rights without determined legal and nonviolent pressure. Lamentably, it is an historical fact that privileged groups seldom give up their privileges voluntarily. Individuals may see the moral light and voluntarily give up their unjust posture; but, as Reinhold Niebuhr[2] has reminded us, groups tend to be more immoral than individuals.

We know through painful experience that freedom is never voluntarily given by the oppressor; it must be demanded by the oppressed. Frankly, I have yet to engage in a direct-action campaign that was "well timed" in the view of those who have not suffered unduly from the disease of segregation. For years now I have heard the word "Wait!" It rings in the ear of every Negro with piercing familiarity. This "Wait" has almost always meant "Never." We must come to see, with one of our distinguished jurists, that "justice too long delayed is justice denied."

We have waited for more than 340 years for our constitutional and God-given rights. The nations of Asia and Africa are moving with jetlike speed toward gaining political independence, but we still creep at horse-and-buggy pace toward gaining a cup of coffee at a lunch counter. Perhaps it is easy for those who have never felt the stinging darts of segregation to say, "Wait." But when you have seen vicious mobs lynch your mothers and fathers at will and drown your sisters and brothers at whim; when you have seen hate-filled policemen curse, kick, and even kill your black brothers and sisters; when you see the vast majority of your twenty million Negro brothers smothering in an airtight cage of poverty in the midst of an affluent society; when you suddenly find your tongue twisted and your speech stammering as you seek to explain to your six-year-old daughter why she can't go to the public amusement park that has just been advertised on television, and see tears welling up in her eyes when she is told that Funtown is closed to colored children, and see ominous clouds of inferiority beginning to form in her little mental sky, and see her beginning to distort her personality by developing an unconscious bitterness toward white people; when you have to concoct an answer for a five-year-old son who is asking, "Daddy, why do white people treat colored people so mean?"; when you take a cross-country drive and find it necessary to sleep night after night in the uncomfortable corners of your automobile because no motel will accept you; when you are humiliated day in and day out by nagging signs reading "white" and "colored"; when your first name becomes "nigger," your middle name becomes "boy" (however old you are) and your last name becomes "John," and your wife

2. American Protestant theologian (1892–1971).

and mother are never given the respected title "Mrs."; when you are harried by day and haunted by night by the fact that you are a Negro, living constantly at tiptoe stance, never quite knowing what to expect next, and are plagued with inner fears and outer resentments; when you are forever fighting a degenerating sense of "nobodiness"—then you will understand why we find it difficult to wait. There comes a time when the cup of endurance runs over, and men are no longer willing to be plunged into the abyss of despair. I hope, sirs, you can understand our legitimate and unavoidable impatience.

15 You express a great deal of anxiety over our willingness to break laws. This is certainly a legitimate concern. Since we so diligently urge people to obey the Supreme Court's decision of 1954 outlawing segregation in the public schools, at first glance it may seem rather paradoxical for us consciously to break laws. One may well ask: "How can you advocate breaking some laws and obeying others?" The answer lies in the fact that there are two types of laws: just and unjust. I would be the first to advocate obeying just laws. One has not only a legal but a moral responsibility to obey just laws. Conversely, one has a moral responsibility to disobey unjust laws. I would agree with St. Augustine[3] that "an unjust law is no law at all."

Now, what is the difference between the two? How does one determine whether a law is just or unjust? A just law is a man-made code that squares with the moral law or the law of God. An unjust law is a code that is out of harmony with the moral law. To put it in the terms of St. Thomas Aquinas:[4] An unjust law is a human law that is not rooted in eternal law and natural law. Any law that uplifts human personality is just. Any law that degrades human personality is unjust. All segregation statutes are unjust because segregation distorts the soul and damages the personality. It gives the segregator a false sense of superiority and the segregated a false sense of inferiority. Segregation, to use the terminology of the Jewish philosopher Martin Buber,[5] substitutes an "I-it" relationship for an "I-thou" relationship and ends up relegating persons to the status of things. Hence segregation is not only politically, economically, and sociologically unsound, it is morally wrong and sinful. Paul Tillich[6] has said that sin is separation. Is not segregation an existential expression of man's tragic separation, his awful estrangement, his terrible sinfulness? Thus it is that I can urge men to obey the 1954 decision of the Supreme Court, for it is morally right; and I can urge them to disobey segregation ordinances, for they are morally wrong.

Let us consider a more concrete example of just and unjust laws. An unjust law is a code that a numerical or power majority group compels a minority group to obey but does not make binding on itself. This is *difference* made legal. By the same token, a just law is a code that a majority compels a minority to follow and that it is willing to follow itself. This is *sameness* made legal.

3. Early Christian church father (354–430).
4. Christian philosopher and theologian (1225–1274).
5. German-born Israeli philosopher (1878–1965).
6. German-born American Protestant theologian (1886–1965).

Let me give another explanation. A law is unjust if it is inflicted on a minority that, as a result of being denied the right to vote, had no part in enacting or devising the law. Who can say that the legislature of Alabama which set up that state's segregation laws was democratically elected? Throughout Alabama all sorts of devious methods are used to prevent Negroes from becoming registered voters, and there are some counties in which, even though Negroes constitute a majority of the population, not a single Negro is registered. Can any law enacted under such circumstances be considered democratically structured?

Sometimes a law is just on its face and unjust in its application. For instance, I have been arrested on a charge of parading without a permit. Now, there is nothing wrong in having an ordinance which requires a permit for a parade. But such an ordinance becomes unjust when it is used to maintain segregation and to deny citizens the First-Amendment privilege of peaceful assembly and protest.

20 I hope you are able to see the distinction I am trying to point out. In no sense do I advocate evading or defying the law, as would the rabid segregationist. That would lead to anarchy. One who breaks an unjust law must do so openly, lovingly, and with a willingness to accept the penalty. I submit that an individual who breaks a law that conscience tells him is unjust, and who willingly accepts the penalty of imprisonment in order to arouse the conscience of the community over its injustice, is in reality expressing the highest respect for law.

Of course, there is nothing new about this kind of civil disobedience. It was evidenced sublimely in the refusal of Shadrach, Meshach, and Abednego to obey the laws of Nebuchadnezzar,[7] on the ground that a higher moral law was at stake. It was practiced superbly by the early Christians, who were willing to face hungry lions and the excruciating pain of chopping blocks rather than submit to certain unjust laws of the Roman Empire. To a degree, academic freedom is a reality today because Socrates practiced civil disobedience.[8] In our own nation, the Boston Tea Party represented a massive act of civil disobedience.

We should never forget that everything Adolf Hitler did in Germany was "legal" and everything the Hungarian freedom fighters[9] did in Hungary was "illegal." It was "illegal" to aid and comfort a Jew in Hitler's Germany. Even so, I am sure that, had I lived in Germany at the time, I would have aided and comforted my Jewish brothers. If today I lived in a Communist country where certain principles dear to the Christian faith are suppressed, I would openly advocate disobeying that country's anti-religious laws.

I must make two honest confessions to you, my Christian and Jewish brothers. First, I must confess that over the past few years I have been gravely

7. Their story is told in Daniel 3.

8. The ancient Greek philosopher Socrates was tried by the Athenians for corrupting their youth through his skeptical, questioning manner of teaching. He refused to change his ways and was condemned to death.

9. In the anti-Communist revolution of 1956, which was quickly put down by the Soviet army.

disappointed with the white moderate. I have almost reached the regrettable conclusion that the Negro's great stumbling block in his stride toward freedom is not the White Citizen's Counciler or the Ku Klux Klanner, but the white moderate, who is more devoted to "order" than to justice; who prefers a negative peace which is the absence of tension to a positive peace which is the presence of justice; who constantly says, "I agree with you in the goal you seek, but I cannot agree with your methods of direct action"; who paternalistically believes he can set the timetable for another man's freedom; who lives by a mythical concept of time and who constantly advises the Negro to wait for a "more convenient season." Shallow understanding from people of good will is more frustrating than absolute misunderstanding from people of ill will. Lukewarm acceptance is much more bewildering than outright rejection.

I had hoped that the white moderate would understand that law and order exist for the purpose of establishing justice and that when they fail in this purpose they become the dangerously structured dams that block the flow of social progress. I had hoped that the white moderate would understand that the present tension in the South is a necessary phase of the transition from an obnoxious negative peace, in which the Negro passively accepted his unjust plight, to a substantive and positive peace, in which all men will respect the dignity and worth of human personality. Actually, we who engage in nonviolent direct action are not the creators of tension. We merely bring to the surface the hidden tension that is already alive. We bring it out in the open, where it can be seen and dealt with. Like a boil that can never be cured so long as it is covered up but must be opened with all its ugliness to the natural medicines of air and light, injustice must be exposed, with all the tension its exposure creates, to the light of human conscience and the air of national opinion, before it can be cured.

25 In your statement you assert that our actions, even though peaceful, must be condemned because they precipitate violence. But is this a logical assertion? Isn't this like condemning a robbed man because his possession of money precipitated the evil act of robbery? Isn't this like condemning Socrates because his unswerving commitment to truth and his philosophical inquiries precipitated the act by the misguided populace in which they made him drink hemlock? Isn't this like condemning Jesus because his unique God-consciousness and never-ceasing devotion to God's will precipitated the evil act of crucifixion? We must come to see that, as the federal courts have consistently affirmed, it is wrong to urge an individual to cease his efforts to gain his basic constitutional rights because the quest may precipitate violence. Society must protect the robbed and punish the robber.

I had also hoped that the white moderate would reject the myth concerning time in relation to the struggle for freedom. I have just received a letter from a white brother in Texas. He writes: "All Christians know that the colored people will receive equal rights eventually, but it is possible that you are in too great a religious hurry. It has taken Christianity almost two thousand years to accomplish what it has. The teachings of Christ take time to come to earth." Such an attitude stems from a tragic misconception of time, from the strangely irrational notion that there is something in the very flow of time that will inevitably cure all ills. Actually, time itself is neutral; it can be used either destructively or constructively. More and more I feel that the people of ill will have used time much more effectively than have the people of good will. We will have to repent in this generation not merely for the hateful words and actions of the bad people, but for the appalling silence of the good people. Human progress never rolls in on wheels of inevitability; it comes through the tireless efforts of men willing to be co-workers with God, and without this hard work, time itself becomes an ally of the forces of social stagnation. We must use time creatively, in the knowledge that the time is always ripe to do right. Now is the time to make real the promise of democracy and transform our pending national elegy into a creative psalm of brotherhood. Now is the time to lift our national policy from the quicksand of racial injustice to the solid rock of human dignity.

You speak of our activity in Birmingham as extreme. At first I was rather disappointed that fellow clergymen would see my nonviolent efforts as those of an extremist. I began thinking about the fact that I stand in the middle of two opposing forces in the Negro community. One is a force of complacency, made up in part of Negroes who, as a result of long years of oppression, are so drained of self-respect and a sense of "somebodiness" that they have adjusted to segregation; and in part of a few middle-class Negroes who, because of a degree of academic and economic security and because in some ways they profit by segregation, have become insensitive to the problems of the masses. The other force is one of bitterness and hatred, and it comes perilously close to advocating violence. It is expressed in the various black nationalist groups that are springing up across the nation, the largest and best-known being Elijah Muhammad's Muslim movement.[10] Nourished by the Negro's frustration over the continued existence of racial discrimination, this movement is made up of people who have lost faith in America, who have absolutely repudiated Christianity, and who have concluded that the white man is an incorrigible "devil."

I have tried to stand between these two forces, saying that we need emulate neither the "do-nothingism" of the complacent nor the hatred and despair of the black nationalist. For there is the more excellent way of love and nonviolent protest. I am grateful to God that, through the influence of the Negro church, the way of nonviolence became an integral part of our struggle.

If this philosophy had not emerged, by now many streets of the South would, I am convinced, be flowing with blood. And I am further convinced that if our white brothers dismiss as "rabblerousers" and "outside agitators" those of us who employ nonviolent direct action, and if they refuse to support our nonviolent efforts, millions of Negroes will, out of frustration and despair, seek solace and security in black-nationalist ideologies—a development that would inevitably lead to a frightening racial nightmare.

Oppressed people cannot remain oppressed forever. The yearning for freedom eventually manifests itself, and that is what has happened to the American Negro. Something within has reminded him of his birthright of freedom, and 30

10. Elijah Muhammed (1897–1975) succeeded to the leadership of the Nation of Islam in 1934.

something without has reminded him that it can be gained. Consciously or unconsciously, he has been caught up by the *Zeitgeist*,[11] and with his black brothers of Africa and his brown and yellow brothers of Asia, South America, and the Caribbean, the United States Negro is moving with a sense of great urgency toward the promised land of racial justice. If one recognizes this vital urge that has engulfed the Negro community, one should readily understand why public demonstrations are taking place. The Negro has many pent-up resentments and latent frustrations, and he must release them. So let him march; let him make prayer pilgrimages to the city hall; let him go on freedom rides—and try to understand why he must do so. If his repressed emotions are not released in nonviolent ways, they will seek expression through violence; this is not a threat but a fact of history. So I have not said to my people, "Get rid of your discontent." Rather, I have tried to say that this normal and healthy discontent can be channeled into the creative outlet of nonviolent direct action. And now this approach is being termed extremist.

But though I was initially disappointed at being categorized as an extremist, as I continued to think about the matter I gradually gained a measure of satisfaction from the label. Was not Jesus an extremist for love: "Love your enemies, bless them that curse you, do good to them that hate you, and pray for them which despitefully use you, and persecute you." Was not Amos an extremist for justice: "Let justice roll down like waters and righteousness like an ever-flowing stream." Was not Paul an extremist for the Christian gospel: "I bear in my body the marks of the Lord Jesus." Was not Martin Luther an extremist: "Here I stand; I cannot do otherwise, so help me God." And John Bunyan:[12] "I will stay in jail to the end of my days before I make a butchery of my conscience." And Abraham Lincoln: "This nation cannot survive half slave and half free." And Thomas Jefferson: "We hold these truths to be self-evident, that all men are created equal. . . ." So the question is not whether we will be extremists, but what kind of extremists we will be. Will we be extremists for hate or for love? Will we be extremists for the preservation of injustice or for the extension of justice? In that dramatic scene on Calvary's hill three men were crucified. We must never forget that all three were crucified for the same crime—the crime of extremism. Two were extremists for immorality, and thus fell below their environment. The other, Jesus Christ, was an extremist for love, truth, and goodness, and thereby rose above his environment. Perhaps the South, the nation, and the world are in dire need of creative extremists.

I had hoped that the white moderate would see this need. Perhaps I was too optimistic; perhaps I expected too much. I suppose I should have realized that few members of the oppressor race can understand the deep groans and passionate yearnings of the oppressed race, and still fewer have the vision to see that injustice must be rooted out by strong, persistent, and determined action. I am thankful, however, that some of our white brothers in the South

11. The spirit of the times.

12. Amos, Old Testament prophet; Paul, New Testament apostle; Luther (1483–1546), German Protestant reformer; Bunyan, English preacher and author (1628–1688).

have grasped the meaning of this social revolution and committed themselves to it. They are still all too few in quantity, but they are big in quality. Some—such as Ralph McGill, Lillian Smith, Harry Golden, James McBridge Dabbs, Ann Braden, and Sarah Patton Boyle—have written about our struggle in eloquent and prophetic terms. Others have marched with us down nameless streets of the South. They have languished in filthy, roach-infested jails, suffering the abuse and brutality of policemen who view them as "dirty nigger-lovers." Unlike so many of their moderate brothers and sisters, they have recognized the urgency of the moment and sensed the need for powerful "action" antidotes to combat the disease of segregation.

Let me take note of my other major disappointment. I have been so greatly disappointed with the white church and its leadership. Of course, there are some notable exceptions. I am not unmindful of the fact that each of you has taken some significant stands on this issue. I commend you, Reverend Stallings, for your Christian stand on this past Sunday, in welcoming Negroes to your worship service on a nonsegregated basis. I commend the Catholic leaders of this state for integrating Spring Hill College several years ago.

But despite these notable exceptions, I must honestly reiterate that I have been disappointed with the church. I do not say this as one of those negative critics who can always find something wrong with the church. I say this as a minister of the gospel, who loves the church; who was nurtured in its bosom; who has been sustained by its spiritual blessings and who will remain true to it as long as the cord of life shall lengthen.

When I was suddenly catapulted into the leadership of the bus protest in Montgomery, Alabama, a few years ago,[13] I felt we would be supported by the white church. I felt that the white ministers, priests, and rabbis of the South would be among our strongest allies. Instead, some have been outright opponents, refusing to understand the freedom movement and misrepresenting its leaders; all too many others have been more cautious than courageous and have remained silent behind the anesthetizing security of stained-glass windows. 35

In spite of my shattered dreams, I came to Birmingham with the hope that the white religious leadership of this community would see the justice of our cause and, with deep moral concern, would serve as the channel through which our just grievances could reach the power structure. I had hoped that each of you would understand. But again I have been disappointed.

I have heard numerous southern religious leaders admonish their worshipers to comply with a desegregation decision because it is the law, but I have longed to hear white ministers declare: "Follow this decree because integration is morally right and because the Negro is your brother." In the midst of blatant injustices inflicted upon the Negro, I have watched white churchmen stand on the sideline and mouth pious irrelevancies and sanctimonious trivialities. In the midst of a mighty struggle to rid our nation of racial and economic injustice, I have heard many ministers say: "Those are social issues, with which the gospel has no real concern." And I have watched many churches commit them-

13. In December 1955, when Rosa Parks refused to move to the back of a bus.

selves to a completely otherworldly religion which makes a strange, un-Biblical distinction between body and soul, between the sacred and the secular.

I have traveled the length and breadth of Alabama, Mississippi, and all the other southern states. On sweltering summer days and crisp autumn mornings I have looked at the South's beautiful churches with their lofty spires pointing heavenward. I have beheld the impressive outlines of her massive religious-education buildings. Over and over I have found myself asking: "What kind of people worship here? Who is their God? Where were their voices when the lips of Governor Barnett dripped with words of interposition and nullification? Where were they when Governor Wallace gave a clarion call for defiance and hatred?[14] Where were their voices of support when bruised and weary Negro men and women decided to rise from the dark dungeons of complacency to the bright hills of creative protest?"

Yes, these questions are still in my mind. In deep disappointment I have wept over the laxity of the church. But be assured that my tears have been tears of love. There can be no deep disappointment where there is not deep love. Yes, I love the church. How could I do otherwise? I am in the rather unique position of being the son, the grandson, and the great-grandson of preachers. Yes, I see the church as the body of Christ. But, oh! How we have blemished and scarred that body through social neglect and through fear of being nonconformists.

40 There was a time when the church was very powerful—in the time when the early Christians rejoiced at being deemed worthy to suffer for what they believed. In those days the church was not merely a thermometer that recorded the ideas and principles of popular opinion; it was a thermostat that transformed the mores of society. Whenever the early Christians entered a town, the people in power became disturbed and immediately sought to convict the Christians for being "disturbers of the peace" and "outside agitators." But the Christians pressed on, in the conviction that they were "a colony of heaven," called to obey God rather than man. Small in number, they were big in commitment. They were too God-intoxicated to be "astronomically intimidated." By their effort and example they brought an end to such ancient evils as infanticide and gladiatorial contests.

Things are different now. So often the contemporary church is a weak, ineffectual voice with an uncertain sound. So often it is an archdefender of the status quo. Far from being disturbed by the presence of the church, the power structure of the average community is consoled by the church's silent—and often even vocal—sanction of things as they are.

But the judgment of God is upon the church as never before. If today's church does not recapture the sacrificial spirit of the early church, it will lose its authenticity, forfeit the loyalty of millions, and be dismissed as an irrelevant social club with no meaning for the twentieth century. Every day I meet young people whose disappointment with the church has turned into outright disgust.

14. Ross Barnett (1898–1988), governor of Mississippi, opposed James Meredith's admission to the University of Mississippi; George Wallace (1919–1998), governor of Alabama, opposed admission of several black students to the University of Alabama.

Perhaps I have once again been too optimistic. Is organized religion too inextricably bound to the status quo to save our nation and the world? Perhaps I must turn my faith to the inner spiritual church, the church within the church, as the true *ekklesia*[15] and the hope of the world. But again I am thankful to God that some noble souls from the ranks of organized religion have broken loose from the paralyzing chains of conformity and joined us as active partners in the struggle for freedom. They have left their secure congregations and walked the streets of Albany, Georgia, with us. They have gone down the highways of the South on tortuous rides for freedom. Yes, they have gone to jail with us. Some have been dismissed from their churches, have lost the support of their bishops and fellow ministers. But they have acted in the faith that right defeated is stronger than evil triumphant. Their witness has been the spiritual salt that has preserved the true meaning of the gospel in these troubled times. They have carved a tunnel of hope through the dark mountain of disappointment.

I hope the church as a whole will meet the challenge of this decisive hour. But even if the church does not come to the aid of justice, I have no despair about the future. I have no fear about the outcome of our struggle in Birmingham, even if our motives are at present misunderstood. We will reach the goal of freedom in Birmingham and all over the nation, because the goal of America is freedom. Abused and scorned though we may be, our destiny is tied up with America's destiny. Before the pilgrims landed at Plymouth, we were here. Before the pen of Jefferson etched the majestic words of the Declaration of Independence across the pages of history, we were here. For more than two centuries our forebears labored in this country without wages; they made cotton king; they built the homes of their masters while suffering gross injustice and shameful humiliation—and yet out of a bottomless vitality they continued to thrive and develop. If the inexpressible cruelties of slavery could not stop us, the opposition we now face will surely fail. We will win our freedom because the sacred heritage of our nation and the eternal will of God are embodied in our echoing demands.

Before closing I feel impelled to mention one other point in your statement that has troubled me profoundly. You warmly commended the Birmingham police force for keeping "order" and "preventing violence." I doubt that you would have so warmly commended the police force if you had seen its dogs sinking their teeth into unarmed, nonviolent Negroes. I doubt that you would so quickly commend the policemen if you were to observe their ugly and inhumane treatment of Negroes here in the city jail; if you were to watch them push and curse old Negro women and young Negro girls; if you were to see them slap and kick old Negro men and young boys; if you were to observe them, as they did on two occasions, refuse to give us food because we wanted to sing our grace together. I cannot join you in your praise of the Birmingham police department. 45

It is true that the police have exercised a degree of discipline in handling the demonstrators. In this sense they have conducted themselves rather "non-

15. The Greek New Testament word for the early Christian church.

violently" in public. But for what purpose? To preserve the evil system of segregation. Over the past few years I have consistently preached that nonviolence demands that the means we use must be as pure as the ends we seek. I have tried to make clear that it is wrong to use immoral means to attain moral ends. But now I must affirm that it is just as wrong, or perhaps even more so, to use moral means to preserve immoral ends. Perhaps Mr. Connor and his policemen have been rather nonviolent in public, as was Chief Pritchett in Albany, Georgia, but they have used the moral means of nonviolence to maintain the immoral end of racial injustice. As T. S. Eliot has said, "The last temptation is the greatest treason: To do the right deed for the wrong reason."[16]

I wish you had commended the Negro sit-inners and demonstrators of Birmingham for their sublime courage, their willingness to suffer, and their amazing discipline in the midst of great provocation. One day the South will recognize its real heroes. They will be the James Merediths,[17] with the noble sense of purpose that enables them to face jeering and hostile mobs, and with the agonizing loneliness that characterizes the life of the pioneer. They will be old, oppressed, battered Negro women, symbolized in a seventy-two-year-old woman in Montgomery, Alabama, who rose up with a sense of dignity and with her people decided not to ride segregated buses, and who responded with ungrammatical profundity to one who inquired about her weariness: "My feets is tired, but my soul is at rest." They will be the young high school and college students, the young ministers of the gospel and a host of their elders, courageously and nonviolently sitting in at lunch counters and willingly going to jail for conscience' sake. One day the South will know that when these disinherited children of God sat down at lunch counters, they were in reality standing up for what is best in the American dream and for the most sacred values in our Judaeo-Christian heritage, thereby bringing our nation back to those great wells of democracy which were dug deep by the founding fathers in their formulation of the Constitution and the Declaration of Independence.

Never before have I written so long a letter. I'm afraid it is much too long to take your precious time. I can assure you that it would have been much shorter if I had been writing from a comfortable desk, but what else can one do when he is alone in a narrow jail cell, other than write long letters, think long thoughts, and pray long prayers?

If I have said anything in this letter that overstates the truth and indicates an unreasonable impatience, I beg you to forgive me. If I have said anything that understates the truth and indicates my having a patience that allows me to settle for anything less than brotherhood, I beg God to forgive me.

50 I hope this letter finds you strong in the faith. I also hope that circumstances will soon make it possible for me to meet each of you, not as an integrationist or a civil-rights leader but as a fellow clergyman and a Christian brother.

16. American-born English poet (1888–1965); the lines are from his play *Murder in the Cathedral*.

17. Meredith (b. 1933) was the first black student to enroll at the University of Mississippi.

Let us all hope that the dark clouds of racial prejudice will soon pass away and the deep fog of misunderstanding will be lifted from our fear-drenched communities, and in some not too distant tomorrow the radiant stars of love and brotherhood will shine over our great nation with all their scintillating beauty.

Yours for the cause of Peace and Brotherhood,
MARTIN LUTHER KING JR.

QUESTIONS

1. King addressed the "Letter from Birmingham Jail" to eight fellow clergymen who had written a statement criticizing his activities (see note 1). Where and how, in the course of the "Letter," does he attempt to make common cause with them?

2. King was trained in oral composition, that is, in composing and delivering sermons. One device he uses as an aid to oral comprehension is prediction: he announces, in advance, the organization of what he is about to say. Locate examples of prediction in the "Letter."

3. Describe King's theory of nonviolent resistance.

4. Imagine an unjust law that, to you, would justify civil disobedience. Describe the law, the form your resistance would take, and the penalties you would expect to incur.

RANDALL BALMER *Diversity and Stability: The Paradox of Religious Pluralism*

"CONGRESS SHALL MAKE NO LAW respecting an establishment of religion, or prohibiting the free exercise thereof," the First Amendment to the United States Constitution states straightforwardly, and this simple principle, unprecedented in Western societies, has always attracted a good deal of notice from historians and legal scholars. "Religion in America takes no direct part in the government of society," Alexis de Tocqueville observed, "but nevertheless it must be regarded as the foremost of the political institutions of that country; for if it does not impart a taste for freedom, it facilitates the use of free institutions."[1] De Tocqueville was not the last to remark upon the unique relation of church and state, religion and politics, in American society.

From Blessed Assurance: A History of Evangelicalism in America *(1999), a book that offers a historical perspective on Evangelicalism's abiding importance in American culture and politics.*

1. Alexis de Tocqueville, *Democracy in America*, ed. Henry Steele Commager, trans. Henry Reeve (New York: Oxford University Press, 1947), 200 [Balmer's note]. Tocqueville (1805–1859) was a French political philosopher.

In 1844, historian Robert Baird extolled the voluntary principle in the United States as the "great alternative" to all European societies and their long, troubled history of church-state entanglements. "Religious liberty, fettered by no State enactment," Baird wrote, "is as perfect as it can be."[2] Although Philip Schaff, a native of Germany, harbored some old-fashioned notions about the unity of the church and the ability of Christianity to "leaven and sanctify all spheres of human life," in 1855 he offered grudging admiration for the American configuration of church and state, which he regarded as a "peculiarity in the ecclesiastical condition of North America."[3]

The willingness to give free rein to religious expression, to eschew an establishment, and to countenance the ambiguity arising from that social and political configuration has prompted twentieth-century historian Sidney E. Mead to characterize the relation of church and state in the United States as a "lively experiment."[4] His contemporary Winthrop Hudson defined voluntarism in America and the equilibrium between church and state as the "great tradition of the American churches."[5]

Historians have argued that although it was indeed unprecedented, the impetus for religious disestablishment as embodied in the First Amendment grew out of disparate impulses dating back at least to the Protestant Reformation.[6] Martin Luther's[7] emphasis on the priesthood of believers and each individual's responsibility before God led almost inevitably (if not immediately) to the concession that people might approach God differently, and the splintering of Christianity after the Reformation demanded some sort of accommodation on the part of government and society to religious diversity. Several of the American colonies had done just that; Thomas Jefferson[8] cited the examples of New York and Pennsylvania, which tolerated many denominations, in his *Notes on the State of Virginia,* written in 1781. In other colonies, however, such groups as the Anglicans in Maryland and Virginia, and the Congregationalists

2. Robert Baird, *Religion in America,* abridged edition with an introduction by Henry Warner Bowden (New York: Harper & Row, 1970), 120, 110 [Balmer's note]. Baird (1798–1863) was an American clergyman and historian of religion.

3. Philip Schaff, *America: A Sketch of Its Political, Social, and Religious Character,* ed. Perry Miller (Cambridge, Mass.: Harvard University Press, 1961; original published 1855), 11, 73 [Balmer's note]. Schaff (1819–1893) was a Swiss-born historian and Protestant theologian.

4. Sidney E. Mead, *The Lively Experiment: The Shaping of Christianity in America* (New York: Harper & Row, 1963) [Balmer's note]. Mead (1904–1999) was an American historian of religion.

5. Winthrop S. Hudson, *The Great Tradition of the American Churches* (New York: Harper & Brothers, 1953) [Balmer's note]. Hudson (1911–2001) was a Baptist minister and historian of religion.

6. A sixteenth-century Christian reform movement that led to a proliferation of Christian denominations.

7. Luther (1483–1546) was a leading figure in the Protestant Reformation.

8. Jefferson (1743–1826) was the primary author of the Declaration of Independence (1776) and the third president of the United States (1801–09).

in Massachusetts and Connecticut, stubbornly defended their establishment status. Several historians look to such figures and movements as Isaac Backus and the Separate Baptists in Connecticut or William Livingston and the Presbyterian party in New York as influential opponents of religious establishment.[9] Most often, however, when historians retrace the steps of religious disestablishment in America their paths lead to Roger Williams, in the seventeenth century, and to Jefferson himself.

5

Williams, a Puritan minister at Salem, Massachusetts, had grown increasingly uneasy about the continued identification of New England Puritanism with the Church of England. In 1635, the General Court of Massachusetts brought charges against him for disrupting the social and religious order of New England by proposing that the church at Salem separate completely from the other Massachusetts churches. The General Court banished Williams from the colony, whereupon he fled south, in January 1636, and founded Providence, which eventually became the charter colony of Rhode Island.

In 1644, responding to a letter from John Cotton, a prominent Puritan divine, Williams set out his views regarding the relation of church and state. "When they have opened a gap in the hedge or wall of separation between the garden of the church and the wilderness of the world," he wrote, "God hath ever broke down the wall itself, removed the candlestick, and made His garden a wilderness, as at this day."[10] Williams sought to protect religion from the depredations of the state, and he saw strict separation as the way to accomplish this. If God, Williams believed, "will ever please to restore His garden and paradise again, it must of necessity be walled in peculiarly unto Himself from the world; and that all that shall be saved out of the world are to be transplanted out of the wilderness of the world, and added unto His church or garden."[11]

A little over a hundred years later, Thomas Jefferson appropriated the "wall of separation" metaphor but toward somewhat different ends. Jefferson, a deist and a creature of the Enlightenment, believed passionately that religious beliefs were a private affair, that religious coercion violated natural rights, and that compelling someone "to furnish contributions of money for the propagation of opinions which he disbelieves and abhors" constituted a form of tyranny.[12] Reli-

9. See William G. McLoughlin, *New England Dissent, 1630–1833: The Baptists and the Separation of Church and State,* 2 vols. (Cambridge, Mass.: 1971); William G. McLoughlin, *Isaac Backus and the American Pietistic Tradition* (Boston: Little, Brown, 1967); John M. Mulder, "William Livingston: Propagandist Against Episcopacy," *Journal of Presbyterian History* 54 (1976): 83–104 [Balmer's note]. Backus (1724–1806) was an influential Baptist minister who opposed state-established religion; Livingston (1723–1790) was governor of New Jersey and a signer of the U.S. Constitution.

10. Perry Miller, *Roger Williams: His Contribution to the American Tradition* (Indianapolis, Ind.: Bobbs-Merrill, 1953), 98 [Balmer's note].

11. Ibid [Balmer's note].

12. Jefferson's "Act for Establishing Religious Freedom" (1786), quoted in John F. Wilson and Donald Drakeman, eds., *Church and State in American History,* 2nd ed. (Boston: Beacon Press, 1987), 16 [Balmer's note].

gious disestablishment, Jefferson believed, provided guarantees against such tyranny. Writing nearly two decades after the ratification of the First Amendment (he had been among its principal architects), Jefferson attested to his "solemn reverence for that act of the whole American people which declared that their legislature should 'make no law respecting an establishment of religion, or prohibiting the free exercise thereof,' thus building a wall of separation between church and State."[13]

Although Jefferson had carefully couched his rhetoric so as to appear that he wished merely to provide for the well-being of organized religion by guarding it against political meddling, it is difficult to escape the impression that he was at least equally concerned that religious factionalism and contentiousness might disrupt the functions of government. While serving as president, he considered the "experiment" in religious freedom that he had helped to create in the new Republic and pronounced it good precisely because it had proved conducive to political order and stability. "We have solved by fair experiment, the great and interesting question whether freedom is compatible with order in government, and obedience to the laws," he wrote to a group of Virginia Baptists in 1802. "And we have experienced the quiet as well as the comfort which results from leaving everyone to profess freely and openly those principles of religion which are the inductions of his own reason, and the serious convictions of his own inquiries."[14]

Both Roger Williams and Thomas Jefferson, then, although separated by more than a century, advocated religious disestablishment, albeit out of somewhat different motives. Williams saw the dangers of state interference in the affairs of the church—the wilderness encroaching on the garden—while Jefferson recognized the dangers that religious interests and factions posed to the political order that he and the other founders had so carefully fashioned.

10 I should like to suggest, however, that the configuration of church and state embodied in the First Amendment—the guarantee of free exercise of religion and the proscription against religious establishment—has succeeded over the past two hundred years beyond even the boldest expectations of either Williams or Jefferson. This wall of separation—which more accurately resembles a line in the dust, continually drawn and redrawn—has satisfied Jefferson's concern that confessional agendas not disrupt political stability, and it has also ensured the religious vitality everywhere in evidence throughout American history.

One characteristic of the United States Constitution implicit in all the flummery and celebration that surrounded its bicentennial is the remarkable resiliency of that document forged in the heat of political debate and compromise two hundred years earlier. It is indeed an extraordinary achievement, a tribute not only to the ideas of James Harrington, John Locke, Common Sense Realism, and the example of such documents as the Union of Utrecht, but also to the daring and inventiveness of a group of politicians willing to build those

13. Jefferson's letter to the Danbury Baptists, January 1, 1802, ibid., 79 [Balmer's note].
14. Quoted in Mead, *Lively Experiment,* 59 [Balmer's note].

ideas into a political structure that would hold thirteen disparate colonies together.[15] The writers of the Constitution showed considerable prescience in anticipating some of the problems that the new society might encounter—so much so, in fact, that a Supreme Court nominee in the 1980s could claim that most contemporary legal disputes could be settled by simple recourse to the "original intent" of the framers—but they also crafted a document of great elasticity and adaptability.

The American form of government has endured for more than two hundred years, and that must surely be its singular achievement. But what lies at the heart of that stability? Surely the Constitution itself, with its checks and balances and its representative democracy, forms the foundation, later strengthened by the freedoms provided for in the Bill of Rights—the first ten Amendments—and by the enfranchisement of women and minorities.

The first clause of the First Amendment, with its guarantee of free exercise of religion and the proscription against religious establishment, has made a particular contribution to American political stability, I shall argue, because religious freedom has siphoned off social discontent that might otherwise find expression in the political sphere. In other words, the kind of factionalism that concerned James Madison in *Federalist No. 10*[16] more often than not has flourished in religion rather than politics, with the effect that some of the energy and discontent that might be directed toward political change dissipates in religious bickering. In that respect, the disestablishment of religion has not only reduced religious pressure on the state, it has also meant that religious factionalism has often provided a buffer against political radicalism.

The idea that religion upholds the temporal order and protects the prevailing political and cultural institutions is, of course, a common refrain, repeated approvingly by Niccolò Machiavelli, Thomas Hobbes, Edmund Burke, and various Erastian Anglicans, and not so approvingly by Karl Marx and Friedrich Nietzsche.[17] The notion that religious *pluralism* can sustain the political order,

15. Regarding the influences on the founders, see Garry Wills, *Inventing America: Jefferson's Declaration of Independence* (Garden City, N.Y.: Doubleday, 1978); James Tanis, "From Provinces and Colonies to Federated States: The Dutch-American Example," paper given at the Tenth Rensselaerswyck Seminar, Albany, N.Y., 19 September 1987 [Balmer's note]. Harrington (1611–1677) was an English political philosopher who held that a strong middle class promotes stable democracy; Locke (1632–1704) was a major English empiricist philosopher and advocate of religious tolerance; Common Sense Realism is the philosophical view that things in the world are as we perceive them to be through our senses; Union of Utrecht (1579) was an alliance that led to the emergence of the Netherlands as a modern state.

16. *The Federalist* (1787–1788) is a series of eighty-five essays on republican government by Alexander Hamilton, James Madison, and John Jay; Madison (1751–1836) was a signer of the U.S. Constitution and fourth president of the United States (1809–1817).

17. T. H. Breen and Stephen Foster have argued that religious principles contributed to the stability of Puritan New England from settlement to the revocation of the charter. See their "The Puritans' Greatest Achievement: A Study of Social Cohesion in

however, is a uniquely American construct. Roger Williams and the founders of Rhode Island recognized the salutary effects of religious freedom. A "flourishing civil state may best be maintained," they believed, "with a full religious liberty, and . . . true piety will give the greatest security for sovereignty and true loyalty."[18] William Livingston, inveterate opponent of religious establishment in colonial New York, remarked in 1754 (a century later) that "nothing can tend so much to maintain our freedom and independency in religion as a division into a variety of sects."[19]

15 Not all American clerics recognized the value of disestablishment to religion immediately; some had to be converted. It was only after reflection that John Henry Livingston, a Dutch Reformed minister in New York, decided that in a country "where hearing is promoted & a spirit of enquiry prevails I am not apprehensive that the Christian religion can receive any essential injury from the greatest scope that can be given to religious freedom," adding that "forcing mankind into a union of sentiment by any machine of State is altogether preposterous & has done more harm to the cause of the gospel than the sword of persecution has ever effected."[20]

In New England, where Congregationalism enjoyed the benefits of establishment, the "standing order" of Congregationalist ministers at first bitterly opposed voluntarism, this notion that no one confession would enjoy preferential status, but they came in time to recognize the salutary effects of religious pluralism. Lyman Beecher[21] initially lamented Connecticut's disestablishment of Congregationalism, in 1818, as "a time of great depression and suffering," but shortly thereafter, flushed with a general revival of religion, he changed his tune. "We were thrown on God and on ourselves, and this created that moral coercion which makes men work," he remembered in 1820. "Before we had been standing on what our fathers had done, but now we were obliged to develop all our energy."[22]

Seventeenth-Century Massachusetts," *Journal of American History* 60 (1973): 5–22 [Balmer's note]. Machiavelli (1469–1527), a Florentine political philosopher, wrote *The Prince* (1513), a book famous for its ruthless advice to rulers; Hobbes (1588–1679), an English political philosopher, advanced the idea that governments are based on a "social contract" between individuals and a ruler or state; Burke (1729–1797) was a conservative English political philosopher and member of Parliament; Erastian Anglicans adhered to the view, erroneously attributed to Thomas Erastus (1524–1583), that state authority supersedes that of the church; Marx (1818–1883) was a major German political philosopher and critic of capitalism; Nietzsche (1844–1900) was a major German philosopher and cultural critic.

18. From the charter granted by Charles II on July 8, 1663, quoted in Wilson and Drakeman, *Church and State*, 16 [Balmer's note].

19. Edward T. Corwin, ed., *Ecclesiastical Records: State of New York*, 7 vols. (Albany, N.Y.: J. B. Lyon, 1901–1916), vol. 5, 3460 [Balmer's note].

20. Quoted in Richard W. Pointer, *Protestant Pluralism and the New York Experience: A Study of Eighteenth-Century Religious Diversity* (Bloomington and Indianapolis, Ind.: Indiana University Press, 1988), 88 [Balmer's note].

21. Beecher (1775–1863) was an American Presbyterian minister.

22. In Wilson and Drakeman, *Church and State*, 95 [Balmer's note].

One of the striking features of the United States, as compared with other Western nations, is the steadfastly centrist nature of its politics. Whereas European nations, most of them governed through the parliamentary system, undergo periodic changes—new political parties, ever shifting coalitions—the two political parties in the United States cling tenaciously to the ideological center. The very difficulty of breaking the pattern of two-party alignment (witness the failed efforts of Ross Perot in 1992 and 1996, John B. Anderson in 1980, George Wallace in 1968, Henry A. Wallace in 1948, and Teddy Roosevelt in 1912) attests to the persistence of moderate politics.[23] The United States has no Green Party to speak of, no Communist Party outside of Berkeley and Greenwich Village, no Conservative or Social Democratic Party that mounts a serious challenge to two-party hegemony.[24]

What America has, however, is religious diversity encompassing every conceivable tradition, confession, and ethnic group. The First Amendment gives all of them free rein. No religion is established, and no citizen is required to give allegiance (or monetary support) to any religious group.

And yet Americans do. The 1984 Gallup poll cited in the introduction found that only 9 percent of Americans expressed no religious preference. On the other hand, as noted previously, 56 percent claimed membership in a church or synagogue, and 40 percent said they attended church or synagogue weekly. Such figures are unheard of in England and Europe. In contrast, political participation is much higher there, while Americans are notoriously lackadaisical about exercising their right to vote. In Queens, New York, for instance, fewer than 55 percent of eligible voters are registered, and in the 1988 presidential election only 49.1 percent—less than half—of the voting-age population nationwide bothered to cast their ballots, a decrease from 53.1 percent in 1984.[25]

23. Perot (b. 1930) is an American businessman; Anderson (b. 1922) was a member of the House of Representatives (1961–1981) from Illinois; G. Wallace (1919–1998) served a number of terms as governor of Alabama (1963–1967, 1971–1979, 1983–1987); H. Wallace (1888–1965) was the vice president of the United States (1941–1945); Roosevelt (1858–1919) was president of the United States (1901–1909). Each ran unsuccessfully for president of the United States as an independent, or in the cases of H. Wallace and Roosevelt, as a third-party candidate.

24. The most votes that a Communist Party candidate for president has received was just over 100,000 (out of more than 38,000,000) in the election of 1932; the Communist presidential candidate received 36,386 votes in 1984 (Marvine Howe, "U.S. Communists May Not Field a 1988 Slate," *New York Times,* 20 November 1987) [Balmer's note]. The Green Party, Communist Party, and Social Democratic Party are European political parties associated with environmentalism, communism, and socialism, respectively.

25. "No Excuse Not to Register," *New York Times,* 16 October 1987; Michael Oreskes, "An American Habit: Shunning the Ballot Box," ibid., 31 Jan 1988; "Voter Turnout Up Slightly, Reversing Trend," ibid., 8 November 1984; "Portrait of the Electorate," ibid., 10 November 1988. Religion, of course, also serves as a conservative social force; for an excellent example of this, see Paul E. Johnson, *A Shopkeeper's Millennium: Society and Revivals in Rochester, New York, 1815–1837* (New York: Hill and Wang, 1978). See also Joseph R. Gusfield, *Symbolic Crusade: Status Politics and the American Temperance*

20 In America, then, religion rather than politics may provide the argot and the arena for popular discourse and the expression of discontent. The existence of what I've referred to as a kind of free market of religion, which means that citizen-consumers are free to shop in the unregulated "marketplace," also provides room for entrepreneurs. Anyone at all can gather around him or her a following of believers disenchanted in one way or another with the existing religious options. American history is full of examples: Alexander Campbell, Joseph Smith, Ellen Gould White, Mary Baker Eddy, Noble Drew Ali, J. Gresham Machen.[26] The majority of popular religious movements, I believe, divert social discontent away from the political and into the religious sphere. As such, religion in America has usually served as a conservative political force—that is, its very existence as a safety valve for social discontent tends to protect the state from radical zealots and the paroxysms of revolution.

Indeed, religious sentiments freely subscribed to without the coercion of the government have often served to shore up mainstream political values and the claims of the state.[27] The *McGuffey Reader*[28] of the nineteenth century, with its unabashed celebration of Protestant, middle-class, patriotic values, comes to mind, as do many other examples. The Catholic church in America, eager to shed its immigrant image, has gone out of its way to affirm the political order and to prove itself patriotic in spite of its putative loyalty to a foreign entity. Until recently, Reform Judaism required its rabbis to serve in the military chaplaincy. Most Protestants have taught their children and their congregants about the Christian's duty to the state as outlined in St. Paul's epistle to the Romans. Even the Mormons, after bitter disputes with the United States government in the nineteenth century, have become ardent defenders of the political status quo and a formidable conservative force.

The civil rights movement, deriving much of its energy and leadership from the black churches, was, in many respects, a *conservative* movement, at least in the means chosen to effect social change. Evangelicals, because of their populist theology and their genius at communication, have been particularly successful in the free marketplace of religion in America, and their reentry into the political arena in the mid-seventies—due in part to their contrived mythology

Movement (Urbana, Ill.: University of Illinois Press, 1963); Charles C. Cole, Jr., *The Social Ideas of the Northern Evangelists, 1826–1860* (New York: Columbia University Press, 1954) [Balmer's note].

26. Campbell (1788–1866) founded the Disciples of Christ; Smith (1805–1844) founded the Church of Jesus Christ of Latter-Day Saints, or Mormonism; White (1827–1915) was a founding member and prophet of the Seventh-Day Adventist Church; Eddy (1821–1910) founded the Church of Christian Science; Ali (1886–1929) founded the Moorish Science Temple of America in New Jersey; Machen (1881–1937) founded the Orthodox Presbyterian Church in America.

27. Religious groups have a vested interest in upholding the claims of the state because of the tax exemptions granted to religious organizations by all levels of government [Balmer's note].

28. The *McGuffey Readers* were series of elementary-school books designed by Ohio frontier schoolteacher William Holmes McGuffey (1800–1873).

about America's "Christian" origins—has helped to sustain a conservative swing in American politics.

Both American politicians and foreign observers have acknowledged the extent to which religious sentiment in America upholds the political order. In 1835, de Tocqueville reported that Americans believed a "sincere faith in their religion" was "indispensable to the maintenance of republican institutions," and he noted that "while the law permits the Americans to do what they please, religion prevents them from conceiving, and forbids them to commit, what is rash or unjust."[29] Extolling that connection has ever been a staple of political discourse. "Of all the dispositions and habits which lead to political prosperity," George Washington declared in his Farewell Address, "religion and morality are indispensable supports."[30] In the mid-twentieth century Dwight Eisenhower reasserted that symbiotic relationship bluntly. "Our government makes no sense unless it is founded on a deeply felt religious faith," he has been quoted as saying, "and I don't care what it is."[31]

I do not think there is any kind of mystical connection between religious conviction and the durability of America's political institutions, as de Tocqueville seems to imply. Rather, just as historians of an earlier age believed that the frontier served as a safety valve for social unrest or that a plenitude of wealth ensured a certain equilibrium,[32] I believe that the cornucopia of religious options—and the liberality with which Americans avail themselves of them—has contributed to America's political stability by providing an alternative to political dissent. It strikes me as no accident, for example, that the truly radical political movement of the sixties and early seventies, the student unrest directed against America's involvement in Vietnam, eventually dissipated in a wave of Eastern spirituality. Surely other forces—political, economic, and cultural—contributed as well, but I wonder if the plethora of religions in America, an abundance guaranteed by the First Amendment, did not help to deflect the radical impulses of the day.

Religious agendas do, of course, continue to shape our political debates, as they have always done. The identity of many Americans is tied up with their 25

29. De Tocqueville, *Democracy in America,* 200 [Balmer's note].

30. *Washington's "Farewell Address" in Facsimile, with Transliterations of All the Drafts of Washington, Madison, and Hamilton, Together with their Correspondence and Other Supporting Documents*, ed. Victor Hugo Paltsits (New York: New York Public Library, 1935), 151 [Balmer's note].

31. I express some hesitation about the quotation because it has never been documented that Eisenhower actually said it, although it is frequently attributed to him; see Patrick Henry, "'And I Don't Care What It Is': The Tradition-History of a Civil-Religion Proof Text," *Journal of the American Academy of Religion* 49 (1981): 35–49 [Balmer's note]. Eisenhower (1890–1969) was an army general and the thirty-fourth president of the United States (1953–1961).

32. Breen and Foster argue that the general prosperity of seventeenth-century New England contributed to its stability ("The Puritans' Greatest Achievement") [Balmer's note].

religious affiliations; many socialize almost exclusively within their religious groups and in any priority of self-disclosure would likely identify themselves as Lutheran or Catholic or Orthodox or Methodist before they would identify themselves as Republican or Democrat.

In 1855, Philip Schaff proposed that the religious verve and energy that he and other Europeans found in America could be traced to the voluntary principle, which, he said, "calls forth a mass of individual activity and interest among the laity in ecclesiastical affairs, in the founding of new churches and congregations, colleges and seminaries, in home and foreign missions, and in the promotion of all forms of Christian philanthropy."[33]

Schaff sought to vindicate his claim about the vitality of religion in America by comparing the patterns of religious affiliation in Berlin and New York City. "In Berlin there are hardly forty churches for a population of four hundred and fifty thousand, of whom, in spite of all the union of church and state, only some thirty thousand attend public worship," he wrote. "In New York, to a population of six hundred thousand, there are over two hundred and fifty well-attended churches, some of them quite costly and splendid, especially in Broadway and Fifth Avenue. In the city of Brooklyn, across the East River, the number of churches is still larger in proportion to the population, and in the country towns and villages, especially in New England, the houses of worship average one to every thousand, or frequently even five hundred, souls." And all of these, Schaff marveled, were supported not by public funds or state-enforced taxation, but by free-will offerings.[34] De Tocqueville had made a similar point twenty years earlier: "There are certain populations in Europe whose unbelief is only equaled by their ignorance and debasement," he wrote, "while in America one of the freest and most enlightened nations in the world fulfills all the outward duties of religion with fervor."[35]

The extraordinarily high level of religious belief and participation in America continues to confound Europeans today. By almost any standard, we are still a religious people. More than six Americans out of ten believe that "religion can answer all or most of today's problems," and only 10 percent express little or no confidence in organized religion.[36]

This confidence marks another distinctive characteristic of American religiosity—its lack of cynicism. Even with widespread publicity about the recent shenanigans of certain televangelists and the (sometimes disturbing, even tragic) activities of radical "cults," there seems to be very little anticlericalism—that is, animosity and suspicion toward religious leaders in general—in America today.

33. Schaff, *America,* 79 [Balmer's note].

34. Ibid., 78 [Balmer's note].

35. De Tocqueville, *Democracy in America,* 202 [Balmer's note].

36. "Religion in America: 50 Years: 1935–1985," *The Gallup Report,* no. 236 (May 1985): 18, 50: ibid., no. 222 (March 1984): 28; Richard John Neuhaus, ed., *Unsecular America* (Grand Rapids, Mich.: W. B. Eerdmans, 1986), 119 [Balmer's note].

Indeed, ever since the First Great Awakening,[37] when evangelicals struggled bitterly against religious establishments and protested the European identification of the clergy with the aristocracy, American history has been virtually free of anticlericalism as such. This again derives, no doubt, from the availability of religious options guaranteed by the Constitution. Why put up with a minister, a confession, or a tradition not to your liking when there are so many alternatives for the taking? Religion has remained a force in America precisely because of this ever-changing menu of religious entrées.

England, once again, provides a useful contrast. Recall, for instance, John Lennon's offhanded comment in 1966 that "Christianity will go"—that the Beatles were "more popular than Jesus now." In Britain that observation elicited nary a comment, but in America it triggered a wave of record burnings and anti-Beatles demonstrations across the country, the intensity of which made the young Liverpudlians fear for their lives.[38] Ironically, Lennon, a former chorister at St. Peter's Church in Woolton, was probably correct insofar as his observations applied to Britain. "We are not a very religious people anymore," a woman in London informed me during a recent visit, in a tone more bemused than apologetic, "and so we have tried to devise ways to use some of these old churches creatively." The parish church adjacent to the archbishop of Canterbury's London residence, just across the Thames from Parliament, is now a garden club. Over the past thirty years nearly 2,000 of England's 16,000 Anglican churches have closed for lack of use, and the established Church of England draws only about 3 percent of the population to its worship services.[39] Perhaps after all the internecine religious battles of the Tudor and Stuart periods the English have simply wearied of religion, but I suspect that the relative absence of religious options in England has rendered Anglicanism rather bland and homogenized and that the English look elsewhere for their voluntary affiliations—to the plethora of political parties, for example, or to garden clubs.

Religious disestablishment and the guarantee of free exercise of religion in America, on the other hand, have provided the climate for a vigorous religious culture—one that is anything but bland or homogenized. Because various religious groups must compete to survive in a buyer's market, voluntarism has lent an unmistakably populist cast to religion in America. While an inevitable pandering to popular tastes has sometimes tended, I think, to elevate form over content and to diminish the overall quality of religious belief and commitment, religious freedom has also ensured a rich and variegated spiritual landscape. American religion boasts a diversity and vibrancy unmatched in any Western culture, and we Americans, with our passion for novelty and our notoriously latitudinarian religious beliefs, freely partake of this cornu-

37. A Protestant religious revival that took place in the American colonies from the 1720s through the 1740s.

38. Philip Norman, *Shout! The Beatles in Their Generation* (New York: Simon & Schuster, 1981), 265–66 [Balmer's note].

39. Francis X. Clines, "With Bare Churches, It's Barely England's Church," *New York Times,* 11 May 1987 [Balmer's note].

copia.[40] And, of course, there is always the possibility that if you are dissatisfied with the available options, you can start your own religious group. The First Amendment guarantees that right.

Whereas historian Charles Beard has argued that the U.S. Constitution was a conservative document in that it safeguarded the economic interests of the landed elite, I am suggesting that the Constitution was conservative in a far more subtle way: the First Amendment, by setting up a free market of religion, has not only ensured religious vitality but it has also helped to thwart political radicalism by redirecting malcontents away from the structured public sphere of American politics and into the pliant and more private domain of religion.

Thomas Jefferson and Roger Williams make strange bedfellows, and it is easy to speculate on the issues upon which they would have disagreed. Williams—first a Puritan, then a Baptist, and then a "seeker"—held strict ideas about the importance of the Bible and the need to separate from evil. Jefferson, on the other hand, excised large portions of the Bible that failed to conform to his own rationalistic, Enlightenment notions. While Williams looked forward to a "never-ending harvest of inconceivable joys" in the afterlife,[41] Jefferson fervently believed that Americans would eventually embrace Unitarianism as their religion of choice.

Despite their radical differences in terms of theology, both Williams and Jefferson agreed on the desirability of religious disestablishment, Williams because he sought to maintain a pure church and Jefferson because he sought political stability. I would suggest that after two hundred years, both might take satisfaction in the results of the unprecedented experiment in religious toleration to which they each contributed. It has lent political stability by diverting social discontent into the religious sphere, and it has ensured religious vitality by guaranteeing untrammeled expression in the free marketplace of American religion.

35 It may be too much to assume of Roger Williams and Thomas Jefferson that either anticipated fully the effects of religious disestablishment in America. Most Americans are well aware of Jefferson's manifold contributions to American life—as architect and inventor, as political theorist, diplomat, and politician—while Williams remains a relatively obscure figure. "Why is our candle yet burning," Williams asked rhetorically near the end of his life, but to serve "God by serving the public in our generation?"[42] In insisting on freedom of religion and liberty of conscience, each of these leaders provided a service that extended well beyond his own generation.

40. On American latitudinarianism in religion, see Patricia U. Bonomi, *Under the Cope of Heaven: Religion, Society, and Politics in Colonial America* (New York: Oxford University Press, 1986), 218–20; Robert N. Bellah et al., *Habits of the Heart: Individualism and Commitment in American Life* (Berkeley and Los Angeles: University of California Press, 1985), chap. 9 [Balmer's note].

41. Quoted in Edwin S. Gaustad, *Liberty of Conscience: Roger Williams in America* (Grand Rapids, Mich.: Wm. B. Eerdmans, 1991), 167 [Balmer's note].

42. Quoted ibid., 189 [Balmer's note].

QUESTIONS

1. Balmer subtitles his essay "The Paradox of Religious Pluralism." Why does he characterize religious pluralism as a paradox? How does the idea of paradox structure the essay?

2. Balmer writes in a professional academic style. What are the hallmarks of this style? What might be its advantages or limitations?

3. Balmer holds that American religion has historically protected the state from political unrest by serving as a "safety valve for social discontent" (paragraph 20). Test this assertion against an example or examples from your own experience. Do you see religion working in this way? Write a response either agreeing or disagreeing with Balmer's "safety valve" theory.

STEPHEN CARTER *The Separation of Church and State*

BY NOW, MANY A PATIENT READER will be ready with another objection: it is all very well to talk about allowing the religious to enter the public square to participate in political debate alongside everybody else. But what about the Constitution? What about the separation of church and state? Don't we have longstanding constitutional and philosophical traditions that limit the influence of religious sectarianism on government policy?

The answer to the last question—as so often in the law—is "not exactly." The courts do indeed enforce a separation of church and state, and it is backed by some very impressive legal philosophy, but one must be careful not to misunderstand what the doctrine and the First Amendment that is said to embody it were designed to do. Simply put, the metaphorical separation of church and state originated in an effort to protect religion from the state, not the state from religion. The religion clauses of the First Amendment were crafted to permit maximum freedom to the religious. In modern, religiously pluralistic America, where, as we have seen, the religions play vital roles as independent sources of meaning for their adherents, this means that the government should neither force people into sectarian religious observances, such as classroom prayer in public schools, nor favor some religions over others, as by erecting a crèche paid for with public funds, nor punish people for their religiosity without a very strong reason other than prejudice. It does not mean, however, that people whose motivations are religious are banned from trying to influence government, nor that the government is banned from listening to them. Understanding this distinction is the key to preserving the necessary separation of church and state without resorting to a philosophical rhetoric that treats religion as an inferior way for citizens to come to public judgment.

From The Culture of Disbelief: How American Law and Politics Trivialize Religious Devotion *(1993), a book that defends the centrality of religion in American political life.*

THE SEPARATION METAPHOR

Religion is the first subject of the First Amendment. The amendment begins with the Establishment Clause ("Congress shall make no law respecting an establishment of religion . . .") which is immediately followed by the Free Exercise Clause ("or prohibiting the free exercise thereof"). Although one might scarcely know it from the zeal with which the primacy of the other First Amendment freedoms (free press, free speech) is often asserted, those protections come *after* the clauses that were designed to secure religious liberty, which Thomas Jefferson called "the most inalienable and sacred of all human rights."[1] What this means in practice, however, is often quite complicated.

Consider an example: at a dinner party in New York City a few years ago, I met a Christian minister who told me about a drug-rehabilitation program that he runs in the inner city. His claim—I cannot document it—was that his program had a success rate much higher than other programs. The secret, he insisted, was prayer. It was not just that he and his staff prayed for the drug abusers they were trying to help, he told me, although they naturally did that. But the reason for the program's success, he proclaimed, was that he and his staff taught those who came to them for assistance to pray as well; in other words, they converted their charges, if not to Christianity, then at least to religiosity. But this program, he went on with something close to bitterness, could receive no state funding, because of its religious nature.

5 Well, all right. To decide that the program should not receive any funds, despite the success of its approach, might seem to be a straightforward application of the doctrine holding that the Constitution sets up a wall of separation between church and state. After all, the program is frankly religious: it uses prayer, and even teaches prayer to its clients. What could be more threatening to the separation of church and state than to provide a government subsidy for it? The Supreme Court has said many times that the government may neither "advance" religion nor engage in an "excessive entanglement" with it.[2] On its face, a program of drug-rehabilitation therapy that relies on teaching people to pray would seem to do both.

It is doubtless frustrating to believe deeply that one has a call from God to do what one does, and then to discover that the secular society often will not support that work, no matter how important it is to the individual. Yet that frustration is itself a sign of the robustness of religious pluralism in America. For the most significant aspect of the separation of church and state is not, as some seem to think, the shielding of the secular world from too strong a religious influence; the principal task of the separation of church and state is to secure religious liberty.

1. Thomas Jefferson, "Freedom of Religion at the University of Virginia," in Saul K. Padover, ed., *The Complete Jefferson* (New York: Duell, Sloan & Pierce, 1943), p. 958 [Carter's note]. Thomas Jefferson (1743–1826) was the primary author of the Declaration of Independence (1776) and the third president of the United States (1801–09).

2. The quoted language is from *Lemon v. Kurtzman,* 403 U.S. 602 (1971), discussed later in this chapter [Carter's note].

The separation of church and state is one of the great gifts that American political philosophy has presented to the world, and if it has few emulators, that is the world's loss. Culled from the writings of Roger Williams[3] and Thomas Jefferson, the concept of a "wall of separation" finds its constitutional moorings in the First Amendment's firm statement that the "Congress shall make no law respecting any establishment of religion." Although it begins with the word "Congress," the Establishment Clause for decades has been quite sensibly interpreted by the Supreme Court as applying to states as well as to the federal government.[4]

For most of American history, the principal purpose of the Establishment Clause has been understood as the protection of the religious world against the secular government. A century ago, Philip Schaff of Union Seminary in New York celebrated the clause as "the Magna Carta of religious freedom," representing as it did "the first example in history of a government deliberately depriving itself of all legislative control over religion."[5] Note the wording: not religious control over government—government control over religion. Certainly this voluntary surrender of control is an indispensable separation if the religions are to serve as the independent intermediary institutions that Tocqueville[6] envisioned.

Over the years, the Supreme Court has handed down any number of controversial decisions under the Establishment Clause, many of them landmarks of our democratic culture. The best known are the cases in which the Justices struck down the recital of organized prayer in the public school classrooms, decisions that for three decades have ranked (in surveys) as among the most unpopular in our history.[7] But the decisions were plainly right, for if the state

3. Roger Williams (1603–1683), a proponent of religious freedom, founded the colony of Rhode Island after being banished from Massachusetts.

4. For a thoughtful discussion of the reasons that the Establishment Clause applies to the states, see Justice William Brennan's concurring opinion in *Abington School District v. Schempp,* 374 U.S. 203 (1963). The application of the Establishment Clause to the states has its critics, including, implicitly, two members of the Supreme Court, but for a variety of reasons, most of them linked to the arcana of constitutional interpretation, I am not among them. To put matters most simply, I ally myself with those who believe that many of the rights that American citizens possess against the federal government through the First Amendment became effective against the states with the adoption of the Fourteenth Amendment after the Civil War [Carter's note].

5. Philip Schaff, *Church and State in the United States* (New York: Putnam, 1888), pp. 22–23; quoted in Robert T. Handy, *Undermined Establishment: Church-State Relations in America, 1880–1920* (Princeton, N.J.: Princeton University Press, 1991), p. 20 [Carter's note]. Schaff (1819–1893) was a Swiss-born historian and protestant theologian.

6. Alexis de Tocqueville (1805–1859) was a French political philosopher; he is best known for his study of America's political and social systems, *Democracy in America* (1835, 1840).

7. The decisions of the Supreme Court collectively known as the "school prayer cases" include: *Engel v. Vitale,* 370 U.S. 421 (1962) (no state-drafted prayer in public schools); *Abington School District v. Schempp,* 374 U.S. 203 (1963) (no devotional Bible readings in public schools); *Wallace v. Jaffree,* 472 U.S. 38 (1985) (no moment of silence in public

is either able to prescribe a prayer to begin the school day or to select a holy book from which a prayer must be taken, it is casting exercising control over the religious aspects of the life of its people—precisely what the Establishment Clause was written to forbid. But although the separation of church and state is essential to the success of a vibrant, pluralistic democracy, the doctrine does not entail all that is done in its name. I have already mentioned the school district in Colorado that thought it the better part of valor to forbid a teacher to add books on Christianity to a classroom library that already included works on other religions. The town of Hamden, Connecticut, where I live, briefly ruled that a church group could not rent an empty schoolhouse for Sunday services. (Cooler heads in the end prevailed.) These rulings were both defended as required by the separation of church and state; so is the intermittent litigation to strike the legend IN GOD WE TRUST from America's coins or the phrase "under God" from the Pledge of Allegiance, an effort, if successful, that would wipe away even the civil religion. In short, it is not hard to understand the frequent complaints that the secular world acts as though the constitutional command is that the nation and its people must keep religion under wraps.

10 Proponents of the hostility thesis believe that the Supreme Court bears a heavy burden of responsibility for what they see as the disfavored position of religion in America. Justice Hugo Black, in *Everson v. Board of Education* (1947), often is said to have started the ball rolling when he wrote these words: "The First Amendment has erected a wall between church and state. That wall must be kept high and impregnable. We could not approve the slightest breach."[8] A year later, Justice Stanley Reed warned that "a rule of law should not be drawn from a figure of speech."[9] One critic wrote years later that Black had simply penned a few "lines of fiction."[10] The critics are not quite right, but they are not quite wrong, either. There is nothing wrong with the metaphor of a wall of separation. The trouble is that in order to make the Founders' vision compatible with the structure and needs of modern society, the wall has to have a few doors in it.

SOURING ON *LEMON*

The embarrassing truth is that the Establishment Clause has no theory; that is, the Supreme Court has not really offered guidance on how to tell when the clause is violated. Since 1971, the Justices have relied on the "*Lemon* test," so

---

schools if used as subterfuge for prayer); *Lee v. Weisman,* 112 S. Ct. 2649 (1992) (no school-sponsored spoken prayer at high school graduation) [Carter's note].

8. *Everson v. Board of Education,* 330 U.S. 1, 18 (1947) [Carter's note]. Hugo LaFayette Black (1886–1971) was a U.S. Supreme Court Justice (1937–1971) whose opinions helped to end school segregation and to support the principle of separation of church and state.

9. *McCollum v. Board of Education,* 333 U.S. 203, 247 (1948) (Justice Stanley Reed, dissenting) [Carter's note]. Stanley Reed (1884–1980) served as a U.S. Supreme Court Justice from 1938 to 1957.

10. Robert L. Cord, *Separation of Church and State: Historical Fact and Current Fiction* (New York: Lambeth Press, 1982), p. 49 [Carter's note].

named because it was framed (quite awkwardly, one is compelled to add) in the Court's 1971 decision in *Lemon v. Kurtzman*.[11] The case is so often cited that legal scholars tend to forget what it involved: a state program to reimburse all private schools, including religious schools, for expenses of textbooks, materials, and, in part, salaries used to teach nonreligious subjects. * * * The Court held the program unconstitutional and, in so doing, enunciated the *Lemon* test—a lemon indeed, for it has proved well nigh impossible to apply. In order to pass Establishment Clause muster, the Justices wrote, the statute in question must meet three criteria: "First, the statute must have a secular legislative purpose; second, its principal or primary effect must be one that neither advances nor inhibits religion; finally, the statute must not foster 'an excessive entanglement with religion.'"

Thus conceived, the clause exists less for the benefit of religious autonomy than for the benefit of secular politics; that is, to borrow from the test itself, the Establishment Clause was written to further "a secular legislative purpose," trying to erect around the political process a wall almost impossible to take seriously. It is perhaps needless to add that *Lemon* left the critics in their glory. Did the legislation enacted at the behest of the religiously motivated civil rights movement have a secular purpose? If granting tax relief to parents whose children attend parochial schools advances religion by making the schools cheaper, does refusing to grant them inhibit religion by making the schools more expensive? If competing factions within the same church both seek control of the same church building, does judicial resolution represent an excessive entanglement?

When it promulgates complex multipart tests for constitutional violations, the Supreme Court is almost always luckless, but the *Lemon* test has been extraordinarily unhelpful to the lower courts. Indeed, the courts have reached results that are all over the map—sometimes quite literally, for one of the more interesting cases involved a rather bland "Motorists' Prayer" to God for safety that North Carolina printed on its official state maps. A federal court, missing the significance of America's civil religion, held the practice to be a violation of the Establishment Clause.[12] Another federal court ruled that the clause prohibits religious groups from petitioning the Congress for private laws (available to all other groups) in order to secure copyrights when they are unable to meet the statutory criteria.[13] The list goes on and on—but *Lemon* remains.

The Supreme Court itself has not fared much better than the lower courts in applying its test. The *Lemon* framework might not work too badly, could the courts but take the requirement of a "secular legislative purpose" to mean, as one scholar has proposed, any "political purpose"—that is, any goal the state legitimately is able to pursue. Recently, however, the courts have seemed to

11. *Lemon v. Kurtzmann*, 403 U.S. 602 (1971) [Carter's note].

12. *Bradshaw v. North Carolina Department of Transportation*, 630 F.2d 1018 (4th Cir. 1980), *cert. denied*, 450 U.S. 965 (1981) [Carter's note].

13. See *United Christian Scientists v. Christian Science Board of Directors*, 829 F.2d 1152 (D.C. Cir. 1987) [Carter's note].

fumble this point, confusing the political purpose for which the statute is enacted with the religious sensibilities of legislators or their constituents.

15 A majority of the Supreme Court missed this point in *Edwards v. Aguillard* (1987), with the suggestion that a law requiring schools to teach scientific creationism is unconstitutional because most of its supporters were religiously motivated—a suggestion that would also render unconstitutional the religiously motivated teaching of evolution, or, for that matter, a religiously motivated nuclear arms freeze.[14] A similar suggestion has been made by some pro-choice scholars who have argued that pro-life legislation violates the Establishment Clause because of the religious motivation of many supporters. For the religiously devout citizen, faith may be so intertwined with personality that it is impossible to tell when one is acting, or not acting, from religious motive—and this is certainly true for legislators, unless we dismiss as hypocritical cynics the entire Congress of the United States, where over 90 percent of the members say that they consult their religious beliefs before voting on important matters. Indeed, by some estimates, an absolute majority of the laws now on the books were motivated, at least in part, by religiously based moral judgments. That is why inquiring into *why* legislators have voted as they have, rather than *what* their legislation does, is almost always a mistake. "That values happen to be religious," New York's Governor Mario Cuomo has warned, "does not deny them acceptability" as part of "the consensus view" needed to support public policy.[15] The result in *Edwards* is probably correct, * * * but not because of the Court's discussion of what was in the minds of the supporters of the statute.

The idea that religious motivation renders a statute suspect was never anything but a tortured and unsatisfactory reading of the clause. As one scholar has put the matter, there is good reason to think that "what the religion clauses of the first amendment were designed to do was not to remove religious values from the arena of public debate, but to keep them there."[16] The Establishment Clause by its terms forbids the imposition of religious belief by the state, not statements of religious belief in the course of public dialogue.[17] The distinction is one of more than semantic significance.

Consider the call by Reinhold Niebuhr and others back in the 1920s for the "Christianization" of American industry.[18] Their use of the word

14. 482 U.S. 578 (1987) [Carter's note].

15. Mario M. Cuomo, "Religious Belief and Public Morality: A Catholic Governor's Perspective," *Notre Dame Journal of Law, Ethics, and Public Policy* 1 (1984): 13, 19 [Carter's note]. Cuomo (b. 1932) was a Democratic governor of New York from 1983 to 1994.

16. Robert N. Van Wyk, "Liberalism, Religion and Politics," *Public Affairs Quarterly* (July 1987): 59, 68, Franklin J. Gramwell, "Religion and Reason in American Politics," *Journal of Law and Religion* 2 (1984): 326 [Carter's note].

17. See Michael W. McConnell, "Why 'Separation' Is Not the Key to Church-State Relations," *Christian Century,* 1989, p. 43 [Carter's note].

18. See Richard Fox, *Reinhold Niebuhr: A Biography* (San Francisco: Harper & Row, 1985), pp. 62–192. For a discussion of the "social gospel" movement among liberal Protestants, a movement Niebuhr largely disdained, see Robert T. Handy, *Undermined Establishment: Church-State Relations in America* (Princeton, NJ: Princeton University

"Christianization" did not mean the imposition of ritual and doctrine; it meant, rather, the transformation of industry into a new form that would accord with a principle of respect for the human spirit that Niebuhr and the rest found lacking in industrial organizations of the day. Critics called it socialism, or perhaps communism. But whatever it was, religious faith was plainly at its heart.

Niebuhr struck a chord, not only with any number of left-leaning Protestants, but also with a good number of socialists, many of them Jews, and with other reformers of no religious persuasion. (A well-known support group was Atheists for Niebuhr.) Suppose the response had been greater, that public support had burgeoned; suppose that legislatures had begun enacting programs that matched the socialist spirit of Christianization. This reform legislation would be purely secular in operation and could certainly be justified in secular terms. But under an establishment clause that is read to equate *acting* out of religious motivation with *imposing* religious belief, the programs might be unconstitutional, because both those who proposed them and many of those who voted for them would have done so out of religious conviction.

That should be a deeply troubling result. A rule holding that the religious convictions of the proponents are enough to render a statute constitutionally suspect represents a sweeping rejection of the deepest beliefs of millions of Americans, who are being told, in effect, that their views do not matter. In a nation that prides itself on cherishing religious freedom, it would be something of a puzzle to conclude that the Establishment Clause means that a Communist or a Republican may try to have his or her world view reflected in the nation's law, but a religionist can not. Although some critics fear we are already at that point, the truth is that we have a good long way to go; but we are heading in the wrong direction in our jurisprudence, and if the courts continue to read *Lemon* as they have, the Establishment Clause might well end up not antiestablishment but antireligion.

20

Recognizing this danger, the Justices, and the scholars who support their Establishment Clause jurisprudence, have simply ignored the rules of *Lemon v. Kurtzman* when applying them might prove too disruptive.[19] In particular, they have tried to tiptoe around many widely accepted practices that seem to run afoul of *Lemon*. But squaring *Lemon*'s rules with the accepted usages of the society's civil religion often requires some fancy footwork. How, for example, does one justify the expenditure of government funds to provide armed forces chaplains, which looks like government sponsorship of religion? Answers one observer; "This is not so much 'setting up a church' as providing access to

Press, 1991), pp. 58–67, 104–125. For an argument that the theology underlying the liberal social gospel movement was closely linked to the theology underlying that of Christian imperialism, see William R. Hutchison, *Errand to the World: American Protestant Thought and Foreign Missions* (Chicago: University of Chicago Press, 1987) [Carter's note]. Reinhold Niebuhr (1892–1971) was an American theologian who advocated "realism" in American international relations.

19. Jesse Choper, "Church, State and the Supreme Court: Current Controversy," *Arizona Law Review* 29 (1987): 551, 552 [Carter's note].

churches already existing for those removed by government action from their normal communities."[20] Okay, but how to explain the use of public funds during the Christmas season to build and maintain a crèche, which celebrates the nativity of Jesus Christ? The Court itself tackled that one: "The display engenders a friendly community spirit of good will in keeping with the season" and any advancement of particular religions "is indirect, remote and incidental."[21] Oh, really? Well, what about the offering of prayers at the opening of legislative sessions? The Justices had an answer for that one too: "In light of the unambiguous and unbroken history of more than 200 years, there can be no doubt that the practice of opening legislative sessions with prayer has become part of the fabric of our society."[22]

Part of the fabric of our society—it is easy to see why the Court is reluctant to hold that the fabric of society includes some threads of unconstitutionality, but it is difficult to imagine how that can be the right test. Racial segregation was once part of the fabric of our society; so was prohibiting the women's vote, and corrupt patronage politics in the big cities. The idea, for example, that a crèche does not advance religion is ridiculous; the point of the crèche is to celebrate the birth of the Lord. So if the Court is willing to ignore *Lemon* and hold that government funds can pay for one, it is simply not doing its job.[23] If the Justices dare not even follow their own rules, it may be time to find a new way to look at these problems. Yet the Supreme Court, although hinting around the edges, has not yet decided to make a full retreat.

Part of the problem is figuring out where the Justices can possibly retreat to. For even if the Court's *Lemon* test is insupportable, it is far from clear what should be put in its place. On this point, not surprisingly, there is a considerable scholarly battle, in which it is healthiest to be a spectator. Michael McConnell has proposed a standard based on coercion of belief, which he has labeled the "lost element" of Establishment Clause jurisprudence.[24] Douglas Laycock has shot back that this test would leave the Establishment Clause void of content.[25] Justice Sandra Day O'Connor has proposed a test asking whether the

20. Dean M. Kelley, *Why Churches Should Not Pay Taxes* (New York: Harper & Row, 1977), p. 143 [Carter's note].

21. *Lynch v. Donnelly,* 465 U.S. 668 (1984) [Carter's note].

22. *Marsh v. Chambers,* 463 U.S. 783 (1983) [Carter's note].

23. For a useful discussion of the Court's failures on this issue, see Alan M. Dershowitz, *Chutzpah* (Boston: Little, Brown, 1991), pp. 331–34 [Carter's note].

24. See Michael W. McConnell, "Coercion: The Lost Element of Establishment," *William and Mary Law Review* 27 (1986): 933 [Carter's note]. McConnell (b. 1955) was a judge on the U.S. Court of Appeals for the Tenth Circuit (2002–09) and is currently director of the Stanford Constitutional Law Center.

25. See Douglas Laycock, "'Noncoercive' Support for Religion: Another False Claim about the Establishment Clause," *Virginia Law Review* 26 (1991): 37 [Carter's note]. Laycock (b. 1948), a legal scholar known for his work on religious liberty, is a professor at the University of Virginia School of Law.

government is endorsing religious belief or not.[26] Mark Tushnet has answered that Christian judges in a Christian-dominated society are not in the best position to tell whether a message of endorsement is being sent.[27] Steven D. Smith, distinguishing between religious individuals and their organizations, has suggested prohibiting only concerted action by state and religious institutions.[28] Kathleen Sullivan has taken the opposite position, proposing to use the clause to guarantee a secular public order.[29] And one could go on this way at some considerable length.

Constitutional provisions all too rarely, alas, have easily discernible meanings, and there are elements of truth in all these readings of the Establishment Clause. Yet what is most vital, in coming to a sensible understanding of the clause, is to avoid the ahistorical conclusion that its principal purpose is to protect the secular from the religious, an approach that, perhaps inevitably, carries us down the road toward a new establishment, the establishment of religion as a hobby, trivial and unimportant for serious people, not to be mentioned in serious discourse. And nothing could be further from the constitutional, historical, or philosophical truth.

* * *

26. See *Lynch v. Donnelly,* 465 U.S. 668, 688 (1984) (Justice Sandra Day O'Connor, concurring) [Carter's note]. O'Connor (b. 1930) was the first woman to sit on the U.S. Supreme Court (1981–2006).

27. See Mark Tushnet, *Red, White, and Blue: A Critical Analysis of Constitutional Law* (Cambridge, MA: Harvard University Press, 1988), pp. 256–57, *n* 31 [Carter's note]. Tushnet (b. 1945) is a professor at the Harvard Law School associated with the Critical Legal Studies movement.

28. Steven D. Smith, "Separation and the 'Secular': Reconstructing the Disestablishment Decision," *Texas Law Review* 67 (1989): 955 [Carter's note]. Smith (b. 1952) is a professor at the University of San Diego School of Law.

29. Kathleen M. Sullivan, "Religion and Liberal Democracy," *University of Chicago Law Review* 59 (1992): 195 [Carter's note]. Sullivan (b. 1955) is a professor at, and former dean of, the Stanford Law School.

QUESTIONS

1. Carter observes that "the wall [between church and state] has to have a few doors in it" (paragraph 10). What sorts of doors does Carter advocate? Why?

2. Carter adopts a historical perspective toward the Establishment Clause and the separation of church and state. How does this perspective shape his argument?

3. Carter's prose is generally formal and academic, but he adopts a more casual tone repeatedly in the essay. What are the effects of this stylistic choice?

4. Locate and read the text of one of the Supreme Court opinions Carter discusses. What do you think the opinion is saying about the separation of church and state? Write about the ways in which your interpretation of the opinion supports or challenges Carter's.

Spoken Words

Martin Luther King Jr. *I Have a Dream*

Five score years ago,[1] a great American, in whose symbolic shadow we stand, signed the Emancipation Proclamation. This momentous decree came as a great beacon light of hope to millions of Negro slaves who had been seared in the flames of withering injustice. It came as a joyous daybreak to end the long night of captivity.

But one hundred years later, we must face the tragic fact that the Negro is still not free. One hundred years later, the life of the Negro is still sadly crippled by the manacles of segregation and the chains of discrimination. One hundred years later, the Negro lives on a lonely island of poverty in the midst of a vast ocean of material prosperity. One hundred years later, the Negro is still languishing in the corners of American society and finds himself an exile in his own land. So we have come here today to dramatize an appalling condition.

In a sense we have come to our nation's capital to cash a check. When the architects of our republic wrote the magnificent words of the Constitution and the Declaration of Independence, they were signing a promissory note to which every American was to fall heir. This note was a promise that all men would be guaranteed the inalienable rights of life, liberty, and the pursuit of happiness.

It is obvious today that America has defaulted on this promissory note insofar as her citizens of color are concerned. Instead of honoring this sacred obligation, America has given the Negro people a bad check which has come back marked "insufficient funds." But we refuse to believe that the bank of justice is bankrupt. We refuse to believe that there are insufficient funds in the great vaults of opportunity of this nation. So we have come to cash this check—a check that will give us upon demand the riches of freedom and the security of justice. We have also come to this hallowed spot to remind America of the fierce urgency of *now*. This is no time to engage in the luxury of cooling off or to take the tranquilizing drug of gradualism. *Now* is the time to rise from the dark and desolate valley of segregation to the sunlit path of racial justice. *Now* is the time to open the doors of opportunity to all of God's children. *Now* is the time to lift our nation from the quicksands of racial injustice to the solid rock of brotherhood.

Delivered on the steps of the Lincoln Memorial in Washington, D.C., on August 28, 1963, at one of the largest civil rights demonstrations in U.S. history.

1. An echo of Lincoln's Gettysburg Address, "Four score . . ."

It would be fatal for the nation to overlook the urgency of the moment and to underestimate the determination of the Negro. This sweltering summer of the Negro's legitimate discontent[2] will not pass until there is an invigorating autumn of freedom and equality. Nineteen sixty-three is not an end, but a beginning. Those who hope that the Negro needed to blow off steam and will now be content will have a rude awakening if the nation returns to business as usual. There will be neither rest nor tranquility in America until the Negro is granted his citizenship rights. The whirlwinds of revolt will continue to shake the foundations of our nation until the bright day of justice emerges. 5

But there is something that I must say to my people who stand on the warm threshold which leads into the palace of justice. In the process of gaining our rightful place we must not be guilty of wrongful deeds. Let us not seek to satisfy our thirst for freedom by drinking from the cup of bitterness and hatred.

We must forever conduct our struggle on the high plane of dignity and discipline. We must not allow our creative protest to degenerate into physical violence. Again and again we must rise to the majestic heights of meeting physical force with soul force. The marvelous new militancy which has engulfed the Negro community must not lead us to distrust of all white people, for many of our white brothers, as evidenced by their presence here today, have come to realize that their destiny is tied up with our destiny and their freedom is inextricably bound to our freedom. We cannot walk alone.

And as we walk, we must make the pledge that we shall march ahead. We cannot turn back. There are those who are asking the devotees of civil rights, "When will you be satisfied?" We can never be satisfied as long as our bodies, heavy with the fatigue of travel, cannot gain lodging in the motels of the highways and the hotels of the cities. We cannot be satisfied as long as the Negro's basic mobility is from a smaller ghetto to a larger one. We can never be satisfied as long as a Negro in Mississippi cannot vote and a Negro in New York believes he has nothing for which to vote. No, no, we are not satisfied, and we will not be satisfied until justice rolls down like waters and righteousness like a mighty stream.

I am not unmindful that some of you have come here out of great trials and tribulations. Some of you have come fresh from narrow cells. Some of you have come from areas where your quest for freedom left you battered by the storms of persecution and staggered by the winds of police brutality. You have been the veterans of creative suffering. Continue to work with the faith that unearned suffering is redemptive.

Go back to Mississippi, go back to Alabama, go back to Georgia, go back to Louisiana, go back to the slums and ghettos of our northern cities, knowing that somehow this situation can and will be changed. Let us not wallow in the valley of despair. 10

I say to you today, my friends, that in spite of the difficulties and frustrations of the moment, I still have a dream. It is a dream deeply rooted in the American dream.

2. An echo of Shakespeare's *Richard III*: "Now is the winter of our discontent."

I have a dream that one day this nation will rise up and live out the true meaning of its creed: "We hold these truths to be self-evident: that all men are created equal."

I have a dream that one day on the red hills of Georgia the sons of former slaves and the sons of former slaveowners will be able to sit down together at a table of brotherhood.

I have a dream that one day even the state of Mississippi, a desert state, sweltering with the heat of injustice and oppression, will be transformed into an oasis of freedom and justice.

15 I have a dream that my four children will one day live in a nation where they will not be judged by the color of their skin but by the content of their character.

I have a dream today.

I have a dream that one day the state of Alabama, whose governor's lips are presently dripping with the words of interposition and nullification,[3] will be transformed into a situation where little black boys and black girls will be able to join hands with little white boys and white girls and walk together as sisters and brothers.

I have a dream today.

I have a dream that one day every valley shall be exalted, every hill and mountain shall be made low, the rough places will be made plain, and the crooked places will be made straight, and the glory of the Lord shall be revealed, and all flesh shall see it together.[4]

20 This is our hope. This is the faith with which I return to the South. With this faith we will be able to hew out of the mountain of despair a stone of hope. With this faith we will be able to transform the jangling discords of our nation into a beautiful symphony of brotherhood. With this faith we will be able to work together, to pray together, to struggle together, to go to jail together, to stand up for freedom together, knowing that we will be free one day.

This will be the day when all of God's children will be able to sing with a new meaning, "My country, 'tis of thee, sweet land of liberty, of thee I sing. Land where my fathers died, land of the pilgrim's pride, from every mountainside, let freedom ring."

And if America is to be a great nation this must become true. So let freedom ring from the prodigious hilltops of New Hampshire. Let freedom ring from the mighty mountains of New York. Let freedom ring from the heightening Alleghenies of Pennsylvania!

Let freedom ring from the snowcapped Rockies of Colorado!

Let freedom ring from the curvaceous peaks of California!

25 But not only that; let freedom ring from Stone Mountain of Georgia![5]

3. George Wallace (1919–1998), Alabama's segregationist governor, used big legal terms such as "interposition" and "nullification" in his unsuccessful attempt to prevent the integration of the University of Alabama.

4. From Isaiah 40.4–5, familiar to many through Handel's *Messiah*.

5. Site of a large Confederate memorial near Atlanta.

Let freedom ring from Lookout Mountain of Tennessee![6]

Let freedom ring from every hill and every molehill of Mississippi. From every mountainside, let freedom ring.

When we let freedom ring, when we let it ring from every village and every hamlet, from every state and every city, we will be able to speed up that day when all of God's children, black men and white men, Jews and Gentiles, Protestants and Catholics, will be able to join hands and sing in the words of the old Negro spiritual, "Free at last! free at last! thank God Almighty, we are free at last!"

6. Site of a Civil War battle, now part of Chickamauga-Chattanooga Military Park.

Questions

1. What elements of a sermon do you notice in King's speech? Why do you think King invokes a sermonic mode?

2. What are the benefits King derives from posing matters in the form of a dream? Are there any losses?

3. King's address has a "modular" form, meaning it has distinct, separate parts. What are the "modules" in King's speech? What would be changed if some parts were omitted?

Eleanor Roosevelt

On the Universal Declaration of Human Rights

The long and meticulous study and debate of which this Universal Declaration of Human Rights is the product means that it reflects the composite views of the many men and governments who have contributed to its formulation. Not every man nor every government can have what he wants in a document of this kind. There are of course particular provisions in the declaration before us with which we are not fully satisfied. I have no doubt this is true of other delegations, but taken as a whole the Delegation of the United States[1] believes that this [is] a good document—even a great document—and we propose to give it our full support. The position of the United States on the various parts of the declaration is a matter of record in the Third Committee. I shall

Given before the General Assembly of the United Nations on December 9, 1948, the day before the U.N. adopted the "Universal Declaration of Human Rights." The speaker was the wife of the late president Franklin Delano Roosevelt and U.S. delegate to the U.N. The "Preamble to the Universal Declaration" is reprinted after the speech.

1. The representatives of the United States to the United Nations.

not burden the Assembly, and particularly my colleagues of the Third Committee, with a restatement of that position here.

Certain provisions of the declaration are stated in such broad terms as to be acceptable only because of the limitations in article 29[2] providing for limitation on the exercise of the rights for the purpose of meeting the requirements of morality, public order, and the general welfare. An example of this is the provision that everyone has the right of equal access to the public service in his country. The basic principle of equality and of nondiscrimination as to public employment is sound, but it cannot be accepted without limitations. My government, for example, would consider that this is unquestionably subject to limitation in the interest of public order and the general welfare. It would not consider that the exclusion from public employment of persons holding subversive political beliefs and not loyal to the basic principles and practices of the constitution and laws of the country would in any way infringe upon this right.

Likewise, my Government has made it clear in the course of the development of the declaration that it does not consider that the economic and social and cultural rights stated in the declaration imply an obligation on governmental action. This was made quite clear in the Human Rights Commission text of article 23[3] which served as a so-called "umbrella" article to the articles on economic and social rights. We consider that the principle has not been affected by the fact that this article no longer contains a reference to the articles which follow it. This in no way affects our whole-hearted support for the basic principles of economic, social, and cultural rights set forth in these articles.

In giving our approval to the declaration today it is of primary importance that we keep clearly in mind the basic character of the document. It is not a treaty; it is not an international agreement. It is not and does not purport to be a statement of basic principles of law or legal obligation. It is a declaration of basic principles of human rights and freedoms, to be stamped with the approval of the General Assembly[4] by formal vote of its members, and to serve as a common standard of achievement for all peoples of all nations.

5 We stand today at the threshold of a great event both in the life of the United Nations and in the life of mankind, that is the approval by the General Assembly of the Universal Declaration of Human Rights recommended by the

2. One of thirty articles in the Declaration.

3. Article 23 states: "1. Everyone has the right to work, to free choice of employment, to just and favourable conditions of work and to protection against unemployment. 2. Everyone, without any discrimination, has the right to equal pay for equal work. 3. Everyone who works has the right to just and favourable remuneration ensuring for himself and his family an existence worthy of human dignity, and supplemented, if necessary, by other means of social protection. 4. Everyone has the right to form and to join trade unions for the protection of his interests."

4. A gathering of representatives from all United Nations constituents and the site of debate and decision-making for the organization.

Eleanor Roosevelt and the United Nations Universal Declaration of Human Rights in Spanish text.

Third Committee. This declaration may well become the international Magna Carta[5] of all men everywhere.

We hope its proclamation by the General Assembly will be an event comparable to the proclamation of the Declaration of the Rights of Man by the French people in 1789,[6] the adoption of the Bill of Rights by the people of the United States,[7] and the adoption of comparable declarations at different times in other countries. At a time when there are so many issues on which we find it difficult to reach a common basis of agreement, it is a significant fact that 58 states[8] have found such a large measure of agreement in the complex field of human rights. This must be taken as testimony of our common aspiration first voiced in the Charter of the United Nations[9] to lift men everywhere to a higher standard of life and to a greater enjoyment of freedom.

5. English legal document, written in 1215, that bound the king to law and thus laid the foundation for constitutional government.

6. French legal document, adopted in 1789, proclaiming the existence of inalienable human rights and thereby setting the stage for the French Revolution.

7. The first ten amendments to the American Constitution, drafted by James Madison in 1789.

8. I.e., nations, countries.

9. The constitution of the United Nations, which lays out the rules that bind the constituent countries and states that those rules trump those set forth in other treaties.

Man's desire for peace lies behind this declaration.

The realization that the flagrant violation of human rights by Nazi and Fascist countries[10] sowed the seeds of the last world war has supplied the impetus for the work which brings us to the moment of achievement here today.

In a recent speech in Canada, Gladstone Murray[11] said: "The central fact is that man is fundamentally a moral being, that the light we have is imperfect does not matter so long as we are always trying to improve it . . . we are equal in sharing the moral freedom that distinguishes us as men. Man's status makes each individual an end in himself. No man is by nature simply the servant of the state or of another man . . . the ideal and fact of freedom—and not technology—are the true distinguishing marks of our civilization."

10 This declaration is based upon the spiritual fact that man must have freedom in which to develop his full stature and through common effort to raise the level of human dignity.

We have much to do to fully achieve and to assure the rights set forth in this declaration. But having them put before us with the moral backing of 58 nations will be a great step forward.

As we here bring to fruition our labors on this Declaration of Human Rights, we must at the same time rededicate ourselves to the unfinished task which lies before us. We can now move on with new courage and inspiration to the completion of an international covenant on human rights and of measures for the implementation of human rights.

In conclusion I feel that I cannot do better than to repeat the call to action by Secretary Marshall[12] in his opening statement to this Assembly:

> "Let this third regular session of the General Assembly approve by an overwhelming majority the Declaration of Human Rights as a statement of conduct for all; and let us, as Members of the United Nations, conscious of our own short-comings and imperfections, join our effort in all faith to live up to this high standard."

PREAMBLE TO THE UNIVERSAL DECLARATION OF HUMAN RIGHTS

Whereas recognition of the inherent dignity and of the equal and inalienable rights of all members of the human family is the foundation of freedom, justice and peace in the world,

Whereas disregard and contempt for human rights have resulted in barbarous acts which have outraged the conscience of mankind, and the advent of a world in which human beings shall enjoy freedom of speech and belief and freedom from fear and want has been proclaimed as the highest aspiration of the common people,

10. Primarily Germany and Italy.

11. First General Manager of the Canadian Broadcasting Corporation.

12. George Marshall (1880–1959), American military leader and Secretary of State, was also author of the Marshall Plan, which helped reconstruct Europe after World War II.

Whereas it is essential, if man is not to be compelled to have recourse, as a last resort, to rebellion against tyranny and oppression, that human rights should be protected by the rule of law,

Whereas it is essential to promote the development of friendly relations between nations,

Whereas the peoples of the United Nations have in the Charter reaffirmed their faith in fundamental human rights, in the dignity and worth of the human person and in the equal rights of men and women and have determined to promote social progress and better standards of life in larger freedom, 5

Whereas Member States have pledged themselves to achieve, in cooperation with the United Nations, the promotion of universal respect for and observance of human rights and fundamental freedoms,

Whereas a common understanding of these rights and freedoms is of the greatest importance for the full realization of this pledge,

Now, therefore, The General Assembly proclaims This Universal Declaration of Human Rights.

Questions

1. In this speech, Eleanor Roosevelt is not expressing her own personal opinions but is representing the United States as a delegate to the United Nations. How, in her opening remarks, does she make clear her government's position on the declaration? Why does she begin with these qualifying remarks?

2. In explaining the importance of the declaration, Roosevelt makes comparisons with other historical documents: the Magna Carta (paragraph 5), the Declaration of the Rights of Man (paragraph 6), the Bill of Rights (paragraph 6), and the Charter of the United Nations (paragraph 6). Why does she choose these documents? What effect do her comparisons have?

3. Toward the middle of the speech, Roosevelt proclaims: "Man's desire for peace lies behind this declaration" (paragraph 7). How does the end of the speech develop this theme?

4. Compare this speech with another speech given on an official occasion (for example, Abraham Lincoln's second inaugural address or John F. Kennedy's inaugural address, both in "Politics and Government"). What similarities do you find? What differences?

Al Gore

The Climate Emergency

April 13, 2004

I'M AL GORE. I used to be the next president of the United States.[1] This has been an interesting period of my life. I wanted to start by inviting you to put yourselves in my shoes for a minute. It hasn't been easy, you know. For eight years I flew on Air Force II,[2] and now I have to take off my shoes to get on an airplane.

Not long after Tipper[3] and I left the White House, we were driving from our home in Nashville to a small farm we have fifty miles east of Nashville. We were driving ourselves. I looked in the rear view mirror and all of a sudden it just hit me that there was no motorcade. Some of you may have heard of phantom limb pain.[4]

It was mealtime, so we looked for a place to eat. We pulled off the interstate highway and finally found a Shoney's Restaurant, a low-cost, family restaurant chain. We walked in and sat down. The waitress came over and made a big commotion over Tipper. She took our order and then went to the couple in the booth next to us, and lowered her voice so much I had to really strain to hear what she was saying: "Yes, that's former Vice President Al Gore and his wife Tipper." And the man said, "He's come down a long way, hasn't he?"

The very next day, continuing a true story, I got on a plane and flew to Africa, to Nigeria, to the city of Lagos, to make a speech about energy. I began my speech by telling that story, that had just happened the day before back in Tennessee, and I told it pretty much the same way I just told it here. They laughed. Then I went on and gave my speech and went back to the airport and flew back toward the U.S. I fell asleep on the plane, and was awakened in the middle of the night when we were landing on the Azores Islands out in the middle of the Atlantic. They opened the door of the plane to let some fresh air in, and I looked out, and here came a man running across the runway waving a piece of paper saying "Call Washington, call Washington."

Gore gave this speech during the 2004 presidential campaign; it became the basis of his documentary film and book, An Inconvenient Truth *(2006). This version was given with extensive illustrations, charts, and graphs on April 13, 2004, at the Yale School of Forestry and Environmental Science, and was included in a collection of speeches,* Red, White, Blue and Green: Politics and the Environment in the 2004 Election *(2004), edited by members of YSFES, James R. Lyons, Heather S. Kaplan, Fred Strebeigh, and Kathleen E. Campbell.*

1. Gore ran for president in 2000 and won more popular votes than George W. Bush, who was nonetheless elected because of his majority in the electoral college.
2. Part of the presidential fleet of airplanes.
3. Tipper Gore (b. 1948), Gore's wife at the time.
4. The sensation of pain in a missing limb.

I thought—what in the world, in the middle of the night, in the middle of the Atlantic, what in the world could be wrong in Washington? And then I remembered it could be a bunch of things. But what it turned out to be was that my staff back in Washington was very, very upset. A wire service reporter in Lagos had written a story about my speech, and it had already been transmitted to the U.S. and printed all over the country. The story began: "Former Vice President Al Gore announced in Nigeria yesterday 'My wife Tipper and I opened a low-cost family restaurant named Shoney's and we are running it ourselves.'" Before I could get back to U.S. soil, the late-night comics Leno and Letterman[5] had already started in on me. They had me in a big white chef's hat and Tipper was taking orders—"One more with fries!" Three days later I got a nice long handwritten letter from my friend Bill Clinton[6] that said "Congratulations on the new restaurant, Al!" We like to celebrate each other's successes in life.

5

Anyway, it really is an honor to be here and to share some words about the climate issue. The title I chose for this speech is not a misprint. The phrase "climate emergency" is intended to convey what it conveys—that this is a crisis with an unusual sense of urgency attached to it, and we should see it as an emergency. The fact that we don't, or that most people don't, is part of what I want to cover here.

CLIMATE CHANGE: IMPACTS AND EVIDENCE

There is a very famous picture called Earth Rise. A young astronaut named William Anders took it on December 24, 1968.[7] This mission, Apollo 7, was the first one to go around the moon. It went on Christmas Eve, and they had just been on the dark side of the moon, coming back around, seeing the earth for the first time. Anders—the rookie astronaut, without a big fancy camera—took this snapshot and it instantly became an icon. Many people believe that this one picture, Earth Rise, in many ways was responsible for the birth of the modern environmental movement. Less than two years after this picture was printed, the first Earth Day[8] was organized. This picture became a powerful force in changing the way people thought about the earth and about the environment.

The environment is often felt to be relatively invulnerable because the earth is so big. People tend to assume that the earth is so big that we as human beings can't possibly have any impact on it. That is a mistake. The most vulnerable part of earth's environment is the atmosphere. It's astonishingly thin, as any image from space shows. The space is so small that we are able to fill it up

5. Jay Leno (b. 1950) and David Letterman (b. 1947), contemporary American comedians.

6. Bill Clinton (b. 1946), forty-second American president (1993–2001); Gore was his vice president.

7. William Anders (b. 1933), United States Air Force officer and astronaut on the Apollo 8 (not 7) mission, took this famous photograph depicting the moon, partially in light, off the edge of the Earth.

8. An annual celebration of the environment, intended to increase awareness and activism, and held at different points around the world.

with greenhouse gases, such as CO_2,[9] which form a thick blanket of gas surrounding the earth, trapping some of the sun's radiation. This process, called the "greenhouse effect," is what leads to increased global temperatures or what most refer to as climate change.

In Europe during the summer of 2003, we experienced an extreme heat wave that killed an estimated 20,000 people, and many predict such events will be much more commonplace as a result of increasing temperatures. The anomaly was extreme, particularly in France, with consequences that were well reported in the press. Year-to-year, decade-to-decade there's variation, but the overall upward trend worldwide since the American Civil War is really clear and really obvious, at least to me.

10 If you look at the glaciers around the world, you see that many are melting away. A friend of mine named Lonnie Thompson of Ohio State studies glaciers, and he reports that 15 to 20 years from now there will be no more snows of Kilimanjaro. This shrinking of glaciers is happening all around the world, including Latin America, China, and the U.S. In our own Glacier National Park, all of the glaciers are predicted to be gone within 15 to 20 years.

One of the remarkable things about glaciers is that they really could care less about politics. They either melt or freeze. Rhetoric has no impact on them whatsoever. A few years ago some hikers in the Alps between Austria and Italy were walking along and they ran across what looked like a 5,000-year-old man. Actually he was from 3,000 B.C., and you don't see that every day. The reason you don't is that the ice there hasn't melted for 5,000 years. Every mountain glacier in the entire world, with the exception of a few in Scandinavia that are affected by the Gulf Stream patterns, is melting rapidly.

Lonnie Thompson and his team of researchers don't just watch glaciers melt. They drill down into the glaciers and pull up columns of ice. Then they study the bubbles of air trapped in the ice, and they can do that year by year because every year there's a new layer. In Antarctica the layers are paper-thin and they stack up 400,000 years back. Ninety-five percent of all the fresh water in the world is locked up as ice in Antarctica. It's two miles high.

When Lonnie and his team drill down through Antarctica, they're able to get 400,000 years worth of ice. They can then look at the little bubbles of atmosphere and measure the CO_2 content, and they can also measure temperature by comparing the ratio of different oxygen isotopes.[10] However that works, it's extremely accurate and not controversial. And here's what that record shows where carbon dioxide is concerned:

Now, there are two points here. The first is: Do those lines—the line for level of temperature and the line for concentration of CO_2—look like they go together to you? They do to me. The second point is: Here in New Haven,[11] on the temperature line, the difference of approximately 15°C of average temperature is the difference between a nice day and having one mile of ice over your

9. Carbon dioxide.
10. Different forms of chemical elements.
11. City in Connecticut where this speech was given.

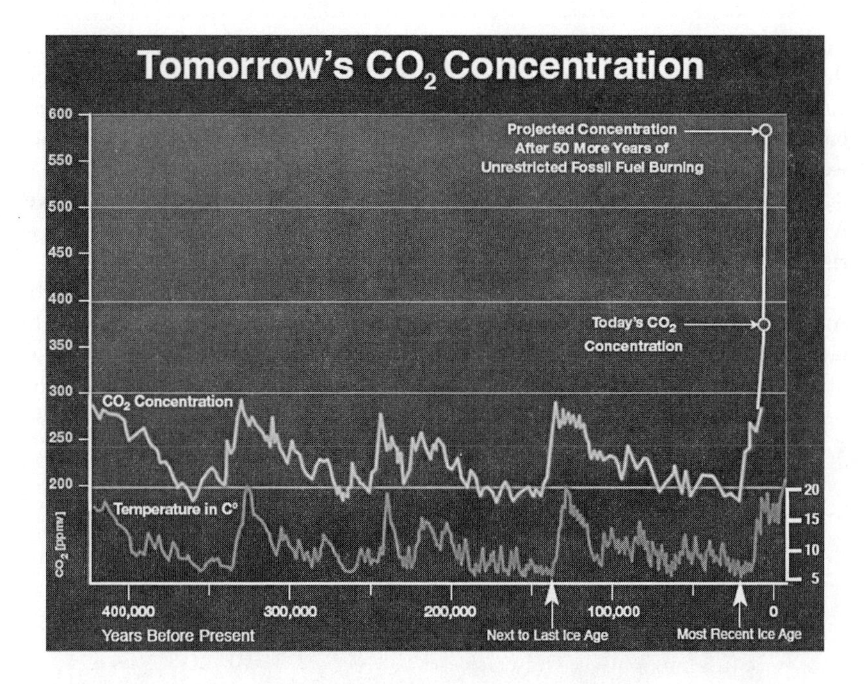

head. What has been happening lately is that the concentration of CO_2 is approaching 380 parts per million. So that's way, way above anything that has been seen for as far back as we can measure—400,000 years. And within fifty years it's going to approach 600 parts per million. So if a difference of approximately 200 parts per million of CO_2 on the cold side is a mile of ice over your head, what does that much difference represent on the warm side?

Or to state the question another way, is it perfectly sane and rational and reasonable to go ahead and do this? Or is it in fact crazy? It is crazy, but that is what the world is doing right now. And fifty years is not a long time. Unless we make decisions very soon, we will reach much higher levels. So, when I use the phrase *climate emergency*, I have partly in mind the fact that this is happening right now. And it carries with it, unless we do something, catastrophic consequences for all civilization.

In Antarctica you've heard about ice shelves the size of Rhode Island[12] coming off and calving. There are actually a bunch of them in the Antarctic, and also in Greenland. Incidentally, there was a flurry of publicity on April 9th about a new study showing that if greenhouse gas emissions continue to rise at current rates the disappearance of Greenland's ice sheet is inevitable, unless we act fairly soon.

When ice melts in mountains and in Antarctica and Greenland—when land-based ice melts—it raises sea level. When you have rivers that are close to

12. Rhode Island is about 37 miles wide by 48 miles long.

the ocean like the Thames River in London, the water level goes up, and it threatens the lower lying areas. London, in 1983, built barriers to protect the city against flooding from higher sea level and thus higher storm surges. These barriers had to be closed only once in 1983. Twenty years later, in 2003, they were closed 19 times. Again, the same pattern shows up wherever you look.

An area of Bangladesh is due to be flooded where ten million people live. A large area of Florida is due to be flooded. The Florida Keys are very much at risk. The Everglades are at risk.

Now the Arctic is very different from the Antarctic because, while the Antarctic is land surrounded by ocean, the Arctic is ocean surrounded by land. And the ice in the Arctic is floating on top of the ocean, so it doesn't get

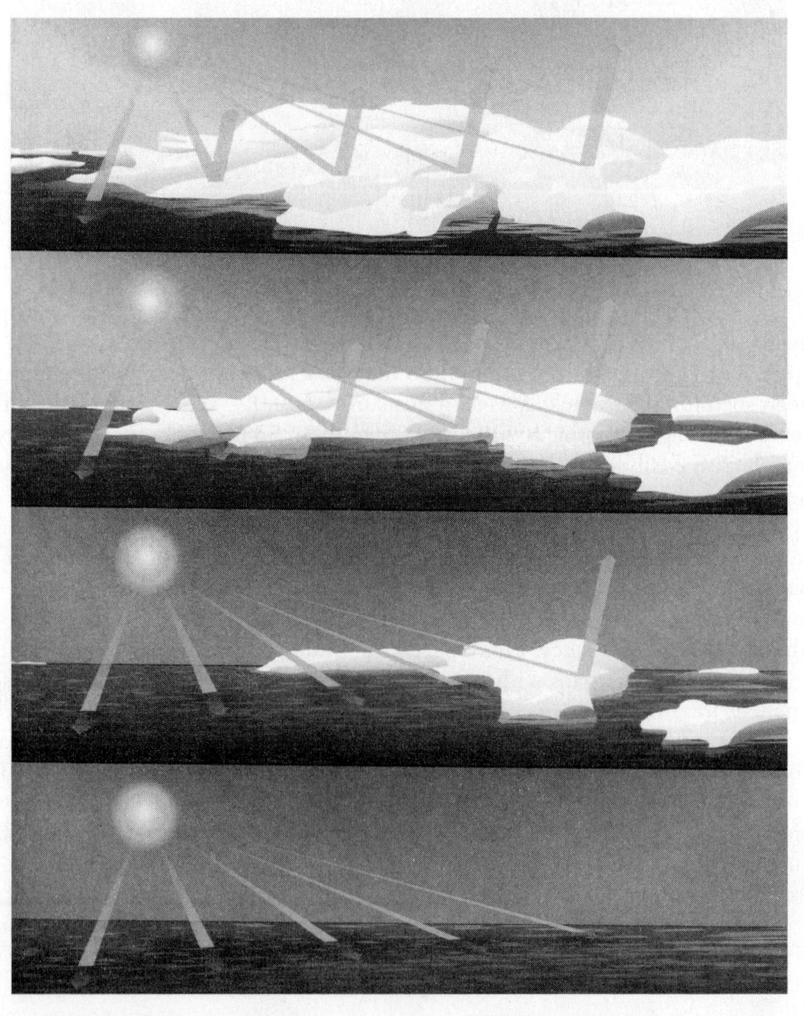

Effect of global warming on Arctic ice cap.

nearly as thick. Instead of two miles thick, it's only ten feet thick—that is, it used to be ten feet. Just in the last few decades it has melted quite a bit. I went up there twice in a submarine. They have these specially designed submarines where the wings rotate vertically so that they can cut through the ice. Ice in water, or thinner ice, melts more rapidly and leads to temperature increases because, as soon as a little bit of ice melts, the water absorbs a lot more temperature. This effect is now happening to the entire Arctic Ocean. The Arctic ice cap has thinned by 40 percent in the last 40 years. Let me repeat that. Listen to that number. The Arctic ice cap has thinned 40 percent in 40 years. Within 50 years it may be entirely gone.

That's a big problem because when the sun hits the ice cap, 95 percent of the energy bounces off like a big mirror. But when it hits the open ocean more than 90 percent is absorbed. So it's a phase change, it's not a gradual change. Ice is that way—the difference between 33F° and 31F° is not just two degrees. That puts more energy into the system and it changes the amount of evaporation off the oceans, so you get more rain and snow but it comes at different times and you get more soil erosion as well. You get simultaneously more flooding and more droughts, which is really a bad thing. You get more precipitation in one-time storm events. More of it comes at one time in big storms. 20

The trend is very clear. What's behind it all? I've come to believe that global warming, the disappearance of the ocean fisheries, the destruction of the rain forests, the stratospheric ozone depletion problem, the extinction crisis, all of these are really symptoms of an underlying cause. The underlying cause is a collision between our civilization and the earth. The relationship between the human species and our planet has been completely changed. All of our culture, all of our literature, all of our history, everything we've learned, was premised on one relationship between the earth and us, and now we have a different one.

Three Leading Causes: Population Growth, Technology, and Our Way of Thinking

The new relationship between humankind and the earth has been caused by a confluence of three factors.

The first is population, which has been growing rapidly. The population crisis has actually been a success story in some ways. We've slowed it down, but the momentum of the population increases is really incredible. Say the scientists are right and we emerged as a species 160,000 years ago. It took from that time, almost 160,000 years until the end of World War II, before we got to a population of 2 billion. Since I've been alive, as part of the baby boom generation, it has gone from 2 billion to 6.3 billion. So if it takes more than 10,000 generations to reach 2 billion and one human lifetime to go from 2 to 6, and if I live to the demographic average of the baby boom generation, it'll go close to 9 billion. That is one of the reasons why the relationship between our species and the earth is different now than ever before.

Some of the other global patterns, species loss for example, match the human population pattern. Most importantly, however, the increase in the pop-

First modern humans

160,000 BC 100,000 BC 10,000 BC 7000 BC 6000 BC 5000 BC 4000 BC

Population Growth Throughout History

ulation of developing nations is driving food demand, water demand, and energy demand, creating intense pressures on human resources. We are seeing a pattern of devastation and destruction that is simply driven by those factors. And it really is a political issue. We in the U.S. are responsible for more greenhouse gas emissions than Africa, South America, Central America, India, and China combined. The world average is way below where we are. Just to recap—this is 1,000 years of carbon emissions, CO_2 concentrations, and temperature. This is not rocket science. Those lines match up.

The second factor that changes the relationship between humans and the earth is technology. In many ways, it is more powerful and significant than the population explosion because new technologies have increased our power beyond imagination. That's a good thing often in areas like medicine or communications—you can fill in the blanks. There are all kinds of great

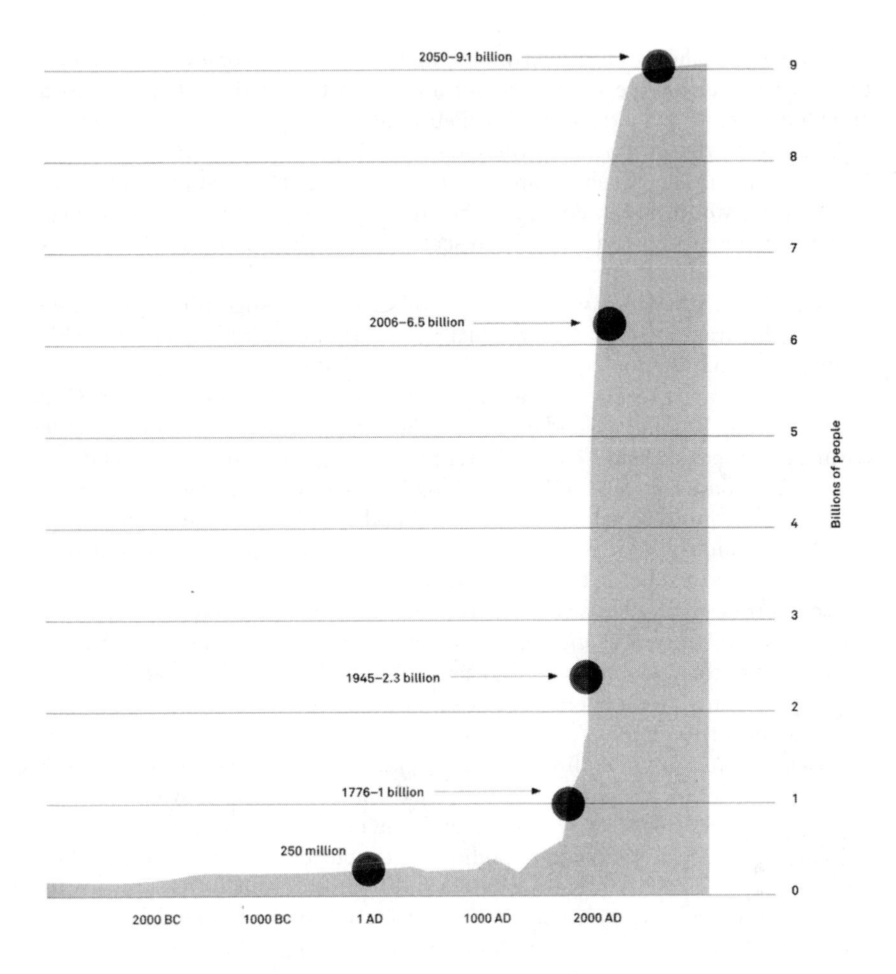

things that represent progress. Even cleaning up the environment with new technology. There are a lot of great things that have come out of this, but when we don't examine habits that have persisted for a long time, and then use the same habits with new technology and don't take into account the new power that we have, then the consequences can get away from us. One quick example: warfare was one thing with swords and bows and arrows and even muskets, but when nuclear weapons were created, the consequences of war were utterly transformed. So we had to think differently about war. And what happened? The cold war emerged and unfortunately the other kind didn't completely go away, but we're in the midst of rethinking that age-old habit of warfare. We just have to, because the new technologies make it unthinkable to continue as we were doing in the past.

Now think about that pattern: old habits, new technologies. Think about the subsistence that we have always drawn from the earth. The plow was a great advance, as was irrigation. But then we began to get more powerful with these tools. At the Aral Sea[13] in Russia, something as simple as irrigation on a large scale led to the virtual disappearance of the fourth largest inland body of water in the world. We're changing the surface of the earth, and technology sometimes seems to dwarf our human scale. We now have to try to change this pattern.

The third factor is our way of thinking. We have to change our way of thinking. One illustration comes from the fact that, as I said earlier, we have these big assumptions that we don't question. I had a classmate in the sixth grade. Every time our geography teacher put a map of the world up he would mutter. One time, he got up his courage and pointed to the outline of South America and the outline of Africa and said, "Did they ever fit together?" And the teacher said "Of course not. That's the most ridiculous thing I've ever heard." In fact, until about the 1960s, the guy who talked about continental drift was thought to be a kook because he said that Africa and South America fit together. It turns out that they did, but the teacher in this story had an assumption in his mind. Continents are so big they obviously don't move, thereby illustrating the old philosopher's saying that "What gets us into trouble is not what we don't know. It's what we know for sure that just ain't so" (Yogi Berra).[14] We know for sure that the earth is so big we can't have a big impact on it, but that's just not so.

You know this cliché, I'm sure: That a frog's nervous system is such that if it's dropped into a pot of boiling water it will jump right out because it perceives the contrast, but if it's put in a pot of tepid water which is slowly heated, it doesn't jump out unless it's rescued. Here's the deeper meaning of that cliché: the frog did perceive the sudden boiling water, but did not perceive the slow process.

Global warming seems to be gradual in the context of a human life, but it is actually fairly sudden. Another problem with our thinking is that there are people who are paid money by some coal companies and oil companies to go out and pretend that the science says something that it doesn't say. These are scientific camp followers who are willing to do things for money. And some of the very same individuals who are doing this now (i.e., trying to persuade people that global warming is not a problem) were some of the same people who took money from the tobacco companies after the Surgeon General's report came out warning of the dangers of smoking. The tobacco companies hired these scientific camp followers to go out and try to confuse the public into thinking that the science wasn't clear. They produced marketing campaigns like "More doctors smoke Camels." On a similar note, the Republican pollster Frank Luntz advised the White House that the issue of the environment is important, but the way to deal with it is to make the lack of scientific certainty a primary issue by finding people who are willing to say that it's confusing when it's really not.

13. A landlocked Central Asian sea.

14. Berra (b. 1925), famous New York Yankee and wordsmith.

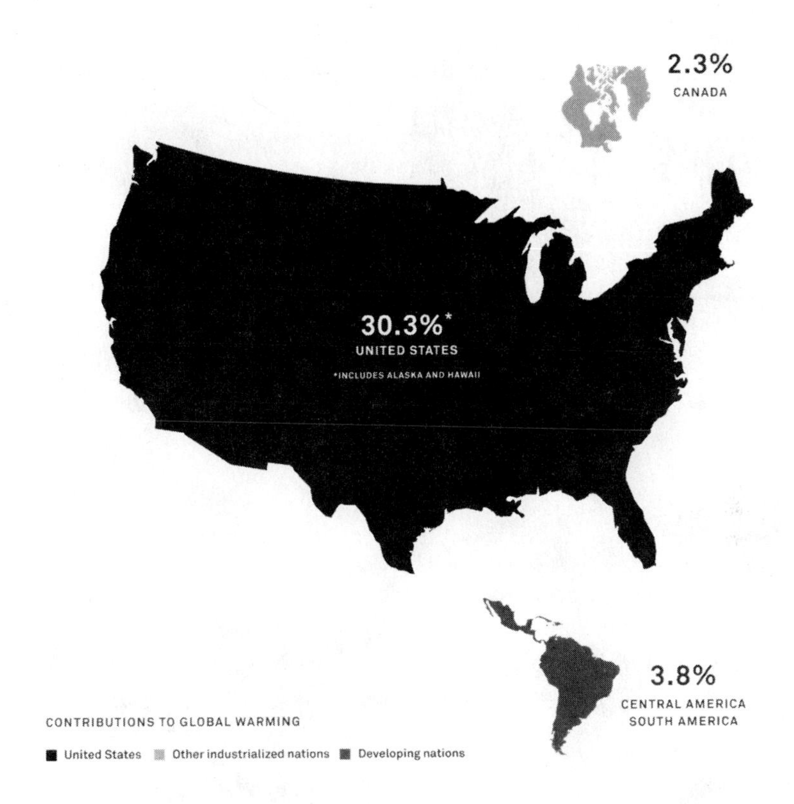

There's another assumption that needs to be questioned. In contrast to the idea that the earth is so big that we can't have any impact on it, there are others who assume that the climate change problem is so big we can't solve it. I, however, believe that we can if we put our minds to it. We had a problem with the ozone hole, a big global problem that seemed too big to solve. In response, we had political leadership and the world passed a treaty outlawing chlorofluorocarbons, the chemicals that caused this problem. 30

The United States led the way, and we brought about a dramatic drop in CFCs and are now in the process of solving that problem. We now have the ability to buy hybrid cars like the Toyota Prius and the marketplace for new sources of energy is increasing dramatically. We're also seeing new efficiencies with energy savings. If we have political leadership and the collective political will to say it is important to solve this problem, we can not only solve it, we can create more jobs, we can create higher incomes, a better way of life, and a higher quality of life by solving the problem.

And finally, it's an issue of values. Back when I was in the Senate, the first President Bush[15] was trying to fend off some of the attacks by myself and many

15. George H. W. Bush (b. 1924), forty-first American president; his son, George W. Bush (b. 1946), followed in his footsteps as forty-third president.

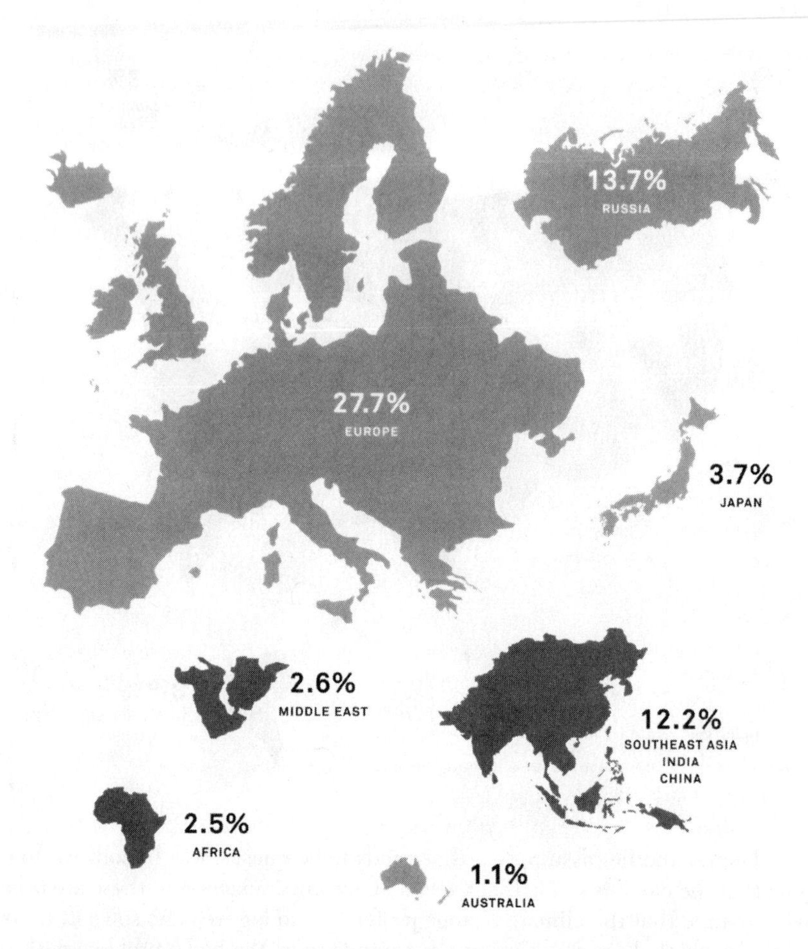

SOURCE: U.S. DEPARTMENT OF ENERGY, ENERGY INFORMATION ADMINISTRATION, CARBON DIOXIDE INFORMATION ANALYSIS CENTER

others in Congress who were saying we have to solve this global warming problem. So they had a White House conference on global stewardship. One of their view graphs caught my attention. Their view of the global environmental crisis was represented by a scale with money, in the form of gold bars on one side, and on the other side of the scales was the entire planet. The point they were trying to make was that we have to find a balance between our monetary wealth and the well being of the entire planet. Boy, that's a tough one! It's a false choice—because you're not going to have much wealth if you lose the planet and there is wealth to be made in saving it. We have to get our perspective right.

Everything we have ever known—and Carl Sagan[16] made a beautiful long statement about this—all the wars, all the heartbreak, all the romance, every

16. American astronomer (1934–1996).

triumph, every mistake, everything we've ever known is contained in this small planet. If we keep the right perspective and keep our eyes on the prize, we *can* solve this problem, we *will* solve this problem, we *must* solve this problem. It really is up to you.

Questions

1. This speech begins with a self-introduction. Why does Al Gore, a well-known public figure, introduce himself to the audience? How do his humorous tactics aid in his presentation of the serious part of his speech?

2. Gore's serious presentation of the climate emergency begins with the section "Climate Change: Impacts and Evidence." (The section headings were added by the editors of *Red, White, Blue and Green.*) Where does he define "climate emergency"? What examples does he give as evidence?

3. Gore introduces and interprets a graph to make a point about temperature change (paragraphs 12–14)—a technique used in scientific writing. Yet Gore's interpretation is not "scientific" in style. How does he make clear to the audience the meaning of this graph?

4. Gore gives three leading causes of the climate emergency: population growth, technology, and our way of thinking. List the kinds of evidence and examples he uses in this part of his speech, and suggest how the diversity of evidence and examples helps him communicate with his audience.

5. Write a speech about a current crisis, drawing on a variety of examples and, if possible, using illustrations, charts, and graphs.

William Faulkner *Nobel Prize Award Speech*

I feel that this award was not made to me as a man but to my work—a life's work in the agony and sweat of the human spirit, not for glory and least of all for profit, but to create out of the materials of the human spirit something which did not exist before. So this award is only mine in trust. It will not be difficult to find a dedication for the money part of it commensurate with the purpose and significance of its origin. But I would like to do the same with the acclaim too, by using this moment as a pinnacle from which I might be listened to by the young men and women already dedicated to the same anguish and

On acceptance of the Nobel Prize in Literature for 1949, Faulkner gave this speech at a banquet in City Hall, Stockholm, Sweden, on December 10, 1950 (the anniversary of the death of Alfred Nobel, founder of the prize). The Nobel Prizes are presented by the king of Sweden, then King Gustaf VI Adolf (1882–1973).

travail, among whom is already that one who will some day stand here where I am standing.

Our tragedy today is a general and universal physical fear so long sustained by now that we can even bear it. There are no longer problems of the spirit. There is only the question: When will I be blown up? Because of this, the young man or woman writing today has forgotten the problems of the human heart in conflict with itself which alone can make good writing because only that is worth writing about, worth the agony and the sweat.

He must learn them again. He must teach himself that the basest of all things is to be afraid; and, teaching himself that, forget it forever, leaving no room in his workshop for anything but the old verities and truths of the heart, the old universal truths lacking which any story is ephemeral and doomed—love and honor and pity and pride and compassion and sacrifice. Until he does so, he labors under a curse. He writes not of love but of lust, of defeats in which nobody loses anything of value, of victories without hope and, worst of all, without pity or compassion. His griefs grieve on no universal bones leaving no scars. He writes not of the heart but of the glands.

Until he relearns these things, he will write as though he stood alone and watched the end of man. I decline to accept the end of man. It is easy enough to say that man is immortal simply because he will endure; that when the last ding-dong of doom has clanged and faded from the last worthless rock hanging tideless in the last red and dying evening, that even then there will still be one more sound: that of his puny inexhaustible voice, still talking. I refuse to accept this. I believe that man will not merely endure; he will prevail. He is immortal, not because he alone among creatures has an inexhaustible voice but because he has a soul, a spirit capable of compassion and sacrifice and endurance. The poet's, the writer's, duty is to write about these things. It is his privilege to help man endure by lifting his heart, by reminding him of the courage and honor and hope and pride and compassion and pity and sacrifice which have been the glory of his past. The poet's voice need not merely be the record of man, it can be one of the props, the pillars to help him endure and prevail.

QUESTIONS

1. Writers accepting the Nobel Prize in literature usually feel obligated to explain what literature and the arts can do for humankind. How does Faulkner's speech meet this obligation?

2. Faulkner gave his speech in the aftermath of World War II. How does he address, directly or indirectly, the work of writers in healing the scars of war?

3. Write a speech that you imagine expresses a writer's sense of the value of literature.

Barack Obama *A New Beginning*

THANK YOU VERY MUCH. Good afternoon. I am honored to be in the timeless city of Cairo, and to be hosted by two remarkable institutions. For over a thousand years, Al-Azhar[1] has stood as a beacon of Islamic learning; and for over a century, Cairo University has been a source of Egypt's advancement. And together, you represent the harmony between tradition and progress. I'm grateful for your hospitality, and the hospitality of the people of Egypt. And I'm also proud to carry with me the goodwill of the American people, and a greeting of peace from Muslim communities in my country: *Assalaamu alaykum.*[2]

We meet at a time of great tension between the United States and Muslims around the world—tension rooted in historical forces that go beyond any current policy debate. The relationship between Islam and the West includes centuries of coexistence and cooperation, but also conflict and religious wars. More recently, tension has been fed by colonialism that denied rights and opportunities to many Muslims, and a Cold War in which Muslim-majority countries were too often treated as proxies without regard to their own aspirations. Moreover, the sweeping change brought by modernity and globalization led many Muslims to view the West as hostile to the traditions of Islam.

Violent extremists have exploited these tensions in a small but potent minority of Muslims. The attacks of September 11, 2001, and the continued efforts of these extremists to engage in violence against civilians has led some in my country to view Islam as inevitably hostile not only to America and Western countries, but also to human rights. All this has bred more fear and more mistrust.

So long as our relationship is defined by our differences, we will empower those who sow hatred rather than peace, those who promote conflict rather than the cooperation that can help all of our people achieve justice and prosperity. And this cycle of suspicion and discord must end.

I've come here to Cairo to seek a new beginning between the United States and Muslims around the world, one based on mutual interest and mutual respect, and one based upon the truth that America and Islam are not exclusive and need not be in competition. Instead, they overlap, and share common principles—principles of justice and progress; tolerance and the dignity of all human beings. 5

Speech delivered by U.S. President Barack Obama in Cairo on June 4, 2009, fulfilling a campaign promise to deliver a major speech from a Muslim capital early in his presidency.

1. Center of Islamic scholarship in Cairo founded around 970; nationalized as Al-Azhar University in 1961.
2. "Peace be upon you."

I do so recognizing that change cannot happen overnight. I know there's been a lot of publicity about this speech, but no single speech can eradicate years of mistrust, nor can I answer in the time that I have this afternoon all the complex questions that brought us to this point. But I am convinced that in order to move forward, we must say openly to each other the things we hold in our hearts and that too often are said only behind closed doors. There must be a sustained effort to listen to each other; to learn from each other; to respect one another; and to seek common ground. As the Holy Koran tells us, "Be conscious of God and speak always the truth." That is what I will try to do today—to speak the truth as best I can, humbled by the task before us, and firm in my belief that the interests we share as human beings are far more powerful than the forces that drive us apart.

Now part of this conviction is rooted in my own experience. I'm a Christian, but my father came from a Kenyan family that includes generations of Muslims. As a boy, I spent several years in Indonesia and heard the call of the *azaan*[3] at the break of dawn and at the fall of dusk. As a young man, I worked in Chicago communities where many found dignity and peace in their Muslim faith.

As a student of history, I also know civilization's debt to Islam. It was Islam—at places like Al-Azhar—that carried the light of learning through so many centuries, paving the way for Europe's Renaissance and Enlightenment.[4] It was innovation in Muslim communities that developed the order of algebra; our magnetic compass and tools of navigation; our mastery of pens and printing; our understanding of how disease spreads and how it can be healed. Islamic culture has given us majestic arches and soaring spires; timeless poetry and cherished music; elegant calligraphy and places of peaceful contemplation. And throughout history, Islam has demonstrated through words and deeds the possibilities of religious tolerance and racial equality.

I also know that Islam has always been a part of America's story. The first nation to recognize my country was Morocco. In signing the Treaty of Tripoli[5] in 1796, our second President, John Adams, wrote, "The United States has in itself no character of enmity against the laws, religion or tranquility of Muslims." And since our founding, American Muslims have enriched the United States. They have fought in our wars, they have served in our government, they have stood for civil rights, they have started businesses, they have taught at our universities, they've excelled in our sports arenas, they've won Nobel Prizes, built our tallest building, and lit the Olympic Torch. And when the first Muslim American was recently elected to Congress, he took the oath to defend our Constitution using

3. Summons to prayer.

4. The European Renaissance, a period of humanistic intellectual and cultural development, began in Italy in the fourteenth century; the Enlightenment, a period characterized by faith in human reason, extended from the mid-seventeenth century through the eighteenth century.

5. First treaty between the United States and Tripoli, formally the *Treaty of Peace and Friendship between the United States and the Bey and Subjects of Tripoli of Barbary.*

the same Holy Koran that one of our Founding Fathers—Thomas Jefferson[6]—kept in his personal library.

So I have known Islam on three continents before coming to the region where it was first revealed. That experience guides my conviction that partnership between America and Islam must be based on what Islam is, not what it isn't. And I consider it part of my responsibility as President of the United States to fight against negative stereotypes of Islam wherever they appear.

But that same principle must apply to Muslim perceptions of America. Just as Muslims do not fit a crude stereotype, America is not the crude stereotype of a self-interested empire. The United States has been one of the greatest sources of progress that the world has ever known. We were born out of revolution against an empire. We were founded upon the ideal that all are created equal, and we have shed blood and struggled for centuries to give meaning to those words—within our borders, and around the world. We are shaped by every culture, drawn from every end of the Earth, and dedicated to a simple concept: E pluribus unum—"Out of many, one."

Now, much has been made of the fact that an African American with the name Barack Hussein Obama could be elected President. But my personal story is not so unique. The dream of opportunity for all people has not come true for everyone in America, but its promise exists for all who come to our shores—and that includes nearly 7 million American Muslims in our country today who, by the way, enjoy incomes and educational levels that are higher than the American average.

Moreover, freedom in America is indivisible from the freedom to practice one's religion. That is why there is a mosque in every state in our union, and over 1,200 mosques within our borders. That's why the United States government has gone to court to protect the right of women and girls to wear the hijab and to punish those who would deny it.

So let there be no doubt: Islam is a part of America. And I believe that America holds within her the truth that regardless of race, religion, or station in life, all of us share common aspirations—to live in peace and security; to get an education and to work with dignity; to love our families, our communities, and our God. These things we share. This is the hope of all humanity.

Of course, recognizing our common humanity is only the beginning of our task. Words alone cannot meet the needs of our people. These needs will be met only if we act boldly in the years ahead; and if we understand that the challenges we face are shared, and our failure to meet them will hurt us all.

For we have learned from recent experience that when a financial system weakens in one country, prosperity is hurt everywhere. When a new flu infects one human being, all are at risk. When one nation pursues a nuclear weapon, the risk of nuclear attack rises for all nations. When violent extremists operate in one stretch of mountains, people are endangered across an ocean. When

6. Jefferson (1743–1826) was the primary author of the Declaration of Independence (1776) and the third president of the United States (1801–09).

innocents in Bosnia and Darfur are slaughtered, that is a stain on our collective conscience. That is what it means to share this world in the 21st century. That is the responsibility we have to one another as human beings.

And this is a difficult responsibility to embrace. For human history has often been a record of nations and tribes—and, yes, religions—subjugating one another in pursuit of their own interests. Yet in this new age, such attitudes are self-defeating. Given our interdependence, any world order that elevates one nation or group of people over another will inevitably fail. So whatever we think of the past, we must not be prisoners to it. Our problems must be dealt with through partnership; our progress must be shared.

Now, that does not mean we should ignore sources of tension. Indeed, it suggests the opposite: We must face these tensions squarely. And so in that spirit, let me speak as clearly and as plainly as I can about some specific issues that I believe we must finally confront together.

The first issue that we have to confront is violent extremism in all of its forms.

20 In Ankara, I made clear that America is not—and never will be—at war with Islam. We will, however, relentlessly confront violent extremists who pose a grave threat to our security—because we reject the same thing that people of all faiths reject: the killing of innocent men, women, and children. And it is my first duty as President to protect the American people.

The situation in Afghanistan demonstrates America's goals, and our need to work together. Over seven years ago, the United States pursued al Qaeda and the Taliban with broad international support.[7] We did not go by choice; we went because of necessity. I'm aware that there's still some who would question or even justify the events of 9/11. But let us be clear: Al Qaeda killed nearly 3,000 people on that day. The victims were innocent men, women, and children from America and many other nations who had done nothing to harm anybody. And yet al Qaeda chose to ruthlessly murder these people, claimed credit for the attack, and even now states their determination to kill on a massive scale. They have affiliates in many countries and are trying to expand their reach. These are not opinions to be debated; these are facts to be dealt with.

Now, make no mistake: We do not want to keep our troops in Afghanistan. We seek no military bases there. It is agonizing for America to lose our young men and women. It is costly and politically difficult to continue this conflict. We would gladly bring every single one of our troops home if we could be confident that there were not violent extremists in Afghanistan and now Pakistan determined to kill as many Americans as they possibly can. But that is not yet the case.

And that's why we're partnering with a coalition of 46 countries. And despite the costs involved, America's commitment will not weaken. Indeed,

7. Al Qaeda is a militant Sunni group responsible for attacks on the World Trade Center and the Pentagon on September 11, 2001; the Taliban is an ultraconservative political and religious movement that controlled Afghanistan in the late 1990s and early 2000s and is now experiencing a resurgence.

none of us should tolerate these extremists. They have killed in many countries. They have killed people of different faiths—but more than any other, they have killed Muslims. Their actions are irreconcilable with the rights of human beings, the progress of nations, and with Islam. The Holy Koran teaches that whoever kills an innocent is as—it is as if he has killed all mankind. And the Holy Koran also says whoever saves a person, it is as if he has saved all mankind. The enduring faith of over a billion people is so much bigger than the narrow hatred of a few. Islam is not part of the problem in combating violent extremism—it is an important part of promoting peace.

Now, we also know that military power alone is not going to solve the problems in Afghanistan and Pakistan. That's why we plan to invest $1.5 billion each year over the next five years to partner with Pakistanis to build schools and hospitals, roads and businesses, and hundreds of millions to help those who've been displaced. That's why we are providing more than $2.8 billion to help Afghans develop their economy and deliver services that people depend on.

Let me also address the issue of Iraq. Unlike Afghanistan, Iraq was a war of choice that provoked strong differences in my country and around the world. Although I believe that the Iraqi people are ultimately better off without the tyranny of Saddam Hussein, I also believe that events in Iraq have reminded America of the need to use diplomacy and build international consensus to resolve our problems whenever possible. Indeed, we can recall the words of Thomas Jefferson, who said: "I hope that our wisdom will grow with our power, and teach us that the less we use our power the greater it will be." 25

Today, America has a dual responsibility: to help Iraq forge a better future—and to leave Iraq to Iraqis. And I have made it clear to the Iraqi people that we pursue no bases, and no claim on their territory or resources. Iraq's sovereignty is its own. And that's why I ordered the removal of our combat brigades by next August. That is why we will honor our agreement with Iraq's democratically elected government to remove combat troops from Iraqi cities by July, and to remove all of our troops from Iraq by 2012. We will help Iraq train its security forces and develop its economy. But we will support a secure and united Iraq as a partner, and never as a patron.

And finally, just as America can never tolerate violence by extremists, we must never alter or forget our principles. Nine-eleven was an enormous trauma to our country. The fear and anger that it provoked was understandable, but in some cases, it led us to act contrary to our traditions and our ideals. We are taking concrete actions to change course. I have unequivocally prohibited the use of torture by the United States, and I have ordered the prison at Guantánamo Bay[8] closed by early next year.

So America will defend itself, respectful of the sovereignty of nations and the rule of law. And we will do so in partnership with Muslim communities which are also threatened. The sooner the extremists are isolated and unwelcome in Muslim communities, the sooner we will all be safer.

8. U.S. detention camp at Guantánamo Bay Naval Base in Cuba for "enemy combatants" captured in Afghanistan and Iraq.

The second major source of tension that we need to discuss is the situation between Israelis, Palestinians and the Arab world.

30 America's strong bonds with Israel are well known. This bond is unbreakable. It is based upon cultural and historical ties, and the recognition that the aspiration for a Jewish homeland is rooted in a tragic history that cannot be denied.

Around the world, the Jewish people were persecuted for centuries, and anti-Semitism in Europe culminated in an unprecedented Holocaust. Tomorrow, I will visit Buchenwald,[9] which was part of a network of camps where Jews were enslaved, tortured, shot and gassed to death by the Third Reich. Six million Jews were killed—more than the entire Jewish population of Israel today. Denying that fact is baseless, it is ignorant, and it is hateful. Threatening Israel with destruction—or repeating vile stereotypes about Jews—is deeply wrong, and only serves to evoke in the minds of Israelis this most painful of memories while preventing the peace that the people of this region deserve.

On the other hand, it is also undeniable that the Palestinian people—Muslims and Christians—have suffered in pursuit of a homeland. For more than 60 years they've endured the pain of dislocation. Many wait in refugee camps in the West Bank, Gaza, and neighboring lands for a life of peace and security that they have never been able to lead. They endure the daily humiliations—large and small—that come with occupation. So let there be no doubt: The situation for the Palestinian people is intolerable. And America will not turn our backs on the legitimate Palestinian aspiration for dignity, opportunity, and a state of their own.

For decades then, there has been a stalemate: two peoples with legitimate aspirations, each with a painful history that makes compromise elusive. It's easy to point fingers—for Palestinians to point to the displacement brought about by Israel's founding, and for Israelis to point to the constant hostility and attacks throughout its history from within its borders as well as beyond. But if we see this conflict only from one side or the other, then we will be blind to the truth: The only resolution is for the aspirations of both sides to be met through two states, where Israelis and Palestinians each live in peace and security.

That is in Israel's interest, Palestine's interest, America's interest, and the world's interest. And that is why I intend to personally pursue this outcome with all the patience and dedication that the task requires. The obligations—the obligations that the parties have agreed to under the road map[10] are clear. For peace to come, it is time for them—and all of us—to live up to our responsibilities.

35 Palestinians must abandon violence. Resistance through violence and killing is wrong and it does not succeed. For centuries, black people in America suffered the lash of the whip as slaves and the humiliation of segregation. But it was not violence that won full and equal rights. It was a peaceful and determined insistence upon the ideals at the center of America's founding. This

9. Nazi concentration camp.

10. The Road Map for Peace was a plan developed in 2002 by the United States, the European Union, Russia, and the United Nations to end the Israeli–Palestinian conflict.

same story can be told by people from South Africa to South Asia; from Eastern Europe to Indonesia. It's a story with a simple truth: that violence is a dead end. It is a sign neither of courage nor power to shoot rockets at sleeping children, or to blow up old women on a bus. That's not how moral authority is claimed; that's how it is surrendered.

Now is the time for Palestinians to focus on what they can build. The Palestinian Authority must develop its capacity to govern, with institutions that serve the needs of its people. Hamas does have support among some Palestinians, but they also have to recognize they have responsibilities.[11] To play a role in fulfilling Palestinian aspirations, to unify the Palestinian people, Hamas must put an end to violence, recognize past agreements, recognize Israel's right to exist.

At the same time, Israelis must acknowledge that just as Israel's right to exist cannot be denied, neither can Palestine's. The United States does not accept the legitimacy of continued Israeli settlements. This construction violates previous agreements and undermines efforts to achieve peace. It is time for these settlements to stop.

And Israel must also live up to its obligation to ensure that Palestinians can live and work and develop their society. Just as it devastates Palestinian families, the continuing humanitarian crisis in Gaza does not serve Israel's security; neither does the continuing lack of opportunity in the West Bank. Progress in the daily lives of the Palestinian people must be a critical part of a road to peace, and Israel must take concrete steps to enable such progress.

And finally, the Arab states must recognize that the Arab Peace Initiative[12] was an important beginning, but not the end of their responsibilities. The Arab-Israeli conflict should no longer be used to distract the people of Arab nations from other problems. Instead, it must be a cause for action to help the Palestinian people develop the institutions that will sustain their state, to recognize Israel's legitimacy, and to choose progress over a self-defeating focus on the past.

America will align our policies with those who pursue peace, and we will say in public what we say in private to Israelis and Palestinians and Arabs. We cannot impose peace. But privately, many Muslims recognize that Israel will not go away. Likewise, many Israelis recognize the need for a Palestinian state. It is time for us to act on what everyone knows to be true. 40

Too many tears have been shed. Too much blood has been shed. All of us have a responsibility to work for the day when the mothers of Israelis and Palestinians can see their children grow up without fear; when the Holy Land of the three great faiths is the place of peace that God intended it to be; when

11. The Palestinian Authority has been the governing Palestinian body in the West Bank and the Gaza Strip since 1994. Hamas is a militant Palestinian movement founded in 1987; its name is an acronym for "Harakat al-Muqāwamat al-Islāmiyyah" ("Islamic Resistance Movement").

12. A 2002 proposal by Crown Prince (now King) Abdullah of Saudi Arabia to end the Arab–Israeli conflict, reiterated in 2007.

Jerusalem is a secure and lasting home for Jews and Christians and Muslims, and a place for all of the children of Abraham to mingle peacefully together as in the story of Isra, when Moses, Jesus, and Mohammed, peace be upon them, joined in prayer.

The third source of tension is our shared interest in the rights and responsibilities of nations on nuclear weapons.

This issue has been a source of tension between the United States and the Islamic Republic of Iran. For many years, Iran has defined itself in part by its opposition to my country, and there is in fact a tumultuous history between us. In the middle of the Cold War, the United States played a role in the overthrow of a democratically elected Iranian government. Since the Islamic Revolution, Iran has played a role in acts of hostage-taking and violence against U.S. troops and civilians. This history is well known. Rather than remain trapped in the past, I've made it clear to Iran's leaders and people that my country is prepared to move forward. The question now is not what Iran is against, but rather what future it wants to build.

I recognize it will be hard to overcome decades of mistrust, but we will proceed with courage, rectitude, and resolve. There will be many issues to discuss between our two countries, and we are willing to move forward without preconditions on the basis of mutual respect. But it is clear to all concerned that when it comes to nuclear weapons, we have reached a decisive point. This is not simply about America's interests. It's about preventing a nuclear arms race in the Middle East that could lead this region and the world down a hugely dangerous path.

45 I understand those who protest that some countries have weapons that others do not. No single nation should pick and choose which nation holds nuclear weapons. And that's why I strongly reaffirmed America's commitment to seek a world in which no nations hold nuclear weapons. And any nation—including Iran—should have the right to access peaceful nuclear power if it complies with its responsibilities under the nuclear Non-Proliferation Treaty.[13] That commitment is at the core of the treaty, and it must be kept for all who fully abide by it. And I'm hopeful that all countries in the region can share in this goal.

The fourth issue that I will address is democracy.

I know—I know there has been controversy about the promotion of democracy in recent years, and much of this controversy is connected to the war in Iraq. So let me be clear: No system of government can or should be imposed by one nation by any other.

That does not lessen my commitment, however, to governments that reflect the will of the people. Each nation gives life to this principle in its own way, grounded in the traditions of its own people. America does not presume to know what is best for everyone, just as we would not presume to pick the outcome of a peaceful election. But I do have an unyielding belief that all people yearn for certain things: the ability to speak your mind and have a say in how you are governed; confidence in the rule of law and the equal administration of justice;

13. Treaty ratified by 189 nations intended to restrict the spread of nuclear weapons.

government that is transparent and doesn't steal from the people; the freedom to live as you choose. These are not just American ideas; they are human rights. And that is why we will support them everywhere.

Now, there is no straight line to realize this promise. But this much is clear: Governments that protect these rights are ultimately more stable, successful and secure. Suppressing ideas never succeeds in making them go away. America respects the right of all peaceful and law-abiding voices to be heard around the world, even if we disagree with them. And we will welcome all elected, peaceful governments—provided they govern with respect for all their people.

This last point is important because there are some who advocate for democracy only when they're out of power; once in power, they are ruthless in suppressing the rights of others. So no matter where it takes hold, government of the people and by the people sets a single standard for all who would hold power: You must maintain your power through consent, not coercion; you must respect the rights of minorities, and participate with a spirit of tolerance and compromise; you must place the interests of your people and the legitimate workings of the political process above your party. Without these ingredients, elections alone do not make true democracy. 50

The fifth issue that we must address together is religious freedom.

Islam has a proud tradition of tolerance. We see it in the history of Andalusia and Córdoba during the Inquisition.[14] I saw it firsthand as a child in Indonesia, where devout Christians worshiped freely in an overwhelmingly Muslim country. That is the spirit we need today. People in every country should be free to choose and live their faith based upon the persuasion of the mind and the heart and the soul. This tolerance is essential for religion to thrive, but it's being challenged in many different ways.

Among some Muslims, there's a disturbing tendency to measure one's own faith by the rejection of somebody else's faith. The richness of religious diversity must be upheld—whether it is for Maronites in Lebanon or the Copts in Egypt.[15] And if we are being honest, fault lines must be closed among Muslims, as well, as the divisions between Sunni and Shia[16] have led to tragic violence, particularly in Iraq.

Freedom of religion is central to the ability of peoples to live together. We must always examine the ways in which we protect it. For instance, in the United States, rules on charitable giving have made it harder for Muslims to fulfill their religious obligation. That's why I'm committed to working with American Muslims to ensure that they can fulfill *zakat*.[17]

14. Andalusia is a region of Spain, parts of which were under Islamic rule from the early eighth through the late fifteenth centuries; Córdoba, an Andalusian city, was an Islamic capital from the early eighth to the early thirteenth centuries; the Spanish Inquisition was a tribunal established in the fifteenth century to enforce Catholic orthodoxy.

15. The Maronites are Eastern-rite Catholics, predominantly Lebanese; the Copts are Egyptian Christians.

16. Sunni and Shia Islam are the two largest branches of that religion.

17. Obligation to give alms, one of the Five Pillars of Islam.

55 Likewise, it is important for Western countries to avoid impeding Muslim citizens from practicing religion as they see fit—for instance, by dictating what clothes a Muslim woman should wear. We can't disguise hostility towards any religion behind the pretence of liberalism.

In fact, faith should bring us together. And that's why we're forging service projects in America to bring together Christians, Muslims, and Jews. That's why we welcome efforts like Saudi Arabian King Abdullah's interfaith dialogue and Turkey's leadership in the Alliance of Civilizations.[18] Around the world, we can turn dialogue into interfaith service, so bridges between peoples lead to action—whether it is combating malaria in Africa, or providing relief after a natural disaster.

The sixth issue—the sixth issue that I want to address is women's rights. I know—I know—and you can tell from this audience, that there is a healthy debate about this issue. I reject the view of some in the West that a woman who chooses to cover her hair is somehow less equal, but I do believe that a woman who is denied an education is denied equality. And it is no coincidence that countries where women are well educated are far more likely to be prosperous.

Now, let me be clear: Issues of women's equality are by no means simply an issue for Islam. In Turkey, Pakistan, Bangladesh, Indonesia, we've seen Muslim-majority countries elect a woman to lead. Meanwhile, the struggle for women's equality continues in many aspects of American life, and in countries around the world.

I am convinced that our daughters can contribute just as much to society as our sons. Our common prosperity will be advanced by allowing all humanity—men and women—to reach their full potential. I do not believe that women must make the same choices as men in order to be equal, and I respect those women who choose to live their lives in traditional roles. But it should be their choice. And that is why the United States will partner with any Muslim-majority country to support expanded literacy for girls, and to help young women pursue employment through micro-financing that helps people live their dreams.

60 Finally, I want to discuss economic development and opportunity.

I know that for many, the face of globalization is contradictory. The Internet and television can bring knowledge and information, but also offensive sexuality and mindless violence into the home. Trade can bring new wealth and opportunities, but also huge disruptions and change in communities. In all nations—including America—this change can bring fear. Fear that because of modernity we lose control over our economic choices, our politics, and most importantly our identities—those things we most cherish about our communities, our families, our traditions, and our faith.

But I also know that human progress cannot be denied. There need not be contradictions between development and tradition. Countries like Japan and South Korea grew their economies enormously while maintaining distinct cultures. The same is true for the astonishing progress within Muslim-majority

18. A U.N. initiative, proposed in 2005 by Spain and cosponsored by Turkey, to promote understanding between Islamic and Western nations.

countries from Kuala Lumpur to Dubai. In ancient times and in our times, Muslim communities have been at the forefront of innovation and education.

And this is important because no development strategy can be based only upon what comes out of the ground, nor can it be sustained while young people are out of work. Many Gulf states have enjoyed great wealth as a consequence of oil, and some are beginning to focus it on broader development. But all of us must recognize that education and innovation will be the currency of the 21st century—and in too many Muslim communities, there remains underinvestment in these areas. I'm emphasizing such investment within my own country. And while America in the past has focused on oil and gas when it comes to this part of the world, we now seek a broader engagement.

On education, we will expand exchange programs, and increase scholarships, like the one that brought my father to America. At the same time, we will encourage more Americans to study in Muslim communities. And we will match promising Muslim students with internships in America; invest in online learning for teachers and children around the world; and create a new online network, so a young person in Kansas can communicate instantly with a young person in Cairo.

65

On economic development, we will create a new corps of business volunteers to partner with counterparts in Muslim-majority countries. And I will host a Summit on Entrepreneurship this year to identify how we can deepen ties between business leaders, foundations and social entrepreneurs in the United States and Muslim communities around the world.

On science and technology, we will launch a new fund to support technological development in Muslim-majority countries, and to help transfer ideas to the marketplace so they can create more jobs. We'll open centers of scientific excellence in Africa, the Middle East and Southeast Asia, and appoint new science envoys to collaborate on programs that develop new sources of energy, create green jobs, digitize records, clean water, grow new crops. Today I'm announcing a new global effort with the Organization of the Islamic Conference[19] to eradicate polio. And we will also expand partnerships with Muslim communities to promote child and maternal health.

All these things must be done in partnership. Americans are ready to join with citizens and governments; community organizations, religious leaders, and businesses in Muslim communities around the world to help our people pursue a better life.

The issues that I have described will not be easy to address. But we have a responsibility to join together on behalf of the world that we seek—a world where extremists no longer threaten our people, and American troops have come home; a world where Israelis and Palestinians are each secure in a state of their own, and nuclear energy is used for peaceful purposes; a world where governments serve their citizens, and the rights of all God's children are respected. Those are mutual interests. That is the world we seek. But we can only achieve it together.

19. International organization of 57 primarily Muslim states.

I know there are many—Muslim and non-Muslim—who question whether we can forge this new beginning. Some are eager to stoke the flames of division, and to stand in the way of progress. Some suggest that it isn't worth the effort—that we are fated to disagree, and civilizations are doomed to clash. Many more are simply skeptical that real change can occur. There's so much fear, so much mistrust that has built up over the years. But if we choose to be bound by the past, we will never move forward. And I want to particularly say this to young people of every faith, in every country—you, more than anyone, have the ability to reimagine the world, to remake this world.

70 All of us share this world for but a brief moment in time. The question is whether we spend that time focused on what pushes us apart, or whether we commit ourselves to an effort—a sustained effort—to find common ground, to focus on the future we seek for our children, and to respect the dignity of all human beings.

It's easier to start wars than to end them. It's easier to blame others than to look inward. It's easier to see what is different about someone than to find the things we share. But we should choose the right path, not just the easy path. There's one rule that lies at the heart of every religion—that we do unto others as we would have them do unto us. This truth transcends nations and peoples—a belief that isn't new; that isn't black or white or brown; that isn't Christian or Muslim or Jew. It's a belief that pulsed in the cradle of civilization, and that still beats in the hearts of billions around the world. It's a faith in other people, and it's what brought me here today.

We have the power to make the world we seek, but only if we have the courage to make a new beginning, keeping in mind what has been written.

The Holy Koran tells us: "O mankind! We have created you male and a female; and we have made you into nations and tribes so that you may know one another."

The Talmud tells us: "The whole of the Torah is for the purpose of promoting peace."

75 The Holy Bible tells us: "Blessed are the peacemakers, for they shall be called sons of God."

The people of the world can live together in peace. We know that is God's vision. Now that must be our work here on Earth.

Thank you. And may God's peace be upon you. Thank you very much. Thank you.

QUESTIONS

1. Obama begins his speech with a long introduction that is simultaneously political, historical, and personal. How does this introduction prepare for the discussions of specific issues that follow?

2. In the body of his speech, Obama discusses seven specific tensions or issues affecting the current relationship between the United States and Muslim nations. Select one of these sections and examine it in detail. How does Obama develop his argument so that it will appeal to various audiences?

3. Compare the introduction and the conclusion. How does Obama's stance toward the relationship between Americans and Muslims change from the beginning to the end of the speech?

4. Obama concludes with a call to action directed especially toward the world's youth: "And I want to particularly say this to young people of every faith, in every country—you, more than anyone, have the ability to reimagine the world, to remake this world" (paragraph 68). Write a paper in which you discuss ways you personally might respond to this call.

Science and Technology

Jacob Bronowski *The Nature of Scientific Reasoning*

What is the insight in which the scientist tries to see into nature? Can it indeed be called either imaginative or creative? To the literary man the question may seem merely silly. He has been taught that science is a large collection of facts; and if this is true, then the only seeing which scientists need to do is, he supposes, seeing the facts. He pictures them, the colorless professionals of science, going off to work in the morning into the universe in a neutral, unexposed state. They then expose themselves like a photographic plate. And then in the darkroom or laboratory they develop the image, so that suddenly and startlingly it appears, printed in capital letters, as a new formula for atomic energy.

Men who have read Balzac and Zola[1] are not deceived by the claims of these writers that they do no more than record the facts. The readers of Christopher Isherwood[2] do not take him literally when he writes "I am a camera." Yet the same readers solemnly carry with them from their school-days this foolish picture of the scientist fixing by some mechanical process the facts of nature. I have had of all people a historian tell me that science is a collection of facts, and his voice had not even the ironic rasp of one filing cabinet reproving another.

It seems impossible that this historian had ever studied the beginnings of a scientific discovery. The Scientific Revolution can be held to begin in the year 1543 when there was brought to Copernicus, perhaps on his deathbed, the first printed copy of the book he had finished about a dozen years earlier. The thesis of this book is that the earth moves around the sun. When did Copernicus go out and record this fact with his camera? What appearance in nature prompted his outrageous guess? And in what odd sense is this guess to be called a neutral record of fact?

Less than a hundred years after Copernicus, Kepler published (between 1609 and 1619) the three laws which describe the paths of the planets. The

First delivered as a lecture at the Massachusetts Institute of Technology and then reprinted as part of Bronowski's book Science and Human Values *(1956).*

1. Honoré de Balzac (1799–1850) and Émile Zola (1840–1902), nineteenth-century French novelists.

2. English novelist and playwright (1904–1986) whose writing was the basis for the musical *Cabaret*.

work of Newton and with it most of our mechanics spring from these laws.[3] They have a solid, matter-of-fact sound. For example, Kepler says that if one squares the year of a planet, one gets a number which is proportional to the cube of its average distance from the sun. Does anyone think that such a law is found by taking enough readings and then squaring and cubing everything in sight? If he does, then, as a scientist, he is doomed to a wasted life; he has as little prospect of making a scientific discovery as an electronic brain has.

5 It was not this way that Copernicus and Kepler thought, or that scientists think today. Copernicus found that the orbits of the planets would look simpler if they were looked at from the sun and not from the earth. But he did not in the first place find this by routine calculation. His first step was a leap of imagination—to lift himself from the earth, and put himself wildly, speculatively into the sun. "The earth conceives from the sun," he wrote; and "the sun rules the family of stars." We catch in his mind an image, the gesture of the virile man standing in the sun, with arms outstretched, overlooking the planets. Perhaps Copernicus took the picture from the drawings of the youth with outstretched arms which the Renaissance teachers put into their books on the proportions of the body. Perhaps he had seen Leonardo's[4] drawings of his loved pupil Salai. I do not know. To me, the gesture of Copernicus, the shining youth looking outward from the sun, is still vivid in a drawing which William Blake[5] in 1780 based on all these: the drawing which is usually called *Glad Day.*

Kepler's mind, we know, was filled with just such fanciful analogies; and we know what they were. Kepler wanted to relate the speeds of the planets to the musical intervals. He tried to fit the five regular solids into their orbits. None of these likenesses worked, and they have been forgotten; yet they have been and they remain the stepping stones of every creative mind. Kepler felt for his laws by way of metaphors, he searched mystically for likenesses with what he knew in every strange corner of nature. And when among these guesses he hit upon his laws, he did not think of their numbers as the balancing of a cosmic bank account, but as a revelation of the unity in all nature. To us, the analogies by which Kepler listened for the movement of the planets in the music of the spheres are farfetched. Yet are they more so than the wild leap by which Rutherford and Bohr[6] in our own century found a model for the atom in, of all places, the planetary system?

No scientific theory is a collection of facts. It will not even do to call a theory true or false in the simple sense in which every fact is either so or not so. The Epicureans held that matter is made of atoms two thousand years ago and we are now tempted to say that their theory was true. But if we do so we confuse

3. Nicolaus Copernicus (1473–1543), Polish astronomer; Johannes Kepler (1571–1630), German astronomer; Isaac Newton (1642–1727), English physicist and mathematician.

4. Leonardo da Vinci (1452–1519), Italian artist, inventor, and designer.

5. English poet, artist, and engraver (1757–1827).

6. Ernest Rutherford (1871–1937), British physicist; Niels Bohr (1885–1962), Danish physicist.

their notion of matter with our own. John Dalton[7] in 1808 first saw the structure of matter as we do today, and what he took from the ancients was not their theory but something richer, their image: the atom. Much of what was in Dalton's mind was as vague as the Greek notion, and quite as mistaken. But he suddenly gave life to the new facts of chemistry and the ancient theory together, by fusing them to give what neither had: a coherent picture of how matter is linked and built up from different kinds of atoms. The act of fusion is the creative act.

All science is the search for unity in hidden likenesses. The search may be on a grand scale, as in the modern theories which try to link the fields of gravitation and electromagnetism. But we do not need to be browbeaten by the scale of science. There are discoveries to be made by snatching a small likeness from the air too, if it is bold enough. In 1935 the Japanese physicist Hideki Yukawa wrote a paper which can still give heart to a young scientist. He took as his starting point the known fact that waves of light can sometimes behave as if they were separate pellets. From this he reasoned that the forces which hold the nucleus of an atom together might sometimes also be observed as if they were solid pellets. A schoolboy can see how thin Yukawa's analogy is, and his teacher would be severe with it. Yet Yukawa without a blush calculated the mass of the pellet he expected to see, and waited. He was right; his meson was found, and a range of other mesons, neither the existence nor the nature of which had been suspected before. The likeness had borne fruit.

The scientist looks for order in the appearances of nature by exploring such likenesses. For order does not display itself of itself; if it can be said to be there at all, it is not there for the mere looking. There is no way of pointing a finger or camera at it; order must be discovered and, in a deep sense, it must be created. What we see, as we see it, is mere disorder.

10 This point has been put trenchantly in a fable by Karl Popper.[8] Suppose that someone wished to give his whole life to science. Suppose that he therefore sat down, pencil in hand, and for the next twenty, thirty, forty years recorded in notebook after notebook everything that he could observe. He may be supposed to leave out nothing: today's humidity, the racing results, the level of cosmic radiation and the stockmarket prices and the look of Mars, all would be there. He would have compiled the most careful record of nature that has ever been made; and, dying in the calm certainty of a life well spent, he would of course leave his notebooks to the Royal Society. Would the Royal Society thank him for the treasure of a lifetime of observation? It would not. The Royal Society would treat his notebooks exactly as the English bishops have treated Joanna Southcott's box.[9] It would refuse to open them at all, because it would

7. British chemist and physicist (1766–1844) who developed the atomic theory of matter and thus is considered a father of modern physical science.

8. Austrian-born British philosopher (1902–1994).

9. Southcott was a nineteenth-century English farm servant who claimed to be a prophet. She left behind a box that was to be opened in a time of national emergency in the presence of all the English bishops. In 1927, a bishop agreed to officiate; when the box was opened, it was found to contain only some odds and ends.

know without looking that the notebooks contain only a jumble of disorderly and meaningless items.

Science finds order and meaning in our experience, and sets about this in quite a different way. It sets about it as Newton did in the story which he himself told in his old age, and of which the schoolbooks give only a caricature. In the year 1665, when Newton was twenty-two, the plague broke out in southern England, and the University of Cambridge was closed. Newton therefore spent the next eighteen months at home, removed from traditional learning, at a time when he was impatient for knowledge and, in his own phrase, "I was in the prime of my age for invention." In this eager, boyish mood, sitting one day in the garden of his widowed mother, he saw an apple fall. So far the books have the story right; we think we even know the kind of apple; tradition has it that it was a Flower of Kent. But now they miss the crux of the story. For what struck the young Newton at the sight was not the thought that the apple must be drawn to the earth by gravity; that conception was older than Newton. What struck him was the conjecture that the same force of gravity, which reaches to the top of the tree, might go on reaching out beyond the earth and its air, endlessly into space. Gravity might reach the moon: this was Newton's new thought; and it might be gravity which holds the moon in her orbit. There and then he calculated what force from the earth (falling off as the square of the distance) would hold the moon, and compared it with the known force of gravity at tree height. The forces agreed; Newton says laconically, "I found them answer pretty nearly." Yet they agreed only nearly: the likeness and the approximation go together, for no likeness is exact. In Newton's science modern science is full grown.

It grows from a comparison. It has seized a likeness between two unlike appearances; for the apple in the summer garden and the grave moon overhead are surely as unlike in their movements as two things can be. Newton traced in them two expressions of a single concept, gravitation: and the concept (and the unity) are in that sense his free creation. The progress of science is the discovery at each step of a new order which gives unity to what had long seemed unlike.

* * *

Questions

1. Mark the generalizations Bronowski makes in the course of "The Nature of Scientific Reasoning"; for example, "No scientific theory is a collection of facts" (paragraph 7). Where is the information that supports them?

2. Bronowski tells the well-known story of Newton and the apple (paragraphs 11–12). How many of his generalizations does it exemplify, and how?

3. "The scientist," Bronowski observes, "looks for order in the appearances of nature" (paragraph 9). Is this operation unique to scientists? Consider the operations of "knowers" in humanities and social science disciplines such as history, literature, psychology, and sociology.

4. Bronowski sets up an adversary, a literary person who believes that scientists observe, collect, and record facts, and writes his essay as a refutation. Adapt his rhetorical strategy in an essay of your own: explain your beliefs about something by refuting the beliefs of someone who disagrees with them.

ISAAC ASIMOV

The Eureka Phenomenon

IN THE OLD DAYS, when I was writing a great deal of fiction, there would come, once in a while, moments when I was stymied. Suddenly, I would find I had written myself into a hole and could see no way out. To take care of that, I developed a technique which invariably worked.

It was simply this—I went to the movies. Not just any movie. I had to pick a movie which was loaded with action but which made no demands on the intellect. As I watched, I did my best to avoid any conscious thinking concerning my problem, and when I came out of the movie I knew exactly what I would have to do to put the story back on the track.

It never failed.

In fact, when I was working on my doctoral dissertation, too many years ago, I suddenly came across a flaw in my logic that I had not noticed before and that knocked out everything I had done. In utter panic, I made my way to a Bob Hope movie—and came out with the necessary change in point of view.

5 It is my belief, you see, that thinking is a double phenomenon like breathing.

You can control breathing by deliberate voluntary action: you can breathe deeply and quickly, or you can hold your breath altogether, regardless of the body's needs at the time. This, however, doesn't work well for very long. Your chest muscles grow tired, your body clamors for more oxygen, or less, and you relax. The automatic involuntary control of breathing takes over, adjusts it to the body's needs and unless you have some respiratory disorder, you can forget about the whole thing.

Well, you can think by deliberate voluntary action, too, and I don't think it is much more efficient on the whole than voluntary breath control is. You can deliberately force your mind through channels of deductions and associations in search of a solution to some problem and before long you have dug mental furrows for yourself and find yourself circling round and round the same limited pathways. If those pathways yield no solution, no amount of further conscious thought will help.

On the other hand, if you let go, then the thinking process comes under automatic involuntary control and is more apt to take new pathways and make

First published in The Magazine of Fantasy and Science Fiction *(June 1971); later included in* The Left Hand of the Electron.

erratic associations you would not think of consciously. The solution will then come while you *think* you are *not* thinking.

The trouble is, though, that conscious thought involves no muscular action and so there is no sensation of physical weariness that would force you to quit. What's more, the panic of necessity tends to force you to go on uselessly, with each added bit of useless effort adding to the panic in a vicious cycle.

It is my feeling that it helps to relax, deliberately, by subjecting your mind to material complicated enough to occupy the voluntary faculty of thought, but superficial enough not to engage the deeper involuntary one. In my case, it is an action movie; in your case, it might be something else. 10

I suspect it is the involuntary faculty of thought that gives rise to what we call "a flash of intuition," something that I imagine must be merely the result of unnoticed thinking.

Perhaps the most famous flash of intuition in the history of science took place in the city of Syracuse in third-century B.C. Sicily. Bear with me and I will tell you the story—

About 250 B.C., the city of Syracuse was experiencing a kind of Golden Age. It was under the protection of the rising power of Rome, but it retained a king of its own and considerable self-government; it was prosperous; and it had a flourishing intellectual life.

The king was Hieron II, and he had commissioned a new golden crown from a goldsmith, to whom he had given an ingot of gold as raw material. Hieron, being a practical man, had carefully weighed the ingot and then weighed the crown he received back. The two weights were precisely equal. Good deal!

But then he sat and thought for a while. Suppose the goldsmith had subtracted a little bit of the gold, not too much, and had substituted an equal weight of the considerably less valuable copper. The resulting alloy would still have the appearance of pure gold, but the goldsmith would be plus a quantity of gold over and above his fee. He would be buying gold with copper, so to speak, and Hieron would be neatly cheated. 15

Hieron didn't like the thought of being cheated any more than you or I would, but he didn't know how to find out for sure if he had been. He could scarcely punish the goldsmith on mere suspicion. What to do?

Fortunately, Hieron had an advantage few rulers in the history of the world could boast. He had a relative of considerable talent. The relative was named Archimedes and he probably had the greatest intellect the world was to see prior to the birth of Newton.

Archimedes was called in and was posed the problem. He had to determine whether the crown Hieron showed him was pure gold, or was gold to which a small but significant quantity of copper had been added.

If we were to reconstruct Archimedes' reasoning, it might go as follows. Gold was the densest known substance (at that time). Its density in modern terms is 19.3 grams per cubic centimeter. This means that a given weight of gold takes up less volume than the same weight of anything else! In fact, a given weight of pure gold takes up less volume than the same weight of *any* kind of impure gold.

20 The density of copper is 8.92 grams per cubic centimeter, just about half that of gold. If we consider 100 grams of pure gold, for instance, it is easy to calculate it to have a volume of 5.18 cubic centimeters. But suppose that 100 grams of what looked like pure gold was really only 90 grams of gold and 10 grams of copper. The 90 grams of gold would have a volume of 4.66 cubic centimeters, while the 10 grams of copper would have a volume of 1.12 cubic centimeters; for a total value of 5.78 cubic centimeters.

The difference between 5.18 cubic centimeters and 5.78 cubic centimeters is quite a noticeable one, and would instantly tell if the crown were of pure gold, or if it contained 10 per cent copper (with the missing 10 per cent of gold tucked neatly in the goldsmith's strongbox).

All one had to do, then, was measure the volume of the crown and compare it with the volume of the same weight of pure gold.

The mathematics of the time made it easy to measure the volume of many simple shapes: a cube, a sphere, a cone, a cylinder, any flattened object of simple regular shape and known thickness, and so on.

We can imagine Archimedes saying, "All that is necessary, sire, is to pound that crown flat, shape it into a square of uniform thickness, and then I can have the answer for you in a moment."

25 Whereupon Hieron must certainly have snatched the crown away and said, "No such thing. I can do that much without you; I've studied the principles of mathematics, too. This crown is a highly satisfactory work of art and I won't have it damaged. Just calculate its volume without in any way altering it."

But Greek mathematics had no way of determining the volume of anything with a shape as irregular as the crown, since integral calculus had not yet been invented (and wouldn't be for two thousand years, almost). Archimedes would have had to say, "There is no known way, sire, to carry through a nondestructive determination of volume."

"Then think of one," said Hieron testily.

And Archimedes must have set about thinking of one, and gotten nowhere. Nobody knows how long he thought, or how hard, or what hypotheses he considered and discarded, or any of the details.

What we do know is that, worn out with thinking, Archimedes decided to visit the public baths and relax. I think we are quite safe in saying that Archimedes had no intention of taking his problem to the baths with him. It would be ridiculous to imagine he would, for the public baths of a Greek metropolis weren't intended for that sort of thing.

30 The Greek baths were a place for relaxation. Half the social aristocracy of the town would be there and there was a great deal more to do than wash. One steamed one's self, got a massage, exercised, and engaged in general socializing. We can be sure that Archimedes intended to forget the stupid crown for a while.

One can envisage him engaging in light talk, discussing the latest news from Alexandria and Carthage, the latest scandals in town, the latest funny jokes at the expense of the country-squire Romans—and then he lowered himself into a nice hot bath which some bumbling attendant had filled too full.

The water in the bath slopped over as Archimedes got in. Did Archimedes notice that at once, or did he sigh, sink back, and paddle his feet awhile before noting the water-slop. I guess the latter. But, whether soon or late, he noticed, and that one fact, added to all the chains of reasoning his brain had been working on during the period of relaxation when it was unhampered by the comparative stupidities (even in Archimedes) of voluntary thought, gave Archimedes his answer in one blinding flash of insight.

Jumping out of the bath, he proceeded to run home at top speed through the streets of Syracuse. He did *not* bother to put on his clothes. The thought of Archimedes running naked through Syracuse has titillated dozens of generations of youngsters who have heard this story, but I must explain that the ancient Greeks were quite lighthearted in their attitude toward nudity. They thought no more of seeing a naked man on the streets of Syracuse, than we would on the Broadway stage.

And as he ran, Archimedes shouted over and over, "I've got it! I've got it!" Of course, knowing no English, he was compelled to shout it in Greek, so it came out, "*Eureka! Eureka!*"

35 Archimedes' solution was so simple that anyone could understand it—once Archimedes explained it.

If an object that is not affected by water in any way, is immersed in water, it is bound to displace an amount of water equal to its own volume, since two objects cannot occupy the same space at the same time.

Suppose, then, you had a vessel large enough to hold the crown and suppose it had a small overflow spout set into the middle of its side. And suppose further that the vessel was filled with water exactly to the spout, so that if the water level were raised a bit higher, however slightly, some would overflow.

Next, suppose that you carefully lower the crown into the water. The water level would rise by an amount equal to the volume of the crown, and that volume of water would pour out the overflow and be caught in a small vessel. Next, a lump of gold, known to be pure and exactly equal in weight to the crown, is also immersed in the water and again the level rises and the overflow is caught in a second vessel.

If the crown were pure gold, the overflow would be exactly the same in each case, and the volume of water caught in the two small vessels would be equal. If, however, the crown were of alloy, it would produce a larger overflow than the pure gold would and this would be easily noticeable.

40 What's more, the crown would in no way be harmed, defaced, or even as much as scratched. More important, Archimedes had discovered the "principle of buoyancy."

And was the crown pure gold? I've heard that it turned out to be alloy and that the goldsmith was executed, but I wouldn't swear to it.

How often does this "Eureka phenomenon" happen? How often is there this flash of deep insight during a moment of relaxation, this triumphant cry of

"I've got it! I've got it!" which must surely be a moment of the purest ecstasy this sorry world can afford?

I wish there were some way we could tell. I suspect that in the history of science it happens *often;* I suspect that very few significant discoveries are made by the pure technique of voluntary thought; I suspect that voluntary thought may possibly prepare the ground (if even that), but that the final touch, the real inspiration, comes when thinking is under involuntary control.

But the world is in a conspiracy to hide the fact. Scientists are wedded to reason, to the meticulous working out of consequences from assumptions to the careful organization of experiments designed to check those consequences. If a certain line of experiments ends nowhere, it is omitted from the final report. If an inspired guess turns out to be correct, it is *not* reported as an inspired guess. Instead, a solid line of voluntary thought is invented after the fact to lead up to the thought, and that is what is inserted in the final report.

45 The result is that anyone reading scientific papers would swear that *nothing* took place but voluntary thought maintaining a steady clumping stride from origin to destination, and that just can't be true.

It's such a shame. Not only does it deprive science of much of its glamour (how much of the dramatic story in Watson's *Double Helix* do you suppose got into the final reports announcing the great discovery of the structure of DNA?),[1] but it hands over the important process of "insight," "inspiration," "revelation" to the mystic.

The scientist actually becomes ashamed of having what we might call a revelation, as though to have one is to betray reason—when actually what we call revelation in a man who has devoted his life to reasoned thought, is after all merely reasoned thought that is not under voluntary control.

Only once in a while in modern times do we ever get a glimpse into the workings of involuntary reasoning, and when we do, it is always fascinating. Consider, for instance, the case of Friedrich August Kekule von Stradonitz.

In Kekule's time, a century and a quarter ago, a subject of great interest to chemists was the structure of organic molecules (those associated with living tissue). Inorganic molecules were generally simple in the sense that they were made up of few atoms. Water molecules, for instance, are made up of two atoms of hydrogen and one of oxygen (H_2O). Molecules of ordinary salt are made up of one atom of sodium and one of chlorine (NaCl), and so on.

50 Organic molecules, on the other hand, often contained a large number of atoms. Ethyl alcohol molecules have two carbon atoms, six hydrogen atoms, and an oxygen atom (C_2H_6O); the molecule of ordinary cane sugar is $C_{12}H_{22}O_{11}$, and other molecules are even more complex.

Then, too, it is sufficient, in the case of inorganic molecules generally, merely to know the kinds and numbers of atoms in the molecule; in organic molecules, more is necessary. Thus, dimethyl ether has the formula C_2H_6O, just

1. I'll tell you, in case you're curious. None! [Asimov's note]. How Francis Crick and James Watson discovered the molecular structure of this vital substance is told in Watson's autobiographical book, *The Double Helix*.

as ethyl alcohol does, and yet the two are quite different in properties. Apparently, the atoms are arranged differently within the molecules—but how to determine the arrangements?

In 1852, an English chemist, Edward Frankland, had noticed that the atoms of a particular element tended to combine with a fixed number of other atoms. This combining number was called "valence." Kekule in 1858 reduced this notion to a system. The carbon atom, he decided (on the basis of plenty of chemical evidence) had a valence of four; the hydrogen atom, a valence of one; and the oxygen atom, a valence of two (and so on).

Why not represent the atoms as their symbols plus a number of attached dashes, that number being equal to the valence. Such atoms could then be put together as though they were so many Tinker Toy units and "structural formulas" could be built up.

It was possible to reason out that the structural formula of ethyl alcohol was

$$\begin{array}{ccccccccc} & & \mathrm{H} & & \mathrm{H} & & & & \\ & & | & & | & & & & \\ \mathrm{H} & — & \mathrm{C} & — & \mathrm{C} & — & \mathrm{O} & — & \mathrm{H}, \\ & & | & & | & & & & \\ & & \mathrm{H} & & \mathrm{H} & & & & \end{array}$$

while that of dimethyl ether was

$$\begin{array}{ccccccccc} & & \mathrm{H} & & & & \mathrm{H} & & \\ & & | & & & & | & & \\ \mathrm{H} & — & \mathrm{C} & — & \mathrm{O} & — & \mathrm{C} & — & \mathrm{H}. \\ & & | & & & & | & & \\ & & \mathrm{H} & & & & \mathrm{H} & & \end{array}$$

In each case, there were two carbon atoms, each with four dashes attached; six hydrogen atoms, each with one dash attached; and an oxygen atom with two dashes attached. The molecules were built up of the same components, but in different arrangements.

Kekule's theory worked beautifully. It has been immensely deepened and elaborated since his day, but you can still find structures very much like Kekule's Tinker Toy formulas in any modern chemical textbook. They represent oversimplifications of the true situation, but they remain extremely useful in practice even so.

The Kekule structures were applied to many organic molecules in the years after 1858 and the similarities and contrasts in the structures neatly matched similarities and contrasts in properties. The key to the rationalization of organic chemistry had, it seemed, been found.

Yet there was one disturbing fact. The well-known chemical benzene wouldn't fit. It was known to have a molecule made up of equal numbers of carbon and hydrogen atoms. Its molecular weight was known to be 78 and a single carbon-hydrogen combination had a weight of 13. Therefore, the benzene molecule had to contain six carbon-hydrogen combinations and its formula had to be C_6H_6.

But that meant trouble. By the Kekule formulas, the hydrocarbons (molecules made up of carbon and hydrogen atoms only) could easily be envisioned as chains of carbon atoms with hydrogen atoms attached. If all the valences of the carbon atoms were filled with hydrogen atoms, as in "hexane," whose molecule looks like this—

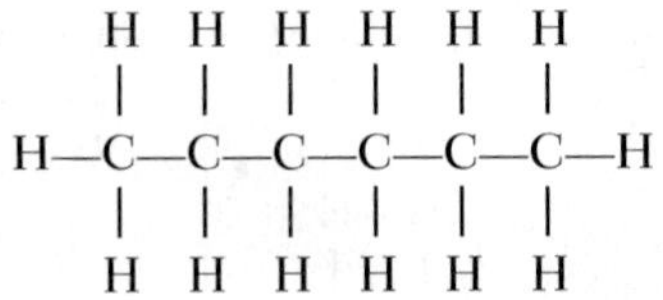

```
    H  H  H  H  H  H
    |  |  |  |  |  |
 H—C—C—C—C—C—C—H
    |  |  |  |  |  |
    H  H  H  H  H  H
```

the compound is said to be saturated. Such saturated hydrocarbons were found to have very little tendency to react with other substances.

60

If some of the valences were not filled, unused bonds were added to those connecting the carbon atoms. Double bonds were formed as in "hexene"—

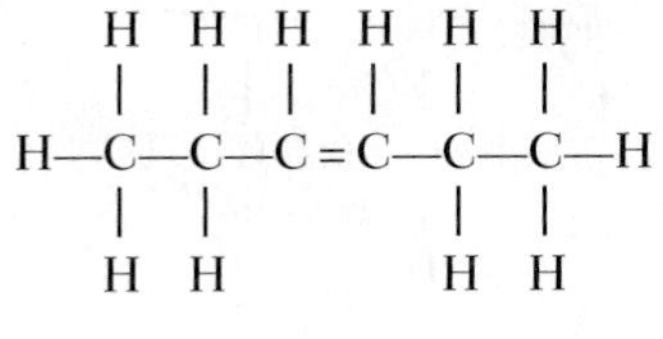

```
    H  H  H  H  H  H
    |  |  |  |  |  |
 H—C—C—C=C—C—C—H
    |  |        |  |
    H  H        H  H
```

Hexene is unsaturated, for that double bond has a tendency to open up and add other atoms. Hexene is chemically active.

When six carbons are present in a molecule, it takes fourteen hydrogen atoms to occupy all the valence bonds and make it inert—as in hexane. In hexene, on the other hand, there are only twelve hydrogens. If there were still fewer hydrogen atoms, there would be more than one double bond; there might even be triple bonds, and the compound would be still more active than hexene.

Yet benzene, which is C_6H_6 and has eight fewer hydrogen atoms than hexane, is *less* active than hexene, which has only two fewer hydrogen atoms than hexane. In fact, benzene is even less active than hexane itself. The six hydrogen atoms in the benzene molecule seem to satisfy the six carbon atoms to a greater extent than do the fourteen hydrogen atoms in hexane.

For heaven's sake, why?

This might seem unimportant. The Kekule formulas were so beautifully suitable in the case of so many compounds that one might simply dismiss benzene as an exception to the general rule.

Science, however, is not English grammar. You can't just categorize something as an exception. If the exception doesn't fit into the general system, then the general system must be wrong.

Or, take the more positive approach. An exception can often be made to fit into a general system, provided the general system is broadened. Such broadening generally represents a great advance and for this reason, exceptions ought to be paid great attention.

For some seven years, Kekule faced the problem of benzene and tried to puzzle out how a chain of six carbon atoms could be completely satisfied with as few as six hydrogen atoms in benzene and yet be left unsatisfied with twelve hydrogen atoms in hexene.

Nothing came to him!

And then one day in 1865 (he tells the story himself) he was in Ghent, Belgium, and in order to get to some destination, he boarded a public bus. He was tired and, undoubtedly, the droning beat of the horses' hooves on the cobblestones, lulled him. He fell into a comatose half-sleep.

In that sleep, he seemed to see a vision of atoms attaching themselves to each other in chains that moved about. (Why not? It was the sort of thing that constantly occupied his waking thoughts.) But then one chain twisted in such a way that head and tail joined, forming a ring—and Kekule woke with a start.

To himself, he must surely have shouted "Eureka," for indeed he had it. The six carbon atoms of benzene formed a ring and not a chain, so that the structural formula looked like this:

```
              H
              |
  H         C          H
    \     /   \\     /
      C           C
      ||          |
      C           C
    /   \       //  \
  H         C          H
            |
            H
```

To be sure, there were still three double bonds, so you might think the molecule had to be very active—but now there was a difference. Atoms in a ring might be expected to have different properties from those in a chain and double bonds in one case might not have the properties of those in the other. At least, chemists could work on that assumption and see if it involved them in contradictions.

It didn't. The assumption worked excellently well. It turned out that organic molecules could be divided into two groups: aromatic and aliphatic. The former had the benzene ring (or certain other similar rings) as part of the structure and the latter did not. Allowing for different properties within each group, the Kekule structures worked very well.

For nearly seventy years, Kekule's vision held good in the hard field of actual chemical techniques, guiding the chemist through the jungle of reactions that led to the synthesis of more and more molecules. Then, in 1932, Linus Pauling applied quantum mechanics to chemical structure with sufficient subtlety to explain just why the benzene ring was so special and what had proven correct in practice proved correct in theory as well.

75 Other cases? Certainly.

In 1764, the Scottish engineer James Watt was working as an instrument maker for the University of Glasgow. The university gave him a model of a Newcomen steam engine, which didn't work well, and asked him to fix it. Watt fixed it without trouble, but even when it worked perfectly, it didn't work well. It was far too inefficient and consumed incredible quantities of fuel. Was there a way to improve that?

Thought didn't help; but a peaceful, relaxed walk on a Sunday afternoon did. Watt returned with the key notion in mind of using two separate chambers, one for steam only and one for cold water only, so that the same chamber did not have to be constantly cooled and reheated to the infinite waste of fuel.

The Irish mathematician William Rowan Hamilton worked up a theory of "quaternions" in 1843 but couldn't complete that theory until he grasped the fact that there were conditions under which $p \times q$ was *not* equal to $q \times p$. The necessary thought came to him in a flash one time when he was walking to town with his wife.

The German physiologist Otto Loewi was working on the mechanism of nerve action, in particular, on the chemicals produced by nerve endings. He awoke at 3 A.M. one night in 1921 with a perfectly clear notion of the type of experiment he would have to run to settle a key point that was puzzling him. He wrote it down and went back to sleep. When he woke in the morning, he found he couldn't remember what his inspiration had been. He remembered he had written it down, but he couldn't read his writing.

80 The next night, he woke again at 3 A.M. with the clear thought once more in mind. This time, he didn't fool around. He got up, dressed himself, went straight to the laboratory and began work. By 5 A.M. he had proved his point and the consequences of his findings became important enough in later years so that in 1936 he received a share in the Nobel prize in medicine and physiology.

How very often this sort of thing must happen, and what a shame that scientists are so devoted to their belief in conscious thought that they so consistently obscure the actual methods by which they obtain their results.

QUESTIONS

1. Consider Asimov's narrative of Archimedes' and Kekule's discoveries. What elements does he heighten and how? How does he include the scientific information necessary to understand them? How does he make (or attempt to make) this information accessible to nonscientists?

2. Scientists, Asimov concludes, "are so devoted to their belief in conscious thought that they . . . consistently obscure the actual methods by which they obtain their results" (paragraph 81). Consider your own experiments in science courses and the way you have been taught to report them. Do you agree or disagree with Asimov? Why?

3. Have you ever had a "Eureka" experience? Does Asimov's account of the "Eureka phenomenon" help you to understand it? Write about your experience with reference to Asimov's essay.

THOMAS S. KUHN *The Route to Normal Science*

IN THIS ESSAY, "normal science" means research firmly based upon one or more past scientific achievements, achievements that some particular scientific community acknowledges for a time as supplying the foundation for its further practice. Today such achievements are recounted, though seldom in their original form, by science textbooks, elementary and advanced. These textbooks expound the body of accepted theory, illustrate many or all of its successful applications, and compare these applications with exemplary observations and experiments. Before such books became popular early in the nineteenth century (and until even more recently in the newly matured sciences), many of the famous classics of science fulfilled a similar function. Aristotle's *Physica*, Ptolemy's *Almagest*, Newton's *Principia* and *Opticks*, Franklin's *Electricity*, Lavoisier's *Chemistry*, and Lyell's *Geology*—these and many other works served for a time implicitly to define the legitimate problems and methods of a research field for succeeding generations of practitioners. They were able to do so because they shared two essential characteristics. Their achievement was sufficiently unprecedented to attract an enduring group of adherents away from competing modes of scientific activity. Simultaneously, it was sufficiently open-ended to leave all sorts of problems for the redefined group of practitioners to resolve.

Achievements that share these two characteristics I shall henceforth refer to as "paradigms," a term that relates closely to "normal science." By choosing it, I mean to suggest that some accepted examples of actual scientific practice—

From The Structure of Scientific Revolutions *(1962), one of the most influential books ever written on the history and philosophy of science.*

examples which include law, theory, application, and instrumentation together—provide models from which spring particular coherent traditions of scientific research. These are the traditions which the historian describes under such rubrics as "Ptolemaic astronomy" (or "Copernican"), "Aristotelian dynamics" (or "Newtonian"), "corpuscular optics" (or "wave optics"), and so on. The study of paradigms, including many that are far more specialized than those named illustratively above, is what mainly prepares the student for membership in the particular scientific community with which he will later practice. Because he there joins men who learned the bases of their field from the same concrete models, his subsequent practice will seldom evoke overt disagreement over fundamentals. Men whose research is based on shared paradigms are committed to the same rules and standards for scientific practice. That commitment and the apparent consensus it produces are prerequisites for normal science, i.e., for the genesis and continuation of a particular research tradition.

Because in this essay the concept of a paradigm will often substitute for a variety of familiar notions, more will need to be said about the reasons for its introduction. Why is the concrete scientific achievement, as a locus of professional commitment, prior to the various concepts, laws, theories, and points of view that may be abstracted from it? In what sense is the shared paradigm a fundamental unit for the student of scientific development, a unit that cannot be fully reduced to logically atomic components which might function in its stead? There can be a sort of scientific research without paradigms, or at least without any so unequivocal and so binding as the ones named above. Acquisition of a paradigm and of the more esoteric type of research it permits is a sign of maturity in the development of any given scientific field.

If the historian traces the scientific knowledge of any selected group of related phenomena backward in time, he is likely to encounter some minor variant of a pattern here illustrated from the history of physical optics. Today's physics textbooks tell the student that light is photons, i.e., quantum-mechanical entities that exhibit some characteristics of waves and some of particles. Research proceeds accordingly, or rather according to the more elaborate and mathematical characterization from which this usual verbalization is derived. That characterization of light is, however, scarcely half a century old. Before it was developed by Planck, Einstein, and others early in this century, physics texts taught that light was transverse wave motion, a conception rooted in a paradigm that derived ultimately from the optical writings of Young and Fresnel in the early nineteenth century.[1] Nor was the wave theory the first to be embraced by almost all practitioners of optical science. During the eighteenth century the paradigm for this field was provided by Newton's *Opticks*, which taught that light was material corpuscles. At that time physicists sought evidence, as the early wave theorists had not, of the pressure exerted by light particles impinging on solid bodies.

1. Max Planck (1858–1947), German physicist; Albert Einstein (1879–1955), German physicist famous for his theory of relativity; Thomas Young (1773–1829), English physician and physicist; Augustin-Jean Fresnel (1788–1827), French physicist.

5

These transformations of the paradigms of physical optics are scientific revolutions, and the successive transition from one paradigm to another via revolution is the usual developmental pattern of mature science. It is not, however, the pattern characteristic of the period before Newton's work, and that is the contrast that concerns us here. No period between remote antiquity and the end of the seventeenth century exhibited a single generally accepted view about the nature of light. Instead there were a number of competing schools and sub-schools, most of them espousing one variant or another of Epicurean, Aristotelian, or Platonic theory.[2] One group took light to be particles emanating from material bodies; for another it was a modification of the medium that intervened between the body and the eye; still another explained light in terms of an interaction of the medium with an emanation from the eye; and there were other combinations and modifications besides. Each of the corresponding schools derives strength from its relation to some particular metaphysic, and each emphasized, as paradigmatic observations, the particular cluster of optical phenomena that its own theory could do most to explain. Other observations were dealt with by *ad hoc*[3] elaborations, or they remained as outstanding problems for further research.

At various times all these schools made significant contributions to the body of concepts, phenomena, and techniques from which Newton drew the first nearly uniformly accepted paradigm for physical optics. Any definition of the scientist that excludes at least the more creative members of these various schools will exclude their modern successors as well. Those men were scientists. Yet anyone examining a survey of physical optics before Newton may well conclude that, though the field's practitioners were scientists, the net result of their activity was something less than science. Being able to take no common body of belief for granted, each writer on physical optics felt forced to build his field anew from its foundations. In doing so, his choice of supporting observation and experiment was relatively free, for there was no standard set of methods or of phenomena that every optical writer felt forced to employ and explain. Under these circumstances, the dialogue of the resulting books was often directed as much to the members of other schools as it was to nature. That pattern is not unfamiliar in a number of creative fields today, nor is it incompatible with significant discovery and invention. It is not, however, the pattern of development that physical optics acquired after Newton and that other natural sciences make familiar today.

The history of electrical research in the first half of the eighteenth century provides a more concrete and better known example of the way a science develops before it acquires its first universally received paradigm. During that period there were almost as many views about the nature of electricity as there were important electrical experimenters, men like Hauksbee, Gray, Desaguliers, Du Fay, Nollett, Watson, Franklin,[4] and others. All their numerous concepts of

2. The reference is to the three principal worldviews of ancient Greek philosophy.

3. For a particular purpose; literally, toward this (Latin).

4. Francis Hauksbee the Elder (d. c. 1713) and Francis Hauksbee the Younger (1687–1763), Stephen Gray (1666–1736), Jean-Théophile Desaguliers (1683–1744), Charles-

electricity had something in common—they were partially derived from one or another version of the mechanico-corpuscular philosophy that guided all scientific research of the day. In addition, all were components of real scientific theories, of theories that had been drawn in part from experiment and observation and that partially determined the choice and interpretation of additional problems undertaken in research. Yet though all the experiments were electrical and though most of the experimenters read each other's works, their theories had no more than a family resemblance.

One early group of theories, following seventeenth-century practice, regarded attraction and frictional generation as the fundamental electrical phenomena. This group tended to treat repulsion as a secondary effect due to some sort of mechanical rebounding and also to postpone for as long as possible both discussion and systematic research on Gray's newly discovered effect, electrical conduction. Other "electricians" (the term is their own) took attraction and repulsion to be equally elementary manifestations of electricity and modified their theories and research accordingly. (Actually, this group is remarkably small—even Franklin's theory never quite accounted for the mutual repulsion of two negatively charged bodies.) But they had as much difficulty as the first group in accounting simultaneously for any but the simplest conduction effects. Those effects, however, provided the starting point for still a third group, one which tended to speak of electricity as a "fluid" that could run through conductors rather than as an "effluvium" that emanated from non-conductors. This group, in its turn, had difficulty reconciling its theory with a number of attractive and repulsive effects. Only through the work of Franklin and his immediate successors did a theory arise that could account with something like equal facility for very nearly all these effects and that therefore could and did provide a subsequent generation of "electricians" with a common paradigm for its research.

Excluding those fields, like mathematics and astronomy, in which the first firm paradigms date from prehistory and also those, like biochemistry, that arose by division and recombination of specialties already matured, the situations outlined above are historically typical. Though it involves my continuing to employ the unfortunate simplification that tags an extended historical episode with a single and somewhat arbitrarily chosen name (e.g., Newton or Franklin), I suggest that similar fundamental disagreements characterized, for example, the study of motion before Aristotle and of statics before Archimedes, the study of heat before Black, of chemistry before Boyle and Boerhaave, and of historical geology before Hutton.[5] In parts of biology—the study of heredity, for example—the first universally received paradigms are still more recent; and it

François de Cisternay Du Fay (1698–1739), Jean-Antoine Nollett (1700–1770), William Watson (1715–1787), and Benjamin Franklin (1706–1790) all made important discoveries about electricity.

5. The scientists referred to include the Greek philosopher-physicists Aristotle (384–322 B.C.E.) and Archimedes (c. 287–211 B.C.E), the British chemists Joseph Black (1728–1799) and Robert Boyle (1627–1691), the Dutch physician and chemist Hermann Boerhaave (1668–1738), and the Scottish geologist James Hutton (1726–1797).

remains an open question what parts of social science have yet acquired such paradigms at all. History suggests that the road to a firm research consensus is extraordinarily arduous.

History also suggests, however, some reasons for the difficulties encountered on the road. In the absence of a paradigm or some candidate for paradigm, all of the facts that could possibly pertain to the development of a given science are likely to seem equally relevant. As a result, early fact-gathering is a far more nearly random activity than the one that subsequent scientific development makes familiar. Futhermore, in the absence of a reason for seeking some particular form of more recondite information, early fact-gathering is usually restricted to the wealth of data that lie ready to hand. The resulting pool of facts contains those accessible to casual observation and experiment together with some of the more esoteric data retrievable from established crafts like medicine, calendar making, and metallurgy. Because the crafts are one readily accessible source of facts that could not have been casually discovered, technology has often played a vital role in the emergence of new sciences. 10

But though this sort of fact-collecting has been essential to the origin of many significant sciences, anyone who examines, for example, Pliny's encyclopedic writings or the Baconian[6] natural histories of the seventeenth century will discover that it produces a morass. One somehow hesitates to call the literature that results scientific. The Baconian "histories" of heat, color, wind, mining, and so on, are filled with information, some of it recondite. But they juxtapose facts that will later prove revealing (e.g., heating by mixture) with others (e.g., the warmth of dung heaps) that will for some time remain too complex to be integrated with theory at all. In addition, since any description must be partial, the typical natural history often omits from its immensely circumstantial accounts just those details that later scientists will find sources of important illumination. Almost none of the early "histories" of electricity, for example, mention that chaff, attracted to a rubbed glass rod, bounces off again. That effect seemed mechanical, not electrical. Moreover, since the casual fact-gatherer seldom possesses the time or the tools to be critical, the natural histories often juxtapose descriptions like the above with others, say, heating by antiperistasis (or by cooling), that we are now quite unable to confirm.[7] Only very occasionally, as in the cases of ancient statics, dynamics, and geometrical optics, do facts collected with so little guidance from pre-established theory speak with sufficient clarity to permit the emergence of a first paradigm.

This is the situation that creates the schools characteristic of the early stages of a science's development. No natural history can be interpreted in the

6. *Historia naturalis*, the one surviving work of the Roman naturalist Pliny the Elder (c. 23–79 B.C.E.), attempts to deal with the physical universe, geography, anthropology, zoology, botany, and mineralogy. In *Novum Organum*, the English philosopher, essayist, and statesman Francis Bacon (1561–1626) presented his scientific method.

7. Bacon [in the *Novum Organum*] says, "Water slightly warm is more easily frozen than quite cold" [Kuhn's note]; antiperistasis: an old word meaning a reaction caused by the action of an opposite quality or principle—here, heating through cooling.

absence of at least some implicit body of intertwined theoretical and methodological belief that permits selection, evaluation, and criticism. If that body of belief is not already implicit in the collection of facts—in which case more than "mere facts" are at hand—it must be externally supplied, perhaps by a current metaphysic, by another science, or by personal and historical accident. No wonder, then, that in the early stages of the development of any science different men confronting the same range of phenomena, but not usually all the same particular phenomena, describe and interpret them in different ways. What is surprising, and perhaps also unique in its degree to the fields we call science, is that such initial divergences should ever largely disappear.

For they do disappear to a very considerable extent and then apparently once and for all. Furthermore, their disappearance is usually caused by the triumph of one of the pre-paradigm schools, which, because of its own characteristic beliefs and pre-conceptions, emphasized only some special part of the too sizable and inchoate pool of information. Those electricians who thought electricity a fluid and therefore gave particular emphasis to conduction provide an excellent case in point. Led by this belief, which could scarcely cope with the known multiplicity of attractive and repulsive effects, several of them conceived the idea of bottling the electrical fluid. The immediate fruit of their efforts was the Leyden jar,[8] a device which might never have been discovered by a man exploring nature casually or at random, but which was in fact independently developed by at least two investigators in the early 1740's. Almost from the start of his electrical researches, Franklin was particularly concerned to explain that strange and, in the event, particularly revealing piece of special apparatus. His success in doing so provided the most effective of the arguments that made his theory a paradigm, though one that was still unable to account for quite all the known cases of electrical repulsion.[9] To be accepted as a paradigm, a theory must seem better than its competitors, but it need not, and in fact never does, explain all the facts with which it can be confronted.

What the fluid theory of electricity did for the subgroup that held it, the Franklinian paradigm later did for the entire group of electricians. It suggested which experiments would be worth performing and which, because directed to secondary or to overly complex manifestations of electricity, would not. Only the paradigm did the job far more effectively, partly because the end of interschool debate ended the constant reiteration of fundamentals and partly because the confidence that they were on the right track encouraged scientists to undertake more precise, esoteric, and consuming sorts of work.[10] Freed from

8. A kind of capacitor (or condenser), a device for storing electrical charge.

9. The troublesome case was the mutual repulsion of negatively charged bodies [Kuhn's note].

10. It should be noted that the acceptance of Franklin's theory did not end quite all debate. In 1759 Robert Symmer proposed a two-fluid version of that theory, and for many years thereafter electricians were divided about whether electricity was a single fluid or two. But the debates on this subject only confirm what has been said above about the manner in which a universally recognized achievement unites the profession.

the concern with any and all electrical phenomena, the united group of electricians could pursue selected phenomena in far more detail, designing much special equipment for the task and employing it more stubbornly and systematically than electricians had ever done before. Both fact collection and theory articulation became highly directed activities. The effectiveness and efficiency of electrical research increased accordingly, providing evidence for a societal version of Francis Bacon's acute methodological dictum: "Truth emerges more readily from error than from confusion."

We shall be examining the nature of this highly directed or paradigm-based research in the next section, but must first note briefly how the emergence of a paradigm affects the structure of the group that practices the field. When, in the development of a natural science, an individual or group first produces a synthesis able to attract most of the next generation's practitioners, the older schools gradually disappear. In part their disappearance is caused by their members' conversion to the new paradigm. But there are always some men who cling to one or another of the older views, and they are simply read out of the profession, which thereafter ignores their work. The new paradigm implies a new and more rigid definition of the field. Those unwilling or unable to accommodate their work to it must proceed in isolation or attach themselves to some other group.[11] Historically, they have often simply stayed in the departments of philosophy from which so many of the special sciences have been spawned. As these indications hint, it is sometimes just its reception of a paradigm that transforms a group previously interested merely in the study of nature into a profession or, at least, a discipline. In the sciences (though not in fields like medicine, technology, and law, of which the principal *raison d'être*[12] is an external social need), the formation of specialized journals, the foundation of specialists' societies, and the claim for a special place in the curriculum have usually been associated with a group's first reception of a single paradigm. At least this was the case between the time, a century and a half ago, when the institutional pattern of scientific specialization first developed and the very recent time when the paraphernalia of specialization acquired a prestige of their own.

15

Electricians, though they continued divided on this point, rapidly concluded that no experimental tests could distinguish the two versions of the theory and that they were therefore equivalent. After that, both schools could and did exploit all the benefits that the Franklinian theory provided [Kuhn's note].

11. The history of electricity provides an excellent example which could be duplicated from the careers of Priestley, Kelvin, and others. Franklin reports that Nollet, who at mid-century was the most influential of the Continental electricians, "lived to see himself the last of his Sect, except Mr. B.—his *Eleve* [pupil] and immediate Disciple." More interesting, however, is the endurance of whole schools in increasing isolation from professional science. Consider, for example, the case of astrology, which was once an integral part of astronomy. Or consider the continuation in the late eighteenth and early nineteenth centuries of a previously respected tradition of "romantic" chemistry [Kuhn's note].

12. Reason for being (French).

The more rigid definition of the scientific group has other consequences. When the individual scientist can take a paradigm for granted, he need no longer, in his major works, attempt to build his field anew, starting from first principles and justifying the use of each concept introduced. That can be left to the writer of textbooks. Given a textbook, however, the creative scientist can begin his research where it leaves off and thus concentrate exclusively upon the subtlest and most esoteric aspects of the natural phenomena that concern his group. And as he does this, his research communiqués will begin to change in ways whose evolution has been too little studied but whose modern end products are obvious to all and oppressive to many. No longer will his researches usually be embodied in books addressed, like Franklin's *Experiments . . . on Electricity* or Darwin's *Origin of Species*, to anyone who might be interested in the subject matter of the field. Instead they will usually appear as brief articles addressed only to professional colleagues, the men whose knowledge of a shared paradigm can be assumed and who prove to be the only ones able to read the papers addressed to them.

Today in the sciences, books are usually either texts or retrospective reflections upon one aspect or another of the scientific life. The scientist who writes one is more likely to find his professional reputation impaired than enhanced. Only in the earlier, pre-paradigm, stages of the development of the various sciences did the book ordinarily possess the same relation to professional achievement that it still retains in other creative fields. And only in those fields that still retain the book, with or without the article, as a vehicle for research communication are the lines of professionalization still so loosely drawn that the layman may hope to follow progress by reading the practitioners' original reports. Both in mathematics and astronomy, research reports had ceased already in antiquity to be intelligible to a generally educated audience. In dynamics, research became similarly esoteric in the latter Middle Ages, and it recaptured general intelligibility only briefly during the early seventeenth century when a new paradigm replaced the one that had guided medieval research. Electrical research began to require translation for the layman before the end of the eighteenth century, and most other fields of physical science ceased to be generally accessible in the nineteenth. During the same two centuries similar transitions can be isolated in the various parts of the biological sciences. In parts of the social sciences they may well be occurring today. Although it has become customary, and is surely proper, to deplore the widening gulf that separates the professional scientist from his colleagues in other fields, too little attention is paid to the essential relationship between that gulf and the mechanisms intrinsic to scientific advance.

Ever since prehistoric antiquity one field of study after another has crossed the divide between what the historian might call its prehistory as a science and its history proper. These transitions to maturity have seldom been so sudden or so unequivocal as my necessarily schematic discussion may have implied. But neither have they been historically gradual, coextensive, that is to say, with the entire development of the fields within which they occurred. Writers on electricity during the first four decades of the eighteenth century possessed far more information about electrical phenomena than had their sixteenth-century predecessors. During the half-century after 1740, few new sorts of electrical phenomena were added to their lists. Nevertheless, in important respects, the electrical writings of Cavendish, Coulomb, and Volta[13] in the last third of the eighteenth century seem further removed from those of Gray, Du Fay, and even Franklin than are the writings of these early eighteenth-century electrical discoverers from those of the sixteenth century.[14] Sometime between 1740 and 1780, electricians were for the first time enabled to take the foundations of their field for granted. From that point they pushed on to more concrete and recondite problems, and increasingly they then reported their results in articles addressed to other electricians rather than in books addressed to the learned world at large. As a group they achieved what had been gained by astronomers in antiquity and by students of motion in the Middle Ages, of physical optics in the late seventeenth century, and of historical geology in the early nineteenth. They had, that is, achieved a paradigm that proved able to guide the whole group's research. Except with the advantage of hindsight, it is hard to find another criterion that so clearly proclaims a field a science.

13. Henry Cavendish (1731–1810), Charles-Augustin de Coulomb (1736–1806), and Alessandro Giuseppe Antonio Anastasio Volta (1745–1827) made important discoveries about electricity.

14. The post-Franklinian developments include an immense increase in the sensitivity of charge detectors, the first reliable and generally diffused techniques for measuring charge, the evolution of the concept of capacity and its relation to a newly refined notion of electric tension, and the quantification of electrostatic force [Kuhn's note].

Questions

1. Mark the important terms in this selection from *The Structure of Scientific Revolutions* and Kuhn's definitions of them. How many terms does he illustrate as well as define? Why does he both define and illustrate?

2. What are prevailing paradigms in sciences other than those Kuhn discusses? You might consider biology, chemistry, psychology, and sociology. Are you aware of older paradigms in these sciences, or have they and the work based on them, as Kuhn says (paragraph 15), disappeared?

3. Without a paradigm, Kuhn writes, "all of the facts that could possibly pertain to the development of a given science are likely to seem equally relevant" (paragraph 10). What, according to Edward O. Wilson in "Intelligent Evolution" (p. 949) or Stephen Jay Gould in "Darwin's Middle Road" (p, 959), was the paradigm that enabled Darwin to discriminate among his facts? How can he be said to have made a "scientific revolution"?

Stephen Hawking *Is Everything Determined?*

In the play *Julius Caesar,* Cassius tells Brutus, "Men at some times are masters of their fate." But are we really masters of our fate? Or is everything we do determined and preordained? The argument for preordination used to be that God was omnipotent and outside time, so God would know what was going to happen. But how then could we have any free will? And if we don't have free will, how can we be responsible for our actions? It can hardly be one's fault if one has been preordained to rob a bank. So why should one be punished for it?

In recent times, the argument for determinism has been based on science. It seems that there are well-defined laws that govern how the universe and everything in it develops in time. Although we have not yet found the exact form of all these laws, we already know enough to determine what happens in all but the most extreme situations. Whether we will find the remaining laws in the fairly near future is a matter of opinion. I'm an optimist: I think there's a fifty-fifty chance that we will find them in the next twenty years. But even if we don't, it won't really make any difference to the argument. The important point is that there should exist a set of laws that completely determines the evolution of the universe from its initial state. These laws may have been ordained by God. But it seems that He (or She) does not intervene in the universe to break the laws.

The initial configuration of the universe may have been chosen by God, or it may itself have been determined by the laws of science. In either case, it would seem that everything in the universe would then be determined by evolution according to the laws of science, so it is difficult to see how we can be masters of our fate.

The idea that there is some grand unified theory that determines everything in the universe raises many difficulties. First of all, the grand unified theory is presumably compact and elegant in mathematical terms. There ought to be something special and simple about the theory of everything. Yet how can a certain number of equations account for the complexity and trivial detail that we see around us? Can one really believe that the grand unified theory has determined that Sinead O'Connor will be the top of the hit parade this week, or that Madonna will be on the cover of *Cosmopolitan?*[1]

5 A second problem with the idea that everything is determined by a grand unified theory is that anything we say is also determined by the theory. But why should it be determined to be correct? Isn't it more likely to be wrong,

From Black Holes and Baby Universes and Other Essays *(1994), an eclectic collection of essays on a range of scientific, political, philosophical, and personal topics from one of the world's leading physicists.*

1. O'Connor (b. 1966), Grammy-winning Irish singer; Madonna (b. 1958), the twentieth century's top-selling female rock musician.

because there are many possible incorrect statements for every true one? Each week, my mail contains a number of theories that people have sent me. They are all different, and most are mutually inconsistent. Yet presumably the grand unified theory has determined that the authors think they were correct. So why should anything I say have any greater validity? Aren't I equally determined by the grand unified theory?

A third problem with the idea that everything is determined is that we feel that we have free will—that we have the freedom to choose whether to do something. But if everything is determined by the laws of science, then free will must be an illusion, and if we don't have free will, what is the basis for our responsibility for our actions? We don't punish people for crimes if they are insane, because we have decided that they can't help it. But if we are all determined by a grand unified theory, none of us can help what we do, so why should anyone be held responsible for what they do?

These problems of determinism have been discussed over the centuries. The discussion was somewhat academic, however, as we were far from a complete knowledge of the laws of science, and we didn't know how the initial state of the universe was determined. The problems are more urgent now because there is the possibility that we may find a complete unified theory in as little as twenty years. And we realize that the initial state may itself have been determined by the laws of science. What follows is my personal attempt to come to terms with these problems. I don't claim any great originality or depth, but it is the best I can do at the moment.

To start with the first problem: How can a relatively simple and compact theory give rise to a universe that is as complex as the one we observe, with all its trivial and unimportant details? The key to this is the uncertainty principle of quantum mechanics, which states that one cannot measure both the position and speed of a particle to great accuracy; the more accurately you measure the position, the less accurately you can measure the speed, and vice versa. This uncertainty is not so important at the present time, when things are far apart, so that a small uncertainty in position does not make much difference. But in the very early universe, everything was very close together, so there was quite a lot of uncertainty, and there were a number of possible states for the universe. These different possible early states would have evolved into a whole family of different histories for the universe. Most of these histories would be similar in their large-scale features. They would correspond to a universe that was uniform and smooth, and that was expanding. However, they would differ on details like the distribution of stars and, even more, on what was on the covers of their magazines. (That is, if those histories contained magazines.) Thus the complexity of the universe around us and its details arose from the uncertainty principle in the early stages. This gives a whole family of possible histories for the universe. There would be a history in which the Nazis won the Second World War, though the probability is low. But we just happen to live in a history in which the Allies won the war and Madonna was on the cover of *Cosmopolitan*.

I now turn to the second problem: If what we do is determined by some grand unified theory, why should the theory determine that we draw the right conclusions about the universe rather than the wrong ones? Why should anything we say have any validity? My answer to this is based on Darwin's idea of natural selection.[2] I take it that some very primitive form of life arose spontaneously on earth from chance combinations of atoms. This early form of life was probably a large molecule. But it was probably not DNA, since the chances of forming a whole DNA molecule by random combinations are small.

10 The early form of life would have reproduced itself. The quantum uncertainty principle and the random thermal motions of the atoms would mean that there were a certain number of errors in the reproduction. Most of these errors would have been fatal to the survival of the organism or its ability to reproduce. Such errors would not be passed on to future generations but would die out. A very few errors would be beneficial, by pure chance. The organisms with these errors would be more likely to survive and reproduce. Thus they would tend to replace the original, unimproved organisms.

The development of the double helix structure of DNA may have been one such improvement in the early stages. This was probably such an advance that it completely replaced any earlier form of life, whatever that may have been. As evolution progressed, it would have led to the development of the central nervous system. Creatures that correctly recognized the implications of data gathered by their sense organs and took appropriate action would be more likely to survive and reproduce. The human race has carried this to another stage. We are very similar to higher apes, both in our bodies and in our DNA; but a slight variation in our DNA has enabled us to develop language. This has meant that we can hand down information and accumulated experience from generation to generation, in spoken and eventually in written form. Previously, the results of experience could be handed down only by the slow process of it being encoded into DNA through random errors in reproduction. The effect has been a dramatic speed-up of evolution. It took more than three billion years to evolve up to the human race. But in the course of the last ten thousand years, we have developed written language. This has enabled us to progress from cave dwellers to the point where we can ask about the ultimate theory of the universe.

There has been no significant biological evolution, or change in human DNA, in the last ten thousand years. Thus, our intelligence, our ability to draw the correct conclusions from the information provided by our sense organs, must date back to our cave dweller days or earlier. It would have been selected for on the basis of our ability to kill certain animals for food and to avoid being killed by other animals. It is remarkable that mental qualities that were selected for these purposes should have stood us in such good stead in the very different circumstances of the present day. There is probably not much survival advantage to be gained from discovering a grand unified theory or answering

2. Darwin (1809–1882), English naturalist who developed the theory of natural selection.

questions about determinism. Nevertheless, the intelligence that we have developed for other reasons may well ensure that we find the right answers to these questions.

I now turn to the third problem, the questions of free will and responsibility for our actions. We feel subjectively that we have the ability to choose who we are and what we do. But this may just be an illusion. Some people think they are Jesus Christ or Napoleon, but they can't all be right. What we need is an objective test that we can apply from the outside to distinguish whether an organism has free will. For example, suppose we were visited by a "little green person" from another star. How could we decide whether it had free will or was just a robot, programmed to respond as if it were like us?

The ultimate objective test of free will would seem to be: Can one predict the behavior of the organism? If one can, then it clearly doesn't have free will but is predetermined. On the other hand, if one cannot predict the behavior, one could take that as an operational definition that the organism has free will.

One might object to this definition of free will on the grounds that once we find a complete unified theory we will be able to predict what people will do. The human brain, however, is also subject to the uncertainty principle.[3] Thus, there is an element of the randomness associated with quantum mechanics in human behavior. But the energies involved in the brain are low, so quantum mechanical uncertainty is only a small effect. The real reason why we cannot predict human behavior is that it is just too difficult. We already know the basic physical laws that govern the activity of the brain, and they are comparatively simple. But it is just too hard to solve the equations when there are more than a few particles involved. Even in the simpler Newtonian theory of gravity,[4] one can solve the equations exactly only in the case of two particles. For three or more particles one has to resort to approximations, and the difficulty increases rapidly with the number of particles. The human brain contains about 10^{26} or a hundred million billion billion particles. This is far too many for us ever to be able to solve the equations and predict how the brain would behave, given its initial state and the nerve data coming into it. In fact, of course, we cannot even measure what the initial state was, because to do so we would have to take the brain apart. Even if we were prepared to do that, there would just be too many particles to record. Also, the brain is probably very sensitive to the initial state—a small change in the initial state can make a very large difference to subsequent behavior. So although we know the fundamental equations that govern the brain, we are quite unable to use them to predict human behavior.

This situation arises in science whenever we deal with the macroscopic system, because the number of particles is always too large for there to be any

3. In quantum theory, the principle that a particle's momentum and location cannot be determined absolutely precisely at the same time.

4. Newton (1643–1727), English mathematician and physicist whose theory of gravity is that the gravitational attraction between two particles is proportional to the product of their masses and inversely proportional to the square of the distance between them.

chance of solving the fundamental equations. What we do instead is use effective theories. These are approximations in which the very large number of particles are replaced by a few quantities. An example is fluid mechanics. A liquid such as water is made up of billions of billions of molecules that themselves are made up of electrons, protons, and neutrons. Yet it is a good approximation to treat the liquid as a continuous medium, characterized just by velocity, density, and temperature. The predictions of the effective theory of fluid mechanics are not exact—one only has to listen to the weather forecast to realize that—but they are good enough for the design of ships or oil pipelines.

I want to suggest that the concepts of free will and moral responsibility for our actions are really an effective theory in the sense of fluid mechanics. It may be that everything we do is determined by some grand unified theory. If that theory has determined that we shall die by hanging, then we shall not drown. But you would have to be awfully sure that you were destined for the gallows to put to sea in a small boat during a storm. I have noticed that even people who claim that everything is predestined and that we can do nothing to change it look before they cross the road. Maybe it's just that those who don't look don't survive to tell the tale.

One cannot base one's conduct on the idea that everything is determined, because one does not know what has been determined. Instead, one has to adopt the effective theory that one has free will and that one is responsible for one's actions. This theory is not very good at predicting human behavior, but we adopt it because there is no chance of solving the equations arising from the fundamental laws. There is also a Darwinian reason that we believe in free will: A society in which the individual feels responsible for his or her actions is more likely to work together and survive to spread its values. Of course, ants work well together. But such a society is static. It cannot respond to unfamiliar challenges or develop new opportunities. A collection of free individuals who share certain mutual aims, however, can collaborate on their common objectives and yet have the flexibility to make innovations. Thus, such a society is more likely to prosper and to spread its system of values.

The concept of free will belongs to a different arena from that of fundamental laws of science. If one tries to deduce human behavior from the laws of science, one gets caught in the logical paradox of self-referencing systems. If what one does could be predicted from the fundamental laws, then the fact of making that prediction could change what happens. It is like the problems one would get into if time travel were possible, which I don't think it ever will be. If you could see what is going to happen in the future, you could change it. If you knew which horse was going to win the Grand National,[5] you could make a fortune by betting on it. But that action would change the odds. One only has to see *Back to the Future*[6] to realize what problems could arise.

20 This paradox about being able to predict one's actions is closely related to the problem I mentioned earlier. Will the ultimate theory determine that we come to the right conclusions about the ultimate theory? In that case, I argued

5. Famous British horse race.

6. A 1985 comic film involving time travel.

that Darwin's idea of natural selection would lead us to the correct answer. Maybe the correct answer is not the right way to describe it, but natural selection should at least lead us to a set of physical laws that work fairly well. However, we cannot apply those physical laws to deduce human behavior for two reasons. First, we cannot solve the equations. Second, even if we could, the fact of making a prediction would disturb the system. Instead, natural selection seems to lead to us adopting the effective theory of free will. If one accepts that a person's actions are freely chosen, one cannot then argue that in some cases they are determined by outside forces. The concept of "almost free will" doesn't make sense. But people tend to confuse the fact that one may be able to guess what an individual is likely to choose with the notion that the choice is not free. I would guess that most of you will have a meal this evening, but you are quite free to choose to go to bed hungry. One example of such confusion is the doctrine of diminished responsibility: the idea that persons should not be punished for their actions because they were under stress. It may be that someone is more likely to commit an antisocial act when under stress. But that does not mean that we should make it even more likely that he or she commit the act by reducing the punishment.

One has to keep the investigation of the fundamental laws of science and the study of human behavior in separate compartments. One cannot use the fundamental laws to deduce human behavior, for the reasons I have explained. But one might hope that we could employ both the intelligence and the powers of logical thought that we have developed through natural selection. Unfortunately, natural selection has also developed other characteristics, such as aggression. Aggression would have given a survival advantage in cave dweller days and earlier and so would have been favored by natural selection. The tremendous increase in our powers of destruction brought about by modern science and technology, however, has made aggression a very dangerous quality, one that threatens the survival of the whole human race. The trouble is, our aggressive instincts seem to be encoded in our DNA. DNA changes by biological evolution only on a time scale of millions of years, but our powers of destruction are increasing on a time scale for the evolution of information, which is now only twenty or thirty years. Unless we can use our intelligence to control our aggression, there is not much chance for the human race. Still, while there's life, there's hope. If we can survive the next hundred years or so, we will have spread to other planets and possibly to other stars. This will make it much less likely that the entire human race will be wiped out by a calamity such as a nuclear war.

To recapitulate: I have discussed some of the problems that arise if one believes that everything in the universe is determined. It doesn't make much difference whether this determination is due to an omnipotent God or to the laws of science. Indeed, one could always say that the laws of science are the expression of the will of God.

I considered three questions: First, how can the complexity of the universe and all its trivial details be determined by a simple set of equations? Alternatively, can one really believe that God chose all the trivial details, like who should be on the cover of *Cosmopolitan*? The answer seems to be that the uncertainty principle of quantum mechanics means that there is not just a single history for the universe but a whole family of possible histories. These histories may be similar on very large scales, but they will differ greatly on normal, everyday scales. We happen to live on one particular history that has certain properties and details. But there are very similar intelligent beings who live on histories that differ in who won the war and who is Top of the Pops.[7] Thus, the trivial details of our universe arise because the fundamental laws incorporate quantum mechanics with its element of uncertainty or randomness.

The second question was: If everything is determined by some fundamental theory, then what we say about the theory is also determined by the theory—and why should it be determined to be correct, rather than just plain wrong or irrelevant? My answer to this was to appeal to Darwin's theory of natural selection: Only those individuals who drew the appropriate conclusions about the world around them would be likely to survive and reproduce.

25 The third question was: If everything is determined, what becomes of free will and our responsibility for our actions? But the only objective test of whether an organism has free will is whether its behavior can be predicted. In the case of human beings, we are quite unable to use the fundamental laws to predict what people will do, for two reasons. First, we cannot solve the equations for the very large number of particles involved. Second, even if we could solve the equations, the fact of making a prediction would disturb the system and could lead to a different outcome. So as we cannot predict human behavior, we may as well adopt the effective theory that humans are free agents who can choose what to do. It seems that there are definite survival advantages to believing in free will and responsibility for one's actions. That means this belief should be reinforced by natural selection. Whether the language-transmitted sense of responsibility is sufficient to control the DNA-transmitted instinct of aggression remains to be seen. If it does not, the human race will have been one of natural selection's dead ends. Maybe some other race of intelligent beings elsewhere in the galaxy will achieve a better balance between responsibility and aggression. But if so, we might have expected to be contacted by them, or at least to detect their radio signals. Maybe they are aware of our existence but don't want to reveal themselves to us. That might be wise, given our record.

In summary, the title of this essay was a question: Is everything determined? The answer is yes, it is. But it might as well not be, because we can never know what is determined.

7. A British pop-music television program (1964–2006).

QUESTIONS

1. Hawking chooses a question for his title and draws attention to this choice in his conclusion. Why a question? How is the essay's title related to its structure?

2. Hawking concludes, "So as we cannot predict human behavior, we may as well adopt the effective theory that humans are free agents who can choose what to do" (paragraph 25). What does Hawking mean by this statement? What are its practical implications?

4. Hawking is a professional scientist, but he has written this essay for a general audience. How is that choice of audience reflected in the essay's style?

5. Hawking is a physicist, but the concept of "natural selection" (paragraph 9) figures prominently in his essay. Write an analysis of the role this concept plays in Hawking's argument.

NICHOLSON BAKER *The Charms of Wikipedia*

WIKIPEDIA IS JUST an incredible thing. It's fact-encirclingly huge, and it's idiosyncratic, careful, messy, funny, shocking, and full of simmering controversies—and it's free, and it's fast. In a few seconds you can look up, for instance, "Diogenes of Sinope," or "turnip," or "Crazy Eddie," or "Bagoas," or "quadratic formula," or "Bristol Beaufighter," or "squeegee," or "Sanford B. Dole," and you'll have knowledge you didn't have before. It's like some vast aerial city with people walking briskly to and fro on catwalks, carrying picnic baskets full of nutritious snacks.

More people use Wikipedia than Amazon or eBay—in fact it's up there in the top-ten Alexa rankings[1] with those moneyed funhouses MySpace, Facebook, and YouTube. Why? Because it has 2.2 million articles, and because it's very often the first hit in a Google search, and because it just feels good to find something there—even, or especially, when the article you find is maybe a little clumsily written. Any inelegance, or typo, or relic of vandalism reminds you that this gigantic encyclopedia isn't a commercial product. There are no banners for E*Trade or Classmates.com, no side sprinklings of AdSense.

It was constructed, in less than eight years, by strangers who disagreed about all kinds of things but who were drawn to a shared, not-for-profit purpose. They were drawn because for a work of reference Wikipedia seemed unusually humble. It asked for help, and when it did, it used a particularly affecting word: "stub." At the bottom of a short article about something, it would say, "This article about X is a stub. You can help Wikipedia by expanding it." And you'd think: That poor sad stub: I will help. Not right now, because I'm writing a book, but someday, yes, I will try to help.

And when people did help they were given a flattering name. They weren't called "Wikipedia's little helpers," they were called "editors." It was like a giant community leaf-raking project in which everyone was called a groundskeeper. Some brought very fancy professional metal rakes, or even back-mounted leaf-

From the New York Review of Books *(March 20, 2008), an American magazine that publishes not only reviews of current books but also articles on literature, the arts, and contemporary social and political issues.*

1. A ranking of Web sites by traffic compiled by Alexa Internet, Inc.

blowing systems, and some were just kids thrashing away with the sides of their feet or stuffing handfuls in the pockets of their sweatshirts, but all the leaves they brought to the pile were appreciated. And the pile grew and everyone jumped up and down in it having a wonderful time. And it grew some more, and it became the biggest leaf pile anyone had ever seen anywhere, a world wonder. And then self-promoted leaf-pile guards appeared, doubters and deprecators who would look askance at your proffered handful and shake their heads, saying that your leaves were too crumpled or too slimy or too common, throwing them to the side. And that was too bad. The people who guarded the leaf pile this way were called "deletionists."

5 But that came later. First it was just fun. One anonymous contributor wrote, of that early time:

> I adored the Wikipedia when it was first launched and I contributed to a number of articles, some extensively, and always anonymously. The Wikipedia then was a riot of contributors, each adding bits and pieces to the articles they were familiar with, with nary an admin or editor in sight.

It worked and grew because it tapped into the heretofore unmarshaled energies of the uncredentialed. The thesis procrastinators, the history buffs, the passionate fans of the alternate universes of Garth Nix, *Robotech*, Half-Life, P. G. Wodehouse, *Battlestar Galactica, Buffy the Vampire Slayer*, Charles Dickens, or *Ultraman*—all those people who hoped that their years of collecting comics or reading novels or staring at TV screens hadn't been a waste of time—would pour the fruits of their brains into Wikipedia, because Wikipedia added up to something. This wasn't like writing reviews on Amazon, where you were just one of a million people urging a tiny opinion and a Listmania list onto the world—this was an effort to build something that made sense apart from one's own opinion, something that helped the whole human cause roll forward.

Wikipedia was the point of convergence for the self-taught and the expensively educated. The cranks had to consort with the mainstreamers and hash it all out—and nobody knew who really knew what he or she was talking about, because everyone's identity was hidden behind a jokey username. All everyone knew was that the end product had to make legible sense and sound encyclopedic. It had to be a little flat—a little generic—fair-minded—compressed—unpromotional—neutral. The need for the outcome of all edits to fit together as readable, unemotional sentences muted—to some extent—natural antagonisms.

So there was this exhilarating sense of mission—of proving the greatness of the Internet through an unheard-of collaboration. Very smart people dropped other pursuits and spent days and weeks and sometimes years of their lives doing "stub dumps," writing ancillary software, categorizing and linking topics, making and remaking and smoothing out articles—without getting any recognition except for the occasional congratulatory barnstar on their user page and the satisfaction of secret fame. Wikipedia flourished partly because it was a shrine to altruism—a place for shy, learned people to deposit their trawls.

But it also became great because it had a head start: from the beginning the project absorbed articles from the celebrated 1911 edition of the *Encyclopedia Britannica*, which is in the public domain. And not only the 1911 *Britannica*. Also absorbed were Smith's *Dictionary of Greek and Roman Biography*, Nuttall's 1906 *Encyclopedia*, Chamber's *Cyclopedia*, Aiken's *General Biography*, Rose's *Biographical Dictionary*, Easton's *Bible Dictionary*, and many others. In August 2001, a group of articles from W. W. Rouse Ball's *Short Account of the History of Mathematics*—posted on the Net by a professor from Trinity College, Dublin—was noticed by an early Wikipedian, who wrote to his co-volunteers: "Are they fair game to grab as source material for our wikipedia? I know we are scarfing stuff from the 1911 encyclopedia, this is from 1908, so it should be under the same lack of restrictions . . ." It was. Rouse Ball wrote that Pierre Varignon

> was an intimate friend of Newton, Leibnitz and the Bernoullis, and, after l'Hospital, was the earliest and most powerful advocate in France of the use of differential calculus.

In January 2006, Wikipedia imported this 1908 article, with an insertion and a few modernizing rewordings, and it now reads: 10

> Varignon was a friend of Newton, Leibnitz, and the Bernoulli family. Varignon's principal contributions were to graphic statics and mechanics. Except for l'Hôpital, Varignon was the earliest and strongest French advocate of differential calculus.

But the article is now three times longer, barnacled with interesting additions, and includes a link to another article discussing Varignon's mechanical theory of gravitation.

The steady influx of top-hat-and-spatted sources elevated Wikipedia's tone. This wasn't just a school encyclopedia, a backyard *Encarta*[2]—this was drinks at the faculty club. You looked up Diogenes and bang, you got something wondrously finished-sounding from the 1911 *Britannica*. That became Diogenes' point of departure. And then all kinds of changes happened to the Greek philosopher, over many months and hundreds of revisions—odd theories, prose about the habits of dogs, rewordings, corrections of corrections. Now in Wikipedia there is this summary of Diogenes' provocations:

> Diogenes is said to have eaten (and, once, masturbated) in the marketplace, urinated on some people who insulted him, defecated in the theatre, and pointed at people with his middle finger.

And yet amid the modern aggregate, some curvy prose from the 1911 Britannica still survives verbatim:

> Both in ancient and in modern times, his personality has appealed strongly to sculptors and to painters.

2. A digital encyclopedia developed by Microsoft (1993–2009).

The fragments from original sources persist like those stony bits of classical buildings incorporated in a medieval wall.

But the sources and the altruism don't fully explain why Wikipedia became such a boom town. The real reason it grew so fast was noticed by co-founder Jimmy "Jimbo" Wales in its first year of life. "The main thing about Wikipedia is that it is fun and addictive," Wales wrote. Addictive, yes. All big Internet successes—e-mail, AOL chat, Facebook, Gawker, Second Life, YouTube, Daily Kos, World of Warcraft[3]—have a more or less addictive component—they hook you because they are solitary ways to be social: you keep checking in, peeking in, as you would to some noisy party going on downstairs in a house while you're trying to sleep.

Brion Vibber,[4] who was for a while Wikipedia's only full-time employee, explained the attraction of the encyclopedia at a talk he gave to Google employees in 2006. For researchers it's a place to look stuff up, Vibber said, but for editors "it's almost more like an online game, in that it's a community where you hang out a bit, and do something that's a little bit of fun: you whack some trolls, you build some material, etcetera." Whacking trolls[5] is, for some Wikipedia editors, a big part of why they keep coming back.

Say you're working away on the Wikipedia article on aging. You've got some nice scientific language in there and it's really starting to shape up:

> After a period of near perfect renewal (in Humans, between 20 and 50 years of age), organismal senescence is characterized by the declining ability to respond to stress, increasing homeostatic imbalance and increased risk of disease. This irreversible series of changes inevitably ends in Death.

Not bad!

15 And then somebody—a user with an address of 206.82.17.190, a "vandal"—replaces the entire article with a single sentence: "Aging is what you get when you get freakin old old old." That happened on December 20, 2007. A minute later, you "revert" that anonymous editor's edit, with a few clicks; you go back in history to the article as it stood before. You've just kept the aging article safe, for the moment. But you have to stay vigilant, because somebody might swoop in again at any time, and you'll have to undo their harm with your power reverter ray. Now you're addicted. You've become a force for good just by standing guard and looking out for juvenile delinquents.

Some articles are so out of the way that they get very little vandalism. (Although I once fixed a tiny page about a plant fungus, *Colletotrichum trichellum*, that infects English ivy; somebody before me had claimed that 40 percent of the humans who got it died.) Some articles are vandalized a lot. On January 11, 2008, the entire fascinating entry on the aardvark was replaced with "one

3. AOL, America Online, an internet service provider; *Gawker*, a New York–based celebrity gossip website; Second Life, a virtual world; *Daily Kos*, political news Web site; World of Warcraft, fantasy role-playing game.

4. Brion Vibber (b. 1982), the lead developer of MediaWiki software until 2009.

5. Banning disruptive users of an Internet forum.

ugly animal"; in February the aardvark was briefly described as a "medium-sized inflatable banana." On December 7, 2007, somebody altered the long article on bedbugs so that it read like a horror movie:

> Bedbugs are generally active only at dawn, with a peak attack period about an hour before dawn, though given the opportunity, they may attempt to feed at your brain at other times.

A few weeks later, somebody replaced everything with:

> BED BUGS MOTHER FUCKER THEY GON GET YO MOTHA FUCKING ASS BRAAAAAAAT FOOL BRAAAAAAAAAAAAAAAP.

A piece of antivandalism software, VoABot II, reverted that edit, with a little sigh, less than a minute after it was made.

Vandalism spiked in August 2006 after comedian Stephen Colbert—in the wake of Stacy Schiff's[6] excellent but slightly frosty *New Yorker* article about Wikipedia—invited viewers of his show to post made-up facts about the increase in the population of African elephants, as proof of the existence of something that was not reality but "wikiality"—a cheap shot, but mildly funny. People repeatedly went after the elephant page, and it was locked for a while. But not for very long. The party moved on.

The Pop-Tarts page is often aflutter. Pop-Tarts, it says as of today (February 8, 2008), were discontinued in Australia in 2005. Maybe that's true. Before that it said that Pop-Tarts were discontinued in Korea. Before that Australia. Several days ago it said: "Pop-Tarts is german for Little Iced Pastry O' Germany." Other things I learned from earlier versions: More than two trillion Pop-Tarts are sold each year. George Washington invented them. They were developed in the early 1960s in China. Popular flavors are "frosted strawberry, frosted brown sugar cinnamon, and semen." Pop-Tarts are a "flat Cookie." No: "Pop-Tarts are a flat Pastry, KEVIN MCCORMICK is a FRIGGIN LOSER notto mention a queer inch." No: "A Pop-Tart is a flat condom." Once last fall the whole page was replaced with "NIPPLES AND BROCCOLI!!!!!"

This sounds chaotic, but even the Pop-Tarts page is under control most of the time. The "unhelpful" or "inappropriate"—sometimes stoned, racist, violent, metalheaded—changes are quickly fixed by human stompers and algorithmicized helper bots. It's a game. Wikipedians see vandalism as a problem, and it certainly can be, but a Diogenes-minded observer would submit that Wikipedia would never have been the prodigious success it has been without its demons.

This is a reference book that can suddenly go nasty on you. Who knows whether, when you look up Harvard's one-time warrior-president, James Bryant Conant, you're going to get a bland, evenhanded article about him, or whether the whole page will read (as it did for seventeen minutes on April 26, 2006): "HES A BIG STUPID HEAD." James Conant was, after all, in some important ways, a big stupid head. He was studiously anti-Semitic, a strong believer in wonder- 20

6. Stacy Schiff (b. 1960), Pulitzer Prize–winning American writer.

weapons—a man who was quite as happy figuring out new ways to kill people as he was administering a great university. Without the kooks and the insulters and the spray-can taggers, Wikipedia would just be the most useful encyclopedia ever made. Instead it's a fast-paced game of paintball.

Not only does Wikipedia need its vandals—up to a point—the vandals need an orderly Wikipedia, too. Without order, their culture-jamming lacks a context. If Wikipedia were rendered entirely chaotic and obscene, there would be no joy in, for example, replacing some of the article on Archimedes with this:

Archimedes is dead.

He died.

Other people will also die.

All hail chickens.

The Power Rangers say "Hi"

The End.

Even the interesting article on culture jamming has been hit a few times: "Culture jamming," it said in May 2007, "is the act of jamming tons of cultures into 1 extremely hot room."

When, last year, some computer scientists at the University of Minnesota studied millions of Wikipedia edits, they found that most of the good ones—those whose words persisted intact through many later viewings—were made by a tiny percentage of contributors. Enormous numbers of users have added the occasional enriching morsel to Wikipedia—and without this bystander's knowledge the encyclopedia would have gone nowhere—but relatively few users know how to frame their contribution in a form that lasts.

So how do you become one of Wikipedia's upper crust—one of the several thousand whose words will live on for a little while, before later verbal fumarolings erode what you wrote? It's not easy. You have to have a cool head, so that you don't get drawn into soul-destroying disputes, and you need some practical writing ability, and a quick eye, and a knack for synthesis. And you need lots of free time—time to master the odd conventions and the unfamiliar vocabulary (words like "smerge," "POV warrior," "forum shopping," "hatnote," "meat puppet," "fancruft," and "transclusion"),[7] and time to read through guidelines and policy pages and essays and the endless records of old skirmishes—and time to have been gently but firmly, or perhaps rather sharply, reminded by other editors how you should behave. There's a long apprenticeship of trial and error.

7. Smerge—a jerk or jerk-like behavior; POV warrior—point-of-view warrior, a wiki editor who violates the convention of objectivity or neutrality; forum shopping—originally, seeking an amenable jurisdiction for a law case, now used generally; hatnote—a note at the top of a Wikipedia article calling attention to related articles; meatpuppet (usually one word)—in Wikipedia a new editor recruited specifically to support the recruiting editor's view; fancruft—information of interest only to a small number of users; transclusion—insertion of one document into another via a reference link.

At least, that's how it used to be. Now there's a quicker path to proficiency: John Broughton's *Wikipedia: The Missing Manual*, part of the Missing Manual series, overseen by the *New York Times*'s cheery electronics expert, David Pogue. "This Missing Manual helps you avoid beginners' blunders and gets you sounding like a pro from your first edit," the book says on the back. In his introduction, Broughton—who has himself made more than 15,000 Wikipedia edits, putting him in the elite top 1,200 of all editors—promises "the information you absolutely need to avoid running afoul of the rules." And it's true: this manual is enlightening, well organized, and full of good sense. Its arrival may mark a new, middle-aged phase in Wikipedia's history; some who read it will probably have wistful longings for the crazy do-it-yourself days when the whole project was just getting going. In October 2001, the first Wikipedian rule appeared. It was:

> Ignore all rules: If rules make you nervous and depressed, and not desirous of participating in the wiki, then ignore them entirely and go about your business.

The "ignore all rules" rule was written by co-founder Larry Sanger and signed by co-founder Jimbo Wales, along with WojPob, AyeSpy, OprgaG, Invictus, Koyaanis Qatsi, Pinkunicorn, sjc, mike dill, Taw, GWO, and Enchanter. There were two dissenters listed, tbc and AxelBoldt. 25

Nowadays there are rules and policy banners at every turn—there are strongly urged warnings and required tasks and normal procedures and notability guidelines and complex criteria for various decisions—a symptom of something called *instruction creep:* defined in Wikipedia as something that happens "when instructions increase in number and size over time until they are unmanageable." John Broughton's book, at a mere 477 pages, cuts through the creep. He's got a whole chapter on how to make better articles ("Don't Suppress or Separate Controversy") and one on "Handling Incivility and Personal Attacks."

Broughton advises that you shouldn't write a Wikipedia article about some idea or invention that you've personally come up with; that you should stay away from articles about things or people you really love or really hate; and that you shouldn't use the encyclopedia as a PR vehicle—for a new rock band, say, or an aspiring actress. Sometimes Broughton sounds like a freshman English comp teacher, a little too sure that there is one right and wrong way to do things: Strunk without White.[8] But honestly, Wikipedia can be confusing, and you need that kind of confidence coming from a user's guide.

The first thing I did on Wikipedia (under the username Wageless) was to make some not-very-good edits to the page on bovine somatotropin. I clicked the "edit this page" tab, and immediately had an odd, almost lightheaded feeling, as if I had passed through the looking glass and was being allowed to fiddle with some huge engine or delicate piece of biomedical equipment. It seemed

8. William Strunk, Jr. (1869–1946) and E. B. White (1899–1985) were the authors of the famous manual, *The Elements of Style*, first published in 1918 by Strunk and revised in 1959 by White.

much too easy to do damage; you ask, Why don't the words resist me more? Soon, though, you get used to it. You recall the central Wikipedian directive: "Be Bold." You start to like life on the inside.

After bovine hormones, I tinkered a little with the plot summary of the article on *Sleepless in Seattle*, while watching the movie. A little later I made some adjustments to the intro in the article on hydraulic fluid—later still someone pleasingly improved my fixes. After dessert one night my wife and I looked up recipes for cobbler, and then I worked for a while on the cobbler article, though it still wasn't right. I did a few things to the article on periodization. About this time I began standing with my computer open on the kitchen counter, staring at my growing watchlist, checking, peeking. I was, after about a week, well on my way to a first-stage Wikipedia dependency.

30 But the work that really drew me in was trying to save articles from deletion. This became my chosen mission. Here's how it happened. I read a short article on a post-Beat poet and small-press editor named Richard Denner, who had been a student in Berkeley in the Sixties and then, after some lost years, had published many chapbooks on a hand press in the Pacific Northwest. The article was proposed for deletion by a user named PirateMink, who claimed that Denner wasn't a notable figure, whatever that means. (There are quires, reams, bales of controversy over what constitutes notability in Wikipedia: nobody will ever sort it out.) Another user, Stormbay, agreed with PirateMink: no third-party sources, ergo, not notable.

Denner was in serious trouble. I tried to make the article less deletable by incorporating a quote from an interview in the Berkeley *Daily Planet*—Denner told the reporter that in the Sixties he'd tried to be a street poet, "using magic markers to write on napkins at Café Med for espressos, on girls' arms and feet." (If an article bristles with some quotes from external sources these may, like the bushy hairs on a caterpillar, make it harder to kill.) And I voted "keep" on the deletion-discussion page, pointing out that many poets publish only chapbooks: "What harm does it do to anyone or anything to keep this entry?"

An administrator named Nakon—one of about a thousand peer-nominated volunteer administrators—took a minute to survey the two "delete" votes and my "keep" vote and then killed the article. Denner was gone. Startled, I began sampling the "AfDs" (the Articles for Deletion debate pages) and the even more urgent "speedy deletes" and "PRODs" (proposed deletes) for other items that seemed unjustifiably at risk; when they were, I tried to save them. Taekwang Industry—a South Korean textile company—was one. A user named Kusunose had "prodded" it—that is, put a red-edged banner at the top of the article proposing it for deletion within five days. I removed the banner, signaling that I disagreed, and I hastily spruced up the text, noting that the company made "Acelan" brand spandex, raincoats, umbrellas, sodium cyanide, and black abaya fabric. The article didn't disappear: wow, did that feel good.

So I kept on going. I found press citations and argued for keeping the Jitterbug telephone, a large-keyed cell phone with a soft earpiece for elder callers; and Vladimir Narbut, a minor Russian Acmeist poet whose second book, *Halleluia*, was confiscated by the police; and Sara Mednick, a San Diego neuroscientist and author of *Take a Nap! Change Your Life*; and Pyro Boy, a minor celebrity who turns himself into a human firecracker on stage. I took up the cause of the Arifs, a Cyprio-Turkish crime family based in London (on LexisNexis I found that the *Irish Daily Mirror* called them "Britain's No. 1 Crime Family"); and Card Football, a pokerlike football simulation game; and Paul Karason, a suspender-wearing guy whose face turned blue from drinking colloidal silver; and Jim Cara, a guitar restorer and modem-using music collaborationist who badly injured his head in a ski-flying competition; and writer Owen King, son of Stephen King; and Whitley Neill Gin, flavored with South African botanicals; and Whirled News Tonight, a Chicago improve troupe; and Michelle Leonard, a European songwriter, co-writer of a recent glam hit called "Love Songs (They Kill Me)."

All of these people and things had been deemed nonnotable by other editors, sometimes with unthinking harshness—the article on Michelle Leonard was said to contain "total lies." (Wrongly—as another editor, Bondegezou, more familiar with European pop charts, pointed out.) When I managed to help save something I was quietly thrilled—I walked tall, like Henry Fonda in *Twelve Angry Men*.[9]

At the same time as I engaged in these tiny, fascinating (to me) "keep" tussles, hundreds of others were going on, all over Wikipedia. I signed up for the Article Rescue Squadron, having seen it mentioned in Broughton's manual: the ARS is a small group that opposes "extremist deletion." And I found out about a project called WPPDP (for "WikiProject Proposed Deletion Patrolling") in which people look over the PROD lists for articles that shouldn't be made to vanish. Since about 1,500 articles are deleted a day, this kind of work can easily become life-consuming, but some editors (for instance, a patient librarian whose username is DGG) seem to be able to do it steadily week in and week out and stay sane. I, on the other hand, was swept right out to the Isles of Shoals. I stopped hearing what my family was saying to me—for about two weeks I all but disappeared into my screen, trying to salvage brief, sometimes overly promotional but nevertheless worthy biographies by recasting them in neutral language, and by hastily scouring newspaper databases and Google Books for references that would bulk up their notability quotient. I had become an "inclusionist."

That's not to say that I thought that every article should be fought for. Someone created an article called Plamen Ognianov Kamenov. In its entirety, the article read: "Hi my name is Plamen Ognianov Kamenov. I am Bulgarian. I am smart." The article is gone—understandably. Someone else, evidently a child, made up a lovely short tale about a fictional woman named Empress Alamonda, who hated her husband's chambermaids. "She would get so jealous she would faint," said the article. "Alamonda died at 6:00 pm in her room. On august 4 1896." Alamonda is gone, too.

9. Henry Fonda (1905–1982), an American actor, played the main character in *Twelve Angry Men* (1957), a film in which a single member of a jury convinces the other jurors of a defendant's innocence.

Still, a lot of good work—verifiable, informative, brain-leapingly strange—is being cast out of this paperless, infinitely expandable accordion folder by people who have a narrow, almost grade-schoolish notion of what sort of curiosity an online encyclopedia will be able to satisfy in the years to come.

Anybody can "pull the trigger" on an article (as Broughton phrases it)—you just insert a double-bracketed software template. It's harder to improve something that's already written, or to write something altogether new, especially now that so many of the *World Book*–sanctioned encyclopedic fruits are long plucked. There are some people on Wikipedia now who are just bullies, who take pleasure in wrecking and mocking people's work—even to the point of laughing at nonstandard "Engrish." They poke articles full of warnings and citation-needed notes and deletion prods till the topics go away.

In the fall of 2006, groups of editors went around getting rid of articles on webcomic artists—some of the most original and articulate people on the Net. They would tag an article as nonnotable and then crowd in to vote it down. One openly called it the "web-comic articles purge of 2006." A victim, Trev-Mun, author of a comic called *Ragnarok Wisdom*, wrote: "I got the impression that they enjoyed this kind of thing as a kid enjoys kicking down others' sand castles." Another artist, Howard Tayler, said: "'Notability purges' are being executed throughout Wikipedia by empire-building, wannabe tin-pot dictators masquerading as humble editors." Rob Balder, author of a webcomic called *Partially-Clips*, likened the organized deleters to book burners, and he said: "Your words are polite, yeah, but your actions are obscene. Every word in every valid article you've destroyed should be converted to profanity and screamed in your face."

40 As the deletions and ill-will spread in 2007—deletions not just of webcomics but of companies, urban places, Web sites, lists, people, categories, and ideas—all deemed to be trivial, "NN" (nonnotable), "stubby," undersourced, or otherwise unencyclopedic—Andrew Lih, one of the most thoughtful observers of Wikipedia's history, told a Canadian reporter: "The preference now is for excising, deleting, restricting information rather than letting it sit there and grow." In September 2007, Jimbo Wales, Wikipedia's panjandrum—himself an inclusionist who believes that if people want an article about every Pokemon character, then hey, let it happen—posted a one-sentence stub about Mzoli's, a restaurant on the outskirts of Cape Town, South Africa. It was quickly put up for deletion. Others saved it, and after a thunderstorm of vandalism (e.g., the page was replaced with "I hate Wikipedia, it's a far-left propaganda instrument, some far-left gangs control it"), Mzoli's is now a model piece, spiky with press citations. There's even, as of January, an article about "Deletionism and inclusionism in Wikipedia"—it too survived an early attempt to purge it.

My advice to anyone who is curious about becoming a contributor—and who is better than I am at keeping his or her contributional compulsions under control—is to get Broughton's *Missing Manual* and start adding, creating, rescuing. I think I'm done for the time being. But I have a secret hope. Someone recently proposed a Wikimorgue—a bin of broken dreams where all rejects could still be read, as long as they weren't libelous or otherwise illegal. Like other middens, it would have much to tell us over time. We could call it the Deletopedia.

QUESTIONS

1. Baker notes that Wikipedia is among the ten most popular Web sites. To what does he attribute this popularity?

2. Contrast the visions of Wikipedia embraced by "deletionists" (paragraph 4) and "inclusionists" (paragraph 35). What is at stake in the struggle between these groups?

3. A strain of nostalgia, a sentimental longing for the past, runs through Baker's essay. How is this nostalgia evident in his argument? In his style?

4. Baker notes that Brion Vibber, one of the developers of Wikipedia, once described Wikipedia as "like an online game" (paragraph 13). Is Vibber's comparison apt? Test it by writing a comparison of Wikipedia as Baker describes it to an online game you know well.

HENRY WECHSLER, ANDREA DAVENPORT, GEORGE DOWDALL, BARBARA MOEYKENS, AND SONIA CASTILLO

Health and Behavioral Consequences of Binge Drinking in College: A National Survey of Students at 140 Campuses

Objective.—To examine the extent of binge drinking by college students and the ensuing health and behavioral problems that binge drinkers create for themselves and others on their campus.

Design.—Self-administered survey mailed to a national representative sample of US 4-year college students.

Setting.—One hundred forty US 4-year colleges in 1993.

Participants.—A total of 17,592 college students.

Main Outcome Measures.—Self-reports of drinking behavior, alcohol-related health problems, and other problems.

Results.—Almost half (44%) of college students responding to the survey were binge drinkers, including almost one fifth (19%) of the students who were frequent binge drinkers. Frequent binge drinkers are more likely to experience serious health and other consequences of their drinking behavior than other students. Almost half (47%) of the frequent binge drinkers experienced five or more different drinking-related problems, including injuries and engaging in unplanned sex, since the beginning of the school year. Most binge drinkers do not consider themselves to be problem drink-

Originally published as "Health and Behavioral Consequences of Binge Drinking in College," Journal of the American Medical Association *(December 7, 1994). The authors' notes are collected at the end as "References," in the style of* JAMA.

ers and have not sought treatment for an alcohol problem. Binge drinkers create problems for classmates who are not binge drinkers. Students who are not binge drinkers at schools with higher binge rates were more likely than students at schools with lower binge rates to experience problems such as being pushed, hit, or assaulted or experiencing an unwanted sexual advance.

Conclusions.—Binge drinking is widespread on college campuses. Programs aimed at reducing this problem should focus on frequent binge drinkers, refer them to treatment or educational programs, and emphasize the harm they cause for students who are not binge drinkers (*JAMA*, 1994; 272:1672–1677).

Heavy episodic or binge drinking poses a danger of serious health and other consequences for alcohol abusers and for others in the immediate environment. Alcohol contributes to the leading causes of accidental death in the United States, such as motor vehicle crashes and falls.[1] Alcohol abuse is seen as contributing to almost half of motor vehicle fatalities, the most important cause of death among young Americans.[2] Unsafe sex—a growing threat with the spread of acquired immunodeficiency syndrome (AIDS) and other sexually transmitted diseases—and unintentional injuries have been associated with alcohol intoxication.[3–5] These findings support the view of college presidents who believe that alcohol abuse is the No. 1 problem on campus.[6]

Despite the fact that alcohol is illegal for most undergraduates, alcohol continues to be widely used on most college campuses today. Since the national study by Straus and Bacon in 1949,[7] numerous subsequent surveys have documented the overwhelming use of alcohol by college students and have pointed to problem drinking among this group.[8–10] Most previous studies of drinking by college students have been conducted on single college campuses and have not used random sampling of students.[9–12] While these studies are in general agreement about the prevalence and consequences of binge drinking, they do not provide a national representative sample of college drinking.

A few large-scale, multicollege surveys have been conducted in recent years. However, these have not selected a representative national sample of colleges, but have used colleges in one state[3] or those participating in a federal program,[5] or have followed a sample of high school seniors through college.[1,3]

In general, studies of college alcohol use have consistently found higher rates of binge drinking among men than women. However, these studies used the same definition of binge drinking for men and women, without taking into account sex differences in metabolism of ethanol or in body mass.[3,5,9–12,14–17]

5 The consequences of binge drinking often pose serious risks for drinkers and for others in the college environment. Binge drinking has been associated with unplanned and unsafe sexual activity, physical and sexual assault, unintentional injuries, other criminal violations, interpersonal problems, physical or cognitive impairment, and poor academic performance.[3–5]

This study examines the nature and extent of binge drinking among a representative national sample of students at 140 US 4-year colleges and details the problems such drinking causes for drinkers themselves and for others on their college campus. Binge drinking is defined through a sex-specific measure to take into account sex differences in the dosage effects of ethanol.

Methods

The Colleges

A national sample of 179 colleges was selected from the American Council on Education's list of 4-year colleges and universities accredited by one of the six regional bodies covering the United States. The sample was selected using probability proportionate to enrollment size sampling. All full-time undergraduate students at a university were eligible to be chosen for this study, regardless of the college in which they were enrolled. This sample contained few women-only colleges and few colleges with less than 1000 students. To correct for this problem, an oversample of 15 additional colleges with enrollments of less than 1000 students and 10 all-women's colleges were added to the sample. Nine colleges were subsequently dropped because they were considered inappropriate. These included seminary schools, military schools, and allied health schools.

One hundred forty (72%) of the final sample of 195 colleges agreed to participate. The primary reason stated for nonparticipation by college administrators was inability to provide a random sample of students and their addresses within the time requirements of the study. The 140 participating colleges are located in 40 states and the District of Columbia. They represent a cross-section of US higher education. Two thirds of the colleges sampled are public and one third are private. Approximately two thirds are located in a suburban or urban setting and one third in a small town/rural setting. Four percent are women-only, and 4% are predominantly black institutions.

When the 55 nonparticipating schools were compared with the 140 in the study, the only statistically significant difference found was in terms of enrollment size. Proportionately fewer small colleges (fewer than 1000 students) participated in the study. Since these were oversampled, sufficient numbers are present for statistical analysis.

Sampling Procedures

Colleges were sent a set of specific guidelines for drawing a random sample of students based on the total enrollment of full-time undergraduates. Depending on enrollment size, every *x*th student was selected from the student registry using a random starting point. A sample of undergraduate students was provided by each of the 140 participating colleges: 215 students at each of 127 colleges, and 108 at each of 13 colleges (12 of which were in the oversample). The final student sample included 28,709 students. 10

The Questionnaire

The 20-page survey instrument asked students a number of questions about their drinking behavior as well as other health issues. Whenever possible, the survey instrument included questions that had been used previously in other national or large-scale epidemiological studies.[13,14] A drink was defined as a

12-oz (360-mL) can (or bottle) of beer, a 4-oz (120-mL) glass of wine, a 12-oz (360-mL) bottle (or can) of wine cooler, or a shot (1.25 oz [37-mL]) of liquor straight or in a mixed drink. The following four questions were used to assess binge drinking: (1) sex; (2) recency of last drink ("never," "not in past year," "within last year but more than 30 days ago," "within 30 days but more than 1 week ago," or "within week"); (3) "Think back over the last two weeks. How many times have you had five or more drinks in a row?" (The use of this question, without specification of time elapsed in a drinking episode, is consistent with standard practice in recent research on alcohol use among this population.[3,5,13,18]); and (4) "During the last two weeks, how many times have you had four drinks in a row (but no more than that) (for women)?" Missing responses to any of these four questions excluded the student from the binging analyses.

Students were also asked the extent to which they had experienced any of the following 12 problems as a consequence of their drinking since the beginning of the school year: have a hangover; miss a class; get behind in schoolwork; do something you later regretted; forget where you were or what you did; argue with friends; engage in unplanned sexual activity; not use protection when you had sex; damage property; get into trouble with campus or local police; get hurt or injured; or require medical treatment for an alcohol overdose. They were also asked if, since the beginning of the school year, they had experienced any of the following eight problems caused by other students' drinking: been insulted or humiliated; had a serious argument or quarrel; been pushed, hit, or assaulted; had your property damaged; had to "babysit" or take care of another student who drank too much; had your studying or sleep interrupted; experienced an unwanted sexual advance; or had been a victim of sexual assault or date rape.

The Mailing

The initial mailing of questionnaires to students began on February 5, 1993. By the end of March, 87% of the final group of questionnaires had been received, with another 10% in April and 2% in May and June. There are no discernible differences in binging rates among questionnaires received in each of the 5 months of the survey. Mailings were modified to take into account spring break, so that students would be responding about their binge drinking behavior during a 2-week time on campus. Responses were voluntary and anonymous. Four separate mailings, usually 10 days apart, were sent at each college: a questionnaire, a reminder postcard, a second questionnaire, and a second reminder postcard. To encourage students to respond, the following cash awards were offered: one $1000 award to a student whose name was drawn from among students responding within 1 week, and one $500 award and ten $100 awards to students selected from all those who responded.

The Response Rate

The questionnaires were mailed to 28,709 students. Overall, 3,082 students were eliminated from the sample because of school reports of incorrect addresses, withdrawal from school, or leaves of absence, reducing the sample size to 25,627. A total of 17,592 students returned questionnaires, yielding an overall student response rate of approximately 69%. The response rate is likely to be underestimated since it does not take into account all of the students who may not have received questionnaires. At 104 of the colleges, response rates were between 60% and 80%, and only six colleges had response rates less than 50%. Response rate was not associated with the binging rate (i.e., the Pearson correlation coefficient between the binge drinking rate at the college and the response rate was 0.06 with a *P* value of .46).

When responses of early and late responders to the survey were compared, there were no significant differences in the percent of nondrinkers, nonbinge drinkers, and binge drinkers. In the case of 11,557 students who could be classified as early or late responders, there was no significant differences in terms of binge drinking (43% for the early responders vs. 42% for the late responders). An additional short form of the questionnaire was mailed to a segment of students who had failed to return the questionnaire. The rate of binge drinking of these nonresponders did not differ from that of responders to the original student survey. 15

Data Analysis

All statistical analyses were carried out using the current version of SAS.[19]* Comparisons of unweighted and weighted sample results suggested little difference between them, so unweighted results are reported here. Chi-square analyses among students who had a drink in the past year were used to compare nonbinge drinkers, infrequent binge drinkers, and binge drinkers. Binge drinking was defined as the consumption of five or more drinks in a row for men and four or more drinks in a row for women during the 2 weeks prior to the survey. An extensive analysis showed that this sex-specific measure accurately indicates an equivalent likelihood of alcohol-related problems. In this article, the term "binge drinker" is used to refer to students who binged at least once in the previous 2 weeks. Frequent binge drinkers were defined as those who binged three or more times in the past 2 weeks and infrequent binge drinkers as those who binged one or two times in the past 2 weeks. Nonbinge drinkers were those who had consumed alcohol in the past year, but had not binged.

Logistic regression analyses were used to examine how much more likely frequent binge drinkers were to experience an alcohol-related problem or driving behavior compared with nonbinge drinkers, and to compare infrequent binge drinkers with nonbinge drinkers. Odds ratios were adjusted for age, sex, race, marital status, and parents' college education.

In examining secondary binge effects, schools were divided into three groups on the basis of the percentage of students who were binge drinkers at each school. The responses of students who had not binged in the past 2 weeks (including those who had never had a drink) and who resided in dormitories, fraternities, or sororities were compared through χ^2† analyses across the three

*A standard social science statistical program.

†Chi-square.

school types. High-level binge schools (where 51% or more students were binge drinkers) included 44 schools with 6,084 students; middle-level binge schools (36% to 50% of students were binge drinkers) included 53 schools with 6,455 students; and low-level binge schools (35% or less of students were binge drinkers) included 43 schools with 5,043 students (for 10 students, information regarding school of attendance was missing). For two of the problems that occurred primarily or almost exclusively to women (sexual assault and experiencing an unwanted sexual advance), only women were included in the analyses.

RESULTS

Characteristics of the Student Sample

This analysis is based on data from 17,592 undergraduate students at 140 US 4-year colleges. The student sample includes more women (58%) than men (42%), due in part to the inclusion of six all-women's institutions. This compares with national 1991 data that report 51% of undergraduates at 4-year institutions are women.[20] The sample is predominantly white (81%). This coincides exactly with national 1991 data that report 81% of undergraduates at 4-year institutions are white.[20] Minority groups included Asian/Pacific Islander (7%), Spanish/Hispanic (7%), black/African American (6%), and Native American (1%). The age of the students was distributed as follows: 45% younger than 21 years, 38% aged 21 to 23 years, and 17% aged 24 years or more. There were slightly more juniors (25%) and seniors (26%) in the sample than freshmen (20%) and sophomores (19%), probably because 30% of the students were transfers from other institutions. Ten percent of the students were in their fifth undergraduate year of school or beyond. Religious affiliation was discerned by asking students in which of the following religions they were raised: Protestant (44%), Catholic (36%), Jewish (3%), Muslim (1%), other (4%), and none (12%). Religion was cited as an important to very important activity among 36% of the students. Approximately three of five students (59%) worked for pay. Approximately half (49%) of the students had a grade-point average of A, A–, or B+.

Extent of Binge Drinking

20

Because of missing responses, there were 496 students excluded from binging analyses (i.e., 17,096 were included). Most students drank alcohol during the past year. Only about one of six (16%) were nondrinkers (15% of the men and 16% of the women). About two of five students (41%) drank but were nonbinge drinkers (35% of the men and 45% of the women). Slightly fewer than half (44%) of the students were binge drinkers (50% of the men and 39% of the women). About half of this group of binge drinkers, or about one in five students (19%) overall, were frequent binge drinkers (overall, 23% of the men and 17% of the women).

Binge Drinking Rates at Colleges

The Figure shows that binge drinking rates vary extensively among the 140 colleges in the study. While 1% of the students were binge drinkers at the school with the lowest rate of binge drinkers, 70% of students were binge drinkers at the school with the highest rate. At 44 schools, more than half of the responding students were binge drinkers.

When the 140 colleges were divided into levels of binging rate, χ^2 analyses showed that several college characteristics were individually associated (at $P<.05$) with binging rate. Colleges located in the Northeast or North Central regions of the United States (compared with those in the West or South) or those that were residential (compared with commuter schools, where 90% or more of the students lived off campus)[21] tended to have higher rates of binging. In addition, traditionally black institutions and women's colleges had lower binge rates than schools that were not traditionally black or were coeducational colleges. Other characteristics, such as whether the college was public or private and its enrollment size, were not related to binge drinker rates.

Examination of whether college alcohol programs and policies have any association with binge drinking will be presented in a separate publication. There is little evidence to conclude that current policies have had strong impacts on overall drinking levels. Preliminary analyses suggest that individual binge drinking is less likely if the institution does not have any alcohol outlets within 1 mile of campus, or if it prohibits alcohol use for all persons (even those older than 21 years) on campus.

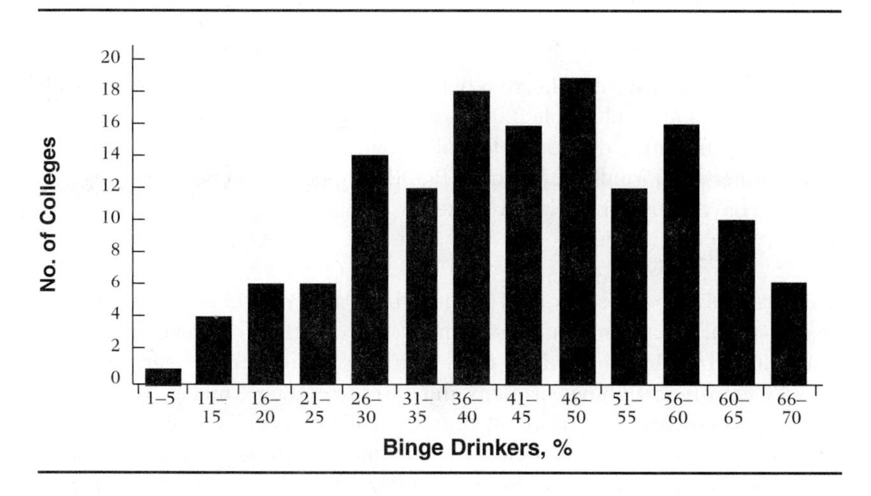

Distribution of colleges by percentage of binge drinkers.

Drinking Patterns of Binge Drinkers

Table 1 indicates that our designations of binge drinker and frequent binge drinker are strongly indicative of a drinking style that involves more frequent and heavier drinking. Furthermore, intoxication (often intentional) is associated with binge drinking in men and women.

25 Binge drinking is related to age. Students who are in the predominant college age group (between 17 and 23 years) have much higher binging rates than older students. However, within the predominant college age group, students who are younger than the legal drinking age of 21 years do not differ in binging rates from students aged 21 to 23 years. In contrast to the modest effects of age, there is no relationship between year in school and binging, with rates of binge drinking virtually identical among students across the years of college attendance.

Alcohol-Related Health and Other Problems

There is a strong, positive relationship between the frequency of binge drinking and alcohol-related health and other problems reported by the students (Table 2). Among the more serious alcohol-related problems, the frequent binge drinkers were seven to 10 times more likely than the nonbinge drinkers to not use protection when having sex, to engage in unplanned sexual activity, to get into trouble with campus police, to damage property, or to get hurt or injured. A similar comparison between the infrequent binge drinkers and nonbinge drinkers also shows a strong relationship.

Men and women reported similar frequencies for most of the problems, except for damaging property or getting into trouble with the campus police. Among the frequent binge drinkers, 35% of the men and 9% of the women reported damaging property, and 16% of the men and 6% of the women reported getting into trouble with the campus police.

Drinking and Driving

There is also a positive relationship between binge drinking and driving under the influence of alcohol (Table 3). A large proportion of the student population reported driving after drinking alcohol. Binge drinkers, particularly frequent binge drinkers, reported significantly ($P<.001$) higher frequencies of dangerous driving behaviors than nonbinge drinkers.

Number of Problems

Nearly half (47%) of the frequent binge drinkers reported having experienced five or more of the 12 problems listed in Table 2 (omitting hangover and including driving after drinking) since the beginning of the school year, compared with 14% of infrequent binge drinkers and 3% of nonbinge drinkers. The adjusted odds ratios indicate that frequent binge drinkers were 25 times more likely than nonbinge drinkers to experience five or more of these problems, while the infrequent binge drinkers were five times more likely than nonbinge drinkers to experience five or more problems.

TABLE 1

DRINKING STYLES OF STUDENTS WHO WERE NONBINGE DRINKERS, INFREQUENT BINGE DRINKERS, OR FREQUENT BINGE DRINKERS*

	Nonbinge Drinkers, %†		*Infrequent Binge Drinkers, %‡*		*Frequent Binge Drinkers, %§*	
Drinking Styles	*Men* (*n*=2,539)	*Women* (*n*=4,400)	*Men* (*n*=1,968)	*Women* (*n*=2,130)	*Men* (*n*=1,630)	*Women* (*n*=1,684)
Drank on 10 or more occasions in the past 30 days‖	3	1	11	6	61	39
Usually binges when drinks	4	4	43	45	83	82
Was drunk three or more times in past month	2	1	17	13	70	55
Drinks to get drunk¶	22	18	49	44	73	68

*Chi-square comparisons of students who were nonbinge drinkers, infrequent binge drinkers, and frequent binge drinkers and each of the four drinking styles were significant for men and women separately at $P<.001$. Sample sizes vary slightly for each question because of missing values. Binging is defined as four or more drinks for women and five or more drinks for men.

†Students who consumed alcohol in the past year, but did not binge.

‡Students who binged one or two times in a 2-week period.

§Students who binged three or more times in a 2-week period.

‖Question asked, "On how many occasions have you had a drink of alcohol in the past 30 days?" Response categories were 1 to 2 occasions, 3 to 5 occasions, 6 to 9 occasions, 10 to 19 occasions, 20 to 39 occasions, and 40 or more occasions.

¶Says that to get drunk is an important reason for drinking.

TABLE 2
RISK OF ALCOHOL-RELATED PROBLEMS COMPARING STUDENTS WHO WERE INFREQUENT BINGE DRINKERS OR FREQUENT BINGE DRINKERS WITH STUDENTS WHO WERE NONBINGE DRINKERS AMONG COLLEGE STUDENTS WHO HAD A DRINK IN THE PAST YEAR*

Reporting Problem	Nonbinge Drinkers, % (n=6,894)	Infrequent Binge Drinkers % (n=4,090	Infrequent Binge Drinkers Adjusted OR (95% CI)†	Frequent Binge Drinkers % (n=3,291)	Frequent Binge Drinkers Adjusted OR (95% CI)‡
Have a hangover	30	75	6.28 (5.73–6.87)	90	17.62 (15.20–20.04)
Do something you regret	14	37	3.31 (3.00–3.64)	63	8.98 (8.11–9.95)
Miss a class	8	30	4.66 (4.15–5.24)	61	16.58 (14.73–18.65)
Forget where you were or what you did	8	26	3.62 (3.22-4.06)	54	11.23 (10.05–12.65)
Get behind in school work	6	21	3.70 (3.26–4.20)	46	11.43 (10.09–12.94)
Argue with friends	8	22	3.06 (2.72–3.46)	42	7.77 (6.90–8.74)
Engage in unplanned sexual activity	8	20	2.78 (2.46–3.13)	41	7.17 (6.37–8.06)
Get hurt or injured	2	9	3.65 (3.01–4.13)	23	10.43 (8.70–12.52)
Damage property	2	8	3.09 (2.53–3.77)	22	9.49 (7.86–11.43)
Not use protection when having sex	4	10	2.90 (2.45–3.42)	22	7.11 (6.07–8.34)
Get into trouble with campus or local police	1	4	2.50 (1.92–3.26)	11	6.92 (5.44–8.81)
Require medical treatment of alcohol overdose	<1	<1	NS	1	2.81 (1.39–5.68)
Have five or more alcohol-related problems since the beginning of the school year§	3	14	4.95 (4.17-5.89)	47	25.10 (21.30-29.58)

*Problem occurred not at all or one or more times. Chi-square comparisons of nonbinge drinkers, infrequent binge drinkers, and frequent binge drinkers and each of the problems are significant at $P<.001$, except for alcohol overdose ($P=.002$). Sample sizes vary slightly for each problem of missing values. OR indicates odds ratio; CI, confidence interval. See Table 1 for explanation of drinking classification.

†Adjusted ORs of infrequent binge drinkers vs. nonbinge drinkers are significant at $P<.001$.

‡Adjusted ORs of frequent binge drinkers vs. nonbinge drinkers are significant at $P<.001$, except for alcohol overdose, $P<.01$.

§Excludes hangover and includes driving after drinking as one of the problems.

TABLE 3

ALCOHOL-RELATED DRIVING BEHAVIOR FOR A 30-DAY PERIOD COMPARING STUDENTS WHO WERE INFREQUENT BINGE DRINKERS OR FREQUENT BINGE DRINKERS WITH STUDENTS WHO WERE NONBINGE DRINKERS*

	Nonbinge Drinkers		*Infrequent Binge Drinkers*			*Frequent Binge Drinkers*		
Drinking Behavior	*Men, %* (n=2,531)	*Women, %* (n=4,393)	*Men, %* (n=1,975)	*Women, %* (n=2,132)	*Adjusted OR* 95% CI)†	*Men, %* (n=1,630)	*Women, %* (n=1,684)	*Adjusted OR* (95% CI)‡
Drove after drinking alcohol	20	13	47	33	5.13 (4.67–5.64)	62	49	10.33 (9.34–11.42)
Drove after having five or more drinks	2	1	18	7	22.23 (16.89–29.26)	40	21	74.30 (56.56–97.58)
Rode with a driver who was high or drunk	7	7	23	22	4.73 (4.20–5.32)	t53	48	15.97 (14.22–17.95)

*Chi-square comparisons of nonbinge drinkers, infrequent binge drinkers, and frequent binge drinkers and each of the three driving behaviors were all significant for men and women separately at $P<.001$. Sample sizes vary slightly for each question because of missing values. OR indicates odds ratio; CI, confidence interval. See Table 1 for explanation of drinking classification.

†Adjusted OR of infrequent binge drinkers vs. nonbinge drinkers (sex combined) are significant at $P<.001$.

‡Adjusted OR of frequent binge drinkers vs. nonbinge drinkers (sex combined) are significant at $P<.001$.

Self-assessment of Drinking Problem

30 Few students describe themselves as having a drinking problem. When asked to classify themselves in terms of their current alcohol use, less than 1% of the total sample (0.2%), including only 0.6% of the frequent binge drinkers, designated themselves as problem drinkers. In addition, few students have ever sought treatment for a problem with alcohol.

A somewhat larger proportion of students indicated that they had ever had a drinking problem. Slightly more than one fifth (22%) of the frequent binge drinkers thought that they ever had a drinking problem, compared with 12% of the infrequent binge drinkers and 7% of the nonbinge drinkers.

Secondary Binge Effects

Table 4 reports on the percentage of nonbinging students who experienced "secondary binge effects," each of eight types of problems due to other students' drinking at each of the three different school types (i.e., schools with high, middle, and low binge levels). For seven of the eight problems studied, students

TABLE 4
STUDENTS EXPERIENCING SECONDARY BINGE EFFECTS
(BASED ON STUDENTS WHO WERE NOT BINGE DRINKERS AND LIVING IN DORMITORIES, FRATERNITIES, OR SORORITIES)*

	School's Binging Level				
		Middle		High	
Secondary Binge Effect	Low, % (n=801)	% (n=1,115)	Adjusted OR (95% CI)†	% (n=1,064)	Adjusted OR (95% CI)‡
Been insulted or humiliated	21	30	1.6 (1.3-2.1)	34	1.9 (1.5-2.3)
Had a serious argument or quarrel	13	18	1.3 (1.0-1.7)	20	1.5 (1.1-2.0)
Been pushed, hit, or assaulted	7	10	1.4 (1.0-2.1)	13	2.0 (1.4-2.8)
Had your property damaged	6	13	2.0 (1.4-2.8)	15	2.3 (1.6-3.2)
Had to take care of drunken student	31	47	1.9 (1.6-2.3)	54	2.5 (2.0-3.0)
Had your study/sleep interrupted	42	64	2.3 (1.9-2.8)	68	2.6 (2.2-3.2)
Experienced an unwanted sexual advance§	15	21	1.7 (1.2-2.3)	26	2.1 (1.5-2.8)
Been a victim of sexual assault or date rape§	2	1	NS	2	NS
Experienced at least one of the above problems	62	82	2.8 (2.3-3.5)	87	4.1 (3.2-5.2)

*OR indicates odds ratio; CI, confidence interval.

†Adjusted OR of students at schools with middle levels of binging vs. students at schools with low levels are significant at $P<.05$.

‡Adjusted OR of students at schools with high levels of binging vs. students at schools with low levels are significant at $P<.05$.

§Based on women only.

at schools with high and middle binge levels were more likely than students at schools with low binge levels to experience problems as a result of the drinking behaviors of others. Odds ratios (adjusted for age, sex, race, marital status, and parents' college education) indicated that nonbinging students at schools with the high binge levels were more likely than nonbinging students at schools with low binge levels to experience secondary binge effects.

The odds of experiencing at least one of the eight problems was roughly 4:1 when students at schools with high binge levels were compared with students at schools with low binge levels.

Binge Drinking in High School

Most students reported the same drinking behavior in high school as in college. Almost half (47%) had not been binge drinkers in high school and did not binge in college, while one fifth (22%) binged in high school and in college. One fifth (22%) of the students were binge drinkers in college but not in high school, while 10% were not binge drinkers at the time of the survey in college, but reported having been binge drinkers in high school.

Comment

To our knowledge, this is the first study that has used a representative national sample, and the first large-scale study to measure binge drinking under a sex-specific definition. Forty-four percent of the college students in this study were classified as binge drinkers. This finding is consistent with the findings of other national studies such as the University of Michigan's Monitoring the Future Project, which found that 41% of college students were binge drinkers,[1,3] and the Core Alcohol and Drug Survey, which found that 42% of college students were binge drinkers.[5] All three studies used a definition of binging over a 2-week period, but the other studies used the same five-drink measure for both sexes. Binge drinking was defined in terms of the number of drinks consumed in a single episode. No attempt was made to specify the duration of time for each episode. Future research might examine whether subgroup differences exist in duration and whether such differences are linked to outcomes. 35

A possible limitation of surveys using self-reports of drinking behavior pertains to the validity of responses; however, a number of studies have confirmed the validity of self-reported of alcohol and substance use.[22–24] Findings indicate that if a self-report bias exists, it is largely limited to the heaviest use group[2,5] and should not affect such a conservative estimate of heavy volume as five drinks.

The results confirm that binge drinking is widespread on college campuses. Overall, almost half of all students were binge drinkers. One fifth of all students were frequent binge drinkers (had three or more binge drinking occasions in the past 2 weeks) and were deeply involved in a lifestyle characterized by frequent and deliberate intoxication. Frequent binge drinkers are much more likely to experience serious health and other consequences of their drinking behavior than other students. Almost half of them have experienced five or more alcohol-related problems since the beginning of the school year, one of three report they were hurt or injured, and two in five engaged in unplanned sexual activity. Frequent binge drinkers also report drinking and driving. Three of five male frequent binge drinkers drove after drinking some alcohol in the 30 days prior to the survey, and two of five drove after having five or more drinks. A recent national report that reviewed published studies concluded that alcohol was involved in two thirds of college student suicides, in 90% of campus rapes, and in 95% of violent crime on campus.[2,6]

Almost a third of the colleges in the study have a majority of students who binge. Not only do these binge drinkers put themselves at risk, they also create problems for their fellow students who are not binge drinking. Students who did not binge and who reside at schools with high levels of binge drinkers were up to three times as likely to report being bothered by the drinking-related behaviors of other students than students who did not binge and who reside at schools with lower levels of binge drinkers. These problems included being pushed, hit, or assaulted and experiencing an unwanted sexual advance.

Effective interventions face a number of challenges. Drinking is not typically a behavior learned in college and often continues patterns established earlier. In fact, one of three students in the present study was already a binge drinker in the year before college.

40

The prominence of drinking on college campuses reflects its importance in the wider society, but drinking has traditionally occupied a unique place in campus life. Despite the overall decline in drinking in US society, recent time-trend studies have failed to show a corresponding decrease in binge drinking on college campuses.[3,13] The variation in binge drinking rates among the colleges in this study suggests that colleges may create and unwittingly perpetuate their own drinking cultures through selection, tradition, policy, and other strategies. On many campuses, drinking behavior that would elsewhere be classified as alcohol abuse may be socially acceptable, or even socially attractive, despite its documented implication in automobile crashes, other injury, violence, suicide, and high-risk sexual behavior.

The scope of the problem makes immediate results of any interventions highly unlikely. Colleges need to be committed to large-scale and long-term behavior change strategies, including referral of alcohol abusers to appropriate treatment. Frequent binge drinkers on college campuses are similar to other alcohol abusers elsewhere in their tendency to deny that they have a problem. Indeed, their youth, the visibility of others who drink the same way, and the shelter of the college community may make them less likely to recognize the problem. In addition to addressing the health problems of alcohol abusers, a major effort should address the large group of students who are not binge drinkers on campus who are adversely affected by the alcohol-related behavior of binge drinkers.

This study was supported by the Robert Wood Johnson Foundation. We wish to thank the following persons who assisted with the project: Lloyd Johnston, PhD, Thomas J. Mangione, PhD, Anthony M. Roman, MD, Nan Laird, PhD, Jeffrey Hansen, Avtar Khalsa, MSW, and Marianne Lee, MPA.

REFERENCES

1. US Dept of Health and Human Services, ***Alcohol and Health.*** Rockville, Md: National Institute on Alcohol Abuse and Alcoholism: 1990.

2. Robert Wood Johnson Foundation. ***Substance Abuse: The Nation's Number One Health Problem. Key Indicators for Policy.*** Princeton, NJ: Robert Wood Johnson Foundation; October 1993.

3. Wechsler H, Isaac N. 'Binge' drinkers at Massachusetts colleges: prevalence, drinking styles, time trends, and associated problems. ***JAMA.*** 1992; 267:2929–2931.

4. Hanson DJ, Engs RC. College students' drinking problems: a national study, 1982–1991. ***Psychol Rep.*** 1992;71:39–42.

5. Presley CA, Meilman PW, Lyerla R. ***Alcohol and Drugs on American College Campuses: Use, Consequence, and Perceptions of the Campus Environment, Volume I: 1989–1991.*** Carbondale, Ill: The Core Institute: 1993.

6. The Carnegie Foundation for the Advancement of Teaching. ***Campus Life: In Search of Community.*** Princeton, NJ: Princeton University Press: 1990.

7. Straus R, Bacon SD. ***Drinking in College.*** New Haven, Conn: Yale University Press: 1953.

8. Berkowitz AD, Perkins HW. Problem drinking among college students: a review of recent research. ***J Am Coll Health.*** 1986;35:21–28.

9. Saltz R, Elandt D. College student drinking studies: 1976–1986. ***Contemp Drug Probl.*** 1986;13:117–157.

10. Haworth-Hoeppner S, Globetti G, Stem J, Morasco F. The quantity and frequency of drinking among undergraduates at a southern university. ***Int J Addict.*** 1989;24:829–857.

11. Liljestrand P. Quality in college student drinking research: conceptual and methodological issues. ***J Alcohol Drug Educ.*** 1993;38:1–36.

12. Hughes S, Dodder R. Alcohol consumption patterns among college populations. ***J Coll Student Personnel.*** 1983;20:257–264.

13. Johnston LD, O'Malley PM, Bachman JG. ***Drug Use Among American High School Seniors, College Students, and Young Adults,*** 1975–1990, Volume 2. Washington, DC: Government Printing Office; 1991. US Dept of Health and Human Services publication ADM 91-1835.

14. Wechsler H, McFadden M. Drinking among college students in New England. ***J Stud Alcohol.*** 1979; 40:969–996.

15. O'Hare TM. Drinking in college: consumption patterns, problems, sex differences, and legal drinking age. ***J Stud Alcohol.*** 1990; 51:536–541.

16. Engs RC, Hanson DJ. The drinking patterns and problems of college students: 1983. ***J Alcohol Drug Educ.*** 1985; 31:65–83.

17. Brennan AF, Walfish S, AuBuchon P. Alcohol use and abuse in college students, I: a review of individual and personality correlates. ***Int J Addict.*** 1986; 21:449–474.

18. Room R. Measuring alcohol consumption in the US: methods and rationales. In: Clark WB, Hilton ME, eds. ***Alcohol in America: Drinking Practices and Problems.*** Albany: State University of New York Press, 1991:26–50.

19. SAS Institute Inc. ***SAS/STAT User's Guide, Release 6.03*** ed. Cary, NC: SAS Institute Inc; 1988.

20. US Dept of Education. ***Digest of Educational Statistics.*** Washington, DC: National Center of Educational Statistics: 1993:180, 205.

21. ***Barron's Profiles of American Colleges.*** Hauppauge, NY: Barron's Educational Series Inc: 1992.

22. Midanik L. Validity of self-reported alcohol use: a literature review and assessment. *Br J Addict.* 1988; 83:1019–1030.

23. Cooper AM, Sobell MB, Sobell LC, Maisto SA. Validity of alcoholics' self-reports: duration data. *Int J Addict.* 1981;16:401–406.

24. Reinisch OJ, Bell RM, Ellickson PL. *How Accurate Are Adolescent Reports of Drug Use?* Santa Monica, Calif: RAND; 1991. RAND publication N-3189-CHF.

25. Room R. Survey versus sales data for the US. *Drink Drug Pract Surv.* 1971; 3:15–16.

26. CASA Commission on Substance Abuse at Colleges and Universities. *Rethinking Rites of Passage: Substance Abuse on America's Campuses.* New York, NY: Columbia University; June 1994.

QUESTIONS

1. This article's conclusions depend on the wording of the questions asked. A central question is "Think back over the last two weeks. How many times have you had five or more drinks in a row?" What do you think "in a row" means? Do you think the question is precise or fuzzy? Why was it asked this way?

2. How do you and people you know define "binge drinking"? How close is your definition to the definition used by Wechsler et al.?

3. At 44 of the 140 colleges surveyed, more than 50 percent of the students were binge drinkers. Does that sound alarming? Accurate? What might some of those colleges be?

4. Compare this scientific article with the op-ed Wechsler and his colleagues wrote for the *Chronicle of Higher Education* (p. 336). Note the important changes you see between this article and the op-ed. Are they changes in style? In audience? In format? In details? Which changes matter most to the overall impact of the essays?

MELVIN KONNER *Why the Reckless Survive*

IN A RECENT ELECTION Massachusetts rescinded its seat-belt law.[1] As a result some hundreds of citizens of that commonwealth have in the past year gone slamming into windshields instead of getting a pain in the neck from the shoulder belt. Quite a few are unnecessarily brain-damaged or dead. Such laws in fact make a difference. Americans in general use seat belts at a rate of about 20 percent; but in Texas, where failure to wear one can cost you not only your life but also fifty dollars, nearly seven people in ten wear them habitually—a fivefold increase since the law was passed in 1985. Having lived in Massachusetts for fifteen years, I considered it—wrongly, perhaps—the most

From Konner's book Why the Reckless Survive, and Other Secrets of Human Nature *(1990), an anthropological analysis of risk taking and adventure seeking.*

1. Massachusetts rescinded its seat belt law in 1986 and reimposed it in 1994.

sensible state in the union, so I was rather amazed by its recent collective decision.

But I shouldn't have been. All I needed to do was to look at my own behavior. I have, while coauthoring a book on health, sat at my word processor at three A.M. guzzling coffee and gobbling Oreo cookies by the dozen, pecking solemnly away about our need to take better care of ourselves. I could almost feel the fat from the cookies sinking into the arteries of my brain, the coffee laying the groundwork for future cardiac arrhythmias.

Why can't we follow our own advice, or others', even when we know it's right? Is it the heedless child in us, or the perverse, destructive teenager, or only the antiauthoritarian, freedom-loving adult that says, *I will do as I please, thank you*? Or could it be that there is something inevitable—even something good—about the taking of all these chances?

People don't think clearly about risk. This is no mere insult, but a conclusion that emerges from attempts by behavioral scientists to understand how people make decisions. In part these studies were sparked by the unprecedented demand for risk reduction that has emerged in recent years. How many cases of cancer do people consider acceptable nationally as a result of the widespread use of a food additive or an industrial chemical? None. How many accidents or near-accidents at nuclear power plants? None. How many airline crashes per decade? Basically, none.

5 We may consider the change good: doesn't it reflect a healthy increase in awareness of real risks? But consider that this is the same American public that, after years of education, wears seat belts at the rate of 20 percent and has reduced its cigarette smoking only somewhat. The widespread success of lotteries alone shows that people do not think or act rationally, even in their own self-interest.

So we ignore some risks and overestimate others. The conundrum for an evolutionist is simple. Natural selection should have relentlessly culled systematic biases in decision making, producing a rational organism that hews to the order of real cost-benefit analysis—an organism that behaves efficiently to minimize those ratios. How can evolution, with its supposedly relentless winnowing out of error, have preserved this bewildering array of dangerous habits?

We are highly sensitive to certain dangers. A Harris poll conducted in 1980 showed that 78 percent of the American public (as opposed to roughly half of business and government leaders) thought that risks in general were greater than they had been twenty years before. The greatest perceived risks were in the areas of crime and personal safety, international and domestic political stability, energy sources, and "the chemicals we use." Comfortable majorities of the general public (but only small minorities of the leadership groups) agreed with the statements "Society has only perceived the tip of the iceberg with regard to the risks associated with modern technology" and "Unless technological development is restrained, the overall safety of society will be jeopardized significantly in the next twenty years."

But the logic of our concerns is problematic. People are willing to pay indirectly large sums of money to reduce the risk of a nuclear accident or a cancer death from a chemical to levels they consider acceptably low. But they will not pay a much smaller amount for air bags in automobiles, that, inflating on impact, will save many more lives; and they will not stop smoking, although this risk-reducing measure would actually save money, both immediately and in the long term.

Apparently, irrational factors are at work. But before we consider them, and why we may be subject to them, it is worth looking at the realities of risk. John Urquhart and Klaus Heilmann, both physicians, have reviewed some of these realities in their book *Riskwatch: The Odds of Life*. There is a genuine hierarchy of danger. For example, the number of deaths linked to cigarette smoking in the United States is equivalent to three jumbo jets full of passengers crashing daily, day in and day out. We have fifty thousand traffic fatalities a year—almost the number of deaths we suffered during our entire involvement in Vietnam. Half involve drunk drivers, and a large proportion would be prevented by seat belts or air bags.

10 Yet neither of these sources of risk evokes the interest—indeed the fear—shown in response to possible nuclear accidents, or to toxic-shock syndrome caused by tampons, or even to homicide, all (for most of us) trivial risks by comparison to smoking or driving. If you tremble when you strap yourself into the seat of an airliner, you ought to really shudder when you climb onto your bicycle, since that is much more dangerous as a regular activity. As for homicide, the people most afraid of it are the ones least likely to be victimized. And the millions of women who stopped taking birth-control pills because of the risk of death from stroke did so in response to an annual probability of dying equal to about one fourth their routine risk of death in an automobile.

Urquhart and Heilmann deal with this quirkiness in our response to risk by developing a Safety-Degree Scale analogous to the Richter scale for earthquake severity. The units are logarithms of the cohort size necessary for one death to occur. Thus lightning, which kills fewer than one person per million exposed, has a safety degree of more than six, while motorcycling, which kills one in a thousand, has a safety degree of three; motorcycling is three orders of magnitude more dangerous. But they aren't perceived in that relation. In general, people will accept one to two orders of magnitude more danger in voluntary risks than they will in involuntary ones. And that is only one aspect of the quirkiness. Risks that result in many deaths at once will be perceived as worse than probabilistically equal risks that kill in a more distributed way. And any bad outcome that is reported unexpectedly—especially if its shock value is exploited—increases fear.

Chronic departures from rationality have been the subject of a major line of thought in economics, in which the most distinguished name is Herbert Simon's. Simon, a winner of the Nobel Memorial prize in economics, has for years criticized and occasionally ridiculed the economic decision theory known as subjective expected utility, or SEU. According to this classic approach, individuals face their life choices with full knowledge of the probability and value of all possible outcomes, and furthermore they possess an unambiguous value scale to measure utility—in plain English, they know a great deal, in advance, about the consequences of their choices, and, more important, they know what they want. In the real world, Simon points out, no such knowledge exists. Whether in the choices of executives or in those of consumers, knowledge is imperfect and values (at least to some extent) indeterminate and mercurial.

A similar point was demonstrated in laboratory experiments by psychologists Amos Tversky and Daniel Kahnemann, in which people are shown to be rather feeble in their abilities to choose among various outcomes. They are readily confused by differences in the language in which a problem is posed. In one study, Tversky and Kahnemann asked physicians to choose among possible programs to combat a hypothetical disease that was on the verge of killing six hundred people. The physicians favored a program guaranteed to save *two hundred lives* over one that had a one-third probability of saving everyone and a two-thirds probability of saving no one. Yet a second group of physicians favored the riskier program over one described as resulting in exactly *four hundred deaths*. They were, of course, rejecting the same alternative the previous group had chosen. The only difference was that it was now being described in terms of victims rather than survivors. Human decision making is rife with such framing errors, and analyzing them has become a cottage industry.

At least equally interesting is a new psychological view—advanced by Lola Lopes among others—that certain "errors" may not be errors at all. Lottery players can be shown to be irrational by multiplying the prize by the probability of winning, and comparing that number to the cost of the ticket. But that does not take into account the subjective value placed on becoming rich, or the fact that this may be someone's only chance for that outcome. Nor, of course, does it consider the thrill of playing.

15 But another aspect of this behavior clearly is irrational: people—especially, but not only, compulsive gamblers—have unrealistically high expectations of winning. On the average, in the larger game of life, they also have unrealistically high expectations of protection against losing. Linda Perloff and others have shown that people—average people—think that they will live longer than average, that they will have fewer diseases than average, and even that their marriages will last longer than average. Since average people are likely to have average rates of disease, death, and divorce, they are (in these studies) underestimating their risks—a tendency Lionel Tiger has summarized as a ubiquitous, biologically based human propensity to unwarranted optimism.

While these results fit well with the prevalence of risky behavior, they seem to contradict the findings about people's *over*estimate of the risk of violent crime, or terrorist attacks, or airline crashes, or nuclear-plant accidents. Part of this is resolvable by reference to the principle that risks beyond our control are more frightening than those we consider ourselves in charge of. So we drink and drive, and buckle the seat belt behind us, and light up another cigarette, on the strength of the illusion that to *these* risks at least, we are invulnerable; and we cancel the trip to Europe on the one-in-a-million chance of an Arab terrorist attack.

Three patterns, then, emerge in our misestimates. First, we prefer voluntary risks to involuntary ones—or, put another way, risks that we feel we have some control over to those that we feel we don't. By the way we drive and react to cues on the road, we think, we reduce our risk to such a low level that seat belts add little protection. But in the case of the terrorist attack or the nuclear-plant accident, we feel we have no handle on the risks. (We seem especially to resent and fear risks that are imposed on us by others, especially if for their own benefit. If I want to smoke myself to death, we seem to say, it's my own business; but if some company is trying to put something over on me with asbestos or nerve gas, I'll be furious.)

Second, we prefer familiar risks to strange ones. The homicide during a mugging, or the airliner hijacked in Athens, or the nerve gas leaking from an armed forces train, get our attention and so loom much larger in our calculations than they should in terms of real risk. Third, deaths that come in bunches—the jumbo-jet crash of the disaster movie—are more frightening than those that come in a steady trickle, even though the latter may add up to more risk when the counting is done. This principle may be related in some way to the common framing error in which people in Tversky and Kahnemann's studies will act more strongly to prevent two hundred deaths in six hundred people than they will to guarantee four hundred survivors from the same group. Framing the risk in terms of death rather than survival biases judgment.

But there is yet another, more interesting complication. "The general public," "average people," "human" rational or irrational behavior—these categories obscure the simple fact that people differ in these matters.

20 Average people knowingly push their cholesterol levels upward, but only a third pay essentially no attention to doctors' orders when it comes to modifying their behavior (smoking, or eating a risky diet) in the setting of an established illness worsened by that behavior. Average people leave their seat belts unbuckled, but only some people ride motorcycles, and fewer still race or do stunts with them. Average people play lotteries, friendly poker, and church bingo, but an estimated one to four million Americans are pathological gamblers, relentlessly destroying their lives and the lives of those close to them by compulsively taking outrageous financial risks.

Psychologists have only begun to address these individual differences, but several different lines of research suggest that there is such a thing as a risktaking or sensation-seeking personality. For example, studies of alcohol, tobacco, and caffeine abuse have found these three forms of excess to be correlated, and also to be related to various other measures of risk taking.

For many years psychologist Marvin Zuckerman, of the University of Delaware, and his colleagues have been using the Sensation Seeking Scale, a questionnaire designed to address these issues directly. Empirically, the questions fall along four dimensions: *thrill and adventure seeking,* related to interest in physical risk taking, as in skydiving and mountain climbing; *experience seeking,* reflecting a wider disposition to try new things, in art, music, travel, friendship, or even drugs; *disinhibition,* the hedonistic pursuit of pleasure through activities like social drinking, partying, sex, and gambling; and *boredom susceptibility,* an aversion to routine work and dull people.

At least the first three of these factors have held up in many samples, of both sexes and various ages, in England and America, but there are systematic differences. Males always exceed females, and sensation seeking in general declines in both sexes with age. There is strongly suggestive evidence of a genetic predisposition: 233 pairs of identical twins had a correlation of 0.60 in sensation seeking, while 138 nonidentical twin pairs had a corresponding correlation of only 0.21.

More interesting than these conventional calculations is a series of studies showing that sensation seeking, as measured by the questionnaire, has significant physiological correlates. For example, heart-rate change in reaction to novelty is greater in sensation seekers, as is brain-wave response to increasingly intense stimulation. The activity of monoamine oxidase (MAO), an enzyme that breaks down certain neurotransmitters (the chemicals that transmit signals between brain cells), is another correlate. Sensation seekers have less MAO activity, suggesting that neurotransmitters that might be viewed as stimulants may persist longer in their brains. Finally, the sex hormones, testosterone and estrogen, show higher levels in sensation seekers.

But in addition this paper-and-pencil test score correlates with real behavior. High scores engage in more frequent, more promiscuous, and more unusual sex; consume more drugs, alcohol, cigarettes, and even spicy food; volunteer more for experiments and other unusual activities; gamble more; and court more physical danger. In the realm of the abnormal, the measure is correlated with hypomania, and in the realm of the criminal, with psychopathy. 25

In other words, something measured by this test has both biological and practical significance. Furthermore, independent studies by Frank Farley and his colleagues at the University of Wisconsin, using a different instrument and a somewhat distinct measure they call thrill seeking, have confirmed and extended these findings. For example, in prison populations fighting and escape attempts are higher in those who score high on thrill seeking. But Farley also emphasizes positive outcomes—a well-established correlation between sensation seeking and the extraverted personality underscores the possibility that some such people are well primed for leadership.

We can now return to the main question: how could all this irrationality have been left untouched by natural selection? Herbert Simon, in an accessible, even lyrical, summary of his thought, the 1983 book *Reason in Human Affairs,* surprised some of us in anthropology and biology who are more or less constantly railing against the un-Darwinian musings of social scientists. He shows a quite incisive understanding of Darwin's theories and of very recent significant refinements of them.

But my own anthropological heart was most warmed by passages such as this one: "If this [situation] is not wholly descriptive of the world we live in today . . . it certainly describes the world in which human rationality evolved: the world of the cavemen's ancestors, and of the cavemen themselves. In that world . . . periodically action had to be taken to deal with hunger, or to flee danger, or to secure protection against the coming winter. Rationality could focus on dealing with one or a few problems at a time. . . ." The appeal to the world of our ancestors, the hunters and gatherers, is as explicit as I could wish. As Simon recognizes, this is the world in which our rationality, limited as it is, evolved. It could not be much better now than it needed to be then, because less perfect rationality would not have been selected against; and we, the descendants of those hunters and gatherers, would have inherited their imperfections.

The result is what Simon calls "bounded rationality"—a seat-of-the-pants, day-by-day sort of problem solving that, far from pretending to assess all possible outcomes against a clear spectrum of values, attempts no more than to get by. "Putting out fires" is another way of describing it; and it follows directly from the concept of economic behavior that made Simon famous: "satisficing," the notion that people are just trying to solve the problem at hand in a way that is "good enough"—his practical answer to those too-optimistic constructions of economists, "maximizing" and "optimizing."

30 Simon has perceived that the basic human environment did not call for optimal decision making, in the modern risk-benefit sense of the phrase; thus our imperfection, this "bounded rationality." But this does not explain the systematic departures from rationality—the preference for "controllable" or familiar rather than "uncontrollable" or strange risks, or the particular fear attached to large disasters. And it does not explain, especially, the sense of invulnerability of risk takers. Certain kinds of recklessness are easy to handle by looking at the specific evolutionary provenance of certain motives. Kristin Luker, a sociologist at the University of California at San Diego, studied contraceptive risk taking and uncovered what often seemed an unconscious desire for a baby. It is no challenge to reconcile this with evolutionary theory; a Darwinian couple ought to take such risks right and left. Sexual indiscretions in general could be covered by a similar line of argument: sexy sensation seekers perpetuate their genes. Slightly more interesting are the specific risks involved in certain human culinary preferences. We overdo it on fats and sweets because our ancestors were rewarded for such excesses with that inch of insulation needed to carry them through shortages. Death by atherosclerosis may be a pervasive threat today, but for most of the past three million years it was a consummation devoutly to be wished.

But we are still far from the comprehensive explanation of recklessness we need. For this we must look to the darker side of human nature, as expressed in that same ancestral environment. Martin Daly and Margo Wilson, both psychologists at McMaster University in Ontario, explore this matter directly in a book called *Homicide*. Although their analysis is restricted to only one highly dramatic form of risk taking, it is paradigmatic of the problem.

Homicides occur in all human societies, and a frequent cause is a quarrel over something seemingly trivial—an insult, a misunderstanding, a disagreement about a fact neither combatant cares about. Of course, these conflicts are never *really* trivial; they are about status and honor—which in practical terms means whether and how much you can be pushed around. And on this will depend your access to food, land, women (the participants are almost always male)—in short, most of what matters in life and in natural selection. In societies where heads are hunted or coups counted, the process is more formalized, but the principle is similar.

If you simulate, as Daly and Wilson do, a series of fights in which individuals with different risk propensities—low, medium, and high—encounter each other, the high-risk individuals invariably have the highest mortality. But any assumption that winning increases Darwinian fitness—virtually certain to be correct in most environments—leads to predominance of high- or medium-risk individuals. Their candles burn at both ends, but they leave more genes.

The underlying assumption is that the environment is a dangerous one, but this assumption is sensible. The environments of our ancestors must have been full of danger. "Nothing ventured, nothing gained" must have been a cardinal rule; and yet venturing meant exposure to grave risk: fire, heights, cold, hunger, predators, human enemies. And all this risk has to be seen against a background of mortality from causes outside of human control—especially disease. With an average life expectancy at birth of thirty years, with a constant high probability of dying from pneumonia or malaria—the marginal utility, in economic terms, of strict avoidance of danger would have been much lower than it is now, perhaps negligible. In Oscar Lewis's studies of the Mexican "culture of poverty" and in Eliot Liebow's studies of poor black street-corner men, the point is clearly made: the failure of such people to plan for the future is not irrational—they live for the day because they know that they have no future.

35 To die, in Darwinian terms, is not to lose the game. Individuals risk or sacrifice their lives for their kin. Sacrifice for offspring is ubiquitous in the animal world, and the examples of maternal defense of the young in mammals and male death in the act of copulation in insects have become familiar. But great risks are taken and sacrifices made for other relatives as well. Consider the evisceration of the worker honeybee in the act of stinging an intruder and the alarm call of a bird or ground squirrel, calling the predator's attention to itself while warning its relatives. During our own evolution small, kin-based groups might have gained much from having a minority of reckless sensation seekers in the ranks—people who wouldn't hesitate to snatch a child from a pack of wild dogs or to fight an approaching grass fire with a counterfire.

In any case, both sensation seekers and people in general should have taken their risks selectively. They may have found it advantageous to take risks with the seemingly controllable and familiar, even while exaggerating the risk of the unknown, and hedging it around with all sorts of taboo and ritual. It is difficult to imagine a successful encounter with a volcano, but an early human would have had at least a fighting chance against a lion. And we, their descendants, fear toxic nuclear waste but leave our seat belts unbuckled.

Why can't we adjust our personal behavior to our modern middle-class spectrum of risks? Because we are just not built to cut it that finely. We are not designed for perfectly rational calculations, or to calibrate such relatively unimpressive risks. For many of us, life seems compromised by such calculations; they too have a cost—in effort, in freedom, in self-image, in fun. And the fun is not incidental. It is evolution's way of telling us what we were designed for.

Sensation seeking fulfills two of the three cardinal criteria for evolution by natural selection: it varies in the population, and the varieties are to some extent inheritable. In any situation in which the varieties give rise in addition to different numbers of offspring, evolution will occur. The notion that riskier types, because they suffer higher mortality, must slowly disappear is certainly wrong for many environments, and it may still be wrong even for ours.

Ideally, of course, one would want a human organism that could take the risks that—despite the dangers—enhance fitness, and leave aside the risks that don't. But life and evolution are not that perfect. The result of the vastly long evolutionary balancing act is a most imperfect organism. The various forms of personal risk taking often hang together; you probably can't be the sort of person who makes sure to maintain perfectly safe and healthy habits, and yet reflexively take the risks needed to ensure survival and reproductive success in the basic human environment. If you are designed, emotionally, for survival and reproduction, then you are not designed for perfect safety.

40 So when my father buckles his seat belt behind him, and my brother keeps on smoking, and my friend rides her motorcycle to work every day, it isn't because, or only because, they somewhat underestimate the risks. My father wants the full sense of competence and freedom that he has always had in driving, since long before seat belts were dreamed of. My brother wants the sense of calm that comes out of the cigarette. My friend wants to hear the roar of the Harley and feel the wind in her hair. And they want the risk, because risk taking, for them, is part of being alive.

As for me, when I avoid those risks, I feel safe and virtuous but perhaps a little cramped. And I suspect that, like many people who watch their diet carefully—despite the lapses—and exercise more or less scrupulously and buckle up religiously, I am a little obsessed with immortality, with the prospect of controlling that which cannot be controlled. I know I am doing the sensible thing—my behavior matches, most of the time, the spectrum of real probabilities. But against what scale of value? I sometimes think that the more reckless among us may have something to teach the careful about the sort of immortality that comes from living fully every day.

QUESTIONS

1. Mark the research and the researchers' disciplines that Konner relies on. How many kinds of studies does he bring together? What are they?

2. Konner is interested in the effects of biology on human behavior. Locate the evidence he draws from biology and explain his uses of it.

3. Konner introduces and concludes this essay with autobiographical material; he stations himself with respect to his subject. What does the autobiographical material contribute to this essay?

4. Write an essay in which you describe your own or someone else's irrational behavior and speculate about its causes.

Edward O. Wilson *Intelligent Evolution*

> We must acknowledge, as it seems to me, that man with all his noble qualities, with sympathy which feels for the most debased, with benevolence which extends not only to other men but to the humblest living creature, with his god-like intellect which has penetrated into the movements and constitution of the solar system—with all these exalted powers—Man still bears in his bodily frame the indelible stamp of his lowly origin.
>
> —Charles Darwin[1]
> *The Descent of Man, and Selection in Relation to Sex* (1871)

Great scientific discoveries are like sunrises. They illuminate first the steeples of the unknown, then its dark hollows. Such expansive influence has been enjoyed by the scientific writings of Charles Darwin. For over 150 years his books * * * have spread light on the living world and the human condition. They have not lost their freshness: more than any other work in history's scientific canon, they are both timeless and persistently inspirational.

The four classics, flowing along one to the next like a well-wrought narrative, trace the development of Darwin's thought across almost all of his adult life. The first, *Voyage of the Beagle* (1845), one of literature's great travel books, is richly stocked with observations in natural history of the kind that were to guide the young Darwin toward his evolutionary worldview. Next comes the "one long argument," as he later put it, of *On the Origin of Species* (1859), arguably history's most influential book. In it the now middle-aged Darwin massively documents the evidences of organic evolution and introduces the theory of natural selection. *The Descent of Man* (1871) then addresses the burning topic foretold in *On the Origin of Species*: "Light will be thrown on the origin of man and his history." Finally, *The Expression of the Emotions in Man and Animals* (1872) draws close to the heart of the matter that concerns us all: the origin and nature of mind, the "citadel" that Darwin could see but knew that science at the time could not conquer.

The adventure that Darwin launched on all our behalf, and which continues into the twenty-first century, is driven by a deceptively simple idea, of

First published in Harvard Magazine *(November/December 2005); a slightly different version appeared as a general introduction to* From So Simple a Beginning: The Four Great Books of Charles Darwin *(2005). The drawings come from the American edition of Charles Darwin's* The Descent of Man, and Selection in Relation to Sex *(1871).*

1. English naturalist (1809–1882) who theorized that living beings evolve through natural selection.

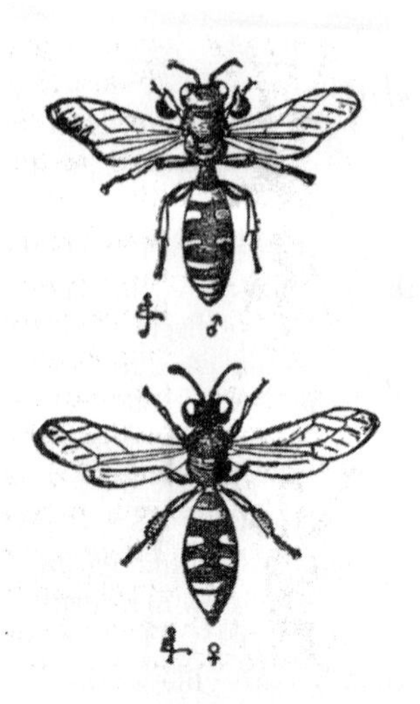

Crabo cribrarius.

which Darwin's friend and staunch supporter Thomas Henry Huxley[2] said, and spoke for many to follow, "How extremely stupid of me not to have thought of that!" Evolution by natural selection is perhaps the only one true law unique to biological systems, as opposed to nonliving physical systems, and in recent decades it has taken on the solidity of a mathematical theorem. It states simply that if a population of organisms contains multiple hereditary variants in some trait (say, red versus blue eyes in a bird population), and if one of these variants succeeds in contributing more offspring to the next generation than the other variants, the overall composition of the population changes, and *evolution has occurred*. Further, if new genetic variants appear regularly in the population (by mutation or immigration), *evolution never ends*. Think of red-eyed and blue-eyed birds in a breeding population, and let the red-eyed birds be better adapted to the environment. The population will in time come to consist mostly or entirely of red-eyed birds. Now let green-eyed mutants appear that are even better adapted to the environment that the red-eyed form. As a consequence the species eventually becomes green-eyed. Evolution has thus taken two more small steps.

The full importance of Darwin's theory can be better understood by realizing that modern biology is guided by two overwhelmingly powerful and creative ideas. The first is that all biological processes are ultimately obedient to even though far from fully explained by, the laws of physics and chemistry. The second is that all biological processes arose through evolution of these physicochemical systems through natural selection. The first principle is concerned with the *how* of biology. The second is concerned with the ways the systems adapted to the environment over periods of time long enough for evolution to occur—in other words the *why* of biology.

5

Knowledge addressing the first principle is called functional biology; that addressing the second is called evolutionary biology. If a moving automobile were an organism, functional biology would explain how it is constructed and operates, while evolutionary biology would reconstruct its origin and history—how it came to be made and its journey thus far.

The impact of the theory of evolution by natural selection, nowadays grown very sophisticated (and often referred to as the Modern Synthesis), has been profound. To the extent it can be upheld, and the evidence to date has done so compellingly, we must conclude that life has diversified on Earth

2. English scientist (1825–1895) who defended and popularized Darwin's theory of evolution.

autonomously without any kind of external guidance. Evolution in a pure Darwinian world has no goal or purpose: the exclusive driving force is random mutations sorted out by natural selection from one generation to the next.

What then are we to make of the purposes and goals obviously chosen by human beings? They are, in Darwinian interpretation, processes evolved as adaptive devices by an otherwise purposeless natural selection. Evolution by natural selection means, finally, that the essential qualities of the human mind also evolved autonomously. Humanity was thus born of Earth. However elevated in power over the rest of life, however exalted in self-image, we were descended from animals by the same blind force that created those animals, and we remain a member species of this planet's biosphere.

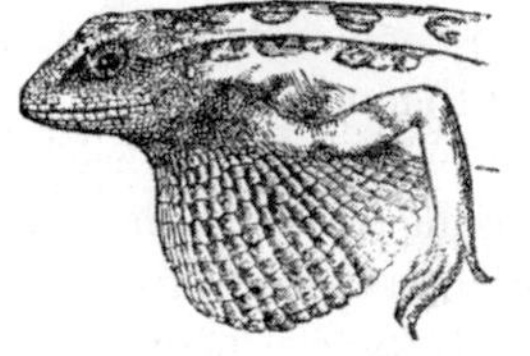

Top: *Tragelaphus strepsiceros.* Bottom: *Sitana minor* (male with the gular pouch expanded).

The revolution in astronomy begun by Nicolaus Copernicus[3] in 1543 proved that Earth is not the center of the universe, nor even the center of the solar system. The revolution begun by Darwin was even more humbling: it showed that humanity is not the center of creation, and not its purpose either. But in freeing our minds from our imagined demigod bondage, even at the price of humility, Darwin turned our attention to the astounding power of the natural creative process and the magnificence of its products:

> There is grandeur in this view of life, with its several powers, having been originally breathed into a few forms or into one; and that, whilst this planet has gone cycling on according to the fixed law of gravity, from so simple a beginning endless forms most beautiful and most wonderful have been, and are being, evolved.
>
> Darwin, *On the Origin of Species* (first edition, 1859)

---

3. Polish astronomer (1473–1543) who posited that the solar system is heliocentric, with the sun rather than the earth at its center.

> If I lived twenty more years and was able to work, how I should have to modify the *Origin*, and how much the views on all points will have to be modified! Well, it is a beginning, and that is something.
>
> —CHARLES DARWIN
> Letter to J. D. Hooker,[4] 1869

Darwin lived thirteen more years after writing this letter to Joseph Hooker, and he did manage to modify the theory of evolution by natural selection, expanding it in *The Descent of Man* (1871) to include human origins and in *The Expression of the Emotions in Man and Animals* (1872) to address the evolution of instinct. The ensuing 130 years have seen an enormous growth of the Darwinian heritage. Joined with molecular and cellular biology, that accumulated knowledge is today a large part of modern biology. Its centrality justifies the famous remark made by the evolutionary geneticist Theodosius Dobzhansky[5] in 1973 that "nothing in biology makes sense except in the light of evolution." In fact, nothing in science as a whole has been more firmly established by interwoven factual documentation, or more illuminating, than the universal occurrence of biological evolution. Further, few natural processes have been more convincingly explained than evolution by the theory of natural selection or, as it is popularly called, Darwinism.

10 Thus it is surpassingly strange that half of Americans recently polled (2004) not only do not believe in evolution by natural selection but do not believe in evolution at all. Americans are certainly capable of belief, and with rocklike conviction if it originates in religious dogma. In evidence is the 60 percent that accept the prophecies of the Book of Revelation[6] as truth, and yet in more evidence is the weight that faith-based positions hold in political life. Most of the religious Right opposes the teaching of evolution in public schools, either by an outright ban on the subject or, at the least, by insisting that it be treated as "only a theory" rather than a "fact."

Yet biologists, particularly those statured by the peer review and publication of substantial personal research on the subject in leading journals of science, are unanimous in concluding that evolution is a *fact*. The evidence they and thousands of others have adduced over 150 years falls together in intricate and interlocking detail. The multitudinous examples range from the small changes in DNA[7] sequences observed as they occur in real time to finely graded sequences within larger evolutionary changes in the fossil record. Further, on the basis of comparably firm evidence, natural selection grows ever stronger as the prevailing explanation of evolution.

4. English botanist (1817–1911) and champion of Darwin's evolutionary theory.
5. Ukrainian evolutionary biologist and geneticist (1900–1975).
6. The final book of the New Testament, which contains visions of apocalypse.
7. Deoxyribonucleic acid, which contains and encodes genetic information in living organisms.

Top: *Cercopithecus petaurista.*
Bottom, from left to right: *Semnopithecus comatus, Cebus capucinus, Ateles marginatus,* and *Cebus vellerosus.*

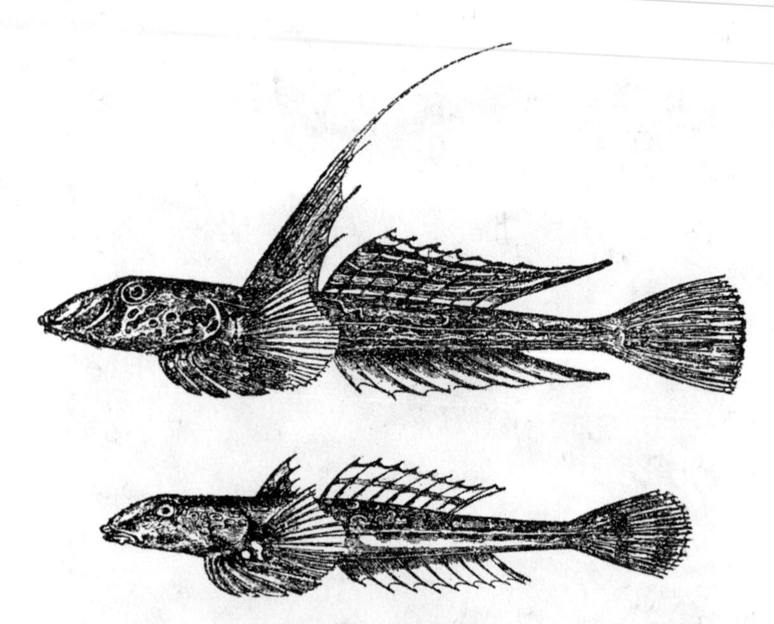

Callionymus lyra (upper figure, male; lower figure, female).

Many who accept the fact of evolution cannot, however, on religious grounds, accept the operation of blind chance and the absence of divine purpose implicit in natural selection. They support the alternative explanation of intelligent design. The reasoning they offer is not based on evidence but on the lack of it. The formulation of intelligent design is a default argument advanced in support of a non sequitur. It is in essence the following: There are some phenomena that have not yet been explained and that (and most importantly) the critics personally cannot imagine being explained; therefore there must be a supernatural designer at work. The designer is seldom specified, but in the canon of intelligent design it is most certainly not Satan and his angels, nor any god or gods conspicuously different from those accepted in the believer's faith.

Flipping the scientific argument upside down, the intelligent designers join the strict creationists (who insist that no evolution ever occurred in the first place) by arguing that scientists resist the supernatural theory because it is counter to their own personal secular beliefs. This may have a kernel of truth; everybody suffers from some amount of bias. But in this case bias is easily overcome. The critics forget how the reward system in science works. Any researcher who can prove the existence of intelligent design within the accepted framework of science will make history and achieve eternal fame. He will prove at last that *science and religious dogma are compatible!* Even a combined Nobel Prize and Templeton Prize (the latter designed to encourage search for just such harmony) would fall short as proper recognition. Every scientist would like to accomplish such an epoch-making advance. But no one has even come close, because unfortunately there is no evidence, no theory, and no criteria for proof that even marginally might pass for science. There is

Dog "in a humble and affectionate frame of mind."

only the residue of hoped for default, which steadily shrinks as the science of biology expands.

In all of the history of science only one other disparity of comparable magnitude to evolution has occurred between a scientific event and the impact it has had on the public mind. This was the discovery by Copernicus that Earth and therefore humanity are not the center of the universe, and the universe is not a closed spherical bubble. Copernicus delayed publication of his masterwork *On the Revolution of the Heavenly Spheres* until the year of his death (1543). For his extension of the idea subsequently, Bruno was burned at the stake, and for its documentation Galileo was shown the instruments of torture at Rome and remained under house arrest for the remainder of his life.[8]

Today we live in a less barbaric age, but an otherwise comparable disjunction between science and religion, the one born of Darwinism, still roils the public mind. Why does such intense and pervasive resistance to evolution continue 150 years after the publication of *The Origin of Species*, and in the teeth of the overwhelming accumulated evidence favoring it? The answer is simply that the Darwinian revolution, even more than the Copernican revolution, challenges the prehistoric and still-regnant self-image of humanity. Evolution by natural selection, to be as concise as possible, has changed everything.

In the more than slightly schizophrenic circumstances of the present era, global culture is divided into three opposing images of the human condition, each logically consistent within its own, independent premises. The dominant of these hypotheses, exemplified by the creation myths of the Abrahamic mono-

8. Giordano Bruno (1548–1600), Italian astronomer, priest, and philosopher burned at the stake for his unconventional beliefs, including in the existence of planets outside our solar system; Galileo Galilei (1564–1642), Italian astronomer whose research supported Copernicus's heliocentric view of the universe.

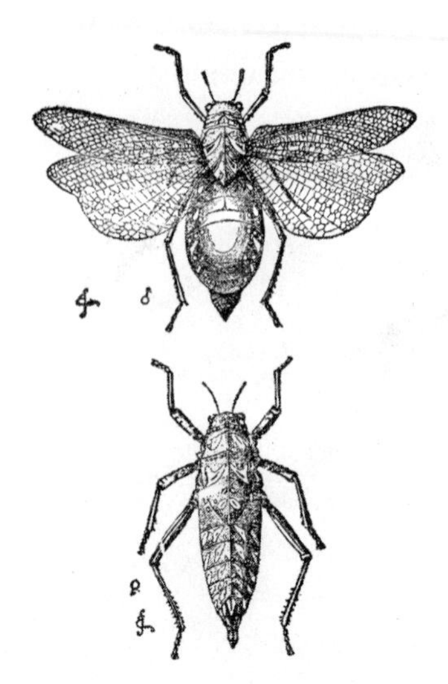

Pneumora.

theistic religions[9] (Judaism, Christianity, and Islam), sees humanity as a creation of God. He brought us into being and He guides us still as father, judge, and friend. We interpret his will from sacred scriptures and the wisdom of ecclesiastical authorities.

The second worldview is that of political behaviorism. Still beloved by the now rapidly fading Marxist-Leninist[10] states, it says that the brain is largely a blank slate devoid of any inborn inscription beyond reflexes and primitive bodily urges. As a consequence the mind originates almost wholly as a result of learning, and it is the product of a culture that itself evolves by historical contingency. Because there is no biologically based "human nature," people can be molded to the best possible political and economic system, namely, as urged upon the world through most of the twentieth century, communism.[11] In practical politics, this belief has been repeatedly tested and, after economic collapses and tens of millions of deaths in a dozen dysfunctional states, is generally deemed a failure.

Both of these worldviews, God-centered religion and atheistic communism, are opposed by a third and in some ways more radical worldview, scientific humanism. Still held by only a tiny minority of the world's population, it considers humanity to be a biological species that evolved over millions of years in a biological world, acquiring unprecedented intelligence yet still guided by complex inherited emotions and biased channels of learning. Human nature exists, and it was self-assembled. It is the commonality of the hereditary responses and propensities that define our species. Having arisen by evolution during the far simpler conditions in which humanity lived during more than 99 percent of its existence, it forms the behavioral part of what, in *The Descent of Man*, Darwin called the indelible stamp of our lowly origin.

To understand biological human nature in depth is to drain the fever swamps of religious and blank-slate dogma.[12] But it also imposes the heavy burden of individual choice that goes with intellectual freedom.

9. Jewish, Christian, and Muslim faiths that trace their lineage to the ancient Hebrew Abraham (ca. 2000 B.C.E.–1500 B.C.E.).

10. Socialist thinking in the style or tradition of German thinker Karl Marx (1818–1883) and Russian politician Vladimir Lenin (1870–1924).

11. A social philosophy that seeks to eliminate class structure and private property in favor of common ownership.

12. The idea that humans are born without personality or knowledge and that their experience is entirely responsible for forming them.

Rhynchaea capensis.

Such was the long journey for Darwin, the architect of the naturalistic worldview. He began his voyage on the *Beagle* as a devout Christian who trained for the ministry. "Whilst on board the *Beagle* I was quite orthodox," he wrote much later in his autobiography, "and I remember being heartily laughed at by several of the officers (though themselves orthodox) for quoting the Bible as an unanswerable authority on some point of morality." His later drift from the religion of his birth was stepwise and slow. Still on H.M.S. *Beagle* during its circumnavigation of the globe (1831–1836) he came to believe that the "false history" and reports of God's vengeful feelings made the Old Testament "no more to be trusted than the sacred books of the Hindoos,[13] or the beliefs of any barbarian." The miracles of Jesus seemed to him to suggest that people living at the time of the Gospels were "ignorant and credulous to a degree almost incomprehensible by us." The growth of disbelief was so slow that Darwin felt no distress. In a striking passage of his autobiography he expressed his final and complete rejection of Christian dogma based solely on blind faith: 20

13. Hindus.

> I can indeed hardly see how anyone ought to wish Christianity to be true; for if so the plain language of the text seems to show that the men who do not believe, and this would include my Father, Brother and almost all my best friends, will be everlastingly punished. And that is a damnable doctrine.

Did Charles Darwin recant in his last days, as some religious critics have hopefully suggested? There is not a shred of evidence that he did or that he was presented with any reason to do so. Further, it would have been wholly contrary to the deliberate, careful manner with which he approached every subject.

The great naturalist did not abandon Abrahamic and other religious dogmas because of his discovery of evolution by natural selection, as one might reasonably suppose. The reverse occurred. The shedding of blind faith gave him the intellectual fearlessness to explore human evolution wherever logic and evidence took him. And so he set forth boldly, in *The Descent of Man* to track the origin of humanity, and in *The Expression of the Emotions in Man and Animals* to address the evolution of instinct. Thus was born scientific humanism, the only worldview compatible with science's growing knowledge of the real world and the laws of nature.

So, will science and religion find common ground, or at least agree to divide the fundamentals into mutually exclusive domains? A great many well-meaning scholars believe that such rapprochement is both possible and desirable. A few disagree, and I am one of them. I think Darwin would have held to the same position. The battle line is, as it has ever been, in biology. The inexorable growth of this science continues to widen, not to close, the tectonic gap between science and faith-based religion.

Rapprochement may be neither possible nor desirable. There is something deep in religious belief that divides people and amplifies societal conflict. In the early part of this century, the toxic mix of religion and tribalism has become so dangerous as to justify taking seriously the alternative view, that humanism based on science is the effective antidote, the light and the way at last placed before us.

25 In any case, the dilemma to be solved is truly profound. On the one side the input of religion on human history has been beneficent in many ways. It has generated much of which is best in culture, including the ideals of altruism and public service. From the beginning of history it has inspired the arts. Creation myths were in a sense the beginning of science itself. Fabricating them was the best the early scribes could do to explain the universe and human existence.

Yet the high risk is the ease with which alliances between religions and tribalism are made. Then comes bigotry and the dehumanization of infidels. Our gods, the true believer asserts, stand against your false idols, our spiritual purity against your corruption, our divinely sanctioned knowledge against your errancy. In past ages the posture provided an advantage. It united each tribe during life-and-death struggles with other tribes. It buoyed the devotees with a sense of superiority. It sacralized tribal laws and mores, and encouraged altruistic behaviors. Through sacred rites it lent solemnity to the passages of life.

And it comforted the anxious and afflicted. For all this and more it gave people an identity and purpose, and vouchsafed tribal fitness—yet, unfortunately, at the expense of less united or otherwise less fortunate tribes.

Religions continue both to render their special services and to exact their heavy costs. Can scientific humanism do as well or better, at a lower cost? Surely that ranks as one of the great unanswered questions of philosophy. It is the noble yet troubling legacy that Charles Darwin left us.

Questions

1. As the contextual note explains, Edward Wilson wrote this essay to introduce a new edition of the scientific works of Charles Darwin. What parts of the essay provide information about Darwin and his work? What parts extend Darwin's theories to present-day debates about evolution and intelligent design? Why does Wilson arrange these parts in the order they appear?

2. Wilson uses similes (comparisons with *like* or *as*) and metaphors (comparisons without connectives) to explain key concepts. Analyze the similes in paragraphs 1 (sunrises), 5 (automobile), and 13 (designers), and explain their function in the argument.

3. In the last section of the essay, Wilson defines three worldviews: religious, Marxist-Leninist, and scientific. How does he define each? How do his classifications and definitions help advance his argument in this essay?

4. Choose one of Darwin's four books or one of the scientists Wilson mentions. Do research about your choice, and write a brief account of its importance in the history of science.

Stephen Jay Gould *Darwin's Middle Road*

"We began to sail up the narrow strait lamenting," narrates Odysseus. "For on the one hand lay Scylla, with twelve feet all dangling down; and six necks exceeding long, and on each a hideous head, and therein three rows of teeth set thick and close, full of black death. And on the other mighty Charybdis sucked down the salt sea water.[1] As often as she belched it forth, like a cauldron on a great fire she would seethe up through all her troubled deeps." Odysseus managed to swerve around Charybdis, but Scylla grabbed six of his finest

For many years Gould wrote a monthly column for the magazine Natural History. *This essay appeared there in December 1979 and was reprinted in Gould's collection* The Panda's Thumb *(1980).*

1. Scylla was a female monster who lived in a cave and threatened Odysseus and his sailors in the *Odyssey*. Located opposite it was Charybdis, a whirlpool in the narrow channel of the Strait of Messina between Sicily and mainland Italy.

men and devoured them in his sight—"the most pitiful thing mine eyes have seen of all my travail in searching out the paths of the sea."

False lures and dangers often come in pairs in our legends and metaphors—consider the frying pan and the fire, or the devil and the deep blue sea. Prescriptions for avoidance either emphasize a dogged steadiness—the straight and narrow of Christian evangelists—or an averaging between unpleasant alternatives—the golden mean of Aristotle. The idea of steering a course between undesirable extremes emerges as a central prescription for a sensible life.

The nature of scientific creativity is both a perennial topic of discussion and a prime candidate for seeking a golden mean. The two extreme positions have not been directly competing for allegiance of the unwary. They have, rather, replaced each other sequentially, with one now in the ascendency, the other eclipsed.

The first—inductivism—held that great scientists are primarily great observers and patient accumulators of information. For new and significant theory, the inductivists claimed, can only arise from a firm foundation of facts. In this architectural view, each fact is a brick in a structure built without blueprints. Any talk or thought about theory (the completed building) is fatuous and premature before the bricks are set. Inductivism once commanded great prestige within science, and even represented an "official" position of sorts, for it touted, however falsely, the utter honesty, complete objectivity, and almost automatic nature of scientific progress towards final and incontrovertible truth.

5 Yet, as its critics so rightly claimed, inductivism also depicted science as a heartless, almost inhuman discipline offering no legitimate place to quirkiness, intuition, and all the other subjective attributes adhering to our vernacular notion of genius. Great scientists, the critics claimed, are distinguished more by their powers of hunch and synthesis, than their skill in experiment or observation. The criticisms of inductivism are certainly valid and I welcome its dethroning during the past thirty years as a necessary prelude to better understanding. Yet, in attacking it so strongly, some critics have tried to substitute an alternative equally extreme and unproductive in its emphasis on the essential subjectivity of creative thought. In this "eureka" view, creativity is an ineffable something, accessible only to persons of genius. It arises like a bolt of lightning, unanticipated, unpredictable and unanalyzable—but the bolts strike only a few special people. We ordinary mortals must stand in awe and thanks. (The name refers, of course, to the legendary story of Archimedes running naked through the streets of Syracuse shouting eureka [I have discovered it] when water displaced by his bathing body washed the scales abruptly from his eyes and suggested a method for measuring volumes.)

I am equally disenchanted by both these opposing extremes. Inductivism reduces genius to dull, rote operations; eurekaism grants it an inaccessible status more in the domain of intrinsic mystery than in a realm where we might understand and learn from it. Might we not marry the good features of each view, and abandon both the elitism of eurekaism and the pedestrian qualities of inductivism? May we not acknowledge the personal and subjective character of creativity, but still comprehend it as a mode of thinking that emphasizes or exaggerates capacities sufficiently common to all of us that we may at least understand if not hope to imitate?

In the hagiography of science, a few men hold such high positions that all arguments must apply to them if they are to have any validity. Charles Darwin, as the principal saint of evolutionary biology, has therefore been presented both as an inductivist and as a primary example of eurekaism. I will attempt to show that these interpretations are equally inadequate, and that recent scholarship on Darwin's own odyssey towards the theory of natural selection supports an intermediate position.

So great was the prestige of inductivism in his own day, that Darwin himself fell under its sway and, as an old man, falsely depicted his youthful accomplishments in its light. In an autobiography, written as a lesson in morality for his children and not intended for publication, he penned some famous lines that misled historians for nearly a hundred years. Describing his path to the theory of natural selection, he claimed: "I worked on true Baconian principles, and without any theory collected facts on a wholesale scale."[2]

The inductivist interpretation focuses on Darwin's five years aboard the *Beagle* and explains his transition from a student for the ministry to the nemesis of preachers as the result of his keen powers of observation applied to the whole world. Thus, the traditional story goes, Darwin's eyes opened wider and wider as he saw, in sequence, the bones of giant South American fossil mammals, the turtles and finches of the Galapagos, and the marsupial fauna of Australia. The truth of evolution and its mechanism of natural selection crept up gradually upon him as he sifted facts in a sieve of utter objectivity.

The inadequacies of this tale are best illustrated by the falsity of its conventional premier example—the so-called Darwin's finches of the Galapagos. We now know that although these birds share a recent and common ancestry on the South American mainland, they have radiated into an impressive array of species on the outlying Galapagos. Few terrestrial species manage to cross the wide oceanic barrier between South America and the Galapagos. But the fortunate migrants often find a sparsely inhabited world devoid of the competitors that limit their opportunities on the crowded mainland. Hence, the finches evolved into roles normally occupied by other birds and developed their famous set of adaptations for feeding—seed crushing, insect eating, even grasping and manipulating a cactus needle to dislodge insects from plants. Isolation—both of the islands from the mainland and among the islands themselves—provided an opportunity for separation, independent adaptation, and speciation. 10

According to the traditional view, Darwin discovered these finches, correctly inferred their history, and wrote the famous lines in his notebook: "If there is the slightest foundation for these remarks the zoology of Archipelagoes will be worth examining; for such facts would undermine the stability of Species." But, as with so many heroic tales from Washington's cherry tree to the

2. Francis Bacon (1561–1626), English philosopher, statesman, and essayist, and the first apostle of inductivism.

piety of Crusaders, hope rather than truth motivates the common reading. Darwin found the finches to be sure. But he didn't recognize them as variants of a common stock. In fact, he didn't even record the island of discovery for many of them—some of his labels just read "Galapagos Islands." So much for his immediate recognition of the role of isolation in the formation of new species. He reconstructed the evolutionary tale only after his return to London, when a British Museum ornithologist correctly identified all the birds as finches.

The famous quotation from his notebook refers to Galapagos tortoises and to the claim of native inhabitants that they can "at once pronounce from which Island any Tortoise may have been brought" from subtle differences in size and shape of body and scales. This is a statement of different, and much reduced, order from the traditional tale of finches. For the finches are true and separate species—a living example of evolution. The subtle differences among tortoises represent minor geographic variation within a species. It is a jump in reasoning, albeit a valid one as we now know, to argue that such small differences can be amplified to produce a new species. All creationists, after all, acknowledged geographic variation (consider human races), but argued that it could not proceed beyond the rigid limits of a created archetype.

I don't wish to downplay the pivotal influence of the *Beagle* voyage on Darwin's career. It gave him space, freedom and endless time to think in his favored mode of independent self-stimulation. (His ambivalence towards university life, and his middling performance there by conventional standards, reflected his unhappiness with a curriculum of received wisdom.) He writes from South America in 1834: "I have not one clear idea about cleavage, stratification, lines of upheaval. I have no books, which tell me much and what they do I cannot apply to what I see. In consequence I draw my own conclusions, and most gloriously ridiculous ones they are." The rocks and plants and animals that he saw did provoke him to the crucial attitude of doubt—midwife of all creativity. Sydney, Australia—1836. Darwin wonders why a rational God would create so many marsupials on Australia since nothing about its climate or geography suggests any superiority for pouches: "I had been lying on a sunny bank and was reflecting on the strange character of the animals of this country as compared to the rest of the World. An unbeliever in everything beyond his own reason might exclaim, 'Surely two distinct Creators must have been at work.'"

Nonetheless, Darwin returned to London without an evolutionary theory. He suspected the truth of evolution, but had no mechanism to explain it. Natural selection did not arise from any direct reading of the *Beagle*'s facts, but from two subsequent years of thought and struggle as reflected in a series of remarkable notebooks that have been unearthed and published during the past twenty years. In these notebooks, we see Darwin testing and abandoning a number of theories and pursuing a multitude of false leads—so much for his later claim about recording facts with an empty mind. He read philosophers, poets, and economists, always searching for meaning and insight—so much for the notion that natural selection arose inductively from the *Beagle*'s facts. Later, he labelled one notebook as "full of metaphysics on morals."

Yet if this tortuous path belies the Scylla of inductivism, it has engendered an equally simplistic myth—the Charybdis of eurekaism. In his maddeningly misleading autobiography, Darwin does record a eureka and suggests that natural selection struck him as a sudden, serendipitous flash after more than a year of groping frustration: 15

> In October 1838, that is, fifteen months after I had begun my systematic inquiry, I happened to read for amusement Malthus on Population,[3] and being well prepared to appreciate the struggle for existence which everywhere goes on from long-continued observation of the habits of animals and plants, it at once struck me that under these circumstances favorable variations would tend to be preserved, and unfavorable ones to be destroyed. The result of this would be the formation of new species. Here, then, I had at last got a theory by which to work.

Yet, again, the notebooks belie Darwin's later recollections—in this case by their utter failure to record, at the time it happened, any special exultation over his Malthusian insight. He inscribes it as a fairly short and sober entry without a single exclamation point, though he habitually used two or three in moments of excitement. He did not drop everything and reinterpret a confusing world in its light. On the very next day, he wrote an even longer passage on the sexual curiosity of primates.

The theory of natural selection arose neither as a workmanlike induction from nature's facts, nor as a mysterious bolt from Darwin's subconscious, triggered by an accidental reading of Malthus. It emerged instead as the result of a conscious and productive search, proceeding in a ramifying but ordered manner, and utilizing both the facts of natural history and an astonishingly broad range of insights from disparate disciplines far from his own. Darwin trod the middle path between inductivism and eurekaism. His genius is neither pedestrian nor inaccessible.

Darwinian scholarship has exploded since the centennial of the *Origin*[4] in 1959. The publication of Darwin's notebooks and the attention devoted by several scholars to the two crucial years between the *Beagle*'s docking and the demoted Malthusian insight has clinched the argument for a "middle path" theory of Darwin's creativity. Two particularly important works focus on the broadest and narrowest scales. Howard E. Gruber's masterful intellectual and psychological biography of this phase in Darwin's life, *Darwin on Man,* traces all the false leads and turning points in Darwin's search. Gruber shows that Darwin was continually proposing, testing, and abandoning hypotheses, and that he never simply collected facts in a blind way. He began with a fanciful theory involving the idea that new species arise with a prefixed life span, and worked his way gradually, if fitfully, towards an idea of extinction by competition in a

3. Thomas Malthus (1766–1834), whose book *An Essay on the Principle of Population* was published under several titles between 1798 and 1817.

4. *The Origin of Species* (1859).

world of struggle. He recorded no exultation upon reading Malthus, because the jigsaw puzzle was only missing a piece or two at the time.

Silvan S. Schweber has reconstructed, in detail as minute as the record will allow, Darwin's activities during the few weeks before Malthus ("The Origin of the *Origin* Revisited," *Journal of the History of Biology*, 1977). He argues that the final pieces arose not from new facts in natural history, but from Darwin's intellectual wanderings in distant fields. In particular, he read a long review of social scientist and philosopher Auguste Comte's most famous work, the *Cours de philosophie positive.* He was particularly struck by Comte's insistence that a proper theory be predictive and at least potentially quantitative. He then turned to Dugald Stewart's *On the Life and Writing of Adam Smith,*[5] and imbibed the basic belief of the Scottish economists that theories of overall social structure must begin by analyzing the unconstrained actions of individuals. (Natural selection is, above all, a theory about the struggle of individual organisms for success in reproduction.) Then, searching for quantification, he read a lengthy analysis of work by the most famous statistician of his time—the Belgian Adolphe Quetelet. In the review of Quetelet, he found, among other things, a forceful statement of Malthus's quantitative claim—that population would grow geometrically and food supplies only arithmetically, thus guaranteeing an intense struggle for existence. In fact, Darwin had read the Malthusian statement several times before; but only now was he prepared to appreciate its significance. Thus, he did not turn to Malthus by accident, and he already knew what it contained. His "amusement," we must assume, consisted only in a desire to read in its original formulation the familiar statement that had so impressed him in Quetelet's secondary account.

20 In reading Schweber's detailed account of the moments preceding Darwin's formulation of natural selection, I was particularly struck by the absence of deciding influence from his own field of biology. The immediate precipitators were a social scientist, an economist, and a statistician. If genius has any common denominator, I would propose breadth of interest and the ability to construct fruitful analogies between fields.

In fact, I believe that the theory of natural selection should be viewed as an extended analogy—whether conscious or unconscious on Darwin's part I do not know—to the laissez faire economics of Adam Smith. The essence of Smith's argument is a paradox of sorts: if you want an ordered economy providing maximal benefits to all, then let individuals compete and struggle for their own advantages. The result, after appropriate sorting and elimination of the inefficient, will be a stable and harmonious polity. Apparent order arises naturally from the struggle among individuals, not from predestined principles or higher control. Dugald Stewart epitomized Smith's system in the book Darwin read:

5. *Cours de philosophie positive* (Course in positivist philosophy) (1830–1842). Dugald Stewart (1753–1828) wrote a brief biography of Adam Smith in 1811, which was frequently included in editions of Smith's *The Wealth of Nations* (1776).

> The most effective plan for advancing a people . . . is by allowing every man, as long as he observes the rules of justice, to pursue his own interest in his own way, and to bring both his industry and his capital into the freest competition with those of his fellow citizens. Every system of policy which endeavors . . . to draw towards a particular species of industry a greater share of the capital of the society than would naturally go to it . . . is, in reality, subversive of the great purpose which it means to promote.

As Schweber states: "The Scottish analysis of society contends that the combined effect of individual actions results in the institutions upon which society is based, and that such a society is a stable and evolving one and functions without a designing and directing mind."

We know that Darwin's uniqueness does not reside in his support for the idea of evolution—scores of scientists had preceded him in this. His special contribution rests upon his documentation and upon the novel character of his theory about how evolution operates. Previous evolutionists had proposed unworkable schemes based on internal perfecting tendencies and inherent directions. Darwin advocated a natural and testable theory based on immediate interaction among individuals (his opponents considered it heartlessly mechanistic). The theory of natural selection is a creative transfer to biology of Adam Smith's basic argument for a rational economy: the balance and order of nature does not arise from a higher, external (divine) control, or from the existence of laws operating directly upon the whole, but from struggle among individuals for their own benefits (in modern terms, for the transmission of their genes to future generations through differential success in reproduction).

Many people are distressed to hear such an argument. Does it not compromise the integrity of science if some of its primary conclusions originate by analogy from contemporary politics and culture rather than from data of the discipline itself? In a famous letter to Engels, Karl Marx identified the similarities between natural selection and the English social scene:

> It is remarkable how Darwin recognizes among beasts and plants his English society with its division of labor, competition, opening up of new markets, 'invention,' and the Malthusian 'struggle for existence.' It is Hobbes' *bellum omnium contra omnes* (the war of all against all).[6]

Yet Marx was a great admirer of Darwin—and in this apparent paradox lies resolution. For reasons involving all the themes I have emphasized here—that inductivism is inadequate, that creativity demands breadth, and that analogy is a profound source of insight—great thinkers cannot be divorced from their social background. But the source of an idea is one thing; its truth or fruitfulness is another. The psychology and utility of discovery are very different subjects indeed. Darwin may have cribbed the idea of natural selection from economics, but it may still be right. As the German socialist Karl Kautsky wrote in 1902: "The fact that an idea emanates from a particular class, or accords with their interests, of course proves nothing as to its truth or falsity." In this case, it is

6. From *Leviathan* (1651), by the English philosopher Thomas Hobbes.

ironic that Adam Smith's system of laissez faire does not work in his own domain of economics, for it leads to oligopoly and revolution, rather than to order and harmony. Struggle among individuals does, however, seem to be the law of nature.

Many people use such arguments about social context to ascribe great insights primarily to the indefinable phenomenon of good luck. Thus, Darwin was lucky to be born rich, lucky to be on the *Beagle*, lucky to live amidst the ideas of his age, lucky to trip over Parson Malthus—essentially little more than a man in the right place at the right time. Yet, when we read of his personal struggle to understand, the breadth of his concerns and study, and the directedness of his search for a mechanism of evolution, we understand why Pasteur made his famous quip that fortune favors the prepared mind.[7]

7. Louis Pasteur (1822–1895), French chemist and microbiologist.

QUESTIONS

1. What, according to Gould, constituted Darwin's scientific research? How and why did he depict it falsely in his autobiography (paragraph 8)?

2. Rather than isolating scientific research from social and political experience, Darwin, Gould explains, was influenced by a social scientist, an economist, and a statistician (paragraph 20). Identify each one and explain what he contributed to Darwin's theory of natural selection.

3. Consider a recent experience of writing an essay. Did you, while thinking and writing, shuttle between inductivism and prediction as Gould claims Darwin did? Describe your experience using Gould's analytic vocabulary.

Literature, the Arts, and Media

Eudora Welty — *One Writer's Beginnings*

I learned from the age of two or three that any room in our house, at any time of day, was there to read in, or to be read to. My mother read to me. She'd read to me in the big bedroom in the mornings, when we were in her rocker together, which ticked in rhythm as we rocked, as though we had a cricket accompanying the story. She'd read to me in the diningroom on winter afternoons in front of the coal fire, with our cuckoo clock ending the story with "Cuckoo," and at night when I'd got in my own bed. I must have given her no peace. Sometimes she read to me in the kitchen while she sat churning, and the churning sobbed along with *any* story. It was my ambition to have her read to me while *I* churned; once she granted my wish, but she read off my story before I brought her butter. She was an expressive reader. When she was reading "Puss in Boots,"[1] for instance, it was impossible not to know that she distrusted *all* cats.

It had been startling and disappointing to me to find out that story books had been written by *people,* that books were not natural wonders, coming up of themselves like grass. Yet regardless of where they came from, I cannot remember a time when I was not in love with them—with the books themselves, cover and binding and the paper they were printed on, with their smell and their weight and with their possession in my arms, captured and carried off to myself. Still illiterate, I was ready for them, committed to all the reading I could give them.

Neither of my parents had come from homes that could afford to buy many books, but though it must have been something of a strain on his salary, as the youngest officer in a young insurance company, my father was all the while carefully selecting and ordering away for what he and Mother thought we children should grow up with. They bought first for the future.

From a set of three lectures delivered at Harvard University in April 1983, to inaugurate the William E. Massey lecture series, and later published in One Writer's Beginnings *(1984).*

1. A fairy tale.

Besides the bookcase in the livingroom, which was always called "the library," there were the encyclopedia tables and dictionary stand under windows in our diningroom. Here to help us grow up arguing around the diningroom table were the Unabridged Webster, the Columbia Encyclopedia, Compton's Pictured Encyclopedia, the Lincoln Library of Information, and later the Book of Knowledge. And the year we moved into our new house, there was room to celebrate it with the new 1925 edition of the Britannica, which my father, his face always deliberately turned toward the future, was of course disposed to think better than any previous edition.

5 In "the library," inside the mission-style bookcase with its three diamond-latticed glass doors, with my father's Morris chair and the glass-shaded lamp on its table beside it, were books I could soon begin on—and I did, reading them all alike and as they came, straight down their rows, top shelf to bottom. There was the set of Stoddard's Lectures, in all its late nineteenth-century vocabulary and vignettes of peasant life and quaint beliefs and customs, with matching halftone illustrations: Vesuvius erupting, Venice by moonlight, gypsies glimpsed by their campfires. I didn't know then the clue they were to my father's longing to see the rest of the world. I read straight through his other love-from-afar: the Victrola Book of the Opera, with opera after opera in synopsis, with portraits in costume of Melba, Caruso, Galli-Curci, and Geraldine Farrar,[2] some of whose voices we could listen to on our Red Seal records.

My mother read secondarily for information; she sank as a hedonist into novels. She read Dickens in the spirit in which she would have eloped with him. The novels of her girlhood that had stayed on in her imagination, besides those of Dickens and Scott and Robert Louis Stevenson,[3] were *Jane Eyre, Trilby, The Woman in White, Green Mansions, King Solomon's Mines.*[4] Marie Corelli's[5] name would crop up but I understood she had gone out of favor with my mother, who had only kept *Ardath* out of loyalty. In time she absorbed herself in Galsworthy, Edith Wharton, above all in Thomas Mann of the *Joseph* volumes.[6]

St. Elmo[7] was not in our house; I saw it often in other houses. This wildly popular Southern novel is where all the Edna Earles in our population started coming from. They're all named for the heroine, who succeeded in bringing a dissolute, sinning roué and atheist of a lover (St. Elmo) to his knees. My mother

2. Nellie Melba (1861–1931), Enrico Caruso (1837–1921), Amelita Galli-Curci (1889–1964), Geraldine Farrar (1882–1967), all opera stars.

3. Charles Dickens (1812–1870), Sir Walter Scott (1771–1832), Robert Louis Stevenson (1850–1894). The first was English, the others Scottish.

4. Respectively by Charlotte Brontë (1816–1855), George Du Maurier (1834–1896), Wilkie Collins (1824–1889), William Henry Hudson (1841–1922), Sir H. Rider Haggard (1856–1925). All were British.

5. The pen name of Mary Mills Mackay (1855–1924), a popular and prolific British novelist.

6. John Galsworthy (1867–1933), British; Edith Wharton (1862–1937), American; Thomas Mann (1875–1955), German, whose *Joseph* novels appeared in four parts, from 1933 to 1943.

7. By Augusta Jane Evans (1835–1909).

was able to forgo it. But she remembered the classic advice given to rose growers on how to water their bushes long enough: "Take a chair and *St. Elmo.*"

To both my parents I owe my early acquaintance with a beloved Mark Twain. There was a full set of Mark Twain and a short set of Ring Lardner in our bookcase,[8] and those were the volumes that in time united us all, parents and children.

Reading everything that stood before me was how I came upon a worn old book without a back that had belonged to my father as a child. It was called *Sanford and Merton.* Is there anyone left who recognizes it, I wonder? It is the famous moral tale written by Thomas Day in the 1780s, but of him no mention is made on the title page of *this* book; here it is *Sanford and Merton in Words of One Syllable* by Mary Godolphin. Here are the rich boy and the poor boy and Mr. Barlow, their teacher and interlocutor, in long discourses alternating with dramatic scenes—danger and rescue allotted to the rich and the poor respectively. It may have only words of one syllable, but one of them is "quoth." It ends with not one but two morals, both engraved on rings: "Do what you ought, come what may," and "If we would be great, we must first learn to be good."

This book was lacking its front cover, the back held on by strips of pasted paper, now turned golden, in several layers, and the pages stained, flecked, and tattered around the edges; its garish illustrations had come unattached but were preserved, laid in. I had the feeling even in my heedless childhood that this was the only book my father as a little boy had had of his own. He had held onto it, and might have gone to sleep on its coverless face: he had lost his mother when he was seven. My father had never made any mention to his own children of the book, but he had brought it along with him from Ohio to our house and shelved it in our bookcase. 10

My mother had brought from West Virginia that set of Dickens; those books looked sad, too—they had been through fire and water before I was born, she told me, and there they were, lined up—as I later realized, waiting for *me.*

I was presented, from as early as I can remember, with books of my own, which appeared on my birthday and Christmas morning. Indeed, my parents could not give me books enough. They must have sacrificed to give me on my sixth or seventh birthday—it was after I became a reader for myself—the ten-volume set of Our Wonder World. These were beautifully made, heavy books I would lie down with on the floor in front of the diningroom hearth, and more often than the rest volume 5, *Every Child's Story Book,* was under my eyes. There were the fairy tales—Grimm, Andersen, the English, the French, "Ali Baba and the Forty Thieves"; and there was Aesop and Reynard the Fox; there were the myths and legends, Robin Hood, King Arthur, and St. George and the Dragon, even the history of Joan of Arc; a whack of *Pilgrim's Progress* and a long piece of *Gulliver.*[9] They all carried their classic illustrations. I located myself in these pages and could go straight to the stories and pictures I loved; very often

8. Mark Twain, the pen name of Samuel Langhorne Clemens (1835–1910); Ring (Ringgold Wilmer) Lardner (1885–1933). Both were American.

9. *The Pilgrim's Progress* by John Bunyan (1628–1688) and *Gulliver's Travels* by Jonathan Swift (1667–1745).

"The Yellow Dwarf" was first choice, with Walter Crane's Yellow Dwarf in full color making his terrifying appearance flanked by turkeys.[10] Now that volume is as worn and backless and hanging apart as my father's poor *Sanford and Merton*. The precious page with Edward Lear's "Jumblies"[11] on it has been in danger of slipping out for all these years. One measure of my love for Our Wonder World was that for a long time I wondered if I would go through fire and water for it as my mother had done for Charles Dickens; and the only comfort was to think I could ask my mother to do it for me.

I believe I'm the only child I know of who grew up with this treasure in the house. I used to ask others, "Did you have Our Wonder World?" I'd have to tell them The Book of Knowledge could not hold a candle to it.

I live in gratitude to my parents for initiating me—and as early as I begged for it, without keeping me waiting—into knowledge of the word, into reading and spelling, by way of the alphabet. They taught it to me at home in time for me to begin to read before starting to school. I believe the alphabet is no longer considered an essential piece of equipment for traveling through life. In my day it was the keystone to knowledge. You learned the alphabet as you learned to count to ten, as you learned "Now I lay me" and the Lord's Prayer and your father's and mother's name and address and telephone number, all in case you were lost.

15 My love for the alphabet, which endures, grew out of reciting it but, before that, out of seeing the letters on the page. In my own story books, before I could read them for myself, I fell in love with various winding, enchanting-looking initials drawn by Walter Crane at the heads of fairy tales. In "Once upon a time," an "O" had a rabbit running it as a treadmill, his feet upon flowers. When the day came, years later, for me to see the Book of Kells,[12] all the wizardry of letter, initial, and word swept over me a thousand times over, and the illumination, the gold, seemed a part of the word's beauty and holiness that had been there from the start.

Learning stamps you with its moments. Childhood's learning is made up of moments. It isn't steady. It's a pulse.

In a children's art class, we sat in a ring on kindergarten chairs and drew three daffodils that had just been picked out of the yard; and while I was drawing, my sharpened pencil and the cup of the yellow daffodil gave off whiffs just alike. That the pencil doing the drawing should give off the same smell as the flower it drew seemed a part of the art lesson—as shouldn't it be? Children, like animals, use all their senses to discover the world. Then artists come along and discover it the same way, all over again. Here and there, it's the same world. Or now and then we'll hear from an artist who's never lost it.

10. A fairy tale illustrated by Walter Crane (1845–1915), popular illustrator of children's books.

11. A narrative poem about creatures called Jumblies who went to sea in a sieve. Edward Lear (1812–1888), British, wrote nonsense poems for children.

12. An illustrated Irish manuscript of the four Gospels from the eighth or ninth century.

In my sensory education I include my physical awareness of the *word.* Of a certain word, that is; the connection it has with what it stands for. At around age six, perhaps, I was standing by myself in our front yard waiting for supper, just at that hour in a late summer day when the sun is already below the horizon and the risen full moon in the visible sky stops being chalky and begins to take on light. There comes the moment, and I saw it then, when the moon goes from flat to round. For the first time it met my eyes as a globe. The word "moon" came into my mouth as though fed to me out of a silver spoon. Held in my mouth the moon became a word. It had the roundness of a Concord grape Grandpa took off his vine and gave me to suck out of its skin and swallow whole, in Ohio.

This love did not prevent me from living for years in foolish error about the moon. The new moon just appearing in the west was the rising moon to me. The new should be rising. And in early childhood the sun and moon, those opposite reigning powers, I just as easily assumed rose in east and west respectively in their opposite sides of the sky, and like partners in a reel they advanced, sun from the east, moon from the west, crossed over (when I wasn't looking) and went down on the other side. My father couldn't have known I believed that when, bending behind me and guiding my shoulder, he positioned me at our telescope in the front yard and, with careful adjustment of the focus, brought the moon close to me.

The night sky over my childhood Jackson[13] was velvety black. I could see the full constellations in it and call their names; when I could read, I knew their myths. Though I was always waked for eclipses, and indeed carried to the window as an infant in arms and shown Halley's Comet[14] in my sleep, and though I'd been taught at our diningroom table about the solar system and knew the earth revolved around the sun, and our moon around us, I never found out the moon didn't come up in the west until I was a writer and Herschel Brickell, the literary critic, told me after I misplaced it in a story. He said valuable words to me about my new profession: "Always be sure you get your moon in the right part of the sky." 20

My mother always sang to her children. Her voice came out just a little bit in the minor key. "Wee Willie Winkie's" song was wonderfully sad when she sang the lullabies.

"Oh, but now there's a record. She could have her own record to listen to," my father would have said. For there came a Victrola record of "Bobby Shafftoe" and "Rock-a-Bye Baby,"[15] all of Mother's lullabies, which could be played to take her place. Soon I was able to play her my own lullabies all day long.

Our Victrola stood in the diningroom. I was allowed to climb onto the seat of a diningroom chair to wind it, start the record turning, and set the needle

13. Jackson, Mississippi, where Welty grew up.

14. A comet named after Edmund Halley (1656–1742), English astronomer.

15. "Wee Willie Winkie," a nursery rhyme of 1841 in which sleep is personified; "Bobby Shafftoe," a traditional sea chantey dating from about 1750; "Rock-a-Bye Baby," words from *Mother Goose's Melodies* (1765), set to music in 1884.

playing. In a second I'd jumped to the floor, to spin or march around the table as the music called for—now there were all the other records I could play too. I skinned back onto the chair just in time to lift the needle at the end, stop the record and turn it over, then change the needle. That brass receptacle with a hole in the lid gave off a metallic smell like human sweat, from all the hot needles that were fed it. Winding up, dancing, being cocked to start and stop the record, was of course all in one the act of *listening*—to "Overture to *Daughter of the Regiment*," "Selections from *The Fortune Teller*," "Kiss Me Again," "Gypsy Dance from *Carmen*," "Stars and Stripes Forever," "When the Midnight Choo-Choo Leaves for Alabam," or whatever came next.[16] Movement must be at the very heart of listening.

Ever since I was first read to, then started reading to myself, there has never been a line read that I didn't *hear*. As my eyes followed the sentence, a voice was saying it silently to me. It isn't my mother's voice, or the voice of any person I can identify, certainly not my own. It is human, but inward, and it is inwardly that I listen to it. It is to me the voice of the story or the poem itself. The cadence, whatever it is that asks you to believe, the feeling that resides in the printed word, reaches me through the reader-voice. I have supposed, but never found out, that this is the case with all readers—to read as listeners—and with all writers, to write as listeners. It may be part of the desire to write. The sound of what falls on the page begins the process of testing it for truth, for me. Whether I am right to trust so far I don't know. By now I don't know whether I could do either one, reading or writing, without the other.

25 My own words, when I am at work on a story, I hear too as they go, in the same voice that I hear when I read in books. When I write and the sound of it comes back to my ears, then I act to make my changes. I have always trusted this voice.

16. *Daughter of the Regiment*, an opera (1840) by the Italian composer Gaetano Donizetti; *The Fortune Teller*, an operetta (1898) by the American Victor Herbert; "Kiss Me Again," a song from Herbert's *Mlle. Modiste* (1905); *Carmen*, an opera (1875) by the French composer Georges Bizet; "Stars and Stripes Forever," a march (1897) by the American John Philip Sousa; "When the Midnight Choo-Choo Leaves for Alabam," a popular song (1912) by the American Irving Berlin.

QUESTIONS

1. In the opening paragraphs Welty speaks of what she later calls her "sensory education." What does she mean? What examples does she give?

2. Throughout her essay Welty lists the titles of books that she and her mother read. What is the effect of these lists? Have you read any of the books? Or books like them? How important were they to you?

3. Welty concludes her essay by talking of the writer's voice—of "testing it for truth" and "trust[ing] this voice" (paragraphs 24 and 25). What meanings does she give the key words "truth" and "trust"?

4. Read John Holt's essay "How Teachers Make Children Hate Reading" (p. 358). Write an essay of your own, entitled "How Children Learn to Love Reading," drawing your evidence from Welty's "One Writer's Beginnings" and your experience, observation, and reading.

5. Welty grew up before the advent of television. How does television affect a child's "sensory education"? Write an essay comparing a modern child's sensory education with Welty's.

Vladimir Nabokov *Good Readers and Good Writers*

"How to be a Good Reader" or "Kindness to Authors"—something of that sort might serve to provide a subtitle for these various discussions of various authors, for my plan is to deal lovingly, in loving and lingering detail, with several European masterpieces. A hundred years ago, Flaubert[1] in a letter to his mistress made the following remark: *Comme l'on serait savant si l'on connaissait bien seulement cinq à six livres:* "What a scholar one might be if one knew well only some half a dozen books."

In reading, one should notice and fondle details. There is nothing wrong about the moonshine of generalization when it comes *after* the sunny trifles of the book have been lovingly collected. If one begins with a ready-made generalization, one begins at the wrong end and travels away from the book before one has started to understand it. Nothing is more boring or more unfair to the author than starting to read, say, *Madame Bovary,* with the preconceived notion that it is a denunciation of the bourgeoisie. We should always remember that the work of art is invariably the creation of a new world, so that the first thing we should do is to study that new world as closely as possible, approaching it as something brand new, having no obvious connection with the worlds we already know. When this new world has been closely studied, then and only then let us examine its links with other worlds, other branches of knowledge.

Another question: Can we expect to glean information about places and times from a novel? Can anybody be so naive as to think he or she can learn anything about the past from those buxom best-sellers that are hawked around by book clubs under the heading of historical novels? But what about the masterpieces? Can we rely on Jane Austen's[2] picture of landowning England with baronets and landscaped grounds when all she knew was a clergyman's parlor?

A lecture delivered to Nabokov's undergraduate class at Cornell University, where he taught from 1948 to 1959; published in Lectures on Literature *in 1980.*

1. Gustave Flaubert (1821–1880), French novelist, author of *Madame Bovary.*
2. British novelist (1775–1817).

And *Bleak House*,[3] that fantastic romance within a fantastic London, can we call it a study of London a hundred years ago? Certainly not. And the same holds for other such novels in this series. The truth is that great novels are great fairy tales—and the novels in this series are supreme fairy tales.

Time and space, the colors of the seasons, the movements of muscles and minds, all these are for writers of genius (as far as we can guess and I trust we guess right) not traditional notions which may be borrowed from the circulating library of public truths but a series of unique surprises which master artists have learned to express in their own unique way. To minor authors is left the ornamentation of the commonplace: these do not bother about any reinventing of the world; they merely try to squeeze the best they can out of a given order of things, out of traditional patterns of fiction. The various combinations these minor authors are able to produce within these set limits may be quite amusing in a mild ephemeral way because minor readers like to recognize their own ideas in a pleasing disguise. But the real writer, the fellow who sends planets spinning and models a man asleep and eagerly tampers with the sleeper's rib, that kind of author has no given values at his disposal: he must create them himself. The art of writing is a very futile business if it does not imply first of all the art of seeing the world as the potentiality of fiction. The material of this world may be real enough (as far as reality goes) but does not exist at all as an accepted entirety: it is chaos, and to this chaos the author says "go!" allowing the world to flicker and to fuse. It is now recombined in its very atoms, not merely in its visible and superficial parts. The writer is the first man to map it and to name the natural objects it contains. Those berries there are edible. That speckled creature that bolted across my path might be tamed. That lake between those trees will be called Lake Opal or, more artistically, Dishwater Lake. That mist is a mountain—and that mountain must be conquered. Up a trackless slope climbs the master artist, and at the top, on a windy ridge, whom do you think he meets? The panting and happy reader, and there they spontaneously embrace and are linked forever if the book lasts forever.

5 One evening at a remote provincial college through which I happened to be jogging on a protracted lecture tour, I suggested a little quiz—ten definitions of a reader, and from these ten the students had to choose four definitions that would combine to make a good reader. I have mislaid the list, but as far as I remember the definitions went something like this. Select four answers to the question what should a reader be to be a good reader:

1. The reader should belong to a book club.
2. The reader should identify himself or herself with the hero or heroine.
3. The reader should concentrate on the social-economic angle.

3. Novel by Charles Dickens (1812–1870) that alternates scenes in London and the country and includes a satire on the British judicial system.

4. The reader should prefer a story with action and dialogue to one with none.
5. The reader should have seen the book in a movie.
6. The reader should be a budding author.
7. The reader should have imagination.
8. The reader should have memory.
9. The reader should have a dictionary.
10. The reader should have some artistic sense.

The students leaned heavily on emotional identification, action, and the social-economic or historical angle. Of course, as you have guessed, the good reader is one who has imagination, memory, a dictionary, and some artistic sense—which sense I propose to develop in myself and in others whenever I have the chance.

Incidentally, I use the word *reader* very loosely. Curiously enough, one cannot *read* a book: one can only reread it. A good reader, a major reader, an active and creative reader is a rereader. And I shall tell you why. When we read a book for the first time the very process of laboriously moving our eyes from left to right, line after line, page after page, this complicated physical work upon the book, the very process of learning in terms of space and time what the book is about, this stands between us and artistic appreciation. When we look at a painting we do not have to move our eyes in a special way even if, as in a book, the picture contains elements of depth and development. The element of time does not really enter in a first contact with a painting. In reading a book, we must have time to acquaint ourselves with it. We have no physical organ (as we have the eye in regard to a painting) that takes in the whole picture and then can enjoy its details. But at a second, or third, or fourth reading we do, in a sense, behave towards a book as we do towards a painting. However, let us not confuse the physical eye, that monstrous masterpiece of evolution, with the mind, an even more monstrous achievement. A book, no matter what it is—a work of fiction or a work of science (the boundary line between the two is not as clear as is generally believed)—a book of fiction appeals first of all to the mind. The mind, the brain, the top of the tingling spine, is, or should be, the only instrument used upon a book.

Now, this being so, we should ponder the question how does the mind work when the sullen reader is confronted by the sunny book. First, the sullen mood melts away, and for better or worse the reader enters into the spirit of the game. The effort to begin a book, especially if it is praised by people whom the young reader secretly deems to be too old-fashioned or too serious, this effort is often difficult to make; but once it is made, rewards are various and abundant. Since the master artist used his imagination in creating his book, it is natural and fair that the consumer of a book should use his imagination too.

There are, however, at least two varieties of imagination in the reader's case. So let us see which one of the two is the right one to use in reading a book. First, there is the comparatively lowly kind which turns for support to the simple emotions and is of a definitely personal nature. (There are various sub-varieties here, in this first section of emotional reading.) A situation in a book is intensely felt because it reminds us of something that happened to us or to someone we know or knew. Or, again, a reader treasures a book mainly because it evokes a country, a landscape, a mode of living which he nostalgically recalls as part of his own past. Or, and this is the worst thing a reader can do, he identifies himself with a character in the book. This lowly variety is not the kind of imagination I would like readers to use.

So what is the authentic instrument to be used by the reader? It is impersonal imagination and artistic delight. What should be established, I think, is an artistic harmonious balance between the reader's mind and the author's mind. We ought to remain a little aloof and take pleasure in this aloofness while at the same time we keenly enjoy—passionately enjoy, enjoy with tears and shivers—the inner weave of a given masterpiece. To be quite objective in these matters is of course impossible. Everything that is worthwhile is to some extent subjective. For instance, you sitting there may be merely my dream, and I may be your nightmare. But what I mean is that the reader must know when and where to curb his imagination and this he does by trying to get clear the specific world the author places at his disposal. We must see things and hear things, we must visualize the rooms, the clothes, the manners of an author's people. The color of Fanny Price's eyes in *Mansfield Park*[4] and the furnishing of her cold little room are important.

10 We all have different temperaments, and I can tell you right now that the best temperament for a reader to have, or to develop, is a combination of the artistic and the scientific one. The enthusiastic artist alone is apt to be too subjective in his attitude towards a book, and so a scientific coolness of judgment will temper the intuitive heat. If, however, a would-be reader is utterly devoid of passion and patience—of an artist's passion and a scientist's patience—he will hardly enjoy great literature.

Literature was born not the day when a boy crying wolf, wolf came running out of the Neanderthal valley with a big gray wolf at his heels: literature was born on the day when a boy came crying wolf, wolf and there was no wolf behind him. That the poor little fellow because he lied too often was finally eaten up by a real beast is quite incidental. But here is what is important. Between the wolf in the tall grass and the wolf in the tall story there is a shimmering go-between. That go-between, that prism, is the art of literature.

Literature is invention. Fiction is fiction. To call a story a true story is an insult to both art and truth. Every great writer is a great deceiver, but so is that arch-cheat Nature. Nature always deceives. From the simple deception of propagation to the prodigiously sophisticated illusion of protective colors in butterflies or birds, there is in Nature a marvelous system of spells and wiles. The writer of fiction only follows Nature's lead.

4. Novel by Jane Austen published in 1814.

Going back for a moment to our wolf-crying woodland little woolly fellow, we may put it this way: the magic of art was in the shadow of the wolf that he deliberately invented, his dream of the wolf; then the story of his tricks made a good story. When he perished at last, the story told about him acquired a good lesson in the dark around the camp fire. But he was the little magician. He was the inventor.

There are three points of view from which a writer can be considered: he may be considered as a storyteller, as a teacher, and as an enchanter. A major writer combines these three—storyteller, teacher, enchanter—but it is the enchanter in him that predominates and makes him a major writer.

15 To the storyteller we turn for entertainment, for mental excitement of the simplest kind, for emotional participation, for the pleasure of traveling in some remote region in space or time. A slightly different though not necessarily higher mind looks for the teacher in the writer. Propagandist, moralist, prophet—this is the rising sequence. We may go to the teacher not only for moral education but also for direct knowledge, for simple facts. Alas, I have known people whose purpose in reading the French and Russian novelists was to learn something about life in gay Paree or in sad Russia. Finally, and above all, a great writer is always a great enchanter, and it is here that we come to the really exciting part when we try to grasp the individual magic of his genius and to study the style, the imagery, the pattern of his novels or poems.

The three facets of the great writer—magic, story, lesson—are prone to blend in one impression of unified and unique radiance, since the magic of art may be present in the very bones of the story, in the very marrow of thought. There are masterpieces of dry, limpid, organized thought which provoke in us an artistic quiver quite as strongly as a novel like *Mansfield Park* does or as any rich flow of Dickensian sensual imagery. It seems to me that a good formula to test the quality of a novel is, in the long run, a merging of the precision of poetry and the intuition of science. In order to bask in that magic a wise reader reads the book of genius not with his heart, not so much with his brain, but with his spine. It is there that occurs the telltale tingle even though we must keep a little aloof, a little detached when reading. Then with a pleasure which is both sensual and intellectual we shall watch the artist build his castle of cards and watch the castle of cards become a castle of beautiful steel and glass.

QUESTIONS

1. Make a list of the qualities that Nabokov believes "good readers" should have; then make a list of the qualities he believes "good writers" should have. Do they correspond? Why or why not?

2. Nabokov, as he points out in the conclusion to his essay (paragraphs 14–16), considers the writer from three points of view: as storyteller, as teacher, and as enchanter. He has not, however, organized his essay by these points of view. Where and how does he discuss each one? Why does he consider the last the most important?

3. Take Nabokov's quiz (paragraph 5). Write an essay in which you explain your "right" answers (as Nabokov sees "good readers") and defend your "wrong" ones.

4. How would Eudora Welty (see "One Writer's Beginnings") do on Nabokov's quiz? Give what you think would be her answers and explain, using information from her essay, what you think her reasons would be.

ALLEGRA GOODMAN *Pemberley Previsited*

THE FIRST TIME I read *Pride and Prejudice*[1] I was nine. I was a pert, excitable, giggly reader. My school librarian couldn't stand me. She had already spoken to me about saving books for when you were older, and suggested ominously that the novel would be ruined for me later on. "Someday," she predicted, "you're going to get too big for your britches."

I'm sure she wouldn't have let me take the novel out of her library, but of course it didn't come from her shelves. I'd found it at the University of Hawaii. My mother was the chair of women's studies there, and my sister and I spent hours after school in the small program library with the books by women authors, the anthropological studies, and, particularly, the variorum edition of *Wonder Woman*.[2] I knew my mother loved Jane Austen, so when I came upon *Pride and Prejudice*, I curled up on a couple of floor cushions in the lounge and began to read.

My school librarian was not entirely wrong. There was a good deal in the book I was too young to understand. I skipped over hard words and long epistolary passages. Nuances of character and the delicate mechanics of plot were lost on me. Like a water insect I skated the surface of the text, scarcely dimpling the rippling current underneath. But I do remember laughing as I read. "Come here, child," Mr. Bennet tells Elizabeth, after her mother orders her to reconsider the odiously officious Mr. Collins. "An unhappy alternative is before you. . . . From this day you must be a stranger to one of your parents. Your mother will never see you again if you do *not* marry Mr. Collins, and I will never see you again if you *do*." I understood that wry proposition perfectly. If nothing else, Austen's buoyant wit came through.

First published in the American Scholar *(Spring 2004) and collected in* Rereadings *(ed. Anne Fadiman, 2006). Goodman's recent book,* The Cookbook Collector *(2010), is a retelling of Jane Austen's* Sense and Sensibility.

1. Jane Austen's 1813 novel follows the story of Elizabeth Bennet and her four sisters as they try to find husbands in spite of having little money.

2. A variorum edition collates all known versions of a text. The comic book *Wonder Woman* was created by William Moulton Marston in 1941 for DC Comics.

The second time I read the book I was in high school and taking a summer English course that sandwiched *Pride and Prejudice* unappetizingly between *Of Mice and Men* and *The Catcher in the Rye*.[3] Laughter had given way to diligence, three-to-five-page essays, and much class discussion about the individual and the community. I do not remember the text this time as much as the small print and the pulpy paper. I had oral surgery the week we "did" Jane Austen, and I read the book while lying on my pink bed, in my pink carpeted bedroom, with tea bags packed into my mouth to stop the bleeding. Sliding mirror doors on my closet reflected a swollen-mouthed and melancholy fifteen-year-old. I stood out among the Polynesian and Asian kids at school because of my extremely fair skin. "Why are you so white?" everyone asked me; if my classmates were in a mood to tease, they called me "shark bait." I tried to imagine myself among the fair-skinned girls in *Pride and Prejudice*, but such escapism cut into my self-pity, so I didn't allow myself to enter Austen's world for long. Surely, I thought, Elizabeth's younger sisters would have dismissed me as a "freckled little thing."

I did not open *Pride and Prejudice* again until I was in college. I had exchanged the tropical island of my childhood for the bricks and snow of Cambridge, where I was an English and philosophy concentrator at Harvard. I had many friends in college, and to my great joy, my complexion was no longer a topic of conversation. My first story had been accepted for publication; I had earned advanced standing and placed into a sophomore English tutorial. All this had restored my self-confidence. Once again a precocious initiate into the mysteries of English literature, I now looked at Jane Austen from a critical perspective. My tutor was a Henry James[4] specialist, and my father had given me a volume of the novelist's book reviews, in which, always incisive but rarely generous, James turned a jaundiced eye on his literary predecessors. It was in college, with James on my reading list and my own professional aspirations in mind, that I began to consider the strengths and weaknesses of *Pride and Prejudice*—the liveliness of Lizzie and her sisters, against the inarticulate stiffness of Darcy.

Granted, Darcy is supposed to be proud and rigid, silent in his dignity, but on this reading I faulted Austen for failing to provide a better view of his mind and heart. I felt she spent more time describing the contents of Darcy's house than developing his character. Darcy is shown early as a figure of unapproachable hauteur and later as a Prince Charming. His motives and interests are objects of intense speculation, but he himself remains a cipher. I began to think him a weak point in the novel, to feel that, as James says of Daniel Deronda,[5] "He is not a man at all," but a construct. Even at the end of the book, when his

3. Classic American novels by John Steinbeck (1939) and J. D. Salinger (1951), respectively.

4. American novelist (1843–1916) known for novels of great psychological complexity and for strong, inquisitive heroines.

5. Title character of George Eliot's 1876 novel, her last, which explores the hidden world of English Jews in the Victorian Age.

transformation is complete, Darcy cannot, or, more accurately, is not allowed to, explain how he came to love Elizabeth. She insists on speaking for him, telling him exactly why he was attracted to her. "The fact is, that you were sick of civility, of deference, of officious attention. You were disgusted with the women who were always speaking and looking, and thinking for *your* approbation alone. I roused, and interested you, because I was so unlike *them*." Elizabeth's bossy, authorial little speech only calls attention to the shameless fairy-tale ending Austen has set up. The novel originally titled "First Impressions" leaves the reader with a final impression that the noble, handsome, fabulously wealthy Darcy is indeed a figment of his author's lively, feminine imagination. He has moved from grudging to admiring appreciation of Elizabeth's performances. But he is always quiet—a passive character, if an excellent audience.

My professors taught me to consider the cultural context of literary works, the social mores delineated, and the position of the author in her world. The more I learned about Jane Austen's England, the more I understood how unrealistic Darcy's second proposal is. The more I learned of Austen's own life, the more I understood how improbable Elizabeth's conquest would have been. At nine, I'd loved *Pride and Prejudice* for its humor; at fifteen, I'd read it with melancholy; but in college, I spurned it with feelings akin to those of my roommate when she broke up with her high-school sweetheart. Henry James was so much darker, so much more worldly, so sophisticated. Austen's art seemed merely sunny. She was a watercolorist, while James was the brilliant mannerist, dazzling with his chiaroscuro. *The Portrait of a Lady* numbed me, then stung me, and finally overwhelmed me. *The Wings of the Dove* entirely turned my head.[6] *Pride and Prejudice* slipped, along with *Huckleberry Finn*,[7] into the pile of slim books from home that I'd enjoyed when I was younger. I glanced through it only to dismiss it, and then I left it behind—seemingly forever.

I'd written books and more stories of my own, drafted my dissertation on Samuel Johnson's edition of Shakespeare, married, had two children, and moved back to Cambridge by the time I picked up *Pride and Prejudice* again. I'd just come home from my mother's funeral. I was twenty-nine and had never felt so old. My mother had died of brain cancer soon after turning fifty-one.

It was October, raining hard, and I was alone in the house with our baby. My brother-in-law was getting married that weekend, but I'd found I couldn't force myself to go to the wedding. My husband flew with our four-year-old to Philadelphia.

10 The rain poured down all the first night and kept coming the next day. It was too wet to take the baby out, so he played on the floor and I listened to the rain. It rattled on the skylight in the stairwell and thrummed the roof, and I began to reread *Pride and Prejudice*. I read the book slowly and uncritically, lying on our new blue sofa in our new sparsely furnished town house. I read it because my mother had loved Jane Austen and because rereading it for solace

6. Novels by Henry James, published in 1881 and 1902, respectively.

7. Mark Twain's classic 1885 novel about a boy's adventures on the Mississippi River.

was something she might have done. I read it because my mother was like Jane Austen in her wit, her love of irony, and her concision. My mother was shrewd like Austen, and ingenious; she flourished in difficult professional situations. And like Austen, my mother had died young with her work unfinished.

It rained all day, and I kept reading steadily. I didn't laugh, but I smiled at Mr. Bennet and Mr. Collins and Lady Catherine de Bourgh. Mr. Darcy didn't bother me at all, but strode into the book, a dashing hero brooking no doubt or literary disappointment. Perhaps he was only a figure of romance, and perhaps Pemberley was just Austen's castle in the air. The romance and the castle were no less powerful for their escapist construction. Indeed, what I found irresistible this time was the way Austen combines astute social satire with fairy tale. The combination did not seem awkward to me, but inspired. The satire is exquisite, while the fairy tale is viscerally satisfying. How delightful to watch Elizabeth rise like Cinderella above the impediments of her mother and her younger sisters! Her mother is not wicked, but she is thoughtless and vulgar. Her sisters, with the exception of Jane, are pedantic, insipid, and lusty, and, as such, throw as many obstacles in Elizabeth's way as if sabotage had been their intent. And, of course, Mr. Bingley's sisters supply their own venom. Naturally, the obstacles make Elizabeth's victory more delicious. Here is the triumph of wit over vulgarity, self-respect over sycophancy. Until this reading, I had never appreciated Austen's fairy tale so well, but perhaps I had never needed it so much. No one dies in *Pride and Prejudice*—not even of embarrassment, as feckless Lydia and Wickham demonstrate. I no longer faulted the book for its cheerfulness or made invidious comparisons with Henry James. A dark imagination is, perhaps, more appealing before you know anything about darkness.

It is the joining of satire and fairy tale that continues to draw me to *Pride and Prejudice*, and I have been thinking about this aspect recently, after my fifth reading. This time, Elizabeth's tour of Pemberley with her aunt and uncle drew me particularly. I wondered at Austen's extensive discussion of the house—"a large, handsome, stone building, standing well on rising ground, and backed by a ridge of high woody hills"—and grounds, which are described both from the perspective of the visitors driving into the estate and through Elizabeth's eyes as she looks out a window at "the hill, crowned with wood, from which they had descended."

Austen does not generally layer on description. Her chapters are airy, uncluttered rooms, not the heavily draped, fringed, and flocked apartments of Dickens.[8] Thus, the detail she devotes to Darcy's estate is striking. Certainly, Austen is providing a catalog of all the riches Elizabeth has refused. She allows Elizabeth to contemplate the beauties of Pemberley with a poignant mixture of admiration, defensive pride, and regret. As Elizabeth and the Gardiners visit and then revisit Pemberley at Darcy's invitation, Austen reports on the stream

8. Charles Dickens, British novelist (1812–1870), best known for serial novels, usually set in London, with complex plots, many characters from all walks of life, and genial social criticism.

stocked with fish, the fine woods, and even the splendid food served: "cold meat, cake, and a variety of all the finest fruits in season." All these demonstrate Darcy's wealth, and also his graciousness, as he extends an invitation to Mr. Gardiner to come fishing, takes the ladies walking, and insists on bringing Elizabeth to meet his sister. Before, these scenes at Pemberley had seemed to me unduly fanciful. I'd felt the action slow, and grown tired of the contrivances by which Austen brings Elizabeth back to Darcy. On this reading, however, they seemed to me the most interesting in the novel, for here Austen truly defines the union between Elizabeth and Darcy, joining liveliness and formality, the bourgeois and the aristocratic, new forms and old in a utopian reworking of the world.

As I read the description of Pemberley, I saw Austen adopting the grand literary tradition of the country-house poem to describe Darcy's noble countryseat. Through Elizabeth's admiring eyes, Pemberley is nothing less than a Penshurst[9] in its natural beauty, order, and elegance. Ben Jonson had praised Penshurst as a house not "built to envious show," and Pemberley succeeds as well in surpassing lesser, and newer, estates like Lady Catherine's Rosings, which are merely ostentatious and fashionable, filled with "uselessly fine" furniture. Pemberley has every virtue that Jonson listed as essential for the great country house: the grounds, the woods, the fish, the fruit in season, the bounty of nature tamed into proportion and elegance.

15 I had read "To Penshurst" in college, and again in graduate school, but I'd never made the connection between the poem and Austen's book. As a student of the novel, I had always looked forward. I'd studied the "rise" of the novel, the development and growth and refinement of the genre. My forward thinking was also the product of my own impatience and ambition as a writer—my eagerness to dart onto the literary stage. As a reader, I've looked forward so much that I've been surprised recently by how pleasurable it can be to look back again to earlier forms, and, as Austen might have said, to rediscover the elegant and pleasing landscapes to be found there.

Like Penshurst, Pemberley is staffed with grateful servants and surrounded by respectful townspeople. It is both a productive estate and a symbol of order for the larger society. The only thing Pemberley lacks is a mistress, and in Elizabeth, Austen provides one. Elizabeth moves Darcy to show that he can be not merely great but gracious and good. This joining of greatness and goodness defines true nobility for Austen, just as it did for Jonson. And yet she goes much further than Jonson, for in her novelistic version of the country-house poem, it is not only the lord who can say he dwells there, but the middle-class admirer who will succeed in dwelling there as well. Elizabeth, the cataloger of Pemberley's beauties—and, by extension, Austen, Elizabeth's author—take possession of them. Elizabeth, who grows to appreciate Darcy's virtues—and, by extension, the reader, Elizabeth's confidant—comes to marry him. Ah, the wish fulfillment here is wonderful indeed, once you begin unfolding the wish in earnest.

9. Ben Jonson's 1616 poem, "To Penshurst," praises the greatness of the Sidney family's estate (and, by extension, the family itself) and is widely considered the great example of the country-house poem.

I think unfolding is what rereading is about. Like pleated fabric, the text reveals different parts of its pattern at different times. And yet every time the text unfolds, in the library, or in bed, or upon the grass, the reader adds new wrinkles. Memory and experience press themselves into each reading so that each encounter informs the next.

Is it possible that if you read *Pride and Prejudice* too young, the book is ruined for you? At what age should you read Jane Austen? At fifteen? Or twenty-nine? At thirty-six? Austen wrote the novel when she was just twenty. It would be strange for the reader to wait until she was older than the author. Can children grow into or out of books, as they grow into and out of clothes? I reread the novel because I read it at nine. I return to it not because it is the best novel I have read, or the most important, but because of the memories and wishes I've folded in its pages—because on every reading I see old things in it.

Questions

1. What does Goodman value about the differences among her experiences of reading *Pride and Prejudice*? Does one reading seem truer than others? Why? Is a definitive reading of a beloved book even possible?

2. Goodman offers a vivid scene of each of her readings of *Pride and Prejudice*. How does the context contribute to the meaning the book had for her?

3. Is there a right age for reading certain books? Are there books you read too early or too late? What are the advantages of reading a book at the "wrong" time?

4. Goodman says that, for Jane Austen, true nobility combines being great with being good. Using examples from this essay, discuss the meaning of each term.

5. Following Goodman's episodic structure, write an essay about a book or movie you have read or seen multiple times. How has its meaning changed for you? What do those changes tell you about yourself and your values?

Northrop Frye *The Motive for Metaphor*

For the past twenty-five years I have been teaching and studying English literature in a university. As in any other job, certain questions stick in one's mind, not because people keep asking them, but because they're the questions inspired by the very fact of being in such a place. What good is the study of literature? Does it help us to think more clearly, or feel more sensitively, or live a better life than we could without it? What is the function of the teacher and

Originally delivered as a speech and then included in Frye's book The Educated Imagination *(1964).*

scholar, or of the person who calls himself, as I do, a literary critic? What difference does the study of literature make in our social or political or religious attitude? In my early days I thought very little about such questions, not because I had any of the answers, but because I assumed that anybody who asked them was naïve. I think now that the simplest questions are not only the hardest to answer, but the most important to ask, so I'm going to raise them and try to suggest what my present answers are. I say try to suggest, because there are only more or less inadequate answers to such questions—there aren't any right answers. The kind of problem that literature raises is not the kind that you ever "solve." Whether my answers are any good or not, they represent a fair amount of thinking about the questions. As I can't see my audience, I have to choose my rhetorical style in the dark, and I'm taking the classroom style, because an audience of students is the one I feel easiest with.

There are two things in particular that I want to discuss with you. In school, and in university, there's a subject called "English" in English-speaking countries. English means, in the first place, the mother tongue. As that, it's the most practical subject in the world: you can't understand anything or take any part in your society without it. Wherever illiteracy is a problem, it's as fundamental a problem as getting enough to eat or a place to sleep. The native language takes precedence over every other subject of study: nothing else can compare with it in its usefulness. But then you find that every mother tongue, in any developed or civilized society, turns into something called literature. If you keep on studying "English," you find yourself trying to read Shakespeare and Milton. Literature, we're told, is one of the arts, along with painting and music, and, after you've looked up all the hard words and the Classical allusions and learned what words like imagery and diction are supposed to mean, what you use in understanding it, or so you're told, is your imagination. Here you don't seem to be in quite the same practical and useful area: Shakespeare and Milton, whatever their merits, are not the kind of thing you must know to hold any place in society at all. A person who knows nothing about literature may be an ignoramus, but many people don't mind being that. Every child realizes that literature is taking him in a different direction from the immediately useful, and a good many children complain loudly about this. Two questions I want to deal with, then, are, first: what is the relation of English as the mother tongue to English as a literature? Second: What is the social value of the study of literature, and what is the place of the imagination that literature addresses itself to, in the learning process?

Let's start with the different ways there are of dealing with the world we're living in. Suppose you're shipwrecked on an uninhabited island in the South Seas. The first thing you do is to take a long look at the world around you, a world of sky and sea and earth and stars and trees and hills. You see this world as objective, as something set over against you and not yourself or related to you in any way. And you notice two things about this objective world. In the first place, it doesn't have any conversation. It's full of animals and plants and insects going on with their own business, but there's nothing that responds to you: it has no morals and no intelligence, or at least none that you can grasp. It may have a shape and a meaning, but it doesn't seem to be a human shape or a human meaning. Even if there's enough to eat and no dangerous animals, you feel lonely and frightened and unwanted in such a world.

In the second place, you find that looking at the world, as something set over against you, splits your mind in two. You have an intellect that feels curious about it and wants to study it, and you have feelings or emotions that see it as beautiful or austere or terrible. You know that both these attitudes have some reality, at least for you. If the ship you were wrecked in was a Western ship, you'd probably feel that your intellect tells you more about what's really there in the outer world, and that your emotions tell you more about what's going on inside you. If your background were Oriental, you'd be more likely to reverse this and say that the beauty or terror was what was really there, and that your instinct to count and classify and measure and pull to pieces was what was inside your mind. But whether your point of view is Western or Eastern, intellect and emotion never get together in your mind as long as you're simply looking at the world. They alternate, and keep you divided between them.

5

The language you use on this level of the mind is the language of consciousness or awareness. It's largely a language of nouns and adjectives. You have to have names for things, and you need qualities like "wet" or "green" or "beautiful" to describe how things seem to you. This is the speculative or contemplative position of the mind, the position in which the arts and sciences begin, although they don't stay there very long. The sciences begin by accepting the facts and the evidence about an outside world without trying to alter them. Science proceeds by accurate measurement and description, and follows the demands of the reason rather than the emotions. What it deals with is there, whether we like it or not. The emotions are unreasonable: for them it's what they like and don't like that comes first. We'd be naturally inclined to think that the arts follow the path of emotion, in contrast to the sciences. Up to a point they do, but there's a complicating factor.

That complicating factor is the contrast between "I like this" and "I don't like this." In this Robinson Crusoe life I've assigned you,[1] you may have moods of complete peacefulness and joy, moods when you accept your island and everything around you. You wouldn't have such moods very often, and when you had them, they'd be moods of identification, when you felt that the island was a part of you and you a part of it. That is not the feeling of consciousness or awareness, where you feel split off from everything that's not your perceiving self. Your habitual state of mind is the feeling of separation which goes with being conscious, and the feeling "this is not a part of me" soon becomes "this is not what I want." Notice the word "want": we'll be coming back to it.

So you soon realize that there's a difference between the world you're living in and the world you want to live in. The world you want to live in is a human world, not an objective one: it's not an environment but a home; it's not the world you see but the world you build out of what you see. You go to work to

1. Referring to *Robinson Crusoe* (1719), a novel by Daniel Defoe (1660–1731) about a man shipwrecked on an island.

build a shelter or plant a garden, and as soon as you start to work you've moved into a different level of human life. You're not separating only yourself from nature now, but constructing a human world and separating it from the rest of the world. Your intellect and emotions are now both engaged in the same activity, so there's no longer any real distinction between them. As soon as you plant a garden or a crop, you develop the conception of a "weed," the plant you don't want in there. But you can't say that "weed" is either an intellectual or an emotional conception, because it's both at once. Further, you go to work because you feel you have to, and because you want something at the end of the work. That means that the important categories of your life are no longer the subject and the object, the watcher and the things being watched: the important categories are what you have to do and what you want to do—in other words, necessity and freedom.

One person by himself is not a complete human being, so I'll provide you with another shipwrecked refugee of the opposite sex and an eventual family. Now you're a member of a human society. This human society after a while will transform the island into something with a human shape. What that human shape is, is revealed in the shape of the work you do: the buildings, such as they are, the paths through the woods, the planted crops fenced off against whatever animals want to eat them. These things, these rudiments of city, highway, garden, and farm, are the human form of nature, or the form of human nature, whichever you like. This is the area of the applied arts and sciences, and it appears in our society as engineering and agriculture and medicine and architecture. In this area we can never say clearly where the art stops and the science begins, or vice versa.

The language you use on this level is the language of practical sense, a language of verbs or words of action and movement. The practical world, however, is a world where actions speak louder than words. In some way it's a higher level of existence than the speculative level, because it's doing something about the world instead of just looking at it, but in itself it's a much more primitive level. It's the process of adapting to the environment, or rather of transforming the environment in the interests of one species, that goes on among animals and plants as well as human beings. The animals have a good many of our practical skills: some insects make pretty fair architects, and beavers know quite a lot about engineering. In this island, probably, and certainly if you were alone, you'd have about the ranking of a second-rate animal. What makes our practical life really human is a third level of the mind, a level where consciousness and practical skill come together.

10 This third level is a vision or model in your mind of what you want to construct. There's that word "want" again. The actions of man are prompted by desire, and some of these desires are needs, like food and warmth and shelter. One of these needs is sexual, the desire to reproduce and bring more human beings into existence. But there's also a desire to bring a social human form into existence: the form of cities and gardens and farms that we call civilization. Many animals and insects have this social form too, but man knows that he has it: he can compare what he does with what he can imagine being done.

So we begin to see where the imagination belongs in the scheme of human affairs. It's the power of constructing possible models of human experience. In the world of the imagination, anything goes that's imaginatively possible, but nothing really happens. If it did happen, it would move out of the world of imagination into the world of action.

We have three levels of the mind now, and a language for each of them, which in English-speaking societies means an English for each of them. There's the level of consciousness and awareness, where the most important thing is the difference between me and everything else. The English of this level is the English of ordinary conversation, which is mostly monologue, as you'll soon realize if you do a bit of eavesdropping, or listening to yourself. We can call it the language of self-expression. Then there's the level of social participation, the working or technological language of teachers and preachers and politicians and advertisers and lawyers and journalists and scientists. We've already called this the language of practical sense. Then there's the level of imagination, which produces the literary language of poems and plays and novels. They're not really different languages, of course, but three different reasons for using words.

On this basis, perhaps, we can distinguish the arts from the sciences. Science begins with the world we have to live in, accepting its data and trying to explain its laws. From there, it moves towards the imagination: it becomes a mental construct, a model of a possible way of interpreting experience. The further it goes in this direction, the more it tends to speak the language of mathematics, which is really one of the languages of the imagination, along with literature and music. Art, on the other hand, begins with the world we construct, not with the world we see. It starts with the imagination, and then works towards ordinary experience: that is, it tries to make itself as convincing and recognizable as it can. You can see why we tend to think of the sciences as intellectual and the arts as emotional: one starts with the world as it is, the other with the world we want to have. Up to a point it is true that science gives an intellectual view of reality, and that the arts try to make the emotions as precise and disciplined as sciences do the intellect. But of course it's nonsense to think of the scientist as a cold unemotional reasoner and the artist as somebody who's in a perpetual emotional tizzy. You can't distinguish the arts from the sciences by the mental processes the people in them use: they both operate on a mixture of hunch and common sense. A highly developed science and a highly developed art are very close together, psychologically and otherwise.

Still, the fact that they start from opposite ends, even if they do meet in the middle, makes for one important difference between them. Science learns more and more about the world as it goes on: it evolves and improves. A physicist today knows more physics than Newton did, even if he's not as great a scientist. But literature begins with the possible model of experience, and what it produces is the literary model we call the classic. Literature doesn't evolve or improve or progress. We may have dramatists in the future who will write plays as good as *King Lear,* though they'll be very different ones, but drama as a whole will never get better than *King Lear. King Lear* is it, as far as drama is concerned; so is *Oedipus Rex,* written two thousand years earlier than that,[2] and both will be models of dramatic writing as long as the human race endures. Social conditions may improve: most of us would rather live in nineteenth-century United States than in thirteenth-century Italy, and for most of us Whitman's celebration of democracy makes a lot more sense than Dante's *Inferno.*[3] But it doesn't follow that Whitman is a better poet than Dante: literature won't line up with that kind of improvement.

So we find that everything that does improve, including science, leaves the literary artist out in the cold. Writers don't seem to benefit much by the advance of science, although they thrive on superstitions of all kinds. And you certainly wouldn't turn to contemporary poets for guidance or leadership in the twentieth-century world. You'd hardly go to Ezra Pound, with his fascism and social credit and Confucianism and anti-semitism. Or to Yeats, with his spiritualism and fairies and astrology. Or to D. H. Lawrence, who'll tell you that it's a good thing for servants to be flogged because that restores the precious current of blood-reciprocity between servant and master. Or to T. S. Eliot, who'll tell you that to have a flourishing culture we should educate an élite, keep most people living in the same spot, and never disestablish the Church of England.[4] The novelists seem to be a little closer to the world they're living in, but not much. When Communists talk about the decadence of bourgeois culture, this is the kind of thing they always bring up. Their own writers don't seem to be any better, though; just duller. So the real question is a bigger one. Is it possible that literature, especially poetry, is something that a scientific civilization like ours will eventually outgrow? Man has always wanted to fly, and thousands of years ago he was making sculptures of winged bulls and telling stories about people who flew so high on artificial wings that the sun melted them off.[5] In an Indian play fifteen hundred years old, *Sakuntala,* there's a god who flies around in a chariot that to a modern reader sounds very much like a private aeroplane. Interesting that the writer had so much imagination, but do we need such stories now that we have private aeroplanes?

15 This is not a new question: it was raised a hundred and fifty years ago by Thomas Love Peacock,[6] who was a poet and novelist himself, and a very brilliant one. He wrote an essay called *Four Ages of Poetry,* with his tongue of course in

2. The first is a tragedy by Shakespeare (1564–1616), the second a tragedy by Sophocles (496?–406? B.C.E.).

3. Walt Whitman (1819–1892), American poet; see "Death of Abraham Lincoln" (p. 716). Dante Alighieri (1265–1321); the *Inferno* is the first part of his *Divine Comedy.*

4. Ezra Pound (1885–1972), an American-born poet, supported Mussolini's fascist regime in Italy and the right-wing economic doctrine of social credit. William Butler Yeats (1865–1939), Irish poet and dramatist; see, for example, his prose work *A Vision.* D. H. Lawrence (1885–1930), British author; see his short story "The Prussian Officer." T. S. Eliot (1888–1965), American-born poet who emigrated to England; see his prose work *The Idea of a Christian Society.*

5. An allusion to the Greek myth of Icarus, who flew too close to the sun on wings made of wax by his father, Daedalus.

6. British author (1785–1866).

his cheek, in which he said that poetry was the mental rattle that awakened the imagination of mankind in its infancy, but that now, in an age of science and technology, the poet has outlived his social function. "A poet in our times," said Peacock, "is a semi-barbarian in a civilized community. He lives in the days that are past. His ideas, thoughts, feelings, associations, are all with barbarous manners, obsolete customs, and exploded superstitions. The march of his intellect is like that of a crab, backwards." Peacock's essay annoyed his friend Shelley,[7] who wrote another essay called *A Defence of Poetry* to refute it. Shelley's essay is a wonderful piece of writing, but it's not likely to convince anyone who needs convincing. I shall be spending a good deal of my time on this question of the relevance of literature in the world of today, and I can only indicate the general lines my answer will take. There are two points I can make now, one simple, the other more difficult.

The simple point is that literature belongs to the world man constructs, not to the world he sees; to his home, not his environment. Literature's world is a concrete human world of immediate experience. The poet uses images and objects and sensations much more than he uses abstract ideas; the novelist is concerned with telling stories, not with working out arguments. The world of literature is human in shape, a world where the sun rises in the east and sets in the west over the edge of a flat earth in three dimensions, where the primary realities are not atoms or electrons but bodies, and the primary forces not energy or gravitation but love and death and passion and joy. It's not surprising if writers are often rather simple people, not always what we think of as intellectuals, and certainly not always any freer of silliness or perversity than anyone else. What concerns us is what they produce, not what they are, and poetry, according to Milton,[8] who ought to have known, is "more simple, sensuous and passionate" than philosophy or science.

The more difficult point takes us back to what we said when we were on that South Sea island. Our emotional reaction to the world varies from "I like this" to "I don't like this." The first, we said, was a state of identity, a feeling that everything around us was part of us, and the second is the ordinary state of consciousness, or separation, where art and science begin. Art begins as soon as "I don't like this" turns into "this is not the way I could imagine it." We notice in passing that the creative and the neurotic minds have a lot in common. They're both dissatisfied with what they see; they both believe that something else ought to be there, and they try to pretend it is there or to make it be there. The differences are more important, but we're not ready for them yet.

At the level of ordinary consciousness the individual man is the center of everything, surrounded on all sides by what he isn't. At the level of practical sense, or civilization, there's a human circumference, a little cultivated world with a human shape, fenced off from the jungle and inside the sea and the sky. But in the imagination anything goes that can be imagined, and the limit of the imagination is a totally human world. Here we recapture, in full consciousness,

7. Percy Bysshe Shelley (1792–1822), British poet.

8. John Milton (1608–1674), British poet; from a prose work, *Tractate of Education*.

that original lost sense of identity with our surroundings, where there is nothing outside the mind of man, or something identical with the mind of man. Religions present us with visions of eternal and infinite heavens or paradises which have the form of the cities and gardens of human civilization, like the Jerusalem and Eden of the Bible, completely separated from the state of frustration and misery that bulks so large in ordinary life. We're not concerned with these visions as religion, but they indicate what the limits of the imagination are. They indicate too that in the human world the imagination has no limits, if you follow me. We said that the desire to fly produced the aeroplane. But people don't get into planes because they want to fly; they get into planes because they want to get somewhere else faster. What's produced the aeroplane is not so much a desire to fly as a rebellion against the tyranny of time and space. And that's a process that can never stop, no matter how high our Titovs and Glenns[9] may go.

For each of these six talks I've taken a title from some work of literature, and my title for this one is "The Motive for Metaphor," from a poem of Wallace Stevens.[10] Here's the poem:

> You like it under the trees in autumn,
> Because everything is half dead.
> The wind moves like a cripple among the leaves
> And repeats words without meaning.
>
> In the same way, you were happy in spring,
> With the half colors of quarter-things,
> The slightly brighter sky, the melting clouds,
> The single bird, the obscure moon—
>
> The obscure moon lighting an obscure world
> Of things that would never be quite expressed,
> Where you yourself were never quite yourself
> And did not want nor have to be,
>
> Desiring the exhilarations of changes:
> The motive for metaphor, shrinking from
> The weight of primary noon,
> The A B C of being,
>
> The ruddy temper, the hammer
> Of red and blue, the hard sound—
> Steel against intimation—the sharp flash,
> The vital, arrogant, fatal, dominant X.

9. Gherman S. Titov, Russian astronaut, first man to make a multi-orbital flight (1961); John H. Glenn, American astronaut, first American to make an orbital flight (1962), later became a senator from Ohio.

10. American poet (1879–1955).

What Stevens calls the weight of primary noon, the A B C of being, and the dominant X is the objective world, the world set over against us. Outside literature, the main motive for writing is to describe this world. But literature itself uses language in a way which associates our minds with it. As soon as you use associative language, you begin using figures of speech. If you say this talk is dry and dull, you're using figures associating it with bread and breadknives. There are two main kinds of association, analogy and identity, two things that are like each other and two things that are each other. You can say with Burns,[11] "My love's like a red, red rose," or you can say with Shakespeare:

> Thou that art now the world's fresh ornament
> And only herald to the gaudy spring.

One produces the figure of speech called the simile; the other produces the figure called metaphor.

20 In descriptive writing you have to be careful of associative language. You'll find that analogy, or likeness to something else, is very tricky to handle in description, because the differences are as important as the resemblances. As for metaphor, where you're really saying "this *is* that," you're turning your back on logic and reason completely, because logically two things can never be the same thing and still remain two things. The poet, however, uses these two crude, primitive, archaic forms of thought in the most uninhibited way, because his job is not to describe nature, but to show you a world completely absorbed and possessed by the human mind. So he produces what Baudelaire[12] called a "suggestive magic including at the same time object and subject, the world outside the artist and the artist himself." The motive for metaphor, according to Wallace Stevens, is a desire to associate, and finally to identify, the human mind with what goes on outside it, because the only genuine joy you can have is in those rare moments when you feel that although we may know in part, as Paul says, we are also a part of what we know.[13]

11. Robert Burns (1759–1796), Scottish poet.
12. Charles Baudelaire (1821–1867), French poet.
13. An allusion to 1 Corinthians 13.9–10: "For we know in part, and we prophecy in part. But when that which is perfect is come, then that which is in part shall be done away with."

QUESTIONS

1. At what point in his essay does Frye come to the meaning of his title? What is his conception of the motive for metaphor? Why does he wait to explain it?

2. Frye describes three kinds of English, or, rather, he describes one English and three uses to which we put it. What are they?

3. Frye describes metaphor, forcibly, as nonsense (paragraph 20). How, then, do we make sense of it?

4. Why, according to Frye, doesn't literature improve the way science does? What happens to old science? Read Thomas S. Kuhn's "The Route to Normal Science" (p. 899), and do additional research if necessary. Then write an essay in which you compare the fates of old literature and old science.

MARK DOTY *Souls on Ice*

IN THE STOP 'N SHOP in Orleans, Massachusetts, I was struck by the elegance of the mackerel in the fresh-fish display. They were rowed and stacked, brilliant against the white of the crushed ice; I loved how black and glistening the bands of dark scales were, and the prismed sheen of the patches between, and their shining flat eyes. I stood and looked at them for a while, just paying attention while I leaned on my cart—before I remembered where I was and realized that I was standing in someone's way.

Our metaphors go on ahead of us, they know before we do. And thank goodness for that, for if I were dependent on other ways of coming to knowledge I think I'd be a very slow study. I need something to serve as a container for emotion and idea, a vessel that can hold what's too slippery or charged or difficult to touch. Will doesn't have much to do with this; I can't choose what's going to serve as a compelling image for me. But I've learned to trust that part of my imagination that gropes forward, feeling its way toward what it needs; to watch for the signs of fascination, the sense of compelled attention (*Look at me*, something seems to say, *closely*) that indicates that there's something I need to attend to. Sometimes it seems to me as if metaphor were the advance guard of the mind; something in us reaches out, into the landscape in front of us, looking for the right vessel, the right vehicle, for whatever will serve.

Driving home from the grocery, I found myself thinking again about the fish, and even scribbled some phrases on an envelope in the car, something about stained glass, soapbubbles, while I was driving. It wasn't long—that same day? the next?—before I was at my desk, trying simply to describe what I had seen. I almost always begin with description, as a way of focusing on that compelling image, the poem's "given." I know that what I can see is just the proverbial tip of the iceberg; if I do my work of study and examination, and if I am lucky, the image which I've been intrigued by will become a metaphor, will yield depth and meaning, will lead me to insight. The goal here is inquiry, the attempt to get at what it is that's so interesting about what's struck me. Because it isn't just beauty; the world is full of lovely things and that in itself wouldn't compel me to write. There's something else, some gravity or charge to this image that makes me need to investigate it.

Originally published in Introspections: American Poets on One of Their Own Poems, *ed. Robert Pack and Jay Parini, in 1997.*

Exploratory description, then; I'm a scientist trying to measure and record what's seen. The first two sentences of the poem attempt sheer observation, but by the second's list of tropes (abalone, soapbubble skin, oil on a puddle) it's clear to me that these descriptive terms aren't merely there to chronicle the physical reality of the object. Like all descriptions, they reflect the psychic state of the observer; they aren't "neutral," though they might pretend to be, but instead suggest a point of view, a stance toward what is being seen. In this case one of the things suggested by these tropes is interchangeability; if you've seen one abalone shell or prismy soapbubble or psychedelic puddle, you've seen them all.

And thus my image began to unfold for me, in the evidence these terms provided, and I had a clue toward the focus my poem would take. Another day, another time in my life, the mackerel might have been metaphor for something else; they might have served as the crux for an entirely different examination. But now I began to see why they mattered for *this* poem; and the sentence that follows commences the poem's investigative process: 5

> Splendor, and splendor,
> and not a one in any way
>
> distinguished from the other
> —nothing about them
> of individuality.

There's a terrific kind of exhilaration for me at this point in the unfolding of a poem, when a line of questioning has been launched, and the work has moved from evocation to meditation. A direction is coming clear, and it bears within it the energy that the image contained for me in the first place. Now, I think, we're getting down to it. This élan carried me along through two more sentences, one that considers the fish as replications of the ideal, Platonic Mackerel, and one that likewise imagines them as the intricate creations of an obsessively repetitive jeweler.

Of course my process of unfolding the poem wasn't quite this neat. There were false starts, wrong turnings that I wound up throwing out when they didn't seem to lead anywhere. I can't remember now, because the poem has worked the charm of its craft on my memory; it convinces me that it is an artifact of a process of inquiry. The drama of the poem is its action of thinking through a question. Mimicking a sequence of perceptions and meditation, it tries to make us think that this feeling and thinking and knowing is taking place even as the poem is being written. Which, in a way, it *is*—just not this neatly or seamlessly! A poem is always a *made* version of experience.

Also, needless to say, my poem was full of repetitions, weak lines, unfinished phrases and extra descriptions, later trimmed, I like to work on a computer, because I can type quickly, put everything in, and still read the results later on, which isn't always true of my handwriting. I *did* feel early on that the poem seemed to want to be a short-lined one, I liked breaking the movement of these extended sentences over the clipped line, and the spotlight-bright focus the short line puts on individual terms felt right. "Iridescent, watery," for instance, pleased me as a line-unit, as did this stanza:

> prismatics: think abalone,
> the wildly rainbowed
> mirror of a soapbubble sphere,

Short lines underline sonic textures, heightening tension. The short a's of *prismatics* and *abalone* ring more firmly, as do the o's of *abalone, rainbowed* and *soapbubble.* The rhyme of mirror and sphere at beginning and end of line engages me, and I'm also pleased by the way in which these short lines slow the poem down, parceling it out as it were to the reader, with the frequent pauses introduced by the stanza breaks between tercets adding lots of white space, a meditative pacing.

And there, on the jeweler's bench, my poem seemed to come to rest, though it was clear there was more to be done. Some further pressure needed to be placed on the poem's material to force it to yield its depths. I waited a while, I read it over. Again, in what I had already written, the clues contained in image pushed the poem forward.

10 *Soul, heaven* . . . The poem had already moved into the realm of theology, but the question that arose ("Suppose we could iridesce . . .") startled me nonetheless, because the notion of losing oneself "entirely in the universe / of shimmer" referred both to these fish and to something quite other, something overwhelmingly close to home. The poem was written some six months after my partner of a dozen years had died of AIDS, and of course everything I wrote—everything I *saw*—was informed by that loss, by the overpowering emotional force of it. Epidemic was the central fact of the community in which I lived. Naively, I hadn't realized that my mackerel were already of a piece with the work I'd been writing for the previous couple of years—poems that wrestled, in one way or another, with the notion of limit, with the line between being someone and no one. What did it mean to be a self, when that self would be lost? To praise the collectivity of the fish, their common identity as "flashing participants," is to make a sort of anti-elegy, to suggest that what matters is perhaps not our individual selves but our brief soldiering in the broad streaming school of humanity—which is composed of us, yes, but also goes on without us.

The one of a kind, the singular, like my dear lover, cannot last.

And yet the collective life, which is also us, shimmers on.

Once I realized the poem's subject-beneath-the-subject, the final stanzas of the poem opened swiftly out from there. The collective momentum of the fish is such that even death doesn't seem to still rob its forward movement; the singularity of each fish more or less doesn't really exist, it's "all for all," like the Three Musketeers. I could not have considered these ideas "nakedly," without the vehicle of mackerel to help me think about human identity. Nor, I think, could

I have addressed these things without a certain playfulness of tone, which appeared first in the archness of "oily fabulation" and the neologism of "iridesce." It's the blessed permission distance gives that allows me to speak of such things at all; a little comedy can also help to hold terrific anxiety at bay. Thus the "rainbowed school / and its acres of brilliant classrooms" is a joke, but one that's already collapsing on itself, since what is taught there—the limits of "me"—is our hardest lesson. No verb is singular because it is the school that acts, or the tribe, the group, the species; or every verb is singular because the only I there *is* is a we.

The poem held one more surprise for me, which was the final statement—it came as a bit of a shock, actually, and when I'd written it I knew I was done. It's a formulation of the theory that the poem has been moving toward all along: that our glory is not our individuality (much as we long for the Romantic self and its private golden heights) but our commonness. I do not like this idea. I would rather be one fish, sparkling in my own pond, but experience does not bear this out. And so I have, tried to convince myself, here, that beauty lies in the whole and that therefore death, the loss of the part, is not so bad—is, in fact, almost nothing. What does our individual disappearance mean—or our love, or our desire—when, as the Marvelettes[1] put it, "There's too many fish in the sea . . . ?"

I find this consoling, strangely, and maybe that's the best way to think of this poem—an attempt at cheering oneself up about the mystery of being both an individual and part of a group, an attempt on the part of the speaker in the poem (me) to convince himself that losing individuality, slipping into the life of the world, could be a good thing. All attempts to console ourselves, I believe, are doomed, because the world is more complicated than we are. Our explanations will fail, but it is our human work to make them. And my beautiful fish, limited though they may be as parable, do help me; they are an image I return to in order to remember, in the face of individual erasures, the burgeoning, good, common life. Even after my work of inquiry, my metaphor may still know more than I do; the bright eyes of those fish gleam on, in memory, brighter than what I've made of them. 15

A Display of Mackerel

They lie in parallel rows,
on ice, head to tail,
each a foot of luminosity

barred with black bands,
which divide the scales' 5
radiant sections

1. Motown's first hit-making girl group had a hit with the song "Too Many Fish in the Sea" (1964).

like seams of lead
in a Tiffany window.
Iridescent, watery

10 prismatics: think abalone,
the wildly rainbowed
mirror of a soapbubble sphere,

think sun on gasoline.
Splendor, and splendor,
15 and not a one in any way

distinguished from the other
—nothing about them
of individuality. Instead

they're *all* exact expressions
20 of one soul,
each a perfect fulfillment

of heaven's template,
mackerel essence. As if,
after a lifetime arriving

25 at this enameling, the jeweler's
made uncountable examples,
each as intricate

in its oily fabulation
as the one before.
30 Suppose we could iridesce,

like these, and lose ourselves
entirely in the universe
of shimmer—would you want

to be yourself only,
35 unduplicatable, doomed
to be lost? They'd prefer,

plainly, to be flashing participants,
multitudinous. Even now
they seem to be bolting

40 forward, heedless of stasis.
They don't care they're dead
and nearly frozen,

just as, presumably,
they didn't care that they were living:
45 all, all for all,

the rainbowed school
and its acres of brilliant classrooms,
in which no verb is singular,

or every one is. How happy they seem,
50 even on ice, to be together, selfless,
which is the price of gleaming.

QUESTIONS

1. What does Doty mean by the subject beneath the subject? How does he find it?

2. Look at how Doty analyzes his own favorite stanza. Read "A Display of Mackerel" again. Choose and analyze the language of your favorite stanza.

3. Doty claims not to like the poem's message, that "our glory is . . . our commonness." Which aspects of the essay and poem celebrate individuality and which celebrate commonness? Which do you think Doty prefers? How do you see the relation between the two?

4. Go to a grocery store, a cafeteria, or some other ordinary spot and look for an image that arrests you. Describe it and then write until you find your own subject beneath the subject. Why did this image capture your attention?

NGŨGĨ WA THIONG'O *Decolonizing the Mind*

I WAS BORN into a large peasant family: father, four wives and about twenty-eight children. I also belonged, as we all did in those days, to a wider extended family and to the community as a whole.

We spoke Gĩkũyũ[1] as we worked in the fields. We spoke Gĩkũyũ in and outside the home. I can vividly recall those evenings of storytelling around the fireside. It was mostly the grown-ups telling the children but everybody was interested and involved. We children would re-tell the stories the following day to other children who worked in the fields picking the pyrethrum[2] flowers, tea-leaves or coffee beans of our European and African landlords.

The stories, with mostly animals as the main characters, were all told in Gĩkũyũ. Hare, being small, weak but full of innovative wit and cunning, was our hero. We identified with him as he struggled against the brutes of prey like

Published in Decolonising the Mind: The Politics of Language in African Literature *(1986), a collection of essays reflecting on the relations of modern African literature to its European heritage and arguing for a new, independent African tradition.*

1. Language spoken by the Kikuyu people, the majority of Kenyans.
2. Type of chrysanthemum, often used as an insecticide or for medicinal purposes.

on, leopard, hyena. His victories were our victories and we learned that the apparently weak can outwit the strong. We followed the animals in their struggle against hostile nature—drought, rain, sun, wind—a confrontation often forcing them to search for forms of co-operation. But we were also interested in their struggles amongst themselves, and particularly between the beasts and the victims of prey. These twin struggles, against nature and other animals, reflected real-life struggles in the human world.

Not that we neglected stories with human beings as the main characters. There were two types of characters in such human-centered narratives: the species of truly human beings with qualities of courage, kindness, mercy, hatred of evil, concern for others; and a man-eat-man two-mouthed species with qualities of greed, selfishness, individualism and hatred of what was good for the larger co-operative community. Co-operation as the ultimate good in a community was a constant theme. It could unite human beings with animals against ogres and beasts of prey, as in the story of how dove, after being fed with castor-oil seeds, was sent to fetch a smith working far away from home and whose pregnant wife was being threatened by these man-eating two-mouthed ogres.

There were good and bad story-tellers. A good one could tell the same story over and over again, and it would always be fresh to us, the listeners. He or she could tell a story told by someone else and make it more alive and dramatic. The differences really were in the use of words and images and the inflection of voices to effect different tones.

We therefore learned to value words for their meaning and nuances. Language was not a mere string of words. It had a suggestive power well beyond the immediate and lexical meaning. Our appreciation of the suggestive magical power of language was reinforced by the games we played with words through riddles, proverbs, transpositions of syllables, or through nonsensical but musically arranged words. So we learned the music of our language on top of the content. The language, through images and symbols, gave us a view of the world, but it had a beauty of its own. The home and the field were then our pre-primary school but what is important, for this discussion, is that the language of our evening teach-ins, and the language of our immediate and wider community, and the language of our work in the fields were one.

And then I went to school, a colonial school, and this harmony was broken. The language of my education was no longer the language of my culture. I first went to Kamaandura, missionary run, and then to another called Maanguuũ run by nationalists grouped around the Gĩkũyũ Independent and Karinga Schools Association. Our language of education was still Gĩkũyũ. The very first time I was ever given an ovation for my writing was over a composition in Gĩkũyũ. So for my first four years there was still harmony between the language of my formal education and that of the Limuru peasant community.

It was after the declaration of a state of emergency over Kenya in 1952 that all the schools run by patriotic nationalists were taken over by the colonial regime and were placed under District Education Boards chaired by Englishmen. English became the language of my formal education. In Kenya, English became more than a language: it was *the* language, and all the others had to bow before it in deference.

Thus one of the most humiliating experiences was to be caught speaking Gĩkũyũ in the vicinity of the school. The culprit was given corporal punishment—three to five strokes of the cane on bare buttocks—or was made to carry a metal plate around the neck with inscriptions such as I AM STUPID or I AM A DONKEY. Sometimes the culprits were fined money they could hardly afford. And how did the teachers catch the culprits? A button was initially given to one pupil who was supposed to hand it over to whoever was caught speaking his mother tongue. Whoever had the button at the end of the day would sing who had given it to him and the ensuing process would bring out all the culprits of the day. Thus children were turned into witch-hunters and in the process were being taught the lucrative value of being a traitor to one's immediate community.

10 The attitude to English was the exact opposite: any achievement in spoken or written English was highly rewarded; prizes, prestige, applause; the ticket to higher realms. English became the measure of intelligence and ability in the arts, the sciences, and all the other branches of learning. English became *the* main determinant of a child's progress up the ladder of formal education.

As you may know, the colonial system of education in addition to its apartheid racial demarcation had the structure of a pyramid: a broad primary base, a narrowing secondary middle, and an even narrower university apex. Selections from primary into secondary were through an examination, in my time called Kenya African Preliminary Examination, in which one had to pass six subjects ranging from Maths to Nature Study and Kiswahili.[3] All the papers were written in English. Nobody could pass the exam who failed the English language paper no matter how brilliantly he had done in the other subjects. I remember one boy in my class of 1954 who had distinctions in all subjects except English, which he had failed. He was made to fail the entire exam. He went on to become a turn boy[4] in a bus company. I who had only passes but a credit in English got a place at the Alliance High School, one of the most elitist institutions for Africans in colonial Kenya. The requirements for a place at the University, Makerere University College, were broadly the same: nobody could go on to wear the undergraduate red gown, no matter how brilliantly they had performed in all the other subjects unless they had a credit—not even a simple pass!—in English. Thus the most coveted place in the pyramid and in the system was only available to the holder of an English language credit card. English was the official vehicle and the magic formula to colonial elitedom.

Literary education was now determined by the dominant language while also reinforcing that dominance. Orature (oral literature) in Kenyan languages stopped. In primary school I now read simplified Dickens and Stevenson alongside Rider Haggard. Jim Hawkins, Oliver Twist, Tom Brown[5]—not Hare, Leopard

3. Swahili, a major East African language.

4. A tout; someone who brings in customers.

5. Charles Dickens (1812–1870), British novelist, author of *Oliver Twist*; Robert Louis Stevenson (1850–1894), Scottish novelist, creator of Jim Hawkins in *Treasure Island*;

and Lion—were now my daily companions in the world of imagination. In secondary school, Scott and G. B. Shaw vied with more Rider Haggard, John Buchan, Alan Paton, Captain W. E. Johns.[6] At Makerere I read English: from Chaucer to T.S. Eliot with a touch of Grahame Greene.[7]

Thus language and literature were taking us further and further from ourselves to other selves, from our world to other worlds.

What was the colonial system doing to us Kenyan children? What were the consequences of, on the one hand, this systematic suppression of our languages and the literature they carried, and on the other the elevation of English and the literature it carried? To answer those questions, let me first examine the relationship of language to human experience, human culture, and the human perception of reality.

15 Language, any language, has a dual character: it is both a means of communication and a carrier of culture. Take English. It is spoken in Britain and in Sweden and Denmark. But for Swedish and Danish people English is only a means of communication with non-Scandinavians. It is not a carrier of their culture. For the British, and particularly the English, it is additionally, and inseparably from its use as a tool of communication, a carrier of their culture and history. Or take Swahili in East and Central Africa. It is widely used as a means of communication across many nationalities. But it is not the carrier of a culture and history of many of those nationalities. However in parts of Kenya and Tanzania, and particularly in Zanzibar,[8] Swahili is inseparably both a means of communication and a carrier of the culture of those people to whom it is a mother-tongue.

Language as communication has three aspects or elements. There is first what Karl Marx[9] once called the language of real life, the element basic to the whole notion of language, its origins and development: that is, the relations people enter into with one another in the labor process, the links they necessarily establish among themselves in the act of a people, a community of human beings, producing wealth or means of life like food, clothing, houses. A human community really starts its historical being as a community of co-operation in production through the division of labor; the simplest is between man, woman and child within a household; the more complex divisions are between branches of produc-

H. Rider Haggard (1856–1925), British adventure novelist; Tom Brown, chief character in *Tom Brown's Schooldays* in the novel by Thomas Hughes (1822–1896).

6. Sir Walter Scott (1771–1832), Scottish poet and novelist; George Bernard Shaw (1856–1950), Irish-born playwright; Buchan (1875–1940), Scottish adventure novelist, author of *The Thirty-Nine Steps,* and also governor general of Canada; Paton (1903–1988), South African novelist; Johns (1893–1968), British writer, famous for the Biggles stories for boys.

7. Geoffrey Chaucer (c. 1343–1400), English poet, author of *The Canterbury Tales*; Eliot (1888–1965), American-born poet; Greene (1904–1991), British novelist.

8. Island off the east coast of Africa; part of Tanzania since 1964.

9. German political philosopher (1818–1883).

tion such as those who are sole hunters, sole gatherers of fruits or sole workers in metal. Then there are the most complex divisions such as those in modern factories where a single product, say a shirt or a shoe, is the result of many hands and minds. Production is co-operation, is communication, is language, is expression of a relation between human beings and it is specifically human.

The second aspect of language as communication is speech and it imitates the language of real life, that is communication in production. The verbal signposts both reflect and aid communication or the relation established between human beings in the production of their means of life. Language as a system of verbal signposts makes that production possible. The spoken word is to relations between human beings what the hand is to the relations between human beings and nature. The hand through tools mediates between human beings and nature and forms the language of real life: spoken words mediate between human beings and form the language of speech.

The third aspect is the written signs. The written word imitates the spoken. Where the first two aspects of language as communication through the hand and the spoken word historically evolved more or less simultaneously, the written aspect is a much later historical development. Writing is representation of sounds with visual symbols, from the simplest knot among shepherds to tell the number in a herd or the hieroglyphics among the Agĩkũyũ gicaandi[10] singers and poets of Kenya, to the most complicated and different letter and picture writing systems of the world today.

In most societies the written and the spoken languages are the same, in that they represent each other: what is on paper can be read to another person and be received as that language, which the recipient has grown up speaking. In such a society there is broad harmony for a child between the three aspects of language as communication. His interaction with nature and with other men is expressed in written and spoken symbols or signs which are both a result of that double interaction and a reflection of it. The association of the child's sensibility is with the language of his experience of life.

But there is more to it: communication between human beings is also the basis and process of evolving culture. In doing similar kinds of things and actions over and over again under similar circumstances, similar even in their mutability, certain patterns, moves, rhythms, habits, attitudes, experiences and knowledge emerge. Those experiences are handed over to the next generation and become the inherited basis for their further actions on nature and on themselves. There is a gradual accumulation of values which in time become almost self-evident truths governing their conception of what is right and wrong, good and bad, beautiful and ugly, courageous and cowardly, generous and mean in their internal and external relations. Over a time this becomes a way of life distinguishable from other ways of life. They develop a distinctive culture and history. Culture embodies those moral, ethical and aesthetic values, the set of spiritual eyeglasses, through which they come to view themselves and their

10. Agĩkũyũ, another term for Kikuyu, the group that forms the majority of the Kenyan population; gicaandi, a particular Kenyan song genre.

place in the universe. Values are the basis of a people's identity, their sense of particularity as members of the human race. All this is carried by language. Language as culture is the collective memory bank of a people's experience in history. Culture is almost indistinguishable from the language that makes possible its genesis, growth, banking, articulation and indeed its transmission from one generation to the next.

Language as culture also has three important aspects. Culture is a product of the history which it in turn reflects. Culture in other words is a product and a reflection of human beings communicating with one another in the very struggle to create wealth and to control it. But culture does not merely reflect that history, or rather it does so by actually forming images or pictures of the world of nature and nurture. Thus the second aspect of language as culture is as an image-forming agent in the mind of a child. Our whole conception of ourselves as a people, individually and collectively, is based on those pictures and images which may or may not correctly correspond to the actual reality of the struggles with nature and nurture which produced them in the first place. But our capacity to confront the world creatively is dependent on how those images correspond or not to that reality, how they distort or clarify the reality of our struggles. Language as culture is thus mediating between me and my own self; between my own self and other selves; between me and nature. Language is mediating in my very being. And this brings us to the third aspect of language as culture. Culture transmits or imparts those images of the world and reality through the spoken and the written language, that is through a specific language. In other words, the capacity to speak, the capacity to order sounds in a manner that makes for mutual comprehension between human beings is universal. This is the universality of language, a quality specific to human beings. It corresponds to the universality of the struggle against nature and that between human beings. But the particularity of the sounds, the words, the word order into phrases and sentences, and the specific manner, or laws, of their ordering is what distinguishes one language from another. Thus a specific culture is not transmitted through language in its universality but in its particularity as the language of a specific community with a specific history. Written literature and orature are the main means by which a particular language transmits the images of the world contained in the culture it carries.

Language as communication and as culture are then products of each other. Communication creates culture: culture is a means of communication. Language carries culture, and culture carries, particularly through orature and literature, the entire body of values by which we come to perceive ourselves and our place in the world. How people perceive themselves affects how they look at their culture, at their politics and at the social production of wealth, at their entire relationship to nature and to other beings. Language is thus inseparable from ourselves as a community of human beings with a specific form and character, a specific history, a specific relationship to the world.

So what was the colonialist imposition of a foreign language doing to us children?

The real aim of colonialism was to control the people's wealth: what they produced, how they produced it, and how it was distributed; to control, in other words, the entire realm of the language of real life. Colonialism imposed its control of the social production of wealth through military conquest and subsequent political dictatorship. But its most important area of domination was the mental universe of the colonized, the control, through culture, of how people perceived themselves and their relationship to the world. Economic and political control can never be complete or effective without mental control. To control a people's culture is to control their tools of self-definition in relationship to others.

For colonialism this involved two aspects of the same process: the destruction or the deliberate undervaluing of a people's culture, their art, dances, religions, history, geography, education, orature and literature, and the conscious elevation of the language of the colonizer. The domination of a people's language by the languages of the colonizing nations was crucial to the domination of the mental universe of the colonized. 25

Take language as communication. Imposing a foreign language, and suppressing the native languages as spoken and written, were already breaking the harmony previously existing between the African child and the three aspects of language. Since the new language as a means of communication was a product of and was reflecting the "real language of life" elsewhere, it could never as spoken or written properly reflect or imitate the real life of that community. This may in part explain why technology always appears to us as slightly external, *their* product and not *ours*. The word "missile" used to hold an alien faraway sound until I recently learnt its equivalent in Gĩkũyũ, *ngurukuhĩ* and it made me apprehend it differently. Learning, for a colonial child, became a cerebral activity and not an emotionally felt experience.

But since the new, imposed languages could never completely break the native languages as spoken, their most effective area of domination was the third aspect of language as communication, the written. The language of an African child's formal education was foreign. The language of the books he read was foreign. The language of his conceptualization was foreign. Thought, in him, took the visible form of a foreign language. So the written language of a child's upbringing in the school (even his spoken language within the school compound) became divorced from his spoken language at home. There was often not the slightest relationship between the child's written world, which was also the language of his schooling, and the world of his immediate environment in the family and the community. For a colonial child, the harmony existing between the three aspects of language as communication was irrevocably broken. This resulted in the disassociation of the sensibility[11] of that child from his natural and social environment, what we might call colonial alienation. The alienation became reinforced in the teaching of history, geography, music, where bourgeois Europe was always the center of the universe.

11. An echo of T. S. Eliot's famous term "dissociation of sensibility," a break from the past, when thought and feeling were unified.

The disassociation, divorce, or alienation from the immediate environment becomes clearer when you look at colonial language as a carrier of culture.

Since culture is a product of the history of a people which it in turn reflects, the child was now being exposed exclusively to a culture that was a product of a world external to himself. He was being made to stand outside himself to look at himself. *Catching Them Young* is the title of a book on racism, class, sex, and politics in children's literature by Bob Dixon.[12] "Catching them young" as an aim was even more true of a colonial child. The images of his world and his place in it implanted in a child take years to eradicate, if they ever can be.

30 Since culture does not just reflect the world in images but actually, through those images, conditions a child to see that world a certain way, the colonial child was made to see the world and where he stands in it as seen and defined by or reflected in the culture of the language of imposition.

And since those images are mostly passed on through orature and literature it meant the child would now only see the world as seen in the literature of his language of adoption. From the point of view of alienation, that is of seeing oneself from outside oneself as if one was another self, it does not matter that the imported literature carried the great humanist tradition of the best Shakespeare, Goethe, Balzac, Tolstoy, Gorky, Brecht, Sholokhov,[13] Dickens. The location of this great mirror of imagination was necessarily Europe and its history and culture and the rest of the universe was seen from that center.

But obviously it was worse when the colonial child was exposed to images of his world as mirrored in the written languages of his colonizer. Where his own native languages were associated in his impressionable mind with low status, humiliation, corporal punishment, slow-footed intelligence and ability or downright stupidity, non-intelligibility and barbarism, this was reinforced by the world he met in the works of such geniuses of racism as a Rider Haggard or a Nicholas Monsarrat;[14] not to mention the pronouncement of some of the giants of western intellectual and political establishment, such as Hume (". . . The negro is naturally inferior to the whites . . ."), Thomas Jefferson (". . . The blacks . . . are inferior to the whites on the endowments of both body and mind . . ."), or Hegel[15] with his Africa comparable to a land of childhood still enveloped in the dark mantle of the night as far as the development of self-

12. Bob Dixon's *Catching Them Young* appeared in two volumes: *Sex, Race, and Class in Children's Fiction* and *Political Ideas in Children's Fiction*.

13. William Shakespeare (1564–1616), English playwright; Johann Wolfgang von Goethe (1749–1832), German novelist and playwright; Honoré de Balzac (1799–1850), French novelist; Leo (Count Lev Nikolayerich) Tolstoy (1828–1910), Russian novelist; Maxim Gorky (1868–1936), Russian dramatist; Bertolt Brecht (1898–1956), German dramatist; Mikhail Aleksandrovich Sholokhov (1905–1984), Russian novelist.

14. British novelist Nicholas Monsarrat's *The Tribe That Lost Its Head* (1956) was a satirical look at British colonialism and the African independence movement.

15. David Hume (1711–1776), Scottish philosopher; Jefferson (1743–1826), third U.S. president, 1801–9; Georg Wilhelm Friedrich Hegel (1770–1831), German philosopher.

conscious history was concerned. Hegel's statement that there was nothing harmonious with humanity to be found in the African character is representative of the racist images of Africans and Africa such a colonial child was bound to encounter in the literature of the colonial languages. The results could be disastrous.

Questions

1. The last paragraphs of Thiong'o's essay contain the names of many classic and contemporary European writers. Why do you think he chose to include them? Can you relate their inclusion to the way Thiong'o chooses to present himself in this essay?

2. What literary writers did you read in secondary school? What values were your teachers (or school) imparting in selecting those writers in particular?

3. Thiong'o experienced a particularly stark contrast between the values contained within the oral stories of his family and the written English of school. Discuss the different value systems. Have you noticed differences between what your extended family values and what your school seemed to want you to value?

4. Imagine an English class for a bilingual or bicultural community. Write a paper justifying the ideal balance between texts from the second language or culture (in translation or not) and English.

Virginia Woolf — *In Search of a Room of One's Own*

It was disappointing not to have brought back in the evening some important statement, some authentic fact. Women are poorer than men because—this or that. Perhaps now it would be better to give up seeking for the truth, and receiving on one's head an avalanche of opinion hot as lava, discolored as dish-water. It would be better to draw the curtains; to shut out distractions; to light the lamp; to narrow the enquiry and to ask the historian, who records not opinions but facts, to describe under what conditions women lived, not throughout the ages, but in England, say in the time of Elizabeth.

For it is a perennial puzzle why no woman wrote a word of that extraordinary literature when every other man, it seemed, was capable of song or sonnet. What were the conditions in which women lived, I asked myself; for fiction, imaginative work that is, is not dropped like a pebble upon the ground,

From chapter three of Woolf's A Room of One's Own *(1929), a long essay that began as lectures given at Newnham College and Girton College, women's colleges at Cambridge University, in 1928. In chapter one, Woolf advances the proposition that "a woman must have money and a room of her own if she is to write fiction." In chapter two, she describes a day spent at the British Museum (now the British Library) looking for information about the lives of women.*

as science may be; fiction is like a spider's web, attached ever so lightly perhaps, but still attached to life at all four corners. Often the attachment is scarcely perceptible; Shakespeare's plays, for instance, seem to hang there complete by themselves. But when the web is pulled askew, hooked up at the edge, torn in the middle, one remembers that these webs are not spun in midair by incorporeal creatures, but are the work of suffering human beings, and are attached to grossly material things, like health and money and the houses we live in.

I went, therefore, to the shelf where the histories stand and took down one of the latest, Professor Trevelyan's *History of England.* Once more I looked up Women, found "position of," and turned to the pages indicated. "Wife-beating," I read, "was a recognised right of man, and was practised without shame by high as well as low. . . . Similarly," the historian goes on, "the daughter who refused to marry the gentleman of her parents' choice was liable to be locked up, beaten and flung about the room, without any shock being inflicted on public opinion. Marriage was not an affair of personal affection, but of family avarice, particularly in the 'chivalrous' upper classes. . . . Betrothal often took place while one or both of the parties was in the cradle, and marriage when they were scarcely out of the nurses' charge." That was about 1470, soon after Chaucer's time. The next reference to the position of women is some two hundred years later, in the time of the Stuarts. "It was still the exception for women of the upper and middle class to choose their own husbands, and when the husband had been assigned, he was lord and master, so far at least as law and custom could make him. Yet even so," Professor Trevelyan concludes, "neither Shakespeare's women nor those of authentic seventeenth-century memoirs, like the Verneys and the Hutchinsons, seem wanting in personality and character." Certainly, if we consider it, Cleopatra must have had a way with her; Lady Macbeth, one would suppose, had a will of her own; Rosalind, one might conclude, was an attractive girl. Professor Trevelyan is speaking no more than the truth when he remarks that Shakespeare's women do not seem wanting in personality and character. Not being a historian, one might go even further and say that women have burnt like beacons in all the works of all the poets from the beginning of time—Clytemnestra, Antigone, Cleopatra, Lady Macbeth, Phèdre, Cressida, Rosalind, Desdemona, the Duchess of Malfi, among the dramatists; then among the prose writers: Millamant, Clarissa, Becky Sharp, Anna Karenina, Emma Bovary, Madame de Guermantes—the names flock to mind, nor do they recall women "lacking in personality and character." Indeed, if woman had no existence save in the fiction written by men, one would imagine her a person of the utmost importance; very various; heroic and mean; splendid and sordid; infinitely beautiful and hideous in the extreme; as great as a man, some think even greater.[1] But this is woman in fiction. In fact, as

1. "It remains a strange and almost inexplicable fact that in Athena's city, where women were kept in almost Oriental suppression as odalisques or drudges, the stage should yet have produced figures like Clytemnestra and Cassandra, Atossa and Antigone, Phèdre and Medea, and all the other heroines who dominate play after play of the 'misogynist' Euripides. But the paradox of this world where in real life a respectable woman could

Professor Trevelyan points out, she was locked up, beaten and flung about the room.

A very queer, composite being thus emerges. Imaginatively she is of the highest importance; practically she is completely insignificant. She pervades poetry from cover to cover; she is all but absent from history. She dominates the lives of kings and conquerors in fiction; in fact she was the slave of any boy whose parents forced a ring upon her finger. Some of the most inspired words, some of the most profound thoughts in literature fall from her lips; in real life she could hardly read, could scarcely spell, and was the property of her husband.

It was certainly an odd monster that one made up by reading the historians first and the poets afterwards—a worm winged like an eagle; the spirit of life and beauty in a kitchen chopping up suet. But these monsters, however amusing to the imagination, have no existence in fact. What one must do to bring her to life was to think poetically and prosaically at one and the same moment, thus keeping in touch with fact—that she is Mrs. Martin, aged thirty-six, dressed in blue, wearing a black hat and brown shoes; but not losing sight of fiction either—that she is a vessel in which all sorts of spirits and forces are coursing and flashing perpetually. The moment, however, that one tries this method with the Elizabethan woman, one branch of illumination fails; one is held up by the scarcity of facts. One knows nothing detailed, nothing perfectly true and substantial about her. History scarcely mentions her. And I turned to Professor Trevelyan again to see what history meant to him. I found by looking at his chapter headings that it meant— 5

"The Manor Court and the Methods of Open-field Agriculture . . . The Cistercians and Sheep-farming . . . The Crusades . . . The University . . . The House of Commons . . . The Hundred Years' War . . . The Wars of the Roses . . . The Renaissance Scholars . . . The Dissolution of the Monasteries . . . Agrarian and Religious Strife . . . The Origin of English Seapower . . . The Armada . . ." and so on. Occasionally an individual woman is mentioned, an Elizabeth, or a Mary; a queen or a great lady. But by no possible means could middle-class women with nothing but brains and character at their command have taken part in any one of the great movements which, brought together, constitute the historian's view of the past. Nor shall we find her in any collection of anecdotes. Aubrey[2] hardly mentions her. She never writes her own life and scarcely keeps

hardly show her face alone in the street, and yet on the stage woman equals or surpasses man, has never been satisfactorily explained. In modern tragedy the same predominance exists. At all events, a very cursory survey of Shakespeare's work (similarly with Webster, though not with Marlowe or Jonson) suffices to reveal how this dominance, this initiative of women, persists from Rosalind to Lady Macbeth. So too in Racine; six of his tragedies bear their heroines' names; and what male characters of his shall we set against Hermione and Andromaque, Bérénice and Roxane, Phèdre and Athalie? So again with Ibsen; what men shall we match with Solveig and Nora, Hedda and Hilda Wangel and Rebecca West?"—F. L. LUCAS, Tragedy, pp. 114–15 [Woolf's note].

2. John Aubrey (1626–1697), whose biographical writings were published posthumously as *Brief Lives.*

a diary; there are only a handful of her letters in existence. She left no plays or poems by which we can judge her. What one wants, I thought—and why does not some brilliant student at Newnham or Girton supply it?—is a mass of information; at what age did she marry; how many children had she as a rule; what was her house like; had she a room to herself; did she do the cooking; would she be likely to have a servant? All these facts lie somewhere, presumably, in parish registers and account books; the life of the average Elizabethan woman must be scattered about somewhere, could one collect it and make a book of it. It would be ambitious beyond my daring, I thought, looking about the shelves for books that were not there, to suggest to the students of those famous colleges that they should re-write history, though I own that it often seems a little queer as it is, unreal, lop-sided; but why should they not add a supplement to history? calling it, of course, by some inconspicuous name so that women might figure there without impropriety? For one often catches a glimpse of them in the lives of the great, whisking away into the background, concealing, I sometimes think, a wink, a laugh, perhaps a tear. And, after all, we have lives enough of Jane Austen; it scarcely seems necessary to consider again the influence of the tragedies of Joanna Baillie upon the poetry of Edgar Allan Poe; as for myself, I should not mind if the homes and haunts of Mary Russell Mitford[3] were closed to the public for a century at least. But what I find deplorable, I continued, looking about the bookshelves again, is that nothing is known about women before the eighteenth century. I have no model in my mind to turn about this way and that. Here am I asking why women did not write poetry in the Elizabethan age, and I am not sure how they were educated; whether they were taught to write; whether they had sitting-rooms to themselves; how many women had children before they were twenty-one; what, in short, they did from eight in the morning till eight at night. They had no money evidently; according to Professor Trevelyan they were married whether they liked it or not before they were out of the nursery, at fifteen or sixteen very likely. It would have been extremely odd, even upon this showing, had one of them suddenly written the plays of Shakespeare, I concluded, and I thought of that old gentleman, who is dead now, but was a bishop, I think, who declared that it was impossible for any woman, past, present, or to come, to have the genius of Shakespeare. He wrote to the papers about it. He also told a lady who applied to him for information that cats do not as a matter of fact go to heaven, though they have, he added, souls of a sort. How much thinking those old gentlemen used to save one! How the borders of ignorance shrank back at their approach! Cats do not go to heaven. Women cannot write the plays of Shakespeare.

Be that as it may, I could not help thinking, as I looked at the works of Shakespeare on the shelf, that the bishop was right at least in this; it would have been impossible, completely and entirely, for any woman to have written the plays of Shakespeare in the age of Shakespeare. Let me imagine, since facts

3. Austen (1775–1817), English novelist; Baillie (1762–1851), Scottish dramatist and poet; Poe (1809–1849), American poet; Mitford (1787–1855), English novelist and essayist.

are so hard to come by, what would have happened had Shakespeare had a wonderfully gifted sister, called Judith, let us say. Shakespeare himself went, very probably—his mother was an heiress—to the grammar school, where he may have learnt Latin—Ovid, Virgil and Horace—and the elements of grammar and logic. He was, it is well known, a wild boy who poached rabbits, perhaps shot a deer, and had, rather sooner than he should have done, to marry a woman in the neighborhood, who bore him a child rather quicker than was right. That escapade sent him to seek his fortune in London. He had, it seemed, a taste for the theatre; he began by holding horses at the stage door. Very soon he got work in the theatre, became a successful actor, and lived at the hub of the universe, meeting everybody, knowing everybody, practicing his art on the boards, exercising his wits in the streets, and even getting access to the palace of the queen. Meanwhile his extraordinarily gifted sister, let us suppose, remained at home. She was as adventurous, as imaginative, as agog to see the world as he was. But she was not sent to school. She had no chance of learning grammar and logic, let alone of reading Horace and Virgil. She picked up a book now and then, one of her brother's perhaps, and read a few pages. But then her parents came in and told her to mend the stockings or mind the stew and not moon about with books and papers. They would have spoken sharply but kindly, for they were substantial people who knew the conditions of life for a woman and loved their daughter—indeed, more likely than not she was the apple of her father's eye. Perhaps she scribbled some pages up in an apple loft on the sly, but was careful to hide them or set fire to them. Soon, however, before she was out of her teens, she was to be betrothed to the son of a neighboring wool-stapler. She cried out that marriage was hateful to her, and for that she was severely beaten by her father. Then he ceased to scold her. He begged her instead not to hurt him, not to shame him in this matter of her marriage. He would give her a chain of beads or a fine petticoat, he said; and there were tears in his eyes. How could she disobey him? How could she break his heart? The force of her own gift alone drove her to it. She made up a small parcel of her belongings, let herself down by a rope one summer's night and took the road to London. She was not seventeen. The birds that sang in the hedge were not more musical than she was. She had the quickest fancy, a gift like her brother's, for the tune of words. Like him, she had a taste for the theatre. She stood at the stage door; she wanted to act, she said. Men laughed in her face. The manager—a fat, loose-lipped man—guffawed. He bellowed something about poodles dancing and women acting—no woman, he said, could possibly be an actress.[4] He hinted—you can imagine what. She could get no training in her craft. Could she even seek her dinner in a tavern or roam the streets at midnight? Yet her genius was for fiction and lusted to feed abundantly upon the lives of men and women and the study of their ways. At last—for she was very young, oddly like Shakespeare the poet in her face, with the same grey eyes and rounded brows—at last Nick Greene the actor-manager took pity on her; she found herself with child by that gentleman and so—who shall measure the heat and vio-

4. In the Elizabethan theater boys played women's parts.

lence of the poet's heart when caught and tangled in a woman's body?—killed herself one winter's night and lies buried at some cross-roads where the omnibuses now stop outside the Elephant and Castle.[5]

That, more or less, is how the story would run, I think, if a woman in Shakespeare's day had had Shakespeare's genius. But for my part, I agree with the deceased bishop, if such he was—it is unthinkable that any woman in Shakespeare's day should have had Shakespeare's genius. For genius like Shakespeare's is not born among laboring, uneducated, servile people. It was not born in England among the Saxons and the Britons. It is not born today among the working classes. How, then, could it have been born among women whose work began, according to Professor Trevelyan, almost before they were out of the nursery, who were forced to it by their parents and held to it by all the power of law and custom? Yet genius of a sort must have existed among women as it must have existed among the working classes. Now and again an Emily Brontë or a Robert Burns blazes out and proves its presence.[6] But certainly it never got itself on to paper. When, however, one reads of a witch being ducked, of a woman possessed by devils, of a wise woman selling herbs, or even of a very remarkable man who had a mother, then I think we are on the track of a lost novelist, a suppressed poet, of some mute and inglorious Jane Austen,[7] some Emily Brontë who dashed her brains out on the moor or mopped and mowed about the highways crazed with the torture that her gift had put her to. Indeed, I would venture to guess that Anon, who wrote so many poems without signing them, was often a woman. It was a woman Edward Fitzgerald,[8] I think, suggested who made the ballads and the folk-songs, crooning them to her children, beguiling her spinning with them, or the length of the winter's night.

This may be true or it may be false—who can say?—but what is true in it, so it seemed to me, reviewing the story of Shakespeare's sister as I had made it, is that any woman born with a great gift in the sixteenth century would certainly have gone crazed, shot herself, or ended her days in some lonely cottage outside the village, half witch, half wizard, feared and mocked at. For it needs little skill in psychology to be sure that a highly gifted girl who had tried to use her gift for poetry would have been so thwarted and hindered by other people, so tortured and pulled asunder by her own contrary instincts, that she must have lost her health and sanity to a certainty. No girl could have walked to London and stood at a stage door and forced her way into the presence of actor-managers without doing herself a violence and suffering an anguish which may have been irrational—for chastity may be a fetish invented by certain societies for unknown reasons—but were none the less inevitable. Chastity had then, it

5. A prominent landmark in London, south of the Thames.

6. Woolf's examples are Emily Brontë (1818–1848), the English novelist, and Robert Burns (1759–1796), the Scottish poet.

7. Woolf alludes to Thomas Gray's "Elegy Written in a Country Churchyard": "Some mute inglorious Milton here may rest."

8. Edward Fitzgerald (1809–1883), poet and translator of the *Rubáiyát of Omar Khayyám*.

has even now, a religious importance in a woman's life, and has so wrapped itself round with nerves and instincts that to cut it free and bring it to the light of day demands courage of the rarest. To have lived a free life in London in the sixteenth century would have meant for a woman who was poet and playwright a nervous stress and dilemma which might well have killed her. Had she survived, whatever she had written would have been twisted and deformed, issuing from a strained and morbid imagination. And undoubtedly, I thought, looking at the shelf where there are no plays by women, her work would have gone unsigned. That refuge she would have sought certainly. It was the relic of the sense of chastity that dictated anonymity to women even so late as the nineteenth century. Currer Bell, George Eliot, George Sand,[9] all the victims of inner strife as their writings prove, sought ineffectively to veil themselves by using the name of a man. Thus they did homage to the convention, which if not implanted by the other sex was liberally encouraged by them (the chief glory of a woman is not to be talked of, said Pericles,[10] himself a much-talked-of man), that publicity in women is detestable. Anonymity runs in their blood. The desire to be veiled still possesses them. They are not even now as concerned about the health of their fame as men are, and, speaking generally, will pass a tombstone or a signpost without feeling an irresistible desire to cut their names on it, as Alf, Bert or Chas. must do in obedience to their instinct, which murmurs if it sees a fine woman go by, or even a dog, Ce chien est à moi.[11] And, of course, it may not be a dog, I thought, remembering Parliament Square, the Sieges Allee and other avenues; it may be a piece of land or a man with curly black hair. It is one of the great advantages of being a woman that one can pass even a very fine negress without wishing to make an Englishwoman of her.

That woman, then, who was born with a gift of poetry in the sixteenth century, was an unhappy woman, a woman at strife against herself. All the conditions of her life, all her own instincts, were hostile to the state of mind which is needed to set free whatever is in the brain. But what is the state of mind that is most propitious to the act of creation, I asked. Can one come by any notion of the state that furthers and makes possible that strange activity? Here I opened the volume containing the Tragedies of Shakespeare. What was Shakespeare's state of mind, for instance, when he wrote *Lear* and *Antony and Cleopatra*? It was certainly the state of mind most favorable to poetry that there has ever existed. But Shakespeare himself said nothing about it. We only know casually and by chance that he "never blotted a line."[12] Nothing indeed was ever said by the artist himself about his state of mind until the eighteenth century 10

9. The pseudonyms of Charlotte Brontë (1816–1855), English novelist; Mary Ann Evans (1819–1880), English novelist; and Amandine Aurore Lucie Dupin, Baronne Dudevant (1804–1876), French novelist.

10. Pericles (d. 429 B.C.E.), Athenian statesman.

11. That dog is mine (French).

12. As recorded by his contemporary Ben Jonson in *Timber, or Discoveries Made upon Men and Matter.*

perhaps. Rousseau perhaps began it.[13] At any rate, by the nineteenth century self-consciousness had developed so far that it was the habit for men of letters to describe their minds in confessions and autobiographies. Their lives also were written, and their letters were printed after their deaths. Thus, though we do not know what Shakespeare went through when he wrote *Lear,* we do know what Carlyle went through when he wrote the *French Revolution*; what Flaubert went through when he wrote *Madame Bovary*; what Keats was going through when he tried to write poetry against the coming of death and the indifference of the world.

And one gathers from this enormous modern literature of confession and self-analysis that to write a work of genius is almost always a feat of prodigious difficulty. Everything is against the likelihood that it will come from the writer's mind whole and entire. Generally material circumstances are against it. Dogs will bark; people will interrupt; money must be made; health will break down. Further, accentuating all these difficulties and making them harder to bear is the world's notorious indifference. It does not ask people to write poems and novels and histories; it does not need them. It does not care whether Flaubert finds the right word or whether Carlyle scrupulously verifies this or that fact. Naturally, it will not pay for what it does not want. And so the writer, Keats, Flaubert, Carlyle, suffers, especially in the creative years of youth, every form of distraction and discouragement. A curse, a cry of agony, rises from those books of analysis and confession. "Mighty poets in their misery dead"[14]—that is the burden of their song. If anything comes through in spite of all this, it is a miracle, and probably no book is born entire and uncrippled as it was conceived.

But for women, I thought, looking at the empty shelves, these difficulties were infinitely more formidable. In the first place, to have a room of her own, let alone a quiet room or a sound-proof room, was out of the question, unless her parents were exceptionally rich or very noble, even up to the beginning of the nineteenth century. Since her pin money, which depended on the good will of her father, was only enough to keep her clothed, she was debarred from such alleviations as came even to Keats or Tennyson or Carlyle,[15] all poor men, from a walking tour, a little journey to France, from the separate lodging which, even if it were miserable enough, sheltered them from the claims and tyrannies of their families. Such material difficulties were formidable; but much worse were the immaterial. The indifference of the world which Keats and Flaubert and other men of genius have found so hard to bear was in her case not indifference but hostility. The world did not say to her as it said to them, Write if you choose; it makes no difference to me. The world said with a guffaw, Write? What's the good of your writing? Here the psychologists of Newnham and

13. Jean-Jacques Rousseau (1712–1778), whose *Confessions* were published posthumously.

14. From William Wordsworth's poem "Resolution and Independence."

15. John Keats (1795–1821) and Alfred, Lord Tennyson (1809–1892) were English poets; Thomas Carlyle (1795–1881) was a Scottish essayist.

Girton might come to our help, I thought, looking again at the blank spaces on the shelves. For surely it is time that the effect of discouragement upon the mind of the artist should be measured, as I have seen a dairy company measure the effect of ordinary milk and Grade A milk upon the body of the rat. They set two rats in cages side by side, and of the two one was furtive, timid and small, and the other was glossy, bold and big. Now what food do we feed women as artists upon? I asked, remembering, I suppose, that dinner of prunes and custard.[16] To answer that question I had only to open the evening paper and to read that Lord Birkenhead is of opinion—but really I am not going to trouble to copy out Lord Birkenhead's opinion upon the writing of women. What Dean Inge says I will leave in peace. The Harley Street specialist may be allowed to rouse the echoes of Harley Street with his vociferations without raising a hair on my head. I will quote, however, Mr. Oscar Browning,[17] because Mr. Oscar Browning was a great figure in Cambridge at one time, and used to examine the students at Girton and Newnham. Mr. Oscar Browning was wont to declare "that the impression left on his mind, after looking over any set of examination papers, was that, irrespective of the marks he might give, the best woman was intellectually the inferior of the worst man." After saying that Mr. Browning went back to his rooms—and it is this sequel that endears him and makes him a human figure of some bulk and majesty—he went back to his rooms and found a stable-boy lying on the sofa—"a mere skeleton, his cheeks were cavernous and sallow, his teeth were black, and he did not appear to have the full use of his limbs. . . . 'That's Arthur' [said Mr. Browning]. 'He's a dear boy really and most high-minded.'" The two pictures always seem to me to complete each other. And happily in this age of biography the two pictures often do complete each other, so that we are able to interpret the opinions of great men not only by what they say, but by what they do.

But though this is possible now, such opinions coming from the lips of important people must have been formidable enough even fifty years ago. Let us suppose that a father from the highest motives did not wish his daughter to leave home and become writer, painter or scholar. "See what Mr. Oscar Browning says," he would say; and there was not only Mr. Oscar Browning; there was the *Saturday Review*; there was Mr. Greg[18]—the "essentials of a woman's being," said Mr. Greg emphatically, "are that *they are supported by, and they minister to, men*"—there was an enormous body of masculine opinion to the effect that nothing could be expected of women intellectually. Even if her father did not

16. In chapter 1, Woolf contrasts the lavish dinner—partridge and wine—she ate as a guest at a men's college at Cambridge University with the plain fare—prunes and custard—served at a women's college.

17. In chapter 2, Woolf lists the fruits of her day's research on the lives of women, which include Lord Birkenhead's, Dean Inge's, and Mr. Oscar Browning's opinions of women; she does not, however, quote them. Harley Street is where fashionable medical doctors in London have their offices.

18. Mr. Greg does not appear on Woolf's list (see preceding note).

read out loud these opinions, any girl could read them for herself; and the reading, even in the nineteenth century, must have lowered her vitality, and told profoundly upon her work. There would always have been that assertion—you cannot do this, you are incapable of doing that—to protest against, to overcome. Probably for a novelist this germ is no longer of much effect; for there have been women novelists of merit. But for painters it must still have some sting in it; and for musicians, I imagine, is even now active and poisonous in the extreme. The women composer stands where the actress stood in the time of Shakespeare. Nick Greene, I thought, remembering the story I had made about Shakespeare's sister, said that a woman acting put him in mind of a dog dancing. Johnson repeated the phrase two hundred years later of women preaching.[19] And here, I said, opening a book about music, we have the very words used again in this year of grace, 1928, of women who try to write music. "Of Mlle. Germaine Tailleferre one can only repeat Dr. Johnson's dictum concerning a woman preacher, transposed into terms of music. 'Sir, a woman's composing is like a dog's walking on his hind legs. It is not done well, but you are surprised to find it done at all.'"[20] So accurately does history repeat itself.

Thus, I concluded, shutting Mr. Oscar Browning's life and pushing away the rest, it is fairly evident that even in the nineteenth century a woman was not encouraged to be an artist. On the contrary, she was snubbed, slapped, lectured and exhorted. Her mind must have been strained and her vitality lowered by the need of opposing this, of disproving that. For here again we come within range of that very interesting and obscure masculine complex which has had so much influence upon the woman's movement; that deep-seated desire, not so much that *she* shall be inferior as that *he* shall be superior, which plants him wherever one looks, not only in front of the arts, but barring the way to politics too, even when the risk to himself seems infinitesimal and the suppliant humble and devoted. Even Lady Bessborough, I remembered, with all her passion for politics, must humbly bow herself and write to Lord Granville Leveson-Gower[21]: ". . . notwithstanding all my violence in politics and talking so much on that subject, I perfectly agree with you that no woman has any business to meddle with that or any other serious business, farther than giving her opinion (if she is ask'd)." And so she goes on to spend her enthusiasm where it meets with no obstacle whatsoever upon that immensely important subject, Lord Granville's maiden speech in the House of Commons. The spectacle is certainly a strange one, I thought. The history of men's opposition to women's emancipation is more interesting perhaps than the story of that emancipation

19. Johnson's opinion is recorded in James Boswell's *The Life of Samuel Johnson, L.L.D.* Woolf, in her tale of Judith Shakespeare, imagines the manager bellowing "something about poodles dancing and women acting."

20. *A Survey of Contemporary Music,* Cecil Gray, p. 246 [Woolf's note].

21. Henrietta, countess of Bessborough (1761–1821), and Lord Granville Leveson Gower, first Earl Granville (1773–1846). Their correspondence, edited by Castalia Countess Granville, was published as his *Private Correspondence, 1781 to 1821,* in 1916.

itself. An amusing book might be made of it if some young student at Girton or Newnham would collect examples and deduce a theory—but she would need thick gloves on her hands, and bars to protect her of solid gold.

But what is amusing now, I recollected, shutting Lady Bessborough, had to be taken in desperate earnest once. Opinions that one now pastes in a book labelled cock-a-doodle-dum and keeps for reading to select audiences on summer nights once drew tears, I can assure you. Among your grandmothers and great-grandmothers there were many that wept their eyes out. Florence Nightingale shrieked aloud in her agony.[22] Moreover, it is all very well for you, who have got yourselves to college and enjoy sitting-rooms—or is it only bed-sitting-rooms?—of your own to say that genius should disregard such opinions; that genius should be above caring what is said of it. Unfortunately, it is precisely the men or women of genius who mind most what is said of them. Remember Keats. Remember the words he had cut on his tombstone. Think of Tennyson;[23] think—but I need hardly multiply instances of the undeniable, if very unfortunate, fact that it is the nature of the artist to mind excessively what is said about him. Literature is strewn with the wreckage of men who have minded beyond reason the opinions of others.

15

And this susceptibility of theirs is doubly unfortunate, I thought, returning again to my original enquiry into what state of mind is most propitious for creative work, because the mind of an artist, in order to achieve the prodigious effort of freeing whole and entire the work that is in him, must be incandescent, like Shakespeare's mind, I conjectured, looking at the book which lay open at *Antony and Cleopatra*. There must be no obstacle in it, no foreign matter unconsumed.

For though we say that we know nothing about Shakespeare's state of mind, even as we say that, we are saying something about Shakespeare's state of mind. The reason perhaps why we know so little of Shakespeare—compared with Donne or Ben Jonson or Milton[24]—is that his grudges and spites and antipathies are hidden from us. We are not held up by some "revelation" which reminds us of the writer. All desire to protest, to preach, to proclaim an injury, to pay off a score, to make the world the witness of some hardship or grievance was fired out of him and consumed. Therefore his poetry flows from him free and unimpeded. If ever a human being got his work expressed completely, it was Shakespeare. If ever a mind was incandescent, unimpeded, I thought, turning again to the bookcase, it was Shakespeare's mind.

22. See *Cassandra,* by Florence Nightingale, printed in *The Cause,* by R. Strachey [Woolf's note]. Florence Nightingale (1820–1910), English nurse and philanthropist.

23. Keats's epitaph reads "Here lies one whose name was writ in water." Tennyson was notably sensitive to reviews of his poetry.

24. John Donne (1572–1631), Jonson (1572–1637), and John Milton (1608–1674) were English poets and, in contrast to Shakespeare, all learned men.

QUESTIONS

1. At the beginning of her essay, Woolf wonders about the conditions in which women lived that made it difficult, if not impossible, for them to produce literature (paragraph 2). What does she reveal about those conditions in the course of her essay?

2. Throughout her essay Woolf supplies many examples of the obstacles faced by women writers. Choose two or three that you find particularly effective and explain why they are effective.

3. How does the phrase "A Room of One's Own" suggest a solution to the problems Woolf has enumerated for women writers?

4. What obstacles face writers in the twenty-first century? How do those obstacles vary based on the writer's background or identity? Write an essay, based on research and/or interviews, in which you argue the extent to which Woolf's argument is still relevant for a specific twenty-first century population.

MICHAEL CHABON *Kids' Stuff*

FOR AT LEAST THE FIRST FORTY YEARS of their existence, from the Paleozoic pre-Superman era of *Famous Funnies* (1933) and *More Fun Comics* (1936), comic books were widely viewed, even by those who adored them, as juvenile: the ultimate greasy kids' stuff. Comics were the literary equivalent of bubblegum cards, to be poked into the spokes of a young mind, where they would produce a satisfying—but entirely bogus—rumble of pleasure. But almost from the first, fitfully in the early days, intermittently through the fifties, and then starting in the mid-sixties with increasing vigor and determination, a battle has been waged by writers, artists, editors, and publishers to elevate the medium, to expand the scope of its subject matter and the range of its artistic styles, to sharpen and increase the sophistication of its language and visual grammar, to probe and explode the limits of the sequential panel, to give free rein to irony, tragedy, autobiography, and other grown-up-type modes of expression.

Also from the first, a key element—at times the central element—of this battle has been the effort to alter not just the medium itself but the public perception of the medium. From the late, great Will Eisner's lonely insistence, in an interview with the *Baltimore Sun* back in 1940 (*1940!*), on the artistic credibility of comics, to the nuanced and scholarly work of recent comics theorists, both practitioners and critics have been arguing passionately on behalf of comics' potential to please—in all the aesthetic richness of that term—the most sophisticated of readers.

Originally the keynote address at the 2004 ComicCon (the largest comic book convention in the Western Hemisphere). Collected in Maps and Legends: Reading and Writing along the Borderlands *(2009).*

The most sophisticated, that is, of *adult* readers. For the adult reader of comic books has always been the holy grail, the promised land, the imagined lover who will greet the long-suffering comic-book maker, at the end of the journey, with open arms, with acceptance, with approval.

A quest is often, among other things, an extended bout of inspired madness. Over the years this quest to break the chains of childish readership has resulted, like most bouts of inspired madness, in both folly and stunning innovation. Into the latter category we can put the work of Bernard Krigstein or Frank Miller, say, with their attempts to approximate, through radical attack on the conventions of panel layouts, the fragmentation of human consciousness by urban life; or the tight, tidy, miniaturized madness of Chris Ware.[1] Into the former category—the folly—we might put all the things that got Dr. Frederic Wertham[2] so upset about EC Comics in the early fifties, the syringe-pierced eyeballs and baseball diamonds made from human organs; or the short-lived outfitting of certain Marvel titles in 1965 with a label that boasted "A Marvel Pop Art Production"; or the hypertrophied, tooth-gnashing, blood-letting quote-unquote heroes of the era that followed Miller's *The Dark Knight Returns*. An excess of the desire to appear grown up is one of the defining characteristics of adolescence. But these follies were the inevitable missteps and overreaching in the course of a campaign that was, in the end, successful.

Because the battle has now, in fact, been won. Not only are comics appealing to a wider and older audience than ever before, but the idea of comics as a valid art form on a par at least with, say, film or rock and roll is widely if not quite universally accepted. Comics and graphic novels are regularly reviewed and debated in *Entertainment Weekly*, the *New York Times Book Review*, even in the august pages of the *New York Review of Books*. Ben Katchor won a MacArthur Fellowship, and Art Spiegelman a Pulitzer Prize.[3]   5

But the strange counterphenomenon to this indisputable rise in the reputation, the ambition, the sophistication, and the literary and artistic merit of many of our best comics over the past couple of decades, is that over roughly the same period comics readership has declined. Some adults are reading better comics than ever before; but fewer people overall are reading any—far fewer, certainly, than in the great sales heyday of the medium, the early fifties, when by some estimates[4] as many as 650 million comic books were sold annually (compared

1. Barnard Krigstein (1919–1990), comic book artist and painter famous for his daring and varied styles; Frank Miller (b. 1957), comic book artist and film director known for *Batman: The Dark Knight Returns;* Chris Ware (b. 1967), comic book artist best known for his Acme Library Novelty Series.

2. Frederic Wertham (1895–1981), a psychiatrist and crusader against comic books. His *Seduction of the Innocent* (1954) led to a congressional investigation of comics as a dangerous influence on adolescents.

3. Ben Katchor (b. 1951), the first comic book artist to win a MacArthur Genius Grant; Art Spiegelman (b. 1948), best known for his graphic memoir, *Maus* (1986), which recounts his father's experience during the Holocaust.

4. See, for example, www.comichron.com [Chabon's note].

to somewhere in the neighborhood of 80 million today). The top ten best-selling comic books in 1996, primarily issues making up two limited series, Marvel's *Civil Wars* and DC's *Infinite Crisis,* were all superhero books, and, like the majority of superhero books in the post–*Dark Knight*, post-*Watchmen* era, all of them dealt rather grimly, and in the somewhat hand-wringing fashion that has become obligatory, with the undoubtedly grown-up issues of violence, freedom, terrorism, vigilantism, political repression, mass hysteria, and the ambivalent nature of heroism. Among the top ten best-selling titles in 1960 (with an aggregate circulation, for all comics, of 400 million) one finds not only the expected *Superman* and *Batman* (decidedly sans ambivalence) but *Mickey Mouse, Looney Tunes*, and the classic sagas of *Uncle Scrooge*. And nearly the whole of the list for that year, from top to bottom, through *Casper the Friendly Ghost* (#14) and *Little Archie* (#25) to *Felix the Cat* (#47), is made up of kids' stuff, more or less greasy.

To recap—Days when comics were aimed at kids: huge sales. Days when comics are aimed at adults: not so huge sales, and declining.

The situation is more complicated than that, of course. Since 1960 there have been fundamental changes in a lot of things, among them the way comics are produced, licensed, marketed, and distributed. But maybe it is not too surprising that for a while now, fundamental changes and all, some people have been wondering: what if there were comic books for children?

Leaving aside questions of creator's rights, paper costs, retail consolidation, the explosive growth of the collector market, and direct-market sales, a lot of comic-book people will tell you that there is simply too much competition for the kid dollar these days and that, thrown into the arena with video games, special-effects-laden films, the Internet, iPods, etc., comics will inevitably lose out. I find this argument unconvincing, not to mention a cop out. It is, furthermore, an example of our weird naïveté, in this generation, about how sophisticated we and our children have become vis-à-vis our parents and grandparents, of the misguided sense of retrospective superiority we tend to display toward them and their vanished world. As if in 1960 there was not a *ton* of cool stuff besides comic books on which a kid could spend his or her considerably less constricted time and considerably more limited funds. In the early days of comics, in fact, unlike now, a moderately adventuresome child could find all kinds of things to do that were not only fun (partly because they took place with no adult supervision or mediation), but absolutely free. The price of fun doesn't get any more competitive than that.

10 I also refuse to accept as explanation for anything the often-tendered argument that contemporary children are more sophisticated, that the kind of comics that pleased a seven-year-old in 1960 would leave an ultracool kid of today snickering with disdain. Even if we accept this argument with respect to "old-fashioned" comics, it would seem to be invalidated by the increasing sophistication of comic books over the past decades. But I reject its very premise. The supposed sophistication—a better term would be *knowingness*—of modern children is largely, I believe, a matter of style, a pose which they have adapted from and modeled on the rampant pose of knowingness, of being wised up, that

characterizes the contemporary American style, and has done at least since the late fifties–early sixties heyday of *Mad* magazine (a publication largely enjoyed, from the beginning, by children). Even in their irony and cynicism there is something appealingly insincere, maladroit, and, well, *childish* about children. What is more, I have found that even my own children, as knowing as they often like to present themselves, still take profound pleasure in the old comics that I have given them to read. My older son has still not quite recovered from the heartbreak he felt, when he was seven, reading an old "archive edition" of *Legion of Superheroes,* at the tragic death of Ferro Lad.

Children did not abandon comics; comics, in their drive to attain respect and artistic accomplishment, abandoned children. And for a long time the lovers and partisans of comics were afraid, after so many years of struggle and hard work and incremental gains, to pick up that old jar of greasy kid stuff again, and risk undoing all the labor of so many geniuses and revolutionaries and ordinary, garden-variety artists. Comics have always been an arriviste art form, and all upstarts are to some degree ashamed of their beginnings. But shame, anxiety, the desire to preserve hard-won gains—such considerations no longer serve to explain the disappearance of children's comics. The truth is that comic-book creators have simply lost the habit of telling stories to children. And how sad is that?

When commentators on comics address this question, in the hope of encouraging publishers, writers, and artists to produce new comic books with children in mind, they usually try formulating some version of the following simple equation: create more child readers now, and you will find yourselves with more adult readers later on. Hook them early, in other words. But maybe the equation isn't so simple after all. Maybe what we need, given the sophistication of children (if we want to concede that point) and the competition for their attention and their disposable income (which has always been a factor), is not simply *more* comics for kids, but more *great* comics for kids.

Easy, I suppose, for me to say. So although I am certain that there are many professional creators of comics—people with a good ear and a sharp eye for and a natural understanding of children and their enthusiasms—who would be able to do a far better job of it, having thrown down the finned, skintight gauntlet, I now feel obliged to offer, at the least, a few tentative principles and one concrete suggestion on how more great comics for kids might be teased into the marketplace, even by amateurs like me. I have drawn these principles, in part, from my memories of the comics I loved when I was young, but I think they hold true as well for the best and most successful works of children's literature.

1) Let's not tell stories that we think "kids of today" might like. That is a route to inevitable failure and possible loss of sanity. *We should tell stories that we would have liked as kids.* Twist endings, the unexpected usefulness of unlikely knowledge, nobility and bravery where it's least expected, and the sudden emergence of a thread of goodness in a wicked nature, those were the kind of stories told by the writers and artists of the comic books that I liked.

15 2) Let's tell stories that, over time, build up an intricate, involved, involving mythology that is also accessible and comprehensible at any point of entry. The *intricacy*, the accretion of lore over time, should be both inventive and familiar, founded in old mythologies and fears but fully reinterpreted, reimagined. It will demand, it will ache, to be mastered by a child's mythology-mastering imagination. The *accessibility* will come from our making a commitment to tell a full, complete story, or a complete piece of a story, in every issue. This kind of layering of intricate lore and narrative completeness was a hallmark of the great "Superman-family" books (*Adventure, Jimmy Olsen, Superboy*) under the editorship of Mort Weisinger.[5]

3) Let's cultivate an unflagging readiness as storytellers to retell the same stories *with endless embellishment*. Anybody who thinks that kids get bored by hearing the same story over and over again has never spent time telling stories to kids. The key, as in baroque music, is repetition with *variation*. Again the Mort Weisinger–edited *Superman* books, written by unflagging story-tellers like Edmond Hamilton and Otto Binder,[6] were exemplary in this regard. The proliferation of theme and variation there verges, at times, on sheer, splendid madness.

4) Let's blow their little minds. A mind is not blown, in spite of whatever Hollywood seems to teach, merely by action sequences, things exploding, thrilling planetscapes, wild bursts of speed. Those are all good things; but a mind is blown when something that you always feared but knew to be impossible turns out to be true; when the world turns out to be far vaster, far more marvelous or malevolent than you ever dreamed; when you get proof that everything is connected to everything else, that everything you know is wrong, that you are both the center of the universe and a tiny speck sailing off its nethermost edge.

So much for my principles: here is my concrete suggestion. If it seems a little obvious, or has already been tried and failed, then I apologize. But I cannot help noticing that in the world of children's *literature*, an overwhelming preponderance of stories are stories *about* children. The same is true of films for children: the central characters are nearly always a child, or a pair or group of children. Comic books, however, even those theoretically aimed at children, are almost always about adults or teenagers. Doesn't that strike you as odd? I suggest that a publisher should try putting out a truly thrilling, honestly observed and remembered, richly imagined, involved and yet narratively straight-forward comic book for children, *about children*.

My oldest son is ten now, and he likes comic books. In 1943, if you were a ten-year-old, you probably knew a dozen other kids your age who were into Captain Marvel and the Submariner and the Blue Beetle. When I was ten, in 1973,

5. Mort Weisinger (1915–1978), editor of the DC Comic *Superman* series; served as story editor for the 1950s Superman television show.

6. Edmond Hamilton (1904–1977), a science fiction writer who, in his work for DC Comics, specialized in stories for Batman and Superman; Otto Binder (1911–1974) wrote Captain Marvel comics for Fawcett and several classic Superman storylines for DC.

I knew three or four. But in his class, in his world, my son is all but unique; he's the only one he knows who reads them, studies them, seeks to master and be worthy of all the rapture and strangeness they still contain. Now, comic books are so important to me—I have thought, talked, and written about them so much—that if my son did not in fact like them, I think he would be obliged to loathe them. I have pretty much *forced* comics on my children. But those of us who grew up loving comic books can't afford to take this handcrafted, one-kid-at-a-time approach anymore. We have to sweep them up and carry them off on the flying carpets of story and pictures on which we ourselves, in entire generations, were borne aloft, on carpets woven by Curt Swan and Edmond Hamilton, Jack Kirby and Stan Lee, Chris Claremont and John Byrne.[7] Those artists did it for us; we who make comics today have a solemn debt to pass it on, to weave bright carpets of our own. It's our duty, it's our opportunity, and I really do believe it will be our pleasure.

7. Curt Swan (1920–1996), a comic book artist best known for drawing Superman comics, often written by Edmond Hamilton. Jack Kirby (1917–1994), a comic book artist, and Stan Lee (b. 1922), a writer, are best known for their collaboration at Marvel Comics. Chris Claremont (b. 1950) and John Byrne (b. 1950) collaborated on the *X-Men* series.

Questions

1. Chabon's essay contrasts the comic book writer's desire for respect with the diminishing audience for comics. Discuss the relationships that link artistic sophistication to both public respect and sales. Do you find Chabon's explanation persuasive? Is he missing something?

2. This essay begins with statistics about the readership of comics, moves to narrative about the evolution of the form, and ends with a manifesto on how to get more kids to read comics. Analyze how each section builds on the others. How does Chabon make the transition from one to another?

3. Chabon is clearly passionate about comics. Choose a passage in which he most effectively conveys that passion, and analyze why it works.

4. Write your own list of principles for how to get kids to love something that you loved as a kid. What elements go into making a comic (or a videogame, toy, collectible, or cartoon) great?

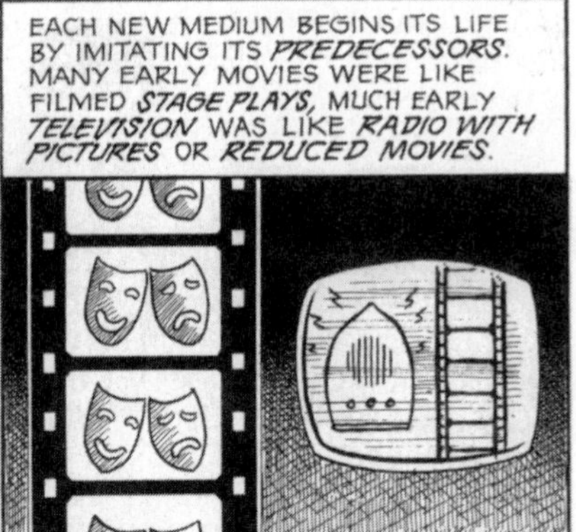

From Understanding Comics, *a graphic book published in 1994.*

WORDS AND PICTURES IN COMBINATION MAY NOT BE MY *DEFINITION* OF COMICS, BUT THE COMBINATION HAS HAD *TREMENDOUS INFLUENCE* ON ITS *GROWTH*.

A HUGE RANGE OF HUMAN EXPERIENCES CAN BE *PORTRAYED* IN COMICS THROUGH EITHER WORDS OR PICTURES.

AS A RESULT--AND DESPITE ITS MANY *OTHER* POTENTIAL USES -- COMICS HAVE BECOME *FIRMLY IDENTIFIED* WITH THE ART OF *STORYTELLING*.

AND *INDEED,* WORDS AND PICTURES HAVE *GREAT* POWERS TO TELL STORIES WHEN CREATORS FULLY EXPLOIT THEM *BOTH*.
DADA
HORROR
SURREALISM
ROMANCE
BLANK VERSE
HISTORICAL FICTION
EPIC POETRY
FOLK TALES
SOCIAL ALLEGORY
SEQUENTIAL ART
EROTICA
MYSTERY
ADAPTATIONS
RELIGIOUS TOPICS
STREAM OF CONSCIOUSNESS
SATIRE

AND SO FAR, WE'VE ONLY SEEN THE *TIP OF THE ICEBERG!*

AS CHILDREN, WE "SHOW AND TELL" *INTERCHANGEABLY,* WORDS AND IMAGES COMBINING TO TRANSMIT A *CONNECTED SERIES OF IDEAS*.
IT'S GOT ONE OF *THESE* THINGS.

THE DIFFERENT WAYS IN WHICH WORDS AND PICTURES CAN *COMBINE* IN COMICS IS VIRTUALLY *UNLIMITED*.

BUT LET'S TRY TO BREAK IT DOWN INTO SOME DISTINCT *CATEGORIES*.

FIRST, WE HAVE THE *WORD SPECIFIC* COMBINATIONS, WHERE PICTURES *ILLUSTRATE*, BUT DON'T SIGNIFICANTLY *ADD* TO A LARGELY *COMPLETE* TEXT.

WE STUMBLED BACK TO THE APARTMENT SHORTLY BEFORE DAWN, *VOMITING* EVERY 20 YARDS.
JUDY GAVE ME HER KEYS AND SMILED.
THE *UNITED STATES CONSTITUTION* WAS ADOPTED BY THE *SECOND CONTINENTAL CONGRESS* IN 1787 AND PUT INTO EFFECT IN 1789.

THEN THERE ARE *PICTURE SPECIFIC* COMBINATIONS WHERE WORDS DO LITTLE MORE THAN ADD A *SOUNDTRACK* TO A VISUALLY TOLD SEQUENCE.

HE DID IT!
MMM...
MMM...

AND, OF COURSE, *DUO-SPECIFIC* PANELS IN WHICH BOTH WORDS AND PICTURES SEND ESSENTIALLY THE *SAME MESSAGE*.

GRIM-FACED, GEORGE LIFTED HIS LOLLYPOP.
BUT THE CAPTAIN'S MIGHTY BLOW **MISSES** ITS INTENDED TARGET!
BLAST! HE DODGED MY PUNCH AND I STRUCK THIS **BRICK WALL!**
HA! I DODGED
I FEEL SO *SAD!*
...THOUGHT AMY.

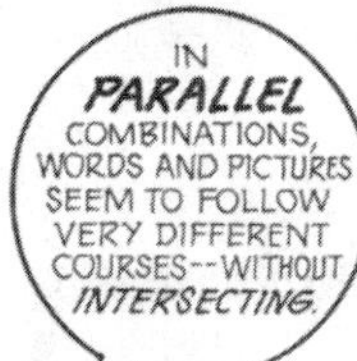

STILL ANOTHER OPTION IS THE ***MONTAGE*** WHERE WORDS ARE TREATED AS INTEGRAL *PARTS* OF THE PICTURE.

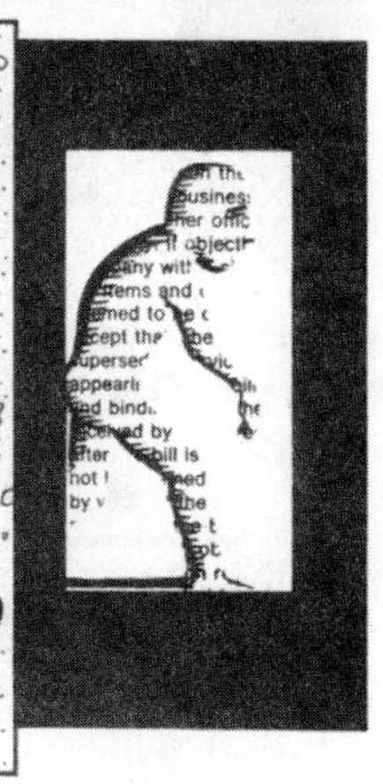

PERHAPS THE MOST COMMON TYPE OF WORD/PICTURE COMBINATION IS THE INTER-DEPENDENT, WHERE WORDS AND PICTURES GO HAND IN HAND TO CONVEY AN IDEA THAT NEITHER COULD CONVEY ALONE.

MEANWHILE...
DID ANYONE SEE YOU?
THIS IS ALL I NEED TO STOP HIM!
I ASK YOU, DOES THIS GUY LOOK LIKE A C.E.O. TO YOU??
"AND JUST GUESS WHO DROVE UP IN BOB'S TRUCK AN HOUR LATER!"
HEY, MARGE!
OH, MY GOD!
HE'S LYING.
UH-HUH.
"AFTER COLLEGE, I PURSUED A CAREER IN HIGH FINANCE."
HURRY UP, WILLYA?!

INTERDEPENDENT COMBINATIONS AREN'T ALWAYS AN EQUAL BALANCE THOUGH AND MAY FALL ANYWHERE ON A SCALE BETWEEN TYPES ONE AND TWO.
P
W
P
W
GENERALLY SPEAKING, THE MORE IS SAID WITH WORDS, THE MORE THE PICTURES CAN BE FREED TO GO EXPLORING AND VICE VERSA.

W
P

IN COMICS AT ITS BEST, WORDS AND PICTURES ARE LIKE PARTNERS IN A DANCE AND EACH ONE TAKES TURNS LEADING.

WHEN BOTH PARTNERS TRY TO LEAD, THE COMPETITION CAN SUBVERT THE OVERALL GOALS...
YOW!

...THOUGH A LITTLE PLAYFUL COMPETITION CAN SOMETIMES PRODUCE ENJOYABLE RESULTS.

BUT WHEN THESE PARTNERS EACH KNOW THEIR ROLES--

--AND SUPPORT EACH OTHER'S STRENGTHS--

--COMICS CAN MATCH ANY OF THE ART FORMS IT DRAWS SO MUCH OF ITS STRENGTH FROM.

QUESTIONS

1. Scott McCloud announces in his title that he wants to help the reader "understand comics." What features of comics does McCloud explain? How do the features of the comic strip form itself aid in that explanation?

2. Choose a frame in which you think word and image work well together, and analyze why they do so. Use one or more of McCloud's categories of analysis.

3. Using the categories that McCloud introduces in the second half of this selection, analyze how a comic strip in your local newspaper works. If relevant, suggest how it might work even better.

SUSAN SONTAG *A Century of Cinema*

CINEMA'S HUNDRED YEARS appear to have the shape of a life cycle: an inevitable birth, the steady accumulation of glories, and the onset in the last decade of an ignominious, irreversible decline. This doesn't mean that there won't be any more new films one can admire. But such films will not simply be exceptions; that's true of great achievement in any art. They will have to be heroic violations of the norms and practices which now govern moviemaking everywhere in the capitalist and would-be capitalist world—which is to say, everywhere. And ordinary films, films made purely for entertainment (that is, commercial) purposes, will continue to be astonishingly witless; already the vast majority fail resoundingly to appeal to their cynically targeted audiences. While the point of a great film is now, more than ever, to be a one-of-a-kind achievement, the commercial cinema has settled for a policy of bloated, derivative filmmaking, a brazen combinatory or re-combinatory art, in the hope of reproducing past successes. Every film that hopes to reach the largest possible audience is designed as some kind of remake. Cinema, once heralded as *the* art of the twentieth century, seems now, as the century closes numerically, to be a decadent art.

Perhaps it is not cinema which has ended but only cinephilia—the name of the distinctive kind of love that cinema inspired. Each art breeds its fanatics. The love movies aroused was more imperial. It was born of the conviction that cinema was an art unlike any other: quintessentially modern; distinctively accessible; poetic and mysterious and erotic and moral—all at the same time. Cinema had apostles (it was like religion). Cinema was a crusade. Cinema was a world view. Lovers of poetry or opera or dance don't think there is *only* poetry or

Written in 1995 for the German newspaper Frankfurter Rundschau *and published in shortened form in the* New York Times Magazine *(February 25, 1996); later reprinted in a small circulation American journal* Parnassus *(1997) and, with editorial changes, in Sontag's collection of essays* Where the Stress Falls *(2001).*

opera or dance. But lovers of cinema could think there was only cinema. That the movies encapsulated everything—and they did. It was both the book of art and the book of life.

As many have noted, the start of moviemaking a hundred years ago was, conveniently, a double start. In that first year, 1895, two kinds of films were made, proposing two modes of what cinema could be: cinema as the transcription of real, unstaged life (the Lumière brothers) and cinema as invention, artifice, illusion, fantasy (Méliès).[1] But this was never a true opposition. For those first audiences watching the Lumière brothers' *The Arrival of a Train at La Ciotat Station*, the camera's transmission of a banal sight was a fantastic experience. Cinema began in wonder, the wonder that reality can be transcribed with such magical immediacy. All of cinema is an attempt to perpetuate and to reinvent that sense of wonder.

"The Arrival of a Train at La Ciotat Station," 1895.

Everything begins with that moment, one hundred years ago, when the train pulled into the station. People took movies into themselves, just as the public cried out with excitement, actually ducked, as the train seemed to move toward *them*. Until the advent of television emptied the movie theatres, it was from a weekly visit to the cinema that you learned (or tried to learn) how to strut, to smoke, to kiss, to fight, to grieve. Movies gave you tips about how to be attractive, such as . . . it looks good to wear a raincoat even when it isn't raining. But whatever you took home from the movies was only a part of the larger experience of losing yourself in faces, in lives that were *not* yours—which is the more inclusive form of desire embodied in the movie experience. The strongest experience was simply to surrender to, to be transported by, what was on the screen. You wanted to be kidnapped by the movie.

5 The prerequisite of being kidnapped was to be overwhelmed by the physical presence of the image. And the conditions of "going to the movies" secured that experience. To see a great film only on television isn't to have really seen that film. (This is equally true of those made for TV, like Fassbinder's *Berlin*

1. Lumière brothers, Auguste (1864–1948) and Louis Jean (1862–1954), French inventors who in 1895 patented and demonstrated the Cinématographe, the first device for photographing, printing, and projecting films; Georges Méliès (1861–1938), early French experimenter with motion pictures, the first to film fictional narratives.

"Nana," 1926.

Alexanderplatz and the two *Heimat* films of Edgar Reitz.)[2] It's not only the difference of dimensions: the superiority of the larger-than-you image in the theatre to the little image on the box at home. The conditions of paying attention in a domestic space are radically disrespectful of film. Since film no longer has a standard size, home screens can be as big as living room or bedroom walls. But you are still in a living room or a bedroom, alone or with familiars. To be kidnapped, you have to be in a movie theatre, seated in the dark among anonymous strangers.

No amount of mourning will revive the vanished rituals—erotic, ruminative—of the darkened theatre. The reduction of cinema to assaultive images, and the unprincipled manipulation of images (faster and faster cutting) to be more attention-grabbing, have produced a disincarnated, lightweight cinema that doesn't demand anyone's full attention. Images now appear in any size and on a variety of surfaces: on a screen in a theatre, on home screens as small as the palm of your hand or as big as a wall, on disco walls and megascreens hanging above sports arenas and the outsides of tall public buildings. The sheer ubiquity of moving images has steadily undermined the standards people once had both for cinema as art at its most serious and for cinema as popular entertainment.

In the first years there was, essentially, no difference between cinema as art and cinema as entertainment. And *all* films of the silent era—from the masterpieces of Feuillade, D. W. Griffith, Dziga Vertov, Pabst, Murnau, King Vidor[3] to the most formula-ridden melodramas and comedies—look, are, better than most of what was to follow. With the coming of sound, the image-making

2. Rainer Werner Fassbinder (1946–1982) and Reitz (b. 1932), both German film directors.

3. Feuillade (1873–1925), French film director who developed short adventure films and screen serials in the period around World War I; David Wark Griffith (1875–1948), American film director who innovated cross-cutting, close-ups, long shots, and flashbacks in such films as *The Birth of a Nation* (1915); Dziga Vertov (Denis Arkadyevich Kaufman, 1896–1954), Soviet film director who developed the "film-eye" theory, which made the camera operate as an instrument much like the human eye; Georg Wilhelm Pabst (1885–1967), German film director who developed "montage" in such works as *The Joyless Street* (1925) and *The Threepenny Opera* (1931); Friedrich Wilhelm Murnau (1889–1931), German film director whose works include *Nosferatu* (1922), *The Last Laugh* (1924), and *Sunrise* (1927); King Vidor (1894–1982), American film director who

"Napoleon," 1927.

lost much of its brilliance and poetry, and commercial standards tightened. This way of making movies—the Hollywood system—dominated filmmaking for about twenty-five years (roughly from 1930 to 1955). The most original directors, like Erich von Stroheim and Orson Welles,[4] were defeated by the system and eventually went into artistic exile in Europe—where more or less the same quality-defeating system was in place with lower budgets; only in France were a large number of superb films produced throughout this period. Then, in the mid-1950s, vanguard ideas took hold again, rooted in the idea of cinema as a craft pioneered by the Italian films of the early postwar era. A dazzling number of original, passionate films of the highest seriousness got made with new actors and tiny crews, went to film festivals (of which there were more and more), and from there, garlanded with festival prizes, into movie theatres around the world. This golden age actually lasted as long as twenty years.

It was at this specific moment in the hundred-year history of cinema that going to movies, thinking about movies, talking about movies became a passion among university students and other young people. You fell in love not just with actors but with cinema itself. Cinephilia had first become visible in the 1950s in France: its forum was the legendary film magazine *Cahiers du Cinéma* (fol-

created *The Crowd* (1928) and later *The Citadel* (1938), the black-and-white scenes of *The Wizard of Oz* (1939), *The Fountainhead* (1949), and *War and Peace* (1956).

4. Erich von Stroheim (1885–1957), German filmmaker, most famous for *Greed* (1925); Orson Welles (1915–1985), American film director, most famous for *Citizen Kane* (1941).

"The 400 Blows," 1959.

lowed by similarly fervent magazines in Germany, Italy, Great Britain, Sweden, the United States, Canada). Its temples, as it spread throughout Europe and the Americas, were the cinematheques and film clubs specializing in films from the past and directors' retrospectives. The 1960s and early 1970s were the age of feverish moviegoing, with the full-time cinephile always hoping to find a seat as close as possible to the big screen, ideally the third row center. "One can't live without Rossellini," declares a character in Bertolucci's *Before the Revolution* (1964)—and means it.

Cinephilia—a source of exultation in the films of Godard and Truffaut and the early Bertolucci and Syberberg;[5] a morose lament in the recent films of Nanni Moretti[6]—was mostly a Western European affair. The great directors of "the other Europe" (Zanussi in Poland, Angelopoulos in Greece, Tarkovsky and Sokurov in Russia, Jancsó and Tarr in Hungary) and the great Japanese directors (Ozu, Mizoguchi, Kurosawa, Naruse, Oshima, Imamura) have tended not to be cinephiles, perhaps because in Budapest or Moscow or Tokyo or Warsaw

5. Jean-Luc Godard (b. 1930), French film director known for *Breathless* (1959), among others; François Truffaut (1932–1984), French director whose films include *The 400 Blows* (1959), *Day for Night* (1973), and *The Last Métro* (1980); Bernardo Bertolucci (b. 1940), Italian filmmaker whose work includes *Last Tango in Paris* (1973) and *The Last Emperor* (1987); Hans-Jurgen Syberberg (b. 1935), German director and critic, known for his *Parsifal* (1988) and his book *Hitler: A Film from Germany* (1982), for which Sontag wrote the English preface.

6. Italian filmmaker, best known for *Caro Diario* (Dear diary, 1993).

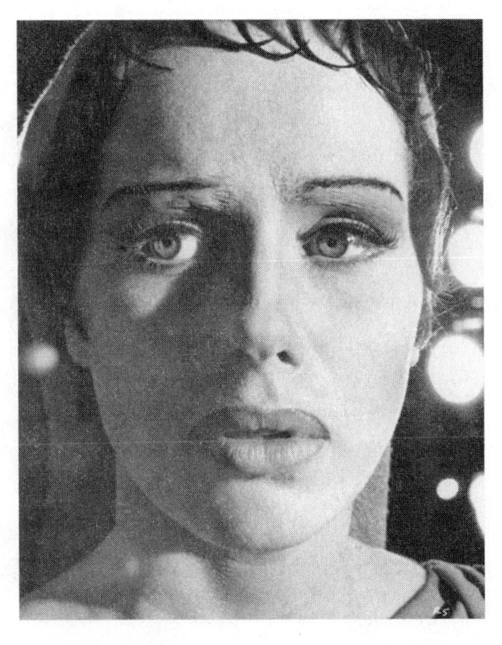
"Persona," 1967.

or Athens there wasn't a chance to get a cinematheque education. The distinctive thing about cinephile taste was that it embraced both "art" films and popular films. Thus, European cinephilia had a romantic relation to the films of certain directors in Hollywood at the apogee of the studio system: Godard for Howard Hawks, Fassbinder for Douglas Sirk. Of course, this moment—when cinephilia emerged—was also the moment when the Hollywood studio system was breaking up. It seemed that moviemaking had re-won the right to experiment; cinephiles could *afford* to be passionate (or sentimental) about the old Hollywood genre films. A host of new people came into cinema, including a generation of young film critics from *Cahiers du Cinéma;* the towering figure of that generation, indeed of several decades of filmmaking anywhere, was Jean-Luc Godard. A few writers turned out to be wildly talented filmmakers: Alexander Kluge in Germany, Pier Paolo Pasolini in Italy. (The model for the writer who turns to filmmaking actually emerged earlier, in France, with Pagnol in the 1930s and Cocteau in the 1940s; but it was not until the 1960s that this seemed, at least in Europe, normal.) Cinema appeared to be reborn.

For some fifteen years there was a profusion of masterpieces, and one allowed oneself to imagine that this would go on forever. To be sure, there was always a conflict between cinema as an industry and cinema as an art, cinema as routine and cinema as experiment. But the conflict was not such as to make impossible the making of wonderful films, sometimes within and sometimes outside of mainstream cinema. Now the balance has tipped decisively in favor of cinema as an industry. The great cinema of the 1960s and 1970s has been thoroughly repudiated. Already in the 1970s Hollywood was plagiarizing and banalizing the innovations in narrative method and editing of successful new European and ever-marginal independent American films. Then came the catastrophic rise in production costs in the 1980s, which secured the worldwide reimposition of industry standards of making and distributing films on a far more coercive, this time truly global, scale. The result can be seen in the melancholy fate of some of the greatest directors of the last decades. What place is there today for a maverick like Hans Jurgen Syberberg, who has stopped

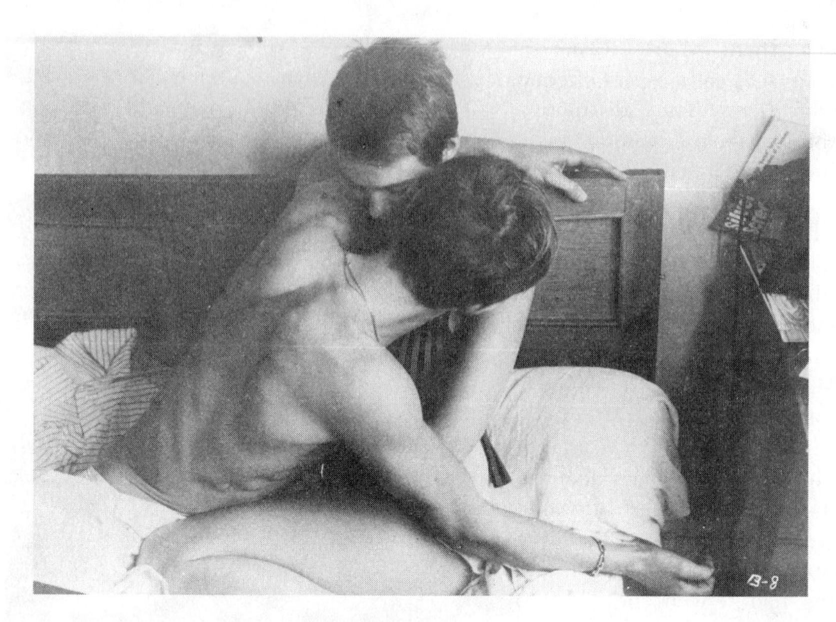

"Breathless," 1959.

making films altogether, or for the great Godard, who now makes films about the history of film on video? Consider some other cases. The internationalizing of financing and therefore of casts was a disaster for Andrei Tarkovsky[7] in the last two films of his stupendous, tragically abbreviated career. And these conditions for making films have proved to be as much an artistic disaster for two of the most valuable directors still working: Krzysztof Zanussi (*The Structure of Crystals, Illumination, Spiral, Contract*) and Theo Angelopoulos (*Reconstruction, Days of '36, The Travelling Players*). And what will happen now to Béla Tarr (*Damnation, Satantango*)? And how will Aleksandr Sokurov (*Save and Protect, Days of Eclipse, The Second Circle, Stone, Whispering Pages*) find the money to go on making films, his sublime films, under the rude conditions of Russian capitalism?[8]

Predictably, the love of cinema has waned. People still like going to the movies, and some people still care about and expect something special, necessary from a film. And wonderful films are still being made: Mike Leigh's *Naked*, Gianni Amelio's *Lamerica*, Hou Hsiao-hsien's *Goodbye South, Goodbye*,

7. Soviet film director (1932–1986), whose work was censored at home but won acclaim in the West. His *Katok i skripka* (The steamroller and the violin, 1960) won a prize at the New York Film Festival, and his first full-length feature film, *Ivanovo detstvo* (Ivan's childhood, 1962), established his international reputation.

8. Zanussi (b. 1939), Polish film director; Angelopolous (b. 1935), Greek film director; Tarr (b. 1955), Hungarian filmmaker; Sokurov (b. 1951), Russian filmmaker who in 1997 produced the award-winning *Mat i syn* (Mother and son).

and Abbas Kiarostami's *Close-Up* and Koker trilogy. But one hardly finds anymore, at least among the young, the distinctive cinephilic love of movies, which is not simply love of but a certain *taste* in films (grounded in a vast appetite for seeing and re-seeing as much as possible of cinema's glorious past). Cinephilia itself has come under attack, as something quaint, outmoded, snobbish. For cinephilia implies that films are unique, unrepeatable, magic experiences. Cinephilia tells us that the Hollywood remake of Godard's *Breathless* cannot be as good as the original. Cinephilia has no role in the era of hyperindustrial films. For by the very range and eclecticism of its passions, cinephilia cannot help but sponsor the idea of the film as, first of all, a poetic object; and cannot help but incite those outside the movie industry, like painters and writers, to want to make films, too. It is precisely this that must be defeated. That has been defeated.

If cinephilia is dead, then movies are dead . . . no matter how many movies, even very good ones, go on being made. If cinema can be resurrected, it will only be through the birth of a new kind of cine-love.

Questions

1. In her essay Sontag summarizes one hundred years of film history, from 1895 to 1995. Diagram her periodization of this history. Locate her moviegoing period (she was born in 1933) and yours on it. Which of the older films Sontag mentions have you seen? If you have seen other films made before you began going to the movies, name some of them. How did you see them—in a film-studies course, for example, or on your own?

2. What is Sontag's definition of a "cinephile"? Are you one? Is Susan Allen Toth one? See her "Going to the Movies," the essay that follows (p. 1036).

3. Sontag has harsh things to say about contemporary films: they are "astonishingly witless," "bloated, derivative," "a brazen combinatory or re-combinatory art" (paragraph 1), reduced to "assaultive images, and the unprincipled manipulation of images (faster and faster cutting) to be more attention-grabbing" and, at the same time, "disincarnated, lightweight," and they don't "demand anyone's full attention" (paragraph 6). Using at least three contemporary films that you have seen, write an essay in which you agree with, disagree with, or modify her charges.

4. Write an essay in which you compare what Sontag and Toth look for in film.

SUSAN ALLEN TOTH *Going to the Movies*

AARON TAKES ME only to art films. That's what I call them, anyway: strange movies with vague poetic images I don't always understand, long dreamy movies about a distant Technicolor past, even longer black-and-white movies about the general meaninglessness of life. We do not go unless at least one reputable critic has found the cinematography superb. We went to *The Devil's Eye,*[1] and Aaron turned to me in the middle and said, "My God, this is *funny.*" I do not think he was pleased.

When Aaron and I go to the movies, we drive our cars separately and meet by the box office. Inside the theater he sits tentatively in his seat, ready to move if he can't see well, poised to leave if the film is disappointing. He leans away from me, careful not to touch the bare flesh of his arm against the bare flesh of mine. Sometimes he leans so far I am afraid he may be touching the woman on his other side instead. If the movie is very good, he leans forward too, peering between the heads of the couple in front of us. The light from the screen bounces off his glasses; he gleams with intensity, sitting there on the edge of his seat, watching the screen. Once I tapped him on the arm so I could whisper a comment in his ear. He jumped.

After *Belle de Jour*[2] Aaron said he wanted to ask me if he could stay overnight. "But I can't," he shook his head mournfully before I had a chance to answer, "because I know I never sleep well in strange beds." Then he apologized for asking. "It's just that after a film like that," he said, "I feel the need to assert myself."

II

Bob takes me only to movies that he thinks have a redeeming social conscience. He doesn't call them films. They tend to be about poverty, war, injustice, political corruption, struggling unions in the 1930s, and the military-industrial complex. Bob doesn't like propaganda movies, though, and he doesn't like to be too depressed, either. We stayed away from *The Sorrow and the Pity;*[3] it would be, he said, just too much. Besides, he assured me, things are never that hopeless. So most of the movies we see are made in Hollywood. Because they are always very topical, these movies offer what Bob calls "food for thought." When

Originally published in Harper's Magazine *(May 1980) as "Cinematypes"; retitled and included in Toth's collection* How to Prepare for Your High School Reunion, and Other Essays *(1988).*

1. Swedish film (1960) about seduction, directed by Ingmar Bergman.
2. French film (1967) about erotic fantasies, directed by Luis Buñuel.
3. French documentary (1972) about the Nazi occupation of France.

we saw *Coming Home,*[4] Bob's jaw set so firmly with the first half hour that I knew we would end up at Poppin' Fresh Pies afterward.

When Bob and I go to the movies, we take turns driving so no one owes anyone else anything. We park far away from the theater so we don't have to pay for a space. If it's raining or snowing, Bob offers to let me off at the door, but I can tell he'll feel better if I go with him while he parks, so we share the walk too. Inside the theater Bob will hold my hand when I get scared if I ask him. He puts my hand firmly on his knee and covers it completely with his own hand. His knee never twitches. After a while, when the scary part is past, he loosens his hand slightly and I know that is a signal to take mine away. He sits companionably close, letting his jacket just touch my sweater, but he does not infringe. He thinks I ought to know he is there if I need him.

One night after *The China Syndrome*[5] I asked Bob if he wouldn't like to stay for a second drink, even though it was past midnight. He thought awhile about that, considering my offer from all possible angles, but finally he said no. Relationships today, he said, have a tendency to move too quickly.

III

Sam likes movies that are entertaining. By that he means movies that Will Jones in the *Minneapolis Tribune* loved and either *Time* or *Newsweek* rather liked; also movies that do not have sappy love stories, are not musicals, do not have subtitles, and will not force him to think. He does not go to movies to think. He liked *California Suite* and *The Seduction of Joe Tynan,*[6] though the plots, he said, could have been zippier. He saw it all coming too far in advance, and that took the fun out. He doesn't like to know what is going to happen. "I just want my brain to be tickled," he says. It is very hard for me to pick out movies for Sam.

When Sam takes me to the movies, he pays for everything. He thinks that's what a man ought to do. But I buy my own popcorn, because he doesn't approve of it; the grease might smear his flannel slacks. Inside the theater, Sam makes himself comfortable. He takes off his jacket, puts one arm around me, and all during the movie he plays with my hand, stroking my palm, beating a small tattoo on my wrist. Although he watches the movie intently, his body operates on instinct. Once I inclined my head and kissed him lightly just behind his ear. He beat a faster tattoo on my wrist, quick and musical, but he didn't look away from the screen.

When Sam takes me home from the movies, he stands outside my door and kisses me long and hard. He would like to come in, he says regretfully, but his steady girlfriend in Duluth wouldn't like it. When the *Tribune* gives a movie four stars, he has to save it to see with her. Otherwise her feelings might be hurt.

4. American film (1978) about a Vietnam veteran.

5. American film (1979) about a disaster in a nuclear power plant.

6. The first, American film (1978) with a script by Neil Simon; the second, American film (1979) about politics.

IV

10 I go to some movies by myself. On rainy Sunday afternoons I often sneak into a revival house or a college auditorium for old Technicolor musicals, *Kiss Me Kate, Seven Brides for Seven Brothers, Calamity Jane,* even, once, *The Sound of Music.*[7] Wearing saggy jeans so I can prop my feet on the seat in front, I sit toward the rear where no one will see me. I eat large handfuls of popcorn with double butter. Once the movie starts, I feel completely at home. Howard Keel and I are old friends; I grin back at him on the screen, admiring all his teeth. I know the sound tracks by heart. Sometimes when I get really carried away I hum along with Kathryn Grayson, remembering how I once thought I would fill out a formal like that. Skirts whirl, feet tap, acrobatic young men perform impossible feats, and then the camera dissolves into a dream sequence I know I can comfortably follow. It is not, thank God, Bergman.

If I can't find an old musical, I settle for Hepburn and Tracy, vintage Grant or Gable, on adventurous days Claudette Colbert or James Stewart. Before I buy my ticket I make sure it will all end happily. If necessary, I ask the girl at the box office. I have never seen *Stella Dallas* or *Intermezzo.*[8] Over the years I have developed other peccadilloes: I will, for example, see anything that is redeemed by Thelma Ritter. At the end of *Daddy Long Legs*[9] I wait happily for the scene when Fred Clark, no longer angry, at last pours Thelma a convivial drink. They smile at each other, I smile at them, I feel they are smiling at me. In the movies I go to by myself, the men and women always like each other.

7. The first three were made in the 1950s, the fourth in the 1960s.
8. The first, American film (1937) about a mother's love for her daughter; the second, American film (1939), a love story in which Ingrid Bergman made her American debut.
9. American film (1955) about a May–December romance.

QUESTIONS

1. Toth describes four kinds of movies by describing the men she sees them with: Aaron, Bob, Sam, and finally no man. Make a list of the adjectives or descriptive phrases she includes for each man. How do such descriptions convey, by implication, her attitudes toward the movies?

2. Which kind of movie does Toth like best—or does she like them all equally? How do you know?

3. Using Toth as a model, write an account of going to some event or participating in some activity by describing the person(s) you go with. Like Toth, convey your response to the event by means of your description of the person(s).

Aaron Copland *How We Listen*

We all listen to music according to our separate capacities. But, for the sake of analysis, the whole listening process may become clearer if we break it up into its component parts, so to speak. In a certain sense we all listen to music on three separate planes. For lack of a better terminology, one might name these: (1) the sensuous plane, (2) the expressive plane, (3) the sheerly musical plane. The only advantage to be gained from mechanically splitting up the listening process into these hypothetical planes is the clearer view to be had of the way in which we listen.

The simplest way of listening to music is to listen for the sheer pleasure of the musical sound itself. That is the sensuous plane. It is the plane on which we hear music without thinking, without considering it in any way. One turns on the radio while doing something else and absentmindedly bathes in the sound. A kind of brainless but attractive state of mind is engendered by the mere sound appeal of the music.

You may be sitting in a room reading this book. Imagine one note struck on the piano. Immediately that one note is enough to change the atmosphere of the room—proving that the sound element in music is a powerful and mysterious agent, which it would be foolish to deride or belittle.

The surprising thing is that many people who consider themselves qualified music lovers abuse that plane in listening. They go to concerts in order to lose themselves. They use music as a consolation or an escape. They enter an ideal world where one doesn't have to think of the realities of everyday life. Of course they aren't thinking about the music either. Music allows them to leave it, and they go off to a place to dream, dreaming because of and apropos of the music yet never quite listening to it.

5 Yes, the sound appeal of music is a potent and primitive force, but you must not allow it to usurp a disproportionate share of your interest. The sensuous plane is an important one in music, a very important one, but it does not constitute the whole story.

There is no need to digress further on the sensuous plane. Its appeal to every normal human being is self-evident. There is, however, such a thing as becoming more sensitive to the different kinds of sound stuff as used by various composers. For all composers do not use that sound stuff in the same way. Don't get the idea that the value of music is commensurate with its sensuous appeal or that the loveliest sounding music is made by the greatest composer. If that were so, Ravel would be a greater creator than Beethoven.[1] The point is that the sound element varies with each composer, that his usage of sound

From Copland's classic guide, What to Listen For in Music *(1957).*

1. Maurice Ravel (1875–1937), French composer; Ludwig van Beethoven (1770–1827), German composer.

forms an integral part of his style and must be taken into account when listening. The reader can see, therefore, that a more conscious approach is valuable even on this primary plane of music listening.

The second plane on which music exists is what I have called the expressive one. Here, immediately, we tread on controversial ground. Composers have a way of shying away from any discussion of music's expressive side. Did not Stravinsky[2] himself proclaim that his music was an "object," a "thing," with a life of its own, and with no other meaning than its own purely musical existence? This intransigent attitude of Stravinsky's may be due to the fact that so many people have tried to read different meanings into so many pieces. Heaven knows it is difficult enough to say precisely what it is that a piece of music means, to say it definitely, to say it finally so that everyone is satisfied with your explanation. But that should not lead one to the other extreme of denying to music the right to be "expressive."

My own belief is that all music has an expressive power, some more and some less, but that all music has a certain meaning behind the notes and that that meaning behind the note constitutes, after all, what the piece is saying, what the piece is about. This whole problem can be stated quite simply by asking, "Is there a meaning to music?" My answer to that would be, "Yes." And "Can you state in so many words what the meaning is?" My answer to that would be, "No." Therein lies the difficulty.

Simple-minded souls will never be satisfied with the answer to the second of these questions. They always want music to have a meaning, and the more concrete it is the better they like it. The more the music reminds them of a train, a storm, a funeral, or any other familiar conception the more expressive it appears to be to them. This popular idea of music's meaning—stimulated and abetted by the usual run of musical commentator—should be discouraged wherever and whenever it is met. One timid lady once confessed to me that she suspected something seriously lacking in her appreciation of music because of her inability to connect it with anything definite. That is getting the whole thing backward, of course.

10 Still, the question remains, How close should the intelligent music lover wish to come to pinning a definite meaning to any particular work? No closer than a general concept, I should say. Music expresses, at different moments, serenity or exuberance, regret or triumph, fury or delight. It expresses each of these moods, and many others, in a numberless variety of subtle shadings and differences. It may even express a state of meaning for which there exists no adequate word in any language. In that case, musicians often like to say that it has only a purely musical meaning. They sometimes go farther and say that *all* music has only a purely musical meaning. What they really mean is that no appropriate word can be found to express the music's meaning and that, even if it could, they do not feel the need of finding it.

But whatever the professional musician may hold, most musical novices still search for specific words with which to pin down their musical reactions.

2. Igor Stravinsky (1882–1971), Russian-born American composer.

That is why they always find Tchaikovsky[3] easier to "understand" than Beethoven. In the first place, it is easier to pin a meaning-word on a Tchaikovsky piece than on a Beethoven one. Much easier. Moreover, with the Russian composer, every time you come back to a piece of his it almost always says the same thing to you, whereas with Beethoven it is often quite difficult to put your finger right on what he is saying. And any musician will tell you that that is why Beethoven is the greater composer. Because music which always says the same thing to you will necessarily soon become dull music, but music whose meaning is slightly different with each hearing has a greater chance of remaining alive.

Listen, if you can, to the forty-eight fugue themes of Bach's *Well Tempered Clavichord*.[4] Listen to each theme, one after another. You will soon realize that each theme mirrors a different world of feeling. You will also soon realize that the more beautiful a theme seems to you the harder it is to find any word that will describe it to your complete satisfaction. Yes, you will certainly know whether it is a gay theme or a sad one. You will be able, in other words, in your own mind, to draw a frame of emotional feeling around your theme. Now study the sad one a little closer. Try to pin down the exact quality of its sadness. Is it pessimistically sad or resignedly sad; is it fatefully sad or smilingly sad?

Let us suppose that you are fortunate and can describe to your own satisfaction in so many words the exact meaning of your chosen theme. There is still no guarantee that anyone else will be satisfied. Nor need they be. The important thing is that each one feel for himself the specific expressive quality of a theme or, similarly, an entire piece of music. And if it is a great work of art, don't expect it to mean exactly the same thing to you each time you return to it.

Themes or pieces need not express only one emotion, of course. Take such a theme as the first main one of the *Ninth Symphony*,[5] for example. It is clearly made up of different elements. It does not say only one thing. Yet anyone hearing it immediately gets a feeling of strength, a feeling of power. It isn't a power that comes simply because the theme is played loudly. It is a power inherent in the theme itself. The extraordinary strength and vigor of the theme results in the listener's receiving an impression that a forceful statement has been made. But one should never try to boil it down to "the fateful hammer of life," etc. That is where the trouble begins. The musician, in his exasperation, says it means nothing but the notes themselves, whereas the nonprofessional is only too anxious to hang on to any explanation that gives him the illusion of getting closer to the music's meaning.

Now, perhaps, the reader will know better what I mean when I say that music does have an expressive meaning but that we cannot say in so many words what that meaning is. 15

3. Peter Ilyich Tchaikovsky (1840–1893), Russian composer.

4. A work composed by Johann Sebastian Bach (1685–1750) in which forty-eight themes are presented by themselves and then elaborated in three voices.

5. Composed by Beethoven.

The third plane on which music exists is the sheerly musical plane. Besides the pleasurable sound of music and the expressive feeling that it gives off, music does exist in terms of the notes themselves and of their manipulation. Most listeners are not sufficiently conscious of this third plane. * * *

Professional musicians, on the other hand, are, if anything, too conscious of the mere notes themselves. They often fall into the error of becoming so engrossed with their arpeggios and staccatos that they forget the deeper aspects of the music they are performing. But from the layman's standpoint, it is not so much a matter of getting over bad habits on the sheerly musical plane as of increasing one's awareness of what is going on, in so far as the notes are concerned.

When the man in the street listens to the "notes themselves" with any degree of concentration, he is most likely to make some mention of the melody. Either he hears a pretty melody or he does not, and he generally lets it go at that. Rhythm is likely to gain his attention next, particularly if it seems exciting. But harmony and tone color are generally taken for granted, if they are thought of consciously at all. As for music's having a definite form of some kind, that idea seems never to have occurred to him.

It is very important for all of us to become more alive to music on its sheerly musical plane. After all, an actual musical material is being used. The intelligent listener must be prepared to increase his awareness of the musical material and what happens to it. He must hear the melodies, the rhythms, the harmonies, the tone colors in a more conscious fashion. But above all he must, in order to follow the line of the composer's thought, know something of the principles of musical form. Listening to all of these elements is listening on the sheerly musical plane.

20 Let me repeat that I have split up mechanically the three separate planes on which we listen merely for the sake of greater clarity. Actually, we never listen on one or the other of these planes. What we do is to correlate them—listening in all three ways at the same time. It takes no mental effort, for we do it instinctively.

Perhaps an analogy with what happens to us when we visit the theater will make this instinctive correlation clearer. In the theater, you are aware of the actors and actresses, costumes and sets, sounds and movements. All these give one the sense that the theater is a pleasant place to be in. They constitute the sensuous plane in our theatrical reactions.

The expressive plane in the theater would be derived from the feeling that you get from what is happening on the stage. You are moved to pity, excitement, or gayety. It is this general feeling, generated aside from the particular words being spoken, a certain emotional something which exists on the stage, that is analogous to the expressive quality in music.

The plot and plot development is equivalent to our sheerly musical plane. The playwright creates and develops a character in just the same way that a composer creates and develops a theme. According to the degree of your awareness of the way in which the artist in either field handles his material will you become a more intelligent listener.

It is easy enough to see that the theatergoer never is conscious of any of these elements separately. He is aware of them all at the same time. The same is true of music listening. We simultaneously and without thinking listen on all three planes.

25 In a sense, the ideal listener is both inside and outside the music at the same moment, judging it and enjoying it, wishing it would go one way and watching it go another—almost like the composer at the moment he composes it; because in order to write his music, the composer must also be inside and outside his music, carried away by it and yet coldly critical of it. A subjective and objective attitude is implied in both creating and listening to music.

What the reader should strive for, then, is a more *active* kind of listening. Whether you listen to Mozart or Duke Ellington,[6] you can deepen your understanding of music only by being a more conscious and aware listener—not someone who is just listening, but someone who is listening *for* something.

6. Wolfgang Amadeus Mozart (1756–1791), Austrian composer; Edward Kennedy ("Duke") Ellington (1899–1974), American jazz composer and band leader.

Questions

1. List Copland's "three planes" of listening to music and explain what each entails. Are these three planes comprehensive? Is there another you would add?

2. In paragraphs 21–24, Copland uses the experience of going to the theater to illustrate his three planes of listening. Can you think of other artistic experiences that can be divided up into different "planes"? To what extent would the planes be the same as Copland's?

3. Copland uses classical music as examples in his explanation of the way humans listen to music. Write an essay about the ways you listen to another kind of music: folk, rap, jazz, hip-hop, pop, or rock.

Gene Weingarten *Pearls before Breakfast*

He emerged from the Metro at the L'Enfant Plaza Station and positioned himself against a wall beside a trash basket. By most measures, he was nondescript: a youngish white man in jeans, a long-sleeved T-shirt and a Washington Nationals baseball cap. From a small case, he removed a violin. Placing the open case at his feet, he shrewdly threw in a few dollars and pocket change as seed money, swiveled it to face pedestrian traffic, and began to play.

Originally published in the Washington Post *(April 2007), where Weingarten is a Pulitzer prize–winning reporter; reprinted in Dave Eggers, ed.,* The Best American Non-Required Reading *(2008).*

It was 7:51 A.M. on Friday, January 12, the middle of the morning rush hour. In the next forty-three minutes, as the violinist performed six classical pieces, 1,097 people passed by. Almost all of them were on the way to work, which meant, for almost all of them, a government job. L'Enfant Plaza is at the nucleus of federal Washington, and these were mostly mid-level bureaucrats with those indeterminate, oddly fungible titles: policy analyst, project manager, budget officer, specialist, facilitator, consultant.

Each passerby had a quick choice to make, one familiar to commuters in any urban area where the occasional street performer is part of the cityscape. Do you stop and listen? Do you hurry past with a blend of guilt and irritation, aware of your cupidity but annoyed by the unbidden demand on your time and your wallet? Do you throw in a buck, just to be polite? Does your decision change if he's really bad? What if he's really good? Do you have time for beauty? Shouldn't you? What's the moral mathematics of the moment?

On that Friday in January, those private questions would be answered in an unusually public way. No one knew it, but the fiddler standing against a bare wall outside the Metro in an indoor arcade at the top of the escalators was one of the finest classical musicians in the world, playing some of the most elegant music ever written on one of the most valuable violins ever made. His performance was arranged by the *Washington Post* as an experiment in context, perception, and priorities—as well as an unblinking assessment of public taste: in a banal setting at an inconvenient time, would beauty transcend?

5 The musician did not play popular tunes whose familiarity alone might have drawn interest. That was not the test. These were masterpieces that have endured for centuries on their brilliance alone, soaring music befitting the grandeur of cathedrals and concert halls.

The acoustics proved surprisingly kind. Though the arcade is of utilitarian design, a buffer between the Metro escalator and the outdoors, it somehow caught the sound and bounced it back round and resonant. The violin is an instrument that is said to be much like the human voice, and in this musician's masterly hands, it sobbed and laughed and sang—ecstatic, sorrowful, importuning, adoring, flirtatious, castigating, playful, romancing, merry, triumphal, sumptuous.

So, what do you think happened?

Hang on, we'll get you some expert help.

Leonard Slatkin, music director of the National Symphony Orchestra, was asked the same question. What did he think would occur, hypothetically, if one of the world's great violinists had performed incognito before a traveling rush-hour audience of one-thousand-odd people?

10 "Let's assume," Slatkin said, "that he is not recognized and just taken for granted as a street musician. . . . Still, I don't think that if he's really good, he's going to go unnoticed. He'd get a larger audience in Europe . . . but, okay, out of one thousand people, my guess is there might be thirty-five or forty who will recognize the quality for what it is. Maybe seventy-five to one hundred will stop and spend some time listening."

So, a crowd would gather?

"Oh, yes."

And how much will he make?

"About $150."

Thanks, Maestro. As it happens, this is not hypothetical. It really happened. 15

"How'd I do?"

We'll tell you in a minute.

"Well, who was the musician?"

Joshua Bell.

"NO!!!" 20

A onetime child prodigy, at thirty-nine Joshua Bell has arrived as an internationally acclaimed virtuoso. Three days before he appeared at the Metro station, Bell had filled the house at Boston's stately Symphony Hall, where merely pretty good seats went for $100. Two weeks later, at the Music Center at Strathmore, in North Bethesda, he would play to a standing-room-only audience so respectful of his artistry that they stifled their coughs until the silence between movements. But on that Friday in January, Joshua Bell was just another mendicant, competing for the attention of busy people on their way to work.

Bell was first pitched this idea shortly before Christmas, over coffee at a sandwich shop on Capitol Hill. A New Yorker, he was in town to perform at the Library of Congress and to visit the library's vaults to examine an unusual treasure: an eighteenth-century violin that once belonged to the great Austrian-born virtuoso and composer Fritz Kreisler. The curators invited Bell to play it; good sound, still.

"Here's what I'm thinking," Bell confided, as he sipped his coffee. "I'm thinking that I could do a tour where I'd play Kreisler's music . . ."

He smiled.

". . . on Kreisler's violin." 25

It was a snazzy, sequined idea—part inspiration and part gimmick—and it was typical of Bell, who has unapologetically embraced showmanship even as his concert career has become more and more august. He's soloed with the finest orchestras here and abroad, but he's also appeared on *Sesame Street,* done late-night talk TV, and performed in feature films. That was Bell playing the soundtrack on the 1998 movie *The Red Violin.* (He body-doubled, too, playing to a naked Greta Scacchi.) As composer John Corigliano accepted the Oscar for Best Original Dramatic Score, he credited Bell, who, he said, "plays like a god."

When Bell was asked if he'd be willing to don street clothes and perform at rush hour, he said:

"Uh, a stunt?"

Well, yes. A stunt. Would he think it . . . unseemly?

Bell drained his cup. 30

"Sounds like fun," he said.

Bell's a heartthrob. Tall and handsome, he's got a Donny Osmond[1]–like dose of the cutes, and, onstage, cute elides into *hott.* When he performs, he is usually the only man under the lights who is not in white tie and tails—he walks out to a standing O, looking like Zorro, in black pants and an untucked black dress shirt, shirttail dangling. That cute Beatles-style mop top is also a strategic asset: because his technique is full of body—athletic and passionate—he's almost dancing with the instrument, and his hair flies.

He's single and straight, a fact not lost on some of his fans. In Boston, as he performed Max Bruch's dour Violin Concerto in G Minor, the very few young women in the audience nearly disappeared in the deep sea of silver heads. But seemingly every single one of them—a distillate of the young and pretty—coalesced at the stage door after the performance, seeking an autograph. It's like that always, with Bell.

Bell's been accepting over-the-top accolades since puberty: *Interview* magazine once said his playing "does nothing less than tell human beings why they bother to live." He's learned to field these things graciously, with a bashful duck of the head and a modified "pshaw."

For this incognito performance, Bell had only one condition for participating. The event had been described to him as a test of whether, in an incongruous context, ordinary people would recognize genius. His condition: "I'm not comfortable if you call this genius." *Genius* is an overused word, he said: It can be applied to some of the composers whose work he plays, but not to him. His skills are largely interpretive, he said, and to imply otherwise would be unseemly and inaccurate.

It was an interesting request, and under the circumstances, one that will be honored. The word will not again appear in this article.

It would be breaking no rules, however, to note that the term in question, particularly as applied in the field of music, refers to a congenital brilliance—an elite, innate, preternatural ability that manifests itself early, and often in dramatic fashion.

One biographically intriguing fact about Bell is that he got his first music lessons when he was a four-year-old in Bloomington, Indiana. His parents, both psychologists, decided formal training might be a good idea after they saw that their son had strung rubber bands across his dresser drawers and was replicating classical tunes by ear, moving drawers in and out to vary the pitch.

To get the Metro from his hotel, a distance of three blocks, Bell took a taxi. He's neither lame nor lazy: he did it for his violin.

Bell always performs on the same instrument, and he ruled out using another for this gig. Called the Gibson ex Huberman, it was handcrafted in 1713 by Antonio Stradivari[2] during the Italian master's "golden period," toward the

1. American pop singer and a teen idol in his youth (b. 1957).
2. Stradivari (1644–1737), widely considered the greatest violin maker.

end of his career, when he had access to the finest spruce, maple, and willow, and when his technique had been refined to perfection.

"Our knowledge of acoustics is still incomplete," Bell said, "but he, he just . . . *knew.*"

Bell doesn't mention Stradivari by name. Just "he." When the violinist shows his Strad to people, he holds the instrument gingerly by its neck, resting it on a knee. "He made this to perfect thickness at all parts," Bell says, pivoting it. "If you shaved off a millimeter of wood at any point, it would totally imbalance the sound." No violins sound as wonderful as Strads from the 1710s, still.

The front of Bell's violin is in nearly perfect condition, with a deep, rich grain and luster. The back is a mess, its dark reddish finish bleeding away into a flatter, lighter shade and finally, in one section, to bare wood.

"This has never been refinished," Bell said. "That's his original varnish. People attribute aspects of the sound to the varnish. Each maker had his own secret formula." Stradivari is thought to have made his from an ingeniously balanced cocktail of honey, egg whites, and gum arabic from sub-Saharan trees.

45 Like the instrument in *The Red Violin,* this one has a past filled with mystery and malice. Twice, it was stolen from its illustrious prior owner, the Polish virtuoso Bronislaw Huberman. The first time, in 1919, it disappeared from Huberman's hotel room in Vienna but was quickly returned. The second time, nearly twenty years later, it was pinched from his dressing room in Carnegie Hall. He never got it back. It was not until 1985 that the thief—a minor New York violinist—made a deathbed confession to his wife and produced the instrument.

Bell bought it a few years ago. He had to sell his own Strad and borrow much of the rest. The price tag was reported to be about $3.5 million.

All of which is a long explanation for why, in the early morning chill of a day in January, Josh Bell took a three-block cab ride to the Orange Line and rode one stop to L'Enfant.

As Metro stations go, L'Enfant Plaza is more plebeian than most. Even before you arrive, it gets no respect. Metro conductors never seem to get it right: "Lehfahn." "Layfont." "El'phant."

At the top of the escalators are a shoeshine stand and a busy kiosk that sells newspapers, lottery tickets, and a wall full of magazines with titles such as *Mammazons* and *Girls of Barely Legal.* The skin mags move, but it's that lottery ticket dispenser that stays the busiest, with customers queuing up for Daily 6 lotto and Powerball and the ultimate suckers' bait, those pamphlets that sell random number combinations purporting to be "hot." They sell briskly. There's also a quick-check machine to slide in your lotto ticket, post-drawing, to see if you've won. Beneath it is a forlorn pile of crumpled slips.

50 On Friday, January 12, the people waiting in the lottery line looking for a long shot would get a lucky break—a free, close-up ticket to a concert by one of the world's most famous musicians—but only if they were of a mind to take note.

Bell decided to begin with "Chaconne" from Johann Sebastian Bach's Partita No. 2 in D Minor. Bell calls it "not just one of the greatest pieces of music ever written, but one of the greatest achievements of any man in history. It's a spiritually powerful piece, emotionally powerful, structurally perfect. Plus, it was written for a solo violin, so I won't be cheating with some half-assed version."

Bell didn't say it, but Bach's "Chaconne" is also considered one of the most difficult violin pieces to master. Many try; few succeed. It's exhaustingly long—fourteen minutes—and consists entirely of a single, succinct musical progression repeated in dozens of variations to create a dauntingly complex architecture of sound. Composed around 1720, on the eve of the European Enlightenment, it is said to be a celebration of the breadth of human possibility.

If Bell's encomium to "Chaconne" seems overly effusive, consider this from the nineteenth-century composer Johannes Brahms, in a letter to Clara Schumann:[3] "On one stave, for a small instrument, the man writes a whole world of the deepest thoughts and most powerful feelings. If I imagined that I could have created, even conceived the piece, I am quite certain that the excess of excitement and earth-shattering experience would have driven me out of my mind."

So, that's the piece Bell started with.

55 He'd clearly meant it when he promised not to cheap out this performance: He played with acrobatic enthusiasm, his body leaning into the music and arching on tiptoes at the high notes. The sound was nearly symphonic, carrying to all parts of the homely arcade as the pedestrian traffic filed past.

Three minutes went by before something happened. Sixty-three people had already passed when, finally, there was a breakthrough of sorts. A middle-aged man altered his gait for a split second, turning his head to notice that there seemed to be some guy playing music. Yes, the man kept walking, but it was *something.*

A half-minute later, Bell got his first donation. A woman threw in a buck and scooted off. It was not until six minutes into the performance that someone actually stood against a wall, and listened.

Things never got much better. In the three-quarters of an hour that Joshua Bell played, seven people stopped what they were doing to hang around and take in the performance, at least for a minute. Twenty-seven gave money, most of them on the run—for a total of $32 and change. That leaves the 1,070 people who hurried by, oblivious, many only three feet away, few even turning to look.

No, Mr. Slatkin, there was never a crowd, not even for a second.

60 It was all videotaped by a hidden camera. You can play the recording once or fifteen times, and it never gets any easier to watch. Try speeding it up, and it becomes one of those herky-jerky World War I–era silent newsreels. The people scurry by in comical little hops and starts, cups of coffee in their hands, cell phones at their ears. ID tags slapping at their bellies, a grim *danse macabre* to indifference, inertia, and the dingy, gray rush of modernity.

3. Johannes Brahms (1833–1897), German composer and pianist; Clara Schumann (1819–1896), German composer and pianist, wife of composer Robert Schumann, and friend and early supporter of Brahms.

Even at this accelerated pace, though, the fiddler's movements remain fluid and graceful; he seems so apart from his audience—unseen, unheard, otherworldly—that you find yourself thinking that he's not really there. A ghost.

Only then do you see it: He is the one who is real. They are the ghosts.

If a great musician plays great music but no one hears . . . was he really any good?

It's an old epistemological debate, older, actually, than the koan about the tree in the forest. Plato weighed in on it, and philosophers for two millennia afterward: What is beauty? Is it a measurable fact (Gottfried Leibniz), or merely an opinion (David Hume), or is it a little of each, colored by the immediate state of mind of the observer (Immanuel Kant)?[4]

We'll go with Kant, because he's obviously right, and because he brings us pretty directly to Joshua Bell, sitting there in a hotel restaurant, picking at his breakfast, wryly trying to figure out what the hell had just happened back there at the Metro. 65

"At the beginning," Bell says, "I was just concentrating on playing the music. I wasn't really watching what was happening around me . . ."

Playing the violin looks all-consuming, mentally and physically, but Bell says that for him the mechanics of it are partly second nature, cemented by practice and muscle memory: it's like a juggler, he says, who can keep those balls in play while interacting with a crowd. What he's mostly thinking about as he plays, Bell says, is capturing emotion as a narrative: "When you play a violin piece, you are a storyteller, and you're telling a story."

With "Chaconne," the opening is filled with a building sense of awe. That kept him busy for a while. Eventually, though, he began to steal a sidelong glance.

"It was a strange feeling, that people were actually, ah . . ."

The word doesn't come easily. 70

". . . *ignoring* me."

Bell is laughing. It's at himself.

"At a music hall, I'll get upset if someone coughs or if someone's cell phone goes off. But here, my expectations quickly diminished. I started to appreciate *any* acknowledgment, even a slight glance up. I was oddly grateful when someone threw in a dollar instead of change." This is from a man whose talents can command $1,000 a minute.

Before he began, Bell hadn't known what to expect. What he does know is that, for some reason, he was nervous.

4. Plato (c. 428–348 B.C.E.), Greek philosopher whose allegory of the cave emphasized humanity's overreliance on the senses and consequent misapprehension of reality; Leibniz (1646–1716), German philosopher, a master logician who developed calculus; David Hume (1711–1776), Scottish philosopher, who broke from tradition to argue that sentiment, more than reason, governs human behavior; Immanuel Kant (1724–1834), German philosopher of the Enlightenment whose monumental *Critique of Pure Reason* (1781) argued for the power and order of our ability to reason.

75 "It wasn't exactly stage fright, but there were butterflies," he says. "I was stressing a little."

Bell has played, literally, before crowned heads of Europe. Why the anxiety at the Washington Metro?

"When you play for ticket-holders," Bell explains, "you are already validated. I have no sense that I need to be accepted. I'm already accepted. Here, there was this thought: *What if they don't like me? What if they resent my presence . . .*"

He was, in short, art without a frame. Which, it turns out, may have a lot to do with what happened—or, more precisely, what didn't happen—on January 12.

Mark Leithauser has held in his hands more great works of art than any king or pope or Medici ever did. A senior curator at the National Gallery, he oversees the framing of the paintings. Leithauser thinks he has some idea of what happened at that Metro station.

80 "Let's say I took one of our more abstract masterpieces, say an Ellsworth Kelly, and removed it from its frame, marched it down the fifty-two steps that people walk up to get to the National Gallery, past the giant columns, and brought it into a restaurant. It's a $5 million painting. And it's one of those restaurants where there are pieces of original art for sale, by some industrious kids from the Corcoran School, and I hang that Kelly on the wall with a price tag of $150. No one is going to notice it. An art curator might look up and say: 'Hey, that looks a little like an Ellsworth Kelly. Please pass the salt.'"

Leithauser's point is that we shouldn't be too ready to label the Metro passersby unsophisticated boobs. Context matters.

Kant said the same thing. He took beauty seriously: In his *Critique of Aesthetic Judgment,* Kant argued that one's ability to appreciate beauty is related to one's ability to make moral judgments. But there was a caveat. Paul Guyer of the University of Pennsylvania, one of America's most prominent Kantian scholars, says the eighteenth-century German philosopher felt that to properly appreciate beauty, the viewing conditions must be optimal.

"Optimal," Guyer said, "doesn't mean heading to work, focusing on your report to the boss, maybe your shoes don't fit right."

So, if Kant had been at the Metro watching as Joshua Bell play to a thousand unimpressed passersby?

85 "He would have inferred about them," Guyer said, "absolutely nothing."

And that's that.

Except it isn't. To really understand what happened, you have to rewind that video and play it back from the beginning, from the moment Bell's bow first touched the strings.

White guy, khakis, leather jacket, briefcase. Early thirties. John David Mortensen is on the final leg of his daily bus-to-Metro commute from Reston. He's heading up the escalator. It's a long ride—one minute and fifteen seconds if you don't walk. So, like most everyone who passes Bell this day, Mortensen gets a good earful of music before he has his first look at the musician. Like most of them, he notes that it sounds pretty good. But like very few of them, when he gets to the top, he doesn't race past as though Bell were some nuisance to be avoided. Mortensen is that first person to stop, that guy at the six-minute mark.

It's not that he has nothing else to do. He's a project manager for an international program at the Department of Energy; on this day, Mortensen has to participate in a monthly budget exercise, not the most exciting part of his job: "You review the past month's expenditures," he says, "forecast spending for the next month, if you have X dollars, where will it go, that sort of thing."

On the video, you can see Mortensen get off the escalator and look around. He locates the violinist, stops, walks away but then is drawn back. He checks the time on his cell phone—he's three minutes early for work—then settles against a wall to listen. 90

Mortensen doesn't know classical music at all; classic rock is as close as he comes. But there's something about what he's hearing that he really likes.

As it happens, he's arrived at the moment that Bell slides into the second section of "Chaconne." ("It's the point," Bell says, "where it moves from a darker, minor key into a major key. There's a religious, exalted feeling to it.") The violinist's bow begins to dance; the music becomes upbeat, playful, theatrical, big.

Mortensen doesn't know about major or minor keys: "Whatever it was," he says, "it made me feel at peace."

So, for the first time in his life, Mortensen lingers to listen to a street musician. He stays his allotted three minutes as ninety-four more people pass briskly by. When he leaves to help plan contingency budgets for the Department of Energy, there's another first. For the first time in his life, not quite knowing what had just happened but sensing it was special, John David Mortensen gives a street musician money.

There are six moments in the video that Bell finds particularly painful to relive: "The awkward times," he calls them. It's what happens right after each piece ends: nothing. The music stops. The same people who hadn't noticed him playing don't notice that he has finished. No applause, no acknowledgment. So Bell just saws out a small, nervous chord—the embarrassed musician's equivalent of, "Er, okay, moving right along . . ."—and begins the next piece. 95

After "Chaconne," it is Franz Schubert's "Ave Maria,"[5] which surprised some music critics when it debuted in 1825: Schubert seldom showed religious feeling in his compositions, yet "Ave Maria" is a breathtaking work of adoration of the Virgin Mary. What was with the sudden piety? Schubert dryly answered: "I think this is due to the fact that I never forced devotion in myself and never compose hymns or prayers of that kind unless it overcomes me unawares: but

5. Schubert (1797–1828), Austrian composer whose style straddles the Classical and Romantic eras; he composed the song for a German translation of Walter Scott's hymn from *The Lady of the Lake*.

then it is usually the right and true devotion." This musical prayer became among the most familiar and enduring religious pieces in history.

A couple of minutes into it, something revealing happens. A woman and her preschooler emerge from the escalator. The woman is walking briskly and, therefore, so is the child. She's got his hand.

"I had a time crunch," recalls Sheron Parker, an IT director for a federal agency. "I had an 8:30 A.M. training class, and first I had to rush Evvie off to his teacher, then rush back to work, then to the training facility in the basement."

Evvie is her son, Evan. Evan is three.

100 You can see Evan clearly on the video. He's the cute black kid in the parka who keeps twisting around to look at Joshua Bell, as he is being propelled toward the door.

"There was a musician," Parker says, "and my son was intrigued. He wanted to pull over and listen, but I was rushed for time."

So Parker does what she has to do. She deftly moves her body between Evan's and Bell's, cutting off her son's line of sight. As they exit the arcade, Evan can still be seen craning to look. When Parker is told what she walked out on, she laughs.

"Evan is very smart!"

The poet Billy Collins once laughingly observed that all babies are born with a knowledge of poetry, because the lub–dub of the mother's heart is in iambic meter. Then, Collins said, life slowly starts to choke the poetry out of us. It may be true with music, too.

105 There was no ethnic or demographic pattern to distinguish the people who stayed to watch Bell, or the ones who gave money, from that vast majority who hurried on past, unheeding. Whites, blacks, and Asians, young and old, men and women, were represented in all three groups. But the behavior of one demographic remained absolutely consistent. Every single time a child walked past, he or she tried to stop and watch. And every single time, a parent scooted the kid away.

If there was one person on that day who was too busy to pay attention to the violinist, it was George Tindley. Tindley wasn't hurrying to get to work. He was at work.

The glass doors through which most people exit the L'Enfant Station lead into an indoor shopping mall, from which there are exits to the street and elevators to office buildings. The first store in the mall is an Au Bon Pain, the croissant and coffee shop where Tindley, in his forties, works in a white uniform busing the tables, restocking the salt and pepper packets, taking out the garbage. Tindley labors under the watchful eye of his bosses, and he's supposed to be hopping, and he was.

But every minute or so, as though drawn by something not entirely within his control, Tindley would walk to the very edge of the Au Bon Pain property, keeping his toes inside the line, still on the job. Then he'd lean forward, as far out into the hallway as he could, watching the fiddler on the other side of the glass doors. The foot traffic was steady, so the doors were usually open. The sound came through pretty well.

"You could tell in one second that this guy was good, that he was clearly a professional," Tindley says. He plays the guitar, loves the sound of strings, and has no respect for a certain kind of musician.

"Most people, they play music; they don't feel it," Tindley says. "Well, that man was *feeling* it. That man was moving. Moving into the sound."

A hundred feet away, across the arcade, was the lottery line, sometimes five or six people long. They had a much better view of Bell than Tindley did, if they had just turned around. But no one did. Not in the entire forty-three minutes. They just shuffled forward toward that machine spitting out numbers. Eyes on the prize.

J. T. Tillman was in that line. A computer specialist for the Department of Housing and Urban Development, he remembers every single number he played that day—ten of them, $2 a piece, for a total of $20. He doesn't recall what the violinist was playing, though. He says it sounded like generic classical music, the kind the ship's band was playing in *Titanic,* before the iceberg.

"I didn't think nothing of it," Tillman says, "just a guy trying to make a couple of bucks." Tillman would have given him one or two, he said, but he spent all his cash on lotto.

When he is told that he stiffed one of the best musicians in the world, he laughs.

"Is he ever going to play around here again?"

"Yeah, but you're going to have to pay a lot to hear him."

"Damn."

Tillman didn't win the lottery, either.

Bell ends "Ave Maria" to another thunderous silence, plays Manuel Ponce's sentimental "Estrellita," then a piece by Jules Massenet, and then begins a Bach gavotte, a joyful, frolicsome, lyrical dance. It's got an Old World delicacy to it; you can imagine it entertaining bewigged dancers at a Versailles ball, or—in a lute, fiddle, and fife version—the boot-kicking peasants of a Pieter Bruegel painting.[6]

Watching the video weeks later, Bell finds himself mystified by one thing only. He understands why he's not drawing a crowd, in the rush of a morning workday. But: "I'm surprised at the number of people who don't pay attention at all, as if I'm invisible. Because, you know what? I'm makin' a lot of noise!"

He is. You don't need to know music at all to appreciate the simple fact that there's a guy there, playing a violin that's throwing out a whole bucket of sound; at times, Bell's bowing is so intricate that you seem to be hearing two instruments playing in harmony. So those head-forward, quick-stepping passersby are a remarkable phenomenon.

6. Pieter Bruegel (c. 1525/30–1569), Dutch painter known for exuberant, heavily populated, and highly detailed scenes of peasant life.

Bell wonders whether their inattention may be deliberate: If you don't take visible note of the musician, you don't have to feel guilty about not forking over money; you're not complicit in a rip-off.

It may be true, but no one gave that explanation. People just said they were busy, had other things on their mind. Some who were on cell phones spoke louder as they passed Bell, to compete with that infernal racket.

And then there was Calvin Myint. Myint works for the General Services Administration. He got to the top of the escalator, turned right and headed out a door to the street. A few hours later, he had no memory that there had been a musician anywhere in sight.

125 "Where was he, in relation to me?"

"About four feet away."

"Oh."

There's nothing wrong with Myint's hearing. He had buds in his ear. He was listening to his iPod.

For many of us, the explosion in technology has perversely limited, not expanded, our exposure to new experiences. Increasingly, we get our news from sources that think as we already do. And with iPods, we hear what we already know; we program our own playlists.

130 The song that Calvin Myint was listening to was "Just Like Heaven," by the British rock band The Cure. It's a terrific song, actually. The meaning is a little opaque, and the Web is filled with earnest efforts to deconstruct it. Many are far-fetched, but some are right on point: It's about a tragic emotional disconnect. A man has found the woman of his dreams but can't express the depth of his feeling for her until she's gone. It's about failing to see the beauty of what's plainly in front of your eyes.

"Yes, I saw the violinist," Jackie Hessian says, "but nothing about him struck me as much of anything."

You couldn't tell that by watching her. Hessian was one of those people who gave Bell a long, hard look before walking on. It turns out that she wasn't noticing the music at all.

"I really didn't hear that much," she said. "I was just trying to figure out what he was doing there, how does this work for him, can he make much money, would it be better to start with some money in the case, or for it to be empty, so people feel sorry for you? I was analyzing it financially."

What do you do, Jackie?

135 "I'm a lawyer in labor relations with the United States Postal Service. I just negotiated a national contract."

The best seats in the house were upholstered. In the balcony, more or less. On that day, for $5, you'd get a lot more than just a nice shine on your shoes.

Only one person occupied one of those seats when Bell played. Terence Holmes is a consultant for the Department of Transportation, and he liked the music just fine, but it was really about a shoeshine: "My father told me never to wear a suit with your shoes not cleaned and shined."

Holmes wears suits often, so he is up in that perch a lot, and he's got a good relationship with the shoeshine lady. Holmes is a good tipper and a good talker, which is a skill that came in handy that day. The shoeshine lady was upset about something, and the music got her more upset. She complained, Holmes said, that the music was too loud, and he tried to calm her down.

Edna Souza is from Brazil. She's been shining shoes at L'Enfant Plaza for six years, and she's had her fill of street musicians there; when they play, she can't hear her customers, and that's bad for business. So she fights.

Souza points to the dividing line between the Metro property, at the top of the escalator, and the arcade, which is under control of the management company that runs the mall. Sometimes, Souza says, a musician will stand on the Metro side, sometimes on the mall side. Either way, she's got him. On her speed dial, she has phone numbers for both the mall cops and the Metro cops. The musicians seldom last long. 140

What about Joshua Bell?

He was too loud, too, Souza says. Then she looks down at her rag, sniffs. She hates to say anything positive about these damned musicians, but: "He was pretty good, that guy. It was the first time I didn't call the police."

Souza was surprised to learn he was a famous musician, but not that people rushed blindly by him. That, she said, was predictable. "If something like this happened in Brazil, everyone would stand around to see. Not here."

Souza nods sourly toward a spot near the top of the escalator: "Couple of years ago, a homeless guy died right there. He just lay down there and died. The police came, an ambulance came, and no one even stopped to see or slowed down to look.

"People walk up the escalator, they look straight ahead. Mind your own business, eyes forward. Everyone is stressed. Do you know what I mean?" 145

What is this life if, full of care,
We have no time to stand and stare.
—from "Leisure," by W. H. Davies

Let's say Kant is right. Let's accept that we can't look at what happened on January 12 and make any judgment whatever about people's sophistication or their ability to appreciate beauty. But what about their ability to appreciate life?

We're busy. Americans have been busy, as a people, since at least 1831, when a young French sociologist named Alexis de Tocqueville[7] visited the States and found himself impressed, bemused, and slightly dismayed at the degree to which people were driven, to the exclusion of everything else, by hard work and the accumulation of wealth.

* * *

In his 2003 book, *Timeless Beauty: In the Arts and Everyday Life*, British author John Lane writes about the loss of the appreciation for beauty in the

7. French historian and political thinker (1805–1859) best known for *Democracy in America* (1835 and 1840) based on his travels in the newly independent United States.

modern world. The experiment at L'Enfant Plaza may be symptomatic of that, he said—not because people didn't have the capacity to understand beauty, but because it was irrelevant to them.

"This is about having the wrong priorities," Lane said.

150 If we can't take the time out of our lives to stay a moment and listen to one of the best musicians on Earth play some of the best music ever written; if the surge of modern life so overpowers us that we are deaf and blind to something like that—then what else are we missing?

That's what the Welsh poet W. H. Davies meant in 1911 when he published those two lines that begin this section. They made him famous. The thought was simple, even primitive, but somehow no one had put it quite that way before.

Of course, Davies had an advantage—an advantage of perception. He wasn't a tradesman or a laborer or a bureaucrat or a consultant or a policy analyst or a labor lawyer or a program manager. He was a hobo.

The cultural hero of the day arrived at L'Enfant Plaza pretty late, in the unprepossessing figure of one John Picarello, a smallish man with a baldish head.

Picarello hit the top of the escalator just after Bell began his final piece, a reprise of "Chaconne." In the video, you see Picarello stop dead in his tracks, locate the source of the music, and then retreat to the other end of the arcade. He takes up a position past the shoeshine stand, across from that lottery line, and he will not budge for the next nine minutes.

155 Like all the passersby interviewed for this article, Picarello was stopped by a reporter after he left the building and was asked for his phone number. Like everyone, he was told only that this was to be an article about commuting. When he was called later in the day, like everyone else, he was first asked if anything unusual had happened to him on his trip into work. Of the more than forty people contacted, Picarello was the only one who immediately mentioned the violinist.

"There was a musician playing at the top of the escalator at L'Enfant Plaza."

Haven't you seen musicians there before?

"Not like this one."

What do you mean?

160 "This was a superb violinist. I've never heard anyone of that caliber. He was technically proficient, with very good phrasing. He had a good fiddle, too, with a big, lush sound. I walked a distance away, to hear him. I didn't want to be intrusive on his space."

Really?

"Really. It was that kind of experience. It was a treat, just a brilliant, incredible way to start the day."

Picarello knows classical music. He is a fan of Joshua Bell but didn't recognize him; he hadn't seen a recent photo, and besides, for most of the time Picarello was pretty far away. But he knew this was not a run-of-the-mill guy out there, performing. On the video, you can see Picarello look around him now and then, almost bewildered.

"Yeah, other people just were not getting it. It just wasn't registering. That was baffling to me."

When Picarello was growing up in New York, he studied violin seriously, intending to be a concert musician. But he gave it up at eighteen, when he decided he'd never be good enough to make it pay. Life does that to you sometimes. Sometimes, you have to do the prudent thing. So he went into another line of work. He's a supervisor at the U.S. Postal Service. Doesn't play the violin much, anymore. 165

When he left, Picarello says, "I humbly threw in $5." It *was* humble: You can actually see that on the video. Picarello walks up, barely looking at Bell, and tosses in the money. Then, as if embarrassed, he quickly walks away from the man he once wanted to be.

Does he have regrets about how things worked out?

The postal supervisor considers this.

"No. If you love something but choose not to do it professionally, it's not a waste. Because, you know, you still have it. You have it forever."

Bell thinks he did his best work of the day in those final few minutes, in the second "Chaconne." And that also was the first time more than one person at a time was listening. As Picarello stood in the back, Janice Olu arrived and took up a position a few feet away from Bell. Olu, a public trust officer with HUD, also played the violin as a kid. She didn't know the name of the piece she was hearing, but she knew the man playing it has a gift. 170

Olu was on a coffee break and stayed as long as she dared. As she turned to go, she whispered to the stranger next to her, "I *really* don't want to leave." The stranger standing next to her happened to be working for the *Washington Post*.

In preparing for this event, editors at the *Post Magazine* discussed how to deal with likely outcomes. The most widely held assumption was that there could well be a problem with crowd control: In a demographic as sophisticated as Washington, the thinking went, several people would surely recognize Bell. Nervous "what-if" scenarios abounded. As people gathered, what if others stopped just to see what the attraction was? Word would spread through the crowd. Cameras would flash. More people flock to the scene; rush-hour pedestrian traffic backs up; tempers flare; the National Guard is called; tear gas, rubber bullets, etc.

As it happens, exactly one person recognized Bell, and she didn't arrive until near the very end. For Stacy Furukawa, a demographer at the Commerce Department, there was no doubt. She doesn't know much about classical music, but she had been in the audience three weeks earlier, at Bell's free concert at the Library of Congress. And here he was, the international virtuoso, sawing away, begging for money. She had no idea what the heck was going on, but whatever it was, she wasn't about to miss it.

Furukawa positioned herself ten feet away from Bell, front row, center. She had a huge grin on her face. The grin, and Furukawa, remained planted in that spot until the end.

175 "It was the most astonishing thing I've ever seen in Washington," Furukawa says. "Joshua Bell was standing there playing at rush hour, and people were not stopping, and not even looking, and some were flipping quarters at him! Quarters! I wouldn't do that to *anybody*. I was thinking, *Omigosh, what kind of a city do I live in that this could happen*?"

When it was over, Furukawa introduced herself to Bell, and tossed in a twenty. Not counting that—it was tainted by recognition—the final haul for his forty-three minutes of playing was $32.17. Yes, some people gave pennies.

"Actually," Bell said with a laugh, "that's not so bad, considering. That's forty bucks an hour. I could make an okay living doing this, and I wouldn't have to pay an agent."

These days, at L'Enfant Plaza, lotto ticket sales remain brisk. Musicians still show up from time to time, and they still tick off Edna Souza. Joshua Bell's latest album, *The Voice of the Violin,* has received the usual critical acclaim. ("Delicate urgency." "Masterful intimacy." "Unfailingly exquisite." "A musical summit." "Will make your heart thump and weep at the same time.")

Bell headed off on a concert tour of European capitals. But he is back in the States this week. He has to be. On Tuesday, he will be accepting the Avery Fisher Prize, recognizing the Flop of L'Enfant Plaza as the best classical musician in America.

QUESTIONS

1. Weingarten offers several explanations for why so few people stopped to listen to Joshua Bell play. Which one is the most persuasive to you and why?

2. Music is notoriously difficult to describe. Choose a brief passage describing a specific piece of music or Bell's playing style that you find particularly evocative. Analyze and explain why it works. Then listen to a recording of Bach's "Chaconne" or Schubert's "Ave Maria" and try to describe it yourself.

3. Do we have time for beauty? Do you? What is the place of beauty—especially artistic beauty—in daily life? What does this experiment teach us?

4. Conduct your own version of Weingarten's experiment and write an essay describing and analyzing your findings. Observe a street artist in your community or recruit a friend to perform at a busy spot on campus. How many people stop and for how long? Compare your results to those of Weingarten.

Philosophy and Religion

Langston Hughes *Salvation*

I was saved from sin when I was going on thirteen. But not really saved. It happened like this. There was a big revival at my Auntie Reed's church. Every night for weeks there had been much preaching, singing, praying, and shouting, and some very hardened sinners had been brought to Christ, and the membership of the church had grown by leaps and bounds. Then just before the revival ended, they held a special meeting for children, "to bring the young lambs to the fold." My aunt spoke of it for days ahead. That night I was escorted to the front row and placed on the mourners' bench[1] with all the other young sinners, who had not yet been brought to Jesus.

My aunt told me that when you were saved you saw a light, and something happened to you inside! And Jesus came into your life! And God was with you from then on! She said you could see and hear and feel Jesus in your soul. I believed her. I had heard a great many old people say the same thing and it seemed to me they ought to know. So I sat there calmly in the hot, crowded church, waiting for Jesus to come to me.

The preacher preached a wonderful rhythmical sermon, all moans and shouts and lonely cries and dire pictures of hell, and then he sang a song about the ninety and nine safe in the fold, but one little lamb was left out in the cold.[2] Then he said: "Won't you come? Won't you come to Jesus? Young lambs, won't you come?" And he held out his arms to all us young sinners there on the mourners' bench. And the little girls cried. And some of them jumped up and went to Jesus right away. But most of us just sat there.

A great many old people came and knelt around us and prayed, old women with jet-black faces and braided hair, old men with work-gnarled hands. And the church sang a song about the lower lights are burning, some poor sinners to be saved. And the whole building rocked with prayer and song.

From The Big Sea *(1940), Hughes's account of his early life.*

1. A place in the front where potential converts sat during an evangelical service.

2. "The Ninety and Nine" and "Let the Lower Lights Be Burning," mentioned in the next paragraph, are the titles of famous evangelical hymns collected by Ira Sankey (1840–1908).

5 Still I kept waiting to *see* Jesus.

Finally all the young people had gone to the altar and were saved, but one boy and me. He was a rounder's[3] son named Westley. Westley and I were surrounded by sisters and deacons praying. It was very hot in the church, and getting late now. Finally Westley said to me in a whisper: "God damn! I'm tired o' sitting here. Let's get up and be saved." So he got up and was saved.

Then I was left all alone on the mourners' bench. My aunt came and knelt at my knees and cried, while prayers and songs swirled all around me in the little church. The whole congregation prayed for me alone, in a mighty wail of moans and voices. And I kept waiting serenely for Jesus, waiting, waiting—but he didn't come. I wanted to see him, but nothing happened to me. Nothing! I wanted something to happen to me, but nothing happened.

I heard the songs and the minister saying: "Why don't you come? My dear child, why don't you come to Jesus? Jesus is waiting for you. He wants you. Why don't you come? Sister Reed, what is this child's name?"

"Langston," my aunt sobbed.

10 "Langston, why don't you come? Why don't you come and be saved? Oh, Lamb of God! Why don't you come?"

Now it was really getting late. I began to be ashamed of myself, holding everything up so long. I began to wonder what God thought about Westley, who certainly hadn't seen Jesus either, but who was now sitting proudly on the platform, swinging his knickerbockered legs and grinning down at me, surrounded by deacons and old women on their knees praying. God had not struck Westley dead for taking his name in vain or for lying in the temple. So I decided that maybe to save further trouble, I'd better lie, too, and say that Jesus had come, and get up and be saved.

So I got up.

Suddenly the whole room broke into a sea of shouting, as they saw me rise. Waves of rejoicing swept the place. Women leaped in the air. My aunt threw her arms around me. The minister took me by the hand and led me to the platform.

When things quieted down, in a hushed silence, punctuated by a few ecstatic "Amens," all the new young lambs were blessed in the name of God. Then joyous singing filled the room.

15 That night, for the last time in my life but one—for I was a big boy twelve years old—I cried. I cried, in bed alone, and couldn't stop. I buried my head under the quilts, but my aunt heard me. She woke up and told my uncle I was crying because the Holy Ghost had come into my life, and because I had seen Jesus. But I was really crying because I couldn't bear to tell her that I had lied, that I had deceived everybody in the church, and I hadn't seen Jesus, and that now I didn't believe there was a Jesus any more, since he didn't come to help me.

3. A rounder was a loafer or wastrel.

Questions

1. Hughes describes how he lost his faith in Jesus at the age of twelve. How did the grown-ups in his life contribute to the experience?

2. Hughes expected to "see" Jesus. How did he understand the word "see"? How did he need to understand it?

3. Hughes was twelve ("going on thirteen") when the event he describes in first-person narration took place. How careful is he to restrict himself to the point of view of a twelve-year-old child? How does he ensure that we, as readers, understand things that the narrator does not?

4. Write a first-person narrative in which you describe a failure—yours or someone else's—to live up to the expectations of parents or other authority figures.

Rita Dove

The Epistle of Paul the Apostle to the Ephesians

On the mysteries of vision, H.D.[1] writes: "We begin with sympathy of thought." One of the last great modern mystics, H.D. scribbled her *Notes on Thoughts and Vision* in a notebook marked "July, Scilly Islands" in 1919, when she retreated to these islands off the coast of Cornwall in order to recuperate—from war, from illness and the breakup of her marriage, from the death of her brother and the hazardous birth of her daughter Perdita. Sea air and salt light to heal a wounded spirit: "The doctor prescribes rest."

I am reading H.D. on a grassy knoll overlooking the grounds of the Villa Serbelloni, the "Study and Conference Center" of the Rockefeller Foundation on Lake Como in northern Italy, trying to ignore a niggling restlessness I've had ever since my arrival. Do I feel displaced in the serenity of this splendid retreat, high above the tourist traffic of the village of Bellagio, here where terraced hills plunge into clear waters and cypresses slope into the mists at evening? Five weeks of hydrangeas and tiger lilies, white-coated butlers and silver candlesticks—what sumptuous reward for all the hours spent hunched in a sixty-watt circle of light, smudging my way through a wilderness of words! At last no meals to cook or phones to answer, little mail, no children; a room of one's own, a study in the woods, and all around, beauty . . . but I'm not writing.

Included in the collection Incarnation: Contemporary Writers on the New Testament *(1990), edited by the poet Alfred Corn.*

1. Pen name of the American poet Hilda Doolittle (1886–1961).

I've told myself it takes time to unwind, and I try to relax by reading afternoons when the *breva*[2] sweeps the fog from the lake, freshening the shore. I read sprawled in a rattan chair set up outside, next to my study, hoping the sun will burn off the stress and fill the emptiness with magic.

While browsing in the villa library this morning I talked with a poet from Canada; he was convinced that the jewellike medieval painting of Saul on the way to Damascus[3] that's mounted near the dictionaries is an unsigned Bono. Unsure who Bono was but unwilling to show my ignorance, I scrutinized the canvas for a signature—nothing in the tufted grass, the parched and rutted road, no scrawls in the surreal blue heaven or bright curls of the seraphim—and before I remembered to put on my museum demeanor I was captivated by the wistful sincerity of the scene before me. Saul looked utterly terrified, his horse rearing and his fellow travelers baffled by such strange behavior on an ordinary day. How devastating an experience for a man so certain of his convictions! No wonder he spent three days in darkness afterward, emptied of himself, until Ananias came to claim him in the name of Christianity. No wonder his name changed, the same sound but a different beginning.

5 H.D.'s *Notes* drop to the grass. A few yards away, three goldfish hidden under the lily pads send up their perky semaphores: I hear this infinitesimal percolation even as wild birds overhead belt out Italian chorales and a speedboat growls across the lake. So that's what's been bothering me: the germ of a poem dealing with religion. But, as if I were a Jewish dyer trading in royal purple, I struggle against the notion of Christianity acquiring a poem from me—just as I struggle against the ideologue who has haunted me since adolescence, whose stony gaze I still feel whenever I rail against the strictures of institutional belief.

Life before Paul was milk and honey, grapes and warm bread, cardboard-and-glitter crèches. In those early Sunday-school years we were fed on floods and famines, raining roads and babies in baskets. Come twelve and the age of accountability, Christ appeared in the Temple and there followed a progression of sun-drenched miracles—Lazarus rising from his shroud, fish gleaming on proliferating hunks of bread. We loved the repetition of blessings, the palms fanning above the stolid head of a donkey, even the thirty pieces of silver. Blood and vinegar on the cross was swept over quickly, and Sunrise Services emphasized the rock rolled away, shining wings, astonishment, and His Glorious Resurrection. That was what a miracle was, after all: absence and light.

I was thirteen when the man who would introduce me to the apostle Paul walked into our senior Sunday-school class. He was tall, dark, and hellishly

2. A strong wind that blows across Lake Como in the afternoons and only starts to weaken at sunset.

3. According to the New Testament (Acts 9:1–9), Saul of Tarsus was traveling on the road to Damascus to destroy the Christian community there, when he was blinded by a brilliant light and heard the voice of Jesus saying, "Saul, Saul, why persecutest thou me?" This story recounts Saul's conversion to Christianity and his name change to Paul.

handsome, severely dressed in a matte-black narrow suit and black shirt from which rose a ring of shocking white, like a slipped halo. Never before had I seen a clerical collar (our minister wore standard suits with striped ties which peeked from his velvet-trimmed "preaching" robe); I thought the collar was his own invention, a kind of symbolic leash worn as a token of his service to God. He was the new assistant minister, straight out of theological school in the South (an exotic country to us in Akron, Ohio), and would take over the twelve-to-fifteen-year-olds, leaving our former teacher with the less unruly high schoolers.

Of course all the girls developed an immediate crush on him. We followed him breathlessly across the hall to a smaller, pale green classroom and without being asked formed a semicircle around the table he leaned against, like a male model from *Ebony* magazine, pinstriped trousers draping elegantly just above the buffed black wingtips. On his left hand glinted, to our disappointment, a large wedding band.

"What do you know of mortal sin?" he asked.

We goggled at him and tittered nervously. "Mortal" sounded all right to us. He frowned, straightening the crease in his pant leg, then patiently unveiled to us the concepts of irretrievable error and purgatory. Since we were past the age of twelve, he explained, we were accountable for our sins against the Ten Commandments, which were inviolable. And our transgressions against any of those laws—whether actual or committed *in thought only*—were unforgivable except through Jesus Christ.

We barely heard the Jesus Christ part. We were doomed, for we had just coveted another woman's husband; we had also disobeyed our parents, stolen, lied, cursed—and if one counted thinking (how can you control your thoughts?) as well, then we committed these transgressions all the time. In an instant, flirting had changed from harmless entertainment to hellfire.

Our church was A.M.E. Zion. The acronym stands for African Methodist Episcopal, an appellation that contains all the contradictions and acclimatizations black Americans have gone through to accommodate both the African memory and the American dream. Basically Methodist, our church believed in a moderate liturgy (responsive readings) but did not tolerate kneeling or chanting; the "Episcopal" distinguished us from the Baptists not only in decorum—we baptized with a few drops of water on a baby's forehead—but in class. Determinedly of the bourgeoisie ("boojy" we called our parents, among them dentists, general practitioners, dry-cleaning moguls), we did not approve of hee-hawing sermons, though the minister was permitted to shout out the last sixth of his text.

"African" meant many things. Sometimes it was the license to wear proud colors and hats piled high, as extravagant as platters—unlike the drab skirt-and-blouse attire of the white Lutherans one street over. "African" also referred to our intimate relationship with God and Christ, the permission to wipe Christ's sweat from our brows and talk to him like a brother, to identify our lot with that of the Israelites under Pharaoh. Martin Luther King, Jr. was our Moses, charged with delivering his people across the Selma bridge. "African" bore the very cadences of nostalgia for our lost homeland, wherever it may have been—

though in those turbulent years of Miriam Makeba and Malcolm X there was an edge to that nostalgia as well, a defiant hope from those who wished for mercy but just might choose, if pressed, to prevail by whatever means necessary.

But "African" always meant righteous singing. I particularly loved the "old hundred" hymns, standard oldies sung during the formal catechism of the service, before the sermon, as well as the choral outbursts from the white-clad women in the front pew.

15 Ah, the deaconesses! Mostly widows with massive bosoms, all ancient, these women put on their blinding white shirtwaists, their chalky nylons, and Shinola-white shoes every Sunday. Some wore tiny starched bonnets, very much like nurses or pilgrims, and others preferred the pure ornament of a scrubbed dark face lifted to the Lord. They were the self-appointed brides of Christ and the acknowledged mothers of the church, the arbiters of the Holy Spirit, and they disapproved of flash and frivolity and black militancy. (Though they never complained about Afros, since several of them had let their hair "go back" to furry halos.) The deaconesses were already seated when the rest of the congregation trickled in. Usually they were bent in prayer, humming vigorously to the mumbled supplications of a deacon, usually the oldest male, who by virtue of his sex and age was permitted to kneel on the first step leading to the altar.

The deaconesses were also intimate with what W. E. B. Du Bois[4] called the Sorrow Songs—older hymns, prehistoric canons that resembled nothing familiar or comforting. They had very few words and were frightening in their near-inarticulate misery. For at least a half hour before the processional signaled the official start of the service, the old women hummed, rocked, wailed these chants as parishioners arrived and drifted into the pews. Unlike gospel, "big with all the wrongs done done," these songs reeked with unappeasable loss and pain. They were the moans of slavery, the rhythms of an existence dulled by rote and brutality and hopelessness, an isolation so complete there could be no words.

The deaconesses led the congregation in that complex courtship between the Holy Spirit and mortal endeavor; the give and take, the surge and ebb between the minister's sermon and their shouted counterpoint was our clue to how well the minister was doing in bringing us closer to holiness, indeed, bringing us *in Christ*, in Paul's complex, mystical phrase, until heat and pinching waistbands dropped away and the message from the pulpit entered us directly, like an injection.

What is the mystery of grace? What does it mean to be *in Christ*? I watched the older women of the church "get happy"; I could see them gathering steam, pushing out the seams of their composure until it dropped down, the Holy Spirit, falling upon them like a hatchet from heaven. Instead of crumbling they rose up, incandescent, to perform amazing feats—they tightroped the backs of pews, skipped along the aisles, threw off ushers and a half-dozen able-bodied men with every shout. (Men rarely got happy; when they did theirs was a decorous performance, hardly an experience at all.) A woman "full of the Spirit" was

4. American civil rights leader, educator, historian, and author (1868–1963).

indomitable; one could almost see sunbeams glancing off the breastplate of righteousness, the white wings twinkling on the sandals of faith. And when it was over, they were not diminished but serene, as if they'd been given a tonic.

Why couldn't I be filled, transfused with glory? The most I'd experienced was a "quickening"—a mini-transformation characterized by shortened breath and an intense longing for the indefinite . . . what? I was tongue-tied, hopelessly guilt-ridden and self-conscious to boot. The most I could do was get teary-eyed. In the face of those bolder ecstasies, I'd fall back into my own ashes, quenched.

Witnessing these transformations usually made me churlish for the rest 20 of the day. I decided God didn't like intelligence. And though we hadn't been meant to sample the Tree of Knowledge, surely we couldn't be blamed for the intelligence we'd been saddled with.

Sunday evenings after "60 Minutes" my father would push off his slippers and shrug into his overcoat, keys jangling. We knew the signal: another trip to Grandma's on the East Side. It was a long way through town, along the gorge and then the slow climb up Market Street, past the defunct oats silos and the Fir Hill Conservatory of Music, then down Arlington and into the purgatorial Furnace Street, where the smoke and brimstone miraculously began, spewing from Plant One of the Goodyear Rubber Company and the smaller infernos of Mohawk and General Tire. This was the part of the journey I waited for. The backlit plumes of smoke and murky variations of exhaust and light were exciting, a negative snapshot of power and hope; the mere sight of a belching smokestack at night made me think of evening gowns and diamond lavaliers.

All across town the accompaniment was radio—the staid ministerial admonitions of a local Presbyterian congregation on the way, and afterward the surging gospels of Shiloh Baptist, my grandmother's own church, whose evening service she attended faithfully via the airwaves, rocking in her armchair in the back bedroom. I was awed by so much fervor: that one could go to church on Sunday morning and still have ardor left over to attend an evening service seemed strange, yet weirdly desirable. How simple life would be if one could believe that much! Later, in bed, I'd tuck my transistor radio under the pillow and tune into the Catholic broadcast at ten—after Shiloh Baptist's creaking ship of lamentations what a relief, a balm, *Hail Mary full of grace Blessed art thou among women and blessed is the fruit of thy womb Jesus* whispered over and over until I dozed off, safe for another night.

Into the intact world of childhood, Paul had introduced Doubt, and I resisted. As far as I was concerned, Saul/Paul was altogether too fervent—his persecution of the Christians too single-minded, his conversion too spectacular, his teachings too humorless. It wasn't the gaudiness of his martyr's life I distrusted (John's vision of the Apocalypse, in contrast, seemed absolute to me and vividly *correct*); rather, it was the contradiction between his life and his words. "Do as I say, not as I do"—we'd learned in Sunday school to nod, straight-faced, when reciting the commandments but to watch as scandals erupted in that orchestrated adult world: a senior usher ogling a pair of fine hips rolling under orange shantung, the occasional girl burgeoning under her choir robes. We waited for public recriminations, but all went on as before. We had a saying: Saints can backslide, but never trust a person who can't dance. Paul couldn't dance, but he shore could talk. Our assistant minister felt it his duty to initiate us into the world of words, the irretrievability of a vow.

I also distrusted the name change, from the Jew Saul to the astringent. New Age Paul. Paul—a name without history. Somehow I suspected him of abandoning with his born name the Old Testament, where Sauls and Jeremiahs flourished, and his desert treks and prison tenure had no aura. He was a traveling salesman, his epistles little more than shtick.

25 And Paul had no music; neither did he make a joyful noise before the Lord. He despised pageantry and silver ornament. His was a ministry of noon—no shadows or respite from the all-reaching rays of righteousness. I could not think of Paul without imagining parched mesas and the emblazoned killing ground of a Colosseum. Even the olives he preferred must have been sharp with rosemary, chewy and bitter.

But the god I knew understood the value of a wink. He was nothing like this Paul with his blind stare, his frozen faith burning in his eyes. Leave such clenched fervor to human beings; gods and angels are casual. No wonder he saw life in terms of architecture, and the body become church, a sacred building you entered silently and where you'd better not spit. And farther up the wine-dark aisle, the path of blood transfixed, this sacrificial artery leading to the plateau where no body lived but Thought reigned, gold and wax and velvet, paltry adornment designed to render palpable to the congregation the ineffable integrity of the spirit. This, then, was Christ presiding over the church, and Man presiding over Wife.

The mystery of Paul's ideology is revealed through his metaphors: comparing the church to a marriage. To be saved, to establish a mystical and *ongoing* spiritual strength, one does not try to become Christ or to identify with Christ; instead, one develops a *relationship to* him. This is a "primitive" concept: the ancient Greeks mingled freely with their gods and goddesses, with sometimes disastrous (poor Leda),[5] sometimes beneficent (Odysseus guided to Ithaca by Pallas Athene) results. African slaves in America transferred their attitudes toward divinities to the abstract figures of Christianity, telling Mary not to weep, exhorting Jonah not to despair, and rejoicing that Christ had personally reached down to lift them up. Black worshipers sat down to talk with God as with an old friend. When I was in my early teens, black disc jockeys favored a popular song that went: "I had a talk with my man last night; / He reassured me everything was all right." It was years before I heard the gospel song that had been its inspiration: "I had a talk with God last night." I was not as shocked by this discovery as perhaps I should have been; I was already on the way to secular humanism. After all, I had been talking to God for several years, bargaining and wheedling from the cave of my pillow, protesting my good intentions.

Human agency. I rolled the phrase around in my mouth as I perched on the curved lip of the pew, willing myself to remember the words through the

5. In Greek mythology, a mortal who was seduced by Zeus in the form of a swan and who gave birth to Helen of Troy.

sermon's climax and the preacher's ecstatic Call to Altar so that I might carry them home and find a use for them. *Human agency* was the key I'd been looking for in the rigid latticework the New Testament had raised around my daily living. Obedient though I was, I could not believe the thoughts that entered my daydreams so easily were forbidden. To hold the mind accountable—surely this wasn't what God had meant. Surely he did not want robots as children; surely a doll's house would be a bore for such a mighty spectator.

The world is protean. Every adolescent knows this, lives this . . . and is astonished at adults' ability to fasten onto the order of things with smug attentions. How can they skim the surface of such stormy oceans? Mother snapping her facial compact shut with a satisfied click, Father Turtle-waxing the Ford on Saturday afternoon: where is the pleasure to be located in these routines when the ultimate pleasure (as every adolescent discovers) is sexual—the disintegrating joy of a French kiss, the utterly selfish desire of the body to *know more?* Of course, we didn't understand the concept of guilt, major guilt—the kind that can't be erased from heart and mind, that distresses even ten, fifteen years later, whenever buried incidents float unbidden to the surface. How could we? We hadn't lived very much.

Saul watched as Stephen was stoned to death; Paul was celibate in order to serve his Christ more ardently. Aren't these flip sides of the same coin? And if not, where did Saul go? Who, if anyone, was in the body that sat three days in darkness in Damascus, who spoke before the crowds, who crouched in that dark prison cell and built up the body of Christian thought into a white and pillared building? Did he remember Saul at all—or had he, as Paul, burned away his past self so completely that with it fled the childhood words for stone and bread? What initially fills the void when the old self is struck down and out—what rushes in before the light, what rides the arrow tip of redemption into the benighted soul? 30

In the rattan chair beside the lily pond, far above the unspeakably blue waters of Lake Como, the poem for Paul takes shape:

On the Road to Damascus

They say I was struck down by the voice of an angel:
        flames poured through the radiant fabric of heaven
as I cried out and fell to my knees.

My first recollection was of Unbroken Blue,
        but two of the guards have already sworn by
the tip of my tongue set ablaze. As an official,

I recognize the lure of a good story:
        useless to suggest that my mount
had stumbled, that I was pitched into a clump

of wild chamomile, its familiar stink
        soothing even as my palms sprang blisters
under the nicked leaves. I heard shouts,

the horse pissing in terror—but my eyes
had dropped to my knees, and I saw nothing.
I was a Roman and had my business

among the clouded towers of Damascus.
I had not counted on earth rearing,
honey streaming down a parched sky,

a spear skewering me to the dust of the road
on the way to the city I would never
enter now, her markets steaming with vendors

and compatriots in careless armor lifting a hand
in greeting as they call out my name,
only to find no one home.

Paul's first visit to Ephesus lasted over two years, during which time he argued in the synagogue and converted "divers souls." Afterward he made for Jerusalem, sending back to Ephesus two disciples to keep the flame burning. In Paul's absence, the disciples met resistance from the silversmiths, who had a hefty business in shrines to the goddess Diana and naturally resented the loss in trade the new iconless religion would occasion. Led by the silversmith Demetrius, the people rose up in defense of their goddess; when the disciples tried to speak, the crowd outshouted them, for two hours chanting "Great is Diana of the Ephesians." Forced to retreat, the disciples were recalled by Paul, who "embraced them" and set out himself for Ephesus, where he gave the heretics "much exhortation" (Acts 20:1–2).

Did Paul's harsh words succeed at Ephesus, or did Diana prevail? The Bible is curiously silent on this point. In fact, the authorship of the Epistle to the Ephesians is heavily disputed among theological scholars—and it was almost certainly not written for the Ephesians, though of course we have other testimonies of his ministry there. It hardly matters whether Paul wrote this epistle or not—the spirit of his thought is still intact. We know from Acts that Paul appeared at Ephesus with a bag of tricks, handkerchiefs emerging from his sleeves to heal the sick and raise the dead . . . and yet the artisans with their silver statuettes of Diana were still able to rouse the people: We want Diana, thousand-breasted deity, they told Paul's disciples, who were forced to retreat. Was the light in Paul's eyes too empty? Or was it simply that two mysticisms—the matriarchal vision of fertility and wholeness, the patriarchal vision of order and clarity—were insisting on their separate paths to glory?

When I was a teenager Paul seemed to be a hard man with an unrealistically severe code of sacrifice, a fanatic who devised silly laws of diet, dress codes, and impossible rules of behavior; an ideologue who equated belief with ethics and transformation with institutional rhetoric. This was the world view our assistant minister promulgated; Paul was his boogeyman.

I see now that Paul's proclamations were demanded of him. At that time Christianity was still a heresy within a larger tradition; Saul's persecution of

Christians, his conversion, and his consequent wrangles with the priests of the Temple—these events were all in the family, so to speak. At the time when the Pauline Epistles were written, the biggest question for the new religion was whether or not to accept Gentiles; once that quandary was settled, more mundane issues (Can they remain uncircumcised? Must they obey the Judaic rules of diet?) were the order of the day. The disciples attempted to thread a path through the existing Old Testament laws; they sought an extension, and fulfillment, of Judaism. Paul's public needed concrete rules, so he gave them restrictions to hold on to: Wife, obey your husband; husband, love your wife—just as you obey Christ and He loves you. Children, obey your parents. Servants (this is the tricky one), obey your masters—followed by a telling conditional: "according to the flesh, with fear and trembling, in singleness of your heart, as unto Christ" (Ephesians 6:5–6). And because pictures are worth a thousand words, he gave them metaphors: the Church as a bride, Christ as bridegroom, and martial imagery sure to delight a city devoted to the huntress Diana. Gird the loins with truth, slip the feet into the Gospel of peace, take up the breastplate of righteousness and the shield of faith! Blatant theatrics, but it worked.

Yet Paul *was* a mystic. Only a mystic would address the newly converted with "And you *hath he quickened*, who were dead in trespasses and sins." Or: "the fulness of him that filleth all in all." Devising a system for connecting and reflection, a guide for conducting a life of energized joy—this is Paul's abiding light. 35

Whenever I move to a new place, the first thing I usually do is "cozy up" my study; I throw down rugs, mount marionettes on the walls, place a crystal or a hand-carved elephant on a shelf where my fidgety gaze might fall for a moment and rest. This time, though, it was different. After leaving the Rockefeller Study and Conference Center in Bellagio, I moved into what was easily the most nondescript room I have ever written poetry in—white brick, gray industrial-strength carpet—and yet, six months later I still could not bear to tack up so much as a single poster.

It was as if the photographs and paintings that used to provide companionship in my solitary hours of composition had ceased to serve as windows and begun to block the view. It seemed I required no distraction from the void. To put it less negatively: I no longer felt the need to focus in on an object in order to allow my thoughts free rein, unsupervised—a window had opened in me.

I was nearly finished writing "On the Road to Damascus" before I understood what about the gold-leaf-and-lapis universe in the painting the Canadian poet attributed to Bono had so moved me that morning in the Villa Serbelloni. Saul was terrified because the eyes that had studied the Law and looked calmly on at the slaying of another man had for the first time failed their owner. The Roman world, once as compact and manageable as the toylike apparition of the city of Damascus hovering on the horizon, had split apart, and he was falling into a mystery, bottomless and widening.

Paul's account of his conversion, on the other hand, is essentially the story of a seduction. He has been entered by Christ the Bridegroom and remade in the image of his Love. Then, as in any marriage, one must work at redemption; one must learn to forgive oneself.

40 H.D. writes: "We must be 'in love' before we can understand the mysteries of vision." This does not mean penetrating the mysterious, nor does it mean being taken by storm. Grace is a state of being, not an assault; and enlightenment, unlike epiphany, is neither brief nor particularly felicitous. The Saul in the painting knew better. Anyone who feels the need to connect the outside world with an interior presence must *absorb* the mysterious into the tangle of contradictions and longings that form each one of us. That's hard, ongoing work, and it never ends.

Questions

1. Reread Dove's last two sentences and see if they apply to her essay as a whole. What's hard about the work she describes?

2. How does Dove's framing her thoughts on Paul with scenes from her stay in Bellagio affect the presentation of her points? Could her points be made without this framing, or is it essential to her argument?

3. How seriously do Dove's twelve- to fifteen-year-olds take the idea of mortal sin? Dove says they've all sinned, but do you believe her? To what extent have they sinned?

4. Write about learning some moral lesson in your own life, using Dove as your model.

JAMES VAN THOLEN *Surprised by Death*

While we were still weak, at the right time Christ died for the ungodly. . . . But God proves his love for us in that while we still were sinners God died for us.
—ROMANS 5:6, 8, NRSV[1]

THIS IS A STRANGE DAY—for all of us. Most of you know that today marks my return to this pulpit after seven months of dealing with an aggressive and deadly form of cancer. Now, with the cancer vacationing for a little while, I am back. And of course, I'm glad to be back. But I can't help feeling how strange this day is—especially because I want to ignore my absence, and I want to pretend everybody has forgotten the reason for it.

A 1999 Sunday sermon, preached as Van Tholen returned to his Rochester, N.Y., pulpit after months of cancer treatment. He died eighteen months later. His sermon was published in Christianity Today, *a moderate evangelical weekly; it was reprinted in* Best American Spiritual Writing *(2001).*

1. New Revised Standard Version, a modern translation of the Bible.

But we can't do that. We can't ignore what has happened. We can rise above it; we can live through it; but we can't ignore it. If we ignore the threat of death as too terrible to talk about, then the threat wins. Then we are overwhelmed by it, and our faith doesn't apply to it. And if that happens, we lose hope.

We want to worship God in this church, and for our worship to be real, it doesn't have to be fun, and it doesn't have to be guilt-ridden. But it does have to be honest, and it does have to hope in God. We have to be honest about a world of violence and pain, a world that scorns faith and smashes hope and rebuts love. We have to be honest about the world, and honest about the difficulties of faith within it. And then we still have to hope in God.

So let me start with the honesty. The truth is that for seven months I have been scared. Not of the cancer, not really. Not even of death. Dying is another matter—how long it will take and how it will go. Dying scares me. But when I say that I have been scared, I don't mean that my thoughts have centered on dying. My real fear has centered somewhere else. Strange as it may sound, I have been scared of meeting God.

How could this be so? How could I have believed in the God of grace and still have dreaded to meet him? Why did I stand in this pulpit and preach grace to you over and over, and then, when I myself needed the grace so much, why did I discover fear where the grace should have been? 5

I think I know the answer now. As the wonderful preacher John Timmer[2] has taught me over the years, the answer is that grace is a scandal. Grace is hard to believe. Grace goes against the grain. The gospel of grace says that there is nothing I can *do* to get right with God, but that God has made himself right with me through Jesus' bloody death. And that is a scandalous thing to believe.

God comes to us before we go to him. John Timmer used to say that this is God's habit. God came to Abraham when there was nothing to come to, just an old man at a dead end. But that's God for you. That's the way God likes to work. He comes to old men and to infants, to sinners and to losers. That's grace, and a sermon without it is no sermon at all.

So I've tried to preach grace, to fill my sermons up with grace, to persuade you to believe in grace. And it's wonderful work to have—that is, to stand here and preach grace to people. I got into this pulpit and talked about war and homosexuality and divorce. I talked about death before I knew what death really was. And I tried to bring the gospel of grace to these areas when I preached. I said that God goes to people in trouble, that God receives people in trouble, that God is a God who *gets* into trouble because of his grace. I said what our Heidelberg Catechism[3] says: that our only comfort in life and in death is that we are not our own but belong to our faithful Savior, Jesus Christ.

I said all those things, and I meant them. But that was before I faced death myself. So now I have a silly thing to admit: I don't think I ever realized the

2. Pastor of the Christian Reformed Church; author of many books of sermons.

3. One of the major statements of faith of the Christian Reformed Church in Europe and the United States. It received its name from the place of its origin, Heidelberg, Germany.

shocking and radical nature of God's grace—even as I preached it. And the reason I didn't get it where grace is concerned, I think, is that I assumed I still had about forty years left. Forty years to unlearn my bad habits. Forty years to let my sins thin down and blow away. Forty years to be good to animals and pick up my neighbors' mail for them when they went on vacation.

But that's not how it's going to go. Now I have months, not years. And now I have to meet my creator who is also my judge—I have to meet God not later, but sooner. I haven't enough time to undo my wrongs, not enough time to straighten out what's crooked, not enough time to clean up my life.

And that's what has scared me.

So now, for the first time, I have to preach grace and know what I'm talking about. I have to preach grace and not only believe it, but rest on it, depend on it, stake my life on it. And as I faced the need to do this I remembered one of the simplest, most powerful statements in the entire Bible.

You may have thought that the reason for my choice of Romans 5 lay in the wonderful words about how suffering produces endurance, and endurance produces character, and character produces hope. Those are beautiful words, true words, but I'm not so sure they apply to me. I'm not sure I've suffered so much or so faithfully to claim that my hope has arisen through the medium of good character. No, many of you know far more about good character than I do, and more about suffering, too.

It wasn't that beautiful chain with character as the main link that drew my attention to Romans 5; instead, it was just one little word in verses 6 and 8. It's the Greek word *eti*, and it has brought comfort to my soul. The word means "yet" or "still," and it makes all the difference between sin and grace. Paul writes that "while we were *still* weak Christ died for the ungodly." He wants us to marvel at the Christ of the gospel, who comes to us in our weakness and in our need. Making sure we get the point, Paul uses the word twice in verse 6 in a repetitious and ungrammatical piling up of his meaning: "*Still* while we were *still* weak, at the right time Christ died for the ungodly."

I'm physically weak, but that's not my main weakness, my most debilitating weakness. What the last half year has proved to me is that my weakness is more of the soul than the body. This is what I've come to understand as I have dwelled on one question: How will I explain myself to my God? How can I ever claim to have been what he called me to be?

And, of course, the scary truth is that I can't. That's the kind of weakness Paul is talking about. And that's where *eti* comes in—while we were *still* weak, while we were *still* sinners, while we were *still* enemies of God, we were reconciled with him through the death of his Son. I find it unfathomable that God's love propelled him to reach into our world with such scandalous grace, such a way out, such hope. No doubt God has done it, because there's no hope anywhere else. I know. I've been looking. And I have come to see that the hope of the world lies only inside the cradle of God's grace.

This truth has come home to me as I've been thinking what it will mean to die. The same friends I enjoy now will get together a year, and three years, and twenty years from now, and I will not be there, not even in the conversation. Life will go on. In this church you will call a new minister with new gifts and a new future, and eventually I'll fade from your mind and memory. I understand. The same thing has happened to my own memories of others. When I was saying something like this a few months ago to a friend of mine, he reminded me of those poignant words of Psalm 103:15–16: "As for mortals, their days are like grass; they flourish like a flower of the field; for the wind passes over it, and it is gone, and its place knows it no more." For the first time I felt those words in my gut; I understood that my place would know me no more.

In his poem "Adjusting to the Light," Miller Williams[4] explores the sense of awkwardness among Lazarus's friends and neighbors just after Jesus has resuscitated him. Four days after his death, Lazarus returns to the land of the living and finds that people have moved on from him. Now they have to scramble to fit him back in:

> Lazarus, listen, we have things to tell you.
> We killed the sheep you meant to take to market.
> We couldn't keep the old dog, either.
> He minded you. The rest of us he barked at.
> Rebecca, who cried two days, has given her hand
> to the sandalmaker's son. Please understand
> we didn't know that Jesus could do this.
> We're glad you're back. But give us time to think.
> Imagine our surprise. . . . We want to say
> we're sorry for all of that. And one thing more.
> We threw away the lyre. But listen, we'll pay
> whatever the sheep was worth. The dog, too.
> And put your room the way it was before.

Miller Williams has it just right. After only a few days, Lazarus's place knew him no more. Before cancer, I liked Williams's poem, but now I'm living it. Believe me: hope doesn't lie in our legacy; it doesn't lie in our longevity; it doesn't lie in our personality or our career or our politics or our children or, heaven knows, our goodness. Hope lies in *eti*.

So please don't be surprised when in the days ahead I don't talk about my cancer very often. I've told a part of my story today, because it seemed right to do it on the first day back after seven months. But what we must talk about here is not me. I cannot be our focus, because the center of my story—*our* story—is that the grace of Jesus Christ carries us beyond every cancer, every divorce, every sin, every trouble that comes to us. The Christian gospel is the story of Jesus, and that's the story I'm called to tell. 20

I'm dying. Maybe it will take longer instead of shorter; maybe I'll preach for several months, and maybe for a bit more. But I am dying. I know it, and I hate it, and I'm still frightened by it. But there is hope, unwavering hope. I

4. Professor at the University of Arkansas (b. 1930) who read one of his poems at President Clinton's second inauguration, in 1997.

have hope not in something I've done, some purity I've maintained, or some sermon I've written. I hope in God—the God who reaches out for an enemy, saves a sinner, dies for the weak.

That's the gospel, and I can stake my life on it. I must. And so must you.

Questions

1. Van Tholen takes a biblical text for his sermon: two verses from the New Testament letter of St. Paul to the Romans (see epigraph, p. 1070). How does he explain and apply these verses in his account of his own life? Specifically, how does he apply the Greek word *eti* (paragraph 14)?

2. In paragraph 6, Van Tholen states that "grace is a scandal." What does he mean by the concept of "grace"? Why is it a "scandal"?

3. Many sermons have a "modular" form, meaning that they are made up of distinct but linked parts. What are the modules in this sermon? How are they organized, and why do you suppose Van Tholen chose this order?

4. Write a brief account of how someone you know faced death or, alternatively, how you believe you would face death. If relevant, draw upon the religious or philosophical beliefs that inform your perspective.

Steven Weinberg *Without God*

In his celebrated 1837 Phi Beta Kappa Oration at Harvard, titled "The American Scholar," Ralph Waldo Emerson[1] predicted that a day would come when America would end what he called "our long apprenticeship to the learning of other lands." His prediction came true in the twentieth century, and in no area of learning more so than in science. This surely would have pleased Emerson. When he listed his heroes he would generally include Copernicus and Galileo and Newton along with Socrates and Jesus and Swedenborg.[2] But I think that Emerson would have had mixed feelings about one consequence of

The New York Review of Books *often prints long "think pieces" like Weinberg's. Here this Nobel Prize–winning nuclear physicist and Harvard professor is writing outside his normal field of expertise.*

1. American writer and philosopher (1803–1882), the father of Transcendentalism.

2. Nicolaus Copernicus (1473–1543), Galileo Galilei (1564–1642), and Isaac Newton (1643–1727) were astronomers who made groundbreaking discoveries; Socrates (c. 469–399 B.C.E.) and Jesus (c. 5 B.C.E.–c. 30 C.E.) were groundbreaking thinkers for the Greeks and Jews, respectively. Swedenborg (1688–1772) was a Swedish theologian and mystic, who also pursued a career as an inventor and scientist.

the advance of science here and abroad—that it has led to a widespread weakening of religious belief.[3]

Emerson was hardly orthodox—according to Herman Melville,[4] he felt "that had he lived in those days when the world was made, he might have offered some valuable suggestions"—but he was for a while a Unitarian minister, and he usually found it possible to speak favorably of the Almighty. Emerson grieved over what he saw in his own time as a weakening of belief, as opposed to mere piety and churchgoing, in America and even more so in England, though I can't say that he attributed it to the advance of science.

The idea of a conflict between science and religion has a long pedigree. According to Edward Gibbon,[5] it was the view of the Byzantine church that "the study of nature was the surest symptom of an unbelieving mind." Perhaps the best-known portrayal of this conflict is a book published in 1896 by Cornell's first president, Andrew Dickson White,[6] with the title *A History of the Warfare of Science with Theology in Christendom.*

In recent times there has been a reaction against talk of warfare between science and religion. White's "conflict thesis" was attacked in a 1986 paper by Bruce Lindberg and Ronald Numbers,[7] both well-known historians of science, who pointed out many flaws in White's scholarship. The Templeton Foundation offers a large prize to those who argue that there is no conflict between science and religion.[8] Some scientists take this line because they want to protect science education from religious fundamentalists. Stephen Jay Gould[9] argued that there could be no conflict between science and religion, because science deals only with facts and religion only with values. This certainly was not the view held in the past by most adherents of religion, and it is a sign of the decay of belief in the supernatural that many today who call themselves religious would agree with Gould.

Let's grant that science and religion are not incompatible—there are after all some (though not many) excellent scientists, like Charles Townes and Francis Collins,[10] who have strong religious beliefs. Still, I think that between sci- 5

3. This essay is based on the Phi Beta Kappa Oration given at Harvard University on June 3, 2008, and draws briefly on some of my other lectures and reviews [Weinberg's note].

4. American novelist (1819–1891), author of *Moby-Dick.*

5. British historian (1737–1794), author of *The Decline and Fall of the Roman Empire.*

6. White (1832–1918), founding president of Cornell University.

7. David [not Bruce] Lindberg (b. 1935) is Hilldale Professor Emeritus of Science and Medicine at the University of Wisconsin at Madison. Ronald Numbers (b. 1942) is Hilldale Professor of the History of Science and Medicine at the University of Wisconsin, Madison. Together they are editing the eight-volume *Cambridge History of Science.*

8. Founded in 1987 to address what it terms "Big Questions" about human purpose, the Templeton Foundation sponsors work reconciling science and religion.

9. Harvard paleontologist (1941–2002) noted for his historical studies of Darwin and opposition to creationism.

10. Charles Townes (b. 1915), Nobel Prize–winning physicist honored by the Templeton Foundation for his contributions to the understanding of religion; Francis Collins

ence and religion there is, if not an incompatibility, at least what the philosopher Susan Haack[11] has called a tension, that has been gradually weakening serious religious belief, especially in the West, where science has been most advanced. Here I would like to trace out some of the sources of this tension, and then offer a few remarks about the very difficult question raised by the consequent decline of belief, the question of how it will be possible to live without God.

1.

I do not think that the tension between science and religion is primarily a result of contradictions between scientific discoveries and specific religious doctrines. This is what chiefly concerned White, but I think he was looking in the wrong direction. Galileo remarked in his famous letter to Grand Duchess Christina[12] that "the intention of the Holy Ghost is to teach us how to go to heaven, not how heaven goes," and this was not just his opinion; he was quoting a prince of the Church, Cardinal Baronius, the Vatican librarian.[13] Contradictions between scripture and scientific knowledge have occurred again and again, and have generally been accommodated by the more enlightened among the religious. For instance, there are verses in both the Old and New Testament that seem to show that the earth is flat, and as noted by Copernicus (quoted by Galileo in the same letter to Christina) these verses led some early Church fathers like Lactantius[14] to reject the Greek understanding that the earth is a sphere, but educated Christians long before the voyages of Columbus and Magellan had come to accept the spherical shape of the earth. Dante found the interior of the spherical earth a convenient place to store sinners.

What was briefly a serious issue in the early Church has today become a parody. The astrophysicist Adrian Melott of the University of Kansas,[15] in a fight with zealots who wanted equal time for creationism in the Kansas public schools, founded an organization called FLAT (Families for Learning Accurate Theories). His society parodied creationists by demanding equal time for flat earth geography, arguing that children should be exposed to both sides of the controversy over the shape of the earth.

But if the direct conflict between scientific knowledge and specific religious beliefs has not been so important in itself, there are at least four sources of tension between science and religion that have been important.

(b. 1950), currently the director of the National Institutes of Health and author of *The Language of God: A Scientist Presents Evidence for Belief* (2006).

11. British-born philosopher (b. 1945) now teaching at the University of Miami.

12. Christina of Lorraine (1565–1637), the Grand Duchess of Tuscany by marriage; Galileo wrote his 1615 letter to explain the relation between the revelations of the Bible and the new discoveries made by scientists.

13. Cardinal Baronius (1538–1607), eminent historian of Christianity.

14. North African–born rhetorician and apologist for Christianity (c. 240–320); not universally considered a Church father.

15. Melott (b. 1947), professor of physics at the University of Kansas who specializes in questions of the formation of the universe.

The first source of tension arises from the fact that religion originally gained much of its strength from the observation of mysterious phenomena—thunder, earthquakes, disease—that seemed to require the intervention of some divine being. There was a nymph in every brook, and a dryad in every tree. But as time passed more and more of these mysteries have been explained in purely natural ways. Explaining this or that about the natural world does not of course rule out religious belief. But if people believe in God because no other explanation seems possible for a whole host of mysteries, and then over the years these mysteries were one by one resolved naturalistically, then a certain weakening of belief can be expected. It is no accident that the advent of widespread atheism and agnosticism among the educated in the eighteenth century followed hard upon the birth of modern science in the previous century.

10

From the beginning, the explanatory power of science worried those who valued religion. Plato was so horrified at the attempt of Democritus and Leucippus[16] to explain nature in terms of atoms without reference to the gods (even though they did not get very far with this) that in Book Ten of the Laws he urged five years of solitary confinement for those who deny that the gods exist or that they care about humans, with death to follow if the prisoner is not reformed. Isaac Newton, offended by the naturalism of Descartes,[17] also rejected the idea that the world could be explained without God. He argued for instance in a letter to Richard Bentley[18] that no explanation but God could be given for the distinction we observe between bright matter, the sun and stars, and dark matter, like the earth. This is ironic, because of course it was Newton and not Descartes who was right about the laws of motion. No one did more than Newton to make it possible to work out thoroughly nontheistic explanations of what we see in the sky, but Newton himself was not in this sense a Newtonian.

Of course, not everything has been explained, nor will it ever be. The important thing is that we have not observed anything that seems to require supernatural intervention for its explanation. There are some today who cling to the remaining gaps in our understanding (such as our ignorance about the origin of life) as evidence for God. But as time passes and more and more of these gaps are filled in, their position gives an impression of people desperately holding on to outmoded opinions.

The problem for religious belief is not just that science has explained a lot of odds and ends about the world. There is a second source of tension: that these explanations have cast increasing doubt on the special role of man, as an actor created by God to play a starring part in a great cosmic drama of sin and salvation. We have had to accept that our home, the earth, is just another planet circling the sun; our sun is just one of a hundred billion stars in a galaxy

16. Plato (429–347 B.C.E.), classical Greek philosopher; Democritus (c. 460–370 B.C.E.) and Leucippus (early fifth-century B.C.E.), pre-Socratic Greek philosophers who were the first to develop a theory of atoms.

17. René Descartes (1596–1650), French philosopher, mathematician, and physicist.

18. Bentley (1662–1742), England's first great textual scholar and the master of Trinity College, Cambridge.

that is just one of billions of visible galaxies; and it may be that the whole expanding cloud of galaxies is just a small part of a much larger multiverse, most of whose parts are utterly inhospitable to life. As Richard Feynman has said, "The theory that it's all arranged as a stage for God to watch man's struggle for good and evil seems inadequate."[19]

Most important so far has been the discovery by Charles Darwin and Alfred Russel Wallace[20] that humans arose from earlier animals through natural selection acting on random heritable variations, with no need for a divine plan to explain the advent of humanity. This discovery led some, including Darwin, to lose their faith. It's not surprising that of all the discoveries of science, this is the one that continues most to disturb religious conservatives. I can imagine how disturbed they will feel in the future, when at last scientists learn how to understand human behavior in terms of the chemistry and physics of the brain, and nothing is left that needs to be explained by our having an immaterial soul.

Note that I refer here to *behavior*, not consciousness. Something purely subjective, like how we feel when we see the color red or discover a physical theory, seems so different from the objective world described by science that it is difficult to see how they can ever come together. As Colin McGinn[21] has said:

> The problem is how to integrate the conscious mind with the physical brain—how to reveal a unity beneath this apparent diversity. That problem is very hard, and I do not believe anyone has any good ideas about how to solve it.[22]

On the other hand, both brain activity and behavior (including what we say about our feelings) are in the same world of objective phenomena, and I know of no intrinsic obstacle to their being integrated in a scientific theory, though it is clearly not going to be easy. This does not mean that we can or should forget about consciousness, and like B. F. Skinner[23] with his pigeons concern ourselves only with behavior. We know, as well as we know anything, that our behavior is partly governed by our consciousness, so understanding behavior will necessarily require working out a detailed correspondence between the objective and subjective. This may not tell us how one arises from the other, but at least it will confirm that there is nothing supernatural about the mind.

19. Richard Feynman, American physicist (1918–1988), winner of the Nobel Prize in 1965. The quotation comes from "The Relation of Science and Religion," a talk given by Dr. Feynman at the Caltech YMCA Lunch Forum on May 2, 1956.

20. Charles Darwin (1809–1882) and Alfred Russel Wallace (1823–1913) both independently developed a theory of evolution.

21. British-born philosopher (b. 1950), now teaching at the University of Miami, who specializes in the philosophy of mind.

22. "Can We Ever Understand Consciousness?," the *New York Review*, June 10, 1999 [Weinberg's note].

23. Harvard psychology professor and proponent of radical behaviorism (1904–1990); many of his experiments involved training pigeons.

Some nonscientists seize on certain developments in modern physics that suggest the unpredictability of natural phenomena, such as the advent of quantum mechanics or chaos theory, as signs of a turn away from determinism, of the sort that would make an opening for divine intervention or an incorporeal soul. These theories have forced us to refine our view of determinism, but not I think in any way that has implications for human life. 15

A third source of tension between science and religious belief has been more important in Islam than in Christianity. Around 1100, the Sufi philosopher Abu Hamid al-Ghazzali[24] argued against the very idea of laws of nature, on the grounds that any such law would put God's hands in chains. According to al-Ghazzali, a piece of cotton placed in a flame does not darken and smolder because of the heat of the flame, but because God wants it to darken and smolder. Laws of nature could have been reconciled with Islam, as a summary of what God usually wants to happen, but al-Ghazzali did not take that path.

Al-Ghazzali is often described as the most influential Islamic philosopher. I wish I knew enough to judge how great was the impact on Islam of his rejection of science. At any rate, science in Muslim countries, which had led the world in the ninth and tenth centuries, went into a decline in the century or two after al-Ghazzali. As a portent of this decline, in 1194 the Ulama of Córdoba[25] burned all scientific and medical texts.

Nor has science revived in the Islamic world. There are talented scientists who have come to the West from Islamic countries and do work of great value here, among them the Pakistani Muslim physicist Abdus Mohammed Salam,[26] who in 1979 became the first Muslim scientist to be awarded a Nobel Prize, for work he did in England and Italy. But in the past forty years I have not seen any paper in the areas of physics or astronomy that I follow that was written in an Islamic country and was worth reading. Thousands of scientific papers are turned out in these countries, and perhaps I missed something. Still, in 2002 the periodical *Nature* carried out a survey of science in Islamic countries, and found just three areas in which the Islamic world produced excellent science, all three directed toward applications rather than basic science. They were desalination, falconry, and camel breeding.

Something like al-Ghazzali's concern for God's freedom surfaced for a while in Christian Europe, but with very different results. In Paris and Canterbury in the thirteenth century there was a wave of condemnations of those teachings of Aristotle[27] that seemed to limit the freedom of God to do things like create a vacuum or make several worlds or move the heavens in straight lines.

24. Persian-born Sunni philosopher and theologian (1058–1111).

25. Ulama were Islamic scholars who interpreted sharia law while Spain was under Muslim domination.

26. Pakistani nuclear physicist (1926–1996) and Nobel Prize laureate (with Weinberg) in 1979.

27. The ancient world's most wide-ranging philosopher (384–322 B.C.E.), who dominated Western learning for well over a thousand years.

The influence of Thomas Aquinas and Albertus Magnus[28] saved the philosophy of Aristotle for Europe, and with it the idea of laws of nature. But although Aristotle was no longer condemned, his authority had been questioned—which was fortunate, since nothing could be built on his physics. Perhaps it was the weakening of Aristotle's authority by reactionary churchmen that opened the door to the first small steps toward finding the true laws of nature at Paris and Lisieux and Oxford in the fourteenth century.

20 There is a fourth source of tension between science and religion that may be the most important of all. Traditional religions generally rely on authority, whether the authority is an infallible leader, such as a prophet or a pope or an imam, or a body of sacred writings, a Bible or a Koran. Perhaps Galileo did not get into trouble solely because he was expressing views contrary to scripture, but because he was doing so independently, rather than as a theologian acting within the Church.

Of course, scientists rely on authorities, but of a very different sort. If I want to understand some fine point about the general theory of relativity, I might look up a recent paper by an expert in the field. But I would know that the expert might be wrong. One thing I probably would not do is to look up the original papers of Einstein,[29] because today any good graduate student understands general relativity better than Einstein did. We progress. Indeed, in the form in which Einstein described his theory it is today generally regarded as only what is known in the trade as an effective field theory; that is, it is an approximation, valid for the large scales of distance for which it has been tested, but not under very cramped conditions, as in the early big bang.

We have our heroes in science, like Einstein, who was certainly the greatest physicist of the past century, but for us they are not infallible prophets. For those who in everyday life respect independence of mind and openness to contradiction, traits that Emerson admired—especially when it came to religion—the example of science casts an unfavorable light on the deference to authority of traditional religion. The world can always use heroes, but could do with fewer prophets.

The weakening of religious belief is obvious in Western Europe, but it may seem odd to talk about this happening in America. No one who expressed doubt about the existence of God could possibly be elected president of the United States. Nevertheless, though I don't have any scientific evidence on this point, on the basis of personal observation it seems to me that while many Americans fervently believe that religion is a good thing, and get quite angry when it is criticized, even those who feel this way often do not have much in the way of clear religious belief. Occasionally I have found myself talking with friends, who identify themselves with some organized religion, about what they think of life after

28. Thomas Aquinas (1225–1274), the Catholic Church's primary philosopher and theologian, best known for his *Summa Theologica*; Albertus Magnus (c. 1200–1280), German-born theologian and Aquinas's teacher.

29. Albert Einstein (1879–1955), a theoretical physicist and philosopher who represents the iconic scientist.

death, or of the nature of God, or of sin. Most often I've been told that they do not know, and that the important thing is not what you believe, but how you live. I've heard this even from a Catholic priest. I applaud the sentiment, but it's quite a retreat from religious belief.

Though I can't prove it, I suspect that when Americans are asked in polls whether they believe in God or angels or heaven or hell they feel that it is a religious duty to say that they do, whatever they actually believe. And of course hardly anyone today in the West seems to have even the slightest interest in the great controversies—Arians vs. Athanasians, monophysites vs. monothelites,[30] justification by faith or by works[31]—that used to be taken so seriously that they set Christians at each other's throats.

I have been emphasizing religious belief here, the belief in facts about God or the afterlife, though I am well aware that this is only one aspect of the religious life, and for many not the most important part. Perhaps I emphasize belief because as a physicist I am professionally concerned with finding out what is true, not what makes us happy or good. For many people, the important thing about their religion is not a set of beliefs but a host of other things: a set of moral principles; rules about sexual behavior, diet, observance of holy days, and so on; rituals of marriage and mourning; and the comfort of affiliation with fellow believers, which in extreme cases allows the pleasure of killing those who have different religious affiliations.

25

For some there is also a sort of spirituality that Emerson wrote about, and which I don't understand, often described as a sense of union with nature or with all humanity, that doesn't involve any specific beliefs about the supernatural. Spirituality is central to Buddhism, which does not call for belief in God. Even so, Buddhism has historically relied on belief in the supernatural, specifically in reincarnation. It is the desire to escape the wheel of rebirth that drives the search for enlightenment. The heroes of Buddhism are the bodhisattvas,[32] who, having attained enlightenment, nevertheless return to life in order to show the way to a world shrouded in darkness. Perhaps in Buddhism too there has been a decline of belief. A recent book by the Dalai Lama barely mentions reincarnation, and Buddhism is now in decline in Japan, the Asian nation that has made the greatest progress in science.

The various uses of religion may keep it going for a few centuries even after the disappearance of belief in anything supernatural, but I wonder how

30. Arians, early Christian heretical sect founded by Arius (c. 250–336), who believed that Christ was created by God the Father and thus inferior to him. Athanasians, Orthodox Christians who followed Athanasius of Alexandria (293–373) and attacked the Arian heresy. Monophysites, fifth-century heretics who claimed that Christ had only a single nature, the divine. Monothelites, seventh-century heretics who believed that Christ had two natures (human and divine) but only one will.

31. Justification by faith is the doctrine that humans can be saved by belief in Christ. Opposed to it is the belief that some combination of faith and works is necessary for salvation.

32. Bodhisattvas: Weinberg refers to a tradition of Buddhism in which the already enlightened aid those still seeking enlightenment.

long religion can last without a core of belief in the supernatural, when it isn't about anything external to human beings. To compare great things with small, people may go to college football games mostly because they enjoy the cheerleading and marching bands, but I doubt if they would keep going to the stadium on Saturday afternoons if the only things happening there were cheerleading and marching bands, without any actual football, so that the cheerleading and the band music were no longer about anything.

2.

It is not my purpose here to argue that the decline of religious belief is a good thing (although I think it is), or to try to talk anyone out of their religion, as eloquent recent books by Richard Dawkins, Sam Harris, and Christopher Hitchens have.[33] So far in my life, in arguing for spending more money on scientific research and higher education, or against spending on ballistic missile defense or sending people to Mars, I think I have achieved a perfect record of never having changed anyone's mind. Rather, I want just to offer a few opinions, on the basis of no expertise whatever, for those who have already lost their religious beliefs, or who may be losing them, or fear that they will lose their beliefs, about how it is possible to live without God.

First, a warning: we had better beware of substitutes. It has often been noted that the greatest horrors of the twentieth century were perpetrated by regimes—Hitler's Germany, Stalin's Russia, Mao's China—that while rejecting some or all of the teachings of religion, copied characteristics of religion at its worst: infallible leaders, sacred writings, mass rituals, the execution of apostates, and a sense of community that justified exterminating those outside the community.

30 When I was an undergraduate I knew a rabbi, Will Herberg,[34] who worried about my lack of religious faith. He warned me that we must worship God, because otherwise we would start worshiping each other. He was right about the danger, but I would suggest a different cure: we should get out of the habit of worshiping anything.

I'm not going to say that it's easy to live without God, that science is all you need. For a physicist, it is indeed a great joy to learn how we can use beautiful mathematics to understand the real world. We struggle to understand nature, building a great chain of research institutes, from the Museum of Alexandria and the House of Wisdom of Baghdad to today's CERN and Fermilab.[35] But we

33. Richard Dawkins (b. 1941), Oxford biologist who wrote *The God Delusion* (2006), a popular book advocating atheism; Sam Harris (b. 1967), author of *The End of Faith* (2004) and *Letter to a Christian Nation* (2006), both books advocating atheism; Christopher Hitchens (b. 1949), British-born cultural critic and author of *God Is Not Great* (2007), a book attacking organized religion.

34. American Jewish social philosopher (1901–1977). There is no record of him being ordained as a rabbi.

35. CERN, the European Center for Nuclear Research, situated in a suburb of Geneva, is the world's biggest particle physics laboratory. Fermilab, located in Batavia, Illinois, outside of Chicago, contains the world's second largest particle accelerator.

know that we will never get to the bottom of things, because whatever theory unifies all observed particles and forces, we will never know why it is that that theory describes the real world and not some other theory.

Worse, the worldview of science is rather chilling. Not only do we not find any point to life laid out for us in nature, no objective basis for our moral principles, no correspondence between what we think is the moral law and the laws of nature, of the sort imagined by philosophers from Anaximander and Plato to Emerson.[36] We even learn that the emotions that we most treasure, our love for our wives and husbands and children, are made possible by chemical processes in our brains that are what they are as a result of natural selection acting on chance mutations over millions of years. And yet we must not sink into nihilism or stifle our emotions. At our best we live on a knife-edge, between wishful thinking on one hand and, on the other, despair.

What, then, can we do? One thing that helps is humor, a quality not abundant in Emerson. Just as we laugh with sympathy but not scorn when we see a one-year-old struggling to stay erect when she takes her first steps, we can feel a sympathetic merriment at ourselves, trying to live balanced on a knife-edge. In some of Shakespeare's greatest tragedies, just when the action is about to reach an unbearable climax, the tragic heroes are confronted with some "rude mechanical" offering comic observations: a gravedigger, or a doorkeeper, or a pair of gardeners, or a man with a basket of figs. The tragedy is not lessened, but the humor puts it in perspective.

Then there are the ordinary pleasures of life, which have been despised by religious zealots, from Christian anchorites in the Egyptian deserts to today's Taliban and Mahdi Army. Visiting New England in early June, when the rhododendrons and azaleas are blazing away, reminds one how beautiful spring can be. And let's not dismiss the pleasures of the flesh. We who are not zealots can rejoice that when bread and wine are no longer sacraments, they will still be bread and wine.

There are also the pleasures brought to us by the high arts. Here I think we are going to lose something with the decline of religious belief. Much great art has arisen in the past from religious inspiration. For instance, I can't imagine the poetry of George Herbert or Henry Vaughn or Gerard Manley Hopkins being written without sincere religious belief.[37] But nothing prevents those of us who have no religious belief from enjoying religious poetry, any more than not being English prevents Americans from enjoying the patriotic speeches in *Richard II* or *Henry V*.

35

We may be sad that no more great religious poetry will be written in the future. We see already that little English-language poetry written in the past few decades owes anything to belief in God, and in some cases where religion

36. Anaximander (c. 610–546 B.C.E.), one of the earliest pre-Socratic Greek philosophers; [see footnote 1 on p. 1074.]

37. George Herbert (1593–1633), Welsh-born Anglican priest, noted for his metaphysical poetry; Henry Vaughan (1622–1695), Welsh-born physician and poet, known for his mystical writings; Gerard Manley Hopkins (1844–1889), English Jesuit known for his original, experimental poetry.

does enter, as with poets like Stevie Smith or Philip Larkin,[38] it is the rejection of religion that provides their inspiration. But of course very great poetry can be written without religion. Shakespeare provides an example; none of his work seems to me to show the slightest hint of serious religious inspiration. Given Ariel and Prospero,[39] we see that poets can do without angels and prophets.

I do not think we have to worry that giving up religion will lead to a moral decline. There are plenty of people without religious faith who live exemplary moral lives (as for example, me), and though religion has sometimes inspired admirable ethical standards, it has also often fostered the most hideous crimes. Anyway, belief in an omnipotent omniscient creator of the world does not in itself have any moral implications—it's still up to you to decide whether it is right to obey His commands. For instance, even someone who believes in God can feel that Abraham in the Old Testament was wrong to obey God in agreeing to sacrifice Isaac, and that Adam in *Paradise Lost* was right to disobey God and follow Eve in eating the apple, so that he could stay with her when she was driven from Eden. The young men who flew airplanes into buildings in the US or exploded bombs in crowds in London or Madrid or Tel Aviv were not just stupid in imagining that these were God's commands; even thinking that these were His commands, they were evil in obeying them.

The more we reflect on the pleasures of life, the more we miss the greatest consolation that used to be provided by religious belief: the promise that our lives will continue after death, and that in the afterlife we will meet the people we have loved. As religious belief weakens, more and more of us know that after death there is nothing. This is the thing that makes cowards of us all.

Cicero offered comfort in *De Senectute* by arguing that it was silly to fear death.[40] After more than two thousand years his words still have not the slightest power to console us. Philip Larkin was much more convincing about the fear of death:

> This is a special way of being afraid[41]
> No trick dispels. Religion used to try,
> That vast moth-eaten musical brocade
> Created to pretend we never die,
> And specious stuff that says no rational being
> Can fear a thing it will not feel, not seeing
> That this is what we fear—no sight, no sound,

38. Stevie Smith (1902–1971), prolific English poet and author of the 1958 essay "The Necessity of Not Believing." Philip Larkin (1922–1985), English poet noted for his gloomy persona and traditional style.

39. Characters in Shakespeare's play *The Tempest*.

40. Cicero (106–43 B.C.E.), Rome's greatest orator, among whose most notable works was his extended essay, *De Senectute (Of Old Age)*.

41. From Larkin's "Aubade," traditionally, a song sung when lovers part.

> No touch or taste or smell, nothing to think with,
> Nothing to love or link with,
> The anaesthetic from which none come round.

Living without God isn't easy. But its very difficulty offers one other consolation—that there is a certain honor, or perhaps just a grim satisfaction, in facing up to our condition without despair and without wishful thinking—with good humor, but without God. 40

QUESTIONS

1. Of the four sources of tension Weinberg notes between science and religion, which strikes you as the most serious? Why?

2. How would you describe Weinberg's tone in his essay? Why does he adopt such a tone?

3. What do you think of Weinberg's conclusion? How does it compare with what you know of traditional Christian beliefs about the afterlife? Write an essay that compares and contrasts Weinberg's views with Christian beliefs or those of another religion you know well.

REG SANER

My Fall into Knowledge

DAILY, AND IN apparently causeless moments, I'm aware of being—though ever so briefly—alive in a place called "the world." Whereupon the oddness in simultaneously feeling hyperordinary yet cosmic throws me into interrogative mode.

Recently, during just such a moment, and because I'm incorrigibly religious, I found myself wondering, "Throughout history, just how many creeds have there been? And the god population—how many deities, now or ever?" An accurate inventory would of course be impossible. Not only do eternal truths come and go, some gods take early retirement. Moreover, ancient tribes, whether of prehistoric Greece or North America's Hopi mesas, occasionally adopted supernatural beings from neighboring peoples into their own cultures. That ecumenical outlook, plus the polytheism factor, means no census could be as simple as one religion, one god. *Impossible* seemed the right word.

Then, as if with a life of its own, the question kept widening: "How many gods are currently in service throughout this galaxy-rich universe?" And sud-

Published in the Georgia Review *(Spring 2010), a small-circulation quarterly magazine. Saner uses the occasion of a debate with an anti-Darwinian to write about a subject that means a great deal to him.*

denly it dawned on me that I'd just invented a new field of study: astrotheology. We already have astrobiology, in case some life-harboring, extraterrestrial planet should be discovered. Sooner or later, where there's life there will be divinities, a natural offshoot.

However, natural is as natural does. All it takes is a planet whose thinking species, upon looking around at the various life forms, concludes, instead of the usual "Some*one* has done this," that "Some*thing* has done this." The ultimate principle of causation on that planet would be considered natural instead of supernatural.

My logic felt rock solid, but hairsplitters may quibble. In any case, future astrotheologians will surely pursue the quasi-infinite possibilities of this new field. Perhaps they will even conjecture a religious war on certain planets, with devotees of Someone-ism righteously deploying fire and sword to destroy forever the infidel Something-ists.

Apropos of the Big Questions, doesn't every child eventually ask, "Mommy, where did I come from?" These days, however, with low-rider jeans, some mothers dressing their ten-year-old daughters like French tarts, boy-girl dialogues of single entendre, and teens copulating as if humans were an endangered species, no parent could invoke the stork and keep a straight face. Is there one mother left who tells her child, "Why, sweetie pie, we found you under a cabbage leaf"?

Way back in the psychedelic sixties, my friend Jo Ann said nothing of the kind. For her five-year-old, Chris, she went into physiologic detail. She didn't just refer vaguely to "certain body parts." She named names. His eyes widened. She implicated his father. Said that she and he had been in cahoots on it. The boy was stunned, revolted, aghast. These were people he had respected. The very people who kept telling him to behave himself. Then, remembering he had a younger sister, he cried out in dismay, "You don't mean you did it *twice?*"

If ever there were a "fall into knowledge" it's that one. It changes the child by putting him further into the real than he had dreamed or wanted to be—a strange new context of animality. Small wonder that many children, perhaps most, prefer not to think of their parents as sex mates.

There are plenty of things we adults don't like to ponder. For example, the size of all we belong to and the pitiful brevity of our visit. Post-Darwin, our biological status is another aspect some among us would rather not dwell on. Like little Chris, surprising numbers of adults vehemently deny their double nature as fur-bearing critters with vestigial claws on hands and feet—animals who talk and think, yet who, like our mammalian kin, also copulate and give suck. In a nutshell, some people simply can't stand the facts of life. That's why they throw hissy fits at the mention of evolution.

A memory lapse explains why a few years ago I accepted an invitation to debate an anti-Darwinian. My friend Jane Bock, a biologist, had been the initial recipient of that invitation. She and other biologists often receive such challenges but routinely ignore them as a waste of time. Then, looking at me, Jane's mischievous streak kicked in. "How about you?" she said, knowing of my intense admiration for Darwin. "Do you want to take them on?" Never in my adult life had I encountered a creationist. Now here was an opportunity to practice my favorite occupation: going forth to see for myself. I said, "Okay, I'll do it." Why? Well, fools do rush in.

Alas, my eagerness to trade verities with a proponent of biblical inerrancy before the breed went extinct led me to forget I had been a creationist for years and years, and would be again, though in a very different way.

At precisely what age I allowed myself to be gathered to the bosom of creationism I can't recall, yet it must have occurred by the time I was five and in first grade. My memory of just how it happened remains clear as the image of tall Sister Mary Daniel in her great black wimple and Dominican[1] habit of ankle-length white linen, as she tested us first graders with the very first question in the *Baltimore Catechism*,[2] "Who made us?"

On cue, we chirruped like a classroom of sparrows, "God made us."

To say Sister did the asking and we the believing would, however, be quite false. Belief implies the possibility of disbelief, a thing literally unthinkable at that age. Children may be finicky eaters, yet when it comes to religion they down whatever's set before them. If your parents follow Jainism,[3] you follow them. Besides, anything Sister Mary Daniel said was true.

15 It wasn't so much that she wore holy clothes covering all but her face and hands, nor that all the mothers including mine spoke to her as to a Very Special Person. It wasn't even because she always seemed so clean and gave off such a nice soapy fragrance. What Sister Mary Daniel said was true because she was tall, patient, soft-spoken, and kind to every one of us children.

Was she pretty? I don't remember—just that she was beautiful.

Surprising as it should have been for me to learn I'd been made by a God, it never entered my noddle to ask why. That just seemed to be what God did. He made things. Unlike the grown-up kind of creationist, I didn't at the least mention of Darwin grind my teeth and spit. I was proud of my spitting, but hadn't yet heard of evolution, so there was no need for righteous saliva. All the same, as we children grew older we did learn that a hellish fate awaited that soul guilty of willfully doubting things the *Baltimore Catechism* said were eternally true, and its pages clearly gave top billing to the Creator.

Me disagree with the catechism? Only heretics did that. Even if I didn't quite know what a heretic was, I did know it was the baddest thing you could ever become. Maybe the word's sound caused me to picture a hairy man in grubby clothes—a swarthy, red-eyed man who stood glaring at me and without lifting a finger was unspeakably wicked.

1. Dominican, the Roman Catholic order founded by St. Dominic in the thirteenth century.

2. The standard Roman Catholic book of religious instruction until the late 1960s.

3. Ancient Indian religion that prescribes a strict doctrine of nonviolence.

A despondent lass in an old play says, "We know what we are, but know not what we may be." Well, the skinny little blue-eyed kid I once was is now himself a full-grown, double-damned heretic—though not particularly hairy. It happened the day I awoke to the single fact of life rendering our human situation inexhaustibly fascinating: no one knows what this world is, much less has the answer to "Why?" Sadly enough, that limitation has always impelled members of our species to claim knowledge they don't have, and I claim to be one of their victims. Hence, my activist interest in those old reliables, the supersize, cosmic questions.

20 Historically speaking, there have been many mystery religions—think Orpheus, think Isis—but only one mystery: the answer to "Why?"

For my showdown with Binford Pyle, a hard-core fundamentalist if ever there was one, I turned up on schedule at the Bethany Church ready for action.[4] True, I had no debate experience and only the vaguest idea of the creationist mind. So what? Biological fact was firmly on my side, wasn't it? Not that I'm a biologist. Far from it. I'm merely an ink-stained wretch puzzled by the millions of adults who seem to believe the facts of life are ungodly.

In addition to my respect for Darwin's achievement, there was a moral dimension in my agreeing to a debate. The people hoping to foist creationism off onto biology courses in our public schools have employed blatantly immoral tactics, and have done so while claiming to be champions of morality. Their hypocrisy deserved a comeuppance. Even more germane, they daily enact our species' peculiar ability to believe the unbelievable, a trait I've always found fascinating.

On entering the church's large vestibule I found dozens of earlier arrivals studying creationist displays, and a wide screen overhead flashing a projected sequence of anti-Darwinian power points. Their techno-effect was unexpectedly hip. "Hm-m," I thought, "and me with only a few handwritten notes." The church's Baptist congregation, drawn from one of Denver's working-class suburbs, would surely be impressed by the electronic look of cutting-edge info. Already I felt a bit daunted.

As each slide brightened, then dissolved into the next one, I hadn't time to read more than a few. Yet visually snappy as they were, they paraded the same old junk science and untruths that, nonetheless, have found a home in the hearts of countless devotees who take the biblical description of creation literally.

25 Why do we believe the unbelievable? Agreed, the answer is obvious: we do because we want to, but saying so addresses only the why, not the how. It's the how that intrigues me.

No sooner had I left the vestibule's displays and entered the church proper, where adult murmuring mingled with adolescent chatter, than I became dismayed by the sight of so many young faces, including quite a few children. I'd assumed the entire audience would be grown-ups. To undercut parental authority was the last thing I, with my straight-arrow midwestern upbringing, wanted to do. That reluctance led me to scrap the main argument of my opening

4. Names of both person and place have been changed [Saner's note].

remarks: a critique of the fundamentalist dogma on the Bible's inerrancy, plus comments on the blood lust of the God its Old Testament describes. Intellectually, my spur-of-the-moment decision to back off was indefensible. I didn't care. Children's respect for their parents' judgment seemed more important, so I chose to extemporize.

On a brightly lit, carpeted platform, Binford Pyle and I sat opposite, each of us behind a small table covered with red cloth. Though Pyle was a man of large girth, he carried his weight well, was soberly attired in a dark blue suit, and made quite a good appearance, while the open laptop before him continued the cutting-edge implications. These he further enhanced by setting it on the podium each time his turn came to speak or rebut. My few handwritten notes seemed so slight by comparison I ditched them and decided to wing it.

From the Internet I had learned of Pyle's speaking engagements and videos; learned too of his conceiving and leading, with others, something called Scriptural Tours in science museums, so as to correct the unbiblical information infesting such places; learned as well of his connection to the Farview Academy, which trains young fundamentalists.

Between us at the podium, in marked contrast to Mr. Pyle, stood our moderator, a man in his late twenties, one Jeremy Higgins. What with his abundant beard, flowing brown hair, and bulky figure, his teddy-bear aspect made his role as the church's youth director seem natural. Into the microphone he explained how the debate would proceed. Each of us would give a ten-minute opening argument. These would be followed by two rebuttals, the first for eight minutes, the second for five minutes. Each of us would then make a five-minute closing argument, after which we'd respond to questions from the audience.

Just before Pyle and I had mounted the platform we stood momentarily face to face long enough for me to ask if he took the creation story in Genesis literally. His reply was edgy, as if long since weary of that issue. "The Creator," he said, "made the world in six days of twenty-four hours."

Temptation overcame me. I asked, "What took him so long?"

He didn't answer that one, so after an ominous pause I tried again. "Well . . . how can you tell whether a given biblical passage is figurative or literal?"

In the same dismissive tone he said, "You can tell by the context," which on the one hand is true enough, but on the other sounds like dealer's choice. I was about to press the point when the moderator asked us to take our places.

To avoid being typecast as one of those university professors fond of destroying young souls with their godless ideas, I had worn a cowboy-style vest woven with Indian designs. Furthermore, I topped it off with a black, broad-brimmed Stetson and choke strap, such as bad guys always wore in the dime movies of my boyhood Saturday afternoons.

During Mr. Higgins' preliminaries I doffed the Stetson, but when my turn came to speak, I put it back on and, in a bantering manner, began with something like the following: "Lest anybody be confused, my hat should clarify the situation. Creationists here can relax. Though Mr. Pyle isn't wearing a white hat, we know the man in the black hat always loses. To further simplify things, I advise those who are satisfied with their beliefs not to credit a word I say."

Then, after pointing out the impossibility of a debate between faith and fact, I sketched my position without raising my voice. Especially before an audience of working-class Baptists, soft-spoken was the only way to go.

Creationists can never lose, owing to the well-known fact that scripture cannot err, which is proven by its being divinely inspired, which is in turn proven by the fact that people who lived eons ago have said so. With that as bedrock, everything creationism—including its clone, intelligent design—has to say passes between twin pillars: the falsehood inscribed on one pillar reads, "Without the Bible and Christ there can be no morality"; the whopper chiseled into that other pillar says, "Evolution is atheistic." Binford Pyle bludgeoned us with those twin fallacies and implied the atheistic bent of evolution by saying, "Evolution claims nature is all there is." It of course does no such thing. Like all science it merely restricts itself to observable phenomena and testable evidence. Oddly, large numbers of laypersons interpret those limits as proof that science has it in for religion.

Saying that morality is impossible without the Bible and Christ requires not only perfect ignorance of the ancient world, but also creationism's foundational denial of our species' prehistory. Owing to the survival value of cooperative behavior within species, morality simply evolved—like everything else. Even our deities are better behaved now than they used to be.

"Evolved?" boggled Pyle, who insisted that the moral truth of the Bible was "eternal and unchanging." Such a remark made me wonder, "Has he read it?" Without such a moral absolute, he continued, "There would be no reason why I shouldn't wrap an airplane around myself and fly into a building."

Directing a baleful glare at the audience, he angrily added, "If you're an evolutionist and you're upset about 9/11, get over it." Considering our presumably decent congregation of believers, I forbore quoting on that topic of malevolence the insight by Steven Weinberg, a Nobel laureate in physics: "With or without religion, good people can behave well and bad people can do evil; but for good people to do evil—that takes religion."[5]

40 Though persons of goodwill can and often do strenuously disagree on an issue, Pyle's righteous indignation on all topics Darwinian seemed to be tinged with some darker animus. I wondered what his life had been before its born-again phase.

"All men," he said, "are flawed and must be restrained." The worse we are, the better for Pyle's exhorting our fallen natures to rise up from the muck. What good is a cure if there's no disease? Unsurprisingly, therefore, he insisted no mire could be blacker than that in the Darwinian morass. Later, however, he surprised me by backing off long enough to say, "Evolution doesn't *make* people wicked, people *are* wicked."

Would we humans, unless compelled by a divine Sky Cop to behave ourselves, lapse into bestiality? Oh, yes! In fact, this alleged degeneracy of

5. The quotation is from "A Designer Universe" in Weinberg's *Facing Up: Science and Its Cultural Adversaries* (Cambridge, MA: Harvard University Press, 2001), 231 [Saner's note]. For Weinberg's statement of his own views, see his essay, "Without God," in this section, pp. 1074–85.

humankind's postlapsarian state seemed oddly dear to the man's heart, and not just because he was selling the cure.

It's true the Pauline Epistles[6] are pervaded by insistent references to our sinful flesh and Satan's activism among us. After all, Christianity's main claim is that our fallen species desperately needed a Redeemer. But Paul's better angel also frequently moved him to exhort his hearers on the value of their communal bond, and of love. Could creationists' gloomy view of our nature, I continued to wonder, be rooted in themselves as well as the Bible? At times in our debate—as if his hearers' salvation were imperiled—Pyle's nostrils flared and his eyes glowered warningly at the audience.

Whether he did so from personal truculence or religious zeal I couldn't know, but I had no doubt what my fate would be if he or any cult of like-minded zealots had the power to inflict rack and stake on misbelievers. I easily imagined them torching Joan of Arc to improve her character.

Blaise Pascal, a seventeenth-century thinker and scientist whose native France had been bloodied by religious wars, commented on such righteousness gone wrong: "Men never do evil so fully and so happily as when they do it for conscience's sake." Or so fully and happily as when they spread untruths. Thanks to Binford Pyle, I now know that "racism is promoted by evolution," that morality comes from a creationist worldview whereas "evolution is inherently selfish, it is self-centered," and it "thrives on death." I learned, too, that "genocide becomes a natural out-flowing of the evolutionary model when applied to human relations." Oh, all manner of Darwinian-induced degeneracy fueled Pyle's rancor. He spoke of evolution as if it weren't based on science but an amoral conspiracy so dangerous that some creationists call it "devilution," a satanic cult roaming the world on cloven hooves and seeking the destruction of souls. 45

Most vividly of all, I remember his claim that an "evolutionist" is bound to condone Hitler's grisly eugenic experiments, an assertion as illogical as saying Pasteur would favor germ warfare.[7] I also recall how my eyes widened and my mouth gaped when he read a quote from Der Führer by way of implying that the author of *Mein Kampf* spoke for Darwinians! What's more, he twice followed former congressman Tom DeLay's lead in linking the bloody murders at Columbine High School[8] to the teaching of evolution: "Evolution kills people," declared Binford Pyle. "If you don't believe me, just look at Columbine!" Then he added, "Those two students learned their lessons well . . . and applied those lessons appropriately."[9]

Given the time constraints on rebuttals, I couldn't begin to point out more than a few absurdities in Mr. Pyle's stream of grievances. Certainly the most

6. Part of the New Testament, representing letters Paul wrote to early Christian congregations.

7. Louis Pasteur (1822–1895), French chemist and microbiologist who proposed the germ theory of disease.

8. Colorado site of a deadly massacre perpetrated by two of the school's students.

9. Eric Harris and Dylan Klebold, the two responsible for the Columbine slaughter, the one born a psychopath, the other seriously depressed. See David Cullen, *Columbine* (New York: Twelve, 2009), passim [Saner's note].

dramatic among them was his charge that Hitler's evolutionist worldview led to the Holocaust.

It seems Darwin's "survival of the fittest" was the culprit. It had authorized blitzkrieg and mass murder.[10] Such an inexhaustibly fallacious statement betrayed gross ignorance of evolutionary fitness, *the* key concept in *On the Origin of Species*. Darwin did not say, as Binford Pyle explicitly claimed, that survival depends on strength and cunning. Rather, evolutionary fitness stems from an organism's ability to adapt biologically to changing environmental conditions. Mighty dinosaurs may perish and tiny mammals thrive.

The charge that Hitlerian evil was merely Darwinism in action has become a favorite whopper among those on the religious right. In August 2006, the Rev. D. James Kennedy—dubbed by blogger Pam Spaulding "the Talibangelist titan of Florida-based Coral Ridge Ministries"—offered TV viewers a sixty-minute documentary on *Darwin's Deadly Legacy*. It hyped the (false) analogy between Nazi eugenics and Darwin's theory of natural selection, thus sharing Pyle's stunning misconception of the theory he so decried.[11] Furthermore, selective breeding was an ancient practice, so Nazi eugenics didn't need Darwin to inspire it. In point of fact, World War II revealed the Nazi unfitness to survive, inasmuch as Nazism reduced Germany to rubble and ashes. Nazi unfitness, however, wasn't the kind Darwin was talking about.

50 As if to produce a crescendo effect, Mr. Pyle began totting up the separate body counts attributable to Hitler, Stalin, and Chairman Mao, with a bonus estimate of lives unborn, owing to Margaret Sanger's promotion of birth control.[12] "That's over 190 million people," he said, "who have been purposely sacrificed on the altar of evolution!"

I flashed on a headline, DARWIN KILLS 190 MILLION, and reeled. But that wasn't the nadir. Either his misunderstanding or his willful misrepresentation of the evolution he so deplored gave birth to this *pièce de résistance*: "If your brain evolves," he asked the audience, "how can you trust your own thinking?"

"At least," I thought but didn't say, "it would be headed in the right direction."

Our debate had become a carnival attraction. I was still tottering over evolution's Slaughter of the Innocents when Mr. Pyle informed the audience that so long as I embraced evolution I was destined for eternal torment. He said it grieved him that I was, though I didn't hear grief in his tone.

10. The catchphrase "survival of the fittest" originated with Herbert Spencer, a contemporary of Darwin—who then borrowed it ill-advisedly, according to Arthur Peacocke, a scientist and Anglican priest [Saner's note].

11. A year later, on 5 August 2007, I listened to an address by D. James Kennedy in a nationally televised hour sponsored by the Coral Ridge Ministries, during which he recited the same mendacities voiced by Binford Pyle in his calumny of Darwin and evolution [Saner's note].

12. Margaret Sanger Slee (1879–1966), birth control activist and founder of the American Birth Control League.

Just then, and mercifully, our robust moderator, Mr. Higgins, signaled an end to the fray and the beginning of a brief Q&A period. Without exception, the queries addressed specifically to me raised points I had already dwelt on in some detail. It was as if everything I had said was so peculiar it needed repeating.

A sampling given here in my paraphrase will indicate their drift: "How can an evolutionist be moral?"; "How can intricate life forms come from chaos without God's help?"; "Is evolution a religion?"; "Why can't a person believe in God *and* natural selection?"; "Should evolution and creationism both be taught in schools?"; "What about those fossils?"; "Where did the universe come from?"; "If you don't believe in anything, what happens when you die?" 55

Hadn't I predicted the man in the black hat always loses? Our not-so-great debate had at least brought me face to face with what I've called our peculiar gift for believing the unbelievable.

My stunned wonder at the echolocation of bats can trigger a sort of free-fall astonishment, with my mind plummeting back through the evolutionary epochs needed to develop an ultrasound system so exquisitely and finely tuned. Lying all about and within us, nature's smallest details abound with time's ingenuities. Every strawberry for my breakfast granola has bedecked itself with minuscule time capsules disguised as seeds. That's cunning indeed, but time's genius as encapsulated by each human cell staggers the mind. Our cells are more impressive than we are.

Thanks to Darwin our imagination can wander billions of years within a droplet of blood. Or, in pondering raven plumage—with its barbules, barbicels, and hooklets[13] so cunningly contrived from an original squiggle of keratin[14]—can be rapt by the depth of time in a feather.

Unfortunately, the extent of gone time, because literally unimaginable, remains therefore unreal for all too many, especially the anti-Darwinians. Surely it's the immeasurable spans of evolutionary time they cannot conceive of, nor can they conceive how, to cite a seminal phrase by the eighteenth-century gentleman geologist James Hutton,[15] "little causes, long continued" could have wrought in all life forms and land forms such enormous effects.

"Long continued" in the case of Earth *life* comes to some 3.5 billion years. Those who don't believe the human eye could have evolved are incredulous partly because they have no clear concept of the words *million* and *billion*. 60

Suppose your doctor should look up from her clipboard to say, "I'm afraid the test results are not good." Naturally you'll wonder, "How long have I got?" Answering your thought she breaks the news, "You have, I'm sorry to say, only a million seconds to live." Time enough to drive to your favorite coffee house for a last latte? Yes, and to spare. Almost twelve full days. Now imagine, having mis-

13. Barbules are small structures growing out of the barbs of a bird's feather, overlapping to make the feather rigid; barbicels are hook-like structures that link adjoining barbules.

14. The material that makes up the outer layer of skin.

15. Scottish scientist (1726–1797) regarded as the father of modern geology.

read her own writing, she corrects herself. "Did I say 'million'? Sorry about that! I meant to say billion. Give or take a few, you've got a billion seconds before the end."

How many more days would that give you? Plenty. In fact, just over thirty-two years. Despite all the bandying of large numbers in the media, people can't grasp how "long continued" a span of 3.5 billion years really is.

Years ago a Grand Canyon ranger told me the average visitation time there was a mere four hours. I suggested that the park service post signs at turnouts along the rim: KINDLY ALLOW THE DUST OF YOUR ARRIVAL TO SETTLE BEFORE YOU DEPART. Such hurry-up visits prove that the views from the South Rim serve mainly as photo ops allowing tourists to say, "Been there, done that." Besides, after hearing about the place for years, a person's first look may not live up: "Grand? Kind of, I guess." Given all the blather, everyone expects more.

Yet nowhere better exemplifies the difference between scenery and nature than the Grand Canyon. From the rim it's a scenic postcard. And traffic. However, by descending even a skimpy eight hundred feet or so, you cross a threshold into that tremendous realm we call nature. Scenery is what you're apart from, nature's what you're a part of. Thus the canyon is really all about you, and the deeper the truer, offering an experience that can feel like identity theft. For visitors wanting more than snapshots, therefore, signage of a different sort might be posted: THOSE WHO DESCEND MAY NEVER CLIMB OUT.

65 That is, any receptive self, descending, won't be the self that ascends. Being contextualized by millions of years made stone will work changes in such a person. For some, that alteration is considerable. Lifelong in my case. Day after incomparable day spent inhaling geological time gradually led me to see everything differently and further accelerated my fall into knowledge.

Way back in 1794, a geo-theologian named Richard Kirwan[16] fired off a critical blast at James Hutton's *Theory of the Earth* for claiming Earth to be unimaginably old. Like our present-day creationists, Kirwan took Genesis literally; thus he argued that Hutton's theory not only contradicts scripture, it threatens all religion and morality—and he added that it hurls humankind into deeps of geological time "from which human reason recoils."

Hutton, called by an admirer "the man who invented time," was a deist who certainly believed in a Creator but ruefully predicted that Earth's true age would produce culture shock:

> It is not any part of the process that will be disputed; but after allowing all the parts, the whole will be denied; and for what?—only because we are not disposed to allow that quantity of time which the ablution of so much wasted mountain might require.[17]

16. Irish scientist (1733–1812), who argued against Hutton's theory of the Earth's ancient origins.

17. As cited from Hutton's *Theory of the Earth* in Sir Archibald Geikie's *Landscape in History*, vol. 1 (New York: Macmillan and Co., 1905), 137 [Saner's note].

Time's quantity? Even today, to use Kirwan's word, we "recoil."

Arriving at the Grand Canyon from Chicago, Japan, Hungary, Savannah, England, Switzerland, Kansas City, France, or wherever, we do just that. Gazing into its depths we feel ourselves missing from our own planet.

"When I was a child," wrote St. Paul, "I spoke like a child, I thought like a child, I reasoned like a child; when I became a man, I gave up childish ways."[18]

So true. As a child I was the handiwork of a god. Was even made in that deity's image, and—along with everybody else—was the be-all and end-all of creation. How much more important can you get? Yet no sooner had I grown up than my status plummeted to that of just another nano-speck adrift in a wilderness of stars—because of my fall. When Adam and Eve fell, at least God and his fiery-sword-wielding angels hung around ever after. 70

But not for willful ones like me. Thus I had to watch while nine flavors of angels, the entire floral-scented bouquet of blessed saints, the world-mothering Madonna, and heaven's trio of deities slowly melted from a suitably pastel-colored cloud to the black of interstellar void. So much for Sky City. Unlike one mistakenly disillusioned young Englishman, however, I didn't reel from ale shop to ale shop claiming Darwin's *On the Origin of Species* had destroyed my life. Still, when the center of your world drops out . . . well, that does take some adjusting.

After the Almighty evaporated on me, I must admit that—human ills aside—nature and the universe itself began to seem far more interesting than some All-Everything supernatural. Without a presiding deity, the world's origin and raison d'être, if any, became—and remains—inexhaustibly fascinating. Nothing so challenges the finite reach of human thought as the unknowable depth and breadth of all we belong to. Even my neutrino-size unimportance within it acquired the freaky grandeur of being that radically dwarfed. In short, if you love living a mystery as I do, alive is the place to be.

On the down side, however, my fall entailed more than the loss of Cloud Nine. It caused the unimaginable scale of cosmic immensity to shrink me to a geometrical point having location but no magnitude—quite a comedown from once being watched over by angels, by all the saints in heaven, and by a three-person God. Still, forgoing my postmortem flight to Paradise wasn't nearly so hard to handle as was facing up to a human world in which those who endure unspeakable pain, squalor, or crushing injustice can expect no otherworldly redress, ever. Triggered by the terrible helplessness we feel in the presence of great suffering, the impulse to beg divine intervention for *les miserables* explains why our polytheist ancestors felt you can never have too many gods. One for every occasion seems little enough.

My psychotherapist friend Charles Proudfit tells me there's such a thing as existential depression. And how not? The cataclysmic randomness of sidereal[19]

18. Saner quotes I Corinthians 13.11.

19. Related to a star.

collisions, black holes, star hatcheries, and supernova explosions going on all the time in the soul-numbing vastitudes surrounding us can shade any human enterprise with the gray-scale of futility. "What's the point of writing? As far as that goes, why do anything?" Which is why any life worth living must contain something of great value that we know isn't there.

75 Meanwhile, swimming in cosmically deep waters without a life preserver adds more than a touch of adventure to any existence—provided we understand that's where we are and what we are doing. Given the combined mass of inanimate matter in the universe, our merely being alive and aware, and neither on fire nor in a black hole, means each of us is, as the astrophysicists put it, in "a highly improbable state." I love that wording. It feels so much more elegant than "abnormal." In fact, it feels like a promotion. Yet there remains, in relation to "the world," an inevitable "Why is there one?" That insuppressibly pesky "Why?" is how, after my fall into knowledge, I came to discover astrotheology.

What's more, if—however briefly—we're among the vanishingly small percent of matter that has consciousness, we may as well pay attention. But consciousness is no life jacket either, and staying afloat in waters unfathomably deep isn't for the faint of heart. As to the point of it all, must there be one? Besides, aren't "the point of it all" and "meaningful" really synonyms for "payday"? As if doing your best, lifelong, both to understand where we are and what we are weren't plenty meaningful enough.

Admittedly, there are sad afternoons when nothing works and reality feels too true to be good. As anodyne for watching my loftiest thoughts get downsized to the height of a dust mite, I sometimes welcome even the desperate comfort of Pascal. He felt himself pitifully finite and daunted by existing between what he called "two infinities," the microscopically small and the astronomically large. Yet he reasoned thus: "Though the universe crush him, man is nobler than the forces that kill him. He understands his mortal nature, whereas the universe knows nothing of it."[20]

Hardly a hip-hip-hooray, but quite a cut above thumb sucking or Linus' blanket.[21] The era is long past when our species can fatten self-esteem by believing its own publicity, yet a modest, astrophysical excuse for chest thumping does remain available. Owing to the subtle intricacies of the phenomenon called life, the lowliest living critter among us, even a gnat, is more complex than the sun that begot it.

Factor human intelligence into the comparison, and the assertion grows all the truer. Each thoughtful person who possesses so much as a vague sense of our location between Pascal's infinities is a more considerable speck than all the mindlessly blazing matter in the universe.

80 If, however, we put our consciousness to no better use than getting through the day, we've ignored the chance of a lifetime, unmindful that being here and alive is the one strangest thing that can ever happen. Considering the innumerable galaxies overhead and underfoot every living moment, our very ennui is

20. From the *Pensées* of Blaise Pascal (1623–1662), no. 347.

21. Linus, the character in the comic strip *Peanuts* who clings to his security blanket.

weird. Actually, our mayfly longevity[22] makes boredom a left-handed mercy, enabling the illusion we live a long time. Surrealism?[23] That was just an art movement, whereas, rightly seen, each of us is a walking, talking surrealist. Because the ultimate truth of our cosmic context remains unknown, we can never truly be who we are nor where we are.

My own favorite moments for letting that surreality happen come while facing sunrises. Just watching the sun's bubble ascend puts me, body and soul, in a cosmos. However, the duality in everything means that the most gorgeous of dawns doesn't lessen the difference between the sun's longevity and mine, just lightens it wonderfully. That same duality supplies my awareness that our daystar has only nuclear fusion at heart with an opposite realization: I owe it everything—including my sadness at knowing it, too, is mortal.

Occasionally at sunrise, to get even better perspective on myself, I swap my stance on the mesa slope near my house for one on the sun. Afloat on the surface of its photosphere I look back toward Earth's pinprick of shine, not quite swallowed up by the blackness of space, and wish others could share the view.

Not only that. I once briefly believed that if on some miraculous day we humans fully faced and accepted our actual situation, we'd take better care of our planet and each other. I know. It's still my favorite fantasy that won't happen, but, as the song says, "I can dream, can't I?" So, while standing on the sun and looking toward Earth, I occasionally imagine, despite humanity's checkered past and present flaws, that my wishful figment may one day be realized. There we'll be, all of us, companionably riding our planet's tiny brightness, and gazing silently out into the question of questions.

22. Mayflies are short-lived, with life spans from a few minutes to a few days.

23. A twentieth-century artistic movement aimed at disrupting traditional forms of rationality and exploring underlying psychological states.

Questions

1. Into what knowledge does Saner actually fall? Why does he call it a "fall"?

2. Saner gives his opponents pseudonyms. Why do you think he chooses "Binford Pyle" for the anti-Darwinian (paragraph 21)? What does the name suggest?

3. Can you pin down Saner's religious beliefs? Describe them as precisely as you can.

4. Write about a debate you had with someone over a strongly held belief or position, describing how your opponent argued as well as how successfully you expressed your view.

Henry David Thoreau *Where I Lived, and What I Lived For*

When I first took up my abode in the woods, that is, began to spend my nights as well as days there, which, by accident, was on Independence day, or the fourth of July, 1845, my house was not finished for winter, but was merely a defence against the rain, without plastering or chimney, the walls being of rough weather-stained boards, with wide chinks, which made it cool at night. The upright white hewn studs and freshly planed door and window casings gave it a clean and airy look, especially in the morning, when its timbers were saturated with dew, so that I fancied that by noon some sweet gum would exude from them. To my imagination it retained throughout the day more or less of this auroral character, reminding me of a certain house on a mountain which I had visited the year before. This was an airy and unplastered cabin, fit to entertain a travelling god, and where a goddess might trail her garments. The winds which passed over my dwelling were such as sweep over the ridges of mountains, bearing the broken strains, or celestial parts only, of terrestrial music. The morning wind forever blows, the poem of creation is uninterrupted; but few are the ears that hear it. Olympus[1] is but the outside of the earth every where.

The only house I had been the owner of before, if I except a boat, was a tent, which I used occasionally when making excursions in the summer, and this is still rolled up in my garret; but the boat, after passing from hand to hand, has gone down the stream of time. With this more substantial shelter about me, I had made some progress toward settling in the world. This frame, so slightly clad, was a sort of crystallization around me, and reacted on the builder. It was suggestive somewhat as a picture in outlines. I did not need to go out doors to take the air, for the atmosphere within had lost none of its freshness. It was not so much within doors as behind a door where I sat, even in the rainiest weather. The Harivansa[2] says, "An abode without birds is like a meat without seasoning." Such was not my abode, for I found myself suddenly neighbor to the birds; not by having imprisoned one, but having caged myself near them. I was not only nearer to some of those which commonly frequent the garden and the orchard, but to those wilder and more thrilling songsters of the forest which never, or rarely, serenade a villager,—the wood-thrush, the veery, the scarlet tanager, the field-sparrow, the whippoorwill, and many others.

I was seated by the shore of a small pond, about a mile and a half south of the village of Concord and somewhat higher than it, in the midst of an extensive

From Thoreau's most famous book, Walden *(1854), an account of his life in a small cabin on Walden Pond, outside the village of Concord, Massachusetts; in* Walden *Thoreau not only describes his life in the woods but also develops a philosophy for living.*

1. The mountain where the Greek gods dwell.
2. Fifth-century epic poem about the Hindu god Krishna.

wood between that town and Lincoln, and about two miles south of that our only field known to fame, Concord Battle Ground;[3] but I was so low in the woods that the opposite shore, half a mile off, like the rest, covered with wood, was my most distant horizon. For the first week, whenever I looked out on the pond it impressed me like a tarn high up on the side of a mountain, its bottom far above the surface of other lakes, and, as the sun arose, I saw it throwing off its nightly clothing of mist, and here and there, by degrees, its soft ripples or its smooth reflecting surface was revealed, while the mists, like ghosts, were stealthily withdrawing in every direction into the woods, as at the breaking up of some nocturnal conventicle. The very dew seemed to hang upon the trees later into the day than usual, as on the sides of mountains.

This small lake was of most value as a neighbor in the intervals of a gentle rain storm in August, when, both air and water being perfectly still, but the sky overcast, mid-afternoon had all the serenity of evening, and the wood-thrush sang around, and was heard from shore to shore. A lake like this is never smoother than at such a time; and the clear portion of the air above it being shallow and darkened by clouds, the water, full of light and reflections, becomes a lower heaven itself so much the more important. From a hill top near by, where the wood had been recently cut off, there was a pleasing vista southward across the pond, through a wide indentation in the hills which form the shore there, where their opposite sides sloping toward each other suggested a stream flowing out in that direction through a wooded valley, but stream there was none. That way I looked between and over the near green hills to some distant and higher ones in the horizon, tinged with blue. Indeed, by standing on tiptoe I could catch a glimpse of some of the peaks of the still bluer and more distant mountain ranges in the north-west, those true-blue coins from heaven's own mint, and also of some portion of the village. But in other directions, even from this point, I could not see over or beyond the woods which surrounded me. It is well to have some water in your neighborhood, to give buoyancy to and float the earth. One value even of the smallest well is, that when you look into it you see that earth is not continent but insular. This is as important as that it keeps butter cool. When I looked across the pond from this peak toward the Sudbury meadows, which in time of flood I distinguished elevated perhaps by a mirage in their seething valley, like a coin in a basin, all the earth beyond the pond appeared like a thin crust insulated and floated even by this small sheet of intervening water, and I was reminded that this on which I dwelt was but *dry land*.

Though the view from my door was still more contracted, I did not feel crowded or confined in the least. There was pasture enough for my imagination. The low shrub-oak plateau to which the opposite shore arose, stretched away toward the prairies of the West and the steppes of Tartary,[4] affording ample room for all the roving families of men. "There are none happy in the world but 5

3. Site of the famous Battle of Concord, April 19, 1775, considered the start of the American Revolution.

4. A region that includes what is today northern Pakistan.

beings who enjoy freely a vast horizon,"—said Damodara,[5] when his herds required new and larger pastures.

Both place and time were changed, and I dwelt nearer to those parts of the universe and to those eras in history which had most attracted me. Where I lived was as far off as many a region viewed nightly by astronomers. We are wont to imagine rare and delectable places in some remote and more celestial corner of the system, behind the constellation of Cassiopeia's Chair, far from noise and disturbance. I discovered that my house actually had its site in such a withdrawn, but forever new and unprofaned, part of the universe. If it were worth the while to settle in those parts near to the Pleiades or the Hyades, to Aldebaran or Altair,[6] then I was really there, or at an equal remoteness from the life which I had left behind, dwindled and twinkling with as fine a ray to my nearest neighbor, and to be seen only in moonless nights by him. Such was that part of creation where I had squatted;—

> "There was a shepherd that did live,
> And held his thoughts as high
> As were the mounts whereon his flocks
> Did hourly feed him by."[7]

What should we think of the shepherd's life if his flocks always wandered to higher pastures than his thoughts?

Every morning was a cheerful invitation to make my life of equal simplicity, and I may say innocence, with Nature herself. I have been as sincere a worshipper of Aurora[8] as the Greeks. I got up early and bathed in the pond; that was a religious exercise, and one of the best things which I did. They say that characters were engraven on the bathing tub of king Tching-thang[9] to this effect: "Renew thyself completely each day; do it again, and again, and forever again." I can understand that. Morning brings back the heroic ages. I was as much affected by the faint hum of a mosquito making its invisible and unimaginable tour through my apartment at earliest dawn, when I was sitting with door and windows open, as I could be by any trumpet that ever sang of fame. It was Homer's[10] requiem; itself an Iliad and Odyssey in the air, singing its own wrath and wanderings. There was something cosmical about it; a standing advertisement, till forbidden, of the everlasting vigor and fertility of the world. The morning, which is the most memorable season of the day, is the awakening hour. Then there is least somnolence in us; and for an hour, at least, some part

5. One of the many names of Krishna, the Hindu god.

6. Cassiopeia's Chair, the Pleiades, and the Hyades are constellations; Aldebaran and Altair are stars.

7. Lines from "The Shepherd's Love for Philladay," from Thomas Evan's *Old Ballads* (1810).

8. Goddess of the dawn.

9. Confucius (551–479 B.C.E.), Chinese philosopher.

10. Greek epic poet (eighth century B.C.E.), author of the *Odyssey* and the *Iliad*.

of us awakes which slumbers all the rest of the day and night. Little is to be expected of that day, if it can be called a day, to which we are not awakened by our Genius, but by the mechanical nudgings of some servitor, are not awakened by our own newly-acquired force and aspirations from within, accompanied by the undulations of celestial music, instead of factory bells, and a fragrance filling the air—to a higher life than we fell asleep from; and thus the darkness bear its fruit, and prove itself to be good, no less than the light. That man who does not believe that each day contains an earlier, more sacred, and auroral hour than he has yet profaned, has despaired of life, and is pursuing a descending and darkening way. After a partial cessation of his sensuous life, the soul of man, or its organs rather, are reinvigorated each day, and his Genius tries again what noble life it can make. All memorable events, I should say, transpire in morning time and in a morning atmosphere. The Vedas[11] say, "All intelligences awake with the morning." Poetry and art, and the fairest and most memorable of the actions of men, date from such an hour. All poets and heroes, like Memnon,[12] are the children of Aurora, and emit their music at sunrise. To him whose elastic and vigorous thought keeps pace with the sun, the day is a perpetual morning. It matters not what the clocks say or the attitudes and labors of men. Morning is when I am awake and there is a dawn in me. Moral reform is the effort to throw off sleep. Why is it that men give so poor an account of their day if they have not been slumbering? They are not such poor calculators. If they had not been overcome with drowsiness they would have performed something. The millions are awake enough for physical labor; but only one in a million is awake enough for effective intellectual exertion, only one in a hundred millions to a poetic or divine life. To be awake is to be alive. I have never yet met a man who was quite awake. How could I have looked him in the face?

We must learn to reawaken and keep ourselves awake, not by mechanical aids, but by an infinite expectation of the dawn, which does not forsake us in our soundest sleep. I know of no more encouraging fact than the unquestionable ability of man to elevate his life by a conscious endeavor. It is something to be able to paint a particular picture, or to carve a statue, and so to make a few objects beautiful; but it is far more glorious to carve and paint the very atmosphere and medium through which we look, which morally we can do. To affect the quality of the day, that is the highest of arts. Every man is tasked to make his life, even in its details, worthy of the contemplation of his most elevated and critical hour. If we refused, or rather used up, such paltry information as we get, the oracles would distinctly inform us how this might be done.

I went to the woods because I wished to live deliberately, to front only the essential facts of life, and see if I could not learn what it had to teach, and not, when I came to die, discover that I had not lived. I did not wish to live what was not life, living is so dear, nor did I wish to practise resignation, unless it was

11. Sacred texts that contain hymns, incantations, and rituals from ancient India.

12. Son of Aurora, the goddess of dawn, and a mortal, Memnon was king of the Ethiopians; he was slain by Achilles while fighting the Greeks in Troy. When he died, his sad mother's tears formed the morning dew.

quite necessary. I wanted to live deep and suck out all the marrow of life, to live so sturdily and Spartan-like as to put to rout all that was not life, to cut a broad swath and shave close, to drive life into a corner, and reduce it to its lowest terms, and, if it proved to be mean, why then to get the whole and genuine meanness of it, and publish its meanness to the world; or if it were sublime, to know it by experience, and be able to give a true account of it in my next excursion. For most men, it appears to me, are in a strange uncertainty about it, whether it is of the devil or of God, and have *somewhat hastily* concluded that it is the chief end of man here to "glorify God and enjoy him forever."

10 Still we live meanly, like ants; though the fable tells us that we were long ago changed into men;[13] like pygmies we fight with cranes;[14] it is error upon error, and clout upon clout, and our best virtue has for its occasion a superfluous and evitable wretchedness. Our life is frittered away by detail. An honest man has hardly need to count more than his ten fingers, or in extreme cases he may add his ten toes, and lump the rest. Simplicity, simplicity, simplicity! I say, let your affairs be as two or three, and not a hundred or a thousand; instead of a million count half a dozen, and keep your accounts on your thumb nail. In the midst of this chopping sea of civilized life, such are the clouds and storms and quicksands and thousand-and-one items to be allowed for, that a man has to live, if he would not founder and go to the bottom and not make his port at all, by dead reckoning, and he must be a great calculator indeed who succeeds. Simplify, simplify. Instead of three meals a day, if it be necessary eat but one; instead of a hundred dishes, five; and reduce other things in proportion. Our life is like a German Confederacy, made up of petty states, with its boundary forever fluctuating, so that even a German cannot tell you how it is bounded at any moment. The nation itself, with all its so called internal improvements, which, by the way, are all external and superficial, is just such an unwieldy and overgrown establishment, cluttered with furniture and tripped up by its own traps, ruined by luxury and heedless expense, by want of calculation and a worthy aim, as the million households in the land; and the only cure for it as for them is in a rigid economy, a stern and more than Spartan simplicity of life and elevation of purpose. It lives too fast. Men think that it is essential that the *Nation* have commerce, and export ice, and talk through a telegraph, and ride thirty miles an hour, without a doubt, whether *they* do or not; but whether we should live like baboons or like men, is a little uncertain. If we do not get our sleepers, and forge rails, and devote days and nights to the work, but go to tinkering upon our *lives* to improve *them*, who will build railroads? And if railroads are not built, how shall we get to heaven in season? But if we stay at home and mind our business, who will want railroads? We do not ride on the railroad; it rides upon us. Did you ever think what those sleepers are that underlie the railroad? Each one is a man, an Irishman, or a Yankee man. The rails are laid

13. In a Greek fable Aeacus asks Zeus to increase a scanty population by turning ants into men.

14. From the *Iliad*, Book III, lines 2–6, in which the Trojans are represented as the cranes.

on them, and they are covered with sand, and the cars run smoothly over them. They are sound sleepers, I assure you. And every few years a new lot is laid down and run over; so that, if some have the pleasure of riding on a rail, others have the misfortune to be ridden upon. And when they run over a man that is walking in his sleep, a supernumerary sleeper in the wrong position, and wake him up, they suddenly stop the cars, and make a hue and cry about it, as if this were an exception. I am glad to know that it takes a gang of men for every five miles to keep the sleepers down and level in their beds as it is, for this is a sign that they may sometime get up again.

Why should we live with such hurry and waste of life? We are determined to be starved before we are hungry. Men say that a stitch in time saves nine, and so they take a thousand stitches to-day to save nine to-morrow. As for *work*, we haven't any of any consequence. We have the Saint Vitus' dance,[15] and cannot possibly keep our heads still. If I should only give a few pulls at the parish bell-rope, as for a fire, that is, without setting the bell, there is hardly a man on his farm in the outskirts of Concord, notwithstanding that press of engagements which was his excuse so many times this morning, nor a boy, nor a woman, I might almost say, but would forsake all and follow that sound, not mainly to save property from the flames, but, if we will confess the truth, much more to see it burn, since burn it must, and we, be it known, did not set it on fire,—or to see it put out, and have a hand in it, if that is done as handsomely; yes, even if it were the parish church itself. Hardly a man takes a half hour's nap after dinner, but when he wakes he holds up his head and asks, "What's the news?" as if the rest of mankind had stood his sentinels. Some give directions to be waked every half hour, doubtless for no other purpose; and then, to pay for it, they tell what they have dreamed. After a night's sleep the news is as indispensable as the breakfast. "Pray tell me any thing new that has happened to a man any where on this globe,"—and he reads it over his coffee and rolls, that a man has had his eyes gouged out this morning on the Wachito River;[16] never dreaming the while that he lives in the dark unfathomed mammoth cave of this world, and has but the rudiment of an eye himself.

For my part, I could easily do without the post-office. I think that there are very few important communications made through it. To speak critically, I never received more than one or two letters in my life—I wrote this some years ago—that were worth the postage. The penny-post is, commonly, an institution through which you seriously offer a man that penny for his thoughts which is so often safely offered in jest. And I am sure that I never read any memorable news in a newspaper. If we read of one man robbed, or murdered, or killed by accident, or one house burned, or one vessel wrecked, or one steamboat blown up, or one cow run over on the Western Railroad, or one mad dog killed, or one lot of grasshoppers in the winter,—we never need read of another. One is enough. If you are acquainted with the principle, what do you care for a myriad instances and

15. A nervous disorder marked by jerky, spasmodic movements that occurs in cases of rheumatic fever involving the connective tissue of the brain.

16. In southern Arkansas.

applications? To a philosopher all *news*, as it is called, is gossip, and they who edit and read it are old women over their tea. Yet not a few are greedy after this gossip. There was such a rush, as I hear, the other day at one of the offices to learn the foreign news by the last arrival, that several large squares of plate glass belonging to the establishment were broken by the pressure,—news which I seriously think a ready wit might write a twelvemonth or twelve years beforehand with sufficient accuracy. As for Spain, for instance, if you know how to throw in Don Carlos and the Infanta, and Don Pedro and Seville and Granada, from time to time in the right proportions,—they may have changed the names a little since I saw the papers,—and serve up a bull-fight when other entertainments fail, it will be true to the letter, and give us as good an idea of the exact state of ruin of things in Spain as the most succinct and lucid reports under this head in the newspapers: and as for England, almost the last significant scrap of news from that quarter was the revolution of 1649;[17] and if you have learned the history of her crops for an average year, you never need attend to that thing again, unless your speculations are of a merely pecuniary character. If one may judge who rarely looks into the newspapers, nothing new does ever happen in foreign parts, a French revolution not excepted.

What news! how much more important to know what that is which was never old! "Kieou-he-yu (great dignitary of the state of Wei) sent a man to Khoung-tseu to know his news. Khoung-tseu caused the messenger to be seated near him, and questioned him in these terms: What is your master doing? The messenger answered with respect: My master desires to diminish the number of his faults, but he cannot come to the end of them. The messenger being gone, the philosopher remarked: What a worthy messenger! What a worthy messenger!" The preacher, instead of vexing the ears of drowsy farmers on their day of rest at the end of the week,—for Sunday is the fit conclusion of an ill-spent week, and not the fresh and brave beginning of a new one,—with this one other draggle-tail of a sermon, should shout with thundering voice,—"Pause! Avast! Why so seeming fast, but deadly slow?"

Shams and delusions are esteemed for soundest truths, while reality is fabulous. If men would steadily observe realities only, and not allow themselves to be deluded, life, to compare it with such things as we know, would be like a fairy tale and the Arabian Nights' Entertainments. If we respected only what is inevitable and has a right to be, music and poetry would resound along the streets. When we are unhurried and wise, we perceive that only great and worthy things have any permanent and absolute existence,—that petty fears and petty pleasures are but the shadow of the reality. This is always exhilarating and sublime. By closing the eyes and slumbering, and consenting to be deceived by shows, men establish and confirm their daily life of routine and habit every where, which still is built on purely illusory foundations. Children, who play life, discern its true law and relations more clearly than men, who fail to live it worthily,

17. Sometimes called the Cromwellian Interlude, the period in British history between 1649 and 1660 in which the monarchy was replaced by the Commonwealth and Oliver Cromwell became Lord Protector.

but who think that they are wiser by experience, that is, by failure. I have read in a Hindoo book, that "There was a king's son, who, being expelled in infancy from his native city, was brought up by a forester, and, growing up to maturity in that state, imagined himself to belong to the barbarous race with which he lived. One of his father's ministers having discovered him, revealed to him what he was, and the misconception of his character was removed, and he knew himself to be a prince. So soul," continues the Hindoo philosopher, "from the circumstances in which it is placed, mistakes its own character, until the truth is revealed to it by some holy teacher, and then it knows itself to be *Brahme*."[18] I perceive that we inhabitants of New England live this mean life that we do because our vision does not penetrate the surface of things. We think that that *is* which *appears* to be. If a man should walk through this town and see only the reality, where, think you, would the "Mill-dam"[19] go to? If he should give us an account of the realities he beheld there, we should not recognize the place in his description. Look at a meeting-house, or a court-house, or a jail, or a shop, or a dwelling-house, and say what that thing really is before a true gaze, and they would all go to pieces in your account of them. Men esteem truth remote, in the outskirts of the system, behind the farthest star, before Adam and after the last man. In eternity there is indeed something true and sublime. But all these times and places and occasions are now and here. God himself culminates in the present moment, and will never be more divine in the lapse of all the ages. And we are enabled to apprehend at all what is sublime and noble only by the perpetual instilling and drenching of the reality that surrounds us. The universe constantly and obediently answers to our conceptions; whether we travel fast or slow, the track is laid for us. Let us spend our lives in conceiving then. The poet or the artist never yet had so fair and noble a design but some of his posterity at least could accomplish it.

15 Let us spend one day as deliberately as Nature, and not be thrown off the track by every nutshell and mosquito's wing that falls on the rails. Let us rise early and fast, or break fast, gently and without perturbation; let company come and let company go, let the bells ring and the children cry,—determined to make a day of it. Why should we knock under and go with the stream? Let us not be upset and overwhelmed in that terrible rapid and whirlpool called a dinner, situated in the meridian shallows. Weather this danger and you are safe, for the rest of the way is down hill. With unrelaxed nerves, with morning vigor, sail by it, looking another way, tied to the mast like Ulysses. If the engine whistles, let it whistle till it is hoarse for its pains. If the bell rings, why should we run? We will consider what kind of music they are like. Let us settle ourselves, and work and wedge our feet downward through the mud and slush of opinion, and prejudice, and tradition, and delusion, and appearance, that alluvion which covers the globe, through Paris and London, through New York and Boston and Concord, through church and state, through poetry and philosophy and religion, till we come to a hard bottom and rocks in place, which we can

18. The supreme soul, the essence of all being, in Hinduism.

19. A dam built in 1635 in the town of Concord on the site of an Indian fishing weir.

call *reality*, and say, This is, and no mistake; and then begin, having a *point d'appui,*[20] below freshet and frost and fire, a place where you might found a wall or a state, or set a lamp-post safely, or perhaps a gauge, not a Nilometer,[21] but a Realometer, that future ages might know how deep a freshet of shams and appearances had gathered from time to time. If you stand right fronting and face to face to a fact, you will see the sun glimmer on both its surfaces, as if it were a cimeter,[22] and feel its sweet edge dividing you through the heart and marrow, and so you will happily conclude your mortal career. Be it life or death, we crave only reality. If we are really dying, let us hear the rattle in our throats and feel cold in the extremities; if we are alive, let us go about our business.

Time is but the stream I go a-fishing in. I drink at it; but while I drink I see the sandy bottom and detect how shallow it is. Its thin current slides away, but eternity remains. I would drink deeper; fish in the sky, whose bottom is pebbly with stars. I cannot count one. I know not the first letter of the alphabet. I have always been regretting that I was not as wise as the day I was born. The intellect is a cleaver; it discerns and rifts its way into the secret of things. I do not wish to be any more busy with my hands than is necessary. My head is hands and feet. I feel all my best faculties concentrated in it. My instinct tells me that my head is an organ for burrowing, as some creatures use their snout and forepaws, and with it I would mine and burrow my way through these hills. I think that the richest vein is somewhere hereabouts; so by the divining rod and thin rising vapors I judge; and here I will begin to mine.

QUESTIONS

1. Thoreau's title might be rephrased as two questions: "Where did I live?" and "What did I live for?" What answers does Thoreau give to each?

2. Throughout this essay Thoreau poses questions—for example, "Why is it that men give so poor an account of their day if they have not been slumbering?" (paragraph 7) or "Why should we live with such hurry and waste of life?" (paragraph 11). To what extent does he answer them? Why might he leave some unanswered or only partially answered?

3. Thoreau is known for his aphorisms (short, witty nuggets of wisdom). Find one you like and explain what it means.

4. If you have ever chosen to live unconventionally at some period of your life, even if only briefly, write about your decision, including the reasons and the consequences.

20. Reference point.

21. A gauge placed in the Nile River in ancient times to measure the rise of the water.

22. A saber with a curved blade, usually spelled "scimitar."

VIRGINIA WOOLF *The Death of the Moth*

MOTHS THAT FLY by day are not properly to be called moths; they do not excite that pleasant sense of dark autumn nights and ivy-blossom which the commonest yellow-underwing asleep in the shadow of the curtain never fails to rouse in us. They are hybrid creatures, neither gay like butterflies nor sombre like their own species. Nevertheless the present specimen, with his narrow hay-colored wings, fringed with a tassel of the same color, seemed to be content with life. It was a pleasant morning, mid-September, mild, benignant, yet with a keener breath than that of the summer months. The plough was already scoring the field opposite the window, and where the share had been, the earth was pressed flat and gleamed with moisture. Such vigor came rolling in from the fields and the down beyond that it was difficult to keep the eyes strictly turned upon the book. The rooks too were keeping one of their annual festivities; soaring round the tree tops until it looked as if a vast net with thousands of black knots in it had been cast up into the air; which, after a few moments sank slowly down upon the trees until every twig seemed to have a knot at the end of it. Then, suddenly, the net would be thrown into the air again in a wider circle this time, with the utmost clamor and vociferation, as though to be thrown into the air and settle slowly down upon the tree tops were a tremendously exciting experience.

The same energy which inspired the rooks, the ploughmen, the horses, and even, it seemed, the lean bare-backed downs, sent the moth fluttering from side to side of his square of the window-pane. One could not help watching him. One was, indeed, conscious of a queer feeling of pity for him. The possibilities of pleasure seemed that morning so enormous and so various that to have only a moth's part in life, and a day moth's at that, appeared a hard fate, and his zest in enjoying his meagre opportunities to the full, pathetic. He flew vigorously to one corner of his compartment, and, after waiting there a second, flew across to the other. What remained for him but to fly to a third corner and then to a fourth? That was all he could do, in spite of the size of the downs, the width of the sky, the far-off smoke of houses, and the romantic voice, now and then, of a steamer out at sea. What he could do he did. Watching him, it seemed as if a fiber, very thin but pure, of the enormous energy of the world had been thrust into his frail and diminutive body. As often as he crossed the pane, I could fancy that a thread of vital light became visible. He was little or nothing but life.

Yet, because he was so small, and so simple a form of the energy that was rolling in at the open window and driving its way through so many narrow and intricate corridors in my own brain and in those of other human beings, there was something marvellous as well as pathetic about him. It was as if someone

The title essay of Woolf's collection The Death of the Moth, and Other Essays *(1942), compiled after her death in 1941.*

had taken a tiny bead of pure life and decking it as lightly as possible with down and feathers, had set it dancing and zig-zagging to show us the true nature of life. Thus displayed one could not get over the strangeness of it. One is apt to forget all about life, seeing it humped and bossed and garnished and cumbered so that it has to move with the greatest circumspection and dignity. Again, the thought of all that life might have been had he been born in any other shape caused one to view his simple activities with a kind of pity.

After a time, tired by his dancing apparently, he settled on the window ledge in the sun, and, the queer spectacle being at an end, I forgot about him. Then, looking up, my eye was caught by him. He was trying to resume his dancing, but seemed either so stiff or so awkward that he could only flutter to the bottom of the window-pane; and when he tried to fly across it he failed. Being intent on other matters I watched these futile attempts for a time without thinking, unconsciously waiting for him to resume his flight, as one waits for a machine, that has stopped momentarily, to start again without considering the reason of its failure. After perhaps a seventh attempt he slipped from the wooden ledge and fell, fluttering his wings, on to his back on the window sill. The helplessness of his attitude roused me. It flashed upon me that he was in difficulties; he could no longer raise himself; his legs struggled vainly. But, as I stretched out a pencil, meaning to help him to right himself, it came over me that the failure and awkwardness were the approach of death. I laid the pencil down again.

5 The legs agitated themselves once more. I looked as if for the enemy against which he struggled. I looked out of doors. What had happened there? Presumably it was midday, and work in the fields had stopped. Stillness and quiet had replaced the previous animation. The birds had taken themselves off to feed in the brooks. The horses stood still. Yet the power was there all the same, massed outside indifferent, impersonal, not attending to anything in particular. Somehow it was opposed to the little hay-colored moth. It was useless to try to do anything. One could only watch the extraordinary efforts made by those tiny legs against an oncoming doom which could, had it chosen, have submerged an entire city, not merely a city, but masses of human beings; nothing, I knew, had any chance against death. Nevertheless after a pause of exhaustion the legs fluttered again. It was superb this last protest, and so frantic that he succeeded at last in righting himself. One's sympathies, of course, were all on the side of life. Also, when there was nobody to care or to know, this gigantic effort on the part of an insignificant little moth, against a power of such magnitude, to retain what no one else valued or desired to keep, moved one strangely. Again, somehow, one saw life, a pure bead. I lifted the pencil again, useless though I knew it to be. But even as I did so, the unmistakable tokens of death showed themselves. The body relaxed, and instantly grew stiff. The struggle was over. The insignificant little creature now knew death. As I looked at the dead moth, this minute wayside triumph of so great a force over so mean an antagonist filled me with wonder. Just as life had been strange a few minutes before, so death was now as strange. The moth having righted himself now lay most decently and uncomplainingly composed. O yes, he seemed to say, death is stronger than I am.

QUESTIONS

1. Trace the sequence in which Woolf comes to identify with the moth. How does she make her identification explicit? How is it implicit in the language she uses to describe the moth?

2. Choose one of the descriptions of a small living creature or creatures in Annie Dillard's "Sight into Insight," below, and compare it with Woolf's description of the moth. Does a similar identification take place in Dillard's essay? If so, how; if not, why not?

3. Henry David Thoreau, in "The Battle of the Ants" (p. 758), also humanizes small living creatures. How do his strategies differ from Woolf's?

4. Write two descriptions of the same living creature, one using Woolf's strategies, the other using Thoreau's. Or, alternatively, write an essay in which you analyze the differences between them.

ANNIE DILLARD

Sight into Insight

WHEN I WAS SIX OR SEVEN YEARS OLD, growing up in Pittsburgh, I used to take a penny of my own and hide it for someone else to find. It was a curious compulsion; sadly, I've never been seized by it since. For some reason I always "hid" the penny along the same stretch of sidewalk up the street. I'd cradle it at the roots of a maple, say, or in a hole left by a chipped-off piece of sidewalk. Then I'd take a piece of chalk and, starting at either end of the block, draw huge arrows leading up to the penny from both directions. After I learned to write I labeled the arrows "SURPRISE AHEAD" or "MONEY THIS WAY." I was greatly excited, during all this arrowdrawing, at the thought of the first lucky passerby who would receive in this way, regardless of merit, a free gift from the universe. But I never lurked about. I'd go straight home and not give the matter another thought, until, some months later, I would be gripped by the impulse to hide another penny.

There are lots of things to see, unwrapped gifts and free surprises. The world is fairly studded and strewn with pennies cast broadside from a generous hand. But—and this is the point—who gets excited by a mere penny? If you follow one arrow, if you crouch motionless on a bank to watch a tremulous ripple thrill on the water, and are rewarded by the sight of a muskrat kit paddling from its den, will you count that sight a chip of copper only, and go your rueful way? It is very dire poverty indeed for a man to be so malnourished and fatigued that he won't stoop to pick up a penny. But if you cultivate a healthy poverty and simplicity, so that finding a penny will make your day, then, since the world

Originally published in Harper's Magazine *(February 1974), an American monthly that explores "the issues and ideas in politics, science, and the arts that drive our national conversation"; included in Dillard's Pulitzer Prize–winning book,* Pilgrim at Tinker Creek (1974).

is in fact planted in pennies, you have with your poverty bought a lifetime of days. What you see is what you get.

Unfortunately, nature is very much a now-you-see-it, now-you-don't affair. A fish flashes, then dissolves in the water before my eyes like so much salt. Deer apparently ascend bodily into heaven; the brightest oriole fades into leaves. These disappearances stun me into stillness and concentration; they say of nature that it conceals with a grand nonchalance, and they say of vision that it is a deliberate gift, the revelation of a dancer who for my eyes only flings away her seven veils.

For nature does reveal as well as conceal: now-you-don't-see-it, now-you-do. For a week this September migrating red-winged blackbirds were feeding heavily down by Tinker Creek at the back of the house. One day I went out to investigate the racket; I walked up to a tree, an Osage orange, and a hundred birds flew away. They simply materialized out of the tree. I saw a tree, then a whisk of color, then a tree again. I walked closer and another hundred blackbirds took flight. Not a branch, not a twig budged: the birds were apparently weightless as well as invisible. Or, it was as if the leaves of the Osage orange had been freed from a spell in the form of redwinged blackbirds; they flew from the tree, caught my eye in the sky, and vanished. When I looked again at the tree, the leaves had reassembled as if nothing had happened. Finally I walked directly to the trunk of the tree and a final hundred, the real diehards, appeared, spread, and vanished. How could so many hide in the tree without my seeing them? The Osage orange, unruffled, looked just as it had looked from the house, when three hundred red-winged blackbirds cried from its crown. I looked upstream where they flew, and they were gone. Searching, I couldn't spot one. I wandered upstream to force them to play their hand, but they'd crossed the creek and scattered. One show to a customer. These appearances catch at my throat; they are the free gifts, the bright coppers at the roots of trees.

5 It's all a matter of keeping my eyes open. Nature is like one of those line drawings that are puzzles for children: Can you find hidden in the tree a duck, a house, a boy, a bucket, a giraffe, and a boot? Specialists can find the most incredibly hidden things. A book I read when I was young recommended an easy way to find caterpillars: you simply find some fresh caterpillar droppings, look up, and there's your caterpillar. More recently an author advised me to set my mind at ease about those piles of cut stems on the ground in grassy fields. Field mice make them; they cut the grass down by degrees to reach the seeds at the head. It seems that when the grass is tightly packed, as in a field of ripe grain, the blade won't topple at a single cut through the stem; instead, the cut stem simply drops vertically, held in the crush of grain. The mouse severs the bottom again and again, the stem keeps dropping an inch at a time, and finally the head is low enough for the mouse to reach the seeds. Meanwhile the mouse is positively littering the field with its little piles of cut stems into which, presumably, the author is constantly stumbling.

If I can't see these minutiae, I still try to keep my eyes open. I'm always on the lookout for ant lion traps in sandy soil, monarch pupae near milkweed, skipper larvae in locust leaves. These things are utterly common, and I've not seen one. I bang on hollow trees near water, but so far no flying squirrels have appeared. In flat country I watch every sunset in hopes of seeing the green ray. The green ray is a seldom-seen streak of light that rises from the sun like a spurting fountain at the moment of sunset; it throbs into the sky for two seconds and disappears. One more reason to keep my eyes open. A photography professor at the University of Florida just happened to see a bird die in midflight; it jerked, died, dropped, and smashed on the ground.

I squint at the wind because I read Stewart Edward White: "I have always maintained that if you looked closely enough you could *see* the wind—the dim, hardly-made-out, fine débris fleeing high in the air." White was an excellent observer, and devoted an entire chapter of *The Mountains* to the subject of seeing deer: "As soon as you can forget the naturally obvious and construct an artificial obvious, then you too will see deer."

But the artificial obvious is hard to see. My eyes account for less than 1 percent of the weight of my head; I'm bony and dense; I see what I expect. I once spent a full three minutes looking at a bullfrog that was so unexpectedly large I couldn't see it even though a dozen enthusiastic campers were shouting directions. Finally I asked, "What color am I looking for?" and a fellow said, "Green." When at last I picked out the frog, I saw what painters are up against: the thing wasn't green at all, but the color of wet hickory bark.

The lover can see, and the knowledgeable. I visited an aunt and uncle at a quarter-horse ranch in Cody, Wyoming. I couldn't do much of anything useful, but I could, I thought, draw. So, as we all sat around the kitchen table after supper, I produced a sheet of paper and drew a horse. "That's one lame horse," my aunt volunteered. The rest of the family joined in: "Only place to saddle that one is his neck"; "Looks like we better shoot the poor thing, on account of those terrible growths." Meekly, I slid the pencil and paper down the table. Everyone in that family, including my three young cousins, could draw a horse. Beautifully. When the paper came back it looked as though five shining, real quarter horses had been corraled by mistake with a papier-mâché moose; the real horses seemed to gaze at the monster with a steady, puzzled air. I stay away from horses now, but I can do a creditable goldfish. The point is that I just don't know what the lover knows; I just can't see the artificial obvious that those in the know construct. The herpetologist asks the native, "Are there snakes in that ravine?" "Nosir." And the herpetologist comes home with, yessir, three bags full. Are there butterflies on that mountain? Are the bluets in bloom, are there arrowheads here, or fossil shells in the shale?

Peeping through my keyhole I see within the range of only about 30 percent of the light that comes from the sun; the rest is infrared and some little ultraviolet, perfectly apparent to many animals, but invisible to me. A nightmare network of ganglia, charged and firing without my knowledge, cuts and splices what I do see, editing it for my brain. Donald E. Carr points out that the sense impressions of one-celled animals are *not* edited for the brain: "This is philosophically interesting in a rather mournful way, since it means that only the simplest animals perceive the universe as it is." 10

A fog that won't burn away drifts and flows across my field of vision. When you see fog move against a backdrop of deep pines, you don't see the fog itself, but streaks of clearness floating across the air in dark shreds. So I see only tatters of clearness through a pervading obscurity. I can't distinguish the fog from the overcast sky; I can't be sure if the light is direct or reflected. Everywhere darkness and the presence of the unseen appalls. We estimate now that only one atom dances alone in every cubic meter of intergalactic space. I blink and squint. What planet or power yanks Halley's Comet out of orbit? We haven't seen it yet; it's a question of distance, density, and the pallor of reflected light. We rock, cradled in the swaddling band of darkness. Even the simple darkness of night whispers suggestions to the mind. This summer, in August, I stayed at the creek too late.

Where Tinker Creek flows under the sycamore log bridge to the tear-shaped island, it is slow and shallow, fringed thinly in cattail marsh. At this spot an astonishing bloom of life supports vast breeding populations of insects, fish, reptiles, birds, and mammals. On windless summer evenings I stalk along the creek bank or straddle the sycamore log in absolute stillness, watching for muskrats. The night I stayed too late I was hunched on the log staring spellbound at spreading, reflected stains of lilac on the water. A cloud in the sky suddenly lighted as if turned on by a switch; its reflection just as suddenly materialized on the water upstream, flat and floating, so that I couldn't see the creek bottom, or life in the water under the cloud. Downstream, away from the cloud on the water, water turtles smooth as beans were gliding down with the current in a series of easy, weightless push-offs, as men bound on the moon. I didn't know whether to trace the progress of one turtle I was sure of, risking sticking my face in one of the bridge's spider webs made invisible by the gathering dark, or take a chance on seeing the carp, or scan the mudbank in hope of seeing a muskrat, or follow the last of the swallows who caught at my heart and trailed it after them like streamers as they appeared from directly below, under the log, flying upstream with their tails forked, so fast.

But shadows spread and deepened and stayed. After thousands of years we're still strangers to darkness, fearful aliens in an enemy camp with our arms crossed over our chests. I stirred. A land turtle on the bank, startled, hissed the air from its lungs and withdrew to its shell. An uneasy pink here, an unfathomable blue there, gave great suggestion of lurking beings. Things were going on. I couldn't see whether that rustle I heard was a distant rattlesnake, slit-eyed, or a nearby sparrow kicking in the dry flood debris slung at the foot of a willow. Tremendous action roiled the water everywhere I looked, big action, inexplicable. A tremor welled up beside a gaping muskrat burrow in the bank and I caught my breath, but no muskrat appeared. The ripples continued to fan upstream with a steady, powerful thrust. Night was knitting an eyeless mask over my face, and I still sat transfixed. A distant airplane, a delta wing out of nightmare, made a gliding shadow on the creek's bottom that looked like a stingray cruising upstream. At once a black fin slit the pink cloud on the water, shearing it in two. The two halves merged together and seemed to dissolve before my eyes. Darkness pooled in the cleft of the creek and rose, as water collects in a well.

Untamed, dreaming lights flickered over the sky. I saw hints of hulking underwater shadows, two pale splashes out of the water, and round ripples rolling close together from a blackened center.

At last I stared upstream where only the deepest violet remained of the cloud, a cloud so high its underbelly still glowed, its feeble color reflected from a hidden sky lighted in turn by a sun halfway to China. And out of that violet, a sudden enormous black body arced over the water. Head and tail, if there was a head and tail, were both submerged in cloud. I saw only one ebony fling, a headlong dive to darkness; then the waters closed, and the lights went out.

I walked home in a shivering daze, up hill and down. Later I lay openmouthed in bed, my arms flung wide at my sides to steady the whirling darkness. At this latitude I'm spinning 836 miles an hour round the earth's axis; I feel my sweeping fall as a breakneck arc like the dive of dolphins, and the hollow rushing of wind raises the hairs on my neck and the side of my face. In orbit around the sun I'm moving 64,800 miles an hour. The solar system as a whole, like a merry-go-round unhinged, spins, bobs, and blinks at the speed of 43,200 miles an hour along a course set east of Hercules. Someone has piped, and we are dancing a tarantella until the sweat pours. I open my eyes and I see dark, muscled forms curl out of water, with flapping gills and flattened eyes. I close my eyes and I see stars, deep stars giving way to deeper stars, deeper stars bowing to deepest stars at the crown of an infinite cone. 15

"Still," wrote Van Gogh[1] in a letter, "a great deal of light falls on everything." If we are blinded by darkness, we are also blinded by light. Sometimes here in Virginia at sunset low clouds on the southern or northern horizon are completely invisible in the lighted sky. I only know one is there because I can see its reflection in still water. The first time I discovered this mystery I looked from cloud to no-cloud in bewilderment, checking my bearings over and over, thinking maybe the ark of the covenant[2] was just passing by south of Dead Man Mountain. Only much later did I learn the explanation: polarized light from the sky is very much weakened by reflection, but the light in clouds isn't polarized. So invisible clouds pass among visible clouds, till all slide over the mountains; so a greater light extinguishes a lesser as though it didn't exist.

In the great meteor shower of August, the Perseid, I wail all day for the shooting stars I miss. They're out there showering down committing hara-kiri in a flame of fatal attraction, and hissing perhaps at last into the ocean. But at dawn what looks like a blue dome clamps down over me like a lid on a pot. The stars and planets could smash and I'd never know. Only a piece of ashen moon occasionally climbs up or down the inside of the dome, and our local star without surcease explodes on our heads. We have really only that one light, one source for all power, and yet we must turn away from it by universal decree. Nobody here on the planet seems aware of this strange, powerful taboo, that we

1. Vincent van Gogh (1853–1890), Dutch Postimpressionist painter.

2. Repository for the stone tablets of the Ten Commandments, carried by the ancient Israelites during their desert wanderings.

all walk about carefully averting our faces, this way and that, lest our eyes be blasted forever.

Darkness appalls and light dazzles; the scrap of visible light that doesn't hurt my eyes hurts my brain. What I see sets me swaying. Size and distance and the sudden swelling of meanings confuse me, bowl me over. I straddle the sycamore log bridge over Tinker Creek in the summer. I look at the lighted creek bottom: snail tracks tunnel the mud in quavering curves. A crayfish jerks, but by the time I absorb what has happened, he's gone in a billowing smoke screen of silt. I look at the water; minnows and shiners. If I'm thinking minnows, a carp will fill my brain till I scream. I look at the water's surface: skaters, bubbles, and leaves sliding down. Suddenly, my own face, reflected, startles me witless. Those snails have been tracking my face! Finally, with a shuddering wrench of the will, I see clouds, cirrus clouds. I'm dizzy, I fall in.

This looking business is risky. Once I stood on a humped rock on nearby Purgatory Mountain, watching through binoculars the great autumn hawk migration below, until I discovered that I was in danger of joining the hawks on a vertical migration of my own. I was used to binoculars, but not, apparently, to balancing on humped rocks while looking through them. I reeled. Everything advanced and receded by turns; the world was full of unexplained foreshortenings and depths. A distant huge object, a hawk the size of an elephant, turned out to be the browned bough of a nearby loblolly pine. I followed a sharp-shinned hawk against a featureless sky, rotating my head unawares as it flew, and when I lowered the glass a glimpse of my own looming shoulder sent me staggering. What prevents the men at Palomar[3] from falling, voiceless and blinded, from their tiny, vaulted chairs?

20 I reel in confusion: I don't understand what I see. With the naked eye I can see two million light-years to the Andromeda galaxy. Often I slop some creek water in a jar, and when I get home I dump it in a white china bowl. After the silt settles I return and see tracings of minute snails on the bottom, a planarian or two winding round the rim of water, roundworms shimmying, frantically, and finally, when my eyes have adjusted to these dimensions, amoebae. At first the amoebae look like *muscae volitantes,* those curled moving spots you seem to see in your eyes when you stare at a distant wall. Then I see the amoebae as drops of water congealed, bluish, translucent, like chips of sky in the bowl. At length I choose one individual and give myself over to its idea of an evening. I see it dribble a grainy foot before it on its wet, unfathomable way. Do its unedited sense impressions include the fierce focus of my eyes? Shall I take it outside and show it Andromeda, and blow its little endoplasm? I stir the water with a finger, in case it's running out of oxygen. Maybe I should get a tropical aquarium with motorized bubblers and lights, and keep this one for a pet. Yes, it would tell its fissioned descendants, the universe is two feet by five, and if you listen closely you can hear the buzzing music of the spheres.

Oh, it's mysterious, lamplit evenings here in the galaxy, one after the other. It's one of those nights when I wander from window to window, looking for a

3. An astronomical observatory in California.

sign. But I can't see. Terror and a beauty insoluble are a riband of blue woven into the fringe of garments of things both great and small. No culture explains, no bivouac offers real haven or rest. But it could be that we are not seeing something. Galileo[4] thought comets were an optical illusion. This is fertile ground: since we are certain that they're not, we can look at what our scientists have been saying with fresh hope. What if there are *really* gleaming, castellated cities hung up-side-down over the desert sand? What limpid lakes and cool date palms have our caravans always passed untried? Until, one by one, by the blindest of leaps, we light on the road to these places, we must stumble in darkness and hunger. I turn from the window. I'm blind as a bat, sensing only from every direction the echo of my own thin cries.

I chanced on a wonderful book called *Space and Sight,* by Marius Von Senden. When Western surgeons discovered how to perform safe cataract operations, they ranged across Europe and America operating on dozens of men and women of all ages who had been blinded by cataracts since birth. Von Senden collected accounts of such cases; the histories are fascinating. Many doctors had tested their patients' sense perceptions and ideas of space both before and after the operations. The vast majority of patients, of both sexes and all ages, had, in Von Senden's opinion, no idea of space whatsoever. Form, distance, and size were so many meaningless syllables. A patient "had no idea of depth, confusing it with roundness." Before the operation a doctor would give a blind patient a cube and a sphere; the patient would tongue it or feel it with his hands, and name it correctly. After the operation the doctor would show the same objects to the patient without letting him touch them; now he had no clue whatsoever to what he was seeing. One patient called lemonade "square" because it pricked on his tongue as a square shape pricked on the touch of his hands. Of another post-operative patient the doctor writes, "I have found in her no notion of size, for example, not even within the narrow limits which she might have encompassed with the aid of touch. Thus when I asked her to show me how big her mother was, she did not stretch out her hands, but set her two index fingers a few inches apart."

For the newly sighted, vision is pure sensation unencumbered by meaning. When a newly sighted girl saw photographs and paintings, she asked, "'Why do they put those dark marks all over them?' 'Those aren't dark marks,' her mother explained, 'those are shadows. That is one of the ways the eye knows that things have shape. If it were not for shadows, many things would look flat.' 'Well, that's how things do look,' Joan answered. 'Everything looks flat with dark patches.'"

In general the newly sighted see the world as a dazzle of "color-patches." They are pleased by the sensation of color, and learn quickly to name the colors, but the rest of seeing is tormentingly difficult. Soon after his operation a patient "generally bumps into one of these color-patches and observes them to be substantial, since they resist him as tactual objects do. In walking about it also strikes him—or can if he pays attention—that he is continually passing in

4. Italian astronomer (1564–1642).

between the colors he sees, that he can go past a visual object, that a part of it then steadily disappears from view; and that in spite of this, however he twists and turns—whether entering the room from the door, for example, or returning back to it—he always has a visual space in front of him. Thus he gradually comes to realize that there is also a space behind him, which he does not see."

25 The mental effort involved in these reasonings proves overwhelming for many patients. It oppresses them to realize that they have been visible to people all along, perhaps unattractively so, without their knowledge or consent. A disheartening number of them refuse to use their new vision, continuing to go over objects with their tongues, and lapsing into apathy and despair.

On the other hand, many newly sighted people speak well of the world, and teach us how dull our own vision is. To one patient, a human hand, unrecognized, is "something bright and then holes." Shown a bunch of grapes, a boy calls out, "It is dark, blue and shiny. . . . It isn't smooth, it has bumps and hollows." A little girl visits a garden. "She is greatly astonished, and can scarcely be persuaded to answer, stands speechless in front of the tree, which she only names on taking hold of it, and then as 'the tree with the lights in it.'" Another patient, a twenty-two-year-old girl, was dazzled by the world's brightness and kept her eyes shut for two weeks. When at the end of that time she opened her eyes again, she did not recognize any objects, but "the more she now directed her gaze upon everything about her, the more it could be seen how an expression of gratification and astonishment overspread her features; she repeatedly exclaimed: 'Oh God! How beautiful!'"

I saw color-patches for weeks after I read this wonderful book. It was summer; the peaches were ripe in the valley orchards. When I woke in the morning, color-patches wrapped round my eyes, intricately, leaving not one unfilled spot. All day long I walked among shifting color-patches that parted before me like the Red Sea and closed again in silence,[5] transfigured, wherever I looked back. Some patches swelled and loomed, while others vanished utterly, and dark marks flitted at random over the whole dazzling sweep. But I couldn't sustain the illusion of flatness. I've been around for too long. Form is condemned to an eternal danse macabre with meaning: I couldn't unpeach the peaches. Nor can I remember ever having seen without understanding; the color-patches of infancy are lost. My brain then must have been smooth as any balloon. I'm told I reached for the moon; many babies do. But the color-patches of infancy swelled as meaning filled them; they arrayed themselves in solemn ranks down distance which unrolled and stretched before me like a plain. The moon rocketed away. I live now in a world of shadows that shape and distance color, a world where space makes a kind of terrible sense. What Gnosticism[6] is this, and what physics? The fluttering patch I saw in my nursery window—silver and green and shapeshifting blue—is gone; a row of Lombardy poplars takes its place, mute, across the distant lawn. That humming oblong creature pale as light that stole along

5. According to the Bible, the Red Sea parted for the Israelites and closed over the Egyptians pursuing them (Exodus 15).

6. Promise of secret knowledge of the divine.

the walls of my room at night, stretching exhilaratingly around the corners, is gone, too, gone the night I ate of the bittersweet fruit, put two and two together and puckered forever my brain. Martin Buber[7] tells this tale: "Rabbi Mendel once boasted to his teacher Rabbi Elimelekh that evenings he saw the angel who rolls away the light before the darkness, and mornings the angel who rolls away the darkness before the light. 'Yes,' said Rabbi Elimelekh, 'in my youth I saw that too. Later on you don't see these things anymore.'"

Why didn't someone hand those newly sighted people paints and brushes from the start, when they still didn't know what anything was? Then maybe we all could see color-patches too, the world unraveled from reason, Eden before Adam gave names. The scales would drop from my eyes; I'd see trees like men walking; I'd run down the road against all orders, hallooing and leaping.

Seeing is of course very much a matter of verbalization. Unless I call my attention to what passes before my eyes, I simply won't see it. If Tinker Mountain erupted, I'd be likely to notice. But if I want to notice the lesser cataclysms of valley life, I have to maintain in my head a running description of the present. It's not that I'm observant; it's just that I talk too much. Otherwise, especially in a strange place, I'll never know what's happening. Like a blind man at the ball game, I need a radio.

When I see this way I analyze and pry. I hurl over logs and roll away stones; 30 I study the bank a square foot at a time, probing and tilting my head. Some days when a mist covers the mountains, when the muskrats won't show and the microscope's mirror shatters, I want to climb up the blank blue dome as a man would storm the inside of a circus tent, wildly, dangling, and with a steel knife claw a rent in the top, peep, and, if I must, fall.

But there is another kind of seeing that involves a letting go. When I see this way I sway transfixed and emptied. The difference between the two ways of seeing is the difference between walking with and without a camera. When I walk with a camera I walk from shot to shot, reading the light on a calibrated meter. When I walk without a camera, my own shutter opens, and the moment's light prints on my own silver gut. When I see this second way I am above all an unscrupulous observer.

It was sunny one evening last summer at Tinker Creek; the sun was low in the sky, upstream. I was sitting on the sycamore log bridge with the sunset at my back, watching the shiners the size of minnows who were feeding over the muddy sand in skittery schools. Again and again, one fish, then another, turned for a split second across the current and flash! the sun shot out from its silver side. I couldn't watch for it. It was always just happening somewhere else, and it drew my vision just as it disappeared: flash! like a sudden dazzle of the thinnest blade, a sparking over a dun and olive ground at chance intervals from every direction. Then I noticed white specks, some sort of pale petals, small, floating from under my feet on the creek's surface, very slow and steady. So I blurred my eyes and gazed toward the brim of my hat and saw a new world. I saw the pale

7. Jewish religious philosopher (1878–1965).

white circles roll up, roll up, like the world's turning, mute and perfect, and I saw the linear flashes, gleaming silver, like stars being born at random down a rolling scroll of time. Something broke and something opened. I filled up like a new wineskin. I breathed an air like light; I saw a light like water. I was the lip of a fountain the creek filled forever; I was ether, the leaf in the zephyr; I was flesh-flake, feather, bone.

When I see this way I see truly. As Thoreau[8] says, I return to my senses. I am the man who watches the baseball game in silence in an empty stadium. I see the game purely; I'm abstracted and dazed. When it's all over and the white-suited players lope off the green field to their shadowed dugouts, I leap to my feet, I cheer and cheer.

But I can't go out and try to see this way. I'll fail, I'll go mad. All I can do is try to gag the commentator, to hush the noise of useless interior babble that keeps me from seeing just as surely as a newspaper dangled before my eyes. The effort is really a discipline requiring a lifetime of dedicated struggle; it marks the literature of saints and monks of every order east and west, under every rule and no rule, discalced[9] and shod. The world's spiritual geniuses seem to discover universally that the mind's muddy river, this ceaseless flow of trivia and trash, cannot be dammed, and that trying to dam it is a waste of effort that might lead to madness. Instead you must allow the muddy river to flow unheeded in the dim channels of consciousness; you raise your sights; you look along it, mildly, acknowledging its presence without interest and gazing beyond it into the realm of the real where subjects and objects act and rest purely, without utterance. "Launch into the deep," says Jacques Ellul,[10] "and you shall see."

35 The secret of seeing, then, is the pearl of great price. If I thought he could teach me to find it and keep it forever I would stagger barefoot across a hundred deserts after any lunatic at all. But although the pearl may be found, it may not be sought. The literature of illumination reveals this above all: although it comes to those who wait for it, it is always, even to the most practiced and adept, a gift and a total surprise. I return from one walk knowing where the killdeer nests in the field by the creek and the hour the laurel blooms. I return from the same walk a day later scarcely knowing my own name. Litanies hum in my ears; my tongue flaps in my mouth, *Alim non,* alleluia![11] I cannot cause light; the most I can do is try to put myself in the path of its beam. It is possible, in deep space, to sail on solar wind. Light, be it particle or wave, has force: you rig a giant sail and go. The secret of seeing is to sail on solar wind. Hone and spread your spirit till you yourself are a sail, whetted, translucent, broadside to the merest puff.

8. Henry David Thoreau (1817–1862), American writer; see "Where I Lived, and What I Lived For" (p. 1098).

9. Shoeless, as the order of the Discalced Carmelites.

10. French Protestant theologian and critic of technology (1912–1994).

11. To paraphrase, "A Muslim learned man no, praise ye Jehovah!"

When her doctor took her bandages off and led her into the garden, the girl who was no longer blind saw "the tree with the lights in it." It was for this tree I searched through the peach orchards of summer, in the forests of fall and down winter and spring for years. Then one day I was walking along Tinker Creek thinking of nothing at all and I saw the tree with the lights in it. I saw the backyard cedar where the mourning doves roost charged and transfigured, each cell buzzing with flame. I stood on the grass with the lights in it, grass that was wholly fire, utterly focused and utterly dreamed. It was less like seeing than like being for the first time seen, knocked breathless by a powerful glance. The flood of fire abated, but I'm still spending the power. Gradually the lights went out in the cedar, the colors died, the cells unflamed and disappeared. I was still ringing. I had been my whole life a bell, and never knew it until at that moment I was lifted and struck. I have since only very rarely seen the tree with the lights in it. The vision comes and goes, mostly goes, but I live for it, for the moment when the mountains open and a new light roars in spate through the crack, and the mountains slam.

Questions

1. Dillard works by accumulation: she heaps up examples. Sometimes, not always, they are accompanied by a terse, apothegmatic general statement, such as "nature is very much a now-you-see-it, now-you-don't affair" (paragraph 3). Locate other examples of these accumulations; mark the general statements that accompany them. What uses do these accumulations serve? In what kinds of writing are they appropriate, in what kinds inappropriate?

2. How does the kind of seeing Dillard describes at the end of her essay differ from the kind of seeing she describes at the beginning? How does the material that appears in the sections on sight help her describe insight?

3. Take one of Dillard's terse, apothegmatic general statements and write your own accumulation of examples for it.

4. Dillard says, "I see what I expect" (paragraph 8). Write a description of something familiar, paying attention to how you "edit" your seeing. Then write a parallel description of it as if you were seeing it "unedited," as Dillard tries to see "color-patches" like the newly sighted do (paragraph 27).

Plato

The Allegory of the Cave

And now, I said, let me show in a figure how far our nature is enlightened or unenlightened: Behold! human beings living in an underground den, which has a mouth open toward the light and reaching all along the den; here they have been from their childhood, and have their legs and necks chained so that they cannot move, and can only see before them, being prevented by the chains from turning round their heads. Above and behind them a fire is blazing at a distance, and between the fire and the prisoners there is a raised way; and you will see, if you look, a low wall built along the way, like the screen which marionette players have in front of them, over which they show the puppets.

I see.

And do you see, I said, men passing along the wall carrying all sorts of vessels, and statues and figures of animals made of wood and stone and various materials, which appear over the wall? Some of them are talking, others silent.

You have shown me a strange image, and they are strange prisoners.

5 Like ourselves, I replied; and they see only their own shadows, or the shadows of one another, which the fire throws on the opposite wall of the cave?

True, he said; how could they see anything but the shadows if they were never allowed to move their heads?

And of the objects which are being carried in like manner they would only see the shadows?

Yes, he said.

And if they were able to converse with one another, would they not suppose that they were naming what was actually before them?

10 Very true.

And suppose further that the prison had an echo which came from the other side, would they not be sure to fancy when one of the passers-by spoke that the voice which they heard came from the passing shadow?

No question, he replied.

To them, I said, the truth would be literally nothing but the shadows of the images.

That is certain.

15 And now look again, and see what will naturally follow if the prisoners are released and disabused of their error. At first, when any of them is liberated and compelled suddenly to stand up and turn his neck round and walk and look toward the light, he will suffer sharp pains; the glare will distress him and he will be unable to see the realities of which in his former state he had seen the shadows; and then conceive some one saying to him, that what he saw before was an illusion, but that now, when he is approaching nearer to being and his

From the Republic, *a dialogue in ten books written by Plato in the early years of his Academy, a school he founded (c. 380* B.C.E.*) to give a philosophical education to men embarking on political careers. In this section Socrates questions Glaucon, a student.*

eye is turned toward more real existence, he has a clearer vision—what will be his reply? And you may further imagine that his instructor is pointing to the objects as they pass and requiring him to name them—will he not be perplexed? Will he not fancy that the shadows which he formerly saw are truer than the objects which are now shown to him?

Far truer.

And if he is compelled to look straight at the light, will he not have a pain in his eyes which will make him turn away to take refuge in the objects of vision which he can see, and which he will conceive to be in reality clearer than the things which are now being shown to him?

True, he said.

And suppose once more, that he is reluctantly dragged up a steep and rugged ascent, and held fast until he is forced into the presence of the sun himself, is he not likely to be pained and irritated? When he approaches the light his eyes will be dazzled and he will not be able to see anything at all of what are now called realities.

Not all in a moment, he said. 20

He will require to grow accustomed to the sight of the upper world. And first he will see the shadows best, next the reflections of men and other objects in the water, and then the objects themselves; then he will gaze upon the light of the moon and the stars and the spangled heaven; and he will see the sky and the stars by night better than the sun or the light of the sun by day?

Certainly.

Last of all he will be able to see the sun, and not mere reflections of him in the water, but he will see him in his own proper place, and not in another; and he will contemplate him as he is.

Certainly.

He will then proceed to argue that this is he who gives the season and the years, and is the guardian of all that is in the visible world, and in a certain way the cause of all things which he and his fellows have been accustomed to behold? 25

Clearly, he said, he would first see the sun and then reason about him.

And when he remembered his old habitation, and the wisdom of the den and his fellow-prisoners, do you not suppose that he would felicitate himself on the change, and pity them?

Certainly, he would.

And if they were in the habit of conferring honors among themselves on those who were quickest to observe the passing shadows and to remark which of them went before, and which followed after, and which were together; and who were therefore best able to draw conclusions as to the future, do you think that he would care for such honors and glories, or envy the possessors of them? Would he not say with Homer,

> Better to be the poor servant of a poor master,

and to endure anything, rather than think as they do and live after their manner?

30 Yes, he said, I think that he would rather suffer anything than entertain these false notions and live in this miserable manner.

Imagine once more, I said, such an one coming suddenly out of the sun to be replaced in his old situation; would he not be certain to have his eyes full of darkness?

To be sure, he said.

And if there were a contest, and he had to compete in measuring the shadows with the prisoners who had never moved out of the den, while his sight was still weak, and before his eyes had become steady (and the time which would be needed to acquire this new habit of sight might be very considerable) would he not be ridiculous? Men would say of him that up he went and down he came without his eyes; and that it was better not even to think of ascending; and if any one tried to loose another and lead him up to the light, let them only catch the offender, and they would put him to death.

No question, he said.

35 This entire allegory, I said, you may now append, dear Glaucon, to the previous argument; the prison-house is the world of sight, the light of the fire is the sun, and you will not misapprehend me if you interpret the journey upwards to be the ascent of the soul into the intellectual world according to my poor belief, which, at your desire, I have expressed—whether rightly or wrongly God knows. But, whether true or false, my opinion is that in the world of knowledge the idea of good appears last of all, and is seen only with an effort; and, when seen, is also inferred to be the universal author of all things beautiful and right, parent of light and of the lord of light in this visible world, and the immediate source of reason and truth in the intellectual; and that this is the power upon which he who would act rationally either in public or private life must have his eye fixed.

I agree, he said, as far as I am able to understand you.

Moreover, I said, you must not wonder that those who attain to this beatific vision are unwilling to descend to human affairs; for their souls are ever hastening into the upper world where they desire to dwell; which desire of theirs is very natural, if our allegory may be trusted.

Yes, very natural.

And is there anything surprising in one who passes from divine contemplations to the evil state of man, misbehaving himself in a ridiculous manner; if, while his eyes are blinking and before he has become accustomed to the surrounding darkness, he is compelled to fight in courts of law, or in other places, about the images or the shadows of images of justice, and is endeavoring to meet the conceptions of those who have never yet seen absolute justice?

40 Anything but surprising, he replied.

Any one who has common sense will remember that the bewilderments of the eyes are of two kinds, and arise from two causes, either from coming out of the light or from going into the light, which is true of the mind's eye, quite as much as of the bodily eye; and he who remembers this when he sees any one whose vision is perplexed and weak, will not be too ready to laugh; he will first ask whether that soul of man has come out of the brighter life, and is unable to see because unaccustomed to the dark, or having turned from darkness to the day is dazzled by excess of light. And he will count the one happy in his condition and state of being, and he will pity the other; or, if he have a mind to laugh at the soul which comes from below into the light, there will be more reason in this than in the laugh which greets him who returns from above out of the light into the den.

That, he said, is a very just distinction.

Questions

1. This essay uses Socratic dialogue, a question-and-answer form in which characters discuss moral and philosophical problems, usually with a philosopher-teacher instructing a student. Locate the key questions the teacher poses, and answer them in your own terms. Do your answers correspond with those of Glaucon, the Platonic student? If not, why?

2. Plato begins with an analogy (or allegory) in which he likens human knowledge to visual sight in an underground den. Locate Plato's interpretation of this allegory. What points does he derive from it?

3. Try writing an allegory in which you characterize some aspect of human existence, and embed your interpretation within your essay.

Jesus

Parables of the Kingdom

The Ten Virgins

Then shall the kingdom of heaven be likened unto ten virgins, which took their lamps, and went forth to meet the bridegroom.

And five of them were wise, and five were foolish.

They that were foolish took their lamps, and took no oil with them:

But the wise took oil in their vessels with their lamps.

While the bridegroom tarried, they all slumbered and slept. 5

And at midnight there was a cry made, Behold, the bridegroom cometh; go ye out to meet him.

Then all those virgins arose, and trimmed their lamps.

And the foolish said unto the wise, Give us of your oil; for our lamps are gone out.

But the wise answered, saying Not so; lest there be not enough for us and you: but go ye rather to them that sell, and buy for yourselves.

And while they went to buy, the bridgroom came; and they that were ready went in with him to the marriage: and the door was shut. 10

Afterward came also the other virgins, saying, Lord, Lord, open to us.

From Jesus's teachings, as written in Matthew 25 and Luke 15, King James Bible (1611).

But he answered and said, Verily I say unto you, I know you not.

Watch therefore, for ye know neither the day nor the hour wherein the Son of man cometh.

The Ten Talents

For the kingdom of heaven is as a man travelling into a far country, who called his own servants, and delivered unto them his goods.

And unto one he gave five talents,[1] to another two, and to another one; to every man according to his several ability; and straightway took his journey.

Then he that had received the five talents went and traded with the same, and made them other five talents.

And likewise he that had received two, he also gained other two.

5 But he that had received one went and digged in the earth, and hid his lord's money.

After a long time the lord of those servants cometh, and reckoneth with them.

And so he that had received five talents came and brought other five talents, saying, Lord, thou deliveredst unto me five talents: behold, I have gained beside them five talents more.

His lord said unto him, Well done, thou good and faithful servant: thou hast been faithful over a few things, I will make thee ruler over many things: enter thou into the joy of thy lord.

He also that had received two talents came and said, Lord, thou deliverdst unto me two talents: behold, I have gained two other talents beside them.

10 His lord said unto him, Well done, good and faithful servant; thou hast been faithful over a few things, I will make thee ruler over many things: enter thou into the joy of thy lord.

Then he which had received the one talent came and said, Lord, I knew thee that thou art an hard man, reaping where thou hast not sown, and gathering where thou hast not strawed:

And I was afraid, and went and hid thy talent in the earth: lo, there thou hast that is thine.

His lord answered and said unto him, Thou wicked and slothful servant, thou knewest that I reap where I sowed not, and gather where I have not strawed:

Thou oughtest therefore to have put my money to the exchanges, and then at my coming I should have received mine own with usury.

15 Take therefore the talent from him, and give it unto him which hath ten talents.

For unto every one that hath shall be given, and he shall have abundance: but from him that hath not shall be taken away even that which he hath.

And cast ye the unprofitable servant into outer darkness: there shall be weeping and gnashing of teeth.

1. A talent was a Middle Eastern coin.

When the Son of man shall come in his glory, and all the holy angels with him, then shall he sit upon the throne of his glory:

And before him shall be gathered all nations: and he shall separate them one from another, as a shepherd divideth his sheep from the goats:

And he shall set the sheep on his right hand, but the goats on the left. 20

Then shall the King say unto them on his right hand, Come, ye blessed of my Father, inherit the kingdom prepared for you from the foundation of the world:

For I was an hungred, and ye gave me meat: I was thirsty, and ye gave me drink: I was a stranger, and ye took me in:

Naked, and ye clothed me: I was sick, and ye visited me: I was in prison, and ye came unto me.

Then shall the righteous answer him, saying, Lord, when saw we thee an hungred, and fed thee? or thirsty, and gave thee drink?

When saw we thee a stranger, and took thee in? or naked, and clothed thee? 25

Or when saw we thee sick, or in prison, and came unto thee?

And the King shall answer and say unto them, Verily I say unto you, Inasmuch as ye have done it unto one of the least of these my brethren, ye have done it unto me.

Then shall he say also unto them on the left hand, Depart from me, ye cursed, into everlasting fire, prepared for the devil and his angels:

For I was an hungred, and ye gave me no meat: I was thirsty, and ye gave me no drink.

I was a stranger, and ye took me not in: naked, and ye clothed me not: sick, and in prison, and ye visited me not. 30

Then shall they also answer him, saying, Lord, when saw we thee an hungred, or athirst, or a stranger, or naked, or sick, or in prison, and did not minister unto thee?

Then shall he answer them, saying, Verily I say unto you, Inasmuch as ye did it not to one of the least of these, ye did it not to me.

And these shall go away into everlasting punishment: but the righteous into life eternal.

The Prodigal Son

And he said, A certain man had two sons;

And the younger of them said to his father, Father, give me the portion of goods that falleth to me. And he divided unto them his living.

And not many days after that, the younger son gathered all together, and took his journey into a far country, and there wasted his substance with riotous living.

And when he had spent all, there arose a mighty famine in that land; and he began to be in want.

And he went and joined himself to a citizen of that country; and he sent him into his fields to feed swine. 5

And he would fain have filled his belly with the husks that the swine did eat; and no man gave unto him.

And when he came to himself, he said, How many of my father's hired servants have bread enough and to spare, and I perish with hunger!

I will arise and go to my father, and will say unto him, Father, I have sinned against heaven, and before thee,

And am no more worthy to be called thy son; make me as one of thy hired servants.

10 And he arose, and came to his father. But when he was yet a great way off, his father saw him, and had compassion, and ran, and fell on his neck, and kissed him.

And the son said unto him, Father, I have sinned against heaven, and in thy sight, and am no more worthy to be called thy son.

But the father said to his servants, Bring forth the best robe, and put it on him; and put a ring on his hand, and shoes on his feet.

And bring the fatted calf, and kill it; and let us eat, and be merry.

For this, my son, was dead, and is alive again; he was lost, and is found. And they began to be merry.

15 Now his elder son was in the field; and as he came and drew nigh to the house, he heard music and dancing.

And he called one of the servants, and asked what these things meant.

And he said unto him, Thy brother is come; and thy father hath killed the fatted calf, because he hath received him safe and sound.

And he was angry, and would not go in; therefore came his father out, and entreated him.

And he, answering, said to his father, Lo, these many years do I serve thee, neither transgressed I at any time thy commandment; and yet thou never gavest me a kid, that I might make merry with my friends.

20 But as soon as this, thy son, was come, who hath devoured thy living with harlots, thou hast killed for him the fatted calf.

And he said unto him, Son, thou art ever with me, and all that I have is thine.

It was meet that we should make merry, and be glad; for this, thy brother, was dead, and is alive again; and was lost, and is found.

QUESTIONS

1. Many parables end with a moral explicitly stated. What explicit lessons does Jesus append to his parables?

2. Is it possible to deduce more than one moral from a biblical parable? Try writing additional or alternative morals that you might draw from one of Jesus' parables.

3. Write a parable that, while using narrative form, has a moral or lesson embedded within it.

Zen Parables

Muddy Road

Tanzan and Ekido were once traveling together down a muddy road. A heavy rain was still falling.

Coming around a bend, they met a lovely girl in a silk kimono and sash, unable to cross the intersection.

"Come on, girl," said Tanzan at once. Lifting her in his arms, he carried her over the mud.

Ekido did not speak again until that night when they reached a lodging temple. Then he no longer could restrain himself. "We monks don't go near females," he told Tanzan, "especially not young and lovely ones. It is dangerous. Why did you do that?"

"I left the girl there," said Tanzan. "Are you still carrying her?" 5

A Parable

Buddha told a parable in a sutra:

A man traveling across a field encountered a tiger. He fled, the tiger after him. Coming to a precipice, he caught hold of the root of a wild vine and swung himself down over the edge. The tiger sniffed at him from above. Trembling, the man looked down to where, far below, another tiger was waiting to eat him. Only the vine sustained him.

Two mice, one white and one black, little by little started to gnaw away the vine. The man saw a luscious strawberry near him. Grasping the vine with one hand, he plucked the strawberry with the other. How sweet it tasted!

Learning to Be Silent

The pupils of the Tendai school used to study meditation before Zen entered Japan. Four of them who were intimate friends promised one another to observe seven days of silence.

On the first day all were silent. Their meditation had begun auspiciously, but when night came and the oil lamps were growing dim one of the pupils could not help exclaiming to a servant: "Fix those lamps."

The second pupil was surprised to hear the first one talk. "We are not supposed to say a word," he remarked.

"You two are stupid. Why did you talk?" asked the third.

"I am the only one who has not talked," concluded the fourth pupil.

Zen Buddhists use parables, called koans, *as a means to enlightenment. These translations come from* Zen Flesh, Zen Bones *(1957).*

QUESTIONS

1. Although some parables end with an explicitly stated moral, Zen parables often do not. Which parables include an explicit lesson? Which require the reader to deduce a lesson?

2. Is it possible to deduce more than one moral from a Zen parable? Try writing two different lessons that you might draw from one Zen parable.

3. Write a Zen-like parable that uses narrative form, includes two characters, and ends with a surprising lesson.

JEAN-PAUL SARTRE *Existentialism*

MAN IS NOTHING ELSE but what he makes of himself. Such is the first principle of existentialism. It is also what is called subjectivity, the name we are labeled with when charges are brought against us. But what do we mean by this, if not that man has a greater dignity than a stone or table? For we mean that man first exists, that is, that man first of all is the being who hurls himself toward a future and who is conscious of imagining himself as being in the future. Man is at the start a plan which is aware of itself, rather than a patch of moss, a piece of garbage, or a cauliflower; nothing exists prior to this plan; there is nothing in heaven; man will be what he will have planned to be. Not what he will want to be. Because by the word "will" we generally mean a conscious decision, which is subsequent to what we have already made of ourselves. I may want to belong to a political party, write a book, get married; but all that is only a manifestation of an earlier, more spontaneous choice that is called "will." But if existence really does precede essence, man is responsible for what he is. Thus, existentialism's first move is to make every man aware of what he is and to make the full responsibility of his existence rest on him. And when we say that a man is responsible for himself, we do not only mean that he is responsible for his own individuality, but that he is responsible for all men.

The word "subjectivism" has two meanings, and our opponents play on the two. Subjectivism means, on the one hand, that an individual chooses and makes himself; and, on the other, that it is impossible for man to transcend human subjectivity. The second of these is the essential meaning of existentialism. When we say that man chooses his own self, we mean that every one of us does likewise; but we also mean by that that in making this choice he also chooses all men. In fact, in creating the man that we want to be, there is not a single one of our acts which does not at the same time create an image of man

From Sartre's classic 1947 statement of his philosophy, L'existentialisme est un humanisme *(translated variously as* Existentialism, Existentialism and Humanism, *or* Existentialism and Human Emotions*). The version printed here was translated by Bernard Frechtman.*

as we think he ought to be. To choose to be this or that is to affirm at the same time the value of what we choose, because we can never choose evil. We always choose the good, and nothing can be good for us without being good for all.

If, on the other hand, existence precedes essence, and if we grant that we exist and fashion our image at one and the same time, the image is valid for everybody and for our whole age. Thus, our responsibility is much greater than we might have supposed, because it involves all mankind. If I am a workingman and choose to join a Christian trade union rather than be a Communist, and if by being a member, I want to show that the best thing for man is resignation, that the kingdom of man is not of this world, I am not only involving my own case—I want to be resigned for everyone. As a result, my action has involved all humanity. To take a more individual matter, if I want to marry, to have children, even if this marriage depends solely on my own circumstances or passion or wish, I am involving all humanity in monogamy and not merely myself. Therefore, I am responsible for myself and for everyone else. I am creating a certain image of man of my own choosing. In choosing myself, I choose man.

This helps us understand what the actual content is of such rather grandiloquent words as anguish, forlornness, despair. As you will see, it's all quite simple.

First, what is meant by anguish? The existentialists say at once that man is anguish. What that means is this: the man who involves himself and who realizes that he is not only the person he chooses to be, but also a lawmaker who is, at the same time, choosing all mankind as well as himself, cannot help escape the feeling of his total and deep responsibility. Of course, there are many people who are not anxious; but we claim that they are hiding their anxiety, that they are fleeing from it. Certainly, many people believe that when they do something, they themselves are the only ones involved, and when someone says to them, "What if everyone acted that way?" they shrug their shoulders and answer, "Everyone doesn't act that way." But really, one should always ask himself, "What would happen if everybody looked at things that way?" There is no escaping this disturbing thought except by a kind of double-dealing. A man who lies and makes excuses for himself by saying "not everybody does that" is someone with an uneasy conscience, because the act of lying implies that a universal value is conferred upon the lie. 5

Anguish is evident even when it conceals itself. This is the anguish that Kierkegaard[1] called the anguish of Abraham. You know the story: an angel has ordered Abraham to sacrifice his son; if it really were an angel who has come and said, "You are Abraham, you shall sacrifice your son," everything would be all right. But everyone might first wonder, "Is it really an angel, and am I really Abraham? What proof do I have?"

There was a madwoman who had hallucinations; someone used to speak to her on the telephone and give her orders. Her doctor asked her, "Who is it who talks to you?" She answered, "He says it's God." What proof did she really have that it was God? If an angel comes to me, what proof is there that it's an

1. Søren Kierkegaard (1813–1855), Danish religious philosopher.

angel? And if I hear voices, what proof is there that they come from heaven and not from hell, or from the subconscious, or a pathological condition? What proves that they are addressed to me? What proof is there that I have been appointed to impose my choice and my conception of man on humanity? I'll never find any proof or sign to convince me of that. If a voice addresses me, it is always for me to decide that this is the angel's voice; if I consider that such an act is a good one, it is I who will choose to say that it is good rather than bad.

Now, I'm not being singled out as an Abraham, and yet at every moment I'm obliged to perform exemplary acts. For every man, everything happens as if all mankind had its eyes fixed on him and were guiding itself by what he does. And every man ought to say to himself, "Am I really the kind of man who has the right to act in such a way that humanity might guide itself by my actions?" And if he does not say that to himself, he is masking his anguish.

There is no question here of the kind of anguish which would lead to quietism, to inaction. It is a matter of a simple sort of anguish that anybody who has had responsibilities is familiar with. For example, when a military officer takes the responsibility for an attack and sends a certain number of men to death, he chooses to do so, and in the main he alone makes the choice. Doubtless, orders come from above, but they are too broad; he interprets them, and on this interpretation depend the lives of ten or fourteen or twenty men. In making a decision he cannot help having a certain anguish. All leaders know this anguish. That doesn't keep them from acting; on the contrary, it is the very condition of their action. For it implies that they envisage a number of possibilities, and when they choose one, they realize that it has value only because it is chosen. We shall see that this kind of anguish, which is the kind that existentialism describes, is explained, in addition, by a direct responsibility to the other men whom it involves. It is not a curtain separating us from action, but is part of action itself.

10 When we speak of forlornness, a term Heidegger[2] was fond of, we mean only that God does not exist and that we have to face all the consequences of this. This existentialist is strongly opposed to a certain kind of secular ethics which would like to abolish God with the least possible expense. About 1880, some French teachers tried to set up a secular ethics which went something like this: God is a useless and costly hypothesis; we are discarding it; but, meanwhile, in order for there to be an ethics, a society, a civilization, it is essential that certain values be taken seriously and that they be considered as having an *a priori*[3] existence. It must be obligatory, *a priori,* to be honest, not to lie, not to beat your wife, to have children, etc., etc. So we're going to try a little device which will make it possible to show that values exist all the same, inscribed in a heaven of ideas, though otherwise God does not exist. In other words—and this, I believe, is the tendency of everything called reformism in France—nothing will be changed if God does not exist. We shall find ourselves with the

2. Martin Heidegger (1889–1976), German philosopher of existential phenomenology.
3. Without examination or analysis (Latin).

same norms of honesty, progress, and humanism, and we shall have made of God an outdated hypothesis which will peacefully die off by itself.

The existentialist, on the contrary, thinks it very distressing that God does not exist, because all possibility of finding values in a heaven of ideas disappears along with Him; there can no longer be an *a priori* Good, since there is no infinite and perfect consciousness to think it. Nowhere is it written that the Good exists, that we must be honest, that we must not lie; because the fact is we are on a plane where there are only men. Dostoievsky[4] said, "If God didn't exist, everything would be possible." That is the very starting point of existentialism. Indeed, everything is permissible if God does not exist, and as a result man is forlorn, because neither within him nor without does he find anything to cling to. He can't start making excuses for himself.

If existence really does precede essence, there is no explaining things away by reference to a fixed and given human nature. In other words, there is no determinism, man is free, man is freedom. On the other hand, if God does not exist, we find no values or commands to turn to which legitimize our conduct. So, in the bright realm of values, we have no excuse behind us, nor justification before us. We are alone, with no excuses.

That is the idea I shall try to convey when I say that man is condemned to be free. Condemned, because he did not create himself, yet, in other respects is free; because, once thrown into the world, he is responsible for everything he does. The existentialist does not believe in the power of passion. He will never agree that a sweeping passion is a ravaging torrent which fatally leads a man to certain acts and is therefore an excuse. He thinks that man is responsible for his passion.

The existentialist does not think that man is going to help himself by finding in the world some omen by which to orient himself. Because he thinks that man will interpret the omen to suit himself. Therefore, he thinks that man, with no support and no aid, is condemned every moment to invent man. Ponge,[5] in a very fine article, has said, "Man is the future of man." That's exactly it. But if it is taken to mean that this future is recorded in heaven, that God sees it, then it is false, because it would really no longer be a future. If it is taken to mean that, whatever a man may be, there is a future to be forged, a virgin future before him, then this remark is sound. But then we are forlorn.

15 To give you an example which will enable you to understand forlornness better, I shall cite the case of one of my students who came to see me under the following circumstances: his father was on bad terms with his mother, and, moreover, was inclined to be a collaborationist,[6] his older brother had been killed in the German offensive of 1940, and the young man, with somewhat immature but generous feelings, wanted to avenge him. His mother lived alone

4. Fyodor Dostoyevsky (1821–1888), Russian novelist.

5. François Ponge (1899–1988), French surrealist poet.

6. After the defeat of France by Germany in 1940, a French government headquartered in Vichy collaborated with the Germans; the French National Committee of Liberation (Free French), headquartered in London, fought with the Allies against them.

with him, very much upset by the half-treason of her husband and the death of her older son; the boy was her only consolation.

The boy was faced with the choice of leaving for England and joining the Free French forces—that is, leaving his mother behind—or remaining with his mother and helping her to carry on. He was fully aware that the woman lived only for him and that his going off—and perhaps his death—would plunge her into despair. He was also aware that every act that he did for his mother's sake was a sure thing, in the sense that it was helping her to carry on, whereas every effort he made toward going off and fighting was an uncertain move which might run aground and prove completely useless; for example, on his way to England he might, while passing through Spain, be detained indefinitely in a Spanish camp; he might reach England or Algiers and be stuck in an office at a desk job. As a result, he was faced with two very different kinds of action: one, concrete, immediate, but concerning only one individual; the other concerned an incomparably vaster group, a national collectivity, but for that very reason was dubious, and might be interrupted en route. And, at the same time, he was wavering between two kinds of ethics. On the one hand, an ethics of sympathy, of personal devotion; on the other, a broader ethics, but one whose efficacy was more dubious. He had to choose between the two.

Who could help him choose? Christian doctrine? No. Christian doctrine says, "Be charitable, love your neighbor, take the more rugged path, etc., etc." But which is the more rugged path? Whom should he love as a brother? The fighting man or his mother? Which does the greater good, the vague act of fighting in a group, or the concrete one of helping a particular human being to go on living? Who can decide *a priori*? Nobody. No book of ethics can tell him. The Kantian[7] ethics says, "Never treat any person as a means, but as an end." Very well, if I stay with my mother, I'll treat her as an end and not as a means; but by virtue of this very fact, I'm running the risk of treating the people around me who are fighting, as means; and, conversely, if I go to join those who are fighting, I'll be treating them as an end, and, by doing that, I run the risk of treating my mother as a means.

If values are vague, and if they are always too broad for the concrete and specific case that we are considering, the only thing left for us is to trust our instincts. That's what this young man tried to do; and when I saw him, he said, "In the end, feeling is what counts. I ought to choose whichever pushes me in one direction. If I feel that I love my mother enough to sacrifice everything else for her—my desire for vengeance, for action, for adventure—then I'll stay with her. If, on the contrary, I feel that my love for my mother isn't enough, I'll leave."

But how is the value of a feeling determined? What gives his feeling for his mother value? Precisely the fact that he remained with her. I may say that I like so-and-so well enough to sacrifice a certain amount of money for him, but I may say so only if I've done it. I may say "I love my mother well enough to remain with her" if I have remained with her. The only way to determine the value of this affection is, precisely, to perform an act which confirms and defines it. But,

7. Immanuel Kant (1724–1804), German philosopher.

since I require this affection to justify my act, I find myself caught in a vicious circle.

On the other hand, Gide[8] has well said that a mock feeling and a true feeling are almost indistinguishable; to decide that I love my mother and will remain with her, or to remain with her by putting on an act, amount somewhat to the same thing. In other words, the feeling is formed by the acts one performs; so, I cannot refer to it in order to act upon it. Which means that I can neither seek within myself the true condition which will impel me to act, nor apply to a system of ethics for concepts which will permit me to act. You will say, "At least, he did go to a teacher for advice." But if you seek advice from a priest, for example, you have chosen this priest; you already knew, more or less, just about what advice he was going to give you. In other words, choosing your adviser is involving yourself. The proof of this is that if you are a Christian, you will say, "Consult a priest." But some priests are collaborating, some are just marking time, some are resisting. Which to choose? If the young man chooses a priest who is resisting or collaborating, he has already decided on the kind of advice he's going to get. Therefore, in coming to see me he knew the answer I was going to give him, and I had only one answer to give: "You're free, choose, that is, invent." No general ethics can show you what is to be done; there are no omens in the world. The Catholics will reply, "But there are." Granted—but, in any case, I myself choose the meaning they have.

When I was a prisoner,[9] I knew a rather remarkable young man who was a Jesuit. He had entered the Jesuit order in the following way: he had had a number of very bad breaks; in childhood, his father died, leaving him in poverty, and he was a scholarship student at a religious institution where he was constantly made to feel that he was being kept out of charity; then, he failed to get any of the honors and distinctions that children like; later on, at about eighteen, he bungled a love affair; finally, at twenty-two, he failed in military training, a childish enough matter, but it was the last straw.

This young fellow might well have felt that he had botched everything. It was a sign of something, but of what? He might have taken refuge in bitterness or despair. But he very wisely looked upon all this as a sign that he was not made for secular triumphs, and that only the triumphs of religion, holiness, and faith were open to him. He saw the hand of God in all this, and so he entered the order. Who can help seeing that he alone decided what the sign meant?

Some other interpretation might have been drawn from this series of setbacks; for example, that he might have done better to turn carpenter or revolutionist. Therefore, he is fully responsible for the interpretation. Forlornness implies that we ourselves choose our being. Forlornness and anguish go together.

As for despair, the term has a very simple meaning. It means that we shall confine ourselves to reckoning only with what depends upon our will, or on the ensemble of probabilities which make our action possible. When we want some-

8. André Gide (1864–1951), French novelist and dramatist.

9. Sartre, who served in the French army during World War II, was a prisoner of war from 1940 to 1941.

thing, we always have to reckon with probabilities. I may be counting on the arrival of a friend. The friend is coming by rail or streetcar; this supposes that the train will arrive on schedule, or that the streetcar will not jump the track. I am left in the realm of possibility; but possibilities are to be reckoned with only to the point where my action comports with the ensemble of these possibilities, and no further. The moment the possibilities I am considering are not rigorously involved by my action, I ought to disengage myself from them, because no God, no scheme, can adapt the world and its possibilities to my will. When Descartes[10] said, "Conquer yourself rather than the world," he meant essentially the same thing.

25 The Marxists to whom I have spoken reply, "You can rely on the support of others in your action, which obviously has certain limits because you're not going to live forever. That means: rely on both what others are doing elsewhere to help you, in China, in Russia, and what they will do later on, after your death, to carry on the action and lead it to its fulfillment, which will be the revolution. You even *have* to rely upon that, otherwise you're immoral." I reply at once that I will always rely on fellow-fighters insofar as these comrades are involved with me in a common struggle, in the unity of a party or a group in which I can more or less make my weight felt; that is, one whose ranks I am in as a fighter and whose movements I am aware of at every moment. In such a situation, relying on the unity and will of the party is exactly like counting on the fact that the train will arrive on time or that the car won't jump the track. But, given that man is free and that there is no human nature for me to depend on, I cannot count on men whom I do not know by relying on human goodness or man's concern for the good of society. I don't know what will become of the Russian revolution; I may make an example of it to the extent that at the present time it is apparent that the proletariat plays a part in Russia that it plays in no other nation. But I can't swear that this will inevitably lead to a triumph of the proletariat. I've got to limit myself to what I see.

Given that men are free and that tomorrow they will freely decide what man will be, I cannot be sure that, after my death, fellow-fighters will carry on my work to bring it to its maximum perfection. Tomorrow, after my death, some men may decide to set up Fascism, and the others may be cowardly and muddled enough to let them do it. Fascism will then be the human reality, so much the worse for us.

Actually, things will be as man will have decided they are to be. Does that mean that I should abandon myself to quietism? No. First, I should involve myself; then, act on the old saw, "Nothing ventured, nothing gained." Nor does it mean that I shouldn't belong to a party, but rather that I shall have no illusions and shall do what I can. For example, suppose I ask myself, "Will socialization, as such, ever come about?" I know nothing about it. All I know is that I'm going to do everything in my power to bring it about. Beyond that, I can't count on anything. Quietism is the attitude of people who say, "Let others do what I can't do." The doctrine I am presenting is the very opposite of quietism, since it

10. René Descartes (1596–1650), French philosopher, scientist, and mathematician.

declares, "There is no reality except in action." Moreover, it goes further, since it adds, "Man is nothing else than his plan; he exists only to the extent that he fulfills himself; he is therefore nothing else than the ensemble of his acts, nothing else than his life."

According to this, we can understand why our doctrine horrifies certain people. Because often the only way they can bear their wretchedness is to think, "Circumstances have been against me. What I've been and done doesn't show my true worth. To be sure, I've had no great love, no great friendship, but that's because I haven't met a man or woman who was worthy. The books I've written haven't been very good because I haven't had the proper leisure. I haven't had children to devote myself to because I didn't find a man with whom I could have spent my life. So there remains within me, unused and quite viable, a host of propensities, inclinations, possibilities, that one wouldn't guess from the mere series of things I've done."

Now, for the existentialist there is really no love other than one which manifests itself in a person's being in love. There is no genius other than one which is expressed in works of art; the genius of Proust is the sum of Proust's works; the genius of Racine is his series of tragedies.[11] Outside of that, there is nothing. Why say that Racine could have written another tragedy, when he didn't write it? A man is involved in life, leaves his impress on it, and outside of that there is nothing. To be sure, this may seem a harsh thought to someone whose life hasn't been a success. But, on the other hand, it prompts people to understand that reality alone is what counts, that dreams, expectations, and hopes warrant no more than to define a man as a disappointed dream, as miscarried hopes, as vain expectations. In other words, to define him negatively and not positively. However, when we say, "You are nothing else than your life," that does not imply that the artist will be judged solely on the basis of his works of art; a thousand other things will contribute toward summing him up. What we mean is that a man is nothing else than a series of undertakings, that he is the sum, the organization, the ensemble of the relationships which make up these undertakings.

When all is said and done, what we are accused of, at bottom, is not our pessimism, but an optimistic toughness. If people throw up to us our works of fiction in which we write about people who are soft, weak, cowardly, and sometimes even downright bad, it's not because these people are soft, weak, cowardly, or bad; because if we were to say, as Zola did,[12] that they are that way because of heredity, the workings of environment, society, because of biological or psychological determinism, people would be reassured. They would say, "Well, that's what we're like, no one can do anything about it." But when the existentialist writes about a coward, he says that this coward is responsible for his cowardice. He's not like that because he has a cowardly heart or lung or

11. Marcel Proust (1871–1922), French novelist; Jean Baptiste Racine (1639–1699), French dramatist who wrote only tragedies.

12. Émile Zola (1840–1902), French writer whose novels about a single family, *Les Rougon-Macquart*, probed the influences of heredity and environment.

brain; he's not like that on account of his physiological make-up; but he's like that because he has made himself a coward by his acts. There's no such thing as a cowardly constitution; there are nervous constitutions; there is poor blood, as the common people say, or strong constitutions. But the man whose blood is poor is not a coward on that account, for what makes cowardice is the act of renouncing or yielding. A constitution is not an act; the coward is defined on the basis of the acts he performs. People feel, in a vague sort of way, that this coward we're talking about is guilty of being a coward, and the thought frightens them. What people would like is that a coward or a hero be born that way.

From these few reflections it is evident that nothing is more unjust than the objections that have been raised against us. Existentialism is nothing else than an attempt to draw all the consequences of a coherent atheistic position. It isn't trying to plunge man into despair at all. But if one calls every attitude of unbelief despair, like the Christians, then the word is not being used in its original sense. Existentialism isn't so atheistic that it wears itself out showing that God doesn't exist. Rather, it declares that even if God did exist, that would change nothing. There you've got our point of view. Not that we believe that God exists, but we think that the problem of His existence is not the issue. In this sense existentialism is optimistic, a doctrine of action, and it is plain dishonesty for Christians to make no distinction between their own despair and ours and then to call us despairing.

QUESTIONS

1. "Existence precedes essence": this concept is central to Sartre's existential philosophy. What does he mean by it?

2. Sartre develops his essay by definition: existentialism, he says, enables us to understand the "actual content" of three terms: "anguish," "forlornness," and "despair" (paragraph 4). What are Sartre's definitions of these three terms? How does he distinguish among them?

3. Sartre says, "when we say that a man is responsible for himself, we do not only mean that he is responsible for his own individuality, but that he is responsible for all men" (paragraph 1). Write an essay explaining how, in the framework of existentialist beliefs, this paradoxical statement is true.

Authors

Edward Abbey (1927–1989)
American essayist, novelist, and self-described "agrarian anarchist." Born in Pennsylvania, Abbey lived in the Southwest from 1948, when he began his studies at the University of New Mexico, until his death. He took as his most pervasive theme the beauty of the Southwestern desert and the ways it has been despoiled by government, business, and tourism. Abbey's novels include *Fire on the Mountain* (1963), *Good News* (1980), and *The Monkey Wrench Gang* (1975), which is credited with helping to inspire the radical environmentalist movement. He published several collections of essays, among them *Abbey's Road* (1979), *Beyond the Wall: Essays from the Outside* (1984), *One Life at a Time, Please* (1988), and, most famously, *Desert Solitaire* (1968), drawing on his years as a ranger in the national parks of southern Utah. See also abbeyweb.net.

Philip Alcabes (b. 1954)
American epidemiologist and essayist. Alcabes earned his B.S. at Union College, his M.A. at the University of California, Berkeley, his M.P.H. at Columbia University, and his Ph.D. at Johns Hopkins University. He is a professor at Hunter College of the City University of New York and a consultant on public health issues such as AIDS prevention. Alcabes has published in scholarly journals such as the *Journal of the American Medical Association*, the *American Journal of Epidemiology*, and the *New England Journal of Medicine*. Known for his willingness to challenge prevailing public health orthodoxies, Alcabes's essays have appeared in *The American Scholar*, *The Chronicle of Higher Education*, and the *Washington Post*. See also philipalcabes.com.

Sherman Alexie (b. 1966)
American poet, novelist, and short story writer. Alexie left the Spokane Indian Reservation in Wellpinit, Washington, to pursue his education at a high school where the only other Indian was the school mascot. He then attended Gonzaga University and graduated from Washington State University in Pullman. His first collection of poems, *The Business of Fancydancing* (1991), was named a *New York Times* Notable Book of the Year in 1992. Since then he has depicted the lives of contemporary Native Americans in eleven more volumes of poetry, three novels including *Flight* (2007), several collections of short stories such as *The Lone Ranger and Tonto Fistfight in Heaven* (1994), and a National Book Award–winning novel for young adults, *The Absolutely True Diary of a Part-Time Indian* (2007). Alexie's screenplay for the film *Smoke Signals* (1999) was based on one of his short stories. See also fallsapart.com.

Maya Angelou (b. 1928)
African American memoirist, poet, essayist, and playwright. Born Marguerite Ann Johnson in St. Louis, Angelou attended public schools in Arkansas and California before studying music and dance. In a richly varied life, she has been a cook, streetcar conductor, singer, actress, dancer, teacher, and director, with her debut film *Down in the Delta* (1998). Author of numerous volumes of poetry (her *Complete Collected Poems* was published in 1994) and ten plays (stage, screen, and television), Angelou may be best known for *I Know Why the Caged Bird Sings* (1970), the first volume of her autobiography, one of the fullest accounts of the African American woman's experience in contemporary literature. Angelou published her sixth volume of autobiography, *A Song Flung Up to Heaven*, in 2002. See also mayaangelou.com.

Gloria Anzaldúa (1942–2004)
Chicana American lesbian-feminist poet and writer. Anzaldúa was born to Mexican American parents and worked on the family ranch in southern Texas until attending Pan American University as the first woman from her family to attend college. She received an M.A. in English from the University of Texas, Austin, and embarked on a career as a writer, college instructor, independent scholar, and social activist. Her most ambitious work, *Borderlands/La Frontera: The New Mestiza* (1987), examines

"border women" like herself who grew up estranged from both their Mexican Indian heritage and also the Anglo-American society that considers them outsiders. Her other works include the anthology *This Bridge Called My Back* (co-edited with Cherrie Moraga, 1981); *Making Face, Making Soul/Haciendo Caras* (1990); and *La Prieta* (1997), an autobiographical essay written in her characteristic "Spanglish," a mixture of Spanish and English. See also voices.cla.umn.edu/artistpages/anzaldua.php.

Hannah Arendt (1906–1975)
German American political theorist and philosopher. Born in Hanover, Germany, and educated at the University of Heidelberg, Arendt began her academic career in Germany but was forced to flee when Hitler came to power. Arriving in the United States in 1940, she became chief editor for a major publisher and a frequent lecturer on college campuses. Arendt taught at a number of American colleges and universities, finishing her career at the New School for Social Research in New York City. She published over a dozen books, including *The Origins of Totalitarianism* (1951), *The Human Condition* (1958), and *On Revolution* (1965). In *Eichmann in Jerusalem* (1963), Arendt coined the famous phrase "the banality of evil" to suggest how moral responsibility extends to those who, like Adolf Eichmann, insist that they are only "following orders," as well as those who passively stand by while evil is perpetrated. See also plato.stanford.edu/entries/arendt.

Isaac Asimov (1920–1992)
American biochemist, science writer, and novelist. Born in Russia, Asimov was educated in the United States and received a Ph.D. in biochemistry from Columbia University. In 1949 he became a member of the faculty at the School of Medicine, Boston University, where he taught biochemistry. An extraordinarily prolific author, Asimov wrote or edited more than 500 books on topics as diverse as mathematics, astronomy, physics, chemistry, biology, geography, mythology, and Shakespeare; his science fiction works include some of the most famous and influential in that genre, particularly the short story collection *I, Robot* (1950) and the *Foundation Trilogy* of novels (1951, 1952, 1953). Among his many works of nonfiction are *The Intelligent Man's Guide to Science* (1965), *Lecherous Limericks* (1976), *The Road to Infinity* (1979), the memoir *In Joy Still Felt* (1980), and *Asimov's Guide to the Bible*, Volumes I and II (1981). See also asimovonline.com.

Francis Bacon (1561–1626)
English civil servant, politician, statesman, scientist, and philosopher. Trained as a lawyer, Bacon served as a member of Parliament during the reign of Queen Elizabeth I. After her death, he found favor with King James I and advanced in government service to the position of lord chancellor. His career was cut short in 1621 when he was convicted of accepting bribes. Retired, he married and devoted the rest of his life to study and to writing philosophical works; in his *Novum Organum* (1620) he describes a systematic procedure for investigating natural phenomena that is considered the basis of the modern scientific method. Bacon's other books include *The Advancement of Learning* (1605) and *Essays* (1597, rev. 1612 and 1625). See also plato.stanford.edu/entries/francis-bacon.

Nicholson Baker (b. 1957)
American novelist and essayist. Born in New York City, Baker grew up in Rochester, New York, and earned a B.A. in philosophy at Haverford College. Since then he has devoted himself to writing cerebral fictions as well as numerous articles and book-length essays espousing pacifism, the pleasures of reading, and the need to preserve libraries. His first novel, *The Mezzanine* (1988), set the template for much of his fiction: little action, but a close examination of moment-to-moment consciousness, intricately depicted in a text embellished with copious footnotes. His eight novels include *Vox* (1992) and, most recently, *The Anthologist* (2009), a rumination on poets and poetry. Baker presently lives in Maine and is a professor at the European Graduate School in Switzerland. See also egs.edu.

James Baldwin (1924–1987)
African American essayist, novelist, and social activist. Baldwin was born in Harlem, became a minister at fourteen, and grew to maturity in an America disfigured by racism and homophobia. He moved to Paris in 1948 believing that only outside the United States could he be read as "not merely a Negro; or, even, merely a Negro writer." Both his first published novel, *Go Tell It on the Mountain* (1953), and his first play, *The Amen Corner* (1955), are autobiographical explorations of race and identity. Although he would write other

plays, Baldwin concentrated his energies on essays and novels such as *Giovanni's Room* (1956) and *Another Country* (1962). His stories are collected in *Going to Meet the Man* (1965); his essay collections, including *Notes of a Native Son* (1955) and *The Fire Next Time* (1963), demonstrate Baldwin's skills as a social critic of insight and passion. See also kirjasto.sci.fi/jbaldwin.htm.

Randall Balmer (b. 1954)
American author, educator, filmmaker, and Episcopal priest. Born in Chicago, Balmer received an extensive religious education culminating in a Ph.D. from Princeton University in 1985 and his ordination as an Episcopal priest in 2006. He has authored many articles and more than a dozen books, including *Religion in Twentieth Century America* (2001) and a memoir, *Growing Pains: Learning to Love My Father's Faith* (2001). His most recent book is *The Making of Evangelicalism: From Revivalism to Politics and Beyond* (2010). Balmer made an Emmy-nominated documentary of his second book, *Mine Eyes Have Seen the Glory: A Journey into the Evangelical Subculture in America* (1989, 4th ed. 2006), and he has produced documentaries on the life of evangelist Billy Graham and the creation-evolution debate. The editor of *Christianity Today*, Balmer is a professor of American religious history at Barnard College, Columbia University. See also columbia.edu/cu/religion/faculty-data/randall-balmer/faculty.html.

Dennis Baron (b. 1944)
American scholar and author. A lifelong teacher since completing his Ph.D. in English at the University of Michigan in 1971, Baron is presently a professor of English and linguistics at the University of Illinois at Urbana-Champaign. As a much-sought-after expert on the English language, he has appeared on radio and television and has published numerous essays and articles, both in academic journals and in newspapers such as the *New York Times* and the *Chicago Tribune*. Among his seven books are *Grammar and Good Taste: Reforming the American Language* (1982), *Grammar and Gender* (1986), and *Guide to Home Language Repair* (1994). His most recent, *A Better Pencil: Readers, Writers, and the Digital Revolution* (2009), explores how the practices of reading and writing shape communication technology and are shaped by it in turn. See also english.illinois.edu.

Roland Barthes (1915–1980)
French literary theorist and cultural critic. Born in the French town of Cherbourg, Barthes grew up in Normandy and later Paris. Despite showing great promise as a student of French literature and the classics, he suffered from ill health that hampered his education and made him something of an outsider in academia. His best-known essay, "The Death of the Author" (1968), draws upon the intellectual currents of his day—existentialism, Marxism, semiology, and structuralism, for example—to assert that literary texts exist outside authorial intention or control; thus readers, not writers, create meaning. Barthes's fiercely anti-bourgeois views on modern society and literature—developed in essay collections such as *Mythologies* (1957) and *S/Z* (1970)—were controversial when first published, but his methods have greatly informed those employed by contemporary cultural critics. See also egs.edu/library/roland-barthes/biography.

Ambrose Bierce (1842–1914?)
American journalist, satirist, and short story writer. Bierce was born the tenth child of a poor Ohio family. After serving in the Civil War and working as a journalist in San Francisco, he went to England, where he wrote satiric sketches. In 1876 he returned to San Francisco as a reporter and editorialist for William Randolph Hearst's *Examiner*, where he cultivated a misanthropic persona as "Bitter Bierce." Following divorce and the death of his two sons, Bierce traveled to Mexico, where he reportedly rode with Pancho Villa's revolutionaries; he disappeared and is presumed to have died there. He is best known for *The Devil's Dictionary* (1906), a collection of darkly comic definitions, but his literary reputation rests on his Civil War stories, particularly "An Occurrence at Owl Creek Bridge." Bierce's twelve-volume *Collected Works* (1909–1912) contains his tales, essays, poems, and fables. See also biercephile.com.

Caroline Bird (b. 1915)
American journalist, public-relations specialist, and writer. Bird attended Vassar College, graduated from the University of Toledo, and received her M.A. from the University of Wisconsin (1939). She worked as a researcher at *Newsweek* and *Fortune* in the 1940s, then moved into public relations, which she left after twenty years to write books that tracked the challenges faced by the women of her

generation: *The Invisible Scar* (1966), a study of the lingering effects of the Great Depression; *Born Female: The High Cost of Keeping Women Down* (1968); *Enterprising Women: Their Contribution to the American Economy, 1776–1976* (1976); *Second Careers: New Ways to Work after Fifty* (1992); and *Lives of Our Own: Secrets of a Salty Old Woman* (1995). Her best-known book, *The Case against College* (1975), argues that college is, for many students, an overpriced waste of time. See also mysite.verizon.net/vze3rtj5/id4.html.

William Blake (1757–1827)
English poet and artist. The son of a London haberdasher, Blake first studied drawing at age ten and apprenticed with an engraver at fourteen. As a young man he established a printing shop in London, where he engraved and printed his second volume of poems, *Songs of Innocence* (1789). Blake's poems and illuminations reflect an independent spirit seeking freedom from repression; they take their inspiration from nature and religion, both being transformed into a deeply personal and unorthodox vision. His major works include *The Marriage of Heaven and Hell* (1793), *Songs of Experience* (1794), *The Four Zoas* (1803), *Milton* (1804), and *Jerusalem* (1809). Although Blake died impoverished and obscure, he is now seen as one of the great English Romantic poets. See also poets.org.

Jacob Bronowski (1908–1974)
English mathematician, scientist, and essayist. Born in Poland and educated in England, in 1933 he received a Ph.D. in mathematics from Cambridge University, where he also co-edited an avant-garde literary magazine. Bronowski served as a university lecturer before entering government service during World War II; in 1945 he was an official observer of the atomic bombings of Hiroshima and Nagasaki. Throughout the 1950s he was head of research for Britain's National Coal Board, and from 1964 until his death he was a resident fellow at the Salk Institute, La Jolla, California. The author of many books, among them *Science and Human Values* (1956; 1965), *Nature and Knowledge* (1969), and *Magic, Science, and Civilization* (1978), Bronowski is best remembered in Britain for the thirteen-part BBC television series "The Ascent of Man" (1973–1974). See also drbronowski.com.

David Brooks (b. 1961)
Canadian-born essayist and news commentator. Brooks was born in Toronto, grew up in New York City, and graduated from the University of Chicago in 1983 with a degree in history. Presently a columnist for the *New York Times* and commentator on *PBS NewsHour*, he was previously a writer and editor for the *Wall Street Journal* and then the senior editor of the neo-conservative *Weekly Standard*. Brooks is the author of *Bobos in Paradise: The New Upper Class and How They Got There* (2000) and *On Paradise Drive: How We Live Now (and Always Have) in the Future Tense* (2004). Brooks himself reports that he was politically liberal before "coming to my senses" as a young man; since then he has frequently broken with fellow conservatives by espousing moderate views on social issues. See also nytimes.com.

Kenneth A. Bruffee (b. 1934)
American teacher, scholar, and essayist. Bruffee graduated from Wesleyan University, earned his Ph.D. at Northwestern University, and is currently a professor of English and director of the Scholars Program and the Honors Academy at Brooklyn College, City University of New York. A scholar of Romantic poetry, Bruffee is also known for his work on composition, collaborative learning, peer tutoring, and liberal education. His books include *A Short Course in Writing* (1993) and *Collaborative Learning: Higher Education, Interdependence, and the Authority of Knowledge* (1999). See also academic.brooklyn.cuny.edu/english/bruffee.

Anthony Burgess (1917–1993)
English novelist, playwright, editor, and composer. Born John Burgess Wilson in Manchester, England, he graduated from Manchester University and became a lecturer and teacher of English until 1954, when he was hired as an education officer in the Colonial Service and stationed in Malaya. He began writing while there, but when told in 1959 that he had a year to live, he returned to England and wrote five novels in one year, publishing as Anthony Burgess. The diagnosis proved wrong, and he lived to write several dozen more, including *A Clockwork Orange* (1962), which was made into a film by Stanley Kubrick; *Nothing Like the Sun* (1964); *M/F* (1971); *Earthly Powers* (1980); *Any Old Iron* (1989); and *A Dead Man in Deptford* (1993). In addition, Burgess wrote highly acclaimed critical studies

of James Joyce and D. H. Lawrence and composed over 250 musical works. See also anthonyburgess.org.

Colby Buzzell (b. 1976)
American author, blogger, and former U.S. Army soldier. Born and raised in California, Buzzell joined the army at the age of twenty-six and was sent to Iraq in 2003 as an infantryman. As the war there escalated, Buzzell began writing an anonymous blog entitled "CBFTW" (standing for "Colby Buzzell Fuck The War") in which he vividly described the daily experiences of an ordinary soldier. The blog soon attracted an avid and growing readership, but after just eight weeks Army authorities discovered the blogger's identity and ordered him to cease. Upon returning from Iraq, Buzzell wove his wartime blog postings, journal entries, and e-mails together and published them as *My War: Killing Time in Iraq* (2005), which won the 2007 Lulu Blooker Prize for the best book based on a blog. See also cbftw.blogspot.com.

Nicholas Carr (b. 1959)
American journalist and author. Carr received his B.A. from Dartmouth College and an M.A. in English from Harvard University, where he was executive editor of the *Harvard Business Review*. After nearly two decades as a management consultant, Carr published his first book, *Does IT Matter? Information Technology and the Corrosion of Competitive Advantage* (2004), earning him a reputation as a contrarian in an age of great excitement about technological change. *The Big Switch: Rewiring the World, from Edison to Google* (2008) and his latest book, *The Shallows: What the Internet Is Doing to Our Brains* (2010), both argue that the explosion of innovation in information technology is already having widespread and unforeseen effects—not necessarily for the better—on commerce, culture, and human intelligence. Carr's detailed analysis of Wikipedia, declaring innumerable entries to be inaccurate and questioning the very idea of "wiki" or "crowdsourced" production, has won him a seat on the *Encyclopedia Britannica*'s editorial board of advisors. See also nicholasgcarr.com.

Rachel Carson (1907–1964)
American marine biologist and writer. Born on her family's farm near Springdale, Pennsylvania, Carson received a B.A. from Pennsylvania College for Women (now Chatham College) and an M.A. from Johns Hopkins University. She joined the U.S. Bureau of Fisheries in 1936, and wrote highly-acclaimed books on sea life: *Under the Sea Wind* (1941), *The Sea Around Us* (1951), and *The Edge of the Sea* (1954). Her most influential book, *Silent Spring* (1962), exposed the dangers of the use of pesticides, particularly DDT. This work led to a presidential commission that recommended a ban on the use of DDT in American agriculture, and eventually to the establishment of the Environmental Protection Agency. Revered as a founder of the modern environmental movement, Carson was posthumously awarded the Presidential Medal of Freedom. See also rachelcarson.org.

Stephen L. Carter (b. 1954)
American law professor, novelist, and essayist. Born in Washington, D.C., Carter grew up in Washington, New York City, and Ithaca, New York. While earning a B.A. in history at Stanford University, he became managing editor of the *Stanford Daily*; at Yale University, where he received his J.D. in 1979, he was an editor of the *Yale Law Journal*. Carter's many articles about law and society have appeared in publications as varied as the *New York Times*, the *Wall Street Journal*, and *Christianity Today*. His seven nonfiction books include the autobiographical *Reflections of an Affirmative Action Baby* (1991) and *The Dissent of the Governed: A Meditation on Law, Religion, and Loyalty* (1998). Carter's first novel, *The Emperor of Ocean Park* (2002), was an enormous best seller; his latest thriller is *Jericho's Fall* (2009). Since 1982 Carter has taught at the Yale Law School. See also stephencarterbooks.com.

Michael Chabon (b. 1963)
American novelist and essayist. Born in Pittsburgh, Chabon grew up there and in Columbia, Maryland. He was educated at Carnegie Mellon University, the University of Pittsburgh, and the University of California, Irvine, where he received an M.F.A. in creative writing. The commercial and critical success of his first novel, *The Mysteries of Pittsburgh* (1988), written as his master's thesis, was followed by his second novel, *Wonder Boys* (1995). *The Amazing Adventures of Kavalier & Clay* (2000), a Pulitzer Prize winner, features Chabon's characteristic themes: family ties, a search for Jewish identity, and a fascination with "lowbrow" genre fiction and comic books. Subsequent books have included the novel *The Yiddish Policemen's*

Union (2007) and the essay collections *Maps and Legends* (2008) and *Manhood for Amateurs* (2009). See also michaelchabon.com.

Judith Ortiz Cofer (b. 1952)
Puerto Rican American novelist, poet, and essayist. Born in Hormigueros, Puerto Rico, Cofer spent much of her childhood traveling between her Puerto Rican home and Paterson, New Jersey. Educated at Augusta College, Florida Atlantic University, and Oxford University, Cofer is currently a professor of English and creative writing at the University of Georgia. *Silent Dancing* (1990) reflects her ongoing efforts to explore her bicultural and bilingual roots as a member of what she calls "the Puerto Rican diaspora." Her other books include *The Latin Deli: Prose and Poetry* (1995), *Woman in Front of the Sun: On Becoming a Writer* (2000), *The Meaning of Consuelo* (2003), the young adult novel *Call Me Maria* (2006), and *A Love Story Beginning in Spanish: Poems* (2005). See also judithortizcofer.english.uga.edu.

Aaron Copland (1900–1990)
American composer, conductor, and writer. Born and raised in Brooklyn, Copland studied music theory and practice in Paris in the early 1920s, then returned to New York to compose, organize concert series, publish American scores, and further the cause of the American composer. His experiments with adapting jazz to classical composition gradually led Copland to develop a distinctly American style. He incorporated American folk songs and legends into many of his works, including three ballet scores: *Billy the Kid* (1938), *Rodeo* (1942), and *Appalachian Spring* (1944), winner of the Pulitzer Prize. His other popular works include *Lincoln Portrait* (1942), for narrator and orchestra; *Fanfare for the Common Man* (1942); and *Connotations for Orchestra* (1962). An avid reader throughout his long life, he also wrote music criticism and essays. In his later years Copland was celebrated as "the Dean of American Music." See also coplandhouse.org.

William Cronon (b. 1954)
American environmental historian. Born in Connecticut and raised in Wisconsin, Cronon was a double major in history and English at the University of Wisconsin. After winning a Rhodes scholarship and completing a degree at Oxford University, Cronon earned a Ph.D. from Yale University, where he taught for over a decade. He later returned to the University of Wisconsin, where he teaches American environmental history and the history of the American West. His books, all of which concern the way humans shape the natural world and are in turn shaped by it, include *Changes in the Land: Indians, Colonists, and the Ecology of New England* (1983), *Nature's Metropolis: Chicago and the Great West* (1991), *Under an Open Sky: Rethinking America's Western Past* (1992), and *Uncommon Ground: Rethinking the Human Place in Nature* (1995). See also williamcronon.net.

Amy Cunningham (b. 1955)
American journalist and essayist. Cunningham studied English at the University of Virginia and has been a freelance writer since she graduated in 1977. She has written on yoga, meditation, spirituality, feminism, and healthy living for magazines such as *Glamour*, *Mademoiselle*, *Parenting*, and the *Washington Post Sunday Magazine*, as well as for several online journals. She has also written a blog, "ChatteringMind," for the Web site Beliefnet.com. See also chatteringmind.com.

Debra Dickerson (b. 1960)
African American lawyer and essayist. Raised in St. Louis, Missouri, Dickerson earned degrees from the University of Maryland and Harvard Law School. She has been an officer in the U.S. Air Force, a senior editor at *U.S. News and World Report*, and a lawyer for the NAACP Legal Defense Fund. She is a Senior Fellow at the New American Foundation in Washington, D.C. Her writing has appeared in the *New Republic*, the *New York Times*, and the *Nation*, among other periodicals; she is also a blogger for *Mother Jones*. Her books, focusing on the role of race in American life, include the memoir *An American Story* (2000) and *The End of Blackness* (2004). See also debradickerson.com.

Joan Didion (b. 1934)
American novelist, essayist, and screenwriter. A native of California, Didion studied at the University of California at Berkeley. After winning *Vogue* magazine's Prix de Paris contest for excellence in writing, she began working for the magazine, and left in 1963, the year her first novel, *Run River*, was published. Since then, she has written five more novels, most recently *The Last Thing He Wanted*

(1996). The essays collected in *Slouching Towards Bethlehem* (1969) and *The White Album* (1979) captured the spirit of the 1960s and 1970s, respectively, and put Didion in the forefront of American essayists. Her recent works of nonfiction include *Fixed Ideas: America since 9.11* (2003) and *The Year of Magical Thinking* (2005), winner of the National Book Award. *We Tell Ourselves Stories in Order to Live* (2006) collects her first seven volumes of nonfiction. See also joan-didion .info.

Annie Dillard (b. 1945)
American nature writer, poet, and novelist. Born in Pittsburgh, Pennsylvania, Dillard received her B.A. and M.A. from Hollins College. Known both for her close observation of the natural world and her poet's sensibility, she has published books that range from the poetry of her first book, *Tickets for a Prayer Wheel* (1974), to the nature meditation *Holy the Firm* (1977), the memoir *An American Childhood* (1987), the literary theory in *Living by Fiction* (1982), the essay collection *Teaching a Stone to Talk* (1982), and the novels *The Living* (1992) and *The Maytrees* (2007). In her Pulitzer Prize–winning nonfiction narrative *Pilgrim at Tinker Creek* (1974), Dillard recounts years she spent living in seclusion in the natural world, much like Henry David Thoreau. In *The Writing Life* (1989) she muses on her life's work—"to examine all things intensely and relentlessly." See also anniedillard.com.

Michael Dirda (b. 1948)
American journalist and literary critic. Born to a working-class family in Lorain, Ohio, Dirda was educated at Oberlin College and Cornell University, where he earned a Ph.D. in comparative literature. A lifelong reader and book lover, he has served since 1983 as senior editor of the *Washington Post*'s literary supplement, *Book World*. In 1993 his reviews and essays won him the Pulitzer Prize for distinguished criticism; selections of his literary journalism are collected in *Readings: Essays and Entertainments* (2003) and *Book by Book: Notes on Reading and Life* (2006). Dirda has also published a memoir, *An Open Book: Coming of Age in the Heartland* (2004), as well as two volumes of essays on "great writers and their books": *Bound to Please* (2005) and *Classics for Pleasure* (2007). See also washing tonpost.com.

John Donne (1572–1631)
English poet, essayist, and cleric. Born into a Roman Catholic family at a time when Catholicism was barely tolerated in England, Donne attended Oxford and Cambridge universities, but could not receive a degree because he was not a member of the Church of England. Donne studied law, though he never practiced, and, after quietly abandoning Catholicism sometime during the 1590s, entered government service. In 1615 he became an Anglican minister, and in 1621 he was named dean of St. Paul's Cathedral in London. Donne's literary reputation rests on his poetry as well as on his devotions and sermons. As a poet, he is renowned for both the "metaphysical" wit and sincere ardor of his early love lyrics and later religious verse. As a preacher, he was regarded as one of the greatest orators of his age. See also luminarium.org.

Mark Doty (b. 1953)
American poet and memoirist. Doty was born in Maryville, Tennessee, and educated at Drake University and Goddard College. The only American recipient of Britain's T. S. Eliot Prize for poetry, Doty has published nine collections; his volume *Fire to Fire: New and Selected Poems* won the National Book Award for Poetry in 2008. Nearly as prolific in prose as in verse, Doty has published five works of nonfiction, including the memoir *Firebird* (1999), which recalls his childhood in the South and in Arizona. In 1989 Doty's life was profoundly altered when his partner, Wally Roberts, was diagnosed with AIDS, the subject of Doty's memoir *Heaven's Coast* (1996); Roberts's death in 1994 is recounted in a third memoir, the best-selling *Dog Years* (2007). Presently Doty lives in New York City and teaches at Rutgers University. See also markdoty.org.

Frederick Douglass (1818–1895)
African American abolitionist, orator, journalist, and memoirist. Born a slave in Maryland, Douglass learned at a young age how to read and write, a remarkable feat since it was against the law to teach literacy to a slave. In 1836 he escaped from his master and fled to the North with Anna Murray, a free black woman, whom he later married. Douglass soon became an important orator in the abolitionist movement and, with the publication of his first autobiography, *A Narrative of the Life of Frederick Douglass* (1845), an international spokesman for freedom. Douglass

founded the antislavery newspaper the *North Star* in 1847 and actively recruited black soldiers to join the Union Army at the outbreak of the Civil War. He continued his autobiography in *My Bondage and My Freedom* (1855) and *Life and Times of Frederick Douglass* (1881, rev. 1892). See also memory.loc.gov/ammem/doughtml.

Rita Dove (b. 1952)
American poet and author. Born in Akron, Ohio, Dove graduated summa cum laude from Miami University. After studying in Germany as a Fulbright scholar, she earned her M.F.A. at the University of Iowa. She has published numerous volumes of poetry, most recently *Sonata Mulattica* (2009); *Thomas and Beulah* (1986), a collection of poems loosely based on the lives of her grandparents, won the 1987 Pulitzer Prize in Poetry. She has also published a book of short stories, *Fifth Sunday* (1985); a novel, *Through the Ivory Gate* (2004); a book of essays, *The Poet's World* (1995); and a verse play, *The Darker Face of the Earth* (1994). From 1993 to 1995 Dove served as the first African American Poet Laureate of the United States. She is currently Commonwealth Professor of English at the University of Virginia. See also people.virginia.edu/~rfd4b.

Brian Doyle (b. 1956)
American essayist, editor, and fiction writer. Born in New York City, Doyle received his B.A. from the University of Notre Dame in 1978. After working on various magazines and newspapers in Chicago and Boston, since 1991 he has edited the University of Portland's *Portland Magazine*. A prolific writer of essays, stories, and the prose poems he calls "proems," Doyle has published ten books, including the essay collection *Spirited Men* (2004), about male musicians and writers; *The Wet Engine* (2005), about "hearts and how they work and do not work and get repaired and patched, for a while"; and *The Grail* (2006), about a year in an Oregon vineyard. His most recent book is what he calls a "sprawling epic elephantine serpentine" novel, *Mink River* (2010). See also up .edu/portlandmag/support.html.

Barbara Ehrenreich (b. 1941)
American journalist, essayist, and novelist. Born in Butte, Montana, the daughter of a copper miner, Ehrenreich studied physics at Reed College and cellular biology at Rockefeller University, where she earned a Ph.D. Opting for a life of social activism rather than science, she campaigned against the war in Vietnam and became a committed socialist, union organizer, and journalist. In addition to many articles, she has published a novel, *Kipper's Game* (1993), and many works of nonfiction, including *The Worst Years of Our Lives: Irreverent Notes from a Decade of Greed* (1990), *Nickel and Dimed: On (Not) Getting By in America* (2001), and most recently, *Bright-sided: How the Relentless Promotion of Positive Thinking Has Undermined America* (2009). In 1998 the American Humanist Association named Ehrenreich the Humanist of the Year. See also barbaraehrenreich.com.

Lars Eighner (b. 1948)
American essayist and novelist. Born in Corpus Christi, Texas, Eighner attended the University of Texas, in Austin, where he now lives. A self-described "skeptical Democrat," Eighner has worked in hospitals and drug-crisis programs despite ongoing struggles with illness and homelessness. His book *Travels with Lizbeth* (1993), which describes his three years of surviving on the streets with his dog, was a best seller. He has also published *Elements of Arousal* (1994), a how-to guide on writing gay erotica, and the comic novel *Pawn to Queen Four* (1995), about the gay subculture of a Texas town. See also larseighner.com.

Ralph Waldo Emerson (1803–1882)
American poet, essayist, philosopher, and lecturer. Emerson was born in Boston, the son of a Unitarian minister. He entered Harvard University at fourteen; after graduating in 1821, he taught school for several years before beginning theological studies in 1825. In 1829 he was ordained a Unitarian minister. Although he enjoyed delivering sermons, his Christian faith began to waver under the influence of the Romantic philosophers. In 1832 he resigned his pastorate and retired to Concord, Massachusetts, to a life of study and reflection. With the publication of his first book, *Nature* (1836), Emerson's gradually evolving philosophy, which he called transcendentalism, began to attract adherents and became an important expression of American spirituality. Emerson's occasional lectures at Harvard and the publication of his *Essays* (1841), which includes the classic "Self-Reliance," secured his reputation as a dominant force in American literature and one of the most influential American essayists. See also emerson. tamu.edu/index.html.

Nora Ephron (b. 1941)
American journalist, director, and screenwriter. Born in New York City, Ephron grew up in Beverly Hills, California, the daughter of two screenwriters. Soon after graduating from Wellesley College in 1962, she began writing for the *New York Post*, *Esquire*, the *New York Times Magazine*, and *New York* magazine. In the mid-1970s she turned from journalism to screenplays and has since been nominated for three Academy Awards for best original screenplay, for *Silkwood* (1983), *When Harry Met Sally* (1989), and *Sleepless in Seattle* (1993). In the 1990s she began directing films, including *You've Got Mail* (1998), *Lucky Numbers* (2000), and *Julie & Julia* (2009). Her books include the novel *Heartburn* (1996) and the essay collections *Wallflower at the Orgy* (1970), *Crazy Salad* (1975), *Scribble, Scribble: Notes on the Media* (1978), and *I Feel Bad About My Neck* (2006). See also imdb.com.

Anne Fadiman (b. 1953)
American essayist and editor. Born in New York City, Fadiman attended Harvard University and graduated from Radcliffe College in 1975. She worked as an editor for *Life* and the *American Scholar*, and was founding editor of the magazine *Civilization*, a publication of the Library of Congress; she has been a frequent contributor to magazines such as *Harper's* and the *New Yorker*. Her first book, *The Spirit Catches You and You Fall Down* (1997), about a family of Hmong refugees, won a National Book Critics Circle Award. Her second, *Ex Libris: Confessions of a Common Reader* (1998), is a collection of essays about Fadiman's love of literature and language. Her most recent collection is *At Large and At Small* (2007). Fadiman currently teaches nonfiction writing at Yale University. See also barclayagency.com.

William Faulkner (1897–1962)
American novelist and short story writer. Apart from a short time in military service and a period spent writing screenplays in Hollywood, Faulkner lived his whole life in his native Mississippi. He attended the University of Mississippi, in the town of Oxford, and much of his writing depicts life in fictional Yoknapatawpha County, an imaginative reconstruction of the area near Oxford. With the help of the author Sherwood Anderson, Faulkner published his first novel, *Soldier's Pay*, in 1926. His major novels include *The Sound and the Fury* (1929), *As I Lay Dying* (1930), *Sanctuary* (1931), *Light in August* (1932), and *Absalom! Absalom!* (1936). His *Collected Stories* (1950) won the National Book Award, as did *A Fable* (1954); he also twice received the Pulitzer Prize for fiction. In 1949 Faulkner was awarded the Nobel Prize for literature. See also nobelprize.org/nobel_prizes/literature/laureates/1949/faulkner-bio.html.

M. F. K. Fisher (1908–1992)
American gastronome and food writer. Born in Albion, Michigan, Mary Frances Kennedy grew up in Whittier, California, and attended the University of California, Berkeley, where she met her first husband, Alfred Young Fisher. The couple spent the early years of their marriage in France; it was in Dijon, which she would later describe as "the gastronomical capital of the world," that she became immersed in the culinary arts that would be her lifelong passion. Not long after returning to the United States she wrote her first book about food and the art of living well, *Serve It Forth* (1937). Among the many books that followed, the best known are *Consider the Oyster* (1941), *The Art of Eating* (1954), and two memoirs, *The Gastronomical Me* (1943) and *Long Ago in France* (1991). See also mfkfisher.com.

Frances FitzGerald (b. 1940)
American journalist and author. FitzGerald was born in New York City to a prominent political family; her father was a deputy director of the CIA, her mother an ambassador to the United Nations. Since graduating from Radcliffe College in 1962, FitzGerald has worked as a freelance journalist and regularly contributed to such periodicals as the *New Yorker*, the *Nation*, *Rolling Stone*, and the *New York Review of Books*. Her reporting in Vietnam at the height of the war there in 1966 resulted in her first book, *Fire in the Lake: The Vietnamese and the Americans in Vietnam* (1972); it won both the Pulitzer Prize and the National Book Award for nonfiction. Her later books include *America Revised: History Schoolbooks in the Twentieth Century* (1979) and *Way Out There in the Blue: Reagan, Star Wars, and the End of the Cold War* (2000). See also albany.edu.

Benjamin Franklin (1706–1790)
American statesman, inventor, writer, and diplomat. Born in Boston, Franklin was apprenticed at twelve to his brother, a printer. He resettled in Philadelphia and

at twenty-four was editor and publisher of the *Pennsylvania Gazette*. In 1733 he began writing *Poor Richard's Almanack*, a collection of aphorisms and advice. Retiring from business at forty-two to devote himself to study and research, he soon found himself involved in colonial politics. From 1757 until 1763 he represented the colonies in England. He served on the committee appointed to draft the Declaration of Independence and later was both minister to France and delegate to the Paris peace conference that officially concluded the Revolutionary War. Revered as "the First American," late in his life he became an advocate for the abolition of slavery. His posthumously published *Autobiography* is a classic memoir. See also tigger.uic.edu/~rjensen/franklin.htm.

H. Bruce Franklin (b. 1934)
American scholar and critic. Born in Brooklyn, Franklin was educated at Amherst College and Stanford University. After stints as a tugboat deckhand and a military intelligence officer, Franklin returned to Stanford as a scholar of Herman Melville; he was the first tenured professor to be fired from Stanford after he urged his students to occupy the campus computer center in protest against the Vietnam War. Since then he has written books on a great variety of subjects, ranging from the media's role in wartime to prison literature to science fiction to commercial fishing. His many books include *Prison Literature in America: The Victim as Criminal and Artist* (1982), *War Stars: The Superweapon in the American Imagination* (1988), and *The Most Important Fish in the Sea: Menhaden and America* (2007). Franklin is a professor of English and American studies at Rutgers University, Newark, New Jersey. See also ncs.rutgers.edu/~hbf/.

Joey Franklin (b. 1980)
American graduate student and essayist. Franklin earned his B.A. in English at Brigham Young University and an M.A. in creative nonfiction at Ohio University. His essay "Working at Wendy's" won the 2006 Random House Twentysomething Essays by Twentysomething Writers contest and appears in an anthology of the same name. More of his work can be seen online at *Brevity: Journal of Concise Nonfiction*. Currently, Franklin is working on his doctorate in English at Texas Tech University. See also creativenonfiction.org/brevity.

Ian Frazier (b. 1951)
American essayist and humorist. Born in Hudson, Ohio, Frazier studied at Western Reserve Academy and Harvard University, where he cut his teeth as a humorist at the satirical *Harvard Lampoon*. Since his graduation from Harvard in 1973 many of his humorous pieces have appeared first in the *New Yorker* and then been collected in such volumes as *Dating Your Mom* (1986), *Coyote v. Acme* (1996), and *Lamentations of the Father* (2008). Frazier's best-known work of nonfiction is *Great Plains* (1989); like the autobiographical *Family* (1994) and *On the Rez* (2000), it is based on both extensive research and his own experiences after moving to Montana in 1982. Since relocating with his family to the East Coast he has published *Gone to New York: Adventures in the City* (2005). See also us.macmillan.com/author/ianfrazier.

Thomas Friedman (b. 1953)
American journalist and author. Born in St. Louis Park, Minnesota, Friedman was educated at the University of Minnesota, Brandeis University, and Oxford University, where received a master's degree in Middle Eastern Studies. He worked in Beirut for both United Press International and the *New York Times*; his reporting from Lebanon won him a Pulitzer Prize in 1983. Reassigned by the *Times* to Jerusalem, he won a second Pulitzer in 1988. Friedman's twice-weekly op-ed column in the *Times*, begun in 1994, earned him a third Pulitzer in 2002, mainly for his commentary on the new challenges posed by international terrorism. Friedman's books include *The Lexus and the Olive Tree: Understanding Globalization* (rev. ed. 2000), the best-selling *The World Is Flat: A Brief History of the Twenty-first Century* (2005), and his most recent, *Hot, Flat, and Crowded* (2008). See also thomaslfriedman.com.

Northrop Frye (1912–1991)
Canadian literary critic and educator. A graduate of the University of Toronto's Victoria College and Oxford University, Frye served as a member of the faculty at Victoria College from 1939 until his death. A specialist in Renaissance and Romantic literature, he launched his career with *Fearful Symmetry* (1947), which led to a radical reevalution of the works of English poet William Blake. His best-known work, *Anatomy of Criticism* (1957), represents his lifelong project: to make the criticism

of literature as rigorously systematic as science. The critic's chief task, he argues, is not to evaluate a work of literature but to discern the archetypes that inform the work. Frye would go on to write more than forty books that apply his theories to subjects ranging from Shakespeare's comedies and Milton's epics to Canadian culture and the Bible as literature. See also fryeblog.blog.lib.mcmaster.ca.

Paul Fussell (b. 1924)
American literary and cultural historian. Born in Pasadena, California, Fussell was twice decorated for his service in the U.S. Army in World War II, earned a Ph.D. at Harvard University, and became an instructor of English at Connecticut College. In 1955 he was hired by the University of Pennsylvania, where he is now a professor emeritus. Fussell's early books deal with poetic theory and eighteenth-century literature. With the publication of *The Great War and Modern Memory* (1975), a National Book Award winner, Fussell became better known as a critic of the glorification of war in popular culture. In *Class: A Guide through the American Status System* (1983), he reveals a sharp eye for the nuances of social class. Fussell has also edited *The Norton Book of Travel* (1987) and *The Norton Book of Modern War* (1990). See also mystfx.ca/pinstitutes/bronfman/paulfussellbiography.htm.

Henry Louis Gates, Jr. (b. 1950)
African American scholar and literary critic. Born and raised in West Virginia, Gates was educated at Yale and Cambridge Universities. Now a professor at Harvard University, Gates balances his time between editing African American literature, writing literary criticism, and writing for general audiences. He has created a number of television documentaries, including "African American Lives" (2006), and his essays have appeared in the *New Yorker*, *Newsweek*, *Sports Illustrated*, and the *New York Times*. Gates's many books include *Figures in Black: Words, Signs, and the "Racial" Self* (1987); *The Signifying Monkey* (1988), winner of the National Book Award; his best-selling autobiography, *Colored People* (1994); *Wonders of the African World* (1999); and most recently, *America Behind the Color Line: Dialogues with African Americans* (2004). Gates is the general co-editor of *The Norton Anthology of African American Literature* (2nd ed. 2004). See also aaas.fas.harvard.edu.

Atul Gawande (b. 1965)
American surgeon, teacher, and essayist. Born in Brooklyn to Indian immigrant parents, Gawande grew up in Athens, Ohio. He earned his B.A. at Stanford University, studied at Oxford University as a Rhodes Scholar, and after a stint advising President Bill Clinton about health-care policy, graduated from the Harvard Medical School in 1995. In addition to scholarly studies published in the *New England Journal of Medicine*, his articles about health care and the medical profession have appeared frequently in *Slate* and the *New Yorker*. Gawande's first book, *Complications: A Surgeon's Notes on an Imperfect Science* (2002), and his second, *Better: A Surgeon's Notes on Performance* (2007), were both widely praised for the elegance and clarity with which they illuminated a complex, technical subject for a general readership. His most recent book is *The Checklist Manifesto: How to Get Things Right* (2009). See also gawande.com.

Malcolm Gladwell (b. 1963)
Canadian journalist and essayist. Born in England and raised in Canada, Gladwell graduated from the University of Toronto in 1984 and soon began his career as a journalist, writing for various publications including the *Washington Post*. Since joining the staff of the *New Yorker* in 1996, he has contributed articles on an astonishingly broad array of topics, from the "science of shopping" to highway safety to the SAT to mammography. His books, all international best sellers, include *The Tipping Point: How Little Things Can Make a Big Difference* (2000), *Blink: The Power of Thinking without Thinking* (2005), *Outliers: The Story of Success* (2008), and most recently, *What the Dog Saw* (2009), a collection of Gladwell's articles in the *New Yorker*. See also gladwell.com.

Pumla Gobodo-Madikizela (b. 1955)
South African psychologist. Gobodo-Madikizela was educated at Fort Hare University, Rhodes University, and the University of Cape Town, where she earned her Ph.D. After three years as a research fellow at Harvard University, she returned to South Africa and joined the faculty at the University of Cape Town. Best known for her work on South Africa's post-apartheid Truth and Reconciliation Committee, she is also a founder of Women Waging Peace, an international organization dedicated to nonviolent resolution of conflict. Gobodo-Madikizela is

the author of *A Human Being Died That Night: A Story of Forgiveness* (2003), an award-winning account of what her work has taught her about the nature of forgiveness. See also uct.ac.za/depts/psychology/staff/gobodo.html.

J. J. Goode (b.1981)
American food and travel writer. Goode covers just about every aspect of food and drink: pancakes and pasta, salsa and sushi, cocktails and coffee. A former editor of Epicurious.com, his reviews and recipes have appeared in the *New York Times*, *Gourmet*, *Bon Appétit*, *Time Out New York*, the *Village Voice*, and many other publications. He provided the introduction to *Morimoto: The New Art of Japanese Cooking* (2007) and co-wrote, along with Adam Perry Lang, the best-selling *Serious Barbecue* (2009). He is presently working with the chef Roberto Santibanez on a Mexican cookbook. See also jjgoode.com.

Adam Goodheart (b. 1970)
American historian and essayist. Born in Philadelphia, Goodheart received an A.B. in American history at Harvard University in 1992. Goodheart's book reviews, travel articles, and essays on culture have appeared in many publications, including the *Atlantic Monthly*, *National Geographic*, the *New York Times*, *Outside*, and Salon .com. He was a founding editor of *Civilization* magazine and is a member of the editorial board of the *American Scholar*. In 2006 Washington College named Goodheart the new director of the C. V. Starr Center for the Study of the American Experience. See also history.washcoll.edu.

Allegra Goodman (b. 1967)
American novelist and essayist. Born in Brooklyn and raised in Hawaii, where her parents were professors at the University of Hawaii, Goodman earned her A.B. at Harvard University and her Ph.D. in English at Stanford University. She launched her career in fiction with two short story collections, *Total Immersion* (1989) and *The Family Markowitz* (1996); since then she has published a string of warmly received novels that depict the manners and mores of contemporary Jewish American life, from *Kaaterskill Falls* (1998) to *The Cookbook Collector* (2010). See also allegragoodman.com.

Al Gore (b. 1948)
American politician, environmentalist, and author. Gore was born in Washington, D.C. Like his father, Gore represented Tennessee in Congress, serving in both the House of Representatives (1977–1985) and the Senate (1985–1993). As vice president throughout the two-term Clinton administration (1993–2000), he was an important advocate for the North American Free Trade Agreement (NAFTA), deficit reduction, and improvements in government efficiency. Gore was the Democratic nominee for president in 2000, and won the popular vote while losing the electoral vote in one of the closest and most controversial elections in U.S. history. Currently he manages his business interests and lectures widely; his talk on the topic of global warming was made into the 2006 Academy Award–winning documentary, *An Inconvenient Truth*. Gore is the author of three best-selling books: *Earth in the Balance* (1992), *An Inconvenient Truth* (2006), and *The Assault on Reason* (2007). In 2007 Gore and the UN's Intergovernmental Panel on Climate Change won the Nobel Peace Prize. See also algore.com.

Stephen Jay Gould (1941–2002)
American paleontologist, essayist, and educator. Raised in New York City, Gould graduated from Antioch College and received a Ph.D. from Columbia University in 1967. That same year he joined the faculty of Harvard University as a professor of geology and zoology and taught courses in paleontology, biology, and the history of science. Witty and fluent, Gould demystified science for lay readers in the essays he wrote for a regular column in *Natural History* magazine; many of these were collected in *Ever Since Darwin* (1977), *Hen's Teeth and Horse's Toes* (1983), and *Eight Little Piggies* (1993). Gould's *The Mismeasure of Man* (1981), which questioned traditional ways of testing intelligence, won the National Book Critics Circle Award for essays and criticism. A renowned neo-Darwinian, Gould championed the theory of evolution throughout his career; his last book on this subject, *The Structure of Evolutionary Theory*, appeared in 2002. See also stephenjaygould.org.

Philip Gourevitch (b. 1961)
American journalist and editor. Born in Philadelphia, Gourevitch was educated at Cornell University and Columbia University, where he earned an M.F.A. in fiction. After a decade as a freelance journalist, he joined the staff of the *New Yorker* in 1997. Gourevitch spent several years

investigating the genocide in Rwanda and published his observations in his first book, *We Wish to Inform You That Tomorrow We Will Be Killed with Our Families: Stories from Rwanda* (1988). *A Cold Case* (2002) concerns the investigation of an unsolved murder in New York City. His most recent work, *Standard Operating Procedure* (2008, reissued as *The Ballad of Abu Ghraib*), co-written with documentary filmmaker Errol Morris, describes the misconduct of American soldiers in Iraq. Gourevitch was named editor of the *Paris Review* in 2005. See also newyorker.com.

David Guterson (b. 1956)
American novelist and essayist. Born in Seattle, Guterson earned his B.A. and M.F.A. degrees at the University of Washington before teaching high school English for twelve years, all the while writing the short stories collected in *The Country Ahead of Us, the Country Behind* (1989) and the essays collected in *Family Matters: Why Homeschooling Makes Sense* (1992). Guterson has published four novels: *Snow Falling on Cedars* (1994), winner of the PEN/Faulkner Award; *East of the Mountains* (1999); *Our Lady of the Forest* (2003); and *The Other* (2008). Guterson is a contributing editor to *Harper's* and has published in the *New York Times Magazine*, *Esquire*, *Sports Illustrated*, and elsewhere. Guterson says that he writes out of an "ethical and moral duty . . . to tell stories that inspire readers to consider more deeply who they are." See also dcn.davis.ca.us/~gizmo/cedars.html.

Stephen Hawking (b. 1942)
British physicist and author. Born in Oxford and raised in London, Hawking earned his B.A. at Oxford University and his Ph.D. at Cambridge University, where for three decades he held the professorship of mathematics once held by Sir Isaac Newton. Hawking is a renowned theoretical physicist; his work has contributed greatly to the modern scientific understanding of cosmology, quantum gravity, and black holes. In addition to a wealth of highly specialized scientific publications, his *A Brief History of Time* (1988) introduced millions of readers to contemporary ideas about the physical universe; Hawking's most recent book, *The Grand Design* (2010), co-written with American physicist Leonard Mlodinow, discusses attempts to combine Einstein's theory of general relativity with quantum physics to create a "Theory of Everything." See also hawking.org.uk.

Ernest Hemingway (1899–1961)
American journalist and novelist. Born and raised in Oak Park, Illinois, Hemingway began his professional writing career immediately after graduation from high school, reporting for newspapers in Kansas City and Toronto. He was wounded while serving as an ambulance driver in World War I. In the 1920s he lived in Paris as part of the expatriate "Lost Generation"; it was there that he developed the terse, understated literary style for which he is renowned. Hemingway's reputation rests on such short story collections as *In Our Time* (1925) and *Men without Women* (1927), and on his classic novels, including *The Sun Also Rises* (1926), *A Farewell to Arms* (1929), and *For Whom the Bell Tolls* (1940). *The Old Man and the Sea* (1952) was the last work published during his lifetime. Hemingway received the Nobel Prize for literature in 1954. See also hemingwaysociety.org.

Jack Hitt (b. 1957)
American journalist and radio commentator. Born and raised in Charleston, South Carolina, Hitt got his start by contributing to and editing his elementary school's literary magazine. Now his feature articles appear in such publications as *Rolling Stone*, *GQ*, *Wired*, *Harper's*, and the *New York Times Magazine*, where he writes about everything from amateur space travel to endangered languages. Hitt is probably best known for his contributions to the National Public Radio program *This American Life*, which has featured his stories about growing up with a transgendered woman, a production of *Hamlet* put on by the inmates of a maximum-security prison, and many other subjects. The author of *Off the Road: A Modern-Day Walk Down the Pilgrim's Route into Spain* (1994), Hitt has also edited *The Harper's Forum Book: What Are We Talking About?* (1991). See also ideas.theatlantic.com.

John Holt (1923–1985)
American teacher and education theorist. Born in New York City, Holt attended boarding schools in New England, served aboard a submarine in World War II, and taught for many years, first in high schools in Colorado and Massachusetts and then at Harvard University and the University of California at Berkeley. Throughout his career he was a firm believer in the natural

human ability to learn, a harsh critic of the damaging effects of schools on children, and an enthusiastic proponent of home-schooling. His numerous books include *How Children Fail* (1964), *How Children Learn* (1967), *The Underachieving School* (1967), *Teach Your Own* (1981), and *Escape from Childhood* (1984). At the age of forty he took up the cello, a learning adventure he recounted in *Never Too Late: My Musical Life Story* (1979). See also holtgws.com.

Langston Hughes (1902–1967)
African American poet, playwright, and fiction writer. Born in Joplin, Missouri, Hughes grew up in the American Midwest before coming to New York City to attend Columbia University. Appalled by the racial discrimination there, he left Columbia to pursue his own writing, especially the "jazz poetry" that became his hallmark. After a period of travel and living abroad, he returned to the United States to complete his B.A. at Pennsylvania's Lincoln University. He returned to New York and soon emerged as a key figure in the Harlem Renaissance of the 1920s and 1930s, beginning with his collection of poems, *The Weary Blues*, in 1926. In his lifetime he would publish sixteen more volumes of poetry as well as two novels, seven collections of short stories, twenty-six plays, and seven works of nonfiction, including the memoir *The Big Sea* (1940). See also poetryfoundation.org.

Zora Neale Hurston (1891–1960)
African American anthropologist, folklorist, and writer. A central figure of the Harlem Renaissance of the 1920s and 1930s, Hurston was born in Notasuga, Alabama, and grew up in Eatonville, Florida, the daughter of a Baptist preacher and a seamstress. She attended Howard University and in 1928 received a B.A. from Barnard College, where she studied anthropology and developed an interest in black folk traditions and in oral history. Hurston's writing draws on her knowledge of folklore and uses a vigorous, rhythmical, direct prose style that influenced many later American writers. Her works include the play *Mule Bone: A Comedy of Negro Life in Three Acts* (1931), written with Langston Hughes, the novel *Their Eyes Were Watching God* (1937), and her autobiography, *Dust Tracks on a Road* (1942), as well as her *Collected Stories* (1995) and *Collected Plays* (2008). See also zoranealehurston .com.

Molly Ivins (1944–2007)
American newspaper columnist and essayist. Born in California and raised in Houston, Texas, Ivins received a B.A. from Smith College and an M.A. in journalism from Columbia University. She worked on the staffs of the *Houston Chronicle*, the *Minneapolis Tribune*, the *Texas Observer*, the *New York Times*, and the *Dallas Times Herald*; she became nationally famous as a syndicated political columnist at the *Fort Worth Star-Telegram*. An unapologetic liberal, Ivins used humor to address serious issues and delighted especially in exposing politics at its worst. Her collections include *Molly Ivins Can't Say That, Can She?* (1991) and *You Got to Dance with Them What Brung You* (1998). Her books include *Shrub: The Short but Happy Political Life of George W. Bush* (2000), *Bushwhacked: Life in George W. Bush's America* (2003), and *Who Let the Dogs In? Incredible Political Animals I Have Known* (2004). See also mollyivins .com.

Thomas Jefferson (1743–1826)
American lawyer, architect, and writer; governor of Virginia (1779–1781), secretary of state to George Washington (1789–1793), vice president to John Adams (1797–1801), and third president of the United States (1801–1809). A learned man of significant accomplishments in many fields, Jefferson became a lawyer and was elected to Virginia's House of Burgesses, where he argued the cause of American independence. After completing his second term as president of the United States, he founded the University of Virginia, designing both the buildings and the curriculum. A fluent stylist, Jefferson authored Virginia's Statute of Religious Freedom and wrote books on science, religion, architecture, and even Anglo-Saxon grammar. He is probably best known for writing the Declaration of Independence; his preliminary drafts were edited by a committee that included Benjamin Franklin and John Adams before Jefferson prepared the final revision. See also sc94 .ameslab.gov/tour/tjefferson.html.

Jesus (c. 4 B.C.E.–c. 30 C.E.)
Jesus of Nazareth, first-century spiritual teacher. The central, foundational figure of the Christian religion, worshipped by most Christians as the Son of God and the Messiah, Jesus spent his brief public career in Palestine, preaching to his fellow Jews a message of repentance, conversion,

and loving-kindness. Jesus' life and teachings are known principally through the four canonical gospels of the New Testament, written and assembled by his followers in the decades after his execution in Jerusalem by the Roman authorities. One of his favorite teaching devices was the parable, a literary form with a long history, used extensively in the rabbinical tradition. The parables of Jesus, despite their seeming simplicity and grounding in the world of everyday experience, often convey subtle, highly nuanced moral and spiritual teachings that have intrigued scholars and lay believers alike for two millennia. See also rc.net/wcc/parables.htm.

Samuel Johnson (1709–1784)
English poet, critic, essayist, and lexicographer. In spite of childhood poverty, poor eyesight, and a neuropsychiatric condition that was probably Tourette syndrome, Johnson achieved renown in his day as a wit, a conversationalist, and an astute observer of the human experience. In 1737, having withdrawn from Oxford University for lack of funds and then failing as a schoolmaster, he sought his fortune in London, where he began contributing essays and poems to the *Gentleman's Magazine*. In 1750 he founded the *Rambler*, a popular periodical containing essays, fables, and criticism. One of the greatest prose stylists of the English language, Johnson won fame for *Rasselas* (1759), a didactic tale; *The Lives of the Poets* (1779–1781); and the monumental *Dictionary of the English Language* (1755). *The Life of Samuel Johnson* (1791), written by his friend and travel companion, James Boswell, is English literature's most famous biography. See also samueljohnson.com.

Ben Jonson (1572–1637)
English essayist, poet, and playwright. The stepson of a London bricklayer, Jonson rose from childhood poverty to become England's first poet laureate. Irascible, vain, and deeply learned, he courted a life of controversy that included barbed attacks on fellow poets and playwrights, imprisonment for "leude and mutynous" behavior, the murder of an actor in a duel, and a Privy Council trial for allegations of "popery and treason" in his play *Sejanus*. He was best known in his own time for popular comedies such as *Every Man in His Humour* (1598), *Volpone* (c. 1605), and *The Alchemist* (1610). The twenty-four masques that Jonson produced to entertain the court of King James I are considered the pinnacle of this now-extinct art form. The 1616 publication of Jonson's *Works* confirmed his renown as a professional author, perhaps the first in England to earn his living solely by his pen. See also poets.org.

Garrison Keillor (b. 1942)
American radio host, humorist, and essayist. Born in Anoka, Minnesota, Keillor graduated from the University of Minnesota in 1966. He is the creator and, since 1971, the host of the popular weekly NPR radio program *A Prairie Home Companion*, a live revue featuring comic skits, spoof advertisements, nationally renowned musicians, and Keillor's trademark monologues, "the news from Lake Wobegon." *The Writer's Almanac*, Keillor's daily NPR radio program, highlights literary history, especially poetry. He has contributed humorous stories to the *New Yorker*, the *Atlantic Monthly*, and Salon .com, and is the author of many books, including *Happy to Be Here* (1981) and the political manifesto *Homegrown Democrat* (2004), as well as the best-selling *Lake Wobegon* series, most recently *Life among the Lutherans* (2009) and *Pilgrims: A Wobegon Romance* (2009). See also prairiehome.publicradio.org.

John Fitzgerald Kennedy (1917–1963)
American writer, politician, and thirty-fifth president of the United States. Born in Brookline, Massachusetts, Kennedy graduated from Harvard University and developed his senior thesis into the best-selling *Why England Slept* (1940). He received the Navy and Marine Corps Medal for his service in World War II. At twenty-nine Kennedy was elected to the U.S. House of Representatives; six years later he narrowly won a seat in the U.S. Senate, representing Massachusetts. His book *Profiles in Courage* (1956), detailing notable instances of political integrity by U.S. senators, won the Pulitzer Prize and added to his growing fame. In 1960 his eloquence and poise in televised debates against Richard Nixon helped Kennedy win the presidency. His inaugural address, calling for all citizens' participation in the affairs of their nation, is one of the best-known speeches in American history. On November 22, 1963, Kennedy was assassinated in Dallas, Texas. See also whitehouse.gov/about/presidents.

Jamaica Kincaid (b. 1949)
Caribbean American journalist, novelist, and garden writer. Born Elaine Richardson in St. John's, Antigua, Kincaid moved to New York City when she was seventeen and worked first as a domestic helper and then as a fact-checker for *Forbes* magazine, a role that eventually led her to the *New Yorker*, where she became a staff writer in 1976. Publishing as Jamaica Kincaid because her family disapproved of her writing, she has produced a collection of short stories, *At the Bottom of the River* (1983); such novels as *Annie John* (1985), *Lucy* (1990), *The Autobiography of My Mother* (1995), and *Mr. Potter* (2002); and several books on gardening, including *My Garden* (2001), a collection of essays. *Among Flowers: A Walk in the Himalayas* (2005) chronicles Kincaid's journey in search of rare plants to bring home to her Vermont garden. Kincaid presently teaches literature at Claremont McKenna College. See also voices.cla.umn.edu.

Martin Luther King, Jr. (1929–1968)
African American clergyman and civil rights leader. By the age of twenty-six, the Atlanta-born King had completed his undergraduate education, finished divinity school, and received a Ph.D. in religion from Boston University. In 1956 King took a public stand to support blacks boycotting segregated buses in Montgomery, Alabama, marking his entry into the civil rights struggle. Soon he became a major figure in the civil rights movement, advocating nonviolent protest in the spirit of Jesus' teachings and Mahatma Gandhi's principles of passive resistance. In 1963, Birmingham, Alabama, perhaps the most segregated city in the South, became the focal point for violent racial confrontations; 2,400 civil rights workers, King among them, were jailed, occasioning his now-famous "Letter from Birmingham Jail." In 1964, at thirty-five, he became the youngest-ever recipient of the Nobel Peace Prize. King was assassinated on April 14, 1968, in Memphis, Tennessee. See also thekingcenter.org.

Stephen King (b. 1947)
American fiction writer. Born in Portland, Maine, King grew up fascinated with horror comics and began writing macabre tales while still a teenager. Not long after graduating with a degree in English from the University of Maine in 1970, he began his first novel, *Carrie* (1973), a best-selling supernatural thriller soon followed by *Salem's Lot* (1975), *The Shining* (1977), and the serialized fantasy *The Dark Tower: The Gunslinger* (1977–1981). Today King is a publishing phenomenon; his forty-nine novels, five nonfiction books, and nine collections of short stories have sold more than 500 million copies worldwide. Even after sustaining severe injuries in a 1999 road accident, he has managed to fulfill his daily quota of 2,000 words. See also stephenking.com.

Maxine Hong Kingston (b. 1940)
Chinese American memoirist and novelist. Born in Stockton, California, to a Chinese immigrant family, Kingston grew up in a culture in which English was a second language; friends and relatives regularly gathered at her family's laundry to tell stories in Chinese and reminisce about their native country. After graduating from the University of California at Berkeley, Kingston taught school in California and Hawaii and began publishing poetry, stories, and articles in magazines such as the *New Yorker*, *New West*, *Ms.*, and the *New York Times Magazine*. Her best-known works, *The Woman Warrior: Memoirs of a Girlhood among Ghosts* (1973) and the National Book Award–winning *China Men* (1980), artfully combine memoir, family legends, and fiction. She has also published a novel, *Tripmaster Monkey: His Fake Book* (1989). Kingston is a professor emeritus of English at the University of California, Berkeley. See also uncp.edu.

Melvin Konner (b. 1946)
American anthropologist, biologist, educator, and physician. Born in Brooklyn, New York, Konner graduated from Brooklyn College, City University of New York, and received his Ph.D. at Harvard University, where he began his teaching career as an anthropologist; he now holds a joint appointment in the departments of anthropology and medicine at Emory University. Konner's concerns range from the crisis in health care to the future of Israel and the health benefits of returning to the so-called caveman diet. His books include *The Tangled Wing: Biological Constraints on the Human Spirit* (1982, 2002), *Becoming a Doctor: A Journey of Initiation in Medical School* (1988), and *Unsettled: An Anthropology of the Jews*. His most recent book, *The Evolution of Childhood* (2009), is a comprehensive study of childhood throughout human history. See also melvinkonner.com.

Jonathan Kozol (b. 1936)
American teacher, education theorist, and social activist. Born in Boston, Kozol was educated at Harvard University and, as a Rhodes Scholar, Oxford University. He taught in Boston-area public schools, an experience he described in his first book, the nonfictional *Death at an Early Age* (1967), a National Book Award winner. His interest in education reform, theories of learning, and social justice have informed all of his twelve books, including *Rachel and Her Children: Homeless Families in America* (1988), *Savage Inequalities: Children in America's Schools* (1991), *Amazing Grace: The Lives of Children and the Conscience of a Nation* (1995), *The Shame of the Nation: The Restoration of Apartheid Schooling in America* (2005), and his most recent book, *Letters to a Young Teacher* (2007). See also learntoquestion.com/seevak/groups/2002.

Nicholas D. Kristof (b. 1959)
American journalist and author. Raised on a sheep farm in Yamhill, Oregon, Kristof was educated at Harvard University and at Magdalen College, Oxford, where he was a Rhodes scholar. He joined the *New York Times* in 1984 and has been an international correspondent, an associate editor, and, since 2001, a regular columnist. Specialists on East Asia, he and his wife, Sheryl WuDunn, have co-authored *China Wakes: The Struggle for the Soul of a Rising Power* (1994), *Thunder from the East: Portrait of a Rising Asia* (2000), and *Half the Sky: Turning Oppression into Opportunity for Women Worldwide* (2009). In 1990, Kristof and WuDunn were awarded the Pulitzer Prize for International Reporting in recognition of their coverage of China's pro-democracy movement, which climaxed with the Tiananmen Square protests. In 2006 Kristof won the Pulitzer Prize for Commentary for his columns on the genocide in Darfur. See also nytimes.com.

Elisabeth Kübler-Ross (1926–2004)
Swiss American psychologist. Born and educated in Switzerland, Kübler-Ross came to the United States in 1958 to continue her medical studies. She discovered her life's mission when, assigned to a psychiatric hospital, she was appalled by the treatment of dying patients. Her first book, *On Death and Dying* (1969), expressed her outrage and outlined the Five Stages of Grief that made her famous. She devoted the rest of her life to understanding the psychology of death, improving care for the terminally ill, and supporting the hospice movement. Her twenty-three books include *On Children and Death* (1983), *AIDS: The Ultimate Challenge* (1987), *The Wheel of Life: A Memoir of Living and Dying* (1997), and, with David Kessler, *On Grief and Grieving: Finding the Meaning of Grief through the Five Stages of Loss* (2005). See also ekrfoundation.org.

Thomas S. Kuhn (1922–1996)
American physicist, philosopher, and historian. Educated at Harvard University, where he earned a Ph.D. in physics, Kuhn was a specialist in the history and philosophy of science. The author of *The Copernican Revolution* (1957) and *The Essential Tension: Selected Studies in Scientific Tradition and Change* (1977), he taught the history of science at Harvard from 1948 to 1956, when he moved to the University of California at Berkeley. Kuhn is perhaps best known for *The Structure of Scientific Revolutions* (1962; 1970; 1996), in which he argued that scientific understanding is determined by frameworks or "paradigms" that periodically are shown to be outmoded and are replaced in "paradigm shifts." Before his death, Kuhn was Laurence S. Rockefeller Professor of Philosophy at the Massachusetts Institute of Technology. Much of his later work is collected in *The Road since Structure: Philosophical Essays, 1970–1993* (2000). See also des.emory.edu/mfp/Kuhnsnap.html.

Jhumpa Lahiri (b. 1967)
Indian American short story writer and novelist. Lahiri was born in London to Bengali Indian immigrant parents who, when she was three years old, moved the family to the United States and settled in Kingston, Rhode Island. She earned her B.A. from Barnard College; at Boston University she earned three master's degrees and a Ph.D. in Renaissance Studies. After her short stories were rejected for publication they were collected in *The Interpreter of Maladies* (1999), a winner of the 2000 Pulitzer Prize. In her novel *The Namesake* (2003) and her second story collection, *Unaccustomed Earth* (2008), Lahiri continues to focus on the experience of Indian immigrants and their children. See also randomhouse.com/kvpa/jhumpalahiri.

Charles Lamb (1775–1835)
English poet and essayist. Born in London, Lamb left school at age fourteen and found work in an accountant's office

where he was employed for twenty-five years. Along with his older sister Mary, Lamb wrote the popular children's book *Tales from Shakespeare* (1807), editions of which are still available today. As a poet Lamb received encouragement from his childhood friend Samuel Taylor Coleridge, but his poems never garnered the attention that Lamb hoped for; as an essayist, though, writing under the pen name "Elia," he published frequently in the *London Magazine* and became one of England's most admired authors, collecting his work in *Essays of Elia* (1823) and *Last Essays of Elia* (1833). See also gutenberg.org.

Chang-Rae Lee (b. 1965)
Korean American novelist. When he was three, Lee and his family left South Korea for the United States, settling in Westchester, New York. He received his B.A. from Yale in 1987 and spent a year as an equities analyst before pursuing his M.F.A. at the University of Oregon. Lee's first novel, *Native Speaker* (1995), examines a Korean American's search for identity; his second, *A Gesture Life* (1999), focuses on a Japanese American, a former medic, who recalls treating "comfort women"—Korean women forced to have sex with Japanese soldiers in World War II. In Lee's 2004 novel, *Aloft*, the main character is a wealthy white Long Island suburbanite, whose perspective allows Lee to approach issues of race and "Americanness" from new angles. Since 2002 Lee has taught creative writing at Princeton University. See also princeton.edu.

Michael Levin (b. 1943)
American philosopher and educator. Educated at Michigan State University and Columbia University, Levin taught philosophy at Columbia from 1968 until 1980. He is currently a professor of philosophy at City College of the City University of New York, pursuing his research interests in theories of knowledge and the heritability of racial differences. The author of a number of scholarly articles, Levin has published *Metaphysics and the Mind-Body Problem* (1979), *Feminism and Freedom* (1987), *Why Race Matters: Race Differences and What They Mean* (1997), and *Sexual Orientation and Human Rights* (1999). Throughout his career Levin has courted controversy, taking contrarian stands on such diverse matters as homosexual rights, feminism, racial differences, and the acceptability of torture. See also gc.cuny.edu.

Abraham Lincoln (1809–1865)
American lawyer, orator, legislator, and sixteenth president of the United States. Born in Kentucky, Lincoln was largely self-made and self-taught. In 1830 his family moved to Illinois, where Lincoln prepared himself for a career in law. In 1834 he was elected to the first of four terms in the Illinois state legislature, and in 1847, to the U.S. Congress. Elected president in 1860, Lincoln guided the Union through the Civil War while pressing for passage of the Thirteenth Amendment (1865), which outlawed slavery "everywhere and forever" in the United States. His most famous speech, the Gettysburg Address (1863), was delivered at the site of one of the Civil War's bloodiest battles. Shortly after his reelection and with the war drawing to a close, Lincoln gave his Second Inaugural Address (1865), an eloquent appeal for reconciliation and peace. He was assassinated a little more than a month later. See also whitehouse.gov/about/presidents.

Niccolò Machiavelli (1469–1527)
Florentine statesman and political philosopher. An aristocrat who held public office while Florence was a republic, Machiavelli fell from favor when the Medici family returned to power in 1512. He was tortured during a brief imprisonment; upon his release he retired to a life of studying philosophy and wrote the treatises that would become seminal works of modern political science. Machiavelli's most famous work, *The Prince* (1513), not published until after his death, has exerted considerable literary and political influence within the Western tradition. Because *The Prince* is such a clear-eyed, unsentimental description of the politics of his era, the term "Machiavellian" has come to mean manipulative, deceitful, and amoral. In fact, Machiavelli himself was a trusted civil servant and an admired philosopher. See also philosophypages.com.

Nancy Mairs (b. 1943)
American poet and essayist. Mairs was born in Long Beach, California, and grew up in Boston. Married at nineteen, she completed her B.A. at Wheaton College, had a child, and earned M.F.A. and Ph.D. degrees from the University of Arizona. The personal difficulties that inform her writing include suffering a near-suicidal bout of agoraphobia and anorexia that led to six months spent in a state mental hospital and the later discovery that she was afflicted with multiple sclerosis. She found salvation both in writing and

in Roman Catholicism, to which she converted in her thirties. Her first book was a collection of poems, *In All the Rooms in the Yellow House* (1984). The eight books of essays and memoirs Mairs has written since include *Plaintext: Deciphering a Woman's Life* (1986), *Carnal Acts* (1990), *Waist-High in the World: A Life among the Nondisabled* (1997), *Voice Lessons: On Becoming a (Woman) Writer* (1997), and, most recently, *A Dynamic God: Living an Unconventional Catholic Faith* (2007). See also nancymairs.com.

Alberto Manguel (b. 1948)
Canadian writer, translator, and editor. Born in Argentina, Manguel spent his youth in Israel, where his father was the Argentine ambassador, and in Buenos Aires, where, as a teenager, he regularly read aloud to the nearly blind writer Jorge Luis Borges. Following the publication of his first major book, *The Dictionary of Imaginary Places* (1980), Manguel worked as an editor for brief periods in Tahiti, Paris, and rural England before settling in Toronto, where he became a Canadian citizen and wrote his first novel, *News from a Foreign Country Came* (1992). In 2000 Manguel moved to France, renovating a medieval chapel to house his 30,000-book library. Throughout this peripatetic life Manguel has published a torrent of literary anthologies as well as his own novels, essays about the pleasures of reading, and biographies of writers such as Borges and Rudyard Kipling. See also alberto.manguel.com.

Peter Matthiessen (b. 1927)
American novelist, nonfiction writer, and environmentalist. Matthiessen was born in New York City, earned degrees at Yale University and the University of Paris, and went on to a life of adventure travel, environmental activism, and tremendous literary productivity. In 1957, while working for the CIA in France, he helped found the *Paris Review*, a legendary literary magazine. *Wildlife in America* (1959) detailed the human-caused extinction of various animal species and was one of the first books to discuss the effects of global warming. Matthiessen's trek through the Himalayas provided the basis for *The Snow Leopard* (1978), winner of the National Book Award. His best-known novels include *At Play in the Fields of the Lord* (1965), depicting American missionaries in South America, and *Shadow Country* (2008), chronicling the life and death of the legendary Florida figure Edgar Watson, which won him his second National Book Award. See also albany.edu.

Scott McCloud (b. 1960)
American cartoonist and comics theorist. McCloud was born in Boston, Massachusetts, and earned a B.F.A. in illustration at Syracuse University. The creator of the science fiction/superhero comic book series *Zot!*, McCloud has also done the artwork for many issues of *Superman* as well as his own *Destroy!!*, which he describes as "a deliberately over-the-top, oversized single-issue comic book, intended as a parody of formulaic superhero fights," and the graphic novel *The New Adventures of Abraham Lincoln* (1998). In 1993, he published *Understanding Comics*, a scholarly work on the definition, history, and methodology of comics, done entirely in comics form. He followed this study with *Reinventing Comics* (2000) and *Making Comics* (2006). See also scottmcloud.com.

Bill McKibben (b. 1960)
American environmentalist and nature writer. Born in Lexington, Massachusetts, McKibben attended Harvard University, where he was president of the *Harvard Crimson* newspaper. He then worked as a staff writer at the *New Yorker*, which serialized his first book, *The End of Nature* (1989), an introduction to climate change and a plea for a reformed attitude to nature. Since then he has written about a broad array of environmental topics, earning him *Time* magazine's description as "the world's best green journalist." McKibben's books include *Hope, Human and Wild: True Stories of Living Lightly on the Earth* (1995); *The Comforting Whirlwind: God, Job, and the Scale of Creation* (2005); *Deep Economy: The Wealth of Communities and the Durable Future* (2007), an attempt to envision a more localized and more sustainable economic system; and most recently the best-selling *Eaarth: Making a Life on a Tough New Planet* (2010), about the inevitability of climate change. See also billmckibben.com.

John McPhee (b. 1931)
American nonfiction author. McPhee was born in Princeton, New Jersey, and educated at Princeton University and Cambridge University. He began his writing career at *Time* magazine; since 1965 he has been a staff writer for the *New Yorker*, which has serialized many of his twenty-nine books. McPhee's output is famously eclectic. His first book, *A Sense of Where*

You Are (1965), profiled then-college basketball player Bill Bradley. His subsequent books include *Encounters with the Archdruid* (1971), a portrait of Sierra Club founder David Brower; *Coming into the Country*, a look at life in Alaska; and *Annals of the Former World* (1998), a tetralogy about geology, which was awarded the Pulitzer Prize. His most recent book is *Silk Parachute* (2010). For decades he has taught a creative writing course, "The Literature of Fact," at Princeton. See also johnmcphee.com.

James McPherson (b. 1936)
American Civil War historian. Born in Valley City, North Dakota, McPherson earned his B.A. at Gustavus Adolphus College and in 1958 his Ph.D. at Johns Hopkins University. McPherson has published nineteen historical works about the war and its era, some scholarly, some written for a more general readership. His *Battle Cry of Freedom* (1989) won a Pulitzer Prize and is regarded by many as the best one-volume history of the Civil War. Other books include *Marching toward Freedom: The Negro in the Civil War, 1861–1865* (1968), *Ordeal by Fire: The Civil War and Reconstruction* (1982, 1992, 2001, 2009), *For Cause and Comrades: Why Men Fought in the Civil War* (1997), and *Tried by War: Abraham Lincoln as Commander in Chief* (2008). A professor emeritus at Princeton University, McPherson was the first recipient of the Pritzker Military Library Literature Award for lifetime achievement in military history. See also neh.gov.

John Hamilton McWhorter (b. 1965)
American linguist and cultural commentator. Born in Philadelphia, McWhorter was educated at Simon's Rock College, Rutgers University, New York University, and Stanford University, where he earned his Ph.D. in linguistics in 1993. He was a Senior Fellow at the Manhattan Institute and has taught at Columbia University since 2008. A frequent guest commentator on radio and television, McWhorter is sought out for his perspectives on matters of race relations and language. He is the author of thirteen books, including *Word on the Street: Debunking the Myth of "Pure" Standard English* (1998), *The Power of Babel: A Natural History of Language* (2001), *Winning the Race: Beyond the Crisis in Black America* (2005), and *Our Magnificent Bastard Tongue: The Untold Story of English* (2008). See also manhattan-institute.org/html/mcwhorter.htm.

Jessica Mitford (1917–1996)
Anglo-American memoirist, journalist, and social activist. Born into one of England's most famous aristocratic families, "Decca" Mitford had little formal education but read widely; she would later describe her privileged upbringing in the memoir *Daughters and Rebels* (1960). She emigrated to the United States in 1939, eventually marrying a prominent civil rights lawyer. During the 1960s she established herself as an investigative reporter with a talent for pungent social criticism. Her study of the American funeral industry, *The American Way of Death* (1963, 1998), was followed by *The Trial of Dr. Spock* (1969), *Kind and Unusual Punishment: The Prison Business* (1973), and *The American Way of Birth* (1992). Her memoir *A Fine Old Conflict* (1977) recounts her youthful enthusiasm for and subsequent disillusionment with the Communist Party; *The Making of a Muckraker* (1979) describes her career as a journalist. See also mitford.org.

N. Scott Momaday (b. 1934)
Native American poet, writer, and artist. Momaday grew up on several reservations in the Southwest, but he drew the greatest influence from the Kiowa people of his native Oklahoma. After studying at the University of New Mexico and Stanford University, he began a teaching career that led him to the University of Arizona, where he is currently a professor of humanities. Momaday's Pulitzer Prize–winning novel, *House Made of Dawn* (1968), was a breakthrough not only for him but for American Indian writers in general. Momaday has written several volumes of poetry, including *The Gourd Dancer* (1976) and *In the Presence of the Sun* (1992); autobiographical works including *The Names: A Memoir* (1976) and *The Man Made of Words: Essays, Stories, Passages* (1997); and two collections of Kiowa folktales, *The Way to Rainy Mountain* (1969) and *In the Bear's House* (1999). See also english.illinois.edu/maps.

Toni Morrison (b. 1931)
American novelist. Born to working-class parents and raised in Lorain, Ohio, Morrison received her undergraduate education at Howard University before completing her master's degree at Cornell University. She worked as an editor for a decade before beginning to publish her own writing, much of which centers on the complexities of race and gender. By the time she won the Pulitzer Prize for

Beloved in 1987, she had published four other novels: *The Bluest Eye* (1970), *Sula* (1973), *Song of Solomon* (1977), and *Tar Baby* (1981). After the publication of *Jazz* (1992) she received the 1993 Nobel Prize for literature. Her most recent novels are *Paradise* (1997) and *Love* (2003). Morrison held teaching positions at Howard, Yale, and Rutgers universities before moving to Princeton University, where she is currently a fellow in the Council of the Humanities. See also luminarium.org.

John Muir (1838–1914)
American naturalist and environmentalist. Muir's family emigrated from Scotland to the United States in 1849 and settled in Wisconsin. An avid student of nature, Muir studied geology and botany at the University of Wisconsin, though he left without taking a degree. As a young man, Muir traveled widely in the western United States to study its flora and fauna. He became a vocal advocate for what was then called "preservationism," co-founding the Sierra Club in 1882 to promote the protection of wilderness areas from development. Muir's efforts are largely responsible for the creation of Yosemite National Park; in 1976 the California Historical Society voted him "The Greatest Californian." His writings, which celebrate wilderness and extol the natural beauty of the American West, include such classics as *The Mountains of California* (1894) and *My First Summer in the Sierra* (1911). See also sierraclub.org/john_muir_exhibit.

Vladimir Nabokov (1899–1977)
Russian American poet, novelist, and educator. Born to a wealthy and prominent St. Petersburg family that barely escaped the 1917 revolution, Nabokov was educated at Cambridge University. He settled into the Russian émigré communities of Germany and later France, becoming known as a poet, novelist, and critic. In 1940 Nabokov came to the United States, where he taught literature at Wellesley College and Cornell University, and, now writing in flawless English, published four more novels and numerous essays, stories, and poems. He became an international celebrity and literary icon in 1958, when his controversial novel *Lolita* (1955) was finally published in America. With the earnings from *Lolita* Nabokov retired from teaching and moved into a luxury hotel in Switzerland to devote himself to writing such classic novels as *Pale Fire* (1962) and *Ada* (1969), as well as translating his early Russian novels into English. See also nabokov.com.

Gloria Naylor (b. 1950)
African American fiction writer and essayist. Naylor was born in New York City to parents from Southern sharecropping families who, wanting better opportunities for their daughter, stressed reading and urged her to keep a journal from an early age. She was a member of the Jehovah's Witnesses as a teenager and young adult, but she left the church in 1975. She earned her B.A. from Brooklyn College and began writing her first novel, *The Women of Brewster Place* (1982), winner of the National Book Award for Best First Novel. She then earned an M.A. in Afro-American studies from Yale University and resumed her career as a novelist known for her strong portrayals of black women. Her books include *Linden Hills* (1985), *Mama Day* (1988), *Bailey's Café* (1992), and *The Men of Brewster Place* (1998). Naylor's most recent work, *1996*, was published in 2005. See also aalbc.com.

Ngũgĩ wa Thiong'o (b. 1938)
Kenyan novelist, playwright, and social critic. Born in what was then British East Africa, Ngũgĩ grew up amidst colonialism, revolution, and the emergence of independent Kenya in 1963. His first novel, *Weep Not, Child* (1964), and his second, *A Grain of Wheat* (1967), depict the Mau Mau Uprising against the British. His 1977 play, *Ngaahika Ndeenda*, written in his native Gĩkũyũ and translated by the author as *I Will Marry When I Want* (1982), was critical of the Kenyan government, resulting in Ngũgĩ's year-long imprisonment. He has since lived in self-imposed exile in the United States and is currently a professor of comparative literature at the University of California, Irvine. His books include *Decolonising the Mind* (1986), which argues for the use of native languages; *Wizard of the Crow* (2006), a novel; and *Dreams in a Time of War: A Childhood Memoir* (2010). See also ngugiwathiongo.com.

Barack Obama (b. 1961)
American author, politician, and forty-fourth president of the United States. Born in Honolulu to an American mother and a Kenyan father, Obama grew up in Hawaii and Indonesia before earning degrees at Columbia University and the Harvard Law School. He worked as a community organizer in Chicago and

taught constitutional law at the University of Chicago Law School. Before his election to the U.S. presidency, he served in the Illinois State Senate and the U.S. Senate. Obama is the author of two books: his memoir, *Dreams from My Father* (1995), and a political manifesto, *The Audacity of Hope* (2006). His keynote speech at the 2004 Democratic National Convention catapulted him to national attention; his speech at Cairo University, soon after his inauguration, marked a "new beginning" in U.S. relations with the rest of the world. In 2009 Obama was awarded the Nobel Peace Prize. See also whitehouse.gov/about/presidents.

Mary Oliver (b. 1935)
American poet and essayist. Born in Cleveland, Ohio, Oliver began writing poems during her teenage years. She briefly attended Ohio State University and Vassar College without receiving a degree, choosing instead to concentrate on writing poetry. Today Oliver is the best-selling poet in the United States. Her work, because of its detailed and appreciative attention to nature, is often compared to that of Walt Whitman and Henry David Thoreau; much of her imagery is drawn from her daily walks in Provincetown, Massachusetts, her home for over forty years. Her many books include *Voyage, and Other Poems* (1963); *American Primitive* (1984), winner of the Pulitzer Prize; *Dreamwork* (1986); *New and Selected Poems* (1992), winner of the National Book Award; *Why I Wake Early: New Poems* (2004); *Long Life: Essays and Other Writings* (2004); and *Swan: Poems and Prose Poems* (2010). See also maryoliver.net.

George Orwell (1903–1950)
Pen name of Eric Blair, English journalist, essayist, novelist, and social critic. Born in India and educated in England, Orwell was an officer in the Indian Imperial Police in Burma (1922–1927), an experience he later recounted in the novel *Burmese Days* (1934). In 1927 he went to Europe to pursue his career as a writer. His first book, *Down and Out in Paris and London* (1933), depicts his years of poverty and struggle while working as a dishwasher and day laborer. Orwell's experiences fighting in the Spanish Civil War are the subject of the memoir *Homage to Catalonia* (1938). Of his seven novels, the satiric *Animal Farm* (1945) and the dystopian *Nineteen Eighty-Four* (1949), both indictments of totalitarianism, have become classics. Orwell, one of the most polished and respected stylists in the English language, published five collections of essays, including *Shooting an Elephant and Other Essays* (1950). See also george-orwell.org.

Henry Petroski (b. 1942)
American engineer, author, and educator. A New York City native, Petroski received his bachelor's degree from Manhattan College and his doctorate in mechanics from the University of Illinois at Urbana-Champaign. Currently he teaches civil engineering and history at Duke University, specializing in failure analysis. Having a particular knack for explaining engineering to the nonspecialist, Petroski delights in revealing the technological complexity behind everyday objects like pencils and toothpicks. He is a frequent contributor to the magazines *American Scientist* and *Prism*; his dozen books include *To Engineer Is Human: The Role of Failure in Successful Design* (1985), *The Pencil: A History of Design and Circumstance* (1990), *Invention by Design: How Engineers Get from Thought to Thing* (1996), and a memoir, *Paperboy: Confessions of a Future Engineer* (2002). Petroski's most recent book is *The Essential Engineer: Why Science Alone Will Not Solve Our Global Problems* (2010). See also cee.duke.edu.

Jo-Ann Pilardi (b. 1941)
American philosopher and educator. Pilardi earned her B.A. in English at Duquesne University, her M.A. in philosophy at Pennsylvania State University, and her Ph.D. in humanities at Johns Hopkins University. A longtime activist in the women's liberation movement, Pilardi helped to develop the Women's Studies Program at Maryland's Towson University, where today she is professor emerita of Philosophy and Women's Studies. Her works include *Simone de Beauvoir Writing the Self: Philosophy Becomes Autobiography* (1999) as well as articles on feminism, abortion rights, and social and political philosophy. Most recently she published "From 'Alien' to 'Guest': A Philosophical Scrutiny of the Bush Administration's Guest Worker Initiative," a work of political philosophy that appeared in *Radical Philosophy Today: Philosophy against Empire* (2006). See also towson.edu.

Steven Pinker (b. 1954)
Canadian American experimental psychologist and author. Born in an English-speaking Jewish community of Montreal, Canada, Pinker earned his B.A. in psychology at McGill University and his Ph.D. at Harvard University, where he now teaches. A specialist in the psychology of language and cognition, he has conducted much of his research in the ways that children acquire language. In addition to his scholarly work, Pinker chairs the Usage Panel of the *American Heritage Dictionary* and writes frequently for a general readership, publishing articles in periodicals such as *Time* and the *New York Times.* He is the author of five books: *The Language Instinct* (1994), *How the Mind Works* (1997), *Words and Rules: The Ingredients of Language* (1999), *The Blank Slate: The Modern Denial of Human Nature* (2002), and *The Stuff of Thought: Language as a Window into Human Nature* (2007). See also harvard.edu.

Sylvia Plath (1932–1963)
American poet and novelist. Born in Boston to an Austrian American mother and a German immigrant father who taught at Boston University, Plath was only eight years old when her first poem was published in the *Boston Herald*. While an undergraduate at Smith College, she won a coveted internship at *Mademoiselle* magazine in New York City, an experience she later recounted in her autobiographical novel *The Bell Jar* (1963), a harrowing chronicle of mental illness. Shortly after receiving her B.A. in English, Plath won a Fulbright Scholarship to study at Cambridge University, where she met her future husband, the poet Ted Hughes. In her short lifetime she published only one volume of poetry, *The Colossus and Other Poems* (1960); her second collection, *Ariel* (1963), came out shortly after her death by suicide and immediately secured her place among the greatest American poets of the twentieth century. See also sylvia plath.info.

Plato (c. 428–c. 348 B.C.E.)
Greek philosopher, mathematician, and teacher. Born to an aristocratic family, probably in Athens, Plato was among the most ardent students of the philosopher Socrates. After Socrates was executed in 399 B.C.E., Plato is believed to have traveled throughout the Mediterranean before returning in the 380s to found the Academy, the Western world's first formally constituted institution of higher learning. Most of Plato's known writings are dialogues featuring Socrates in vigorous pursuit of the truth of human existence through tireless questioning. The best-known of these Socratic dialogues, the *Republic*, probes the nature of justice, the relationship between the individual and society, and the ideal "forms" that are, Plato believed, the ultimate reality beyond the world we experience with our senses. Plato remains enormously influential; his teachings were carried on by his student Aristotle, and indeed all of Western philosophy has been called "footnotes to Plato." See also plato.standford.edu.

Michael Pollan (b. 1955)
American journalist, environmentalist, and educator. The son of two writers, Pollan was educated at Bennington College, Oxford University, and Columbia University, where he earned his M.A. in English. Pollan's first book, *Second Nature: A Gardener's Education* (1991), sets the template for a career focused mainly on food—not only as a source of nutrition and pleasure for the individual but also as a critical factor in science, economics, politics, and culture. An outspoken critic of modern industrial agriculture, he has explored these themes in numerous articles and in books such as *The Botany of Desire: A Plant's-Eye View of the World* (2001), *In Defense of Food: An Eater's Manifesto* (2005), and *The Omnivore's Dilemma: A Natural History of Four Meals* (2006). Pollan is a professor of journalism at the University of California, Berkeley. See also michaelpollan.com.

Anna Quindlen (b. 1953)
American journalist and novelist. Born in Philadelphia, Quindlen graduated from Barnard College and immediately began writing for the *New York Post*. Three years later she moved to the *New York Times*, where she would eventually win a Pulitzer Prize for the regular column she once described as "taking things personally for a living." These columns have been collected in *Living Out Loud* (1988) and *Thinking Out Loud* (1993). After twenty years Quindlen left the *Times* to devote herself to writing fiction and has since published six novels, including *Object Lessons* (1991); *One True Thing* (1994), which was made into a movie in 1998; *Black and Blue* (1998); *Blessings* (2002); and *Every Last One* (2010). *How Books Changed My Life* (1998) is her memoir

about the importance of reading. She currently writes a bi-weekly column for *Newsweek*. See also annaquindlen.net.

Jonathan Rauch (b. 1960)
American author and journalist. Born in Phoenix, Arizona, Rauch earned a B.A. at Yale University before commencing his journalism career at the *Winston-Salem Journal* in North Carolina. Now a contributing editor for the *National Journal* in Washington, D.C., Rauch writes about the contemporary American political scene. His essays have appeared in the *New Republic*, the *Atlantic Monthly*, the *New York Times*, and the *Wall Street Journal*. His books include *The Outnation: A Search for the Soul of Japan* (1992), *Kindly Inquisitors: The New Attacks on Free Thought* (1993), *Government's End: Why Washington Stopped Working* (1994, 2000), and most recently *Gay Marriage: Why It Is Good for Gays, Good for Straights, and Good for America* (2004). An outspoken gay activist, Rauch is a vice president of the Independent Gay Forum. See also jonathanrauch.com.

Tom Regan (b. 1938)
American philosopher and teacher. Born in Pittsburgh, Regan earned his B.A. at Thiel College in Pennsylvania and his Ph.D. in philosophy from the University of Virginia. He has spent most of his career teaching philosophy at North Carolina State University, where he is now professor emeritus. His research in theoretical and applied ethics led him to the teachings of Mohandas Gandhi, whom Regan credits for his interest in the ethical treatment of animals. Today Regan is regarded as one of the leading intellectuals in the animal rights movement. His works include *All That Dwell Therein: Essays on Animal Rights and Environmental Ethics* (1982); *The Case for Animal Rights* (1983, 1985, 2004); his autobiography, *The Bird in the Cage: A Glimpse of My Life* (1991); and *Empty Cages: Facing the Challenge of Animal Rights* (2004). See also ncsu.edu.

Adrienne Rich (b. 1929)
American poet and essayist. Born in Baltimore, Maryland, Rich grew up reading and writing poetry from an early age. She published her first volume of poems, *A Change of World* (1951), even before completing her B.A. at Radcliffe College. Her many subsequent collections, reflecting her emergence as a fiercely outspoken feminist, include *Snapshots of a Daughter-in-Law* (1963), the National Book Award–winning *Diving into the Wreck* (1974), *The Fact of a Doorframe: Poems Selected and New, 1950–1984* (1984), *Midnight Salvage* (1999), and *Telephone Ringing in the Labyrinth* (2007). A selection of her essays, *Arts of the Possible: Essays and Conversations*, was published in 2001; her most recent collection is *Tonight No Poetry Will Serve: Poems 2007–2010* (2011). The recipient of many honors, Rich was awarded the National Book Foundation's Medal for Distinguished Contribution to American Letters in 2006. See also poets .org.

Alberto Alvaro Ríos (b. 1952)
American poet, fiction writer, and memoirist. Ríos was born in Nogales, Arizona, to an English mother and a Mexican father. As a child Ríos spoke Spanish and English, but he was chastised by teachers for using Spanish and "forgot" the language until he encountered more encouraging mentors in high school. He earned a B.A. in literature, another in psychology, and an M.F.A. in creative writing, all from the University of Arizona. He currently teaches creative writing at Arizona State University. Ríos is the author of nine books and chapbooks of poetry, including *The Smallest Muscle in the Human Body* (2002) and *The Theater of Night* (2006), along with three collections of short stories. His memoir *Capirotada* (1999) won the Latino Literary Hall of Fame Award. See also asu.edu.

Richard Rodriguez (b. 1944)
American essayist and educator. Born in San Francisco to Mexican American immigrant parents, Rodriguez learned to speak English in a Catholic grammar school in Sacramento, California, and went on to earn a B.A. from Stanford University and an M.A. from Columbia University. Once a doctoral candidate in English literature at the University of California at Berkeley, Rodriguez opted instead to pursue his own path as a teacher, journalist, and author. He now works for the Pacific News Service and is a regular guest on *PBS NewsHour*. In *Hunger of Memory: The Education of Richard Rodriguez* (1982), he recounts his sometimes painful assimilation into mainstream American society. His second book, *Days of Obligation: A Letter to My Mexican Father* (1992), further explores the tensions between his Mexican and his American selves. His most recent book is *Brown: The Last Discovery of America* (2002). See also pbs.org.

Betty Rollin (b. 1936)
American journalist, television reporter, and nonfiction writer. Born in New York City, Rollin spent several years as a stage and television actress before beginning her career in journalism, first at *Vogue* and then at *Look*. In 1971, she became a television news correspondent, chiefly for NBC, where her series on the American Indians on South Dakota's Pine Ridge Reservation won an Emmy. Rollin is the author of seven books, including *First, You Cry* (1976), detailing her bouts with breast cancer; *Am I Getting Paid for This? A Romance about Work* (1982); *Last Wish* (1985), about her terminally ill mother's assisted suicide; and *Here's the Bright Side: Of Failure, Fear, Cancer, Divorce, and Other Bum Raps* (2007), with illustrations by cartoonist Jules Feiffer. See also harrywalker.com/speaker/Betty-Rollin.cfm?Spea_ID=193.

Eleanor Roosevelt (1884–1962)
American first lady and political activist. Roosevelt was born in New York City and educated by tutors until age fifteen, when she was sent to the Allenswood Academy for girls in England. When she was twenty she married future U.S. president Franklin Delano Roosevelt, a distant cousin, and went on to become perhaps the most important and influential first lady in American history. Roosevelt was a strong supporter of her husband's New Deal legislation and of civil rights, and she continued to work actively for these and other causes after his death in 1945. A devoted suffragist, she was committed to improving the status of working women, though she opposed the Equal Rights Amendment, which she felt would be detrimental to women. She was a leading supporter of the United Nations and chaired the committee that drafted and approved the Universal Declaration of Human Rights. See also firstladies.org.

Mike Rose (b. 1944)
American educator and author. Born to Italian immigrant parents in Altoona, Pennsylvania, Rose grew up in Los Angeles. Because of an administrative error at his high school, he was placed in the "vocational track" for academic underachievers; an alert teacher discovered the error, and Rose went on to excel as a student, earning his B.A. from Loyola University and a Ph.D. in education from UCLA. Rose has made a career of championing the academic potential of the poor and underprivileged. A teacher for forty years, he is presently a professor at the UCLA Graduate School of Education and Information Studies. His ten books include *Lives on the Boundary* (1989), which argues that poor preparation, not lack of intelligence, hampers most underachieving students, and *The Mind at Work: Valuing the Intelligence of the American Worker* (2004). See also mikerosebooks.com.

Scott Russell Sanders (b. 1945)
American novelist, essayist, and teacher. Born in Memphis, Tennessee, and educated at Brown and Cambridge Universities, Sanders has spent his teaching career at Indiana University at Bloomington, where he is professor of English. The author of four novels, two short story collections, and seven children's books, he is best known for his nature writing and his eloquent, quietly insightful personal essays. Among his many books are *Wilderness Plots: Tales about the Settlement of the American Land* (1983, 2007); *The Paradise of Bombs* (1987), a collection of essays about violence in the United States; *Staying Put: Making a Home in a Restless World* (1994); *The Force of Spirit* (2001), a collection of meditations on family and the passage of time; *A Private History of Awe* (2006), a spiritual memoir; and *A Conservationist Manifesto* (2009). See also scottrussellsanders.com.

Reg Saner (b. 1931)
American poet and essayist. Born in Jacksonville, Illinois, Saner earned a B.A. at St. Norbert College in Wisconsin. After serving in the U.S. army during the Korean War, he studied at the University of Illinois and the University of Florence in Italy. Saner began teaching creative writing at the University of Colorado at Boulder soon after returning to the United States and retired after thirty-seven years in the classroom. His poems have appeared in, by his own count, 140 journals, and he has authored many collections since his first volume, *Climbing into the Roots* (1976), won the first Walt Whitman Award conferred by the Academy of American Poets. His best-known book is *The Four-Cornered Falcon: Essays on the Interior West and the Natural Scene* (1983); his latest essay collection is *The Dawn Collector: On My Way to the Natural World* (2005). See also pw.org/content/reg_saner_1.

Jean-Paul Sartre (1905–1980)
French philosopher, novelist, playwright, critic, and political activist. Sartre was born

in Paris and earned his doctorate in philosophy at the École Normale Supérieure. While serving as a provincial schoolmaster, he produced a flood of philosophical essays and seminal works, such as the novel *Nausea* (1938) and the short story collection *The Wall* (1939), which embodied the philosophy of radical freedom Sartre called existentialism. Described by the *New York Times* as "a rebel of a thousand causes, a modern Don Quixote," Sartre was a major force in the intellectual life of post–World War II Europe, and existentialism influenced generations of artists and thinkers. Steadfastly independent, Sartre refused the Nobel Prize for literature in 1964. His major works include the plays *The Flies* (1943) and *No Exit* (1944), as well as the essays *Being and Nothingness* (1943) and *Critique of Dialectical Reason* (1960). See also sartre.org.

Chief Seattle (c. 1780–1866)
Native American leader. A fierce young man, Seattle (also Seathl or Sealth) was chief of the Suquamish, Duwamish, and allied Salish tribes of the Pacific Northwest. He was baptized a Roman Catholic in 1848 and, foreseeing the unstoppable influx of whites, became an advocate of peace. Local settlers honored him and his work by naming their town Seattle, an Anglicization of Si'ahl (his name in his native language, Lushootseed). His famous "Address" is a reply to an offer to buy over two million acres of Indian land around Puget Sound, proffered in 1854 by Isaac Stevens, governor of the newly created Washington Territory. (No authenticated translation of the speech exists; the most common version was first published thirty-three years after the fact.) Because of Seattle's example, his people avoided the bloody warfare that afflicted the territory from 1855 until 1870. See also chiefseattle.com.

Peter Singer (b. 1946)
Australian author, philosopher, and ethicist. Born in Melbourne, Australia, to Austrian parents fleeing Nazi persecution of Jews, Singer was educated at Melbourne University and at England's Oxford University. Throughout his subsequent academic career, during which he has held professorships in England, Australia, and the United States, Singer has generated controversy and even outrage for his application of utilitarianism—"the greatest good of the greatest number"—to a wide variety of ethical issues, ranging from euthanasia and abortion to economic justice and animal rights. A prolific author, Singer's principal works include *Animal Liberation* (1975), *Practical Ethics* (1979), and *Rethinking Life and Death* (1994). He is currently a professor of bioethics at Princeton University. See also princeton.edu.

Jennifer Sinor (b. 1969)
American teacher and author. Sinor received her B.A. at the University of Nebraska, her M.A. at the University of Hawaii, and her Ph.D. at the University of Michigan. Presently she teaches creative writing at Utah State University, where she directs the Literature and Writing program. Her essays have appeared in literary journals such as *Fourth Genre*, the *American Scholar*, and *Brevity*. She is the author of *The Extraordinary Work of Ordinary Writing* (2002), based on the diary of Annie Ray, a nineteenth-century settler in the Dakota Territory who was one of Sinor's forebears. She is co-editor of an anthology, *Placing the Academy: Essays on Landscape and Academic Identity* (2007). See also english.usu.edu.

Jane Smiley (b. 1949)
American novelist and essayist. Smiley was born in Los Angeles and grew up in the suburbs of St. Louis, Missouri. She earned a B.A. at Vassar College, and both an M.F.A. and a Ph.D. at the University of Iowa. Her first novel, *Barn Blind*, appeared in 1980; since then she has published twelve more novels, including the Pulitzer Prize–winning *A Thousand Acres* (1985), a contemporary retelling of Shakespeare's *King Lear* set on an Iowa farm. Her latest, *Private Life* (2010), is an intimate depiction of the life of a woman who comes of age in post–Civil War Missouri. Smiley's nonfiction includes the biography *Charles Dickens* (2003), *A Year at the Races: Reflections on Horses, Humans, Love, Money, and Luck* (2004), and *Thirteen Ways of Looking at the Novel* (2005), a consideration of the history of the novel. See also web.mac.com/therealjanesmiley.

Rebecca Solnit (b. 1961)
American journalist and author. Born in San Francisco, Solnit skipped high school altogether, instead passing the GED exam at sixteen, taking classes in a junior college, living for a time in Paris, and, at the age of twenty, completing her B.A. at San Francisco State University. She earned her master's in journalism at the University of

California, Berkeley, in 1984. Since then she has been a journalist, an activist for environmental and human-rights causes, and the author of a dozen books. Solnit's subjects span a remarkable range, from art history to human wanderlust to utopian projects. Her *River of Shadows* (2003), a study of the pioneering nineteenth-century photographer Eadweard Muybridge, won the National Book Critics Circle Award for criticism. Solnit's most recent book is *A Paradise Built in Hell: The Extraordinary Communities That Arise in Disaster* (2009). See also believermag.com.

Susan Sontag (1933–2004)
American essayist, art critic, and filmmaker. Born in New York City, Sontag grew up in Tucson, Arizona, and Los Angeles. After graduating from high school at fifteen, she started classes at the University of California at Berkeley, later earning philosophy degrees from the University of Chicago and Harvard University and studying further at Oxford University and the University of Paris. Sontag's collection of essays *Against Interpretation* (1966) staked out her place as a serious intellectual, just as *Trip to Hanoi* (1968) established her reputation as a political and cultural critic. After a near-fatal bout with breast cancer, she wrote *Illness as Metaphor* (1978), followed by *AIDS and Its Metaphors* (1988). Sontag considered herself foremost a novelist; her novels include *The Volcano Lover* (1992) and the National Book Award–winning *In America* (2001). Her last collection of essays, *Where the Stress Falls*, appeared in 2001. See also susansontag.com.

Elizabeth Cady Stanton (1815–1902)
American abolitionist and women's rights activist. Born in Johnstown, New York, she excelled academically at Johnstown Academy, but because of her sex, was barred from nearby Union College. She married the prominent abolitionist Henry B. Stanton, and the two spent their honeymoon at the World's Anti-Slavery Convention in London. In 1848 Stanton joined Lucretia Mott and others to organize the first American convention for women's rights, held in Seneca Falls, New York, where Stanton presented her draft of "The Declaration of Sentiments and Resolutions," now seen as a founding document of modern feminism. Three years later she was introduced to Susan B. Anthony, who became her lifelong friend and colleague; together they founded the National Woman Suffrage Association in 1869. Stanton spent the rest of her life campaigning for women's suffrage and legislation that would make divorce laws more favorable to women. See also nps.gov.

Brent Staples (b. 1951)
African American journalist and essayist. Born in Chester, Pennsylvania, Staples earned his B.A. from Widener University and his Ph.D. in psychology from the University of Chicago. After several years teaching college psychology, he began his career in journalism with a brief stint at the *Chicago Sun-Times* before joining the *New York Times* in 1983. Staples has often written about the role of race in American culture, striving to broaden the consideration of the "black experience"—an expression he says he despises—beyond stereotypes of poverty and crime. Indeed, a list of his recent *New York Times* articles includes topics as diverse as plagiarism, gardening, and urban wildlife. In 1990 he joined the *Times* editorial board. His memoir, *Parallel Time: Growing Up in Black and White*, was published in 1994. See also nyt.com.

Gloria Steinem (b. 1934)
American journalist, editor, and feminist. Steinem was born in Toledo, Ohio, to a father who was an itinerant antique-dealer and a mother whose mental instability Steinem would later attribute in part to sexism. After receiving a B.A. from Smith College, Steinem spent two years studying in India and returned to the United States fiercely committed to social justice. While working as a freelance journalist, she helped to found *New York* magazine in 1968; in 1971, by then an influential spokesperson for the women's movement, Steinem became founding editor of *Ms.* magazine. Her books include two collections of her essays, *Outrageous Acts and Everyday Rebellions* (1983) and *Moving Beyond Words: Age, Rage, Sex, Power, Money, Muscles: Breaking the Boundaries of Gender* (1995); *Marilyn: Norma Jean* (1986), a biography of Marilyn Monroe; *Revolution from Within: A Book of Self-Esteem* (1992); and, as editor, *The Reader's Companion to Women's History* (1999). See also gloriasteinem.com.

Sandra Steingraber (b. 1959)
American biologist, poet, and essayist. A native of Illinois, Steingraber received her B.A. in biology from Illinois Wesleyan University, her M.A. in English from Illinois

State University, and her Ph.D. in biology from the University of Michigan. Since a near-fatal bout with bladder cancer when she was in her twenties, Steingraber has devoted her career to exploring the connections between the environment and human health. Her first book was a volume of intimately personal poems, *Post-Diagnosis* (1995). In *Living Downstream: An Ecologist Looks at Cancer and the Environment* (1997, 2010), she examines the links between industrial chemicals and increased risks of cancer; following its publication, Steingraber was hailed as "the new Rachel Carson" by the Sierra Club. *Having Faith: An Ecologist's Journey to Motherhood* (2001) explores "the intimate ecology of motherhood." Steingraber currently teaches at Cornell University in Ithaca, New York. See also steingraber.com.

Fred Strebeigh (b. 1951)
American nonfiction writer and teacher. Born in New York City and raised in Nonquitt, Massachusetts, Strebeigh attended Yale University, where he now teaches nonfiction writing in the English department and the School of Forestry and Environmental Studies. His work, ranging from natural and environmental history to the legal system, has appeared in the *Atlantic Monthly*, *Audubon*, *Legal Affairs*, the *New Republic*, *Smithsonian*, the *New York Times Magazine*, and *Sierra* magazine. In 2009 Strebeigh published the book *Equal: Women Reshape American Law*. See also strebeigh.com.

Andrew Sullivan (b. 1963)
English journalist, editor, and author. Born and raised south of London, Sullivan earned his B.A. at Oxford University and a Ph.D. in government from Harvard University. His "traditional conservatism," as he calls it, combining elements of both left- and right-wing ideologies, has won a large readership for his insightful and sometimes acerbic commentary on the American political scene. A former editor of the *New Republic*, Sullivan began his politics blog, The Daily Dish, in 2000 and was soon attracting over 300,000 visits each month; The Daily Dish is currently hosted on The Atlantic Online, the *Atlantic Monthly*'s online presence. Sullivan's five books include *Virtually Normal: An Argument about Homosexuality* (1995), which makes the case for same-sex marriage; *Love Undetectable: Notes on Friendship, Sex, and Survival* (1998); and *The Conservative Soul: How We Lost It, How to Get It Back* (2006). See also andrewsullivan.theatlantic.com.

Jonathan Swift (1667–1745)
Anglo-Irish poet, satirist, and cleric. Born to English parents who resided in Ireland, Swift studied at Trinity College, Dublin, and then moved to London in 1689. There he became part of the literary and political worlds, beginning his career by writing political pamphlets in support first of the Whigs, then the Tories. Swift earned a master's degree at Oxford University before returning to Ireland. Ordained in the Church of Ireland in 1695, he was appointed dean of St. Patrick's Cathedral, Dublin, in 1713 and held the post until his death. One of the master satirists of the English language, he wrote several scathing attacks on extremism and anti-Irish bigotry, including *The Battle of the Books* (1704), *A Tale of a Tub* (1704), and *A Modest Proposal* (1729), but he is probably best known for the imaginative worlds he created in *Gulliver's Travels* (1726). See also online-literature.com.

Paul Theroux (b. 1941)
American novelist, essayist, and travel writer. Born in Medford, Massachusetts, Theroux earned a B.A. at the University of Massachusetts before teaching in Malawi as a Peace Corps volunteer, and at Uganda's Makerere University and the University of Singapore. Since then he has lived mainly in England when not traveling all over the world—by train whenever possible. Theroux's novels include *Waldo* (1967), *Saint Jack* (1973), *The Mosquito Coast* (1981), and *Dr. Slaughter* (1984), each made into a movie. He is best known for his travel books, particularly *The Great Railway Bazaar: By Train through Asia* (1975), *The Old Patagonian Express: By Train through the Americas* (1979), *Riding the Iron Rooster* (1988), *The Happy Isles of Oceania* (1992), *Dark Star Safari* (2002), *A Dead Hand: A Crime in Calcutta* (2009). See also paultheroux.com.

Lewis Thomas (1913–1993)
American physician, science writer, and teacher. Educated at Princeton University and Harvard Medical School, Thomas specialized in pediatrics, public health, and cancer research. From 1973 to 1980 he served as president of Memorial Sloan-Kettering Cancer Center in New York City. In 1970 Thomas began writing occa-

sional essays for the *New England Journal of Medicine*. A number of these were gathered in *The Lives of a Cell* (1974), a National Book Award winner that established Thomas's reputation as a science writer. Other collections include *The Medusa and the Snail* (1979), *Late Night Thoughts on Listening to Mahler's Ninth Symphony* (1983), *Et Cetera, Et Cetera: Notes of a Word Watcher* (1991), and *The Fragile Species* (1992). Thomas's autobiography, *The Youngest Science: Notes of a Medicine-Watcher* (1983), traces the history of modern medicine, much of which developed during the course of his lifetime. See also vcu.edu.

Henry David Thoreau (1817–1862)
American philosopher, essayist, naturalist, and poet. A graduate of Harvard University, Thoreau worked at a number of jobs—schoolmaster, house painter, employee in his father's pencil factory—before becoming a writer. He befriended Emerson and joined the Transcendental Club, contributing frequently to its journal, the *Dial*. Drawn to the natural world, he wrote his first book, *A Week on the Concord and Merrimac Rivers* (1849), about a canoe trip with his brother. Thoreau's abolitionist stance against slavery led to his arrest for refusing to pay the Massachusetts poll tax (an act of protest against the Mexican War, which he viewed as serving the interests of slaveholders). His eloquent essay defending this act, "Civil Disobedience" (1849); his probing meditation on the solitary life, *Walden* (1854); and his speech "A Plea for Captain John Brown" (1859) are classics of American literature. See also vcu.edu.

Sallie Tisdale (b. 1957)
American nurse and essayist. Born in Eureka, California, Tisdale earned a nursing degree from the University of Portland in 1983. She has worked as a registered nurse and taught at Reed College, Northwestern University, and New York University. A largely self-taught writer on health and medical issues, Tisdale has contributed to the *Antioch Review*, *Esquire*, *Harper's*, and many other publications. "I am really a generalist," she writes, "drawn to a variety of subjects and points of view, but memoir and the first-person essay are the core of all I do." Her books include *The Sorcerer's Apprentice: Tales of the Modern Hospital* (1986), *Lot's Wife* (1988), *Talk Dirty to Me* (1994), *The Best Thing I Ever Tasted: The Secret of Food* (2000), and *Women of the Way: Discovering 2,500 Years of Buddhist Wisdom* (2006). She is a contributing editor at *Harper's* and Salon.com. See also inlander.com.

Susan Allen Toth (b. 1940)
American essayist, memoirist, and travel writer. Born in Ames, Iowa, Toth was educated at Smith College, the University of California at Berkeley, and the University of Minnesota. She taught English at Macalester College until she was in her mid-thirties, when she became a freelance travel writer and autobiographer. Her memoirs include *Blooming: A Small-Town Girlhood* (1981), *Ivy Days: Making My Own Way Back East* (1984), and *Leaning into the Wind: A Memoir of Midwest Weather* (2003). Toth frequently writes about her travels in England for the *New York Times* and has published three books about this favorite destination: *My Love Affair with England: A Traveler's Memoir* (1992), *England as You Like It* (1995), and *England for All Seasons* (1997). Her personal essays are collected in *How to Prepare for Your High School Reunion and Other Midlife Musings* (1988). See also dcn.davis.ca.us/~gizmo/toth.html.

Barbara Tuchman (1912–1989)
American historian. After graduating from Radcliffe College in 1933, Tuchman worked as a research assistant for the Institute of Pacific Relations, an experience that later found expression in the Pulitzer Prize–winning *Stilwell and the American Experience in China* (1971). During the 1930s and 1940s she wrote on politics for the *Nation*, covered the Spanish Civil War as a journalist, and after the Japanese attack on Pearl Harbor took a job with the U.S. Office of War Information. Critical and public acclaim followed the publication of two books on the origins of World War I: *The Zimmerman Telegram* (1958) and *The Guns of August* (1962), her first Pulitzer Prize winner. Her other books include *The Proud Tower* (1966), *A Distant Mirror: The Calamitous Fourteenth Century* (1978), *The March of Folly: From Troy to Vietnam* (1984), and *Practicing History* (1981), a collection of articles, reviews, and talks. See also kirjasto.sci.fi/tuchman.htm.

Mark Twain (1835–1910)
Pen name of Samuel Clemens, American journalist, novelist, and humorist. Twain grew up in Hannibal, Missouri, beside the river that he would later immortalize in

the memoir *Life on the Mississippi* (1883) and in *The Adventures of Huckleberry Finn* (1885), one of the greatest American novels. First apprenticed as a printer, he was by turns a riverboat pilot, a Confederate soldier (for two weeks), a gold prospector, and a journalist. His short story "The Celebrated Jumping Frog of Calaveras County" (1867) made him famous; during his lifetime he was enormously popular, lecturing widely to great acclaim and publishing a flood of articles, essays, stories, and novels. Many of his books, including the memoir *Roughing It* (1872) and the novel *The Adventures of Tom Sawyer* (1876), are classics. William Faulkner called Twain "the father of American literature." See also mtwain.com.

Laurel Thatcher Ulrich (b. 1938)
American historian. Raised on a farm in eastern Idaho, Ulrich studied at the University of Utah, Simmons College, and the University of New Hampshire, where she earned her Ph.D. and became a professor of history. In her Pulitzer Prize–winning study, *A Midwife's Tale: The Life of Martha Ballard, Based on Her Diary, 1785–1812* (1991), Ulrich wrote that "well-behaved women seldom make history," a phrase that took on a life of its own, appearing on T-shirts, bumper stickers, and other commercial paraphernalia. Ulrich has continued writing scholarly works such as *The Age of Homespun: Objects and Stories in the Creation of an American Myth* (2001); her most recent book, *Well-Behaved Women* (2007), returns to her famous phrase and explores the myriad ways women have affected the course of history. Ulrich currently teaches at Harvard University. See also history.fas.harvard.edu.

James van Tholen (1964–2001)
American pastor. Van Tholen attended Calvin Theological Seminary before becoming the pastor of Rochester Christian Reformed Church in Rochester, New York, at the age of thirty-one. Just two years later he was diagnosed with a severe and fatal form of cancer that forced him to leave his congregation for seven months while he underwent an array of aggressive treatments. When the sermon he gave upon returning to the pulpit, "Surprised by Death," was published in *Christianity Today*, it was immediately recognized as a classic assertion of spiritual courage in the face of mortality. A collection of Van Tholen's sermons was published posthumously as *Where All Hope Lies: Sermons for the Liturgical Years* (2003). See also christianitytoday.com.

Alice Walker (b. 1944)
African American poet, novelist, essayist, and social activist. Born to a sharecropping family in rural Georgia, Walker attended Spelman College and Sarah Lawrence College, where she wrote her first book of poems, *Once* (1968). As an editor for *Ms.* magazine, Walker championed a revival of interest in the work of Zora Neale Hurston before receiving widespread fame for her third novel, *The Color Purple* (1982), winner of both the Pulitzer Prize and the National Book Award. Walker's subsequent novels include *The Temple of My Familiar* (1989) and *Possessing the Secret of Joy* (1992). Her essays have been collected in numerous volumes, including *In Search of Our Mothers' Gardens: Womanist Prose* (1983) and *Overcoming Speechlessness* (2010). She lives in San Francisco, where she runs the publishing company Wild Tree Press. See also alicewalkersgarden.com.

David Foster Wallace (1962–2008)
American novelist and nonfiction writer. Born in Ithaca, New York, Wallace grew up in Champaign and Urbana, Illinois, the son of two college professors. He earned a B.A. in English and philosophy at Amherst College; his English thesis would become his first novel, *The Broom of the System* (1987). He went on to earn an M.F.A. in creative writing at the University of Arizona. His second novel, the massive *Infinite Jest* (1996), showcases Wallace's penchant for experimental metafiction, baroque language, ironic detachment, and layered footnotes. Wallace's ten books include the short story collections *Brief Interviews with Hideous Men* (1999) and *Oblivion* (2004), and the essay collections *A Supposedly Fun Thing I'll Never Do Again* (1997) and *Consider the Lobster* (2005). Wallace received a MacArthur Foundation Grant in 1997. His third novel, *The Pale King*, was unfinished when he took his own life in 2008. See also davidfosterwallace.com.

Henry Wechsler (b. 1932)
American research psychologist and educator. Wechsler was born in Warsaw, Poland, and immigrated with his family to the United States during World War II. He received an A.B. from Washington and Jefferson College and an M.A. and a Ph.D. in social psychology from Harvard Univer-

sity. Wechsler has written numerous articles and contributed to books on medical and psychological topics. He is currently a lecturer of social psychology at the Harvard School of Public Health, where since 1992 he has been principal investigator for the nationwide College Alcohol Study. His research group has conducted a number of controversial studies about the effects of alcohol policies and high-risk behaviors such as binge drinking, a term that Wechsler has been credited with popularizing. See also harvard.edu.

Steven Weinberg (b. 1933)
American physicist. Born in New York City, Weinberg earned his B.A. at Cornell University, studied at Copenhagen's Niels Bohr Institute, and in 1957 completed his Ph.D. in physics at Princeton University. His research in particle physics—the study of natural forces that govern the material universe at the very smallest scale—won Weinberg the Nobel Prize in 1979. Since 1982 he has taught at the University of Texas at Austin. His writings include two of the most important textbooks in contemporary science: *Gravitation and Cosmology* (1972) and *The Quantum Theory of Fields* (1995, 1996, 2003). *The First Three Minutes: A Modern View of the Origin of the Universe* (1977, 1993) is one of the most highly regarded explanations for the nonspecialist of current scientific thinking in cosmology. An outspoken atheist, Weinberg has written that "the more the universe seems comprehensible, the more it seems pointless." See also nobelprize.org.

Gene Weingarten (b. 1951)
American journalist. Born in New York City, Weingarten studied psychology at New York University because, he says, "it was the easiest major"; nevertheless, he became so immersed in his work for the school newspaper that he never completed his degree. Instead, he went to work for the *Miami Herald*'s Sunday magazine, *Tropic*, which won two Pulitzer Prizes during his tenure as editor. Since joining the *Washington Post*, he has contributed the weekly humor column "Below the Beltway," and his feature articles have won him two Pulitzer Prizes of his own: one in 2008 for his story "Pearls before Breakfast," about a busking violin virtuoso, and another in 2010 for "Fatal Distraction," about the perils of leaving children unattended in cars. His books include *The Hypochondriac's Guide to Life And Death* (1998) and *The Fiddler in the Subway* (2010). See also washingtonpost.com.

Eudora Welty (1909–2001)
American writer, critic, and photographer. Born and raised in Jackson, Mississippi, Welty became one of the South's leading literary voices. After graduating from the University of Wisconsin in 1929 and studying for a year at Columbia University's School of Business, she returned to Jackson and became a publicity agent for the Works Progress Administration, a New Deal social agency. With the help of Robert Penn Warren and Cleanth Brooks, she published several short stories that launched her literary career. Best known for her masterly short fiction—her *Collected Stories* came out in 1982—Welty's work includes such novellas and novels as *The Robber Bridegroom* (1942) and *The Optimist's Daughter* (Pulitzer Prize, 1972); two volumes of photographs; and an acclaimed collection of critical essays, *The Eye of the Story* (1978). Three lectures delivered at Harvard University in April 1983 were published as *One Writer's Beginnings* (1984). See also eudorawelty.org.

E. B. White (1899–1985)
American poet, journalist, editor, and essayist. Elwyn Brooks White was born in Mount Vernon, New York. Just three years after graduating from Cornell University in 1921, he began a sixty-year career on the staff of the *New Yorker*, contributing poems and articles and serving as a discreet and helpful editor. Among his many books, three written for children earned him lasting fame: *Stuart Little* (1945), *Charlotte's Web* (1952), and *The Trumpet of the Swan* (1970). Renowned for his graceful prose, White revised and edited William Strunk's text *The Elements of Style* (1919, 1959), a classic guide to writing still widely known as "Strunk and White." The collected *Essays of E. B. White* was published in 1977; a year later White was awarded a Pulitzer Prize for a lifetime of literary achievement. See also kirjasto.sci.fi/ebwhite.htm.

Walt Whitman (1819–1892)
American poet and essayist. Born on Long Island and raised in Brooklyn, New York, Whitman received scant formal education before going to work at age eleven in a newspaper office. He taught school and worked at several government posts during his lifetime, but Whitman considered

himself primarily a writer, publishing poetry, stories, and newspaper articles from the age of nineteen. In 1855 he published *Leaves of Grass*, a series of twelve poems notable for their expansive spirit, use of free verse, and the almost biblical cadences of their clear, colloquial language. As it evolved through its various editions, *Leaves of Grass* came to include well over 100 poems, including "Song of Myself," "Crossing Brooklyn Ferry," and "Out of the Cradle Endlessly Rocking." In his poetry and prose, Whitman exuberantly celebrates the landscape and people of the United States. See also whitman archive.org.

Patricia Williams (b. 1951)
American legal scholar and critic. Williams received her B.A. from Wellesley College and her J.D. from Harvard Law School. Currently a professor at Columbia Law School, she is a leading proponent of critical race theory, which argues that race is a principal determinant in the legal system and in culture generally. Williams writes a regular column for the *Nation* titled "Diary of a Mad Law Professor." Her books include *The Alchemy of Race and Rights: A Diary of a Law Professor* (1991), *The Rooster's Egg* (1995), *Seeing a Color-Blind Future: The Paradox of Race* (1997), and *Open House: Of Family, Friends, Food, Piano Lessons, and the Search for a Room of My Own* (2004). She has received a MacArthur Foundation Fellowship, along with numerous other honors. See also thenation.com.

Terry Tempest Williams (b. 1955)
American poet, nature writer, and environmental activist. Born to a Mormon family in Corona, California, Williams grew up surrounded by the vast desert landscape of Utah; she holds degrees in both English and environmental education from the University of Utah. Her first book, *Pieces of White Shell: A Journey to Navajoland* (1984), is a personal exploration of Native American myths. Her much-reprinted essay, "The Clan of One-Breasted Women," became the final section of the autobiographical *Refuge: An Unnatural History of Family and Place* (1991). Her subsequent books include *An Unspoken Hunger: Stories from the Field* (1994), *Red: Passion and Patience in the Desert* (2001), *The Open Space of Democracy* (2004), and *Finding Beauty in a Broken World* (2008). Williams is a frequent contributor to the *New York Times*, the *New Yorker*, and *Orion Magazine*. See also terrytempestwilliams.com.

Edward O. Wilson (b. 1929)
American biologist, ecologist, and author. Born in Birmingham, Alabama, Wilson earned his B.S. and M.S. degrees at the University of Alabama and his Ph.D. from Harvard University, where he is a research professor of evolutionary biology. His lifelong study of ants has provided the foundation of a new scientific field he calls sociobiology, "the systematic study of the biological basis of all social behavior"; he has been called "the father of biodiversity" for his contributions to ecology. Wilson's many books include *Sociobiology: The New Synthesis* (1975); *The Diversity of Life* (1992); *Naturalist* (1994), his memoir; *Consilience: The Unity of Knowledge* (1998), in which Wilson coined the phrase "scientific humanism"; *The Creation: An Appeal to Save Life on Earth* (2006); and *Anthill* (2010), a novel. Wilson has twice won the Pulitzer Prize, for *On Human Nature* (1979) and *The Ants* (with Bert Hölldobler, 1991). See also encyclopediaofalabama.org.

Tom Wolfe (b. 1931)
American journalist, essayist, and novelist. A native of Richmond, Virginia, Wolfe earned a B.A. at Washington and Lee University and a Ph.D. in American studies from Yale. Working as a traditional journalist at the *Washington Post* and the *New York Herald Tribune*, Wolfe started to utilize techniques derived from narrative fiction, creating what became known as "the New Journalism." Books such as *The Kandy-Kolored Tangerine-Flake Streamline Baby* (1965), *The Electric Kool-Aid Acid Test* (1968), and *From Bauhaus to Our House* (1981) established his reputation as a witty social critic and historian of popular culture. Wolfe's National Book Award–winning chronicle of the American space program, *The Right Stuff* (1979), was made into a popular film. His ambitiously sprawling satiric novels—*Bonfire of the Vanities* (1987), *A Man in Full* (1998), and *I Am Charlotte Simmons* (2005)—aim to depict the breadth of American society. See also tomwolfe.com.

Mary Wollstonecraft (1759–1797)
English social critic, philosopher, and novelist. Born in London to a troubled family with dwindling fortunes, Wollstonecraft had little formal schooling but read widely. She left home early and, with

her sisters and her best friend, started a school, which soon closed. By 1787, as she began channeling her ideas into prose, she suffered the devastating losses of both her mother and her best friend. In the years that followed, Wollstonecraft published essays, translations, novels, and a children's book. *A Vindication of the Rights of Men* (1790), which supported the republican principles of the French Revolution, was an instant success and established her reputation in literary and political circles. *A Vindication of the Rights of Women* (1792), an important early feminist treatise, presents a radical yet tightly reasoned argument for social and educational equality between women and men. See also plato.stanford.edu.

Virginia Woolf (1882–1941)
English novelist, critic, and essayist. The London-born daughter of the eminent philosopher Sir Leslie Stephen, Woolf was mainly self-educated through her unrestricted reading in her father's substantial library. For decades she was at the center of the Bloomsbury Group, a celebrated collection of artists, scholars, and writers that included both Woolf and her husband, socialist writer Leonard Woolf. Together, the Woolfs founded and operated the Hogarth Press, whose publications included many of her works. A foremost modernist, Woolf employed penetrating psychological insight, lyrical intensity, and experimental literary techniques in her fiction; her nine novels include the now-classic *Mrs. Dalloway* (1925), *To the Lighthouse* (1927), and *The Waves* (1931). Her numerous essays are collected in four volumes; they include *A Room of One's Own* (1929), a historical investigation of women and creativity; and *Three Guineas* (1938), philosophical dialogues that explore issues of war and feminism. See also www.virginiawoolfsociety.co.uk.

William Zinsser (b. 1922)
American journalist, editor, and educator. Born in New York City, Zinsser graduated from Princeton University and then served in the army for two years at the end of World War II. In 1946 he joined the staff of the *New York Herald Tribune*, first as a features editor, then as a drama editor and film critic, and finally as an editorial writer. A freelancer throughout the 1960s, Zinsser contributed to *Life*, *Look*, the *New York Times Magazine*, and other publications. In the 1970s he joined the English faculty at Yale University, where he taught nonfiction writing and edited the alumni magazine. Zinsser wrote seventeen books ranging from travel to jazz to baseball, but he is best known for *On Writing Well* (1976, 1998), a classic guide to clear, economical nonfiction writing. Recently, he has published the memoir *Writing Places: The Life Journey of a Writer and Teacher* (2009). See also williamzinsserwriter.com.

Permissions Acknowledgments

TEXT:

Edward Abbey: "The Serpents of Paradise" from *Desert Solitaire* by Edward Abbey. Reprinted by permission of Don Congdon Associates, Inc. Copyright © 1968 by Edward Abbey, renewed © 1996 by Clarke Abbey.

Philip Alcabes: "The Bioterrorism Scare" from *The American Scholar* 73.2 (2004) is reprinted by permission of International Creative Management, Inc. Copyright © 2004 by Philip Alcabes.

Sherman Alexie: "Superman and Me" from the *Los Angeles Times,* series "The Joy of Reading and Writing", Apr. 19, 1998. Copyright © 1998 by Sherman Alexie. Used by permission of the author. All rights reserved.

Maya Angelou: Selection entitled "Graduation" (retitled) from *I Know Why The Caged Bird Sings* by Maya Angelou. Copyright © 1969 and renewed 1997 by Maya Angelou. Reprinted by permission of Random House, Inc.

Gloria Anzaldua: "How to Tame a Wild Tongue" from *Borderlands: La Frontera, The New Mestiza.* Copyright © 1987, 1999, 2007 by Gloria Anzaldua. Reprinted by permission of Aunt Lute Books.

Hannah Arendt: "Deportations from Western Europe" from *Eichmann in Jerusalem* by Hannah Arendt, copyright © 1963, 1964 by Hannah Arendt. Used by permission of Viking Penguin, a division of Penguin Group (USA) Inc.

Isaac Asimov: "The Eureka Phenomenon" by Isaac Asimov, copyright © by Isaac Asimov. Reprinted by permission of the Estate of Isaac Asimov.

Nicholson Baker: "The Charms of Wikipedia" first appeared in *The New York Review of Books.* Copyright © 2008 by Nicholson Baker. Reprinted with permission of Melanie Jackson Agency, LLC.

James Baldwin: "Stranger in the Village" from *Notes of a Native Son* by James Baldwin. Copyright © 1955, renewed © 1983, by James Baldwin. Reprinted by permission of Beacon Press, Boston.

Randall Balmer: "Diversity and Stability: The Paradox of Religious Pluralism" from *Blessed Assurance: A History of Evangelicalism in America,* copyright © 1999 by Beacon Press. Reprinted with permission of Beacon Press via Copyright Clearance Center.

Dennis Baron: "Yes, We Want—Who Owns Global English?" is reprinted by permission of the author from *The Web of Language,* online, Apr. 21, 2010.

Roland Barthes: "Toys" from *Mythologies* by Roland Barthes, trans. by Annette Lavers. Translation copyright © 1972 by Jonathan Cape Ltd. Reprinted by permission of Hill and Wang, a division of Farrar, Straus and Giroux, LLC and Random House Group Ltd.

Caroline Bird: "College Is a Waste of Time and Money" from *The Case Against College* (1975) by Caroline Bird. Reprinted by permission of the author.

Jacob Bronowski: *Human Values* by Jacob Bronowski. Copyright © 1956, 1965 by Jacob Bronowski. Copyright © renewed 1954, 1993 by Rita Bronowski. All rights reserved. Reprinted by permission of Scribner, a division of Simon &: Schuster, Inc.

David Brooks: "The Gender Gap at School" from *The New York Times,* June 11, 2006, copyright © 2006 by The New York Times. All rights reserved. Used by permission and protected by the Copyright Laws of the United States. The printing, copying, redistribution, or retransmission of the material without written permission is prohibited.

Ken Bruffee: "Binge Drinking as a Substitute for a Community of Learning" by Ken Brufee from *Chronicle of Higher Education* Feb. 9, 1999 is reprinted by permission of the author.

Anthony Burgess: "Is America Falling Apart?" by Anthony Burgess from *The New York Times Magazine*, Nov. 7, 1971 is reprinted by permission of the Literary Estate of Anthony Burgess. Copyright © The Estate of Anthony Burgess.

Colby Buzzell: From *My War: Killing Time in Iraq*, copyright © 2005 by Colby Buzzell. Used by permission of G.P. Putnam's Sons, a division of Penguin Group (USA) Inc.

Nicholas Carr: "Is Google Making Us Stupid?" from the atlantic.com July/August 2008 is reprinted by permission of the author. Copyright © 2008 by Nicholas Carr.

Rachel Carson: "The Moving Tides" from *The Sea Around Us*. Copyright © 1950 by Rachel L. Carson. Reprinted by permission of Frances Collin, Trustee.

Stephen Carter: "The Separation of Church and State" from *The Culture of Disbelief: How American Law and Politics Trivialize Religion* Copyright © 1993 Stephen L Carter. Reprinted by permission of Basic Books, a member of the Perseus Books Group via Copyright Clearance Center.

Michael Chabon: "Kids' Stuff" from *Maps & Legends: Reading and Writing Along the Borderlands* (McSweeney's Books). Copyright © 2008 by Michael Chabon. All Rights Reserved. Reprinted by arrangement with Mary Evans, Inc.

Aaron Copland: "How We Listen" from *What to Listen for in Music* by Aaron Copland. Reprinted by permission of Aaron Copland Fund for Music, Inc., copyright owner.

William Cronon: "The Trouble with Wilderness, or, Getting Back to the Wrong Nature" by William Cronon from *Uncommon Ground*, ed. by William Cronon. Copyright © 1995 by William Cronon. Used by permission of W. W. Norton & Company, Inc.

Amy Cunningham: "Why Women Smile" first appeared, in different form, in *Lear's Magazine* 1993, is reprinted by permission of the author.

Debra Dickerson: "Who Shot Johnny?: A Day in the Life of Black America" by Debra Dickerson from *The New Republic* Jan. 1, 1996, is reprinted by permission of the author.

Joan Didion: "On Going Home" and "On Keeping a Notebook" from *Slouching Towards Bethlehem* by Joan Didion. Copyright © 1966, 1968, renewed 1996 by Joan Didion. Reprinted by permission of Farrar, Straus, and Giroux, LLC.

Annie Dillard: From *An American Childhood* by Annie Dillard, copyright © 1987 by Annie Dillard, is reprinted by permission of HarperCollins Publishers. "Sight into Insight' by Annie Dillard from *Harper's Magazine*, Feb. 1974, is reprinted by permission of the author and Blanche C. Gregory, Inc.

Michael Dirda: "In Wildness Is the Preservation of the World" from *Book by Book: Notes on Reading and Life* by Michael Dirda. Copyright © 2006 by Michael Dirda. Reprinted by arrangement with Henry Holt and Company, LLC.

Mark Doty: "Soul on Ice" from www.poets.com, was later published in slightly different form in *Introspections: Contemporary American Poets on one of Their Own Poems*, ed. by Robert Pack and Jay Parini (1997). Reprinted by permission of the publisher and author, copyright © University Press of New England, Lebanon, NH.

Rita Dove: "The Epistle of Paul the Apostle to the Ephesians" from *Incarnation: Contemporary Writers on the New Testament*, Viking Press, © 1990 by Rita Dove. Reprinted by permission of the author.

Brian Doyle: "Joyas Voladoras" is reprinted by permission of the publisher from *The American Scholar*, vol. 73, No. 4, Autumn 2004. Copyright © 2004 by the author.

Barbara Ehrenreich: "Guys Just Want to Have Fun" from *Time* magazine July 23, 2006. Copyright © 2006 by Time Inc. Reprinted by permission. TIME is a registered trademark of Time Inc. Inc. All rights reserved."

Lars Eighner: "On Dumpster Diving" from *Travels with Lisbeth: Three Years on the Road and on the Streets* by Lars Eighner. Copyright © 1993 by Lars Eighner. Reprinted by permission of St. Martin's Press.

Nora Ephron: "The Boston Photographs" by Nora Ephron is reprinted by permission of International Creative Management, Inc. Copyright © 1975 by Nora Ephron.

Anne Fadiman: "Night Owl" from *At Large and at Small*. Copyright © 2007 by Anne Fadiman. Reprinted by permission of Farrar, Straus and Giroux, LLC.

William Faulkner: "Nobel Prize Award Speech" from *Essays, Speeches and Public Letters* by William Faulkner, ed. by James Merriwether. Copyright © 1965 by Random House, Inc. Reprinted by permission.

M. F. K. Fisher: "Young Hunger" from *As They Were* by M. F. K. Fisher, copyright © 1955, 1961, 1979, 1981, 1982 by M. F. K. Fisher. Used by permission of Alfred A. Knopf, a division of Random House, Inc.

Frances FitzGerald: "Rewriting American History" from *America Revised: History Schoolbooks in the Twentieth Century*. Published by Little Brown and Company. Copyright © 1979, 1980 by Frances Fitzgerald. Reprinted by permission of Lescher & Lescher, Ltd. All rights reserved.

H. Bruce Franklin: From "Realism to Virtual Reality: Images of America's Wars" by H. Bruce Franklin from *The Georgia Review*, Spring 1994. Copyright © 1994 by H. Bruce Franklin. Reprinted by permission of the author.

Joey Franklin: "Working at Wendy's" by Joey Franklin, copyright © 2006 by Joey Franklin, from *20 Something Essays by 20 Something Writers*, ed. by Matt Kellog and Jillian Quint. Used by permission of Random House Trade Paperbacks, a division of Random House, Inc.

Ian Frazier: "Take the F" from *Gone to New York*. Copyright © 2005 by Ian Frazier. Reprinted by permission of Farrar, Straus and Giroux, LLC.

Thomas Friedman: "America's Real Dream Team" from *The New York Times*, March 21, 2010, copyright © 2010 by The New York Times. All rights reserved. Used by permission and protected by the Copyright Laws of the United States. The printing, copying, redistribution, or retransmission of the Material without express written permission is prohibited.

Northrop Frye: "The Motive for Metaphor" from *The Educated Imagination* by Northrop Frye. Copyright © 1963 by Northrop Frye and the Canadian Broadcasting Corporation. Reprinted with permission of Indiana University Press and House of Anansi Press., www.anansi.ca

Paul Fussell: "Thank God for the Atom Bomb" from *The New Republic*, Aug. 22 and Aug. 29 1981. Copyright © 1981 The New Republic, Inc. Reprinted by permission of the publisher.

Henry Louis Gates, Jr.: "In the Kitchen" from *Colored People: A Memoir* by Henry Gates, Jr., copyright © 1994 by Henry Louis Gates, Jr. Used by permission of Alfred A. Knopf, a division of Random House, Inc.

Atul Gawande: "When Doctors Make Mistakes" from *Complications: a Surgeon's Notes on an Imperfect Science*. Copyright © 2002 by Atul Gawande. Reprinted by arrangement with Henry Holt and Company, LLC.

Malcolm Gladwell: "Java Man" by Malcolm Gladwell from *The New Yorker*, July 30, 2001, is reprinted by permission of the author.

Pumla Gobodo-Madikizela: "Language Rules": Witnessing about Trauma in South Africa's TRC" is reprinted with permission from *River Teeth: A Journal of Nonfiction Narrative*, Spring 2007; Vol. 8, No. 2, 25–33 via Copyright Clearance Center.

J. J. Goode: "Single-Handed Cooking" first published in *Gourmet*, copyright © 2009 by Condé Nast. All rights reserved. Reprinted by permission.

Adam Goodheart: "The Skyscraper and the Airplane" copyright@ 2002 by Adam Goodheart. Originally published in *The American Scholar*, Winter 2002, vol. 71 #1. Reprinted with permission of The Wylie Agency LLC.

Allegra Goodman: "Pemberley Previsited" is reprinted from *The American Scholar*, 73 Spring 2004. Copyright © 2004 by Allegra Goodman.

Al Gore: "The Climate Emergency" by Al Gore is reprinted from *Red, White, Blue and Green* (Yale School of Forestry and Environmental Studies, 2004) by permission of the author and publisher.

Stephen Jay Gould: "Darwin's Middle Road," copyright © 1979 by Stephen Jay Gould, from *The Panda's Thumb: More Reflections in Natural History* is used by permission of W. W. Norton & Co., Inc.

Philip Gourevitch: "After the Genocide" from *We Wish to Inform You that Tomorrow We Will Be Killed With our Families* by Phlip Gourevitch. Copyright © 1998 by Philip Gourevitch. Reprinted by permission of Farrar, Straus and Giroux, LLC.

David Guterson: "Enclosed. Encyclopedic, Endured: One Week at the Mall of America" by David Guterson. Copyright © 1993 by David Guterson. Reprinted by permission of Georges Borchardt, Inc., for the author. Originally appeared in *Harper's Magazine*, Vol. 287, Aug. 1993.

Stephen Hawking, "Is Everything Determined?" From *Black Holes and Baby Universes and Other Essays* by Stephen W. Hawking, copyright © 1993 by Stephen W. Hawking. Used by permission of Bantam Books, a division of Random House, Inc.

Ernest Hemingway: Reprinted with permission of Scribner, a Division of Simon & Schuster, Inc., from *A Farewell to Arms* by Ernest Hemingway. Copyright © 1929 by Charles Scribner's Sons; renewed copyright © renewed 1957 by Ernest Hemingway.

Jack Hitt: "The Battle of the Binge" by Jack Hitt from *The New York Times Magazine*, Oct. 24, 1999, p. 31–32 is reprinted by permission of the author.

John Holt: "How Teachers Make Children Hate Reading" from *The Under-Achieving School* by John Holt. Copyright © 1994 by Holt Associates, Inc. Reprinted by permission of Holt Associates, Inc.

Langston Hughes: "Salvation" from *The Big Sea* by Langston Hughes. Copyright © 1940 by Langston Hughes. Copyright renewed 1968 by Arna Bontemps and George Houston Bass. Reprinted by permission of Hill and Wag, a division of Farrar, Straus and Giroux, LLC.

Zora Neale Hurston: "How It Feels To Be Colored Me" first published in *The World Tomorrow* (1928) is reprinted by permission Edgar Hurston for the Estate of Zora Neale Hurston.

Molly Ivins: "Get a Knife, Get a Dog, but Get Rid of Guns" From *Nothin' but Good Times Ahead* by Molly Ivins. Copyright © 1993 by Molly Ivins. Reprinted by permission of Random House, Inc.

Garrison Keillor: "Postcards" from *We Are Still Married: Stories and Letters* by Garrison Keillor, copyright © 1982, 1983, 1984, 1985, 1986, 1987, 1988, 1989, 1990 by Garrison Keillor. Used by permission of Viking Penguin, a division of Penguin Croup (USA) Inc. and Penguin Group (Canada), a division of Pearson Canada Inc. "How to Write a Personal Letter" from *We Are Still Married: Stories and Letters* by Garrison Keillor. Copyright © 1987 by International Paper Co. Reprinted by permission of Garrison Keillor.

Jamaica Kincaid: "Sowers and Reapers" first published in *The New Yorker*, Jan. 22, 2001, copyright © 2001 by Jamaica Kincaid, reprinted with permission of The Wylie Agency LLC.

Martin Luther King, Jr.: "Letter from Birmingham Jail" and "I Have a Dream" speech by Dr. Martin Luther King, Jr. Copyright © 1963 by Martin Luther King, Jr. and copyright renewed 1991 by Coretta Scott King. Reprinted by arrangement with The Heirs to the Estate of Martin Luther King, Jr. c/o Writers House as agent for the proprietor New York, NY.

Stephen King: "On Writing" from *On Writing: A Memoir of the Craft*. Copyright © 2000 by Stephen King. All rights reserved. Reprinted with the permission of Scribner, a Division of Simon & Schuster, Inc.

Maxine Hong Kingston: "Tongue-Tied" from *The Woman Warrior* by Maxine Hong Kingston, copyright © 1975, 19976 by Maxine Hong Kingston. Used by permission of Alfred A. Knopf, a division of Random House, Inc.

Melvin Konner: "Why the Reckless Survive" from *Why the Reckless Survive*, copyright © 1990 by Melvin Konner. Used by permission of Viking Penguin, a division of Penguin Group (USA) Inc.

Jonathan Kozol: "Fremont High School" from *The Shame of the Nation* by Jonathan Kozol, copyright © 2005 by Jonathan Kozol. Used by permission of Crown Publishers, a division of Random House, Inc.

Nicholas D. Kristof: "Saudis in Bikinis" by Nicholas Kristof from *The New York Times*, Oct. 25, 2002. Copyright © 2002 by The New York Times. All rights reserved. Used by permission and protected by the Copyright Laws of the United States. The printing, copying, redistribution, or retransmission of the Material without express written permission is prohibited.

Elisabeth Kubler-Ross: "On the Fear of Death" from *On Death and Dying* by Elizabeth Kubler-Ross. Copyright © 1969 by Elisabeth Kubler-Ross. Copyright © renewed 1997 by Elisabeth Kubler-Ross. All rights reserved. Reprinted with the permission of Scribner, a division of Simon & Schuster, Inc.

Thomas S. Kuhn: "The Route to Normal Science" from *The Structure of Scientific Revolutions* by Thomas S. Kuhn is reprinted by permission of the University of Chicago Press. Copyright © 1993 by the University of Chicago.

Jhumpa Lahiri. "Rhode Island" from *State by State: A Panoramic Portrait of America* by Matt Weiland and Sean Wilsey, eds. Copyright © 2008 by Trim Tables, LLC. Reprinted by permission of HarperCollins Publishers.

Chang-Rae Lee: "Coming Home Again" by Chang-rae Lee is reprinted by permission of International Creative Management, Inc. Copyright © 1995 by Chang-Rae Lee.

Michael Levin: "The Case for Torture" by Michael Levin from *Newsweek*, June 7, 1982, copyright © 1982, is reprinted by permission of the author.

Niccolo Machiavelli: From *The Prince: A Norton Critical Edition*, Second Edition, trans. by Robert M. Adams. Copyright © 1977 by W. W. Norton & Company, Inc. Used by permission of W. W. Norton & Co., Inc.

Nancy Mairs: "On Being a Cripple" from *Plaintext* by Nancy Mairs. Copyright © 1986 The Arizona Board of Regents. Reprinted by permission of the University of Arizona Press.

Alberto Manguel. "The Library as Survival" from *The Library at Night* is reprinted by permission of the publisher Yale University Press. Copyright 2006 by Alberto Manguel.

Peter Matthiessen, From *Tigers in the Snow*, copyright © 2000 by Peter Matthiessen. Reprinted by permission of Donadio & Olson, Inc.

Scott McCloud: Pages 151–156 from *Understanding Comics* by Scott McCloud, copyright © 1993, 1994 by Scott McCloud. Reprinted by permission of HarperCollins Publishers.

Bill McKibben: "The Case for Single-Child Families" by Bill McKibben is reprinted with permission from the May 13, 1998, issue of *The Christian Century*. Copyright © 1998 by The Christian Century.

John McPhee. "Under the Snow" from *Table of Contents*, copyright © 1985 by John McPhee. Reprinted by permission of Farrar, Straus and Giroux, LLC.

James. M . McPherson. "How Lincoln Won the War with Metaphors" from *Abraham Lincoln and the Second American Revolution* (1991) is reprinted by permission of the author.

John Hamilton McWhorter. "The Cosmopolitan Tongue: The Universality of English" from *World Affairs*, Fall 2009, Vol. 173 no. 2, pp. 61–68. Copyright © 2009. Reprinted with permission of the World Affairs Institute. www.WorldAffairs.Journal.org

Jessica Mitford: From *The American Way of Death* by Jessica Mitford is reprinted by permission of The Estate of Jessica Mitford. Copyright © 1963, 1978 by Jessica Mitford. All rights reserved.

N. Scott Momaday: from *The Way to Rainy Mountain*. Copyright © 1969 by The University of New Mexico Press. Reprinted by permission.

Toni Morrison: "Strangers" by Toni Morrison is reprinted by permission of International Creative Management, Inc. Copyright © 1998 by Toni Morrison.

Vladimir Nabokov: "Good Readers and Good Writers" from *Lectures on Literature* by Vladimir Nabokov, copyright © 1980 by the Estate of Vladimir Nabokov, reprinted by permission of Harcourt, Inc.

Gloria Naylor: "Mommy, What Does Nigger Mean?" is reprinted by permission of SLL/Sterling Lord Literistic, Inc. Copyright © 1986 by Gloria Naylor. The author wants it understood that the use of the word "nigger" is reprehensible in today's society. This essay speaks to a specific time and place when that word was utilized to empower African Americans; today it is used to degrade them even if spoken from their own mouths.

Ngugi wa Thiong'o: "Decolonizing the Mind" from *Decolonising the Mind* (1986) is reprinted by permission of Boydell & Brewer Ltd.

Mary Oliver: "Waste Land: An Elegy" from *Long Life* by Mary Oliver, copyright © 2004 by Mary Oliver, is reprinted by permission of Perseus Books Group via Copyright Clearance Center.

Judith Ortiz Cofer: "More Room" from *Silent Dancing: A Partial Remembrance of a Puerto Rican Childhood* by Judith Ortiz Cofer is reprinted with permission from the publisher, copyright © 1990 by Arte Publico Press-University of Houston.

George Orwell: "Shooting an Elephant" and "Politics and the English Language" from *Shooting an Elephant and Other Essays* by George Orwell, copyright 1950 by Sonia Bronwell Orwell and renewed 1978 by Sonia Pitt-Rivers. Reprinted by permission of Harcourt, Inc.

Henry Petroski: "Falling Down is Part of Growing Up" from *To Engineer Is Human: The Role of Failure in Successful Design*, copyright © 1985 by Henry Petroski. Reprinted by permission of St. Martin's Press, LLC.

Jo-Ann Pilardi: "The Immigration Problem is About Us, Not them" is reprinted from *The Baltimore Sun*, June 7, 2006, by permission of the author.

Steven Pinker: "The Moral Instinct" from *The New York Times Magazine* Jan. 13, 2008, copyright © 2008 The New York Times. All rights reserved. Used by permission and protected by the Copyright Laws of the United States. The printing, copying, redistribution, or retransmission of the Material without express written permission is prohibited.

Sylvia Plath: From *The Journals of Sylvia Plath* by Ted Hughes, ed., copyright © 1982 by Ted Hughes as Executor of the Estate of Sylvia Plath. Used by permission of Doubleday, a division of Random House, Inc.

Michael Pollan: "An Animal's Place" by Michael Pollan is reprinted by permission of International Creative Management, Inc. Copyright © 2002 by Michael Pollan.

Anna Quindlen: "Between the Sexes, a Great Divide" from *The New York Times*, Feb. 24, 1988, copyright © 1988 by The New York Times. All rights reserved. Used by permission and protected by the Copyright Laws of the United States. The printing, copying, redistribution, or retransmission of the Material without express written permission is prohibited. "Stuff is not Salvation" is reprinted by permission of International Creative Management, Inc. Copyright © 2008 by Anna Quindlen.

Jonathan Rauch: "In Defense of Prejudice: Why Incendiary Speech Must Be Protected" by Jonathan Rauch, copyright © 1995 by *Harper's Magazine*. All rights reserved. Reproduced from the May issue by special permission.

Tom Regan: "The Case for Animal Rights" from *In Defense of Animals* by Tom Regan. Copyright © 1985 by Tom Regan. Reprinted by permission of Blackwell Publishing, Ltd.

Paul Reps: "Muddy Road, A Parable, Learning to be Silent" from *Zen Flesh Zen Bones* by Paul Reps. Reprinted by permission of the publisher, Tuttle Publishing. www.tuttlepublishing.com

Adrienne Rich: "Taking Women Students Seriously," "When We Dead Awaken: Writing as Re-Vision" from *On Lies, Secrets, and Silence: Selected Prose 1966–1978*. Copyright © 1979 by W. W. Norton & Company, Inc. Used by permission of the author and W. W. Norton & Company, Inc.

Alberto Alvaro Rios: "Green Cards" by Alberto Rios, from the *Indiana Review* Oct. 1995, copyright © 1995 by Albert Alvaro Rios. Reprinted by permission of the author.

Richard Rodriguez: From *Hunger of Memory: The Education of Richard Rodriguez* by Richard Rodriguez is reprinted by permission of David R. Godine, Publisher, Inc. Copyright © 1982 by Richard Rodriguez.

Betty Rollin: "Motherhood: Who Needs It?" from *Look* magazine, Sept. 22, 1970. Copyright © 1869 by WESH-TV Broadcasting Company.

Mike Rose. "Blue-Collar Brilliance" is reprinted by permission of the publisher from *The American Scholar,* Vol. 78, No. 3, Summer 2009. Copyright © 2009 by Mike Rose.

Scott Russell Sanders: "Looking at Women" from *Secrets of the Universe* by Scott Russell Sanders. Copyright © 1991 by Scott Russell Sanders. Reprinted by permission of Beacon Press via Copyright Clearance Center. "Under the Influence," copyright © 1989 by Harper's magazine. Reprinted from the November issue by special permission. All rights reserved. Lines from "My Papa's Waltz" by Theodore Roethke, copyright 1942 by Hearst Magazines, Inc. from *The Collected Poems of Theodore Roethke*.

Reg Saner. "My Fall into Knowledge" originally appeared in *The Georgia Review,* Vol. LXIV, No. 1, Spring 2010, copyright © 2010 by Reg Saner. Reprinted by permission of Reg Saner and *The Georgia Review*.

Sartre, Jean-Paul Sartre "Existentialism" from *Existentialism* (1947), tr. Bernard Frechtman. Reprinted by permission of Philosophical Library.

Peter Singer. "What Should a Billionaire Give—and What Should You?" from *The New York Times Magazine*, December 17, 2006, copyright © 2006 by The New York Times. All rights reserved. Used by permission and protected by the Copyright Laws of the United States. The printing, copying, redistribution, or retransmission of the Material without express written permission is prohibited.

Jennifer Sinor. "Confluences" is reprinted by permission of the publisher from The American Scholar, vol. 77, No. 1 Winter 2008. Copyright © 2007 by Jennifer Sinor.

Jane Smiley. "Belly, Dancing, Belly, Aching, Belly, Beasts" from *Body*, Sharon Sloan Fiffer and Steve Fiffer, eds. (Avon 1999), is reprinted by permission of Jane Smiley.

Rebecca Solnit. "Locked Horns" from *Storming the Gates of Paradise: Landscapes for Politics*, copyright © 2007. Reprinted with permission of the University of California Press via Copyright Clearance Center.

Susan Sontag: "A Century of Cinema" from *Where the Stress Falls*, copyright © 2001 by Susan Sontag. Reprinted by permission of Farrar, Straus and Giroux, LLC.

Brent Staples: "Why Colleges Shower Their Students with A's" from *The New York Times*, March 8, 1998. Copyright © 1998 by The New York Times. All rights reserved. Used by permission and protected by the Copyright Laws of the United States. The printing, copying, redistribution, or retransmission of the Material without express written permission is prohibited. "Black Men and Public Space" first appeared as "Just Walk On By" in *Ms.* magazine, Sept. 1986. Copyright © 1986 by Brent Staples. Reprinted by permission.

Gloria Steinem: "The Good News Is: These Are Not the Best Years of Your Life" from *Ms.* magazine, Sept. 1979. Copyright © 1979 by Gloria Steinam. Reprinted by permission.

Sandra Steingraber "Tune of the Tuna Fish" was first published in *Orion* Jan/ Feb. 2006 Vol. 25 # 1. Reprinted by permission of Sandra Steingraber, www.steingraber.com.

Fred Strebeigh: "The Wheels of Freedom: The Bicycle in China" from *Bicycling* magazine, April 1991. Copyright © 1991 by Fred Strebeigh. Reprinted by permission of the author.

Andrew Sullivan: "What Is a Homosexual?" from *Virtually Normal* by Andrew Sullivan, copyright © 1005 by Andrew Sullivan. Used by permission of Alfred A. Knopf, a division of Random House, Inc.

Paul Theroux: "Being a Man" from *Sunrise with Seamonsters*, copyright © 1985 by Cape Cod Scriveners Co. Reprinted by permission of Houghton Mifflin Harcourt Publishing Company. All rights reserved.

Lewis Thomas: "Notes on Punctuation" from *The Medusa and the Snail*, copyright © 1979 by Lewis Thomas. Used by permission of Viking Penguin, a division of Penguin Group (USA) Inc.

Sallie Tisdale "We Do Abortions Here" from *Harper's Magazine*, Oct. 1990. Copyright © 1990 by Sallie Tisdale. Reprinted by permission of the author.

Susan Allen Toth: "Going to the Movies" from *How to Prepare for Your High School Reunion* by Susan Toth. Reprinted by permission of the Aaron Priest Literary Agency.

Barbara Tuchman: "This is the End of the World: The Black Death" from *A Distant Mirror* by Barbara W. Tuchman, text copyright © 1978 by Barbara W. Tuchman. Maps copyright © 1978 by Anita Karl. Used by permission of Alfred A. Knopf, a division of Random House, Inc.

Laurel Thatcher Ulrich. "The Slogan" from *Well-Behaved Women Seldom Make History* by Laurel Thatcher Ulrich, copyright © 2007 by Laurel Thatcher Ulrich. Used by permission of Alfred A. Knopf, a division of Random House, Inc. First verse and refrain from the lyrics to "Well-Behaved Women Rarely Make History" written by Jill Conner Browne and Kacey Jones. Copyright © 2003 by Mamalama Music Publishing (ASCP). Used by permission. International Copyright Secured.

James Van Tholen: "Surprised by Death" was published as "Where All Hope Lies" by James Van Tholen in *Christianity Today*. Copyright © 1999 by Wm. B. Eerdmans Publishing Company. Reprinted by permission of the publisher. All Rights Reserved.

Alice Walker: "Beauty: When the Other Dancer is the Self" from *In Search of our Mothers' Gardens: Womanist Prose*, copyright © 1983 by Alice Walker, reprinted by permission of Harcourt, Inc.

David Foster Wallace: From *Consider the Lobster* by David Foster Wallace. Copyright © 2005 by David Foster Wallace. First published by *Gourmet Magazine*. Reprinted by permission of Little, Brown and Co.

Henry Wechsler et al.: "Too Many Colleges are Still in Denial about Alcohol Abuse" from *The Chronicle of Higher Education*, April 14, 1995. Copyright © 1995 by Henry Wechsler. Reprinted by permission of Henry Wechsler. "Health and Behavioral Consequences of Binge Drinking" from *Journal Of The American Medical Association* Dec. 7, 1994. Reprinted by permission of the American Medical Association.

Steven Weinberg: "Without God" from *The New York Review of Books* Sep. 25, 2008. Copyright © 2008 Steve Weinberg. Reprinted by permission of Steven Weinberg. Excerpt from "Aubade" from *Collected Poems*, by Philip Larkin, copyright © 1988, 2003 by the Estate of

Philip Larkin. Reprinted by permission of Farrar Straus and Giroux, LLC and Faber & Faber Ltd.

Gene Weingarten: "Pearls Before Breakfast" from *The Washington Post* April 8, 2007, copyright © 2007 The Washington Post. All rights reserved. Used by permission and protected by the Copyright Laws of the United States. The printing, copying, redistribution, or retransmission of the Material without express written permission is prohibited.

Eudora Welty: "One Writer's Beginnings" and "Clamorous to Learn" are reprinted by permission of the publisher from *One Writer's Beginnings* by Eudora Welty, pp. 5–12, 22–29, Cambridge, Mass.: Harvard University Press, copyright © 1983, 1984 by Eudora Welty.

E. B. White: "Once More to the Lake" from *One Man's Meat* by E. B. White. Copyright © 1941 by E. B. White, copyright renewed. Reprinted by permission of Tilbury House, Publishers, Gardiner, Maine.

Patricia J. Williams: "The Death of the Profane" reprinted by permission of the publisher from *The Alchemy of Race and Rights: Diary of a Law Professor* by Patricia J. Williams, pp. 44–51, Cambridge, Mass.: Harvard University Press, copyright © 1991 by the President and Fellows of Harvard College.

Terry Tempest Williams: "The Clan of One-Breasted Women" from Witness vol. iii # 4 (Winter 1989), is reprinted by permission of the publishers.

Edward O. Wilson: Introduction from *From So Simple a Beginning: Darwin's Four Great Books*, ed. by Edward O. Wilson. Copyright © 2006 by Edward O. Wilson. Used by permission of W. W. Norton & Company, Inc.

Tom Wolfe: From "Yeager" from *The Right Stuff* by Tom Wolfe. Copyright © 1979 by Tom Wolfe. Reprinted by permission of Farrar, Straus and Giroux, LLC.

Virginia Woolf: "The Death of the Moth" from *The Death of The Moth and Other Essays* by Virginia Woolf, copyright 1942 by Harcourt, Inc. and renewed 1970 by Marjorie T. Parsons, Executrix. Chapter Three from *A Room of One's Own*, copyright 1929 by Harcourt, Inc. and renewed 1957 by Leonard Woolf. Reprinted by permission of Houghton Mifflin Harcourt Publishing Company.

William Zinsser: "College Pressures" by William K. Zinsser from *Blair & Ketchum's Country Journal*, Vol. VI, no. 4, April 1979. Copyright © 1979 by William K. Zinsser. Reprinted by permission of the author.

ILLUSTRATIONS:

120-122 Copyright © N. Scott Momaday. From *The Way to Rainy Mountain*, University of New Mexico Press; **136-137** Four photographs reprinted by permission of the photographer, Robert Bergman. Originally printed in color in his book, *A Kind of Rapture*; **161** Judy Griesedieck/Contact Press Images; **163** Judy Griesedieck/Contact Press Images; **165** Judy Griesedieck/Contact Press Images; **227** © 2011 Guy Billout. First published in *The Atlantic*; **277** Reprinted by kind permission of Fred Strebeigh. Copyright © Fred Strebeigh; **280** Reprinted by kind permission of Fred Strebeigh. Copyright © Fred Strebeigh; **281** (left) Reprinted by kind permission of Fred Strebeigh. Copyright © Fred Strebeigh; **281** (right) Reprinted by kind permission of Fred Strebeigh. Copyright © Fred Strebeigh; **283** Reprinted by kind permission of Fred Strebeigh. Copyright © Fred Strebeigh; **285** © Peter Turnley/Corbis; **394** Photo courtesy of Mike Rose; **397** Photo courtesy of Mike Rose; **436** Courtesy of Madrid.com; **437** By Steve Leggat/ Flickr; **439** Courtesy of Madrid .com; **496** Drawings by Peter Parnall; **497** Drawings by Peter Parnall; **499** Drawings by Peter Parnall; **516** Alamy; **526** From *A Wind-storm in the Forests* by John Muir; **658-660** Stanleyformanphotos.com; **693** Scala/Art Resource, NY; **694** Snark/Art Resource, NY; **703** bottom and bottom Réunion des Musées Nationaux/Art Resource, NY; **742** Collection of Melissa A. Goldthwaite **745** Auschwitz-Birkenau State Museum Archives; **749** Jacob Edelstein, The image of Jacob Edelstein neg 5144; **750** Library in Theresienstadt Ghetto, Author's collection; **762** Library of Congress; **770** AP/Wide World Photos; **771** Still from Michael Cimino's *The Deer Hunter* (1978). Courtesy of Photofest; **772** Courtesy of Canon Films; **773** © 1995 Marvel Entertainment Group, Inc. All rights reserved.; **774** © 1995 Marvel Entertainment Group, Inc. All rights reserved.; **857** Franklin D. Roosevelt Presidential Library and Museum; **863** Courtesy Al Gore, *Red, White,*

Blue and Green: Politics and the Environment in the 2004 Election; **864** Reprinted from: *An Inconvenient Truth* by Al Gore. Copyright © 2006 by Al Gore. Permission granted by Rodale, Inc., Emmaus, PA 18098; **867** Reprinted from: *An Inconvenient Truth* by Al Gore. Copyright © 2006 by Al Gore. Permission granted by Rodale, Inc., Emmaus, PA 18099; **869** Reprinted from: *An Inconvenient Truth* by Al Gore. Copyright © 2006 by Al Gore. Permission granted by Rodale, Inc., Emmaus, PA 18100; **870** Reprinted from *An Inconvenient Truth* by Al Gore. Copyright © 2006 by Al Gore. Permission granted by Rodale, Inc., Emmaus, PA 18100; **931** Journal of the American Medical Association, 271.21 (1994), Copyright ©1994 American Medical Association. All rights reserved.; **933-936** Journal of the American Medical Association, 271.21 (1994), Copyright ©1994 American Medical Association. All rights reserved.; **950, 951** *The Descent of Man*, and Selection in Relation to Sex, by Charles Darwin; **953-957** *The Descent of Man*, and Selection in Relation to Sex, by Charles Darwin; **1022-1027** Understanding Comics, by Scott McCloud; **1030** Still from Jean Renoir's Nana (1962). Courtesy of Photofest; **1031** Still from Abel Gance's *Napoleon* (1927). Courtesy of Photofest; **1032** Still from Francois Tuffaut's *The 400 Blows* (1959). Courtesy of Photofest; **1033** Still from Ingmar Bergman's *Persona* (1967). Courtesy of Photofest; **1034** Still from Jean-Luc Godard's *Breathless* (1959). Courtesy of Photofest.

Chronological Index

380BC Plato: *The Allegory of the Cave* 1120
1513 Niccolo Machiavelli: *The Morals of the Prince* 797
1597 Francis Bacon: *Of Youth and Age* 475
1611 Jesus: *Parables of the Kingdom* 1123
1623 John Donne: *No Man Is an Island* 479
1729 Jonathan Swift: *A Modest Proposal* 790
1732 Benjamin Franklin: from *Poor Richard's Almanack* 481
1740 Ben Jonson: *To Write Well* 477
1750 Samuel Johnson: *Against Wicked Characters* 479
1776 Thomas Jefferson and Others: *The Declaration of Independence* 804
Original Draft of the Declaration of Independence 807
1790 William Blake: *Proverbs of Hell* 483
1791 Benjamin Franklin: *Learning to Write* 440
1792 Mary Wollstonecraft: from *A Vindication of the Rights of Woman* 480
1819 Ralph Waldo Emerson: from *Journals* 90
1822 Charles Lamb: *A Dissertation upon Roast Pig* 266
1837 Henry David Thoreau: from *Journal* 93
1845 Frederick Douglass: *Learning to Read* 346
1854 Henry David Thoreau: *The Battle of the Ants* 758
1854 Henry David Thoreau: *Where I Lived, and What I Lived For* 1098
1863 Abraham Lincoln: *The Gettysburg Address* 486
1865 Abraham Lincoln: *Second Inaugural Address* 813
1881 Elizabeth Cady Stanton: *Declaration of Sentiments and Resolutions* 811
1882 Walt Whitman: *The Death of Lincoln* 716
1882 Mark Twain: *Advice to Youth* 550
1894 John Muir: *A Wind-Storm in the Forests* 525
1906 Ambrose Bierce: from *The Devil's Dictionary* 484
1928 Zora Neale Hurston: *How It Feels to Be Colored Me* 12
1929 Virginia Woolf: *In Search of a Room of One's Own* 1005
1929 Ernest Hemingway: from *A Farewell to Arms* 486
1936 George Orwell: *Shooting an Elephant* 784
1940 Langston Hughes: *Salvation* 1059
1941 E. B. White: *Once More to the Lake* 79
1942 Virginia Woolf: *The Death of the Moth* 1107
1943 M. F. K. Fisher: *Young Hunger* 206
1947 Jean-Paul Sartre: *Existentialism* 1128
1948 Eleanor Roosevelt: *On the Universal Declaration of Human Rights* 855
1950 George Orwell: *Politics and the English Language* 463
1950 William Faulkner: *Nobel Prize Award Speech* 871

1951 Rachel Carson: *Tides* 519
1955 James Baldwin: *Stranger in the Village* 304
1956 Jacob Bronowski: *The Nature of Scientific Reasoning* 886
1957 Zen Parables: *Muddy Road, A Parable, Learning to Be Silent* 1127
1957 Aaron Copland: *How We Listen* 1039
1957 Roland Barthes: *Toys* 274
1961 John F. Kennedy: *Inaugural Address* 815
1962 Thomas S. Kuhn: *The Route to Normal Science* 899
1963 Martin Luther King Jr.: *I Have a Dream* 852
1963 Martin Luther King Jr.: *Letter from Birmingham Jail* 818
1963 Jessica Mitford: *Behind the Formaldehyde Curtain* 254
1963 Hannah Arendt: *Deportations from Western Europe* 736
1964 Northrop Frye: *The Motive for Metaphor* 983
1966 Joan Didion: *On Going Home* 1
1966 Joan Didion: *On Keeping a Notebook* 84
1967 N. Scott Momaday: *The Way to Rainy Mountain* 119
1968 Edward Abbey: *The Serpents of Paradise* 496
1969 Elisabeth Kübler-Ross: *On the Fear of Death* 219
1969 John Holt: *How Teachers Make Children Hate Reading* 358
1970 Betty Rollin: *Motherhood: Who Needs It?* 286
1970 Maya Angelou: *Graduation* 15
1971 Anthony Burgess: *Is America Falling Apart?* 235
1971 Isaac Asimov: *The Eureka Phenomenon* 890
1974 Annie Dillard: *Sight into Insight* 1109
1975 Nora Ephron, *The Boston Photographs* 657
1975 Caroline Bird: *College Is a Waste of Time and Money* 372
1976 Maxine Hong Kingston: *Tongue-Tied* 401
1977 Chief Seattle: *Letter to President Pierce, 1855* 532
1978 Adrienne Rich: *Taking Women Students Seriously* 386
1978 Barbara Tuchman: *"This Is the End of the World": The Black Death* 692
1979 Gloria Steinem: *The Good News Is: These Are Not the Best Years of Your Life* 213
1979 Lewis Thomas: *Notes on Punctuation* 451
1979 Frances FitzGerald: *Rewriting American History* 776
1979 Tom Wolfe: *Yeager* 126
1979 Stephen Jay Gould: *Darwin's Middle Road* 959
1979 William Zinsser: *College Pressures* 380
1980 Vladimir Nabokov: *Good Readers and Good Writers* 973
1980 Susan Allen Toth: *Going to the Movies* 1036
1981 Paul Fussell: *Thank God for the Atom Bomb* 664
1982 Richard Rodriguez: *Aria* 405
1982 Sylvia Plath: from *The Journals of Sylvia Plath* 95
1982 Michael Levin: *The Case for Torture* 647
1983 Eudora Welty: *One Writer's Beginnings* 967

1983 Alice Walker: *Beauty: When the Other Dancer Is the Self* 55
1983 Eudora Welty: *Clamorous to Learn* 350
1983 John McPhee: *Under the Snow* 504
1985 Henry Petroski: *Falling Down Is Part of Growing Up* 199
1985 Paul Theroux: *Being a Man* 176
1985 Tom Regan: *The Case for Animal Rights* 608
1986 Brent Staples: *Black Men and Public Space* 314
1986 Ngugi Wa Thiong'o: *Decolonizing the Mind* 997
1986 Gloria Naylor: *"Mommy, What Does 'Nigger' Mean?"* 420
1986 Nancy Mairs: *On Being a Cripple* 46
1987 Annie Dillard: from *An American Childhood* 110
1987 Gloria Anzaldúa: *How to Tame a Wild Tongue* 411
1988 Anna Quindlen: *Between the Sexes, a Great Divide* 174
1989 Garrison Keillor: *How to Write a Letter* and *Postcards* 446, 449
1989 Scott Russell Sanders: *Looking at Women* 179
1989 Terry Tempest Williams: *The Clan of One-Breasted Women* 543
1989 Scott Russell Sanders: *Under the Influence* 100
1990 Rita Dove: *The Epistle of Paul the Apostle to the Ephesians* 1061
1990 Sallie Tisdale: *We Do Abortions Here: A Nurse's Story* 650
1990 Melvin Konner: *Why the Reckless Survive* 940
1990 Judith Ortiz Cofer: *More Room* 116
1991 James McPherson: *How Lincoln Won the War with Metaphors* 723
1991 Fred Strebeigh: *The Wheels of Freedom: Bicycles in China* 276
1991 Patricia Williams: *The Death of the Profane: The Rhetoric of Race and Rights* 423
1993 Amy Cunningham: *Why Women Smile* 189
1993 David Guterson: *Enclosed. Encyclopedic. Endured: The Mall of America* 161
1993 Lars Eighner: *On Dumpster Diving* 31
1993 Stephen Carter: *The Separation of Church and State* 843
1993 Molly Ivins: *Get a Knife, Get a Dog, but Get Rid of Guns* 323
1994 Philip Gourevitch: *After the Genocide* 752
1994 Stephen Hawking: *Is Everything Determined?* 908
1994 Henry Wechsler et al.: *Health and Behavioral Consequences of Binge Drinking* 925
1994 Henry Louis Gates, Jr.: *In the Kitchen* 260
1994 H. Bruce Franklin: *From Realism to Virtual Reality: Images of America's Wars* 761
1994 Scott McCloud: *Understanding Comics* 1022
1995 William Cronon: *The Trouble with Wilderness* 533
1995 Susan Sontag: *A Century of Cinema* 1028
1995 Alberto Alvaro Ríos: *Green Cards* 40
1995 Andrew Sullivan: *What Is a Homosexual?* 195
1995 Chang-Rae Lee: *Coming Home Again* 3

1995 Jonathan Rauch: *In Defense of Prejudice* 569
1995 Henry Wechsler et al.: *Too Many Colleges Are Still in Denial about Alcohol Abuse* 336
1995 Ian Frazier: *Take the F* 154
1996 Debra Dickerson: *Who Shot Johnny?* 316
1997 Sherman Alexie: *Superman and Me* 355
1997 Mark Doty: *Souls on Ice* 992
1998 Bill McKibben: *The Case for Single-Child Families* 295
1998 Brent Staples: *Why Colleges Shower Their Students with A's* 329
1998 Toni Morrison: *Strangers* 135
1999 Atul Gawande: *When Doctors Make Mistakes* 590
1999 Anne Fadiman: *Night Owl* 62
1999 James van Tholen: *Surprised by Death* 1070
1999 Jack Hitt: *The Battle of the Binge* 340
1999 Randall Balmer: *Diversity and Stability* 831
1999 Jane Smiley: *Belly, Dancing, Belly, Aching, Belly, Beasts* 209
1999 Kenneth A. Bruffee: *Binge Drinking as a Substitute for a "Community of Learning"* 343
2000 Peter Matthiessen: *Tigers in the Snow* 510
2000 Stephen King: *On Writing* 443
2001 Jamaica Kincaid: *Sowers and Reapers* 139
2001 Malcolm Gladwell: *Java Man* 248
2002 Michael Pollan: *An Animal's Place* 619
2002 Adam Goodheart: *9.11.01: The Skyscraper and the Airplane* 241
2002 Nicholas D. Kristof: *Saudis in Bikinis* 272
2003 Mary Oliver: *Waste Land: An Elegy* 537
2003 Rebecca Solnit: *Locked Horns* 453
2004 Brian Doyle: *Joyas Voladoras* 502
2004 Al Gore: *The Climate Emergency* 860
2004 David Foster Wallace: *Consider the Lobster* 635
2004 Philip Alcabes: *The Bioterrorism Scare: A Historical Perspective* 705
2004 Allegra Goodman: *Pemberley Previsited* 978
2004 Michael Chabon: *Kids' Stuff* 1016
2005 Edward O. Wilson: *Intelligent Evolution* 949
2005 Colby Buzzell: *Killing Time in Iraq* 97
2005 Michael Dirda: *In Wildness Is the Preservation of the World* 663
2005 Jonathan Kozol: *Fremont High School* 367
2006 Barbara Ehrenreich: *Guys Just Want to Have Fun* 331
2006 Sandra Steingraber: *Tune of the Tuna Fish* 540
2006 Alberto Manguel: *The Library as Survival* 741
2006 David Brooks: *The Gender Gap at School* 333
2006 Jo-Ann Pilardi: *Immigration Problem Is About Us, Not Them* 325
2006 Joey Franklin: *Working at Wendy's* 25
2007 Gene Weingarten: *Pearls before Breakfast* 1043

2007 Peter Singer: *What Should a Billionaire Give?* 578
2007 Laurel Thatcher Ulrich: *The Slogan: "Well-Behaved Women Seldom Make History"* 678
2007 Pumla Gobodo-Madikizela: *"Language Rules": Witnessing about Trauma in South Africa* 456
2008 Steven Pinker: *The Moral Instinct* 552
2008 Anna Quindlen: *Stuff Is Not Salvation* 321
2008 Steven Weinberg: *Without God* 1074
2008 Jennifer Sinor: *Confluences* 69
2008 Nicholson Baker: *The Charms of Wikipedia* 915
2008 Jumpa Lahiri: *Rhode Island* 144
2008 Nicholas Carr: *Is Google Making Us Stupid?* 226
2009 J. J. Goode: *Single-Handed Cooking* 43
2009 John McWhorter: *The Cosmopolitan Tongue: The Universality of English* 429
2009 Barack Obama: *A New Beginning* 873
2009 Mike Rose: *Blue-Collar Brilliance* 393
2010 Dennis Baron: *Who Owns Global English?* 435
2010 Reg Saner: *My Fall into Knowledge* 1085
2010 Thomas Friedman: *America's Real Dream Team* 327

Genres Index

Argument

Randall Balmer: Diversity and Stability 831
Dennis Baron: Who Owns Global English? 435
Nicholas Carr: Is Google Making Us Stupid? 226
Stephen Carter: The Separation of Church and State 843
Michael Chabon: Kids' Stuff 1016
William Cronon: The Trouble with Wilderness 533
Thomas Friedman: America's Real Dream Team 327
Stephen Hawking: Is Everything Determined? 908
Thomas Jefferson: Original Draft of the Declaration of Independence 807
Thomas Jefferson and Others: The Declaration of Independence 804
Martin Luther King Jr.: Letter from Birmingham Jail 818
Michael Levin: The Case for Torture 647
John McWhorter: The Cosmopolitan Tongue 429
Barack Obama: A New Beginning 873
Henry Petroski: Falling Down Is Part of Growing Up 199
Steven Pinker: The Moral Instinct 552
Michael Pollan: An Animal's Place 619
Jonathan Rauch: In Defense of Prejudice 569
Tom Regan: The Case for Animal Rights 608
Mike Rose: Blue-Collar Brilliance 393
Peter Singer: What Should a Billionaire Give? 578
Elizabeth Cady Stanton: Declaration of Sentiments and Resolutions 811
Sallie Tisdale: We Do Abortions Here: A Nurse's Story 650
Steven Weinberg: Without God 1074

Cultural Analysis

Nicholson Baker: The Charms of Wikipedia 915
James Baldwin: Stranger in the Village 304
Roland Barthes: Toys 274
Nicholas Carr: Is Google Making Us Stupid? 226
Amy Cunningham: Why Women Smile 189
Debra Dickerson: Who Shot Johnny? 316
Anne Fadiman: Night Owl 62
Joey Franklin: Working at Wendy's 25
Henry Louis Gates, Jr.: In the Kitchen 260
Atul Gawande: When Doctors Make Mistakes 590
Malcolm Gladwell: Java Man 248

Adam Goodheart: 9.11.01: The Skyscraper and the Airplane 241
Nicholas D. Kristof: Saudis in Bikinis 272
Charles Lamb: A Dissertation upon Roast Pig 266
Jessica Mitford: Behind the Formaldehyde Curtain 254
Gloria Naylor: "Mommy, What Does 'Nigger' Mean?" 420
Betty Rollin: Motherhood: Who Needs It? 286
Mike Rose: Blue-Collar Brilliance 393
Scott Russell Sanders: Looking at Women 179
Andrew Sullivan: What Is a Homosexual? 195
Susan Sontag: A Century of Cinema 1028
Brent Staples: Black Men and Public Space 314
Fred Strebeigh: The Wheels of Freedom: Bicycles in China 276
Paul Theroux: Being a Man 176
Laurel Thatcher Ulrich: The Slogan: "Well-Behaved Women Seldom Make History" 678
Gene Weingarten: Pearls before Breakfast 1043

HISTORICAL NARRATIVES

Hannah Arendt: Deportations from Western Europe 736
H. Bruce Franklin: From Realism to Virtual Reality: Images of America's Wars 761
Paul Fussell: Thank God for the Atom Bomb 664
Pumla Gobodo-Madikizela "Language Rules": Witnessing about Trauma in South Africa 456
Philip Gourevitch: After the Genocide 752
Alberto Manguel: The Library as Survival 741
Barbara Tuchman: "This Is the End of the World": The Black Death 692
Walt Whitman: Death of Abraham Lincoln 716

LITERACY NARRATIVES

Sherman Alexie: Superman and Me 355
Frederick Douglass: Learning to Read 346
Ben Franklin: Learning to Write 440
Allegra Goodman: Pemberley Previsited 978
Maxine Hong Kingston: Tongue-Tied 401
Richard Rodriguez: Aria 405
Eudora Welty: Clamorous to Learn 350
Eudora Welty: One Writer's Beginnings 967

MEMOIRS AND AUTOBIOGRAPHICAL ESSAYS

Maya Angelou: Graduation 15
Annie Dillard: Sight into Insight 1109

Lars Eighner: On Dumpster Diving 31
Langston Hughes: Salvation 1059
Zora Neale Hurston: How It Feels to Be Colored Me 12
Chang-Rae Lee: Coming Home Again 3
Nancy Mairs: On Being a Cripple 46
George Orwell: Shooting an Elephant 784
Alberto Alvaro Ríos: Green Cards 40
Henry David Thoreau: Where I Lived, and What I Lived For 1098
Alice Walker: Beauty: When the Other Dancer Is the Self 55
E. B. White: Once More to the Lake 79

Natural History

Edward Abbey: The Serpents of Paradise 496
Rachel Carson: Tides 519
Brian Doyle: Joyas Voladoras 502
Peter Matthiessen: Tigers in the Snow 510
John Muir: A Wind-Storm in the Forests 525
Henry David Thoreau: The Battle of the Ants 758
Henry David Thoreau: from Journal 93
Virginia Woolf: The Death of the Moth 1107

Op-Eds

David Brooks: The Gender Gap at School 333
Kenneth A. Bruffee: Binge Drinking as a Substitute for a "Community of Learning" 343
Barbara Ehrenreich: Guys Just Want to Have Fun 331
Thomas Friedman: America's Real Dream Team 327
Jack Hitt: The Battle of the Binge 340
Molly Ivins: Get a Knife, Get a Dog, but Get Rid of Guns 323
Nicholas D. Kristof: Saudis in Bikinis 272
Bill McKibben: The Case for Single-Child Families 295
Jo-Ann Pilardi: Immigration Problem Is About Us, Not Them 325
Anna Quindlen: Stuff Is Not Salvation 321
Brent Staples: Why Colleges Shower Their Students with A's 329
Henry Wechsler et al.: Too Many Colleges Are Still in Denial about Alcohol Abuse 336

Parables

Jesus: Parables of the Kingdom 1123
Plato: The Allegory of the Cave 1120
Zen Parables: Muddy Road, A Parable, Learning to be Silent 1127

PROFILE OF A PERSON, MINI-BIOGRAPHY

Annie Dillard: from An American Childhood 110
Scott Russell Sanders: Under the Influence 100
Gene Weingarten: Pearls before Breakfast 1043
Tom Wolfe: Yeager 126

PROFILE OF A PLACE

Joan Didion: On Going Home 1
Ian Frazier: Take the F 154
David Guterson: Enclosed. Encyclopedic. Endured: The Mall of America 161
Jonathan Kozol: Fremont High School 367
Jhumpa Lahiri: Rhode Island 144
Peter Matthiessen: Tigers in the Snow 510
N. Scott Momaday: The Way to Rainy Mountain 119
John Muir: A Wind-Storm in the Forests 525
Mary Oliver: Waste Land: An Elegy 537

PROPOSALS

Nicholson Baker: The Charms of Wikipedia 915
Michael Chabon: Kids' Stuff 1016
Niccolò Machiavelli: The Morals of the Prince 797
George Orwell: Politics and the English Language 463
Adrienne Rich: Taking Women Students Seriously 386
Jonathan Swift: A Modest Proposal 790

REPORTS

Jonathan Kozol: Fremont High School 367
Henry Wechsler et al.: Health and Behavioral Consequences
of Binge Drinking in College
A National Survey of Students at 140 Campuses 925

SPEECHES AND ORATIONS

Al Gore: The Climate Emergency 860
John F. Kennedy: Inaugural Address 815
Martin Luther King Jr.: I Have a Dream 852
Abraham Lincoln: The Gettysburg Address 486
Abraham Lincoln: Second Inaugural Address 813
Barack Obama: A New Beginning 873
Eleanor Roosevelt: On the Universal Declaration of Human Rights 855
James Van Tholen: Surprised by Death 1070

Textual Analysis

Rita Dove: The Epistle of Paul the Apostle to the Ephesians 1061
Allegra Goodman: Pemberley Previsited 978
James McPherson: How Lincoln Won the War with Metaphors 723
Ngũgĩ wa Thiong'o: Decolonizing the Mind 997
George Orwell: Politics and the English Language 463
Henry Petroski: Falling Down Is Part of Growing Up 199
Laurel Thatcher Ulrich: The Slogan: "Well-Behaved Women Seldom Make History" 678

Visual Analysis

Sherman Alexie: Superman and Me 355
Nora Ephron: The Boston Photographs 657
H. Bruce Franklin: From Realism to Virtual Reality: Images of America's Wars 761
Scott McCloud: Understanding Comics 1022
Toni Morrison: Strangers 135

Modes Index

Narration

Sherman Alexie: Superman and Me 355
Maya Angelou: Graduation 15
Nicholson Baker: The Charms of Wikipedia 915
Colby Buzzell: Killing Time in Iraq 97
Judith Ortiz Cofer: More Room 116
Annie Dillard: from An American Childhood 110
Frederick Douglass: Learning to Read 346
M. F. K. Fisher: Young Hunger 206
Joey Franklin: Working at Wendy's 25
Atul Gawande: When Doctors Make Mistakes 590
Pumla Gobodo-Madikizela: "Language Rules": Witnessing about Trauma in South Africa 456
J. J. Goode: Single-Handed Cooking 43
Langston Hughes: Salvation 1059
Stephen King: On Writing 443
Jonathan Kozol: Fremont High School 367
Jhumpa Lahiri: Rhode Island 144
Charles Lamb: A Dissertation upon Roast Pig 266
Chang-Rae Lee: Coming Home Again 3
Alberto Manguel: The Library as Survival 741
Peter Matthiessen: Tigers in the Snow 510
N. Scott Momaday: The Way to Rainy Mountain 119
Toni Morrison: Strangers 135
John Muir: A Wind-Storm in the Forests 525
Alberto Alvaro Ríos: Green Cards 40
Scott Russell Sanders: Under the Influence 100
Reg Saner: My Fall into Knowledge 1085
Jennifer Sinor: Confluences 69
Fred Strebeigh: The Wheels of Freedom: Bicycles in China 276
Henry David Thoreau: Where I Lived, and What I Lived For 1098
Sallie Tisdale: We Do Abortions Here: A Nurse's Story 650
Barbara Tuchman: "This Is the End of the World": The Black Death 692
Laurel Thatcher Ulrich: The Slogan: "Well-Behaved Women Seldom Make History" 678
Alice Walker: Beauty: When the Other Dancer Is the Self 55
Gene Weingarten: Pearls before Breakfast 1043
E. B. White: Once More to the Lake 79

Patricia Williams: The Death of the Profane: The Rhetoric of Race and Rights 423
Terry Tempest Williams: The Clan of One-Breasted Women 543

DESCRIPTION

Edward Abbey: The Serpents of Paradise 496
Sherman Alexie: Superman and Me 355
Roland Barthes: Toys 274
Joan Didion: On Going Home 1
Annie Dillard: from An American Childhood 110
Mark Doty: Souls on Ice 992
Brian Doyle: Joyas Voladoras 502
Lars Eighner: On Dumpster Diving 31
Nora Ephron: The Boston Photographs 657
Anne Fadiman: Night Owl 62
Joey Franklin: Working at Wendy's 25
Ian Frazier: Take the F 154
Henry Louis Gates, Jr.: In the Kitchen 260
Atul Gawande: When Doctors Make Mistakes 590
Philip Gourevitch: After the Genocide 752
David Guterson: Enclosed. Encyclopedic. Endured: The Mall of America 161
Jonathan Kozol: Fremont High School 367
Jhumpa Lahiri: Rhode Island 144
Charles Lamb: A Dissertation upon Roast Pig 266
Nancy Mairs: On Being a Cripple 46
Alberto Manguel: The Library as Survival 741
Peter Matthiessen: Tigers in the Snow 510
John McPhee: Under the Snow 504
Toni Morrison: Strangers 135
Mary Oliver: Waste Land: An Elegy 537
George Orwell: Shooting an Elephant 784
Mike Rose: Blue-Collar Brilliance 393
Jennifer Sinor: Confluences 69
Rebeccas Solnit: Locked Horns 453
David Foster Wallace: Consider the Lobster 635
Gene Weingarten: Pearls before Breakfast 1043
Tom Wolfe: Yeager 126

EXPOSITION

ANALYZING CAUSE AND EFFECT

Randall Balmer: Diversity and Stability 831
Dennis Baron: Who Owns Global English? 435

Kenneth A. Bruffee: Binge Drinking as a Substitute for a "Community of Learning" 343
Nicholas Carr: Is Google Making Us Stupid? 226
Michael Chabon: Kids' Stuff 1016
Amy Cunningham: Why Women Smile 189
Debra Dickerson: Who Shot Johnny? 316
Joan Didion: On Keeping a Notebook 84
Paul Fussell: Thank God for the Atom Bomb 664
Atul Gawande: When Doctors Make Mistakes 590
Pumla Gobodo-Madikizela: "Language Rules": Witnessing about Trauma in South Africa 456
Adam Goodheart: 9.11.01: The Skyscraper and the Airplane 241
Al Gore: The Climate Emergency 860
Stephen Hawking: Is Everything Determined? 908
Jack Hitt: The Battle of the Binge 340
Melvin Konner: Why the Reckless Survive 940
Charles Lamb: A Dissertation upon Roast Pig 266
John McWhorter: The Cosmopolitan Tongue 429
George Orwell: Politics and the English Language 463
George Orwell: Shooting an Elephant 784
Reg Saner: My Fall into Knowledge 1085
Chief Seattle: Letter to President Pierce, 1855 532
Peter Singer: What Should a Billionaire Give? 578
Gloria Steinem: The Good News Is: These Are Not the Best Years of Your Life 213
Sandra Steingraber: Tune of the Tuna Fish 540
Henry David Thoreau: The Battle of the Ants 758
Steven Weinberg: Without God 1074
Gene Weingarten: Pearls before Breakfast 1043
Terry Tempest Williams: The Clan of One-Breasted Women 543
Mary Wollstonecraft: from A Vindication of the Rights of Woman 480

Classifying and Dividing

Gloria Anzaldúa: How to Tame a Wild Tongue 411
Rachel Carson: Tides 519
Aaron Copland: How We Listen 1039
Anne Fadiman: Night Owl 62
H. Bruce Franklin: From Realism to Virtual Reality: Images of America's Wars 761
Northrop Frye: The Motive for Metaphor 983
Stephen Hawking: Is Everything Determined? 908
Jamaica Kincaid: Sowers and Reapers 139
Steven Pinker: The Moral Instinct 552
Peter Singer: What Should a Billionaire Give? 578

Susan Allen Toth: Going to the Movies 1036
Steven Weinberg: Without God 1074
Edward O. Wilson: Intelligent Evolution 949
William Zinsser: College Pressures 380

COMPARING AND CONTRASTING

Francis Bacon: Of Youth and Age 475
Brian Doyle: Joyas Voladoras 502
Anne Fadiman: Night Owl 62
Frances FitzGerald: Rewriting American History 776
Adam Goodheart: 9.11.01: The Skyscraper and the Airplane 241
Allegra Goodman: Pemberley Previsited 978
Al Gore: The Climate Emergency 860
Jamaica Kincaid: Sowers and Reapers 139
Jonathan Kozol: Fremont High School 367
James M. McPherson: How Lincoln Won the War with Metaphors 723
John McWhorter: The Cosmopolitan Tongue 429
Michael Pollan: An Animal's Place 619
Anna Quindlen: Between the Sexes, a Great Divide 174
Chief Seattle: Letter to President Pierce, 1855 532
Rebeccas Solnit: Locked Horns 453
Virginia Woolf: In Search of a Room of One's Own 1005

DEFINING

Francis Bacon: Of Youth and Age 475
Jacob Bronowski: The Nature of Scientific Reasoning 886
Annie Dillard: Sight into Insight 1109
Lars Eighner: On Dumpster Diving 31
Pumla Gobodo-Madikizela: "Language Rules": Witnessing about Trauma in South Africa 456
Langston Hughes: Salvation 1059
Garrison Keillor: Postcards 449
Thomas S. Kuhn: The Route to Normal Science 899
Nancy Mairs: On Being a Cripple 46
Vladimir Nabokov: Good Readers and Good Writers 973
Gloria Naylor: "Mommy, What Does 'Nigger' Mean?" 420
Steven Pinker: The Moral Instinct 552
Jean-Paul Sartre: Existentialism 1128
Andrew Sullivan: What Is a Homosexual? 195
Paul Theroux: Being a Man 176
Lewis Thomas: Notes on Punctuation 451
Alice Walker: Beauty: When the Other Dancer Is the Self 55
Gene Weingarten: Pearls before Breakfast 1043

Explaining a Process

Nicholson Baker: The Charms of Wikipedia 915
Mark Doty: Souls on Ice 992
Atul Gawande: When Doctors Make Mistakes 590
Pumla Gobodo-Madikizela: "Language Rules": Witnessing about Trauma in South Africa 456
J. J. Goode: Single-Handed Cooking 43
John Holt: How Teachers Make Children Hate Reading 358
Garrison Keillor: How to Write a Letter 446
Stephen King: On Writing 443
Elisabeth Kübler-Ross: On the Fear of Death 219
Charles Lamb: A Dissertation upon Roast Pig 266
Ngũgĩ wa Thiong'o: Decolonizing the Mind 997
Mike Rose: Blue-Collar Brilliance 393
Susan Sontag: A Century of Cinema 1028
Sandra Steingraber: Tune of the Tuna Fish 540
Barbara Tuchman: "This Is the End of the World": The Black Death 692

Persuasion/Argument

Hannah Arendt: Deportations from Western Europe 736
Nicholson Baker: The Charms of Wikipedia 915
Randall Balmer: Diversity and Stability 831
Dennis Baron: Who Owns Global English? 435
Caroline Bird: College Is a Waste of Time and Money 372
David Brooks: The Gender Gap at School 333
Kenneth A. Bruffee: Binge Drinking as a Substitute for a "Community of Learning" 343
Anthony Burgess: Is America Falling Apart? 235
Nicholas Carr: Is Google Making Us Stupid? 226
Stephen Carter: The Separation of Church and State 843
Michael Chabon: Kids' Stuff 1016
William Cronon: The Trouble with Wilderness 533
Michael Dirda: In Wildness Is the Preservation of the World 663
Anne Fadiman: Night Owl 62
Thomas Friedman: America's Real Dream Team 327
Paul Fussell: Thank God for the Atom Bomb 664
Atul Gawande: When Doctors Make Mistakes 590
Pumla Gobodo-Madikizela: "Language Rules": Witnessing about Trauma in South Africa 456
Allegra Goodman: Pemberley Previsited 978
Stephen Hawking: Is Everything Determined? 908
Jack Hitt: The Battle of the Binge 340
Molly Ivins: Get a Knife, Get a Dog, but Get Rid of Guns 323

Thomas Jefferson: Original Draft of the Declaration of Independence 807
Thomas Jefferson and Others: The Declaration of Independence 804
Martin Luther King Jr.: Letter from Birmingham Jail 818
Jonathan Kozol: Fremont High School 367
Michael Levin: The Case for Torture 647
Abraham Lincoln: The Gettysburg Address 486
Abraham Lincoln: Second Inaugural Address 813
James M. McPherson: How Lincoln Won the War with Metaphors 723
John McWhorter: The Cosmopolitan Tongue 429
Ngũgĩ wa Thiong'o: Decolonizing the Mind 997
Barack Obama: A New Beginning 873
Henry Petroski: Falling Down Is Part of Growing Up 199
Jo-Ann Pilardi: Immigration Problem Is About Us, Not Them 325
Steven Pinker: The Moral Instinct 552
Michael Pollan: An Animal's Place 619
Anna Quindlen: Stuff Is Not Salvation 321
Jonathan Rauch: In Defense of Prejudice 569
Tom Regan: The Case for Animal Rights 608
Betty Rollin: Motherhood: Who Needs It? 286
Mike Rose: Blue-Collar Brilliance 393
Reg Saner: My Fall into Knowledge 1085
Chief Seattle: Letter to President Pierce, 1855 532
Peter Singer: What Should a Billionaire Give? 578
Elizabeth Cady Stanton: Declaration of Sentiments and Resolutions 811
Brent Staples: Black Men and Public Space 314
Brent Staples: Why Colleges Shower Their Students with A's 329
Jonathan Swift: A Modest Proposal 790
Henry David Thoreau: Where I Lived, and What I Lived For 1098
Laurel Thatcher Ulrich: The Slogan: "Well-Behaved Women Seldom Make History" 678
Henry Wechsler et al.: Too Many Colleges Are Still in Denial about Alcohol Abuse 336
Steven Weinberg: Without God 1074
Terry Tempest Williams: The Clan of One-Breasted Women 543
Edward O. Wilson: Intelligent Evolution 949
Mary Wollstonecraft: from A Vindication of the Rights of Woman 480

THEMATIC INDEX

GENDER AND SEXUALITY

Judith Ortiz Cofer: More Room 116
Amy Cunningham: Why Women Smile 189
Barbara Ehrenreich: Guys Just Want to Have Fun 331
Allegra Goodman: Pemberley Previsited 978
Nicholas D. Kristof: Saudis in Bikinis 272
Anna Quindlen: Between the Sexes, a Great Divide 174
Adrienne Rich: Taking Women Students Seriously 386
Betty Rollin: Motherhood: Who Needs It? 286
Scott Russell Sanders: Looking at Women 179
Jane Smiley: Belly, Dancing, Belly, Aching, Belly, Beasts 209
Gloria Steinem: The Good News Is: These Are Not the Best Years of Your Life 213
Andrew Sullivan: What Is a Homosexual? 195
Paul Theroux: Being a Man 176
Laurel Thatcher Ulrich: The Slogan: "Well-Behaved Women Seldom Make History" 678

RACE, CLASS, AND ETHNICITY

Sherman Alexie: Superman and Me 355
Gloria Anzaldúa: How to Tame a Wild Tongue 411
James Baldwin: Stranger in the Village 304
Judith Ortiz Cofer: More Room 116
Debra Dickerson: Who Shot Johnny? 316
Thomas Friedman: America's Real Dream Team 327
Philip Gourevitch: After the Genocide 752
Zora Neale Hurston: How It Feels to Be Colored Me 12
Maxine Hong Kingston: Tongue-Tied 401
Jonathan Kozol: Fremont High School 367
Chang-Rae Lee: Coming Home Again 3
Alberto Manguel: The Library as Survival 741
Gloria Naylor: "Mommy: What Does 'Nigger' Mean?" 420
Ngũgĩ wa Thiong'o: Decolonizing the Mind 997
Jo-Ann Pilardi: Immigration Problem Is About Us, Not Them 325
Jonathan Rauch: In Defense of Prejudice 569
Mike Rose: Blue-Collar Brilliance 393
Alberto Alvaro Ríos: Green Cards 40

Richard Rodriguez: Aria 405
Brent Staples: Black Men and Public Space 314

CRIME AND VIOLENCE

Colby Buzzell: Killing Time in Iraq 97
Debra Dickerson: Who Shot Johnny? 316
Philip Gourevitch: After the Genocide 752
Molly Ivins: Get a Knife, Get a Dog, but Get Rid of Guns 323
Michael Levin: The Case for Torture 647
George Orwell: Shooting an Elephant 784

WAR AND ITS EFFECTS

Hannah Arendt: Deportations from Western Europe 736
Colby Buzzell: Killing Time in Iraq 97
H. Bruce Franklin: From Realism to Virtual Reality: Images of America's Wars 761
Paul Fussell: Thank God for the Atom Bomb 664
Pumla Gobodo-Madikizela: "Language Rules": Witnessing about Trauma in South Africa 456
Philip Gourevitch: After the Genocide 752
Alberto Manguel: The Library as Survival 741
Rebeccas Solnit: Locked Horns 453
Walt Whitman: Death of Abraham Lincoln 716

LAW AND JUSTICE

Randall Balmer: Diversity and Stability 831
Stephen Carter: The Separation of Church and State 843
Debra Dickerson: Who Shot Johnny? 316
Pumla Gobodo-Madikizela: "Language Rules": Witnessing about Trauma in South Africa 456
Thomas Jefferson and Others: The Declaration of Independence 804
Thomas Jefferson: Original Draft of the Declaration of Independence 807
John F. Kennedy: Inaugural Address 815
Martin Luther King Jr.: I Have a Dream 852
Martin Luther King Jr.: Letter from Birmingham Jail 818
Michael Levin: The Case for Torture 647
Jo-Ann Pilardi: Immigration Problem Is About Us, Not Them 325
Michael Pollan: An Animal's Place 619
Tom Regan: The Case for Animal Rights 608
Eleanor Roosevelt: On the Universal Declaration of Human Rights 855
Peter Singer: What Should a Billionaire Give? 578
Elizabeth Cady Stanton: Declaration of Sentiments and Resolutions 811

Illness, Death, and Dying

Atul Gawande: When Doctors Make Mistakes 590
Pumla Gobodo-Madikizela: "Language Rules": Witnessing about Trauma in South Africa 456
Melvin Konner: Why the Reckless Survive 940
Elisabeth Kübler-Ross: On the Fear of Death 219
Chang-Rae Lee: Coming Home Again 3
Nancy Mairs: On Being a Cripple 46
Jennifer Sinor: Confluences 69
James van Tholen: Surprised by Death 1070
Barbara Tuchman: "This Is the End of the World": The Black Death 692
Virginia Woolf: The Death of the Moth 1107

Religion and Spirituality

Randall Balmer: Diversity and Stability 831
Annie Dillard: Sight into Insight 1109
Rita Dove: The Epistle of Paul the Apostle to the Ephesians 1061
Stephen Carter: The Separation of Church and State 843
Stephen Hawking: Is Everything Determined? 908
Langston Hughes: Salvation 1059
Jesus: Parables of the Kingdom 1123
Alberto Manguel: The Library as Survival 741
Reg Saner: My Fall into Knowledge 1085
James van Tholen: Surprised by Death 1070
Steven Weinberg: Without God 1074
Zen Parables 1127

Food

Mark Doty: Souls on Ice 992
Lars Eighner: On Dumpster Diving 31
M. F. K. Fisher: Young Hunger 206
Joey Franklin: Working at Wendy's 25
Malcolm Gladwell: Java Man 248
J. J. Goode: Single-Handed Cooking 43
Charles Lamb: A Dissertation upon Roast Pig 266
Chang-Rae Lee: Coming Home Again 3
Michael Pollan: An Animal's Place 619
Sandra Steingraber: Tune of the Tuna Fish 540
David Foster Wallace: Consider the Lobster 635

HOME AND FAMILY

Judith Ortiz Cofer: More Room 116
Joan Didion: On Going Home 1
Annie Dillard: from An American Childhood 110
Ian Frazier: Take the F 154
Henry Louis Gates, Jr.: In the Kitchen 260
Pumla Gobodo-Madikizela: "Language Rules": Witnessing about Trauma in South Africa 456
Jhumpa Lahiri: Rhode Island 144
Chang-Rae Lee: Coming Home Again 3
Bill McKibben: The Case for Single-Child Families 295
N. Scott Momaday: The Way to Rainy Mountain 119
Richard Rodriguez: Aria 405
Scott Russell Sanders: Under the Influence 100
Jennifer Sinor: Confluences 69
Jane Smiley: Belly, Dancing, Belly, Aching, Belly, Beasts 209
Henry David Thoreau: Where I Lived, and What I Lived For 1098

FOREIGN PLACES AND OTHER CULTURES

James Baldwin: Stranger in the Village 304
Dennis Baron: Who Owns Global English? 435
Colby Buzzell: Killing Time in Iraq 97
Pumla Gobodo-Madikizela: "Language Rules": Witnessing about Trauma in South Africa 456
Peter Matthiessen: Tigers in the Snow 510
Alberto Manguel: The Library as Survival 741
John McWhorter: The Cosmopolitan Tongue
Ngũgĩ wa Thiong'o: Decolonizing the Mind 997
George Orwell: Shooting an Elephant 784
Fred Strebeigh: The Wheels of Freedom: Bicycles in China 276

EDUCATION, SCHOOLS, AND LIBRARIES

Maya Angelou: Graduation 15
Caroline Bird: College Is a Waste of Time and Money 372
Frederick Douglass: Learning to Read 346
Barbara Ehrenreich: Guys Just Want to Have Fun 331
Benjamin Franklin: Learning to Write 440
Thomas Friedman: America's Real Dream Team 327
Allegra Goodman: Pemberley Previsited 978
John Holt: How Teachers Make Children Hate Reading 358
Jonathan Kozol: Fremont High School 367
Alberto Manguel: The Library as Survival 741

Reg Saner: My Fall into Knowledge 1085
Brent Staples: Why Colleges Shower Their Students with A's 329
Mary Wollstonecraft: from A Vindication of the Rights of Women 480
William Zinsser: College Pressures 380

Work

Caroline Bird: College Is a Waste of Time and Money 372
Barbara Ehrenreich: Guys Just Want to Have Fun 331
Joey Franklin: Working at Wendy's 25
Henry Louis Gates, Jr.: In The Kitchen 260
Atul Gawande: When Doctors Make Mistakes 590
Alberto Alvaro Ríos: Green Cards 40
Betty Rollin: Motherhood: Who Needs It? 286
Mike Rose: Blue-Collar Brilliance 393
Tom Wolfe: Yeager 126

INDEX

Abbey, Edward, 496
Advice to Youth, 550
After the Genocide, 752
Against Wicked Characters, 479
Alcabes, Philip, 705
Alexie, Sherman, 355
Allegory of the Cave, The, 1120
America's Real Dream Team, 327
American Childhood, An, *from,* 110
analytic genres, xxxii, xliii
Angelou, Maya, 15
Animal's Place, An, 619
annotating, xxxvii
annotations, xxv
Anzaldúa, Gloria, 411, 490
Arendt, Hannah, 736
argumentative genres, xxxiv, xliii
Aria, 405
Asimov, Isaac, 890
audience, xxi, xli
author, xxiii
autobiographical essay, xxvii
autobiography, see *autobiographical essay*

Bacon, Francis, 476
Baker, Nicholson, 915
Baldwin, James, 304
Balmer, Randall, 831
Baron, Dennis, 435
Barthes, Roland, 274
Battle of the Ants, The, 758
Battle of the Binge, The, 340
Beauty: When the Other Dancer Is the Self, 55
Behind the Formaldehyde Curtain, 254
Being a Man, 176
Belly, Dancing, Belly, Aching, Belly, Beasts, 209
Between the Sexes, a Great Divide, 174
Bierce, Ambrose, 484
Binge Drinking as a Substitute for a "Community of Learning," 343
biographical narrative, xxviii
biographical profile, see *profile of a person*
biographical sketch, see *profile of a person*
Bioterrorism Scare: A Historical Perspective, The, 705
Bird, Caroline, 372
Black Men and Public Space, 314
Blake, William, 483
Blue-Collar Brilliance, 393
Boston Photographs, The, 657
brainstorming, see *generating ideas*
Bronowski, Jacob, 886
Brooks, David, 333
Bruffee, Kenneth A., 343
Burgess, Anthony, 235
Buzzell, Colby, 97

Carr, Nicholas, 226
Carson, Rachel, 519
Carter, Stephen, 843
Case for Animal Rights, The, 608
Case for Single-Child Families, The, 295
Case for Single-Child Families, The, *from,* 494
Case for Torture, The, 647
Castillo, Sonia, 925
cause and effect, analyzing, xliv
Century of Cinema, A, 1028
citing sources, lii
Chabon, Michael, 1016
Charms of Wikipedia, The, 915
Clamorous to Learn, 350
Clan of One-Breasted Women, The, 543
classifying and dividing, xlv
Climate Emergency, The, 860
close reading, xxxii
Cofer, Judith Ortiz, 116
College Is a Waste of Time and Money, 372
College Pressures, 380
Coming Home Again, 3
Confluences, 69
Consider the Lobster, 635
contextual notes, xxi
conventions, xxvi
Copland, Aaron, 1039
The Cosmopolitan Tongue: The Universality of English, 429
Cronon, William, 533
cultural analysis, xxxiii
Cunningham, Amy, 189

Darwin's Middle Road, 959
Davenport, Andrea, 925
Death of Abraham Lincoln, 716
Death of the Moth, The, 1107
Death of the Profane: The Rhetoric of Race and Rights, The, 423
Declaration of Independence, Original Draft of the, 807
Declaration of Independence, The, 804
Declaration of Sentiments and Resolutions, 811
Decolonizing the Mind, 997

defining, xlvi
Deportations from Western Europe, 736
describing, xlvi
descriptive genres, xxix, xliii
Deutsch, Charles, 336
Devil's Dictionary, The, *from*, 48
Dickerson, Debra, 316
Didion, Joan, 1, 84, 488
Dillard, Annie, 110, 1109
Dirda, Michael, 663
Dissertation upon Roast Pig, A, 266
Diversity and Stability: The Paradox of Religious Pluralism, 831
Donne, John, 479
Doty, Mark, 992
Douglass, Frederick, 346
Dove, Rita, 1061
Dowdall, George, 336, 925
Doyle, Brian, 502
drafting, lii; see also *revising*

editing, lv
editorials, xxxv
Ehrenreich, Barbara, 331
Eighner, Lars, 31
Emerson, Ralph Waldo, 90
Enclosed. Encyclopedic. Endured: The Mall of America, 161
Ephron, Nora, 657
Epistle of Paul the Apostle to the Ephesians, The, 1061
Eureka Phenomenon, The, 890
evidence, xxv, l, liv
Existentialism, 1128

Fadiman, Anne, 62
Falling Down Is Part of Growing Up, 199
Farewell to Arms, A, *from*, 486
Faulkner, William, 871
Fisher, M. F. K., 206
FitzGerald, Frances, 776
Franklin, Benjamin, 440, 481
Franklin, H. Bruce, 493, 761
Franklin, Joey, 25
Frazier, Ian, 154, 492
freewriting, lii
Fremont High School, 367
Friedman, Thomas 327
From Realism to Virtual Reality, *from*, 493
From Realism to Virtual Reality: Images of America's Wars, 761
Frye, Northrop, 983
Fussell, Paul, 664

Gates, Henry Louis Jr., 260
Gawande, Atul, 590
Gender Gap at School, The, 333
generating ideas, xlviii
genre, xxvi, xliii
Get a Knife, Get a Dog, but Get Rid of Guns, 323
Get a Knife, Get a Dog, but Get Rid of Guns, *from*, 491
Gettysburg Address, The, 486
Gladwell, Malcolm, 248
Gobodo-Madikizela, Pumla, 456
Going to the Movies, 1036
Good News Is: These Are Not the Best Years of Your Life, The, 213
Good Readers and Good Writers, 973
Goode, J. J., 43
Goodheart, Adam, 241
Goodman, Allegra, 978
Gore, Al, 860
Gould, Stephen Jay, 959
Gourevitch, Philip, 752
Graduation, 15
Green Cards, 40
Guterson, David, 161
Guys Just Want to Have Fun, 331

Hawking, Stephen, 908
Health and Behavioral Consequences of Binge Drinking: A National Survey of Students at 140 Campuses, 925
Hemingway, Ernest, 486
historical narrative, xxviii
Hitt, Jack, 340
Holt, John, 358
How It Feels to Be Colored Me, 12
How Lincoln Won the War with Metaphors, 723
How Teachers Make Children Hate Reading, 358
How to Tame a Wild Tongue, 411
How to Tame a Wild Tongue, *from*, 490
How to Write a Letter, 446
How We Listen, 1039
Hughes, Langston, 1059
Hurston, Zora Neale, 12

I Have a Dream, 852
I Have a Dream, *from*, 487
illustrations, analyzing, xxxvii
Immigration Problem Is About Us, Not Them, 325
In Defense of Prejudice, 569
In Search of a Room of One's Own, 1005
In the Kitchen, 260
In Wilderness Is the Preservation of the World, 663
Inaugural Address, 815
Intelligent Evolution, 949
Is America Falling Apart? 235
Is Everything Determined? 908
Is Google Making Us Stupid? 226
Ivins, Molly, 323, 491

Java Man, 248
Jefferson, Thomas, 807
Jefferson, Thomas, and Others, 804
Jesus, 1123

Johnson, Samuel, 479
Jonson, Ben, 477
Journal, *from* (Thoreau), 93
Journals, *from* (Emerson), 90
Journals of Sylvia Plath, The, *from*, 95
Joyas Voladoras, 502

Keillor, Garrison, 446, 449
Kennedy, John F., 815
Kids' Stuff, 1016
Killing Time in Iraq, 97
Kincaid, Jamaica, 139, 491
King, Martin Luther Jr., 487, 818, 852
King, Stephen, 443
Kingston, Maxine Hong, 401
Konner, Melvin, 940
Kozol, Jonathan, 367
Kristof, Nicholas D., 272
Kübler-Ross, Elisabeth, 219
Kuhn, Thomas S., 899

Lahiri, Jhumpa, 144
Lamb, Charles, 266
"Language Rules": Witnessing about Trauma in South Africa, 456
Learning to Read, 346
Learning to Write, 440
Lee, Chang-Rae, 3
Letter from Birmingham Jail, 818
Letter to President Pierce, 532
Levin, Michael, 647
Library as Survival, The, 741
Lincoln, Abraham, 486, 813
literacy narrative, xxvii
Locked Horns, 453
Looking at Women, 179

Machiavelli, Niccolò, 797
Mairs, Nancy, 46
Manguel, Alberto, 741
Matthiessen, Peter, 510
McCloud, Scott, 1022
McKibben, Bill, 295, 494
McPhee, John, 490, 504
McPherson, James M., 723
McWhorter, John, 429
memoir, see *autobiographical essay*
mini-autobiography, see *autobiographical essay*
mini-biography, see *profile of a person*
Mitford, Jessica, 254
Modest Proposal, A, 790
Moeykens, Barbara, 925
Momaday, N. Scott, 119
"Mommy, What Does 'Nigger' Mean?" 420
Moral Instinct, The, 552
Morals of the Prince, The, 797
More Room, 116
Morrison, Toni, 135
Motherhood: Who Needs It? 286
Motive for Metaphor, The, 983
Muir, John, 525
My Fall Into Knowledge, 1085

Nabokov, Vladimir, 973
narrating, xlvii
narrative genres, xxvii, xliii
natural history, xxxi
Nature of Scientific Reasoning, The, 886
Naylor, Gloria, 420
New Beginning, A, 873
Ngũgĩ wa Thiong'o, 997
Night Owl, 62
9.11.01: The Skyscraper and the Airplane, 241
No Man Is an Island, 479
Nobel Prize Award Speech, 871
Notes on Punctuation, 451

Obama, Barack, 873
Of Youth and Age, 475
Oliver, Mary, 537
On Being a Cripple, 46
On Dumpster Diving, 31
On Going Home, 1
On Going Home, *from*, 488
On Keeping a Notebook, 84
On the Fear of Death, 219
On the Universal Declaration of Human Rights, 855
On Writing, 443
Once More to the Lake, 79
One Writer's Beginnings, 967
op-eds, xxxv
orations, xxxv
organizing ideas, l, liv
Orwell, George, 463, 784

parables, xxxvi
Parables of the Kingdom, 1123
paraphrasing, liii
Pearls before Breakfast, 1043
peer review, see *revising*
Pemberley Previsited, 978
personal narrative, see *autobiographical essay*
Petroski, Henry, 199
Pilardi, Jo-Ann, 325
Pinker, Steven, 552
place essay, see *profile of a place*
plagiarism, liii
Plath, Sylvia, 95
Plato, 1120
Politics and the English Language, 463
Pollan, Michael, 619
Poor Richard's Almanack, *from*, 481
Postcards, 449
previewing, xxxvii
process, explaining a, xlvii

profile of a person, xxix
profile of a place, xxx
proofreading, lv
Proverbs of Hell, 483
purpose, xxiv, xl

Quindlen, Anna, 174, 321

Rauch, Jonathan, 569
reading, strategies for, xxxvii
Regan, Tom, 608
revising, liii
Rewriting American History, 776
rhetorical context, xxiv
rhetorical modes, xliv
rhetorical occasion, xxiv
rhetorical situation, xxiv
rhetorical strategies, using, xliv
Rhode Island, 144
Rich, Adrienne, 386
Ríos, Alberto Alvaro, 40
Rodriguez, Richard, 405
Rollin, Betty, 286
Roosevelt, Eleanor, 855
Rose, Mike, 393
Route to Normal Science, The, 899

Salvation, 1059
Sanders, Scott Russell, 100, 179
Saner, Reg, 1085
Sartre, Jean-Paul, 1128
Saudis in Bikinis, 272
Seattle, Chief, 532
Second Inaugural Address, 813
Separation of Church and State, The, 843
Serpents of Paradise, The, 496
Shooting an Elephant, 784
Sight into Insight, 1109
Single-Handed Cooking, 43
Singer, Peter, 578
Sinor, Jennifer, 69
Slogan: "Well-Behaved Women Seldom Make History," The, 678
Smiley, Jane, 209
Solnit, Rebecca, 453
Sontag, Susan, 1028
Souls on Ice, 992
Sowers and Reapers, 139
Sowers and Reapers, *from,* 491
speeches, public, xxxv
Stanton, Elizabeth Cady, 811
Staples, Brent, 314, 329
Steinem, Gloria, 213
Steingraber, Sandra, 540
Stranger in the Village, 304
Strangers, 135
Strebeigh, Fred, 276
Stuff Is Not Salvation, 321
subject, finding a, xli
summarizing, xxxviii
Sullivan, Andrew, 195
Superman and Me, 355
Surprised by Death, 1070
Swift, Jonathan, 790
synthesizing, lii

Take the F, 154
Take the F, *from,* 492
Taking Women Students Seriously, 386
textual analysis, xxxii
Thank God for the Atom Bomb, 664
Theroux, Paul, 176
thesis, xlix
"This Is the End of the World": The Black Death, 692
Thomas, Lewis, 451
Thoreau, Henry David, 93, 758, 1098
Tides, 519
Tigers in the Snow, 510
Tisdale, Sallie, 650
To Write Well, 477
tone, liv
Tongue-Tied, 401
Too Many Colleges Are Still in Denial about Alcohol Abuse, 336
Toth, Susan Allen, 1036
Toys, 274
Trouble with Wilderness, The, 533
Tuchman, Barbara, 692
Tune of the Tuna Fish, 540
Twain, Mark, 550

Ulrich, Laurel Thatcher, 678
Under the Influence, 100
Under the Snow, 504
Under the Snow, *from,* 490
Understanding Comics, 1022

van Tholen, James, 1070
Vindication of the Rights of Woman, A, *from,* 480
visual analysis, xxxii

Walker, Alice, 55
Wallace, David Foster, 635
Waste Land: An Elegy, 537
Way to Rainy Mountain, The, 119
We Do Abortions Here: A Nurse's Story, 650
Wechsler, Henry, 336, 925
Weinberg, Steven, 1074
Weingarten, Gene, 1043
Welty, Eudora, 350, 967
What Is a Homosexual? 195
What Should a Billionaire Give—and What Should You? 578
Wheels of Freedom: Bicycles in China, The, 276
When Doctors Make Mistakes, 590
Where I Lived, and What I Lived For, 1098

White, E. B., 79
Whitman, Walt, 716
Who Owns Global English? 435
Who Shot Johnny? 316
Why Colleges Shower Their Students with A's, 329
Why the Reckless Survive, 940
Why Women Smile, 189
Williams, Patricia, 423
Williams, Terry Tempest, 543
Wilson, Edward O., 949
Wind-Storm in the Forests, A, 525
Without God, 1074
Wolfe, Tom, 126, 488
Wollstonecraft, Mary, 480
Woolf, Virginia, 1005, 1107
Working at Wendy's, 25
writing, strategies for, xlviii; see also *rhetorical strategies*

Yeager, 126
Yeager, *from*, 488
Young Hunger, 206

Zen Parables, 1127
Zinsser, William, 380

About the Authors

Linda Peterson (Ph.D., Brown University), General Editor, is a professor of English at Yale University and has published widely on nonfiction prose, notably autobiography and women's authorship. She co-directed the Bass Writing Program at Yale for twenty-five years and has served as president of the Council of Writing Program Administrators.

John Brereton (Ph.D., Rutgers University) is a professor of English, emeritus, at the University of Massachusetts, Boston. Previously he served as executive director of the Calderwood Writing Initiative at the Boston Athenæum. He has taught writing at Harvard University, Wayne State University, Brandeis University, and the City University of New York. His scholarship focuses on the history of teaching English literature and composition.

Joseph Bizup (Ph.D., Indiana University) is an associate professor of English and director of the Arts and Sciences Writing Program at Boston University. He previously taught and directed writing programs at Yale University and Columbia University in the City of New York. His scholarly interests include nineteenth-century literature, especially nonfiction prose, and writing studies, especially genre, style, and argumentation.

Anne Fernald (Ph.D., Yale University) directs the first year writing program at Fordham University's Lincoln Center campus, where she is an associate professor of English and women's studies. She is the author of *Virginia Woolf: Feminism and the Reader* (Palgrave 2006) and is currently at work on the Cambridge University Press edition of *Mrs. Dalloway*. She has published articles on Woolf, Lawrence, and modernism as well as essays in *Guernica*, *Open Letters Monthly*, and *H.O.W.* Her personal blog is *Fernham*.

Melissa Goldthwaite (Ph.D., The Ohio State University), professor of English at Saint Joseph's University, teaches creative writing and rhetorical theory. Her books include *The Norton Pocket Book of Writing by Students* (W. W. Norton, 2010), *Surveying the Literary Landscapes of Terry Tempest Williams* (University of Utah Press, 2003), and the fifth and sixth editions of *The St. Martin's Guide to Teaching Writing* (Bedford/St. Martin's, 2003 and 2007).